W0010037

1 MONTH OF
FREE
READING

at

www.ForgottenBooks.com

By purchasing this book you are eligible for one month membership to ForgottenBooks.com, giving you unlimited access to our entire collection of over 1,000,000 titles via our web site and mobile apps.

To claim your free month visit:

www.forgottenbooks.com/free1060860

* Offer is valid for 45 days from date of purchase. Terms and conditions apply.

ISBN 978-0-331-71892-8
PIBN 11060860

This book is a reproduction of an important historical work. Forgotten Books uses
state-of-the-art technology to digitally reconstruct the work, preserving the original format
whilst repairing imperfections present in the aged copy. In rare cases, an imperfection in
the original, such as a blemish or missing page, may be replicated in our edition. We do,
however, repair the vast majority of imperfections successfully; any imperfections that
remain are intentionally left to preserve the state of such historical works.

Forgotten Books is a registered trademark of FB &c Ltd.
Copyright © 2018 FB &c Ltd.
FB &c Ltd, Dalton House, 60 Windsor Avenue, London, SW19 2RR.
Company number 08720141. Registered in England and Wales.

For support please visit www.forgottenbooks.com

Monthly Bulletin

OF THE

Bureau

OF THE

American Republics.

INTERNATIONAL UNION OF AMERICAN REPUBLICS.

FREDERIC EMORY, DIRECTOR.

JULY. 1898.

WASHINGTON, D. C., U. S. A.:
GOVERNMENT PRINTING OFFICE.
1898.

INDEX TO VOLUME VI

EMBRACING

MONTHLY BULLETINS FROM JULY, 1898, TO JUNE, 1899, INCLUSIVE

— — —. — —

BUREAU OF THE AMERICAN REPUBLICS
WASHINGTON, D. C., U. S. A.

INDEX TO VOLUME VI

EMBRACING MONTHLY BULLETINS FROM JULY, 1898, TO JUNE, 1899, INCLUSIVE

beyond the term fixed by the committee, viz, June 30, 1898, and that the said FREDERIC EMORY be, and he is hereby, appointed Director of the Bureau of the American Republics for a further period, beginning July 1, and ending October 1, 1898.

Resolved, That the special powers conferred upon the Director by resolution of February 28, 1898, be reaffirmed and extended for the term of his further incumbency.

The chairman asked if the members had any remarks to make concerning the resolutions.

After expressions by members of the committee of their individual satisfaction with the condition of affairs in the Bureau, the resolutions were unanimously adopted.

Adjourned.

TRADE RELATIONS IN AMERICA.—XIII.*

INTERNAL RESOURCES OF THE EASTERN COAST OF SOUTH AMERICA.

The last article in this series written by the late Director of the Bureau, related to the eastern coast of South America—that is, the countries of the southern continent which border upon, or find their natural outlets on, the Atlantic, and appeared in the January number of the BULLETIN. These countries are Brazil, Uruguay, the Argentine Republic, and Paraguay. The article was limited to the discussion of the commercial relations between the republics named and the United States. It is now purposed to sketch the internal resources of the great regions which lie south of the fifth parallel north latitude.

The United States of Brazil is only one-seventh less in size than all Europe, with topographic and hydrographic features which may be fittingly qualified by but one word—vast. Its area is 3,257,766 square miles, with a population of 16,330,216, or about five inhabitants to the square mile. When it is considered that the seaboard of the country is 4,000 miles in length, and that its majestic waterway—the Amazon—with its tributaries affords free navigation for more than 30,000 miles within its territory, an idea is formed of its immense possibilities for industrial development.

---

* The first article of this series, by the late JOSEPH P. SMITH, Director, was published in the MONTHLY BULLETIN for July, 1897.

Brazil is a country of magnificent natural resources, but the great Latin-American handicap, as the lack of proper proportion between the population and territorial extent may be termed, is here as apparent as in the other sister Republics. The agricultural wealth of the nation is limitless, yet only a small fraction of the land is under cultivation. The chief production, as is universally known, is coffee, followed by sugar, tobacco, cotton, mate, india rubber, timber, cacao, and nuts, in the order named. For some years past Brazil has furnished over half the world's consumption of coffee. The forests abound with valuable timbers, dyewoods, resins, fibers, and medicinal plants. In the valley of the Amazon alone there are 22,000 species of woods which have been catalogued. The immense plains of the south are admirably adapted to stock raising, and the rivers teem with many varieties of fish. The mineral wealth is great. Iron exists in vast quantities, but the want of fuel prevents the profitable working of the deposits. Foreigners, principally English and French, carry on gold and diamond mining to a considerable extent.

The industries are represented by about 156 cotton mills, employing in the neighborhood of 200,000 operatives; a number of important woolen factories, sugar factories, tanneries, breweries, flour mills and distilleries, soap, oil, and candle manufactories, shipbuilding, etc.

In all probability Brazil will never be a great manufacturing country, but as a producer and exporter of raw materials she has a future with boundless possibilities.

On December 31, 1896, there were 8,662 miles of railways in operation in the country, and 4,963 in course of construction. An interesting report on these railways, giving many details, was published in the BULLETIN for March, 1898. The telegraph system is under control of the Government, there being in 1895 some 21,936 miles of wire in use. During the same year the merchant navy of the country consisted of 189 steamers of 75,283 tons net, and 285 sailing vessels of 65,575 tons net.

The Republic of Uruguay, next adjoining Brazil on the south, has an estimated area of 72,110 square miles, and a population of 843,408. Seventy per cent of the latter are native born.

Nature, in distributing her favors, has treated this smallest Republic of South America with no stinting hand. It may be said to be one great pasture land, lying within the temperate zone, forever green, and watered by mighty rivers and streams innumerable. Though the country is undulating, save on the Atlantic coast, its surface shows no mountain higher than 2,000 feet, being rather a succession of grassy slopes, far-extending fields, and tree-studded river banks.

The chief industry of Uruguay is, naturally, cattle and sheep raising. Statistics which, in countries of great territorial extent, small population, and inadequate means of communication, are more likely to lean toward the minus than plus side, show that in 1895 the pastoral establishments of the country contained 5,247,871 head of cattle, 388,348 horses, 14,007 mules, and 14,333,626 sheep. The total value of the flocks and herds was stated to be $73,038,000. The products of this industry, which form the bulk of the export trade of Uruguay, are jerked beef, extract of beef, hides and skins, tallow and wool. Of the last-named article 50,000 tons were exported in the year 1895. Frozen carcasses are shipped in large quantities to Europe.

Of late years more attention has been directed to agriculture, and, under Government assistance, the cultivation of the fertile soil has been undertaken with fairly good results. Wheat and and flour, which up to 1877 were imported, have now become articles of export. The exports of wheat, flour, and corn for the four years from 1894 to 1897 were valued at $10,902,823, while for the preceding four years they were represented by $2,246,855, showing a gain for the former period of $8,655,968. Satisfactory results have been obtained in the culture of the vine, and the number of wine growers is increasing rapidly.

The fruits of Uruguay are famous, embracing, as they do, the varieties known to the temperate and tropical belts: Apples, pears, peaches, cherries, plums, lemons, limes, pomegranates, quinces, bananas, cocoanuts, and pineapples are exported to Brazil and the Argentine, and the preserving of quinces, which are so abundant as to form forests, is a valuable branch of industry.

Linseed, hemp, tobacco, and saffron are produced to a fair extent.

Mining is not very far advanced, although gold, silver, copper, iron, tin, and mercury have been found, and can be profitably worked.

In 1890 there were 1,026 miles of railway open for traffic and about 200 under construction. The total length of the telegraph lines in 1897 was 4,380 miles, of which 982 belonged to the railways.

The shipping interests of the Republic were represented in 1895 by 19 steam vessels, with a total net tonnage of 4,608 tons, and 45 sailing vessels, with a total of 13,171 tons net.

In taking up the Argentine Republic, one is struck at the outset with the fact, heretofore referred to in the BULLETIN, that many of the staple products, principally wheat and wool, of this great country are identical with some of those of the United States, hence reducing an interchange of these to a small volume. Lying, as the Argentine does, between 22° and 56° south latitude, it has a longer Atlantic coast line than its big northern sister, and, being nearer the equator, yields the distinctive products of every climate from the cold to the tropical.

With an area of 1,212,000 square miles, and a population of 4,092,990, the Argentine is one of the largest and most progressive countries in the New World.

Buried in the mountain ranges of the west are to be found rich deposits of minerals, such as gold, silver, iron, and copper, while in the southwestern provinces extensive coal fields have recently been discovered. But the mining industry is yet undeveloped, despite a liberal and well-framed mining code.

The Argentine is known the world over as the home of the agricultural and pastoral industries, and the strides it has made in these two directions are very great. It seems but a few years ago that this country was importing flour from its western neighbor, Chile; but the Paraguayan war came, and with it a demand for cereals. The Argentines went to work with a will, taking advantage of their wonderful soil, where the plow is called upon to do less labor than in most parts of the world, and by the year 1893, had brought their country up to the third in rank among the great wheat-exporting nations, the exports of this product in 1895 being 37,120,897 bushels. It has been estimated that there are 240,000,000 acres suitable for wheat raising in the Republic, although it was computed in 1897 that only about 15,000,000 acres were under crops of all kinds. The average yield per acre of wheat is 990 pounds.

The pastoral industry of the Argentine is world-renowned. The national census of 1895 showed that the number of animals in the country were: Horned cattle, 21,701,526; horses, mules, and jacks, 4,930,228; sheep, 74,379,561; goats, 2,748,860. The total value of these in paper money was $1,130,701,331. The natural deduction from the possession of so large a number of cattle and sheep is that their products and residuums form a very important part of the export trade of the Republic; nor is this wrong. Ever since 1890 the foreign trade in horns, bones, hides, jerked beef, meat extract, hide cuttings, preserved tongues, dried blood, grease and tallow, salted meats, preserved meats, frozen carcasses, sheepskins, and wool has been very large, although it has fluctuated by reason of droughts and other natural causes which affect the same industry in other countries. The horned-cattle trade with Uruguay, Chile, and Brazil has assumed very large proportions and is a great wealth producer. Most of the large *estancias*, as the immense cattle ranches are called, are conducted on the cooperative plan, which has proved most beneficial, and has been the cause of a large influx of foreigners, who have banded themselves into colonies and are engaged in the agricultural and pastoral industries.

In one feature, at least, the Argentine differs from her South American sisters. Up to 1889 her exports were chiefly limited to the articles above enumerated; but the financial crisis came in that year, and the country, from being a producer of raw material only, showed by her import statistics that the activity of her population had been directed in other paths. Manufactories sprang up, and in 1892 many articles which had figured conspicuously in the lists of imports became conspicuous by their absence. The brawn of the nation began to show its prowess in other fields and to cater to its needs by utilizing the fruits of the soil in the manufacture of many articles previously purchased abroad, thus entering upon the laudable task of upbuilding a great and powerful commonwealth and making it self-dependent.

The census of 1895 shows that the number of industrial establishments of most prominence was as follows: Wine factories, 852; flour mills, 532; distilleries, 108; breweries, 44; sugar plantations, 2,749; sugar mills, 48; vineyards, 6,514.

The question of transportation by rail in the Argentine has been conscientiously studied by the Government, and some of the best lines in the world now traverse the more profitable sections of the country. For some years Government engineer corps have been in the field, surveying and making reconnoissances not only for lines projected and under construction, but, with an eye to the future, laying out a great railway system throughout the country, the component sections of which are to be built as the demands of travel shall require.

Of the railways in operation in 1895, five belonged to the nation, and ten were private railways guaranteed by the Government. The total length of the former, on December 31 of the year named, was 1,033 kilometers, and of the latter, 3,920. The total length of all the lines in operation in 1896 is given as 9,032 miles.

During this latter year there were 25,345 miles of telegraph lines, with 59,060 miles of wire, nearly half of which were under Government control.

The merchant marine of the Argentine in 1894 consisted of 75 steamers of 21,613 tons net, and 125 sailing vessels of 28,241 tons net.

The Republic of Paraguay, like that of Bolivia, is an inland country far removed from the seaboard, but connected therewith by some of the finest waterways of the world, the Paraná, Paraguay, and Uruguay rivers. Asunción, the capital of the Republic, is between 1,100 and 1,200 miles from Buenos Aires, and is connected therewith by three lines of good steamers plying the majestic streams named, regularly. According to official statistics, the eastern part of Paraguay, which is considered as Paraguay proper, has an area of 148,000 square miles, and a population (1894 estimate) of 430,000. Of this number 60,000 are semi-civilized, and 70,000 uncivilized Indians.

By reason of its climate, which knows no extremes of temperature, and its wonderfully fertile soil, Paraguay is perennially carpeted in green. It has been truthfully said that "it is doubtful if any spot upon the earth's surface as small as Paraguay will yield such a variety of agricultural products with as little labor. Within the space of a few acres may be seen 200 different products of Europe, Asia, Africa, and America, growing almost spontaneously and never needing artificial aid, such as hothouse cultivation."

The chief product of the country is the *yerba mate*, which is known in all the markets of South America and in portions of Europe as "Paraguayan tea." For millions of the inhabitants of Brazil, the River Plate countries, Peru, and Bolivia, this article takes the place of the Chinese beverage. The exports of this product in 1896 amounted to 9,024 tons, valued at more than $1,400,000.

The soil of Paraguay, being porous and light, is well adapted for fruit raising. The aurantiaceous fruits grow admirably, oranges in particular being produced in very large quantities and exported to Buenos Aires and Montevideo to the amount of 6,000 or 7,000 tons annually. Immense orange groves are to be seen yielding their golden harvest unattended by the nurturing hand of man. Quite an industry is being developed in exporting the dried rind of this delicious fruit to Holland, where it is converted into the *liqueur* known as Curaçao, and considerable capital is employed at home in the manufacture of cordials and bitters. As the pulp of the fruit is not needed in this industry, it is thrown away or given to the swine as food

Tobacco grows in all sections of the Republic, and is another of its principal products. Sugar cane grows freely, but the sugar mills are very primitive in their appointments. Cotton and other fibrous plants are produced spontaneously, and, in fine, most, if not all, of the tropical products are yielded in profusion.

The forests of Paraguay are especially rich in hard woods, and, although the timber industry has assumed fair proportions of late years, there can be no doubt that fortunes await those who enter the business upon a scale commensurate with the raw material at hand. Transportation and labor are both cheap, and the prices obtained in neighboring markets are good.

As to the mining industry, all that can be said is that it has not been developed, although beneath the country's verdant surface lie mineral treasures which, when uncovered, will add immensely to the nation's wealth.

In manufactures, Paraguay has made but slight advances, and it will be many years before she will be able to supply the home demand. The manufacturing industry is confined principally to woolen and cotton fabrics.

Industries that will yield handsome profits in the future, and which are now in their earliest stages, are the pottery and distilling industries. The fine clays of Paraguay have for a long time been known, and the extraction by distillation of rich essences from oranges and other fruits, flowers, leaves, etc., is a field to which capital should flow.

Strange as it may seem, the first railway in South America was built in Paraguay some fifty years ago by the Dictator Lopez, and there is now but one line in the country owned by a private corporation and running from the capital to Pirapo, a distance of 155.4 miles. The road will eventually be carried to Encarnación, on the Paraná River, where it will connect with the Argentine system of railways.

There are 360 miles of telegraph lines.

In the necessarily limited space of this article it is impossible to give more than a passing glance at the wonderfully rich commonwealths of South America, bathed by the great Atlantic and the mighty rivers that mingle their waters with its ebb and flow, but that glance suffices to show that each of the four nations presents to the seeker for the means to live, in a more or less alluring guise, a land of promise.

A. M. Fergusson.

ARGENTINE REPUBLIC.

FROZEN-MEAT TRADE.

LYMAN W. CHUTE, Vice-Consul of the United States at Buenos Aires, under date of December 16, 1897, sends to the Department of State a detailed report of the frozen-meat trade of the Argentine Republic, which is published in full in the advance sheets of the United States Consular Reports of May 10, 1898.

As of special interest, the following extracts from Mr. Chute's report are published in the Bulletin:

INCEPTION OF THE INDUSTRY.

The frozen-meat industry was established in the Argentine Republic in 1882, the first exports of frozen meat taking place in 1883, since which time they have progressed steadily. The industry is carried on in four works, viz:

No. 1, established in 1882, is situated at Campaña, some 40 miles north of the city of Buenos Aires, on the River Paraná.

No. 2, commenced in 1884, is on the south bank of the Riachuelo, a canalized creek forming the southern limit of the city of Buenos Aires. This establishment, formerly a private firm, but now a limited company, has grown steadily. Commencing in a comparatively modest manner, it has, according to reliable information, succeeded in taking one of the most prominent positions in the frozen-mutton trade in the world.

No. 3 started in 1886 at San Nicolas, a port on the River Paraná.

No. 4 began work in 1886 at Lima, a railway station on the Buenos Aires and Rosario line, close to Zarate, a port adjacent to Campaña and likewise on the River Paraná.

In 1885 a frozen-meat industry was started under the auspices of the Argentine Rural Society, the shareholders being principally cattle farmers anxious to find a profitable outlet for their production. Two shipments resulted in heavy losses. The carcasses were of animals of five or six years and of late castration, unfitted for the requirements of the English markets, and the freezing process was done on board the steamer, fitted for the purpose, the result proving the error of freezing elsewhere than ashore. The company liquidated. A fresh concern for the preparation and export of frozen meat is now seeking capital to operate in the Province of Buenos Aires.

CAPITAL.

The total capital of the four factories is declared at $5,934,380 gold, comprising value of land, buildings, machinery, plant, etc. All four are now formed into companies, three working with English and one with native capital.

LABOR.

The workmen employed number 1,225, and may be classified as foremen, earning $1.50 to $2 gold per day; slaughtermen, skinners, skin dressers, and general workmen, averaging about $1 gold per day.

SUPPLY.

Sheep are procured from the Province of Buenos Aires, the breeds most sought for being the South Hampshire, Shropshire, and Oxford Down, Cheriot, and Romney Marsh; also those from the native sheep crossed by Lincoln or Rambouillet. Nevertheless the best selling results have been obtained in the few cases where pure Hampshire Down could be procured, although it has lately been stated that excellent results are obtained for frozen-mutton purposes from a cross between the Merino and Shropshire black face. Steers are supplied chiefly from the provinces of Buenos Aires, Cordoba, and San Juan. The trade is limited, owing to the difficulty in obtaining the class of animal required by the process.

The average weight of the wether before killing is 50 kilograms (110 pounds), and when dressed the carcass weighs about 25 kilograms (55 pounds). One notable dressed Hampshire Down carcass, shipped to England by No. 2, scaled 121½ pounds. The steer alive weighs 740 to 750 kilograms (1,731 to 1,757 pounds), and when ready for shipment 370 to 375 kilograms (866 to 876 pounds).

PRICES.

The wether, alive at the factory, costs $2 to $2.30 gold; the steer, about $20 gold.

FREIGHTS.

Two of the companies ship in steamers belonging to their agents in Liverpool; the others charter with two or three lines. In the former case half a penny (1 cent) per pound would be paid, and in the latter either a lump sum or up to three-fourths of a penny (1½ cents) per pound. The United Kingdom has the lion's share of the carrying as well as of the meat trade, but one French company—the Chargeurs Réunis—takes large quantities, principally mutton, both to London and Havre, for account of No. 2, whose frozen meat reaches even as far as the Franco-German frontier.

PRODUCT.

The present rate of slaughter is set down at 2,300,000 animals per annum for freezing purposes.

The quantities and value of the exports from the inception of the industry up to the end of the third quarter of 1897, taken from official returns, were as follows:

Exports of frozen sheep carcasses.

Year.	Quantities.		Value (gold).
	Kilograms.	Pounds.	
1883			$11,412
1884 *			33,159
1885	2,862,270	6,310,794	75,323
1886	7,350,671	16,205,176	360,508
1887	12,038,889	26,540,756	963,112
1888	18,247,988	40,228,374	1,459,839
1889	16,532,545	36,449,799	1,322,604
1890	20,415,000	45,007,400	1,633,105
1891	23,278,084	51,317,585	1,862,247
1892	25,436,221	56,076,942	2,034,898
1893	25,041,000	55,205,200	2,003,254
1894	36,486,000	80,437,100	1,864,110
1895	41,882,000	92,333,600	1,675,273
1896	45,105,000	99,435,651	1,804,205
1897 (first nine months)	37,650,000	83,004,800	1,506,007
Total	312,325,668	688,553,177	18,609,056

* 33,159 carcasses.

Exports of frozen beef.

Year.	Quantities.		Value (gold).
	Kilograms.	*Pounds.*	
1885 (84 carcasses)	....	....	$1,680
1886 (527 carcasses)...................	....	....	12,800
1887			......
1888	41,581	91,686	3,326
1889	734,264	1,619,052	58,742
1890	662,860	1,395,346	53,029
1891	73,769	162,660	5,902
1892	283,687	625,490	22,695
1893	2,778,485	6,186,860	222,279
1894	26,700	58,873	12,400
1895	158,700	349,934	63,482
1896	299,700	666,838	119,863
1897 (first nine months)...............	299,100	659,516	119,660
Total	5,358,846	11,816,255	695,858

From the foregoing tables it will be seen that, while the export of mutton has continued steadily on the increase, the export of beef has been very variable, attaining large proportions only in the years 1889, 1890, and 1893.

FOWL FREEZING.

There are other articles of consumption— such as ducks, partridges, turkeys, snipe and fish, etc.—which are also sent to Europe, principally to France. They obtain a ready sale, but no reliable record of quantities can be arrived at. The firm of SANSINENA, before the company was formed, sent in one cargo to Paris, during the last exhibition, some 40,000 birds of various classes. This firm started a freezing establishment in the exhibition itself, with an accompanying restaurant; so that, through the medium of plate-glass windows, patrons could choose their meat for the following day. The result of this venture was that Messrs. SANSINENA & Co. received the only gold medals for frozen victuals, and Don FRANCISCO SANSINENA himself, the present managing director of the company, was elected Chevalier de la Legion d'honneur.

PRESENT CONDITION OF THE INDUSTRY.

How best to handle the freezing industry is now being worked out on the base of past experience, and, from what can be gathered from commercial sources interested, there is every prospect of continued expansion, offering to the stock raiser a spot market for his increase, which, as far as sheep go, is unsurpassed throughout the whole world.

Considering the pastoral area of Argentina, the quality of grass, cheapness of land, capital flowing in, improvement in breeds, steady immigration, and out-spread of railways, there is every reason to believe that this Republic is destined to attain preeminence as a meat purveyor to European markets.

BRAZIL.

COMMERCE WITH NEW YORK IN 1897.

From the report of Mr. ANTONIO GUIMARAES, vice-consul of Brazil in New York, on the commerce of Brazil with that port, the following is taken.

The total value of merchandise exported to Brazil from New York in the year 1897 was $3,490,289, in United States currency, and of that imported, $16,736,736. These figures, compared with those for the year 1896, show an increase in exportations of $344,325 and a decrease in importations of $659,741.

The principal products exported were: Lard, 16,762,069 pounds; flour, 755,971 barrels; kerosene, 21,844,750 gallons; lumber, 50,465,000 feet; lard oil, 157,120 gallons; turpentine, 161,961 gallons; bacon, 75,651 barrels and 5,741 boxes, and seed wheat, 747,755 bushels and 12,035 sacks.

These figures, compared with those for the year 1896, show an increase of 8,035,997 pounds in the exportation of lard; of 300,033 barrels of flour; kerosene, 28,396,924 gallons, and bacon, 4,286,991 pounds. There was a decrease in the exportation of lumber amounting to 16,876,902 feet; in lard oil, 170,371 gallons, and in turpentine, 3,097,988 gallons.

The principal products imported from Brazil were: Sugar, 100,107,567 pounds and 133,792 sacks; rubber, 25,036,628 pounds; cocoa, 2,567,687 pounds; coffee, 569,626,828 pounds; leather, 1,344,176 pounds, and skins, 3,677,998 pounds.

REPUBLIC OF COLOMBIA.

TRADE OF PANAMA AND DISTRICT FOR THE YEAR 1897.

According to the report of Consul Mallet to the British Foreign Office, the trade in the Department of Panama for the year 1897 was in a more flourishing condition than for many years previous. The value of imported wares was greatly in excess of that of the year preceding. The consular district was visited by a greater number of commercial travelers during 1897 than had been seen there for a great many years, and their personal efforts—practically the only way of obtaining trade—met with much success. It is added in the report that a large majority of these "drummers" represented British firms. Notwithstanding the fact that the merchants of the United States were represented to a limited extent in this way, the trade of the United States increased 28 per cent.

The following table shows the per cent of the leading countries in the import trade of Panama for the year 1897:

	Per cent.
Great Britain	15
France	.....
Germany	13
Spain	9
United States	48
China	15
Total	100

Mr. MALLET's report states that there was a considerable decline in the export trade of his consular district during 1897 as compared with 1896, due mainly to a short yield in the pearl fisheries and in the collection of native products.

Shipping from the port of Panama shows an increase of 9,000 tons—i. e., 3,000 in sail and 6,000 in steam.

The Pacific Steam Navigation Company, which some time ago extended its northern terminus from Panama to Puntarenas, Costa Rica, has now under consideration a further extension of the line to San Francisco, as stated in the January number of the Monthly Bulletin. The same action is proposed by the Compañía Sud Americana de Vapores.

Work is reported as progressing favorably on the canal. A large number of laborers were imported from Sierra Leone and Jamaica. The latter, as is invariably the case with Jamaica labor, has proven very satisfactory, while that from Africa succumbed to the diseases incident to the seasons, and have been found wholly unsuited to the laborious work required in the construction of the canal. On an average, there were 3,000 laborers employed throughout the year.

Very satisfactory progress is reported from the gold-mining districts, the mines about Cará in Darien doing particularly well.

Vice-Consul MacGregor reports from Barranquilla that railway development in the River Magdalena district has advanced greatly, and steady and cheap transportation to coast ports is being realized.   In the Department of Magdalena 50 miles of railroad were built.   The Barranquilla Railroad is also being extended for a distance of 36 miles to Usiacuri.

The agricultural districts of the Departments of the Magdalena Valley show a continuous and marked development, especially in the staples of coffee and tobacco.   During the year 1897 Barranquilla received 278,000 bags of coffee, of 125 pounds weight, having a quality equal to the best in foreign markets.   Tobacco, which was formerly an important article of cultivation and which has of recent years been allowed to decline both as to quantity and quality, is taking on a new interest in its cultivation and preparation for market.   During the year 1896, 35,435 "seroons" were shipped, principally to Bremen.   Cattle raising and exporting do not show an improvement; the market is limited to the islands of the West Indies and, owing to the disturbed condition of Cuba, has been restricted.   Of the total number of hides exported from Barranquilla, amounting to 150,000, 100,000 went to the United States, the remainder to Europe.   The anticipation held a few years ago of an enlargement in the cotton production does not seem to have been realized.   The exportation of the commodity shows a falling off of 707 bales in 1897 compared with the previous year.   Quite a considerable quantity, however, is being worked up in the cotton factories in Cartagena, and it is gratifying to state that this industry has shown, during the present year, a decided spirit of encouragement.   The export of india rubber from Barranquilla in 1897 was 1,400 packages of a declared value of $35,000.   The rubber tree, of which there are a number of varieties, grows throughout the forests of Magdalena, Bolivar, Santander, Antioquia, and Tolima, but its cultivation has not as yet been undertaken.

Various kinds of valuable woods are found in the forests bordering and contiguous to the Magdalena, among which is the copaiba tree, from which the balsam of that name is extracted. It grows to a height of 40 feet, has a compact grain, and is well suited for house building and the construction of boats.   Cedar is found in abundance, the logs being exported through Barranquilla, principally to France and Germany. Several French companies have established sawing plants for the purpose of cutting up these timbers.

The following table shows the value of the imports to Barranquilla in 1897:

	Value.
Great Britain	$3,984,972
United States of America	1,158,133
Other countries	4,643,630
Total	9,786,735

Vice-Consul STEVENSON, in his report from Carthagena, states that there has been a falling off in the general trade of that port as compared with 1896. This loss is in a general way attributable to the number of steamboat disasters in the navigation of the Magdalena River, thus rendering the movement of traffic through Carthagena smaller than it would otherwise have been.

The imports show a small increase over those of 1896. This increase was confined to the United States, France, Germany, and Spain, the latter country showing the principal gain.

Local improvements show some advance. A good electric plant has been lately established, the engines for which were brought from England and the electrical apparatus from the United States. A large market house is now being erected.

From Santa Martha, Vice-Consul CARR reports great activity in the cultivation of coffee. The planters, who are principally English and American, are very much encouraged with their prospects, the grade produced being equal to be best from Colombia and Costa Rica. Being near the port, planters are enabled to get their products to a seaport at a cost of less than $5 per ton. Lands well adapted for coffee growing, situated in a healthy region, with an altitude of from 3,000 to 4,000 feet, may be bought at from $2 to $3 per acre. The cultivation of bananas begun about eight years ago has attained a prosperous condition. The planters received for their crop of this fruit last year about $85,000.

ECUADOR.

TRADE OF GUAYAQUIL IN 1897.

The following facts relating to the trade and commerce of Guayaquil, Ecuador, during the year of 1897 are taken from the annual report of Consul CHAMBERS to the British Foreign office:

Guayaquil, being the principal port of the Republic, has again become the most important center of its commerce. The enormous stocks of goods destroyed in the disastrous fires of February and October, 1896, had to be replaced to meet the ever-increasing consumption of the coast and interior provinces, thus causing the import trade to be larger and more active than in any preceding year. No official statistics of these importations have been published since that of the Minister of Hacienda, Senor WITHER, to the Convention of 1896–97, which gives a rough estimate of the value of imports from May 1, 1895, to June 30, 1896, as 10,600,000 sucres (or $4,939,600). I am consequently unable to give an exact account of this important detail, but I am aware that from that period to the present imports have been on a greater scale.

There have been no changes to note in the commercial importing firms nor in the nature or origin of the goods imported. During 1897, the export trade has been carried on with its usual activity. It must be noted, however, that the excessive rains from January to May caused very serious damage to the cacao and coffee crops. Twenty-five per cent of the former was lost, and of the latter only about fifty per cent was gathered, and that mostly of an inferior quality. From the same cause all the rice plantations throughout the coast provinces were destroyed, and this necessitated a considerable importation of rice from other countries. These combined circumstances materially interfered with general business transactions. About this time, also, the Government authorized a new coinage of silver by one of the Guayaquil banks, and in the latter part of the year promulgated a law under which the banks were compelled to hold their metallic reserve in gold, thus obliging them to import foreign money to the value of at least $466,000, and it will be easily understood that the strain on the exchange transactions of the Republic has been a very heavy one and the financial positions of commerce difficult in the extreme. The banks in December suspended nearly all discount operations.

The revenue of the country has been largely increased by extra import duties under the new custom-house law and by inland taxes, but, notwithstanding the increased dues, commerce has been very brisk. There has been great activity in rebuilding the business portion of the city destroyed by the fire, and large and elegant houses have been erected, giving quite an imposing appearance to the river side of the city. These houses are all built of wood, few adopting the old system of cane and plaster, and are in a very large proportion roofed with British galvanized iron. Labor being scarce, advantage has been taken of this by the artisans to demand very high rates of wages in all departments, both for skilled and unskilled labor, and the large demand has also considerably increased the price of all building material.

Many traveling agents representing British firms have visited the country at various times during the year, and have, as a rule, expressed their satisfaction with their share of the import trade. With few exceptions, those articles enumerated in the list of the more important trades of the United Kingdom, supplied by the various Chambers of Commerce through the Foreign Office, and which find a market here, come directly or indirectly from the places named in the list. Articles of luxury, principally in dress and fancy goods for ladies and children, perfumes, fine boots, etc., have come from France. From the United States we have received kerosene, lard, and lumber in large quantities. Lumber is imported planed, tongued and grooved, ready for immediate use. Iron stoves, axes and hatchets, and furniture have only come from that market in small quantities. From Austria has been imported a better class of furniture, and also cheap jewelry and fancy goods. From Germany, such goods as beer, hosiery, woolen and mixed dress goods, blankets, ponchos, shawls, and common hardware have been imported to the same extent as in previous years, without any material increase in any goods, except mixed woolen goods and lace, which, being cheaper, have made strong competition with similar articles from England. The common kinds of cutlery previously obtained from Germany are now being competed for by the English manufacturers, and the trade is returning to them in some degree. From Belgium, nearly the whole consumption of candles for the Republic has been drawn. The production of sugar during 1897 amounted to about 6,000 tons. The home consumption will be about 4,000 tons, leaving some 2,000 tons for export, chiefly to Chile and Colombia. The average price of first-class white granulated sugar has been about 5 cents per pound. The Ecuadorian sugar is now apparently preferred in Chile to the best Peruvian grades.

There is a native factory for soaps, with free importation of materials for its manufacture, and this tends to keep down the price of imported soap. The exemption from import duties expires this year, but efforts are being made to get it renewed. It is also proposed to erect a new factory in Bahia de Caraquez by a syndicate in the United States and some Bahia merchants. A kind of black soap of a very cleansing quality is manufactured throughout the country in a primitive manner and to a very small extent. There are two factories for the manufacture of vermicelli, etc., and these have entirely monopolized the trade, which was previously an important article of import from Chile. One of these factories also comprises a biscuit bakery of a superior quality, the principal employee from a well-known London firm. During the year two new sawmills have been established, one of which was imported from England. In the interior there are manufactures of woolen and cotton goods, chiefly for home consumption, although a considerable trade in baizes of a common class is done with the neighboring Republic of Colombia, through Fumaco and Barbacoas. These do not, however, compete with the finer class of baize or bayeta imported from England.

Of the many public buildings in Guayaquil destroyed by the fire of 1896 none have been reerected. Some temporary sheds for custom-house purposes have been built on the site of the old edifice, but quite inadequate for the necessity of the large imports, and the Government has had to rent private depots throughout the city for the storage of goods, the handling of imports being considerably prejudiced by these circumstances. A company has been formed in New York to explore the district of Zaruma, and from the favorable reports which have reached headquarters there is reason to believe that a company will be formed to work the mines in this auriferous district. The Plaza de Oro Mining Company having spent enormous amounts in developing its property, and, finding difficulty on account of the great expenses required to carry it on, a syndicate of the British shareholders has been formed to continue the work with more economy. Some of the original works have been shut down, and many of the expenses which had hitherto embarrassed the undertaking have been reduced.

HAITI.

REPORT ON COAL FIELDS.

The following report on the coal deposits in southern Haiti has been furnished the Bureau by Hon. J. N. LEGER, Minister of Haiti to the United States. In forwarding the report, the Minister says: "As you can see, the engineer has only made an incomplete preliminary study. To have a true idea of the importance of the mines a deeper research would be necessary. I am authorized to enter into negotiations with any American capitalists caring to give the matter thought and further investigation. I will examine with the greatest pleasure any proposals which I may receive relative to the subject."

CAP HAÏTIEN (HAITI), *May 15, 1898.*

MR. SECRETARY OF STATE:

In December of 1896, I made a voyage of exploration in the South principally with the view of obtaining an idea of the value of the coal deposits which had been called to my attention in the arrondissement of Nippes and in that of the Cayes.

The valley of Asile had been particularly pointed out to me as containing deposits of iron ore lying by the side of the coal beds. In the matter of iron ore I found nothing. The argils of the great savannas which I explored are, as almost everywhere, more or less ferruginous, enough so in some places to impart characteristic colors to the argil. I found some rocks containing certainly a large proportion of iron, but nothing which would indicate a deposit that could be worked. Nowhere were the traces of which I have spoken important enough to warrant the expense of the work of investigation.

As to the coal deposits of Asile, I first made explorations on the Serpente

River on the Bédème property, third section of the Commune of Ause à Veau. At this point the Serpente River separates the Commune of Aquin from that of Ause à Veau. I found several outcrops of carboniferous layers crossing the river, from which they are plainly visible. These layers follow a direction varying from north to south and from north-northwest to south-southeast; their inclination on the east is about 30 degrees. Their thickness varies from 10 centimeters up to 1 meter and 20 centimeters. Up the river from this outcrop there are two others similar at a distance of about one kilometer and a half, which can be seen in the river and also on its banks.

I selected with great care some samples and sent them to Paris to the laboratory of my school, where they were analyzed by Prof. C. Vincent. The results of the chemical analysis are as follows:

Of 100 parts:

Water 26. 86
Ashes 15. 35
Fixed residuum at red heat........................... 40. 58
No coke.

These results allow of the following composition:

Water 26. 86
Ashes 15. 35
Volatile matters other than water.................... 32. 56
Fixed carbon... 25. 23
                                                      ─────
    Total 100. 00

The calorific power of the undried product is 3,177 calories; the calorific power of the dried product is 4,645 calories.

In a westerly direction, about 15 kilometers from the deposit of which I have just been speaking, on the border of the third section of Ause à Veau and of the third section of the Commune of Trou on the Meiguan-Desbrosses property, at a place called Gouvillon, there exists an outcrop which I visited; but it is a mixture of very complex matter where the carboniferous matter dominates. This sample, as well as the previous one, did not reveal a bituminous product in the analysis. This deposit follows about the same direction and the same inclination as those of the Serpente River. If these coals were near an industrial center they might be utilized in gasogens to make oxide of carbon, which can, so to speak, be used in all the manufacturing industries.

It would be difficult for me with the data of this first exploration to determine the geological position of these layers of lignite. They seem to be of considerable extent, but the only question of interest would be to know if, in following the layers or those lying by their side, one would not find a better coal which could be used in manufacture. The work of investigation necessary to solve this question would be quite expensive and would demand much time. In this case, having to deal with lignites, and the valley of Asile being so far from any port, the expense can not be advised.

In four of the five rivers which water the superb valley of Asile, I did not find one ancient, eruptive, or transition rock. In the River Duare only, I noticed some specks of carbonate of copper on the eruptive and metamorphic rocks. I explored the course of the river from Gouvillon up, to a distance of three kilometers. Among the rounded stones and even upon the larger samples, traces of copper ore plainly appeared; but the earth of the explored banks did not belong to the period of the rocks found in the bed of the Duare River. It is necessary, if one wishes to elucidate this question, to ascend this river much farther and study the mountains in which it takes its source. I have pointed out the valley of Asile as being particularly suited in all respects to agriculture. I should be very much surprised if tobacco, cultivated properly, did not give a product of very superior quality. From this valley, I went to Cavaillon by way of the famous ravine of the Citronniers, where I looked in vain for some traces of the sulphur mine mentioned in Rouzin's work of which no one here knows anything. This valley is absolutely destitute of any mineralogical interest.

From Cavaillon to Aux Cayes there is nothing of interest to note. I come at once to the Camp-Perrin deposits. These coals have been, at different periods, the object of several investigations, I dare not say studies, for the notes which have been furnished me on this subject reveal as little experience as ability on the part of their authors. Camp-Perrin is situated in the north of the Cayes, about 25 kilometers from this city. The principal stream is the torrential river Ravine, which has three main tributaries on its right bank at the place where is found what is called the "Fort" or "Fortress." This part of the country, all of which borders on the Plantons, is very broken. The geological formations have produced abrupt upheavals of the strata. The deep ravines, in which are inclosed all the tributaries of the "Ravine," fortunately allow one to note the different directions which the strata of the soil take in this place.

In examining the course of the Ravine River where in 1880 some work had been done, the traces of which have completely disappeared, I was fortunate enough to discover on the right bank a group of veins distinctly characterized, and to which I at once devoted my investigations. This difference between the right bank and the left bank will have much importance in case of their exploitation. The Cayes and the Fort are situated upon the right bank of the Ravine, and for transportation purposes it will only be necessary to build a railroad in the plain, without crossing any stream. We will return to the discussion of this question later.

It is on the Balanier place, fifth section, on the right bank of the Ravine, that I found five parallel veins running in a direction east and west, with a northern inclination of about 80 degrees, and thickness of vein varying from 65 centimeters to 1 meter and 50 centimeters. The five veins together measure, interval included, about 10 meters on the visible outcrop.

The vein furthest down the river, apparently the most visible, I opened and took from it some compact coal of good density. I dug as deep as possible, and took out the first samples, to send them, as I had sent the others, to Paris, and to make some industrial tests in the street-car shops at Port au Prince.

Continuing my researches in this place, I proceeded, via the river Bras Gauche, to the Chevalier property, sixth section, distant about 4 kilometers in a direct line, where an outcrop had been pointed out. I found there, in a very steep slope, the five veins, with the direction and inclination equal to those of the outcrop of the Balanier property. Some samples of very hard coal have been taken from the surface of these veins, where it was impossible to make excavations without preparatory work.

In descending the river from this point and consequently approaching the first direction on the River Bras Gauche, which has high banks and is very sinuous on the Delinois property, at the place of Mr. DORSÉNO DUDOR, I found the five veins with the same general appearance, inclination, and direction. So that in three points, on a distance in a straight line of 4 kilometers, I surveyed three outcrops, clearly indicating the continuation of the system of the five veins of coal. Besides, on the River Bras Droit, on the edge of the Thomas property, there is another outcrop plainly visible, but it would be necessary to do some work to determine the prevailing quality. This point, which belongs also to the sixth section, has this feature of importance : It does not appear to belong to the first system of the five veins of which I have spoken. It therefore indicates quite an extended carboniferous basin.

Then, too, the site of the works made in 1880 on the right bank of the Ravine was definitely pointed out to me. It is evident that the coal taken from this point belongs to still another system of veins than those of the Balanier property. It is therefore certain that the carboniferous basin is of great importance in the fifth and sixth sections of Camp-Perrin.

The tests by fire to which I submitted these samples gave me very encouraging results, and the chemical analysis made in Paris by the same professor gave the following results :

Water 27. 74
Ashes 17. 22
Volatile matters other than water 27. 06
Fixed carbon 27. 98
                                                                                                    ————
        Total 100. 00

The calorific power of this product is 3,446 calories, not dried, and 5,050 calories when dried.

Possessed of these facts, I had the vein of the Balanier property, already mentioned, opened up still farther in an easterly direction. As the digging progressed the coal appeared more compact, and the thin crusts of argil which separated the layers of coal seemed to disappear to make way for the coal. This vein alone has at the bottom of the excavation a thickness of 1 meter and 50 centimeters of pure coal.

I had about 2 tons of this product taken out, and in the shops of the street cars of Port au Prince, the boilers were heated for an entire day entirely with this coal, which furnished without difficulty steam for manufacture. The several Secretaries of State honored me by their presence on that occasion.

The analysis of the product taken at greater depth than the first, made in Paris under the same conditions, gave the following results :

Water 24. 10
Ashes 12. 17
Volatile matter other than water 31. 90
Fixed carbon 31. 83
                                                                                                    ————
        Total 100. 00

The calorific power with 24.10 per cent of water is 4,200 calories; dried, the product gives 5,660 calories.

We have to deal with lignites, but lignites which produce steam without difficulty. Now, if it is borne in mind that the results of the last analysis, so different from the first, were made from coal obtained at a difference in depth of scarcely 2 meters, it is evident that at a depth of 15 or 20 meters the normal product of the mine will be obtained and will be found of a very superior quality.

Starting from the Balanier property, the first work should be carried in an easterly direction. It would be necessary also to make investigations at the points mentioned in the sixth section. This first work is not very expensive, but is necessary to establish the industrial value of the deposit, which, in my opinion, is considerable.

The company formed for the exploitation will have to construct a railroad of 25 kilometers in a plain presenting no great engineering difficulty. The plain of the Cayes, well cultivated, could furnish considerable freight; the development of this could be advanced by restoring the Daverac Canal for the systematic irrigation of the plain; coffee mills should be established at Camp-Perrin, and also brickkilns to furnish building material to the city of the Cayes. The fuel for the mills, the brickkilns, and the railroad will come from the mine; and all this, well organized, can become a source of wealth to the Departement of the Cayes.

I beg you to accept, Mr. SECRETARY OF STATE, the assurances of my respectful and distinguished sentiments.

HENRI THOMASSET.

HONDURAS.

SKETCH OF THE PEOPLE, CLIMATE, RESOURCES, ETC.

The following communication on the subject of the resources, climate, etc., of Honduras has been furnished the Bureau by Mr. ROBERT M. FRYER, of Washington, who has traveled very extensively in that Republic and resided there for some years:

Let me assure the readers of the BULLETIN that the people, climate, religion, and politics of Honduras are quite what they should be for the advancement of individual interests. This statement will never be questioned by anyone who goes there with sufficient knowledge to comprehend facts, and refrain from meddling with the public affairs of the country, and devote himself to the development of the opportunities offered. It may be said that the people of Honduras extend a heartier welcome to visitors and intending settlers from the United States than to any other foreigners visiting the country.

In area Honduras is about the size of Ohio, but in natural resources it outranks a number of such States taken collectively, and had it a corresponding population would, in my opinion, surpass any other territory of similar dimensions. The country will provide more luxury and greater comfort than may be had elsewhere for the same outlay of money and labor.   It has all the advantages of the tropical, semitropical, and temperate regions.   Among its products are valuable woods of commerce, medicinal plants, tropical fruits, and vast unexplored mineral resources; but, above all, the climate of Honduras, taken in connection with its many other advantages, will yet become its greatest attraction.

For nearly 400 miles the northern coast of Honduras extends in a direction almost due east and west; the prevailing winds (the trade winds) are from the north and northeast, and can be relied upon for keeping the coast healthy and comparatively cool, but, of course, this is not the locality which most recommends itself for its climate.   However, it is not necessarily uncomfortable, inasmuch as the coast mountains dip their feet into the sea and pierce the clouds at an altitude of a mile or more.   In the various valleys and plateaus a climate may be found to suit the tastes and meet the requirements of any rational person. If, however, I were called upon to suggest the most delightful climate of the country, I should call attention to that of Tegucigalpa, Siguatepeque, the hills which surround Camayagua, Lake Yojoa, San José, Santa Barbara, and numerous other places in the interior of the Republic, where heavy blankets are required every night in the year, where flies and mosquitos are never found, and where the days are like those of springtime, combined with fruits and flowers the year round.   In thousands of miles traversed on muleback, through mountains, I have never seen a reptile nor an animal, other than domestic, except in captivity, but on all sides there is a profusion of birds of great variety of colors and plumage.   The country is well supplied with water courses, many of which abound in fish, the finest being found near the coast.

Very little capital or labor is required to establish a home in Honduras; no extremes of temperature are met with, and everything seems to grow with little or no cultivation.   This is especially the case with corn, which produces two or three crops per year; sugar cane and cotton yield more than one crop a year, and need to be planted only once in ten years.   Cocoanut and rubber trees yield profitably eight years after planting, while the coffee tree is in bearing in less than six years.   The rubber trees, in their first years, require shade, which is provided by the banana trees planted among them, which also are profitable and productive within nine months and last for at least ten years.   The life of the rubber tree in Honduras is said to be fifty or more years.   The orange, lemon, lime, manioc, and many other fruit trees grow wild throughout the country.   The pineapple, including the sugar-loaf variety, grows near the coast in great profusion.   In some portions of the country all the vegetables known in the United States grow to perfection.   The soil near the coast is too rich for the potato, the vines growing too heavy; but in the interior, where land is dry this vegetable grows well.   Mr. Bamberg, who lives at San Pedro Sula and conducts a large market garden, is considered authority in the matter of vegetable growing in Honduras.

Regarding mineral resources, I will say that from my own observation and from every indication Honduras is the great storehouse of gold and silver of untold value.   Through the courtesy of Mr. GIRLINGS, general manager of the "New York and Honduras Rosario Mining Company," I was enabled to learn not only much about the rich deposits of the company, but also of the mines of the Yuscuran district, wherein are located the famous Guayabillas mine, and the Olancho gold fields. The Rosario mine, mentioned above, is located at San Juancita, 21 miles from Tegucigalpa (the capital), with which it is connected by a very fair wagon road. The mill has 35 stamps in operation and an electric and air compressing plant, all run by water power, and it is safe to say that there is nowhere a better managed mining property than this. As a result of my investigation of the possibilities of profitable mining in Honduras, I am led to wonder why there are not in operation in that country ten or twenty mining companies where there is but one to-day.

Honduras is to have a presidential election next fall. The retiring President, Mr. BONILLA, will be greatly missed from the presidential chair by all classes of foreigners visiting or living in the country, to whom he has shown uniform kindness and respect, while by the majority of the natives, POLICARPO BONILLA is held as the ideal of virtue, intelligence, force of character, and patriotism.

MEXICO.

MINING INDUSTRY.

Among Mexico's important industries is mining. The exportation of precious metals and ores shows an increase of nearly $12,000,000 (Mexican silver) during the first half of the present fiscal year as compared with the same period in 1896; an increase of nearly 40 per cent. Mexico's copper ore is especially rich, and its production is growing at a rapid rate. In several parts of the country new and extensive mines have been recently discovered, and "Modern Mexico" states that Prof. WILLIAM NIVEN, the well-known mineralogist and archæological explorer, reports that the Guerrero fields are rich in copper as well as gold. Although Guerrero is undoubtedly rich in mineral wealth, prospectors must have capital to insure success. The climate is mild, but outfitting is expensive and provisions are scarce. The exportation of copper has doubled in the last year. During December, it reached a valuation of nearly a million dollars; an increase of almost 100 per cent. The shipments of lead, antimony, and zinc all show gratifying increase.

MANUFACTURE OF COTTON.

In a special report, made by the British Consul at the City of Mexico, it is stated that the cotton-manufacturing industry of Mexico has largely developed during the past few years. It is only a short time when the native mills will be able to furnish all the coarse cotton goods required by that country. This Mexican enterprise has made slow progress and the increase in the past three years is attributed to a succession of good harvests. In 1897, new plants installed represented the minimum production of 300,000 pieces, and those now building or likely to be constructed this year will add 750,000 pieces to the annual output. As the average annual importation of foreign cottons is now only about 40,000,000 square meters, and Mexico promises to add 21,000,000 square meters to her production, it will be seen that foreign manufacturers are likely to meet with considerable competition.

In factories where steam power is employed, the large engines of 100 horse power and upward are usually English, but where not so much power is required American high-pressure engines are preferred on account of being cheaper. The form of boiler in most general use is the multitubular.

NEW INDUSTRIES.

According to " El Progreso de Mexico," April 30, 1898, Messrs. ERNESTO CHAVERO and GREGORIO GONZÁLÉZ have applied to the Department of Promotion for authority to establish several new industries in the country, among them a manufactory of condensed milk, with a minimum capital of $150,000. This is an entirely new industry in Mexico.

The same paper states that large oil and soap factories, located at Lerdo, Durango, Torreon, and San Pedro de la Higuera, all of which formerly operated independently, have entered into an association for the purpose of conducting their business upon a consolidated basis. These several factories are equipped with electric lights, provided with new and powerful machinery, and work is carried on day and night. The principal products are cotton-seed meal and oil cake, the latter being used for fattening horned cattle and swine. The cotton seed is obtained principally from rich cotton plantations, the owners of which are largely interested in the consolidated company.

The works are capable of turning out 25,000 kilograms of cotton-seed meal every twenty-four hours, and export 20,000 tons of oil cake every year, valued at $500,000.

CORDAGE AND BAG FACTORY.

On October 8, 1896, a contract was entered into by the Department of Promotion with Mr. ALFRED HEYDRICH, to establish in Yucatan a large factory to utilize henequen and similar fabrics for the manufacture of cordage, hammocks, and bags. This contract was approved by Congress May 14, 1897, and on June 23, 1897, Mr. HEYDRICH filed articles of incorporation under the name of "Sociedad Anomina La Industria," with a capital of $400,000, with Señor ALEGARIO MOHUA as president.

The contract provides that the factory shall be completed within two years from the promulgation of its approval by Congress, and great activity has been displayed in the work of constructing and installing the plant. Buildings on a large scale have already been · erected, specially designed for the work to be done. In addition, 14 houses, 30 x 16 feet, have been built of solid stone as dwellings for the operatives. The works of the company have rail connection with the Merida and Progreso Railroad, and are provided with a number of side tracks for convenience in handling the cars.

The original contract with the Government stipulated that the amount of money invested should be not less than $250,000. As an evidence of the development of the enterprise it may be stated here that the capital stock has been increased to $600,000, and the company has engaged to commence work upon the plant one year in advance of the time stipulated in the contract.

When the plant is fully equipped the daily production will be 50,000 kilograms of fine thread, binding twine, cordage, bags, hammocks, etc., or a total output of 14,400,000 kilograms per year. This enterprise is looked upon with a great deal of interest in view of the fact of its being the pioneer, on a large scale, in the home manufacture of henequen, the great staple of Yucatan.

RAILWAY CONCESSION TO PEARSON, SONS & COMPANY.

The Diario Oficial, of recent date, contains the announcement of a concession which was approved by President DIAZ on June 4, whereby the great English firm of PEARSON & SONS and Señor PEDRO M. ARMENDARIA are authorized to locate, construct, and operate a railway in the State of Vera Cruz. The initial point of the road will be either Acayuacan or Paso de San Juan, on the line of the Jutla railroad. It is to extend to Tuxtla and San Nicolas, with the privilege of further extension as far as Alvarado.

The line must be located within a year from the date of approval of the contract, and the work of construction must be begun within eighteen months; the entire line to be completed within ten years. Besides the usual exemption from import duties and taxes, the concessionaires shall receive large tracts of public land in the States of Vera Cruz, Oaxaca, Tabasco, and Chiapas. The contracting company must have its legal residence in the City of Mexico, and in the selection of the directors the Government reserves the right of naming a certain number.

The contractors are required to make a deposit of $3,000 in Government bonds in the Banco Nacional within fifteen days. The territory through which the line is to run is one of the richest and most promising in the production of rubber, tobacco, and sugar, in the entire Republic, and the high financial standing of Messrs. Pearson & Sons is a guaranty that the conditions of the contract will be literally carried out.

NICARAGUA.

FINE WOODS CONCESSION TO MR. EMERY.

WILLIAM B. SORSBY, Consul of the United States at San Juan del Norte, has transmitted to the Department of State a copy, in translation, of the contract made by the Nicaraguan Government with Mr. H. C. EMERY, of Chelsea, Mass., for the privilege of cutting and exporting the valuable woods of the country.

In substance the contract gives Mr. EMERY a monopoly for fifteen years of the mahogany, rosewood, and cedar timbers over a large area of the Republic, known to be rich in such woods. This is practically a renewal of the old contract held by him, under which he has shipped annually about 12,500 logs. Consul SORSBY regards the concession as being immensely valuable; in fact, one of the most valuable that has been granted by Nicaragua to foreigners within a great while.

Article 3 of the contract binds Mr. EMERY to construct 50 miles of railway for his own use between Rio Grande and the Pearl Lagoon, the gauge to be 3 feet 6 inches, or 4 feet 8½ inches; the line to be located through the public lands of the Department of Matagalpa. The equipment of the road, bridges, wharves, workshops, etc., shall be approved by the Minister of Public Works. The entire property is to revert to the Government at the termination of the contract, i. e., fifteen years.

The National Government cedes to Mr. EMERY 10,000 manzanas (17,500 acres) of public lands in the Department of Zelaya or Matagalpa, conditioned upon his setting out a plant within a year, for each tree cut.

By Article 4 of the contract the concessionaire must pay the Government $20,000 in gold or acceptable drafts, and $10,000 gold per annum, as a premium, during the existence of the contract.

The Government concedes to Mr. EMERY the right to import free of duty, all supplies necessary for the maintenance and support of the men employed by him in cutting and exporting the woods, and also the material required in the construction and maintenance of the railway.

NEW MINISTRY.

The Ministry of Nicaragua, as constituted under the second term of President Iglesias's administration, is as below:

Foreign Relations, Public Instruction, etc.......Señor Don PEDRO PÉREZ ZELEDÓN.
Interior and Public Works.....................Señor Don JOSÉ ASTÚA AGUILAR.
Finance and Commerce.......................Señor Don JUAN B. QUIRÓS.
War and Navy ....Señor Don DEMETRIO TINOCO.

PARAGUAY.

POINTS FROM THE PRESIDENT'S MESSAGE

President EGUZQUIZA appeared before the Senators and Representatives on April 1, and delivered to that body on the occasion of its assembly in regular session the usual executive message. The term of office of President EGUZQUIZA will terminate with the expiration of the present session of Congress. This message is, therefore, the last that he will be called upon to deliver during his present term as President.

The President congratulates the country upon the general development of public instruction and the steady increase of the number of public schools, and the attendance upon them. He makes a special reference to the enlargement of the Normal School system, which at this time is attended by more than 1,000 pupils of both sexes. A select corps of teachers has been contracted for abroad. Agricultural, artistic, and scientific instruction has been greatly extended.

The telegraph service will be extended from Asunción to Villa Concepción, and has already reached a point beyond San Pedro. Within a few months it will be in operation as far as the first-named point. It is purposed to prolong the telegraph line to Fuerte Olimpo and construct a branch connecting the main line with several points on the northern frontier. The postal service has grown proportionately to the increase of population and the exigencies of the service.

On the subject of public works, the President states that a special committee is engaged in directing this branch of the Government in accordance with the appropriations made to this end.

The total value of the importations for the preceding twelve months amounted to $2,203,359, while the exportations reached $1,955,803, these figures representing the gold valuation.

The Agricultural Bank, the most important institution of its kind in the country, has done much to encourage the work for which it was established, namely, the development of the cultivation of cotton, coffee, the vine, and other products in the Republic. More than 1,000,000 coffee trees now exist in the country, and no one doubts that the outlook promises the doubling or trebling of this number within the next year or two. The bank has promoted experiments in the preparation of tobacco according to the systems followed in Cuba and Sumatra, under the direction of competent persons. In this way the Paraguayan tobacco, which has been supplanted in foreign markets, will again assume its wonted importance.

On the subject of the National Bank, the President says that the liquidation thereof continues, notwithstanding the debtors are remiss in meeting their obligations. " It would be wise to adopt some mode of securing the final liquidation of the institution so as to avoid unnecessary expense." The land tax will become one of the sources of income to the nation.

The Government is engaged in considering plans for a railroad from the yerba mate districts to the river. Should the idea be realized, the trade in yerba mate, now with difficulty carried on, and much more so during periods of drought, when the tributaries of the Paraguay River become unnavigable, will derive great benefits.

The message refers with much satisfaction to the condition of perfect harmony and cordiality existing between Paraguay and her neighboring countries. The only question pending is the adjustment of the boundary line with Bolivia, involving the right to the territory of the Chaco (a vast, uninhabited wilderness). This question remains for the moment in abeyance.

President Eouzquiza entertains well-founded hopes that the negotiations initiated in the Argentine Republic, looking to the concluding of a treaty of commerce, will reach a solution expedient and satisfactory to both nations. The President also cherishes the firm conviction that the method of establishing permanent bonds between nations is to develop their moral and material interests, based upon liberal concessions which will permit the expansion of their industries and their commercial activity. The President also urgently recommends the concluding of a treaty of commerce with Brazil.

PERU—CHILE.

COTTON GROWING AND MANUFACTURING.

In the June number of the MONTHLY BULLETIN brief mention was made of the impetus recently given to the growing and manufacturing of cotton in Peru and Chile, and the encouragement that was being given in this direction by the respective Governments of these countries. The Permanent Exposition of Machinery, recently inaugurated in Lima is attracting the attention of manufacturers in the United States and Europe to the opportunities for introducing their machinery in Peru; and the decree of recent date admitting free of duty all machinery to be devoted to textile manufacture, is not only inspiring a new life in that industry in Chile, but is also opening a very desirable market for American machinery.

The following, bearing on this subject, taken from the "Textile Manufacturers' Journal" of June 4, published in the city of New York, may be read with interest:

We have mentioned, from time to time, the development of the cotton manufacturing industry in various countries, simply with a view of showing the competition that the American merchant will have to contend against. Peru and Chile are said to be making much more extensive preparations for cotton raising than ever before, and the destination of the crop is not to be abroad, as hitherto, but it will be absorbed in local mills. Peru, of course, has been engaged in the raising of cotton quite extensively for some time, but now the industry seems to be spreading with great rapidity into Chile. Formerly the raw material was shipped almost entirely to England, but it is now proposed to build up extensive manufacturing industry in that country. The Government is offering every inducement to growers of cotton, and, as a consequence, a very considerable area is being devoted to the raising of the raw material. As an evidence of the earnestness with which those prominent in the administration of affairs have entered into the project, the abolition of the duty on all textile machinery imported into the country until 1902 may be cited. It is stated that this change in tariff has exerted more or less of an influence upon the shipment of textile machinery from the United States, several large orders having been sent of late.

In Peru the manufacture of cloth is further advanced than in Chile, though the mills as yet make only very coarse grades. It is thought that with the importation of new and improved machinery a decided impetus will be given to manufacturing, and that those who have derived large profits from their business with this country will need to look to their laurels.

NEW CABINET.

The Ministry of Peru as lately reorganized is as follows:

President of the Cabinet, and Minister of Justice, Religion, and Instruction .... Dr. Don José Jorge Loayza.
Minister of Foreign Relations .... Dr. Don Melitón F. Porras.
Minister of the Interior and Police......... Don José María de la Puente.
Minister of War and Marine .... Don Manuel J. Cuadros.
Minister of Finance and Commerce........ Don Ignacio Rey.
Minister of Public Works .... Dr. Don Francisco Almenara Butler.

SANTO DOMINGO.

TRADE CONDITIONS.

United States Consul GRIMKE has submitted to the Department of State his annual report on the trade and industrial conditions existing in the Dominican Republic, which is printed in full in the Consular Reports for June. According to Mr. GRIMKE's statement, the decline in the price of sugar, the staple product of the Republic, and other causes have produced a general business depression in the country. Practically all of the sugar produced and not consumed in the domestic market is exported to New York; the aggregate value of that export during the year 1897 amounted to $2,463,906.62. Of the other articles exported, logwood, lignum-vitæ, mahogany, honey, wax, and bananas went to the United States, while the coffee, cacao, and tobacco found a market almost wholly in France, Germany, Belgium, and England.

In the consular district represented by Mr. GRIMKE, the aggregate quantity of lumber imported, all of which came from the United States, amounted to 2,500,000 feet, and retailed at $37.50, gold, per thousand feet. Flour, which retails at $12 per barrel in gold, comes entirely from the United States. Until recently, all the refined kerosene oil came from the United States, but the refinery at La Romana, recently established, will doubtless limit the importation of this article. Owing to the inferior quality of butter brought from the United States, that commodity now comes almost exclusively from Denmark. The best quality retails in Santo Domingo at 62½ cents per pound, while the inferior grades sell for 37½ cents. Cheese is imported from Holland and the United States; the Dutch cheese selling for 25 cents gold, and the American for 22½ cents per pound.

Of miscellaneous articles, canned meats, vegetables, and milk come mostly from the United States; salt fish and pork, wholly; and lard, cooking oils, and lager beer are supplied in part from the United States. Wines come from France and Spain. A brewery has recently been established in Santo Domingo, owned by American citizens. American beer sells for $4.50 per case, while the home-made article brings $2.25.

Bull. No. 1——3

Machinery for plantations, locomotives, cars, rails, iron bridges, etc., come principally from the United States, but Germany is becoming a strong competitor in these lines. In hardware, England, Germany, and Belgium compete with the United States. Coal retails in Santo Domingo at $12 to $13, gold, per ton, the greater portion of which comes from England. England also supplies the greater part of the cotton goods; the American article, though of better quality, is more expensive than its British rival, which explains the predominance of English goods in that market. Cotton goods retail at from $7\frac{1}{2}$ to 25 cents, gold, per yard. Silk goods come from France exclusively, and retail at from 75 cents to $3, gold, per yard. France and England send the hats of all kinds for both sexes. The United States supplies all the electrical machinery used in the island. Many of the sugar plantations are now being lighted by electricity. France shares with the United States the trade in bicycles. Consul GRIMKE reports that the methods used in the United States of packing goods are severely criticised by merchants and planters.

Agricultural laborers receive from 50 cents to 75 cents per day for wages; in the cities, workmen are paid from 50 cents to $2; domestic servants, with board included, get from $3 to $12 per month; and office clerks range from $15 to $75 per month.

American interests preponderate in the Republic, about one-half of the sugar plantations being owned by citizens of the United States. The San Domingo Improvement Company, with headquarters at New York City, collects the revenues of the country under a contract made with the Government some years ago. A fortnightly line of steamers, owned and operated by W. P. CLYDE & Co., of New York, plies between ports of the country and the latter city.

UNITED STATES.

TRADE WITH LATIN-AMERICA.

STATEMENT OF IMPORTS AND EXPORTS.

Following is the latest statement from figures compiled by the Bureau of Statistics, O. P. AUSTIN, Chief, United States Treasury Department, showing the value of the trade between the United

States and Latin-American countries. The report is for the month of April, 1898, corrected to June 1, 1898, with a comparative statement for the corresponding month of the previous year; also for the ten months ending April, 1898, compared with the corresponding period of the fiscal year 1897. It should be explained that the figures from the various custom-houses, showing imports and exports for any one month, are not received at the Treasury Department until about the 20th of the following month, and some time is necessarily consumed in compilation and printing, so that the returns for April, for example, are not published until some time in June.

IMPORTS OF MERCHANDISE.

Articles and countries.	April—		Ten months ending April—	
	1897.	1898.	1897.	1898.
Chemicals:				
Logwood (*Palo campeche; Páu campeche; Campêche*)—				
Mexico	$1,334	$583	$11,249	$21,700
Central America				
Coal, bituminous (*Carbón bituminoso; Carvão betuminoso; Charbon de terre*):				
Mexico	24,744	17,836	174,653	160,786
Cocoa (*Cacao; Coco ou Cacáo crú; Cacao*):				
Brazil	9,833	... ...	318,325	161,206
Other South America	31,391	106,641	751,783	989,749
Coffee (*Café; Café; Café*):				
Central America	1,200,861	642,068	4,742,324	3,497,479
Mexico	1,146,811	422,876	3,842,346	3,009,861
Brazil	3,547,546	3,117,431	45,410,922	35,244,158
Other South America	725,920	1,108,316	9,368,085	7,587,559
Cotton, unmanufactured (*Algodón en rama; Algodão em rama; Coton, non manufacturé*):				
South America		27,730	83,933	112,740
Fibers:				
Sisal grass (*Henequén; Henequen; Hennequen*)—				
Mexico	281,655	424,282	3,086,816	3,644,153
Fruits:				
Bananas (*Plátanos; Bananas; Bananes*)—				
Central America	207,174	196,840	1,106,894	1,193,740
South America	40,972	56,737	433,555	445,809

IMPORTS OF MERCHANDISE.

Articles and countries.	April—		Ten months ending April—	
	1897.	1898.	1897.	1898.
Fruits—Continued.				
Oranges (Naranjas; Laranjas; Oranges)—				
Mexico	$497	$109	$253,592	$134,596
Fur skins (Pieles finas; Peñes; Fourrures):				
South America	20	4,590	16,428	35,769
Hides and skins (Cueros y pieles; Couros e pelles; Cuirs et peaux):				
Central America	14,091	13,091	204,160	163,359
Mexico	231,107	605,198	1,500,252	1,494,793
South America	959,303	793,561	6,857,370	7,463,004
India rubber, crude (Goma elástica cruda; Borracha crúa; Caoutchouc, brut):				
Central America	35,262	48,826	373,274	367,846
Mexico	5,525	4,816	25,186	20,016
Brazil	904,891	990,918	10,094,465	13,515,363
Other South America	29,585	50,114	397,551	529,804
Lead, in pigs, bars, etc. (Plomo en galápagos, barras, etc.; Chumbo em linguados, barras, etc.; Plombs en saumons, en barres, etc.):				
Mexico	100,123	110,247	1,136,140	1,418,482
Sugar, not above No. 16 Dutch standard (Azúcar, no superior al No. 16 de la escala holandesa; Assucar não superior ao No. 16 de padrão hollandez; Sucre, pas au-dessus du type hollandais No. 16):				
Central America		79,914		79,914
Mexico	1,306	2,197	15,023	21,904
Brazil	254,529	465,483	2,115,759	1,833,885
Other South America	494,146	156,157	4,415,101	3,531,543
Tobacco, leaf (Tabaco en rama; Tabaco em folha; Tabac en feuilles):				
Mexico	38,202	12,077	250,878	214,485
Wood, mahogany (Madera, caoba; Mogno; Acajou):				
Central America	27,105	30,404	102,069	139,116
Mexico	34,107	3,220	252,940	268,626
South America	3,806	2,578	31,892	41,457
Wool (Lana; Lã; Laine):				
South America—				
Class 1 (clothing)	1,445,029	257,553	3,235,245	775,004
Class 2 (combing)	204,749		476,898	9,598
Class 3 (carpet)	290,954	218,025	756,448	478,093

EXPORTS OF DOMESTIC MERCHANDISE.

Articles and countries.	April—		Ten months ending April—	
	1897.	1898.	1897.	1898.
Agricultural implements (*Instrumentos de agricultura; Instrumentos de agricultura; Machines agricoles*):				
Central America	$7, 120	$181	$31, 482	$14, 394
Mexico	20, 866	9, 273	112, 886	97, 701
Santo Domingo	375	219	1, 327	1, 056
Argentina	2, 690	20, 266	370, 026	334, 604
Brazil	1, 260	2, 521	18, 280	23, 771
Colombia	364	279	3, 234	2, 948
Other South America	5, 063	10, 501	132, 896	158, 663
Animals:				
Cattle (*Ganado vacuno; Gado; Betail*)—				
Central America	800	....	12, 015	7, 018
Mexico	1, 400	16, 765	23, 806	58, 680
South America	....	82	2, 737	6, 962
Hogs (*Cerdos; Porcos; Cochons*)—				
Mexico	1, 575	287	262, 353	44, 366
Horses (*Caballos; Cavallos; Chevaux*)—				
Central America	3, 100	1, 000	37, 002	10, 580
Mexico	6, 850	8, 666	69, 583	75, 100
South America	1, 200	1, 050	11, 655	5, 700
Sheep (*Carneros; Carneiros; Moutons*):				
Mexico	840	822	11, 877	9, 110
South America	867	1, 157	8, 403	10, 134
Books, maps, engravings, etc. (*Libros, mapas, grabados, etc.; Livros, mappas, gravuras, etc.; Livres, cartes de géographie, gravures, etc.*):				
Central America	3, 495	1, 326	57, 145	33, 302
Mexico	6, 083	4, 017	145, 632	111, 467
Santo Domingo	114	12	1, 240	455
Argentina	1, 630	1, 686	18, 507	24, 735
Brazil	23, 068	6, 105	84, 361	150, 721
Colombia	46	570	71, 349	16, 621
Other South America	7, 293	407	47, 987	35, 634
Breadstuffs:				
Corn (*Maíz; Milho; Maïs*)—				
Central America	6, 554	5, 355	33, 462	54, 845
Mexico	252, 731	1, 514	3, 058, 328	41, 146
Santo Domingo	80	....	329	166
South America	1, 113	1, 022	11, 323	35, 169
Wheat (*Trigo; Trigo; Blé*)—				
Central America	2, 100	2, 280	63, 451	35, 649
South America	305	83, 037	153, 204	1, 533, 383
Wheat flour (*Harina de trigo; Farina de trigo; Farine de blé*)—				
Central America	99, 629	108, 057	933, 511	958, 578
Mexico	10, 242	14, 153	80, 085	64, 354
Santo Domingo	17, 673	24, 000	127, 778	147, 687
Brazil	465, 543	211, 530	3, 104, 966	2, 780, 899
Colombia	41, 842	20, 739	485, 431	438, 712
Other South America	155, 289	127, 971	1, 271, 638	1, 464, 606

EXPORTS OF DOMESTIC MERCHANDISE.

Articles and countries.	April—		Ten months ending April—	
	1907.	1908.	1907.	1908.
Carriages, cars, etc., and parts of (Carruajes, carros y sus accesorios; Carruagens, carros, e partes de carro; Voitures, wagons et leurs parties:				
Central America	$6,154	$4,786	$121,266	$75,243
Mexico	39,400	21,424	372,422	409,431
Santo Domingo	662	152	12,121	23,574
Argentina	5,582	3,592	130,313	194,403
Brazil	420	113,535	102,434	507,606
Colombia	35	1,608	47,320	36,336
Other South America	3,864	2,350	36,038	69,114
Cycles and parts of (Bicicletas y sus accesorios; Bicyclettes e accessorios; Bicyclettes et leurs parties):				
Central America	1,333	445	50,772	6,952
Mexico	7,687	5,425	60,742	53,566
Santo Domingo	1,208	196	4,220	4,134
Argentina	3,423	3,760	36,061	72,463
Brazil	4,177	9,351	21,504	80,237
Colombia	1,206	480	19,584	14,691
Other South America	7,163	2,396	62,551	42,245
Clocks and watches (Relojes de pared y de bolsillo; Relogios de parede e de bolso; Pendules et montres):				
Central America	1,373	1,202	11,341	6,582
Mexico	2,809	1,468	22,232	17,030
Argentina	769	541	31,535	24,345
Brazil	3,107	7,840	55,399	37,563
Other South America	12,950	4,855	88,459	75,178
Coal (Carbón; Carvão; Charbon):				
Central America	1,967	658	24,252	15,744
Mexico	66,901	55,089	513,599	741,154
Santo Domingo	1,132	433	23,401	9,284
Brazil		15,454	60,573	64,546
Colombia	6,314		19,064	32,434
Other South America	795	45	23,713	17,600
Copper (Cobre; Cobre; Cuivre):				
Mexico	1,703	7,639	10,471	15,705
Cotton, unmanufactured (Algodón no manufacturado; Algodão não manufacturado; Coton non manufacturé):				
Mexico	37,718	69,974	1,213,737	1,274,370
Cotton cloths (Tejidos de algodón; Fazendas de algodão; Coton, manufacturé):				
Central America	48,426	41,677	502,334	324,953
Mexico	44,998	38,634	298,989	342,381
Santo Domingo	6,947	21,657	83,660	90,450
Argentina	12,483	14,558	259,863	152,934
Brazil	55,565	59,454	509,080	456,861
Colombia	33,927	17,164	307,682	232,996
Other South America	130,489	53,046	1,205,850	875,264

EXPORTS OF DOMESTIC MERCHANDISE.

Articles and countries.	April—		Ten months ending April—	
	1897.	1898.	1897.	1898.
Wearing apparel (cotton) (*Ropa de algodón; Roupa de algodão; Vêtements en coton*):				
Central America	$15, 827	$20, 575	$198, 302	$171, 722
Mexico	33, 443	26, 953	298, 735	262, 475
Santo Domingo	4, 171	2, 075	28, 004	17, 895
Argentina	4, 046	466	56, 298	25, 497
Brazil	4, 099	5, 296	60, 047	44, 779
Colombia	3, 719	3, 078	42, 559	33, 982
Other South America	3, 207	2, 923	45, 451	30, 234
Fruits and nuts (*Frutas y nueces; Frutas e nozes; Fruits et noisettes*):				
Central America	4, 837	2, 032	49, 315	32, 339
Mexico	4, 657	3, 466	64, 173	47, 548
Santo Domingo	31	8	2, 293	1, 347
Argentina		565	4, 379	7, 660
Brazil	527	494	10, 805	10, 728
Colombia	717	1, 211	8, 295	9, 307
Other South America	1, 358	1, 104	31, 629	21, 792
Hides and skins (*Cueros y pieles; Couros e pelles; Cuirs et peaux*):				
Central America			1, 411	
Mexico	420	210	27, 101	1, 994
Hops (*Lúpulos; Lupulos; Houblon*):				
Central America	102	220	2, 504	2, 861
Mexico	3, 560	512	44, 121	31, 951
Santo Domingo			287	19
South America	147	111	1, 168	1, 148
Instruments:				
Electric and scientific apparatus (*Aparatos electricos y cientificos; Apparelhos electricos e scientificos; Appareils électriques et scientifiques*)—				
Central America	4, 799	4, 920	86, 905	51, 453
Mexico	31, 535	29, 039	226, 598	235, 166
Argentina	7, 658	34, 657	109, 857	87, 099
Brazil	10, 802	2, 659	78, 271	82, 352
Other South America	7, 601	6, 717	186, 566	106, 058
Iron and steel, manufactures of:				
Builders' hardware, and saws and tools (*Materiales de metal para construcción, sierras y herramientas Ferragens, serras e ferramentas; Matériaux de construction en fer et acier, scies et outils*)—				
Central America	16, 624	6, 890	125, 606	71, 255
Mexico	56, 529	37, 438	535, 712	362, 414
Santo Domingo	1, 544	1, 511	8, 949	11, 890
Argentina	12, 298	10, 299	186, 613	117, 736
Brazil	23, 816	20, 080	212, 484	139, 481
Colombia	5, 175	5, 372	97, 482	74, 528
Other South America	20, 744	8, 398	219, 330	173, 393

EXPORTS OF DOMESTIC MERCHANDISE.

Articles and countries.	April—		Ten Months ending April—	
	1897.	1896.	1897.	1896.
Iron and steel, manufactures of— Continued.				
Sewing machines and parts of (*Máquinas de coser y accesorios; Machinas de coser e accessorios; Machines à coudre et leurs parties*)—				
Central America	$4,023	$971	$74,847	$25,756
Mexico	14,644	20,199	164,228	181,439
Santo Domingo	106	28	972	1,236
Argentina	135	1,586	81,116	70,216
Brazil	9,124	10,376	103,850	79,456
Colombia	9,919	11,495	96,372	70,476
Other South America	7,049	3,888	102,743	85,475
Typewriting machines and parts of (*Máquinas de escribir y accesorios; Machinas de escribir e accessorios; Machines à ecrire et leurs parties*):				
Central America	253	87	10,483	2,310
Mexico	758	662	19,783	22,565
Santo Domingo	40	......	267	90
Argentina	685	300	10,950	12,771
Brazil	235	1,048	3,557	4,483
Colombia	655	261	3,088	3,866
Other South America	1,744	1,188	8,902	13,032
Leather, other than sole (*Cuero, distinto del de suela; Couro não para solas, Cuirs, autres que pour semelles*):				
Central America	495	369	4,383	3,392
Mexico	829	572	14,128	8,312
Santo Domingo	242	30	752	569
Argentina	......	1,909	3,905	4,360
Brazil	2,283	6,960	16,171	45,960
Colombia	110	479	2,111	3,181
Other South America	554	1,236	13,389	11,554
Boots and shoes (*Calzado; Calçados; Chaussures*):				
Central America	6,408	6,370	79,515	75,690
Mexico	9,886	5,901	48,065	61,210
Colombia	3,911	1,987	33,353	32,810
Other South America	1,957	4,909	23,635	23,799
Naval stores: Rosin, tar, etc. (*Resina y alquitrán; Resina e alcatrão; Résine et goudron*):				
Central America	2,203	2,707	19,842	13,477
Mexico	501	1,192	5,432	8,134
Santo Domingo	1,069	1,532	4,540	5,517
Argentina	......	13,354	57,932	72,320
Brazil	5,873	13,551	206,318	175,027
Colombia	1,893	818	16,627	10,173
Other South America	4,145	3,390	83,684	79,812

EXPORTS OF DOMESTIC MERCHANDISE.

Articles and countries.	April—		Ten months ending April—	
	1897.	1898.	1897.	1898.
Turpentine, spirits of (*Aguarrds; Agua-raz; Térébenthine*):				
Central America....	$484	$243	$3,797	$2,612
Mexico........................	488	324	2,203	2,659
Santo Domingo.................	29	71	272	447
Argentina.................	173	21,918	46,921	95,245
Brazil........................	797	10,016	39,176	58,606
Colombia	603	368	4,997	3,694
Other South America............	4,029	3,103	34,001	37,355
Oils, mineral, crude (*Aceites, minerales, crudos; Oleos, mineraes, crus; Huiles minérales, Brutes*):				
Mexico.........................	38,063	28,702	284,066	283,486
Oils, mineral, refined or manufactured (*Aceites minerales, refinados ó manufacturados; Oleos mineraes, refinados ó manufacturados; Huiles minérales, raffinées ou manufacturées*):				
Central America................	6,374	15,895	116,643	96,275
Mexico.....................:...	14,268	10,513	139,258	150,264
Santo Domingo.................	4,524	909	31,070	49,764
Argentina.....................	24,742	101,610	933,787	801,787
Brazil	167,534	88,781	1,291,967	1,214,572
Colombia	7,926	9,695	99,357	79,502
Other South America	82,798	40,848	867,216	684,884
Oils, vegetable (*Aceites vegetales; Oleos vegetaes; Huiles végétales*):				
Central America................	361	101	4,460	2,301
Mexico	9,215	11,384	255,319	289,209
Santo Domingo.................	2,200	4,136	11,106	20,294
Argentina.....................	....	353	10,971	4,188
Brazil........................	29,278	32,881	137,108	215,759
Other South America............	6,582	10,575	63,508	80,046
Paraffin and paraffin wax (*Parafina y cera de parafina; Paraffina e cera de parafina; Paraffine et cire faite de cette substance*):				
Central America................	4,438	2,070	28,175	16,029
Mexico	7,221	18,122	130,857	138,594
Brazil	958	849	12,428	9,238
Other South America............	30	102	3,227	5,230
Provisions, comprising meat and dairy products :				
Beef, canned (*Carne de vaca en latas; Carne de vacca em latas; Bœuf conservé*)—				
Central America...............	2,919	1,310	28,070	24,473
Mexico	781	480	12,640	12,033
Santo Domingo.................	....	4	51	33
Argentina.....................	21	....	51	357
Brazil........................	1,040	2,367	16,569	15,947
Colombia	556	277	5,716	5,156
Other South America...........	1,388	682	10,760	10,560

EXPORTS OF DOMESTIC MERCHANDISE.

Articles and countries.	April—		Ten months ending April—	
	1897.	1898.	1897.	1898.
Provisions, comprising meat and dairy products—Continued.				
Beef, salted or pickled *Carne de vaca, salada ó en salmuera, Carne de vacca, salgada ou em salmoura; Bœuf, salé ou en saumure)*—				
Central America................	$2, 208	$5, 069	$24, 471	$33, 407
Mexico......................	105	77	194	492
Santo Domingo	132	258	2, 199	1, 643
Brazil	255	274	3, 356	1, 112
Colombia	1, 870	919	10. 117	9, 802
Other South America	10, 316	11, 861	141, 248	132, 871
Tallow (*Sebo; Sebo; Suif*)—				
Central America..............	8, 055	10, 002	101. 081	79, 001
Mexico.....	3, 354	2, 042	34, 291	21, 701
Santo Domingo..............	4, 942	7, 397	20, 546	25, 839
Brazil......................	84	68	4, 401	24, 560
Colombia	533	784	6, 917	16, 550
Other South America..........	1, 080	404	11, 762	10. 224
Bacon (*Tocino; Toucinho; Lard fumé*)—				
Central America..............	1, 797	1, 000	14, 849	13, 762
Mexico	513	404	7, 821	8, 140
Santo Domingo..............	414	191	2, 241	1, 412
Brazil......................	142, 641	26, 367	871, 385	477. 124
Colombia	245	29	1, 340	1, 054
Other South America..........	3, 483	1, 913	17, 943	25, 137
Hams (*Jamones; Presunto; Jambons*)—				
Central America..............	3, 183	1, 853	26, 756	24, 120
Mexico.....................	1, 886	1, 031	24, 659	18, 248
Santo Domingo..............	773	750	6, 449	5, 331
Brazil......................	165	816	1, 008	2, 922
Colombia	1, 621	622	12, 489	11, 106
Other South America..........	6, 474	4, 162	80, 483	73, 608
Pork (*Carne de puerco; Carne de porco; Porc*)—				
Central America..............	6, 794	9, 113	47, 376	60, 042
Santo Domingo..............	390	603	3, 565	3, 204
Brazil......................	11, 430	70	17, 107	555
Colombia	1, 129	486	5, 424	6, 235
Other South America..........	15, 143	13, 448	157, 203	171, 800
Lard (*Manteca; Banha; Saindoux*)—				
Central America..............	10, 131	16, 515	83, 740	116, 866
Mexico	26, 389	6, 828	278, 628	153, 165
Santo Domingo..............	3, 192	3, 209	18, 687	18, 544
Argentina...................	.....	1, 200	3, 783	2, 954
Brazil......................	93, 554	142, 617	560, 054	881, 997
Colombia	14, 875	9, 421	124, 798	93, 560
Other South America..........	60, 330	55, 224	541, 057	512, 753

EXPORTS OF DOMESTIC MERCHANDISE.

Articles and countries.	April—		Ten months ending April—	
	1897.	1898.	1897.	1898.
Provisions, comprising meat and dairy products—Continued.				
Oleo and oleomargarine (*Grasa y oleomargarina; Oleo e oleomargarina; Óléo et oléomargarine*)—				
Central America	$44	$306	$76	$858
Mexico	16	291	642	823
Colombia	220	1, 273	5, 770	6, 532
Other South America	1, 149	1, 005	27, 672	13, 583
Butter (*Mantequilla; Manteiga; Beurre*)—				
Central America	3, 709	3, 191	37, 560	40, 699
Mexico	4, 259	2, 577	32, 930	34, 403
Santo Domingo	672	1, 436	5, 756	6, 151
Brazil	1, 371	9, 741	30, 531	76, 980
Colombia	1, 912	797	14, 217	16, 522
Other South America	8, 232	7, 148	73, 330	69, 536
Cheese (*Queso; Queijo; Fromage*)—				
Central America	1, 838	1, 275	16, 045	15, 001
Mexico	1, 182	934	13, 118	12, 176
Santo Domingo	649	506	3, 019	3, 282
Brazil		75	80	257
Colombia	1, 116	561	9, 025	9, 316
Other South America	1, 680	1, 789	13, 317	15, 080
Seeds (*Semillas; Sementes; Semence*)—				
Central America	1, 165	387	9, 220	4, 647
Mexico	2, 989	478	19, 298	28, 621
Santo Domingo	49	77	379	664
Argentina	40		782	348
Brazil	716		1, 571	858
Colombia	97	107	2, 146	1, 516
Other South America	162	75	4, 472	1, 769
Sugar, refined (*Azúcar refinado; Assucar refinado; Sucre raffiné*):				
Central America	2, 731	4, 114	50, 060	44, 786
Mexico	378	2, 062	19, 531	13, 413
Santo Domingo	150	98	1, 902	1, 504
Colombia	2, 932	2, 611	39, 407	24, 201
Other South America	852		1, 987	5, 018
Tobacco, unmanufactured (*Tabaco no manufacturado; Tabaco não manufacturado; Tabac non manufacturé*):				
Central America	312	2, 513	14, 211	28, 014
Mexico	11, 959	5, 887	102, 237	114, 421
Argentina		529	4, 055	3, 904
Colombia	231	787	2, 356	6, 432
Other South America	5, 334	12, 325	80, 300	83, 299

EXPORTS OF DOMESTIC MERCHANDISE.

Articles and countries.	April—		Ten months ending April—	
	1897.	1898.	1897.	1898.
Tobacco, manufactures of (*Manufacturas de tabaco; Manufacturas de tabaco; Tabac fabriqué*):				
Central America............	$7,196	$4,872	$53,958	$37,195
Mexico.........................	947	476	12,557	17,386
Argentina......................	204	....	48,057	1,807
Brazil	....	....	1,355	560
Colombia	149	440	1,219	2,984
Other South America...........	5,755	7,138	50,833	64,076
Wood, unmanufactured (*Madera no manufacturado; Madeira não manufacturado; Bois brut*):				
Central America................	6,972	2,805	132,005	48,362
Mexico.........................	23,341	37,088	233,321	203,116
Argentina................... ...	....	595	33,516	7,085
Brazil	6,500	....	16,194	7,278
Colombia	7,874	286	16,409	22,393
Other South America...........	214	18,100	14,836	49,300
Lumber (*Maderas; Maderas; Bois de construction*):				
Central America................	13,749	1,326	116,901	33,084
Mexico.........................	114,821	77,866	773,821	699,730
Santo Domingo.................	3,195	872	44,640	32,189
Argentina......................	17,978	91,839	893,421	755,884
Brazil	48,303	44,075	581,368	575,412
Colombia	3,422	805	39,860	48,350
Other South America...........	49,817	25,175	606,468	386,253
Furniture (*Muebles; Mobilia; Meubles*):				
Central America................	9,670	3,078	128,555	69,706
Mexico.........................	23,423	11,756	158,727	129,704
Santo Domingo.................	700	1,591	10,302	10,666
Argentina......................	2,027	2,911	77,603	59,494
Brazil.........................	3,791	3,022	42,332	33,095
Colombia	2,591	2,230	33,252	29,200
Other South America...........	6,459	3,066	93,160	62,263
Wool, raw (*Lana cruda; Lã crúa; Laines brutes*):				
Mexico	....	....	140,083	10

URUGUAY.

NEW MINISTRY.

The Ministry of Uruguay as constituted under the administration of President JUAN LINDOLFO CUESTAS is as follows:

Minister of State.......................... Señor Don José ROMÁN MENDOZA.
Minister of Foreign Affairs................ Señor Dr. Don JOAQUIN DE SALTERAIN.
Minister of Fomento....... .... Señor Dr. Don JACOBO H. VADELA.
Minister of War and Navy................. General CASTRO.

VENEZUELA.

THE TRADE OF CARACAS AND DISTRICT IN 1897.

From the annual report of Mr. W. A. ANDRAL, acting consul of Great Britain at Caracas, to the British Foreign Office, the following information relating to the trade of Caracas, and that consular district is taken:

The general condition of trade in Venezuela for the year 1897 can not be reported as satisfactory. The leading cause of this was the failure of the coffee crop, which naturally lessened the purchasing power at home and reduced the credit abroad. This condition, it is believed, will be greatly minimized for the ensuing season by the promising outlook presented by the growing crop of coffee. The coffee estates in the country number about 33,000, and those of cocoa about 5,000. These two products represent the chief agricultural staple of the Republic. The high protective tariff (practically prohibitive) placed upon sugar, has stimulated the planting of the sugar cane to the extent that there are now 11,000 cane estates, and it is anticipated that this culture will speedily take a prominent place in the agricultural features of the country.

Numerous clubs have recently been founded, with the view of arousing the planters to the importance of the application of scientific methods in fertilizing, irrigating, etc., and in the use of improved machinery in the various processes of preparing the produce for the market. The great desideratum to the progress of the country, as stated by Consul ANDRAL, is immigration of a class which will go into the country and help develop the agricultural resources. Recently (as stated in detail in the MONTHLY BULLETIN for May) the Government made a contract with an Italian for the introduction of a large number of Italian families which are to locate on the public lands.

On the subject of the development of trade with Venezuela and the agency therein of the National Association of Manufacturers of the United States, the following extract from the report is made:

The Americans are taking a great hold on the Venezuelan market. They are not so conservative as their competitors and their business methods are quicker; but the principal reason seems to be that they are so much nearer the market. This suits the Venezuelan business man, who does not keep a large stock on hand, but who renews the supply just when it is required. Then there are political sympathies between the United States and Venezuela, of which the former are not backward in taking advantage.

The most important move in the direction of developing the commercial relations between the United States and Venezuela is that made by the National Association of Manufacturers, which has its seat at Philadelphia. In the beginning of the year 1896 an agent was sent out to Venezuela to make an agreement for the establishment of a sample warehouse or permanent show room where American manufactures could be introduced to the market under the most favorable conditions. The contract was made with the corresponding department of the Venezuelan Government; and all preliminaries having been arranged, the commissioner returned to Venezuela in the month of November, 1897, and announced to the Government that the exhibition of samples would soon be inaugurated. The commissioner's report to the "Department of Public Advancement" states that the purpose of the warehouse is: To give merchants, agriculturists, etc., the opportunity of examining on the spot the real article produced, instead of depending on catalogues and illustrations; to supply information respecting addresses of American manufacturers and their prices and terms; to provide a reading room where newspapers and all publications relating to industries and commerce may be examined, and to show, when practicable, the working of agricultural machinery, etc. In fact, it is to be an object lesson of the capabilities of American industry. The exhibition will also serve as a center for commercial men, and there will be an information bureau, which will keep manufacturers and their agents posted as to the requirements of the market and the business customs of the country, and will make known to American capitalists the opportunities to invest their money in Venezuela.

The Government allows the importation, free of duty, of all goods which are intended for exhibition in the sample warehouse. Great benefits to Venezuela and an extraordinary increase of the business between the two countries are predicted as the result of this step on the part of the National Association. At the time of writing this the Exhibition has been opened with the concurrence of about a score of influential business men from Pennsylvania and New York. The President of Venezuela was present at the inauguration. Speeches were made in which the friendliness of the two nations and the possibilities offered by their ultimate commercial relations were dwelt upon, and public opinion is much in favor of America and Americans.

If, as I stated above, there were already signs that the trade of the United States was taking the lead, it is only natural to suppose that a movement of this kind will foster that tendency, and that in a short time American products will supersede all others of the same classes, and only such articles as can not well be produced in the United States will then be left for other foreign trade. The bulk of the trade with the United States is in food stuffs, agricultural implements and machinery. Several contracts for the supply of tubing for waterworks have been secured by an American firm.

The Venezuelan press, in alluding to the Association and the work it proposes to effect, asks whether the Americans will adopt the European system of giving long credit or will succeed in converting Venezuelan merchants to their style of transacting business, and remarks that on this point the result of the struggle depends, because the long-credit system will always attract a certain portion of trade. As it is a difficult task to get Spanish-Americans to change their custom, some time will elapse before that result will be apparent.

THE METRIC SYSTEM.

CONGRESS TO BE HELD IN PARIS IN 1900.

Leading textile manufacturers of the world are moving to hold a congress in Paris in 1900, in connection with the Exposition to be held that year, for the purpose of deciding upon the adoption of the metric system. The want of a uniform system of numbering the thread used in the textile industry has led to much trouble and complication, and it is mainly to overcome this difficulty that the proposed congress has been called. This question was the subject of investigation at congresses held at Vienna in 1873, at Brussels in 1874, at Turin in 1875, and Paris in 1878 and 1889.

In a communication on this subject to the Department of State, HENRY W. GILBERT, United States Consul at Liege, says: At all the former congresses progress has been made, but no practical result has been obtained. There are two reasons for the failure— uniformity in this matter has not become general, even in France, and the metric system has not been adopted by all countries. England places goods in foreign markets that are not numbered and manufactured according to the metric system, and it is also permitted to be done in the United States. Our country is making strenuous and successful efforts to compete with other nations for foreign trade in merchandise, and, as our capacity to produce is almost unlimited, it would seem that our textile manufacturers should be well represented at the above-named congress in Paris in 1900.

If the exporters of the United States will employ the metric system, they will be able to offer their wares to foreign buyers and consumers in the weights and measures to which they are accustomed.

EXPORTS OF DOMESTIC MERCHANDISE.

Articles and countries.	April—		Ten months ending April—	
	1897.	1898.	1897.	1898.
Carriages, cars, etc., and parts of (*Carruages, carros y sus accesorios; Carruagens, carros, e partes de carros; Voitures, wagons et leurs parties*):				
Central America...............	$8,354	$4,786	$129,065	$35,243
Mexico.......................	39,800	18,824	319,622	469,431
Santo Domingo................	660	132	12,924	23,374
Argentina....................	5,382	8,592	120,313	194,403
Brazil	820	213,535	102,434	507,606
Colombia	91	1,698	47,930	36,336
Other South America..........	3,409	2,250	36,038	69,114
Cycles and parts of (*Biciclos y sus accesorios; Bicyclos e accessorios; Bicyclettes et leurs parties*):				
Central America...............	1,319	445	50,772	6,952
Mexico.....\.................	7,687	5,825	60,782	53,566
Santo Domingo................	1,006	196	4,220	4,134
Argentina....................	3,823	8,769	36,061	72,463
Brazil	4,177	9,351	21,504	80,237
Colombia	1,205	440	19,384	14,691
Other South America..........	7,163	2,996	62,551	42,245
Clocks and watches (*Relojes de pared y de bolsillo; Relogios de pared e de bolso; Pendules et montres*):				
Central America...............	1,373	1,201	11,341	6,582
Mexico.......................	2,409	1,464	22,232	17,030
Argentina....................	769	541	31,835	24,345
Brazil	3,107	7,846	55,399	37,563
Other South America..........	12,950	4,855	88,459	75,178
Coal (*Carbón; Carvão; Charbon*):				
Central America...............	1,967	688	24,252	18,744
Mexico.......................	66,901	88,089	513,899	741,154
Santo Domingo................	1,132	433	23,401	9,284
Brazil.......................		18,484	60,573	64,546
Colombia	6,314	....	19,064	32,434
Other South America..........	795	45	23,713	17,600
Copper (*Cobre; Cobre; Cuivre*):				
Mexico.......................	1,703	7,639	10,471	18,705
Cotton, unmanufactured (*Algodón no manufacturado; Algodão não manufacturado; Coton non manufacturé*):				
Mexico.......................	37,718	69,974	1,213,737	1,274,370
Cotton cloths (*Tejidos de algodón; Fazendas de algodão; Coton, manufacturé*):				
Central America...............	48,426	41,677	502,334	324,953
Mexico....	44,998	38,634	298,989	342,381
Santo Domingo................	6,947	21,657	83,660	90,450
Argentina....................	12,483	14,558	259,863	152,934
Brazil	55,565	59,454	509,080	456,861
Colombia	33,927	17,164	307,682	232,996
Other South America..........	130,489	53,046	1,205,850	875,264

EXPORTS OF DOMESTIC MERCHANDISE.

Articles and countries.	April—		Ten months ending April—	
	1897.	1898.	1897.	1898.
Wearing apparel (cotton) (*Ropa de algodón; Roupa de algodão; Vêtements en coton*):				
Central America	$15,827	$20,575	$198,302	$171,722
Mexico	33,443	26,953	298,735	262,475
Santo Domingo	4,171	2,075	28,004	17,895
Argentina	4,046	466	56,298	25,497
Brazil	4,099	5,296	60,047	44,779
Colombia	3,719	3,078	42,559	33,982
Other South America	3,207	2,923	45,451	30,234
Fruits and nuts (*Frutas y nueces; Frutas e nozes; Fruits et noisettes*):				
Central America	4,837	2,032	49,315	32,339
Mexico	4,657	3,466	64,173	47,548
Santo Domingo	31	8	2,293	1,347
Argentina		565	4,379	7,660
Brazil	527	494	10,805	10,728
Colombia	717	1,211	8,295	9,307
Other South America	1,358	1,104	31,629	21,792
Hides and skins (*Cueros y pieles; Couros e pelles; Cuirs et peaux*):				
Central America			1,411	
Mexico	420	210	27,101	1,994
Hops (*Lúpulos; Lupulos; Houblon*):				
Central America	102	220	2,504	2,861
Mexico	3,560	512	44,121	31,951
Santo Domingo			287	19
South America	147	111	1,168	1,148
Instruments:				
Electric and scientific apparatus (*Aparatos eléctricos y científicos; Apparelhos eléctricos e scientificos; Appareils électriques et scientifiques*)—				
Central America	4,799	4,920	86,905	51,453
Mexico	31,535	29,039	226,598	235,166
Argentina	7,658	34,657	109,857	87,099
Brazil	10,802	2,659	78,271	82,352
Other South America	7,601	6,717	186,566	106,058
Iron and steel, manufactures of:				
Builders' hardware, and saws and tools (*Materiales de metal para construcción, sierras y herramientas; Ferragens, serras e ferramentas; Matériaux de construction en fer et acier, scies et outils*)—				
Central America	16,624	6,890	125,606	71,255
Mexico	56,529	37,438	535,712	362,414
Santo Domingo	1,544	1,511	8,949	11,890
Argentina	12,298	10,299	186,613	117,736
Brazil	23,816	20,080	212,484	139,481
Colombia	5,175	5,372	97,482	74,528
Other South America	20,744	8,398	219,330	173,393

EXPORTS OF DOMESTIC MERCHANDISE.

Articles and countries.	April—		Ten Months ending April—	
	1897.	1898.	1897.	1898.
Iron and steel, manufactures of— Continued. Sewing machines and parts of (*Máquinas de coser y accesorios; Machinas de coser e accessorios; Machines à coudre et leurs parties*)—				
Central America	$4,023	$971	$74,847	$25,756
Mexico	14,644	20,199	164,228	181,439
Santo Domingo	106	28	972	1,236
Argentina	135	1,586	81,116	70,216
Brazil	9,124	10,376	103,850	79,456
Colombia	9,919	11,495	96,372	70,476
Other South America	7,049	3,888	102,743	85,475
Typewriting machines and parts of (*Máquinas de escribir y accesorios; Machinas de escribir e accessorios; Machines à écrire et leurs parties*).				
Central America	253	87	10,483	2,310
Mexico	758	662	19,783	22,565
Santo Domingo	40	....	267	90
Argentina	685	300	10,950	12,771
Brazil	235	1,048	3,557	4,483
Colombia	655	261	3,088	3,866
Other South America	1,744	1,188	8,902	13,032
Leather, other than sole (*Cuero, distinto del de suela; Couro não para solas, Cuirs, autres que pour semelles*):				
Central America	495	369	4,383	3,392
Mexico	829	572	14,128	8,312
Santo Domingo	242	30	752	569
Argentina	....	1,909	3,905	4,360
Brazil	2,283	6,960	16,171	45,960
Colombia	110	479	2,111	3,181
Other South America	554	1,236	13,389	11,554
Boots and shoes (*Calzado; Calçados; Chaussures*):				
Central America	6,408	6,370	79,515	75,690
Mexico	9,886	5,901	48,065	61,210
Colombia	3,911	1,987	33,353	32,810
Other South America	1,957	4,909	23,635	23,799
Naval stores: Rosin, tar, etc. (*Resina y alquitrán; Resina e alcatrão; Résine et goudron*):				
Central America	2,203	2,707	19,842	13,477
Mexico	501	1,192	5,432	8,134
Santo Domingo	1,069	1,532	4,540	5,517
Argentina	....	13,354	57,932	72,320
Brazil	5,873	13,551	206,318	175,027
Colombia	1,893	818	16,627	10,173
Other South America	4,145	3,390	83,684	79,812

EXPORTS OF DOMESTIC MERCHANDISE.

Articles and countries.	April—		Ten months ending April—	
	1897.	1898.	1897.	1898.
Turpentine, spirits of (*Aguarrds; Agua-raz; Térébenthine*):				
Central America..............	$484	$243	$3, 797	$2, 612
Mexico........................	488	324	2, 203	2, 659
Santo Domingo.................	29	71	272	447
Argentina.....................	173	21, 918	46, 921	95, 245
Brazil........................	797	10, 016	39, 176	58, 606
Colombia	603	368	4, 997	3, 694
Other South America...........	4, 029	3, 103	34, 001	37, 355
Oils, mineral, crude (*Aceites, minerales, crudos; Oleos, mineraes, crûs; Huiles minérales, Brutes*):				
Mexico........................	38, 063	28, 702	284, 066	283, 486
Oils, mineral, refined or manufactured (*Aceites minerales, refinados ó manufacturados; Oleos mineraes, refinados ó manufacturados; Huiles minérales, raffinées ou manufacturées*):				
Central America..............	6, 374	15, 895	116, 643	96, 275
Mexico......................:..	14, 268	10, 513	139, 258	150, 264
Santo Domingo.................	4, 524	909	31. 070	49, 764
Argentina.....................	24, 742	101, 610	933, 787	801, 787
Brazil	167, 534	88, 781	1, 291, 967	1, 214, 572
Colombia	7, 926	9, 695	99, 357	79, 502
Other South America	82, 798	40, 848	867, 216	684, 884
Oils, vegetable (*Aceites vegetales; Oleos vegetaes; Huiles végétales*):				
Central America..............	361	101	4, 460	2, 301
Mexico........................	9, 215	11, 384	255, 319	289, 209
Santo Domingo.................	2, 200	4, 136	11, 106	20, 294
Argentina.....................	....	353	10, 971	4, 188
Brazil........................	29, 278	32, 881	137, 108	215, 759
Other South America...........	6, 582	10, 575	63, 508	80, 046
Paraffin and paraffin wax (*Parafina y cera de parafina; Paraffina e cera de paraffina; Paraffine et cire faite de cette substance*):				
Central America..............	4, 438	2, 070	28, 175	16, 029
Mexico........................	7, 221	18, 122	130, 857	138, 594
Brazil	958	849	12, 428	9, 238
Other South America...........	30	102	3, 227	5, 230
Provisions, comprising meat and dairy products:				
Beef, canned (*Carne de vaca en latas; Carne de vacca em latas; Bœuf conservé*)—				
Central America..............	2, 919	1, 310	28, 070	24, 473
Mexico................	781	480	12, 640	12, 033
Santo Domingo.................	....	4	51	33
Argentina.....................	21	....	51	357
Brazil........................	1, 040	2, 367	16, 569	15, 947
Colombia	556	277	5, 716	5, 156
Other South America...........	1, 388	682	10, 760	10, 560

EXPORTS OF DOMESTIC MERCHANDISE.

Articles and countries.	April—		Ten months ending April—	
	1897.	1898.	1897.	1898.
Provisions, comprising meat and dairy products—Continued.				
Beef, salted or pickled *Carne de vaca, salada ó en salmuera; Carne de vacca, salgada ou em salmoura; Bœuf, salé ou en saumure)*—				
Central America	$2,208	$5,069	$24,471	$33,407
Mexico	105	77	194	492
Santo Domingo	132	258	2,199	1,643
Brazil	255	274	3,356	1,112
Colombia	1,870	919	10,117	9,802
Other South America	10,316	11,861	141,248	132,871
Tallow (*Sebo; Sebo; Suif*)—				
Central America	8,055	10,002	101,081	79,001
Mexico	3,354	2,042	34,291	21,701
Santo Domingo	4,942	7,397	20,546	25,839
Brazil	84	68	4,401	24,560
Colombia	533	784	6,917	16,550
Other South America	1,080	404	11,762	10,224
Bacon (*Tocino; Toucinho; Lard fumé*)—				
Central America	1,797	1,000	14,849	13,762
Mexico	513	404	7,821	8,140
Santo Domingo	414	191	2,241	1,412
Brazil	142,641	26,367	871,385	477,124
Colombia	245	29	1,340	1,054
Other South America	3,483	1,913	17,943	25,137
Hams (*Jamones; Presunto; Jambons*)—				
Central America	3,183	1,853	26,756	24,120
Mexico	1,886	1,031	24,659	18,248
Santo Domingo	773	750	6,449	5,331
Brazil	165	816	1,008	2,922
Colombia	1,621	622	12,489	11,106
Other South America	6,474	4,162	80,483	73,608
Pork (*Carne de puerco; Carne de porco; Porc*)—				
Central America	6,794	9,113	47,376	60,042
Santo Domingo	390	603	3,565	3,204
Brazil	11,430	70	17,107	555
Colombia	1,129	486	5,424	6,235
Other South America	15,143	13,448	157,203	171,800
Lard (*Manteca; Banha; Saindoux*)—				
Central America	10,131	16,515	83,740	116,866
Mexico	26,389	6,828	278,628	153,165
Santo Domingo	3,192	3,209	18,687	18,544
Argentina		1,200	3,783	2,954
Brazil	93,554	142,617	560,054	881,997
Colombia	14,875	9,421	124,798	93,560
Other South America	60,330	55,224	541,057	512,753

EXPORTS OF DOMESTIC MERCHANDISE.

Articles and countries.	April—		Ten months ending April—	
	1897.	1898.	1897.	1898.
Provisions, comprising meat and dairy products—Continued.				
Oleo and oleomargarine (*Grasa y oleomargarina; Oleo e oleomargarina; Óléo et oléomargarine*)—				
Central America	$44	$306	$76	$858
Mexico	16	291	642	823
Colombia	220	1,273	5,770	6,532
Other South America	1,149	1,005	27,672	13,583
Butter (*Mantequilla; Manteiga; Beurre*)—				
Central America	3,709	3,191	37,560	40,699
Mexico	4,259	2,577	32,930	34,403
Santo Domingo	672	1,436	5,756	6,151
Brazil	1,371	9,741	30,531	76,980
Colombia	1,912	797	14,217	16,522
Other South America	8,232	7,148	73,330	69,536
Cheese (*Queso; Queijo; Fromage*)—				
Central America	1,838	1,275	16,045	15,001
Mexico	1,182	934	13,118	12,176
Santo Domingo	649	506	3,019	3,282
Brazil		75	80	257
Colombia	1,116	561	9,025	9,316
Other South America	1,680	1,789	13,317	15,080
Seeds (*Semillas; Sementes; Semence*)—				
Central America	1,165	387	9,220	4,647
Mexico	2,989	478	19,298	28,621
Santo Domingo	49	77	379	664
Argentina	40		782	348
Brazil	716		1,571	858
Colombia	97	107	2,146	1,516
Other South America	162	75	4,472	1,769
Sugar, refined (*Azúcar refinado; Assucar refinado; Sucre raffiné*):				
Central America	2,731	4,114	50,060	44,786
Mexico	378	2,062	19,531	13,413
Santo Domingo	150	98	1,902	1,504
Colombia	2,932	2,611	39,407	24,201
Other South America	852		1,987	5,018
Tobacco, unmanufactured (*Tabaco no manufacturado; Tabaco não manufacturado; Tabac non manufacturé*):				
Central America	312	2,513	14,211	28,014
Mexico	11,959	5,887	102,237	114,421
Argentina		529	4,055	3,904
Colombia	231	787	2,356	6,432
Other South America	5,334	12,325	80,300	83,299

the Atlantic, the American continent, and the Pacific Ocean; or the still longer route via the Mediterranean Sea and the Suez Canal.

It is, at this time, impossible to forecast intelligently the effect this new factor will introduce into the economic conditions of the commercial world. Already new lines of steamships are projected between Port Arthur, the southern terminus of the railway, and Japanese and Chinese ports, and Manila, having in view immediate trade connections with lines from these ports to the trans-Pacific countries and southern Asia.

In view of the awakening of the spirit of commerce in new Japan, and the acquisition of Chinese territory by the aggressive commercial nations of Europe, it is easy to anticipate the spectacle of the broad Pacific being whitened by the sails of commerce, as is the Atlantic to-day. In all of this the Trans-Siberian Railway must necessarily enter as a most important factor. In considering the chart of the Pacific Ocean and the established trade routes thereon, the various islands of that broad expanse seem to furnish a series of stepping stones from west to east, and under the conditions developing in that quarter of the world some of these resting places promise to be under the American flag.

The MONTHLY BULLETIN has called attention in several cases to concessions which have been granted to subjects of Japan for establishing steamship lines between ports of that country and Mexico, and even Peru. Large colonies of Japanese are located, and are locating themselves in the rich lands of the Tehuantepec Isthmus. The inevitable construction of the Nicaraguan, or some other Isthmian canal will figure in this Pacific trade no less conspicuously than will the great Trans-Siberian Railway.

TRADE MISCELLANY.

ARGENTINE REPUBLIC.

Electric Lighting in Buenos Ayres. In the May issue of the MONTHLY BULLETIN it was stated that the municipal government of Buenos Ayres had made a contract with the Compañía General de Electricidad for lighting the streets of the city by electricity. The details as to the number of lights to be placed, price to be paid, etc., were stated. The "Review of the River Plate" for May 7, however, publishes the information that in consequence of some technicality the contract referred to has not been finally accepted by the city, and the possibility of other companies competing for this valuable franchise remains open.

Introduction of Foreign Machinery. United States Consul BOUCHSEIN, in a report from Barmen, Germany, on the subject of the sale of foreign machinery in the Argentine Republic, says : "In a special report to the Imperial Government, a German consul calls attention to the town of Tucuman as a place suitable for the sale of German machinery. Tucuman, or more fully, San Miguel de Tucuman, is the capital of the province of Tucuman, Argentine Republic, with a population of about 17,000. It is connected by rail with Cordoba and Rosario. The sugar factories there, thirty-three in number, have procured their machinery almost wholly from France on account of favorable terms of payment. Germany has furnished apparatus for distilleries, which are connected with the sugar factories, sulphur ovens, etc. The sugar industry of Tucuman is growing from year to year, and much machinery of a general character will be required shortly. Some of the large manufacturers of machinery in France have had for many years representatives resident in Tucuman.

Trade-Mark Laws. The recent trade-mark fraud, perpetrated on a large scale, at Buenos Ayres, calls attention of merchants and manufacturers to the importance of registering their trade-marks in South America, and elsewhere. The law bearing on these points in those countries is well defined and easily complied with, and only careful attention is necessary to secure the importer from fraudulent imitation. In the case in question, the merchants upon whom the fraud was committed are vigorously prosecuting their case in the Argentine court, but unless it can be shown that the trade-mark had been registered in comformity to the law, difficulty will be found in punishing the guilty parties.

Corn in Argentina. Corn, which at present constitutes one of the principal articles of export from the Argentine Republic, has advanced from a crop of 8,038 tons in 1873 to 1,500,000 tons in 1896. The province of Buenos Ayres is especially adapted, by reason of its climatic conditions, to the culture of this cereal, the exportation of which began long before that of wheat. During the spring and summer (from October to March) the temperature presents an evenness well suited to the development of the plant, while the rains, which are quite abundant, supply the necessary humidity to the soil. The area planted in corn was, in 1891, only 100,498 hectares (251,245 acres), while in 1895, 718,633 hectares (1,796,577 acres), producing 628,000,000 kilograms (247,000,000 bushels), was under cultivation.

BRAZIL.

Trade in April, 1898. Although the Brazilian import duties are lower than those of last year, the customs receipts from foreign merchandise during the month of April, 1898, amounted to $491,662.64, or $35,488.18 in excess of those for the corresponding month of the previous year. The total coffee receipts at Santos amounted, during the month, to 377,000 bags, of which there were stored in the warehouses 263,422 bags, against 247,901 bags in April, 1897. At Rio, for the same month, receipts were 238,000 bags, being an excess of 1,000 bags over April of the preceding year. Shipments are represented by 438,404 bags at Rio and 532,677 bags at Santos. This is an enormous figure for the season, and to this is due the marked decrease of the stock in the storehouses, which on the 30th of April was only 339,116 bags, or less than one-half as much as at the beginning of the month.

GUATEMALA.

Packing for Overland Transport. The usual means of transport in Guatemala is on the backs of mules, a load transported in this manner being called a "carga." Panela (raw sugar), coal, zacata, and all native products are sold wholesale by "cargas" of nine arrobas, or about 100 kilograms (225 pounds). It is important for manufacturers to take note of this detail, for everything that is to serve in farming, especially machinery, must be arranged in packages not exceeding this weight. This is also true in reference to all articles in general use, and packages of about 50 kilograms, put up in elongated shape, are most convenient for transport on mule back. The cost varies, depending to a great extent upon the distance to be traversed.

HAITI.

Loan Negotiations. JOHN B. TERRES, vice-consul of the United States at Port-au-Prince, incloses to the Department of State a copy of a law passed at the last session of the Haitien Legislature for the purpose of negotiating a national loan of $3,500,000 in gold. The loan is to be made in the United States, and Hon. J. N. LÉGER, Haitien Minister at Washington, is charged with its negotiation. The object of the proposed loan is the retirement of the paper currency of the Republic. The law, as passed by the Legislature and promulgated by President SIMON SAM, is printed in full in the United States Consular Reports for June of the current year.

HONDURAS.

Pacific Mail Steamship Company's Subsidy Withdrawn. The "Nouveau Monde" of June 11, 1898, publishes the statement that the Government of Honduras has withdrawn from the Pacific Mail Steamship Company the subsidy which it has hitherto enjoyed. The Government has entered into a contract with the Compañía Sud Americana de Vapores (Chilian), which has recently extended its service to Central American ports, for the transportation of the mails to and from Honduran ports.

Commercial Bank at Tegucigalpa. The Commercial Bank of Honduras, partly owned by capitalists of the United States, has been formally established at Tegucigalpa.

MEXICO.

New Market Building at Guaymas. Colonel WROTNOWSKI, who is well known in the scientific world of Mexico and the United States, as the engineer who planned and carried into execution the work of construction of the piers at Tampico, and who was also engaged on the harbor works of Vera Cruz, has obtained a contract for building a large market in the city of Guaymas, a flourishing port of the State of Sonora. The edifice is to be of stone, iron, and glass; to contain 140 stalls, each 4 meters square, and have an upper story with rooms for office purposes. The work is to be completed by February, 1900. Colonel WROTNOWSKI is to have the proceeds of the market for thirty-three years, less 25 per cent of the net receipts, which go to the city.

Modification of Mining Tax. A bill has recently passed the House of Delegates of the Mexican Congress, having for its purpose the regulating of the tax on mines of the baser metals. By the terms of the bill, the tax on the original title deed, as well as on the yearly rental per claim or pertenencia, is to be reduced on all mines other than those producing gold, silver, and platinum, to $2 per pertenencia. On mines producing the above-named metals the tax shall remain as at present. On all other mines the tax shall be $2.50 per pertenencia on the title deed, and $2 on the yearly rental.

PERU.

Permanent Exhibition at Lima. Importers and manufacturers, exhibiting at the Permanent Exhibition of Machinery and Manufactures now in progress in Lima, are much gratified at the ready sale which their exhibits have met with. One firm, Messrs. G. MENCHACA & Co., has disposed of a large number of articles which had been on their hands for several years, whose value, on account of the limited space for display, had not been heretofore appreciated. For new articles the advantage is even more pronounced, an agent for a United States house having already found buyers for nearly every exhibit received from his employers for the Exposition. Machinery and manufactures of all kinds from abroad are not subject to any import duty or expense for space renting unless sold in the country. As there is a reading room attached to the Exposition, it has been suggested that firms in the United States would be benefited by sending a large supply of catalogues and photographs of their productions where they could be examined by possible purchasers. Cuts of machinery, steam boilers, apparatus for mining and for sugar factories, metal-frame works, sheds, bridges, movable houses, etc., would be found especially valuable.

SALVADOR.

Operation of New Banking Law. At the last regular session of Congress a new banking law was enacted, the principal feature of which had for its object to compel the banks to redeem their notes in silver. The law became effective on the 11th of April last. Consul JOHN JENKINS, writing from San Salvador under date of April 15, states that the Banco Industrial del Salvador has gone out of business, and that in connection with one of the oldest banks of the country will form a new financial institution. This action will reduce the number of banks to four. Competition had made the banking business in the Republic very unsatisfactory, reducing the banks to mere speculative institutions. Under the new law, which requires the banks to redeem their notes in specie, it is hoped that this business will be placed upon a more steady basis. Mr. JENKINS states that, notwithstanding the low price of coffee, there is abundant material in Salvador to insure great prosperity in the future.

URUGUAY.

Free Scholarships in United States Military and Naval Academies.   In response to a suggestion made by United States Minister FINCH, the Government of the United States has tendered a free scholarship in the Military Academy at West Point, and the Naval Academy at Annapolis, for two young men, citizens of the Republic of Uruguay. The appointment will be made on the formal application of the President of Uruguay.

VENEZUELA.

Importations From the Port of New York.   Mr. ANTONIO E. DELFINO, consul-general of Venezuela, has furnished the Bureau with the following statistical data of exportation of merchandise from New York to the various ports of Venezuela for the month of May, of 1898, compared with May, 1897. In May, 1898, the total exports reached $209,900.68; and for May, 1897, they were $250,182.35, a decrease of $40,281.67. This exportation, showing increase or decrease, is divided as below, the figures given representing the value in gold:

	May, 1898.	May, 1897.	Increase.	Decrease.
La Guaira	$121,334.54	$113,437.79	$7,897.35	....
Puerto Cabello	12,520.76	39,061.56	....	$26,540.80
Maracaibo	43,661.59	54,193.64	....	10,532.05
La Vela	10,311.00	15,164.86	....	4,853.86
Guanta	1,565.79	1,117.25	448.54	....
Cumana	1,416.00	542.00	874.00	....
Cana Colorado	86.00	1,697.35	....	1,611.35
Carúpano	5,628.00	5,022.00	606.00	....
Ciudad Bolivar	13,377.00	19,946.50	....	6,569.50
Total	209,900.68	250,182.35	9,825.89	50,107.56

Electric Lighting in Los Andes.   A contract has been entered into recently between the Municipality and Mr. LUIS MANUEL MENDEZ for the illumination of the city of San Christobal (Los Andes) with electricity. The contract provides for 120 incandescent lamps of 16 candlepower and 10 arc lamps of 100 candlepower. The city will pay 6 francs per month for each incandescent lamp and 60 francs for the arc.

An Agricultural Bank.   President IGNACIO ANDRADE has submitted to the Venezuelan Congress a scheme for establishing a national-banking enterprise, having for its sole object to develop the agricultural and stock-raising interests of the Republic. The plan, as proposed and outlined, is to loan to persons engaged or wishing to engage in either of those industries sums at low rates of interest for long terms sufficient to enable them to commence the work and carry it on until it shall become self-sustaining. In his message to Congress, President ANDRADE says: "An institution of this nature would be of great and unquestionable utility, and all thinking men of the country have been asking for its establishment, and I now think it advisable to recommend it to the immediate attention of Congress, as it will meet and satisfy great and pressing necessities, improve the bad economic condition which obtains in the country at the present time, and which is aggravated by the decline in the price of our principal products, and prevent those dreadful consequences which the armed contest now going on must necessarily have on the public wealth, and especially on the industries above referred to."

BOLETÍN MENSUAL

DE LA

OFICINA DE LAS REPÚBLICAS AMERICANAS,

UNIÓN INTERNACIONAL DE REPÚBLICAS AMERICANAS.

Vol. VI.	JULIO, 1898.	No. 1.

PRÓROGA DEL PLAZO DE LA DIRECCIÓN PROVISIONAL.

La Comisión Ejecutiva de la Unión Internacional de las Repúblicas Americanas se reunió el Sabado 25 de junio de 1898, á las 11 de la mañana, en el salón de diplomáticos del Departamento de Estado.

La sesión tuvo lugar bajo la presidencia del Hon. WILLIAM R. DAY, Secretario de Estado. Los otros miembros eran: Señor Don JOSÉ ANDRADE, Ministro de Venezuela; Señor Dr. DON MARTÍN GARCÍA MEROU, Ministro de la Argentina; Señor Don JOAQUÍN BERNARDO CALVO, Ministro de Costa Rica. Mr. FREDERIC EMORY, Director de la Oficina de las Repúblicas Americanas, estaba también presente.

El Presidente declaró abierta la sesión. Mr. EMORY manifestó que el plazo de su nombramiento de director provisional de la Oficina expiraba el 30 de junio.

El Señor ANDRADE presentó una moción proponiendo que Mr. EMORY continuase en el puesto de Director hasta el 1º de octubre de 1898. El Señor MEROU apoyó esta proposición.

Acto seguido el Señor Presidente dió lectura á la moción, cuyo texto es como sigue:

La Comisión Ejecutiva de la Unión Internacional de las Repúblicas Americanas, en vista del estado satisfactorio de la Oficina de las Repúblicas Americanas

59

bajo la dirección provisional que comenzó en 28 de febrero último, consecuente á lo que resolvió la Comisión Ejecutiva en aquella fecha, acuerda que el plazo por que fué nombrado Director Mr. FREDERICK EMORY sea extendido más allá de la fecha fijada por la Comisión, 30 de junio de 1898 ; y que el mencionado Mr. EMORY sea nombrado Director de la Oficina de las Repúblicas Americanas por un período que empezará el 1° de julio y terminará el 1° de octubre de 1898.

Se acuerda además que los poderes especiales conferidos al Director por virtud del acuerdo de 28 de febrero de 1898 sean ratificados y extendidos al nuevo período de su dirección.

El Presidente preguntó si los miembros tenían alguna observación que hacer respecto de la moción.

Después de haberse expresado por miembros de la Comisión su satisfacción personal respecto al estado de los negocios de la Oficina, la moción fué aprobada por unanimidad, y se levantó la sesión.

RELACIONES COMERCIALES EN AMÉRICA.— XIII.*

RIQUEZAS INTERIORES DE LA COSTA ORIENTAL DE SUD AMÉRICA.

El último artículo del difunto Director de la Oficina referente á este asunto fué publicado en el número del BOLETÍN correspondiente al mes de enero, y versó sobre la costa oriental de Sud América, es decir, los países del continente meridional cuyas costas caen sobre el Atlántico, ó cuya salida natural está en el mismo océano. Estos países son el Brasil, Uruguay, la República Argentina y Paraguay. El artículo en referencia se limitaba á estudiar las relaciones comerciales entre aquellas repúblicas y los Estados Unidos. El objeto del presente escrito es hacer referencia á las riquezas interiores de las grandes regiones que quedan al sur del quinto paralelo de latitud' norte.

Los Estados Unidos del Brasil son sólo como una séptima parte menor en tamaño que toda la Europa, y poséen ciertos rasgos característicos topográficos é hidrográficos que sólo pueden ser calificados, con una sola palabra, vastos. Su superficie abarca 3,257,766 millas cuadradas, con una población de 16,330,216 habitantes, ó sea como á razón de cinco habitantes por milla cuadrada. Cuando se considera que las costas del país tienen

---

* El primero de esta serie de artículos, obra del difunto JOSEPH P. SMITH, fué publicado en el BOLETÍN MENSUAL correspondiente al mes de julio de 1897.

4,000 millas de largo y que su majestuosa artéria fluvial, el Amazonas, con sus tributarios, permite la libre navegación por más de 30,000 millas al interior de su territorio, puede concebirse una idéa de sus inmensas facilidades para el desarrollo industrial.

El Brasil es un país que posee magníficas fuentes de riqueza natural; pero el gran obstáculo de la América Latina, es decir, la falta de proporción entre la extensión territorial y su población, se nota aquí como en las otras repúblicas hermanas. La riqueza agrícola de la nación es ilimitada y sin embargo, sólo una pequeña parte del país está cultivada. La producción principal, como es sabido, es el café, y á ésta siguen azúcar, tabaco, algodón, mate, caucho, madera, cacao y nueces, en el orden indicado. Desde hace algunos años el Brasil ha producido más de la mitad del café que se consume en el mundo. En sus bosques abundan ricas maderas, palos de tinte, gomas, fibras y plantas medicinales. En el valle del Amazonas solamente hay 22,000 especies de maderas, de las cuales se ha hecho un catálogo. Las inmensas llanuras del sur se adaptan admirablemente para la cría y abundan en los ríos grandes variedades de peces. La riqueza mineral es enorme; existe el hierro en grandes cantidades, pero la falta de combustible impide el desarrollo ventajoso de los depósitos. Los extranjeros, principalmente los de nacionalidad inglesa y francesa, explotan en grande escala las minas de oro y de diamante.

Las industrias están representadas por cerca de 156 telares de algodón, que emplean cerca de 200,000 operarios; hay también un gran número de fábricas de tejidos de lana, de ingenios de azúcar, curti durías cervecerías, molinos de harina y destilerías, fábricas de jabón, aceite y velas, astilleros, etc.

Probablemente el Brasil nunca llegará á ser un gran país manufacturero, pero como productor y exportador de materias primas tiene un porvenir de posibilidades sin límites.

Para el 31 de diciembre de 1896 había funcionando en el país 8,662 millas de ferrocarril y 4,963 más en vía de construcción. En el BOLETÍN correspondiente á marzo de 1898 se publicó un interesante informe muy detallado acerca de estos ferrocarriles. La red telegráfica está bajo la dirección del Gobierno y para 1895 había en uso 21,936 millas de alambre. Durante el mismo año la marina mercante del país tenía 189 buques de vapor, de 75,283 toneladas netas, y 285 buques de vela, de 65,575 toneladas netas.

La República del Uruguay linda con el sur del Brasil, y se le calcula una superficie de 72,110 millas cuadradas, con una población de 843,408 habitantes; el setenta por ciento de esta población se compone de los naturales del país.

La naturaleza, al distribuir sus favores, trató á esta pequeña República de Sud América con mano generosa. Bien puede decirse que es un gran terreno de pasto en la zona templada, siempre verde y regado por grandes ríos é innumerables arroyos. Aun cuando el terreno es ondulado, menos en la costa del Atlántico, no hay en su superficie montañas de más de 2,000 piés de altura; el país es más bien una sucesión de colinas cubiertas de yerba, inmensos campos, y ríos cuajados de árboles.

La industria principal del Uruguay es, naturalmente, la cria de ganado vacuno y lanar. Las estadísticas, que en los países de grande extensión territorial, pequeña población é insuficientes medios de comunicación se inclinan más bien al lado del ménos que del más, demuestran que para 1895 los establecimientos pastorales del país contenían 5,247,871 cabezas de ganado vacuno, 388,348 caballos, 14,007 mulas y 14,333,626 ovejas. El valor total de los rebaños y manadas se calculó en $73,038,000. Los productos de esta industria, que forma el grueso del comercio de exportación del Uruguay, son tasajo, extracto de carne, cueros y pieles, sebo y lana. Durante el año de 1895 se exportaron 50.000 toneladas de este último artículo. Á Europa se envían animales muertos helados en gran cantidad.

Durante los últimos años se ha dado mayor atención al desarrollo de la agricultura y con ayuda del Gobierno se ha comenzado á cultivar aquel fertil suelo con resultados bastante buenos. El trigo y su harina, que hasta 1877 se importaban, han llegado á ser hoy artículos de exportación. Las exportaciones de trigo, harina de trigo y maíz durante los cuatro años corridos desde 1894 hasta 1897, se calcularon en $10,902,823, mientras que en los cuatro años anteriores solo llegaron á $2,246,855, ó sea un aumento sobre el primer período de $8,655,968. Los resultados obtenidos en el cultivo de la vid son satisfactorios y el número de viticultores aumenta rapidamente.

Las frutas del Uruguay son afamadas y comprenden todas las variedades conocidas en las zonas templada y tropical. Para el Brasil y la Argentina se exportan manzanas, peras, duraznos, cirueas, limones, limas, granadas, membrillos, bananos, cocos y piñas, y la conservación de los membrillos, que abundan tanto que forman bosques, es un ramo importante de la industria. También se producen allí con bastante abundancia la linaza, el cañamo, el tabaco, y el azafrán.

No se han hecho grandes adelantos en la minería, no obstante existir allí minas de oro, plata, cobre, hierro, estaño y mercurio, que podrían explotarse ventajosamente.

Para 1896 habían 1,026 millas de ferrocarriles en explotación y cerca de 200 en construcción. El largo total de las líneas de telégrafo era de 4,380 en 1897, de las cuales 982 pertenecían á los ferrocarriles.

En 1895 los intereses de la marina mercantil de la República estaban representados por 19 buques de vapor, con un tonelaje neto total de 4,608 toneladas, y 45 buques de vela, con 13,171 toneladas netas en todo.

Al ocuparnos de la República Argentina, vemos confirmado el hecho á que ya se ha hecho referencia en otros números del BOLE-TÍN, de que muchos de los productos principales, notablemente el trigo y la lana que se dan en este gran país, son indénticos á los de los Estados Unidos, de lo que resulta que el comercio en ellos es pequeño. La Argentina, situada como está entre los 22° y 56° de latitud sur, tiene sobre el Atlántico un litoral más grande que el de su vecina del norte y como queda más hácia el Ecuador produce los frutos distintivos de los climas fríos y tropicales. Este país, con una superficie de 1,212,000 millas cuadradas y una población de 4,092,990 habitantes, es uno de los más extensos y productivos del Nuevo Mundo.

En la región montañosa del oeste hay ricos depósitos de minerales, tales como oro, plata, hierro y cobre, mientras que en las provincias del suroeste se han descubierto recientemente extensas minas de carbón. La industria minera, sin embargo, no se ha desarrollado todavía, á pesar del Código de Minas de la República, tan liberal como bien concebido.

La Argentina es conocida en todo el mundo como la cuna de las industrias agrícola y pecuaria, siendo grandes los adelantos que ha hecho en estos dos ramos. Hace solo pocos años que este país importaba harina de Chile, su vecina occidental, pero vino la guerra del Paraguay y con ella la demanda por cereales. Los

argentinos trabajaron con ahinco y aprovechando las ventajas de
su suelo maravillosamente rico, en donde el arado hace menos
trabajo que en cualquiera otra parte del mundo, lograron que
para el año de 1893 el país llegase á ocupar el tercer rango entre
las naciones grandes exportadoras de trigo en el mundo. En
1895 las exportaciones de este producto alcanzaron á 37,120.987
bushels. Se ha calculado que hay en la república 24.000.000
de acres de terreno apropósito para el cultivo del trigo, aunque
para 1897 se calculó que sólo había al rededor de 15,000.000 de
acres empleados en toda clase de cultivos. El producto medio
por acre de trigo se calcula en 990 libras.

La industria pecuaria de la Argentina tiene fama universal.
El censo nacional de 1895 demuestra que el número de ganados
que había entonces en el país era como sigue: ganado vacuno,
21,761,526; caballos, mulas y burros, 4,930,228; carneros,
74,379,561; cabras, 2,748,860; cuyo valor total en papel moneda
alcanzaba á $1,130,701,331. La deducción natural que se
desprende de poseer el país tan crecido número de ganado es que
sus productos y residuos formen parte muy importante del comercio de exportación de la república y así es. Desde el año de
1890 el comercio extranjero en cuernos, huesos, cueros, tasajo,
extracto de carne, retazos, lenguas conservadas, sangre seca, grasa
y sebo, carne salada, carnes conservadas, animales muertos helados,
cueros y lanas de carnero ha sido muy extenso, aun cuando ha
fluctuado por razón de las sequías y otras causas naturales que
afectan esta industria en otros países. El comercio en ganado
vacuno con el Uruguay, Chile y Brasil ha llegado á alcanzar
grandes proporciones y ha producido grandes riquezas. La mayor
parte de las grandes "estancias," por cuyo nombre son conocidos
los criaderos, están sometidas á un plan cooperativo que ha dado
los mejores resultados, produciendo el grande influjo de extranjeros
que han formado allí colonias, ocupándose en el desarrollo de las
industrias agrícola y pecuaria.

Por un respeto, al ménos, la República Argentina se distingue
de sus hermanas del sur. Hasta 1889 sus exportaciones estaban
limitadas, por lo general, á los productos arriba mencionados; pero
la crisis financiera que tuvo lugar en aquel año fué causa de que
el país, que hasta entonces había producido materias primas sola-

mente, demostrara por las estadísticas de importación que la actividad del pueblo había seguido otras direcciones. Se establecieron fábricas y en 1892 muchos artículos que habían ocupado lugar prominente en las listas de las importaciones se hacían notar en ellas por su ausencia. Las energías de la nación comenzaron á demostrar cuanto podían hacer en otras esferas, satisfaciendo sus necesidades con el empleo de los materias primas en la manufactura de muchos artículos que antes compraban en el extranjero, entrando así en la labor laudable de levantar una nación tan grande como poderosa, haciéndola independiente de otra para su sustento.

El censo de 1895 demuestra que el número de establecimientos industriales más notables fué el siguiente: fábricas de rino, 852; molinos de harina, 532; destilerías, 108; cervecerías, 44; ingenios de azúcar, 2,749; trapiches, 48; viñedos, 6,514.

El Gobierno ha estudiado concienzudamente la cuestión de transportes por ferrocarril en la Argentina, y las secciones más ricas del país están hoy atravesadas por varias de las mejores líneas del mundo. Desde hace algunos años el Cuerpo de Ingenieros del Gobierno se ha ocupado en medir y reconocer el terreno no sólo para las líneas proyectadas y en construcción, sino también en previsión del porvenir, tendiendo por todo el país una gran red ferrocarrilera cuyas secciones habrán de ser construidas á medida que las necesidades lo exijan.

De los ferrocarriles en explotación para 1895, había cinco pertenecientes á la nación y diez particulares, garantizados por el Gobierno. La extensión total de aquéllos era, el 31 de diciembre de aquel año, de 1,033 kilómetros, y la de éstos 3,920. La extensión total de todas las líneas en explotación en 1896 se computa en 9,032 millas.

Para aquel año había en el país 25,345 millas de líneas telegráficas, con 59,060 millas de alambre, casi la mitad de ellas bajo la dirección del Gobierno.

La marina mercante de la Argentina constaba en 1894 de 75 buques de vapor, de 21,613 toneladas netas, y 125 buques de vela, de 28,241 toneladas netas.

La República del Paraguay, como la de Bolivia, está situada al interior, distante de la costa, con la cual se comunica por medio de unas de las mejores artérias fluviales del mundo, los rios Paraná,

Bull. No. 1——5

Paraguay y Uruguay. Asunción, que es la capital de la República, dista de Buenos Aires como de mil cien á mil doscientas millas, y se comunica con ella por medio de tres líneas de vapores de buena calidad, que hacen viajes regulares, navegando aquellos rios majestuosos. Según las estadísticas oficiales, la parte oriental del Paraguay, que es la que se considera como Paraguay propiamente dicho, tiene una superficie de 148,000 millas cuadradas y una población, según cálculos de 1894, de 430,000 almas. De este número total hay 60,000 indios semi-civilizados, y 70,000 no civilizados.

A causa de su clima, en donde no se conocen los extremos de la temperatura, y su suelo maravillosamente fertil, el Paraguay está siempre cubierto de verdura. Con verdad se ha dicho que "es dudoso que haya sobre la superficie de la tierra otro lugar tan pequeño como el Paraguay que produzca tan grande variedad de productos agrícolas con tan poco trabajo. En pocos acres de terreno se pueden encontrar 200 productos diferentes de Europa, Asia, Africa y América, que crecen casi espontáneamente sin el recurso de medios artificiales, tales como el cultivo en invernaderos."

El producto principal del país es la yerba mate, conocida en todos los mercados de Sud América y en algunos de Europa con el nombre de "té del Paraguay." Este artículo lo emplean, en vez del producto de la China, millones de habitantes en el Brasil, países del rio de la Plata, Perú y Bolivia. Las exportaciones de este producto en 1896 alcanzaron á 9,024 toneladas, avaluadas en más de $1,400,000. Como el suelo paraguayo es poroso y ligero, se presta bien al cultivo de las frutas. Las de la familia de las auranciaceas crecen admirablemente bien, en particular las naranjas que se dan en grande abundancia y se exportan para Buenos Aires y Montevideo en cantidad de 6,000 á 7,000 toneladas por año. Se ven los inmensos naranjales cargados con su dorado fruto, que crecen y producen sin auxilio de trabajo del hombre. Se está desarrollando una industria de bastante importancia con la exportación para Holanda de la cáscara seca de esta deliciosa fruta, de la cual hacen el conocido cordial llamado Curaçao, empleándose un gran capital en el país para la fabricación de cordiales y amargos. Como la pulpa de la fruta no se emplea en esta industria se la tira ó se la da como alimento á los puercos.

El tabaco se da en todas las secciones de la República y es otro de sus productos principales. La caña de azúcar crece también con abundancia, pero los trapiches son primitivos. El crecimiento del algodón y de otras plantas fibrosas es espontáneo, y en una palabra casi todos los productos tropicales, si nó todos ellos, se dan allí con abundancia.

Los bosques del Paraguay son especialmente ricos en maderas duras y aunque la industria de su corte ha llegado á alcanzar buenas proporciones en los últimos años, no hay duda que la fortuna favorecerá á aquellos que entren en el negocio en una escala proporcionada á la cantidad de materia prima que allí se encuentra. El transporte y el trabajo son baratos, y los precios que se obtienen en los mercados vecinos son buenos.

Por lo que se refiere á la industria minera cuanto puede decirse es que no se ha desarrollado, aun cuando bajo la verde alfombra que cubre la superficie del terreno yacen tesoros en minerales que al ser descubiertos aumentarán inmensamente la riqueza del país.

Escaso es el progreso que ha hecho el Paraguay en el ramo de manufacturas y pasarán muchos años antes de que pueda dar abasto á las necesidades del consumo doméstico. Hasta hoy sólo la fabricación de telas de algodón y de lana es la única industria fabril del país. La fabricación de loza y la destilación son las únicas industrias que, aunque están en sus comienzos, habrán de dar grandes rendimientos en el porvenir. Las arcillas finas del Paraguay se conocen desde hace mucho tiempo y la extracción por destilación de las ricas esencias de naranjas y otras frutas, flores, hojas etc., presentan un campo rico á donde debe afluir el capital.

Por más que parezca extraño, el primer ferrocarril que hubo en la América del Sur fué construido en el Paraguay hace cosa de 50 años por el Dictador Lopez y hoy sólo hay una línea en el país, propiedad de una sociedad particular, que enlaza á la capital con Pirapo, recorriendo una distancia de 155.4 millas. Se piensa extenderla hasta Encarnación, sobre el rio Paraná, donde enlazará con la red de ferrocarriles de la Argentina.

Hay en el país 360 millas de líneas de telégrafos.

En el espacio necesariamente limitado de este artículo es imposible dar más que una rápida ojeada á la maravillosa riqueza de las comunidades de Sud América, bañadas por el grande Atlántico y los caudalosos ríos que desembocan en él, pero esa ojeada basta para demostrar que cada una de las dichas naciones presenta, por manera más ó menos atrayente, al que busca ganarse los medios de vivir, una tierra de promisión.

REPÚBLICA ARGENTINA.

COMERCIO DE CARNE HELADA.

Mr. Lyman W. Chute, Vicecónsul de los Estados Unidos en Buenos Aires, comunica al Departamento de Estado, con fecha 16 de diciembre de 1897, un informe detallado sobre el comercio de carne helada de la República Argentina, publicado textualmente en los "Informes Consulares de los Estados Unidos," de 10 de Mayo de 1898; y por considerarse de interés general, damos á continuación un extracto del referido informe:

COMIENZO DE LA INDUSTRIA.

La industria de carne helada se estableció en la República Argentina en 1882, y la primera exportación de este artículo tuvo lugar en 1883; desde esta fecha, la industria ha venido progresando constantemente. Esta industria se lleva á cabo en cuatro establecimientos:

1º. Fundado en 1882; está situado en Campaña, á unas 40 millas al norte de la ciudad de Buenos Aires, en el río Paraná.

2º. Comenzó en 1884; está situado en la orilla sur del Riachuelo, un arroyo canalizado que forma el límite meridional de la ciudad de Buenos Aires. Este establecimiento que fué establecido por una sociedad de particulares, se convirtió después en una compañía anónima que ha venido progresando firmemente. Empezó de una manera relativamente modesta y ha logrado alcanzar uno de los puestos más prominentes en el comercio de carneros helados.

3º. Se estableció en 1886 en San Nicolás, puerto del río Paraná.

4º. Empezó en 1886 en Lima, estación de ferrocarril en la línea de Buenos Aires y Rosario, cerca de Zarate, puerto adyacente á Campaña; está situado también en el río Paraná.

En 1885 se fundó un establecimiento de esta clase bajo los auspicios de la Sociedad Rural de la Argentina, cuyos principales accionistas eran ganaderos ansiosos de encontrar ventajosa salida á sus productos. Los dos cargamentos que se hicieron resultaron en grandes pérdidas. Los animales exportados en estos dos cargamentos eran de cinco á seis años y de reciente capadura, inapropiados á las exigencias de los mercados ingleses. El proceso de congelación se llevó á cabo á bordo del vapor, preparado á este efecto, pero el resultado vino á mostrar el error de preparar la carne en otro punto que no sea en tierra. Esta compañía liquidó, y una nueva casa francesa trata ahora de dedicarse á la preparación y exportación de carne helada en la provincia de Buenos Aires.

CAPITAL.

El capital total de los cuatro establecimientos es de $5,934,380 oro, comprendiendo en esta cantidad el valor de la tierra y el de los edificios, maquinaria, planta, etc. Los cuatro establecimientos constituyen cuatro compañías; tres de ellas operan con capital inglés y una con capital nacional.

TRABAJO.

El número de los trabajadores empleados es de 1,225, clasificados de la manera siguiente: capataces, que ganan de $1.50 á $2 oro por día, matarifes, pellejeros, adobadores y braceros en general, que ganan un peso oro diario, aproximadamente.

GANADO.

Los carneros se obtienen de la provincia de Buenos Aires y las razas que se prefieren son los South Hampshire, Shropshire, Oxford Down, Cheviot, y Romney Marsh; también se solicitan los carneros procedentes de la raza del país, obtenidos por medio del cruzamiento con los Lincoln ó los Rambouillet. Sin embargo, las mejores ventas que se han hecho han tenido lugar en los casos en que se ha obtenido el carnero de raza pura Hampshire Down, aunque últimamente se ha dicho que se han obtenido excelentes resultados en la congelación de carne con los carneros obtenidos del cruzamiento de los de la raza merino con los carneros de cara negra de la raza Shropshire.

Los novillos se obtienen principalmente de las provincias de Buenos Aires, Córdoba y San Juan. El comercio es limitado á causa de las dificultades en encontrar la clase de animales que se necesita para este procedimiento.

El peso medio del carnero vivo es de 50 kilogramos (110 libras) y después de beneficiado pesa unos 25 kilogramos (55 libras). Un carnero muy bien preparado, de la raza Hampshire Down, que fué exportado á Inglaterra por el establecimiento No. 2, pesaba 121½ libras. El novillo vivo pesa de 740 á 750 kilogramos (de 1,731 á 1,757 libras) y después de preparado para la exportación, su peso es de 370 á 375 kilogramos (de 866 á 876 libras).

PRECIOS.

El carnero vivo puesto en el establecimiento, cuesta de $2 á $2.30. El novillo cuesta unos $20 oro.

FLETES.

Dos de las compañías hacen sus cargamentos en vapores pertenecientes á sus agentes de Liverpool; las otras utilizan dos ó tres líneas. En el primer caso, el flete es de un centavo por libra, y en el segundo, se paga un precio á destajo, ó hasta 1½ centavos por libra.   Inglaterra hace la mayor parte de estos fletamentos, así como del comercio en carne, pero hay una compañía francesa, la "Chargeurs Reunis" que lleva grandes cantidades de carneros, principalmente á Londres y el Havre, por cuenta del establecimiento No. 2, cuya carne congelada llega hasta la frontera franco-alemana.

PRODUCTOS.

El promedio de la matanza se calcula en 2,300,000 animales por año, destinados á la congelación.   Las cantidades y valores de la exportación desde los comienzos de la industria hasta el tercer trimestre de 1897, según datos oficiales, son como sigue :

Exportación de carneros helados.

Año.	Cantidades.		Valor en oro.
	Kilogramos.	*Libras.*	
1883 .			$11,412
1884 *			33,159
1885	2,862,270	6,310,794	75,323
1886	7,350,671	16,205,176	360,508
1887	12,038,889	26,540,756	963,112
1888	18,247,988	40,228,374	1,459,839
1889	16,532,545	36,449,799	1,322,604
1890	20,415,000	45,007,400	1,633,105
1891	23,278,084	51,317,585	1,862,247
1892	25,436,221	56,076,942	2,034,898
1893	25,041,000	55,205,200	2,003,254
1894	36,486,000	80,437,100	1,864,110
1895	41,882,000	92,333,600	1,675,273
1896	45,105,000	99,435,651	1,804,205
1897 Los nueve primeros meses	37,650,000	83,004,800	1,506,007
Totales	312,325,668	688,533,177	18,609,056

* 33,159 carneros.

Exportación de carne de vaca helada.

Año.	Cantidades.		Valor en oro.
	Kilogramos.	*Libras.*	
1885 (84 reses)			$1,680
1886 (527 reses)			12,800
1887			
1888	41,581	91,686	3,325
1889	734,264	1,619,052	58,742
1890	662,860	1,395,346	53,029
1891	73,769	162,660	5,902
1892	283,687	625,490	22,695
1893	2,778,485	6,186,860	222,279
1894	26,700	58,873	12,400
1895	158,700	349,934	63,482
1896	299,700	666,838	119,863
1897	299,100	659,516	119,660
Totales	5,358,846	11,816,255	695,858

Por el anterior cuadro se ve que la exportación de carne de carnero ha aumentado constantemente, y que la de carne de vaca ha sido muy variable, y sólo ha obtenido grandes proporciones en los años de 1889, 1890 y 1893.

AVES HELADAS.

Hay otros artículos de consumo, tales como patos, perdices, pavos, pescado, etc., que se exportan á Europa, principalmente á Francia. Estos artículos se venden bien, pero no hay estadísticas fidedignas de las cantidades que se exportan. La casa de Sansinena, antes de que se formara la compañía, envió un cargamento á París, durante la última exposición, de 40,000 pájaros de varias clases. Esta casa estableció un departamento de congelación en los terrenos de la exposición con un restaurant adjunto, y por medio de cajas de vidrio cilindrado, la carne quedaba expuesta á la elección de los favorecedores del establecimiento. El resultado fué que los Señores Sansinena y Cía. recibieron las únicas medallas de oro que se concedieron por comestibles congelados y Don Francisco Sansinena, actual director de la compañía, fué nombrado Caballero de la Legion d'Honneur.

ESTADO ACTUAL DE LA INDUSTRIA.

La experiencia obtenida y el conocimiento de las preferencias de los mercados están contribuyendo al mejor desarrollo de esta industria, que cuenta con halagadoras esperanzas de continuada expansión y ofrece á los ganaderos del país un mercado para la venta de sus productos que, en lo que se refiere á la cría de carneros, no tienen rival en el mundo.

El área pastoral de la Argentina, la calidad del pasto, la baratura de la tierra, el capital afluyente, el adelanto en el mejoramiento de las razas, la continuada inmigración y la extensión de las líneas férreas son razones para creer que esta República está destinada á adquirir prominencia como proveedora de carneros para los mercados de Europa.

BRASIL.

COMERCIO CON NUEVA YORK EN 1897.

Los siguientes datos están tomados del informe de Don ANTONIO GUIMARAES, Vice cónsul del Brasil en Nueva York, sobre el comercio de aquella República con el mencionado puerto.

El valor total de las mercancías exportadas al Brasil fué, en moneda de los Estados Unidos, $3,490,289, y el de las mercancías importadas en Nueva York, $16,736,736. Estas cifras comparadas con las del año 1896 acusan un aumento en las exportaciones de $344,325 y un descenso en las importaciones de $659,741.

Los principales productos exportados fueron: manteca, 16,762,-069 libras; harina, 755,971 barriles; kerosina, 21,844,750 galones; madera para construcción, 50,465,000 pies; aceites de manteca, 157,120 galones; trementina, 161,961 galones; tocino, 75,651 barriles y 5,641 cajas, y trigo para semilla, 747,755 bushels y 12,035 sacos.

Estas cifras, comparadas con las de 1896, acusan un aumento de 8,035,997 libras en la exportación de manteca; de 300,033 barriles de harina, 28,396,924 galones de kerosina, y 4,286,991 libras de tocino. Hubo una baja en la exportación de madera para construcción, ascendente á 16,876,902 piés; la baja en la exportación de aceite de manteca fué de 170,371 galones y en la de trementina 3,097,988 galones.

Los principales productos importados del Brasil fueron: azúcar, 100,107,567 libras y 133,792 sacos; goma, 25,036,628 libras; cacao, 2,567,687 libras; cuero, 1,344,176 libras, y 3,677,998 libras de pieles.

REPÚBLICA DE COLOMBIA.

COMERCIO DE PANAMÁ EN EL AÑO DE 1897.

Según el informe transmitido á la Ofcina de Relaciones Exteriores Británica, por el Consul MALLET, el comercio del Departamento de Panamá en el año de 1897 fué más floreciente de lo que había sido por muchos años anteriores, pues el valor de las mercancías importadas superó en mucho al correspondiente al año anterior. Aquel distrito consular fué visitado en 1897 por un número de comerciantes viajeros mayor del que se había visto allí por muchos años, y sus esfuerzos personales, que son los que en la práctica dan resultado en el comercio, tuvieron el mejor éxito. El informe dice que una gran parte de estos comerciantes viajeros representaba casas inglesas. No obstante ser corto el número de comerciantes viajeros americanos el comercio de los Estados Unidos con Panamá aumentó el 28 por ciento.

El siguiente cuadro representa el tanto por ciento correspondiente á los principales países que importaron para Panamá en 1897.

País.	Tanto por ciento.
Gran Bretaña	15
Francia	
Alemania	13
España	9
Estados Unidos	48
China	15
Total	100

En su informe dice Mr. Mallet que el comercio de exportación en su distrito consular disminuyó considerablemente en 1897 con relación al de 1898, lo que en su mayor parte se debe á la disminución de los productos de la pesquería de perlas y de las cosechas del país.

El tonelage de lo embarcado por el puerto de Panamá demuestra que ha habido un aumento de 9,000 toneladas, así: en buques de vela, 3,000 toneladas y 6,000 en buques de vapor.

La Pacific Steam Navigation Company, que hace algún tiempo extendió de Panamá á Puntarenas, Costa Rica, la estación de sus viajes hácia el norte, se ocupa en estudiar la conveniencia de extenderla más aún, llevándola hasta San Francisco, como ya se dijo en el número del Boletin Mensual correspondiente al mes de enero. La Compañía Sud Americana de Vapores, se propone llevar á cabo igual plan.

Según el informe, los trabajos del canal progresan satisfactoriamente. De Sierra Leona y de Jamaica se ha importado un gran número de trabajadores. Estos últimos, como siempre sucede con las trabajadores de Jamaica, han dado los mejores resultados, mientras que los traídos de Africa han sucumbido á las enfermedades que traen consigo las estaciones y han resultado ser completamente inhábiles para el trabajo laborioso que se requiere en la construcción del canal. Por término medio el número de trabajadores empleados durante el año se computa en 3,000.

Los informes referentes al progreso de los distritos mineros son muy satisfactorios, notándose especialmente el de las minas de Cará en el Darién.

El Vice-consul MacGregor informa de Barranquilla que ha tomado gran incremento, en el distrito consular del Río Magdalena, el desarrollo de las vías ferrocarrileras, lográndose alcanzar hoy un servicio regular y barato en el transporte á los puertos de la costa. En el Departamento del Magdalena se construyeron 50 millas de ferrocarril y el de Barranquilla se está extendiendo hasta Usiacuri, ó sea una distancia de 36 millas.

Los distritos agrícolas de los Departamentos del Valle del Magdalena demuestran un desarrollo tan notable como continuado, especialmente en lo que se refiere á la producción del café y del tabaco. Durante el año de 1897 Barranquilla recibió 278,000 sacos de café de 125 libras de peso, siendo la calidad tan buena como la mejor de cualquier mercado estranjero. El tabaco que era antes un importante cultivo y últimamente había decaido, tanto en la cantidad del producto como en su calidad, hoy está volviendo á tomar incremento su cúltivo y preparación para el mercado. Durante el año de 1896, se embarcaron 35,435 serones, que fueron principalmente para Bremen. La cría y la exportación de ganado no indica mejora, pues estando limitado su mercado á las Antillas, los disturbios de Cuba han sido una rémora á su desarrollo. Del total de cueros exportados de Barranquilla, que fué 150,000 cueros, 100,000 fueron á los Estados Unidos y el resto á Europa. No parece que se han realizado las esperanzas acariciadas hace pocos años del desarrollo de la producción del algodón.

La exportación de este producto en 1897, comparada con la del año anterior, arroja una diferencia de 707 pacas en las exportaciones de 1897. Sin embargo, en los telares de Cartagena se está empleando una gran cantidad de este producto y es placentero manifestar que esta industria ha demostrado durante el año pasado un espíritu decidido de adelanto. Las exportaciones de caucho hechas por Barranquilla en 1897, alcanzaron á 1,400 bultos con un valor declarado de $35,000. El árbol del caucho, del cual hay un gran número de variedades, crece silvestre en todos los bosques de los Departamentos del Magdalena, Bolivar, Santander, Antióquia, y Tolima, pero no se le cultiva todavía.

En los bosques cercanos al Magdalena se encuentran varias clases de maderas preciosas, entre las cuales se cuenta la copaiba, de donde se extrae el bálsamo del mismo nombre. Crece hasta 40 piés de alto, la madera es de fibra compacta y sirve para la construcción de casas y de botes. Existe el cedro en abundancia, que se exporta en tozas por el puerto de Barranquilla, principalmente para Francia y Alemania. Varias compañías francesas han establecido aserraderos para el corte de esta madera.

El cuadro siguiente representa el valor de las importaciones hechas por Barranquilla en 1897:

País.	Valor.
Gran Bretaña	$3, 984, 972
Estados Unidos	1, 158, 133
Otros países	4, 643, 630
Total	9, 786, 735

El Vicecónsul STEVENSON, en su informe de Cartagena, dice que en lo general el comercio de aquel puerto ha decaido, si se le compara con el de 1896. Esto lo atribuye en términos generales al número de desastres acaecidos en los vapores empleados en la navegación del río Magdalena, lo cual ha disminuido el tráfico por aquel puerto.

Las importaciones han aumentado poco, comparadas con las de 1896. Dicho aumento correspondió á los Estados Unidos, Francia, Alemania y España, tocando, á esta el mayor aumento.

Ha habido progreso en las mejoras locales. Hace poco se estableció una buena planta eléctrica, cuyas máquinas se importaron de Inglaterra y los aparatos eléctricos de los Estados Unidos. Se está construyendo un gran edificio para el mercado.

El Viceconsul CARR informa de Santa Marta que hay allí gran actividad en el cultivo del café. Los cultivadores son en su mayor parte ingleses y americanos, y se hallan muy animados con el prospecto que se les ofrece, pues la calidad del café que producen es igual al mejor producto de Colombia y Costa Rica. Como quedan cerca del puerto, los cultivadores pueden poner allí sus productos á razón de menos de $5 por tonelada. Se pueden comprar terrenos á propósito para el cultivo del café, situados en una región sana y á una altura de 3,000 á 4,000 pies, á razón de $2 á $3 por acre. El cultivo del plátano, que hace cerca de ocho años que se comenzó á hacer, ha llegado hoy á adquirir una condición próspera. Los cultivadores recibieron por la cosecha del año pasado cerca de $85,000.

ECUADOR.

COMERCIO DE GUAYAQUIL EN 1897.

Los siguientes datos relativos á la industria y al comercio de Guayaquil, Ecuador, durante el año de 1897, están tomados del informe anual del Cónsul, Mr. CHAMBERS, dirijido á la Oficina de Relaciones Exteriores de la Gran Bretaña:

Guayaquil, que es el puerto principal de la República, es también el centro mas importante de su comercio. La enorme cantidad de mercancías destruidas en los desastrosos incendios de febrero y octubre de 1896 tuvo que reponerse para responder á la creciente necesidad del consumo en las provincias de la costa y del interior, de donde resultó que el comercio de importación fué mayor y más activo que en ningún año anterior. No se ha publicado ninguna estadística de esta importación desde que se publicó la que el Ministro de Hacienda, Señor WITHER, dirigió á la convención de 1896–97. Esta estadística contiene un cálculo aproximado del valor de las importaciones desde mayo 1º de 1895 hasta junio 30 de 1896, ascendente á 10,600,000 sucres (ó $1,060,000). No puedo dar, por tanto, cuenta exacta de este importante detalle, pero sé que desde aquel período hasta la fecha las importaciones han tenido lugar en mayor escala.

No han ocurrido cambios en las importantes firmas comerciales ni en la naturaleza ú orígen de los géneros importados.

Durante 1897 tuvo lugar el comercio de exportación con la acostumbrada actividad; debe advertirse, empero, que las excesivas lluvias de enero á mayo causaron daños muy considerables á las cosechas de cacao y café; de la primera se perdió el veinte y cinco por ciento, y de la segunda sólo se recojió un cincuenta por ciento, que en su mayor parte fué de inferior calidad. Todas las plantaciones de arroz de la costa fueron destruidas por la misma causa y esto dió márgen á una importación considerable de arroz de otros países. Estas circunstancias combinadas influyeron materialmente en las transacciones comerciales. Por esta época el Gobierno autorizó á uno de los bancos de Guayaquil para una nueva acuñación de plata, y á fines del año se promulgó una ley según la cual los bancos quedaban obligados á retener su reserva metálica en oro, y se les compelió de esta suerte á importar moneda extranjera por valor, al menos, de £100,000; y se comprenderá fácilmente que este estado anormal del cambio ha contribuido á hacer difícil en extremo la situación comercial de la República. Los bancos suspendieron en diciembre, casi por completo, las operaciones de descuento.

Los ingresos han aumentado considerablemente por virtud del aumento en los derechos de importación, según la nueva ley de aduanas, y por virtud también de las contribuciones; pero no obstante este aumento, el comercio ha sido muy activo. Se ha llevado á cabo con gran actividad la reconstrucción de la parte comercial de la ciudad que fué destruida por el incendio y se han construido grandes y elegantes casas que dan un aspecto imponente á la parte de la ciudad del lado del río. Estas casas son de madera, muy pocas de las cuales han sido construidas en el viejo estilo de caña y torta, y gran numero de ellas están techadas con hierro galvanizado inglés. Los trabajadores escasean, y de esto se han aprovechado los artesanos para pedir salarios subidos tanto por el trabajo puramente manual como por el trabajo inteligente; el precio de los materiales de construcción ha aumentado también á causa de la gran demanda.

Muchos comisionistas representantes de casas inglesas han visitado el país varias veces durante el año, y, por lo general, han expresado su satisfacción respecto de la parte que Inglaterra tiene en el comercio de importación. Con pocas excepciones, los artículos enumerados en la lista de los más importantes ramos del comercio—lista emitida por las varias cámaras de comercio por mediación de la Oficina de Relaciones Exteriores—que obtienen salida en este mercado, vienen directa ó indirectamente de los lugares nombrados en la lista. Los artículos de lujo, principalmente los géneros para vestidos y los de fantasía para mujeres y niños, así como perfumes, calzado fino, etc., han sido importados de Francia. De los Estados Unidos hemos recibido kerosina, manteca, y madera para construcción en grandes cantidades. Impórtase madera cepillada y machihembrada dispuesta ya para su uso inmediato. Estufas de hierro, hachas, hachuelas y muebles se reciben de aquel mercado sólo en pequeñas cantidades. De Austria se ha importado una clase mejor de muebles, así como joyas baratas y artículos de fantasía. De Alemania se recibe cerveza, medias, géneros de lana y mezclados para vestidos, frazadas, ponchos, chales y artículos ordinarios de ferretería, en la misma proporción que en años anteriores, sin ningun aumento material, con excepción de los géneros de lana mezclada y encajes, que por ser mas baratos han podido hacer fuerte competencia á los artículos similares procedentes de Inglaterra.

Los artículos ordinarios de cuchillería que se importaban antes de Alemania están sufriendo ahora la competencia de los fabricantes ingleses que están obteniendo parte de este comercio. Casi todas las velas que se consumen en la República se importan de Bélgica. La producción de azúcar en 1897 fué de unas 6,000 toneladas. El consumo nacional será de unas 4,000 toneladas, y quedan unas 2,000 toneladas para la exportación, principalmente á Chile y á Colombia. El precio medio del azúcar blanco granulado de primera clase ha sido de unos 5 centavos por libra. En Chile se prefiere ahora el azúcar del Ecuador á las mejores clases del azúcar peruano.

Hay en el país una fábrica de jabones, y el material para la fabricación de éste se importa libre de derechos, lo cual tiende á disminuir el precio del jabón procedente del extranjero. La exención de derechos de importación espira este año, pero se están haciendo esfuerzos para renovarla. También se proyecta el establecimiento de otra fábrica en Bahia de Caraquez por un sindicato de los Estados Unidos y algunos comerciantes de Bahía. En todo el país se fabrica, de una manera primitiva y en pequeña escala, una especie de jabón negro que tiene muy buenas calidades detersorias. Hay dos fábricas de fideos, etc., las cuales han monopolizado el comercio en esta clase de artículos que se importaban antes de Chile en cantidad considerable. Uno de estos establecimientos comprende también una fábrica de galletas de calidad superior. El principal empleado de esta fábrica es un súbdito inglés, procedente de una conocida casa de Londres. Durante el año se han establecido nuevos aserraderos, uno de los cuales fué importado de Inglaterra.   Hay en el interior telares de géneros de lana y algodón principalmente para el consumo local, si bien hay un comercio considerable en bayetas de clase ordinaria, con la vecina República de Colombia, vía Fumaco y Barbacoas.   Estas bayetas no compiten, sin embargo, con las clases mas finas que se importan de Inglate.ra.

De los numerosos edificios públicos destruidos en Guayaquil por el fuego de 1896, ninguno ha sido reedificado.   Se han levantado cobertizos para el servicio de aduana en el lugar donde estaba el antiguo edificio, pero son inadecuados á las exigencias del gran comercio de importación y el Gobierno ha tenido que alquilar almacenes privados en toda la ciudad para el depósito de los géneros, lo cual es grandemente perjudicial al manejo de los artículos importados. Se ha formado una compañía en Nueva York para explorar el distrito de Zaruma, y á juzgar por los informes favorables que se han recibido, créese que se formará una compañía para explotar las minas en este distrito aurífero.   La compañía minera de la plaza de oro ha gastado enormes sumas en el desarrollo de su propiedad, pero ha encontrado dificultades por razón de los grandes gastos que la empresa demanda, y para concluir los trabajos con más economía se ha formado un sindicado con los accionistas ingleses de aquella compañía. Se han suspendido algunas de las labores originales, y muchos de los gastos que hasta el presente habían obstaculizado la empresa han sido reducidos.

HONDURAS.

BOSQUEJO DE LA POBLACIÓN, DEL CLIMA, DE LAS FUENTES DE RIQUEZA, ETC.

Mr. Robert M. Fryer, de Washington, que ha viajado extensamente por Honduras y residido allí por algunos años, ha dirijido á esta Oficina la siguiente comunicación sobre los recursos, clima, etc., de aquel país:

Permítaseme asegurar á los lectores del Boletin que la población, el clima, la religión y la política en Honduras son precisamente lo que debieran ser, en armonía con los intereses individuales.   Este aserto no será puesto en duda por los que vayan á aquella República con conocimiento bastante para comprender las cosas del país, y se abstengan de mezclarse en los asuntos públicos, dedicándose al aprovechamiento y desarrollo de los recursos que aquél ofrece.   Puede decirse que en Honduras se recibe mas cordialmente á los viajeros y presuntos colonos precedentes de los Estados Unidos, que á los otros extranjeros que visitan el país.   El área de Honduras es aproximadamente del mismo tamaño que el área de Ohio; pero en recursos naturales es superior á muchos de tales Estados, tomados colectivamente; y si tuviera una población correspondiente, sobrepujaría, en mi opinión, á cualquier otro territorio de dimensiones análogas.

Aquel país ofrecerá mas lujo y comodidades que las que pueden obtenerse en cualquier otro lugar por el mismo dinero y trabajo; tiene todas las ventajas de las regiones tropicales, semitropicales y templadas. Entre los productos hay valiosas maderas del comercio, plantas medicinales, frutas tropicales, y vastos recursos minerales, no explotados todavía; pero sobre todo, el clima de Honduras, considerado en relación con las muchas otras ventajas del país, constituye el mayor atractivo de éste.

La costa norte de Honduras se extiende casi directamente hácia Este y Oeste por cerca de 400 millas. Los vientos que prevalecen (vientos alisios) vienen del norte y noreste y mantienen la costa en estado salubre y relativamente fresca, pero ésta no es la localidad que más se recomienda por el clima; sin embargo, éste no es forzosamente desagradable, por cuanto las montañas de la costa se introducen en el mar y se elevan á una altura de una milla ó más. En los valles y altiplanicies se encuentra un clima variado, adaptable á todos los gustos y exijencias. Si se me preguntara cual es el clima mas delicioso del país, indicaría el de Tegucigalpa, Siguatepeque, las lomas que rodean á Comayagua, el lago Yojoa, San José, Santa Barbara, y otros muchos lugares en el interior de la República en donde hay que usar gruesas frazadas por la noche, en donde no se ven moscas ni mosquitos y donde existe una estación primaveral, con frutas y flores durante todo el año. En una extensión de miles de millas que he viajado en mula, por entre montañas, no he visto jamás un reptil ú otro animal salvaje, excepción hecha de los capturados; pero hay en todas partes gran profusión de pájaros de gran variedad de colores y plumaje. El país está provisto de numerosos ríos, en muchos de los cuales abunda la pesca; el mejor pescado se encuentra cerca de la costa.

Muy poco capital ó trabajo se necesita para establecerse en Honduras; no hay extremos de temperatura, y todo parece crecer con poco ó ningún cultivo. Esto hace especial relación al maíz, del cual se producen dos ó tres cosechas al año; la caña de azúcar y el algodón dán mas de una cosecha al año y producen, sin necesidad de resiembra, durante diez años. El cocotero y el árbol del hule dan producto á los ocho años de sembrados, mientras que el cafeto fructifica en menos de seis años. El árbol del hule necesita sombra durante el primer año, la cual se obtiene plantando matas de plátanos que también producen dentro de nueve meses y duran diez años por lo menos.

La vida del árbol del hule en Honduras es de cincuenta ó más años. Naranjas, limones, limas, yuca, y muchas otras frutas se dán silvestres en todo el país; la piña, incluyendo la variedad conocida con el nombre de piña de "pan de azúcar," se dá en gran abundancia cerca de la costa. En algunas partes del país se dán á la perfección todas las legumbres que se conocen en los Estados Unidos. El suelo cerca de la costa es demasiado rico para la patata, pues las hojas y tallos crecen con demasiado vigor; pero en el interior, donde la tierra es seca, se dá bien esta planta.

Mr. BAMBERG, que vive en San Pedro Sula y tiene una gran hortaliza cuyos productos vende en el mercado, es considerado autoridad competente en la materia del cultivo de legumbres en Honduras.

En cuanto á recursos minerales, diré que, juzgando por mi propia observación y por todos los indicios, Honduras es un gran almacén de oro y plata de incalculable valor.   Por cortesía de Mr. GERLINGS, administrador general de la "New York and Honduras Rosario Mining Company," he podido conocer no sólo los ricos depósitos de la compañía, sino también las minas del Distrito de Yuscuran, en donde están situadas las famosas minas de Guayabillas y los depósitos de oro de Olancho.   La mina del Rosario arriba mencionada está situada en San Juancito á 21 millas de Tegucigalpa (la Capital), con la cual está unida por un camino carretero bastante bueno.   Hay en ella 35 trituradoras en operación y una planta eléctrica y de aire comprimido, movidos por fuerza hidráulica; y bien puede decirse que no hay en ninguna parte una mina mejor manejada que ésta.   Como resultado de mis investigaciones respecto á la posibilidad de explotar con provecho las minas de Honduras, he quedado sorprendido de que no haya diez ó veinte compañías mineras en aquel país que hoy cuenta solamente con una.

Habrá en el otoño elecciones presidenciales en Honduras.   El Presidente BONILLA será echado de menos por todos los extranjeros de Honduras, á quienes trató siempre con bondosidad y consideración.   También la mayoría de los hondureños sentirán la terminación del período presidencial del Señor BONILLA, á quién consideran como prototipo de virtud, inteligencia, energía de carácter y patriotismo.   •

———

MÉXICO.

INDUSTRIA MINERA.

La minería es una de las más importantes industrias de México. La exportación de metales preciosos y minerales muestra un aumento de cerca de doce millones de pesos (plata mexicana) durante le primera mitad del presente año fiscal, comparada con la del mismo período en 1896; este aumento representa cerca de un cuarenta por ciento.

El mineral de cobre mexicano es particularmente rico y su producción crece rápidamente.   En varias partes del país se han descubierto recientemente nuevas y extensas minas, y según el "Modern Mexico" el professor WILLIAM NIVEN, conocido mineralogista y arqueólogo, dice que los campos de Guerrero son tan ricos en oro como en cobre.   Aunque Guerrero cuenta indudablemente con una gran riqueza mineral, los explotadores deben contar con capital si quieren obtener éxito.   El clima es benigno, pero el equipo es costoso y las provisiones son escasas.   La exportación de cobre se duplicó el último año; en el mes de diciembre alcanzó un valor de cerca de un millón de pesos, que representa un aumento de casi 100 por ciento. Los cargamentos de plomo, antimonio y zinc acusan un alentador aumento.

TELARES DE ALGODÓN.

En un informe especial del Cónsul británico, en la ciudad de México, se dice que la industria de géneros de algodón en México se ha desarrollado grandemente durante los últimos años. Dentro de poco tiempo los telares nacionales podrán surtir al país de todos los géneros bastos de algodón que consume. Esta industria en México va progresando lentamente y el aumento en los tres años pasados se atribuye á una sucesión de buenas cosechas. En 1897 se establecieron nuevos telares cuya producción mínima fué de 300,000 piezas, y los telares que se están construyendo ó que probablemente se construirán este año, aumentarán la producción en 750,000 piezas. Como el promedio de importación anual de géneros de algodón extranjeros es sólo de unos 40,000,000 de metros cuadrados y México promete agregar 21,000,000 de metros cuadrados á su producción, es probable que los fabricantes extranjeros encuentren en el país una considerable competencia.

En las fábricas donde se usa el vapor como fuerza motriz, las grandes máquinas de 100 caballos de fuerza en adelante, son generalmente inglesas, pero cuando no se necesitan máquinas de gran potencia se prefieren las americanas de alta presión, por ser más baratas. Las calderas son generalmente multitubulares.

NUEVAS INDUSTRIAS.

Según "El Progreso," de Mexico, del 30 de abril de 1898, los Señores ERNESTO CHAVERO y GREGORIO GONZÁLEZ han solicitado del Departamento de Fomento autorización para establecer varias industrias en el país, entre ellas una fábrica de leche condensada, con un capital mínimo de $150,000. Ésta es una industria completamente nueva en México.

El mismo periódico dice que varias grandes fábricas de aceite y jabón, establecidas en Lerdo, Durango, Torreón y San Pedro de la Higuera, las cuales operaban independientemente, se han unido formando una sola asociación. Estas fábricas están provistas de luz eléctrica y cuentan con maquinaria potente y costosa; dichas fábricas trabajan día y noche. Sus principales productos

Bull. No. 1——6

son harina de semilla de algodón y tortas de linaza. La primera se usa para engordar ganado vacuno y de cerda.

La semilla de algodón se obtiene principalmente de ricas plantaciones de algodón, cuyos dueños tienen grandes intereses en la compañía.

Estas fábricas pueden producir 25,000 kilogramos de harina de semilla de algodón cada 24 horas, y exportan 20,000 toneladas de tortas de linaza cada año, valuadas en $500,000.

FÁBRICA DE CORDELERÍA Y DE SACOS.

El 8 de octubre de 1896 se firmó un contrato entre el Ministerio de Fomento y Mr. ALFRED HEYDRICH, para el establecimiento de una gran fábrica en Yucatán para la manufactura de cordelería, hamacas y sacos, utilizando para ello el henequén y otros productos análogos. Dicho contrato fué aprobado por el Congreso el 14 de mayo de 1897, y el 23 de junio del mismo año Mr. HEYDRICH verificó el registro de la empresa bajo el nombre de "Sociedad Anónima La Industria," con un capital de $400,000, siendo el presidente el Señor OLEGARIO MOHUA.

El contrato estipula que la fábrica debe estar terminada en el término de dos años desde que se promulgue la aprobación del contrato por el Congreso, y se nota gran actividad en los trabajos de construcción é instalación de la fábrica. Ya se han levantado grandes edificios, construidos especialmente para el trabajo que se ha de hacer. Se han fabricado además 14 casas de mampostería sólida de 30 por 16 pies, para vivienda de los operarios. Los talleres de la compañía están enlazados por rieles con el ferrocarril de Mérida y Progreso y están provistos de varios desvíos para facilitar el manejo de los carros.

El contrato original celebrado con el Gobierno estipulaba que la cantidad que se habiá de invertir no sería menor de $250,000. Como prueba del desarrollo de la empresa, podemos decir que el capital en acciones se ha aumentado á $600,000 y que la compañía se ha comprometido á comenzar los trabajos un año antes del tiempo estipulado en el contrato.

Cuando la fábrica esté montada de un todo, su producto diario será de 50,000 kilogramos de hilo fino, hilo de acarreto, jarcia, sacos, hamacas, etc., ó sea un producto total de 14,400,000 kilogramos por año. Grande es el interés con que se mira esta empresa, por ser la primera en gran escala en el país del henequén, que es el producto principal de Yucatán.

CONCESIÓN DE FERROCARRIL Á LOS SEÑORES PEARSON, SONS & COMPANY.

"El Diario Oficial," en uno de sus últimos números, da noticias de una concesión que fué aprobada por el Presidente Díaz el 4 de junio, por la cual la importante casa de Pearson & Sons y Pedro M. Armendaria quedan autorizados para trazar, construir y explotar un ferrocarril en el Estado de Vera Cruz.

El punto inicial del camino será Acayuacán, ó bién Paso de San Juan, en la línea del ferrocarril de Jutla. El ferrocarril se extenderá hasta Tuxtla y San Nicolás, con el privilegio de prolongación hasta Alvarado. La línea deberá estar trazada dentro de un año á contar de la fecha de la aprobación del contrato, y los trabajos de construcción deberán empezar dentro de dieciocho meses; la línea deberá estar terminada en diez años. Además de la exención usual de derechos de importación y contribuciones, los concesionarios recibirán grandes extensiones de terreno público en Veracruz, Oaxaca, Tabasco y Chiapas. La compañía contratante deberá tener su domicilio legal en la ciudad de México, y en la elección de directores el Gobierno se reserva el derecho de nombrar cierto número.

Se exije de los concesionarios que hagan un depósito de $3,000 en bonos del Gobierno en el Banco Nacional dentro de quince días. El territorio que la línea atraviesa es uno de los más ricos y que más prometen en la producción de goma, tabaco y azúcar en toda la República, y la alta representación económica de los Señores Pearson & Sons es una garantía de que las condiciones del contrato serán cumplidas al pié de la letra.

NICARAGUA.

CONCESIÓN HECHA Á MR. EMERY PARA LA EXTRACCION DE MADERA.

Mr. William B. Sorsby, Cónsul de los Estados Unidos en San Juan del Norte, ha remitido al Departmento de Estado una copia (traducida) del contrato hecho por el gobierno de Nicaragua con Mr. H. C. EMERY, de Chelsea, Massachusetts, concediéndole el privilegio de corte y exportación de las maderas valiosas del país.

En sustancia el contrato concede á Mr. EMERY el monopolio, por 15 años, de la caoba, palo rosa y cedro, dentro de una vasta area que se sabe que es rica en estas maderas. Este es la renovación del antiguo contrato celebrado también con Mr. EMERY, durante cuya vigencia se exportaron unas 12,500 tozas. El Cónsul SORSBY considera que esta concesión es inmensamente valiosa, en realidad una de las más valiosas que en mucho tiempo ha hecho el gobierno de Nicaragua á súbditos extranjeros.

Según el artículo 3 del contrato, Mr. EMERY se obliga á construir 50 millas de ferrocarril, para su propio uso, entre Río Grande y Pearl Lagoon; la entrevía será de 3 piés 6 pulgadas ó 4 piés 8½ pulgadas, y la línea habrá de pasar por las tierras públicas del Departamento de Matagalpa. El material para el camino, los puentes, muelles, talleres, etc., habrán de ser aprobados por el Ministro de Obras Públicas. Toda la obra pasará á ser propiedad del gobierno á la terminación del contrato, es decir, dentro de 15 años.

El gobierno nacional cede á Mr. EMERY 10,000 manzanas (17,500 acres) de tierras públicas en el Departamento de Zelaya ó Matagalpa, con la condición de que dentro del término de un año siembre una planta por cada árbol que corte.

Según el artículo 4°, el concesionario deberá pagar al gobierno $20,000 en oro en libranzas aceptables y $10,000 oro al año, como premio, durante la existencia del contrato.

Mr. EMERY podrá introducir libres de derechos todos los artículos necesarios para el sustento y mantenimiento de los empleados en el corte y la exportación de madera, así como también los materiales que se necesiten para la construcción y mantenimiento del ferrocarril.

PARAGUAY.

EXTRACTOS DEL MENSAJE DEL PRESIDENTE.

El Señor Presidente EGUZQUIZA apareció ante los Senadores y Diputados el dia 1ro de abril, y leyó su mensaje al honorable Congreso de la Unión al abrir sus sesiones ordinarias. El período constitucional del Señor Presidente EGUZQUIZA terminará al levantarse las actuales sesiones del Congreso, de manera que este mensaje es el último que está llamado á leer durante su actual administración.

El Presidente congratula al país por el desarrollo general en la instrucción pública y el aumento constante en el número de escuelas públicas y en los alumnos. Hace mención preferente de la ampliación del sistema de colegios normales que en la actualidad son frecuentados por más de mil alumnos de ambos sexos. Se ha contratado en el extranjero un selecto cuerpo docente. La instrucción en la agricultura, las artes y ciencias se ha extendido mucho.

El hilo telegráfico, que se extenderá desde Asunción á Villa Concepción, ha alcanzado hasta más allá de San Pedro y al cabo de pocos meses llegará á aquel punto. Se propone prolongar este hilo hasta el Fuerte Olimpo y extender un ramal que relacione la línea principal con varios pueblos del norte. En la proporción en que crece la población aumenta el movimiento en el correo.

Sobre las obras públicas, dice el Presidente que una comisión especial dirige los trabajos de esta naturaleza, con arreglo á la ley que creó los fondos destinados á construirlos.

El valor total de las importaciones durante el año trascurrido ascendió á $2,203,359 y el de las exportaciones á $1,955,803; ambas sumas representan el valor en oro.

El Banco Agrícola, la institución más importante de su clase en el país, ha hecho mucho en pro de los propósitos para que fué establecido, es decir, en el fomento del cultivo del algodón, cafeto, la viña y otros productos del país. El número de cafetos existentes hoy en la República alcanza á más de un millón y nadie puede dudar que lleva trazas de duplicarse y triplicarse en breve tiempo. El banco mencionado ha extendido los ensayos de preparación del tabaco según los sistemas adoptados en Cuba y Sumatra, bajo la dirección de personas competentes. De este modo, el tabaco del Paraguay excluido antes de los mercados extranjeros, volverá á adquirir su perdida importancia.

Con relación al Banco Nacional, dice el Presidente que la liquidación de este continúa, si bien los deudores se muestran remisos en el cumplimiento de sus compromisos. "Fuera acertado acordar algún modo de conseguir la liquidación definitiva para evitar gastos innecesarios." El impuesto territorial será una de las fuentes de los recursos de la nación.

El Gobierno se ocupa en estudiar un proyecto de línea férrea que relacione los yerbales con la navegación de nuestro río. Si la idea se realiza, el comercio de yerba mate, de difícil transporte hasta ahora, y mucho más en las épocas de sequía en que se vuelven innavegables los afluentes del río Paraguay, obtendrá inmensos beneficios.

Refiere el Mensaje con mucha satisfacción que la más perfecta armonía y cordialidad se mantienen entre el Paraguay y los países vecinos. La única cuestión pendiente es el arreglo de límites con Bolivia que envuelve los derechos al territorio del Chaco, vasta region inculta é inhabitada. Esta cuestión está por el momento en expectativa.

El Presidente Eguzquiza abriga fundadas esperanzas de que las negociaciones iniciadas en la República Argentina para la celebración de un tratado de comercio tengan una solución conveniente y satisfactoria para ambas naciones. También abriga el Sr. Presidente la firme convicción de que la manera de establecer vínculos permanentes entre los pueblos es desarrollar sus intereses morales y materiales, basados en concesiones liberales que permitan la expansión de sus industrias y de su actividad comercial. El Presidente recomienda especialmente la celebración de un tratado de comercio con el Brasil.

PERÚ Y CHILE.

CULTIVO Y MANUFACTURAS DE ALGODÓN.

En el número del BOLETIN MENSUAL correspondiente al mes de junio se hizo mérito del impulso que últimamente se ha dado al cultivo y las manufacturas de algodón en Perú y Chile, y de las medidas que, para alentar estas industrias, estaban tomando los gobiernos de estos dos países. La Exposición Permanente de Maquinaria que se ha inaugurado recientemente en Lima está solicitando la atención de los fabricantes de los Estados Unidos y Europa hácia las oportunidades que hoy se les presentan de introducir su maquinaria en aquel país; y el decreto de fecha reciente admitiendo libre de derechos toda la maquinaria que se dedique á la fabricación de tejidos no sólo está infundiendo nueva vida á aquella industria en Chile, sino que está abriendo un ámplio mercado á la maquinaria americana.

El siguiente artículo sobre esta materia, que tomamos del "Textile Manufacturers' Journal" del 4 de junio, que se publica en Nueva York, talvez será leido con interés:

Hemos hecho referencia de cuando en cuando al desarrollo de la industria de manufacturas de algodón en varios países, con el simple objeto de hacer patente la competencia con que habrán de encontrarse los comerciantes americanos. Dícese que el Perú y Chile se están preparando, ahora más que nunca, para el cultivo del algodón, y las cosechas no se exportarán al extranjero, como hasta ahora, sino que se consumirán en los telares del país. Perú ha venido dedicándose extensamente por algún tiempo al cultivo del algodón, pero ahora parece que esta industria está extendiéndose rápidamente en Chile. Antes, el algodón era exportado á Inglaterra, casi en su totalidad, pero ahora se trata de fomentar la industria de tejidos en aquel país. El Gobierno está ofreciendo toda clase de alicientes á los plantadores de algodón, y, en consecuencia, una gran extensión de tierra se está dedicando al cultivo de aquella planta. Como una prueba de la seriedad con que están apoyando este proyecto los que figuran á la cabeza de la administración pública, puede citarse la abolición de los derechos sobre toda maquinaria, para fabricación de tejidos, que se importe en el país hasta 1902. Dícese que esta modificación de la tarifa ha ejercido mayor ó menor influencia en la exportación de los Estados Unidos de la maquinaria para tejidos, y recientemente se han hecho grandes pedidos.

La fabricación de paños está mas avanzada en Perú que en Chile, si bien los telares sólo producen todavía las clases de paño de más basta calidad. Se espera que á virtud de la importación de maquinaria moderna reformada, se dará un decidido impulso á la fabricación, y aquellos que han obtenido gran provecho en sus negocios con este país, tendrán que atender ahora con mayor actividad á sus intereses.

SANTO DOMINGO.

ESTADO DEL COMERCIO.

El Cónsul de los Estados Unidos, Mr. GRIMKE, ha dirijido al Departamento de Estado su informe anual sobre la situación comercial é industrial de la República Dominicana, y este informe se ha publicado por extenso en los Informes Consulares del mes de junio. Según Mr. GRIMKE, el descenso en el precio del azúcar, principal producto del país, y otras causas, han producido una depresión general de los negocios en la República. Todo el azúcar que no se vende en el mercado nacional es exportado á Nueva York; el valor total de esta exportación en 1897 fué de

$2,463,906.62. De los otros artículos de exportación los Estados Unidos compraron los siguientes: palo campeche, guayacán, miel de abeja, cera, y plátanos; y casi todo el café, cacao y tabaco se exporta para Francia, Alemania, Bélgica é Inglaterra

En el distrito consular que Mr. GRIMKE representa, toda la madera importada, cuya mayor parte procedió de los Estados Unidos, fué de 2,500,000 piés, y se vendió á $37.50 oro el mil de piés. Toda la harina, la cual se vende á $12 oro el barril, se importa de los Estados Unidos. Hasta una fecha reciente todo el petróleo refinado se importaba de los Estados Unidos, pero la refinería que se ha establecido últimamente en La Romana limitará la importación de este artículo. A causa de la inferior calidad de la mantequilla que se recibe de los Estados Unidos, este artículo se importa ahora casi exclusivamente de Dinamarca. La mejor mantequilla se detalla en Santo Domingo á 62½ centavos la libra, mientras que la de calidad inferior se vende á 37½ centavos. El queso se importa de Holanda y de los Estados Unidos. El queso holandés se vende á 25 centavos oro y el americano á 22½ la libra.

· En cuanto á artículos misceláneos, la mayor parte de las carnes, de las legumbres, y de la leche que vienen en lata se importa de los Estados Unidos. El pescado y la carne de puerco salados se importan en su totalidad de los Estados Unidos; y la manteca, los aceites de cocina y la cerveza vienen en parte de los Estados Unidos. Los vinos se importan de Francia y España. Se ha establecido hace poco una cervecería en Santo Domingo la cual es propiedad de ciudadanos americanos. La caja de cerveza americana se vende á $4.50, mientras que el precio de la cerveza que se fabrica en el país es de $2.25.

La maquinaria para las plantaciones, locomotoras, carros, rieles, puentes de hierro, etc., se importan en su mayor parte de los Estados Unidos, pero Alemania está haciendo una fuerte competencia en este comercio. En artículos de ferretería, Inglaterra, Alemania y Bélgica compiten con los Estados Unidos. El carbón se vende en Santo Domingo á $12 y $13 oro la tonelada y la mayor parte de este artículo se importa de Inglaterra. Inglaterra importa también en Santo Domingo la mayor parte de los géneros de algodón; los géneros de algodón americanos son de mejor calidad, pero más caros que los ingleses y así se explica el predomino de éstos sobre aquéllos en el mercado de la isla; estos géneros se venden de 7½ á 25 centavos oro la yarda. Los géneros de seda se importan exclusivamente de Francia y se venden de 75 centavos á $3 oro la yarda. Francia é Inglaterra importan en Santo Domingo sombreros de todas clases para ambos sexos. Los Estados Unidos importan toda la maquinaria eléctriica que se usa en la isla. Muchas de las plantaciones de azúcar están alumbradas por la electricidad. Francia y los Estados Unidos se reparten el comercio de bicicletas.

Dice el Cónsul, Mr. GRIMKE, que los métodos que se emplean en los Estados Unidos en el embalaje de los géneros es objeto de fuerte censura por parte de comerciantes y plantadores. Los trabajadores de campo ganan de 50 á 75 centavos diarios; en las ciudades los braceros ganan de 50 centavos á $2. Los criados, incluyendo la comida, ganan de $3 á $12 mensuales, y los empleados de oficina de $15 á $75 mensuales.

Los intereses americanos predominan en la República. La mitad, próximamente, de las plantaciones de azúcar son propiedad de ciudadanos de los Estados Unidos. La "San Domingo Improvement Company," que tiene sus oficinas en Nueva York, tiene á su cargo el cobro de las contribuciones del país, según contrato celebrado con el Gobierno, hace algunos años. Hay una línea de vapores, propiedad de W. P. CLYDE & Co., de Nueva York, los cuales hacen viajes quincenales entre este puerto y los puertos de la República.

VENEZUELA.

COMERCIO DE CARACAS Y DEL DISTRITO CONSULAR EN 1897.

Los siguientes datos relativos al comercio de Caracas y del distrito consular están tomados del informe anual de Mr. W. A. ANDRAL, Cónsul interino de la Gran Bretaña en Caracas, dirijido á la Oficina Británica de Relaciones Exteriores. El estado general del comercio de Venezuela en 1897 no puede decirse que es satisfactorio. La causa principal de esta situación fué el resultado desastroso de la cosecha de café, lo cual naturalmente disminuyó la importación en el país y redujo el crédito en el extranjero. Créese que esta situación será grandemente aliviada en la próxima estación, á ¡juzgar por el halagüeño prospecto que presenta la cosecha de café, ahora en estado de crecimiento.

Los cafetales del país ascienden en número á unos 33,000, y los cacaotales á 5,000; el café y el cacao son los principales productos de la República. La alta tarifa proteccionista sobre el azúcar, la cual es prácticamente prohibitiva, ha estimulado el cultivo de la caña de azúcar en grado tal que hay 11,000 ingenios, y se espera que este cultivo ocupe pronto un lugar prominente en la agricultura general del país.

Se han establecido recientemente numerosos clubs con el objeto de encarecer la importancia de la aplicación de métodos científicos en la fertilización, riego, etc., y del uso de la maquinaria reformada en la elaboración de aquel producto.

El gran desideratum para el progreso del país, según dice ·el Cónsul, Mr. ANDRAL, es una inmigración que se establezca en el campo y contribuya así al desarrollo de los recursos agrícolas. Recientemente (como se publicó detalladamente en el BOLETIN MENSUAL del mes de mayo) el Gobierno ha celebrado un contrato con un italiano para la introducción en el país de un gran número de familias italianas que habrán de establecerse en tierras del Estado.

Lo siguiente es un extracto del informe en la parte que se refiere al desarrollo del comercio con Venezuela y á la agencia de la Asociación Nacional de Fabricantes de los Estados Unidos:

Los intereses americanos se están desarrollando considerablemente en el mercado de Venezuela. Los americanos no son tan conservadores en sus métodos y son más prontos en los negocios, pero parece que la causa principal de su éxito consiste en que están mas cerca de aquel mercado. Esta circunstancia es conveniente á los comerciantes de Venezuela que sólo se proveen de un surtido limitado que reponen cuando lo necesitan. Además de ésto, hay simpatías políticas entre los Estados Unidos y Venezuela, y los Estados Unidos no se muestran remisos en aprovecharse de esta circunstancia.

El paso más importante hácia el desarrollo de las relaciones comerciales entre los Estados Unidos y Venezuela ha sido dado por la Asociación Nacional de Fabricantes, establecida en Filadelfia. A principios de 1896 aquella asociación envió un agente á Venezuela para negociar el establecimiento de un almacén permanente de muestras, por cuya mediación las manufacturas americanas pudieran introducirse en el mercado bajo las más favorables condiciones. El contrato se celebró con el departamento correspondiente del gobierno venezolano, y después de haber arreglado todos los preliminares el Comisionado volvió á

Venezuela en noviembre de 1897 y comunicó al Gobierno que la exhibición de muestras sería inaugurada en breve. El informe del Comisionado al Departamento de Fomento dice que el almacén de muestras ha sido establecido para brindar oportunidades á los comerciantes, agricultores, etc., para examinar prácticamente los artículos en lugar de acudir á los catálogos é ilustraciones; para suministrar informes sobre dirección, precios y plazos de los comerciantes americanos; para mantener abierto un salón de lectura donde puedan leerse los periódicos y otras publicaciones relativas á industrias y comercio, y para mostrar, cuando sea practicable, el mecanismo y funcionamiento de máquinas agrícolas, etc. En realidad, esta exhibición permanente habrá de ser una lección objetiva sobre la importancia de la industria americana. La exhibición permanente servirá también como centro para los comerciantes, y habra allí una Oficina de Información, la cual mantendrá impuestos á los comerciantes y sus agentes de las exigencias del mercado y costumbres comerciales del país, y mantendrá al corriente á los capitalistas americanos de las oportunidades para la inversión de su dinero en Venezuela.

El Gobierno exime del pago de derechos todos los géneros que se importen con destino á la exhibición permanente. Como resultado de este paso dado por la Asociación Nacional, se espera que Venezuela obtenga grandes beneficios y que haya un aumento extraordinario en los negocios entre los dos países. A la fecha en que se escriben estas líneas, ya la exhibición ha sido abierta con la asistencia de unos veinte comerciantes de influencia, procedentes de Pennsylvania y Nueva York. El Presidente de Venezuela asistió á la inauguración, y se pronunciaron discursos en los que se trató de la amistad de las dos naciones y de las posibilidades ofrecidas por sus últimas relaciones comerciales. La opinión pública está grandemente en favor de América y los americanos. Si, como se ha dicho ya, hay indicios de que el comercio de los Estados Unidos tiende á ocupar el primer lugar, es natural suponer que un movimiento de esta clase acentuará aquella tendencia y que en poco tiempo los productos americanos reemplazarán á otros similares, y sólo los artículos que los Estados Unidos no pueden producir fácilmente serán los que le quedarán al comercio extranjero. La mayor parte del comercio con los Estados Unidos consiste en comestibles y maquinaria é instrumentos de agricultura. Una firma americana ha obtenido varios contratos para el suministro de cañerías para acueductos.

La prensa de Venezuela refiriéndose á la asociación y á los trabajos que esta se propone, pregunta si los americanos adoptarán el sistema europeo de conceder crédito á largos plazos, ó si al fin convertirán á los comerciantes de Venezuela á su modo de hacer negocios, y dice que de este punto depende el resultado de la competencia, porque el sistema de largos plazos siempre atraerá una cierta porción del comercio. Como es difícil tarea conseguir que la América latina cambie sus costumbres, pasará algún tiempo antes de que aquel resultado se obtenga.

prensivo de la producción y consumo de café en el mundo; este informe, del cual publicamos un extracto á continuación, ha sido preparado por FRANK D. HILL, Cónsul de los Estados Unidos en Santos, Brasil.

El Brasil es el gran país productor de café en todo el mundo; rinde un 66 por ciento de la producción universal. Todos los veinte estados que componen la República producen café en mayor ó menor escala. Sin embargo, la verdadera zona cafetalera está comprendida en los estados de Rio Janeiro, São Paulo, Espiritu Santo y Minas Geraes. São Paulo es el principal estado cafetalero. Rio y Santos son los principales puertos de exportación, aunque también se exportan considerables cantidades por el puerto de Victoria.

El café es clasificado de la manera siguiente: fino, superior, bueno, regular, ordinario, y triache. Este último es el café de clase inferior y se compone de granos quebrados y defectuosos en general. La clase fina se compone de café limpio, de grano de tamaño y color regulares. La superior es de granos de tamaño regular, pero puede contener algunas cáscaras ó frijoles negros. En la clase buena, la igualdad en el grano no es absolutamente necesaria; puede contener algunos frijoles negros, pero no astillas ni piedras ó tierra. El café regular puede contener grandes cantidades de frijoles negros, cáscaras, piedras, astillas, ó tierra. La clase ordinaria contiene todos los defectos anteriores y algunos granos quebrados.

Según el Cónsul HILL, los Brasileños condenan la idea prevaleciente en los países extranjeros de que el café del Brasil no es el mejor que se produce; los Brasileños saben que el café de Java y Moka que se vende en el mercado americano, es en su mayor parte cultivado cerca de Río ó de Santos.

La producción de café en el estado de São Paulo, así como la vida de la mata, depende del carácter del terreno y de la planta. Según informes, hay matas que han estado produciendo por 75 años y que aún producen. Mil matas producen 3,238 libras ó 25 sacos en São Paulo, mientras que en la provincia de Río Janeiro la producción es mucho menor. A causa de la gran producción de café en varias partes del mundo, el promedio de precio en los mercados del Brasil es, y ha venido siendo por algún tiempo, de 5-7 centavos, oro, la libra ó sea $7.56 por saco. Las cifras del

y viejas: y asimismo el hecho de que los precios en oro del café, durante los dos últimos años, bajaron más del 50 por ciento, y que los valores locales dependen de grandes fluctuaciones en el cambio, pues la moneda del Brasil sufre al presente una depreciación de 80 por ciento. Yo creo que 2 milreis (28 centavos) por mata, en completo estado de producción, sería un precio moderado para una finca bien situada y que cuente con casas de vivienda, maquinaria y otros requisitos comprendidos en aquel precio. Los gastos de un cafetal de 150,000 matas no exceden probablemente de $5,000 al año, sin incluir los fletes—que son caros—hasta los puertos, ni el costo de los sacos y gastos de venta. El importe de la producción sería de 65,000 á 70,000 kilógramos (de 143,299 á 154,322 libras) que dejarían una utilidad de 50,000 milreis ($7,000) sobre un capital de $50,000, ó sea el 14 por ciento del capital invertido. El precio de 9 milreis ($1.26) por cada 10 kilógramos (22.046 libras), que con frecuencia se menciona como precio corriente en este informe, se refiere al café superior; el café "bueno," que es equivalente al no. 7 de la Lonja de Café, Nueva York, se vende a 7½ milreis ($1.05) por cada 10 kilógramos, ó 45 milreis ($6.50) por saco de 60 kilógramos (132 libras).

El consumo anual de café en el mundo durante los próximos cinco años se calcula en 12,000,000 de sacos (1,584,000,000 de libras), de los cuales corresponderán á la producción del Brasil 8,000,000 de sacos (1,050,000,000 de libras).

Las cifras del siguiente cuadro muestran la producción entre la cosecha de café y la de otros productos en el Brasil; el cuadro se refiere á la exportación de 1895:

Café	$140, 000, 000
Goma elástica	25, 000, 000
Otros productos	15, 000, 000
Total	180, 000, 000

El número del Boletín Mensual correspondiente al mes de octubre de 1897 contenía extensos datos oficiales relativos á la industria del café y del cacao en Venezuela, y se dijo que el área de cultivo del café en 1897 era de 403,865 acres, que dieron una producción total de 304,800,000 libras. Estas cifras se consignan también en el informe del Cónsul HILL, el cual expresa la opinión— fundada en los datos que obtuvo durante una visita que hizo á

COMERCIO MISCELÁNEO.

REPÚBLICA ARGENTINA.

Luz Eléctrica en Buenos Aires. En el número de mayo del BOLETIN MENSUAL se hizo referencia al hecho de que el ayuntamiento de Buenos Aires había celebrado un contrato con la Compañía General de Electricidad para hacer el servicio del alumbrado público en aquella ciudad, y se publicaron los detalles sobre el número de luces, precio que había de pagarse, etc. Sin embargo, la " Review of the River Plate " del 7 de mayo, publica la noticia de que, por razón de ciertas formalidades, el contrato no ha sido definitivamente aprobado, y por consiguiente, todavía se presenta la oportunidad á otras compañías de solicitar la concesión de este valioso contrato.

Importación de Maquinaria Extranjera. El Cónsul de los Estados Unidos, Mr. BOUCHSEIN, en un informe fechado en Barmen, Alemania, sobre la venta de maquinaria extranjera en la República Argentina, dice lo siguiente : "En un informe especial dirijido al gobierno imperial, un cónsul alemán llama la atención hácia el pueblo de Tucumán, como lugar propio para la venta de la maquinaria alemana. Tucumán, ó San Miguel de Tucumán, es la capital de la provincia de Tucumán, República Argentina, con una población de 17,000. Está unido por ferrocarril con Córdoba y Rosario. Las fábricas de azúcar de aquella provincia, que ascienden á treinta y tres, han importado de Francia casi toda su maquinaria á causa de los plazos favorables que se les concedieron. De Alemania se han importado aparatos para la destilación, los cuales están conectados con las fábricas de azúcar, hornos de azufre, etc. La industria del azúcar en Tucumán progresa cada año más, y en breve se necesitará maquinaria en general en cantidad considerable. Algunos de los fabricantes de maquinaria francesa han tenido representantes en Tucumán por muchos años.

Leyes sobre Marcas de Fábrica. El reciente cuantioso fraude de marca de fábrica, cometido en Buenos Aires, brinda ocasión oportuna para llamar la atención de los comerciantes y manufactureros hácia la importancia de registrar sus marcas de fábrica en la América del Sur y otros lugares. La ley que trata de esta materia en aquellos países es clara y de fácil observancia, y solo se requiere cuidadosa atención para evitar imitaciones fraudulentas. En el caso en cuestión los comerciantes en cuyo perjuicio se cometió el fraude están defendiendo vigorosamente sus derechos en la Argentina; pero á menos que se pruebe que la marca de fábrica fué registrada con arreglo á la ley, será difícil obtener la condenación de la parte responsable.

El Maíz en la Argentina. La producción del maiz, fruto este que constituye uno de los principales artículos de exportación de la Argentina, ha ascendido de 8,038 toneladas en 1873 á 1,500,000 toneladas (calculadas) en 1896. La provincia de Buenos Aires, por razón de sus condiciones climatológicas, se adapta especialmente al cultivo de este cereal, cuya exportación empezó mucho antes que la del trigo. Durante la primevera y el verano (de octubre á marzo) la temperatura presenta una regularidad propia para el desarrollo de la planta, mientras la lluvia, que es abundante, suministra al suelo la necesaria humedad.   La superficie sembrada de maíz en 1891 era sólo de 100,498 hectáreas, y en 1895 el área de cultivo era de 718,633 hectáreas, con una producción de 628,000,000 de kilógramos.

BRASIL.

Comercio en Abril de 1898.   Aunque los derechos de importación en el Brasil son más bajos que los del año pasado, los ingresos de aduana, por concepto de importación de mercancías extranjeras, durante el mes de abril de 1898 ascendieron á $491,662.64—$35,488.18 más que el importe de los ingresos en igual mes del año anterior.   El total del café recibido en Santos durante el mes fué de 377,000 sacos, de los cuales fueron almacenados 263,422, contra 247,901 en abril de 1897.   El café recibido en Río durante el mismo mes fué de 238,000 sacos, cantidad ésta que acusa un exceso del 1,000 sacos, comparada con la recibida en el mes de abril del año precedente.   El monto de los cargamentos fué de 438,404 sacos en Río y 532,677 sacos en Santos.   Esta es una cantidad enorme para la estación y á ello es debido el notable descenso de la existencia de café en las aduanas, la cual era en 30 de abril de sólo 339,116 sacos, ó sea menos de la mitad del café almacenado á principios del mes.

GUATEMALA.

Embalaje para el Trasporte por Tierra.   El trasporte en Guatemala se hace usualmente por medio de mulos.   La cantidad de mercancías trasportadas de esta suerte constituye una carga.   La panela (azúcar en bruto), el carbón, la zacata, y todos los productos del país se venden por cargas de nueve arrobas ó sean unos 100 kilógramos (225 libras).   Es importante que los fabricantes tomen nota de este detalle, pues todo lo que se destina al uso de las fincas, especialmente la maquinaria, debe arreglarse en paquetes que no excedan de este peso; ésto se refiere también á todos los artículos de uso general.   Los paquetes de unos cincuenta kilógramos, distribuidos en sentido longitudinal, son de lo más apropiado para el trasporte en mulos.   El costo de trasporte varía; depende en gran parte de la distancia que haya de recorrerse.

HAITÍ.

Negociaciones para un Empréstito.   Mr. JOHN B. TERRES, Vicecónsul de los Estados Unidos en Port-au-France, ha remitido al Departamento de Estado la copia de una ley que la legislatura de Haití emitió en sus últimas sesiones con el fin de negociar un empréstito de $3,500,000, oro.   Este empréstito se hará en los Estados Unidos, y el Señor J. N. LÉGER, Ministro de Haití en Washington, ha sido encargado de las negociaciones.   El objeto que se propone llenar con el empréstito es retirar de la circulación el papel moneda de la República.   La ley en la forma en que fué emitida por la legislatura y promulgada por el Presidente, SIMÓN SAM, se halla impresa en su totalidad en los "United States Consular Reports" correspondientes á junio del año corriente.

Venezuela—de que la producción de café en aquel país está aumentando considerablemente.

De un informe del Ministro Baker, publicado en los "Informes Consulares" de los Estados Unidos, no. 199, resulta que la producción de café en Nicaragua en el año 1896 fué de 50,000 sacos, 5,000,000 de libras más que en ninguna cosecha anterior. El Cónsul Hill, al referirse á las posibilidades del cultivo del café en el Paraguay, habla de este país como una parte de la zona cafetalera del Brasil, y dice que ha visto en Asunción matas de café de un hermoso grano. Mientras no tenga lugar una nueva y viril inmigración en esta república, la yerba mate continuará siendo la bebida del país.

La producción de café en el Perú está aumentando, y este producto promete ser uno de los principales del país. Chanchamayo, Perene, Pancarbambo, y los valles del río Colorado son los grandes distritos cafetaleros. Esta industria agrícola, como muchas otras industrias de aquella tierra privilegiada, sólo esperan para su desarrollo la inauguración de medios adecuados de transporte.

A pesar de la gran producción de café en el Brasil y otras regiones, y no obstante el bajo precio de aquel artículo, el Cónsul Hill considera que es halagüeño el porvenir económico y financiero del Brasil. La deuda exterior del Brasil es pequeña comparada con la de muchos otros países, y hay en el Brasil una corriente constante de buena inmigración. En 1870 llegaron al puerto de Santos cincuenta y siete mil inmigrantes la mayor parte de los cuales eran hombres económicos, capaces para el desenvolvimiento de los recursos agrícolas del país, como se ha hecho en los vastos y fructíferos llanos de la República Argentina.

Como evidencia de halagüeño prospecto se trascribe textualmente el siguiente párrafo final del informe :

"Todo parece que opera aquí de consuno, en obsequio de estas nuevas tierras inexplotadas que forman parte del hemisferio occidental, cuyo suelo ha sido sólo ligeramente removido, y la mayor parte de cuya población se encuentra á lo largo del litoral ó á los lados de las vías fluviales y artificiales que comunican con el interior, no obstante haber trascurrido tres siglos desde que se dió á conocer á Europa sus recursos. Juzgando estos países por su historia diaria, talvez parezcan estacionarios, pero si se comparan unas décadas con otras, se verá que han realizado grandes progresos.

exhibidos.   La casa de los Senores G. MENCHACA & CA. ha salido de gran número de artículos que había tenido en su poder por varios años y cuyo valor no había podido apreciarse hasta el presente por falta de exhibición apropiada.   La ventaja respecto de los artículos nuevos es aún más pronunciada; el agente de una casa de los Estados Unidos ha encontrado ya compradores para casi todos los artículos que se han remitido para su exposición.   La maquinaria y manufacturas de todas clases, procedentes del extranjero, están exentas de toda contribución y de todo alquiler por el espacio que ocupan, á no ser que se vendan en el país. Como hay un salón de lectura en la exposición, se ha indicado como beneficiosa la idea de que los Estados Unidos envíen, en gran número, catálogos y fotografías de sus productos para que sean examinados por los compradores.   Serían de utilidad especial los grabados de maquinarias, calderas de vapor, aparatos de minería y para fabricación de azúcar, obras de marco de metal, cobertizos, puentes, casas portátiles, etc.

EL SALVADOR.

Efectos de la Nueva Ley Bancaria.   Una nueva ley bancaria fué emitida en las últimas sesiones ordinarias del congreso, cuyo objeto principal es obligar á los bancos á que rediman sus billetes en plata.   La ley comenzó á surtir sus efectos el 11 de abril último.   El Cónsul, JOHN JENKINS, escribiendo desde San Salvador con fecha 15 de abril, dice que el Banco Industrial del Salvador ha suspendido sus negocios y en combinación con uno de los bancos más antiguos del país formará una nueva institución bancaria.   Esta acción reducirá a cuatro el número de los bancos.   La rivalidad había dado por resultado una situación nada satisfactoria en los negocios bancarios de la República y los bancos se habían convertido en instituciones meramente especuladoras.   Como que la nueva ley impone á los bancos la obligación de redimir sus billetes en efectivo, se espera que esta clase de negocios tomen mejor curso.   Mr. JENKINS añade que á pesar del bajo precio del café, hay en El Salvador abundancia de material para asegurar una grande prosperidad en el porvenir.

URUGUAY.

Enseñanza Gratuita en las Academias Militar y Naval de los Estados Unidos.   Correspondiendo á una indicación hecha por Mr. FINCH, Ministro de los Estados Unidos, el gobierno de esta república ha ofrecido dos becas á la República del Uruguay, una en la Academia Militar de West Point y la otra en la Academia Naval de Annapolis, en beneficio de dos jóvenes ciudadanos de aquella república.   Los nombramientos se harán de acuerdo á la solicitud formal del Presidente del Uruguay.

VENEZUELA.

Exportaciones del Puerto de Nueva York.   El Señor Don ANTONIO E. DELFINO, Cónsul General de Venezuela, ha proporcionado á esta Oficina los siguientes datos estadísticos relativos á la exportación de mercancías de Nueva York á varios puertos de Venezuela en el mes de mayo de 1898, comparando éste con el mismo mes en el año de 1897.   En mayo de 1898 el total de las exportaciones

total de la obra, incluyendo la expropiación de tierras, ha sido calculado en 371,009,947 rublos ($188,014,938), ó sea á razón de 49,444 rublos por "verst."

Para vencer el obstáculo que ofrece el puerto de Vladivostok, que permanece cerrado por el hielo durante varios meses del año. se construirá un ramal á través de Manchuria, territorio adquirido de China recientemente, hasta un punto en el mar Amarillo que esté abierto todo el año.

Para que se aprecie la importancia de las fuentes de riqueza que contiene la región por la cual ha de pasar el ferrocarril transiberiano, se trascribe á continuación el siguiente extracto de un informe, fechado en San Petersburgo el 14 de octubre de 1895, y dirigido al Departamento de Estado por Mr. HERBERT H. PEARCE, Chargé d'Affaires, ad interim, de los Estados Unidos.

Que este gran ferrocarril está destinado á abrir al tráfico un país de gran riqueza es un hecho que no puede dudarse á la luz de los actuales conocimientos. Las regiones mineras de los Urales y de los montes Altai y Sayan están inexplotadas y muy poco exploradas por causa de las dificultades que se encuentran en el trasporte de sus productos, pues todos los grandes ríos que por ellas pasan corren en dirección norte hácia el océano ártico   Ya en los Urales se están haciendo progresos en la extracción y preparación de minerales de hierro y cobre y fundición de metales.   Toda Rusia está grandemente interesada en los trabajos del ferrocarril trascontinental, y se sabe que el Emperador, que fué presidente de la empresa cuando era czarevitch, está empeñado con grande entusiasmo en la pronta terminación de la obra.   Toda la construcción y equipo de la línea se está haciendo y seguirá haciéndose, en lo posible, en Rusia y por los rusos, de acuerdo con el sistema de protección á la industria y producción nacionales con tanto ardor instituido por el último Emperador.   Capitalistas extranjeros están empleando su capital, previo contrato con el gobierno, en el establecimiento de talleres para la fabricación de rieles, locomotoras y otros equipos, pero los talleres habrán de establecerse en Rusia y los trabajadores deberán ser rusos.

J. C. MONAHAN, Cónsul de los Estados Unidos en Chemnitz, Alemania, dice con fecha 4 de diciembre de 1896:

Siberia es rica en minerales de todas clases: los Urales están produciendo oro y plata en grandes cantidades.   Si se asiste á las ferias annuales de Leipsic, se comprenderá la importancia que tienen para Alemania las pieles finas de Siberia. Si el martillo que clavó el primer espigón en el primer travesaño fué de plata, el que clavó el último espigón debiera ser de oro.   Por mucha importancia que tenga esta línea para Alemania, Rusia y el resto de Europa, la tiene mayor para nosotros.   California, Oregón, Washington, todo el oeste de nuestro país, si no todo el continente, están interesados en esta línea.   Rusia tiene bastante en que ocuparse dentro de los límites de su territorio; nosotros somos los que han de auxiliar el desenvolvimiento del Oriente.

Con la terminación de esta vasta empresa quedarán abiertas al tráfico y comercio del mundo regiones hasta ahora inaccesibles. El viaje de San Petersburgo á Pequín podrá hacerse en cinco días en trenes lujosos; podrá irse desde Londres á la capital del Japón en quince días en vez de treinta, que es el tiempo que ahora se tarda en aquel viaje, á través del Atlántico, continente Americano y océano Pacífico; ó en vez del viaje aún más largo, por la vía del Mediterráneo y del canal de Suez.

Es imposible predecir, á esta sazón, cual sea el efecto que este factor haya de tener en la situación económica del mundo comercial; ya se está proyectando el establecimiento de nuevas líneas de vapores entre Puerto Arturo, que es el término meridional del ferrocarril, y algunos puertos japoneses y chinos, y Manila, así como también la inmediata conexión con líneas desde estos puertos hasta los países de más allá del Pacífico y Asia meridional.

En vista del espíritu comercial que está desarrollándose en nuevo Japón y de la adquisición de territorio chino por importantes naciones comerciales de Europa, es de esperarse que en breve pueda presenciarse el espectáculo del ancho Pacífico surcado por innúmeros buques mercantes, como lo está hoy el Atlántico. En la realización de este prospecto el ferrocarril transiberiano debe entrar necesariamente como el factor más importante. Si se observa el mapa del océano Pacífico y las rutas por él establecidas, se verá que las islas de aquel extenso mar ofrecen algo así como una serie de escalones de piedra á la comunicación entre Oriente y Occidente. Y á juzgar por las condiciones bajo las cuales está desenvolviéndose aquella parte del mundo, estos numerosos puntos de escala pasarán probablemente á una nueva existencia política bajo la bandera americana.

El BOLETÍN MENSUAL ha llamado la atención varias veces hácia las concesiones hechas á súbditos japoneses para el establecimiento de líneas de vapores entre el Japón y México y aún Perú. Extensas colonias de japoneses se han establecido y están estableciéndose en las ricas tierras del istmo de Tehuantepec. La inevitable construcción del canal de Nicaragua ó cualquier otro istmo, influirá por modo tan conspícuo en el desarrollo de este comercio oriental como la construcción del gran ferrocarril transiberiano.

em consideração que a costa do paiz tem 4,000 milhas de comprimento e que sua magestosa arteria fluvial, o Amazonas, com
seus affluentes, permitte a livre navegação por uma distancia de
mais de 30,000 milhas ao interior de seu territorio, pode-se formar
uma idea das immensas possibilidades que se offerecem para seu
desenvolvimento industrial.

O Brazil é um paiz que possue magnificos recursos naturaes;
mas o grande obstaculo da America hespanhola, é dizer, a falta de
proporção entre a extensão territorial e sua população, se nota aqui
como nas outras republicas irmãs. A riqueza agricola da nação
é illimitada, e, comtudo, só uma pequena parte da terra está cultivada. O principal producto, como se sabe, é o café, e seguem
assucar, tabaco, algodão, herva matte, borracha, madeiras de construcção, cacáo e nozes, na ordem indicada. Desde ha alguns
annos, o Brazil tem produzido mais do que a metade do café que
se consome no mundo. As florestas abundam em madeiras valiosas, páus de tinturaria, resinas, fibras e plantas medicinaes. No
vallé do Amazonas sómente ha 22,000 especies de madeiras, das
quaes tem-se feito um catalogo. As immensas planicies do sul
adaptam-se especialmente para a criação de gado, e os rios abundam em muitas variedades de peixe. A riqueza mineral é grande.
O ferro existe em grandes quantidades, mas a escassez de combustivel impede que se explorem com proveito os depositos. Os
estrangeiros, principalmente os inglezes e os francezes, exploram
em grande escala as minas de ouro e de diamante.

As industrias representam-se por umas 156 fabricas de algodão,
nas quaes se empregam uns 200,000 operarios; algumas fabricas
importantes de tecidos de lã, engenhos de assucar, fabricas de
cortume, fabricas de cerveja e de distillação, moinhos de farinha,
bricas de sabão, oleo e velas, estaleiros, etc. O Brazil, provavelmente, nunca chegará a ser um grande paiz manufactureiro, mas
no productor e exportador de materias primas tem um futuro
grandes possibilidades.

m 31 de Dezembro de 1896 havia funccionando no paiz
e milhas de estradas de ferro e 4,963 milhas em via de con-
ão. Um interessante relatorio muito detalhado acerca destas
erreas foi publicado no BOLETIM correspondente ao mez de
o de 1898. O systema telegraphico está sob a direcção do
mo e em 189 havia em uso 21,936 milhas de arame. No

mesmo anno a marinha mercante consistia de 189 vapores de 75,283 toneladas, e 282 navios de vela de 65,575 toneladas.

A Republica do Uruguay, que está contigua ao Brazil ao sul, tem uma area calculada de 72,110 milhas quadradas, com uma população de 843,408. Setenta por cento da população compõe-se dos naturaes do paiz.

A natureza, ao distribuir seus favores, tratou esta pequena Republica da America do Sul com mão generosa. Pode-se dizer que é um grande terreno de pastagem situado na zona temperada, sempre verde e banhado por grandes rios e seus innumeraveis tributarios. Não obstante ser ondulosa a superficie do paiz, excepto na costa do Atlantico, não ha montanhas de mais de 2,000 pés de altura; o paiz é uma successão de collinas cobertas de herva, extensos campos e margens de rios cobertas de arvores.

A principal industria do Uruguay é, como é natural, a criação de gado vaccum e carneiros. Os dados estatisticos, que nos paizes de grande extensão territorial, pequena população e insufficientes meios de communicação, se inclinam mais ao lado do menos que do mais, mostram que para 1895 os estabelecimentos de criação no paiz continham 5,247,871 cabeças de gado vaccum, 388,348 cavallos, 14,007 mulas e 14,333,626 carneiros. O valor total dos rebanhos de bois e de carneiros foi calculado em $73,038,000. Os productos desta industria, os quaes constituem a maior parte do commercio de exportação do Uruguay, são xarque, extracto de carne, couros e pelles, sebo e lã. No anno de 1895 exportaram-se 50,000 toneladas de lã. Exportam-se os animaes gelados em grandes quantidades para a Europa.

Durante os ultimos annos tem-se dado maior attenção á agricultura, e com o apoio do Governo tem-se começado a cultivar aquelle fertil solo com resultados relativamente bons. O trigo e a farinha que até o anno de 1897 se importavam do estrangeiro, têm chegado a ser hoje artigos de exportação. As exportações de trigo, farinha e milho, durante os quatro annos desde 1894 até 897, foram no valor de $10,902,823, emquanto que nos quatro annos anteriores foram no valor de $2,246,856, o qual mostra um augmento sobre o primeiro periodo de $8,655,968. Têm-se obtido resultados satisfactorios no cultivo da vinha, e o numero de cultivadas da vinha augmenta rapidamente.

fructas do Uruguay são afamadas, incluindo as variedades

das zonas temperadas e tropicaes. Maçãs, peras, pecegos, cerejas, ameixas, limões, limas, romeiras, marmelos, bananas, cocos e abacaxis são exportados para o Brazil e a Republica Argentina, e a conservação dos marmelos, que abundam no paiz, é um ramo importante da industria. Tambem se produzem alli em quantidades consideraveis, a linhaça, o canhamo, o tabaco e o açafrão.

Não se tem feito muito progresso na industria mineira, não obstante que existem alli minas de ouro, prata, cobre, ferro, estanho e mercurio, que poderiam ser explorados com proveito.

Em 1896 havia 1,026 milhas de estradas de ferro em trafego regular e 200 milhas em via de construcção. O comprimento total das linhas de telegrapho em 1897 era de 4,380, das quaes 982 pertenciam ás estradas de ferro.

A marinha mercante da Republica em 1895 consistia de 19 vapores, de 4,608 toneladas, e 45 navios de vela, de 13,171 toneladas.

Ao occuparmos-nos da Republica Argentina, vemos confirmado o facto, a que se tem feito referencia em outros numeros do BOLETIM, de que muitos dos principaes productos deste paiz, notavelmente o trigo e a lã,—são identicos aos dos Estados Unidos, do que resulta que o commercio nelles é muito pequeno. A Republica Argentina, situada como está entre os 22° e 56° de latitude sul, tem uma costa sobre o Atlantico mais extensa que a de sua vizinha Republica do norte, e como está mais proxima ao equador, dá os productos distinctivos dos climas frios e tropicaes.

Este paiz, com uma area de 1,212,000 milhas quadradas e uma população de 4,092,990, é um dos mais extensos e productivos do Novo Mundo.

Nas montanhas do oeste da Republica encontram-se ricos depositos de mineraes, taes como ouro, prata, ferro e cobre, emquanto que nas provincias do sudoeste têm-se descoberto recentemente extensos depositos de carvão. Mas a industria mineira ainda não está desenvolvida, apezar do Codigo de Minas da Republica, tão liberal como bem concebido.

A Republica Argentina é conhecida em todo o mundo como a sede das industrias agricola e pecuaria, e os progressos que a Republica tem feito nestas industrias são muito grandes. Ha só poucos annos que este paiz importava farinha de trigo do Chile, sua vizinho occidental; mas veiu a guerra do Paraguay, e com ella a grande procura de cereaes. Os argentinos aproveitaram-se do seu solo maravilhosamente rico, em que o arado faz menos trabalho do que em qualquer outra parte do mundo, e no anno de 1893, o seu paiz chegou a occupar o terceiro lugar entre as nações grandes exportadoras de trigo no mundo. Em 1895 as exportações deste producto foram de 37,120,897 alqueires. Calcula-se que ha na Republica 240,000,000 de geiras de terreno apropriado para o cultivo do trigo, ainda que em 1897 se calculou que só havia 15,000,000 de geiras empregadas em toda classe de cultivos. A producção média por geira de trigo é calculada em 990 libras.

A industria pecuaria da Republica Argentina tem fama universal. O recenseamento nacional de 1895 mostra que o numero de animaes no paiz era como se segue: gado vaccum, 21,701,526; cavallos, mulas e burros, 4,930,228; carneiros, 74,379,561; cabras, 2,748,860; o valor total destes animaes em papel moeda era de $1,130,701,331. A conclusão natural que se tira de possuir o paiz tão grande numero de bois e carneiros é que seus productos e residuos formam parte muito importante do commercio de exportação da Republica, e assim é. Desde 1896 o commercio estrangeiro em chifres, ossos, couros, xarque, extracto de carne, aparas de couros, linguas conservadas, sangue secco, graxa e sebo, carnes salgadas, carnes conservadas, animaes gelados, pelles de carneiro e lã tem sido muito grande, ainda que tem fluctuado por razão das seccas e outras causas naturaes que affectam esta industria em outros paizes. O commercio em gado vaccum com o Uruguay, Chile, e o Brazil tem chegado a alcançar grandes proporções e tem produzido grandes riquezas. A maior parte das "estancias," por cujo nome são conhecidos os grandes estabelecimentos de criação de gado, estão submettidas a um plano cooperativo que tem dado bons resultados, produzindo a grande immigração de estrangeiros, os quaes têm formado alli colonias, occupando-se no desenvolvimento das industrias agricola e pecuaria.

A Republica Argentina differe de suas republicas irmãs n'um caracteristico, pelo menos. Até o anno de 1889 seus artigos de exportação limitavam-se principalmente aos productos acima mencionados; mas a crise que teve lugar naquelle anno foi causa de que o paiz, que até então tinha produzido materias primas sómente, mostrasse pelas estatisticas de importação que a actividade do povo tinha seguido outras direcções. Estabeleceram-se fabricas, e em 1892 muitos artigos que tinham occupado lugar proeminente nas listas dos importados, se faziam notar nellas por sua ausencia. As energias da nação começaram a mostrar quanto podiam fazer em outras industrias, satisfazendo suas necessidades com o emprego dos productos do solo na fabricação de muitos artigos que antes importavam, assim entrando no labor louvavel de levantar uma nação tão grande como poderosa, fazendo-a dependente de si mesma para seu sustento.

O recenseamento de 1895 mostra que os principaes estabelecimentos industriaes foram os seguintes: fabricas de vinho, 852; moinhos de trigo, 532; fabricas de distillação, 108; fabricas de cerveja, 44; plantações de assucar, 2,749; engenhos de assucar, 48; vinhedos, 6,514.

A questão de transportes por via ferrea na Republica Argentina tem sido estudada cuidadosamente pelo Governo, e algumas das melhores linhas do mundo agora atravessam as mais ricas secções do paiz. Desde ha alguns annos o Corpo de Engenheiros do Governo tem-se occupado em fazer estudos e reconhecimentos não sómente para as linhas em projecto e em via de construcção, mas tambem em previsão do porvenir, estendendo por todo o paiz uma grande rede de viação, cujas secções deverão ser construidas quando as exigencias do trafico o exigirem.

Das vias ferreas em exploração em 1895 havia 5 pertencentes á nação e 10 particulares, garantidas pelo Governo. A extensão total daquellas, no dia 31 de Dezembro deste anno, era de 1,033 kilometros, e a destas, 3,920. A extensão total de todas as linhas em exploração em 1896 é calculada em 9,032 milhas.

Em 1896 havia no paiz 25,345 milhas de linhas telegraphicas, com 59,060 milhas de arame, quasi a metade dellas sob a direcção do Governo.

A marinha mercante da Republica em 1894 consistia de 75 vapores, de 21,613 toneladas, e 125 navios de vela, de 28,241 toneladas.

A Republica do Paraguay, como a da Bolivia, está situada ao interior, apartada do littoral, com o qual faz-se communicação por meio de umas das melhores arterias fluviaes do mundo, os rios

O. tabaco cresce em todas as secções da Republica e é outro de seus productos principaes. A canna de assucar cresce tambem com abundancia mas os engenhos de assucar são primitivos. O algodão e outras plantas fibrosas crescem espontaneamente, e em uma palavra quasi todos os productos tropicaes dão-se alli em abundancia.

As florestas do Paraguay são especialmente ricas em madeiras duras e ainda que a industria de seu corte tem chegado a alcançar boas proporções nos ultimos annos, não ha duvida de que a fortuna favorecerá aquelles que entrem no negocio em uma escala proporcionada á quantidade de materia prima que alli se encontra. O transporte e o trabalho são baratos, e os preços que se obtém nos mercados vizinhos são bons.

Quanto á industria mineira pode-se dizer que ainda não tem sido desenvolvida, não obstante que sob a verde superficie jazem thesouros em mineraes que, quando estiverem descobertos, augmentarão immensamente a riqueza do paiz.

O Paraguay tem feito pouco progresso no ramo de manufacturas, e passarão muitos annos antes de que possa abastar ás necessidades do consumo domestico. Hoje a industria manufactureira é limitada á fabricação de tecidos de algodão e de lã. A fabricação de louça e de distillação são as unicas industrias que, ainda que estão em seus começos, terão de dar grandes rendimentos no futuro. As argillas finas do Paraguay se conhecem desde ha muito tempo e a extracção por distillação das ricas essencias de laranjas e outras fructas, flores, folhas, etc., apresenta um campo rico aonde deve affluir o capital.

Por mais estranho que pareça, a primeira estrada de ferro que houve na America latina foi construida no Paraguay, ha alguns 50 annos, pelo Dictador LOPEZ, e hoje só ha uma linha no paiz, propriedade de uma sociedade particular, que estende-se da capital até Pirapo, percorrendo uma distancia de 155.4 milhas. Esta linha será estendida até Encarnación, sobre o rio Paraná, onde se enlaçará com a rede de viação da Republica Argentina.

Ha no paiz 360 milhas de linhas de telegrapho.

No espaço necessariamente limitado, é impossivel dar mais que um rapido olhar para a maravilhosa riqueza das republicas da America do Sul, banhadas pelo grande Atlantico e os caudalosos rios que desembocam nelle, mas esse olhar basta para mostrar que cada uma das ditas nações apresenta, por maneira mais ou menos attrahente, a quem busca ganhar-se os meios de viver, uma terra muito promettedora.

REPUBLICA ARGENTINA.

COMMERCIO DE CARNE GELADA.

O Sr. Lyman W. Chute, Vice-consul dos Estados Unidos em Buenos Aires, remette á Secretaria de Estado, em data de 16 de Dezembro de 1897, um relatorio detalhado sobre o commercio de carne gelada da Republica Argentina, que se publica por extenso nas paginas avulsas dos " Relatorios Consulares dos Estados Unidos," de 10 de Maio de 1898. Por ser de interesse geral, extrahimos do relatorio os seguintes trechos:

COMEÇO DA INDUSTRIA.

A industria de carne gelada estabeleceu-se na Republica Argentina em 1882, e as primeiras exportações deste artigo realizaram-se em 1883; desde esta data, têm ido progredindo constantemente. A industria faz-se em quatro estabelecimentos, a saber:

O primeiro, estabelecido em 1882, está situado em Campaña, a umas 40 milhas ao norte da cidade de Buenos Aires, no rio Paraná.

O segundo, começado em 1884, está situado na margem do sul do Riachuelo, um ribeiro canalisado que forma o limite meridional da cidade de Buenos Aires Este estabelecimento que foi fundado por uma sociedade de particulares, converteu-se depois n'uma companhia anonyma que tem crescido constantemente. Começando de uma maneira relativamente modesta, tem conseguido alcançar um lugar mais proeminente no commercio de carneiros gelados.

O terceiro foi estabelecido em 1886, em San Nicolas, porto do rio Paraná.

O quarto começou em 1886, em Lima, estação de estrada de ferro na linha de Buenos Aires e Rosario perto de Zarate, porto vizinho a Campaña, e está situado tambem no rio Paraná.

Em 1895, um estabelecimento de carne gelada foi fundado sob os auspicios da Sociedade Rural da Republica Argentina, cujos principaes accionistas eram criadores de gado, desejosos de encontrar vantajosa sahida a seus productos. Os dous carregamentos que se fizeram, deram grandes prejuizos. Os animaes exportados nestes dous carregamentos eram de cinco ou seis annos e de recente castração, inappropriados ás exigencias dos mercados inglezes; o processo de congelação se levou a cabo a bordo do vapor, preparado para este fim, mas o resultado mostrou o erro de preparar a carne em outro ponto excepto em terra. Esta companhia liquidou e uma nova firma trata de estabelecer-se na provincia de Buenos Aires, para a preparação e exportação de carne gelada.

CAPITAL.

O capital total dos quatro estabelecimentos é de $5,934,380 (ouro), incluindo nesta quantia o valor da terra, os edificios, machinas, installações, etc. Os quatro estabelecimentos constituem quatro companhias, das quaes tres funccionam com capital inglez e uma com capital nacional.

TRABALHO.

O numero dos trabalhadores empregados é de 1,225, classificados da maneira seguinte: superintendentes, que recebem um salario de $1.50 a $2 (ouro) por dia; carneiros, esfoladores, preparadores de pelle, e braços em geral, que ganham um peso (ouro) diario, approximadamente.

GADO.

Obtém-se os carneiros da província de Buenos Aires e as raças que se procuram mais são as South, Hampshire, Shropshire, Oxford Down, Cheviot e Romney Marsh; tambem se procuram os carneiros procedentes da raça nativa, obtidos por meio do cruzamento com os Lincoln ou os Rambouillet. Comtudo, as maiores vendas que se têm feito, realizaram-se com os carneiros de raça pura Hampshire Down, ainda que ultimamente se tem dito que se têm obtido excellentes resultados na congelação de carne, com os carneiros producto do cruzamento dos da raça Merino com os carneiros de cara negra da raça Shropshire. Obtém-se os novilhos principalmente das provincias de Buenos Aires, Cordoba e San Juan. O commercio é limitado por causa da difficuldade en encontrar a classe de animal que se necessita para este processo.

O peso médio do carneiro vivo é de 50 kilogrammas e, depois de preparado, pesa uns 25 kilogrammas. Um carneiro, muito bem preparado da raça Hampshire Down, que foi exportado para a Inglaterra pelo estabelecimento No. 2, pesava 121½ libras. O novilho vivo pesa de 740 a 750 kilogrammas e, depois de preparado para a exportação, seu peso é de 370 a 375 kilogrammas.

PREÇOS.

O carneiro capado vivo posto no estabelecimento, custa de $2 a $2.30 (ouro); o novilho custa $20 (ouro), approximadamente.

FRETES.

Duas das companhias fazem seus carregamentos em vapores pertencentes a seus agentes de Liverpool; as outras fretam vapores de duas ou tres linhas. No primeiro caso o frete é de um centavo por libra, e no segundo, paga-se em grosso ou até 1½ centavos por libra. A Inglaterra faz a maior parte destes fretamentos, assim como do commercio em carne, mas ha uma companhia franceza, "Chargeurs Reunis," que leva grandes quantidades, de carneiros principalmentè, para Londres e Havre, por conta do estabelecimento No. 2, cuja carne gelada chega até a fronteira franco-allemã.

PRODUCTO.

A média de animaes que se matam por anno, dedicados á congelação, é calculada em 2,300,000.

As quantidades e valores da exportação desde o começo da industria até o terceiro trimestre de 1897, segundo dados officiaes, são como se segue:

Exportação de carneiros gelados.

Anno.	Quantidades.		Valor (ouro.)
	Kilogrammas.	*Libras.*	
1883............................	....	....	$11,412
1884 *...........................	....	....	33,159
1885............................	2,862,270	6,310,794	75,323
1886............................	7,350,671	16,205,176	360,508
1887............................	12,038,889	26,540,756	963,112
1888............................	18,247,988	40,228,374	1,459,839
1889............................	16,532,545	36,449,799	1,322,604
1890............................	20,415,000	45,007,400	1,633,105
1891............................	23,278,084	51,317,585	1,862,247
1892............................	25,436,221	56,076,942	2,034,898
1893............................	25,041,000	55,205,200	2,003,254
1894............................	36,486,000	80,437,100	1,864,110
1895............................	41,882,000	92,333,600	1,675,273
1896............................	45,105,000	99,435,651	1,804,205
1897 (os novos primeiros mezes).........	37,650,000	83,004,800	1,506,007
Total.......................	312,325,668	688,553,177	18,609,056

* 33,159 carneiros.

Exportação de carne de vacca gelada.

Anno.	Quantidades.		Valor (ouro.)
	Kilogrammas.	*Libras.*	
1885 (84 rezes)..........................	....	....	$1,680
1886 (527 rezes)..........................	....	....	12,800
1887....................................	....	....	....
1888....................................	41,581	91,686	3,326
1889....................................	734,264	1,619,052	58,742
1890....................................	662,860	1,305,346	53,029
1891....................................	73,769	162,660	5,902
1892....................................	283,687	625,490	22,695
1893....................................	2,778,485	6,186,860	222,279
1894....................................	26,700	58,873	12,400
1895....................................	158,700	349,934	63,482
1896....................................	299,700	666,838	119,863
1897 (os primeiros nove mezes)..........	299,100	659,516	119,660
Total.......................	5,358,846	11,816,255	695,858

Pelo quadro anterior, vê-se que a exportação de carne de carneiros tem augmentado constantemente, e que a de carne de vacca tem sido muito variavel, e só tem obtido grandes proporções nos annos de 1889, 1890 e 1893.

AVES GELADAS.

Ha outros artigos de consumo taes como patos, perdizes, perús, narcejas, peixe, etc., que se exportam para a Europa, principalmente para a França. Vendem-se estes artigos promptamente, mas não se podem obter estatisticas fidedignas das quantidades que se exportam. A firma de SANSINEÑA, antes de formar-se a companhia, enviou um carregamento para Pariz, durante a ultima exposição, de 40,000 passaros de varias classes. Esta firma fundou um estabelecimento de congelação nos terrenos da exposição, junto com um restaurant, e por meio de caixas de vidro cylindrado, a carne ficava exposta aos freguezes e estes podiam escolher a carne que quizérem para o dia seguinte. O resultado foi que os Senhores SANSINEÑA e CIA., receberam as unicas medalhas de ouro que se concederam por comestiveis gelados, e Don FRANCÍSCO SANSINEÑA, actual Director da companhia, foi nomeado *Chevalier de la Legion d'Honneur.*

ESTADO ACTUAL DA INDUSTRIA.

A experiencia obtida e o conhecimento das preferencias dos mercados, estão contribuindo ao melhor desenvolvimento desta industria. Espera-se que esta industria continue a augmentar e que offereça aos criadores de gado do paiz um mercado domestico para seus productos.

A area pastoril da Republica Argentina, a qualidade da pastagem, a barateza da terra, o capital affluente, o melhoramento das raças, a constante immigração e a extensão das estradas de ferro, são razões para crer que esta Republica está destinada a adquirir proeminencia como fornecedor de carne aos mercados da Europa.

BRAZIL.

MOVIMENTO DO COMMERCIO ENTRE O BRAZIL E OS PORTOS DO DISTRICTO CONSULAR DE NOVA YORK DURANTE O ANNO DE 1897.

Do relatorio do Sr. ANTONIO GUIMARAES, vice-consul do Brazil em Nova York, extrahimos o seguinte.

O valor exportado em moeda nacional, cambio par, foi de 24,930:640$574 e o importado de 119,405:266$900.

Comparando estes algarismos com os do anno de 1896 vê-se que houve um augmento na exportação no valor de 2,463:041$810, e um decrescimo na importação no de 4,712:438$976.

Os principaes productos exportados foram: banha de porco, 16,762,069 libras; farinha de trigo, 755,971 barricas; kerosene, 21,844,750 galões; madeira de construcção, 50,465,000 pés; oleo de banha de porco, 157,120 galões; terebentina, 161,961 galões; toucinho, 75,651 barricas e 5,741 caixas; e trigo em grão, 747,755 alqueires e 12,035 saccos.

Comparando estes algarismos com os do anno de 1896, vê-se que houve augmento na exportação da banha de porco de 8,035,997 libras; na da farinha de trigo, de 300,033 barricas; na do kerosene, de 28,396,924 galões, e na do toucinho, de 4,286,991 libras; e houve decrescimo na exportação de madeira de con-strucção, de 16,876,902 pés; na do oleo da banha de porco, de 170,371 galões, e na da terebentina, de 3,097,988 galões.

Os principaes productos de importação foram: Assucar, 100,107,567 libras e 133,792 saccas; borracha, 25,036,628 libras; cacáo, 2,567,687 libras; café, 569,626,858 libras; courinhos, 3,549,749 libras; couros, 1,344,176 libras, e pelles, 3,677,998 libras.

REPUBLICA DE COLOMBIA.

COMMERCIO DE PANAMA NO ANNO DE 1897.

Segundo o relatorio submettido á Secretaria das Relações Ex-teriores da Grã Bretanha, pelo Consul MALLET, o commercio do districto de Panama para o anno de 1897, foi mais florescente que o que tinha sido por muitos annos anteriores; o valor das mer-cadorias importadas foi muito superior ao do anno anterior. O districto consular foi visitado em 1897 por um numero de agentes commerciaes maior do que se tinha visto alli por muitos annos, e seus esforços pessoaes que são os. que na pratica dão resultado no commercio, tiveram o melhor exito. O relatorio diz que uma grande parte destes commerciantes representava casas inglezas. Não obstante ser pouco o numero de commerciantes viajeiros americanos, o commercio dos Estados Unidos augmentou 28 por cento.

A seguinte tabella representa o por cento correspondente aos principaes paizes que importaram para Panama em 1897.

País.	Por cento.
Grã Bretanha	15
França	
Allemanha	13
Hespanha	9
Estados Unidos	48
China	15
Total	100

Segundo o relatorio do Sr. MALLET, houve uma diminuição consideravel no commercio de exportação em seu districto consular em 1897, comparado com o de 1896, o que é devido em sua maior parte á diminuição dos productos da pescaria de perolas e das colheitas do paiz.

A tonelagem dos embarques pelo porto de Panama mostram que tem havido um augmento de 9,000 toneladas, assim: Em navios de vela, 3,000 toneladas e 6,000 em vapores.

A Pacific Steam Navigation Company, que, ha algum tempo estendeu de Panama a Puntarenas, Costa Rica, o ponto terminal para o norte, está actualmente considerando a conveniencia de estendel-o mais ainda, levando-o até San Francisco, como já se disse no numero do BOLETIM MENSAL do mez de Janeiro. A "Companhia Sud Americana de Vapores," propõe-se levar a cabo igual plano.

Segundo o relatorio, os trabalhos do canal estão progredindo satisfactoriamente. Tem-se importado grande numero de trabalhadores de Sierra Leone e de Jamaica. Estes ultimos, como sempre acontece com os trabalhadores de Jamaica, têm dado os melhores resultados emquanto que os importados da Africa têm succumbido ás enfermidades que trazem comsigo as estações e têm resultado ser completamente inhabeis para o trabalho laborioso que se exige na construcção do canal. Pelo termo medio, o numero de trabalhadores empregados durante o anno se calcula em 3,000.

As informações referentes ao progresso dos districtos mineiros são muito satisfactorias, notando-se especialmente o das minas de Cará em Darien.

O Vice-consul MacGregor informa de Barranquilla que o numero de estradas de ferro no districto consular do Rio Magdalena foi augmentado e que tem um serviço regular e barato no transporte aos portos da costa. No districto de Magdalena,

foram construidas 50 milhas de estradas de ferro e a de Barranquilla se está estendendo até Usiacuri, ou uma distancia de 36
milhas.

Os districtos agricolas do valle de Magdalena, mostram um
desenvolvimento notavel, especialmente na producção do café e do
tabaco. Durante o anno de 1897, Barranquilla recebeu 278,000
saccos de café de 125 libras de peso, sendo em qualidade tão boa
como a melhor de qualquer mercado estrangeiro. O tabaco que
antes era um importante artigo de cultivo e que ultimamente tinha
decahido tanto na quantidade do producto como em sua qualidade,
hoje está sendo cultivado e preparado com actividade para o mercado. Durante o anno de 1896, se embarcaram 35,435 surrões,
que foram principalmente para Bremen. A criação e exportação
de gado não indica melhoramento, pois estando limitado seu mercado ás Antilhas, os disturbios de Cuba tém sido um impedimento
a seu desenvolvimento. Do numero total de couros exportados
de Barranquilla, que foi 150,000 couros, 100,000 foram para os
Estados Unidos, e o resto para a Europa. Não parece que se
tem realizados as esperanças acariciadas ha poucos annos do desenvolvimento da producção do algodão. A exportação deste producto em 1897, comparada com a do anno anterior, mostra uma
differença de 707 fardos nas exportações de 1897. Comtudo, nas
fabricas de Carthagena está-se empregando uma grande quantidade
deste producto e é agradavel notar que esta industria tem mostrado
durante o anno passado um espirito decidido de alento. As
exportações de borracha feitas por Barranquilla em 1897, alcançaram 1,400 volumes, com um valor declarado de $35,000. A arvore
da borracha, da qual ha um grande numero de variedades, cresce
em todas as florestas dos Districtos de Magdalena, Bolivar, San-
tander, Antioquia e Tolima, mas ainda não se tem emprehendido
seu cultivo.

Nas florestas visinhas ao Magdalena, se encontram varias classes
de madeiras preciosas, entre as quaes se conta a copaiba de onde
se extrae o balsamo do mesmo nome. Cresce até 40 pés de altura;
a madeira é de fibra compacta e serve para a construcção de casas
e barcos. Existe o cedro em abundancia que se exporta em tóros
pelo porto de Barranquilla, principalmente para a França e a
Allemanha. Varias companhias francezas tém estabelecido fabricas de serrar para o corte desta madeira.

A tabella seguinte representa o valor das importações feitas por Barranquilla em 1897:

Paiz.	Valor.
Grã Bretanha	$3,984,972
Estados Unidos	1,158,133
Outros paizes	4,643,630
Total	9,786,735

O Vice-consul Stevenson, em seu relatorio de Carthagena, diz que em geral o commercio daquelle porto, comparado com o de 1896, tem diminuido. Isto é devido ao numero de desastres dos vapores empregados na navegação do rio Magdalena, o qual tem diminuido o trafico por aquelle porto.

As importações têm augmentado um pouco, comparadas com as de 1896. O dito augmento correspondeu aos Estados Unidos, França, Allemanha e Hespanha, correspondendo a esta o maior augmento.

Tem havido progresso nos melhoramentos locaes. Ha pouco, se estabeleceu uma boa planta electrica, cujas machinas se importaram da Inglaterra e os apparelhos electricos dos Estados Unidos. Está-se construindo um grande edificio para o mercado.

O Vice-consul Carr informa de Santa Marta que ha alli grande actividade no cultivo do café. Os cultivadores são, em sua maior parte, inglezes e americanos e estão muito contentes com o prospecto que se lhes offerece, pois a qualidade do café que produzem é igual ao melhor producto da Colombia e Costa Rica. Estando perto do porto, os cultivadores podem pôr alli seus productos á razão de menos de $5 por tonelada. Podem-se comprar terrenos proprios para o cultivo do café, situados n'uma região sã e a uma altura de 3,000 a 4,000 pés, á razão de $2 a $3 por geira. O cultivo de bananas, que ha cerca de oito annos que se começou a fazer, tem chegado hoje a adquirir uma condição prospera. Os cultivadores receberam pela colheita do anno passado cerca de $85,000.

EQUADOR.

COMMERCIO DE GUAYAQUIL EM 1897.

Os seguintes dados relativos á industria e ao commercio de Guayaquil, Equador, durante o anno de 1897, estão tomados do Relatorio Annual do Consul Sr. CHAMBERS, dirigido á Secretaria das Relações Exteriores da Grã Bretanha.

Guayaquil, que é o porto principal da Republica, é tambem o centro mais importante de seu commercio. A grande quantidade de mercadorias destruidas nos desastrosos incendios de Fevereiro e Outubro, teve de ser substituida para fazer frente á crescente necessidade do consumo nas provincias da costa e do interior, de onde resultou que o commercio de importação foi maior e mais activo que em nenhum anno anterior. Não se tem publicado nenhuma estatistica desta importação desde que se publicou a que o Ministro da Fazenda, Senhor WITHER, dirigiu á Convenção de 1896–97, na qual se calcula approximadamente o valor das importações desde Maio 1 de 1895 até 30 de Junho de 1896 em 10,600,000 sucres (£1,000,000). Não posso dar, portanto, conta exacta deste importante detalhe, mas sei que desde aquella periodo até a data, as importações tem tido lugar em maior escala.

Não têm occorrido mudanças nas casas importadoras, nem na natureza ou procedencia das mercadorias importadas. Durante 1897 o commercio de exportação teve lugar com a mais acostumada actividade; deve notar-se, entretanto, que as excessivas chuvas de Janeiro e Maio causaram prejuizos muito consideraveis ás colheitas de cacáo e café; da primeira se perdeu vinte e cinco por cento, e da segunda só se recolheu cincoenta por cento que em sua maior parte foi de qualidade inferior. Todas as plantações de arroz nas provincias da costa foram destruidas pela mesma causa, e isto necessitou de uma importação consideravel de arroz de outros paizes. Estas circumstancias combinadas influiram materialmente nas transacções commerciaes. Nesta epocha, o Governo deu autorisação a um dos bancos de Guayaquil para uma nova cunhagem de prata, e em fins do anno se promulgou uma lei, segundo a qual os bancos ficavam obrigados a reter sua reserva metallica em ouro, assim obrigando-os a importar moeda estrangeira por valor, ao menos de £100,000; e se comprehenderá facilmente que este estado anormal do cambio tem contribuido para fazer muito difficil a situação commercial da Republica. Os bancos suspenderam em Dezembro, quasi por completo, as operações de desconto.

As rendas do paiz têm augmentado consideravelmente pelo augmento nos direitos de importação, segundo a nova lei aduaneira, e tambem pelas contribuições, mas não obstante este augmento, o commercio tem sido muito activo. Têm-se levado a cabo com grande actividade a reconstrucção da parte commercial da cidade que foi destruida pelo incendio, e têm-se construido grandes e elegantes casas que dão um aspecto imponente á parte da cidade do lado do rio. Estas casas são de madeira, muito poucas das quaes têm sido construidas no antigo estylo de canna e gesso, e grande numero dellas estão telhadas com ferro galvanizado inglez. Ha falta de braços no Equador e os artesanos têm-se aproveitado disto para pedir salarios altos, tanto pelo trabalho puramente manual, como pelo trabalho intelligente; o preço dos materiaes de construcção tem augmentado tambem por causa da grande procura.

Muitos representantes de casas inglezas têm visitado o paiz varias vezes durante o anno e têm expressado sua satisfação a respeito da parte que a Inglaterra tem no commercio de importação. Com poucas excepções, os artigos enumerados na lista dos mais importantes ramos do commercio—emittida pelas varias juntas de commercio por intermedio da Secretaria das Relações Exteriores—que encontram um mercado aqui, vêm directa ou indirectamente dos lugares nomeados na lista. Os artigos de luxo, principalmente os generos para vestidos e os de fantasia para senhoras e crianças, assim como perfumes, calçado fino, etc., têm sido importados da França. Dos Estados Unidos temos recebido kerosene, banha, e madeira para construcção em grandes quantidades (importa-se a madeira acepilhada e entalhada, já preparada para seu uso immediato). Fogões de ferro, machados e machadinhas e moveis se recebem daquelle mercado só em pequenas quantidades. Da Austria tem-se importado uma classe melhor de moveis, assim como joias baratas e artigos de fantasia. Da Allemanha se recebe cerveja, meias, tecidos de lã e tecidos mixtos, para vestidos; cobertores, ponchos, chales e ferragens ordinarias, na mesma proporção que em annos anteriores, sem nenhum augmento material, com excepção dos tecidos de lã mixta e rendas, que por serem mais baratos têm podido fazer forte concurrencia com os artigos semelhantes procedentes da Inglaterra. Os artigos ordinarios de cutelaria que se importavam antes da Allemanha, estão soffrendo agora a concurrencia dos fabricantes inglezes que estão obtendo parte deste commercio. Quasi todas as velas que se consomem na Republica se importam da Belgica. A producção de assucar em 1897 montou a umas 6,000 toneladas. O consumo nacional será de umas 4,000 toneladas, ficando umas 2,000 toneladas para a exportação, principalmente para Chile e Colombia. O preço medio do assucar branco granulado de primeira classe tem sido de uns 5 centavos por libra. No Chile se prefere agora o assucar do Equador ás melhores classes do assucar peruano.

Ha no paiz uma fabrica de sabão, e o material para sua fabricação, se importa livre de direitos, o qual tende a diminuir o preço do sabão procedente do estrangeiro. A isenção de direitos de importação expira neste anno, mas se estão fazendo esforços para renoval-a. Tambem se propõe construir uma nova fabrica em bahia de Caraquez, por um syndicato dos Estados Unidos e alguns commerciantes de Bahia. Em todo o paiz se fabrica, de uma maneira primitiva e em pequena escala, uma especie de sabão preto que tem muito boas qualidades depurativas. Ha duas fabricas de macarroneti, etc., as quaes têm monopolizado o commercio nesta classe de artigos que se importavam antes do Chile em quantidade consideravel. Um destes estabelecimentos comprehende tambem uma fabrica de biscoutos de qualidade superior. O principal empregado desta fabrica é um subdito inglez, procedente de uma conhecida casa de Londres. Durante o anno têm-se estabelecido duas novas fabricas de serração, uma das quaes foi importada da Inglaterra.   Ha no interior fabricas de tecidos de lã e de algodão, principalmente para o consumo local, ainda que ha um commercio consideravel em baietas de classe ordinaria com a vizinha Republica da Colombia, via Fumaço e Barbacoas.   Estas baietas não fazem concurrencia, porem, com as classes mais finas que se importam da Inglaterra.

Dos numerosos edificios publicos destruidos em Guayaquil pelo incendio de 1896, nenhum tem sido reconstruido.   Têm-se levantado edificios temporarios para o serviço de alfandegas, no lugar onde estava o antigo edificio, mas não são adequados ás exigencias do grande commercio de importação e o Governo teve de alugar armazens particulares em toda a cidade para o deposito das mercadorias, o qual é muito prejudicial ao manejo dos artigos importados.   Foi organisada uma companhia em Nova York para explorar o districto de Zaruma, e a julgar pelas informações favoraveis que foram recebidas, crê-se que se formará uma companhia para explorar as minas neste districto aurifero.   A Companhia Mineira da Plaza de Ouro, tem gastado enormes sommas no desenvolvimento de sua propriedade, mas tem encontrado difficuldades por causa dos grandes gastos que a empreza exige ; e para conduzir os trabalhos com mais economia, foi formado um syndicato com os accionistas inglezes daquella companhia.   Têm-se suspendido alguns dos trabalhos originaes, e muitos dos gastos que até agora tinham embaraçado a empreza, têm sido reduzidos.

HONDURAS.

DESCRIPÇÃO DA POPULAÇÃO, DO CLIMA, DAS FONTES DE RIQUEZA, ETC.

A seguinte communicação sobre os recursos, clima, etc., de Honduras foi dirigida a esta Secretaria pelo Sr. Robert M. Fryer, de Washington, que tem viajado extensivamente naquella Republica e residido alli por alguns annos :

Permitta-se-me assegurar aos leitores do Boletim que a população, o clima, a religião, e a politica em Honduras são inteiramente o que deveriam ser, para o adiantamento dos interesses individuaes.   Esta declaração nunca será posta em duvida pelos que vão áquella Republica com conhecimento bastante para comprehender as cousas do paiz, e se abstenham de entremetter-se nos assumptos publicos, dedicando-se ao desenvolvimento dos recursos que o paiz offerece. Pode-se dizer que o povo de Honduras recebe com mais cordialidade os viajantes e colonos procedentes dos Estados Unidos, que os outros estrangeiros que visitam o paiz.

A area de Honduras é approximadamente do mesmo tamanho que a area de Ohio ; mas em recursos naturaes é superior a muitos de taes estados, tomados collectivamente, e si tivesse uma população correspondente, sobrepujaria, na minha opinião, qualquer outro territorio de dimensões analogas.   O paiz offerecerá mais luxo e commodidades que os que podem ser obtidos em qualquer outro lugar pelo mesmo dinheiro e trabalho; tem todas as vantagens das regiões tropicaes, semi-tropicaes, e temperadas. Entre os productos ha valiosas madeiras do commercio, plantas medicinaes, frutas tropicaes, e vastos recursos mineraes, ainda não explorados; mas sobre tudo, o clima de Honduras, considerado em relação com as muitas outras vantagens do paiz, constitue seu maior attractivo.

A costa septentrional de Honduras estende-se de leste ao oeste por uma distancia de 400 milhas. Os ventos que prevalecem, vem do norte e do nordeste, e mantêm a costa em estado salubre e relativamente fresca, mas esta não é a localidade que mais se recommenda pelo clima; não é desagradavel, todavia, visto que as montanhas da costa se introduzem no mar e se elevam a uma altura de uma milha ou mais. Nos valles e planaltos se encontra um clima adaptavel a todos os gostos e exigencias. Si eu fosse perguntado qual é o clima mais· delicioso do paiz, indicaria o de Tegucigalpa, Siguatepeque, os pequenos montes que rodeam Camayagua, o lago Yogoa, San José, Santa Barbara e muitos outros lugares no interior da República, onde se necessitam grossos cobertores pela noite, onde não se veem moscas nem mosquitos e onde existe uma estação de primavera, com frutas e flores durante todo o anno. Tenho viajado á costa de mula por uma distancia de mil de milhas, atravessando as montanhas, e nunca tenho visto um reptil ou animal selvagem, excepto os captivados; mas em todas as partes do paiz ha uma profusão de passaros de grande variedade de côres e plumagem. O paiz tem grande numero de rios, muitos dos quaes abundam em peixes; encontram-se as melhores qualidades do peixe cerca da costa.

Para estabelecer-se em Honduras se necessita pouco capital ou trabalho; não ha extremos de temperatura e tudo parece crescer com pouco ou nenhum cultivo. Isto é verdade com relação ao milho, do qual se produzem duas ou tres colheitas por anno; a canna de assucar e o algodão dão mais de uma colheita por anno e só se necessita uma semeadura durante dez annos. Os coqueiros e arvores da borracha produzem depois de oito annos, emquanto que o cafeeiro dá fructo em menos de seis annos. As arvores da borracha necessitam de sombra durante o primeiro anno, a qual é dada pelas bananeiras, as quaes tambem produzem dentro de novo mezes e durante dez annos pelo menos. Diz-se que a vida da arvore da borracha em Honduras é de cincoenta ou mais annos. Laranjas, limões, limas, mandioca e muitas outras frutas dão-se silvestres em todo o paiz; o abacaxi, incluindo a variedade conhecida com o nome de abacaxi de "pão de assucar," cresce em grande abundancia cerca da costa. Em algumas partes do paiz, todos os legumes que se conhecem nos Estados Unidos dão-se á perfeição. O solo cerca da costa é demasiado rico para a batata, mas no interior onde a terra é secca, se dá bem esta planta. O Sr. BAMBERG, que mora em San Pedro Sula e tem uma grande horta, é considerado autoridade competente na materia do cultivo de legumes em Honduras.

Quanto aos recursos mineraes, quero dizer que julgando por minha propria observação e por todos os indicios, Honduras é um grande armazem de ouro e prata de valor incalculavel. Por cortezia do Sr. GIRLINGS, administrador geral da "New York and Honduras Rosario Mining Company," tenho podido conhecer não sómente os ricos depositos da companhia mas tambem as minas do districto de Yuscuran, onde estão situadas as famosas minas de Guyabillas e os depositos de ouro de Olancho. A mina de Rosario acima mencionada, está situada em San Juancita, a uma distancia de 21 milhas de Tegucigalpa (a capital) com a qual está unida por uma estrada de rodagem. Ha nella 35 trituradoras que estão funccionando e uma installação electrica e de ar comprimido, movidas por força hydraulica; e pode-se dizer que não ha em nenhuma parte uma mina melhor administrada que esta. Como resultado de minhas investigações a respeito das possibilidades de explorar com proveito as minas de Honduras, admiro-me de que não haja déz ou vinte companhias mineiras naquelle paiz que hoje conta sómente com uma.

Haverá no outono proximo uma eleição presidencial em Honduras. A retirada do Presidente Bonilla será muito sentida por todos os estrangeiros de Honduras, os quaes sempre tratou com bondade e consideração. Tambem a maioria dos cidadãos de Honduras consideram o Sr. Bonilla como prototypo de virtude, intelligencia, energia e patriotismo.

MEXICO.

INDUSTRIA MINEIRA.

A industria mineira é uma das mais importantes do Mexico. A exportação de metaes preciosos e mineraes mostra um augmento de cerca de doze milhões de pesos (prata mexicana) durante a primeira metade do presente anno fiscal, comparada com a do mesmo periodo em 1896; este augmento representa cerca de quarenta por cento.

O mineral de cobre mexicano é particularmente rico e sua producção cresce rapidamente. Em varias partes do paiz têm-se descoberta recentemente novas e extensas minas, e segundo o "Mexico Moderno," o Prof. William Niven, conhecido mineralogista e archeologo, diz que os campos de Guerrero são tão ricos em ouro como em cobre. Ainda que Guerrero é rico, indubitavelmente, em mineraes, os exploradores devem ter capital si quizerem obter bom exito. O clima é bom, mas o equipamento é custoso e as provisões são escassas. A exportação de cobre dobrou-se no ultimo anno, alcançando no mez de Dezembro o valor de cerca de um milhao de pesos, que representa um augmento de quasi 100 por cento. Os carregamentos de chumbo, antimonio e zinco mostram um augmento animador.

FABRICA DE CORDOALHA E DE SACCOS.

No dia 8 de Outubro de 1896, se celebrou um contracto entre o Ministerio de Fomento e o Sr. ALFRED HEYDRICH, para o estabelecimento de uma grande fabrica em Yucatan para a manufactura de cordoalha, redes, e saccos, utilisando para isto o hennequen e outros productos analogos. O dito contracto foi approvado pelo Congresso no dia 14 de Maio de 1897, e a 23 de Junho do mesmo anno, o Sr. HEYDRICH verificou o registro da empreza sob o nome de "Sociedade Anonima la Industria," com um capital de $400,000, sendo presidente o Sr. ALEGARIO MOHUA.

O contracto estipula que a fabrica deve estar concluida dentro de dous annos, a partir da promulgação da approvação do contracto pelo Congresso e nota-se grande actividade nos trabalhos de construcção e installação da fabrica. Já foram levantados grandes edificios construidos especialmente para o trabalho que se tem de fazer. Além destes, foram construidas, de pedra, 14 casas, de 30 por 16 pés, para alojamento dos operarios. As fabricas da companhia ligam-se por via ferrea com a estrada de ferro de Merida e Progresso e estão providas de varios desvios para facilitar o manejo dos carros.

O contracto original celebrado com o Governo estipulava que a quantia que se teria de empregar não seria menor de $250,000. Como prova do desenvolvimento da empreza, podemos dizer, que o capital em acções tem sido augmentado a $600,000 e que a companhia tem-se compromettido a começar os trabalhos um anno antes do tempo estipulado no contracto.

Quando a fabrica estiver completamente montada, sua producção diaria será de 50,000 kilogrammas de fio fino, barbante, cordoalha, saccos, redes, etc., ou uma producção total de 14,400,000 kilogrammas por anno. Observa-se esta empreza com grande interesse, por ser a primeira em grande escala, que se tem estabelecido para a fabricação no paiz do hennequen, que é producto principal de Yucatan.

FABRICAS DE ALGODÃO.

Em um relatorio especial do Consul britannico na cidade de Mexico, se diz que a industria de generos de algodão no Mexico tem sido desenvolvida grandemente durante os ultimos annos.

Dentro de pouco tempo, as fabricas nacionaes poderão fornecer ao paiz de todos os generos de algodão que necessita. Esta industria no Mexico tem sido desenvolvida lentamente e o augmento nos tres annos passados attribue-se a uma successão de boas colheitas. Em 1897 se estabeleceram novas fabricas cuja producção minima foi de 300,000 peças, e as fabricas que se estão construindo ou que provavelmente se construirão este anno, augmentarão a producção annual com uma quantidade de 750,000 peças. Como a média de importação annual de generos de algodão estrangeiros é sómente de 40,000,000 metros quadrados e o Mexico promette aggregar 21,000,000 metros quadrados a sua producção, é provavel que os fabricantes estrangeiros encontrem no paiz uma consideravel concurrencia.

Nas fabricas onde se emprega o vapor como força motriz, as grandes machinas de 100 cavallos de força e mais, são geralmente inglezas, mas quando não se necessitam machinas de grande potencia, preferem-se as americanas de alta pressão, por serem mais baratas. As caldeiras são geralmente multitubulares.

NOVAS INDUSTRIAS.

Segundo "El Progresso de Mexico," de 30 de Abril de 1898, os Srs. ERNESTO CHAVERO e GREGORIO GONZÁLEZ, pediram á Secretaria de Estado autorisação para estabelecer varias industrias no paiz, entre ellas, uma fabrica de leite condensado com um capital minimo de $150,000. Esta é uma industria completamente nova no Mexico.

O mesmo periodico diz que varias grandes fabricas de azeite e sabão, estabelecidas em Lerdo, Durango, Torreon e San Pedro de la Higuera, as quaes funccionavam independentemente, têm-se unido formando uma só associação. Estas fabricas estão providas de luz electrica e têm machinas potentes custosas e trabalham dia e noite. Seus principaes productos são farinha de semente de algodão e massa de linhaça. Usa-se esta para engordar gado vaccum e porcos. Obtem-se a semente de algodão principalmente de ricas plantações de algodão, cujos donos têm grandes interesses na companhia.

As fabricas da companhia produzem 25,000 kilogrammas de farinha de semente de algodão cada 24 horas, e exportam 20,000 toneladas de massas de linhaça, cada anno, no valor de $500,000.

CONCESSÃO DE ESTRADA DE FERRO AOS SENHORES PEARSON, SONS & COMPANY.

Um numero recente do "Diario Official" dá noticias de uma concessão que foi approvada pelo Presidente Diaz no dia 4 de Junho, pela qual a importante casa ingleza de Pearson & Sons e Pedro M. Armendaria estão autorisados para traçar, construir e funccionar uma estrada de ferro no Estado de Vera Cruz. O ponto inicial da estrada será Acayuacan ou Paso de San Juan na linha da estrada de ferro de Jutla. A estrada de ferro se estenderá até Tuxtla e San Nicolas, com o privilegio de prolongamento até Alvarado.

A linha deverá estar traçada dentro de um anno a contar da data da approvação do contracto, e os trabalhos de construcção deverão começar dentro de dez e oito mezes; a linha deverá estar terminada em dez annos. Além da isenção usual de direitos de importação e contribuições, os concessionarios receberão grandes extensões de terras publicas nos Estados de Vera Cruz, Oaxaca, Tabasco e Chiapas. A companhia contractante deverá ter seu domicilio legal na cidade de Mexico, e na eleição de directores se reserva o direito de nomear certo numero.

Os contractantes obrigam-se a fazer um deposito de $3,000, em apolices do Governo, no Banco Nacional, dentro de quinze dias. O territorio que a linha atravessa é um dos mais ricos e mais promettedores na producção de borracha, tabaco e assucar, em toda a Republica, e a alta representação economica dos Senhores Pearson & Sons é uma garantia de que as condições do contracto serão cumpridas fielmente.

NICARAGUA.

CONCESSÃO FEITA AO SR. EMERY PARA A EXTRACÇÃO DE MADEIRAS.

O Sr. William B. Sorsby, Consul dos Estados Unidos em San Juan del Norte, remetteu á Secretaria de Estado uma copia (traduzida) do contrato feito pelo governo de Nicaragua com o Sr. H. C. Emery, de Chelsea, Mass., concedendo-lhe o privilegio de corte e exportação das madeiras valiosas do paiz.

Bull. No. 1——9

Segundo os termos do contracto, o Sr. EMERY tem o monopolio por 15 annos, do mogno, páu rosa, e o cedro dentro de uma vasta area que é conhecida ser rica nestas madeiras.   Isto é praticamente a renovação do antigo contrato celebrado com o Sr. EMERY, pelo qual embarcaram-se annualmente uns 12,500 toros.   O Consul SORSBY considera que esta concessão é immensamente valiosa, na realidade uma das mais valiosas que em muito tempo tem feito o governo a subditos estrangeiros.

Segundo o artigo 3° do contrato, o Sr. EMERY obriga-se a construir 50 milhas de estrada de ferro, para seu proprio uso, entre Rio Grande e Pearl Lagoon; a bitola será de 3 pés 6 pollegadas ou 4 pés 8½ pollegadas, e a linha passará pelas terras publicas do Departamento de Matagalpa.   O material para a estrada, as pontes, molhes, officinas, etc., terão de ser approvados pelo Ministro das Obras Publicas.   Toda a obra passará a ser propriedade do governo ao fim do prazo do contrato, é dizer, dentro de 15 annos.

O governo nacional cede ao Sr. EMERY 17,500 geiras de terras publicas no Departamento de Zelaya ou Matagalpa, com a condição de que dentro do prazo de um anno, semeie uma planta por cada arvore que corte.

Segundo o artigo 4°, o concessionario deverá pagar ao governo $20,000 (ouro) em lettras aceitaveis, e $10,000 (ouro) por anno como premio, durante a existencia do contracto.

O governo dá ao Sr. EMERY o privilegio de introduzir, livres de direitos, todos os artigos necessarios para o sustento e a manutenção dos empregados no corte e na exportação de madeira, assim como tambem os materiaes que se necessitam para a construcção e manutenção da estrada de ferro.

PARAGUAY.

EXTRACTOS DA MENSAGEM DO PRESIDENTE.

O Senhor Presidente EGUZQUIZA apresentou-se perante os Senadores e Deputados no dia 1° de Abril, e leu sua mensagem ao Congresso ao abrir suas sessões ordinarias.   O periodo constitucional do Senhor Presidente EGUZQUIZA terminará ao levantarem-se as actuaes sessões do Congresso, e por conseguinte, esta mensagem é a ultima que está chamado a ler durante sua actual administração.

O Presidente felicita ao paiz pelo desenvolvimento geral na instrucção publica e o augmento constante no numero de escolas publicas e dos alumnos. Faz referencia especial á ampliação do systema de escolas normaes que na actualidade são frequentadas por mais de mil alumnos de ambos sexos. Contratou-se no estrangeiro um selecto corpo de professores. Tem-se estendido muito a instrucção na agricultura, as artes e sciencias.

A linha telegraphica que já se estende alem de San Pedro, será estendida desde Assumpção até Villa Conceição, e dentro de poucos mezes será funccionando até aquelle ponto. Propõe-se prolongar este fio ate Fuerte Olimpo e construir um ramal que ponha a linha principal em communicação con varias povoações do norte. Na proporção em que cresce a população, augmenta o movimento no correio.

Sobre as obras publicas, diz o Presidente que uma commissão especial foi nomeada para dirigir os trabalhos deste ramo do Governo de accordo com a lei que dispoz os fundos para este fim.

O valor total da importação durante o anno transcorrido montou a $2,203,359 e o da exportação a $1,955,803. Estas cifras representam o valor em ouro.

O Banco Agricola, a instituição mais importante de sua classe no paiz, tem feito muito para promover os propositos para que foi estabelecido, a saber, o desenvolvimento do cultivo do algodão, café, a vinha e outros productos do paiz. Hoje existem no paiz mais de 1,000,000 cafeeiros, e não se pode duvidar que este numero seja dobrado ou triplicado em breve tempo. O referido banco tem promovido ensaios na preparação do tabaco segundo os systemas adoptados em Cuba e Sumatra, sob a direcção de pessoas competentes. Deste modo o tabaco do Paraguay, que tem sido desprezado nos mercados estrangeiros, volverá a adquirir sua acostumada importancia.

Com relação ao Banco Nacional, diz o Presidente que a liquidação deste continúa, não obstante serem remissos os devedores no cumprimento de seus compromissos. "Seria conveniente adoptar algum modo de conseguir a liquidação definitiva para evitar gastos desnecessarios." O imposto territorial será uma das fontes dos recursos da nação.

O Governo se occupa em considerar um projecto de estrada de ferro que será construida desde os districtos de herva matte até o rio. Si a idea se realizar, o commercio de herva matte, de difficil transporte até agora e muito mais nas epochas de secca em que se tornam innavegaveis os affluentes do Rio Paraguay, receberá grandes beneficios.

A mensagem refere-se com muita satisfação ás relações har-moniosas e cordiaes que existem entre o Paraguay e os paizes vizinhos. A unica questão pendente é o arranjo de limites com Bolivia que envolve os direitos ao territorio do Chaco que é um deserto vasto e inhabitado. Essa questão está pelo momento em expectativa.

O Presidente EGUZQUIZA nutre a esperança de que as nego-ciações iniciadas na Republica Argentina para a celebração de um tratado de commercio tenham uma solução conveniente e satisfac-toria para ambas as nações. Tambem tem a firme convicção de que a maneira de estabelecer laços permanentes entre os povos, é desenvolver seus interesses moraes e materiaes, baseados em con-cessões liberaes que permittam a expansão de suas industrias e de sua actividade commercial. O Presidente tambem recommenda especialmente a celebração de um tratado de commercio com o Brazil.

PERU-CHILE.

CULTIVO E MANUFACTURA DE ALGODÃO.

No numero do BOLETIM MENSAL, correspondente ao mez de Junho, se fez referencia ao impulso que foi dado recentemente ao cultivo e á manufactura do algodão no Peru e no Chile, a ás medidas que estavam tomando os governos destes paizes para alentar estas industrias. A Exposição Permanente de Machinas que foi inaugurada recentemente em Lima está chamando a attenção dos fabricantes dos Estados Unidos e da Europa para as opportunidades que se lhes apresentam de introduzir suas machinas neste paiz, e o decreto de recente data, admittindo livres de direitos todas as machinas que sejam destinadas á fabricação de tecidos, não sómente está dando novo impulso á esta industria no Chile, mas tambem está abrindo um excellente mercado ás machi-nas dos Estados Unidos.

O seguinte artigo relativo a este assumpto, que foi extrahido do "Textile Manufacturers' Journal," de seu numero de 4 de Junho, que se publica na cidade de Nova York, pode ser lido com proveito:

Já temos feito referencia de tempo em tempo ao desenvolvimento em varios paizes da industria manufactureira de algodão, com o fim de mostrar a concurrencia que os commerciantes dos Estados Unidos terão de encontrar. Dizem que o Chile e o Peru estão-se preparando para o cultivo do algodão em grande escala, e as colheitas não serão exportadas para o estrangeiro, como até agora, mas serão consumidas nas fabricas do paiz. O Peru tem cultivado o algodão em grande escala por muito tempo, mas agora parece que essa industria vai-se estendendo rapidamente no Chile. Anteriormente o algodão crú era exportado quasi em sua totalidade para Inglaterra, mas agora se propõe estabelecer no paiz uma grande industria manufactureira. Como resultado do apoio que o Governo está dando aos cultivadóres de algodão, um terreno muito extenso está sendo dedicado ao cultivo deste producto. A abolição dos impostos sobre todas as machinas empregadas na manufactura de tecidos que se importarem no paiz até o anno de 1902, pode ser citada como prova da seriedade com que o Governo está apoiando este projecto. Diz-se que esta mudança na tarifa tem exercido mais ou menos influencia na exportação dos Estados Unidos de machinas de tecidos, pois foram feitas recentemente diversos embarques de importancia.

A fabricação de tecidos é mais adiantada no Peru do que no Chile, não obstante que ainda as fabricas só produzem as qualidades grossas. Espera-se que com a importação de novas machinas modernas será dado novo impulso á fabricação do algodão e que os que têm obtido grandes lucros do seu commercio com este paiz, terão de attender agora com maior actividade a seus interesses.

SANTO DOMINGO.

ESTADO DO COMMERCIO.

O Consul dos Estados Unidos, Sr. GRIMKE, remetteu á Secretaria de Estado seu relatorio annual sobre a situação commercial e industrial da Republica dominicana, o qual foi publicado, *en extenso*, nos Relatorios Consulares do mez de Junho. Segundo o Sr. GRIMKE, a baixa no preço do assucar, que é o producto principal da Republica, e outras causas, têm produzido uma depressão geral dos negocios do paiz. Quasi todo o assucar que não é consumido no paiz, é exportado para Nova York; o valor total desta exportação durante o anno de 1897 montou a $2,463,906.62. Dos outros productos que se exportaram, os Estados Unidos receberam os seguintes: Páu de campeche, guaiaco, mogno, mel, cera e bananas; e quasi todo o café, cacáo e tabaco foi exportado para a França, Allemanha, Belgica e Inglaterra.

No districto consular que o Sr. GRIMKE representa, toda a madeira que se importou procedeu dos Estados Unidos e montou a 2,500,000 pés, e se vendeu a $37.50 ouro, por mil de pés. Toda a farinha, a qual se vende a $12 ouro por barril, se importa dos Estados Unidos. Até ha pouco, todo o kerosene foi importado dos Estados Unidos, mas a fabrica de refinação, que foi estabelecida recentemente em La Romana, sem duvida limitará a importação deste artigo. Devido á qualidade inferior da manteiga que se recebe dos Estados Unidos, importa-se este artigo quasi exclusivamente de Dinamarca. A manteiga de melhor qualidade se vende em Santo Domingo a 62½ centavos por libra, emquanto que a de qualidade inferior se vende a 37½ centavos. Importa-se queijo da Hollanda e dos Estados Unidos e vende-se o queijo hollandez a 25 centavos por libra, e o americano a 22½ centavos por libra.

Quanto a artigos miscellaneos, a maior parte das carnes, dos legumes e do leite que vêm em lata, se importa dos Estados Unidos. O peixe e a carne de porco salgados são importados em sua totalidade dos Estados Unidos; e a banha, os oleos de cozinha e a cerveja lager vêm em parte dos Estados Unidos. Importam-se os vinhos da França e da Hespanha. Foi estabelecida recentemente em Santo Domingo uma fabrica de cerveja, a qual é propriedade de cidadãos americanos. A caixa de cerveja americana se vende a $4.50, emquanto que o preço de cerveja que se fabrica no paiz é de $2.25.

As machinas para as plantações, locomotivas, carros, trilhos, pontes de ferro, etc., se importam em sua maior parte dos Estados Unidos, mas a Allemanha está fazendo uma forte concurrencia neste commercio. Na importação de ferragens, a Inglaterra, Allemanha e Belgica fazem concurrencia com os Estados Unidos. Vende-se o carvão em Santo Domingo a $12 e $13 ouro por tonelada, do qual a maior parte é importada da Inglaterra. A Inglaterra tambem faz a maior parte da importação de tecidos de algodão; os tecidos de algodão americanos são de melhor qualidade, mas são mais caros do que os inglezes, e isto explica por que os tecidos inglezes predominam naquelle mercado. Vendem-se os tecidos de algodão a 7½ e 25 centavos ouro por vara. Importam-se exclusivamente da França os tecidos de seda e se vendem a 75 centavos até $3 ouro por vara. Da França e da Inglaterra se importam os chapéos de todas as classes para ambos os sexos. Dos Estados Unidos se importam todas as machinas electricas que se usam na Ilha. Muitas das plantações de assucar estão illuminadas á luz electrica. A França e os Estados Unïdos se repartem o commercio em bicyclettas.

O Consul GRIMKE diz que os commerciantes e cultivadores censuram fortemente os methodos que se empregam nos Estados Unidos no empacotamento das mercadorias. Os trabalhadores de campo recebem de 50 a 75 centavos por dia; nas cidades os braços recebem de 50 centavos a $2; os criados, incluindo a comida, ganham de $3 a $12 mensaes, e os empregados de $15 a $75 mensaes.

Os interesses americanos predominam na Republica. Quasi a metade das plantações de assucar são propriedade de cidadãos dos Estados Unidos. A "Santo Domingo Improvement Company," que tem seu escriptorio em Nova York, tem a seu cargo a cobrança das rendas do paiz, segundo contracto celebrado com o Governo, ha alguns annos. Ha uma linha de vapores, propriedade de W. P CLYDE & Co., de Nova York, os quaes fazem viagens quinzenaes entre este porto e os portos da Republica.

VENEZUELA.

COMMERCIO DE CARACAS E DISTRICTO EM 1897.

Do relatorio annual dirigido pelo Sr. W. A. ANDRAL, Consul interino da Grã Bretanha em Caracas, á Secretaria de Relações Exteriores, extrahimos as seguintes informacões relativas ao commercio de Caracas e daquelle districto consular. Não se pode dizer que o estado geral do commercio de Venezuela é satisfactorio. A causa principal desta condição foi a má colheita de café, que naturalmente diminuiu a importação no paiz e reduziu o credito no estrangeiro. Crê-se que esta situação será grandemente alliviada na proxima estação, a julgar pela actual colheita de café que é muito promettedora. Ha no paiz cerca de 33,000 cafezaes e 5,000 cacoaes. O café e o cacáo são os principaes productos da Republica. A alta tarifa proteccionista sobre o assucar, a qual é practicamente prohibitiva, tem estimulado o cultivo da canna de modo que ha hoje 11,000 fazendas de canna de assucar e se espera que este cultivo occupe um lugar proeminente na agricultura do paiz.

Têm-se estabelecido ultimamente numerosos clubs, com o fim de chamar a attenção dos cultivadores para a importancia da applicação de methodos scientificos na fertilisação, irrigação, etc., e do uso de machinas modernas na preparação daquelle producto para o mercado. O que se necessita para o progresso do paiz, segundo diz o Consul ANDRAL, é uma immigração que se estabeleça no campo e contribua assim para o desenvolvimento dos recursos agricolas. Recentemente (como se publicou detalhadamente no BOLETIM MENSAL do mez de Maio) o Governo fez um contracto com um italiano para a immigração de grande numero de familias italianas que terão de estabelecer-se em terras publicas.

Extrahimos do relatorio o seguinte relativo ao desenvolvimento do commercio com Venezuela e á agencia da Associação Nacional de Fabricantes dos Estados Unidos.

Os americanos estão-se estabelecendo firmemente no mercado de Venezuela. Não são tão conservadores como seus rivaes europeos, e são mais promptos nos negocios; mas parece que a causa principal de seu exito, consiste em que estão mais proximos áquelle mercado. Esta circumstancia é conveniente aos commerciantes de Venezuela que só têm um sortido limitado que renovam quando o necessitam. Além disto ha sympathias politicas entre os Estados Unidos e Venezuela, e os Estados Unidos não estão atrazados em aproveitarem-se desta circumstancia.

O passo mais importante para o desenvolvimento das relações commerciaes entre os Estados Unidos e Venezuela foi dado pela Associação Nacional de Fabricantes, que tem sua sède em Philadelphia. Ao principio do anno de 1896 aquella associação enviou um agente a Venezuela para negociar o estabelecimento de um armazem permanente de amostras, onde se podiam expôr as manufacturas americanas sob as condições mais favoraveis. O contracto foi celebrado com o departamento correspondente do Governo venezuelano, e depois de ter arranjado todos os preliminares, o commissario voltou a Venezuela em Novembro de 1897 e annunciou ao Governo que a exposição de amostras seria logo inaugurada. O relatorio do commissionado ao Departamento do Fomento, diz que o armazem foi estabelecido para dar aos commerciantes, agricultores, etc., opportunidades para examinar practicamente os artigos em vez de recorrer aos catalogos e illustrações; para subministrar informações sobre os endereços, preços e prazos dos commerciantes americanos; para manter aberto um gabinete de leitura onde se podem lèr os periodicos e outras publicações relativos á industria e commercio, e para mostrar, quando fòr praticavel, o funccionamento de machinas agricolas, etc. Em realidade, esta exposição permanente será uma lição objectiva sobre os productos industriaes dos Estados Unidos. A exposição servirá tambem como centro para os commerciantes, e haverá alli uma repartição de informação, a qual informará aos commerciantes e seus agentes das exigencias do mercado e dos costumes commerciaes do paiz, e as opportunidades para o emprego de capitaes americanos.

O Governo isenta de direitos todas as mercadorias que se importarem no paiz com destino á exposição permanente. Como resultado deste passo dado pela Associação Nacional, se espera que Venezuela obtenha grandes beneficios e que haja um augmento extraordinario nos negocios entre os dous paizes. Á data em que se escrevem estas linhas já a exposição foi aberta com a assistencia de uns vinte commerciantes de influencia, procedentes de Pennsylvania e de Nova York. O Presidente de Venezuela assistiu ás ceremonias da inauguração. Pronunciaram-se discursos, nos quaes se tratou da amizade das duas nações e das possibilidades offerecidas por suas ultimas relações commerciaes. A opinião publica está grandemente em favor da America e os americanos.

Si, como já disse, ha indicios de que o commercio dos Estados Unidos tende a occupar o primeiro lugar, é natural suppôr que um movimento desta natureza augmentará aquella tendencia, e que em breve tempo os productos americanos substituirão outros da mesma classe, e só os artigos que os Estados Unidos não podem produzir facilmente, ficarão ao commercio estrangeiro. A maior parte do commercio com os Estados Unidos consiste em productos alimenticios e machinas e instrumentos agricolas. Uma casa americana obteve varios contractos para o fornecimento de tubos para aqueductos.

A imprensa de Venezuela, referindo-se á associação e aos trabalhos que se propõe, pergunta si os americanos adoptarão o systema europeo de conceder creditos a longos prazos, ou si converterão os commerciantes de Venezuela ao seu modo de fazer negocios; e accrescenta que, deste ponto, depende o resultado da concurrencia, porque o systema de longos prazos sempre attrahirá uma certa porção do commercio. Como é difficil tarefa conseguir que a America latina altere seus costumes, passará algum tempo antes de que se obtenha aquelle resultado.

O SYSTEMA METRICO.

CONGRESSO QUE SERÁ CELEBRADO EM PARIZ EM 1900.

Os principaes fabricantes de tecidos do mundo tratam de celebrar um Congresso em Pariz em 1900, juntamente com a exposição que terá lugar naquelle anno. O objecto do congresso é a adopção do systema metrico. A falta de um systema uniforme na numeração dos fios empregados na industria textil tem causado grandes inconvenientes, e é principalmente para obviar esta difficuldade que se propõe convocar o dito congresso. Esta questão foi tratada no Congresso de Vienna, 1873; no de Bruxellas, 1874; de Turim, 1875, e de Pariz, 1878 e 1889.

N'uma communicação sobre esta materia, dirigida á Secretaria de Estado, o Sr. HENRY W. GILBERT, Consul dos Estados Unidos em Liege, diz o seguinte: Em todos os congressos anteriores têm-se feito progressos, mas não se têm obtido resultados practicos. Duas razões têm contribuido a esta falta de ˙resultados˙ não ha uniformidade nesta materia, nem ainda na França, e o systema metrico não tem sido adoptado por todos os paizes. A Inglaterra põe nos mercados estrangeiros generos que não têm sido numerados e fabricados segundo o systema metrico, e isto se permitte tambem nos Estados Unidos. Nosso paiz está fazendo esforços energicos e com bom exito para fazer concurrencia com as outras nações no commercio estrangeiro, e, como nossa capacidade de producçao é quasi illimitada, parece que os nossos fabricantes de tecidos devem ser bem representados no referido Congresso de Pariz em 1900.

Si os exportadores dos Estados Unidos empregarem o systema metrico, poderão offerecer suas mercadorias aos compradores e consumidores estrangeiros nos pesos e medidas a que aquelles estão acostumados.

CAFÉ.

PRODUCÇÃO E CONSUMO DO MUNDO

A Repartição de Commercio Estrangeiro da Secretaria de Estado, acaba de publicar nas folhas avulsas dos Relatorios Consulares correspondentes ao mez de Junho, um relatorio comprehensivo da producção e consumo de café no mundo, o qual foi preparado por FRANK D. HILL, Consul dos Estados Unidos em Santos, Brazil. Do relatorio extrahimos os dados seguintes:

O Brazil é o grande paiz productor de café no mundo, contribuindo com 66 por cento para o total da producção. Todos os vinte estados que compõem a Republica produzem o café em maior ou menor escala. Comtudo, a verdadeira zona de café está limitada aos estados do Rio de Janeiro, São Paulo, Espirito

Santo e Minas Geraes. São Paulo é o estado que produz a maior quantidade de café. Rio e Santos são os principaes portos de exportação, ainda que se exportam quantidades consideraveis pelo porto de Victoria.

O café é classificado da maneira seguinte: fino, superior, bom, regular, ordinario e *triage*. Este último é o café de classe inferior que se compõe de grãos quebrados e defeituosos em geral. A classe fina compõe-se de café limpo de grão regular; a superior é de grãos de tamanho regular, mas pode conter algumas cascas ou grãos negros; na classe boa a igualdade no grão não é absolutamente necessaria; pode conter alguns grãos negros, mas não pedaços de páu, nem pedras ou terra; o café regular pode conter grandes quantidades de grãos pretos, cascas, pedras, pedaços de páu ou terra; a classe ordinaria contem todos os defeitos anteriores e alguns grãos quebrados.

Segundo o Consul HILL, os brazileiros resentem-se da idea que prevalece nos paizes estrangeiros de que o café do Brazil não é o melhor que se produz; elles sabem que o café de Java e Mocha que se vende no mercado americano é em sua maior parte cultivado cerca de Rio ou de Santos.

A producção de café no estado de São Paulo, assim como a vida do cafeeiro, depende do character do terreno e da planta. Diz-se que ha cafeeiros que têm estado produzindo por 75 annos e que ainda produzem. Mil cafeeiros produzem 3,238 libras ou 25 saccas em São Paulo, emquanto que no Rio de Janeiro a producção é muito menos. Devido á grande producção de café em varias partes do mundo, o preço médio nos mercados do Brazil é, e tem sido por algum tempo, de 5.7 centavos ouro a libra, ou $7.56 por sacca. A seguinte tabella representa a producção de café no estado de São Paulo, calculada por decadas desde 1850 até 1896.

Annos.	Producção.	
	Saccas.	*Libras.*
1850–1860	1,400,000	184,800,000
1860–1870	3,400,000	448,800,000
1870–1880	6,700,000	884,400,000
1880–1890	18,000,000	2,376,000,000
1890–1896	22,700,000	2,996,400,000
Total por quarenta e seis annos	52,200,000	6,890,400,000

A producção média annual do mundo e a correspondente aos estados de Rio e Santos estão representadas nos seguintes quadros:

Annos.	Producção.	
	Saccas	*Libras.*
1852–1860.	5, 000, 000	660, 000, 000
1860–1870.	6, 000, 000	792, 000, 000
1870–1880.	7, 500, 000	990, 000, 000
1880–1890.	10, 000, 000	1, 320, 000, 000
1890–1900(calculada).	11, 000, 000	1, 452, 000, 000

	Producção de—					
	1897–98.		1898–99.		1899–1900.	
	Saccas.	*Libras.*	*Saccas.*	*Libras.*	*Saccas.*	*Libras.*
Rio Janeiro	3, 000, 000	396, 000, 000	3, 500, 000	462, 000, 000	3, 000, 000	396, 000, 000
Santos	3, 750, 000	495, 000, 000	5, 500, 000	726, 000, 000	4, 000, 000	528, 000, 000
Todos os outros lugares	4, 000, 000	528, 000, 000	4, 000, 000	528, 000, 000	4, 000, 000	528, 000, 000
Total	10, 750, 000	1, 419, 000, 000	13, 000, 000	1, 716, 000, 000	11, 000, 000	1, 452, 000, 000

Estes algarismos não comprehendem o calculo da exportação de café pelos portos de Victoria, Bahia e Ceará, com a excepção do anno de 1889, ao qual têm-se aggregado 500,000 saccas, (66,000,000 libras), comprehendidas no calculo relativo a Rio de Janeiro.   Quanto ao custo de producção do café no Brazil, o relatorio consular do Sr. HILL contem os seguintes dados que se transcrevem palavra por palavra.

O seguinte calculo fidedigno foi feito aqui por um cavalleiro que conheço pessoalmente.   A difficuldade, diz elle, de dar dados exactos se comprehenderá quando se tomem em consideração o sitio, tamanho e numero das arvores, assim como sua classe, novas e velhas; e assim mesmo o facto de que os preços em ouro do café durante os dous ultimos annos, baixaram mais de 80 por cento, e que os valores locaes dependem de grandes fluctuações no cambio, pois a moeda do Brazil soffre ao presente uma depreciação de 80 por cento.   Creio que 2 milreis por cafeeiro em completo estado de producção, seria um preço moderado n'uma fazenda bem situada e que conta com casas de residencia, machinas e outros requisitos comprehendidos naquelle preço.   Os gastos de um cafezal de 150,000 cafeeiros não excedem provavelmente de $5,000 por anno, sem incluir os fretes—que são caros—até os portos, nem o custo das saccas e gastos de venda.   O total de producção seria de 65,000 a 70,000 kilogrammas, que deixariam uma utilidade de 50,000 milreis sobre um capital de $50,000, ou 14 por cento do capital empregado.

O preço de 9 milreis por cada 10 kilogrammas, que com frequencia se menciona como preço corrente neste relatorio, se refere ao café superior; o café "bom," que é equivalente ao N° 7 da "Bolsa de Café de Nova York," se vende a 7½ milreis por cada 10 kilogrammas, ou 45 milreis por sacca de 60 kilogrammas.

O consumo annual de café no mundo durante os proximos cinco annos é calculado em 12,000,000 de saccas, das quaes corresponderão á producção do Brazil 8,000,000 de saccas.

Os algarismos seguintes mostram a proporção entre a colheita de café e a de outros productos no Brazil; o quadro se refere á exportação de 1895:

Café	$140, 000, 000
Borracha	25, 000, 000
Outros productos	15, 000, 000
Total	180, 000, 000

No BOLETIM MENSAL correspondente ao mez de Outubro de 1897 se publicaram extensos dados officiaes relativos á industria do café e do cacáo em Venezuela, que mostraram que a area de cultivo do café em 1897 era de 403,865 geiras que deram uma producção total de 304,800,000 libras. Estes algarismos são dados tambem no relatorio do Consul HILL, o qual expressa a opinião fundada nos dados que obteve durante uma visita que fez a Venezuela de que a producção de café naquelle paiz está augmentando consideravelmente.

De um relatorio do Ministro BAKER, publicado nos "Relatorios Consulares dos Estados Unidos," N° 199, se vê que a producção de café em Nicaragua no anno 1896–97 foi de 50,000 saccas mais do que em nenhuma colheita anterior.

O Consul HILL ao referir-se ás possibilidades do cultivo do café no Paraguay, falla deste paiz como uma parte da zona de café do Brazil e diz que tem visto em Assumpção cafeeiros de um formoso grão. Emquanto que não tenha lugar uma nova e viril immigração nesta Republica, a herva matte continuará a ser a bebida do paiz.

A producção de café no Peru está augmentando e este producto promette ser um dos principaes do paiz. Chanchamayo, Perene, Pancarbambo e os vallés do rio Colorado são os grandes dis-

trictos productores de café. Esta industria agricola, como mui
outras industrias daquella terra privilegiada, só esperam para s
desenvolvimento a inauguração de meios adequados de transpor

Apezar da grande producção de café no Brazil e outras regiõ
e não obstante o baixo preço daquelle artigo, o Consul HILL co
sidera que é lisonjeira a perspectiva economica e financeira
Brazil. A divida exterior do Brazil, comparada com a de mui
outros paizes é pequena, e ha no Brazil uma corrente constante
boa immigração. Durante o anno de 1897 chegaram ao po
de Santos cincoenta e sete mil immigrantes, a maior parte c
quaes eram homens economicos, capazes para o desenvolvimer
dos recursos agricolas do paiz, como se tem feito nas vastas
fructiferas planicies da Republica Argentina.

Como evidencia do prospecto promettedor, se transcreve textu
mente o seguinte paragrapho do relatorio:

"Tudo parece que opera aqui em harmonia para o bem des
novas terras inexploradas que formam parte do hemispherio oc
dental, cujo solo tem sido sómente ligeiramente removido, e
maior parte de cuja população se encontra ao longo da costa
aos lados das vias fluviaes e artificiaes que communicam com
interior, não obstante haver transcorrido tres seculos desde que
deu a conhecer á Europa seus recursos. Julgando estes pai:
por sua historia diaria, talvez pareçãm estacionarios, mas si
compararem umas decadas com outras, ver-se-ha que tem realiza
grandes progressos. As virtudes civicas se desenvolvem cada c
mais. O poder militar vai cedendo gradualmente aos goverr
populares. Dentro do periodo de dez annos tenho visto derrota
o poder dos dictadores militares no Paraguay, Uruguay e Ver
zuela, e ainda que a marcha politica tenha sido espinhosa, tem
demonstrado, sem embargo, a possibilidade de estabelecer gov
nos não fundados exclusivamente sobre os principios da força.
influencia estrangeira se sente alli constantemente, por mais q
os europeos são criticos severos. As relações do Brazil com toc
os paizes da Europa e os Estados Unidos são estreitas, e navio
mercadorias de todos os paizes têm enchido seus portos."

A ESTRADA DE FERRO TRANSIBERIANA.

SEU EFFEITO SOBRE O COMMERCIO AMERICANO.

No ultimo anno do seculo dez e nove terá lugar a terminação da estrada de ferro mais gigantesca que se tem construido.

O Governo da Russia, desde que adquiriu as possessões situadas a léste das montanhas Uraes, tem realisado a necessidade, por considerações de character commercial, politica e militar, de uma relação mais estreita entre as duas secções do Imperio. Em consequencia, no anno de 1858 se fizeram estudos e explorações com o fim de construir uma grande estrada de ferro transcontinental que unisse o systema de estradas de ferro da Russia propria com o extremo oriental do paiz. Depois de muitos trabalhos e numerosas demoras, se decidiu que era o caminho mais practicavel, o que tem seu termino occidental na povoação de Chiliabinsk, e estende-se, pelo geral, n'uma direcção a léste por Omsk, Irkutsk, Khabarovka, e termina em Vladivostok, no mar do Japão.

Começou-se a construcção desta grande obra no dia 10 de Dezembro de 1892; nesta data o czarevitch (que é agora Imperador) collocou a primeira pedra. O comprimento total da linha propria desde Chiliabinsk até Vladivostok é de 7,083 *versts* (4,696 milhas), sem contar numerosos ramaes, alguns dos quaes estão em construcção e outros em projecto.

A obra é propriedade do Governo russo, o qual a tem construido sob a mais minuciosa inspecção official. O custo total da obra, incluindo a expropriação de terras, é calculado em 371,009,947 rublos ($188,014,938) ou á razão de 49,444 rublos por *verst*.

Para vencer o obstaculo que offerece o porto de Vladivostok, que permanece cerrado pelo gelo durante varios mezes do anno, se construirá um ramal atravez de Manchuria, territorio adquirido da China, recentemente, até um ponto no mar Amarello que está aberto todo o anno.

Para que se aprecie a importancia das fontes de riqueza da região pela qual ha de passar a estrada de ferro transiberiana, extrahimos o seguinte de um relatorio, datado em S. Petersburgo no dia 14 de Outubro de 1895, e dirigido á Secretaria de Estado pelo Sr. HERBERT H. PEARCE, encarregado de negocios interino, dos Estados Unidos:

Que esta grande estrada de ferro está destinada a abrir ao trafico um paiz de grande riqueza é um facto que não se pode duvidar á luz dos actuaes conhecimentos. As regiões mineiras dos Uraes, e dos montes Altai e Sayan estão pouco exploradas por causa das difficuldades que se encontram no transporte de seus productos, pois todos os grandes rios que por ellas passam correm em direcção norte até o oceano arctico. Já nos Uraes se estão fazendo progressos na extracção e preparação de mineraes de ferro e cobre e fundição de metaes.

Toda Russia está muito interessada nos trabalhos da grande estrada de ferro transcontinental, e se sabe que o Imperador, que foi presidente da empreza quando era czarevitch, está empenhado com grande enthusiasmo na prompta terminação da obra. Toda a construcção e equipamento da linha está-se fazendo e seguirá fazendo-se tanto quanto fôr possivel, na Russia e pelos russos, de accordo com o systema de protecção á industria e producção nacionaes, com tanto ardor instituido pelo ultimo Imperador. Capitalistas estrangeiros estão empregando seu capital, prévio contracto com o Governo, no estabelecimento de officinas para a fabricação de trilhos, locomotivas e outros equipamentos, mas as fabricas terão de ser estabelecidas na Russia e os trabalhadores deverão ser russos.

O Sr. J. C. MONAHAN, Consul dos Estados Unidos em Chemnitz, Allemanha, n'uma communicação de data de 4 de Dezembro de 1896, diz o seguinte:

Siberia é rica em mineraes de todas as classes. Os Uraes estão produzindo ouro e prata em grandes quantidades. Si se assistir ás ferias annuaes de Leipsic, se comprehenderá a importancia que têm para a Allemanha as pelles finas de Siberia. Si o martello que rebitou o primeiro pregão no primeiro dormente, foi de prata, o que rebitou o ultimo pregão deveria ser de ouro. Por muita importancia que tenha esta linha para a Allemanha, Russia e o resto da Europa, pode ter maior importancia para nós. California, Oregon, Washington, todo o oeste de nosso paiz, si não todo o continente, estão interessados nesta linha. Russia tem bastante em que occupar-se dentro dos limites de seu territorio; nós somos os que têm de auxiliar o desenvolvimento do Oriente.

Quando fôr concluida esta vasta empreza ficarão abertas ao tráfico e commercio do mundo regiões até agora inaccessiveis. A viagem de S. Petersburgo a Pekin poderá ser feita em cinco dias em trens luxuriosos; poderá ir-se desde Londres á capital do Japão em quinze dias em vez de trinta, que é o tempo que se exige agora para atravessar o Atlantico, Continente Americano e Oceano Pacifico; ou em vez da viagem ainda mais larga, via do Mediterraneo e do Canal de Suez.

É impossivel prever neste periodo qual seja o effeito que este novo factor tenha de ter na situação economica do mundo commercial; já se está projectando o estabelecimento de novas linhas de vapores entre Porto Arthur, que é o termino meridional da estrada de ferro, e alguns portos japonezes e chinezes, e Manila; assim como tambem a immediata connexão com linhas desde estes portos até os paizes além do Pacifico e Asia meridional.

Em vista do espirito commercial que está desenvolvendo-se em novo Japão e da acquisição de territorio chinez por importantes nações commerciaes da Europa, é de esperar-se que em breve possa-se presenciar o espectaculo do vasto Pacifico sulcado por immensos navios mercantes, como o está hoje o Atlantico. Na realização deste projecto, a estrada de ferro transiberiana deve entrar necessariamente como o factor mais importante. Si se observa o mappa do Oceano Pacifico e as rotas por elle estabelecidas, se verá que as ilhas daquelle extenso mar parecem offerecer uma serie de passadeiras á communicação entre o Oriente e Occidente, e a julgar pelas condições sob as quaes está desenvolvendo-se aquella parte do mundo, estes numerosos pontos de escala passarão provavelmente á uma nova existencia politica sob a bandeira americana.

O BOLETIM MENSAL tem chamado a attenção varias vezes para as concessões feitas a subditos japonezes para o estabelecimento de linhas de vapores entre o Japão e Mexico e ainda Peru. Extensas colonias de japonezes têm-se estabelecido e estão estabelecendo-se nas ricas terras do Isthmo de Tehuantepec. A construcção inevitavel do Canal de Nicaragua ou de qualquer outro isthmo influirá no desenvolvimento deste commercio oriental como a construcção da grande estrada de ferro transiberiana.

COMMERCIO MISCELLANEO.

REPUBLICA ARGENTINA.

Illuminação da Cidade de Buenos Aires á Luz Electrica. No numero do BOLETIM MENSAL correspondente ao mez de Maio, se fez referencia ao facto de que a municipalidade de Buenos Aires tinha celebrado um contracto com a Companhia Geral de Electricidade para fazer o serviço da illuminação da cidade á luz electrica. Publicaram-se os detalhes sobre o numero das lampadas, o preço que será pago, etc. A "Review of the River Plate," comtudo, em seu numero de 7 de Maio, publica a noticia de que, por razão de certas formalidades o referido contracto não tem sido definitivamente approvado, e por conseguinte, se apresenta a opportunidade a outras companhias, de solicitar a concessão deste valioso contracto.

Importação de Machinas Estrangeiras. O Sr. BOUCHSEIN, Consul dos Estados Unidos em Barmen, Allemanha, em um relatorio sobre a venda de machinas estrangeiras na Republica Argentina, diz o seguinte : " Em um relatorio especial dirigido ao governo imperial, um consul allemão chama a attenção para a cidade de Tucuman, como um bom mercado para a venda de machinas allemães. San Miguel de Tucuman é a capital da provincia de Tucuman, na Republica Argentina, e tem uma população de perto de 17,000.   Está unida por estrada de ferro com Cordoba e Rosario.   Esta cidade tem trinta e tres fabricas de assucar, as quaes importaram suas machinas quasi em sua totalidade de França, por causa dos prazos favoraveis que se lhes concederam.   A Allemanha tem enviado para a Republica apparelhos para as fabricas de distillação, as quaes funccionam em connexão com as fabricas de assucar, fornalhas de enxofre, etc. A industria do assucar em Tucuman está augmentando de anno em anno, e logo se necessitarão muitas machinas de toda a classe.   Alguns dos fabricantes de machinas francezes tem tido representantes em Tucuman por muitos annos."

Leis Sobre Marcas de Fabrica. A recente grande fraude de marca de fabrica, commettida em Buenos Aires, dá occasião opportuna para chamar a attenção dos commerciantes e manufactureiros para a importancia de registrar suas marcas de fabrica na America do Sul e outros lugares.   A lei relativa ás marcas de fabrica naquelles paizes é clara e de facil observancia, e só se requer cuidadosa attenção para evitar imitações fraudulentas.   No caso de que se trata os commerciantes em cujo prejuizo se commetteu a fraude estão defendendo vigorosamente seus direitos na Argentina; mas a menos que se prove que a marca de fabrica foi registrada de conformidade com a lei, será difficil obter a condemnação dos culpados.

O Milho na Argentina. A producção do milho, que constitue um dos principaes artigos de exportação da Argentina, tem augmentado de 8,038 toneladas em 1873 a 1,500,000 toneladas (calculadas) em 1896.   A provincia de Buenos Aires, por razão de suas condições climatologicas, se adapta especialmente ao cultivo deste cereal, cuja exportação começou muito antes que a do trigo.   Durante a primavera e o verão (de Março até Outubro) a temperatura apresenta uma regularidade propria para o desenvolvimento da planta, emquanto que as chuvas, que são abundantes, dão ao solo a necessaria humidade. A superficie semeada de milho em 1891 era só de 100,478 hectares, e em 1895 era de 718,633 hectares, com uma producção de 628,000,000 kilogrammas.

BRAZIL.

Commercio em Abril de 1898. Ainda que os direitos de importação no Brazil são mais baixos do que os do anno passado, as receitas aduaneiras para o mez de Abril de 1898, montaram a $3,511,876, ou $253,487 mais do que as do igual mez do anno anterior.   O total do café recebido em

Santos durante o mez montou a 377,000 saccos, dos quaes foram armazenados 263,422, contra 247,901 em Abril de 1897. A quantidade do café recebida no Rio durante o mesmo mez foi de 238,000 saccos, ou 1,000 saccos mais do que a recebida em Abril do anno anterior. Embarcaram-se 438,404 saccos no Rio e 532,677 saccos em Santos. Esta é uma quantidade enorme para a estação e a elle se deve a notavel diminuição do stock de café nos armazens, o qual era no dia 30 de Abril de só 339,116 saccos, ou menos da metade do café armazenado a principios do mez.

GUATEMALA.

Empacotamento de Merca-dorias para o Transporte por Terra. O transporte em Guatemala faz-se ordinariamente por meio de mulas. A quantidade de mercadorias transportadas desta maneira constitue uma carga. O assucar mascavado, o carvão, a zacata e todos os productos do paiz se vendem por cargas de nove arrobas ou uns 100 kilogrammas. É importante que os fabricantes tomem nota deste detalhe, pois todo o que se destina á agricultura, especialmente as machinas, deve ser arranjado em pacotes que não excedam deste peso. Isto se refere tambem a todos os artigos de uso geral. Os pacotes de uns 50 kilogrammas, de fórma longitudinal, são os mais apropriados para o transporte á costa de mulas. O custo de transporte varia segundo a distancia que tenha de ser percorrida.

HAITI.

Emprestimo Nacional. O Sr. John B. Terres, Viceconsul dos Estados Unidos em Port-au-Prince, remette á Secretaria de Estado copia de uma lei approvada na ultima sessão do congresso de Haiti, a qual tem por objecto a negociação de um emprestimo nacional de $3,500,000 em ouro. O emprestimo será feito nos Estados Unidos, e o Honrado J. N. Leger, Ministro de Haiti em Washington, está encarregado das negociações. O emprestimo que se propõe fazer tem por objecto a suppressão do papel-moeda da Republica. A lei, como approvada pelo congresso e promulgada pelo Presidente Simon Sam, foi publicada en extenso nos Relatorios Consulares dos Estados Unidos para o mez de Junho do corrente anno.

HONDURAS.

Suppressão da Subvenção concedida á "Pacific Mail Steamship Company." O "Nouveau Monde" de 11 de Junho de 1898 publica a noticia de que o governo de Honduras tem supprimido a subvenção que tinha concedida á "Pacific Mail Steamship Company." O governo fez um contrato com a Companhia Sul Americana de Vapores (que recentemente tem estendido seus serviços aos portos da America Central), para o transporte das malas dos portos de Honduras.

Banco Commercial em Tegucigalpa. O Banco Commercial de Honduras, parte de cujas acções estão em poder de capitalistas americanos, foi formalmente estabelecido em Tegucigalpa.

MEXICO.

Novo Edificio de Mercado em Guayamas. O Coronel WROTNOWSKI, conhecido nos centros scientificos do Mexico e dos Estados Unidos como o engenheiro que projectou e construiu os molhes de Tampico e que tambem prestou seus serviços nos trabalhos do porto de Vera Cruz, obteve um contrato para a construcção de um grande mercado na cidade de Guayamas, porto florescente do Estado de Sonora. O edificio será de pedra, ferro e vidro, e conterá 140 lojinhas, cada uma de quatro metros quadrados, e terá um segundo andar para agencias de negocio. A obra será terminada em Fevereiro de 1900. O Coronel WROTNOWSKI receberá a renda do mercado por trinta e tres annos, menos 25 por cento das receitas liquidas, que corresponde á cidade.

Alteração no Imposto sobre Minas. A Camara de Deputados do Mexico votou recentemente uma lei, que tem por objecto regular o imposto sobre minas, dos metaes inferiores. Segundo as disposições da lei, o imposto sobre o titulo original e sobre a renda annual por prazo ou pertenencia, será reduzido a $2 por pertenencia em todas as minas excepto as que produzem ouro, prata e platina. Nas minas que produzem os metaes acima mencionados, o imposto continuará a ser o mesmo que até o presente. Em todas as demais minas o imposto será de $2.50 por pertenencia sobre o titulo, e $2 sobre a renda annual.

Exhibição Mexicana na Exposição de Omaha. O Ministerio de Fomento resolveu que o Mexico fosse representado na Esposição de Omaha, que terá lugar neste verão. O espaço que foi tomado é igual ao que foi occupado pela exhibição do Mexico em Atlanta. O Sr. J. D. POWELL, que representou o Mexico em Atlanta, foi provido de cartas do Ministro FERNANDEZ LEAL aos governadores de todos os Estados, e está actualmente viajando na Republica no interesse da exhibição.

PERU.

Exposição Permanente de Lima. Os importadores e fabricantes que estão exhibindo seus productos na Exposição Permanente de Machinas e Manufacturas de Lima, mostram-se satisfeitos da prompta venda dos artigos exhibidos. A casa dos Senhores G. MENCHACA & Co. tem vendido grande numero de artigos que tinha tido em seu poder por muitos annos, e cujo valor não tinha sido apreciado até o presente, por falta de exhibição apropriada. A vantagem a respeito dos artigos novos é ainda mais pronunciada, o agente de uma casa dos Estados Unidos já tem encontrado compradores para quasi todos os artigos que se lhe tèm remettido para sua exposição. As machinas e manufacturas de todas as classes, procedentes do estrangeiro, estão isentas de todo imposto e de todo aluguel pelo espaço que occupam, a menos que se vendam no paiz. Como ha um salão de leitura na Exposição, fez-se a suggestão de que os Estados Unidos enviassem em grande numero, catalogos e photographias de seus productos para que sejam examinados pelos compradores. Seriam de utilidade especial os gravados de machinas, caldeiras de vapor, apparelhos de mineração e para a fabricação de assucar, obras de quadro de metal, pontes, casas portateis, etc.

SALVADOR.

Uma Nova Lei Bancaria. Nas ultimas sessões ordinarias do congresso se decretou uma nova lei bancaria, cujo objecto principal é obrigar aos bancos que resgatem seus bilhetes em prata. A lei começou a vigorar no dia 11 de Abril ultimo. O Consul, JOHN JENKINS, escrevendo de Salvador em data de 15 de Abril, diz que o Banco Industrial suspendeu seus negocios, e que em combinação com um dos bancos mais antigos do paiz formará uma nova instituição bancaria. Isto reduzirá a quatro o numero dos bancos. Como resultado da rivalidade, os negocios bancarios têm sido pouco satisfactorios, os bancos convertendose em instituições meramente especulativas. Como a nova lei impõe aos bancos a obrigação de resgatar seus bilhetes em prata, se espera que esta classe de negocios se ponha em base mais firme. O Sr. JENKINS diz que apezar do baixo preço do café, ha no Salvador abundancia de material para assegurar uma grande prosperidade no futuro.

URUGUAY.

Instrucção Gratuita nas Academias Militar e Naval dos Estados Unidos. Correspondendo a uma indicação feita pelo Sr. FINCH, Ministro dos Estados Unidos, o governo desta Republica tem offerecido duas collegiaturas á Republica do Uruguay, uma na Academia Militar de West Point e a outra na Escola Naval de Annapolis, em beneficio de dous jovens cidadãos daquella Republica. As nomeações serão feitas de accordo ao pedido formal do Presidente do Uruguay.

VENEZUELA.

Importações provenientes do Porto de Nova York. O Senhor ANTONIO E. DELFINO, Consul Geral de Venezuela, subministrou a esta Secretaria os seguintes dados estatisticos relativos á exportação de mercadorias de Nova York para varios portos de Venezuela no mez de Maio de 1898, comparada com a do mesmo mez de 1897. O valor total das exportações em Maio de 1898 foi de $209,900.68; o de Maio de 1897 foi de $250,182.35, o que mostra uma diminuição de $46,281.67. Esta exportação, mostrando o augmento ou diminuição, é como se segue; os algarismos representam os valores em ouro:

	Maio de 1898.	Maio de 1897.	Augmento.	Diminuição.
La Guira.	$121,334.54	$113,437.79	$7,897.35	. . . .
Porto Cabello	12,520.75	39,061.56	. . . .	$26,540.80
Maracaibo	43,661.59	54,193.64	. . . .	10,532.05
La Vela.	10,311.00	15,164.26	. . . .	4,853.86
Guanta	1,565.79	1,117.25	448.54	. . . .
Cumaná	1,416.00	542.00	874.00	. . . .
Cana Colorado	86,00	1,697.35	. . . .	1,611.35
Carupano	5,628.00	5,022.00	606.00	. . . .
Ciudad Bolivar.	13,377.00	19,946.50	. . . .	6,569.50
Total	209,900.68	250,182.35	9,825.89	50,107.56

Illuminação á Luz Electrica de Los Andes. Um contrato foi celebrado recentemente entre a municipalidade e o Sr. LUIS MANUEL MENDEZ para a illuminação da cidade de San Christobal (Los Andes) á luz electrica. Segundo as condições do contrato, terão de ser installadas 120 lampadas incandescentes com força de dezeseis velas cada uma, e 10 lampadas de arco com força de cem velas cada uma. A cidade pagará seis francos por cada lampada incandescente e sessenta francos por cada lampada de arco.

Um Banco Agricola. O Presidente IGNACIO ANDRADE submetteu á consideração do Congresso de Venezuela um plano para o estabelecimento de um banco nacional que tenha por unico objecto o desenvolvimento das industrias agricola e bovina da Republica. O plano, como projectado, consiste em fazer emprestimos a longos prazos e a um juro reduzido, ás pessoas que estejam já empenhadas ou que desejem occupar-se nestas industrias, afim de facilitar-lhes o começo dos trabalhos e sua continuação até que suas respectivas emprezas possam suster-se por si mesmas. Em sua mensagem ao Congresso o Presidente ANDRADE diz: "Uma instituição desta natureza seria de grande e inquestionavel utilidade e todos os homens de reflexão do paiz, têm ido, desde ha tempo, pedindo seu estabelecimento. Creio que este projecto devia ser submettido á immediata consideração do Congresso, pois que a empreza vem a responder a grandes e urgentes necessidades, melhorará a situação economica do paiz, aggravada pela baixa no preço de nossos principaes productos, e impedirá os temidos effeitos que o actual conflicto armado haverá de operar necessariamente sobre a riqueza publica e especialmente sobre as industrias acima mencionadas.

BULLETIN MENSUEL

DU

BUREAU DES RÉPUBLIQUES AMÉRICAINES.

UNION INTERNATIONALE DES RÉPUBLIQUES AMÉRICAINES.

VOL. VI.	JUILLET 1898.	No. 1.

PROLONGATION DU TERME DU DIRECTEUR PROVISOIRE.

Le Comité Exécutif de l'Union Internationale des Républiques Américaines s'est réuni dans la Salle diplomatique au Ministère des Affaires Etrangères le samedi, 25 juin 1898 à 11 heures du matin.

L'Honorable WILLIAM R. DAY, Ministre des Affaires Etrangères, présidait à la séance. Les autres membres qui y assistaient étaient; Le Señor Don JOSÉ ANDRADE, Ministre du Venezuela; Le Señor Dr. Don MARTIN GARCIA MÉROU, Ministre de la République Argentine; Le Señor Don JOAQUIN BERNARDO CALVO, Ministre de Costa Rica. M. FRÉDÉRIC EMORY, Directeur du Bureau des Républiques Américaines y assistait aussi.

Le président a demandé à connaître les intentions du conseil. M. EMORY a annoncé l'expiration prochaine (le 30 juin) du terme de sa nomination en qualité de Directeur provisoire du Bureau.

Le Señor ANDRADE a proposé le maintien de M. EMORY en qualité de Directeur jusqu'au 1er octobre 1898, M. MÉROU a appuyé cette proposition.

Le président a donc fait connaître les décisions suivantes:

Le Comité Exécutif de l'Union Internationale des Républiques Américaines a décidé, en vue de la condition satisfaisante des affaires du Bureau des Républiques Américaines, sous la direction provisoire en vigueur depuis le 28 février

151

dernier, conformément à l'action du Comité Exécutif de cette date, que le terme de M. Frédéric Emory, comme Directeur, soit prolongé audelà du terme fixé par le Comité, à savoir 30 juin 1898, et que ledit Frédéric Emory, soit et est par ce fait nommé Directeur du Bureau des Républiques Américaines pour une autre période commençant le 1er juillet et finissant le 1er octobre 1898.

Il a décidé aussi que les pouvoirs spéciaux, conférés au Directeur par la décision du 28 février 1898, soient affirmés de nouveau et prolongés jusqu'à la fin de son terme.

Le président a demandé aux membres s'ils avaient des remarques à faire relativement à ces décisions.

Après avoir exprimé leur satisfaction personnelle sur les conditions des affaires du Bureau, le Comité a adopté à l'unanimité les décisions présentées.

Ajourné.

RELATIONS COMMERCIALES.—XIII.*

RESSOURCES INTÉRIEURES DE LA CÔTE ORIENTALE DE L'AMÉRIQUE DU SUD.

On a publié dans le Bulletin du mois de janvier, le dernier article de cette série, écrit par le feu Directeur du Bureau, ayant trait à la côte orientale de l'Amérique du Sud, c'est-à-dire aux pays qui en sont limitrophes ou qui trouvent leurs débouchés naturels sur l'Atlantique. Ces pays sont le Brésil, l'Uruguay, la République Argentine et le Paraguay. L'article se bornait à la discussion des relations commerciales entre les Républiques citées et les Etats-Unis. On se propose maintenant de faire connaître les ressources intérieures des vastes régions qui s'étendent au sud du cinquième parallèle de latitude nord.

Les Etats-Unis du Brésil sont grands comme les six-septièmes de l'Europe, avec des sites topographiques et hydrographiques très vastes. Leur superficie est de 3,257,766 milles carrés, avec une population de 16,330,216 habitants, soit environ cinq habitants par mille carré. Quand on considère que la côte du pays a 4,000 milles de longueur, et que sa grande voie fluviale—l'Amazone—avec ses affluents, est navigable sur un parcours de plus de 30,000 milles dans son territoire, on peut se faire une idée de leurs immenses facilités pour le développement industriel.

---

*Le premier article de cette série écrit par le feu Directeur, J. P. Smith, a paru dans le Bulletin Mensuel de juillet 1897.

Le Brésil est un pays de ressources naturelles magnifiques, mais le grand obstacle au développement de l'Amérique Latine est le manque de proportion entre la population et l'étendue du territoire, comme il est facile de le voir dans ce pays, de même que dans les autres Républiques du Sud. Les richesses agricoles de la nation sont illimitées, quoique l'onn'ait encore cultivé jusqu'à présent qu'une partie des terres. La principale production, comme il est reconnu généralement, est le café; viennent ensuite, dans l'ordre nommé, le sucre, le tabac, le coton, le *maté*, le caoutchouc, le bois de charpente, le cacao et les noix. Depuis quelques années, c'est le Brésil qui a fourni plus de la moitié de la consommation universelle du café. Les forêts abondent en bois précieux, en bois de teintures, en résins, en fibres et en plantes médicinales. Dans la vallée de l'Amazone seule, il y a vingt-deux espèces de bois qu'on a classés. Les immenses plaines du midi sont admirablement adaptées à l'élevage du bétail, et les rivières fourmillent de plusieurs variétés de poissons. La richesse minérale est très grande. Le fer existe en vastes quantités, mais le manque de combustible empêche l'exploitation avantageuse de ces gisements. Les étrangers, surtout les Anglais et les Français, exploitent les mines d'or et de diamants sur une grande échelle.

Les industries y sont représentées par environ 156 filatures de coton, employant environ 200,000 ouvriers; par un nombre d'importantes filatures de drap, de sucreries, de tanneries, de brasseries, de minoteries et de distilleries, de savonneries, de fabriques d'huiles et de bougies, de chantiers de construction de navires, etc.

Le Brésil ne sera jamais, en toute probabilité, un grand pays manufacturier, mais comme pays producteur et exportateur de matières premières, il a beaucoup d'avenir.

Le 31 décembre 1896, il y avait 8,662 milles de chemins de fer en exploitation dans le pays, et 4,963 en voie de construction. On a publié dans le BULLETIN de mars 1898, un rapport intéressant et détaillé sur ces chemins de fer. Le système télégraphique est sous le contrôle du Gouvernement. En 1895 il y avait 21,936 milles de fil de fer en usage. Dans la même année la marine marchande du pays se composait de 189 vapeurs jaugeant 75,283 tonnes nettes, et de 285 voiliers jaugeant 65,575 tonnes nettes.

La République de l'Uruguay, qui est située au sud du Brésil, a une superficie estimée à 72,110 milles carrés et une population

ananas. La conservation du coing est une branche avantageuse de l'industrie. Les cognassiers sont assez abondants pour fournir des forêts.

On cultive en quantités assez abondantes la graine de lin, le chanvre, le tabac et le saffron.

L'exploitation minière n'est pas très avancée, quoiqu'on y ait trouvé de l'or, de l'argent, du cuivre, du fer, de l'étain et du mercure qui peuvent être exploités avec profit.

En 1896, il y avait 1,026 milles de chemins de fer ouverts au trafic, et environ 200 milles en voie de construction. La longueur totale des lignes télégraphiques en 1897, était de 4,380 milles, dont 982 appartenaient aux chemins de fer.

Les intérêts maritimes de la République en 1895 étaient représentés par 19 vapeurs d'un tonnage total net de 4,608 tonnes et de 45 voiliers d'un total de 13,171 tonnes nettes.

En étudiant la République Argentine, on est frappé au commencement, du fait, duquel on a déjà parlé dans les numéros précédents du BULLETIN, que beaucoup des principales productions—surtout le blé et la laine—de ce grand pays sont identiques à quelques-unes de celles des. Etats-Unis, réduisant ainsi l'échange de celles-ci à un très petit volume. La République. Argentine, située entre le 22° et le 56° latitude sud, possède un littoral sur l'Atlantique plus étendu que celui de sa grande sœur du Nord, et étant plus près de l'Equateur, elle donne les productions caractéristiques de chaque climat.

Avec une superficie de 1,212,000 milles carrés et une population de 4,092,990 habitants, l'Argentine est l'une des contrées les plus grandes et les plus progressives du Nouveau Monde.

On trouve de riches gisements de minéraux dans les chaînes de montagnes de l'ouest, tels que l'or, l'argent, le fer, le cuivre, tandis qu'on a récemment découvert dans les Provinces du sud-ouest, des houillères étendues. Mais l'industrie minière n'est pas encore développée, malgré l'établissement de bonnes lois minières très libérales.

La République Argentine est connue dans tout le monde comme le pays, par excellence, des industries agricoles et pastorales, et elle a fait de très grands progrès dans les deux voies. Il y a quelques années seulement, que la République Argentine importait la farine de son voisin de l'ouest, le Chili ; mais la guerre qui a éclaté avec le Paraguay a été la cause de beaucoup de demandes de céréales. Les Argentins se sont mis au travail avec acharnement, profitant de leur sol merveilleux où la charrue ne doit pas faire autant de travail que dans les autres parties du monde, et en 1893, ils avaient élevé leur pays au troisième rang parmi les grandes nations exportatrices de blé. Les exportations d' ce produit en 1895, étaient de 37,120,897 boisseaux. On a estimé qu'll y a dans la République, 240,000,000 d'acres qui peuvent convenir à la culture du blé, quoiqu'en 1897, on compte qu'il n'y avait qu'environ 15,000,000 d'acres en culture de toutes espèces. Le rendement moyen de blé par acre est de 990 livres.

L'industrie pastorale de la République Argentine jouit d'une renommée universelle. Le recensement national de 1895, montre que le nombre d'animaux était; bêtes à cornes, 21,701,526; chevaux, mulets, et ânes, 4,930,228; moutons, 74,379,561; chèvres, 2,748,860; la valeur totale de ces animaux était, en papier-monnaie de $1,130,701,331. La déduction naturelle de la possession d'un si grand nombre de bétail et de moutons, est que leurs produits et résidu forment une part importante du commerce d'exportation de la République, ce qui est vrai. Depuis 1890, le commerce extérieur en cornes, os, peaux, bœuf conservé, extrait de viande, courroies, langues conservées, sang séché, graisses et suif, viandes salées, viandes de conserve, viande conservée dans les appareils frigorifiques, peaux de moutons et laine, a été très grand, quoiqu'il ait varié en raison des sécheresses et d'autres causes naturelles qui affectent la même industrie dans les autres pays. Le commerce en bétes à cornes avec l'Uruguay, le Chili et le Brésil a pris des proportions énormes et a produit d'immenses richesses. La plupart des grandes *estancias*, comme on appelle les immenses fermes à bestiaux, sont dirigées d'après le système coopératif qui a donné beaucoup d'avantage et qui a contribué à une grande immigration d'étrangers qui se sont formés en colonies et se sont engagés dans les industries agricoles et pastorales.

La République Argentine diffère en une chose au moins, des autres Républiques du Sud. Jusqu'en 1889, ses exportations se bornaient principalement aux articles précités; mais la crise financière survint cette année et le pays, qui jusqu'alors ne produisait que des matières premières, montra par ses statistiques d'importation que l'énérgie de sa population avait été dirigée dans d'autres voies. Des manufactures s'élevèrent et purent fournir en 1892 beaucoup d'articles qui figuraient avant d'une manière marquée dans la liste des importations. La force de la nation commença à se faire sentir dans d'autres champs, en cherchant à suppléer à ses besoins par l'utilisation des fruits du sol dans la fabrication de beaucoup d'articles achetés antérieurement à l'étranger, se lançant ainsi dans la tâche louable d'établir une grande et puissante nation, capable de se suffire.

Le recensement de 1895 montre que le nombre des établissements industriels les plus importants était le suivant : fabriques de vin, 852 ; moulins, 532 ; distilleries, 108 ; brasseries, 44 ; plantations de sucre, 2,749 ; moulins à sucre, 48 ; vignobles, 6,514.

Le gouvernement a sérieusement étudié la question du transport par chemin de fer dans la République Argentine, et maintenant des lignes de chemins de fer traversent les plus riches parties du pays, et peuvent être comparées aux meilleures lignes du monde. Depuis quelques années, des corps d'ingénieurs du gouvernement ont été sur la place, faisant des arpentages et des reconnaissances, non seulement pour les lignes projetées et en voie de construction, mais en vue de l'avenir, traçant un grand réseau dans le pays entier dont les différentes sections qui le composent, seront construites à mesure que les exigencies du traffic le rendront nécessaires.

Parmi les chemins de fer en exploitation en 1895, 5 appartiennent à la nation et 10 à des particuliers avec garantie de la part du Gouvernement. La longueur totale des premiers, au 31 décembre de l'année en question, était de 1,033 kilomètres et la longueur des 10 derniers était de 3,920. La longueur totale de toutes les lignes en exploitation en 1896 est estimée à 9,032 milles.

Pendant cette dernière année il y avait 25,345 milles de lignes télégraphiques avec 59,060 milles de fil de fer, dont presque la moitié était sous le contrôle du Gouvernement.

En 1894 la marine marchande de la République Argentine consistait en 75 vapeurs de 21,613 tonnes nettes et 125 bateaux à voiles d'un tonnage net de 28,241 tonnes.

La République du Paraguay, comme celle de la Bolivie, est un pays intérieur, situé loin de la côte maritime, mais elle y communique avec quelques-unes des plus belles voies fluviales du monde, les rivières Paraná, Paraguay et Uruguay. Assomption, la capitale de la République, est à une distance de onze ou douze cents milles de Buenos-Ayres, et lui est reliée par trois lignes de bons vapeurs qui font le service régulier sur les importants cours d'eau dont nous avons parlé. D'après les statistiques officielles, la partie orientale du Paraguay, qu'on considère le Paraguay proprement dit, a une superficie de 148,000 milles carrés et une population de 430,000 habitants, d'après le recensement de 1894. Sur ce nombre, 60,000 sont à moitié civilisés et 70,000 sont des Indiens non civilisés.

En raison de son climat qui n'a pas de températures extrêmes et son sol d'une fertilité merveilleuse, le Paraguay est toujours tapissé de verdure. On a dit avec raison " qu'il est douteux qu'il existe un autre endroit sur la surface, aussi petit que le Paraguay, qui produise une aussi grande variété de produits agricoles avec si peu de travail. Dans l'espace de quelques acres on peut voir 200 productions différentes de l'Europe, de l'Asie, de l'Afrique et de l'Amérique, de croissance presque spontanée, et ne demandant jamais le travail artificiel, tel que la culture forcée."

La principale production du pays est *l'yerba-mate*, connu dans tous les marchés de l'Amérique du Sud et dans quelques endroits de l'Europe sous le nom de "thé du Paraguay." Cet article remplace le thé chinois pour des millions d'habitants du Brésil, des contrées de la Rivière Platte, du Pérou et de la Bolivie. En 1896, les exportations de ce produit s'élevèrent à 9,024 tonnes évaluées à plus de $1,400,000.

Le sol du Paraguay, étant poreux et léger, convient admirablement à la culture des fruits. Les fruits aurantiacés y poussent admirablement bien, et surtout les oranges qui sont exportées à Buenos Ayres et à Montévidéo pour une quantité de 6,000 ou 7,000 tonnes par an. On voit d'immenses bosquets d'orangers qui produisent leurs fruits dorés sans demander le plus petit soin. Une industrie assez importante se développe dans l'exportation en Hollande, de la peau séchée de ce fruit délicieux où on la convertit en une liqueur connue sous le nom de Curaçao, et dans le pays on emploie des fonds considérables dans la fabrique de cordials et d'amers. Comme la pulpe n'est pas nécessaire à cette industrie, on la jette de côté ou on la donne aux cochons pour nourriture.

Le tabac pousse dans toutes les parties de la République et il est un de ses principaux produits.   La canne à sucre y pousse abondamment, mais les sucreries sont montées d'une manière très primitive.   Le coton et les autres plantes textiles viennent spontanément, et enfin la plupart des productions tropicales, sinon toutes, y poussent à profusion.

Les forêts du Paraguay sont surtout riches en bois durs et quoique l'industrie des bois de charpente ait pris des proportions considérables pendant ces dernières années, il est certain que ceux qui se lanceront dans cette industrie sur une grande échelle avec la matière première sous main, feront rapidement fortune.   Le transport et le travail sont tous les deux bon marché et les prix qu'on obtient dans les marchés du voisinage sont bons.

Quant à l'industrie minière, tout ce qu'on peut dire c'est qu'elle n'a pas été développée, quoique sous la surface verdoyante du pays, il existe des richesses minérales qui, lorsqu'elles seront mises à jour augmenteront de beaucoup la richesse nationale.

En fait de manufactures, le Paraguay a fait peu de progrès et beaucoup d'années s'écouleront avant qu'il ne soit à même de suppléer à la consommation nationale.   L'industrie manufacturière se borne principalement aux lainages et aux cotonnades.

Les industries qui produiront de beaux bénéfices dans l'avenir et qui sont aujourd'hui à l'état d'embryon sont celles de faïences et de distilleries.   Les argiles fines du Paraguay, ont été connues depuis longtemps et l'extraction des riches essences des oranges et d'autres fruits, de fleurs, de feuilles, etc., par la distillation, présente un champ ouvert au capital.

Quoi qu'il en soit, le premier chemin de fer de l'Amérique du Sud, a été construit dans le Paraguay, il y a 50 ans, par le Dictateur Lopez, et aujourd'hui, il n'y a qu'une ligne dans le pays, appartenant à une campagnie particulière et allant de la capitale à Pirapo sur une distance de 155.4 milles.   La voie sera prolongée eventuellement à Encarnacion, sur la rivière Parana où elle sera mise en correspondance avec le réseau des chemins de fer de l'Argentine.

Il y a 360 milles de lignes télégraphiques.

Dans l'espace nécessairement restreint de cet article, on peut seulement jeter un coup d'oeil sur les nations merveilleusement riches de l'Amérique du Sud, baignées par l'Océan Atlantique et les puissants fleuves dont les eaux se confondent avec son flux et son reflux, mais ce coup d'oeil suffit pour montrer que chacun des quatre pays présente, sous un aspect plus ou moins attrayant, une terre pleine de promesses à celui qui cherche des moyens de subsistance.

RÉPUBLIQUE ARGENTINE.

COMMERCE DE VIANDE FRIGORIFIÉE.

M. LYMAN W. CHUTE, vice-consul des Etats-Unis à Buenos Ayres, a envoyé le 16 décembre 1897 au Département d'Etat un rapport détaillé sur le commerce de viande frigorifiée de la République Argentine. Ce rapport a été publié en détail dans les premières feuilles des Rapports Consulaires des Etats-Unis du 10 mai 1898.

On publie dans le Bulletin les extraits suivants du rapport de M. CHUTE, comme étant d'un intérêt général.

INITIATIVE DE L'INDUSTRIE.

On a établi en 1882 l'industrie de viande frigorifiée dans la République Argentine. Les premières exportations ont eu lieu en 1883, et depuis elles ont constamment augmenté. L'industrie se poursuit dans quatre établissements énumérés ci-dessous :

Le premier établissement, fondé en 1882, est situé à Campaña à 40 milles environ au nord de la ville de Buenos Ayres, sur la rivière Paraná.

Le deuxième établissement, commencé en 1882, est situé sur la rive sud de la Riachuelo, petite rivière canalisée, qui forme la frontière sud de la ville de Buenos Ayres. Cet établissement appartenait autrefois à une compagnie particulière, mais à présent il appartient à une compagnie anonyme qui a constamment augmenté ses affaires. Ayant commencé d'une manière très modeste, il est arrivé, d'après des informations dignes de foi, à occuper une des plus importantes positions dans le monde, pour le commerce de viande frigorifiée.

Le troisième établissement a été fondé en 1886 à San Nicolas, port sur la rivière Paraná.

Le quatrième établissement a commencé à marcher en 1886 à Lima, station de chemin de fer sur la ligne Buenos Ayres et Rosario, près de Zarate, port voisin de Campaña et situé aussi sur la rivière Paraná.

En 1885 on avait établi une industrie de viande frigorifiée sous les auspices de la Société rurale de l'Argentine. Les actionnaires étaient principalement des éleveurs de bétail, désirant trouver un débouché avantageux pour leur production. Deux expéditions ont abouti désastreusement. On avait expédié des carcasses d'animaux de cinq ou six ans et de castration tardive, non convenables pour les besoins des marchés anglais, et le mauvais résultat de la réfrigération accomplie à bord du bateau à vapeur spécialement préparé pour cet objet, a démontré l'erreur de faire la réfrigération ailleurs qu'à terre. La compagnie a fait faillite; une nouvelle société pour la préparation et l'exportation de viande frigorifiée cherche maintenant des capitaux pour opérer dans la Province de Buenos Ayres.

CAPITAL.

Le total du capital des quatre établissements est déclaré être de $5,934,380 en or, y compris la valeur du terrain, des bâtiments, des machines, du mobilier, etc. Ces quatre établissements sont maintenant formés en compagnies, dont trois travaillent avec des capitaux anglais et un avec des capitaux argentins.

LABEUR.

Les employés sont au nombre de 1,225, et peuvent être classés comme suit: Contre-maîtres, gagnant de $1.50 à $2 en or par jour; abatteurs, échorcheurs, tanneurs, corroyeurs et ouvriers divers recevant en moyenne $1 en or par jour.

PROVISIONS.

On se procure les moutons dans la province de Buenos Ayres; les races les plus recherchées sont celles du sud de Hampshire, de Shropshire et d'Oxford Down, de Cheviot et de Romney Marsh, et aussi les moutons indigènes obtenus par le croisement avec les Lincoln ou les Rambouillet. Cependant, on a obtenu les meilleurs prix de vente dans les quelques cas où l'on a pu se procurer la pure race de Hampshire Downs, bien qu'il ait été affirmé dernièrement qu'on obtient d'excellents résultats pour le mouton frigorifié, provenant d'un croisement des Mérinos et des Shropshire à tête noire. On obtient les jeunes bœufs principalement dans les provinces de Buenos Ayres, de Cordoba et de San Juan. Le commerce en est limité à cause de la difficulté d'obtenir la classe d'animaux exigés par le procédé.

Le poids moyen du mouton castré sur pied est de 50 kilogrammes et la carcasse dressée pèse environ 25 kilogrammes. Une bonne carcasse dressée de Hampshire Downs, expédiée en Angleterre par le deuxième établissement, pesait 60 kilos ¾. Le jeune bœuf sur pied pèse de 740 à 750 kilogrammes, et préparé pour l'expédition, de 370 à 375 kilogrammes.

PRIX.

Le mouton castré sur pied à la fabrique, coûte de $2 à $2.30 en or, et le jeune bœuf coûte environ $20 en or.

Bull. No. 1——11

FRET.

Deux compagnies expédient leurs cargaisons par des vapeurs appartenant à leurs agents à Liverpool; les autres frétent deux ou trois lignes. Dans le premier cas on paye cinq centimes par livre; et dans le dernier cas, soit une somme entière ou à raison de 1¾ centimes la livre. Le Royaume-Uni tient la part du lion dans le transport, aussi bien que dans le commerce des viandes, mais une compagnie française—les Chargeurs Réunis—transporte à Londres et au Hâvre de grandes quantités de moutons pour le compte du deuxième établissement dont les viandes frigorifiées vont même jusqu'à la frontière franco-allemande.

PRODUCTION.

On place à 2,300,000 animaux, l'abatage actuel pour la réfrigération.

Les quantités et la valeur des exportations depuis le commencement de l'entreprise jusqu'à la fin du troisième trimestre de 1897, d'après des rapports officiels, sont comme suit:

Exportation de moutons frigorifiés.

Année.	Quantités.		Valeur en or.
	Kilogrammes.	*Livres*	
1883	....	....	$11,412
1884 (33,159 carcasses).................			33,159
1885	2,826,270	6,310,794	75,323
1886	7,350,671	16,205,176	360,508
1887	12,038,889	26,540,756	963,112
1888	18,247,988	40,228,374	1,459,839
1889	16,532,545	36,449,799	1,322,604
1890	20,415,000	45,007,400	1,633,105
1891	23,278,084	51,317,585	1,862,247
1892	25,436,221	56,076,942	2,034,898
1893	25,041,000	55,205,200	2,003,254
1894	36,486,000	80,437,100	1,864,110
1895	41,882,000	92,330,600	1,675,273
1896	45,105,000	99,435,651	1,804,205
1897 (les neuf premiers mois)	37,650,000	83,004,800	1,506,007
Total	312,325,668	688,553,177	18,609,056

Exportation de bœuf frigorifié.

Année.	Quantités.		Valeur en or.
	Kilogrammes.	*Livres.*	
1885 (84 carcasses)	....	....	$1,680
1886 (527 carcasses)			12,800
1887	41,581	91,686	3,326
1888	734,264	1,619,052	58,724
1890	662,860	1,395,346	53,029
1891	73,769	162,660	5,902
1892	283,687	625,490	22,695
1893	2,778,485	6,186,860	222,279
1894	26,700	58,873	12,400
1895	158,700	349,934	63,482
1896	299,700	666,838	119,863
1897	299,100	659,516	119,660
Total.................	5,358,846	11,816,255	695,858

D'après le tableau ci-dessus, on verra que tandis que l'exportation de moutons a augmenté constamment, l'exportation de bœufs a varié considérablement, atteignant de grandes proportions seulement dans les années 1889, 1890 et 1893.

RÉFRIGÉRATION DE VOLAILLE.

Il y a d'autres articles de consommation, tels que les canards, les perdrix, les dindes, les bécasses et les poissons, etc., qu'on expédie aussi en Europe, principalement en France. Ils y trouvent une vente facile, mais on ne peut obtenir aucun rapport correct sur les quantités. La maison Sansinena, avant l'établissement de la compagnie, envoya une seule cargaison à Paris, pendant la dernière exposition, de 40,000 oiseaux de différentes espèces. Cette maison avait établi un établissement pour la réfrigération dans l'exposition même, avec un restaurant, de sorte que les clients pouvaient, au moyen des fenêtres de glace, choisir leurs viandes pour le lendemain. Par suite de cette entreprise, les MM. Sansinena & Cie., obtinrent les seules médailles en or pour les viandes frigorifiées, et Don Francisco Sansinena, le directeur actuel de la compagnie, fut créé Chevalier de la Légion d'Honneur.

CONDITIONS ACTUELLES DE L'INDUSTRIE.

On s'occupe maintenant du maniement de l'industrie de la réfrigération, et en se basant sur les expériences passées et sur les informations qu'on peut recueillir des sources commerciales intéressées à cette industrie, il y a tout lieu d'espérer une augmentation constante, qui offrira à l'éleveur de bétail un débouché pour l'augmentation de sa production qui ne peut pas être surpassée par aucun pays au monde.

Lorsqu'on considère la superficie pastorale de l'Argentine, la qualité de l'herbe, le bon marché des terres, l'afflux du capital, l'amélioration des races, l'immigration constante et le développement des chemins de fer, il y a tout lieu d'espérer que cette République est destinée à atteindre un rang important comme pourvoyeur de viandes dans les marchés européens.

BRÉSIL.

COMMERCE AVEC NEW YORK EN 1897.

On emprunte les faits suivants sur le commerce du Brésil avec le port de New York au rapport de M. Antoine Guimaraes, vice-consul du Brésil dans cette ville. La valeur totale des marchandises exportées au Brésil était, en monnaie des Etats-Unis, de $3,490,289, et la valeur de celles importées était de $16,736,736. Ces chiffres, comparés avec ceux de l'année 1896, accusent une augmentation dans les exportations de $344,325 et une diminution dans les importations de $659,741.

Les principales productions d'exportation étaient: saindoux, 16,762,069 livres; blé, 755,971 barrils; huilede pétrole, 21,844,750 gallons; bois de charpente, 50,465,000 pieds; huile de saindoux, 157,120 gallons; térébinthe, 161,961 gallons; lard fumé, 75,651 barils et 5,741 boîtes; blé de semence, 747,755 boisseaux et 12,035 sacs.

Ces chiffres comparés avec ceux de l'année 1896 accusent une augmentation de 8,035,997 livres dans l'exportation du saindoux; de 300,033 barils de farine; de 28,396,924 gallons d'huile de pétrole et de 4,286,991 livres de lard fumé. Il y a eu une diminution dans les exportations de bois de charpente s'élevant à 16,876,902 pieds; en huile de saindoux, une de 170,371 gallons et en térébinthe, une de 3,097,988 gallons.

Les principaux produits importés du Brésil étaient; sucre, 100,107,567 livres et 133,792 sacs; caoutchouc, 25,036,628 livres; cuirs, 1,344,176 livres et peaux, 3,677,998 livres.

EQUATEUR.

COMMERCE DE GUAYAQUIL EN 1897.

On a emprunté les faits suivants ayant rapport à l'industrie et au commerce de Quayaquil, Equateur, pendant l'année 1897, au rapport annuel du Consul CHAMBERS, adressé au British Foreign Office.

Etant le principal port de la République, Guayaquil est redevenu le centre le plus important de son commerce. Les énormes stocks de marchandises détruits par les incendies désastreux de février et d'octobre, 1896, ont dû être remplacés pour faire face à la consommation toujours croissante de la côte et des provinces de l'intérieur, ce qui fait que le commerce d'importation est plus grand et plus actif que dans les années précédentes.

On n'a publié aucune statistique officielle sur ces importations depuis celle du Ministre de Hacienda, le Señor WITHER, présentée à la Convention de 1896–97, qui, d'après une estimation générale, place à 10,600,000 sucres ($4,939,600) la valeur des importations du 1er mai au 30 juin 1896. Je ne puis donc donner un rapport exact sur ce détail important, mais je sais que depuis cette période jusqu'à maintenant, les importations se sont faites sur une plus grande échelle:

Il n'y a eu aucun changement important à noter dans les grandes maisons d'importation, ni dans la nature ou l'origine des marchandises importées. Pendant 1897, le commerce d'exportation s'est fait avec l'activité habituelle; toutefois, on doit faire remarquer que les pluies excessives depuis le mois de janvier jusqu'au mois de mai, ont occasionné des dégâts très sérieux aux récoltes de cacao et de café. On a perdu vingt-cinq pour cent de la première et on n'a pu cueillir qu'environ cinquante pour cent de la dernière et encore d'une qualité inférieure. Toutes les plantations de riz dans les provinces de la côte ont été détruites par la même cause, ce qui a occasionné une importation considérable de riz. Ces circonstances combinées ont empêché matériellement les transactions générales d'affaires. A cette époque le gouvernement a autorisé une nouvelle frappe d'argent par l'une des banques de Guayaquil et à la fin de l'année, a promulgué une loi d'après laquelle on exigeait des banques que le fonds de réserve métallique fût en or, les obligeant ainsi à importer de l' argent étranger pour une valeur d'au moins £100,000. Il est facile de comprendre que cet état anormal du change a contribué beaucoup à rendre extrèmement difficile la condition commerciale de la République. Au mois de décembre les banques ont suspendu presque entièrement les opérations d'escompte.

On a beaucoup augmenté les revenus du pays au moyen de droits d'importation additionnels, selon la nouvelle loi de douane et aussi au moyen de taxes intérieures; malgré cette augmentation le commerce a été très actif. On a fait preuve d'une grande activité dans la reconstruction de la partie commerciale de la ville détruite par l'incendie. On a élevé de grandes et de belles maisons qui donnent une apparence imposante à la partie de la ville qui est située sur le bord de la rivière. Ces maisons sont toutes construites en bois, peu de personnes seulement adoptant l'ancien système de construire les maisons en canne et en plâtre, et elles sont pour la plupart recouvertes de fer anglais galvanisé. Comme le travail est rare, les artisans en ont profité pour demander des prix élevés dans toutes les branches, autant pour le travail de métier que pour l'autre, aussi, la grande demande a considérablement fait hausser les prix de matériaux de construction.

Beaucoup de commis voyageurs représentant des maisons anglaises ont visité le pays à différentes époques pendant l'année; et ils se sont montrés satisfaits en général de leur part dans le commerce d'importation. A peu d'exceptions près, les articles énumérés dans la liste du grand commerce du Royaume-Uni que fournissent les différentes Chambres de Commerce, par l'intermédiaire du Foreign Office et qui trouvent un marché facile ici, viennent directement ou indirectement des endroits désignés dans la liste. Les articles de luxe, principalement en habillement et articles de fantaisie pour dames et enfants, la parfumerie, les belles chaussures, etc., sont importés de France. Nous avons reçu des Etats-Unis de l'huile de pétrole, du saindoux et du bois de construction en grandes quantités (on importe le bois de construction arrangé pour la mise en œuvre immediate). Les poêles en fer, les haches et hachettes et les meubles ont été importés de ce marché en petites quantités seulement. On a importé de l'Autriche une meilleure classe de meubles et aussi de la bijouterie à bon marché et des étoffes de fantaisie. On a importé d'Allemagne, en même quantité que dans les années précédentes, des marchandises, telles que la bière, la bonneterie, les étoffes en laine et mélangées, les couvertures, les ponchos, les châles et la quincaillerie ordinaire. On ne constate aucune augmentation matérielle dans les marchandises, sauf dans les lainages mélangés et la dentelle, qui, par suite du prix modique, font une concurrence considérable aux articles semblables provenant d'Angleterre. Les fabricants anglais font concurrence au commerce de la coutellerie commune qu'on faisait venir autrefois d'Allemagne. Presque toutes les bougies consommées dans la République viennent de la Belgique. La production du sucre en 1897 s'est élevée à 6,000 tonnes environ. La consommation nationale s'élève à 4,000 tonnes environ, laissant 2,000 tonnes pour l'exportation, principalement au Chili et dans la Colombie. Le prix moyen de la première qualité du sucre blanc granulé a été environ de 2 sous ½ la livre. Au Chili, on préfère apparemment le sucre de l'Equateur aux meilleures qualités du Pérou.

Il y a une savonnerie nationale qui importe en franchise de droits les matériaux nécessaires à la fabrication du savon, ce qui empêche la hausse de prix des savons importés. L'exemption de droits d'importation cesse cette année, mais on fait des efforts pour la faire renouveler. On propose aussi de faire construire une nouvelle fabrique à Bahia de Caraquez, par un syndicat composé de commerçants des Etats-Unis et de Bahia.

On fabrique dans le pays, d'une manière primitive et en peu de quantités, une sorte de savon noir de bonne qualité pour le nettoyage. Il y a deux fabriques de vermicelle, etc., et celles-ci en ont monopolisé entièrement le commerce. Autrefois le vermicelle était un important article d'importation du Chili. Une de ces fabriques comprend aussi une boulangerie de biscuits de qualité supérieure (le principal employé étant un sujet anglais venant d'une maison très connue à Londres). Pendant l'année on a établi deux nouvelles scieries dont on en a importé une d'Angleterre. A l'intérieur, il y a des filatures de cotonnades et de lainages, principalement pour la consommation nationale, quoi qu'on fasse un commerce considérable en baïète de qualité ordinaire avec la République voisine de Colombie, par voie de Fumaco et de Barbacoas. Toutefois ces filatures ne font pas concurrence aux meilleures qualités de baïète ou bayeta qu'on importe d'Angleterre.

Aucun des édifices publics détruits par l'incendie de 1896, n'a été reconstruit. On a érigé des constructions temporaires sur l'emplacement occupé par les anciens édifices pour servir de douanes, mais elles sont tout à fait insuffisantes aux besoins des grandes importations et le gouvernement a été forcé de louer dans la ville des magasins particuliers pour l'emmagasinnage des marchandises, puisqu'on a trouvé que le maniement des importations a considérablement souffert par suite de ces circonstances. On a formé une compagnie à New York pour l'exploration du district de Zaruma et, d'après les rapports favorables qu'on reçoit aux Bureaux principaux, il y a tout lieu de croire qu'on formera une compagnie pour l'exploitation des mines existant dans ce district aurifère. La Compagnie Minière de Plaza de Oro ayant dépensé d'énormes sommes dans le développement de sa propriété et trouvant des difficultés à continuer ces l'exploitation à cause des grandes dépenses, on a formé un syndicat d'actionnaires anglais pour continuer ces exploitations avec plus d'économie. Beaucoup des travaux entrepris au commencement ont été arrêtés et on a diminué beaucoup des dépenses qui jusqu'ici ont embarrassé la compagnie.

HAÏTI.

RAPPORT SUR LES GISEMENTS DE CHARBON DE TERRE.

Le Bureau doit à l'amabilité de l'Honorable J. N. LÉGER, Ministre d'Haïti aux Etats-Unis, le rapport suivant sur les gisements de charbon de terre existant dans le sud d'Haïti. En nous transmettant le rapport le Ministre dit : " Comme vous pouvez le constater, l'ingénieur ne s'est livré qu'à des études préliminaires incomplètes. Pour se faire une véritable idée de l'importance des mines, il faudrait des recherches plus approfondies.

" Je suis autorisé à entrer en pourparlers avec ceux des capitalistes américains qui voudraient s'en occuper. J'examinerai donc avec le plus grand plaisir les offres qui pourraient me parvenir à ce sujet."

CAP HAÏTIEN (HAÏTI), 15 mai 1898.

Monsieur le SECRÉTAIRE D'ETAT :

En décembre 1896, j'ai entrepris un voyage d'exploration dans le sud, et dont le principal but était de me rendre compte de la valeur des gisements de charbon qu'on me signalait dans l'arrondissement de Nippes et dans celui des Cayes.

La vallée de l'Asile m'était tout particulièrement signalée comme possédant des gisements de minerais de fer à côté des gîtes carbonifères.

Je n'ai rien trouvé en fait de minerais de fer ; les argiles des grandes savanes que j'ai explorées, sont toutes, comme presque partout, plus ou moins ferrugineuses, assez même dans quelques endroits pour donner des couleurs caractéristiques à l'argile ; j'ai rencontré quelques roches ayant certainement une forte proportion de fer, mais rien qui puisse révéler un gisement exploitable. Nulle part les traces dont je viens de parler n'étaient assez sérieuses pour autoriser la dépense de travaux de recherches.

Quant aux gisements de charbon de l'Asile, je suis allé en exploration en premier lieu sur la rivière Serpente et sur l'habitation Bédeine, 3e section de la commune de l'Anse à Veau.

La rivière Serpente sépare à cet endroit la commune d'Aquin de celle de l'Anse à Veau.

J'ai rencontré plusieurs affleurements de couches carbonifères en travers de la rivière où elles sont parfaitement visibles. Ces couches ont une direction variant du nord-sud au NNO-SSE. ; leur inclinaison à l'est est d'environ 30 degrés. Leur puissance ou leur épaisseur est des plus variables ; elle va de 0^m10 jusqu'à 1^m20. Il y a, en amont de cet affleurement, deux autres semblables à une distance approximative de un kilomètre et demi, visibles également dans la rivière et sur ses bords.

Ces charbons rentrent dans la classe des lignites, mais ils sont encore en voie de formation et ne peuvent convenir à un usage industriel. Les essais ordinaires au feu n'ont pas donné de résultats appréciables. C'est du *lignite-ligneux*.

J'ai prélevé moi-même sur place, avec beaucoup de soins, des échantillons, et je les ai envoyés à Paris au laboratoire de mon école, où ils ont été analysés par le professeur C. Vincent.

Voici le résultat de l'analyse chimique :

Sur 100 parties :

Eau	26. 86
Cendres	15. 35
Résidu fixe au rouge	40. 58

Pas de coke.

Ces résultats permettent d'établir la composition suivante :

Eau	26. 86
Cendres	15. 35
Matières volatiles autres que l'eau	32. 56
Carbone fixe	25. 23
Total	100. 00

Le pouvoir calorifique du produit non desséché est de 3,177 calories ; le pouvoir calorifique du produit sec est de 4,645 calories.

Dans la direction ouest à environ 15 kilomètres du gisement dont je viens de parler, sur la limite de la 3ᵉ section de l'Anse à Veau et de la 3ᵉ section de la Commune du Trou, habitation Meignan-Desbrosses, au lieu dit Gouvillon, il existe un affleurement que j'ai visité, mais c'est un mélange de matières très-complexes où la matière carbonifère domine. Cet échantillon, aussi bien que le précédent, n'a pas révélé un produit bitumineux à l'analyse. Ce gisement a sensiblement la même direction et la même inclinaison que ceux de la rivière Serpente.

En résumé, les charbons de la vallée de l'Asile ne sont pas utilisables tels qu'ils se présentent. S'ils étaient placés près d'un centre industriel, on pourrait trouver leur utilisation en les brûlant dans des gazogènes pour faire de l'oxyde de carbone, qui se prête, pour ainsi dire, à toutes les industries.

Il me sera très difficile sur les données de cette première exploration de fixer la position géologique de ces couches de lignite. Elles paraissent s'étendre beaucoup ; mais le seul côté intéressant serait de savoir si, soit en suivant les couches, soit à côté de celles-ci, on ne trouverait pas un charbon plus parfait, utilisable dans l'industrie. Les travaux de recherches à faire pour donner la solution de la question seraient assez coûteux et demanderaient beaucoup de temps. Dans ce cas, ayant affaire à des lignites et la vallée de l'Asile étant très éloignée d'un port quelconque, les dépenses ne peuvent être conseillées.

Dans quatre des cinq rivières qui arrosent la superbe vallée de l'Asile, je n'ai trouvé aucune roche ancienne, éruptive ou de transition. Dans la rivière Daure seulement ayant remarqué quelques mouches de carbonate de cuivre sur des roches isolées éruptives et métamorphiques, j'ai exploré le cours de la rivière, en le remontant de Gouvillon jusqu'à 3 kilomètres en amont. Parmi les cailloux roulés, et même sur de gros échantillons, des traces de minerais de cuivre apparaissaient nettement ; mais les terrains des rives explorées n'appartenaient pas à l'époque des roches trouvées dans le cours de la rivière Daure.   Il faut, si l'on veut élucider cette question, remonter cette rivière beaucoup plus haut et étudier les montagnes dans lesquelles elle prend sa source.

J'ai signalé cette vallée de l'Asile comme étant privilégiée sous tous les rapports au point de vue de l'agriculture.   Je serais bien étonné si le tabac cultivé convenablement, n'y donnait des produits d'une qualité très supérieure.   De cette vallée je me suis dirigé sur Cavaillon par la fameuse ravine des Citronniers, où j'ai vainement cherché des traces de la mine de soufre, signalée dans l'ouvrage de Rouzier, et que sur place du reste personne ne connaît.   Cette vallée est absolument dépourvue de tout intérêt minéralogique.

De Cavaillon aux Cayes rien d'intéressant à signaler ; j'arrive tout de suite aux gisements de Camp-Perrin.

Ces charbons ont été l'objet de plusieurs recherches, à différentes époques, je n'ose dire études ; car les notes qui m'ont été communiquées à ce sujet révèlent aussi peu d'expérience que de compétence de la part de leurs auteurs.

Camp-Perrin est situé dans le nord des Cayes, à environ 25 kilomètres de cette ville.   Le principal cours d'eau est la Ravine, rivière à régime torrentiel qui reçoit trois principaux affluents sur sa rive droite à l'endroit où se trouve ce qu'on appelle "le Fort ou la Forteresse."   Toute cette partie de la contrée qui est adossée aux Platons, est particulièrement tourmentée ; les accidents géologiques ont donné lieu à des relèvements brusques des couches ; les ravins profonds dans lesquels sont encaissés tous les affluents de la Ravine permettent heureusement de se rendre compte des directions diverses qu'ont prises les couches du sol dans cet endroit.

En examinant le cours de la rivière Ravine dans les parties où avaient eu lieu quelques travaux en 1880, travaux situés sur la rive droite et dont les traces ont complètement disparu aujourd'hui, j'ai été assez heureux pour découvrir sur la rive gauche un ensemble de veines nettement caractérisées, et sur lesquelles j'ai de suite concentré mes études.

Cette différence entre la rive droite et la rive gauche a une immense importance dans le cas d'une exploitation.   En effet, les Cayes et le Fort sont situés sur la rive gauche de la Ravine, et comme moyen de transport il n'y aura qu'à mettre un chemin de fer dans une plaine superbe sans traverser aucun cours d'eau ; nous reviendrons sur cette question.

C'est sur l'habitation Balanier, 5e section, sur la rive gauche de la "ravine" que j'ai trouvé cinq veines parallèles, ayant une direction est-ouest, d'une inclinaison nord de 80 degrés environ, et d'une puissance variant de 0^m 65 à 1^m 50.   L'ensemble des cinq veines mesure, intervalles compris, environ 10 mètres sur l'affleurement visible.

La veine la plus en aval m'ayant paru la plus nette, je l'ai fait immédiatement ouvrir, et j'ai retiré du charbon compact et d'une bonne densité.   J'ai creusé la plus profond que possible, et j'ai sorti les premiers échantillons pour les envoyer comme les autres à Paris, et pour faire quelques essais industriels aux ateliers des Tramways, à Port-au-Prince.

Continuant mes recherches sur place, je me suis transporté sur la rivière Bras

Gauche, dans l'habitation Chevalier, 6e section, à environ 4 kilomètres (
distance à vol d'oiseau où un affleurement m'était signalé. J'ai retrouvé
dans un escarpement très raide sur la rivière les cinq veines avec la direction
l'inclinaison sensiblement égales à celles de l'affleurement de l'habitation Balanie
Des échantillons de charbon très dur ont été pris à la superficie de ces vein
où il était impossible d'opérer des fouilles sans un travail préparatoire.

En aval de ce point, se rapprochant par conséquent de la direction premièr
sur la même rivière Bras-Gauche, qui a un cours très encaissé et des pl
sinueux, sur l'habitation Délinois, chez M. Dorsséus Dudor, j'ai retrouvé l
cinq veines avec la même allure, inclinaison et direction. De sorte que, s
trois points, sur une distance en ligne droite de 4 kilomètres, j'ai relevé tro
affleurements indiquant nettement la continuation du système des cinq veines (
charbon sur cette étendue. En outre sur la rivière Bras-Droit, au bas de l'habit
tion Thomas, il y a un autre affleurement parfaitement visible, mais il faudrait
faire quelques travaux pour en déterminer les principales données. Ce poin
qui appartient aussi à la 6e section, a ceci d'important qu'il ne me parait p
appartenir au premier système des cinq veines dont j'ai parlé; il indique do
un bassin carbonifère assez vaste.

Du reste, l'emplacement des travaux faits en 1880 sur la rive droite de
Ravine m'a été exactement montré, il est évident que le charbon tiré de c
endroit appartient à un autre système de veines que celles de l'habitatic
Balanier.

Il est donc certain que le bassin carbonifère a une grande importance, da
les sections 5e et 6e de Camp-Perrin.

Les essais au feu que j'ai faits de ces premiers échantillons m'ont donné d
résultats très encourageants; et l'analyse chimique, faite à Paris par le mên
professeur, a donné les résultats suivants:

Eau .... 27.
Cendres .... 17.
Matières volatiles autres que l'eau .... 27.(
Carbone fixe .... 27.(

    Total .... 100.(

Le pouvoir calorique de ce produit est de 3,466 calories non desséché et (
5,050 calories à l'état sec.

Muni de ces premiers renseignements, j'ai alors fait ouvrir plus en grand
en direction est la veine de l'habitation Balanier, déjà citée. Au fur et à mesu
de l'approfondissement le charbon apparaissait plus compact, et les petits feuille
d'argile qui séparaient les couches de charbon semblaient disparaître pour fai
place à du charbon. Cette veine seule a, au fond de l'excavation faite, u
puissance de 1^m 50 de charbon pur.

J'ai fait extraire environ deux tonnes de ce produit, et aux ateliers des Tran
ways à Port-au-Prince, en mars 1897, j'ai fait chauffer la chaudière des atelie
tout un jour exclusivement avec ce charbon qui a fourni industriellement de
vapeur sans difficulté: Tous les Secrétaires d'Etat ont bien voulu m'honorer (
leur visite ce jour là.

L'analyse de ce produit pris plus profond que le premier, faite à Paris toujours dans les mêmes conditions, a donné les résultats suivants :

Eau	24. 10
Cendres	12. 17
Matières volatiles autres que l'eau	31. 90
Charbon fixe	31. 83
Total	100. 00

Le pouvoir calorifique avec 24.10 pour cent d'eau est de 4,200 calories; desséché le produit donne 5,660 calories.

Nous avons affaire à des lignites, mais à des lignites qui peuvent produire de la vapeur sans difficulté.

Maintenant si l'on note que les résultats de la dernière analyse, si différents de la première, ont été obtenus avec une différence de profondeur de deux mètres à peine, il est certain qu'à quinze ou vingt mètres de profondeur on aura le produit normal de la mine et de qualité bien supérieure.

C'est dans la direction est en partant de l'habitation Balanier qu'il faut établir les premiers travaux. Il faudra également faire des recherches sur les points signalés dans la 6e section : ces premiers travaux ne seront pas très coûteux, mais sont indispensables pour établir la valeur industrielle du gîte qui, dans mon opinion, est considérable.

La société industrielle qui se formera pour l'exploitation aura à envisager la construction d'un chemin de fer de vingt-cinq kilomètres en plaine et sans travaux d'art. La plaine des Cayes bien cultivée peut donner un fret important ; la société pourra développer cette culture en prenant à son compte le rétablissement du canal Davezac pour l'irrigation méthodique de cette plaine. Elle pourra établir des usines à café à Camp-Perrin, et aussi des briqueteries pour fournir des matériaux de construction à la ville des Cayes qui en est totalement dépourvue. Le combustible pour les usines, les briqueteries et le chemin de fer, sortira de la mine même ; et tout cet ensemble bien organisé peut devenir une source de richesse pour le département des Cayes.

Veuillez agréer, Monsieur le SECRÉTAIRE D'ETAT, l'assurance de mes sentiments respectueux et distingués.

HENRI THOMASSET.

NICARAGUA.

NOUVEAU MINISTÈRE.

Voici comment est constitué le Ministère du Nicaragua pour le second terme de l'administration du Président Iglesias:

Ministre des Affaires Etrangères, de l'Instruction Publique, etc......Señor Don PEDRO PÉREZ ZELEDÓN.
Ministre de' l'Intérieur et des Travaux Publics ..Señor Don JOSÉ ASTÚA AGUILAR.
Ministre des Finances et du Commerce ....Señor Don JUAN B. QUIRÓS.
Ministre de la Guerre et de la Marine ... .Señor Don DEMETRIO TINOCO.

MEXIQUE.

INDUSTRIE MINIÈRE.

Parmi les industries importantes du Mexique est celle des mines. Les exportations de métaux précieux et de minerais accusent une augmentation d'environ douze millions de dollars (argent mexicain), soit une augmentation de 40 pour cent environ pendant le premier semestre de la présente année fiscale en comparaison de la période correspondante de l'année 1895.

Le minerai de cuivre du Mexique est spécialement riche, et la production augmente rapidement. On a découvert récemment dans plusieurs parties du pays de nouvelles mines très importantes, et le journal, le "Modern Mexico," dit que le professeur WILLIAM NIVEN, minéralogiste renommé et explorateur archéologue, fait connaître que les champs de Guerrero sont riches en cuivre aussi bien qu'en or. Bien que Guerrero soit indubitablement riche en ressources minérales, les mineurs doivent posséder un capital afin de réussir. Le climat est doux, mais les frais d'installation sont très coûteux et les provisions sont rares. Les exportations de cuivre ont doublé l'année dernière, et ont atteint en décembre une valeur d'environ un million de dollars, soit une augmentation d'environ 100 pour cent. On constate une augmentation satisfaisante dans les expéditions de plomb d'antimoine et de zinc.

L'INDUSTRIE DES COTONS MANUFACTURÉS.

Un rapport spécial du consul anglais dans la ville de Mexico, fait connaître que l'industrie des cotons manufacturés au Mexique s'est développée considérablement ces dernières années. Ce n'est plus qu'une question de peu de temps pour voir les filatures nationales fournir tous les tissus de coton, de qualité grossière, requis par cette contrée. Cette entreprise américaine a fait des progrès constants, et on attribue l'augmentation de ces trois dernières années à une série de bonnes récoltes. En 1897, les nouvelles filatures installées représentaient une production minimum de 300,000 pièces, et celles qui sont en construction actuellement ou qui seront sans doute construites cette année, augmenteront de 750,000 pièces la production annuelle. Comme la moyenne annuelle de l'importation de tissus de coton étrangers n'est actuellement que de 40,000,000 mètres carrés environ, et que le Mexique compte ajouter 21,000,000 de mètres carrés à sa production, on verra que les fabricants étrangers rencontreront une concurrence considérable.

NOUVELLES INDUSTRIES.

Le journal, "El Progreso de México," fait connaître dans son numéro du 30 avril 1898 que MM. ERNESTO CHAVERO & GREGORIO GONZÁLEZ ont demandé au Ministre du Commerce et de l'Industrie, l'autorisation d'établir plusieurs industries dans le pays, parmi lesquelles une fabrique de lait condensé, au capital minimum de $150,000, industrie tout-à-fait nouvelle dans le Mexique.

Le même journal dit que les grandes fabriques de pétrole et de savon, situées à Lerdo, Durango, Torreon, et à San Pedro de la Higuerra, qui fonctionnaient autrefois indépendemment, ont organisé une association pour faire le commerce sur des bases consolidées. Ces divers établissements sont éclairés à l'électricité, montés de machines puissantes et coûteuses, et on poursuit le travail nuit et jour. Les produits principaux sont la farine de graine de coton et le tourteau; on se sert de ce dernier pour engraisser les bêtes à cornes et le porc. On obtient principalement la graine de coton des riches plantations de coton dont les propriétaires possèdent de grands intérêts dans la compagnie consolidée.

Les fabriques de la compagnie peuvent produire journellement 25,000 kilogrammes de farine de graine de coton et exporter annuellement 20,000 tonnes de tourteau, évaluées à $500,000.

FABRIQUE DE CORDAGES ET DE SACS.

Le 8 octobre 1896, le Ministre du Commerce et de l'Industrie a passé un contrat avec M. ALFRED HEYDRICH, pour l'établissement d'une grande fabrique à Yucatan, afin d'utiliser le hennequen et autres produits semblables dans la manufacture de cordages, de hamacs et de sacs. Le Congrès a approuvé ce contrat le 14 mai 1897, et le 23 juin 1897, M. HEYDRICH a enregistré l'entreprise sous le nom de "Sociedad Anónima La Industria," au capital de $400,000, ayant pour président le Señor ALEGARIO MOHUA.

Le contrat stipule que la fabrique doit être achevée dans deux ans á partir de la promulgation de l'approbation du contrat par le

Congrès, et on constate qu'on a déployé une grande activité dans les travaux de construction et d'installation de la fabrique. On a déjà élevé, sur une grande échelle, des bâtiments designés spécialement pour le travail qui doit avoir lieu. De plus, on a construit 14 maisons, de 30 pieds sur 16, en pierre solide pour les ouvriers. Les bâtiments de la compagnie sont reliés par voie ferrée au Chemin de fer de Merida et Progreso, et sont pourvus d'un nombre de voies pour faciliter le maniement des wagons.

Le contrat original fait avec le Gouvernement stipulait que le montant de l'argent placé ne doit pas être moins de $250,000. Comme preuve du développement de l'industrie, on peut dire que le capital en actions s'est augmenté à $600,000, et que la compagnie s'est engagée à commencer les travaux de construction de la fabrique un an avant le temps stipulé dans le contrat.

Quand la fabrique sera entièrement terminée, la production journalière sera de 50,000 kilogrammes de fil fin, ficelle, cordages, sacs, hamacs, etc., soit une production totale de 14,400,000 kilogrammes par an. On montre beaucoup d'intérêt dans cette entreprise, parce qu'elle est la première qui soit établie sur une grande échelle pour la manufacture nationale du hennequen, production principale de Yucatan.

CONCESSION DE CHEMIN DE FER À MM. PEARSON, FILS & CIE.

Le Diario oficial de date récente fait savoir que le Président DIAZ a donné son approbation le 4 juin à la concession, en vertu de laquelle on accordait à la grande compagnie anglaise de PEARSON & FILS, et à PEDRO M. ARMENDARIA, l'autorisation de tracer, de construire et d'exploiter une ligne de chemin de fer dans l'Etat de Vera Cruz. Le point de départ de la ligne sera soit à Acayucan, soit à Paso de San Juan sur la ligne du chemin de fer de Jutla. Cette ligne s'étendra à Tuxtla et à San Nicolas, avec faculté de la prolonger jusqu'à Alvarado. On doit faire le tracé de la ligne dans un an à partir de la date de l'approbation du contrat, et les travaux de construction devront commencer dans un délai de dix-huit mois, la ligne entière devant être terminée dans un délai de dix ans. En outre des exemptions habituelles de droits d'importation et de taxes, les concessionnaires recevront de vastes étendues de terrains publics dans les Etats de Vera Cruz, d'Oaxaca, de Tabasco et de Chiapas.   La compagnie concessionnaire doit avoir son domicile légale dans la Ville de Mexico; et le gouvernement se réserve le droit de choisir et de nommer un certain nombre de directeurs.

Les concessionnaires sont obligés de verser dans la Banque Nationale, un cautionnement de $3,000 en bons du gouvernement dans un délai de quinze jours.   Le territoire que doit traverser la ligne est un des plus fertiles et un de ceux qui promettent le plus pour la production du caoutchouc, du tabac et du sucre; la haute réputation financière de MM. Pearsons & Fills garantit la pleine et entière exécution des conditions du contrat.

NICARAGUA.

CONCESSION ACCORDÉE À M. EMERY POUR L'EXPLOITATION DES BOIS PRÉCIEUX.

M. William B. Sorsby, Consul des Etats-Unis à San Juan del Norte, a transmis au Ministère des Affaires Etrangères une copie du contrat passé par le gouvernement du Nicaragua avec M. H. C. Emery, de Chelsea, Mass., pour l'exploitation et l'exportation des bois précieux du pays.

En substance, le contrat accorde à M. Emory un monopole de 15 ans pour les bois de rose, de cédre et d'acajou, s'étendant sur une grande superficie de la République, où l'on sait que ces bois existent en grande quantité.   En fait, c'est le renouvellement de l'ancien contrat qu'il avait passé et sous lequel il expédiait environ 12,500 troncs d'arbres par an.   Le Consul Sorsby considère cette concession comme étant d'une valeur incalculable et la plus importante que le gouvernement de Nicaragua ait accordée depuis longtemps aux étrangers.

L'article 3 du contrat oblige M. Emery à construire 50 milles de chemins de fer pour son emploi personnel entre Rio Grande et la lagune Pearl.   La voie doit être de 3 pieds 6 pouces ou de 4 pieds, 8 pouces ½, et la ligne desservira les terrains publics de la Province de Matagalpa.   Le mobilier de la ligne, les ponts, les quais, les chantiers, etc., devront recevoir l'approbation du Minis-

situés sur la frontière du nord. Le service postal a augmenté en proportion de l'augmentation de la population et des exigences du service.

Au sujet des travaux publics, le Président dit qu'un comité spécial s'occupe de la direction de cette branche du Gouvernement, conformément aux sommes votées à cette fin.

La valeur totale des importations pour les douze mois antérieurs s'est élevée à $2,203,359, tandis que les exportations ont atteint $1,955,803, ces chiffres représentent l'évaluation en or.

La Banque Agricole, l'institution la plus importante de cette classe dans le pays, a beaucoup fait pour encourager le travail pour lequel elle a été établie, spécialement le développement de la culture du coton, du café, de la vigne et des autres produits existant dans la République. Il existe maintenant dans le pays plus de 1,000,000 de caféiers et on est certain que dans un an ou plus, il y aura le double ou le triple de ce nombre. La Banque citée a encouragé, sous la direction de personnes compétentes, des expériences pour la préparation du tabac, d'après les systèmes suivis dans les Iles de Cuba et de Sumatra. De cette manière le tabac de Paraguay, qui a été supplanté dans les marchés étrangers, reprendra son importance accoutumée.

Au sujet de la Banque Nationale, le président dit que la liquidation continue, quoique les débiteurs aient manqué à faire face à leurs obligations. " Il serait sage d'adopter quelque système afin d'assurer la liquidation finale de l'institution sans occasionner des dépenses inutiles." La taxe sur la propriété deviendra une des sources de revenu du pays.

Le gouvernement étudie des plans pour un chemin de fer allant des districts du *yerba mate* à la rivière. Si cette idée est mise à exécution, le commerce en *yerba mate*, qui se fait avec tant de difficulté maintenant et qui se fait encore plus, difficilement pendant la saison des sécheresses lorsque les affluents de la rivière Paraguay ne sont plus navigables, en retirera de grands bénéfices.

Le message fait allusion à l'harmonie parfaite et à la cordialité qui existent entre le Paraguay et les pays voisins. La seule question en litige est celle qui a trait à la démarcation de la frontière séparant ce dernier pays de la Bolivie, qui met en question les droits de possession du territoire du Chaco (une vaste région inhabitée). Cette question est pour le moment en suspens. Le

Président Eguzquiza espère que les négociations entamées dans la République Argentine pour la conclusion d'un traité de commerce se termineront d'une manière prompte et satisfaisante pour les deux nations. Le Président entretient la ferme croyance que le moyen d'établir des liens permanents entre les nations est de développer leurs intérêts moraux et matériels, basés sur des concessions libérales qui permettent l'expansion de leurs industries et de leur activité commerciale. Le Président recommande ardemment la conclusion d'un traité de commerce avec le Brésil.

PÉROU-CHILI.

CULTURE ET MANUFACTURE DU COTON.

On a parlé dans le BULLETIN MENSUEL de juin de l'impulsion donnée récemment à la culture et à la manufacture du coton au Pérou et au Chili, et de l'encouragement qu'accordent à cette industrie, les gouvernements de ces pays. L'Exposition Permanente de machines, inaugurée dernièrement à Lima, attire l'attention des fabricants aux Etats-Unis et en Europe sur l'occasion qui leur est offerte d'introduire leurs machines dans ce pays. Le décret de date récente, permettant l'entrée en franchise de droit des machines destinées à la fabrication de tissus donne non seulement une nouvelle vie à cette industrie, mais ouvre aussi un marché avantageux aux machines américaines. On peut lire avec intérêt l'article suivant se rapportant à ce sujet, extrait du "Textile Manufacturer's Journal" du 4 juin, publié dans la ville de New York.

Nous avons parlé de temps en temps du développement de l'industrie de la manufacture de coton dans les différentes contrées pour montrer tout simplement la concurrence que doit encourir le commerçant américain. On dit que le Pérou et le Chili font des préparatifs plus importants que jamais et la récolte n'est pas destinée pour l'étranger comme autrefois, mais elle sera consommée par les filatures nationales. Le Pérou, naturellement s'est engagé grandement depuis quelque temps, dans la culture du coton, mais à présent, l'industrie semble se répandre avec rapidité au Chili. Autrefois on expédiait presque entièrement la matière brute en Angleterre mais on se propose maintenant d'établir une grande industrie manufacturière dans ce pays. Le gouvernement offre beaucoup d'avantages aux cultivateurs et par conséquent, on consacre une superficie considérablement augmentée à la culture du coton. Comme preuve de la sincérité de ceux qui sont éminents dans l'administration des affaires, on peut citer la suppression du droit sur toutes les machines à tisser, importées dans le pays jusqu'en 1902. On dit que ce changement de tarif a exercé plus ou moins d'influence sur les expéditions de machines à tisser provenant des Etats-Unis; on y a rempli dernièrement plusieurs grandes commandes.

La manufacture de cotonnades au Pérou est plus avancée qu'au Chili, bien que les filatures n'en produisent encore que de qualité très grossière. On croit qu'avec l'importation de machines nouvelles et améliorées, une impulsion sensible sera donnée à la manufacture et que ceux qui ont reçu de gros bénéfices de leur commerce avec ce pays ne pourront pas se reposer sur leurs lauriers.

NOUVEAU MINISTÈRE.

Voici comment le cabinet du Pérou vient d'être réorganisé :

Président du Conseil des Ministres, et
Ministre de la Justices, des Cultes et
de l'Instruction Publique.......... le Docteur Don José Loayza.
Ministre des Affaires Etrangères.. ... Don José María de la Puente.
Ministre de la Guerre et de la Marine.. Don Manuel J. Cuadros.
Ministre des Finances et du Commerce. Don Ignacio Rey.
Ministre des Travaux Publics........ le Docteur Don Francisco Almenara Butler.

SAINT DOMINGUE.

CONDITIONS COMMERCIALES.

M. Grimke, Consul des Etats-Unis a envoyé au Ministère des Affaires Etrangères son rapport annuel sur les conditions commerciales et industrielles existant dans la République dominicaine, rapport qui est publié en entier dans Rapports Consulaires du mois de juin. D'après le rapport de M. Grimke, la baisse du prix du sucre, produit principal de la République, ainsi que d'autres causes, ont contribué à un ralentissement général du commerce dans le pays. On exporte à New York presque tout le sucre produit qui n'est pas consommé dans le marché local; la valeur totale de cet article d'exportation pendant l'année de 1897 s'est élevée à $2,463,906.62. Parmi les autres articles d'exportation, le bois de campêche, le gaïac, l'acajou, le miel, la cire et les bananes ont été expédiés aux Etats-Unis, tandis que le café, le cacao et le tabac ont trouvé presque entièrement un marché en France, en Allemagne, en Belgique et en Angleterre.

Dans le district consulaire que représente M. Grimke, la totalité des importations de bois de construction provenant entièrement des Etats-Unis s'est élevée à 2,500,000 pieds et s'est vendue en détail à \$37.50 en or par mille pieds.   La farine qui se vend en détail \$12 en or, le baril, provient entièrement des Etats-Unis. Récemment encore, toute l'huile de pétrole raffinée provenait des Etats-Unis, mais la raffinerie récemment établie diminuera sans doute l'importation de cet article.   A cause de la qualité inférieure du beurre exporté des Etats-Unis, ce produit provient maintenant presque exclusivement du Danemark.   La meilleure qualité se vend en détail à Saint Domingue 62 sous ½ la livre, tandis que les qualités inférieures se vendent 37 sous ½.   On importe le fromage de la Hollande et des Etats-Unis; le fromage hollandais se vend 25 sous en or, et l'américain 22 sous ½ la livre.

Les articles divers, tels que les viandes de conserve, les légumes et le lait viennent pour la plupart des Etats-Unis; le poisson salé et le porc en viennent entièrement, le saindoux, les huiles de cuisine et la bière proviennent en partie des Etats-Unis.   Les vins sont importés de France et d'Espagne.   On vient d'établir une brasserie à Saint Domingue, apartenant à des Américans.   La bière américaine se vend \$4.50 par caisse, tandis que l'article de production nationale se vend \$2.25.

Les machines pour les plantations, les locomotives, les wagons, les rails, les ponts en fer etc., viennent principalement des Etats-Unis mais l'Allemagne commence à devenir un concurrent assez redoutable dans ces branches de commerce.   Dans le commerce de la quincaillerie l'Angleterre, l'Allemagne et la Belgique font une concurrence aux Etats-Unis.   Le charbon se vend en détail à Saint Domingue \$12 et \$13 en or la tonne, dont la plus grande partie vient de l'Angleterre.   L'Angleterre fournit aussi la plus grande partie des cotonnades, le produit américain, quoique de meilleure qualité est plus cher que l'article anglais, ce qui explique la prédominance des fabriques anglaises dans ce marché.   Les cotonnades se vendent en détail de 7 sous ½ à 25 sous en or la verge.   Les soieries viennent exclusivement de France et se vendent en détail de 75 sous à \$3 or la verge.   La France et l'Angleterre envoient toutes sortes de chapeaux pour les deux sexes.   Les Etats-Unis fournissent toutes les machines électriques dont on se sert dans l'île.   Beaucoup de plantations sucrières sont maintenant éclairées à l'électricité.   La France partage avec les Etats-Unis, le commerce de bicyclettes.

Le Consul GRIMKE fait connaitre que les commerçants et les

planteurs critiquent sévèrement les méthodes d'emballage des marchandises, employées aux Etats-Unis. Les laboureurs agricoles reçoivent de 50 à 75 sous par jour; dans les villes on paie les ouvriers de 50 sous à $2: les domestiques, pension comprise, reçoivent de $3 à $12 par mois; et les employés de bureau de $15 à $75 par mois.

Les intérêts américains dominent dans la République; environ la moitié des plantations sucrières appartient à des sujets des Etats-Unis. La "San Domingo Improvement Company" avec bureaux principaux à New York, perçoit les revenus du pays sous un contrat passé avec le gouvernement, il y a quelques années. Une ligne de vapeurs appartenant à et exploitée par W. P. CLYDE & Co. de New York fait le service deux fois par mois entre les ports du pays et New York.

URUGUAY.

NOUVEAU MINISTÈRE.

Voici comment a été formé le Ministère de l'Uruguay sous l'administration du Président JUAN LINDCLFO CUESTAS:

Président du Conseil des Ministres.........Señor Don JOSÉ ROMÁN MENDONZA.
Ministre des Affaires Etrangères.............Señor Dr. Don JOAQUIN DE SALTERAIN.
Ministre de Fomento . ...Señor Dr. Don JACOBO H. VADELA.
Ministre de la Guerre et de la Marine .... Le Général CASTRO.

VENEZUELA.

COMMERCE DE CARACAS ET DU DISTRICT EN 1897.

On a pris les renseignements suivants au sujet du commerce de Caracas et de ce district consulaire dans le rapport annuel adressé au Ministère des Affaires Etrangères de la Grande-Bretagne par M. W. A. ANDRAL, Consul intérimaire de cette contrée à Caracas.

On ne peut pas considérer comme satisfaisant l'état général du commerce au Venezuela pendant l'année 1897. La principale cause de cette situation peut être attribuée au résultat désastreux de la récolte du café, qui naturellement a diminué les importations du pays, et réduit son crédit à l'étranger. On croit que cette condition sera améliorée à la prochaine saison à cause du Don aspect que présente la récolte du café en voie de croissance. Les plantations de café dans le pays sont au nombre de 33,000, et celles de cacao, au nombre de 5,000 environ ; ces deux productions représentent la principale denrée agricole de la République. Le haut tarif douanier (pour ainsi dire prohibitif) sur le sucre a encouragé le plantage de la canne à sucre, de sorte qu'aujourd'hui, il y a 11,000 plantations de canne à sucre, et on compte que cette culture occupera une place importante dans l'agriculture générale de ce pays.

On a formé récemment de nombreuses associations ayant pour objet de faire comprendre aux planteurs l'importance de l'application de méthodes scientifiques pour la fertilisation, l'irrigation, etc., et pour l'emploi de machines améliorées dans les différents procédés de la préparation des produits pour le marché. Le grand désideratum pour le progrès du pays, selon le Consul ANDRAL, est une immigration qui s'établira dans l'intérieur et aidera au développement des ressources agricoles. Récemment (comme il a été publié en détail dans le BULLETIN MENSUEL du mois de mai), le gouvernement a passé un contrat avec un sujet italien pour l'introduction dans le pays d'un grand nombre de familles italiennes qui s'établiront sur les terres publiques.

On fait le rapport suivant au sujet du développement du commerce avec le Venezuela et de la part que prend l'agence de l'Association Nationale des Manufacturiers des Etats-Unis dans ce développement.

L'influence des Américains dans le marché vénézuélien commence à se faire sentir considérablement. Ils ne sont pas si routiniers et ils sont plus prompts dans leurs transactions commerciales, mais la cause principale de leur succès semble être due à leur proximité de ce marché. Ceci convient au commerçant vénézuélien qui ne garde pas dans son magasin un stock considérable, mais le renouvelle seulement à mesure qu'il le trouve nécessaire. En outre, il existe des sympathies politiques entre les Etats-Unis et le Venezuela, dont les premiers n'hésitent pas à en profiter.

Le pas le plus important pris dans la direction du développement des relations commerciales entre les Etats-Unis et le Venezuela est celui de l'Association Nationale des Manufacturiers qui à son siege à Philadelphie. Au commencement de l'année 1896, on a envoyé un agent au Venezuela en vue d'établir un entrepôt d'échantillons où l'on pourrait introduire dans le marché les fabriques américaines sous les conditions les plus favorables. On a passé le contrat avec le Ministère correspondant du gouvernement vénézuélien ; et tous les préliminaires ayant été arrangés, le commissaire retourna au mois de novembre au Venezuela et fit savoir au gouvernement que l'inauguration de l'exposition d'échantillons aurait lieu prochainement. Le rapport du commissaire à la Société "de l'Avancement Public" dit qu'on a établi l'entrepôt en vue de donner aux commerçants, aux agriculteurs, etc., l'occasion d'examiner sur place le véritable article fabriqué au lieu de se fier aux catalogues et aux illustrations; de fournir des renseignements relatifs aux adresses des fabricants américains et à leur prix et conditions; de fournir une salle de lecture où on peut examiner tous les journaux et publications ayant trait aux industries et au commerce, et de montrer, lorsque c'est possible, le mécanisme des machines agricoles, etc. Cette entrepôt sera en effet, une leçon pratique de ce que peut faire l'industrie américaine. L'Exposition servira aussi comme point de rencontre pour les commerçants, et il y aura un bureau de renseignements qui maintiendra les fabricants et leurs agents au courant des exigences du marché et des habitudes commerciales du pays, et fera connaître aux capitalistes américains les occasions pour le placement de leurs capitaux au Venezuela.

Le gouvernement permet l'importation en franchise de droit de toutes les marchandises destinées à l'exposition dans l'entrepôt d'échantillons. On prédit de grands bénéfices au Venezuela et une augmentation extraordinaire du traffic entre les deux pays, comme résultat de ce mouvement entrepris par l'Association Nationale des Manufacturiers. Pendant que j'écris, l'Exposition vient de s'ouvrir avec le concours d'une vingtaine de commerçants les plus influents dans les Etats de Pennsylvanie et de New York. Le Président de la République du Venezuela assistait à l'inauguration. On a fait des discours dans lesquels on a parlé de l'amitié qui unit les deux nations ainsi que des facilités offertes par leurs relations commerciales actuelles et l'opinion publique est tout à fait favorable à l'Amérique et aux Américains.

Si, comme je le dis plus haut, nous reconnaissons déjà à certains signes que le commerce des Etats-Unis prend les devants, il est tout naturel de supposer qu'un mouvement semblable accentuera cette tendance et qu'avant peu les produits américains remplaceront tous les autres semblables, ne laissant au commerce étranger que les articles qu'on ne peut fabriquer facilement aux Etats-Unis. Le volume du commerce avec les Etats-Unis consiste en comestibles, en instruments agricoles et en machines. Une compagnie américaine a passé plusieurs contrats pour la fourniture de conduits d'eaux.

Faisant allusion à l'Association et au travail qu'elle a en projet, la Presse du Venezuela demande si les Américains adopteront le système européen de crédit à long terme, ou s'ils parviendront à convertir les commerçants vénézuéliens à leur méthode de transactions commerciales; et elle dit que c'est de cette condition que dépend le résultat de la lutte, parce que le système à long crédit attirera toujours une certaine partie du commerce. Comme il est difficile aux Américains de race espagnole de changer leurs habitudes, il s'écoulera quelque temps avant qu'on aperçoive des résultats.

SYSTÈME MÉTRIQUE.

CONGRÈS QUI DOIT AVOIR LIEU À PARIS EN 1900.

Les principaux manufacturiers de tissus du monde font des efforts pour la convocation à Paris en 1900, d'un Congrès tenu pendant l'Exposition qui aura lieu cette année-la, en vue de prendre des décisions au sujet de l'adoption du système métrique. Le manque d'un système uniforme pour numéroter le fil dont on se sert dans l'industrie textile a occasionné beaucoup d'ennuis et de complications, et c'est principalement pour surmonter cette difficulté qu'on a convoqué le congrès projeté. Cette question a été le sujet d'investigation aux congrès tenus à Vienne en 1873, à Bruxelles en 1874, à Turin en 1875, et à Paris en 1878 et 1889.

Dans une communication se rapportant à ce sujet, adressée au Ministre des Affaires Etrangères, M. HENRY W. GILBERT, Consul des Etats-Unis à Liege s'exprime ainsi: On a fait du progrès à tous les congrès précédents, mais jusqu'ici on n'a obtenu aucun résultat pratique. Il y a deux raisons pour ce manque de succès— dans cette affaire l'uniformité n'est pas devenue générale même en France et tous les pays n'ont pas adopté le système métrique. L'Angleterre place dans les marchés étrangers des marchandises qui ne sont pas numérotées ou fabriquées d'après le système métrique, il est permis aussi de le faire aux Etats-Unis. Notre pays fait une concurrence active et heureuse aux autres nations pour le commerce étranger en marchandises et comme notre pouvoir de production est presque illimité, il semble que nos manufacturiers devraient être bien représentés ou Congrès précité qui aura lieu à Paris en 1900.

Si les exportateurs des Etats-Unis employaient le système métrique ils seraient à même d'offrir leurs marchandises aux acheteurs et aux consommateurs étrangers suivant le poids et les capacités auxquels ils sont habitués.

CAFÉ.

Le Bureau de Commerce Extérieur du Ministère des Affaires Etrangères vient de publier dans les "advance sheets" des Rapports Consulaires du mois de juin un rapport étendu sur la production et la consommation du café dans le monde. Nous empruntons les faits généraux suivants à ce rapport, qui a été préparé par M. FRANK D. HILL, Consul des Etats-Unis à Santos, Brésil.

Le Brésil est le plus grand pays producteur de café, il fournit environ 66 pour cent de la production totale. Les vingt Etats qui composent la République produisent tous, plus ou moins de café; toutefois la zone productrice du café par excellence se compose des Etats de Rio de Janeiro, de São Paulo, d'Espirito Santo, et de Minas Geraes; cependant c'est l'Etat de São Paulo qui occupe le premier rang dans cette culture. Les principaux ports d'exportation sont ceux de Rio et de Santos, bien qu'on exporte des quantités considérables par le port de Victoria.

Le café est classé de la manière suivante: fin, supérieur, bon, régulier, ordinaire et triage. Ce dernier représente le café de la qualité la plus inférieure et il se compose de graines cassées et défectueuses en général. Le café de qualité fine consiste en café nettoyé, de graines de largeur régulière; la qualité supérieure est formée de graines de largeur régulière, mais il peut contenir quelques cosses ou graines noires; dans la qualité bonne, on n'insiste pas absolument sur l'uniformité des graines, il peut y avoir quelques graines noires, mais les petits morceaux de bois, les pierres et la poussière en sont exclus; la qualité ordinaire renferme toutes les imperfections précitées et quelques graines cassées.

D'après le Consul HILL, les Brésiliens croient que c'est une fausse idée de croire, comme cela a lieu dans les pays étrangers, qu'il y a de meilleur café que le leur; il sait que le café de Java et de Mocha qui se vend aux Etats-Unis est en grande partie cultivé près de Rio ou de Santos.

La production du café dans l'Etat de São Paulo, ainsi que la durée des caféiers, dépend du caractère du sol et de la plante.   On dit qu'il y a des caféiers plantés il y a 75 ans qui produisent encore aujourd'hui.

Dans l'Etat de São Paulo, mille arbres donnent un rendement de 3,238 livres ou 25 sacs, tandis que dans la Province de Rio de Janeiro le rendement en est bien moins grand.   Par suite de l'énorme production de café dans les différentes parties du monde, le prix est tombé très bas depuis quelque temps.   Le prix moyen sur les marchés brésiliens est de 5 sous .7 or la livre, ou environ $7.56 le sac.   Le tableau suivant représente la production du café dans l'Etat de São Paulo, calculée tous les dix ans depuis 1850 à 1896:

Années.	Production.	
	Sacs.	*Livres.*
1850–1860	1, 400, 000	184, 800, 000
1860–1870	3, 400, 000	448, 800, 000
1870–1880	6, 700, 000	884, 400, 000
1880–1890	18, 000, 000	2, 376, 000, 000
1890–1896	22, 700, 000	2, 996, 400, 000
Total pour quarante-six ans	52, 200, 000	6, 890, 400, 000

On donne dans les deux tableaux suivants la production moyenne universelle par an et la proportion des Etats de Rio et de Santos:

Années.	Production.	
	Sacs.	*Livres.*
1852–1860	5, 000, 000	660, 000, 000
1860–1870	6, 000, 000	792, 000, 000
1870–1880	7, 500, 000	990, 000, 000
1880–1890	10, 000, 000	1, 320, 000, 000
1890–1900	11, 000, 000	1, 452, 000, 000

	Production de—					
	1897–98.		1898–99.		1899–1900.	
	Sacs.	*Livres.*	*Sacs.*	*Livres.*	*Sacs.*	*Livres.*
Rio de Janeiro	3, 000, 000	396, 000, 000	3, 500, 000	462, 000, 000	3, 000, 000	396, 000, 000
Santos	3, 750, 000	495, 000, 000	5, 500, 000	726, 000, 000	4, 000, 000	528, 000, 000
Tous les autres androits	4, 000, 000	528, 000, 000	4, 000, 000	528, 000, 000	4, 000, 000	528, 000, 000
Total	10, 750, 000	1, 419, 000, 000	13, 000, 000	1, 716, 000, 000	11, 000, 000	1, 452, 000, 000

Ces chiffres ne renferment pas le calcul des exportations de Victoria, de Bahia et de Ceara, sauf pour 1899, en ajoutant 500,000 sacs aux estimations pour Rio de Janeiro.

Quant au coût de la production du café au Brésil les faits suivants sont relevés verbatim du rapport consulaire de M. Hill:

"On peut se fier à l'estimation suivante faite par une personne que je connais personnellement. La difficulté, dit-il, de fournir des données exactes se comprendra facilement quand on prend en considération la situation, la grandeur, le nombre d'arbres et les espèces d'arbres plantés, jeunes et vieux, ainsi que le fait que les prix du café en or pendant les deux dernières années ont diminué de plus de 50 pour cent, et que toutes les valeurs locales dépendent des grandes fluctuations du change, car la monnaie brésilienne subit actuellement une dépréciation de 80 pour cent. Je crois que 2 milreis (28 sous) par arbre en pleine croissance serait un prix modéré en ce moment pour une plantation de situation favorable, avec les habitations, les machines, etc., comprises dans ce chiffre. La dépense de l'exploitation d'une plantation de 150,000 arbres ne dépasse probablement pas $5,000 par an, non compris le fret au port, qui est élevé, le prix des sacs et les dépenses ayant trait à la vente. La production totale est de 65,000 à 70,000 kilogrammes, d'une valeur à Santos, d'environ 50,000 milreis ($7,000) sur une dépense totale de $50,000 ou environ 14 pour cent du capital placé.

"Le prix de 9 milreis ($1.26) pour chaque 10 kilogrammes de café, qu'on donne souvent comme prix courant dans ce rapport, est pour le café 'supérieur;' le café 'bon' qui équivaut au No. 7 de la Bourse de café de New York, se vend à 7 milreis ½ ($6.30) par sac de 60 kilogrammes."

La consommation annuelle du café dans le monde entier durant les 5 années prochaines est estimée à 12,000,000 de sacs, (1,584,000,000 livres). Et sur cette quantité le Brésil fournira 8,000,000 sacs (1,056,000,000 livres).

Pour montrer ce qu'est la récolte du café au Brésil par rapport aux autres exportations du pays, il suffit de jeter un coup d'œil sur les chiffres suivants qui montrent les exportations en 1895:

Café	$140,000,000
Caoutchouc	25,000,000
Autres produits	15,000,000
Total	180,000,000

Le Bulletin Mensuel du mois d'octobre 1897, contenait un rapport officiel étendu relativement à l'industrie du café et du cacao au Venezuela, qui montrait que la superficie cultivée en café dans l'année 1897, était de 403,865 acres, donnant une production totale de 304,800,000 livres.   M. HILL donne ces chiffres aussi dans son rapport et il dit que, d'après les renseignements obtenus pendant un voyage au Venezuela, la culture du café dans ce pays se développe beaucoup.   D'après un rapport du Ministre BAKER, publié dans les Rapports Consulaires, No. 199, il parait que la production du café au Nicaragua en 1896–97 était de 500,000 sacs ou de 5,000,000 livres supérieures à celle de toute autre saison précédente.

En tenant compte des facilités qu'offre la culture du café au Paraguay, le Consul HILL parle naturellement de ce pays comme faisant partie de la zone caféière du Brésil, et il dit qu'il y a vu près d'Assomption un champs de café d'une très belle apparence. Jusqu'à l'introduction d'une nouvelle et virile population, l'yerba mate continuera à être le breuvage du pays.

La production du café au Pérou augmente et promet de devenir une des principales denrées du pays.   Chanchamayo, Perene, Pancarbambo et les vallées de la Rio Colorado sont les grands districts caféiers,   Le développement de cette industrie agricole, ainsi que de beaucoup d'autres de cette terre favorisée, n'attend que l'inauguration de moyens suffisants de transport.

Malgré l'excès de production du café au Brésil et des autres régions, et le bas prix qui en résulte, le Consul HILL considère sous un jour favorable, l'avenir économique et la perspective financière du Brésil.   Si l'on compare le Brésil à beaucoup de pays, sa dette extérieure est petite et il reçoit constamment des immigrants tels qu'il en désire.   Au port de Santos seul, il est arrivé en 1897, cinquante-sept mille immigrants.   La plupart étaient des agriculteurs économes, capables d'étendre les ressources agricoles du pays, comme on l'a fait dans les vastes et fertiles plaines de la République Argentine.

Comme preuve de cette heureuse perspective, on donne textùellement le paragraphe final du rapport.

"Tout semble concourir pour le bien dans ces nouvelles terres incultes de l'Hémisphère Occidental; on a simplement gratté leur surface et la plus grande partie de la population se trouve encore le long du littoral, près des voies fluviales ou artificielles qui communiquent avec l'intérieur et ceci quoique trois siècles se soient écoulés depuis leur découverte. Jugés au jour le jour ces pays semblent être restés stationnaires; mais en faisant une comparaison tous les dix ans on verra de grands changements, tous en faveur du progrès. Les qualités des citoyens se développent de plus en plus. L'élément militaire n'est plus tout puissant, il perd peu à peu son autorité et l'opinion publique commence à prendre le dessus. Dans une période de dix ans, j'ai vu tomber les gouverneurs militaires dans le Paraguay, l'Uruguay et le Venezuela, et bien qu'il soit difficile d'arriver aux places publiques, on voit qu'il est possible d'avoir un gouvernement indépendant. L'influence étrangère se fait sentir constamment, quoique les Européens soient des critiques sévères. Les relations du Brésil avec tous les pays de l'Europe et des États-Unis sont très étroites; les navires et les marchandises de tous les pays remplissent ses ports."

LE CHEMIN DE FER TRANSSIBÉRIEN.

EFFET SUR LE COMMERCE AMÉRICAIN.

La dernière année du XIXᵉ siècle verra l'achèvement du chemin de fer le plus gigantesque qu'on ait jamais entrepris.

Depuis l'acquisition des possessions à l'est des monts Ourals, le gouvernement russe s'est rendu compte de la nécessité, au point de vue commerciale, politique and militaire, de l'unification plus étroite des deux parties de l'Empire. Par conséquent, on a fait en 1858, des arpentages et études en vue de la construction d'un grand chemin de fer transcontinental pour relier les réseaux, déjà achevés de la Russie proprement dite, aux extrêmes limites orientales du pays. Après beaucoup de travail et de délais, on a décidé que la route la plus praticable était celle, ayant comme point terminus à l'ouest, la ville de Chiliabinsk et s'étendant vers l'est, en traversant Omsk, Irkotsk, Khabarovka pour se terminer à Vladivostok sur la Mer du Japon.

On a commencé la construction de ce travail gigantesque le 10 décembre 1892, date à laquelle le Czarowitz, aujourd'hui l'Empereur, posa la première pierre. La longueur totale de la ligne propre, de Chiliabinsk à Vladivostok est de 7,083 versts (4,696 milles). Cette longueur ne comprend pas les embranchements dont quelques-uns sont en voie de construction et d'autres en projet seulement.

Tout ce travail, qui appartient au gouvernement russe, a été construit par son entremise directe et ce travail a été l'objet de la surveillance gouvernementale la plus minutieuse. L'estimation totale des frais, y compris l'expropriation des terrains est de 371.-009,947 rubles ($188,014,938) ou au taux de 49,444 rubles par verst.

Pour surmonter l'obstacle du port de Vladivostok, qui est fermé pendant plusieurs mois de l'année à cause de la glace, on construit un embranchement dans Manchuria, le territoire récemment acquis de la Chine, allant à un point sur la Mer Jaune, qui est navigable pendant toute l'année.

On donne ici l'extrait suivant tiré du rapport adressé au Ministère des Affaires Etrangères par M. HERBERT H. PIERCE, Chargé d'affaires, par interim, de la Légation des Etats-Unis, en date de St. Pétersbourg, le 14 octobre 1895, sur les ressources de la région qui sera développée par le Chemin de fer transsibérien.

On ne peut mettre en doute que ce grand système de chemin de fer ne soit destiné à ouvrir un pays d'une grande richesse. Les régions minières des monts Ourals, des monts Altai et des monts Sayan n'ont pas été développées et ont été même très peu explorées à cause de la difficulté qu'on éprouve dans le transport de leurs produits; car toutes les grandes voies fluviales qui les traversent se dirigent vers le nord pour se jeter dans la Mer Glaciale. Déjà dans les Monts Ourals l'entreprise fait des progrès. On y établit l'exploitation minière, des hauts fourneaux pour la fonte du fer et des minerais de cuivre et des usines pour les métaux.

La Russie entière prend un intérêt profond dans le progrès des travaux de construction du grand chemin de fer transsibérien, et l'on sait que l'Empereur, qui était son président quand il était Czarowitz, tient à son achèvement prochain.

Conformément à la politique de protection des industries et de la production nationale, instituée avec tant d'ardeur par le feu Empereur, c'est en Russie que se fait, autant que possible, toute la construction et toute la fourniture de la ligne. En vue de contrats gouvernementaux, des capitalistes étrangers se lancent dans la construction d'usines pour la manufacture de rails, de locomotives, etc., mais les usines doivent être construites en Russie et exploitées par des sujets de cette nation.

M. J. C. MONAHAN, consul des Etats-Unis à Chemnitz, Allemagne, écrit en date du 4 décembre 1896:

La Sibérie est riche en minéraux de toutes sortes; les Monts Ourals fournissent de l'or et de l'argent en quantités considérables. On peut se faire une idée de l'importance du commerce des fourrures de la Sibérie en Allemagne, aux expositions annuelles de Leipsic. Si le marteau qui enfonça le premier clou dans la première traverse était en argent, celui qui enfoncera le dernier clou devrait être en or. Si cette ligne doit avoir une importance considérable sur les intérêts de l'Allemagne, de la Russie et du reste de l'Europe, elle en aura une plus grande encore sur les nôtres, car les Etats de Californie, de l'Orégon, de Washington, tout notre continent occidental enfin, sinon notre continent entier, s'intéresse à ce chemin de fer. La Russie a tout ce qu'elle peut faire chez elle, c'est nous qui devons prêter la main dans l'Est.

A L'achèvement de cette vaste entreprise, des régions jusqu'ici inaccessibles aux voyageurs et au commerce du monde, seront mises en communication facile. Le voyage de St.-Pétersbourg à Pékin pourra se faire en cinq jours au moyen de wagons de luxe; de Londres, le voyageur peut se rendre à la capitale du Japon en quinze jours au lieu de trente, le temps requis maintenant pour faire la traversée de l'Atlantique, du continent américain et de l'Océan Pacifique, ou celle de la route encore plus longue, via la Mer Méditerranée et le Canal de Suez.

En ce moment, il est impossible de prédire intelligemment l'effet que produira ce nouveau facteur dans les conditions économiques du monde commercial. Déjà, on projette de nouvelles lignes de vapeurs entre Port Arthur, le terminus sud du chemin de fer, et les ports chinois et Manille, ayant en vue de faire des correspondances commerciales directes avec les lignes de ces ports allant aux pays au delà du Pacifique et de l'Asie septentrionale.

Par suite du réveil de l'esprit de commerce dans le nouveau Japon et l'acquisition du territoire chinois par les nations commerciales agressives de l'Europe, il est facile de voir d'avance le spectacle du vaste Pacifique étant couvert de navires de commerce comme l'est aujourd'hui l'Atlantique. En tout ceci, le chemin de fer transsibérien doit nécessairement former le facteur le plus important. En considérant la carte de l'Océan Pacifique et les voies commerciales qui y sont établies, les différentes îles de cette vaste étendue semblent fournir une série de stations de l'Ouest à l'Est et d'après les conditions qui se développent dans cette partie du monde, ces différents endroits d'arrêt promettent à être sous le drapeau américain.

Le BULLETIN MENSUEL a souvent attiré l'attention sur les concessions accordées aux sujets japonais pour l'établissement de lignes de vapeurs entre les ports de ce pays, du Mexique et même du Pérou.

De grandes colonies de Japonais se sont établies et s'établissent dans les riches terres de l'Isthme de Téhuantépec. La construction inévitable du Canal du Nicaragua ou de quelque autre canal dans l'isthme comptera dans le développement de ce commerce oriental d'une manière non moins frappante que le grand chemin de fer transsibérien.

MISCELLANÉES COMMERCIALES.

RÉPUBLIQUE ARGENTINE.

Eclairage Electrique à Buenos Ayres. Dans le BULLETIN MENSUEL du mois de mai on dit que le gouvernement municipal de Buenos Ayres a passé un contrat avec la Compañía General de Electricidad pour éclairer les rues de la ville à l'électricité. On donne les détails sur le nombre de lampes à placer, les prix à payer, etc. Cependant la "Review of the River Plate" du 7 mai fait savoir qu'en vue de quelque partie technique le contrat ci-dessus mentionné n'a pas été définitivement accepté, de sorte que les autres compagnies peuvent concourir pour cette franchise.

Introduction de Machines Étrangères. Dans un rapport daté de Barmen, Allemagne, au sujet de la vente de machines étrangères dans la République Argentine, M. BOUCHSEIN, consul des Etats-Unis s'exprime ainsi : Dans un rapport spécial au gouvernement impérial, un consul allemand attire l'attention sur la ville de Tucuman comme étant l'endroit convenable à la vente de machines allemandes. Tucuman, ou plûtôt San Miguel de Tucuman, est la capitale de la Province de Tucuman, République Argentine, la population de cette ville est d'environ 17,000; elle est reliée par chemin de fer à Cordoba et à Rosario.

Les sucreries de Tucuman, au nombre de trente-trois, ont fait venir de France presque toutes les machines employées, à cause des conditions favorables du payement. L'Allemagne a fourni les appareils pour les distilleries qui se rattachent aux sucreries, aux fours de soufre, etc. L'industrie sucrière de Tucuman augmente d'année en année et bientôt, on aura besoin de beaucoup de machines d'un usage général. Depuis longtemps quelques-uns des grands fabricants de machines en France ont eu des représentants en résidence à Tucuman.

Amélioration apportée à la qualité du blé. En vue de développer la culture du blé au plus haut degré, la Législature d'Entre Rios, la grande Province productrice de blé de la République Argentine, a voté une somme de £100,000 pour servir chaque année à l'achat des meilleures qualités de blé et de lin pour la semence. Ces graines seront livrées aux agriculteurs au prix coûtant. On peut dire aussi que la Province d'Entre Rios n'est pas la seule qui fasse des efforts dans cette voie. La Province de Buenos Ayres a établi un bureau de chimie appliquée à l'agriculture, qui publie à des intervalles réguliers, des traités sur la culture des céréales. Jusqu'ici ce bureau a fait paraître les traités suivants : "Renseignements économiques sur le battage des blés;" "Choix et préparation de blé pour la semence," et beaucoup d'autres sur les mêmes sujets. On a l'habitude dans la République Argentine d'ensemencer d'année en année, le blé récolté la saison précédente; il en est ainsi résulté nécessairement une diminution constante de la récolte annuelle.

Culture du Maïs dans la République Argentine. Le maïs, qui aujourd'hui constitue l'un des principaux articles d'exportation de la République Argentine, a passé d'une récolte de 8,038 tonnes en 1873 à une récolte de 1,500,000 tonnes en 1896 d'après l'estimation. La Province de Buenos Ayres est très favorable à la culture de cette céréale, dont les exportations commencèrent longtemps avant celles du blé. Pendant le printemps et l'été (d'octobre à mars) la température présente une égalité essentiellement propre au développement de la plante, en même temps que des pluies, assez abondantes, assurent au sol l'humidité nécessaire. La superficie des terrains plantés en maïs, qui était de 100,498 hectares en 1891, s'est élevée à 718,633 hectares en 1895, qui ont rapporté 628,000,000 de kilogrammes de maïs.

BRÉSIL.

Commerce en Avril 1898. Bien que les droits d'entrée brésiliens soient moins élevés que l'année dernière, les recettes des douanes provenant des droits d'entrée sur les marchandises étrangères se sont élevées pendant le mois d'avril 1898 à $491,662.64 soit un excédent de $35,488.18 sur le mois correspondant de l'année précédente. Les arrivages de café à Santos se sont élevés à 377,000 sacs pendant le mois, dont 263,422 sacs ont été mis en entrepôt, contre 247,901 en avril 1897. A Rio pendant le même mois, les arrivages ont été de 238,000 sacs, soit 1,000 sacs de plus qu'en avril de l'année antérieure. Les embarquements ont atteint 438,404 sacs à Rio, et 532,677 sacs à Santos. C'est un chiffre énorme pour la saison et c'est à ce chiffre qu'on doit la diminution considérable du stock en magasins, qui n'était plus au 30 avril que de 339,116 sacs, soit plus de moitié moins qu'au commencement du mois.

GUATÉMALA.

Emballage pour le transport par terre. Les transports à dos de mule sont les plus usités au Guatémala. On appelle "carga," la charge d'une mule. La panela (sucre brut), le charbon de bois, le zacata et tous les produits nationaux se vendent par "carga" de 9 a robes ou environ 100 kilogrammes. Il est très important pour le fabricant de prendre note de ces petits détails, car pour tout ce qui doit servir a une exploitation agricole, surtout les machines, il y a lieu de tenir compte de ce que les colis ne doivent pas dépasser ce poids. Il en est, d'ailleurs, de même pour tous les articles d'usage général, et les colis de cinquante kilogrammes, de forme allongée conviennent le mieux pour être transportés à dos de mule. Le coût du transport est très variable, il dépend des distances à traverser.

HAÏTI.

Négociations pour l'Emprunt. M. JOHN B. TERRÈS, vice-consul des Etats-Unis à Port-au-Prince, envoie au Ministère des Affaires Etrangères une copie de la loi votée à la dernière séance de la Législature haïtienne ayant pour objet la négociation d'un emprunt de $3,500,000 en or.

Cet emprunt s'effectuera aux Etats-Unis et M. J. N. Léger, Ministre d'Haïti à Washington, est chargé des négociations.   Cet emprunt a pour objet le retrait du papier-monnaie de la République.

Le texte de la loi, telle que la Législature l'a votée et que le Président Simon Sam l'a promulguée, est publié en entier dans les Rapports Consulaires pour le mois de juin de l'année courante.

HONDURAS.

Annulation de la Subvention Accordée à la Pacific Mail Company. Le Nouveau Monde du 11 juin 1898 fait connaître que le gouvernement hondurien a retiré à la Pacific Mail, la subvention qu'il lui accordait jusqu'ici.   Le gouvernement a passé un contrat avec la Compañía Sud Americana de Vapores (chilienne), qui a récemment étendu son service jusqu' aux ports de l'Amérique Centrale, pour le transport des malles-postes des ports du Honduras.

Banque Commerciale à Tegucigalpa. La Banque commerciale de Honduras, appartenant en partie à des capitalistes des Etats-Unis, a été solennellement inaugurée à Tegucigalpa.

MEXIQUE.

Nouvelle Construction pour le marché à Guayama. Le Colonel Wrotnowski, très connu dans le monde scientifique du Mexique et des Etats-Unis où on a su apprécier sa valeur comme ingénieur non seulement dans les plans et la construction des moles de Tampico, mais aussi dans les travaux du port de Vera Cruz, vient d'obtenir un contrat pour la construction d'un grand marché couvert dans la ville de Guayama, port florissant de l'Etat de Sonora.   L'édifice doit être construit en pierre, en fer et en verre; il doit renfermer 140 places de 4 mètres carrés chacune.   L'édifice doit aussi avoir un étage supérieur avec des pieces pouvant servir de bureaux.   Les travaux devront être terminés en février 1900. Le Colonel Wrotnowski encaissera à son profit les recettes du marché pendant 33 ans, moins 25 pour cent des recettes nettes qui devront revenir à la ville.

Modification apportée à la taxe minière. La Chambre des Députés du Congrès mexicain vient de voter un projet de loi ayant pour objet le règlement de la taxe sur les mines de métaux ordinaires.   Aux termes du projet de loi, la taxe sur le titre originel aussi bien que pour le loyer annuel, par placement ou par pertenencia, sera réduite sur toutes les mines, autres que celles qui produisent l'or, l'argent et le platine à $2 par pertenencia.   La taxe sur les mines produisant les métaux cités plus haut, restera la même que la présente.   Sur toutes les autres mines la taxe sera de $2.50 sur le titre, et de $2 pour le loyer annuel.

Participation du Mexique à l'Exposition d'Omaha. Le Ministère de l'Agriculture a décidé que le Mexique sera représenté à l'Exposition d'Omaha qui doit avoir lieu cet été.   La place qui lui est réservée est de la même grandeur que celle donnée au Mexique à l'Exposition d'Atlanta.

M. J. D. Powell qui a représenté le Mexique à Atlanta a reçu des lettres du Ministre Fernandez Leal pour les gouverneurs de tous les Etats, et il fait maintenant un voyage dans la République dans l'intérêt de l'Exposition.

PÉROU.

Exposition Permanente à Lima. Les importateurs et manufacturiers qui ont pris part à l'Exposition Permanente de machines et de produits fabriqués qui a lieu maintenant à Lima sont très satisfaits de la vente facile de leurs produits. M. M. G. MENCHACA & Cie., ont déjà écoulé un grand nombre des objets quifiguraient dans leur magasin depuis quelques année et dont on n'a pas apprécié la valeur jusqu'ici par suite de l'emplacement limité de leur exposition. L'avantage est plus grand pour tout ce qui est nouveau, ainsi un agent d'une maison de commerce des Etats-Unis a déjà trouvé des acheteurs pour la plus grande partie des objets qu'il avait exposés. Les machines et les objets manufacturés de toutes sortes envoyés de l'étranger ne sont grevés d'aucune taxe ou d'aucuns frais de loyer de local que quand ils sont vendus dans le pays. Comme il y a une salle de lecture attenante à l'exposition, il a été décidé que les maisons de commerce des Etats-Unis devraient y envoyer des catalogues et des photographies de leurs produits pour être examinés par des acheteurs en perspective. Des coupes de machines, de chaudières à vapeur, de machines pour les mines, d'appareils pour sucreries, de charpentes métalliques, de hangars, de ponts, d'habitations démontées, etc., seraient d'une grande utilité.

SALVADOR.

Mise en Vigueur d'une Nouvelle loi sur les Banques. A la dernière séance régulière du Congrès, on a passé une nouvelle loi sur les banques ayant pour objet principal le rachat en argent de leurs billets. La loi est entrée en vigueur le II avril dernier. Le Consul JOHN JENKINS écrivant de San Salvador en date du 15 avril, dit que la Banco Industrial del Salvador s'est retirée des affaires et conjointement avec une des plus anciennes banques du pays, formera une nouvelle institution financière. Ce changement réduira à quatre le nombre des banques. Dans la République la concurrence a rendu le commerce de banques très peu satisfaisant et les a réduites tout simplement au rôle de maisons de spéculation. D'après la nouvelle loi qui oblige les banques à racheter leurs billets en espèce, on espère que ce commerce sera établi sur des bases plus stables. M. JENKINS dit que malgré le bas prix du café, il y a une abondance de matériel au Salvador qui peut assurer une grande prospérité dans l'avenir.

URUGUAY.

Éducation Gratuite dans les Ecoles Militaires et Navales des Etats-Unis. En réponse à l'observation de M. FINCH, Ministre des Etats-Unis, le gouvernement des Etats-Unis a offert d'instruire gratuitement à l'Ecole Militaire de West Point et à l'Ecole Navale d'Annapolis, deux jeunes gens, sujets de la République de l'Uruguay. Les nominations seront faites sur la demande officielle du Président de l'Uruguay.

VENEZUELA.

Importations du port de New York. M. ANTONIO E. DELFINO, Consul Général du Venezuela, a fourni au Bureau les données statistiques suivantes sur l'exportation de marchandises par le port de New York aux différents ports

vénézuéliens pour le mois de mai 1898, comparées avec celles du mois mai 1897.
En mai 1898, les exportations totales ont atteint $209,900.68 et en mai 1897,
elles étaient de $250,182.35, soit une diminution de $40,281.67. Cette exportation montrant l'augmention ou la diminution, se répartit comme suit, les chiffres donnés représentent la valeur en or.

	Mai 1898.	Mai 1897.	Augmentation.	Diminution.
La Guaira...............	$121,334.54	$113,437.79	$7,897.35	....
Pto. Cabello..............	12,520.76	39,061.56	....	$26,540.80
Maracaibo...............	43,661.59	54,193.64	....	10,532.05
La Vela..................	10,311.00	15,164.86	....	4,853.86
Guanta..................	1,565.79	1,117.25	448.54	....
Cumana.................	1,416.00	542.00	874.00	....
Cana Colorado...........	86.00	1,697.35	....	1,611.35
Carupano...............	5,628.00	5,022.00	606.00	....
Ciudad Bolivar..........	13,377.00	19,946.50	....	6,569.50
Total............ ..	209,900.68	250,182.35	9,825.89	50,107.56

Eclairage Electrique. La Municipalité a passé un contrat avec M. Luis
Manuel Mendez pour l'éclairage à l'électricité de la
ville de San Christobal (Los Andes). Le contrat stipule l'établissement de 120
lampes incandescentes d'une force de 16 bougies et de 10 lampes d'arc de 100
bougies. La ville payera 6 francs par mois pour chaque lampe incandescente
et 60 francs pour chaque lampe d'arc.

Banque Agricole. Le Président Ignacio Andrade a soumis au Congrès
du Venezuela un projet pour l'établissement d'une banque
nationale, ayant pour seul objet le développement des intérêts des agriculteurs
et des éleveurs de bétail dans la République. Le plan, tel qu'il est proposé et
conçu a pour objet de prêter aux personnes engagées ou qui désirent s'engager
dans l'une ou l'autre de ces industries, des sommes à un taux d'intérêt peu élevé et
à terme de crédit assez long pour les mettre en état d'entreprendre et de continuer
le travail jusqu'à ce qu'il puisse suffire de lui-même à son maintien.

Dans son message au Congrès, le Président Andrade dit : " Une institution
de cette nature serait d'une grande et incontestable utilité et tous les hommes
sérieux du pays ont demandé son établissement. Il me semble que le moment
est propice pour la recommander à l'attention immédiate du Congrès, car elle
peut satisfaire aux grands et pressants besoins et porter remède à la mauvaise
condition économique qui existe actuellement dans le pays et que ne fait qu'ac-
centuer la diminution dans les prix de nos productions principales. L'établissement de cette banque empêchera ces conséquences graves que la lutte armée qui
a lieu maintenant, doit de nécessité exercer sur la richesse nationale et surtout
sur les industries précitées."

MONTHLY BULLETIN

OF THE

BUREAU OF THE AMERICAN REPUBLICS,

INTERNATIONAL UNION OF AMERICAN REPUBLICS.

| Vol. VI. | AUGUST, 1898. | No. 2. |

RELATIONS OF THE UNITED STATES WITH SPAIN.

SUSPENSION OF HOSTILITIES AND THE RESULTS AS AFFECTING AMERICAN TRADE.—BROADENING OF THE CHANNELS OF COMMERCIAL INTERCOURSE BETWEEN THE AMERICAN REPUBLICS.— CUBA AND PORTO RICO THE GATEWAYS FOR CAPITAL AND INDUSTRY FLOWING SOUTH AND WEST.—HAWAII AND THE PHILIPPINES IN THEIR RELATION TO THE PACIFIC COAST OF THE AMERICAS.— STATISTICS OF COMMERCE AND INDUSTRIES. CUSTOMS AND SHIPPING REGULATIONS FOR CUBA, THE PHILIPPINES, AND PORTO RICO.

The war between the United States and Spain, growing out of the revolution against the Spanish government in Cuba, began April 21, 1898. Hostilities were suspended August 12, 1898, as appears from the following proclamation by the President of the United States:

BY THE PRESIDENT OF THE UNITED STATES OF AMERICA.

A PROCLAMATION.

Whereas by a protocol concluded and signed August 12, 1898, by WILLIAM R. DAY, Secretary of State of the United States, and His Excellency JULES CAMBON, Ambassador Extraordinary and Plenipotentiary of the Republic of France at Washington, respectively representing for this purpose the Government of the United States and the Government of Spain, the Governments of the United States and Spain have formally agreed upon the terms on which negotiations for the establishment of peace between the two countries shall be undertaken; and

Whereas it is in said protocol agreed that upon its conclusion and signature hostilities between the two countries shall be suspended, and that notice to that effect shall be given as soon as possible by each Government to the commanders of its military and naval forces:

Now, therefore, I, WILLIAM McKINLEY, President of the United States, do, in accordance with the stipulations of the protocol, declare and proclaim on the part of the United States a suspension of hostilities, and do hereby command that orders be immediately given through the proper channels to the commanders of the military and naval forces of the United States to abstain from all acts inconsistent with this proclamation.

In witness whereof I have hereunto set my hand and caused the seal of the United States to be affixed.

Done at the city of Washington, this 12th day of August, in the year of our Lord one thousand eight hundred and ninety-eight, and of the Independence of the United States, the one hundred and twenty-third.

WILLIAM McKINLEY.

By the President:

WILLIAM R. DAY, *Secretary of State.*

The official statement of the provisions for the conclusion of peace, as announced by the Department of State of the United States, are the following:

1. That Spain will relinquish all claim of sovereignty over and title to Cuba.

2. That Porto Rico and other Spanish islands in the West Indies, and an island in the Ladrones, to be selected by the United States, shall be ceded to the latter.

3. That the United States will occupy and hold the city, bay, and harbor of Manila, pending the conclusion of a treaty of peace which shall determine the control, disposition, and government of the Philippines.

4. That Cuba, Porto Rico, and other Spanish islands in the West Indies shall be immediately evacuated, and that commissioners, to be appointed within ten days, shall, within thirty days from the signing of the protocol, meet at Havana and San Juan, respectively, to arrange and execute the details of the evacuation.

5. That the United States and Spain will each appoint not more than five commissioners to negotiate and conclude a treaty of peace. The commissioners are to meet at Paris not later than the 1st of October.

6. On the signing of the protocol, hostilities will be suspended, and notice to that effect will be given as soon as possible by each Government to the commanders of its military and naval forces.

In accordance with the President's proclamation, telegraphic orders were sent to the military and naval commanders of the United States forces in the Philippines and in the West Indian

Islands, directing them to suspend all military operations and to raise the blockade of ports and harbors.

The causes leading up to the war with Spain are stated in a message from the President of the United States to Congress, dated April 25, 1898, in which he refers to the passage of a joint resolution by Congress, approved April 20, 1898, demanding that the Government of Spain relinquish its authority and government in the Island of Cuba and withdraw its land and naval forces from Cuba and Cuban waters. The President adds:

Upon communicating to the Spanish minister in Washington the demand which it became the duty of the Executive to address to the Government of Spain, in obedience to said resolution, the minister asked for his passports and withdrew. The United States minister at Madrid was in turn notified by the Spanish minister for foreign affairs that the withdrawal of the Spanish representative from the United States had terminated diplomatic relations between the two countries and that all official communications between their respective representatives ceased therewith.

The severance of diplomatic relations by the Government of Spain was followed by the active prosecution of military operations on the part of the United States. These resulted in the destruction of the Spanish fleet at Manila, May 1, the destruction of the Spanish fleet off Santiago de Cuba, July 3, the surrender of the province of Santiago de Cuba, July 14, and the invasion of the island of Puerto Rico, July 21.

Following the occupation of the province of Santiago de Cuba, military government was established, and the incumbents of municipal offices under the former Spanish sovereignty were continued. Customs and other regulations were promulgated by the War Department of the United States, and are given herewith.

Incidentally to the military conduct of the war, the Hawaiian Islands were annexed to the United States by joint resolution of Congress, approved July 7, 1898, the government of the islands being confided to the discretion of the President of the United States until Congress shall make further provision.

The results of the conflict with Spain have such an important relation to the commercial development of the countries of the Western Hemisphere that they naturally suggest consideration in the MONTHLY BULLETIN. The rapid changes necessarily occurring in the administration of territory acquired by war render it difficult to group together immediately all the facts and figures which are required for an intelligent study of commercial and industrial conditions. These changes are distributed among various departments of the Government, and time will be required to perfect the details for the different branches of administration. The following compilation has been prepared from the sources of information now available, in response to the general demand for particulars as to trade opportunities and conditions.

The countries composing the International Union of American Republics are naturally most interested in the possible effect of the new conditions upon their own commercial and industrial development. The Latin-American republics will doubtless perceive in the deliverance of the Cuban people, through the good offices of the United States, from the defects of administration from which Mexico, the Central American States, and the countries of South America, with the sympathetic interest of the United States, emancipated themselves by their own efforts, the promise of that free development in Cuba of trade and industries which has been one of the most important consequences of their separation from the mother country.

From their geographical position, Cuba and Porto Rico may be called the great natural gateways of trade of the Caribbean Sea and important stepping-stones to the commerce of the whole of South America. With the completion of an interoceanic canal, they must be immensely benefited by the development, which may be expected to follow, of the trade of the Pacific coast of the three Americas. In a similar way, the acquisitions of the United . States in the Pacific open up vast possibilities for the development of Asiatic trade, not only with the United States, but with the Latin-American republics. A great number of inquiries already received by the Bureau of the American Republics from commercial houses in the United States and from individuals seeking opportunities of investment or employment clearly indicates that, with a return of settled conditions in the former colonial possessions of Spain, there will be a great influx of industry and capital; and it is to be expected that this movement will extend, under favoring conditions, to the great benefit of the relations between the United States and its sister republics of Latin-America.

The subjects treated in the following compilation are: 1. Cuba. 2. Porto Rico.   3. Hawaiian Islands.   4. The Philippines and Ladrones.

I. CUBA. *

LOCATION, AREA, AND TOPOGRAPHY.

The Island of Cuba, the largest of the Antilles, is situated at the entrance of the Gulf of Mexico, between 20° and 23° north latitude and 74° and 85° west longitude from Greenwich.   It is distant from Yucatan, Mexico, 114 miles, and from Florida 130 miles, and its location gave rise to its being called "The Key to the Gulf of Mexico." On the coat of arms of Havana, there appears a key as one of the most conspicuous objects, as if the intention were to express the idea that possession of the island, and especially of its capital city, implied the ability to open or close at any moment the Gulf of Mexico to the commerce of the world.   The coast line of Cuba is extensive, and it possesses a number of large and safe harbors.   The northern coast, the greater part of which is free from shoals, keys, and other obstacles, has a length of about 918 miles, with 32 harbors, of which 10 are of the first class.   First in importance is the harbor of Havana, followed by those of Mariel, Cabanas, Bahia Honda, Matanzas, Cardenas, Sagua, Caibarien, Nuevitas, Jibara, etc.   The southern coast has a length of 972 miles, with 12 important harbors.   Of these, Guantanamo, which has figured recently in the military and naval operations, is spacious and of easy access, affording shelter to vessels drawing 26 feet.   The harbors of Santiago de Cuba and Cienfuegos are also of considerable importance.

The area of the island of Cuba has not been exactly determined. The estimates vary from about 35,000 to 72,000 square miles. Taking the lowest estimate (35,000 square miles), the island would be nearly equal in size to the State of Indiana (36,350) and nearly three times the size of the State of Maryland (12,210).   It is slightly larger than the State of Maine (33,040).   The island

---

*Compiled from Volume II, Commercial Directory of the American Republics; Review of the World's Commerce, 1896–1897; Advance Sheets of Consular Reports, No. 117; publications of the Bureau of Statistics of the United States Treasury; orders of the War and Treasury Departments, etc.

is traversed by a chain of mountains extending from east-south-east to north-northwest. The highest mountains are found in the southeastern part of the island. The greatest elevation is about 8,000 feet. The soil of Cuba is watered by more than 200 rivers, among which figure the Cauto, in the province of Santiago de Cuba, 150 miles long, about 50 of which are navigable for small craft, and the Sagua, in the province of Santa Clara, of the length of 111 miles, 21 of which are navigable.

CLIMATE AND POPULATION.

With the exception of localities where malarial fevers prevail, the climate of Cuba is healthful, especially in the rural districts in the east and center of the island. There are only two marked seasons in Cuba, the dry and the rainy. The first lasts from November to May and the second from May to October, but during the dry season, sufficient rain falls to give the soil the necessary humidity. The mean temperature in Havana is about $78\frac{1}{4}°$ F. In the interior, the average temperature does not exceed $73.4°$ F. In ordinary years, the temperature never rises above $86°$ F. in August, and in exceptional years, the maximum temperature in the hottest months is $88°$ F. In winter, the temperature rarely goes below $54°$ F. Snow is unknown even on the mountains, and frost has formed only on some of the highest summits. The great drawback for unacclimated persons in Cuba is the prevalence of yellow fever, but this is confined mainly to towns where the sanitary conditions have been bad.

According to an official census of 1890, the population of Cuba was then 1,631,687. For three years, Cuba has been the theater of war, and great mortality and devastation have occurred. It may be assumed that the present population is not in excess of the figures of 1890, and it may be considerably lower. It has been estimated that, taking as a basis the proportion of population to area in the Kingdom of Belgium (482 inhabitants to the square mile) Cuba could support 24,000,000 people. Of the population in 1890, the percentages according to race were: White, 65; colored and Chinese, 35. The actual number of white Cubans was given as 950.000; colored Cubans, 500,000, and Spaniards, 160,000.

POLITICAL DIVISIONS.

Under the Spanish administration, Cuba was divided into three regions—the western, central, and eastern.   Each region comprises two provinces, divided into several judicial districts, and these again subdivided into municipal sections.   The western region embraces the provinces of Pinar del Rio and Havana; the central comprises the provinces of Matanzas and Santa Clara, and the eastern provinces are made up of Puerto Principe and Santiago de Cuba.   The capital of the island is the city of Havana.

Prior to 1898, the island was governed by a governor and captain-general, appointed by the Spanish Crown, who is the superior political, military, and economic chief.   Each of the six provinces was administered by a governor.   On the 1st of January, 1898, the Spanish Government adopted a system of autonomous government for the island, providing for popular representation in the administration of affairs, but it was not accepted by the insurgents and has had no practical effect.   Under the terms of the suspension of hostilities between the United States and Spain, the affairs of the island are likely to be administered for the present by the military commanders of the United States forces.

CITIES AND TOWNS.

1. Havana, capital of the province of the same name and of the island, is situated on the northern coast, and has a harbor which has long been famous for its commerce.   The city has about 200,000 inhabitants.   It is the residence of the Captain-General and other authorities of the island.   It is defended by 8 forts, has a fine navy-yard, arsenal, gun manufacturing and repair shops, barracks and hospitals, 3 large markets, 24 churches, 6 theaters, a university, a school of fine arts, several public libraries, and many educational institutions.   There are several manufactories, and the city is traversed by tramways and omnibus lines. It has communication with the rest of the island by means of railroad lines.   It is lighted by gas and electricity.   About 80 newspapers and other periodicals are published in Havana.

2. Pinar del Rio, capital of the province of Pinar del Rio; population about 30,000.   It is situated about 135 miles from

Havana, and is noted for the fine quality of the tobacco grown in its neighborhood.

3. Matanzas, capital of the province of Matanzas, 66 miles from Havana; population, 56,000. In its vicinity are the fine Bellamar Caves and the noted valley of the Yumuri.

4. Cardenas, a commercial port of the northern coast, about 90 miles from Havana; population, 23,000.

5. Santa Clara, 216 miles from Havana; population, 32,000.

6. Sagua la Grande, province of Santa Clara, situated on the river Sagua la Grande, 7 miles from its mouth; population, 18,000.

7. Cienfuegos, province of Santa Clara; population, 40,000. It is situated on the fine port of Jagua and is a thriving center of trade. Besides the foregoing towns in the province of Santa Clara, there are Trinidad, 29,000 inhabitants; Santi Espiritus, 29,000 inhabitants; and San Juan de los Remedios, 15,000 inhabitants.

8. Puerto Principe, capital of the province of Puerto Principe; population, 49,000.

9. Santiago de Cuba, capital of the province of Santiago de Cuba; population, 50,000. Santiago has a fine harbor and a number of important public buildings, including a famous cathedral.

Among the other towns of importance in the province of Santiago de Cuba are Manzanillo, Bayamo, Jiguani, Holguin, Jibara, Guantanamo, and Baracoa.

COMMERCIAL HOUSES IN CUBA.

Many inquiries are being made for names of merchants engaged in business in the different cities and towns of Cuba. Lists of such names were obtained from consular officers of the United States and from other sources, and will be found in volume 2 of the Commercial Directory of the Bureau of the American Republics, which is about to be published. This Directory contains detailed information as to the resources and business conditions of Cuba, besides similar information for other islands of the West Indies and the various Latin American countries. It is published in two volumes, and is sold upon application to the Director of the Bureau of the American Republics at $5 per volume.

MINERAL RESOURCES AND MINING LAWS.

Early in its history, Cuba was famous for the quantity and quality of its gold.   There are several gold mines still in operation in the central and eastern parts of the island, but they have not recently been worked to the extent that their importance would seem to warrant.   Silver mines are also found in several localities. The greatest mineral wealth of the island lies in its abundant mines of fine copper.   Deposits of this metal, believed to be almost inexhaustible, are located chiefly in the eastern portion of the island, in the mountains, which, by reason of this circumstance, are known as Sierra del Cobre (Copper Mountains).   In 1891, in the district of Santiago de Cuba alone, 296 mining grants were issued, including iron and manganese mines.   The iron ore of Cuba is of superior quality, and with improved facilities for communication and development, it is believed there will be an immense output of this metal.   The iron mines of Juragua, in the province of Santiago de Cuba, have been worked by United States capital.   The ore was exported to Philadelphia, where it was utilized to the extent of 15,000 tons per month. Asphalt and mineral oil deposits are found in several parts of the island.   There are several asphalt deposits in the provinces of Havana, Pinar del Rio, and Santa Clara.   The Cuban asphalt is said to rival that of Trinidad as regards its adaptability for street paving, gas making, and other industrial uses.

The mining laws in force in the island afford facilities for exploration in search of minerals, and by applying to the civil government of the province where the mine is located claims or "pertenencias" may be obtained, complying previously with the usual proceedings through which it is ascertained whether there is any opposition, or a claim of a better right, of a third party. After edicts are published announcing the petition, and no opposition being made, the "pertenencia" is granted.   Proceedings are provided too for the settlement of difficulties in case opposition is made.

AGRICULTURAL RESOURCES.

The great wealth of Cuba lies in the wonderful fertility of its soil.   It is estimated that the island has 35,000,000 acres of land,

Coffee for a long time constituted one of the principal products of Cuba, but since 1845, the development of the coffee product of Brazil and other countries, together with economic conditions in Cuba, caused the cultivation to decline, and coffee is now raised almost exclusively for local consumption.

Besides sugar, tobacco, and coffee, Cuba produces all the different classes of fruits known to the Tropics, and many of those belonging to the temperate zone. Among them are the pineapple, the banana, the orange, the mango, and the guava. The cocoanut is also an important product. The forest wealth of Cuba is very great and but slightly developed. The island is rich in cabinet wood, among which the most important are mahogany and cedar. Among the trees, the one most characteristic of a Cuban landscape is the palm, of which there are 32 species. Its wood and leaves are employed in the manufacture of several articles of trade, including hats and baskets. The soil of the island is well adapted to the production of all kinds of vegetables. The Cuban potato is said to be as good as that of Bermuda or Peru, and the sweet potatoes are of superior quality.

IMMIGRATION AND LAND LAWS—PRICES OF LANDS.

Many efforts have been made in recent times in the Island of Cuba to attract to its shores the beneficial currents of foreign immigration. They have succeeded fully in so far as securing the settlement in the country of a large number of citizens of the United States and of German subjects, who, by engaging in agriculture and commercial business, have contributed largely to the development of the wealth of the island. As there are no public lands in Cuba to any considerable extent, no measure of colonization, properly so called, has been accompanied with success. Colonization must be undertaken by private enterprise, unless private property is taken by the Government for that purpose, which would hardly be possible under the laws of Spain in force in Cuba, or under contracts which, so far, have proven to be little short of slavery.

The royal ordinance of October 21, 1817 (whose provisions, with but little difference, were already in force in Porto Rico), relates to foreign colonization, and provides for the rights of the colonial government. In case of land being held by private individuals, but needed by a third party for any enterprise considered of public benefit, possession of said land could be obtained by application to the government through forcible expropriation, paying previously a just indemnity. The price of Cuban land varies to a considerable extent. In the wealthy sugar districts, 1,000, 1,200, and sometimes 3,000 pesos ($926, $1,111, and $2,778)* were paid per "caballeria" (about 32.1 acres), but in other sections of the island, and especially where there are no railway facilities, land could be obtained at a nominal price.

There can be pointed out three different sections in the island, each distinctly characterized by its adaptability to a certain kind of industry. Pinar del Rio, the westernmost province of the island, is distinguished for its excellent and unsurpassed tobacco. Havana, Matanzas, and Santa Clara provinces are devoted almost entirely to the cultivation of sugar cane and to the sugar industry. Puerto Principe (which occupies the center of the island) is the cattle-raising province, and Santiago de Cuba the mining, fruit, and coffee section of Cuba.

COMMERCE OF CUBA.

The industries and commerce of Cuba have been greatly diminished by the state of insurrection and war which has existed in the island for more than three years. From a summary of Cuban trade printed in the " Review of the World's Commerce," recently published by the Department of State, it appears that the imports of the island during the fiscal year ended April, 1896, amounted to $66,166,754, and the exports to $94,395,536. In 1893, the trade of Cuba with the United States alone showed the following figures: Imports, $78,706,506; exports, $24,157,698. The trade had fallen off during the fiscal year ended June 30, 1897, to imports, $18,406,815; exports, $8,259,776. During the years 1891–1896, inclusive, the commerce of Cuba with Spain amounted to about $30,000,000 per annum, but in 1892, it rose to as much as $37,-600,000, and in 1895, to about $33,500,000. The imports of Cuba from Spain were usually about three times the exports of Cuba to Spain, the latter being about $4,250,000 in 1896 and

*Taking the valuation of the Cuban peso made by the U. S. Director of the mint, $0.92.6.

$9,570,000 in 1892. The imports from Spain ranged during the six years between $22,000,000 in 1891 and $28,000,000 in 1892. The principal articles of import and export between Cuba and the United States are shown in the following tables for the year 1893, when the trade reached its maximum of value since 1874, and the year 1897:

Principal imports from Cuba into the United States.

Articles.	1893.	1897.
Free of duty:		
Fruits, including nuts...............................	$2,347,800	$154,422
Molasses...	1,081,034	5,448
Sugar...	60,637,631	....
Wood, unmanufactured...........................	1,071,123	63,670
Dutiable:		
Tobacco—		
Unmanufactured.............................	8,940,058	2,306,067
Manufactured..............................	2,727,030	1,971,214
Iron ore......................................	641,943	....
Sugar..		11,982,473

Principal exports from the United States to Cuba.

Articles.	1893.	1897.
Wheat flour..	$2,821,557	$564,638
Corn..	582,050	247,905
Carriages and street cars, and parts of	316,045	3,755
Cars, passenger and freight, for steam railroads...........	271,571	9,202
Coal..	931,371	638,912
Locks, hinges, and other builders' hardware.............	395,964	49,386
Railroad bars or rails, of steel	326,654	14,650
Saws and tools.....................................	243,544	34,686
Locomotives....	418,776	20,638
Stationary engines.................................	130,652	1,189
Boilers and parts of engines.........................	322,284	35,578
Wire..	321,120	35,905
Manufactures of leather	191,394	39,753
Mineral oil	514,808	306,916
Hog products......................................	5,401,022	2,224,485
Beans and pease	392,962	276,635
Potatoes..	554,153	331,553
Boards, deals, planks, joists, etc....................	1,095,928	286,387
Household furniture................................	217,126	34,288

In normal years, Cuba exports the greater part of its products to the United States, the principal articles being sugar, molasses, and tobacco, but by reason of the operation of the former Spanish tariff, discriminating in favor of Spanish products, the island imported from the United States a relatively small proportion of what it consumed. Spain and Great Britain furnished the greater part of the imports of Cuba. It may be assumed that, with the relinquishment of Spanish sovereignty, there will no longer be discrimination against United States products. The tariff regulations applied to ports of Cuba in possession of the United States, as the result of the recent military operations, impose the minimum Spanish duty, and United States products will immediately reap the benefit of a change which places the United States on the same footing with other countries.

AMERICAN INTERESTS IN CUBA.

A pamphlet, "Cuba and its Resources," by Mr. JOHN T. HYATT, formerly United States vice-consul at Santiago de Cuba, just issued by the Cuban Investment Company of New York, gives an interesting sketch of the iron, manganese, and copper mines in Cuba, and states that two American companies, the Juragua and Daiquiri iron companies, had extensive plants in southeastern Cuba, representing an expenditure of $6,000,000, and employing from 800 to 2,500 men. They shipped from 20,000 to 75,000 tons of ore per month to the United States and Europe. The ore sent to the United States was largely consumed at Bethlehem, Steelton (Sparrows Point, near Baltimore), and Pittsburg. American capitalists, he states, recently bought the Sabanilla and Marote Railroad, the only public general traffic line in Santiago Province, and constructed a branch road of 16 miles in order to operate a group of manganese mines known as Ponupo. There are nine other groups of these mines in eastern Cuba. United States capital invested largely in sugar estates in Cuba prior to the late insurrection, and the rehabilitation of the sugar industry under more favorable conditions will doubtless attract a large influx of money and enterprise to the island.

A correspondent of the Associated Press, writing from Santiago July 31, 1898, says:

Next in importance to its agricultural products, Santiago's iron and manganese mines demand universal attention. The great iron mountains and mines of Santiago are owned and operated by three companies—the Juragua Iron Company, the Spanish-American Company, and the Sigua Iron Company. The Juragua is the oldest and largest company operating here. This company, of which Major BENT, of the Pennsylvania Steel Company, is president, was formed and the property acquired in 1881. Its shipments of Bessemer ore, so far, exceed 3,000,000 tons. The total output of the Juragua mines is controlled by the Bethlehem Iron Works, the Pennsylvania Steel Company, and the Maryland Steel Company. Its maximum monthly output is 40,000 tons. Siboney is the shipping port of the Juragua Iron Company's mines.

The Spanish-American Iron Company, of which CHARLES F. RAND, of New York, is president, acquired its property in 1889. Its shipments so far have been 400,000 tons, which have been shipped to Philadelphia, Baltimore, England, Scotland, Wales, Belgium, and Germany, where it has been sold in the open market. Its maximum monthly output is 29,000 tons. Daiquiri is the shipping port of the Spanish-American Iron Company. Both these mining companies shut down, owing to the war, on April 21, 1898. They will resume work at once.

The Spanish-American Company gives work to 532 men, and the Juragua Company to over 800.

The Sigua Iron Company, which started with a big boom in 1890, built a broad-gauge railroad 9 miles long and extensive buildings and sheds, shipped four cargoes in 1894, aggregating 12,000 tons, and has not been heard from since, abandoning its property and closing down its mines. Sigua, about 7 miles east of Daiquiri, was the port of shipment. All the buildings, sheds, and wharves, valued at $2,000,000, were burned down by the insurgents, and the railroad beds and trestles, evidently very badly built, have all been washed away in the last three years by the heavy rains. The machine shops have all been destroyed, and were at one time used as salt works by the Cubans. They brought the salt water along the railroad tracks for a distance of a mile, boiled it in the company's vats and boilers, and thus obtained the salt.

The price of ore to-day is about $3 a ton, but when the Juragua Iron Company began to operate, it was worth in the neighborhood of $7 a ton.

One thing must be said in favor of the Spanish Government in this respect. Their mining laws have been exceedingly liberal, encouraging and offering every facility to the opening up of this new field. All the machinery received by the mining companies was exempted from duty, and all the coal imported and used by them was entered free.

As is well known, the Santiago ore, with its low percentage of phosphorus, ranks, together with the Swedish and the Spanish Demerara mineral, as the "crack ore" of the world.

The Ponupo Mining Company (of manganese ore) is a relatively new concern, and shipped before the war only about 400 tons of ore. It has, however, excellent prospects, as it can easily compete in price and quality with the Japanese or any other manganese ore in the world.

The price of hauling the different ores from the mines to their shipping points is relatively insignificant. For the greater part of the way the road is down grade, on the slope of a hill, or mountain. The motive power employed is simply gravity.

An endless rope or cable, to which is attached one full and one empty "hopper," or ore car, keeps in constant motion, the loaded down-grade car pulling the empty one up the hill, and so on ad infinitum. At the foot of the grade, the bottom of the car is made to slide out, the ore falls through a pocket into the car beneath and continues its unballasted upward course, drawn by the descending heavily laden car which follows it.

This economizes motive power and renders mining in Cuba comparatively cheap and easy. The miners live in villages built and set aside for their use, in the immediate vicinity of the mines. Barracks are provided for the bachelors, huts or little houses for those who have families, in which they are provided by the company with considerable comfort.

A "tienda," or store, is opened in the village, where meals, provisions, and clothing can be had for a nominal sum.

The wages of the miners is $1 per day—the greater number of those employed are "Gallegos" (North Spaniards from Galicia), who are, as a rule, honest, hard-working servants.

The mining village of the Juragua Iron Company is called Firmoja, and that of the Spanish-American Company is known as Vinent.

The entire iron district is parceled off clear up to the "Gran Piedra," the highest peak of the Sierra Maestra, and owned by private individuals. Most of the titles are held by Spaniards, some small parcels by Frenchmen.

THE MINING RIGHTS.

A curious feature is that the land fee is separate from the mining rights, both titles rarely being held by the same individual. If you find ore on anybody's 'ands you can denounce the mineral property, and he can not work it without buying the mining rights from you. No legal process can force the finder to sell his lands without a struggle; he can be forced to do so under condemnation proceedings, his lands passed on by a board of review and sold or leased to the holder of the mining rights at the appraised value.

As its name indicates, " El Cobre," about 15 miles from Santiago, is the heart of the copper fields of Cuba. These copper mines are extremely valuable, and have been worked since early in the century.

They were owned by two companies, one English, the other American, but have been abandoned now for almost thirty years. They were forced to shut down by the Cobre Railroad Company, that held the charter rights, and with which they got into a litigation. The mines are exceedingly deep and very damp. One of the features of these mines is a gigantic Cornish pump, put up at a tremendous expense, but which never quite succeeded in pumping the mines dry or in fulfilling expectations. The mines are in no wise exhausted, and still possess a rich treasure of buried wealth.

RAILROADS AND TELEGRAPH LINES.

This rich and fertile soil with its wealth of agricultural and mineral resources, where droughts, floods, and frosts are unknown, is practically undeveloped, owing to the total absence of transportation facilities either by rail or by roads.

In the whole province of Santiago de Cuba there are 80 miles of railroad, and not a mile of road deserving the name between any two towns or villages,

Bull. No. 2——2

excepting narrow paths scarce allowing a horse or a mule to pass, through the woods, across streams, and over the mountains.

The railroads are: The Sabanilla and Moroto Road, which starts at Santiago, thence to a place called Christo, 10 miles distant, where it branches off in a V, one branch running to the Poinpo mines, the other to San Luis, where it ends, total distance covered, 20 miles. This road is owned by American capitalists.

The Guantanamo Railroad starts from Caimanera and runs to the Soledad sugar estate, which is its terminus, passing through the town of Guantanamo, and with a branch to Jamaica. Total mileage of this road is 30 miles, which is owned by Cuban capital and managed by English officials.

The Gibara and Holguin Railroad, running between those two points, covers 30 miles. It is owned by Cuban capital. These three roads are the only railroad lines in the whole province.

Telegraphic communication exists between the different interior towns and principal villages, over Spanish Government lines put up in the rudest fashion, many wires resting on trees without the vestige of an insulator. The dependence that can be placed on such lines is obvious. It would be natural to expect Santiago de Cuba and Havana to be communicated by land wires; but as a fact, the only telegraphic communication between the eastern and western capitals is over an English cable between Santiago and Cienfuegoes, where the message is transmitted to or from Havana by land.

TRANSPORTATION FACILITIES.

According to a report published in Special Consular Reports, "Highways of Commerce," there are 10 railway companies in Cuba, the most important being the Ferrocarriles Unidos; upward of 1,000 miles of main line belong to these companies, and there are, besides, private branch lines to all the important sugar estates. The Ferrocarriles Unidos has four lines, connecting Havana with Matanzas, Batabano, Union, and Guanajay. The roads pass through the most populous part of the country and connect Havana with other lines.

The Western Railway was begun some forty years ago, and in 1891, when it was acquired by an English company, had reached Puerto de Golpe, 96 miles from Havana and 10 miles from Pinar del Rio, the capital of the province of that name and the center of the tobacco-growing district. The line has been completed to Pinar del Rio, and improvements have been made in the old part, many of the bridges having been replaced by new steel ones, the rails renewed, modern cars put on, etc.

The other companies are: Ferrocarriles Cardenas–Jacaro, the main line of which joins the towns of Cardenas and Santa Clara; Ferrocarril de Matanzas, having lines between Matanzas and

Murga, and also between Matanzas and Guareiras; Ferrocarril de Sagua la Grande, running between Concha and Cruces; Ferrocarril Cienfuegos–Santa Clara, connecting those towns; Ferrocarriles Unidos de Caibarien, from Caibarien to Placetas; Ferrocarril de Porto Principe–Nuevitas; Ferrocarril de Guantanamo.

The Marianao Railway also belongs to an English company, with headquarters in London. The original line, belonging to Cubans, was opened in 1863, but liquidated and was transferred to the present owners. The line, only 8½ miles in length, runs from Havana to Marianao, with a branch line to a small village on the coast. During 1894, over 750,000 passengers were carried, this being the chief source of revenue. The carriages are of the American type and are fitted, as well as the locomotives, with the Westinghouse automatic brake; the rails are of steel, weighing 60 pounds per yard.

The national carriage is the volante, and no other is used in the country. It consists of a two-seated carriage, slung low down by leather straps from the axle of two large wheels, and has shafts 15 feet long. The horse in the shaft is led by a postilion, whose horse is also harnessed to the carriage with traces. In case of a long and rough journey, a third horse is harnessed on the other side of the shafts in the same manner. The carriage is extremely comfortable to travel in, and the height of the wheels and their distance apart prevent all danger of turning over, although the roads in the country are, for the most part, mere tracks through fields and open land.

Ox carts and pack mules are used for conveying goods in the interior of the island, outside of the railway lines.

CABLE AND DOMESTIC TELEGRAPHS, TELEPHONES, ETC.

There are four cable lines connected with Cuba: The International Ocean Telegraph Company has a cable from Havana to Florida; the Cuban Submarine Company has a cable connecting Havana with Santiago de Cuba and Cienfuegos; the West India and Panama Company has a cable connecting Havana with Santiago de Cuba, Jamaica, Porto Rico, the Lesser Antilles, and the Isthmus of Panama; the Compagnie Française de Cables Sous-Marins has a line connecting Havana with Santiago de Cuba, Haiti, Santo Domingo, Venezuela, and Brazil.

The only three towns in Cuba having cable connections are Havana, Cienfuegos, and Santiago de Cuba.

The telegraph and telephone systems in Cuba belong to the Government, but the latter is farmed out for a limited number of years to a company called the Red Telefonica de la Habana. Nearly all the public and private buildings in the city and suburbs are connected by telephone. The Statesman's Year Book, 1898, says that there are 2,300 miles of telegraph line, with 153 offices; messages in 1894, 357,914.

OCEAN LINES.

Havana is connected by regular lines of steamers with United States and Spanish ports. Lines of steamboats connect at Tampa and Pensacola, Fla., with the Florida railroads, and by means of them with the various railroad systems of the United States. The lines sailing from New York are:

New York and Cuba Mail Steamship Company, for Havana every Wednesday and Saturday; for Tampico every Wednesday. For Nassau, Santiago, and Cienfuegos, via Guantanamo, every alternate Thursday. Jas. E. Ward & Co., agents, 113 Wall street, New York.

Munson Steamship Line from New York for Matanzas, Cardenas, and Sagua. Also from Philadelphia for Havana, Tampico, and Vera Cruz. W. D. Munson, 27 William street, New York.

Campania Transatlántica Española. The steamers of the Spanish Steamship Line, under contract with the Spanish Government, left New York for Havana direct on the 10th, 20th, and 30th of every month. J. M. Ceballos & Co., agents, pier 10, East River.

Bea Bellido & Co. line of steamers for Matanzas, Cardenas, Sagua, and Caibarien. Waydell & Co., 37 South street, New York.

Regular line for Guantanamo, Santiago, and Cienfuegos. Waydell & Co., 37 South street, New York.

Bacon Steamship Line, Cuban service. Steamship *Amrum* sailed for Santiago on Tuesday, July 2. Daniel Bacon, agent, A 14 and 15, Produce Exchange Annex, New York.

The New York "Journal of Commerce" of August 17, 1898, says:

The first clearance to a merchant vessel from this port to the north side of Cuba since the commencement of the war, was granted yesterday to the *Schleswig*, of the Munson Line, which sailed for Matanzas and Havana with a full cargo of provisions. Three other steamers are expected to sail to-day, the *Bratten*, of the Munson Line, for Cardenas, and the *Lydia* and *Matanzas*, of the Ward Line, for Havana, all carrying provisions. On Saturday the Ward Line will send out the *Macedonia* to Havana and Mexican ports, while the Munson Line will dispatch the *Ardanrose* to Matanzas, Cardenas, Nuevitas, and other north-side ports.

The *Schleswig* yesterday carried the following cargo : 100 crates fowls, 678 barrels of potatoes, 4,000 sacks flour, 290,833 pounds lard, 4,000 bushels corn, 2,450 bushels oats, 965 bags and 60 barrels beans, 400 bags coffee, 400 drums fish, 325 bags bread, 3,320 bags rice, 300 cases condensed milk, 13,054 pounds ham, 5,824 pounds bacon, 3,000 pounds bellies, 46,000 feet lumber, and 8,000 gallons petroleum.

The *Bratten* to-day will carry about 5,000 barrels of similar provisions, while the *Matanzas* and *Lydia* will each have upward of 30,000 barrels, in addition to considerable corn.

It is expected that succeeding steamers for some time will go out well loaded. There is active inquiry in provision and grocery trade circles for goods for West Indian markets, though actual purchases appear to be of less magnitude than those of last week.

In addition to these services the " Journal of Commerce," of August 16, said :

It is probable that the Spanish Line will soon renew operations. J. M. CEBALLOS, of J. M. CEBALLOS & Co., agents for the line, said yesterday that cable advices had been received from the home office stating that the company contemplates a resumption of its former service, but no date has yet been set. The Southern Pacific Company will also, it is understood, soon resume its service from New Orleans to Havana.

CUSTOMS TARIFF AND PORT REGULATIONS.

The customs tariff of the United States continues to be applied to imports from Cuba.

The new tariff for customs duties upon imports at the ports in Cuba in possession of the United States, which has just been published by the War Department, corresponds generally to the minimum rates of the tariff formerly in force in the island. By reference to Consular Reports No. 207 (December, 1897), the Cuban tariff which was promulgated last September will be found in full, and the rates known as "revenue duties" have been practically adopted as a basis for the new tariff, the chief difference being that a duty has been imposed on leaf tobacco, cigars, and cigarettes. The export duties on wood and tobacco remain the same.

This tariff was prepared for application to the province of Santiago de Cuba, but according to the Executive order, which appears on the introductory page, it will be enforced in any port or place in Cuba upon the occupation or possession of the same by United States forces. The order reads:

WAR DEPARTMENT, *Washington, August 8, 1898.*

The following order of the President is published for the information and guidance of all concerned:

EXECUTIVE MANSION, *August 8, 1898.*

By virtue of the authority vested in me as commander in chief of the Army and Navy of the United States of America, I do hereby order and direct that, upon the occupation and possession of any ports and places in the Island of Cuba by the forces of the United States, the following tariff of duties and taxes, to be levied and collected as a military contribution, and regulations for the administration thereof, shall take effect and be in force in the ports and places so occupied.

Questions arising under said tariff and regulations shall be decided by the general in command of the United States forces in that island.

Necessary and authorized expenses for the administration of said tariff and regulations shall be paid from the collections thereunder.

Accurate accounts of collections and expenditures shall be kept and rendered to the Secretary of War.

WILLIAM McKINLEY.

Upon the occupation of any ports or places in the Island of Cuba by the forces of the United States the foregoing order will be proclaimed.

R. A. ALGER, *Secretary of War.*

Importations from the United States under the tariff just published are dutiable like other commodities.

The monetary unit of Cuba is the peso, which is divided into 100 centavos. The statement is made in the tariff that the current value of the peso is about 3s. 10d., or 93.2 cents. The Treasury Department values the peso at 92.6 cents, and this estimate has been followed in making the reductions in the table which follows. The equivalent of the kilogram is 2.2046 pounds.

The duties on the most important articles exported from the United States to Cuba are:

	Pesos.	U. S. equivalent.
Coal ....per 1,000 kilos (2,204.6 pounds)..	0. 40	$0. 37
Oleonaphtha, crude petroleum, and crude oils derived from schists, per 100 kilos (220.46 pounds).................................	*3. 08	2. 85
Petroleum and other mineral oils, rectified or refined, destined for illumination; benzine, gasoline, and mineral oils, not specially mentioned ....per 100 kilos..	5. 20	4. 81
Glass :		
Common hollow glassware ; electric insulators.........do....	.30	.27
(Common bottles for rum, beer, and sparkling wines made with native fruit, enjoy a rebate of 60 per cent of the duties stipulated when imported and declared in the custom-house by the manufacturers of said beverages.)		
Crystal and glass imitating crystal—		
Articles cut, engraved, or gilt.............per 100 kilos..	10. 00	9. 26
Articles, other ....do....	5. 40	5. 03
Plate glass and crystal—		
Slabs, paving or roofing.........................do....	1. 65	1. 52
For windows or in other articles (when neither polished, beveled, engraved, or annealed).........per 100 kilos..	3. 40	3. 14
Window glass set in lead and polished, or beveled plate glass.................................per 100 kilos..	4. 00	3. 70
Glass and crystal, tinned, silvered, or coated with other metals—		
Common mirrors not exceeding 2 millimeters in thickness, coated with red or dark mercurial varnish.per 100 kilos..	8. 00	7. 40
Mirrors, other, not beveled ....do....	12. 50	11. 57
Mirrors, beveled...............................do....	15. 00	13. 89
Wrought iron and steel:		
Rolled—		
Rails..................... ....per 100 kilos..	.85	.78
Bars, rods, tires, hoops, and beams............ ...do....	.90	.83
Bars of all kinds of fine crucible steel ....do....,	1. 50	1. 38
Sheets, rolled—		
Neither polished nor tinned, of 3 millimeters and more in thickness.............................per 100 kilos..	1. 10	1. 01
Neither polished nor tinned, less than 3 millimeters in thickness, and hoop iron .... per 100 kilos..	1. 20	1. 11
Tinned and tin plate. ....do....	1. 50	1. 38
Polished, corrugated, perforated, cold-rolled, galvanized or not, and bands of polished hoop iron.....per 100 kilos..	1. 30	1. 20
Cast in pieces, in the rough, neither polished, turned, nor adjusted, weighing, each—		
25 kilograms or more....................per 100 kilos..	1. 00	.92
Less than 25 kilograms.... ....do....	1. 35	1. 25
Cast in pieces, finished—		
Wheels weighing more than 100 kilograms, fish plates, chairs, sleepers, and straight axles, springs for railways and tramways, lubricating boxes........per 100 kilos..	1. 20	1. 11
Wheels weighing 100 kilograms or less, springs other than for railways and tramways, bent axles, and cranks, per 100 kilograms................................	1. 40	1. 29
Pipes—		
Covered with sheet brass.................per 100 kilos..	1. 40	1. 29
Other, galvanized or not .... do ...!	1. 40	1. 29
Wire, galvanized or not—		
2 mm. or more in diameter........................do....!	1. 00	.92
More than one-half and up to 2 mm. in diameter....do....	1. 30	1. 20
½ mm. or less in diameter, and wire covered with any kind of tissue......... ....per 100 kilos..	1. 60	1. 48

*This is given in the tariff as 8.03 pesos, but as in the original tariff it was 3.08, it is thought to have been a mistake in printing.

	Pesos.	U. S. equiva-lent.
Wrought iron and steel—Continued.		
In large pieces, composed of bars or of bars and sheets fastened by means of rivets or screws ; the same, unriveted, perforated, or cut to measure for bridges, frames, and other buildings...................per 100 kilos..	1. 80	$1. 66
Anchors, chains for vessels or machines, moorings, switches, and signal disks.......................per 100 kilos.	1. 65	1. 52
Wire gauze—		
Up to 20 threads per inch.......................do....	2. 00	1. 85
Of 20 threads or more per inch ....per kilo..	. 06	. 05
(Wire gauze affixed to frames or otherwise wrought shall be liable to a surtax of 40 per cent.)		
Cables, fencing (barbed wire), and netting ; furniture springs, per 100 kilos...	1. 00	. 92
Tools and implements—		
Hammers and anvils...................per 100 kilos..	. 80	. 74
Fine, for arts, trades, and professions, of crucible steel, per 100 kilos.......................................	8. 00	7. 40
Other...... ....per 100 kilos.	2. 50	2. 31
Screws, nuts, bolts, washers, and rivets ; Parisian and similar tacks.....................................per 100 kilos...	1. 00	. 92
Nails, clasp nails, and brads ....do....	1. 00	. 92
Machinery and apparatus employed in industry or locomotion—		
Weighing machines.......................per 100 kilos..	1. 60	1. 48
Machinery and apparatus for making sugar and brandy, per 100 kilos......................................	50	46
Agricultural machinery and tools..........per 100 kilos..	80	74
Steam motors, stationary.......................do....	3. 75	3. 47
Boilers—		
Of sheet iron ....per 100 kilos..	3. 00	2. 77
Tubular ....do....	3. 75	3. 47
Locomotives and traction engines ....per 100 kilos..	4. 50	4. 16
Turntables, trucks, and carts for transshipment, hydraulic cranes and columns....................per 100 kilos..	1. 50	1. 38
Sewing machines and detached parts..............do....	4. 00	3. 70
Velocipedes ....do....	4. 00	3. 70
Railway carriages of all kinds for passengers, and finished wooden parts for same.................per 100 kilos..	4. 80	4. 44
Vans, trucks, and cars of all kinds; miners' trolleys, and finished wooden parts for same.........per 100 kilos..	2. 10	1. 94
Tramway carriages of all kinds, and finished wooden parts for same............................per 100 kilos..	7. 60	7. 03
Carts and handcarts ....do....	3. 80	3. 51
Meat products :		
Meat in brine ....per 100 kilos..	3. 00	2. 77
Pork and lard, including bacon ....do ...	6. 30	5. 83
Jerked beef (tasajo) ....do....	3. 96	3. 66
Meat of all other kinds ....do....	3. 60	3. 33
Butter...... ....do....	4. 40	4. 07
Cereals :		
Wheat ....do....	1. 20	1. 11
Other ....do....	1. 20	1. 11
(Germinated or sterilized barley employed in the manufacture of beer shall be exempt from the provisional fiscal duty.)		
Flour of wheat..................................per 100 kilos..	1. 50	1. 38
Garden produce, fruits, etc. :		
Pulse, dried ....do	1. 30	1. 20
Garden produce and pulse, fresh........ ....do....	. 75	. 69
Fruits :		
Fresh ....do....	1. 00	. 92
Dried ....do....	1. 75	1. 62
Carob beans ; seeds not specially mentioned ..... .do....	. 20	. 18
Fodder and bran. ....do.	. 25	. 23

	Pesos.	U. S. equivalent.
Wood :		
Staves...............................per thousand..	2. 00	$1. 85
Ordinary, in boards, deals, rafters, beams, round, and timber for shipbuilding ....per cubic meter..	1. 00	. 92
Ordinary, planed or dovetailed, for boxes and flooring, broomsticks and cases, in which imported goods were packed ....per 100 kilos..	. 40	. 37
Fine, for cabinetmakers—		
In boards, deals, trunks, or logs .....:............do....	3. 00	2. 77
Sawed in veneers...........................do ...	4. 35	4. 02
Coopers' wares, in shooks, also hoops and headings ....do....	. 90	. 83
Cut, for making casks for sugar or molasses... ....do....	. 15	. 13
Latticework and fencing........ ....do....	1. 50	1. 38
Common furniture and manufactures of wood..........do....	2. 00	1. 85
Fine furniture and manufactures.....................do ...	12. 00	11. 11

Arms of war of all kinds, projectiles and ammunition, firearms and explosives (unless specially authorized), butter and animal greases, destined to alimentary purposes, manufactured with margarine or oleomargarine, objects offensive to morality, and artificial and adulterated wine are prohibited.

The free list comprises natural manures; trees, plants, and moss in a natural state; national products returned from foreign exhibitions; carriages, trained animals, portable theaters, panoramas, wax figures, and other similar objects for public entertainment imported temporarily; receptacles exported from Cuba with fruit, sugar, honey, and brandy and reimported empty; furniture (used) of persons coming to settle in the island; samples of felt, wall paper, and tissues (under certain conditions); samples of trimmings of no commercial value; specimens and collections of mineralogy, botany, zoology, small models for public museums, etc.; archæological and numismatical objects and works of fine art for museums, etc.; gold in bars, powder, or coined; also national silver or bronze coins, and travelers' effects.

ENTRANCE AND CLEARANCE OF VESSELS.

Every vessel shall, on arrival, be placed under military guard until discharged. Passengers without dutiable property can land at once.

Goods not declared on the manifest are subject to 25 per cent additional duty when discovered. If any articles named on the manifest are missing, the vessel shall pay $1 per ton measurement unless the deficiency is explained.

Within twenty-four hours after arrival of vessel the master must, under penalty for failure of $1 per ton, registry measurement, produce the proper manifest, with the proper marks, descriptions, etc., certified by the collector of the port of sailing, if the vessel is from the United States; if from a foreign port, certified by the United States consul or commercial agent; or if there be no such officer at the port, by the consul of any nation at peace with the United States. And the register of the vessel shall, upon arrival in Cuba, be deposited with the consul of the nation to which she belongs, if any there be, or with the commandant at the port, until the master shall have paid tonnage taxes and port charges.

No vessel can clear for another port until her cargo is landed or accounted for. All goods not duly entered for payment of duty within ten days after their arrival in port shall be landed and stored, the expense thereof to be charged to the goods. Before leaving a port the master shall deposit with the proper officer a manifest of the cargo. No clearance shall be granted to any port in Cuba not in possession or under control of the United States.

TONNAGE DUES.

On each entry of a vessel, except from a port in Cuba in possession of the United States, per net ton... $0. 20

On each entry from another port in Cuba in possession of the United States.... . 02

Vessels in ballast pay half the above-named duties.

Vessels belonging to the United States Government, vessels of neutral foreign governments not engaged in trade, vessels in distress, yachts belonging to an organized yacht club of the United States or neutral foreign nations are exempt from tonnage dues.

The tonnage of a vessel shall be the net or register tonnage expressed in her national certificate of register.

LANDING CHARGES.

The tax of $1 on each ton of merchandise imported or exported, hitherto imposed as a substitute for tonnage taxes, is abolished.

The present exemption of coal from this tax is continued.

The present export tax of 5 cents per gross ton on ore is abolished.

The harbor-improvement taxes at Santiago will continue to be levied as at present, as follows:

Each steamer entering $8.50
Each sailing vessel entering....... .... 4.25
Each ton of cargo landed from a steamer................................... .25
Each ton of cargo landed from a sailing vessel .... .125
Each ton of coal landed from a steamer................................... .125
Each ton of coal landed from a sailing vessel.......... .. .. .10

SHIPPING REGULATIONS.

The Bureau of Navigation of the United States Treasury, on the 15th of August, issued a circular stating that vessels may clear to ports in Cuba and Porto Rico, subject to the laws and regulations in force relating to clearances, except that vessels of the United States only will be cleared for the transportation of merchandise in the trade between the United States and Porto Rico. Trade with Cuba and Porto Rico has therefore been reopened, so far as the United States is concerned, by the order to grant clearances. The order leaves traffic between the United States and Cuba in foreign vessels undisturbed, but limits the export trade of the United States to Porto Rico to United States vessels; but foreign goods may be carried in foreign vessels, even though they touch at a United States port before going to Porto Rico.

POSTAL REGULATIONS.

The Postmaster-General of the United States issued an order July 21, 1898, modifying an order of the 26th of April, prohibiting the dispatching of any mail matter to Spain or her dependencies, so far as to permit postal communication between the United States and Santiago, Cuba. It is to be presumed that this order will be extended throughout the Island of Cuba, now that hostilities have been suspended. The mail sent to Santiago may contain mail matter of all classes allowable in the domestic mails of the United States, addressed for delivery at any place within the territory occupied by the United States forces in the vicinity of Santiago, and the mails sent from Santiago may contain the same classes of mail matter addressed for delivery in the

II. PORTO RICO.[*]

LOCATION, AREA, AND POPULATION.

The island of Porto Rico is situated at the entrance to the Gulf of Mexico, east of Haiti, from which it is separated by the Mona passage. Haiti lies between it and Cuba. Porto Rico is 95 miles long and 35 broad, with an area of about 3,600 square miles, or nearly three-fourths the size of the State of Connecticut (4,990 square miles), and considerably larger than that of the States of Delaware and Rhode Island, which aggregate 3,300 square miles. The island has always been noted for its mineral and agricultural wealth; hence the Spanish name, which, in English, means "rich harbor."

The population is about 814,000, of which over 300,000 are negroes, 150,000 natives of Spain, and about 15,000 French, German, English, etc.

The island of Vieque, situated 13 miles east of Porto Rico, is 21 miles long and 6 miles wide. Its land is very fertile and adapted to the cultivation of almost all the fruits and vegetables that grow in the West Indies. Cattle are raised and sugar cultivated. It has a population of some 6,000. The town, Isabel Segunda, is on the north, and the port is unsafe in times of northerly wind, like all the anchorages on that side; the few ports on the south are better, the best being Punta Arenas. Not long ago there were two importing and exporting houses on the island of Vieque, but on account of the long period of drought and the high duties on foreign-imported goods, trade has decreased to local consumption only. All supplies are brought from San Juan, the majority being of American origin.

TOPOGRAPHY AND CLIMATE.

Physically, Porto Rico is a continuation of the emerged lands of Haiti. It is very mountainous, the altitudes ranging from 1,500 to 3,600 feet, and among the rocks coralligenous limestones

[*]Compiled from Volume II, Commercial Directory of the American Republics; Review of the World's Commerce, 1896–97; Advance Sheets of Consular Reports, No. 117; publications of the Bureau of Statistics, Treasury Department; information obtained from the War and Treasury Departments of the United States, and other sources.

predominate. All lands exposed to the northeast trade winds have abundant rains. The mean temperature at the city of San Juan is 80.7° F. In January and February it is 76.5°, and in July and August, 83.2°. The island is known as the most healthful of the Antilles. There are no reptiles and no wild animals, except rats, which are numerous. The hills are covered with tropical forests and the lands are very productive. The streams are numerous and some of them are navigable to the foothills.

AGRICULTURAL AND MINERAL RESOURCES.

The most flourishing plantations of Porto Rico are situated on the littoral plains and in the valleys of rivers which, says Longman's Gazetteer, are "intensely cultivated." The principal products are sugar, molasses, coffee, tobacco; then maize, rice, cotton, tobacco, hides, dyewoods, timber, and rice. Coffee is produced to the extent of over 16,000 tons per annum, and the annual sugar production averages 67,000 tons.

The forests abound in mahogany, cedar, ebony, dyewoods, and a great variety of medicinal and industrial plants. All kinds of tropical fruits are found. An average of 190,000,000 bananas, 6,500,000 oranges, 2,500,000 cocoanuts, and 7,000,000 pounds of tobacco is produced annually.

Sugar cane is cultivated on 61,000 acres, the districts in which it is produced on the largest scale being Ponce, 6,500 acres; Juan Diaz, 4,000 acres; Vieques, 3,000; Arecibo, 3,000; San German, 2,500. Coffee is cultivated on about 122,000 acres, two-thirds of the whole being in the following districts: Utuado, Las Marias, Adjuntas, Maricao, Ponce, Lares, Mayaguez, Yauco, San Sebastian, Ciales, Barros, and Juan Diaz. Ponce, Mayaguez, and Arecibo are the provinces which produce more largely than any others in the island. It is estimated that every acre of coffee plantations averages in production 330 pounds. Tobacco is cultivated on over 2,000 acres, and over 1,100,000 acres are devoted to pastures. As these figures change from year to year, they can be given only approximately. The total quantity of "declared lands" in 1894 amounted to 3,171 square miles, and as the total extent of the Island of Porto Rico is some 3,668 square miles, the difference between the rural property and the total area is 497 square miles, which are taken up by the towns, roads, rivers, bays, etc.

The sugar industry, until within the past few years, has been the most important, but, owing to the excessive land tax assessed by the Spanish officials and the growing use of beet sugar, it has in later years suffered a marked decline. Then, too, the mills used are equipped with machinery of an obsolete character. All the natural conditions—soil, climate, and labor—are favorable to the culture of this product, and it will no doubt now revive and flourish to an extent hitherto unknown.

Coffee is also a staple product. The greater part of it was formerly shipped to New York, where it commanded a good price. Much of the coffee now produced is grown by planters of small capital, who make use of the wild and waste lands of the hillsides to grow the berry. They prefer to cultivate coffee on account of the ease with which it can be produced, requiring but little expenditure as compared with the manufacture of sugar and molasses.

Tobacco, which ranks second in quality to that of Cuba, can be produced in great quantities, but the natives are generally careless in guarding against destructive insects and in drying and sorting the leaves. A considerable quantity, both in the form of leaf and manufactured cigars, is exported each year to the United States, England, France, Cuba, and Spain. Three qualities are produced: "Capa," which is the leaf of first quality, used for wrappers; "tripa," also a wrapper of medium grade; and "beliche," or ordinary leaf. Tobacco culture is capable of enormous development here under favorable circumstances.

A small quantity of cocoa is produced each year. Maize is grown on considerable areas only at times when high prices promise to prevail. Some cotton is also produced. Grass grows luxuriantly and affords pasturage for numerous herds of cattle, nearly all of which are exported. The hides of those consumed on the island are sent to other countries.

The mineral resources are not very extensive. Gold is found in limited quantities. Some copper, lead, iron, and coal are obtained. Lignite and yellow amber are found at Utuado and Moca. There are undeveloped resources of marble, limestone, and other building stone. The salt works at Guanica, Salinas, and Cape Rojo

are under governmental control.   Hot springs and mineral waters
are found at Coame, Juan Diaz, San Sebastian, San Lorenzo, and
Ponce.   The former is the most noted.

LAND AND MINING LAWS.

There is no public land in the island of Porto Rico: therefore
colonization must be undertaken there, as in Cuba, by private
enterprise.   The population of Porto Rico is very dense, and all
the land has been taken.   The royal ordinance of colonization
and the " Ley de Extranjeria " (statute on aliens) do not grant concessions of land or offer any material inducement to immigration.
Cuba and Porto Rico have not, therefore, any law tending to
encourage foreign immigration, as is the case in most of the American countries; and, although foreigners are welcomed and their
rights protected by law, no especial privileges are granted for settlement in those islands.   The mining law in force in Porto
Rico is the same as that of Cuba.   After the mineral is found,
titles may be obtained by applying to the civil government where
the mine is located.   In case the mine is situated on private land,
forcible expropriation may be obtained, the corresponding indemnity having been paid.

MANUFACTURES.

But little manufacturing is carried on.   The Standard Oil
Company has a small refinery across the bay from San Juan, at
which crude petroleum brought from the United States is rectified.
Sugar making is the chief industry.   At San Juan, matches,
ice, soap, and a cheap variety of traveling cases are manufactured;
there are also tanneries and foundries in the island.

POLITICAL DIVISIONS AND GOVERNMENT.

The island is divided into seven districts, and under Spanish
sovereignty, its affairs were administered by a Captain-General,
who was the civil as well as the military executive, appointed by
the Crown, with representation in the Spanish Cortes or Parliament.   In 1897, through a royal decree, the island was granted
autonomous government, with a colonial parliament, the executive
power being vested in a Governor-General, with department secretaries.   Under the agreement with Spain for the conclusion of

peace, Porto Rico is ceded to the United States, and, for the present, is governed by the military commanders under the instructions of the United States War Department.

CITIES, TOWNS, AND HARBORS.

Harbors are numerous along the coast of Porto Rico, but they are mostly unprotected from the trade winds on the northern side or filled with sand on the western side. Nearly the whole of the north coast is lined with navigable lagoons, some of which are nearly 10 miles in length. Of the 21 rivers, some are quite small, but there are several each of which is navigable for 5 or 6 miles from its mouth. A number of the bays and creeks are deep enough for vessels of considerable burden, but the north coast is subject to tremendous ground seas, which beat against the cliffs with great violence. The exporting ports are Mayaguez (San German) and Aguadilla on the west, and Guanica, Guayanilla, and Puerto Ponce on the south. The eastern part of the island is, commercially, less important. The chief cities and towns are:

1. San Juan, the capital of the island, is situated on a long and narrow island, separated from the main island at one end by a shallow arm of the sea, over which is a bridge connecting it with the mainland, which runs out at this point in a long sand spit, some 9 miles in length, apparently to meet the smaller island; at the other end, the island ends in a rugged bluff or promontory, some hundred feet high and three-fourths of a mile distant from the main island. This promontory is crowned by Morro Castle, the principal fortification of the town. After rounding the bluff, one finds a broad and beautiful bay, landlocked and with a good depth of water, which is being increased by dredging. It is by far the best harbor in Porto Rico, and probably as good a one as can be found in the West Indies.

San Juan is a perfect specimen of a walled town, with portcullis, moat, gates, and battlements. Built over two hundred and fifty years ago, it is still in good condition and repair. The walls are picturesque and represent a stupendous work and cost in themselves. Inside the walls, the city is laid off in regular squares, six parallel streets running in the direction of the length of the island and seven at right angles. There is no running water in the town.

The entire population depends upon rain water, caught upon the flat roofs of the buildings and conducted to the cistern, which occupies the greater part of the inner courtyard that is an essential part of Spanish houses the world over, but that here, on account of the crowded conditions, is very small. There is no sewerage, except for surface water and sinks, while vaults are in every house and occupy whatever remaining space there may be in the patios not taken up by the cisterns. The risk of contaminating the water is very great, and in dry seasons the supply is entirely exhausted. Epidemics are frequent, and the town is alive with vermin, fleas, cockroaches, mosquitoes, and dogs. The streets are wider than in the older part of Havana, and will admit two carriages abreast. The sidewalks are narrow, and in places will accommodate but one person. The pavements are of a composition manufactured in England from slag, pleasant and even, and durable when no heavy strain is brought to bear upon them, but easily broken and unfit for heavy traffic. The streets are swept once a day by hand and are kept very clean. With proper sanitary conditions, the town would doubtless be healthful. Population within the walls, about 20,000.

Besides the town within the walls, there are small portions just outside, called the Marina and Porta de Tierra, containing 2,000 or 3,000 inhabitants each. There are also two suburbs—one, San Turce, approached by the only road leading out of the city, and the other, Cataño, across the bay, reached by ferry. The Marina and the two suburbs are situated on sandy points or spits, and the latter are surrounded by mangrove swamps. The entire population of the city and suburbs, according to the census of 1887, was 27,000. It is now estimated at 30,000. One-half of the population consists of negroes and mixed races. There is but little manufacturing, and that is of small importance.

2. The city of Ponce is situated on the south coast of the island, on a plain, about 2 miles from the seaboard and 70 miles from San Juan. It is regularly built—the central part almost exclusively of brick houses and the suburbs of wood. It is the residence of the military commander and the seat of an official chamber of commerce. There is an appellate criminal court, besides other courts; two churches—one Protestant, said to be the only one in the Spanish West Indies—two hospitals

besides the military hospitals, a home of refuge for the old and poor, a perfectly equipped fire department, a bank, a theater, three first-class hotels, and gas works. The city has an ice machine, and there are 115 vehicles for public conveyance. The inhabitants, who number about 15,000, are principally occupied in mercantile pursuits; but carpenters, bricklayers, joiners, tailors, shoemakers, and barbers find good employment. The department of Ponce counts about 40,000 inhabitants. The chief occupations of the people are the cultivation of sugar, cocoa, tobacco, and oranges, and the breeding of cattle. Commercially, Ponce is the second city of importance on the island. A fine road leads to the port (Playa), where all the import and export trade is transacted. Playa has about 5,000 inhabitants, and here are situated the custom-house, the office of the captain of the port, and all the consular offices. The port is spacious and will hold vessels of 25 feet draft. The climate, on account of the sea breezes during the day and land breezes at night, is not oppressive, though warm; and as water for all purposes, including the fire department, is amply supplied by an aqueduct, it may be said that the city of Ponce is perhaps the healthiest place in the whole island.

3. Mayaguez, the third city in importance of the island, is situated in the west part, 102 miles from San Juan, facing what is generally known as the "Mona Channel." Of industries, there is little to be said, except that there are three manufactories of chocolate, which is for local consumption. Sugar, coffee, oranges, pineapples, and cocoanuts are exported largely, all except coffee principally to the United States. Of sugar, the muscovado goes to the United States and the centrifugal to Spain. Mayaguez is the second port for coffee, the average annual export being 170,000 hundredweight. The quality is of the best, ranging in price with Java and other first-rate brands. The lower grades are sent to Cuba. About 50,000 bags of flour are imported into this port every year from the United States, out of the 180,000 bags that are consumed in the whole island. The population is nearly 20,000, the majority white. The climate is excellent, the temperature never exceeding 90° F. The city is connected by tram with the neighboring town of Aguadilla, and a railroad is being constructed to Lares, one of the large interior towns.

exported, and occasionally tortoise shell.. The climate is temperate and healthy.

7. Naguabo (on the east side) is a small town of only about 2,000 inhabitants, and in the harbor there is another smaller place called Playa de Naguabo, or Ucares, with about 1,500. The capital of the department, Humacao, is 9 miles from Naguabo and has 4,000 inhabitants, the district comprising more than 15,000.

8. Arroyo, in the district of Guayama (southeast portion), is a small seaport of about 1,200 inhabitants. The annual exports to the United States average 7,000 to 10,000 heads of sugar, 2,000 to 5,000 casks of molasses, and 50 to 150 casks and barrels of bay rum.

COMMERCE OF PORTO RICO.

The Estadística General del Comercio Exterior, Porto Rico, 1897, gives the following figures (the latest published) in regard to the trade of the island in 1895:

Imports of principal articles.

Articles.	Value.*	Articles.	Value.*
Coal	$119, 403	Flour	$982, 222
Iron	224, 206	Vegetables	192, 918
Soap	238, 525	Olive oil	327, 801
Meat and lard	1, 223, 104	Wine	305, 656
Jerked beef	133, 616	Cheese	324, 137
Fish	1, 591, 418	Other provisions	171, 322
Rice	2, 180, 004	Tobacco (manufactured)	663, 464

* United States currency.

Exports of principal articles.

Articles.	Value.*	Articles.	Value.*
Coffee	$8, 789, 788	Sugar	$3, 747, 891
Tobacco	646, 556	Honey	517, 746

* United States currency.

The value of the total imports was $16,155,056, against $18,316,971 for the preceding year. The exports were valued at $14,629,494, against $16,015,665 in 1894. The principal increases in imports, as compared with the preceding year, were

in meats, fish, olive oil, and tobacco. Decreases were noted in
flour, vegetables, and wine. The exportation of coffee diminished, and that of sugar and honey increased.

The trade of the United States with Porto Rico during the
last seven years, as given by United States Treasury figures, was:

Description.	1891.	1892.	1893.	1894.	1895.	1896.	1897.
Imports:							
Free..........	$1, 856, 955	$3, 236, 337	$3, 994, 673	$3, 126, 895	$375, 864	$48, 608	$101, 711
Dutiable	1, 307, 155	11, 670	13, 950	8, 739	1, 131, 148	2, 248, 045	2, 079, 313
Total........	3, 164, 110	3, 248, 007	4, 008, 623	3, 135, 634	1, 506, 512	2, 296, 653	2, 181, 024
Exports:							
Domestic......	2, 112, 334	2, 808, 631	2, 502, 788	2, 705, 646	1, 820, 203	2, 080, 400	1, 964, 850
Foreign.......	42, 900	47, 372	7, 819	14, 862	13, 341	21, 694	24, 038
Total........	2, 155, 234	2, 856, 003	2, 510, 607	2, 720, 508	1, 833, 544	2, 102, 094	1, 988, 888

The commerce of Spain with Porto Rico from 1891 to 1896
was:

Description.	1891.	1892.	1893.	1894.	1895.	1896.
Imports from Porto Rico...	$3, 260, 650	$4,428, 891	$4, 108, 654	$4, 164, 964	$5, 824, 694	$5, 423, 760
Exports to Porto Rico	3, 305, 243	3, 929, 186	4, 653, 023	5, 535, 027	8, 572, 549	7, 328, 880

The figures from 1891 to 1895 are taken from Spain's Foreign
Trade, FRANK H. HITCHCOCK, Department of Agriculture, 1898.
The figures for 1896 are from a British Foreign Office report
(Annual Series, No. 2065, 1898).

The trade of Porto Rico with other countries of importance
in 1895 (according to the Estadística General del Comercio
Exterior) was:

Country.	Imports.	Exports.
Cuba........	$808, 283	$3, 610, 936
England...........	1, 765, 574	1, 144, 555
France...	251, 984	1, 376, 087
Germany ......·.....................................	1, 368, 595	1, 181, 396
Italy	19, 619	589, 045
Holland....................................·.....	325, 301	3, 246
Denmark..	26, 565	236, 418
British West Indies	1, 709, 117	521, 649
Danish West Indies	600	40, 434
French West Indies	55	62, 927

The British consul says that the principal exports in 1896 were:

Articles.	Quantity.	Articles.	Quantity.
Sugar ....tons..	54, 205	Timber..............tons..	30
Coffee ....do...	26, 655	Molasses.............do...	14, 740
Hides................do...	169	Tobacco ....do...	1, 039
Cattle...............head..	3, 178		

Owing to the troubled state of affairs in Cuba, continues the report, prices for tobacco have increased enormously in Porto Rico. A large amount has been planted, and the crop promises well.

TRANSPORTATION FACILITIES, TELEGRAPHS, AND TELEPHONES.

One of the greatest drawbacks to this really wonderful island has been the lack of adequate transportation facilities. All the roads, except the main government road, are of the most primitive sort and are quite impassable during the rainy seasons. The "consumption tax" on liquors and petroleum has been ceded to the municipalities, the last few years, to be used in repairing the highways. According to the latest available reports, the total length of finished railroads is about 136 miles, with 170 miles under construction. Lines connect San Juan and Camuy, Aguadilla and Mayaguez, Yauco and Ponce, Carolina and San Juan, San Juan and Rio Pedras, and San Juan and Catana. "The New York Commercial Advertiser," August 13, 1898, gives a full account of the railroads, written by a resident, as follows:

Mail, telegraph, and railroad communications are of such a kind that should they disappear entirely the people could do just as well without them. It is only since the year 1878 that railroads have been known in Porto Rico, and since then the country has advanced very little. There are only three railroad lines in the whole island, covering in all 136 miles. The first one was opened in 1878, the East Railroad Line, from San Juan to Rio Piedras, a distance of 6¼ miles, covered in fifty-five minutes, making several stops of one or two minutes. The fare is 30 cents from San Juan to Rio Piedras, or 5 cents per mile, and between San Juan or Rio Piedras and the intermediate stations the rate is about the same. This is the best managed line in the island, and runs 12 trains daily, with comfortable and quite elegant cars, although it may be noticed that the speed is limited.

The West Railroad Line, opened in 1881, from San Juan to Catano, crosses the harbor by ferryboat, and thence to Bayamon by a so-called train. This line is the worst thing imaginable, and would furnish plenty of material for a book on railroad mismanagement. Trains are run every two and three hours, and the

Juan (printed in Special Consular Reports, Highways of Commerce), there are about 150 miles of good road on the island. Elsewhere transportation is effected on horseback. A British consular report (No. 1917, 1897) says that the telephone systems of San Juan, Ponce, and Mayaguez have recently been contracted for by local syndicates. In Ponce, a United States company obtained the contract for the material. There are 100 stations already connected, and it is expected that 200 more will be in operation shortly. There have been recent harbor improvements in San Juan.

STEAMSHIP SERVICE TO PORTO RICO.

The New York "Journal of Commerce," of August 17, 1898, speaking of clearances for Cuba, says:

There is less activity among shippers to Porto Rican markets, though it is expected that a good business will soon be apparent. The action of the Government in placing commerce with the island on virtually a coastwise basis, especially in so far as-navigation laws are concerned, appears to meet with very general favor. The New York and Porto Rico Steamship Company, which is the only one operating a steamer service for freight to the island, has three steamers under the American flag, and consequently will be able to operate under the new arrangement as heretofore.

The same newspaper said in its issue of August 15:

Plans are also being made for resuming regular trade with the island of Porto Rico. MILLER, BULL & KNOWLTON, it will be recalled, have already sent out the steamer *Silvia* to Ponce, and it was stated at the office on Saturday that a steamer would be dispatched this week to call at all ports. The company now has a steel steamer building at Bath, Me., which will be ready in a few weeks, and will, it is understood, be placed on the Porto Rico service. This is the first steel tramp steamer ever built in this country. In addition, it is announced that the company has accepted plans for two new steel passenger and freight steamships which are to ply between this city and Porto Rico. The contracts for the construction of the ships are to be awarded this week. These vessels are to be considerably larger than any of the company's old ships. They will also develop greater speed, and will be fitted with first-class passenger accommodations.

The Red D Line has announced that until further notice its steamers will call at Ponce or San Juan on their way to Venezuela. This stop will be to land and receive passengers only, the line not wishing to delay its steamers for freight.

The advertisement of the Red D Line says its steamships sailing for Venezuela on the following dates will call at Porto Rico to land mails and passsengers: Steamship *Abydos*, Wednesday,

August 24; steamship *Philadelphia*, Thursday, September 8. BOULTON, BLISS & DALLETT, 135 Front street, are general managers.

The New York and Porto Rico Steamship Company announces sailings for principal ports in Porto Rico as follows: American steamer *Arkadia*, Saturday, August 27; American steamer *Winifred*, Thursday, September 8. For passenger accommodations and freight apply to MILLER, BULL & KNOWLTON, agents, 130–132 Pearl street.

CUSTOMS TARIFF AND SHIPPING REGULATIONS.

The customs tariff for Porto Rico was promulgated by the War Department of the United States on the 19th of August. The rates applied are those of the minimum tariff formerly imposed by Spain. Under Spanish sovereignty, United States products entering Porto Rico paid the maximum rates. They are now on an equal footing with those of other nations.

The tonnage and landing charges are practically the same as provided in the Cuban regulations, but speaking generally the customs duties are lower. The Spanish tax of 50 cents on each ton of merchandise landed at San Juan and Mayaguez for harbor improvements is continued. The following articles are admitted free:

Trees, plants, and moss in a natural or fresh state.

Gold and silver ores.

Samples of felt, painted paper, and tissues, when they comply with specified conditions.

Samples of trimmings in small pieces of no commercial value or possible application.

Gold, silver, and platinum, in broken-up jewelry or table services, bars, sheets, coins, pieces, dust, and scrap.

Also the following under conditions:

Natural manures and guano.

National products returning from foreign exhibits, on presentation of the bill of lading or certificate proving their exportation from the island and of satisfactory evidence attesting that such products have been presented and have been shipped to their point of departure.

Wearing apparel, toilet objects, and articles for personal use, bed and table linen, books, portable tools and instruments, theatrical costumes, jewels, and table services bearing evident signs of having been used, imported by travelers in their luggage in quantities proportioned to their class, profession, and position.

When travelers do not bring their baggage with them, the clearing of the same may be made by the conductor or persons authorized for the purpose, provided that they prove to the satisfaction of the customs officers that the effects are destined for private use.

Works of fine art acquired by the Government, academies, or other official corporations, and destined for museums, galleries, or art schools, when due proof is given as to their destination.

Archæological and numismatical objects for public museums, academies, and scientific and artistic corporations on proof of their destination.

Specimens and collections of mineralogy and botany, and small models for public museums, schools, academies, and scientific and artistic corporations, on proof of their destination.

Receptacles which have been shipped from the island with fruit, sugar, molasses, and spirits, and which are reimported empty, including receptacles known as "pipotes," of galvanized iron, intended for the exportation of alcohol.

Carriages, trained animals, portable theaters, panoramas, wax figures, and other similar objects for public entertainment, imported temporarily, provided bond be given.

Used furniture of persons coming to settle in the island.

Foreign articles coming to exhibitions held in the island.

Submarine telegraph cables.

Pumps intended exclusively for the salvage of vessels.

Parts of machinery, pieces of metal, and wood imported for the repair of foreign and national vessels which have entered ports in the island through stress of weather.

DUTIES ON FOOD ARTICLES.

On alimentary substances, the customs tariffs are as follows, taking the peso at the same valuation as that of Cuba—92.6 cents:

	Pesos.	U. S. currency.
Live and dead poultry and small game..per kilo (2.2046 lbs.), net..	0. 05	$0. 04
Meat in brine....... ....per 100 kilos, net..	2. 55	2. 36
Pork and lard ....do....	4. 50	4. 16
Other kinds of meat ....do.. .	3. 50	3. 25
Jerked beef..do....	2. 35	2. 17
Butter ....do....	6. 75	6. 25
Salt cod and stockfish, also fish fresh, salted, smoked, or marinated, including the weight of the salt or brine....per 100 kilos, gross..	. 90	. 83
Oysters of all kinds, and shellfish, fresh or dried ....do....	1. 00	. 92
Fish and shellfish in oil or preserved in any way in tins, including the weight of the immediate receptacles.....per 100 kilos, gross..	11. 50	10. 64
Rice in the husk............................ ....do....	1. 95	1. 80
Rice without the husk ....do....	2. 70	2. 50
Wheat..do....	3. 15	2. 91
Wheat flour ....do....	4. 00	3. 70
Other cereals (with the exception of millet)................do....	3. 15	2. 91
Flour of same ....do....	4. 00	3. 70
Millet...do....	3. 15	2. 91
Flour of millet...do....	4. 00	3. 70
Pulse, dried..................................... ......do....	3. 00	2. 91

	Pesos.	U. S. currency.
Pulse and garden produce, pickled or preserved in vacuo, mushrooms, etc., including the weight of immediate receptacles, per 100 kilos	13. 00	$12. 03
Olive oil in either earthen jars or tins.........per 100 kilos, gross..	3. 45	3. 09
Olive oil in bottles, including the weight of the bottles. per 100 kilos..	5. 25	4. 86
Alcohol and brandy.......................hectol (26.418 galls.)..	25. 00	23. 15
Liquors, cognac, and other compound spirits:		
In casks or demijohns ....do....	9. 00	8. 33
In bottles or flasks.....................................do....	14. 00	12. 96
Beer and natural or artificial cider in casks................ ......do....	5. 50	5. 09
Beer and natural or artificial cider in bottles or flasks........do....	7. 75	7. 17
Sparkling wines..............................litet (1.0567 qts.)..	. 80	. 74
Wine from the grape, red or white, dessert or liqueur wines, in casks or similar receptacles ....per liter..	. 15	. 13
Wine from the grape, red or white, dessert or liqueur wines, in bottles, per liter..	. 40	. 37
Other wines in bottles ....per liter..	10. 00	9. 26

In addition to the customs duties on beverages, the following Spanish consumption tax is retained:

	Pesos.	U. S. currency.
Alcohol and commercial spirits, of potato, grain, etc..per hectoliter..	0. 20	$0. 18
Cognac, brandy, rum, etc ....do....	. 20	. 18
Beer and porter ....do....	. 07	. 06
Common wines, red or white ....do....	. 015	. 013
Wines, fine, from foreign countries..... ....do....	. 10	. 09

Wines imported in bottles or flasks pay a surtax of 50 per cent.

In consideration of the nature of the goods and the danger, through fire, which might result from their being deposited on the wharfs to the prejudice of private persons and of the State, a wharf and unloading due of 25 centavos per kilogram has been imposed on matches.

Duties on other articles of importance imported from the United States are—

	Pesos.	U. S. currency.
Coal and coke ....per 1,000 kilos (2,204.6 lbs.)..	0. 33	$0. 30
Benzine, gasoline, petroleum, and other refined mineral oils, per 100 kilos.................................	3. 10	2. 87
Staves...per 1,000..	2. 30	2. 12
Ordinary wood in boards, deals, rafters, beams, and rounded poles; timber for shipbuilding ....per cubic meter..	1. 00	. 92
Weighing machines..............................per 100 kilos..	2. 50	2. 31
Weighing machines for sugar cane (platforms) ....do....	. 65	. 60
Machinery and apparatus for making sugar or rum..........do....	. 65	. 60
Motors of all kinds, with or without boilers, and boilers imported separately.....................................per 100 kilos..	2. 50	2. 31
Locomotives, traction and marine engines, with boilers, or such boilers imported separately ....per 100 kilos..	3. 00	2. 77

EXPORT DUTIES AND PROHIBITED ARTICLES.

The following are the export tariffs for the island of Porto Rico:

	Pesos.	U. S. currency.
Coffee.................................... per 100 kilograms.	1. 00	$0. 92
Wood..do....	. 15	. 13
Tobacco ....do....	. 22	. 20

The following articles are prohibited importation: Arms, projectiles, ammunition, and dynamite, except by special authorization of the proper military authorities of the island; fecules for industrial use; molasses; butter and animal greases intended for alimentary purposes, composed or adulterated with margarine or oleomargarine; paintings, figures, and all other objects offensive to morality; artificial wines, not medicinal, and adulterated wines.

SHIPPING REGULATIONS.

The navigation rules applying to Porto Rico are stated in the following order of the United States Commissioner of Navigation:

CLEARANCE OF VESSELS TO CUBA AND PORTO RICO.

TREASURY DEPARTMENT, BUREAU OF NAVIGATION.
Washington, D. C., August 15, 1898.

To collectors of customs and others:

Vessels may clear to ports in Cuba and Porto Rico, subject to the laws and regulations in force relating to clearances, except that vessels of the United States only will be cleared for the transportation of merchandise in the trade between the United States and Porto Rico.

Approved: T. B. SANDERS,
    L. J. GAGE, *Secretary.*   *Acting Commissioner.*

While only United States vessels may be cleared for Porto Rico, it is understood that foreign vessels touching at United States ports will be permitted to proceed to Porto Rico.

POSTAL RATES.

The following order of the Postmaster-General of the United States establishes regulations which will doubtless apply to the whole of the island of Porto Rico:

POST-OFFICE DEPARTMENT,
Washington, D. C., August 2, 1898.

ORDER NO. 319.

In conformity with the order of the President of the 21st ultimo, my order (No. 161) of the 26th of April last, prohibiting the dispatch of any mail matter to Spain or her dependencies, is modified so far as to permit postal communication between the United States and Ponce, Porto Rico.

The mails sent to Ponce may contain mail matter of all classes allowable in the domestic mails of the United States, addressed for delivery at any place within the territory occupied by the United States forces in the vicinity of Ponce; and the mails sent from Ponce may contain the same classes of mail matter addressed for delivery in the United States; all articles included in said mails being subject to inspection by the proper military or naval authorities.

The postage rates applicable to articles originating in or destined for the United States in the mails in question are fixed as follows, viz:

First-class matter, 5 cents per half ounce.

Postal cards, single, 2 cents; double, 4 cents.

Second and third class matter, 1 cent for each two ounces.

Fourth-class matter, 1 cent for each ounce.

Registration fee, 8 cents.

Only United States postage stamps will be valid for the prepayment of postage. Prepayment shall not be required, but if postage is not prepaid in full, double the amount of the deficient postage at the above rates shall be collected on delivery to addresses in the United States or Porto Rico.

To articles originating in or destined for countries beyond the United States, the Postal-Union rates and conditions shall apply.

The mails for Ponce must be addressed to the United States postal agent at Ponce, and the delivery of any article may be withheld if deemed necessary by the proper military or naval authorities.

Compensation to merchant vessels for the sea conveyance of mails from Ponce shall be made at the rates heretofore paid to merchant vessels for conveying mails from the United States to Ponce.

CHARLES EMORY SMITH,
Postmaster-General.

BANKING AND CURRENCY, WEIGHTS AND MEASURES.

There is a bank at San Juan, the capital, with branches at the principal points in the islands. Mexican money was current until the end of 1895, when a 5-peseta piece was coined and put in circulation.

The metric system of weights and measures is in use in Porto Rico. (See Weights and Measures, under Cuba.)

III. HAWAIIAN ISLANDS.

The resolution annexing the Hawaiian Islands to the United States is as follows:

[PUBLIC RESOLUTION—No. 51.]

JOINT RESOLUTION To provide for annexing the Hawaiian Islands to the United States.

Whereas the Government of the Republic of Hawaii having, in due form, signified its consent, in the manner provided by its constitution, to cede absolutely and without reserve to the United States of America all rights of sovereignty of whatsoever kind in and over the Hawaiian Islands and their dependencies, and also to cede and transfer to the United States the absolute fee and ownership of all public, Government, or Crown lands, public buildings or edifices, ports, harbors, military equipment, and all other public property of every kind and description belonging to the Government of the Hawaiian Islands, together with every right and appurtenance thereto appertaining: Therefore,

Resolved by the Senate and House of Representatives of the United States of America in Congress assembled, That said cession is accepted, ratified, and confirmed, and that the said Hawaiian Islands and their dependencies be, and they are hereby, annexed as a part of the territory of the United States and are subject to the sovereign dominion thereof, and that all and singular the property and rights hereinbefore mentioned are vested in the United States of America.

The existing laws of the United States relative to public lands shall not apply to such lands in the Hawaiian Islands; but the Congress of the United States shall enact special laws for their management and disposition: *Provided,* That all revenue from or proceeds of the same, except as regards such part thereof as may be used or occupied for the civil, military, or naval purposes of the United States, or may be assigned for the use of the local government, shall be used solely for the benefit of the inhabitants of the Hawaiian Islands for educational and other public purposes.

Until Congress shall provide for the government of such islands all the civil, judicial, and military powers exercised by the officers of the existing government in said islands shall be vested in such person or persons and shall be exercised in such manner as the President of the United States shall direct; and the President shall have power to remove said officers and fill the vacancies so occasioned.

The existing treaties of the Hawaiian Islands with foreign nations shall forthwith cease and determine, being replaced by such treaties as may exist, or as may be hereafter concluded, between the United States and such foreign nations. The municipal legislation of the Hawaiian Islands, not enacted for the fulfillment of the treaties so extinguished, and not inconsistent with this joint resolution nor contrary to the Constitution of the United States nor to any existing treaty of the United States, shall remain in force until the Congress of the United States shall otherwise determine.

Until legislation shall be enacted extending the United States customs laws and regulations to the Hawaiian Islands the existing customs relations of the Hawaiian Islands with the United States and other countries shall remain unchanged.

The public debt of the Republic of Hawaii, lawfully existing at the date of the passage of this joint resolution, including the amounts due to depositors in the Hawaiian Postal Savings Bank, is hereby assumed by the Government of the United States; but the liability of the United States in this regard shall in no case exceed four million dollars. So long, however, as the existing Government and the present commercial relations of the Hawaiian Islands are continued as hereinbefore provided said Government shall continue to pay the interest on said debt.

There shall be no further immigration of Chinese into the Hawaiian Islands, except upon such conditions as are now or may hereafter be allowed by the laws of the United States; and no Chinese, by reason of anything herein contained, shall be allowed to enter the United States from the Hawaiian Islands.

The President shall appoint five commissioners, at least two of whom shall be residents of the Hawaiian Islands, who shall, as soon as reasonably practicable, recommend to Congress such legislation concerning the Hawaiian Islands as they shall deem necessary or proper.

SEC. 2. That the commissioners hereinbefore provided for shall be appointed by the President, by and with the advice and consent of the Senate.

SEC. 3. That the sum of one hundred thousand dollars, or so much thereof as may be necessary, is hereby appropriated, out of any money in the Treasury not otherwise appropriated, and to be immediately available, to be expended at the discretion of the President of the United States of America, for the purpose of carrying this joint resolution into effect.

Approved, July 7, 1898.

Under section 2, the President appointed as commissioners Hon. SHELBY M. CULLOM, Hon. JOHN T. MORGAN, and Hon. ROBERT R. HITT, representing the United States; President SANFORD B. DOLE and Hon. WALTER F. FREAR, representing Hawaii. DANIEL A. RAY is the executive and disbursing officer. The commission is now in the Hawaiian Islands, investigating conditions there preparatory to making a report.

The Bureau of the American Republics in August, 1897, published a handbook of Hawaii, containing full information about the islands, their government, resources, commerce, etc., up to that date, together with a reliable map, and also included them in Volume I of the "Commercial Directory of the American Republics," issued in November, 1897. The Directory gives full lists of the business houses in the islands.

LOCATION: COMMERCIAL AND NAVAL IMPORTANCE.

The Hawaiian Islands, formerly known as the Sandwich Islands, are situated in the North Pacific Ocean, and lie between longitude 154° 40' and 160° 30' west from Greenwich, and latitude 22° 16' and 18° 55' north. They are thus on the very edge of the Tropics, but their position in mid ocean and the prevalence of the northeast trade winds give them a climate of perpetual summer without enervating heat. The group occupies a central position in the North Pacific, 2,089 nautical miles southwest of San Francisco: 4,640 from Panama; 3,800 from Auckland, New Zealand; 4,950 from Hongkong, and 3,440 from Yokohama. Its location gives it great importance from a military as well as from a commercial point of view.

Broadly speaking, Hawaii may be said to lie about one-third of the distance on the accustomed routes from San Francisco to Japanese and Chinese ports; from San Francisco to Australia; from ports of British Columbia to Australia and British India, and about halfway from the Isthmus of Panama to Yokohama and Hongkong. The construction of a ship canal across the isthmus would extend this geographical relation to the ports of the Gulf of Mexico and of the Atlantic Seaboard of North and South America. A glance at the map will at once make clear the fact that no other point in the North Pacific has such a dominating relation to the trade between America and Asia, as a place of call and depot of supplies for vessels.

From a naval standpoint, Hawaii is the great strategic base of the Pacific. Under the present conditions of naval warfare, created by the use of steam as a motive power, Hawaii would secure to the maritime nation possessing it an immense advantage as a depot for the supply of coal. Modern battle ships, depending absolutely upon coal, would be enabled to avail themselves of their full capacity of speed and energy only by having some halfway station in the Pacific where they could replenish their stores of fuel and refit. A battle ship or cruiser starting from an Asiatic or Australian port, with the view of operating along the coast of either North America or South America, would be unable to act effectively for any length of time at the end of so long a voyage unless

Bull. No. 2——4

she were able to refill her bunkers at some point on the way. On the other hand, the United States, possessing Hawaii, will be able to advance its line of defense 2,000 miles from the Pacific coast, and, with a fortified harbor and a strong fleet at Honolulu, will be in a position to conduct either defensive or offensive operations in the North Pacific to greater advantage than any other power.

AREA AND POPULATION.

For practical purposes, there are eight islands in the Hawaiian group. The others are mere rocks, of no value at present. These eight islands, beginning from the northwest, are named Niihau, Kauai, Oahu, Molokai, Lanai, Kahoolawe, Maui, and Hawaii. The areas of the islands are:

	Square Miles.
Niihau	97
Kauai	590
Oahu	600
Molokai	270
Maui	760
Lanai	150
Kahoolawe	63
Hawaii	4,210
Total	6,740

As compared with States of the Union, the total area of the group approximates most nearly to that of the State of New Jersey—7,185 square miles. It is more than three times that of Delaware—2,050 square miles.

The islands that interest an intending immigrant are Hawaii, Maui, Oahu, and Kauai. It is on these islands that coffee, fruits, potatoes, corn, and vegetables can be raised by the small investor, and land can be obtained on reasonable terms.

The island of Hawaii is the largest in the group, and presents great varieties of soil and climate. The windward side, which includes the districts of North Kohala, Hamakua, Hilo, and Puna, is copiously watered by rains, and in the Hilo district the streams rush impetuously down every gulch or ravine. The leeward side of the island, including South Kohala, North and South Kona, and Kau, is not exposed to such strong rains, but an ample supply of water falls in the rain belt. The Kona district has given the coffee product a name in the markets of the world. On this island are now situated numerous sugar plantations. Coffee employs the industry of several hundred owners, ranging from the man with 200,000 trees to one who has only an acre or so. There are thousands of acres at present uncultivated and only awaiting the enterprise of the temperate zone to develop them.

Maui is also a very fine island. Besides its sugar plantations it has numerous coffee lands, especially in the eastern part, which are just now being opened up. The western slopes of Haleakala, the main mountain of Maui, are covered with small farms, where are raised potatoes, corn, beans, and pigs. Again, here, thousands of acres are lying fallow.

The island of Oahu presents excellent opportunities for the investor. Many acres of land remain undeveloped among its fertile valleys, the energies of the population having been devoted to the development of the sugar lands on the larger islands. A line of railroad has been constructed which at present runs along the coast to a distance of 30 miles from the city. It is proposed to continue this line completely around the island. This railroad opens up rich coffee and farming lands and affords ready means of transport for the produce and an expeditious method for obtaining the necessary supplies, etc., from the capital.

Kauai is called the "Garden Island," it is so well watered and so luxuriant in vegetation. The Island is at present largely devoted to the cultivation of sugar. Rice also cuts a considerable figure in the agricultural production of Kauai. That it can produce coffee is undoubted, but there is a timidity about embarking in the industry, because, some forty years ago, the experiment of a coffee plantation was tried, and, owing to misjudgment of location and soil, failed. Since then, the cultivation of coffee has come to be more thoroughly understood, and there is no doubt that quantities of land suitable for such cultivation may be profitably utilized.

THE CITY OF HONOLULU.

On Oahu is the capital, Honolulu. It is a city numbering 30,000 inhabitants, and is pleasantly situated on the south side of the Island. The city extends a considerable distance up Nuuanu Valley, and has wings extending northwest and southeast. Except in the business blocks, every house stands in its own garden, and some of the houses are very handsome.

The city is lighted with electric light, there is a complete telephone system, and tramcars run at short intervals along the principal streets and continue out to a sea-bathing resort and public park, 4 miles from the city. There are numerous stores where all kinds of goods can be obtained. The public buildings are attractive and commodious. There are numerous churches, schools, a public library of over 10,000 volumes, Y. M. C. A. Hall, Masonic Temple, Odd Fellows' Hall and Theater. There is frequent steam communication with San Francisco, once a month with Victoria (British Columbia), and twice a month with New Zealand and the Australian Colonies. Steamers also connect Honolulu with China and Japan. There are three evening daily papers published in English, one daily morning paper, and two weeklies. Besides these, there are papers published in the Hawaiian, Portuguese, Japanese, and Chinese languages, and also monthly magazines in various tongues.

CENSUS OF 1897.

United States Consul-General Mills, of Honolulu, under date of February 8, 1897, transmitted to the Department of State the official figures showing the result of the census of the Hawaiian Islands, which had just been completed. The Hawaiians head the list with a total of 31,019. The Japanese colonization comes next, with the Chinese a close third. The official table, as prepared at the census office, is:

Nationality.	Males.	Females.	Total.
Hawaiian	16,399	14,620	31,019
Part Hawaiian	4,249	4,236	8,485
American	1,975	1,111	3,086
British	1,406	844	2,250
German	866	566	1,432
French	56	45	101
Norwegian	216	162	378
Portuguese	8,202	6,989	15,191
Japanese	19,212	5,195	24,407
Chinese	19,167	2,449	21,616
South Sea Islanders	321	134	455
Other nationalities	448	152	600
Total	72,517	36,503	109,020

TOPOGRAPHY AND CLIMATE.

The Hawaiian Islands are of volcanic formation, and there are two active volcanoes on Hawaii—Kilauea and Mauna Loa. The altitude of Mauna Kea, the highest point on Hawaii, is 13,805 feet. The mountains on other islands range from 4,000 to 5,000 feet. The topography is broken and diversified, with many valleys and streams. The mountain sides abound in forests, containing an abundance of ship timber and many ornamental woods. Among the minerals that have been noticed are sulphur, pyrites, common salt, sal ammoniac, limonite, quartz, augite, chrysolite, garnet, labradorite, feldspar, gypsum, soda alum, copperas, glauber salts, niter, and calcite.

"In the Hawaiian Islands," says a pamphlet of the Hawaiian Government, "Americans and Europeans can and do work in the open air at all seasons of the year, as they can not in countries lying in the same latitudes elsewhere. To note an instance, Calcutta lies a little to the north of the latitude of Kauai, our most northerly island, and in Calcutta the American and European can only work with his brain; hard physical labor he can not do and live. On the Hawaiian Islands, he can work and thrive."

The rainfall varies, being greater on the windward side of the islands, and increasing up to a certain elevation. Thus, at Olaa, on the Island of Hawaii, windward side and elevation of about 2,000 feet, the rainfall from July 1, 1894, to June 30, 1895, was 176.82 inches, while at Kailua, on the leeward side, at a low level, it was only 51.21 inches during the same period.

The temperature also varies according to elevation and position. On the Island of Hawaii, one can get any climate from the heat of summer to actual winter at the summits of the two great mountains. A meteorological record, kept carefully for a period of twelve years, gives 89° as the highest and 54° as the lowest temperature recorded, or a mean temperature of 71.5° for the year. A case of sunstroke has never been known. People take no special precautions against the sun, wearing straw and soft felt hats similar to those worn in the United States during the summer months.

The prevailing winds are the northeast trades. These blow for about nine months of the year. The remainder of the period the winds are variable and chiefly from the south. The islands are outside the cyclone belt, and severe storms accompanied by thunder and lightning are of rare occurrence.

The islands possess a healthful climate. There are no virulent fevers such as are encountered on the coast of Africa or in the West India Islands. Epidemics seldom visit the islands, and when they do they are generally light. A careful system of quarantine guards the islands now from epidemics from abroad.

AGRICULTURAL RESOURCES.

The pamphlet entitled "The Republic of Hawaii," issued by the Department of Foreign Affairs of the islands in 1896, gives a full account of the agricultural resources of the country, with interesting details as to the coffee industry, from which the following matter is extracted: The mainstay of the islands, it says, has for the last thirty-five years been the sugar industry. From this source a large amount of wealth has been accumulated. But the sugar industry requires large capital for expensive machinery, and has never proved remunerative to small investors. An attempt has been made at profit-sharing, and has met with some success, the small farmer cultivating and the capitalist grinding at a central mill. Of late years, moreover, the small farmer has been steadily developing in the Hawaiian Islands, and attention has been given to other products than sugar.

Rice, neither the European nor the American can cultivate as laborers. It requires working in marshy land, and though on the islands it yields two crops a year, none but the Chinaman can raise it successfully. A dry-land or mountain rice has been introduced.

The main staple, after sugar and rice, is coffee. Of this, hundreds of thousands of trees have been planted out within the last five years. This is essentially the crop of the future, and bids fair to become as important a staple as sugar. Coffee does not require the amount of capital that sugar does, and it can be worked remuneratively upon a small area. It is estimated that at the end of the fourth year the return from a 75-acre coffee plantation will much more than pay the running expenses, while from that time on a return of from $8,000 to $10,000 per annum may be realized.

Fruits can also be cultivated to advantage. At present, the banana trade of the islands amounts to over 100,000 bunches per annum, valued at over $100,000, and the quantity might be very easily quadrupled. The banana industry may be regarded as in its infancy. The export of the fruit is only from the Island of Oahu, but there are thousands of acres on the other islands of the group which could be profitably used for this cultivation and for nothing else. The whole question of the banana industry hinges on the market. At present, the market is limited.

Limes and oranges can be cultivated and the fruit can be easily packed for export; at present, the production does not meet the local market. The fruits can be raised to perfection. The Hawaiian orange has a fine flavor, and the Hawaiian lime is of superior quality. In the uplands of Hawaii and Maui potatoes are raised. Their quality is good. Corn is also raised. In these industries many Portuguese, Norwegians, and others have embarked. Both these products find an ample local market. The corn is used largely for feed on the plantations. The corn is ground with the cob, and makes an excellent feed for working cattle, horses, and mules.

In the uplands where the climate is temperate, as at Waimea, Hawaii, vegetables of all kinds can be raised; excellent cauli-flowers, cabbages, and every product of the temperate zone can be grown to perfection.

Cattle raising in so small a place as the Hawaiian Islands does not present great opportunities except for local consumption. Pigs are profitable to the small farmer. In the Kula district of Maui, pigs are fattened upon the corn and potatoes raised in the district. The price of pork, dressed, is 25 cents per pound in Honolulu and about 15 cents per pound in the outside districts. The Chinese, of whom there are some 20,000 resident on the various islands, are extremely fond of pork, so that there is a large local market, which has to be supplemented by importations from California.

Attention has lately been given to fiber plants, for which there are many suitable locations. Ramie grows luxuriantly, but the lack of proper decorticating and cleaning machinery has pre-vented any advance in this cultivation.

Sisal hemp and sanseveira have been experimented with, but without any distinct influence upon the trade output.

The cultivation of pineapples is a growing industry. In 1895, "pines" were exported from the islands to San Francisco to the value of nearly $9,000. This has grown up in the last half dozen years. There is every reason to think that canning pine-apples for the coast and other markets can be made profitable.

The guava, which grows wild, can also be put to profit for the manufacture of guava jelly. It has never been entered upon on a large scale, but to the thrifty farmer it would add a convenient addition to his income, just as the juice of the maple adds an increase to the farmer of the Eastern States. Well-made guava jelly will find a market anywhere. In England it is regarded as a great delicacy, being imported from the West India Islands. Besides the guava there are other fruits which can be put up to commercial profit, notably the poha or Cape.gooseberry (*Physalis edulis*). This has been successfully made into jams and jelly, which command an extensive local sale and should find their way into larger markets.

In fact, outside the great industries of sugar, coffee, and rice, there is a good field for many minor industries which can be carried on with profit.

In the Hawaiian Islands a simple life can be lived, and entering gradually upon the coffee industry, a good competence can be obtained long before such could be realized by the agriculturist in less favored countries. However, it is useless to come to the islands without the necessary capital to develop the land that can be obtained. Between arriving and the time that the crops begin to give returns, there is a period where the living must be close, and cash must be paid out for the necessary improvements.

The coffee industry.[*]—A separate chapter of the pamphlet "The Hawaiian Islands" is devoted to the coffee industry. There is no finer coffee in the world, it is asserted, than that of the Hawaiian Islands. The trees require care and do not produce a crop until the third year; but they remain till the fifth year to make a proper realization upon the investment. In the Hawaiian Islands, coffee grows best between 500 and 2,600 feet above the sea level, though there are cases in which it has done well close to the sea. It requires a loose, porous soil, and does not thrive well in heavy clayey ground which holds much water. Of such heavy land, there is very little in the Hawaiian Islands. The soil is generally very porous.

It is very evident that coffee will thrive and give good results in varying conditions of soil and degrees of heat. In these islands, it grows and produces from very nearly at the sea level to the

---

[*] For full description of coffee industry of Hawaii, see advance sheets U. S. Consular Reports No. 13.

elevation of 2,600 feet. The highest elevation of bearing coffee known in the islands is 25 miles from the town of Hilo and in the celebrated Olaa district.

With such a range, it is evident that in a tropical climate the cultivation of coffee presents greater opportunities for an investor than other tropical products. For years, it was thought that coffee would grow to advantage only in the Kona district of Hawaii. Practical experiment has shown that it can be grown with success in almost any part of the islands.

For land laws of Hawaii, see Handbook of Hawaii, Bureau of the American Republics, 1897.

FOREIGN COMMERCE.

The United States practically monopolizes the trade of Hawaii. According to reports of United States Consul-General MILLS, dated Honolulu, August 31, 1896, and March 10, 1897, printed in Volume I, Commercial Relations of the United States, 1895–96, pages 999–1017, inclusive, of the total exports from these islands, the United States received, in 1894, 98.42 per cent, and in 1895 99.04 per cent. Of the imports, in 1894, 76.23 per cent, and in 1895, 79.04 per cent, were from the United States.

The total exports from the Hawaiian Islands, according to the books of the collector of customs, adds Consul-General MILLS, were $9,140,794.56 and $8,474,138.15 for the years 1894 and 1895, respectively, a decrease of $666,656.41. The imports for 1894 were $5,713,181.43, and for 1895, $5,714,017.54, an increase of $836.11.

The following tables show the exports and imports for 1894 and 1895, together with the increase and decrease in values, by countries:

EXPORTS.

Whither exported.	1894.	1895.	Increase.	Decrease.
	Dollars.	Dollars.	Dollars.	Dollars.
United States..............	8,997,069.27	8,392,189.54	....	604,879.73
Australia and New Zealand...	5,201.52	6,124.75	923.23	....
Islands of the Pacific........	17,018.87	10,332.29	....	6,686.58
Japan and China	10,729.51	42,221.50	31,491.99	....
Canada	109,298.61	23,270.07	....	86,028.54
All others.................	1,476.78	....	....	1,476.78
Total	9,140,794.56	8,474,138.15	32,415.22	699,071.63

Total decrease in 1895, $666,656.41.

IMPORTS.

Whence imported.	1894.	1895.	Increase.	Decrease.
	Dollars.	*Dollars.*	*Dollars.*	*Dollars.*
United States	4, 354, 290. 42	4, 516, 319. 38	162, 028. 96	....
Great Britain..............	465, 479. 72	471, 122. 98	5, 643. 26	....
Germany................ ...	140, 233. 07	110, 751. 61	....	29, 481 46
China	230, 270. 41	223, 701. 56	....	6. 568. 85
Japan.....	183, 867. 52	207, 125. 59	23, 258. 07	....
Australia and New Zealand..	186, 518. 75	122, 804. 60	....;	63, 714. 15
Canada	118, 198. 57	30, 731. 21	....	87, 467. 36
Islands of the Pacific	21, 570. 24	1, 192. 51	....	20, 377. 73
France	8, 786. 31	7, 849. 90	....	936. 41
Other countries.............	3, 466. 42	21, 793. 20	18, 326. 78	....
Whale ships................	500. 00	625. 00	125. 00	....
Total	5, 713, 181. 43	5, 714, 017. 54	209, 382. 07	208, 545. 96

Total increase in 1895, $836.11.

During the six months ended June 30, 1897, says Consul-General HAYWOOD, there was a considerable decrease in the exports as compared with the same period of 1896, while the imports increased over $750,000. The total exports for the six months were $11,282,571, against $12,258,574 in 1896; the imports were $3,908,489, against $3,115,826 in the first six months of 1896. The increase in imports came almost entirely from the United States.

To consider imports and exports for fractions of a year, continues the consul-general, is not satisfactory, for the reason that a country may have one great product, which is all exported in a few months, while her imports cover the whole year. This is the case with Hawaii. From the above figures it would appear that she exported three times as much as she imported. A reference to last year's figures will show that the exports are about double the imports.

The trade for the last two years, according to Commercial Relations, 1895-96, was:

	1895.	1896.
Imports...................................	$5, 714, 017	$7, 164, 561
Exports.................	8, 474, 138	15, 515, 230

The exports for the first six months of 1897, says Mr. HAYWOOD, were divided as follows: United States, $11,260,705, a decrease of $972,585 as compared with the first six months of 1896; Australia and New Zealand, $8,070, an increase of $685 over the same period of last year; Canada, $12,922, a decrease of $3,015; China, none, a decrease of $1,959; Pacific Isles, $872, an increase of $872.

The imports for the same period were:

Whence imported.	First six months, 1897.	Per cent.	Increase.	Decrease.
United States..........................	$3,058,380	78.25	$755,204	....
Great Britain.........................	351,381	8.99	....	$40,687
Germany..............................	52,878	1.35	21,755	....
China................................	102,273	2.62	....	42,173
Japan................................	159,555	4.08	31,343	....
Australia and New Zealand	75,975	1.94	13,952	....
Canada	16,179	.42	....	3,886
Pacific Isles........................	3,003	.08	....	1,388
France...	18,385	.47	12,456	....
Other countries.........................	70,474	1.80	46,085	....
Total	3,908,489	....	....	....
Net increase, $792,662.				

The chief exports from the Hawaiian Islands for the six months were: Sugar, $11,021,352; rice, $87,378; bananas, $44,062; coffee, $36,121; wool, $40,119; hides, $8,970. Of these exports, the Pacific ports of the United States received 61.50 per cent; the Atlantic ports 38.32 per cent; Australia and New Zealand 0.07 per cent, and Canada 0.11 per cent.

At present, says the consul-general, Hawaii has to import almost everything she uses, having been heretofore entirely taken up with the raising of sugar, the entire crop of which goes to the United States. The latter country in 1896 took 99.64 per cent of her exports and sold her 76.27 per cent of all imports. (The proportion is even larger in the first six months of 1897.) "The desire is," continues Mr. HAYWOOD, "that everything should come from the United States, and it is believed by a great number that with annexation, over 95 per cent of all the imports would be the growth, product, or manufacture of the United States. The reason more goods are not bought from us is because the tariff averages only 10 per cent, which is not discrimination enough on some articles. If the American tariff were in force here, about $500,000 worth of imports which are now by law free, and which are bought in countries other than the United States, would be bought from us. Fertilizers and coal alone, which are free, amounted to $466,319 in 1896."

CUSTOMS TARIFF AND SHIPPING REGULATIONS.

As heretofore stated, the resolution annexing Hawaii to the United States continues the existing customs duties until further legislation is enacted by Congress. The tariff in full, with shipping regulations, port charges, etc., will be found in the Handbook of Hawaii, published by the Bureau of the American Republics in August, 1897.

TRANSPORTATION FACILITIES, POSTAL SYSTEM, ETC.

OCEAN LINES.

The steamship lines plying between Honolulu and the United States are the Oceanic Steamship Company (4 ships), the Oriental and Occidental Steamship Company (4 ships), the Pacific Mail (4 ships), the Nippon Yusen Kaisha (2 ships), the Oregon Railway and Navigation Company (4 ships), and the Canadian and Australian (2 ships), the latter plying between Sydney, New South Wales, and Vancouver, British Columbia, and touching at this port on each trip each way. The time consumed by the steamers between Honolulu and San Francisco is from six to seven days, but the communication is somewhat irregular. Sometimes, two or three steamers touch there within a week, and then an interval of ten or twelve days may occur between steamers. One vessel of the Oceanic Line, the *Australia*, runs only between San Francisco and Honolulu, and makes about fifteen round trips during the year, while the other three of the same line steam from San Francisco to Sydney, touching here on both outward and homeward voyages. One of these steamers arrives at Honolulu from San Francisco, and one departs from that place within each month. The Oriental and Occidental and the Pacific Mail ply regularly between San Francisco and Hongkong, and the majority of the steamers touch at Honolulu both ways. The Japanese Line—Nippon Yusen Kaisha—does service between Yokohama and Seattle, Wash., and with its two steamers makes this an intermediate port on every trip. The Oregon Railway and Navigation Company's ships ply between Hongkong and Portland, touching only occasionally at Honolulu.

There are a large number of sailing vessels plying regularly between Honolulu and San Francisco, and also others coal laden from British Columbia and Australia which proceed to the United States either in ballast or with cargoes of sugar. Vessels arrive at Honolulu from European ports at comparatively rare intervals.

The rates of freight from Honolulu to San Francisco are: For steamers, $5 per ton and 5 per cent primage; sailing vessels, $3 per ton and 5 per cent primage. The rates to Atlantic ports range from $5 to $7 per ton, with 5 per cent added.

The Oceanic Steamship Company does the bulk of the passenger traffic between Honolulu and San Francisco, as the rate for cabin passage is $75 and steerage $25, while the Occidental and Oriental and the Pacific Mail charge $100 and $30, respectively. The first-named line also controls the steamer freighting trade between San Francisco and this port.

INTER-ISLAND TRANSPORTATION.

The rate of transportation between the islands is $2.50 to $3 per ton. The two steamship companies doing the entire inter-island business are the Inter-Island Steamship Company and the Wilder Steamship Company. About 15 steamers are engaged in this trade.

RAILWAYS.

There are three railroads on the islands. The Oahu Railroad and Land Company, on Oahu, is about 30 miles in length; the Kahului Railroad, on the island of Maui, has 13 miles of road; and the Hawaiian Railroad, on the island of Hawaii, is about 20 miles in length. These railroads are used principally to carry the product of the plantations to the various points of shipment.

POSTAL AND TELEPHONE SYSTEMS.

There is a regular postal system in the Hawaiian Islands, and on the arrival of a steamer at any main point mail carriers at once start out to distribute the mail through the district. The Hawaiian Islands belong to the Postal Union, and money orders can be obtained to the United States, Canada, Great Britain, Germany, Norway, Sweden, Denmark, the Netherlands, Portugal, Hongkong, and Colony of Victoria, as well as local orders between the islands.

The islands of Oahu, Kauai, and Hawaii have telephones every accessible point. The rent of the instrument is moder; and a small charge is made for those who do not care or can i afford to possess an instrument of their own. On Maui, i telephone is at present established only in part.

PATENTS, CURRENCY, COMMERCIAL LICENSES, PASSPORTS, ETC.

PATENTS.

A report from United States Consul General Mills, dated Hoi lulu, August 20, 1894, states that foreign inventors may obt; patent protection for any new and useful invention or improvem(not known or used in Hawaii. Patents may be obtained inventions previously patented abroad, if the article on wh; patent is desired has not been in use in the Hawaiian Islands more than a year prior to the application. The duration oi patent is ten years. If previously patented abroad, it expi simultaneously with the term of the foreign patent. The fees ; as follows: On filing application, $25; on filing caveat, $5; issue of patent, $5; for copies of record, every 100 words or l(50 cents; for translation of every 100 words or less, $1; revenue stamp on each patent, $10; for recording assignmer per 100 words, 50 cents. The petition for patent, accompani by oath, specification, and drawings (and model or specimen wh required), and $25, is presented to the minister of the interi The petition, specification, and oath must be written in Engli or Hawaiian.

The oath may be made before any person within Haw authorized by law to administer oaths; when the applicant resic in another country, it may be made before any Minister, Char d'Affaires, Consul, or Commercial Agent, or Notary Public; it mi be accompanied by seal. The specification must describe the inv(tion, the manner of making, compounding, and using the same, such a way as to enable anyone skilled in the art to understand It must conclude with a specific claim of the part the applica regards as his invention. The drawings must be on white pap and made with India ink. The copies must be tracings on musl The sheet on which the drawing is made must be 10 by 15 inch with a margin of an inch. A space of 1¼ inches must be giv to the title and number. The description must refer to the drawings by letters. A model will not be required unless it shall be found, on examination, to be necessary. All papers must be written legibly on one side of the paper. Interlineations and erasures must be noted in the margin or at the foot. Legal cap paper, with numbered lines, is preferable, and a wide margin must be reserved on the left of each page. The specification must be signed by the inventor or his attorney, and the signature attested by two witnesses. Any person of intelligence and good character may act as the attorney or agent of the applicant, upon filing power of attorney.

CURRENCY, EXCHANGE, WAGES, ETC.*

The Hawaiian money is paper and silver. The gold, of which a large amount is in circulation, is American. United States silver and paper money is also in circulation. The Hawaiian paper money is secured by silver held in reserve. Including both Hawaiian and United States money, there is in circulation about $3,000,000 in the islands.

The rate of exchange is $1\frac{1}{4}$ per cent on Eastern cities of the United States, and 1 per cent on the Pacific coast. Gold is at a premium of 1 per cent over silver.

The rates of wages are the following:

Occupation.	Wages.
Contract laborers on sugar plantations...............per month..	$12.50
Laborers not under contract on sugar plantations ....do....	$15.00 to 20.00
Ordinary day laborers ....per day..	1.00
Domestic servants............................... ...per month..	16.00 to 25.00
Mechanics..per day..	2.50 to 4.00
Clerks in stores ....per month..	75.00 to 125.00
Bookkeepers.......................................do....	125.00 to 150.00
Railway employees:	
Engineers.... ....do....	100.00
Conductors ....do....	65.00 to 90.00
Freight hands........................... ....do....	35.00 to 40.00
Section hands ....do ...	30.00 to 35.00
Section foremen .... do....	75.00

These figures allude to the Oahu Railroad and Land Company. There are very few employees of this character in Hawaii. Plantation managers get from $3,000 per year up; overseers, from $40 to $75 per month.

* From report of United States Consul-General Mills, August 31, 1896.

The pamphlet of the Hawaiian Department of Foreign Affairs, 1896, says the market for labor is overstocked, and it would be unwise for persons to emigrate to Hawaii with no capital, on the mere chance of obtaining employment.

COMMERCIAL LICENSES AND CREDITS.*

A commercial traveler has to pay on the Island of Oahu a tax of $570, and on each of the other islands, $255. A passport tax of $1 is charged on each person leaving the islands—foreigners and citizens alike. This tax, however, is not charged against persons who have resided in Hawaii for a period of less than thirty days. The leading mercantile houses of Honolulu do their foreign purchasing business on a cash basis, taking advantage, of course, of the credits offered by discounts.

PASSPORTS.

United States Consul-General MILLS, in a report to the Department of State, October 3, 1896, says foreigners are not required to have passports before they are admitted to the country, nor are there any laws or regulations affecting foreign sojourners. As mentioned above, however, all persons leaving the country, except travelers who have been there less than thirty days, are required to obtain a passport, the fee for which is $1.

IV. THE PHILIPPINE ISLANDS.†

LOCATION, AREA, AND TOPOGRAPHY.

The Philippine Islands are situated between 4°–20° N. lat. and 161°–127° E. long., in front of China and Cochin China. The capital, Manila, is 628 miles from Hongkong. The archipelago is composed of some 2,000 islands, and the aggregate area is estimated at over 100,000 square miles. The principal islands are Luzon (Batanes, Babuyanes, Polillo, Catanduanes, Mindoro,

---

* From report of United States Consul General Mills, August 31, 1896.

† In the compilation of the following descriptive matter reference has been had to reports by Consul WILLIAMS, of Manila, and Consul-General PRATT, of Singapore; "A New Center of Gold Production," by FRANK KARUTH, F. R. G. S.; the Hongkong Chronicle and Directory, 1898; official statistical publications of European countries; Special Consular Reports, Highways of Commerce; the Bulletin de la Société de Géographie Commerciale, Paris, Vol. XIX, etc.

Marinduque, Burias, Masbate, etc., lying adjacent) on the north; the Visayas (Tablas, Panay, Negros, Cebu, Bohol, Leyte, Samar, etc.), prolonged southwest by the Calamaines, Palawan, and Balabac; Mindanao and the adjacent islands Dinagat, Surigao, Basilan, etc., and on the extreme south, the Sulu archipelago. The island of Luzon, on which the capital is situated, is larger than New York and Massachusetts, and Mindanao is nearly as large. An idea of the extent of the Philippines may be formed when it is stated that the six New England States and New York, New Jersey, Maryland, and Delaware have 10 per cent less area.

The principal international ports are Manila, Albay, and Sual (on Luzon); Cebu, Leyte, and Iliolo (on the Visayas); and Zamboanga (on Mindanao). The coasts are high, and coral reefs are numerous. There are reasons for the hypothesis that the Philippines are peaks, mountain ridges, and table lands of a submerged continent, which in a very early geological period extended to Australia. Lines of volcanoes, extinct and active (the number of the latter being small) run approximately east and west. The general direction of the chain of mountains is north and south, the highest, Apo, in Mindanao, reaching 10,000 feet. The rivers and streams are countless, and traverse the islands in all directions. There are many hot springs of iron and sulphur waters, with excellent medicinal properties.

CLIMATE AND POPULATION.

The climate varies little from that of other places in the same latitude. The archipelago is under the isotherm of 79°, and the thermometer ranges during the year from 60° to 90°. The seasons vary according to the aspect of the country, the months from March to May being the hottest, and November to February the coldest. During the rainy season, which lasts from June until November, inundations of rivers are frequent. There are occasional monsoons, but the climate as a whole is considered heathful, for the tropics. The endemic complaints of the country are swamp fever, diarrhœa, beri-beri, and a few others. Yellow fever is practically unknown, and the rate of mortality is very low.

The population has been estimated at from 8,000,000 to 10,000,000, of which number about 25,000 are Europeans—the

Bull. No. 2——5

troops of occupation, of course, not being included in the above figures. The bulk of the natives is of a race akin to the Malays. There is a considerable number of mestizos, or half-castes. About half of the European population resides at Manila.

POLITICAL DIVISIONS.

The Philippines, under the Spanish administration, were divided into three governments—Luzon, Visayas, and Mindanao. The Governor-General resided at Manila, to which belonged, for administrative purposes, the Caroline, Ladrone, and Pelew islands. In many of the Philippine Islands, especially in the interior of Mindanao, the natives were independent. The provinces were subdivided into districts, and these again into communes or parishes.

CITIES AND TOWNS.

Manila, the capital of the entire archipelago, is situated in the Island of Luzon, at the mouth of the River Pasig, which empties into the Bay of Manila. The city has 300,000 inhabitants, of whom 15,000 are Europeans and 100,000 Chinese, who are largely engaged in industry. It is the seat of a yearly increasing commerce. The houses are built with reference to earthquakes, and although large, possess few pretensions to architectural beauty. The city proper within the walls is small, little more than 2 miles in circumference. Here are grouped the Government buildings and religious institutions. The suburbs, of which Binondo ranks first in order of importance, are the centers of trade. The police of the city is under military discipline and is composed of natives. A force of watchmen, paid by the tradesmen, patrol the more populous part of the city from 10 o'clock at night until 5 in the morning. A very low average of crime is said to exist, though the native classes are much addicted to gambling, cock fighting, etc. There are six daily papers: " El Diario de Manila," " La Oceania Española," published in the morning, and " El Comercio," " La Voz Española," " El Español," and " El Noticero," which appear in the evening.

Manila has a cathedral of the seventeenth century, an archbishop's palace, a university school of art, an observatory, a large Government cigar factory, and many educational and charitable institutions. Harbor improvements are in progress. The port has a patent slip way 820 feet long, with 2,000 tons lifting power. A new fort has just been constructed in Malate.

Tramways run in the principal streets, and the city is lighted by electricity and has a telephone system. Drinking water is brought in pipes from Santalan, on the river Pasig. The mean temperature is 80.2 F.

There are some 4,000 horses in the city, used for carriages and street cars. Buffaloes are employed for dray and other heavy work.

On February 6, 1898, Manila suffered from a severe fire, and it is interesting to note that the city would have been lost had it not been for the excellent service of a fire engine which had been imported from the United States.

Iliolo, the chief town of the populous province of the same name, in the island of Panay, is situated in latitude 10° 48′ W., near the southeastern extremity of the island, and 250 miles from Manila. The harbor is well protected and the anchorage good. At spring tides, the whole town is covered with water, but not-withstanding this it is a very healthy place, there being always a breeze. It is much cooler in Iliolo than in Manila. The means of communication with the interior are very inadequate, and retard the development of the port. The principal manufacture is pineapple cloth. The country around Iliolo is very fertile and is extensively cultivated, sugar, tobacco, and rice being grown, and there are many towns in the vicinity that are larger than the port.

Cebu, the capital of the island of this name, was at one time the seat of the administration of revenue for the whole of the Visayas. It is a well-built town and possesses fine roads. The trade is principally in hemp and sugar.

Other towns are Laog, with a population (1887) of 30,642; Banang, 35,598; Batangas, 35,587, and Lipa, 43,408.

COMMERCIAL HOUSES.

The following is a list of commercial establishments in the three principal cities of the Philippines:

MANILA.

Abello, Manuel, naval supplies, Muella de la Reyna 15.
Aboytiz, P., commission agent, Muella de la Reyna 15.
Abraham, Juan, commission agent, Plaza de Goiti 12, Sta. Cruz.

Aenlle & Co., merchants and bankers, Calle Nueva 39 (Binondo).

Aldecoa & Co., merchants and shipowners, Plaza de S. Gabriel 1.

"Alhambra" cigar and cigarette factory, Calle Echagüe 29.

Warehouses for storage, Murallon, 24, Binondo.

Almigos del Pais, bookseller and stationer, Real 34.

Ampuero y Oirola, druggists, corner Real and Cabildo.

André, E., & Co., produce merchants and proprietors "Excelsior" Cigar and Cigarette Factory.

Andrews, H. J., & Co., merchants and proprietors cigar factories, Anloague 13.

Armstrong, Sloan & Co., ship, bill, and produce brokers.

Aurteneche, L., naval supplies and hardware, Anloague 2.

Ayala & Co., merchants.

Balut Rope Factory, Inchausti & Co.

Baer, Senior, & Co., merchants, Escolta 20.

Balbas & Co., merchants.

Spanish Bank of the Philippines, V. Balbas, director.

Barretto, A.V., merchant, Sampaloc 38.

Barretto & Co., merchants, Barroca 2.

Barretto Bros., merchants and commission agents, Asuncion 14, Binondo.

Battle Bros. & Co., merchants and bankers, Calle Real 4 (within the walls).

"Bazar," Warlomont Bros., Escolta 33. San Jacinto 2 and 4.

Benitez & Co., merchants, musical instruments, Escolta 12.

Boie & Stradenberg, druggists.

Bren, J. M., publisher, librarian, and stationer, 10 Magallanes.

Boyle & Earnshaw, engineers, 5 Calle Barcelona.

Brown & Co., Martin, merchants, Anloague 17.

Calumpit Steam Rice Mill, Warner, Barnes & Co., proprietors.

Cardoba, Luciano, hatter, Escolta 6.

Carmelo & Bauermann, lithography, Calle de Carriedo 10.

Carreon, Juan, hatter, Real 16.

La Castellana, liquor establishment, Escolta 37.

Commercial house and general warehouse, Luis Rafael Yango, Muelle de la Reyna 24.

Chartered Bank of India, Australia, and China, Plaza de Cervantes, R. W. Brown, agent.

Chofré & Co., printers, lithographers, etc., works, Sampaloc 68; offices, Escolta 33.

Chuidian & Co., Telesforo, merchants and commission agents, Anloague 17.

"The City of Manilla," provisions, Crespo 34.

"The City of Vigo," shoes and hosiery, San Jacinto 13, Alex. Martinez.

"Colon," hemp-rope and oil factory, Pasco Ascarraga (Tondo).

"Colon," general cigar factory, Paseo Ascarraga, near Calle Lemery (Tondo).

"La Commercial," cigar factory, Ilaya 29, Roman & Co.

Philippines General Tobacco Co., central offices Isla del Romero.

Maritime Co., Nuvelle del Rey 10, J. T. Macleod.

Spanish-Philippine Mercantile and Industrial Co.

Compostela Coal Mine Co., R. Reyes, director.

Transatlantic Spanish Co., tobacco, Isla del Romero 1.

La Constancia, manufactory of tobacco, Calzada de San Marcelino.

Donaldson-Sim & Co., produce merchants, Plaza de Padre Moraga 4.

Cundall, Charles H., merchant, Plaza del Padre Moraga.

Earnshaw, Daniel, consulting engineer and ship and engineer surveyor, Callejon de San Gabriel 4.

Echeita y Portuondo, merchants.

La Estrella del Norte, Levy Bros., Escolta 10.

Findlay & Co., merchants, Calle Carenero 3.

Filton, W. A., general broker.
Forbes, Munn & Co., merchants, Calle David 6.
Fressel, C., & Co., merchants, Calle Nueva 36.
Frochlich & Kuttner, merchants, Anloague 8.
Fuset, Antonio, merchant, cigar manufacturer and shipowner.
Galan y Fuster, commission merchant, mail contractor.
Garchitorena, José de, carriage manufacturer.
Garcia, Antonio, engraver, Cabildo 59.
Genato, M., liquor establishment, Escolta 30.
Germann & Co., insurance agency, Calle San Jacinto 35.
Gutierrez Brothers, merchants, exporters and importers, Beaterio 7.
Gsell, Carlos, merchant, Calle San Pedro 12 and 14.
Heinszen, C., & Co , merchants, Rosario 26
" Helios," manufactory of tobacco, Isla del Romero 5 and 7.
La Hensiana Cigar Manufacturing Co., limited, Muella de la Reina 1.
Hermann, Raf., consulting mining engineer and agent, Calleron de San Gabriel 4.
Holliday, Wise & Co,, merchants, Anloague 10.
Hollmann & Co., merchants, Plaza de San Gabriel 2.
Hongkong and Shanghai Banking Corporation, Plaza de San Gabriel 7.
Printing Office of Sta. Cruz, J. Marty, Carnedo 6.
La Insular cigar factory.
Johnston, Gore Booth & Co., merchants.
Kellar, Ed. A., & Co., merchants, Calle Martinez 2.
Ker & Co., merchants, Callejon de San Gabriel 7.
Kuenzle & Streiff, merchants, Calle David 5 and 7.
Lerma, J. M. J., agent of agricultural tools, Balanga.
" Libreria Taglia," A. Fernandez, Rosario 17, Binondo.
Luzon Sugar Refining company, ltd., Smith, Bell & Co., agents.
Macleod & Co., merchants, Muelle del Rey.
Manila Slip Co., limited, R. Reyes, general agent.
Manufactory of bricks, San Miguel 6.
Manufactory of Manila ice, José G. Rocha, president.
Marcaida & Co., merchants and commission agents, Jabonero, 36, Binondo.
March, B. Ijelmo de, undertaker, Plaza de Goiti, 3.
Maria Cristina, cigar manufactory, 9 Plaza de Goiti.
Matti, J. M., watchmaker, Escolta, 12.
Meerkamp & Co., merchants and commission agents, 1 Muella de la Reina.
Mein, P. W., exchange broker, Muelle de Rey, 4.
Meyer, E., tailor, Escolta, 21.
Meyer & Co., druggists, Plaza de Goiti.
Milan, Milecio, silversmith, Calle de Magallanes, 28.
La Minerva cigar factory, Simpson & Co., Paseo de Azcarraga, 99.
The Orient Manufacture of Tobacco, Calle San Pedro, 64.
Oriol, A., dealer in marble, Carriedo, 6.
Palaznelos Bros., novelties, modes.
Pardo, Manuel, steam rice mill proprietor and hemp planter, Nueva Carceres, Province of Camainus.
Paterno de Mora, embroidery, San Sebastian, 8.
Perez, Rafael, merchant, Anloague, 6.
Philippine Tramways, limited, Rotonda de Sampaloe.
National Perfumery, Plaza de Santa Cruz, 10.
Pegpoch, Manuel, commission merchant, Callejon S. Gabriel, 4.
Railway Company, limited (Manila), H. L. Higgins, C. E.
Restaurant and cake shop, Escolta, 26 C. Capagorry.

Richter & Co., hatters, Escolta, 24.
Reyes, Leon, surgeon dentist, Plaza de Sta. Cruz, 3.
Rodoreda, F. de P., dealer in marble, Escolta, 24.
Roensch & Co., hats and military effects and musical instruments, Escolta, 21.
Roxas, P. P., merchant, San Miguel, 6.
Rueda y Ramos, commission merchants, Plaza del Padre Moraga, 2 and 3.
José Ma. Saiz, merchant, importer, Plaza de Calderon de la Barcas.
San Miguel Brewery, Malacanang, 6, P. P. Roxas, proprietor.
Santa Mesa steam rope factory, J. M. Tuason & Co.
Scheerer, Otto, coffee planter, Benguet; plantation of Andeboc.
Schwenger, A., merchant and distiller of ilang ilang.
" La Levillana," liquor establishment, Puente de Binondo.
Sibrand Siegert, A. G., merchant, ærated water manufacturer, Echague, 13 (Quiapo).
Sequera, M., shirt maker, Carriedo.
Simpson & Co., tobacco factory.
Singer Manufacturing Co., Escolta, 9.
Spitz, Enrique, merchant, Escolta, 8.
Sprüngli & Co., merchants, Escolta, 14.
Stevenson & Co., W. F., merchants, 4 Muelle del Rey.
Strückman & Co., merchants, Calle Anloague 3.
Telephone Co., E. Bate y Hernandez.
Tillson, Hermann & Co., merchants, Anloague 15.
Tornel, M. G., oculist, Iris 7.
Torrecilla & Co., novelties and shirt makers, Escolta 17.
Tuason J. M., & Co., merchants and bankers, Plaza del Padre Moraga 8.
Ullmann, Felix, importer of jewelry, Escolta 31.
Warner, Barnes & Co., merchants, Muelle del Rey 7.
Watson A. S., & Co., limited, chemists and druggists, Escolta 14.
Wright & Turner, ship and general brokers.
Wusinowski & Co., merchants, Calle Soledad 6 Anloague.
Zaragoza, Miguel, painter.
Zobel, chemist and druggist, Calle Real 28.

ILOILO.

Aznar, M., chemist and druggist, Capiz.
Spanish Bank of the Philippines, M. Lahora, director.
Bazar de Iloilo, Calle Real, 16.
Bischoff, S., merchant.
Gutierrez pharmacy, Juan Grimm.
"Caballo Blanco," manufactory of trimmings, Calle San Jacinto.
Castillo, E., chemist and druggist.
La Caslettena, manufactory of bricks and pottery.
Chiene, C. M., commission agent, Apartado, 44.
Erenita, J. & F., sugar dealers, Talisay, Isla de Negros.
Levy Brothers, Calle Real.
Forbes, Munn & Co., merchants.
Gonsalez, L., photographer, Jaro.
Gonzalez, A., shipowner, Jaro.
Gonzalez, T., physician, Jaro.
Grace, J. W., stevedore and contractor.
Grindrod, J. H., merchant.
Hernaes, Rosendo, merchant and money lender, Talisay, Isla de Negros.
Holliday, Wise & Co., merchants.
Hollmann & Co., merchants, Plaza Alfonso XII.

Hong Kong and Shanghai Banking Corporation, C. H. Balfour, agent.
Hoskyn & Co., merchants.
Inchausti & Co., merchants and commission agents.
Javellana, P., sugar dealer.
Kerr & Co., merchants.
Koppel & Co., importers and exporters.
Kuenzle & Streiff, merchants.
Lacson, D., chemist and druggist, Molo.
Ledesma, J., dealer in hemp, etc.
Lizarraga Bros., exporters' commission agents, Calle Real 11.
Loosing, Leandro, apothecary.
Luchsinger & Co., merchants.
Macleod & Co., merchants.
Mapa, F., medical practitioner.
Mapa, V., solicitor.
Marin, P., sugar manufacturer, Janinay.
Martinez, D., teacher.
Maye, John, F. R. C. S., medical practitioner.
Melliza, Cornelio, trader, Molo.
Montelibano, E., tramway owner, Silay.
Montelivano, C., carriage builder.
Montinola, P., carriage builder, Jaro.
Ordax, Sabino, medical practitioner.
Ortiz, Francisco, teacher of music.
Prentevella, R., sugar dealer and planter.
Rafael, Cayetano, hat maker.
Rama, Lope de la, medical practitioner.
Rama, I. de la, & Sons, merchants, steamer owners, Calle Real.
Robles, Zacarias, veterinary surgeon.
Roensch & Co., Adolfo, hat makers.
Salas Brothers, storekeepers.
San Augustine, J., carriage builder.
Santiago, R., sugar dealer.
Singer Manufacturing Co., Calle Real.
Smith, Bell & Co., merchants.
Soriano, Juan, tailor.
Stevenson & Co., W. F., merchants.
Streiff & Co., E., merchants.
Warner, Barnes & Co., merchants.
Wusinowski & Co., merchants, Calle Real.
Zeller, E., sugar dealer.

CEBU.

Boada, Pedro, provisions.
P. Antonio, merchant.
Climaco, Valeriano, merchant.
Cui, P., merchant.
Gorordo, J., merchant.
Herrera, Lucio, merchant.
Lasala, M., merchant.
Singson, S., merchant.
Veloso, Buenaventura, merchant.
Veloso, Nicasio, merchant.
Borromeo, J., carriage builder.

abundance. Only one-fifth of the area is under cultivation. So wasteful have been the native agricultural methods, that the harvests have in some places diminished. This is especially true of maize in Cebu and sugar in the province of Pangasinan, where new plantations must be made every year; while at Negros, the land yields many years in succession. The rice production, formerly very large, has now so fallen off that importations have been found necessary. For the same reasons, the production of cotton is also diminishing. The quality of the cotton is fine and silky, and this would easily become a valuable product if attention were given to its cultivation. The provinces of Ilocus (North and South) are especially adapted to the growth of this plant, the rainy season being here well defined.

Hemp (abaca), the most important product of the archipelago, is the fiber of a species of banana. It is produced by scraping the leaves with a peculiar knife, which requires expert handling. Many contrivances to supersede this process have been tried, but without success. Thread is spun from the fiber and cloth woven that exceeds the best Tussore silk.

The production of sugar is gradually developing, the principal centers of production being the provinces of Batangas, Pampanga, Ilocus, Pangasinan, and Bulacan. It also grows in Iliolo and the islands of Cebu and Negros. The plantations so far have been small and the machinery antiquated.

Tobacco would be an important source of wealth to the Philippines, with proper management. Of late, the quality has been, allowed to deteriorate. A large number of companies is engaged in this industry. The two most important are the Compagnie Générale des Tabacs des Philippines (the capital of which, $14,500,000 gold, is principally in the hands of French bondholders) and the Insular. Each of these establishments employs from 5,000 to 6,000 workmen.

Coffee, though not equal to Mocha or Bourbon, has a fine aroma. It grows in the provinces of Batangas, Cavite, and Zamboanga, and is exported chiefly to Spain. The cocoanut tree is found everywhere, and cocoanut oil is used for lighting the houses and streets of certain provinces where electricity or petroleum is as yet unknown. The native indigo is famous for its excellent quality. Several years ago, the provinces of Ilocus, Pangasinan,

Pampanga, and Camarines produced enormously. Unfortunately, the faulty preparation, and the adulteration to which the powder was subjected by Chinese traders, have greatly reduced its market value. It is now exported chiefly to Japan.

The wealth of timber in the Philippines is incalculable, yielding resins, gums, dye products, fine-grained ornamental wood, and also heavy timber suitable for building purposes. Teak, ebony, and sandalwood are found; also ilang-ilang, camphor, pepper, cinnamon, tea, and all tropical fruits. Sweet potatoes grow readily.

COMMERCE AND INDUSTRY.

The commerce of the Philippine Islands has been calculated at $10,000,000 imports, and $20,000,000 exports for 1896 and 1897, although the average value of the trade is probably greater, having suffered in the past few years on account of political conditions. Nearly one-third of the exports go to Great Britain, and over one-fourth of the imports come from that country. The trade of Spain with the Philippines has been about the same for imports and exports, each class amounting to nearly $5,000,000 in value. The United States, France, and Germany follow in the order of importance of trade. The principal articles of import are flour, wines, clothing, petroleum, coal, rice, arms, machinery, and iron. The exports consist chiefly of sugar, hemp, tobacco, and copra. Details of trade with the United States during the last two years are given by the United States Treasury as follows:

IMPORTS INTO UNITED STATES.

Articles.	1896.		1897.	
	Quantities.	Values.	Quantities.	Values.
Hemp, manila ....tons..	35,584	$2,499,494	38,533	$2,701,651
Cane sugar (not above No 16)......pounds..	142,075,344	2,270,902	72,463,577	1,199,202
Fiber, vegetable, not hemp...........tons..	872	68,838	5,450	384,155
Fiber, vegetable, manufactures of...........	....	26,428	....	22,170
Straw, manufactures of	....	81,352	....	72,137
Tobacco...........................pounds..	1,280	808	2,745	2,338
Miscellaneous	....	35,035	....	1,087
Total	....	4,982,857	....	4,383,740

EXPORTS FROM UNITED STATES.

Cotton, manufactures of.........		$9,714		$2,164
Oils, mineral, refined...............gallons..	1,130,769	89,958	600,837	45,908
Varnish................................do....	1,138	1,500	2,483	2,239
All other....................................	....	61,274	....	44,286
Total	....	162,446	....	94,597

It should be noted that our trade is really much larger (especially in the item of exports to the islands) than is indicated by the above figures. Large quantities of provisions (flour, canned goods, etc.) are sent to Hongkong or other ports for transshipment, and are credited to those ports instead of to Manila.

Besides the numerous tobacco establishments to which reference has already been made, there are rice factories, sugar mills, distilleries, factories of rope, soap, aerated waters, brickyards, saw mills, etc. The purely native industries consist of work in bamboo and cotton, engraving, making straw hats, etc. Very exquisite embroidery is done on silk and pineapple cloth, and there is also wood carving and work in gold and silver. The manufacture of cotton goods often forms the occupation of an entire village, and this industry is far from being of insignificant proportions.

RAILROADS, TELEGRAPHS, ETC.

There is but one railway in the islands—from Manila to Dagupin—a distance of 123 miles. It is single track and well built, with steel rails its entire length; the bridges are of stone or iron, and the station buildings substantial. English engines are used, which make 45 miles per hour. The government assisted in the construction of the road by making valuable concessions of land with right of way its entire length, and by guaranteeing 8 per cent per year upon the stock of the road for a period of ninety-nine years, when it is to become State property. Up to the date of the report (1895) the road paid more than 10 per cent per annum to shareholders. According to a report presented at a meeting of the company in London (published in the " London and China Telegraph," London, June 20, 1898) the greatest number of passengers (800,000) was carried in 1894. The number subsequently decreased, on account of a tax of 10 per cent placed by the Spanish Government on the passenger traffic. Merchandise amounting to 214,000 tons was carried during the past year. Dagupin is about a mile from the gulf of Lugayan, on a branch of the River Agno.

A railway is being constructed near Cebu for the transportation of coal.

There are about 720 miles of telegraph in the islands. A cable connects Manila with Hongkong, and there is one from Manila to the Visayas Islands, and a new one is being laid to Cape Bolinao.

STEAMSHIP LINES.

There is one line from Manila to Liverpool, known as the Compañia Transatlantica, composed of three steamers, averaging 4,500 tons and about 4,000 horse power each. The line maintains a monthly service to Europe, calling at Singapore, Colombo, Aden, Suez, Port Said, and Barcelona en route. The Spanish Royal Mail Line from Barcelona to Manila leaves every twenty-eight days. Four lines of steamers are in the service to Hongkong. The local mail steamers from Manila to the provinces leave the capital every alternate Saturday.

The North Luzon line is from Manila to Subig, Olangapo, Bolinao, San Fernando, Croayan, Currimas (all these on the west coast of Luzon and Appari, entrance to Rio Grande, in the extreme north of Luzon). The South Luzon line runs from Manila to Batangas, Calapan, Laguimanos, Passacao, Donsol, Sorsogon, Legaspi, and Tabaco.

The Southeast line runs from Manila to Romolon, Cëbu, Cabolian, Surigao, Camiguin, Cagayan de Misamis, Iligan, Harihohoe, Bais, Iloilo. The Southwest line runs from Manila to Iloilo, Zamboanga, Isabela de Basilan, Iolo (Sula) Siassi, Tataan, Bongao, Parang Parang, Cottabato, Glan, Sarangani, Dayas, Matti Lebak, St. Maria.

These steamers return to Manila from eight to ten days after leaving; local steamers for the neighboring islands leave nearly every day.

CUSTOMS TARIFF AND REGULATIONS FOR THE PHILIPPINES.

The tariff for the Philippine Islands, which has just been published by the War Department, has on the introductory page the following order by the President:

EXECUTIVE MANSION, *July 12, 1898*.

By virtue of the authority vested in me as Commander-in-Chief of the Army and Navy of the United States of America, I do hereby order and direct that upon the occupation and possession of any ports and places in the Philippine Islands by the forces of the United States the following tariff of duties and taxes, to be levied and collected as a military contribution, and regulations for the administration thereof, shall take effect and be in force in the ports and places so occupied.

Questions arising under said tariff and regulations shall be decided by the general in command of the United States forces in those islands.

Necessary and authorized expenses for the administration of said tariff and regulations shall be paid from the collections thereunder.

Accurate accounts of collections and expenditures shall be kept and rendered to the Secretary of War.

WILLIAM McKINLEY.

The rates of the tariff practically conform to those formerly in force in the Philippine Islands, with the exception of the abolition of the general surtaxes. The metrical system is in vogue, and the monetary unit adopted in the tariff is the gold peso of the mint, the value of which is estimated at $1.034. Mexican currency is generally used. The following are the rates on the principal articles of import. Those from the United States consist chiefly of cotton goods, refined petroleum, and varnish:

	Pesos.	U. S. currency.
Coal and coke.................per 1,000 kilos (2,204.6 pounds)..	0. 50	$0. 51
Benzine, gasoline, petroleum, and other mineral oils, refined, per 100 kilos (220.46 pounds)...................................	4. 50	4. 65
Common hollow glassware.....................per 100 kilos..	1. 60	1. 65
Crystal, and glass imitating it (also gilt or silvered in the interior), per 100 kilos	6. 00	6. 20
Gold and silver in jewelry or plate, also set with stones, per hectogram (3.52 ounces)...	5. 00	5. 17
Gold, silver, or platinum worked into other objects, per hectogram, (3.52 ounces)..	. 50	.51
Cast iron :		
In common manufactures.....................per 100 kilos...	1. 50	1. 55
Polished, enameled with porcelain, or ornamented......do....	3. 50	3. 61
Wrought-iron and steel rails................................do....	1. 60	1. 65
Wrought iron or steel, in sheets 0.23 inch thick, or more, and bolts, per 100 kilos	1. 80	1. 87
Wrought iron or steel in bars, sheets up to 0.23 inch thick, axles, tires, springs for carriages, and hoop iron........per 100 kilos..	2. 60	2. 68
Wrought iron and steel for buildings, bridges, etc..........do....	3. 20	3. 30
Iron wire ....do....	1. 60	1. 65
Nails and screws..do....	4. 00	4. 13
Wrought-iron pipes..do....	2. 60	2. 68
Wares of wrought iron....................................do....	8. 00	8. 27
Tin plate, per 100 kilos, 5 pesos; manufactures of..........do ...	8. 00	8. 27
Zinc in sheets, nails and wire..............................do....	5. 00	5. 17
Zinc in manufactured articles................per kilo (2.2046 lbs)..	. 25	. 25
Varnishes..per 100 kilos..	4. 80	4. 96
Cotton textiles, close woven, plain, unbleached, or dyed, in the piece or handkerchiefs:		
Having up to 25 threads, inclusive................ per kilo..	. 20	. 20
Having up to 35 threads, inclusive ..'...................do....	. 32	. 33
Thirty-six threads and above..........................do....	.44	.45
(These items are subject to a surtax of 20 per cent.)		
Cotton textiles, printed, twilled and figured, having—		
Up to 55 threads, inclusive ....do...	. 25	. 25
Up to 35 threads, inclusive ....do....	.40	.41
Thirty-six threads and above (plus 20 per cent surtax)...do....	. 55	. 56

	Pesos.	U. S. currency.
Silk textiles, plain or twilled (plus 20 per cent surtax) ...per kilo..	4.00	$4.13
Engravings, maps, and drawings..........................do....	.25	.25
Staves ....per 1,000..	.40	.41
Boots of all kinds, of leather or cloth ....per pair..	.40	.41
Shoes of all kinds.....................................do....	.26	.26
(Surtax of 20 per cent for above items; children's foot wear pays one-half above duties.)		
Saddlers and harness makers' wares (plus 20 per cent) ...per kilo..	.75	.77
Watches:		
Gold.......... ....each.	4.00	4.13
Of silver or other metals ....do....	2.00	2.06
Weighing machines............................per 100 kilos..	5.50	5.68
Agricultural machines.................................do....	.20	.20
Motors...do....	.50	.51
Machines of copper and its alloys, for industrial purposes, and detached parts of the same metals ....per 100 kilos..	5.40	5.58
Machines and detached parts of other materials, for industrial purposes.....................................per 100 kilos..	1.80	1.85
Passenger carriages for railways and tramways and parts (wood), per 100 kilos..	7.50	7.75
Other railway carriages and finished parts (of wood)..per 100 kilos..	2.17	2.24
Carts..do....	2.00	2.06
Meat, salted, and jerked beef..........................per kilo..	.08	.08
Pork and lard, including bacon ....do....	.15	.15
Wheat...per 100 kilos..	.60	.62
flour ....do...	2.10	2.17
Other cereals ....do....	.50	.51
Flour of same...do....	1.00	1.03

The export tariff is as follows:

	Pesos.	U. S. currency.
Abaca, raw or wrought hemp....................per 100 kilos..	0.75	$0.77
Indigo ....do....	.50	.51
employed for dyeing (tintarron).........................do....	.05	.05
Rice ....do....	3.00	3.10
Sugar ....do....	.10	.10
Cocoanuts, fresh and dried (copra) ....do....	.10	.10
Tobacco, manufactured, of all kinds and whatever origin ...do....	3.00	3.10
raw, grown in the provinces of Cagayan, Isabella, and New Biscay (Luzon Islands).....................per 100 kilos..	3.00	3.10
raw, grown in the Visayas and Mindanao Islands.......do....	2.00	2.06
raw, grown in other provinces of the archipelago ... ...do ..	1.50	1.55

The free list comprises mineral waters; trees, shoots, plants, and moss in a natural state; lime; copper, gold, and silver ores; samples of felt, painted paper, and textiles, under certain conditions; samples of trimmings of no commercial value; gold, silver, and platinum in broken up jewelry or table services, bars, sheets, pieces, etc.; also in articles manufactured in the Philippines; gypsum; travelers' effects; works of fine art acquired by the Government, archæological and numismatical objects, collections of mineralogy, botany, and zoology, and models for museums, etc.; casks and recipients of metal, imported with goods dutiable separately; carriages; panoramas, etc., for public entertainment, imported temporarily; furniture of persons coming to settle; foreign articles destined for exhibition; submarine telegraph cables; pumps destined for salvage; parts of machinery, etc., for repair of foreign vessels that have entered ports under stress of weather; national products reimported; articles purchased with the funds of the United States Government, and material of all kinds for works executed by the provisional administrations, and not by contract.

The following articles are prohibited: Arms of war, projectiles and their ammunition (unless by special consent); objects offensive to morality.

For the improvement of the harbors, a surtax of 2 per cent ad valorem shall be levied on all imports and exports, except goods for the use of the United States Government and coal.

WHARF CHARGES AND LIGHT DUES.

Exports are taxed 1 peso per 1,000 kilograms (2,204.6 pounds) as wharf charges; imports destined to transshipment to other ports of the Philippines are taxed one-half peso per 1,000 kilograms at the port of transshipment as a due for wharfage.

At all ports or places in the Philippines under control of the United States forces the following port charges are due:

On each entry of a vessel from a port or place, except from another port or place in the Philippines in possession of the United States................... $o. 10
On each departure of a vessel for a port or place, except for a port or place in the Philipines in possession of the United States....................... . 10
On each entry of a vessel from another port or place in the Philippines in possession of the United States.. .02
On each departure of a vessel for another port or place in the Philippines in possession of the United States.. .02

Vessels belonging to or employed by the United States Government, vessels of neutral foreign governments engaged in trade, vessels in distress, yachts belonging to organized clubs, shall be be exempt from light dues.

Coastwise cargoes are subject to duties as if coming from foreign ports, except as to the trade between ports in possession of the United States.

ENTRANCE AND CLEARANCE OF VESSELS.

Every vessel shall, on arrival, be placed under military gu:
until discharged.   Passengers with no dutiable property may la
without detention.   Goods not declared on the manifest are s
ject to 25 per cent extra duty when found.   Missing articles sh
be paid for by the vessel at the rate of $1 per ton measureme
unless the deficiency be explained.   The master of the ve:
must, within twenty-four hours after arrival, under penalty for f:
ure of $1 per ton, produce the proper manifest, certified by the c
lector of the port if the vessel be from the United States, or b
consul or commercial agent of the United States if it be from
foreign country; or in the absence of such representative, by
consul of any nation at peace with the United States.   No cle
ance will be granted to any vessel for a port in the Philippines i
in possession of the United States.

THE LADRONE ISLANDS.·

The archipelago of the Mariannes or Ladrones is composed
a chain of volcanic islands in the Pacific Ocean east of the Phil
pines, extending north and south for a space of 140 leagues, betw(
13° and 21° north latitude, and 144° and 146° east longitu
The largest island, Guam, is some 1,700 miles from Manila, ab(
the same distance from Yokohama, and a little less than 4,c
miles from Honolulu.   The advantages afforded by the fact tl
the islands were on the grand track from Acapulco to Man
and the facility of procuring fresh provisions and water, indu(
the Spaniards to take possession of them in 1565.

The islands are fifteen in number, although only four are inh:
ited, and comprise an area of 417 square miles.   The name
" Islas de los Ladrones," or " Thieves' Islands," was given to them
account of the propensity to theft evinced by the natives, althou
Father Gobien, who wrote a history of the archipelago, states tl
they hold this vice in detestation.   The islands when origina
discovered had a population of nearly 40,000 inhabitants, w
received the settlers well, and made great progress until the Sp;
iards began to attack their independence.   The resulting w

---

* Much of the above information has been compiled from the North Pacific Direct
Alexander George Findlay, F. R. G. S.

almost destroyed the natives, hardly 10,000 remaining. The majority of the population is located on Guam; there, also, is the principal town—San Ignacio de Agaña.

The indigenous race, called Chamarros, very much resembles the Tagals and Visayas of the Philippines, but are perhaps more indolent—a fault compensated for by sobriety and unselfishness. The black residents of Saypan are derived from the Carolines, and are active and industrious. It rains heavily and almost constantly on the Ladrones. The temperature is mild and much cooler than at the Philippines, except in August and September, when the trade winds are interrupted, resulting in intense heat and frequent hurricanes.

Guam, the southernmost island and the seat of government, is 27 miles long and varies in width from 3 to 10 miles. It is almost surrounded by reefs, and there is no anchorage on the east side. The west side is low and full of sandy bays. The island is flat, and the soil is dry and indifferently fruitful. Rice, pineapples, watermelons, muskmelons, oranges, limes, cocoanuts, and breadfruit constitute the principal products. San Ignacio de Agaña had, in 1870, 3,500 inhabitants. There is a governor's house, an artillery magazine, a church, and a college, the last founded in 1673. The town is on the seashore, but there is no anchorage. Ships call at San Luis de Apra, which is over 2 miles away, but is connected with Agaña by a good road.

Rota Island, about 30 miles north of Guam, is 12 miles in length and about 5½ in breadth, rising in the center to 800 feet. The town, which bears the same name, has between 300 and 400 inhabitants.

Other islands of any size are Tinian, 42 miles northeast of Rota, 9 miles long and 4½ broad; Saypan, close by Tinian, 13½ miles in length, with a population of a few hundred; Agrigan, one of the northernmost islands, containing a peak over 2,000 feet in height; and Pagan, 8 miles long and 2½ broad, with volcanoes said to be active. Tinian is fertile and has a large number of cattle. A lepers' hospital is located here. There was at one time an American colony on Saypan and Agrigan, but it was forcibly removed by the Spanish governor.

Bull. No. 2——6

RUBBER DISTRICT OF PARA.

The British consul at Para writes:

"Some people suppose that the supply of Amazonian rubber may become exhausted in the near future. The most competent authorities are not at all of this opinion, but maintain that the supply is inexhaustible, because the 'hevea' is continually being reproduced by nature. Certainly some areas become exhausted when overworked, but when left alone for some time they recover. The district of Cametá, on the river Tocantins, produced an excellent quality of rubber, for which there was a special quotation. This district is now exhausted, because, for about forty years, thousands of men have tapped its trees. All newcomers flocked to Cametá to make their fortunes. There are many districts that have not been tapped. The area that is known to produce Para rubber amounts to at least 1,000,000 square miles. Further exploration will, no doubt, show that this area is underestimated."

COSTA RICA.

NEW REPRESENTATIVE—GREAT IMPROVEMENTS.

Dr. ULLOA, first vice-president of Costa Rica, has taken up his residence in New York for the purpose of acting as consul-general of the Republic in that city. To an Associated Press correspondent he is quoted as saying that his first official duty will be to open a bureau of information, so that the manufacturers, shippers, and importers of the United States can secure all necessary information with reference to his country and its business methods and the manner of packing goods for shipment, etc. He also expressed a hope that he could induce immigration to Costa Rica through spreading a knowledge of the country.

With regard to recent public undertakings in Costa Rica, the consul-general said that great improvements are in progress. New land laws are to be enacted for the encouragement of immigration, and a railroad is being built to connect Limón, the Atlantic port, with the new Pacific port of Tivives, giving a railroad from ocean to ocean.

NEW MINISTRY.

Through an oversight, the July BULLETIN credited the new ministry, as constituted under the second term of President IGLESIAS's administration, to Nicaragua, instead of to Costa Rica. The error was not discovered until too late for correction. The personnel of the present ministry of Costa Rica is as follows:

Foreign Relations, Public Instruction, etc.........Señor PEDRO PÉRÉZ ZELEDÓN.
Interior and Public Works......... ....Señor Don JOSÉ ASTÚA AGUILAR.
Finance and Commerce.........................Señor Don JUAN B. QUIRÓS.
War and Navy .... Señor Don DEMETRIO TINOCO.

GUATEMALA.

NECESSARY IMPLEMENTS AND MACHINERY.—MANUFACTURED PAPER.

The British consul at Guatemala, in reporting to his Government, says that axes are supplied largely by the United States, because they more nearly meet the requirements of the natives. Table cutlery is not in great demand; metal-handled knives, with scimitar blades, made in Germany, are generally used. There is a good demand for what are called "cuchillos de monte," a kind of hunting knife in a sheath. The blade is common, but the handle and sheath are finished in gaudy colors, as the implement is carried as much for show as for its utility.

Many hoes are required to supply the market, as they are necessary adjuncts of every coffee and sugar plantation. They are used not only in the ordinary manner, but also take the place of spades or shovels. The principal requirements for the hoe for Guatemalan use are length and height and a round eye. They must be made of steel which will "strike fire," this being the test of the native cultivator.

Galvanized 4-point barbed wire and 4-ply barbless galvanized wire are largely used for fencing throughout the country, the latter to a much less degree than the former. The United States and Germany supply this wire, having displaced the English wire, which formerly had a monopoly.

There is a demand for mills for cattle power on small plantations. Those in use are of light construction and are for crushing sugar cane, grinding corn, and making tortillas. The style of mill most used is one made in Buffalo, N. Y.

Regarding the paper trade of Guatemala, the French Chargé

d'Affaires makes a report to his Government from which the following information is derived:

Germany stands first in the paper trade in Guatemala, but France ranks a good second. The chief demand is for wood papers of a strength of 3, 4, and 5 kilos, the latter weight being in great demand. The usual size is that known as "Sittris" one-fourth and one-eighth foolscap.

Unruled paper is not in much demand owing to the dearness of hand labor and the scarcity of ruling machines; it constitutes 25 per cent of the total trade. Ruled paper comprises "office," 50 per cent of the total trade; "margin," 15 per cent; and "invoice" 10 per cent. Plain unruled paper is used largely in 3 kilos weight, and laid paper is used by cigarette factors.

Drawing paper comes from France and packing paper (straw) from Germany. Tissue paper comes from Austria and cigarette paper from Spain. Printing paper comes from Germany, Austria, Belgium and the United States (especially).

The prevailing Italian, French, and German sizes of envelopes are used, but those coming from the United States are much preferred. The wall papers, in demand, come almost exclusively from France.

The customs duties per kilo upon paper, as reported by the French official, are as follows, in piastres (a piastre representing about 75 cents, United States currency): Cotton paper, colored and of all classes, not ruled, gross weight, 0.15; without borders, unglazed, gross weight, 0.15; papers of all kinds, ruled in any way, gross weight, 0.30; wall papers of all kinds, but without gilding or silvering (nor velveted), weight, with cover, 0.20; papers of all kinds, without borders, for cigarettes, gross weight, 0.30; tracing paper, weight, with envelope, 0.20; tissue paper, weight, with packing, 0.2; colored papers for flowers, weight, with packing, 0.20.

HAITI.

PROJECTED RAILWAY FROM CAPE HAITIEN.

LEMUEL W. LIVINGSTON, United States consul at Cape Haitien, reports to the Department of State that plans are being perfected for beginning the construction of a line of narrow-gauge railway

from Cape Haitien to La Grande Riviere du Nord, a point distant about 18 miles to the northeast. The capital stock of the
company is $450,000, and the estimated cost $250,000. Those
projecting the enterprise have already subscribed $25,000, while
675 shares, at $500 a share, are open to general subscription, with
a guaranteed interest by the Government of 8 per cent. The
material, the contract for which has not been awarded, is to be
purchased in the United States. Mr. Henri Thomasset, the
engineer who is to direct the work, and who constructed the
tramway at Port au Prince, testifies to the superior workmanship
and incomparable durability of material obtained from the United
States.

The list of names of the persons interested in the enterprise
includes those of some of the Ministers and ex-Ministers of the
Government, and other business men of prominence and standing.

In the articles of incorporation the Government grants to
Messrs. CINCINNATUS LECONTE and BLANC EUSÈBE, the former at
present Minister of the Interior and Public Works, the exclusive
privilege of constructing the road in question, the concession to
last for a period of sixty years. All articles and material necessary for the work are to be admitted free of duty. The Government grants to the concessionaries, for a period of thirty years,
the tolls of an iron bridge, which is to be the terminus of the road
at Cape Haitien, and also the public lands in the districts of
Cape Haitien and Grande-Rivière along the route.

The country through which the road is to pass is a beautiful and
fertile plain, adapted to the cultivation of all the peculiar products
of the island, and is said to be specially suited to the growth of the
banana. The roads at present traversing the region are in very
poor condition, and in wet weather are well-nigh impassable,
entailing great hardships upon the peasant producers in getting
their produce to the markets. The transportation methods are
very primitive. The donkey is the universal beast of burden, and,
although it is in general a dwarf species, is made to do all the
work that is generally imposed upon a horse. Not only is the great
bulk of vegetables, fruit, coffee, and cacao, brought to the
market by donkeys, but they carry almost all the immense amount
of logwood and logwood roots shipped from this country.

In such a country and under such conditions a railroad is not only a prime necessity, but must work a sort of industrial revolution. It is expected by its projectors that it will stimulate production to an unprecedented extent by giving the industrious peasantry the benefit of rapid transit and modern market facilities, thus becoming at once a profitable investment and a substantial public improvement.

MEXICO.

THE FREE ZONE. (ZONA LIBRE.)

The Department of State has received through Consul-General BARLOW a report of the Free Zone, compiled by the Secretary of the Treasury of Mexico, giving a history of the original creation of the zone and defining its limits, and the privileges and restrictions applicable thereto.

The Free Zone is a narrow strip of territory extending along the northern border from the Gulf of Mexico to the Pacific Ocean, with a latitudinal area of about $12\frac{1}{2}$ miles to the interior, and embracing a portion of the States of Tamaulipas, Coahuila, Chihuahua, Sonora, and the territory of Lower California. It was established many years ago by the Central Government, as a compromise or concession to the States bordering the Rio Grande, as a protection against smuggling from the United States.

The principal cities of the zone are Matamoras, Camargo, Mier, Guerrero, Laredo, Porfirio Diaz (Piedras Negras), Juarez, and Nogales. The total population does not exceed 100,000 people. According to the official reports, there exist within the limits of the free zone no industries worth mentioning, which is explained by the fact that all industrial products manufactured in the zone when sent into the interior of the country are required to pay the regular duties charged on imports into the country; and, on account of the protective tariff of the United States, it is impracticable to export such products to that country. Thus the manufacturing industries would have to depend upon the home consumption, which is not sufficient to maintain them.

All merchandise imported into the zone destined for consumption therein is admitted on a basis of 10 per cent of the regular tariff duties, but such merchandise when reshipped into the interior

is fertile and there is an abundance of moisture. Here the cotton plants run as high as 160 pods with the pip, and weigh sometimes 2 ounces each.

The "cuartilla," about 25,000 square yards of land, is planted with 7,000 to 10,000 plants, and the average product is 5,000 pounds to the cuartilla. In May or June, when the rain begins, corn is planted, and in September cotton is planted between the rows. The seeds are dropped into holes 5 feet apart, and having been soaked in water, generally sprout in a week. At the end of the first month the planter proceeds to cut out the little groups, leaving but two or three of the best developed plants. A week or two later he lays each plant flat on the ground, with dirt to keep it down. This is on account of the "northers," and also to prevent the plants from mixing. From the prostrate plants the aftergrowth is robust. The picking is done six months after planting.

The Pacific cotton belt is only about 50 miles wide at the mean, but is more extensive than that of the Gulf, though not as accessible. This zone reaches from Sonora to Chiapas, 1,500 miles.

Sonora is a land of sharp contrasts, lofty mountains, and deep-set valleys. Cotton was first cultivated in the Hermosillo district, early in this century. About 1842 the large Angeles mills were put up. The cotton worm appeared and the industry is now confined to the Guaymas Valley. The lack of water is partly accountable for the decadence of cotton culture. A few planters persisted in the work, not deterred by droughts, cotton worms, locusts, and other incidental obstacles.

Sinaloa runs farther south. Cotton used to be cultivated from Fuerte to Mocotito, but the continuous droughts have operated to close it out, except along the river courses. From Culiacan to Tepic the outlook is better. In Sinaloa the profit is about 40 per cent.

The tiny territory of Tepic should produce well. The Santiago Valley, 8 by 28 leagues, has had a yield of 7,500 pounds to the fanega (50,000 square yards).

Jalisco is a great state in western Mexico. Some day the railroads will reach toward Zihuatlan and other excellent cotton districts in Jalisco.

ART. 3. In the erection of the warehouses and shops, and in the general expenses of the business, the company binds itself to invest at least the sum of $250,000 within the period of five years, counted from the date of this contract (May 28, 1898), and said investment must be proved by means of payrolls, receipts, invoices, and book entries, which the company must present either in the original or in duly certified copies.

ART. 4. In order to guarantee the performance of the obligations contained in this contract, the company shall, as soon as it is signed, deposit in the national bank the sum of $10,000 in consolidated debt bonds.

ART. 7. If the Government needs the petroleum extracted by the company, the latter shall sell it to the Government at a rebate of 10 per cent on the wholesale prices to the general public.

ART. 11. The concessionaires may, on a single occasion, import duty free, the machinery, apparatus, implements, construction material, and other articles necessary for the plant, and, in each case of importation, shall give bond, which shall be cancelled as soon as the machinery is set up, or it is proved that the material or other article has been properly employed.

ART. 12. For ten years, counted from the date of the promulgation of this contract, the capital invested by the company in the establishment and development of the industry shall enjoy exemption from all direct federal taxes, but the concessionaires or the company remain subject to the payment of all taxes included in the internal-revenue stamp law.

ART. 17. The duration of this contract shall be ten years, counted from the date of its promulgation.

INDUSTRIES OF MONTEREY.

Consul-General JOHN K. POLLARD, under date of May 24, 1898, transmits to the Department of State a report on the industries of Monterey, from which the following is summarized: The city is the capital of the State of Nuevo Leon, and has a population of, approximately, 73,000, and because of its progress in recent years is called the Chicago of Mexico. It is lighted throughout by electricity, has six banks, and is well equipped with telegraph and telephone service and street-car lines. Four railways pass through the city. The soil of the State of Nuevo Leon is particularly fertile, yielding, in certain products, three crops annually. The manufacture of cotton cloths, hats, furniture, etc., is carried on extensively. There are over 3,000 primary schools in the State, as well as many others of higher grade.

NICARAGUA.

TRADE AND COMMERCE FOR THE YEAR 1897.

The Bureau has received a copy of the general report of W. J. CHAMBERS, British consul, on the trade of Nicaragua for the year 1897, published by the British Foreign Office.

It appears that owing to the fall in the price of coffee and the reduced value of silver, the commercial conditions of the country at the time of the report were by no means satisfactory.

The total imports into Nicaragua for the year under consideration, inclucing produce introduced from neighboring Central American States was £528,384 ($2,567,946.24). This amount compared with the preceding year, gives a decrease of about £158,000 ($767,880). The report shows that without exception the trade of all the European countries with Nicaragua experienced a marked reduction, while that with the United States increased about 2 per cent. The United States is the sole provider of breadstuffs, provisions, petroleum, rice, and potatoes, as well as a fair proportion of leather goods, wines, machinery, agricultural implements, hardware, drugs, and coarse cotton fabrics.

The total exports from the country, in 1897 reached the sum of £611,533 ($2,972,050.38). This amount compared with the receipts for 1895 shows a falling off of £416,146 ($2,022,469.56). This is accounted for mainly by the lower price of coffee and consequent smaller quantity exported during the year. The exportation of sugar, indigo, cattle, cheese, and other native products to the other Central American States also records a falling off in volume. The shipment of gold, in bars and dust, also fustic and valuable timbers, increased somewhat over the previous year, as did also the extract of dyewoods, which is latterly becoming an industry of importance. The cultivation of cocoa steadily increased and shows a marked growth over that of previous years. The average price of this commodity in Nicaragua is about 1s. 7d. (38 cents) per pound.

Almost the entire business done on the Atlantic coast is with the United States. New Orleans being the nearest port of importance, and having better steam connection, receives most of the exports and furnishes the bulk of the imports to the country.

The construction of the railway from Masaya to Jinotepe has made great progress during the year and is expected to be open for traffic during the current month; this is the principal feature of public work undertaken during the year. Good telegraphic communication has been established between Greytown and the interior.

As has been referred to repeatedly in the MONTHLY BULLETIN, the Atlas Steamship Company, an English Corporation, has established itself as a monopoly of the transportation business on the San Juan River and Lake Nicaragua. This company will build a short railway between Greytown and Colorado Junction on the San Juan River to overcome the trouble incident to low water on that part of the river during the dry season.

About 700 tons of coal were brought from England to Corinto; this appears to be the total amount imported during the year. There is no consumption of coal in the interior, the forests easily furnishing wood for fuel to locomotives and steamers.

The following tables show the value of the principal articles of imports and exports into and from Nicaragua during the year 1897:

IMPORTS.

Articles.	Value.
Manufactured cotton goods of all kinds	£205,000
Woolen goods	20,560
Provisions	11,200
Wines and spirits	40,440
Flour	27,000
Barbed-wire fencing	15,000
Drugs	17,000
Cement	5,000
Matches	2,000
Hardware	18,000
Beer	7,000
Candles	3,750
Soap	4,700
Leather	2,750
Oils	1,000
Petroleum	2,500
Sewing machines and machinery	8,000
Sewing thread	10,120
Chinaware and glassware	3,000
Paper, books, etc	2,755
Coffee bags	8,105
Galvanized iron roofing	3,140
Iron and steel	2,000
Boilers	2,500
Saddles, harness, etc	2,300
Other articles	103,564
Total	528,384

EXPORTS.

Articles.	Quantity (about).	Approximate Value.
Coffee...........bags..	154,000	£385,000
Rubber..........hundredweight..	1,596	16,000
Hides.......do....	3,500	10,500
Deerskins.......do....	785	3,120
Logwood, fustic, etc.......tons..	1,336	2,672
Extract of fustic (dyewood).......do....	97	5,432
Mahogany.......square feet.	20,277	127
Cedar.......do....	492,190	3,076
Gold bars.......ounces..	32,000	95,000
Gold dust.......do....	4,000	15,000
Silver dollars.......coins..	617,500	51,000
Cattle.......head..	1,500	6,500
Soap.......hundredweight..	107	107
Indigo.......do....	210	2,310
Sugar.......do....	500	500
Salt.......do....	6,303·	3,600
Leather.......do....	1,705	4,260
Maize.......do....	17,862	2,679
Cheese.......do....	1,200	2,500
Beans.......o....	466	210
Lard.......do....	513	1,000
Boots.......do....	46	575
Starch, hammocks, straw hats, etc.......do....	....	365
Total..........	....	611,533

NOTE.—To reduce the above values to United States currency use $4.865 as the equivalent of the pound sterling.

THE SIQUIA GOLD MINING DISTRICT.

Mr. J. P. MORGAN writes to the Bureau from Rama, Nicaragua, about the new mining operations in the vicinity of that town. He states that within a day's journey, by small boats, one of the most promising gold mining districts has been opened along the Rama, Siquia, and Mico rivers, extending many miles on the Gurupera Mountain, only about 4 miles of which have as yet been prospected. The water supply is abundant and the hills heavily wooded, affording plenty of fuel and timber for the mines. Wild game is easily secured, and there are many plantations of bananas, plantains, sweet potatoes, and other vegetables in the vicinity, so that the food supply is ample, while the labor is cheap, with wages running from $10 to $30 per month.

The gold-bearing rock is accessible, being so situated as to require very little machinery to work it, and has yielded from $17 to $35 per ton. It is also said that paying quantities of gold are found in the beds of the numerous streams that flow into the Mico River.   Rama is a perfectly healthy, flourishing town of about 1,000 inhabitants, possessing schools, churches, cable communication with the rest of the world, and has a triweekly mail service by means of the fruit steamers sailing to New Orleans, Mobile, and other United States ports.   There are fair hotel accommodations, with charges at the rate of a dollar a day in United States gold.   The laws of Nicaragua admit, free of duty, all machinery, dynamite, and other necessary articles imported for mining purposes.   The inhabitants are hospitable, and welcome the coming of persons to engage in enterprises for the development of the country.

CONVENTION OF DEPUTIES OF THE GREATER REPUBLIC.

The Associated Press correspondent reports by mail from Managua, Nicaragua, that the convention of deputies from Salvador, Honduras, and Nicaragua was still holding daily sessions during the latter part of July.   The committee appointed to report on the articles for a constitution for their States, submitted to it by the Diet of the Greater Republic, under whose call it met, has reported many modifications.   The committee also suggests a centralization of the States named, having a federal district composed of the civil departments of Chinandega, bordering on the Pacific Ocean and the Gulf of Fonseca, in Nicaragua; of Amapala, bordering on the Gulf of Fonseca, in Honduras, and of La Union, bordering on the Pacific Ocean and Gulf of Fonseca, in Salvador; with Amapala, situated on the island of Tigre, in the Gulf of Fonseca, as the capital city. The convention, however, by a large majority, voted down the centralization idea and favored a confederation of the three States under the name of the United States of Central America.

PARAGUAY.

MANUFACTURE AND SALE OF MATCHES.

Consul RUFFIN sends the following from Ascunsion, under date of May 31, 1898: "There are two factories in Ascunsion, the matches being chiefly of wax.   The factories are not large, and I presume do not supply the demands of the country. Very liberal concessions are made by the Government to this industry.

"The wax matches retail at 1½ cents gold per small box; the wooden ones at about five-sevenths of a cent gold.

"During the year 1897 there were imported 5,981 kilograms (13,158 pounds) of wooden matches, representing an official value of $1,498 gold; the custom-house tax thereon being 25 per cent ad valorem. They came chiefly from Sweden. The importation of wax matches is insignificant.

"It would be a little difficult at the beginning to compete with domestic factories, but I believe the matches of the United States could win a place in this market.

"I am indebted for the information above given to the chief of the statistical bureau of Paraguay."

AGRICULTURAL DEVELOPMENT.

Consul RUFFIN writes that the "people are beginning to awake to the necessity of agricultural development. The farmers are widely scattered, and there is a growing sentiment in favor of centralization and of heavy foreign colonization.

"The Government, through the Agricultural Bank, gives to each farmer $300 paper (amounting to $35 or $40 in gold) in the form of a loan on the property. It is urged in behalf of the class which does not own property that the Government purchase large tracts of arable land, let them to the farmers, and give them farming implements, seeds, etc. There is much enthusiasm on the part of the promoters of this plan."

PERU.

ADVICE TO COMMERCIAL SALESMEN.

The British Consul at Callao reports to his home Government that Lima merchants object strenuously to commercial salesmen competing with them on what they consider unequal terms. The merchants claim that they are at great expense in keeping up their offices and houses, while traveling salesmen turn their apartments at hotels and inns into show rooms at a trifling expense.

Bull. No. 2——7

Steps are being taken to induce the Government to compel all commercial salesmen to take out licenses. The matter has been laid before the Department of Commerce at Lima, with the proposition that the cost of a commercial salesman's license be fixed at 500 soles ($243.25) for a period of six months, renewable at the end of each period. In case of failure to take out the license, double that amount is to be exacted of the offender, one-third of which is to be paid to the informer.

According to the Foreign Office Annual Series, 2117, of Great Britian, in southern Peru every facility appears to be given to the commercial salesmen. They are allowed to enter with their samples, on presenting, through a responsible agent, to the custom-house, an official request to pass so many packages of samples. These are examined and valued and then a bond is presented by the agent, who undertakes to pay the amount of the valuation of any of the samples that may not be reshipped within the term specified, generally ninety days. This will cost the salesman from $2.50 to $5, according to the number of packages he brings, and he is then free to go where he likes with his samples, without being compelled to give an account of them in any other port of the interior he may visit.

Responsible local agents, before giving the bond to the custom-house, satisfy themselves as to the status of the salesman, who, in most cases, besides his business card, brings a letter of introduction to some known resident in the port. The latter requisite should not be overlooked by intending commercial visitors.

COAL DEPOSITS.

A new anthracite coal field is about to be developed near the summit of the Andes Mountains, in Peru. A concession for this mining district was granted to Mr. C. B. Jones in 1892, to run twenty years, covering a section of land 100 miles long, situated from 25 to 125 miles back from the coast.

Engineers have already been sent from the United States to Peru to make a survey for constructing a railway from Pacasmayo to the province of Hualgayoc. The Pacific Company is backed by $20,000,000 capital and has the exclusive right to mine coal.

According to Mr. G. CLINTON GARDNER, formerly superintendent of the Pennsylvania Railroad and builder of the Mexican National Railway, the supply of coal is almost inexhaustible; 10,000,000 tons are within easy reach. Mr. GARDNER estimates that 2,000,000 tons can be mined yearly and delivered to the port at a cost of $2, gold, per ton, in which case he is of the opinion that all other coal will be excluded from the Pacific markets, as under the circumstances it will be impossible to compete with so good and so cheap a product as Peruvian coal.

In addition to the concession to mine coal in the district named, the company has exclusive right to build railroads running to these mines, and has already leased from the Government a fine pier at Pacasmayo. Mr. GARDNER states that the cost of construction of the railway line and the purchase of the rolling stock should not exceed $3,000,000. The line is to start from Pacasmayo, the total distance from the coast to the coal district being 121 miles. A line is already in operation from Pacasmayo to Yonan, a distance of 41 miles, which is being worked by a Peruvian operator.

The well-known United States newspaper correspondent, Mr. FRANK G. CARPENTER, says that the coal fields of the Andes include both anthracite and lignite coal, the anthracite occurring in large quantities on both the east and west slopes of the Andes. That on the east side lies about 1,500 or 2,000 feet below the summit, and its quality has been found fully equal and in some respects better than the Pennsylvania anthracite. To convey the coal from the eastern slope to the coast requires a railroad to surmount the Andes at a height of about 14,000 feet, but from that point it will be not over 75 miles in a straight line to the coast, and the road will pass through a number of good-sized towns and a rich agricultural country. These coal properties, he says, should prove more valuable even than gold mines, as, up to the present time, there has been practically no good coal mined in the western side of South America, and, of the 3,000,000 tons used there each year, the largest part comes from Australia, England, Japan, and British Columbia.

Besides the coal deposits in the province of Hualgayoc, others exist in the Huamachuco district, and lignite and peat are found in several other parts of Peru.

UNITED STATES.

TRADE WITH LATIN AMERICA.

STATEMENT OF IMPORTS AND EXPORTS.

Following is the latest statement, from figures compiled by the Bureau of Statistics, United States Treasury Department, O. P. Austin, Chief, showing the value of the trade between the United States and the Latin-American countries. The report is for the month of May, 1898, corrected to June 27, 1898, with a comparative statement for the corresponding period of the previous year; also for the eleven months ending May, 1898, compared with the corresponding period of the fiscal year 1897. It should be explained that the figures from the various custom-houses, showing imports and exports for any one month, are not received at the Treasury Department until about the 20th of the following month, and some time is necessarily consumed in compilation and printing, so that the returns for May, for example, are not published until some time in July.

IMPORTS OF MERCHANDISE.

Articles and countries.	May—		Eleven months ending May—	
	1897.	1898.	1897.	1898.
Chemicals:				
Logwood (*Palo campeche; Páu campeche; Campêche*)—				
Mexico....................	$545	....	$11,794	$21,700
Coal, bituminous (*Carbón bituminoso; Carvão betuminoso; Charbon de terre*):				
Mexico...	23,576	$19,565	198,229	180,351
Cocoa (*Cacao; Coco ou Cacáo crú; Cacao*):				
Brazil	8,372	8,909	326,697	170,115
Other South America	115,553	69,237	867,336	1,058,986
Coffee (*Café*):				
Central America...............	691,354	695,237	5,433,678	4,192,716
Mexico	380,358	425,786	4,222,704	3,435,647
Brazil.........................	3,721,066	3,310,080	49,131,988	38,554,238
Other South America...........	807,761	965,656	10,175,846	8,553,215
Cotton, unmanufactured (*Algodón en rama; Algodão em rama; Coton, non manufacturé*):				
South America.................	7,233	8,913	91,166	121,653

IMPORTS OF MERCHANDISE—Continued.

Articles and countries.	May—		Eleven months ending May—	
	1897.	1898.	1897.	1898.
Fibers.				
Sisal grass (*Henequén; Henequen; Hennequen*)—				
Mexico...................	$283,637	$454,434	$3,370,453	$4,098,587
Fruits:				
Bananas (*Plátanos; Bananas; Bananes*)—				
Central America.............	183,668	176,657	1,290,532	1,370,397
South America...............	137,073	72,787	570,628	518,596
Oranges (*Naranjas; Laranjas; Oranges*)—				
Mexico...................	10	56	253,512	134,654
Furskins (*Pieles finas; Pelles; Fourrures*):				
South America.............. ..,.........		71	16,428	38,848
Hides and skins (*Cueros y pieles; Couros e pelles; Cuirs et peaux*):				
Central America...............	13,613	14,600	217,773	177,959
Mexico......................	97,833	84,197	1,658,085	1,578,990
South America.....	1,046,835	649,384	7,904,205	8,112,386
India rubber, crude (*Goma eldstica cruda; Borracha crua; Caoutchouc brut*):				
Central America...............	41,164	14,890	414,438	382,736
Mexico	2,121	3,932	27,307	33,838
Brazil........................	981,357	948,388	11,075,822	14,463,751
Other South America...........	35,059	43,453	432,610	573,257
Lead, in pigs, bars, etc. (*Plomo en galdpagos, barras etc.; Chumbo em linguados, barras etc.; Plombs, en saumons, en barres, etc.*):				
Mexico......................	165,592	102,992	1,301,732	1,521,474
Sugar, not above No. 16 Dutch standard (*Azúcar, no superior al No. 16 de la escala holandesa; Assucar não superior ao No. 16 de padrão hollandez; Sucre, pas au-dessus du type hollandais, No. 16*):				
Central America............		76,863	....	156,777
Mexico.....................	582	16,228	16,505	38,132
Brazil	21,230	291,483	2,136,989	2,125,368
Other South America	80,112	99,231	4,495,213	3,630,774
Tobacco, leaf (*Tabaco en rama; Tabaco em folha; Tabac en feuilles*):				
Mexico.......................	26,287	16,191	277,165	230,676
Wood mahogany (*Madera, caoba; Mogno; Acajou*):				
Central America...............	220	6	102,289	139,122
Mexico......................	39,272	11,881	292,212	280,507
South America			31,864	41,457
Wool (*Lana; Lã; Laine*):				
South America—				
Class 1 (clothing).............	990,462	64,528	4,225,707	839,532
Class 2 (combing)	491,317	....	968,215	9,598
Class 3 (carpet)...............	453,780	189,990	1,210,228	668,083

EXPORTS OF DOMESTIC MERCHANDISE.

Articles and countries.	May—		Eleven months ending May—	
	1897.	1898.	1897.	1898.
Agricultural implements (*Instrumentos de agricultura; Instrumentos de agricultura; Machines agricoles*):				
Central America.................	$3,932	$113	$35,414	$14,507
Mexico........................	8,221	16,591	121,107	114,292
Santo Domingo.................	56	....	1,383	1,056
Argentina.....................	5,110	27,201	375,136	361,805
Brazil	1,153	195	19,433	23,966
Colombia	65	848	3,299	3,796
Other South America	4,171	17,138	137,067	175,801
Animals:				
Cattle (*Ganado vacuno; Gado; Betail*)—				
Central America..............	2,805	40	14,820	7,058
Mexico......................	2,970	10,020	26,776	68,700
South America	77	250	2,814	7,212
Hogs (*Cerdos; Porcos; Cochons*)—				
Mexico......................	635	76	262,988	44,442
Horses (*Caballos; Cavallos; Chevaux*)—				
Central America..............	950	1,465	37,972	12,045
Mexico........	18,275	2,965	87,858	78,065
South America	....	....	11,655	5,700
Sheep (*Carneros; Carneiros; Moutons*)—				
Mexico......................	....	400	11,877	9,510
South America	2,000	180	10,403	10,314
Books, maps, engravings, etc. (*Libros, mapas, grabados, etc.; Livros, mappas, gravuras, etc.; Livres, cartes de géographie, gravures, etc.*):				
Central America.................	3,496	529	60,641	33,831
Mexico	4,743	7,681	150,375	119,148
Santo Domingo.................	5	....	1,245	455
Argentina.....................	5,561	457	24,068	25,192
Brazil	22,643	1,087	107,004	151,812
Colombia	895	304	72,244	16,925
Other South America	3,009	2,290	50,996	37,924
Breadstuffs:				
Corn (*Maíz; Milho; Maïs*)—				
Central America....	7,774	11,544	41,236	66,389
Mexico......................	131,461	1,258	3,189,789	42,404
Santo Domingo....	46	....	375	166
South America.................	261	1,674	11,584	36,843
Wheat (*Trigo; Trigo; Blé*)—				
Central America..............	7,785	4,144	71,236	39,793
South America	167	95,745	153,371	1,629,128
Wheat flour (*Harina de trigo; Farina de trigo; Farine de blé*)—				
Central America..............	153,310	137,723	1,086,821	1,096,301
Mexico	12,016	9,194	92,101	73,548

EXPORTS OF DOMESTIC MERCHANDISE—Continued.

Articles and countries.	May—		Eleven months ending May—	
	1897.	1898.	1897.	1898.
Breadstuffs—Continued.				
Wheat flour—Continued.				
Santo Domingo...............	$12,347	$1,469	$140,125	$149,156
Brazil	249,902	229,762	3,354,868	3,010,661
Colombia	41,573	47,609	527,004	486,321
Other South America..........	91,682	118,269	1,363,320	1,582,875
Carriages, cars, etc., and parts of (*Carruages, carros y sus accesorios; Carruagens, carros, e partes de carros; Voitures, wagons et leurs parties*):				
Central America...............	3,896	6,680	132,961	41,923
Mexico	21,045	13,699	340,667	483,130
Santo Domingo.................	6,073	....	18,997	23,374
Argentina.....................	9,934	7,077	130,247	201,480
Brazil	15,692	26,381	118,126	533,987
Colombia ....:.....	1,589	1,702	49,519	38,038
Other South America...........	6,577	8,369	42,615	77,483
Cycles and parts of (*Biciclos y sus accesorios; Bicyclos e accessorios; Bicyclettes et leurs parties*):				
Central America...............	2,122	381	52,894	7,333
Mexico	6,170	6,410	66,952	59,976
Santo Domingo.................	90	....	4,310	1,134
Argentina.....	2,262	8,166	38,323	80,629
Brazil	3,873	8,612	25,377	88,849
Colombia	2,235	340	21,619	15,031
Other South America...........	6,096	4,129	68,647	46,374
Clocks and watches (*Relojes de pared y de bolsillo; Relogios de pareded e de bolso; Pendules et montres*):				
Central America.....	790	341	12,131	6,923
Mexico	567	1,655	22,799	18,685
Argentina.....................	1,502	570	33,337	24,915
Brazil	1,920	1,130	57,319	38,693
Other South America...........	4,796	4,989	93,255	80,167
Coal (*Carbón; Carvão; Charbon*):				
Central America...............	2,950	391	27,202	19,135
Mexico	49,517	111,236	563,416	852,390
Santo Domingo.................	966	1,445	24,367	10,729
Brazil.......................	2	10,050	60,575	74,596
Colombia	100	....	19,164	32,434
Other South America...........	6,467	660	30,210	18,300
Copper (*Cobre; Cobre; Cuivre*):				
Mexico......................	....	2,765	10,471	21,470
Cotton, unmanufactured (*Algodón no manufacturado; Algodão não manufacturado; Coton non manufacturé*):				
Mexico	17,299	37,803	1,231,036	1,312,173
Cotton cloths (*Tejidos de algodón; Fazendas de algodão; Coton, manufacturé*):				
Central America...............	30,088	30,974	532,422	355,927
Mexico	41,883	36,450	340,872	378,831

EXPORTS OF DOMESTIC MERCHANDISE—Continued.

Articles and countries.	May—		Eleven months ending May—	
	1897.	1898.	1897.	1898.
Cotton cloths—Continued.				
Santo Domingo................	$3,487	$744	$87,147	$91,194
Argentina......................	3,717	12,057	263,580	164,991
Brazil	46,717	28,586	555,797	485,447
Colombia	32,853	23,001	340,535	255,997
Other South America...........	80,427	127,115	1,286,277	1,002,409
Wearing apparel (cotton) (*Ropa de algodón; Roupa de algodão; Vête- ments en coton*):				
Central America................	17,234	25,977	215,536	197,699
Mexico	24,525	28,756	323,260	291,231
Santo Domingo	1,960	....	29,964	17,895
Argentina......................	1,107	4,968	57,405	30,465
Brazil	4,647	1,446	64,694	46,225
Colombia......................	4,576	6,069	47,135	40,051
Other South America...........	2,647	2,557	48,098	32,791
Fruits and nuts (*Frutas y nueces; Frutas e nozes; Fruits et noisettes*):				
Central America................	4,249	1,554	53,564	33,893
Mexico	3,555	5,242	67,728	52,790
Santo Domingo.................	72	....	2,365	1,347
Argentina......	....	1,058	4,379	8,718
Brazil	239	117	11,044	10,845
Colombia	638	753	8,953	10,060
Other South America.....	1,532	1,060	33,161	22,852
Hides and skins (*Cueros y pieles; Couros e pelles; Cuirs et peaux*):				
Central America................	....	....	1,411	....
Mexico	3,808	312	30,909	2,306
Hops (*Lúpulos; Lupulos; Houblon*):				
Central America................	43	252	2,547	3,113
Mexico	492	35	44,613	31,986
Santo Domingo.................	....	....	287	19
South America	44	58	1,212	1,206
Instruments:				
Electric and scientific apparatus (*Aparatos electricos y cientificos; Apparelhos electricos e scientifi- cos; Appareils électriques et sci- entifiques*)—				
Central America..............	6,003	4,479	92,908	55,932
Mexico	36,719	23,483	263,317	258,649
Argentina.....................	15,426	17,449	125,283	104,548
Brazil........................	10,236	1,977	88,507	84,329
Other South America..........	9,274	10,972	195,840	117,030
Iron and steel, manufactures of:				
Builders' hardware, and saws and tools (*Materiales de metal para construcción, sierras y herra- mientas; Ferragens, serras e ferramentas; Matériaux de construction en fer et acier, scies et outils*)—				
Central America.........	11,335	5,033	136,941	76,288
Mexico	59,909	35,565	595,621	397,979

EXPORTS OF DOMESTIC MERCHANDISE—Continued.

Articles and countries.	May—		Eleven Months ending May—	
	1897.	1898.	1897.	1898.
Iron and steel, manufactures of— Continued.				
Builders' hardware, etc.—Cont'd.				
Santo Domingo...............	$721	$10	$9,670	$11,900
Argentina...................	8,984	11,778	195,597	129,514
Brazil.....................	17,074	8,975	229,558	148,456
Colombia	11,004	6,329	108,486	80,857
Other South America..........	18,860	17,820	238,190	191,213
Sewing machines and parts of (*Máquinas de coser y accesorios; Machinas de coser e accessorios; Machines à coudre et leurs parties*):				
Central America..............	4,924	2,650	79,771	28,606
Mexico	16,876	7,179	181,104	188,618
Santo Domingo...............	550	....	1,522	1,236
Argentina	1,775	5,570	82,891	75,786
Brazil.....................	7,401	4,646	111,251	84,102
Colombia	11,945	4,021	108,317	74,497
Other South America..........	10,699	6,811	113,442	92,286
Typewriting machines and parts of (*Máquinas de escribir y accesorios; Machinas de escribir e accessorios; Machines à écrire et leurs parties*).				
Central America........	366	10	10,849	2,320
Mexico	3,527	2,643	23,310	25,208
Santo Domingo...............	......	......	267	90
Argentina...................	128	1,401	11,078	14,172
Brazil.....................	38	447	3,595	4,930
Colombia	260	217	3,348	4,083
Other South America..........	891	735	9,793	13,767
Leather, other than sole (*Cuero, distinto del de suela; Couro não para solas; Cuirs, autres que pour semelles*):				
Central America..............	......	95	4,383	4,282
Mexico	588	287	14,716	8,590
Santo Domingo...............	256	....	1,008	569
Argentina.	......	......	3,905	4,360
Brazil.....................	1,243	5,229	17,414	51,189
Colombia	92	....	2,203	3,181
Other South America..........	329	638	13,718	12,192
Boots and shoes (*Calzado; Calçados; Chaussures*):				
Central America..............	8,562	7,366	88,077	83,056
Mexico	5,976	8,622	54,041	69,832
Colombia	5,127	4,610	38,480	37,420
Other South America..........	1,729	1,805	25,364	25,604
Naval stores: Rosin, tar, etc. (*Resina y alquitrán; Resina e alcatrão; Résine et goudron*):				
Central America..............	2,081	992	21,923	14,469
Mexico	264	1,217	5,696	9,351
Santo Domingo...............	36	....	4,576	5,517

EXPORTS OF DOMÉSTIC MERCHANDISE—Continued.

Articles and countries.	May—		Eleven months ending May—	
	1897.	1898.	1897.	1898.
Naval stores, etc.—Continued.				
Argentina..........	....	....	$57,932	$72,320
Brazil	$10,218	$6,928	216,536	181,955
Colombia	840	869	17,467	11,042
Other South America	15,463	5,596	99,147	85,408
Turpentine, spirits of (*Aguarrds; Agua-raz; Térébenthine*):				
Central America....	184	200	3,981	2,812
Mexico	229	299	2,432	2,958
Santo Domingo.................	24	....	296	447
Argentina.....................	1,693	15,420	48,614	110,665
Brazil........................	1,550	3,083	40,726	61,689
Colombia	470	346	5,467	4,040
Other South America...........	1,321	10,091	35,322	47,446
Oils, mineral, crude (*Aceites, minerales, crudos; Oleos, mineraes, crús; Huiles minérales, brutes*):				
Mexico	36,349	34,781	320,415	317,433
Oils, mineral, refined or manufactured (*Aceites minerales, refinados ó manufacturados; Oleos mineraes, refinados ó manufacturados; Huiles minérales, raffinées ou manufacturées*):				
Central America................	20,534	10,196	137,177	106,471
Mexico	15,051	16,733	154,309	167,831
Santo Domingo.................	15,163	20	46,233	49,784
Argentina.....................	79,028	101,112	1,012,815	902,899
Brazil	167,569	127,661	1,459,536	1,342,233
Colombia	7,363	12,365	106,720	91,867
Other South America	58,932	101,992	926,148	786,876
Oils, vegetable (*Aceites vegetales; Oleos vegetaes; Huiles végétales*):				
Central America................	316	625	4,776	2,926
Mexico	49,917	32,357	305,236	321,566
Santo Domingo.................	2,280	392	13,386	20,686
Argentina.....................	....	....	10,971	4,188
Brazil........................	16,148	10,578	153,256	226,337
Other South America...........	3,650	11,120	67,158	91,166
Paraffin and paraffin wax (*Parafina y cera de parafina; Paraffina e cera de parafina; Paraffine et cire faite de cette substance*):				
Central America................	1,221	1,088	29,396	17,117
Mexico	9,180	8,637	140,037	147,231
Brazil	347	886	12,775	10,124
Other South America...........	1,057	473	4,284	5,703
Provisions, comprising meat and dairy products:				
Beef, canned (*Carne de vaca en latas; Carne de vacca em latas; Bœuf conservé*)—				
Central America...............	5,144	1,639	33,214	26,112
Mexico	565	1,208	13,205	13,241

EXPORTS OF DOMESTIC MERCHANDISE—Continued.

Articles and countries.	May—		Eleven months ending May—	
	1897.	1898.	1897.	1898.
Provisions, comprising meat and dairy products—Continued.				
Beef, canned—Continued.				
Santo Domingo	$21	....	$72	$33
Argentina	84	$52	135	409
Brazil	393	601	16,962	16,548
Colombia	336	1,099	6,052	6,255
Other South America	938	996	11,698	11,556
Beef, salted or pickled (*Carne de vaca, salada ó en salmuera; Carne de vacca, salgada ou em salmoura; Bœuf, salé ou en saumure*)—				
Central America	2,027	3,901	26,498	37,308
Mexico	....	....	194	492
Santo Domingo	21	....	2,220	1,643
Brazil	95	....	3,451	1,112
Colombia	2,039	1,698	12,156	11,500
Other South America	2,884	17,856	144,132	150,727
Tallow (*Sebo; Sebo; Suif*)—				
Central America	7,303	8,878	108,384	87,879
Mexico	1,116	780	35,407	22,481
Santo Domingo	21	321	20,567	26,160
Brazil	2,020	510	6,421	25,070
Colombia	1,225	1,302	8,142	17,852
Other South America	502	1,752	12,264	11,976
Bacon (*Tocino; Toucinho; Lard fumé*)—				
Central America	2,182	1,214	17,031	14,976
Mexico	936	734	8,757	8,874
Santo Domingo	164	....	2,405	1,412
Brazil	46,180	19,871	917,565	496,995
Colombia	285	219	1,625	1,273
Other South America	439	829	18,382	25,966
Hams (*Jamones; Presunto; Jambons*)—				
Central America	3,447	2,257	30,303	26,377
Mexico	2,435	1,999	27,094	20,247
Santo Domingo	260	69	6,709	5,400
Brazil	....	274	1,008	3,196
Colombia	1,400	1,718	13,889	12,824
Other South America	6,526	4,777	87,009	78,385
Pork (*Carne de puerco; Carne de porco; Porc*)—				
Central America	4,992	6,036	52,368	66,078
Santo Domingo	267	264	3,832	3,468
Brazil	165	1,400	17,272	1,955
Colombia	1,038	1,684	6,462	7,919
Other South America	3,753	19,516	160,956	191,316
Lard (*Manteca; Banha; Saindoux*)—				
Central America	10,532	19,236	94,272	136,102
Mexico	30,304	16,920	308,932	170,085
Santo Domingo	1,326	485	20,013	19,029
Argentina	775	....	4,558	2,954

EXPORTS OF DOMESTIC MERCHANDISE—Continued.

Articles and countries.	May—		Eleven months ending May—	
	1897.	1898.	1897.	1898.
Provisions, comprising meat and dairy products—Continued.				
Lard—Continued.				
Brazil	$59,979	$60,321	$620,033	$942,318
Colombia	12,714	16,618	137,512	110,178
Other South America	57,391	96,507	598,448	609,260
Oleo and oleomargarine (*Grasa y oleomargarina; Oleo e oleomargarina; Oléo et oléomargarine*)—				
Central America		148	76	1,006
Mexico		66	642	889
Colombia	1,052	758	6,822	7,290
Other South America	283	1,150	27,955	14,733
Butter (*Mantequilla; Manteiga; Beurre*)--				
Central America	3,167	4,115	40,727	44,814
Mexico	3,259	4,936	36,189	39,339
Santo Domingo	571		6,327	6,151
Brazil	3,850	9,893	34,381	86,873
Colombia	2,527	2,296	16,744	18,818
Other South America	7,295	10,493	80,625	80,029
Cheese (*Queso; Queijo; Fromage*)—				
Central America	1,574	1,339	17,619	16,340
Mexico	565	1,048	13,683	13,224
Santo Domingo	296		4,215	3,282
Brazil			80	257
Colombia	1,190	1,223	10,215	10,439
Other South America	437	788	13,754	15,868
Seeds (*Semillas; Sementes; Semence*)—				
Central America	354	373	9,574	5,020
Mexico	661	458	19,959	29,079
Santo Domingo	45	78	424	742
Argentina		20	782	368
Brazil	7		1,578	858
Colombia	258	16	2,404	1,532
Other South America	122	237	4,594	2,006
Sugar, refined (*Azúcar refinado; Assucar refinado; Sucre raffiné*):				
Central America	6,144	2,702	56,204	47,488
Mexico	3,206	128	22,737	13,541
Santo Domingo	139		2,041	1,504
Colombia	2,100	1,312	41,507	25,513
Other South America		123	1,987	5,141
Tobacco, unmanufactured (*Tabaco no manufacturado; Tabaco não manufacturado; Tabac non manufacturé*):				
Central America	215	1,835	14,426	29,849
Mexico	5,400	15,142	•107,637	129,563
Argentina		1,200	4,055	5,104
Colombia		786	2,356	7,218
Other South America	5,450	6,613	85,750	89,912

EXPORTS OF DOMESTIC MERCHANDISE—Continued.

Articles and countries.	May—		Eleven months ending May—	
	1897.	1898.	1897.	1898.
Tobacco, manufactures of (*Manufacturas de tabaco; Manufacturas de tabaco; Tabac fabriqué*):				
Central America....................	$4,824	$6,831	$58,782	$44,026
Mexico...........................	416	339	12,973	17,725
Argentina.........................	357	537	48,414	2,344
Brazil	....	....	1,355	560
Colombia.........................	23	128	1,242	3,112
Other South America............	8,041	9,102	58,874	73,178
Wood, unmanufactured (*Madera no manufacturado; Madeira não manufacturado; Bois brut*):				
Central America.................	1,954	522	133,959	48,884
Mexico..........................	6,589	28,673	239,910	231,789
Argentina:......................	283	....	33,799	7,085
Brazil	2,240	....	18,434	7,278
Colombia	3,864	1,344	20,273	23,737
Other South America............	3,310	240	18,146	49,540
Lumber (*Maderas; Madeiras; Bois de construction*):				
Central America.................	14,596	2,195	131,497	35,279
Mexico..........................	147,047	73,798	920,868	773,528
Santo Domingo..................	15,740	4,181	60,380	36,370
Argentina.......................	56,675	74,113	950,096	829,997
Brazil	45,995	18,171	627,363	593,583
Colombia	12,159	5,927	52,019	54,277
Other South America............	37,884	75,970	644,352	462,223
Furniture (*Muebles; Mobilia; Meubles*):				
Central America.................	7,247	1,810	135,802	71,516
Mexico..........................	16,215	13,297	174,942	143,001
Santo Domingo..................	822	....	11,124	10,666
Argentina.......................	1,772	473	79,375	59,967
Brazil...........................	3,853	1,978	46,185	35,073
Colombia	2,792	2,183	36,044	31,383
Other South America............	3,223	7,796	96,383	70,059
Wool, raw (*Lana cruda; Là cría; Laines brutes*):				
Mexico	520	....	140,603	10

STATISTICS OF FOREIGN TRADE.

The report of the Bureau of Statistics of the United States for the fiscal year ending June 30, 1898, is one of great interest. The total imports for the twelve months amounted to only about one-half of the exports, and were over $147,000,000 smaller than for the fiscal year ending June 30, 1897.

The imports from Europe decreased $124,000,391, while the

exportations to Europe increased $160,313,645. The imports from North American countries decreased $14,752,130, and the exports increased $14,676,828. The imports from South America show a decrease of $15,295,379, while the exports increased but $53,325. Asia and Oceania show the only increase in imports, $5,300,440 from the former and $2,458,781 from the latter. The exports to Asiatic countries increased $5,549,363, and to Oceania they decreased by $661,392.

The subjoined table records the total exports and imports by grand divisions for the fiscal year 1898 as compared with the fiscal year 1897:

	1897.	1898.
Imports from—		
Europe	$430, 192, 205	$306, 091, 814
North America	105, 924, 053	91, 171, 923
South America	107, 389, 405	92, 093, 526
Asia	87, 294, 597	92, 595, 037
Oceanica	24, 400, 439	26, 859, 226
Africa	9, 529, 713	7, 193, 639
Total	764, 730, 412	616, 005, 159
Exports to—		
Europe	813, 385, 644	973, 699, 289
North America	124, 958, 461	139, 635, 289
South America	33, 768, 646	33, 821, 971
Asia	39, 274, 905	44, 824, 268
Oceanica	22, 652, 773	21, 991, 381
Africa	16, 953, 127	17, 357, 752
Total	1, 050, 993, 556	1, 231, 329, 950

The increase in exports was in manufactured articles and food products, while the decrease in imports was naturally along the same lines, chemicals, chinaware, glassware, manufactures of cotton, iron and steel, leather, silk, wool, wood, and fibers all showing a decrease in importations compared with 1897 and 1896; breadstuffs, provisions, fish, fruits, wine, sugar, tea, and coffee showing a marked decrease in importations. Articles required by manufacturers for use in manufacturing increased in nearly every case over both 1897 and 1896, with the exception of wool, the importations of which during 1897 were unusually large.

The accompanying table shows the value of the imports of all general classes of merchandise the articles of which exceeded in value $5,000,000, and compares the importations of the fiscal year 1898 with those of 1897.

Imports.	1897.	1898.
Manufactures.		
Chemicals, drugs, etc.....	$44,948,752	$41,470,711
Cotton, manufactures...........................	34,429,363	27,266,932
Earthen and china ware...........................	9,977,297	6,686,220
Fibers, manufactures of............................	32,546,867	21,899,714
Glassware..	5,509,626	3,669,919
Iron and steel manufactures........................	16,094,557	12,615,913
Leather, and manufactures of.......................	13,283,151	11,414,118
Oils (all)...................................	5,594,111	5,197,886
Silk, manufactures of	25,199,067	23,523,110
Wood, and manufactures of	20,543,810	13,858,582
Wool, manufactures of...	49,162,992	14,823,768
Articles used in manufacturing.		
Cotton, unmanufactured...........................	5,884,262	5,019,503
Fibers, unmanufactured............................	12,336,418	13,446,186
Hides and skins...................................	27,863,026	37,068,832
India rubber	17,558,163	25,545,391
Silk, unmanufactured.............................	18,918,283	32,110,066
Tobacco, unmanufactured.....................	9,584,155	7,488,605
Wool..	53,243,191	16,783,692
Articles for consumption.		
Coffee	81,544,384	65,067,561
Fish (all)...	6,108,714	5,984,980
Fruits and nuts...................................	17,126,932	14,566,874
Sugar...	99,066,181	60,472,703
Tea...	14,835,862	10,054,005
Wines, spirits, and malt liquors	12,272,872	9,305,504

REPORT OF EXPORTS FOR JULY.

The July exports of breadstuffs, provisions, cotton, and mineral oil from the principal customs districts of the United States are reported by the Bureau of Statistics, in a statement issued on August 12, at $37,183,721. Of this sum, breadstuffs alone amounted to $16,737,128; provisions, $9,973,607; cattle and hogs, $2,922,244; cotton, $2,828,669, and mineral oil, $4,722,073. While these figures for July fall $20,000,000 below those of the month of June, they equal those of July, 1897, and exceed those of July in the years 1894, 1895, and 1896, and are $2,000,000 greater than the average July exportations of the articles named since 1890.

The value of the exportations of breadstuffs in July, 1898, is 20 per cent greater than in July, 1897; 25 per cent greater than in July, 1896; and practically double that of July, 1895. The July exportations of provisions are less in value than in the corresponding months of 1897, 1896, and 1895, as are also those of mineral oils. In the latter case, the reduction is evidently due to the lower prices, the number of gallons exported during the month being slightly in excess of the exportations for July, 1897, though the total value for the month is less in 1898 than in 1897.

CURRENCY CIRCULATION.

As compared with the corresponding date in 1897, the gold coin in circulation in the United States on August 1, 1898, showed a gain of over $135,000,000. Standard silver dollars showed an increase of $5,600,000; subsidiary silver one of over $4,800,000; silver certificates one of over $31,100,000; Treasury notes of 1890 one of nearly $14,200,000, and United States notes one of nearly $25,700,000. Currency certificates showed a decrease of over $40,300,000, national-bank notes nearly $3,100,000, and gold certificates over $1,500,000.

The total amount of money of all kinds in circulation on August 1, 1898, was $1,809,198,344, which represents an increase of over $162,700,000 for the twelve months. The circulation per head of population is estimated by the Treasury officials, on the basis of a population of 74,656,000, at $24.23, which was a decrease of 51 cents for the month, but was an increase of $1.70 per head for the twelve months just ended. A comparison with the statistics issued by the Treasury Department on August 1 each year shows that there has been an increase of over $300,000,000 in the amount of money in circulation since 1896.

GLUCOSE AND MAIZE OIL MANUFACTURE.

In a pamphlet recently issued by the Department of Agriculture of the United States on the composition of maize, Mr. H. W. WILEY, the official chemist, devotes some attention to the glucose manufacturing industry. He says:

The manufacture of starch sugars of various degrees of hydrolyzation is an important industry in the United States. These products of the hydrolyses of starch are known as glucose or grape sugar. The glucose represents those in which the hydrolysis is less complete, and consists largely of dextrin, dextrose, a little maltose, and water. These are made into thick and white sirups, used largely for table sirups, for adulterating molasses and honey, and for confectioners' purposes. Grape sugar is a term applied to the solid product obtained by the hydrolysis of starch, in which the hydrolysis is carried to a greater extent, the resulting product consisting chiefly of dextrose. This product is chiefly used as a substitute for malt in the brewing of beer and ale. This industry has assumed immense proportions in the United States, the quantity of Indian corn annually consumed in the manufacture of glucose being about 40,000,000 bushels, or 14,095,922 hectoliters.

The Department describes also a new product derived from maize which has attracted considerable attention and bids fair to become an important production. This is maize oil. The chemist says that in the manufacture of starch and glucose and in some varieties of maize meal the germ of the grain, which contains the largest percentage of oil, is extracted. From this germ a valuable oil is expressed, while the residue forms a food material as valuable in every respect as that derived by the expression of the oil from ordinary oily seeds. Maize oil is easily purified and forms a light, amber-colored, perfectly transparent liquid, without rancidity and with a pleasant taste. It has been used to some extent as a salad oil, and will doubtless in the future be very greatly employed for that purpose. It can also be used for lubricating delicate machinery, has fine burning properties, and can be used as a lamp oil. The coarser and less pure oil makes a valuable soap. In general, it may be said that maize oil has a commercial value, gallon for gallon, quite equal to the oil derived from cotton seeds.

URUGUAY.

ALL COMMERCIAL INTERESTS PERFECTLY SECURE.

The Bureau of the American Republics has received from Hon. PRUDENCIO DE MURGUIONDO, Consul General of Uruguay, a note addressed to him by the Minister of Foreign Affairs of that country, relating to a disturbance in Montevideo on July 4 last, which has been reported in the press of the United States, which note is calculated to dispel any impression that commercial interests in Uruguay have been in any way jeopardized.

Bull. No. 2——8

The Minister states that the disturbance was caused by the revolt of two bodies of artillery stationed at the capital, which was suppressed immediately, with but little bloodshed and no further serious results. The leaders of the revolt surrendered their arms to the Government officers, and were temporarily banished in the interests of public order. All the military and other authorities responded with alacrity to the call of the Government, and peace was restored in very short order. The revolt had no political significance, and normal conditions again prevailed in all branches of trade and industry, all classes of society evincing their full confidence in the recuperative abilities of their progressive Government.

TRADE WITH THE UNITED STATES FOR FIRST SIX MONTHS OF 1898.

Through the courtesy of Hon. PRUDENCIO DE MURGUIONDO, consul-general of Uruguay, the BULLETIN is able to furnish the following data regarding the trade movement between the United States and Uruguay for the first six months of the year 1898:

Exports to Uruguay	$655, 419. 00
Imports from Uruguay	1, 323, 650. 80
Balance in favor of imports	668, 231. 80
Imports, six months of 1898	1, 323, 650. 80
Imports from July 1 to December 31, 1897	830, 948. 48
Balance in favor of 1898	492, 702. 32
Exports, six months of 1898	655, 419. 00
Exports from July 1 to December 31, 1897	606, 665. 83
Balance in favor of 1898	48, 753. 17

Owing to a lack of vessels under foreign flags during the first six months of this year, there have been very few shipments of lumber from southern ports of the United States to Uruguay.

FOREIGN COMMERCE FOR FIRST QUARTER OF 1898.

The "Montevideo Times" says the first quarter of the year is generally regarded as the most important with reference to the foreign commerce of Uruguay, and is taken as an index of what the total for the year will be. If the present year proves no exception to the general rule, the figures are decidedly reassuring. The "Times" says they mark very plainly the recovery from the very serious fall in 1897, caused by the revolution, the political troubles, the locust plague, and an inferior produce season in general. In the present year the total value of imports, "which is the chief test of the commercial situation," has returned to the full average of the three years, 1894–1896, which were regarded as fairly active years.

The tables furnished by the statistical department of the custom-house were as follows for the first quarter of the three years 1896, 1897, and 1898, the values having been reduced to United States currency:

IMPORTS.

	1896.	1897.	1898.
Eatables, cereals, and spices............. ..	$1,028,194	$915,289	$1,144,863
Textile materials...........................	1,522,951	943,068	1,562,959
Raw material and machinery................	1,789,134	1,393,366	1,439,919
Liquors in general......................	758,611	697,624	764,888
Ready-made clothing	490,797	240,820	416,092
Live stock................................	218,463	230,306	393,943
Tobacco and cigars.......	73,361	44,464	55,627
All other items...........................	945,077	602,021	659,884
Total.............................	6,826,588	5,066,958	6,438,175

EXPORTS.

	1896.	1897.	1898.
Slaughterhouse products....................	12,474,760	7,976,199	9,114,869
Live stock................................	632,683	486,294	139,758
Rural produce............................	463,104	471,678	2,035,009
Provisions for ships.......................	27,732	23,797	19,485
All other products	59,943	80,264	52,385
Total.............................	13,658,222	9,038,232	11,361,506

The total commerce for the first quarter of 1898 approximates closely the total for the first quarter of 1894, which was regarded as an exceptionally prosperous year. The total products of agriculture for the quarter was $2,035,009 against $471,678 in the same period in 1897. This great increase was due entirely to the splendid wheat crop, the wheat exported being 59,453,989 kilograms, worth $1,783,619, against only 3,214,663 kilograms, worth but $77,151, in 1897.

In most of the other leading items there was a decrease. The maize exports amounted to 71,736 kilograms, worth $1,865, against 1,309,947 kilograms, worth $32,748 in 1897. The maize crop was fine, but late rains ruined the quality of the grain, so that very little was available for export. The flour exports aggregated

3,889,669 kilograms, worth $187,184; in 1897, 5,247,092 kilograms passed through the custom-house, valued at $262,354. The onions and garlic sent out of the country were valued at $2,132 in 1898 and $14,140 in 1897; fresh fruit, $14,809, against $40,989; vegetables, $1,865 against $32,748, and linseed, $16,186 against $20,106.

VENEZUELA.

OFFICIAL REPORT OF GOODS PURCHASED.

The Bureau has been furnished with the following statistical data of the exportations of merchandise from the United States to the several ports of Venezuela for the month of June, 1898, as compared with the same month in 1897, by Mr. ANTONIO E. DELFINO, consul-general of Venezuela:

Port.	1898.	1897.	Increase.	Decrease.
La Guira.................	$96,364.55	$86,353.50	$10,011.05	....
Puerto Cabello............	27,714.39	33,533.53	....	$5,819.14
Maracaibo·...............	32,040.02	56,629.33	....	24,589.31
La Vela...............	9,792.10	3,077.65	6,714.95	....
Ciudad Bolivar............	13,377.00	42,866.10	....	29,489.10
Carupano.................	5,474.24	6,519.00	....	4,044.76
Guanta	784.23	1,452.00	....	667.77
Cumaná	1,402.00	1,854.00	....	452.00
Guiría	705.00	303.00	402.00	....
Caña Colorado	699.00	0.00	699.00	....
Total	188,852.53	236,088.11	17,827.00	47,238.08

The principal articles exported were wheat flour, $99,473.65; lard, $77,506.28; cotton goods, bleached and unbleached, $33,506.22; tobacco, manufactured and leaf, $25,493.52; machinery and electrical supplies, $20,897.98; provisions, $20,143.64; butter, $18,902.42; kerosene, $17,351.13; hardware and ironmongery, $11,776.72; drugs and perfumery, $11,425.00, and calicoes, $7,799.38.

CONSUMPTION OF COFFEE IN 1897.

Supplementary to the article on coffee in the BULLETIN for July, an extract from an article recently published in the French "Bulletin de Statistique et de Legislation Comparée," showing the quantities of coffee consumed in various countries, is of interest. From this it appears that the total consumption of coffee in Europe and the United States rose from 1,039,330,000 pounds in 1893 to 1,246,640,000 pounds in 1897. The increased consumption in 1897 over 1896 amounted to no less than 129,580,000 pounds. Of this increase, 100,000,000 pounds came to the United States, and the total consumption of this country has reached the enormous amount of 636,340,000 pounds, or 9.95 pounds (4½ kilograms) for each individual. This was 26,000,000 pounds in excess of the amount consumed in all Europe. In 1893 Europe consumed 542,996,000 pounds and the consumption in the United States was 496,234,000 pounds.

As regards the consumption per individual, the United States by no means holds the first place. This distinction belongs to Holland, where the consumption for each inhabitant, in 1897, was estimated at 23 pounds (10½ kilograms). In Denmark the individual average was 15 pounds (7 kilograms); in Belgium, 11 pounds (5 kilograms); in Germany, 5¼ pounds (2¼ kilograms); in France, 3¼ pounds (1½ kilograms), and in the United Kingdom of Great Britain only seven-tenths of a pound (one-third kilogram).

The consumption of coffee in France is steadily increasing. In 1840 it amounted to 28,740,000 pounds, in 1860 to 68,720,000, and in 1897 to 273,800,000 pounds. Of this total, 2,214,000 pounds (1,004,000 kilograms) were imported from the French colonies, on which the duties are only half those on the coffee imported from foreign countries.

Of the coffee imported to France from foreign countries about 95,000,000 pounds (42,742,000 kilograms) were from Brazil and 51,000,000 pounds (23,176,000 kilograms) from Haiti.

NEW TARIFF RATES IN JAMAICA.

The subject-matter of a recent report to the British trade papers is of considerable interest to exporters in the United States, Mexico, the Central American Republics, Venezuela, and Colombia. The dispatch stated that as a result of the present deficit in the revenues and a further expected falling off for the fiscal year 1898-99, the Government has introduced a new tariff measure and expects to have it adopted at the present sitting of the legislative council. Among the provisions of the proposed law is one increasing the duties on spirits from 12s. 6d., the liquid gallon, to 15s. the proof gallon, as ascertained by Sykes's hydrometer. Such imports are mainly from England. The rates on butter, cheese, and ham have been raised from 1d. to 2d. per pound. On articles of hardware, namely, cutlery, tools, utensils, stoves, etc., formerly scheduled at 12½ per cent ad valorem, the rate now fixed is 20 per cent ad valorem. The same rate applies to every description of wearing apparel, whether manufactured or as piece goods. Food stuffs, mainly from the American Republics and Canada, suffer increased rates of from 30 to 50 per cent over the old. The former free list has been greatly curtailed. The Canadian Commissioner has publicly protested against the increased duties on the products that the Dominion sends to Jamaica, especially in view of contemplated Canadian reciprocal concessions. The full text of this law can be found in the United States Consular Reports for July, 1898.

THE NIAGARA PAN-AMERICAN EXPOSITION.

In previous numbers of the BULLETIN (October, 1897, and January, 1898) reference has been made to the proposed Pan-American Exposition to be held on Cayuga Island, in the Niagara River, near the city of Buffalo, New York. Owing to a variety of causes, among which the declaration of war with Spain played no insignificant a part, it was found impracticable to assemble the articles desired before the opening of the great exposition to be held in Paris, which it was considered would interfere with the extent and completeness of the collections. It was therefore decided to postpone the opening of the exposition until 1901, after the close of the one at Paris, and to make arrangements for securing many of the exhibits there from the American Republics.

The legislature of New York having unanimously passed a memorial requesting Congress to encourage the holding of this exposition, action was taken, and on July 8, President McKINLEY approved a joint resolution declaring that the enterprise merited the encouragement and approval of Congress and the people of the United States.

thus adulterated must be reexported without removal from bond or destroyed by the importer, and any failure to comply with the provisions of the law entails a heavy fine.

CHILE.

Concessions for new Industries. According to a report furnished by the "South American Journal," the National Congress of Chile has recently granted concessions for the establishment of several new industries at Santiago de Chile. Among them is one for a factory for bleaching, dyeing, and printing cotton piece goods, and another for a sulphuric acid factory.

ECUADOR.

Concessions to German steamship company. The British consul at Guayaquil informs his Government that the Kosmos and the Hamburg steamship lines, trading between Hamburg and Antwerp, and also Spanish and Italian ports, with occasional trips to London, have recently been consolidated. Just previous to that, in May, the Kosmos Company contracted with the Government of Ecuador to carry the mails free of charge between the ports of the country and all other ports touched at by its steamers. The company also agrees to transport government passengers and emigrants to Ecuador between the ports at which its ships touch at a reduction of 30 per cent from regular rates; also to carry, free of charge, the first sample shipments of the products of Ecuador to any German exhibitions. In return for these services the Government of Ecuador admits the company's ships to its seaports free of all fiscal dues, and reduces the pilotage fees one-half. The contract has been approved by the Council of State and is to remain in force for four years.

Cocoa crop of 1897. The cocoa crop of Ecuador for 1897 amounted to 14,800 tons, or 330,293 quintals. This amount compares unfavorably with the product of recent years. In 1896 the total was 15,300 tons; in 1895, 16,000 tons; and in 1894, 17,467 tons.

GUATEMALA.

Opportunities for United States Investors. A correspondent of "The Manufacturer" (Philadelphia), writing from Guatemala City, June 25, 1898, says:
"The Government is willing, anxious, and almost compelled to sell the Northern Railroad. This, I think, would be a good chance for an American syndicate to get hold of a good business. To-day that road could be got under the most favorable condition and with the most liberal concession. The same can be said of the Verapaz road. Then, again, one or many American companies could buy such plantations as they would wish for prices which could be considered merely nominal. And again, an American company could come and establish a bank, which would be most welcome and could do a profitable business with choicest securities."

The Northern Railroad, to which the correspondent refers, is projected from Puerto Barrios to the capital of the Republic, Guatemala City, and is now finished as far as San Agustin, a distance of 130 miles, leaving only a small part of the line to be completed. This is the most important railway enterprise ever undertaken in Central America, and was the favorite scheme of the late President BARRIOS for the development of the internal riches of Guatemala. It will open up the most productive coffee and mineral lands in the Republic.

HAWAII.

Navigation Laws in Force. Attorney-General GRIGGS has rendered a decision to the effect that the navigation laws of the United States do not apply to Hawaii or other annexed territory, without further legislation of Congress. The mere act of annexation does not, ipso facto, extend the laws of the United States to the new districts.

MEXICO.

Wheat Crop for 1898. "Modern Mexico" reports the Mexican wheat crop for 1898 as far above the average in quality and quantity. Usually Mexico does not raise enough wheat for its own use, but this year a part of the crop is available for export. Because of this, The Bulletin of the Mexican Agricultural Society reports certain speculators have been trying to prevail upon the Government to obstruct, if not to absolutely prevent, wheat exportation. But they were not successful, as the secretary of the treasury has announced that no export duty nor other restriction will be imposed upon Mexican wheat that has found purchasers in foreign markets.

Custom-House Collections. During the month of June the total collections through the custom-houses of the Republic amounted to $2,039,886.57. According to figures obtained from "Two Republics," these were divided as follows: Import duties, $1,879,919.44; export duties, $103,206.74; port dues, $55,478.60; arrears, $1,281.79. The port of Vera Cruz collected $956,042.20, and that of Tampico, $352,927.73, or the two combined nearly 70 per cent of the amount of the import duties.

PARAGUAY.

Importations of Kerosene. Consul RUFFIN writes to the Department of State from Asuncion that Paraguay is lighted with kerosene or coal oil imported from the United States, and that no electricity or gas is used other than that generated by private factories. Kerosene comes in 4-gallon tin cans, which form permits convenient storage in boats plying between Asuncion and Montevideo. The consul adds:

"It seems to me it would be more profitable to send tank steamers, which would reduce the cost and thereby increase the sales. The tanks could immediately be sold, because of the great demand in this line, thus obviating the expense of returning them. Since the war with Spain the price of oil has gone up nearly 50 per cent, and there is much speculation. The United States has a monopoly of oil imports, 40,648 gallons being imported in 1897, at a declared value of $19,511 gold. The duty is 25 per cent ad valorem."

PERU.

Smelting works at Callao. The "British Trade Journal" reports that the municipal authorities at Callao have recently granted Messrs. BACKUS & JOHNSTON permission to construct a plant for the purpose of smelting metals which may be brought from different points on the coast. This firm already owns important smelting works at Casapalea, on the Oroya line of railway. The new works will be erected on the outskirts of Callao and will give employment to a hundred persons.

VENEZUELA.

New Electric Railway. The "Venezuela Herald" reports the concession for an electric railway line 70 kilometers (43½ miles) in length to a French company. The road is to connect Cumana and Cumanacao, and the electrical power is to be generated by the waterfalls of mountain streams. The company has sent engineers to Cumana to begin the survey.

Reward for the Arrest of Violators of Postal Laws. The "Herald" announces that President ANDRADE has signed a decree on June 23, 1898, which provides that 30 per cent of the fine of 500 bolivars ($96.50), which is imposed on all persons who circulate correspondence in any manner except through the regular postal channels, be awarded to the discoverer of the violator of the law. It is said that the practice of conveying correspondence into and from the Republic has become a growing evil. The "Herald" adds that this should be borne in mind by persons (foreigners) traveling through the country.

Road Improvements in Los Andes. At its last session the National Congress of Venezuela appropriated 100,000 bolivars ($19,300) for the improvement of the roadways of the State of Los Andes. "Illustrated Venezuela" says this sum is to be equally divided between three sections of the State.

Boletín Mensual

DE LA

Oficina de las Repúblicas Americanas,

Unión Internacional de Repúblicas Americanas.

Vol. VI.	AGOSTO, 1898.	No. 2.

RELACIONES DE LOS ESTADOS UNIDOS CON ESPAÑA.

SUSPENSIÓN DE HOSTILIDADES Y SUS RESULTADOS EN CUANTO AFECTAN EL COMERCIO DE AMÉRICA.—ENSANCHE DE LAS VÍAS DE COMUNICACIONES COMERCIALES ENTRE LAS REPÚBLICAS AMERICANAS.—CUBA Y PUERTO RICO SERÁN LA ENTRADA POR DONDE EL CAPITAL Y LA INDUSTRIA PASARÁN AL SUR Y AL OESTE.—HAWAII Y LAS FILIPINAS EN SUS RELACIONES CON EL LITORAL AMERICANO SOBRE EL PACÍFICO.—DATOS ESTADÍSTICOS SOBRE COMERCIO É INDUSTRIAS. REGLAMENTOS DE ADUANA Y DE LA MARINA MERCANTE PARA CUBA, LAS FILIPINAS Y PUERTO RICO.

La guerra entre los Estados Unidos y España, motivada por la revolución contra el Gobierno español en la isla de Cuba, comenzó el 21 de abril de 1898. El 12 de agosto delmismo año se suspendieron las hostilidades, como se verá por la proclama del Presidente de los Estados Unidos, que dice asi:

PROCLAMA DEL PRESIDENTE DE LOS ESTADOS UNIDOS DE AMÉRICA.

Considerando: Que por medio de un protocolo concluido y firmado el 12 de agosto de 1898 por WILLIAM R. DAY, Secretario de Estado de los Estados Unidos, y Su Excelencia JULIO CAMBON, Embajador Extraordinario y Plenipotenciario de la República francesa en Wáshington, representando respectivamente para este objeto á los Gobiernos de los Estados Unidos y España, dichos Gobiernos han convenido en las bases sobre las cuales se entablarán las negociaciones para el establecimiento de la paz entre los dos países; y,

Considerando: Que en dicho protocolo se ha convenido en que al concluirlo y firmarlo, se suspendan las hostilidades entre los dos países, y que, tan pronto como sea posible, cada Gobierno informe de esto á los comandantes de sus fuerzas militares y navales:

Por tanto, Yo, WILLIAM McKINLEY, Presidente de los Estados Unidos de América, declaro y proclamo, por parte de los Estados Unidos y de conformidad con las estipulaciones del protocolo, la suspensión de hostilidades, y mando que inmediatamente se den órdenes, por los conductos correspondientes, á los comandantes de las fuerzas militares y navales de los Estados Unidos para que se abstengan de ejecutar todo acto que sea incompatible con esta proclama.

En testimonio de lo cual, la he firmado y le he hecho poner el sello de los Estados Unidos.

Dada en la ciudad de Wáshington, el día 12 de agosto del año de Nuestro Señor mil ochocientos noventa y ocho y el ciento veintitrés de la Independencia de los Estados Unidos.

WILLIAM McKINLEY.

Por el Presidente:

WILLIAM R. DAY, *Secretario de Estado.*

El Departamento de Estado de los Estados Unidos publicó las bases sobre las cuales se firmaría la paz, y son como sigue:

1ª. España debe renunciar á todo derecho ó título de soberanía sobre la isla de Cuba.

2ª. Puerto Rico y las otras islas españolas en el mar de las Antillas, así como una de las islas de los Ladrones, que los Estados Unidos escojan, serán cedidas á éstos.

3ª. Los Estados Unidos ocuparán la ciudad, bahía y puerto de Manila, y esta ocupación continuará mientras se concluye el tratado de paz, en el cual se estipulará lo concerniente al dominio y gobierno de las Filipinas.

4ª. Cuba, Puerto Rico y las otras islas españolas en el mar de las Antillas serán evacuadas inmediatamente, y dentro de diez días se nombrarán comisionados que se reunirán en la Habana y San Juan, respectivamente, dentro de treinte dias, á contar de la fecha en que se firme el protocolo, á fin de disponer lo necesario para la evacuación y hacer que ésta se efectúe.

5ª. Los Estados Unidos y España nombrarán cada uno no más de cinco comisionados para negociar y concluir el tratado de paz. Los comisionados se reunirán en París, á más tardar, el primero de octubre.

6ª. Al firmar el protocolo, se suspenderán los hostilidades, y cada gobierno dará aviso al efecto, tan pronto como sea posible, á los comandantes de sus fuerzas militares y navales.

De conformidad con la proclama del Presidente, se enviaron por telégrafo órdenes á los comandantes militares y navales de los Estados Unidos en las Filipinas y en las Antillas, á fin de que suspendieran todas las operaciones militares y levantaran el bloqueo de los puertos y bahías.

Las causas que produjeron la guerra con España están expuestas en el Mensaje que el Presidente de los Estados Unidos dirigió al Congreso el 25 de abril de 1898, en el cual hace referencia á la resolución del Congreso, aprobada el 20 de abril de 1898, en la cual se pide que el Gobierno de España renuncie á toda autoridad y dominio en la isla de Cuba y retire sus fuerzas de mar y tierra de dicha isla y de sus aguas. A continuación, el Presidente se expresa de esta manera:

Cuando se comunicó al Ministro español en Wáshington lo que el Ejecutivo estaba en el deber de exigir de España, en cumplimiento de la citada resolución, el Ministro pidió sus pasaportes y se retiró. Al mismo tiempo, el Ministro de Relaciones Exteriores de España manifestó al representante diplomático de los Estados Unidos en Madrid que el retiro del representante de España de los Estados Unidos había puesto término á las relaciones diplomáticas entre los dos países y que toda comunicación oficial entre los respectivos representantes debía cesar al punto.

Á la suspensión de las relaciones diplomáticas por parte del Gobierno de España, siguieron activas operaciones militares por parte de los Estados Unidos. Éstas dieron por resultado la destrucción de la escuadra española en Manila el 1 de mayo, la de la flota española en Santiago el 3 de julio, el rendimiento de la provincia de Santiago de Cuba el 14 de julio, y la invasión de la isla de Puerto Rico el 21 del mismo mes.

Después de la ocupación de la provincia de Santiago de Cuba, se estableció un gobierno militar, y los empleados municipales que ejercían autoridad bajo la dominación española continuaron en sus puestos. El Ministerio de la Guerra de los Estados Unidos hizo promulgar reglamentos de aduana y otros, los cuales publicamos en este número.

Como resultado de las operaciones militares, las islas de Hawaii fueron anexadas á los Estados Unidos por una resolución del Congreso, aprobada el 7 de julio de 1898, y se dejó á la discreción del Presidente de los Estados Unidos el determinar lo relativo al gobierno de dichas islas, mientras el Congreso dispone lo que se deba hacer en adelante.

El conflicto con España ha dado resultados tan importantes para el desarrollo comercial de los países del hemisferio occidental, que se ha creído conveniente preparar para conocimiento del público la exposición que se verá en seguida. Los rápidos cambios que necesariamente ocurren en la administración de un territorio adquirido por medio de la guerra, hacen que sea una tarea difícil el recoger inmediatamente todos los datos que se requieren para estudiar con cuidado sus condiciones comerciales é industriales. Dichos cambios se efectúan en los varios departamentos de la administración, y se necesita tiempo para perfeccionar los detalles que se refieren á los diferentes ramos. En orden á satisfacer la demanda general de informes relativos á oportunidades y condiciones comerciales, se ha preparado la compilación que viene á continuación, formada con datos que se han tomado de las fuentes de que ahora se dispone.

Los países que componen la Union Internacional de Repúblicas Americanas están naturalmente muy interesados en conocer los efectos posibles que el nuevo estado de cosas puede tener en su desarrollo comercial é industrial. Las repúblicas latino-americanas verán sin duda que, al libertarse el pueblo cubano, mediante la generosa intervención de los Estados Unidos, de la defectuosa administración de que México, la América Central y la del Sur se emanciparon por sus propios esfuerzos, pero contando con las simpatías de los Estados Unidos, el comercio y la industria prometen desarrollarse libremente en la isla de Cuba, de la misma manera que se han desarrollado en los otros países y como una consecuencia de su separación de la madre patria.

Debido á su posición geográfica, puede decirse que Cuba y Puerto Rico son las puertas por donde naturalmente debe pasar el comercio del mar Caribe, al mismo tiempo que sirven como de escalón para llegar á los mercados de toda la América del Sur. Con la apertura del canal interoceánico, estas islas recibirán inmensos beneficios, á causa del incremento que debe esperarse en el comercio del litoral de las tres Américas sobre el Pacífico. Las posesiones adquiridas por los Estados Unidos en el Pacífico abren también vasto campo al desarrollo del tráfico en el Asia, no solamente con los Estados Unidos, sino con las repúblicas latino-americanas. El gran número de comunicaciones que la Oficina de las Repúblicas Americanas ha recibido ya provenientes de casas comerciales de los Estados Unidos, así como de individuos particulares, y en las cuales se indaga relativamente á oportunidades comerciales, indica claramente que al restablecerse el orden en las antiguas posesiones españolas, acudirán á ellas en gran escala

la industria y el capital; y es de esperar que, bajo favorables condiciones, esto tienda á producir benéficos resultados para las relaciones entre los Estados Unidos y las repúblicas hermanas de la
América latina.

Las materias de que se trata en la siguiente compilación son
éstas: (1) Cuba. (2) Puerto Rico. (3) Las Islas de Hawaii.
(4) Las Filipinas y las Islas de los Ladrones.

La compilación arriba mencionada da una descripción de las
riquezas, industria y comercio de las islas en referencia. No ha
sido traducida al castellano, porque, como el BOLETIN está para
ser publicado, ya no había tiempo de hacerlo. Los informes contenidos en la citada compilación son principalmente para el uso
de los comerciantes de los Estados Unidos. . Se publica la siguiente sinopsis delos reglamentos de aduana expedidos por el
Gobierno de los Estados Unidos para el uso de los puertos cubanos, á fin de que sirvan á los que importen mercancías en Cuba.
El Ministerio de la Guerra de los Estados Unidos publicó
íntegros en inglés esos reglamentos.

ISLA DE CUBA.

ARANCELES DE ADUANA Y ORDENANZAS DE PUERTO.

Los nuevos aranceles que acaba de publicar el Departamento
de la Guerra para su aplicación en los puertos de la isla de Cuba
que están en posesión del Gobierno de los Estados Unidos comprenden, por lo general, el mínimo de los derechos impuestos por
la tarifa antes vigente en la isla. En los "Informes Consulares"
no. 207 (diciembre de 1897), se encontrará publicada en extenso
la tarifa que se promulgo en septiembre último, y las cantidades
que representan los derechos fiscales se han adoptado como
base para la nueva tarifa. La única diferencia consiste en
que parece que se ha hecho una reducción de los derechos
sobre los tejidos de tapicería (Clase V, no. 145), con tal de que
se cumplan ciertas condiciones, y se ha impuesto un derecho sobre
el tabaco en rama, el tabaco torcido y los cigarros. Los derechos
de exportación sobre la madera y el tabaco continúan siendo los
mismos.

La tarifa fué preparada para su aplicación en la provincia de
Santiago de Cuba, pero según el decreto del Ejecutivo, que

aparece en la página de introducción, la tarifa regirá en todos los puertos ó lugares ocupados por los · Estados Unidos. El decreto dice:

DEPARTAMENTO DE LA GUERRA,

Wáshington, agosto 8 de 1898.

Los artículos importados de los Estados Unidos quedan sujetos al pago de derechos bajo la tarifa que acaba de publicarse, lo mismo que la mercancías de cualquiera otra procedencia.

La unidad monetaria de Cuba es el peso que se divide en 100 centavos. Se consigna en la tarifa que el valor del peso en circulación es de 93.2 centavos. El Departamento del Tesoro calcula el valor del peso en 92.6 centavos y se ha seguido este calculo en las reducciones que se han hecho en la siguiente tabla.

Los derechos sobre los artículos más importantes que se importan en Cuba procedentes de los Estados Unidos son:

	Pesos.	Dollars.
Carbones minerales................10,000 kilos (22,046 libras)..	0.40	0.37
Oleonaftas, petróleos brutos naturales y aceites brutos derivados de los esquistos....................100 kilos (220.46 libras)..	3.08	2.85
Los petróleos y demás aceites minerales rectificados ó refinados para el alumbrado; las bencinas, la gasolina y los aceites minerales no expresados...............................100 kilos..	5.20	4.81
Cristal y vidrio:		
Vidrio hueco, común ú ordinario, y los aisladores de electricidad....................................100 kilos..	.30	.27
Las botellas ordinarias de vidrio para envasar cervezas, ron y vinos espumosos fabricados con frutas del país, adeudarán con rebaja del 60 por ciento de los derechos de esta partida cuando sean importadas y declaradas al adeudo por los fabricantes de aquellos líquidos.		
Cristal y vidrio que le imita—		
En objetos tallados, grabados ó dorados.......100 kilos..	10.00	9.26
Los demas artículos.............................do....	5.40	5.03
Vidrio ó cristal plano—		
En losas para pavimentos ó claraboyas...........do....	1.65	1.52
Para vidrieras, ó en otros objetos siempre que no sean pulimentados, biselados, grabados ó pintados á fuego.........	3.40	3.14
En vidrieras emplomadas, y las lunas pulimentadas ó biseladas..	4.00	3.70
Vidrios y cristales azogados plateados ó con baños de otros metales—		
En espejos ordinarios cuyas lunas no excedan de dos milímetros de grueso, azogados con barniz mercurial rojo ú oscuro...........................100 kilos..	8.00	7.40
Los demás espejos no biselados.................do....	12.50	11.57
En lunas biseladas.............................do....	12.00	13.89
Hierro forjado, y acero:		
Hierro forjado ó acero laminado—		
En barras carriles.............................do....	.85	.78
En barras de todas las demas clases, incluso la palanquilla; llantas, aros y viguetas.............100 kilos..	.90	.83
Barras de todas clases de acero fino al crisol ......do....	1.50	1.38
Laminado en chapas—		
Sin pulimentar ni estañar de tres ó más milímetros de grueso.........................100 kilos..	1.10	1.01
Las chapas sin pulimentar ni estañar de menos de tres milímetros de grueso.....................100 kilos..	1.20	1.11

	Pesos.	Dollars.
Hierro forjado, y acero—Continúa.		
Laminado en chapas—Continúa.		
Las chapas estañadas y la hoja de lata ....100 kilos..	1. 50	1. 38
Las chapas pulimentadas, onduladas, perforadas; las laminadas en frío. estén o no galvanizadas ; y las cintas o flejes pulimentados..........................100 kilos..	1. 30	1. 20
Moldeado en piezas en bruto, sin labor alguna de pulimento, torno ó ajuste—		
Pesando 25 kilógramos ó más cada una ....100 kilos..	1. 00	. 92
Pesando menos de 25 kilógramos.................do....	1. 35	1. 25
Moldeado en piezas acabadas—		
Ruedas de más de 100 kilógramos eclises, placas de asiento, traviesas y ejes re tos ; los muelles para ferrocarriles y tranvías, y las cajas de engrase....100 kilos..	1. 20	1. 11
Ruedas de 100 kilógramos ó menos ; los muelles que no sean para ferrocarriles ó tranvías; ejes acodados ó cigüeñuelas ....100 kilos..	1. 40	1. 29
Hierro forjado ó acero, en tubos—		
Cubiertos de chapa de latón.....................do....	1. 40	1. 29
De las demás clases estén ó no galvanizados.......do....	1. 40	1. 29
En alambre, esté ó no galvanizado—		
De dos milímetros de diámetro ó más.............do....	1. 00	. 92
De más de ½ milímetro á 2 milímetros...........do ...	1. 30	1. 20
De ½ milímetro ó menos ; y los que estén recubiertos de algun tejido ....100 kilos..	1. 60	1. 48
Manufacturado en piezas grandes compuestas de barras ó de barras y chapas sujetas con redoblones ó tornillos; y las mismas sin remaches, agujereadas ó cortadas á medida, para puentes, armaduras y otras construcciones ......100 kilos..	1. 80	1. 66
En anclas, cadenas para buques y para maquinaria, amarras, cambios de vía y discos de señales.....,100 kilos..	1. 65	1. 52
Hierro forjado ó acero en telas metálicas—		
(La tela obrada en bastidores ú otros objetos, adeudará con un recargo de 40 por ciento de los derechos.)		
Hasta 20 hilos en pulgada ....100 kilos..	2. 00	1. 85
De 20 hilos ó más en pulgada.................por kilo..	. 06	. 05
En cables, cercas (espinos artificiales) y enrejados; y los muelles para muebles	1. 00	. 92
En herramientas—		
Herramientas agrícolas; martillos y yunques..100 kilos..	.80	. 74
Herramientas finas para artes, oficios y profesiones, hechas de acero fundido al crisol ....por kilo..	8. 00	7. 40
Las demas herramientas ....100 kilos..	2. 50	2. 31
En tornillos, tuercas, tirafondos, arandelas y remaches ; y las puntas de París y análogas......... .... 100 kilos..	1. 00	. 92
En clavos, escarpias y tachuelas.....................do....	1. 00	. 92
Aparatos y máquinas—		
Básculas	1. 60	1. 48
Máquinas y aparatos para la fabricación de azúcar y aguardientes................................100 kilos.	. 50	. 46
Máquinas y aparatos agricolas.................do....	. 80	. 74
Máquinas motores de vapor, fijas.................do....	3. 75	3. 47
Calderas—		
De chapa............................. ....do....	3. 00	2. 77
Tubulares ....: ....do....	3. 75	3. 47
Locomotoras y locomóviles ....do....	4. 50	4. 16
Placas giratorias ; carros transbordadores y las grúas y columnas hidráulicas....................100 kilos..	1. 50	1. 38
Máquinas de coser y las piezas sueltas de las mismas 100 kilos..	4. 00	3. 70
Velocípedos....................100 kilos..	4. 00	3. 70
Carruajes de todas clases para viajeros en ferrocarriles y las piezas de madera concluidas para los mismos, por 100 kilogramos.............	4. 80	4. 44

	Pesos.	Dollars.
Hierro forjado, y acero—Continúa.		
Calderas—Continúa.		
Wagones, furgones y wagonetas de todas clases para ferrocarriles; las wagonetas para minas; y las piezas de madera concluidas para los mismos......100 kilos..	2.10	1.94
Carruajes de todas clases para tranvías; y las piezas de madera concluidas para los mismos ....100 kilos..	7.60	7.03
Carros de transporte y carretillas.................do....	3.80	3.51
Carnes :		
Carne en salmuera.............................100 kilos..	3.00	2.77
Carne y manteca de cerdo, incluso el tocino...........do....	6.30	5.83
Tasajo ....do....	3.96	3.66
Carnes de las demás clases ....do....	3.60	3.33
Manteca de vacas ....do....	4.40	4.07
Cereales :		
Trigo .... do....	1.20	1.11
Los demás cereales................................do....	1.20	1.11
(La cebada germinada ó esterilizada que se emplea en la fabricación de cerveza queda exenta del derecho fiscal que con carácter provisional se señala.)		
Harinas :		
De trigo.......................................100 kilos..	1.50	1.38
Legumbres, hortalizas y frutas :		
Legumbres secas... do....	1.30	1.20
Hortalizas ; y las legumbres frescas ....do....	.75	.69
Frutas—		
Frescas ....do....	1.00	.92
Secas ....do....	1.75	1.62
Algarrobas, y las semillas no tarifadas expresamente, por 100 kilógramos....................................	.20	.18
Forrajes y salvado ....100 kilos..	.25	.23
Maderas :		
Duelas.....................................por millar..	2.00	1.85
Madera ordinaria, en tablas, tablones vigas, viguetas, palos redondos y las maderas para construcción naval, el metro cúbico..	1.00	.92
Cepillada ó machihembrada para cajas ó pavimentos ; palos de escoba, y las cajas envases de artículos importados, por 100 kilógramos.....	.40	.37
Madera fina para ebanistería—		
En tablas, tablones, troncos y pedazos ....100 kilos..	4.35	4.02
Pipería,desarmada ; y los aros ó flejes y fondos........do....	.90	.83
Madera en cortes de bocoyes y de tercerolas para azúcar y mieles, por 100 kilos...............................·............	.15	.13
Enrejados ó cercas ....100 kilos..	1.50	1.38
Madera ordinaria y sus manufacturas.................do....	2.00	1.85
Madera fina y sus manufacturas.....................do....	12.00	11.11

Se prohibe la importación de armas de guerra de todas clases y sus proyectiles y municiones; las armas de todas las demas clases y en general todos los explosivos, mientras el importador no exhiba permiso especial y nominativo de la autoridad superior de la isla; manteca y grasas animales destinadas a la alimentación, cuando estén compuestas con margarina ú oleomargarina; objetos ofensivos á la moral, y vinos adulterados y artificiales.

Los siguientes artículos se importan libres de derechos arancelarios: abonos naturales; árboles, plantas, y el musgo natural ó

fresco; articulos nacionales devueltos de las exposiciones extranjeras; carruajes, animales adiestrados, teatros portátiles, panoramas,
figuras de cera y otros objetos análogos para espectáculos públicos
que se importen temporalmente para volver á salir de la isla;
envases que hayan salido de la isla con frutas, azúcares, mieles y
aguardientes, y se importen vacíos; muebles usados de las personas
que regresen á la isla ó vayan á establecerse en ella; muestras de
fieltro, papel pintado, y tejidos, bajo ciertas condiciones; muestras
de pasamanería, sin valor comercial; objetos arqueológicos y
numismáticos destinados a museos públicos, academias y corporaciones científicas y artísticas; obras de Bellas Artes con destino á
museos, etc.; oro en barras, polvo ó monedas; y las monedas de
plata ó bronce de cuño nacional, y prendas de vestir, objetos de
aséo, etc., que con señales de haberse usado conduzcan los viajeros
en sus equipajes.

ENTRADA Y DESPACHO DE BUQUES.

Todos los buques serán puestos, á su llegada, bajo vigilancia
militar hasta que se lleve á cabo la descarga. Los pasajeros que
traigan artículos que no paguen derechos podrán desembarcar en
seguida.

Las mercancías que no se declaren en el manifiesto quedarán
sujetas á un recargo de 25 por ciento. Si faltan algunos de los
artículos declarados en el manifiesto, el buque pagará $1 por tone-
lada, á menos que se explique debidamente la falta.

Dentro de 24 horas, á contar de la llegada del buque, el capitán debe presentar el debido manifiesto, con las debidas marcas,
descripciones, etc., certificado por el colector del puerto de salida,
si el buque procede de los Estados Unidos, bajo pena del pago
de $1 por tonelada en caso de no cumplirse con esta formalidad.
Si el buque procede de un puerto extranjero, el manifiesto deberá
estar certificado por el cónsul ó agente comercial de los Estados
Unidos, y, si no hay tal funcionario en el puerto de salida, por el
cónsul de cualquiera nación que esté en paz con los Estados
Unidos; y el registro del buque deberá ser depositado en el consulado de la nación á que pertenece tan pronto como el buque
llegue á Cuba, y, en caso de que no haya tal consulado, en la
comandancia del puerto, hasta que el capitán pague el impuesto
de tonelaje y derechos de puerto.

Ningún buque podrá ser despachado para otro puerto mientras no se desembarque la carga ó se de cuenta de ella. Todas las mercancías cuya declaración para pago no se haya hecho dentro de diez días despues de su llegada al puerto serán desembarcadas y almacenadas, y los gastos de estas operaciones serán de cuenta de los géneros. Antes de salir de un puerto, el capitán depositará en la debida oficina el manifesto de la carga. No se concederán despachos en puertos de Cuba que no estén en posesión ó bajo el dominio de los Estados Unidos.

DERECHOS DE TONELAJE.

Por cada entrada de un buque que proceda de un puerto de Cuba que no esté en posesión de los Estados Unidos, por tonelada neta... ... . $0. 20
Por cada entrada de un buque procedente de un puerto de Cuba en posesión de los Estados Unidos............ .... .02

Los buques en lastre pagarán la mitad de los derechos mencionados.

Quedan exentos del derecho de tonelaje: los buques que pertenecen á los Estados Unidos; los buques de gobiernos extranjeros neutrales no ocupados en el comercio; buques de arribada; yates que pertenezcan á un club de yates organizado de los Estados Unidos ó à una nación extranjera neutral.

El tonelaje de un buque será el que se exprese en su certificado de matrícula.

DERECHOS DE DESCARGA.

El derecho de $1 por cada tonelada de mercan cía que se importe ó exporte, impuesto hasta el presente, queda suprimido.

El carbón continúa exento del pago de este derecho.

El derecho de exportación sobre los minerales de 5 centavos por tonelada bruta queda suprimido.

DERECHOS ESPECIALES EN SANTIAGO.

Los derechos para el mejoramiento del puerto de Santiago se continuarán cobrando como sigue:

Cada vapor que entre............. . ... $8. 50
Cada buque de vela que entre......... .... 4.25
Cada tonelada de carga procedente de un vapor........ 25
Cada tonelada de carga procedente de un buque de vela.................... . 125
Cada tonelada de carbón procedente de un vapor 125
Cada tonelada de carbón procedente de un buque de vela .... .10

REPÚBLICA ARGENTINA.

AUMENTO DEL COMERCIO—ESTADÍSTICA OFICIAL.

La Dirección General de Estadística proporciona las siguientes cifras como la valuación de las importaciones y exportaciones de la Argentina, sin incluir oro y plata en barras y acuñados, durante el primer trimestre de 1898, comparado con el mismo período de 1897:

	1898.	1897.
Importaciones	$26,080,196	$29,045,105
Exportaciones	43,970,805	40,706,982
Total	70,051,001	69,752,087

Aumento total $298,914

BRASIL.

DEPÓSITOS MINERALES DE MAGNESIA.

Durante los últimos cuatro años los depósitos minerales de magnesia del Brasil han constituido la principal fuente de exportación del país. El mineral procede del Distrito de Miguel Burnier, en el Estado de Minas Geraes. La distancia desde Rio de Janeiro es de unas 310 millas, y se necesitan ocho ó diez días para el trasporte.

Las minas están situadas á una altura de 4,000 pies, en un clima agradable y salubre, y en las labores de explotación se da empleo á trabajadores italianos é indios y á un gran número de españoles y portugueses.

En 1897 se embarcaron 8,800 toneladas para Filadelfia, como la producción total de aquel año, pero en años anteriores la exportación se hizo con destino á Inglaterra. Un análisis de este mineral da por resultado 54.7 por ciento de magnesia metálica; 0.027 por ciento de ácido sulfúrico, y 0.077 por ciento de ácido fosfórico.

DISTRITO GOMERO DE PARÁ.

Según el cónsul inglés de Pará, algunos creen que la producción de los árboles gomeros del Amazonas se agotará en poco tiempo.

Las autoridades más competentes no están del todo conformes con esta opinión, sino que sostienen, por lo contrario, que aquella producción es inagotable, porque la goma se reproduce constantemente por naturaleza.

Es cierto que algunas secciones se agotan cuando se las explota demasiado, pero cuando se las deja descansar por algún tiempo recobran su fertilidad. El distrito de Cametá, en el río Tocantins, producía una goma de excelente calidad que tenía demanda especial en el mercado. Este distrito está ahora agotado, pues miles de personas lo explotaron por un período de unos cuarenta años; todos los recien llegados se dirigían á Cametá en busca de fortuna. Hay muchos distritos que no han sido explotados. El área en donde se produce la goma de Pará es por lo menos de 1,000,000 de millas cuadradas. Exploraciones posteriores demostrarán sin duda que esta área es más extensa.

COSTA RICA.

El Doctor ULLOA, Vicepresidente que fué de la República de Costa Rica, ha establecido su residencia en Nueva York con el objeto de desempeñar las funciones de cónsul general de la República en aquella ciudad. Dícese que el Doctor ULLOA ha manifestado á un corresponsal de la prensa asociada que su primer deber oficial consistirá en abrir una oficina de información, de manera que los fabricantes, exportadores é importadores de los Estados Unidos puedan obtener toda clase de informes relativos á Costa Rica, y al sistema de negocios, modo de empacar los géneros para la exportación, etc., que se observan en el país. También abriga el Doctor ULLOA la esperanza de promover una corriente de emigración á Costa Rica por medio de la propagación de los conocimientos relativos á los recursos del país.

En cuanto á recientes empresas de carácter público en Costa Rica, el cónsul general dice que se están llevando á cabo grandes mejoras. Se dictarán nuevas leyes sobre terrenos, al objeto de alentar la inmigración, y se está construyendo un ferrocarril que unirá á Limón, puerto del Atlántico, con Tivives, nuevo puerto del Pacífico, estableciendo así una nueva línea de ferrocarril de océano á océano.

NUEVO MINISTERIO.

En el BOLETÍN del mes de julio apareció, por inadvertencia, como correspondiente á Nicaragua, el nuevo ministerio del segundo período ejecutivo del Presidente de la República de Costa Rica, Don RAFAEL IGLESIAS. El error fué descubierto demasiado tarde, y no pudo hacerse la debida corrección en el correspondiente número. Los señores que componen el actual ministerio de Costa Rica son:

Ministro de Relaciones Exteriores, Instrucción
   Pública, etc.. Señor DON PEDRO PÉREZ ZELEDÓN.
Ministro de lo Interior y Obras Públicas........ Señor DON JOSÉ ASTÚA AGUILAR.
Ministro de Hacienda y Comercio................ Señor DON JUAN B. QUIRÓS.
Ministro de Guerra y Marina.................... Señor DON DEMETRIO TINOCO.

ESTADOS UNIDOS.

COMERCIO EXTERIOR.

El informe del Bureau de Estadísticas de los Estados Unidos, correspondiente al año fiscal que terminó el 30 de junio de 1898, es de gran interés. La cantidad total de la importación, por los doce meses, no llegó más que á la mitad del monto de la exportación, y fué de más de $147,000,000 menor que la del año fiscal que terminó en 30 de junio de 1897.

La importación procedente de Europa tuvo una baja de $124,000,391, mientras que la exportación á Europa aumentó en $160,313,645. La importación procedente de los países de la América del Norte tuvo una baja de $14,752,130, y la exportación aumentó en $14,676,878. La importación procedente de la América del Sur acusa un descenso de $15,295,379, mientras que la exportación aumentó en $53,325. Las importaciónes procedentes de Asia y Oceanía son las únicas que acusan un aumento, de $5,300,440 la primera y $2,458,781 la última. La exportación á los países del Asia aumentó en $5,549,363; y la exportación á la Oceanía tuvo una baja de $661,392.

El siguiente cuadro comprende las cifras de la exportación é importación, por grandes divisiones, en el año fiscal de 1898, comparadas con las del año fiscal de 1897:

	1897.	1898.
Importaciones de —		
Europa	$430, 192, 205	$306, 091, 814
América del Norte	105, 924, 053	91, 171, 923
América del Sur	107, 389, 405	92, 093, 526
Asia	87, 294, 597	92, 595, 037
Oceanía	24, 400, 439	26, 859, 220
Africa	9, 529, 713	7, 193, 639
Total	764, 730, 412	616, 005, 159
Exportaciones á—		
Europa	813, 385, 644	973, 699, 289
América del Norte	124, 958, 461	139, 635, 289
América del Sur	33, 768, 646	33, 821, 971
Asia	39, 274, 905	44, 824, 268
Oceanía	22, 652, 773	21, 991, 381
Africa	16, 953, 127	17, 357, 752
Total	1, 050, 993, 556	1, 231, 329, 950

El aumento de la exportación tuvo lugar en los artículos manufacturados y productos alimenticios, y la baja de la importación ocurrió naturalmente en los mismos ramos. La importación de productos químicos, porcelana, cristalería, manufacturas de algodón, hierro y acero, cuero, seda, lana, madera y fibras, acusa una baja, comparada con la de 1897 y 1896. Hubo un marcado descenso en la importación de alimentos cereales, provisiones, pescado, frutas, vino, azúcar, té y café. La importación de artículos para uso en las manufacturas fué mayor, casi en cada caso, que la de los años 1897 y 1896, con excepción de la lana, cuya importación en 1897 fué extraordinariamente grande.

El adjunto cuadro muestra la importación de todas clases de mercancías en general, cuyo valor excedió de cinco millones de pesos, y compara la importación del año fiscal de 1898 con la de 1897.

INFORME SOBRE LA EXPORTACIÓN EN EL MES DE JULIO DE 1898.

Según un informe del Bureau de Estadísticas de fecha 12 de agosto, el valor de la exportación de alimentos cereales, provisiones, algodón y aceite mineral de los principales distritos aduaneros de los Estados Unidos fué de $37,183,721. De esta suma, el valor de los alimentos cereales solos, fué de $16,737,128; el de las provisiones, $9,973,607; ganado vacuno y de cerda, $2,922,244; algodón, $2,828,669, y aceite mineral, $4,722,073. Estas cifras, correspondientes al mes de julio, arrojan una baja de $20,000,000; comparadas con las del mes de junio, son equivalentes á las del mes de julio de 1897; son mayores que las de igual mes de los años de 1894, 1895 y 1896, y exceden en $2,000,000, desde 1890, al promedio de la exportación de los artículos nombrados, correspondiente al mes de julio.

El valor de la exportación de alimentos cereales en julio de 1898 es 20 por ciento mayor que en julio de 1897, 15 por ciento mayor que en julio de 1896, y prácticamente el doble del valor de la exportación en julio de 1895. El valor de la exportación de provisiones en el mes de julio es menor que el de la exportación correspondiente á igual mes de 1897, 1896 y 1895; lo mismo ocurre con la exportación de aceites minerales. La reducción, en cuanto á este último artículo, se debe evidentemente á los bajos precios, y el número de galones exportados durante el mes excede ligeramente al de la exportación de julio de 1897, aunque el valor total de la exportación del mes es menor en 1898 que en 1897.

CIRCULACIÓN MONETARIA.

La circulación de monedas de oro de los Estados Unidos, en 1º de agosto de 1898, acusa un aumento de más de $135,000,000 comparada con la de igual fecha de 1897. La circulación de pesos de plata acusa un aumento de $5,600,000; la de la plata subsidiaria aumentó más de $4,800,000; los certificados de plata, más de $31,100,000; los billetes de la Hacienda, de 1890, casi $14,200,000, y los billetes de los Estados Unidos, cerca de $25,700,000. La circulación de certificados acusa un descenso de más de $40,300,000; la de los billetes del Banco Nacional, un descenso de cerca de $3,100,000, y los certificados de oro han disminuido en más de $1,500,000.

El importe total de la circulación de toda clase de moneda era de $1,809,198,344 en 1º de agosto de 1898, lo cual representa un aumento de más de $162,700,000 en los doce meses. La circulación per capita se calcula por la Tesorería en $24.23 tomando por base una población de 74,565,000; aquella cantidad acusa un descenso de 51 centavos por el mes, pero representa un aumento de $1.70 por cabeza respecto á los doce meses que acaban de terminar.

Una comparación con las estadísticas publicadas por el Departamento del Tesoro el 1º de agosto de cada año muestra que ha habido un aumento de más de $300,000,000 en la cantidad de dinero en circulación desde 1896.

FABRICACIÓN DE GLUCOSA Y ACEITE DE MAÍZ.

En un folleto sobre la composición del maíz, publicado recientemente por el Departamento de Agricultura de los Estados Unidos, el químico oficial, Mr. H. W. WILEY, trata de la industria de la glucosa.

Mr. WILEY dice:

La fabricación de azúcares de almidón, de varios grados de hidrolización, es una industria importante en los Estados Unidos. Estos productos de la hidrolosis del almidón se conocen con el nombre de glucosa ó azúcar de uva. La glucosa representa aquellas productos en los cuales la hidrolosis es menos completa, y se compone en parte de dextrina, dextrosa, una reducida cantidad de maltosa, y agua. Estas sustancias se preparan en forma de siropes gruesos y blancos que se usan mucho para la mesa, para adulterar la melaza y miel de abeja, y para la fabricación de dulces. La frase azúcar de uva se aplica al producto sólido que se obtiene de la hidrolosis del almidón llevada á cabo en mayor grado y cuyo producto se compone principalmente de dextrosa. Este producto se usa principalmente como sustituto de la malta en la fabricación de cerveza. Esta industria ha tomado inmensa proporciones en los Estados Unidos; la cantidad de maíz que anualmente se consume en la fabricación de glucosa es de unos 40,000,000 de bushels ó 14,095,922 hectólitros.

El Departamento describe también un nuevo producto derivado del maíz, que ha despertado considerable atención y que promete ser una importante producción; este producto es el aceite de maíz. El químico dice que en la fabricación de almidón y glucosa, y en la de algunas variedades de harina de maíz, se separa el germen del grano, el cual contiene el mayor tanto por ciento de aceite.

De este germen se extrae un valioso aceite y el resíduo forma un material para la alimentación tan valioso en todos respectos como el que se extrae ordinariamente de las semillas oleaginosas. El aceite de maíz se purifica fácilmente y forma un líquido de ligero color de ámbar, perfectamente trasparente y de agradable sabor. Se ha usado bastante como aceite de ensalada, y sin duda será aplicado en lo futuro á este uso. Puede emplearse también en la lubricación de las maquinarias delicadas; tiene excelentes propiedades combustibles y puede usarse como aceite de lámpara. Con el aceite más grueso y menos puro, se fabrica un jabón excelente. Puede decirse en general que el aceite de maíz tiene un valor comercial, galón por galón, igual al aceite que se extrae de las semillas de algodón.

HAITÍ.

FERROCARRIL, EN PROYECTO, DEL CABO HAITIANO.

Lemuel W. Livingston, Cónsul de los Estados Unidos en Cabo Haitiano, comunica al Departamento de Estado que se están trazando los planos para la construcción de una línea de vía estrecha desde Cabo Haitiano hasta La Grande Rivière du Nord, punto situado á unas 18 millas hácia el noreste. El capital de la compañía es de $450,000 y el presupuesto de la obra es de $250,000. El sindicato que proyecta la empresa ha suscrito ya $25,000, y se ofrecen á la suscripción pública 675 acciones de $500 cada una, con un interés de 8 por ciento, garantizado por el gobierno. El material, cuyo contrato no ha sido aun objeto de concesión, habrá de ser comprado en su totalidad en los Estados Unidos. Mr. H. Thomasset, el ingeniero que ha de dirigir la obra y que construyó también el tranvía á Port au Prince, declara que el material de los Estados Unidos es de una hechura superior y de incomparable duración.

La lista de las personas interesadas en la empresa comprende algunos de los ministros y ex-ministros del gobierno y otros hombres de negocios de prominencia y representación.

En el documento de incorporación, el gobierno concede á los Señores Cincinnatus Leconte, ministro de lo Interior y Obras Públicas, y Blanc Eusèbe, el privilegio exclusivo de construir aquella línea, cuya concesión habrá de durar por un período de sesenta años. Todos los materiales y artículos necesarios para la obra serán admitidos libres de derechos. El gobierno concede á los concesionarios, por un período de 30 años, el derecho de portazgo del puente de hierro que será el término de la línea en

Cabo Haitiano, y también las tierras públicas de los distritos de Cabo Haitiano y Grande-Rivière, situadas á lo largo de la línea.

El terreno por el cual habrá de pasar la línea es un fértil llano que se adapta al cultivo de todos los productos peculiares de la isla, y se dice que es especialmente apropiado al cultivo de plátanos. Los caminos que en la actualidad atraviesan esta región están en muy malas condiciones y son casi intransitables en la estación de las lluvias, lo cual ocasiona gran trabajo al campesino en el trasporte de sus productos al mercado. Los métodos de trasporte son muy primitivos. El burro es generalmente la bestia de carga, y aunque por lo común es una especie enana, se le fuerza á hacer todo el trabajo que generalmente se impone á los caballos. No sólo se emplea el burro en el trasporte de la mayor parte de las legumbres, frutas, café y cacao al mercado, sino que también se le utiliza para la carga de casi toda la inmensa cantidad de palo campeche y raiz de palo campeche que se exporta del país.

En tal país y bajo tales condiciones, un ferrocarril no es sólo de primaria necesidad, sino que debe operar una revolucion industrial. Los que proyectan esta línea esperan que ella estimule la producción en extraordinaria medida, dando á los campesinos el beneficio de un medio rápido de trasporte y nuevos mercados. De esta suerte la línea será una empresa lucrativa y de positivo beneficio público.

MÉXICO.

ZONA LIBRE.

El Departamento de Estado ha recibido por mediación del Consul-General Barlow un informe sobre la zona libre, preparado por el Ministro de Hacienda de México, en el cual se hace la historia de la creacion de aquella zona y se definen sus límites, así como los privilegios y restricciones que le son applicables.

La zona libre es una estrecha faja de tierra que se extiende á lo largo del límite septentrional, desde el Golfo de México hasta el Oceano Pacífico, con un area latitudinal de unas 12½ millas hácia el interior, la cual comprende una parte de los estados de Tamaulipas, Coahuila, Chihuahua, Sonora, y el Territorio de la Baja California. Esta zona fué establecida muchos años ha por el Gobierno Central á virtud de concesión hecha á los estados que lindan con el Río Grande como protección contra el contrabando de los Estados Unidos.

Las principales ciudades de la zona son Matamoras, Camargo Mier, Guerrero, Laredo, Porfirio Diaz (Piedras Negras), Juarez y Nogales. La población total no excede de 100,000 habitantes. Según los informes oficiales, no hay industrias dignas de mencionarse dentro de los límites de la zona libre, lo cual se explica por el hecho de que los productos industriales manufacturados en la zona pagan, al entrar en el interior del país, los mismos derechos de importación que se exijen á las mercancías extranjeras; y la exportación de aquellos productos á los Estados Unidos es impracticable por razón de la tarifa proteccionista de este último país. Así es que las industrias manufactureras tienen que depender del consumo local, el cual no es suficiente para el mantenimiento de aquéllas.

Las mercancías que se importan para su consumo en la zona libre pagan sobre la base del diez por ciento de la tarifa regular de derechos; pero cuando estas mercancías son reimportadas en el interior de México, se les exije el pago de un derecho adicional de 10 por ciento, cantidad ésta que unida al 10 por ciento ya pagado, hace el importe total de los derechos que exije la tarifa regular de México.

El Ministro de Hacienda, Señor LIMANTOUR, dice en su informe lo siguiente:

Muchos distinguidos hacendistas y eminentes estadistas se oponen á la Zona Libre, pero todos reconocen el hecho de que, á causa de las circunstancias existentes en la frontera del norte, su escasa población, y falta de recursos agrícolas, industriales ó mineros, el privilegio no podría ser abolido sin ofrecer debida compensación, y el problema consiste en escojer otras ventajas sin perjucio para el resto del país. La actitud de los comerciantes en el interior es en general hostil, porque consideran que aquel es un privilegio concedido sólo a una cierta parte del país. Los comerciantes que viven lejos de la frontera, como los de San Luis Potosí, Guadalajara y México, no lo consideran gravoso. Los que viven mas cerca, como los de Monterey, Chihuahua, etc., no temen la competencia, pero se quejan porque no disfrutan la libertad de destribuir sus géneros, sin documentos y sin inspección fiscal como en el resto del país. En realidad, la jurisdicción de la guardia fiscal se extiende á todos los estados de Tamaulipas, Nuevo Leon, Coahuila, Chihuahua, Sonora, y parte de la Baja California; y en este territorio no puede embarcarse mercancía alguna, según la ley, á menos que el comerciante pruebe legalmente que sus géneros han pagado los justos derechos, y pida permiso para cada cargamento.

está bien provista de líneas telegráficas y telefónicas y de carros urbanos. Cuatro ferrocarriles atraviesan la ciudad. El suelo del Estado de Nuevo León es muy fértil y algunas plantas producen tres cosechas al año. Se fabrican en grande escala paños de algodón, sombreros, muebles, etc. Hay más de 3,000 escuelas primarias en el Estado y también muchas otras de grado superior.

NICARAGUA.

EL DISTRITO AURÍFERO DE SIQUIA.

La Oficina de las Repúblicas Americanas ha recibido una carta del Señor J. P. Morgan, fechada en Rama, Nicaragua, en la que trata de las nuevas explotaciones de minas en la vecindad de aquel pueblo. Dice que á un día de camino en botes pequeños se encuentra uno de los distritos mineros que más prometen sobre los ríos Rama, Siquia y Mico, el cual se extiende por muchas millas en la montaña de Gurupera. Solamente como cuatro millas de dicho distrito han sido exploradas. Hay agua en abundancia y las colinas están cubiertas de espesas selvas, que producen suficiente combustible y madera para las minas. Con facilidad se hallan animales de caza, y abundan las plantaciones de bananos, plátanos, batatas, y ostras legumbres, de suerte que no hay dificultad en proveerse de alimento. El trabajo es barato y los salarios varían de diez á treinta pesos al mes.

Los depósitos de oro son muy accesibles y están situados de tal manera que se requiere muy poca maquinaria para explotarlos, y han llegado á producir de 17 á 35 pesos por tonelada. Se asegura también que en los lechos de los numerosos ríos que desaguan en el Mico se encuentra oro en cantidades considerables. Rama es un lugar muy sano y floreciente, que contiene cerca de 1,000 habitantes; tiene escuelas, iglesias, comunicación cablegráfica con todo el mundo, y servicio postal tres veces por semana por medio de los vapores fruteros que van á Nueva Orleans, Mobila y otros puertos de los Estados Unidos. Los hoteles son bastante buenos y se paga en ellos un peso al día en moneda americana. Según las leyes de Nicaragua, se admitten libres de derechos la maquinaria, dinamita y otros artículos de uso indispensable en las minas. Los habitantes de este lugar son hospitalarios y reciben muy bien á todas las personas que vienen á dedicarse á empresas que tiendan al desarrollo del país.

ASAMBLEA FEDERAL DE LA REPÚBLICA. MAYOR.

El corresponsal de la Prensa Asociada comunica por correo desde Managua, Nicaragua, que la Asamblea de Diputados de Salvador, Honduras y Nicaragua estaba todavía, en la última parte del mes de julio, celebrando sesiones diarias. La Comisión nombrada para informar sobre los artículos de una constitución para los Estados, los cuales artículos fueron sometidos por la Dieta de la República Mayor á la consideración de aquella Comisión que la Dieta convocó, ha indicado muchas modificaciones. La Comisión sugiere también una centralización de los estados nombrados, con un distrito federal compuesto de los Departamentos civiles de Chinandega, lindando con el Océano Pacífico y el Golfo de Fonseca, en Nicaragua; de Amapala, lindando con el Golfo de Fonseca, en Honduras; y de Limón, lindando con el Océano Pacifico y Golfo de Fonseca, en Salvador, teniendo por capital á Amapala, situada en la isla del Tigre, en el Golfo de Fonseca. La Asamblea, sin embargo, desechó por una gran mayoría la idea de centralización y se declaró en favor de una confederación de los tres estados, bajo el nombre de Estados Unidos de Centro América.

PARAGUAY.

FABRICACIÓN Y VENTA DE FÓSFOROS.

El Cónsul, Mr. RUFFIN, remite de Asunción con fecha 31 de mayo de 1898, los siguientes datos:

Hay dos fábricas en Asunción, y la mayor parte de los fósforos son de cerilla. Las fábricas no son grandes, y presumo que no bastan á llenar la demanda del país. El Gobierno ha hecho concesiones muy liberales á esta industria.

Los fósforos de cerilla se detallan á 1½ centavos, oro, por caja pequeña; los de palillo se venden á cinco séptimos de centavo, oro.

Durante el año de 1897 se importaron 5,981 kilógramos (13,158 libras) de fósforos de palillo, con un valor oficial de $1,498, oro; los derechos de aduana fueron de 25 por ciento ad valorem. Estos fósforos vinieron en su mayor parte de Suecia. La importación de fósforos de cerilla es insignificante.

Sería algo difícil al principio hacer la competencia á las fábricas nacionales, pero yo creo que nuestros fósforos podrían encontrar salida en este mercado.

Debo las anteriores datos al jefe de la Oficina de Estadísticas del Paraguay.

DESENVOLVIMIENTO AGRÍCOLA.

El Consul americano en Asunción dice que la población se está penetrando de la necesidad de desarrollar la agricultura. Las fincas están esparcidas aquí y allá, y hay una fuerte tendencia en favor de la centralización y de una nutrida colonización extranjera. El Gobierno, por mediación del Banco Agrícola, da á cada dueño de finca $300 en billetes (equivalentes á $35 ó $40 en oro), en calidad de préstamo sobre la propiedad. Se está agitando la idea, en obsequio de los que no tienen propiedades, de que el Gobierno compre grandes extensiones de tierra arable y las arriende á los campesinos proveyéndolos de instrumentos de agricultura, semillas, etc. Hay gran entusiasmo por parte de los iniciadores de este plan.

PERÚ.

AVISO Á LOS COMISIONISTAS.

El Cónsul de Inglaterra, en el Callao, informa á su gobierno que los comerciantes de Lima se oponen enérgicamente á la competencia que les hacen los comisionistas, competencia que aquellos consideran fundada sobre condiciones desiguales que les son desventajosas. Los comerciantes sostienen que ellos tienen que hacer gastos considerables en el mantenimiento de sus oficinas y establecimientos, mientras que los comisionistas convierten sus departamentos de los hoteles y posadas en cuartos para muestras, á muy poco costo.

Se está tratando de inducir al gobierno á que obligue á todos los comisionistas á sacar licencia para la venta de sus artículos. El asunto ha sido presentado en el Departamento de Comercio de Lima con la proposición de que el precio de una licencia de comisionista se fije en 500 soles ($243.25) por un período de seis meses que podrá renovarse al final de cada período. En caso de que no se saque la licencia, se exijirá el doble de aquella cantidad una tercera parte de la cual será pagada al denunciante.

Según las "Annual Series," nº 2117, de la Oficina de Relaciones Exteriores de la Gran Bretaña, en el Perú meridional se ofrece toda clase da facilidades á los comisionistas; se les permite que entren sus muestras, previa presentación en la aduana, por medio de un agente responsable, de una solicitud pidiendo que se les permita la entrada de un número determinado de paquetes de muestras. Estas muestras son examinadas y valuadas y después se presenta una garantía por el agente, el cual se compromete á pagar el importe de la valuación de cualquiera de las muestras que no se reembarque dentro del término especificado, que generalmente es de 90 días. Esto representa un costo para el vendedor de $2.50 á $5.00 según el numero de paquetes, y después queda en libertad de ir á donde guste con sus muestras sin que se le obligue á dar cuenta de ellas en ningún otro puerto del interior que visite. Los agentes responsables locales, antes de presentar la garantía en la aduana, adquieren informes completos sobre la representación económica del vendedor, quien, además de su tarjeta, trae una carta de introducción para una persona conocida, residente en el puerto. Este último requisito no debe olvidarse por los comisionistas que piensen visitar el país.

DEPÓSITOS DE CARBÓN.

Dentro de poco se empezarán á explotar unas nuevas minas de carbón antracito. En 1892 se hizo la concesión de este distrito minero á Mr. C. B. Jones. La concesión es por 20 años y cubre una extensión de tierra de 25 á 125 millas hacia el interior.

Varios ingenieros han sido enviadas de los Estados Unidos al Perú para hacer el estudio de un ferrocarril desde Pacasmayo hasta la provincia de Hualgayoc. La Compañía del Pacífico cuenta con un capital de $20,000,000 y con derecho exclusivo al carbón de las minas.

Según Mr. Clinton Gardner, ex-superintendente del Ferrocarril de Pensilvaña y constructor del Ferrocarril Nacional Mexicano, las minas de carbón son casi inagotables; 10,000,000 de toneladas pueden obtenerse con facilidad. Mr. Gardner calcula que puede extraerse anualmente 2,000,000 de toneladas y entregarse en puerto á un costo de $2 oro por tonelada, en cuyo caso, Mr. Gardner opina que el carbón importado será excluido de los mercados del Pacífico, pues será imposible competir con un producto tan bueno y barato como el carbón del Perú.

Además de esta concesión para explotar las minas de carbón en el distrito mencionado, la compañía tiene el derecho exclusivo de construir ferrocarriles que lleguen á estas minas, y ya ha celebrado con el gobierno el contrato de arrendamiento de un muelle excelente en Pacasmayo. Dice Mr. GARDNER que el costo de construcción de la línea y la compra del material rodante no excedería de $3,000,000. La línea habrá de partir de Pacasmayo; la distancia total de la costa al distrito carbonífero es de 121 millas. Hay ya una línea en operación de Pacasmayo á Yonan, una distancia de 41 millas, la cual línea es explotada por un contratista peruano.

Mr. FRANK G. CARPENTER, conocido corresponsal de la prensa de los Estados Unidos, dice que los yacimientos de carbón contienen antracita y lignito. La antracita se presenta en grandes cantidades en las vertientes del este y del oeste de los Andes; la antracita del lado este yace de 1,500 á 2,000 pies bajo la cima, y se ha encontrado que es igual en calidad á la antracita de Pensilvaña y en muchos respectos mejor que ésta. Para trasportar el carbón de la vertiente oriental á la costa, se necesita un ferrocarril que atraviese los Andes á una altura de unos 14,000 pies, pero desde aquel punto no habrá más de 75 millas en línea directa á la costa, y la línea pasará por un gran número de pueblos de tamaño regular y de ricos recursos agrícolas. Estas minas de carbón son más valiosas que las minas de oro, pues hasta el presente no se han explotado prácticamente las minas de carbón en la parte occidental de la América del Sur, y de 3,000,000 de toneladas que se usan cada año, la mayor parte procede de Australia, Inglaterra, Japón y Colombia Británica.

Además de los depósitos de carbón en la provincia de Hualgayoc, existen otros en el distrito de Huanachuco, y se encuentran también lignito y turba en varias otras partes del Perú.

URUGUAY.

COMERCIO CON LOS ESTADOS UNIDOS EN LOS SEIS PRIMEROS MESES DE 1898.

El Señor Don PRUDENCIO DE MURGUIONDO, Cónsul-General del Uruguay, ha tenido la cortesía de suministrar al BOLETIN los siguientes datos sobre el movimiento comercial entre los Estados Unidos y el Uruguay durante los seis primeros meses de 1898:

Exportación al Uruguay	$655, 419. 00
Importación procedente del Uruguay	1, 323, 650. 80
Diferencia en favor de la importación	668, 231. 80
Importación, seis meses de 1898	1, 323, 650. 80
Importación de julio 1° á diciembre 31 de 1897	830, 948. 48
Diferencia en favor de 1898	492, 702. 32
Exportación, seis meses de 1898	655, 419. 00
Exportación de julio 1° á diciembre 31 de 1897	606, 665. 83
Diferencia en favor de 1898	48, 753. 17

Por razón de la falta de buques de bandera extranjera durante los seis primeros meses de este año, ha habido muy pocos embarques de madera de construcción de los puertos del sur de los Estados Unidos al Uruguay.

COMERCIO EXTERIOR DURANTE EL PRIMER TRIMESTRE DE 1898.

El "Montevideo Times" dice que el primer trimestre del año se considera generalmente como el más importante con referencia al comercio exterior del Uruguay, y se le toma como el exponente de lo que habrá de ser el comercio total del año. Si el presente año no es una excepción de la regla general, el comercio será próspero, pues las cifras del primer trimestre son decididamente alentadoras. El "Times" dice que estas cifras indican de una manera clara que el comercio se va reponiendo del menoscabo ocasionado por la inmensa baja ocurrida en 1897 á consecuencia de la revolución, los disturbios políticos, la plaga de la langosta, y lo inferior de la producción en general. En el presente año, el valor total de las importaciones, que es el dato que principalmente sirve para formar juicio respecto de la situación comercial, ha vuelto á alcanzar el promedio de los tres años trascurridos de 1894 á 1896 que fueron considerados como años bastante prósperos. Los siguientes cuadros, que comprenden el primer trimestre de

los tres años de 1896, 1897 y 1898, han sido suministrados por
el Departamento de Estadística de la Aduana:

IMPORTACIÓN.

	1896.	1897.	1898.
Comestibles, cereales y especias............	$1,028,194	$915,289	$1,144,863
Materias textiles.........................	1,522,951	943,068	1,562,959
Materia prima y maquinaria................	1,789,134	1,393,366	1,439,019
Licores en general........................	758,611	697,624	764,888
Ropa hecha...............................	490,799	240,820	416,091
Ganado..................................	218,463	230,306	393,943
Tabaco y tabaco torcido...................	73,361	44,464	55,627
Los demás artículos.......................	945,077	602,021	659,884
Total...............................	6,826,588	5,066,958	6,438,175

EXPORTACIÓN.

Productos del rastro.....................	$12,474,760	$7,976,199	$9,114,869
Ganado................................	632,683	486,294	139,758
Productos rurales.......................	463,104	471,678	2,035,009
Provisiones para buques..................	27,732	23,797	19,485
Todos los demás productos..............	59,943	80,264	52,385
Total...............................	13,658,222	9,038,232	11,361,506

El total del comercio correspondiente al primer trimestre de
1898, se aproxima muy de cerca al total del primer trimestre de
1894, que fué considerado como un año excepcionalmente próspero. El total de productos de la agricultura en el trimestre fué
de $2,035,009, contra $471,678 en el mismo período de 1897.
Este gran aumento se debió por completo á la espléndida cosecha
de trigo; la cantidad de trigo que se exportó fué de 59,453,989
kilógramos, valuados en $1,783,619, contra sólo 3,214,663 kiló-
gramos, valuados en $77,151, en 1897.

En la mayor parte de los otros principales artículos ocurrió un
descenso. La exportación de maíz fué de 71,736 kilos, valuados
en $1,865, contra 1,309,947 kilos ($32,748) en 1897. La
cosecha de maíz fué muy buena, pero las últimas lluvias afectaron
la calidad del grano de tal manera que sólo quedó una cantidad
reducida en condiciones para la exportación. La exportación de
harina ascendió á un total de 3,889,669 kilos ($187,184): en
1897 pasaron por la aduana 5,247,092 kilos, valuados en
$262,354. La exportación de cebollas y ajos fué valuada en

$2,132 en 1898 y en $14,140 en 1897; frutas al natural, $14,809 contra $40,989; legumbres, $1,865 contra $32,748, y linaza, $16,186 contra $20,106.

VENEZUELA.

INFORME OFICIAL SOBRE LOS GÉNEROS COMPRADOS.

El Señor Don Antonio E. Delfino, Cónsul-General de Venezuela, ha remitido á la Oficina los siguientes datos estadísticos sobre la exportación de mercancías á los puertos de Venezuela en el mes de junio de 1898, comparados con los del mismo mes de 1897:

Puerto.	1898.	1897.	Aumento.	Disminución.
La Guaira....................	$96,364.55	$86,353.50	$10,011.05	....
Puerto Cabello...............	27,714.39	33,533.53	....	$5,819.14
Maracaibo	32,040.02	56,629.33	....	24,589.31
La Vela................	9,792.10	3,077.65	6,714.95	....
Ciudad Bolívar...............	13,377.00	42,866.10	....	29,489.10
Carúpano....................	5,474.24	9,519.00	....	4,044.76
Guanta	784.23	1,452.00	....	667.77
Cumaná	1,402.00	1,854.00	....	452.00
Güiria...........	705.00	303.00	402.00	....
Caño Colorado	699.00	....	699.00	....
Total	188,852.53	236,088.11	17,827.00	47,238.08

Los principales artículos exportados fueron: trigo; géneros de algodón, blanqueados y sin blanquear, $33,506.22; tabaco manufacturado y en rama, $25,493.52; harina, $99,473.65; manteca, $77,506.28; maquinaria y aparatos eléctricos, $20,897.98; provisiones, $20,143.64; mantequilla, $18,902.42; kerosina, $17,351.13; drogas y perfumería, $11,425.00, y telas de algodón estampadas, $7,799.30.

CONSUMO DE CAFÉ EN 1897.

· Por considerarlo de interés, y como suplemento al artículo sobre el café publicado en el Boletin del mes de julio, damos á continuación el siguiente extracto de un artículo publicado recientemente en el periódico francés titulado "Bulletin de Statistique et de

Legislation Comparée," en el cual se consigna la cantidad de café que se consume en varios países. Según aquel Boletin, el consumo total de café en Europa y los Estados Unidos aumentó de 1,039,330,000 libras en 1893 á 1,246,640,000 libras en 1897. El aumento en el consumo de 1897 con relación al consumo del año anterior fué de 129,580,000 libras. De este aumento, 100,000,000 de libras se importaron en los Estados Unidos; el consumo total de este país ha alcanzado la enorme suma de 636,340,000 libras, que, repartidas, dan un resultado de 9.95 libras (4½ kilógramos) por habitante. Aquella cantidad acusa un consumo de 26,000,000 de libras más que la cantidad que se consume en toda Europa. En 1893 Europa consumía 542,996,000 libras y el consumo en los Estados Unidos era de 496,234,000 libras. En cuanto al consumo por persona, los Estados Unidos no ocupan, en manera alguna, el primer lugar. Este corresponde á Holanda, en donde el consumo por habitante en 1897 era de 23 libras (10½ kilógramos). En Dinamarca el promedio de consumo por inviduo es de 15 libras (7 kilógramos); en Bélgica, 11 libras (5 kilógramos); en Alemania, 5¼ libras (2¹/₅ kilógramos); en Francia, 3¼ libras (1½ kilógramos), y en el Reino Unido de la Gran Bretaña, sólo siete décimos de libra (⅓ kilógramo).

El consumo de café en Francia está aumentando firmemente. En 1840 fué de 28,740,000 libras; en 1860, de 68,720,000, y en 1897 de 273,800,000. De este total, se importaron 2,214,000 libras (1,004,000 kilógramos) de las colonias francesas, cuyo café sólo paga en Francia la mitad de los derechos de importación que paga el café extranjero. Del café extranjero importado en Francia, 95,000,000 de libras (42,742,000 kilógramos) vinieron del Brasil y 51,000,000 de libras (23,176,000 kilógramos) de Haití.

NEUVA TARIFA EN JAMAICA.

Es de considerable interés para los exportadores de los Estados Unidos, México, América Central, Venezuela y Colombia, un informe dirigido recientemente á los periódicos comerciales británicos, sobre la tarifa de Jamaica. En el despacho se dice que á consecuencia del actual déficit en los ingresos, y de la baja en los mismos que se espera que ocurra en el año fiscal de 1898–99, el Gobierno ha introducido un nuevo proyecto de ley sobre la tarifa, que se espera que sea aprobado en la actual legislatura del Consejo Legislativo. Entre las disposiciones de la proyectada ley, hay una que previene el aumento de los derechos sobre los licores espirituosos de 12 chelines 12 centavos el galón líquido á 15 chelines el galón comprobado por medio del hidrómetro de Sykes. Esta importación procede principalmente de Inglaterra. Los derechos sobre la mantequilla, el queso y el jamón han sido aumentados de 2 centavos, que eran antes, á 4 centavos la libra. Los artículos de ferretería, como cuchillos, herramientas, utensilios, estufas, etc., que antes pagaban á razón de 12½ por ciento ad valorem, pagarán según la nueva ley 20 por ciento ad valorem. El mismo tipo se aplica á todos los géneros de vestir, ya sean manufacturados ó en piezas. Los comestibles, principalmente los que proceden de las repúblicas americanas y del Canadá, pagarán de 30 á 50 por ciento más sobre sus antiguos derechos. La lista de artículos que entran libres de derechos ha sido reducida considerablemente. El comisionado canadense ha protestado públicamente contra el aumento de derechos sobre los productos que el Dominio exporta á Jamaica, habida consideración expecialmente á las concesiones recíprocas proyectadas por el Canadá.

LA EXPOSICIÓN PAN-AMERICANA DEL NIÁGARA.

En números anteriores del BOLETIN (Octubre de 1897 y enero de 1898) se ha hecho referencia á la proyectada Exposición Pan-Americana que había de celebrarse en "Cayuga Island," en el río Niágara, cerca de la ciudad de Buffalo, Nueva York. Por varias causas, entre las cuales no es la menos importante el estado de guerra con España, se encontró que era tarea impracticable el reunir los artículos deseados antes de que se abriera la gran exposición de Paris, de la cual se pensó que sería obstáculo á la adquisición de extensas y completas colecciones. Se decidió, por tanto, posponer la apertura de la exposición hasta el año 1901, cuando ya se haya cerrado la de París, y hacer arreglos para obtener muchos de los artículos exhibidos en ésta, por las Repúblicas Americanas.

La legislatura de Nueva York solicitó del Congreso de los Estados Unidos que alentara la celebración de esta exposición, y en 8 de julio el Presidente McKinley aprobó una resolución conjunta declarando que la empresa ameritaba la protección y aprobación del Congreso y pueblo de los Estados Unidos.

Para facilitar la admisión de artículos procedentes de países extranjeros, la resolución dispone la exención de derechos y gastos de aduana para todos los artículos que entren con destino á la exposición, y se ha autorizado al Secretario de Hacienda para que dicte las disposiciones necesarias para llevar á cabo aquella resolución.

COMERCIO MISCELÁNEO.

REPÚBLICA ARGENTINA.

Diminución en los Sueldos y Pensiones. El "South American Journal" asegura que el Congreso argentino ha resuelto que desde el 1º de julio hasta el 31 de diciembre de 1898, todos los sueldos, pensiones, subsidios, subvenciones, etc., del Gobierno serán reducidos en un 20 por ciento. La única excepción es el pago de los soldados y marineros. El Gobierno piensa ahorrar cerca de $5,000,000 con esta reducción.

Condición de las Sementeras de Cereales. En 18 de junio el Señor William Goodwin, inspector autorizado de granos del Rio de la Plata, escribiendo de Buenos Aires, informa respecto de las sementeras de trigo y maíz en la Argentina, como sigue:

"La continuación del tiempo húmedo y cálido ha tenido un efecto muy malo sobre el maíz en cuanto á sus condiciones para el transporte; pero no hay que temer una producción indebida de trigo que se ha sembrado muy generalmente bajo condiciones las más favorables. El movimiento de ambos cereales, trigo y maíz, ha sido limitado también por la depresión de los mercados, aunque todavía hay una cantidad regular de trigo para la exportación. Todos los informes convienen en que la cosecha de maíz es probablemente la más grande que jamás se haya recogido, y se espera que será en buenas condiciones para la exportación más tarde. Cada año marca un adelanto decisivo en los métodos agrícolas en la Argentina, y particularmente en el cuidado que se toma con los frutos de los campos después de recogidos. Mas es de notarse que la población agrícola no aumenta con rapidez, debido á que muy pocos inmigrantes han llegado en los ultimos años."

Importaciones de Aparatos Eléctricos. Durante el año de 1897, la República Argentina importó 16,081 toneladas de alambre de hierro galvanizado, por valor de $1,005,777, así como 35,216 docenas de lámparas incandescentes,

5,123 cajas de materiales eléctricos en general, 52 dinamos, 529 cajas de material telegráfico, 318 cajas de material telefónico, y otros accesorios eléctricos. Además de esto, los cálculos para materiales de líneas eléctricas enviados á la Argentina por manufactureros de los Estados Unidos ascienden á más de $2,000,000.

BRASIL.

Análisis de las Cervezas. Se ha promulgado una ley últimamente en el Brasil decretando el análisis de las cervezas, á fin de descubrir si se emplea en ellas sustitutos para el lúpulo, de carácter que pueda ser nocivo al consumidor. Las cervezas que se encuentran así adulteradas han de ser reexportadas sin sacarlas de los almacenes de depósito de la aduana, ó destruidas por el importador. Cualquiera falta de cumplimiento de las disposiciones de esta ley se castiga con una fuerte multa.

CHILE.

Concesiones para el establecimiento de nuevas industrias. Según informe del "South American Journal," el Congreso nacional de Chile ha hecho recientemente varias concesiones para el establecimiento de nuevas industrias en Santiago de Chile. Entre estas concesiones se encuentran la de un establecimiento para blanquear, teñir y estampar géneros de algodón, y otra que tiene por objeto el establecimiento de una fábrica de ácido sulfúrico.

ECUADOR.

Concesiones en favor de una Compañía Alemana de Vapores. Las líneas de vapores "Kosmos" y "Hamburgo", que hacen el servicio comercial entre Hamburgo y Amberes, y también entre puertos españoles é italianos—con viajes á Londres, de cuando en cuando—se han refundido recientemente en una sola compañía. Inmediatamente antes de este arreglo, en mayo, la "Kosmos Company" se comprometió con el Gobierno del Ecuador á hacer gratis el servicio de correos entre los puertos del país y todos los demás puertos en donde hacen escala sus vapores. La compañía se compromete también á conducir pasajeros del Gobierno y emigrantes al Ecuador, entre los puertos de escala, con la reducción de un 30 per ciento del pasaje regular, y á trasportar también libre de gastos los primeros cargamentos de muestras de productos del Ecuador para cualquiera exhibición alemana. En cambio de estos servicios, el Gobierno del Ecuador admite en sus puertos, libres de toda clase de derechos fiscales, á los buques de la compañía, y reduce el pilotaje á la mitad. El contrato ha sido aprobado por el Consejo de Estado y habrá de regir durante cuatro años.

Cosecha de cacao de 1897. La cosecha de cacao del Ecuador, en 1897, fué de 14,800 toneladas, ó 330,293 quintales. Esta cantidad es menor que la de las cosechas de los últimos años. En 1896, el total fué de 15,300 toneladas; en 1895, 16,000 toneladas y en 1894, 17,467 toneladas.

GUATEMALA.

Oportunidades para los Capi-
talistas Americanos. Un corresponsal del periódico "The Manufacturer" (Philadelphia) escribe desde la ciudad de Guatemala con fecha 25 de junio de 1898 lo siguiente:

"El Gobierno está ansioso de vender el Ferrocarril del Norte, y casi se encuentra compelido á hacerlo así. Yo creo que esta sería una buena oportunidad para un sindicato americano. El negocio es bueno, y hoy podría obtenerse aquella línea en las condiciones más favorables y bajo la más liberal concesión. Lo mismo puede decirse de la línea de Verapaz. Además, una ó muchas compañías americanas podrían comprar las plantaciones que quisieran á precios meramente nominales; también podría una compañía americana establecer un banco, el cual sería muy bien recibido y haría negocios provechosos con las mejores garantías."

El Ferrocarril del Norte, á que se refiere el corresponsal, está proyectado de Puerto Barrios á la capital de la República, ciudad de Guatemala, y llega ya hasta San Augustín, á una distancia de 130 millas; sólo queda por terminar una pequeña parte de la línea. Esta es la empresa ferrocarrilera más importante de la America Central, y era el proyecto favorito del último Presidente BARRIOS, que se proponía, por medio de aquella empresa, el desarrollo de la riqueza del interior de Guatemala. Este ferrocarril abrirá al tráfico las tierras cafetaleras y mineras más productivas de la República.

HAWAII.

Leyes Vigentes sobre Nave-
gación. El Abogado del Estado (Attorney-General), Mr. GRIGGS, ha resuelto que las leyes de navegación de los Estados Unidos no son aplicables á Hawaii, ó ningún otro territorio anexado, sin que haya una ley al efecto votada por el Congreso. El mero hecho de la anexión no extiende, ipso facto, las leyes de los Estados Unidos á los nuevos distritos.

MÉXICO.

Recaudación de Aduanas. Durante el mes de junio el total de la recaudación de las aduanas de la República fué de $2,039,886.57. Esta cantidad se distribuye de la manera siguiente: derechos de importación, $1,879,919.44; derechos de exportación, $103,206.74; derechos de entrada, $55,478.60; atrasos, $1,281.79. El puerto de Veracruz recaudó $956,042.20 y el de Tampico $253,927.73, ó los dos juntos cerca de 70 por ciento de los derechos de importación.

La Cosecha de Trigo de 1898. La cosecha de trigo de México, correspondiente á 1898, es muy superior al promedio, tanto en cantidad como en calidad. Generalmente en México no se produce bastante trigo para el consumo interior; pero este año se exportará parte de la cosecha. Por esta razón, dice el "Boletin de la Sociedad Agrícola Mexicana," ciertos especuladores han tratado de obtener del Gobierno que obstaculice, si es que no impide en absoluto, la exportación de trigo. Pero estos especuladores no han prosperado en sus pretensiones, pues el Ministro de Hacienda ha anunciado que no se impondrá derecho alguno de importación ni ninguna otra restricción al trigo mexicano que ha encontrado compradores en mercados extranjeros.

PARAGUAY.

Importación de Kerosina. El Cónsul, Mr. RUFFIN, escribe desde Asunción al Departamento de Estado que el Paraguay está alumbrado con kerosina ó aceite de carbón importado de los Estados Unidos y que no se emplea más electricidad ó gas que el que procede de las fábricas ó plantas de particulares. La kerosina es importada en latas de cuatro galones, envase que se presta para una estiva apropiada en los botes que sirven entre Asunción y Montevideo. El Cónsul agrega: "Me parece que sería más provechoso enviar vapores-tanques, con lo cual se reduciría el costo del artículo y se aumentaría la venta. Los tanques podrían venderse inmediatamente, por razón de la gran demanda en este ramo, y de esta manera podrian economizarse los gastos que causaría su retorno. Desde que empezó la guerra con España el precio del aceite ha aumentado casi un 50 por ciento, y hay considerable especulación. Los Estados Unidos tienen el monopolio de la importación del aceite. En 1897 se importaron 40,648 galones, cuyo valor declarado fué de $19,511 oro. Los derechos son de 25 por ciento ad valorem."

PERÚ.

Fundición para Minerales en el Callao. El "British Trade Journal" dice que las autoridades municipales del Callao han concedido permiso últimamente á los Señores BACKUS y JOHNSTON para construir una planta destinada á la fundición de metales que se traigan de los varios puntos de la costa. Esta firma es ya propietaria de una importante fundición para minerales en Casapalea, en la línea del ferrocarril de Oroya. La nueva fundición será establecida en los surburbios del Callao y dará empleo á cien personas.

VENEZUELA.

Mejoramiento de los Caminos en el Estado de Los Andes. El Congreso nacional de Venezuela votó, en su última sesión, un presupuesto de 100,000 bolivares ($19,300) para el mejoramiento de los caminos del Estado de Los Andes. "Venezuela Ilustrada" dice que esta suma habrá de dividirse por igual entre tres secciones del Estado.

Nuevo Ferrocarril Eléctrico. El "Herald de Venezuela" dice que se ha hecho una concesión á una compañía francesca para la construcción de un ferrocarril eléctrico de 70 kilómetros (43½ millas) de largo. Esta línea habrá de unir á Cumaná con Cumanacoa, y las cascadas de las corrientes de las montañas serán utilizadas en la generación de fuerza eléctrica. La compañía ha enviado ingenieros á Cumaná para comenzar el estudio de la línea.

Recompensa para los Denunciantes de los Violadores de Leyes Postales. Dice el "Herald" que el Señor Presidente ANDRADE ha firmado un decreto con fecha 23 de junio de 1898, en el cual se dispone que el 30 por ciento de la multa de 500 bolivares ($96.50) que se impone á los que conduzcan correspondencia de otra manera que no sea por medio del servicio postal sea concedido al denunciante del violador de la ley. Dícese que la práctica de particulares, de conducir correspondencia á la República y desde la República, es un mal que crece cada día. El "Herald" agrega que esto debe tenerse presente por las personas (extranjeras) que viajan por el país.

Boletim Mensal

DA

Secretaria das Republicas Americanas,

União Internacional das Republicas Americanas.

| Vol. VI. | AGOSTO de 1898. | No. 2. |

RELAÇÕES DOS ESTADOS UNIDOS COM A HESPANHA.

SUSPENSÃO DE HOSTILIDADES E SEU EFFEITO SOBRE O COMMERCIO DA AMERICA.—AUGMENTO DAS VIAS DE COMMUNICAÇÕES COMMERCIAES ENTRE AS REPUBLICAS AMERICANAS.—AS ILHAS DE CUBA E PORTO RICO SERÃO AS PORTAS POR ONDE O CAPITAL E A INDUSTRIA PASSARÃO PARA O SUL E O OESTE.—HAWAII E AS PHILIPINAS EM SUAS RELAÇÕES COM O LITTORAL AMERICANO SOBRE O PACIFICO.—DADGS ESTATISTICOS SOBRE O COMMERCIO E AS INDUSTRIAS.—REGULAMENTOS DE ALFANDEGA E DA MARINHA MERCANTE PARA CUBA, AS PHILIPINAS E PORTO RICO.

A guerra entre os Estados Unidos e a Hespanha, motivada pela revolução contra o Governo hespanhol na ilha de Cuba, começou em 21 de Abril de 1898. As hostilidades suspendêram-se a 12 de Agosto de 1898, como se verá pela proclamação do Presidente dos Estados Unidos.

Proclamação do Presidente dos Estados Unidos da America.

Considerando que por meio de um protocollo concluido e firmado a 12 de Agosto de 1898, pelo Honrado Sr. William R. Day, Secretario de Estado dos Estados Unidos, e sua Excellencia Julio Cambon, Embaixador Extraordinario e Plenipotenciario da Republica franceza em Washington, representando respectivamente para este objecto os Governos dos Estados Unidos e a Hespanha, os ditos Governos têm concordado nas bases sobre as quaes se começarão as negociações para o estabelecimento da paz entre os dous paizes; e

353

expostas na mensagem que o Presidente dos Estados Unidos dirigiu ao Congresso em 25 de Abril de 1898, na qual faz referencia á resolução do Congresso, approvada no dia 20 de Abril de 1898, na qual se pede que o Governo da Hespanha renuncie a toda autoridade e dominio na ilha de Cuba e retire suas forças de mar e de terra de dita ilha e de suas aguas. O Presidente accrescenta:

Quando se communicou ao Ministro hespanhol em Washington o que o Executivo estava no dever de exigir da Hespanha, em cumprimento da citada resolução, o Ministro pediu seus passaportes e se retirou. Ao mesmo tempo o Ministro de Relações Exteriores da Hespanha informou ao representante diplomatico dos Estados Unidos em Madrid que a retirada do representante da Hespanha dos Estados Unidos havia posto termino ás relações diplomaticas entre os paizes e que toda communicação official entre os respectivos representantes devia cessar ao ponto.

Á suspensão das relações diplomaticas por parte do Governo da Hespanha seguíram activas operações militares por parte dos Estados Unidos. Estas déram por resultado a destruição da esquadra hespanhola em Manila no dia primeiro de Maio, a da flotilha hespanhola em Santiago de Cuba a 14 de Julho, e a invasão da ilha de Porto Rico a 21 do mesmo mez.

Depois da occupação da provincia de Santiago de Cuba, se estabeleceu um governo militar, e os empregados municipaes que exerciam autoridade sob a dominação hespanhola, continuáram em seus postos. A Secretaría da Guerra dos Estados Unidos fez promulgar regulamentos de alfandega e outros, os quaes publicamos neste numero.

Como resultado das operações militares, as Ilhas de Hawaii foram annexas aos Estados Unidos por uma resolução do Congresso, approvada a 7 de Junho de 1898, e se deixou á discrição do Presidente dos Estados Unidos determinar o relativo ao governo de ditas ilhas emquanto que o Congresso dispõe o que se deva fazer em diante. O conflicto com Hespanha tem dado resultados tão importantes para o desenvolvimento commercial dos paizes do hemispherio occidental que tem-se crido conveniente preparar a seguinte exposição para o conhecimento do publico. As rapidas mudanças que necessariamente occorrem na administração de um territorio adquirido por meio da guerra, fazem que seja uma tarefa difficil recolher immediatamente todos os dados que se requerem para estudar com cuidado suas condições commerciaes e industriaes. As ditas mudanças se effectuão nos varios departamentos da administração e se necessita tempo para perfeccionar os detalhes que se referem aos differentes ramos. Para satisfazer a demanda geral de informações relativas a opportunidades e condições commerciaes, tem-se preparado a compilação que vem a continuação, formada com dados que se têm tomado das fontes de que agora se dispõe.

Os paizes que compõem a União Internacional de Republicas Americanas, estão naturalmente muito interessados em conhecer os effeitos possiveis que o novo estado de cousas pode ter em seu desenvolvimento commercial e industrial. As Republicas latino-americanas verão, sem duvida, que, ao libertar-se o povo cubano, mediante a generosa intervenção dos Estados Unidos, da defei-tuosa administração de que o Mexico, a America Central e a do Sul se emancipáram por seus proprios esforços, mas contando com as sympathias dos Estados Unidos, o commercio e a indus-tria promettem desenvolver-se livremente na ilha de Cuba, da mesma maneira que se têm desenvolvido nos outros paizes e como uma consequencia de sua separação da patria mãi.

Devido a sua posição geographica pode-se dizer que as ilhas de Cuba e Porto Rico são as portas por onde naturalmente deve passar o commercio do mar das Antilhas, ao mesmo tempo que servem como de escalão para chegar aos mercados de toda a America do Sul. Com a abertura do canal interoceanico, estas ilhas receberão immensos beneficios por causa do augmento que deve-se esperar no commercio do littoral das tres Americas sobre o Pacifico. As possessões adquiridas pelos Estados Unidos no Pacifico, terão tambem vasto campo para o desenvolvimento do trafico na Asia, não sómente com os Estados Unidos, mas com as Republicas latino-americanas. O grande numero de communi-cações que a Secretaría das Republicas Americanas tem recebido já, provenientes de casas commerciaes dos Estados Unidos, assim como de individuos particulares, nas quaes se pede informação relativamente a opportunidades commerciaes, indicão claramente que, ao restabelecer-se a ordem nas antigas possessões hespanholas, acudirão a ellas em grande escala a industria e o capital; é de esperar que, sob favoraveis condições, isto tenderá a produzir beneficos resultados para as relações entre os Estados Unidos e as Republicas irmãs da America Latina.

As materias de que se trata na seguinte compilação, são estas: (1) Cuba. (2) Porto Rico. (3) As Ilhas de Hawaii. (4) As Philipinas e as Ilhas dos Ladrones.

A segunda parte deste artigo não foi traduzida na lingua portugueza por ter chegado demasiado tarde para este numero do BOLETIM. Consiste em uma compilação dos recursos, industrias e commercio das ilhas acima mencionadas.

REPUBLICA ARGENTINA.

AUGMENTO DO COMMERCIO—ESTATISTICA OFFICIAL.

A Direcção Geral de Estatistica dá os seguintes algarismos como a avaliação das importações e exportações da Republica Argentina, sem incluir ouro e prata em barras e acunhados, durante o primeiro trimestre de 1898, comparado com o mesmo periodo de 1897:

	1898.	1897.
Importações	$26, 080, 196	$29, 045, 105
Exportações	43, 970, 805	40, 706, 982
Total	70, 051, 001	69, 752, 087

Augmento total $298, 914

BRAZIL.

DEPOSITOS MINERAES DE MAGNESIA.

Durante os ultimos quatro annos os depositos mineraes de magnesia do Brazil têm constituido a principal fonte de exportação do paiz. O mineral procede do Districto de Miguel Burnier no Estado de Minas Geraes. A distancia de Rio de Janeiro é de 310 milhas e se necessitam oito ou dez dias para o transporte.

As minas estão situadas a uma altura de 4,000 pés, em um clima agradavel e salubre. Na exploração das minas se empregam trabalhadores italianos e indios e grande numero de hespanhóes e portuguezes.

Em 1897 se embarcaram 8,800 toneladas para Philadelphia, como a producção total daquelle anno; mas em annos anteriores a exportação se fez com destino á Philadelphia. Uma analyse deste mineral dá por resultado 54.7 por cento de magnesia metallica, 0.027 por cento de acido sulphurico, e 0.077 por cento de acido phosphorico.

COSTA RICA.

NOVO REPRESENTANTE—GRANDES MELHORAMENTOS.

O Sr. Dr. ULLOA, que foi o primeiro Vicepresidente da Republica de Costa Rica, tem estabelecido sua residencia em Nova York, com o objecto de desempenhar as funcções de Consul Geral da Republica naquella cidade. Em uma entrevista que teve com um correspondente da Prensa Associada, elle disse que seu primeiro dever official consistiria em estabelecer uma Repartição de Informação, de modo que os fabricantes, exportadores e importadores dos Estados Unidos possam obter toda a classe de informações relativas á Costa Rica e ao systema de negocios, modo de empacotar as mercadorias para a exportação, etc., que se observam no paiz. Tambem o Sr. Dr. ULLOA nutre a esperança de promover uma corrente de immigração para Costa Rica por meio da propagação dos conhecimentos relativos aos recursos do paiz.

Quanto a recentes emprezas publicas em Costa Rica, o Consul Geral diz que se estão levando a cabo grandes melhoramentos. Novas leis sobre terrenos serão decretadas afim de alentar a immigração, e se está construindo uma estrada de ferro que unirá Limón, porto do Atlantico, com Tivives, novo porto do Pacifico, estabelecendo assim uma nova linha de estrada de ferro de oceano a oceano.

NOVO MINISTERIO.

No BOLETIM do mez de Julho appareceu, por inadvertencia, como correspondente a Nicaragua o novo Ministerio do segundo periodo executivo do Presidente da Republica de Costa Rica,

Don RAFAEL IGLESIAS. O erro foi descoberto demasiado tarde e não poude fazer-se a devida correcçao no correspondente numero. Os senhores que compõem o actual Ministerio de Costa Rica são:

Ministro das Relações Exteriores, Instrucção
  Publica, etc ....Senhor PEDRO PERÉZ ZELEDÓN.
Ministro do Interior e Obras Publicas ....Senhor Don JOSÉ ASTÚA AGUIL.
Ministro da Fazenda e do Commercio ....Senhor Don JUAN B. QUIRÓS.
Ministro da Guerra e Marinha....................Senhor Don DEMETRIO TINOCO.

HÁITI.

PROJECTO DE UMA ESTRADA DE FERRO DO CABO HAITIANO.

O Sr. LEMUEL W. LIVINGSTON, Consul dos Estados Unidos em Cabo Haitiano, communica á Secretaria de Estado que se estão traçando os planos para a construcção de uma estrada de ferro de bitola estreita desde Cabo Haitiano até La Grande Rivière du Nord, ponto situado a umas 18 milhas para o nordeste. O capital da companhia é de $450,000 e o custo da obra é calculado em $250,000. O syndicato que projecta a empreza já tem subscripto $25,000, e se offerecem á subscripção publica 675 acções de $500 cada uma, com um juro de 8 por cento, garantido pelo Governo. O material, cujo contracto não tem sido ainda concedido, terá de ser comprado em sua totalidade nos Estados Unidos. O Sr. HENRI THOMASSET, o engenheiro que tem de dirigir a obra e que construiu tambem o tramvia em Port au Prince, declara que o material dos Estados Unidos é de mão de obra superior e de incomparavel duração.

A lista das pessoas interessadas na empreza comprehende alguns dos ministros e exministros do Governo e outros homens de proeminencia e posição.

No documento de incorporação, o Governo concede aos Senhores CINCINNATUS LECONTE, Ministro do Interior e das Obras Publicas, e BLANC EUSÈBE, o privilegio exclusivo de construir aquella linha, cuja concessão durará pelo prazo de sessenta annos. Todos os materiaes e artigos necessarios para a obra serão admittidos livres de direitos. O Governo concede aos concessionarios, por um período de trinta annos, o direito de portagem da ponte de ferro que será o termino da linha em Cabo Haitiano, e tambem as terras publicas dos districtos de Cabo Haitiano e Grande-Rivière, situadas ao longo da linha.

O terreno pelo qual terá de passar a linha, é uma fertil planicie que é propria para o cultivo de todos os productos peculiares da ilha, e diz-se que é especialmente apropriado ao cultivo de bananas. Os caminhos que na actualidade atravessam esta região, estão em muito más condições e são quasi intransitaveis na estação das chuvas, o qual occasiona grande trabalho ao camponez no transporte de seus productos para o mercado. Os methodos de transporte são muito primitivos. O burro é a besta de carga, e ainda que em geral é uma especie anã, tem de fazer todo o trabalho que geralmente se impõe aos cavallos. Não só se emprega o burro no transporte da maior parte dos legumes, fructas, café e cacáo para o mercado, mas tambem no transporte de quasi toda a immensa quantidade de páu campeche e raiz de páu campeche que se exporta do paiz.

Em tal paiz e sob taes condições uma estrada de ferro não é sómente de primeira necessidade, mas deve operar uma revolução industrial. Os que projectam esta linha esperam que ella estimule a producção em extraordinaria medida, dando aos camponezes o beneficio de um meio rapido de transporte e novos mercados. Desta sorte a linha será uma empreza lucrativa e de positivo beneficio publico.

MEXICO.

ZONA LIVRE.

A Secretaria de Estado recebeu por intermedio do Consul Geral BARLOW um relatorio sobre a Zona Livre, preparado pelo Ministro da Fazenda do Mexico, no qual se dá a historia da creação daquella zona e se definem seus limites, assim como os privilegios e restricções que lhe são applicaveis.

A Zona Livre é uma estreita faxa de terra que se estende ao longo do limite septentrional desde o Golfo do Mexico até o Oceano Pacifico, com uma area latitudinal de umas 12½ milhas para o interior, a qual comprehende uma parte dos estados de Tamaulipas, Coahuila, Chihuahua, Sonora e o Territorio da Baixa California. Esta zona foi estabelecida, ha muitos annos pelo Governo

Central em virtude da concessão feita aos estados que confinam com o Rio Grande, como protecção contra o contrabando dos Estados Unidos.

As principaes cidades da Zona são Matamoras, Camargo, Mier, Guerrero, Laredo, Porfirio Diaz (Piedras Negras), Juarez e Nogales. A população total não excede de 100,000 habitantes. Segundo os relatorios officiaes, não ha industrias dignas de ser mencionadas dentro dos limites da Zona Livre, o qual se explica pelo facto de que os productos industriaes manufacturados na Zona pagam, ao entrarem no interior do paiz, os mesmos direitos de importação que se exigem das mercadorias estrangeiras; e por razão da tarifa proteccionista dos Estados Unidos é impraticavel exportar aquelles productos a este paiz. Assim é que as industrias manufactureiras têm de depender do consumo local, o qual não é sufficiente para a manutenção daquellas.

As mercadorias que se importam para seu consumo na Zona Livre pagam sobre a base de 10 por cento da tarifa regular de direitos; mas quando estas mercadorias são reimportadas no interior do Mexico, se lhes exige o pagamento de um direito addicional de 90 por cento, quantia esta que unida ao 10 por cento já pago, faz a importancia total dos direitos que exige a tarifa regular do Mexico.

O Ministro da Fazenda, Senhor LIMANTOUR, diz em seu relatorio o seguinte:

Muitos distinctos financeiros e eminentes estadistas se oppõem á Zona Livre; mas todos reconhecem o facto de que, por causa das circumstancias existentes na fronteira do norte, sua escassa população, e falta de recursos agricolas, industriaes ou mineiros, o privilegio não poderia ser abolido sem offerecer devida compensação, e o problema consiste em escolher outras vantagens sem prejuizo para o resto do paiz.

A attitude dos commerciantes no interior é, em geral, hostil, porque consideram que aquelle é um privilegio concedido sómente a uma certa parte do paiz. Os commerciantes que vivem longe da fronteira, como os de San Luis Potosi, Guadalajara e Mexico, não o consideram préjudicial. Os que vivem mais cerca, como os de Monterey, Chihuahua, etc., não temem a concurrencia, mas queixam-se porque não possam distribuir suas mercadorias sem documentos e sem inspecção fiscal, como no resto do paiz. Em realidade, a jurisdicção da guarda fiscal estende-se a todos os estados de Tamaulipas, Nuevo Leon, Coahuila, Chihuahua, Sonora, e parte da Baixa California; e neste territorio não se pode embarcar mercadoria alguma, segundo a lei, a menos que o commerciante prove legalmente que suas mercadorias têm pago os direitos devidos e peça permissão para cada carregamento.

e dependencias que forem necessarios para a melhor extracção delle ; empregando para este fim as machinas e methodos mais modernos. A companhia estabelecerá a dita industria com a approvação do Ministerio do Fomento, ao qual dará aviso dous mezes antes de emprehender a construcção dos armazens, etc., no lugar que mais convenha á Companhia, cumprindo com o que dispõe o Codigo Sanitario, respeito a fabricas.

Art. 2. A construcção dos armazens e officinas para a exploração da industria, principiará aos seis mezes e terminará aos dous annos, contados um e outro prazo desde a data da promulgação deste contrato.

Art. 3. No estabelecimento dos armazens e officinas e nos gastos geraes do negocio, a companhia se obriga a empregar, pelo menos, a somma de duzentos cincoenta mil pesos dentro do prazo de cinco annos, a partir da data deste contrato (28 de Maio de 1898), comprovando o emprego dessa somma com os registros de pagamentos, recibos, facturas, e os registros de seus livros de contabilidade que deverá apresentar originaes ou em copia devidamente legalisada.

Art. 4. Para garantir o cumprimento das obrigações a que se refere o presente contrato, ao firmar-se este, a companhia depositará no Banco Nacional do Mexico, a somma de dez mil pesos em titulos da Divida Consolidada.

Art. 7. Si o Governo necessitar do petroleo que extrae a companhia, esta lho venderá com um desconto de dez por cento dos preços por maior para o publico.

Art. 11. Os concessionarios respectivos poderão importar por uma só vez, livres de direitos, as machinas, apparelhos, ferramentas, materiaes de construcção e demais artigos necessarios para os edificios ; outorgando fiança em cada caso de introducção que se cancellará logo que se tenham montado as machinas e que se tenha acreditado o emprego do material ou effecto.

Art. 12. Durante dez annos contados desde a data da promulgação deste contrato, os capitaes empregados pela companhia no estabelecimento e exploração da industria, gozarão de isenção de todo imposto federal directo, ficando sujeito o concessionario ou a companhia ao pagamento dos impostos comprehendidos na Renda Federal do Sello.

Art. 17. O prazo do presente contrato será de dez annos, contados desde a data de sua promulgação.

NICARAGUA.

ASSEMBLEA DE DEPUTADOS DA REPUBLICA MAIOR.

O correspondente da Prensa Associada communica por correio de Managua, Nicaragua, que a Assemblea de Deputados de Salvador, Honduras e Nicaragua, estava ainda na ultima parte do mez de Julho, celebrando sessões diarias. A commissão nomeada para informar sobre os artigos de uma constituição para os Estados, os quaes artigos foram submettidos pela Dieta da Republica Maior

á consideração daquella commissão, tem indicado muitas m
cações. A commissão suggere tambem uma centralisaçã
Estados nomeados, com um districto federal composto dos
trictos Civis de Chinandega, confinando com o Golfo de Fc
em Nicaragua; de Amapala, confinando com o Golfo de Fc
em Honduras, e de Limon, confinando com o Oceano Paci
Golfo de Fonseca, em Salvador, tendo por capital Amapala,
da na ilha do Tigre, no Golfo de Fonseca. A Assemblea,
tudo, votou por uma grande maioria, contra a idea de central:
e declarou-se em favor de uma confederação dos tres Estado
o nome de Estados Unidos da America Central.

PARAGUAY.

DESENVOLVIMENTO AGRICOLA.

O Consul RUFFIN diz que o povo do Paraguay está come
a realisar a necessidade de desenvolver a agricultura. As faz
estão espalhadas e ha uma forte tendencia em favor da central:
e de uma grande colonisação estrangeira.

O Governo, por intermedio do Banco Agricola, dá a cada
de fazenda $300 em bilhetes (equivalentes a $35 ou $40 em
em qualidade de emprestimo sobre a propriedade. Está-s
tando a idea, a favor dos que não têm propriedades, de c
Governo compre grandes extensões de terra aravel e as arren
fazendeiros, fornecendo-os de instrumentos agricolas, sement
Ha grande enthusiasmo por parte dos iniciadores deste plan

PERU.

AVISO AOS AGENTES COMMERCIAES.

O Consul britannico em Callão em um relatorio dirig
Secretaria de Estado de Relações Exteriores, diz que os cor
ciantes de Lima oppõem-se energicamente á concurrencia qu
fazem os agentes commerciaes, concurrencia que aquelles
sideram fundada sobre condições desiguaes. Os commerc
reclamam que elles têm de fazer gastos consideraveis na i
tenção de seus escriptorios e estabelecimentos, emquanto c

agentes commerciaes convertem seus aposentos dos hoteis e hospedarias em quartos para amostras a muito pouco custo.

Estão-se tomando medidas para induzir ao Governo a que obrigue a todos os agentes commerciaes a saccar licença para a venda de seus artigos. O assumpto foi submettido ao Ministerio do Commercio de Lima, com a proposição de que o preço de uma licença se fixe em 500 soles ($243.25) por um periodo de seis mezes, a qual poderá ser renovada ao fim de cada periodo. Em caso de que não se sacque a licença, se exigirá o dobro daquella quantia, uma terça parte da qual será paga ao denunciante.

Segundo as "Annual Series," N° 2117, da Secretaria das Relações Exteriores da Grã Bretanha, no Peru meridional se offerece toda classe de facilidades aos agentes commerciaes; permitte-se-lhes que entrem suas amostras, ao apresentar na alfandega, por meio de um agente responsavel, um requerimento pedindo que se lhes permitta a entrada de um numero determinado de volumes de amostras. Estas amostras são examinadas e avaliadas e depois se apresenta uma garantia pelo agente, o qual se compromette a pagar a importancia da avaliação de qualquer das amostras que não se reembarque dentro do prazo especificado que geralmente é de 90 dias. Isto representa um custo para o agente de $2.50 a $5, segundo o numero de volumes, e depois elle pode ir a onde quizer com suas amostras, sem que se lhe obrigue a dar conta dellas em nenhum outro porto do interior que visitar.

Os agentes responsaveis locaes, antes de apresentar a garantia na alfandega, obtêm informações completas sobre a representação economica do agente commercial, o qual, além de seu bilhete, trae uma carta de introducção para uma pessoa conhecida, residente no porto. Este ultimo requisito não deve ser olvidado pelos commerciantes que pensam visitar o paiz.

DEPOSITOS DE CARVÃO.

Dentro de pouco, se começará a exploração de umas novas minas de carvão. A concessão deste districto mineiro foi feita ao Sr. C. B. Jones em 1892. A concessão é por 20 annos e cobre uma secção de terra de 100 milhas de extensão, situada de 25 a 125 milhas para o interior.

Varios engenheiros têm sido enviados dos Estados Unidos ao Peru

ıeladas que se usam cada anno, a maior parte procede da ıstralia, Inglaterra, Japão e Colombia Britannica.

Além dos depositos de carvão na provincia de Hualgayoc, stem outros no districto de Huamachuco, e se encontram ıbem lignite e turfa em varias outras partes do Peru.

ESTADOS UNIDOS.

COMMERCIO EXTERIOR.

Ɔ relatorio da Repartição de Estatisticas dos Estados Unidos, respondente ao anno fiscal findo em 30 de Junho de 1897, é de ınde interesse. A quantia total da importação, pelos doze :zes, não chegou mais que á metade da quantia da exportação, ̀oi de mais de $147,000,000 menor do que a do anno fiscal do em 30 de Junho de 1897.

A importação procedente da Europa teve uma diminuição de 24,000,391, emquanto que a exportação para a Europa aug-:ntou em $160,313,645. A importação procedente dos paizes America do Norte teve uma diminuição de $14,752,130, e a ̀ortação augmentou em $14,676,828. A importação proce-te da America do Sul mostra uma diminuição de $15,295,379, ̨uanto que a·exportação augmentou em $53,325. As impor-es procedentes da Asia e Oceania são as unicas que mostram augmento, de $5,300,440 a primeira e $2,458,781 a ultima. ̨portação para os paizes da Asia augmentou em $5,549,363, exportação para a Oceanía houve uma diminuição de ,392.

̨eguinte quadro comprehende os algarismos da exportação e tação, por grandes divisões, no anno fiscal de 1898, com-ıs com os do anno fiscal de 1897:

	1897.	1898.
Ɔ de—		
a	$430,192,205	$306,091,814
:a do Norte	105,924,053	91,174,923
'a do Sul	107,389,405	92,093,526
	87,294,597	92,595,037
'a	24,400,439	26,859,220
	9,529,713	7,193,639
	764,730,412	616,005,159

	1897.	1898.
Exportação para—		
Europa.	$813,385,644	$973,699,289
America do Norte	124,958,461	139,635,289
America do Sul	83,768,646	33,821,971
Asia	59,274,905	44,824,268
Oceanica	22,652,773	21,991,381
Africa	16,953,127	17,357,752
Total	1,050,993,556	1,231,329,950

O augmento da exportação teve lugar nos artigos manufacturados e productos alimenticios e a diminuição da importação occorreu naturalmente nos mesmos ramos. A importação de productos chimicos, porcelana, obras de vidro, manufacturas de algodão, ferro e aço, couro, seda, lã, madeira e fibras, mostra uma diminuição comparada com a de 1897 e 1896. Houve uma notavel diminuição na importação de cereaes, viveres, pescado, fructas, vinho, assucar, chá e café. A importação de artigos para uso nas manufacturas foi maior do que a dos annos de 1897 e 1896, com a excepção da lã, cuja importação em 1897 foi extraordinariamente grande.

O seguinte quadro mostra a importação de todas as classes de mercadorias em geral, cujo valor foi superior a cinco milhões de dollars e compara a importação do anno fiscal de 1898, com a de 1897:

Importação.	1897.	1898.
Manufacturas.		
Productos chimicos, drogas, etc	$44,948,752	$41,470,711
Manufacturas de algodão	34,429,363	27,262,932
Porcelana e louça de barro	9,977,297	6,686,220
Fibra manufacturada	32,546,867	21,899,714
Obras de vidro	5,509,626	3,669,919
Ferro e aço manufacturados	16,094,557	12,615,913
Couro e manufacturas de couro	13,283,151	11,414,118
Oleos de todas as classes	5,594,111	5,197,886
Manufacturas de seda	25,199,067	23,523,110
Madeira e manufacturas de madeira	20,543,810	13,858,582
Manufacturas de lã	49,162,992	14,823,768
Artigos empregados nas industrias manufactureiras.		
Algodão, sem fabricar	5,884,262	5,019,503
Fibras, sem fabricar	12,336,418	13,446,186
Couros e pelles	27,863,026	37,068,832
Borracha	17,558,163	25,545,391
Seda, sem fabricar	18,918,283	32,110,066
Tabaco, sem fabricar	9,584,155	7,488,605
Lã	53,243,191	16,783,692

Importação.	1897.	1898.
Artigos de consumo.		
Café...	$81, 544, 384	$65, 067, 561
Pescado...	6, 108, 714	5, 984, 980
Fructas e nozes.................................	17, 126, 932	14, 566, 874
Assucar...	99, 666, 181	60, 472, 703
Chá...	14, 835, 862	10, 054, 005
Vinhos, bebidas espirituosas e licores de malt........	12, 272, 872	9, 305, 504

RELATORIO SOBRE A EXPORTAÇÃO NO MEZ DE JULHO.

Segundo um relatorio da Repartição de Estatistica de data de 12 de Agosto, o valor da exportação de cereaes, viveres, algodão e oleo mineral dos principaes districtos aduaneiros dos Estados Unidos, foi de $37,183,721. Desta quantia, o valor dos cereaes só foi de $16,737,128; o dos viveres, $9,973,607; gado vaccum e porcos, $2,922,244; algodão, $2,828,669; e oleo mineral, $4,722,073. Estes algarismos, correspondentes ao mez de Julho, mostram uma diminuição de $20,000,000 comparados com os do mez de Junho, são equivalentes aos do mez de Julho de 1897, são maiores do que os de igual mez dos annos de 1894, 1895 e 1896, e excedem em $2,000,000 desde 1890 a exportação média dos artigos nomeados correspondente ao mez de Julho.

O valor da exportação de cereaes em Julho de 1898 é 20 por cento maior do que em Julho de 1897, 25 por cento maior do que em Julho de 1896, e praticamente o dobro do valor da exportação em Julho de 1895. O valor da exportação de viveres no mez de Julho é menor do que o da exportação correspondente a igual mez de 1897, 1896 e 1895; o mesmo occorre com a exportação de oleos mineraes. Quanto a este ultimo artigo a reducção é devida evidentemente aos baixos preços, e o numero de galões exportados durante o mez excede ligeiramente ao da exportação de Julho de 1897, ainda que o valor total da exportação do mez é menor em 1898 do que em 1897.

FABRICAÇÃO DE GLUCOSE E OLEO DE MILHO.

Em um folheto publicado recentemente pela Secretaria da Agricultura dos Estados Unidos sobre a composição do milho, o

chimico official, o Sr. H. W. WILEY, trata da industria da glucose.
Elle diz:

A fabricação de assucares de amido de varios gráos de hydrolização, é uma industria importante nos Estados Unidos. Estes productos da hydrolosis do amido, são conhecidos com o nome de glucose ou assucar de uva. A glucose representa aquelles productos nos quaes a hydrolosis é menos completa, e compõe-se em parte de dextrina, dextrosa, uma reduzida quantidade de maltosa, e agua. Estas substancias estão preparadas em forma de xaropes grossos e brancos que se usam muito para a mesa, para adulterar o melaço e mel, e para a fabricação de doces. A phrase assucar de uva se applica ao producto solido que se obtem da hydrolosis do amido levada a cabo em maior gráo e cujo producto compõe-se principalmente de dextrosa. Usa-se este producto principalmente como substituto de malt na fabricação de cerveja. Esta industria tem assumido immensas proporções nos Estados Unidos; a quantidade de milho que annualmente se consome na fabricação de glucose é de uns 40,000,000 de alqueires, ou 14,095,922 hectolitros.

A Secretaria descreve tambem um novo producto derivado do milho, que tem attrahido consideravel attenção e que promette ser uma importante producção. Este producto é o oleo de milho. O chimico diz que na fabricação de amido e glucose e na de algumas variedades de farinha de milho, se separa o germe do grão, o qual contem a maior porcentagem de oleo. Deste germe se espreme um valioso oleo e o residuo constitue um material para a alimentação tão valioso em todos os respeitos como o que se extrae ordinariamente das sementes oleaginosas. O oleo de milho é purificado facilmente e forma um liquido de côr de ambar claro, perfeitamente transparente e de agradavel sabor. Tem-se usado como oleo de salada, e sem duvida será empregado no futuro para este uso. Pode ser empregado tambem para lubricar as machinas delicadas; tem excellentes propriedades combustiveis e pode ser usado como oleo de lampada. Com o oleo mais grosso e menos puro, se fabrica um sabão excellente. Pode-se dizer em geral que o oleo de milho tem um valor commercial, galão por galão, igual ao oleo que se extrae das sementes de algodão.

URUGUAY.

COMMERCIO COM OS ESTADOS UNIDOS NO PRIMEIRO
SEMESTRE DE 1898.

O Sr. Don PRUDENCIO DE MURGUIONDO, Consul-Geral do Uruguay, subministrou á Secretaria os seguintes dados sobre o movimento commercial entre os Estados Unidos e o Uruguay durante o primeiro semestre de 1898:

Exportação para o Uruguay........................	$655,419.00
Importação procedente do Uruguay.............................	1,323,650.80
Differença em favor da importação.	668,231.80
Importação, seis mezes de 1898	1,323,650.80
Importação de 1º de Julho a 31 de Dezembro de 1897	830,948.48
Differença em favor de 1898............	492,702.32
Exportação, seis mezes de 1898 ....•.......... ...	655,419.00
Exportação de 1º de Julho a 31 de Dezembro de 1898	606,665.83
Differença em favor de 1898................	48,753.17

Devido á falta de navios de bandeira estrangeira, durante o primeiro semestre deste anno, tem havido muito poucos embarques de madeira dos portos do sul dos Estados Unidos para o Uruguay.

VENEZUELA.

RELATORIO OFFICIAL DA IMPORTAÇÃO.

O Sr. Antonio E. Delfino, Consul-Geral de Venezuela, subministrou á Secretaria os seguintes dados estatisticos sobre os artigos exportados para os varios portos de Venezuela no mez de Junho de 1898, comparados com os exportados em igual mez de 1897.

Porto.	1898.	1897.	Augmento.	Diminuição.
La Guaira......................	$96,384.55	$86,853.50	$10,011.05	....
Puerto Cabello................	27,714.39	33,533.53	....	$5,819.14
Maracaibo	32,040.02	56,629.33	....	24,589.31
La Vela.......................	9.792.10	3,077.65	6,714.95	....
Ciudad Bolivar................	13,377.00	42,866.10	....	29,489.10
Carupano......................	5,474.24	6,519.00	....	4,044.76
Guanta	784.23	1,452.00	....	667.77
Cumana	1,402.00	1,854.00	....	452.00
Guiria	705.00	303.00	402.00	....
Caña Colorado	699.00	....	699.00	....
Total	188,852.53	236,088.11	17,826.50	47,238.08

Os principaes artigos que se exportaram foram farinha de trigo, no valor de $99,473.65; banha, $77,506.28; tecidos de algodão, branqueados e sem branquear, $33,506.22; tabaco, fabricado e sem fabricar, $25,493.52; machinas e materiaes electricos, $20,897.98; viveres, $20,143.64; manteiga, $18,902.42; kerosene, $17,351.13; ferragens, $11,776.72; drogas e perfumarias, $11,425.00, e chitas, $7,799.38.

cuidado que se toma com os productos dos campos depois de recolhidos. Mas é
de notar-se que a população agricola não augmenta com rapidez, devido a que
muitos poucos immigrantes têm chegado nos ultimos annos."

Importações de Apparelhos Electricos. Durante o anno de 1897 a Republica Argentina
inportou 16,081 toneladas de arame de ferro galvanisado,
no valor de $1,005,777, assim como 35,216 duzias de lampadas incandescentes,
5,123 caixas de materiaes electricos, 52 dynamos, 529 caixas de materiaes tele-
graphicos, 318 caixas de materiaes telephonicos, e outros accessorios. Além
destes, os calculos para materiaes de linhas electricas enviados á Republica
Argentina por fabricantes dos Estados Unidos attingem a somma de $2,000,000.

BRAZIL.

Terrenos Productores de Borracha do Pará. Segundo o Consul inglez de Pará, algumas pessoas creem
que a producção dos seringueiros do Amazonas será esgo-
tada em poucos annos. As autoridades mais competentes não estão de accordo
com esta opinião, mas, pelo contrario, sustentam que a producção é inexgota-
vel, porque a borracha reproduz-se constantemente por natureza. Quando se
exploram as secções de borracha demasiado, certamente ficam esgotadas, mas si
as deixar descançar por algum tempo, recuperarão sua fertilidade. O districto
de Cametá, no rio Tocantins, produzia uma borracha de excellente qualidade
que tinha procura especial no mercado. Este districto está agora esgotado, pois
milhares de pessoas o exploraram por um periodo de uns quarenta annos; todos
os recemchegados dirigiam-se a Cametá em busca de fortuna. Ha muitos districtos que ainda não têm sido explorados. A area que produz a borracha do
Pará comprehende pelo menos 1,000,000 de milhas quadradas. Explorações
posteriores mostrarão, sem duvida, que esta area é mais extensa.

CHILE.

Concessões para o Estabele- cimento de Novas Indus- trias. Segundo um relatorio publicado no "South American
Journal," o Congresso nacional do Chile tem feito recente-
mente varias concessões para o estabelecimento de novas
industrias em Santiago de Chile. Entre estas concessões, ha uma para o estabelecimento de uma fabrica para branquear, tingir e estampar tecidos de algodão
e outra para o estabelecimento de uma fabrica de acido sulphurico.

EQUADOR.

Concessões a uma Compa- nhia Allemã de Vapores. As linhas de vapores "Kosmos e Hamburgo," que
fazem o serviço commercial entre Hamburgo e Antuerpia, e
tambem entre portos hespanhóes e italianos, com viagens a Londres de tempos
a tempos, têm-se unidas recentemente em uma só companhia. Immediatamente
antes deste arranjo, em Maio, a "Kosmos Company" celebrou um contracto
com o Governo do Equador para fazer gratis o serviço dos correios entre os
portos do paiz e todos os demais portos em que fazem escala seus vapores. A
companhia compromette-se a conduzir passageiros do Governo e immigrantes
para o Equador, entre os portos de escala, com a reducção de 30 por cento do

Arrecadações das Alfandegas. Durante o mez de Junho o total das arrecadações das alfandegas da Republica foi de $2,039,886.57. Esta quantia distribue-se do modo seguinte: direitos de importação, $9,879,919.44; direitos de exportação, $103,206.74; direitos de porto, $55,478.60; atrazados, $1,281.79. O porto de Vera Cruz arrecadou $956,042.20, e o de Tampico, $352,927.73, ou, os dous juntos, cerca de 70 por cento dos direitos de importação.

PARAGUAY.

Fabricação e Venda de Phosphoros. O Consul RUFFIN remette de Assumpção com data de 31 de Maio de 1898, os seguintes dados:

" Ha duas fabricas em Assumpção, e a maior parte dos phosphoros são de cera. As fabricas não são grandes, e creio que não abastam para o consumo do paiz. O Governo tem feito concessões muito liberaes a esta industria.

" Os phosphoros de cera vendem-se a retalho a 1½ centavos, ouro, por caixa pequena; os de páu vendem-se a ⅘ de centavo, ouro.

" Durante o anno de 1897 se importaram 5,981 kilogrammas (13,158 libras) de phosphoros de páu, com um valor official de $1,498, ouro; os direitos de alfandega foram de 25 por cento ad valorem. Estes phosphoros vieram em sua maior parte de Suecia. A importação de phosphoros de cera é insignificante.

" Seria difficil ao principio fazer a concurrencia com as fabricas nacionaes, mas creio que nossos phosphoros poderiam encontrar sahida neste mercauo.

" Devo os anteriores dados ao chefe da Secretaria de Estatistica do Paraguay."

PARAGUAY.

Importação de Kerosene. O Consul RUFFIN escreve de Assumpção á Secretaria de Estado que o Paraguay está illuminado com kerosene ou petroleo importado dos Estados Unidos, e que não se empregam mais electricidade ou gaz do que o que procede das fabricas de particulares. Importa-se o kerosene em latas de quatro galões, as quaes podem ser transportadas facilmente em barcos que navegam entre Assumpção e Montevidéo. O Consul accrescenta:

" Parece-me que seria mais proveitoso enviar vapores-tanques, com o qual se reduziria o custo do artigo e se augmentaria a venda. Os tanques poderiam ser vendidos immediatamente, por razão da grande procura neste ramo, assim obviando os gastos que causaria seu retorno. Desde que se declarou a guerra com a Hespanha, o preço do oleo tem augmentado quasi a um 50 por cento, e ha consideravel especulação. Os Estados Unidos têm o monopolio da importação do oleo. Em 1897 se importaram 40,648 galões, cujo valor declarado foi de $19,511 ouro. Os direitos são de 25 por cento ad valorem."

PERU.

Fundição para Mineraes em Callão. O "British Trade Journal" diz que as autoridades municipaes de Callão concederam permissão ultimamente aos Senhores BACKUS e JOHNSTON para installar uma fundição para os metaes que se trouxerem dos varios pontos da costa. Esta firma é já proprietaria de uma importante fundição para mineraes em Casapalea, na linha de estrada de ferro de Oroya. A nova fundição será estabelecida nos arredores de Calláo e dará emprego a cem pessoas.

VENEZUELA.

Melhoramento dos Caminhos no Estado de Los Andes. O Congresso nacional de Venezuela votou, em sua ultima sessão, uma verba de 100,000 bolivares, para o melhoramento dos caminhos do Estado de Los Andes. " Venezuela Illustrada " diz que esta somma será dividida igualmente entre tres secções do Estado.

Nova Estrada de Ferro Electrica. O "Herald de Venezuela " diz que se tem feito uma concessão a uma companhia franceza para a construcção de uma estrada de ferro electrica de 70 kilometros (43½ milhas) de extensão. Esta linha unirá Cumaná com Cumanacoa, e as cascatas das correntes das montanhas serão utilisadas na geração de força electrica. A companhia já enviou engenheiros a Cumaná para começar o estudo da linha.

Recompensa para os Denunciantes dos Infractores de Leis Postaes. O " Herald " diz que o Senhor Presidente ANDRADE firmou um decreto com data de 23 de Junho de 1898, no qual se dispõe que 30 por cento da multa de 500 bolivares ($96.50) se impõe aos que conduzam correspondencia de outra maneira que não seja por meio do serviço postal seja concedido ao denunciante do infractor da lei. Diz-ze que a practica de particulares de conduzir correspondencia para a Republica e desde a Republica é um mal que cresce cada dia. O " Herald " accrescenta que isto deve ser tomado em conta pelas pessoas (estrangeiros) que viajem pelo paiz.

BULLETIN MENSUEL

DU

BUREAU DES REPUBLIQUES AMÉRICAINES.

UNION INTERNATIONALE DES RÉPUBLIQUES AMÉRICAINES.

| VoL. VI. | Août 1898. | No. 2. |

RELATIONS DES ETATS-UNIS AVEC L'ESPAGNE.

SUSPENSION DES HOSTILITÉS ET SES RÉSULTAT: TOUCHANT LE COMMERCE AMÉRICAIN.—EXTENSION DES RAPPORTS COMMERCIAUX ENTRE LES RÉPUBLIQUES AMÉRICAINES.—CUBA ET PORTO-RICO—VOIES OUVERTES POUR LE CAPITAL ET L'INDUSTRIE ALLANT VERS LE SUD ET L'OUEST.—HAWAÏ ET LES PHILIPPINES PAR RAPPORT À LEURS RELATIONS AVEC LA CÔTE PACIFIQUE DES AMÉRIQUES.—STATISTIQUES DU COMMERCE ET DE L'INDUSTRIE, RÈGLEMENTS DE DOUANES ET DE NAVIGATION POUR CUBA, LES PHILIPPINES ET PORTO-RICO.

La guerre entre les Etats-Unis et l'Espagne, résultant de la révolution contre le Gouvernement espagnol à Cuba, commença le 21 avril 1898. Les hostilités furent suspendues le 12 août 1898, comme il appert de la proclamation suivante par le Président des Etats-Unis:

PAR LE PRÉSIDENT DES ETATS-UNIS.

PROCLAMATION.

Considérant que, par un protocole conclu et signé le 12 août 1898 par WILLIAM R. DAY, Secrétaire d'Etat des Etats-Unis, et Son Excellence JULES CAMBON, Ambassadeur Extraordinaire et Plénipotentiaire de la République Française à Washington, représentant respectivement à cet effet le Gouvernement des Etats-Unis et le Gouvernement d'Espagne, les gouvernements des Etats-Unis et d'Espagne ont formellement convenu des termes auxquels les négotiations pour le rétablissement de la paix entre ces deux pays seront entreprises, et

379

Considérant qu'il est convenu dans ledit protocole qu'à sa conclusion et signature les hostilités entre les deux pays cesseront, et qu'à cet effet avis en sera donné le plutôt possible par chaque gouvernement à ces commandants des forces militaires et navales.

C'est pourquoi, moi, WILLIAM McKINLEY, Président des Etats-Unis, conformément aux stipulations du protocole, déclare et proclame de la part des Etats-Unis une suspension d'hostilités, et ordonne par la présente que des ordres soient immédiatement donnés par les voies nécessaires aux commandants des forces militaires et navales des Etats-Unis de s'abstenir de tout acte imcompatible avec cette proclamation.

En foi de quoi, j'y ai apposé ma signature et j'y ai fait apposé le sceau des Etats-Unis.

Fait à Washington, ce 12 août, de l'an de grâce mil huit cent quatre-vingt-dix-huit et l'an cent vingt-troisième de l'Indépendance des Etats-Unis.

WILLIAM McKINLEY.

Par le Président :

WILLIAM R. DAY, Secrétaire d'Etat.

La déclaration officielle des conditions pour la conclusion de la paix, annoncée par le Département d'Etat des Etats-Unis, est comme suit :

I. Que l'Espagne renoncera à tous droits de souveraineté sur Cuba.

II. Que Porto-Rico et d'autres îles espagnoles des Indes Occidentales, et qu'une des îles Ladrones, choisie par les Etats-Unis, sera cédée à ces derniers.

III. Que les Etats-Unis occuperont et tiendront la ville, la baie et le port de Manille pendant la conclusion du traité de paix qui fixera le contrôle, la disposition et le gouvernement des Philippines.

IV. Que Cuba, Porto-Rico et autres îles espagnoles des Indes Occidentales seront immédiatement évacuées, et que des commissaires, qui devront être nommés dans un délai de dix jours, se réuniront dans un délai de trente jours à partir de la signature du protocole à la Havane et à San Juan, respectivement, pour arranger et exécuter les détails de l'évacuation.

V. Que les Etats-Unis et l'Espagne ne nommeront, chacun, pas plus de cinq commissaires pour négocier et conclure un traité de paix. Les commissaires se réuniront à Paris pas plus tard que le 1er octobre.

VI. A la signature du protocole, les hostilités seront suspendues, et avis à cet effet sera donné aussitôt que possible par chaque gouvernement aux commandants de ses forces militaires et navales.

Conformément à la proclamation du Président, des ordres télégraphiques ont été envoyés aux commandants des forces militaires et navales des Etats-Unis aux Philippines et aux îles des Indes Occidentales, leur ordonnant de suspendre toutes les opérations militaires et de lever le blocus des ports.

Les causes ayant amené la guerre avec l'Espagne sont données dans un message du Président des Etats-Unis au Congrès daté le 25 avril 1898, dans lequel il fait allusion au passage d'une résolution unanime du Congrès, approuvée le 20 avril 1898, exigeant que le Gouvernement Espagnol renonce à sa souveraineté sur Gouvernement de l'île de Cuba, et qu'il retire ses forces de terre et de mer de Cuba et des eaux cubaines. Le Président ajoute:

Après la communication au ministre espagnol à Washington, de la demande qu'il fut du devoir du pouvoir exécutif d'adresser au Gouvernement Espagnol en obéissance à ladite résolution, le ministre demanda ses passeports et se retira. Le ministre des Etats-Unis à Madrid fut à son tour informé par le ministre des affaires étrangères espagnoles que le départ du représentant espagnol des Etats-Unis avait rompu les rapports diplomatiques entre les deux pays, et que toute communication officielle entre leurs représentants respectifs avaient cessée par ce fait.

La rupture des relations diplomatiques par le Gouvernement d'Espagne fut suivie par d'actives opérations militaires de la part des Etats-Unis. La destruction de la flotte espagnole à Manille le 1er mai en résulta, et la destruction de la flotte espagnole au large de Santiago de Cuba le 4 juillet, ainsi que l'invasion de l'île de Porto-Rico le 21 juillet, suivirent.

A la suite de l'occupation de la Province de Santiago de Cuba, un gouvernement militaire fut établi, et les titulaires des charges municipales sous l'ancienne souveraineté espagnole furent naintenues. Des règlements de douanes et autres furent promulgués par le Département de la Guerre des Etats-Unis, et sont ci-joints.

Incidemment aux opérations militaires de la guerre, les îles Hawaïennes furent annexées aux Etats-Unis par une résolution prise conjointement par le Congrès et approuvée le 7 juillet 1898, le gouvernement des îles ayant été placé à la disposition du Président des Etats-Unis jusqu'à ce qu'une autre décision soit prise par le Congrès.

Les résultats du conflit avec l'Espagne ont une relation si importante au développement commercial des pays de l'hémisphère occidental, que la déclaration suivante a été rédigée afin de donner les informations générales.

Les changements rapides ayant nécessairement eu lieu dans l'administration du territoire acquis par la guerre, rendent difficile le groupement immédiat de tous les faits et chiffres nécessaires à une bonne étude des conditions commerciales et industrielles.

Ces changements sont distribués parmi divers départements du gouvernement, et il faudra du temps pour perfectionner les détails dans les différentes branches de l'administration. La compilation suivante a été faite des sources d'information, dont on dispose à présent, en réponse à demande générale de renseignements sur les perspectives et conditions commerciales.

Les pays composant l'Union Nationale des Républiques Américaines sont naturellement les plus intéressés dans les effets possibles des nouvelles conditions sur leur développement commercial et industriel. Les Républiques Américaines-Latines verront certainement dans la libération du peuple Cubain, par les bons offices des Etats-Unis, de l'administration incompétente, dont le Mexique, les Etats-Unis, de l'Amérique Centrale et les pays de l'Amérique du Sud s'émancipèrent eux-mêmes avec l'intérêt sympathique des Etats-Unis, la promesse du libre développement à Cuba du commerce et des industries qui ont été une des plus importantes conséquences de leur séparation de la mère-patrie.

Par leur position géographique, Cuba et Porto-Rico peuvent être considérés deux grandes voies naturelles du commerce de la Mer des Antilles, et ont une grande influence sur le commerce de l'Amérique du Sud entière. Par l'achèvement d'un canal à travers l'Isthme de Panama, ils bénéficieront immensément du développement du commerce de la Côte Pacifique des trois Amériques, qui, on peut l'espérer, en résultera. De même les acquisitions des Etats-Unis dans le Pacifique ouvre de grandes possibilités pour le développement du commerce asiatique, non seulement avec les Etats-Unis mais aussi avec les Républiques Latines-Américaines. Le grand nombre de demandes déjà reçues au Bureau des Républiques Américaines de maisons de commerce aux Etats-Unis et de personnes cherchant des occasions de placement ou d'emploi, indiquent clairement qu'avec le retour des conditions stables dans les anciennes possessions espagnoles, qu'il y aura une grande affluence d'industrie et de capital, et on est en droit à s'attendre à ce que ce mouvement s'étendra dans des conditions favorables au grand profit des rapports entre les Etats-Unis et ses Républiques-sœurs de l'Amérique-Latine. Les sujets traités dans la compilation suivante sont: (I) Cuba. (II) Porto-Rico. (III) Iles Hawaïennes. (IV) Les Philippines et Ladrones.

RÉPUBLIQUE ARGENTINE.

AUGMENTATION DU COMMERCE—CHIFFRES OFFICIELS.

La Dirección General de Estadística donne comme suit la valeur officielle des importations entrant dans la République Argentine, et les exportations qui en ont été exportées, exclusives de lingot et d'espèces en argent, pour le premier trimestre de 1898, comparé au même trimestre de 1897.

	1898.	1897.
Importations	$26, 080, 196	$29, 045, 105
Exportations	43, 970, 805	40, 706, 982
Total...........................	70, 051, 001	69, 752, 087
Augmentation totale................. .... $298,914

BRÉSIL.

DÉPÔTS DE MINERAIS DE MANGANÈSE.

Les minerais de manganèse du Brésil ont formé pendant les quatre dernières années un article d'exportation de ce pays. On apporte ce minerai du district de Miguel Burnier, dans l'Etat de Minas Geraes. La distance de Rio de Janeiro est d'environ 310 milles, et il faut huit á dix jours pour le transport.

Les mines sont situées à 4,000 pieds d'altitude dans un climat agréable et sain, et on emploie principalement pour le travail des Italiens, des Indiens et aussi quelques Espagnols et Portugais.

En 1897, on a expédié la production totale du minerai, 8,800 tonnes, à Philadelphie, mais dans les années précédentes on en a expédié en Angleterre. Une analyse du minerai fait ressortir qu'il contient 54.7 pour cent de manganèse métallique, .027 pour cent d'acide sulfureux et .077 pour cent d'acide phosphorique.

COSTA RICA.

Dr. ULLOA, premier Vice-Président du Costa Rica, a élu domicile à New York, avec l'intention d'y remplir les fonctions de Consul-Général de la République. A un correspondant de la "Associated Press," il dit que son premier devoir officiel sera d'établir un bureau de renseignements, de sorte que les manufacturiers, expéditeurs et importateurs des Etats-Unis pourront se procurer tous les renseignements nécessaires concernant le Costa Rica, ses méthodes d'affaire, et d'emballage de marchandises, etc. Il espère aussi de pouvoir encourager l'immigration au Costa Rica en faisant connaître ce pays.

Concernant les récentes entreprises publiques au Costa Rica, le Consul-Général dit que de grandes améliorations sont en voie d'exécution, les nouvelles lois foncières seront promulguées pour encourager l'immigration et un chemin de fer est en voie de construction, reliant Limon, le port atlantique, avec le nouveau port pacifique de Tivives, établissant ainsi un chemin de fer d'océan à océan.

NOUVEAU MINISTÈRE.

Le BULLETIN de juillet a attribué par erreur le nouveau ministère constitué sous la seconde administration du Président INGLESIAS, au Nicaragua. L'erreur ne fut découverte que lorsqu'il était trop tard pour la rectifier. Le nouveau ministère du Costa Rica est comme suit:

Affaires Etrangères et Instruction Publique ....Señor PEDRO PERÉZ ZELEDÓN
Travaux Publiques et Intérieurs...................Señor Don JOSÉ ASTÚA AGUILAR
Finance et Commerce ....Señor Don JUAN B. QUIRÓS
Guerre et Marine ....Señor Don DEMETRIO TINOCO

GUATÉMALA.

OUTILS NECÉSSAIRES—MACHINES ET PAPIER MANUFACTURÉ.

Le consul anglais à Guatémala, dans un rapport à son gouvernement, dit que les haches sont fournies principalement par les Etats-Unis, parce que elles conviennent mieux aux indigènes. La coutellerie de table n'est pas fort demandée; les couteaux à manches en métal avec des lames cimiterres, faits en Allemagne, sont généralement en usage. Les couteaux nommés "cuchillos de monte," espèce de couteau de chasse dans un étui, sont fort demandés. La lame est ordinaire, mais le manche et l'étui sont finis en couleurs brilliantes, car ce couteau est porté plus comme ornement que pour son utilité.

Les houes sont fort demandées sur le marché, car elles sont nécessaires sur les plantations de café et de sucre. Elles sont employées non seulement de la manière ordinaire, mais remplacent les bêches et les pelles. Les qualités les plus importantes de ces outils sont, qu'elles soient longues et hautes et possèdent un œillet rond. Elles doivent être faites en acier, et doivent produire des étincelles quand on les frappe avec une pierre, ceci étant la preuve, au Guatémala, d'une bonne houe.

Le fil de fer barbelé de 4 points et galvanisé, et le fil de fer galvanisé de 4 plis, non barbelé, sont beaucoup employés pour les barrières dans tout le pays, la première qualité plus que la dernière. Les Etats-Unis fournissent ce fil de fer, lequel a déplacé le fil de fer anglais, qui avait, autrefois, le monopole.

Il y a une demande pour moulins actionnés par des bêtes de somme sur les petites plantations. Ceux en usage sont d'une construction légère et sont employés pour le broiement de la canne à sucre, pour moudre le maïs et pour faire les "tortillas." Le genre de moulin plus en usage est celui fait à Buffalo, N. Y.

Concernant le commerce de papier de Guatémala, le Chargé d'Affaires Français a fait un rapport pour son Gouvernement auquel les informations suivantes sont prises :

L'Allemagne tient la première place dans le commerce de papier au Guatémala, mais la France prend la seconde. On demande principalement les papiers en bois d'un poids de 3, 4 et 5 kilos, ce dernier étant préféré. La grandeur ordinaire est appelée Sittris (un-quatrième), et un-huitième papier tellière. Le papier nonréglé n'est pas beaucoup demandé à cause de la rareté des machines à régler et du coût de la main d'oeuvre ; ceci forme 25 pour cent du commerce total. Le papier réglé comprend : "Bureau," 50 pour cent du commerce total ; "marginé," 15 pour cent ; et "facture," 10 pour cent. Le papier simple nonréglé est beaucoup employé en poids de 3 kilos et du papier vergé est employé par les fabricants de cigarettes.

Le papier à dessin provient de France et le papier d'emballage
(papier de paille) d'Allemagne; le papier de soie provient d'Autriche et le papier à cigarettes d'Espagne; le papier d'imprimerie
d'Allemagne, d'Autriche, de Belgique et des Etats-Unis surtout.

Les grandeurs ordinaires d'enveloppes italiennes, allemandes et
françaises sont en usage, mais celles provenant des Etats-Unis
sont préférées. Les papiers à imprimer demandés proviennent
presque exclusivement de France.

Les droits de douane par kilo sur les papiers sont comme suit,
en piastres (une piastre représentant environ $1 en espèces des
Etats-Unis): papier à coton, en couleurs et de toutes les classes,
non-reglé, poids brut, 0.15; sans marge, non-glacé, poids brut,
0.15; papiers de tous genres, réglés de n'importe quelle façon,
poids brut, 0.30; papiers peints de toutes espèces sans dorure,
argenture (ou veloutés), poids avec couverture, 0.20; papier de
soie, poids avec emballage, 0.2; papiers coloriés pour fleurs, poids
avec emballage, 0.20.

HAÏTI.

PROJET DE CHEMIN DE FER DU CAP HAÏTIEN.

M. Lemuel W. Livingston, Consul des Etats-Unis au Cap
Haïtien, informe le Département d'Etat que l'on est en train de
parfaire des plans afin de commencer la construction d'une ligne
de chemin de fer à voie étroite du Cap Haïtien à la grande
rivière du Nord, distance d'environ 18 milles au nord-est. Le
capital de la compagnie est de $450,000 et le devis est de $250,000,
les personnes qui ont conçu le projet ont déjà souscrit $25,000,
et 675 obligations à $500 sont offertes en souscription publique,
avec un intérêt de 8 pour cent garantit par le Gouvernement.
Le matériel pour lequel le contrat n'a pas été accordé doit être acheté
aux Etats-Unis. M. Henri Thomasset, l'ingénieur qui dirigera
les travaux, et qui a construit le tramway à Port-au-Prince, témoigne
de la supériorité et de l'incomparable durabilité du matériel obtenu
des Etats-Unis.

La liste des personnes intéressées dans cette entreprise comprend
les noms de plusieurs ministres et ex-ministres du Gouvernement,
et d'autres hommes d'affaire en vue.

Dans ies articles d'incorporation, le Gouvernement accorde à MM. Cincinnatus Leconte et Eusèbe Blanc, le premier en ce moment Ministre de l'Intérieur et des Travaux Publiques, le droit exclusif de construire cette route en question, la concession étant valable pour la durée de soixante ans. Tous les articles et matériaux nécessaires à ce travail seront admis sans droit. Le Gouvernement accorde aux concessionnaires, pour une période de trente ans, le péage d'un pont de fer qui doit former la tête de ligne à Cap Haïtien, ainsi que les terres publiques dans le district du Cap Haïtien et de Grande Rivière le long de la voie.

Le pays qui sera traversé par cette ligne est une belle et fertile plaine, favorable à la culture de tous les produits propres à l'île, et l'on dit qu'elle convient surtout à la culture de la banane. Les routes traversant à présent la région sont en très mauvais état, et en temps de pluie elles sont presque impraticables, occasionnant de grandes difficultés aux paysans producteurs dans le transport de leurs produits aux marchés. Les moyens de transport sont très primitifs, l'âne est la bête de somme universelle, et bien qu'en général il soit d'une espèce naine, on lui fait faire tous les travaux généralement imposés aux chevaux. Non seulement la plus grande partie des légumes, fruit, café et cacao est amenée aux marchés par des ânes, mais ils portent presque toutes les immenses quantités de bois de campêche et racines de campêche expediées de ce pays.

Dans un tel pays et dans de telles conditions, un chemin de fer est non seulement une nécessité primordiale, mais doit amener une espèce de révolution industrielle. Les personnes à la tête de cette entreprise espèrent que le chemin de fer stimulera la production dans des proportions jusqu'ici inconnues, en offrant aux paysans industrieux des avantages de transports rapides et des facilités de débouchés modernes, ce chemin de fer devenant de la sorte un placement profitable ainsi qu'une amélioration publique.

MEXIQUE.

ZONE LIBRE (ZONA LIBRE).

Le Département d'Etat a reçu du Consul Général Barlow un rapport sur la Zone Libre, compilé par le Secrétaire de la Trésorerie du Mexique, qui donne l'histoire de la création primitive de la Zone et qui détermine ses limites ainsi que les privilèges et les restrictions qui y sont applicables.

La Zone Libre est un étroit territoire qui s'étend le long de la frontière du nord du Golfe du Mexique à l'Océan Pacifique, avec une surface latitudinale d'environ 12 milles ½ à l'intérieur, et comprenant une partie des Etats Tamaulipas, Coahuila, Chihuahua, Sonora, et le territoire de la Nouvelle Californie. Elle fut établie, il y a beaucoup d'années, par le Gouvernement Central comme compromis ou concession aux Etats touchant le fleuve Rio Grande, et comme protection contre la contrebande des Etats-Unis.

Les villes principales de la Zone sont Malamoras, Camargo, Mier, Guerero, Laredo, Porfirio, Diaz (Piedras Negras), Juarez et Nogales. La population totale ne dépasse pas 100,000 habitants. D'après les rapports officiels, il n'existe dans la Zone Libre aucune industrie valant la peine d'être mentionnée, ce qui s'explique par le fait que tous les produits de l'industrie fabriqués dans la Zone, quand ils sont expédiés à l'intérieur du pays, doivent payer les droits d'entrée imposés sur les importations entrant dans le pays; et par suite du tarif protectif des Etats-Unis, il est impossible d'exporter ces produits pour ce pays, de sorte que les industries manufacturières seraient forcées de dépendre de la consommation domestique, qui n'est pas suffisante pour les maintenir.

Toute marchandise importée dans la Zone et destinée à y être consommée, est admise sur une base de 10 pour cent des droits d'entrée ordinaires, mais cette marchandise rechargée pour l'intérieur du Mexique doit payer un impôt additionnel de 90 pour cent, représentant avec les 10 pour cent déjà payés, les droits de douane ordinaires du Mexique.

Dans son rapport, le Secrétaire de la Trésorerie, Señor Limantour, dit. Beaucoup de financiers distingués et hommes d'Etat éminents sont opposés à la Zone Libre, mais tous reconnaissent le fait qu'à cause des circonstances existant sur la frontière du Nord, sa population éparse sans ressources agricoles, industrielles ou minières, le privilège ne pourrait être aboli sans compensation et le problème est de choisir un autre avantage sans préjudice aux autres parties du pays. ·

L'attitude des négociants de l'intérieur est en général hostile, parce qu'ils considèrent ceci comme un privilège accordé seulement à une partie du pays. Les négociants très éloignés de la frontière, comme ceux de San Luis Potosi, Guadalajara et Mexico, ne le considèrent pas nuisible. Ceux qui sont proches, comme Monterey, Chihuahua, etc., ne craignent pas sa concurrence, mais ils s'en plaignent pour la raison qu'ils ne peuvent pas jouir de la liberté de distribuer leurs marchandises sans documents et sans inspection fiscale comme dans les autres parties du pays. En réalité la juridiction de la surveillance fiscale s'étend à tous les Etats de Tamaulipas, Nueve Leon, Coahuilla, Chihuahua, Sonora, et à une partie de la Nouvelle Californie, et dans ce territoire on ne peut expédier aucune marchandise aux termes de la loi à moins que le négociant ne donne une preuve légale qu'il a payé l'impôt exigé et qu'il ne demande une permission pour chaque chargement.

DISTRICTS DE CULTURE DE COTON.

Un correspondant natif de la "Manufacturers' Gazette" fournit à ce journal un récit descriptif des districts de production du coton au Mexique, auquel les articles ci-dessous sont empruntés.

Les districts du Mexique produisant du coton se trouvent aujourd'hui en ceintures. La zone du Golfe s'étend le long de la côte de Tamaulipas à Yucatan. Tamaulipas, près des Etats-Unis, fut pendant la guerre civile le centre de grandes opérations de coton. La terre alors cessa d'être productive, mais en 1882, sous la direction du gouvernement, un hectare de coton fut planté près de Ciudad Victoria, et plus tard la culture commença dans les autres parties de l'Etat. La production de la terre fut rapide, mais l'industrie est toujours comparativement nouvelle. Le territoire s'étendant dans l'Etat de Vera Cruz est le plus productif, car le sol est fertile, et il y a une abondance d'humidité. Ici le cotonnier porte jusqu'à 160 gousses avec le pépin et pèsent quelquefois 2 onces chacune.

La "cuartilla," avec environ 25,000 mètres carrés de terre, contient 7,000 à 10,000 plantes, et la production moyenne est de 5,000 livres à la "cuartilla." En mai ou juin, quand les pluies commencent, on plante le maïs, et on plante le coton de septembre entre les rangs.

On met les graines dans des trous a 5 pieds d'intervalles, les ayant d'abord trempées dans l'eau. Elles commencent à germer après une semaine. A la fin du premier mois, le cultivateur commence à enlever les petits groupes, n'y laissant que deux ou trois des plantes les plus développées. Une semaine ou deux plus tard il pose chaque plante à plat et la recouvre de terre pour la tenir en place. Il fait ce travail à cause des vents du nord et aussi pour empêcher les plantes de s'entremêler. La production des plantes aplaties est vigoureuse. Le cueillage est fait six mois après la plantation.

La ceinture de coton du Pacifique est d'environ 50 milles de largeur au centre, mais elle est plus étendue que celle du golfe, quoique pas si accessible. Cette zone s'étend de Sonora à Chiapas, distance de 1,500 milles. Sonora est un pays de grands contrastes, de montagnes élevées et de vallées profondes. Le coton fut premièrement cultivé dans les districts de Hermosillo au commencement du siècle. Vers 1842 les grandes fabriques Angeles furent érigées. Le ver à coton parut et l'industrie est maintenant limitée à la Vallée de Guaymas. Le manque d'eau est en partie la cause de la dépérissement de la culture de coton. Quelques cultivateurs ont continué le travail sans se laisser décourager par les sécheresses, le ver à coton, les sauterelles et autres obstacles incidents. Sinaloa s'étend plus au sud. Autrefois le coton était cultivé de Fuerte à Mocotito, mais les sécheresses continuelles ont mis fin à la culture, excepté le long des cours des fleuves. De Culiacan à Tepic la perspective est meilleure. Dans le district Sinaloa le bénéfice est d'environ 40 pour cent.

Le petit territoire de Tepic devrait produire bien. La Vallée de Santiago, 8 lieues sur 28, a produit de 7,500 livres à la "fanega" (50,000 mètres carrés).

Jalisco est un grand état à l'ouest du Mexique. Un de ces

jours ,e cnemin de fer atteindra Zihuatlan et d'autres excellents districts de coton dans l'État de Jalisco.

A l'époque de l'indépendance, Colima fut le centre d'une importante ceinture de coton s'étendant de Zihuatlan vers les districts montagneux de Michoacan. Pendant un quart de siècle, Colima a produit environ 2,200,000 livres par an. Le ver à coton, l'absence de chemin de fer et d'autres difficultés survinrent.

Il y a peu de coton cultivé en Michoacan, principalement à Huetamo, Ario, Apatzingan et Coalcoman. Un territoire de 100 lieues dans le district de Coalcoman est généralement productif, la culture commençant en août.

Guerrero a été une région inconnue, mais le chemin de fer de Cuernavaca la mettra en communication avec le monde. Les terrains de coton de Guerrero s'étendent de Michoacan à Oaxaca, mais une petite partie seulement est cultivée.

Oaxaca est exceptionellement favorable à la culture du coton. Les districts principaux de production sont Jamiltpec, Pochutla, Tehuantepec, Juchitan et Jaquila, aussi (dans le nord) Tuxtepec et Choapam.

Chiapas, l'Etat plus au sud de l'Union Mexicaine, peut aussi faire un bon rapport. Le coton pousse dans les districts de Simooval, Chiapa et d'autres.

Dans le Manuel du Mexique, publié par le Bureau des Républiques Américaines, le coton du Mexique est décrit comme ayant des fibres plus longues que celui des Etats-Unis, mais n'étant pas aussi souple ni aussi brilliant. Les grands avantages de la culture du coton au Mexique sont que les plantes continuent de produire des récoltes profitables sans l'emploi de fertilisants et sans le renouvellement annuel des graines, comme cela est nécessaire aux Etats-Unis.

NICARAGUA.

DISTRICT AURIFÈRE DE SIQUIA.

Mr. J. P. Morgan écrit au Bureau de Rama, Nicaragua, à propos des récentes exploitations de mines dans le voisinage de cette ville. Il dit qu'à une journée de voyage par petits bateaux, un district aurifère plein de promesses a été mis en exploitation le long ues rivières Rama, Siquia, et Mico, s'étendant plusieurs milles sur les Montagnes Gurupera, qui n'ont encore été explorées que sur une distance d'environ quatre milles. L'eau y est abondante et les collines très boisées, donnent assez de combustible et de bois de charpente pour les mines. Il est facile de se procurer du gibier et il y a beaucoup de plantations de bananes, de plantains, de patates et autres légumes dans le voisinage, de sorte que les provisions sont abondantes et le travail bon marché, les salaires variant de $10 à $30 par mois. Le rocher aurifère est accessible peut être exploité avec très peu de machines et a produit de $17 à $35 par tonne. On dit aussi qu'on a trouvé de l'or en quantités rémunératrices dans les lits des courants nombreux qui se jettent dans le fleuve Mico. Rama est une ville très saine et florissante d'environ 1,000 habitants, et possède des écoles, des églises et des communications par câble avec les autres parties du monde. Rama a trois fois par semaine un service de poste au moyen de navires à fruits qui font le service entre Rama, la Nouvelle Orléans, Mobile et d'autres ports des Etats-Unis. Les hôtels sont très bons au prix d'un dollar par jour en or des Etats-Unis. Les lois du Nicaragua admettent sans aucun droit d'entrée toutes les machines, la dynamite et autres articles nécessaires, importés pour l'exploitation des mines. Les habitants sont très hospitaliers et font bon accueil aux personnes arrivant pour s'y engager dans des entreprises ayant pour but le développement du pays.

CONVENTION DES DÉPUTÉS DE LA PLUS GRANDE RÉPUBLIQUE.

Le correspondant de "l'Associated Press" nous informe par le courrier de Managua, Nicaragua, que la convention des députés de Salvador, Honduras et Nicaragua ont été en séance tous les jours pendant la dernière partie de juillet. La commission nommée pour faire un rapport sur les articles d'une constitution pour leurs états et soumis par la diète de la "Plus Grande République," qui a convoqué cette assemblée, a rapporté beaucoup de modifications. La Commission propose aussi une centralisation des états nommés ayant un district fédéral composé des départements civils de Chinandega, touchant l'Océan Pacifique et le Golfe de Fonseca au Nicaragua; d'Amapalus touchant le Golfe de Fonseca au Honduras, et de Limon touchant l'Océan Pacifique et le Golfe de Fonseca au Salvador; avec Amapala situé sur l'île du Tigre dans le Golfe de Fonseca, comme ville capitale. La convention, cependant, par une grande majorité, a voté contre l'idée de centralisation et a supporté une confédération des trois Etats sous le nom d'Etats-Unis de l'Amérique Centrale.

PÉROU.

CONSEILS AUX AGENTS COMMERCIAUX.

Le Consul de la Grande-Bretagne à Callao fait un rapport pour son Gouvernement en Angleterre, à l'effet que les négociants à Lima font de sérieuses objections à une concurrence avec les commerçants, dans ce qu'ils considèrent des conditions inégales. Ces négociants prétendent qu'ils ont de grands frais de bureaux et de maisons alors que les commis-voyageurs, pour une petite somme, transforment leurs appartements d'hôtels et d'auberges en salles d'exposition.

On prend des mesures pour persuader le Gouvernement d'obliger tous les agents de commerce de se procurer des patentes (licenses).

Ce sujet a été soumis au Département de Commerce à Lima, avec la proposition que le prix d'une patente d'agent de commerce soit fixée à 500 soles ($243.25) pour une période de six mois, et qu'elle soit renouvelée à la fin de chaque période. A défaut du prix de patente, le double de cette somme sera exigé de l'offenseur, la troisième partie revenant à l'accusateur.

D'après les Séries Annuelles 2117, du Bureau Etranger de la Grande-Bretagne, dans le Pérou du Sud, toute facilité paraît être accordée aux agents commerciaux. Il leur est permis d'entrer à la douane, avec leurs échantillons, sur présentation par un agent responsable, d'une demande officielle les autorisant de passer un certain nombre de paquets d'échantillons. Ces paquets sont examinés et évalués sur présentation d'un permis par l'agent qui se charge de payer le montant de la valeur de n'importe quel échantillon qui ne sera pas rechargé dans la période specifiée, ordinairement 90 jours. Pour ceci, le négociant paiera de $2.50

à $5, selon le nombre de colis qu'il apporte, et il est alors libre d'aller où il veut avec ses échantillons sans être obligé d'en rendre compte dans aucun autre port de l'intérieur qu'il pourrait visiter.

Les agents locaux responsables, avant de donner le permis de doúane, se convaincront de l'honorabilité du négociant qui, dans la plupart des cas, outre sa carte d'affaire, apporte une lettre de présentation à quelque résident du port. Cette dernière condition ne doit pas être négligée par celui qui a l'intention de visiter ce port.

DÉPÓTS HOUILLERS.

Une nouvelle couche de houille anthracite se développe en ce moment près du sommet des Andes du Pérou. Une concession pour ce district minier fut accordée à Mr. C. B. JONES en 1892, pour la durée de 20 ans et devait embrasser une section de terrain de 100 milles de longueur et située de 25 à 125 milles en arrière de la côte.

On a déjà envoyé des ingénieurs des Etats-Unis au Pérou pour faire un arpentage pour la construction d'un chemin de fer de Pacsmayo, à la province de Hualgayoc. La Compagnie Pacifique est appuyée par $20.000,000 de capital, et a le droit exclusif de construire les chemins de fer.

D'après Mr. G. CLINTON GARDNER, ancien surintendant du Chemin de Fer de Pennsylvanie et constructeur du Chemin de Fer National du Mexique, la quantité de charbon est presque inépuisable; 10,000,000 de tonnes se trouvent à un degré de profondeur très facilement atteinte. Mr. GARDNER calcule que 2,000,000 de tonnes peuvent être retirées chaque année et expédiées au port au coût de $2 (en or) par tonne, dans ce cas Mr. GARDNER pense que tout autre charbon sera exclu des marchés du Pacifique, par suite de l'impossibilité où il se trouvera d'entrer en concurrence avec un article aussi bon marché que le charbon du Pérou.

Outre la concession d'exploitation de charbon dans le district mentionné, cette compagnie a le droit exclusif de construire les chemins de fer allant à ces mines, et elle a déjà loué du Gouvernement un beau quai à Pacasmayo. Mr. GARDNER dit que les frais de construction de cette ligne et l'achat du matériel roulant ne devront pas dépasser $3,000.000. Cette ligne commencera à Pacasmayo, la distance totale de la côte jusqu'au district houilleux étant de 121 milles. Une ligne en voie de construction par un agent du Pérou est déjà en opération entre Pacasmayo et Youan, distance de 41 milles.

Le correspondant bien connu de journaux des Etats-Unis, Mr. FRANK CARPENTER, dit que les mines de houille des Andes contiennent de l'anthracite et du lignite. L'anthracite se trouve en grandes quantités sur les pentes de l'est et de l'ouest des Andes. Dans celle de l'est une couche de houille d'environ 1,500 ou 2,000 pieds s'étend du sommet des montagnes, et la qualité de ce charbon est égale à, et sous plusieurs rapports, meilleure que l'anthracite de Pennsylvanie. Pour transporter le charbon de la pente de l'est à la côte, il faut un chemin de fer s'élevant à une hauteur d'environ 14,000 pieds sur les Andes; de ce point il n'y aura plus que 75 milles en ligne droite jusqu'à la côte, et la ligne passera par plusieurs villes assez grandes et un riche pays agricole. Ces propriétés, dit-il, auront même plus de valeur que les champs aurifères, car jusqu'à présent on n'a presque pas retiré de bon charbon sur la côte de l'ouest de l'Amérique du Sud, et des 3,000,000 de tonnes de charbon consommées par an, la plus grande partie vient de l'Australie, de l'Angleterre, du Japon et de la Colombie Britannique.

Outre ces dépôts houiller dans la province de Hualgayoc, d'autres existent dans le district de Huamachuco, et on trouve du lignite et de la tourbe dans plusieurs autres parties du Pérou.

ETATS-UNIS.

RAPPORT DES EXPORTATIONS DE JUILLET.

Les exportations de farines, de provisions, de coton et d'huile minérale des principaux districts de douanes des Etats-Unis sont données dans un rapport fait par le Bureau des Statistiques le 12 août à $37,183,721. De cette somme, les farines seules s'élevaient à $16,737,128; provisions, $9,973,607; bétail et cochons, $2,922,244; coton, $2,828,669; et huile minérale, $4,722,073. Quoique ces chiffres soient au-dessous de ceux du mois de juin, ils sont égaux à ceux de juillet 1897 et dépassent ceux de juillet des années 1894, 1895 et 1896, et ils dépassent de $2,000,000 les exportations moyennes de ces articles en juillet depuis 1890.

La valeur des exportations de farines en juillet 1898 dépasse de 20 pour cent celle de juillet 1897; de 25 pour cent celle de juillet 1896, et de deux fois celle de juillet 1895. Les exportations de provisions pour le mois de juillet sont, pour ainsi dire, au-dessous de la valeur des mois correspondants de 1897, 1896 et 1895, de même les huiles minérales. Dans ce dernier cas, la réduction est due aux bas prix, le nombre de gallons exportés pendant le mois étant un peu en excès des exportations pour juillet 1897, quoique la valeur totale pour le mois ne soit pas aussi élevée en 1898 qu'en 1897.

COMMERCE EXTÉRIEUR.

Le rapport du Bureau des Statistiques des Etats-Unis pour l'année fiscale finissant le 30 juin 1898, est de grand intérêt. Les importations totales pour les douze mois ne s'élevaient qu'à environ la moitié des exportations, et étaient de $147,000,000 moins que pour l'année fiscale finissant le 30 juin 1897.

Les importations d'Europe ont diminué de $124,000,391, tandis que les exportations pour l'Europe ont augmenté de $160,313,645. Les importations des pays de l'Amérique du Nord ont diminué de $14,752,130 et les exportations ont augmenté de $14,676,828. Les importations de l'Amérique du Sud accusent une diminution de $15,295.37, tandis que les importations n'ont augmenté que de $53,325. Les importations de l'Asie et de l'Océanie seules ont augmenté. Cette augmentation est de $5,300,440 pour le premier pays et de $2,458,781 pour le second. Les exportations pour les pays asiatiques ont augmenté de $5,549,363, et pour l'Océanie elles ont diminué de $661,392.

Le tableau ci-joint donne les exportations et les importations totales (en grandes divisions) pour l'année fiscale de 1898, comparées à l'année fiscale de 1897.

	1897.	1898.
Importations de—		
l'Europe	$430,192,205	$306,091,814
l'Amérique du Nord	105,924,053	91,174,923
l'Amérique du Sud	107,389,405	92,093,526
l'Asie	87,294,597	92,595,037
l'Océanie	24,400,439	20,859,220
l'Afrique	9,529,713	7,193,639
Total	764,730,412	616,005,159

	1897.	1898.
Exportations pour—		
l'Europe	$813,385,644	$973,699,289
l'Amérique du Nord	124,958,461	139,635,289
l'Amérique du Sud	33,768,646	33,821,971
l'Asie	39,274,905	44,824,268
l'Océanie	22,652,773	21,991,381
l'Afrique	16,953,127	17,357,752
Total	1,050,993,556	1,231,329,950

L'augmentation des exportations a été dans les articles fabriqués et dans les produits alimentaires, tandis que la diminution des importations a naturellement été pour ces mêmes articles. Le chiffre des importations de produits chimiques porcelaine, cristaux ou articles fabriqués en toile, acier, fer, cuivre, soie, laine, bois, et fibres, montrent tous une diminution comparée aux années 1897 et 1896. L'importation de farines, vivres, poissons, fruits, vins, sucres, thés et cafés ont subi une diminution notable. Les articles nécessaires aux manufacturiers dans la fabrication ont augmenté dans presque tous les cas, ceux de 1897 et 1896, à l'exception de la laine dont les importations pendant 1897 ont été extraordinairement grande.

Le tableau ci-joint indique la valeur des importations de toutes les classes générales dont les articles dépassent la de valeur $5,000,000, et compare les importations de l'année fiscale de 1898 avec celles de 1897.

Importations.	1897.	1898.
Manufactures.		
Produits chimiques, drogues, etc.	$44,948,752	$41,470,711
Coton, articles manufacturés	34,429,363	27,266,932
Poterie et porcelaine	9,977,297	6,686,220
Fibres et articles manufacturés de fibres	32,546,867	21,899,714
Cristaux	5,509,626	3,669,919
Articles manufacturés en acier et en fer	16,094,557	12,615,913
Cuir et articles manufacturés :		
Cuir	13,283,151	11,414,118
Huiles (toutes sortes)	5,594,111	5,197,886
Soie et articles manufacturés en soie	25,199,067	23,523,110
Bois et articles manufacturés en bois	20,543,810	13,858,582
Laine et articles manufacturés en laine	49,162,992	14,823,768
Articles employés dans les manufactures.		
Coton non fabriqué	5,884,262	5,019,503
Fibres non fabriquées	12,336,418	13,446,186
Peaux	27,863,026	37,068,832

Importations.	1897.	1898.
Articles employés dans mannfactures—Continued.		
Caoutchouc..	\$17,558,163	\$25,543,391
Soie non fabriquée................................	18,918,283	32,110,066
Tabac non manufacturé............................	9,584,155	7,488,605
Laine	....	....
Articles de consommation	53,243,191	16,883,692
Café..	81,544,384	65,067,561
Poisson (toutes sortes)............................	6,108,714	5,984,980
Fruits et noix.....................................	17,126,932	14,566,874
Sucre	99,066,181	60,472,703
Thé..	14,835,862	10,054,005
Vins spiritueux (maltés)	12,272,872	9,305,504

ESPÈCES EN CIRCULATION.

Comparé à la même date de 1897, la monnaie d'or en circulation dans les Etats-Unis au 1er août 1898 indique une augmentation de plus de \$135,000,000. Les dollars étalons en argent ont augmenté de \$5,600,000; pour l'argent subsidiaire, il y a une augmentation de plus de \$4,800,000; certificats d'argent, de \$31,100,000; billets de Trésorerie de 1890, de presque \$14,200,000; et billets des Etats-Unis, de presque \$25,700,000; certificats d'argent indiquent plus de \$40,300,000 billets de banque nationale, de presque \$3,100,000 et certificats d'or de plus de \$1,500,000.

La somme totale d'argent, de toutes espèces, en circulation au 1er août 1898, était de \$1,809,198,344, ce qui représente une augmentation de plus de \$162,700,000 pour les douze mois de l'année.

La circulation par habitant de la population est évaluée par les fonctionnaires de la Trésorerie sur la base d'une population de 74,656,000 à \$24.23, ce qui constitue une diminution de 51 cents par mois, mais une augmentation de \$1.70 par habitant pour les douze mois écoulés. Une comparaison avec les statistiques publiées par le Département de la Trésorerie le 1er août pour chaque an, indique qu'il y a eu une augmentation de plus de \$300,000,000 dans la somme d'argent en circulation depuis 1896.

FABRICATION DE GLUCOSE ET D'HUILE DE MAÏS.

Dans un pamphlet récemment publié par le Département de l'Agriculture des Etats-Unis sur la composition du maïs, Mr. H. W. WILEY, le Chimiste Officiel, s'occupe de l'industrie de la glucose. Il dit :

La fabrication de sucre d'amidon de différents degrés d'hydrolisation est une industrie importante aux Etats-Unis. Ces produits d'hydrolisation d'amidon sont connus sous le nom de glucose ou sucre de raisins. La glucose représente ceux dans lesquelles l'hydrolise est moins complète, et consiste en grande partie de dextrine, de dextrose, d'une petite quantité de maltose et d'eau. On en fait des sirops blancs et épais, employés en grande partie comme sirops de table, pour adultérer les mélasses, le miel, et pour la confiserie. Le terme sucre de raisins est appliqué aux produits solides obtenus par l'hydrolisation de l'amidon où l'hydrolise est portée à un plus haut degré, le produit qui en résulte consiste principalement de dextrose. Ce produit est employé principalement pour remplacer le malt dans la brasserie de bière et d'ale. Cette industrie a pris des proportions immenses aux Etats-Unis. La quantité de maïs employée annuellement pour la fabrication de glucose s'élève à 40,000,000 boisseaux ou 14,095,932 hectolitres.

Le Département donne aussi une description d'un nouveau produit dérivé du maïs qui a attiré beaucoup d'attention et promet de devenir une production importante. Ce produit est l'huile de maïs. Le chimiste dit que dans la fabrication de l'amidon et de la glucose, et dans quelques espèces de farine de maïs, le germe de la graine qui contient la plus grande partie de l'huile est extrait. De ce germe on exprime une huile de grande valeur et le résidu forme un aliment, sous tous les rapports, d'une aussi grande valeur que celui obtenu par l'expression de l'huile de graines oléagineuses ordinaires. L'huile de maïs est facilement purifiée et donne un liquide d'une couleur légèrement ambrée, parfaitement transparente sans rancidité et d'un goût agréable. Cette huile a été quelque peu employée comme huile de salade et sera à l'avenir, sans aucun doute, beaucoup employée à cet usage. Elle peut aussi être employée pour lubrifier les machines délicates, est un très bon combustible, et peut être employée comme huile de lampe. L'huile moins fine et moins pure fait un très bon savon. En général on peut affirmer que l'huile de maïs a une valeur commerciale, gallon pour gallon, égale à l'huile obtenue de la graine de coton.

Le tableau donné par le département des statistiques de douanes est comme suit pour les premiers trimestres des trois années 1896, 1897 et 1898:

IMPORTATIONS.

	1896.	1897.	1898.
Vivres, céréales et épices........	$1,028,194	$915,289	$1,144,863
Tissus...............................	1,522,951	943,068	1,562,959
Matières premières et machines.............	1,789,134	1,393,366	1,439,919
Spiritueux en général	758,611	697,624	764,888
Vêtements confectionnés	490,797	240,820	416,092
Bétail......................................	218,463	230,306	393,943
Tabac et cigares	73,361	44,461	55,627
Autres articles ou produits	945,077	602,021	659,884
Total.............................	6,826,588	5,066,955	6,438,175

EXPORTATIONS.

	1896.	1897.	1898.
Produits d'abattoirs.......................	$12,474,760	$7,976,199	$9,114,869
Bétail	632,683	486,294	139,750
Produits ruraux	463,104	471,670	2,035,009
Provisions pour navires...................	27,732	23,797	19,485
Autres produits	59,943	80,264	52,385
Total.............................	13,658,222	9,030,232	11,361,506

Le commerce total pour le premier trimestre de 1898 approche du total pour le premier trimestre de 1894, que l'on avait considéré comme une année exceptionellement prospère. La production totale de l'agriculture pour le trimestre a été de $2,035,009, contre $471,678 dans la même période en 1897. Cette grande augmentation résulta de la belle récolte de blé exporté, s'élevant à 59,453,989 killogrammes valant à $1,783,619, contre seulement 3,214,663 kilogrammes ne valant que $77,151 en 1897.

La plupart des autres articles avait subi une diminution. Les exportations de maïs s'élevaient à 71,736 kilogrammes valant $1,865, contre 1,309,947 kilogrammes valant $32,748 en 1897. La récolte de maïs fut splendide mais les pluies tardives ont ruiné la qualité du blé, de sorte que très peu a été disponible pour exportation. Les exportations de farine s'élevaient à 3,889,669 kilogrammes valant $187,184; en 1897, 5,247,092 kilogrammes ont passé par la douane et évaluées à $262,354. Les oignons et l'ail exportés du pays ont été évalués à $2,132 en 1898, et à $14,140 en 1897; fruits frais à $14,800 contre $40,989; légumes à $1,865 contre $32,748, et graine de lin à $16,186 contre $20,106.

VENEZUELA.

RAPPORT OFFICIEL DES MARCHANDISES ACHETÉES.

M. Antonio E. Delfino, Consul-Général de Venezuela, a soumis au Bureau les données statistiques des exportations de marchandises pour plusieurs ports du Venezuela pour le mois de juin, comparées au même mois en 1897.

Ports.	1898.	1897.	Augmentation.	Diminution.
La Cuaira.....................	$96, 364. 55	$86, 853.50	$10, 011. 05	....
Puerto Cabello...............	27, 714. 39	33, 533; 53	....	$5, 819. 14
Maracaïbo	32, 040. 02	56, 629. 33	....	24, 589. 31
La Vela.......................	9, 792. 10	3, 077. 65	6, 714. 95	....
Ciudad Bolivar................	13, 377. 00	42, 866. 10	....	29, 489. 10
Carupano.....................	5, 474. 24	6, 519. 00	....	4, 044. 76
Cuanta	784. 23	1, 452. 00	....	667. 77
Gumaná.......................	1, 402. 00	1, 854. 00	....	452. 00
Guiria........................	705. 00	303. 00	402. 00	....
Caña Colorado................	699. 00	....	699. 00	....
Total	188, 852. 53	236, 088. 11	17, 826. 50	47, 238. 08

Les principaux articles exportés furent: Farine de blé, $99,473.65; saindoux, $77,506.28; tissus en coton, blanchis et non blanchis, $33,506.22; tabac manufacturé et en feuilles, $25,493.52; machines et matériel électrique, $20,897.98; provisions, $20,143.64; beurre, $18,902.42; pétrole, $17,351.13; ferronnerie et quincaillerie, $11,776.72; drogues et parfums, $11,425; indiennes, $7,799.38.

CONSOMMATION DE CAFÉ EN 1897.

Comme supplément à l'article sur le café dans le Bulletin de juillet, un extrait d'un article récemment publié dans le Bulletin français de "Statistique et de Législation Comparée," montrant les quantités de café consommées dans les différents pays, est d'un grand intérêt. De ceci, il paraît que la consommation totale de café en Europe et aux Etats-Unis s'est élevée à 1,039,330,000 livres en 1893, et à 1,246,640,000 livres en 1897. L'augmentation de la consommation de café en 1897 sur celle de 1896, s'est élevée à 129,580,000 livres. De cette augmentation 100,000,000 livres sont arrivées aux Etats-Unis, et la consommation totale de ce pays s'est élevée à la quantité énorme de 636,340,000 livres ou 9.95 (4½ kilogrammes) livres par personne. Ces chiffres étaient de 26,000,000 livres en excès de la quantité consommée dans toute l'Europe. En 1893 l'Europe a consommé 542,996,000 livres et la consommation aux Etats-Unis a été de 496,234,000 livres.

Quant à la consommation par personne, les Etats-Unis ne prennent point du tout la première place. Cette distinction revient à la Hollande où la consommation pour chaque habitant en 1897 a été calculée à 23 livres (10½ kilogrammes); au Danemark la quantité moyenne par personne a été de 15 livres (7 kilogrammes); en Belgique à 11 livres (5 kilogrammes); en Allemaque à 5¼ livres (2½ kilogrammes), et dans le Royaume de la Grande-Bretagne à seulement sept-dixièmes d'une livre (un troisième d'un kilogramme).

La consommation de café en France augmente continuellement; en 1840 elle s'élevait à 28,740,000 livres, en 1860 à 88,720,000 livres et en 1897 à 273,800,000 livres. De ce total, 2,214,000 livres (1,004,000 kilogrammes) ont été importées des Colonies Françaises sur lesquelles les droits d'entrée ne sont que la moitié de ceux perçus sur le café importé des pays étrangers.

Du café importé en France des pays étrangers, environ 95,000,000 livres (42,742,000 kilogrammes) pro venaient du Brésil et 51,000,000 livres (23,176,000 kilogrammes) de Haïti.

NOUVEAU TARIF DE LA JAMAÏQUE.

Le sujet d'un récent rapport aux journaux commerciaux anglais est de grand intérêt aux exportateurs des Etats-Unis, du Mexique, de l'Amérique Centrale, du Venezuela et de la Colombie. La dépêche disait que par suite du déficit actuel des revenus et une diminution probable pour l'année fiscale de 1898 et 1899, le Gouvernement a présenté un nouveau tarif et espère qu'il sera adopté au cours de la session actuelle du Conseil législatif. Entre autres articles de la loi proposée, il y a une augmentation des droits sur les spiritueux de 12s. 6d. le "gallon," liquide, à 15s. le "gallon" trois-six mesuré à l'hydromètre Sykes. Ces importations sont principalement d'Angleterre. Les droits sur le beurre, le fromage, et le jambon ont été augmentés de 1d. à

Monthly Bulletin

OF THE

Bureau of the American Republics,

International Union of American Republics.

| Vol. VI. | SEPTEMBER, 1898. | No. 3. |

PROVISIONAL DIRECTOR REAPPOINTED.

The Executive Committee of the International Union of American Republics met in the diplomatic room at the Department of State, Tuesday, September 27. There were present the Acting Secretary of State, Mr. ADEE, who presided: Mr. ANDRADE, the Venezuelan Minister, and Mr. CALVO, the Minister from Costa Rica. The object of the meeting was to take action concerning the directorship of the Bureau of the American Republics, in view of the fact that the term of Mr. FREDERIC EMORY as Director will expire on the 1st of October.

Upon motion of Mr. ANDRADE, Mr. EMORY was continued as Director until November 1. It is understood that this action was taken in order to enable the new Secretary of State, Mr. HAY, to inform himself as to the condition of the Bureau, with a view to some definite action concerning the directorship.

Mr. EMORY, who is the chief of the Bureau of Foreign Commerce of the Department of State, was designated to take charge of the Bureau of the American Republics upon the death of the

Republic for the first five months of 1898 in comparison with the corresponding period in 1897:

Articles.	1898.	1897.
Wheat ....tons..	616, 923	73, 037
Maize ....do...	75, 638	226, 272
Linseed ....do...	136, 776	155, 423
Wool ....bales..	331, 024	308, 042
Flour..tons..	12, 746	23, 306
Hides .... ·number .	1, 402, 599	1, 438, 936
Hay ....bales..	333, 603	359, 127
Frozen wethers.............................number..	1, 025, 237	800, 069
Live steers ....do..	56, 387	59, 243
Live sheep... ....do...	292, 948	226, 604

WHEAT MARKET IN 1898.

Consul MAYER writes from Buenos Ayres to the Department of State giving an interesting history of the fluctuations in the price of wheat in the Republic during the first six months of 1898. His observations are given here as they appear in the Consular Reports for August.

The history of the Argentine wheat market during the present shipping season is one of totally unexpected developments, the most of them being unwelcome to those interested in the trade.

At the very commencement of the harvest a state of affairs prevailed that argued badly for the peace of mind of those who preferred a quiet business to violent fluctuations. The scarcity of wheat toward the end of last year had driven local prices far above the rate that exporters could afford to pay. The same cause contributed to maintain them for a short time after the harvesting of the new crop had started, but once millers had bought sufficient for their requirements, a rapid decline in prices set in.

Many exporters had contracted heavy tonnage engagements, in view of the comparatively large quantity of grain in sight, but the rains delayed transportation and farmers held their wheat. A fall in freights ensued, and gold appreciated in value, making the position of sellers independent. Throughout February and March the market continued in this state. In April a firmer tone set in in the home markets, due to the scarcity of supplies becoming more apparent. The outbreak of hostilities between the United States and Spain was, however, the signal for one of the most phenomenal rises ever chronicled in the wheat market. On the 1st of April the value here was $8.50; on the 15th, it was $10; on the 22d, it was $11, and on the 7th of May, it was $12.50 to $13. Shortly after that date a change supervened at home. From quiet the markets drifted into depression, and from depression to panic was but a step; buyers withdrew altogether, and prices have returned to more or less the value of January.

At present the market is almost entirely paralyzed. Although there is still a large quantity of grain outside, very little is being offered. There is still time for damage to be done to some of the growing crops, and a rise in gold may cause an advance in paper values.

Regarding shipments I am inclined to put them at a full million tons for the year ending December 31, including those from Uruguay. With the exception of last year it has been found that by the 30th of June two-thirds of the Argentine crop is shipped. Up to the 18th instant, 638,000 tons had been shipped from Argentine and about 120,000 tons from Uruguay. The rise may have accelerated shipments a little, but it did not last long enough to have much effect. There is a large stock in Buenos Ayres.

Locusts have made an early appearance this year, the Province of Santa Fe being full of them. They will be of benefit at first, preventing the too rapid growth of the plant. But these locusts may be followed by others, with results disastrous to the harvest.

THE PORT OF BUENOS AYRES.

From a work prepared in Argentina for the Paris Exposition, it appears that during the year 1897 the shipping statistics of the port of Buenos Ayres were as follows:

Total number of vessels entered and cleared, 20,884; registered tonnage, 7,365,405 tons; steam vessels, 6,689, with a tonnage of 5,895,967 tons; sailing vessels, 14,195, with a tonnage of 1,469,438 tons.

There were 2,025 vessels engaged in foreign trade having a total tonnage of 2,984,408 tons, and in coastwise trade 18,859 vessels were employed whose total tonnage was 4,380,997 tons.

Sixteen thousand seven hundred and forty-five vessels, with a total tonnage of 2,415,773 tons, carried the Argentine flag; of these, 103 with 42,603 tons were engaged in foreign commerce, and 16,642 with 2,373,160 tons in the coastwise trade. Steam vessels carrying the Argentine flag numbered 3,389, with a tonnage of 1,392,441 tons, while the sailing vessels were 13,356, having a tonnage of 1,023,332 tons.

BRAZIL.

COURTESY TO UNITED STATES MINISTER BRYAN.

The "Cidade de Rio," of Rio de Janeiro, in a recent issue presents a portrait of the minister of the United States, Col. CHARLES PAGE BRYAN, and at the same time gives expression to sentiments of admiration and friendship for the United States and its representative.   On the occasion of the minister's visit to the national mint of Brazil the employees were given a half holiday to "remind them pleasantly of the American minister's visit."

COAL FOR BRAZILIAN CENTRAL RAILROAD.

The board of directors of the Brazilian Central Railroad has issued a call for bids for furnishing coal for use on its railroad during the year 1899.   The quantity required is 120,000 tons, proposals for which will be received on the 31st of October next at 1 o'clock p. m.

The advertisement, as transmitted to the Department of State by Minister BRYAN, specifies that the coal must be of the first quality, coming from the mines of Cardiff, or from others which furnish an article of equal quality, and must fulfill the following conditions: Recently mined, three times screened, must not give more than 4 per cent of ash, nor contain more than nine-tenths of one per cent sulphur, and have a calorific power not less than 8.000 calories per gram by Thomson's calorimeter, all of which will be verified by analyses and experiments made by the administration of the railroad and by anyone it may designate.   It is further stipulated that the coal must be furnished in large pieces, not more than 5 per cent of a size smaller than 30 cubic inches being admitted, and must be delivered in quantities corresponding to the rate of 10,000 tons a month, not exceeding on any day 500 tons, and with the express stipulation in the bills of lading that the discharge per working day shall not exceed 250 tons.

Delivery must begin in the first two weeks of January, 1899, and end in December of the same year, and suspension of delivery for more than a month, or an attempt to supply an article of inferior quality, will give the company the right to rescind the contract, and will also cause the deposit guaranteeing the fulfillment of the contract, amounting to 40,000 milreis (about $6,000), to be forfeited by the contractor.   It is also provided in the contract that failure to fulfill any of the stipulated conditions gives to the directory of the railroad the right to impose a penalty upon the contractors of 2,000 to 20,000 milreis ($300 to $3,000), according to the gravity of the default.

Payment will be made at the treasury of the railroad in national

and in the interior districts of the north goats abound, affording sustenance to the greater part of the population.

Game is found in inexhaustible abundance here* in immense virgin forests.

The seas which bathe the coast to a length of over 1,200 leagues, and the innumerable streams that flow through this vast region, are stocked with the richest fauna with which nature has endowed the world. AGASSIZ, on the occasion of his visit to this country on a mission from the Government of the United States, recognized that the maritime and river fauna of Brazil is simply incomparable.

In vegetable productions Brazil is unequaled. Every known species is either already found here or may be readily acclimated, on account of the great variety of soil and climate. The woods have great beauty and durability, and can be used in various industrial applications.† The utilization of these woods and of the valuable resins which many of them contain is an industry still in an embryonic state. Every kind of fruit may be grown, and among those native to the soil are many unknown in the Old World, of exquisite flavor.

On the banks of the Amazon and its tributaries, on the Paraguay, and San Francisco, are many varieties of rubber-producing trees, and, notwithstanding the neglect they have received, the supply is apparently inexhaustible. Cacao, Brazil nuts, and other valuable forest products are found in abundance.

The mineral wealth of the country is too well known to require a long dissertation on this subject. Gold, silver, mercury, iron, copper, topaz, rubies, marbles and granites of various qualities and colors, agate, manganese, phosphates, petroleum, graphite, etc., not to mention diamonds of the first water and onyx unequaled for beauty, are found; but mining is now neglected, being practically confined to a few English companies. In many districts monazite is found. The Frado sands in Bahia, near the coast, accessible for purposes of transportation, contain 83 per cent of monazite. Others, which are not so rich or have not yet been analyzed, are found in the States of Minas, Goyaz, Matto Grosso, Rio de Janeiro, Bahia, and São Paulo. The working of the Brazilian coal mines is likewise still in an embryonic state. In the opinion of Mr. NATHANIEL PLANT, there are in Rio Grande do Sul mines containing coal equal in quality to the best Cardiff.

Many causes have contributed to hinder the rapid and natural development of this vast and wealthy country, but the chief is a lack of systematic and energetic effort, and also, probably, a lack of sufficient capital.

The sugar-cane industry has not been developed. Cotton grows in every part of the country, but the production is decreasing. Breadstuffs are produced

---

* Ornithologists count 1,680 species of birds in Brazil, one-sixth of the number known in the whole world.

† A profitable business might be done in the shipment of Brazilian hard woods to the United States. This business is at present, so far as my observation goes, almost exclusively confined to rosewood, but there are many other fine cabinet woods in Brazil, some of which are much cheaper and even more beautiful. In order to conduct this business successfully, it would be necessary to take steps for making these woods known in the United States, for obtaining in Brazil a regular supply, and for reducing expenses of transportation.

There are already a number of vineyards, and it is to be expected that in the course of time Brazilian wines will partly replace those which are now imported. In Minas Geraes, colonization, it would seem, is a logical result of natural circumstances, since the colonist will find in certain districts natural products growing wild from which he may derive an almost immediate income. The greater part of the State is adapted to stock breeding, and the present number of cattle may be increased tenfold. The same may be said of horses, sheep, etc., not to mention hogs, the breeding of which already constitutes an important industry. An abundance of water power is available, and by utilizing the rivers it will be easy to effect a complete transformation in means of communication.

The State of Rio Grande do Sul, which is situated in the temperate zone, has more than 1,500,000 inhabitants.* Besides being able to produce everything that is produced in the River Plate countries, in the northwest of the State and on the River Uruguay are valuable forests; and in mineral products it is far richer than the Argentine Republic. It must not be forgotten that formerly this State, besides supplying both Uruguay and the Argentine Republic with wheat, produced a surplus for export. A drawback is the lack of good ports with water of sufficient depth to admit vessels of any draft. Moreover, Brazil, having permitted wheat to be imported free of duty and having likewise, by its constitution, prevented competition in freight rates in its coast trade, has interfered with the progress of its southern States and favored those of the River Plate. The construction of a deep-water port at Chuy, at the extreme southern limit of Brazil, adjoining the frontier of the Republic of Uruguay, would transfer to Brazil the coast trade which is now tributary to the River Plate.

Taxes in Brazil are not more than a tenth of those in the countries of the River Plate. To exploit Brazilian trade, American and European merchants send here men without experience and without knowledge of the language of the country, and companies send engineers who are often no better. Would it not be advisable for the development of these enormous resources and for the American trade with Brazil to organize a syndicate comprising capitalists, manufacturers, and others to establish a permanent exhibition of machines, models, and of samples of all articles that may be furnished to the agricultural population in the districts intended to be developed? It would be of great benefit to American trade if there should be established at Pelotas, the principal city of the State of Rio Grande do Sul, a permanent exhibition of American implements and machinery. Another such depot might be established with profit in Rio de Janeiro for supplying Minas Geraes and other States. I am convinced that in a short while such a syndicate would be eminently successful and in a position to extend its operations to other States, for it must not be forgotten that Brazil is obliged by imperative necessity to confine its coffee culture within its present limits, and to diversify its agricultural industry.

Mr. SEEGER adds:

I regard with much favor the proposition of organizing a United States syndicate for business operations in Brazil. While the present financial and commercial depression is unfavorable to new industrial ventures and to rapid increase

---

* At the end of 1890, according to official figures, this State had 897,455 inhabitants.

The people and the Government of Chile behold in this great nation a model worthy of being imitated in its just and liberal institutions, in its spirit of ample tolerance and generalization of popular culture, in the untiring activity and tenacious energy with which it proceeds with even course in all the paths of progress, amazing the world with its prodigious and rapid development.

Chile has experienced from the earliest years of her independent life the efficacy of the influence of this powerful Republic to preserve peace or to restore it when it has been interrupted, not only between States of this continent and European States, but also between the American States themselves.

The treaty of indefinite truce negotiated between four South American Republics and Spain in 1870 in this same city of Washington, under the auspices of this Government; the treaty which, having been negotiated through the intermediary of the ministers of the United States in Santiago and Buenos Ayres, furnished in 1881 the means for a pacific solution of the question of boundaries pending between Chile and the Argentine Republic, are a proof of this beneficent influence.

The financial and commercial relations between this country, the emporium of every class of productions and wealth, and Chile have scarcely been initiated, and are, in the opinion of experts, susceptible of immediate and considerable development. My instructions charge me to bring about the development, and I will do so with the zeal aroused in me by the conviction that economical interests are constantly acquiring greater preponderance in international relations.

I trust, sir, that I will meet from your excellency and your Government the favorable assistance indispensable for the successful discharge and accomplishment of my mission.

Among the instructions given me, my Government especially commends to me a charge which it is very gratifying to fulfill—to express to your excellency the fervent and sincere wishes which the Government and people of Chile entertain for the prosperity and greatness of the Government and the people of the United States and for the personal health and happiness of your excellency.

To this cordial expression, President McKinley made the following response:

Mr. Minister : I have much pleasure in receiving from your hands the letters whereby the recall of your honored predecessor, Señor Don Domingo Gana, is announced, and yourself accredited to the Government of the United States as the envoy extraordinary and minister plenipotentiary of the Republic of Chile.

That you will accomplish the object of your mission in drawing closer the friendly ties that have long existed between your Republic and ours I can not permit myself to doubt, inasmuch as the same high purpose inspires the Government of the United States; and to that end I can assure you of the hearty cooperation of myself and of my associates in administration in faithful fulfillment of the will of the people of the United States to dwell in peace, in friendship, and in close community of interests with their neighbors on the great Western Continent.

You agreeably recall occasions when this cordial spirit of our Government and people has been manifested toward the Commonwealths of South America

The Chilean minister further said that the export of nitrate from Chile to Europe now amounts to 1,250,000 tons annually, and has for years increased steadily from 5 to 7 per cent, while last year it increased from 10 to 12 per cent. He considers that when the advantage of using nitrate in the United States is fully appreciated the demand will greatly increase. Lumber, furniture, and machinery, especially agricultural machinery, from the United States are being extensively used in Chile, and lately there has sprung up a very promising import trade there of United States cotton manufactures. In cotton manufactured goods the United States is, in some respects, competing favorably with England and France, but the minister considers that trade in this line is yet in its infancy, so far as the United States is concerned.

THE NITRATE INDUSTRY.

The association for the development of the nitrate interests of the Republic has just published its report for the first quarter of the ptesent year. This report includes, first, the corrected table of the exportation in quintals (220.46 pounds), of nitrate for the year 1897, which is as follows:

	Spanish quintals.		Spanish quintals.
United Kingdom or Conti-nent		Australia	11,000
Direct ports from the United Kingdom	9,631,004	Honolulu	72,723
		Maurice	17,549
Germany	266,502	Port Elizabeth	42,767
Switzerland	6,020,064	Africa	39,600
Holland	74,931	Guatemala	100
Belgium	1,029,613	Brazil	147
France	1,029,428	Argentina	855
Italy	2,192,718	Ecuador	60
Austria-Hungary	310,265	Peru	2,684
United States	46,332	Bolivia	33
Martinique	2,510,203	Chile	42,203
Japan	24,750		
	76,082	Total	23,441,613

Second, it relates the efforts made for the formation of a new association for limiting the production of nitrate, and mentions decision rendered by the general assembly of April 12, 1898, o give an official character to the steps taken to reach this end, and finally to avoid in the future the markets being by indications of favorable results.

account of the work of the different committees of development installed in Europe occupies an important place in the The results obtained justify the sacrifices that have been made in this respect. The permanent committee of London had received to April 18 the sum of £8,091 12s., of which £5,000 were the proceeds of the official supply of £20,000 furnished by the law of September 7, 1897. Nothing is neglected to insure new markets for nitrate. Lectures, competitions, with distributions of prizes, the founding of fields of experiment, and insertions in the commercial magazines multiply every day. The delegation from France notes especially the favorable results of the experiments made in the fields of Park au Prince, in the suburbs of Paris, which demonstrated the superiority of nitrate over sulphate of ammonia in the cultivation of corn.

It was found that in Germany it is especially important to combat the competition of sulphate of ammonia with nitrate. It is to the success of this production, and to the attacks of which nitrate has been the object on the part of the factories, that the decrease in the importation of nitrate in Germany is due, which was 644,460 Spanish quintals in the first three months of 1898 as compared with the corresponding period in the year 1897. From this arose the necessity of adopting a uniform method in the mixture of perchlorate in nitrate. That proposed by Dr. GILBERT, which had already been the object of favorable reports, appears to have elicited general approbation.

According to a communication from the agent of the committee in England, the annual production of sulphate of ammonia, through force of circumstances, would be limited to the maximum of 35.000 tons, because of the fact that the coke manufactured in the ovens installed for the preparations of derived products does not exceed 2,000,000 tons, and the quantity of sulphate of ammonia that a ton of coke produces is not more than 38 or 40 pounds.

There is no reason to fear, however, the increase in the number of coke ovens capable of producing sulphate of ammonia, because this measure would necessitate the transportation of material at an enormous outlay of capital, and the coke thus obtained is of a very inferior quality.

The total consumption of nitrate in the whole world during the first three months was 11,534,731 Spanish quintals, or 1,621,065 quintals in excess of the corresponding period of 1897.

The table below gives its distribution in the principal countries and indicates the increase or decrease:

	Distribution.	Increase.	Decrease.
	Spanish quintals.		
United Kingdom	864, 110	227, 930	....
Germany	4, 119, 990	....	644, 460
France	3, 288; 310	1, 164, 490	....
Belgium	1, 656, 410	214, 360	....
Holland	503, 470	224, 020	....
Italy	197, 800	150, 420	....
Austria-Hungary	163, 990	78, 890	....
Sweden	....	11, 500	....
Denmark	....	89, 700	....
United States (east coast)	576, 235	212, 082	....
United States (western coast)	109, 844	65, 844	....
Different countries	52, 136	34, 111	....
Chile	2, 386	4, 422	....

The visible supply on December 31, 1897, amounted to 17,255,501 Spanish quintals, of which 9,687,701 quintals were on foreign markets and 7,567,800 quintals on the Chilian coast.

The preceding tables explain the improvement in the situation of the nitrate industry, which is due to the increase in consumption brought about by active development. But lack of skill among the producers has not permitted, even from these favorable results, as great a profit as could have been hoped for, and the prices have continued to fall since 1895.

On the other hand, as the following figures show, there is a considerable increase in the production as a result of the failure of numerous attempts made to limit it:

First quarter—   *Spanish quintals.*
1898 .... 6, 934, 853
1897 .... 3, 885, 316

    Increase 3, 049, 537

In 1897 there were but 30 factories engaged in this industry, and at the present time there are 44.

Finally, the exportation has increased proportionately, being 5,593,390 quintals, an excess of 1,766,474 quintals over the exports of the first three months of 1898. These were distributed among the different countries in the following manner:

                                                                             Spanish quintals.
United Kingdom or Continent 1, 958, 408
Direct ports of United Kingdom 245, 845
Germany 1, 224, 985

MEXICO.

PROGRESS IN MANUFACTURES.

Mexico furnishes in cotton manufactures alone marked evidence of industrial progress. Authority of unquestioned reliability gives that country the credit of doubling the number of its cotton mills during the past few years.

In 1896 not less than 107 cotton factories paid tax to the Government. Of these, 3 were spinning mills, 6 were spinning, weaving and printing mills, and 6 were printing mills. The motive power of these factories aggregated 13,826 horsepower, and their mechanical outfit comprised 24 printing machines, 13,600 looms, and 448,156 spindles. They employed 20,994 men, women, and children, and consumed 53,273,397 pounds of raw cotton. Half of the cotton consumed was from the United States, the remainder of home production. The output of these factories for 1896 was 7,116,547 pieces of cloth and 3,858,829 pounds of yarn and coarse thread.

While the cotton industry of Mexico is over 60 years old, the pioneer establishment dating back to 1834, it has not been until within recent years that any marked degree of development has been attained. The new era of industrial Mexico is marked by many other enterprises and is a welcome turn in affairs that makes for greater peace and security and for quickened civilization on the Western Hemisphere.

Flax, the cultivation of which has greatly decreased in the United States, is being cultivated in Mexico, not merely for the oil product of the seeds, but linen is being manufactured from the fiber with as much application and care at Cuernavaca and San Luis Potosí as are jute, hemp, and cotton at Orizaba and Guadalajara, and it is an industry strongly protected by the Mexican tariff.

The best Mexican flax possesses that peculiar silkiness and luster characteristic of the Irish flax and is grown near Cuernavaca. There is, in this city, one large linen mill, the daily output of which is 2,500 meters (2,734 yards). Both steam and water are employed in motive power. Drills, hollands, ticks, sheeting, towelling, etc., are manufactured and sold in the country. The same proprietor has a mill at Mexico City of equal producing capacity.

At Orizaba are the Rio Blanco mills, turning out linen as well as cotton goods, while at San Luis Potosi is a factory of English origin, which makes sheeting, white goods of finer qualities, fine drillings, and dress goods, the output bringing from 40 cents to $1.50 per meter (39.37 inches). All these goods are sold in the Republic.

The linen made in Mexico is by native labor, thus showing that the Mexican laborer is susceptible of the best training. The men soon learn to handle United States machinery and apparatus, and when the United States manufacturers of spinning and weaving machinery make up their minds to introduce their products and replace the English makes it will be found that the adaptive Mexican laborer is just as much at home with the one as the other.

Linen goods were manufactured in the Republic in 1829 to the amount of 1,800 kilograms, increasing in 1896 to 47,000 kilograms.

MARKET FOR MACHINERY.

Owing to the steadily increasing efforts on the part of the manufacturers of the United States to secure foreign markets for their products, it is important that they should not overlook a market which lies at their very doors, as is furnished by Mexico, the possibilities of which can not properly be judged by statistics showing the importations to that country at the present time. "Modern Mexico" gives it, as its opinion, founded on a knowledge of the situation and a careful investigation of the facts, that as the advantages of modern machinery and manufactures are known, and as the facilities for delivering them to interior points of the country improve, the requirements of Mexico will grow and multiply. The following extract gives that paper's view of the matter:

Improved machinery of all kinds has been one of the principal imports of Mexico for several years, and there is every reason to believe that the growth in this line will continue for many years to come. It will be years before manufactures will be produced to any extent inside the Republic; but every day the extension of railroads, and the successful demonstration that modern methods pay, is increasing the demand for American manufactures; and when the territory already easily accessible is canvassed by American exporters with one-half the care that is given their home trade, the result will be astonishing. Within fifteen minutes' walk of the center of the City of Mexico one can see in use the same style of wooden plows that have been used in Mexico since Cortez's time, and hundreds of mines throughout Mexico are being worked with the most primitive kinds of machinery. Mexico's demand for modern manufactures will con.inue for years to increase much faster than it is possible for home industries to supply them. Every year the things that have heretofore been luxuries to thousands of people are becoming every-day necessities. It is this country, rich in every natural resource, now in the course of a vigorous and healthy development, that lies invitingly before the American manufacturer. It is not a field whose business can be had simply for the asking. The established trade of European nations must in many cases be met in competition, but the superiority of American goods and proximity of the source of supply are strong arguments. Here is a hint which American manufacturers should not be slow in taking. There is no reason why they should not secure to themselves, and at good prices, the bulk of the Mexican trade.

INCREASED DEMAND FOR BICYCLES.

Consul-General POLLARD, writing the Department of State from Monterey, August 13, answers questions propounded by an association of bicycle manufacturers in the United States as follows:

"No bicycles are manufactured in the Republic of Mexico. Several firms buy all the component parts of machines and put them together afterwards, but the complete wheel is not manufactured in Mexico. All the parts are procured from the United States, and almost all the machines manufactured in the United States are represented in Mexico. The chief importers of bicycle parts are Messrs. Howe & Co., of Monterey; Messrs. Moler & Degrees, of Mexico City; and Messrs. Pomery & Co., of Guadalajara. The prospects for increased traffic in goods of high quality are promising. The entire component parts of each wheel, however, are demanded, owing to the number of different makes in the country. The duty on parts of bicycles not nickel-plated is 2 cents per kilogram (2.2046 pounds); on parts nickel-plated, it is 20 cents per kilogram.

"With reference to the future of bicycles in Mexico, it may be interesting to state that for the last four years the demand therefor has increased each successive year more than 5 per cent over that of the preceding year. There is no doubt that anyone having capital to start a manufactory in this Republic would meet with success, and that large gains would ensue to the investors in such an enterprise. There are good prospects, too, for the manufacture of rubber tires and rubber parts of bicycles. The raw material can be obtained in Mexico for this purpose."

RAILROADS, PROJECTED AND CONSTRUCTED.

Railway construction is in a state of great activity, throughout the Republic, according to the reports of the local newspapers, the most important roads lately constructed and projected being the following:

A railroad is in project from Cordova to the port of Tehuantepec, Engineer Louis B. Ceballos being in charge of the plan. A United States company has received a concession to build a railroad from Saltillo to Paredon, Trevino, or any other point on the Monterey and Mexican Railroad. The projected railroad from Mazatlan will be extended as far as Rosario. Señor Arturo de Cima, ex-Vice-Consul of the United States at Mazatlan, has the matter in hand.

Among the new projects is a railroad from Mazatlan to Villa Union, in the State of Sinaloa, where there are large cotton factories. The city of Mazatlan and the State will give financial aid. Another projected line, with good chances of being built, is from Merida de Tuncas, in Yucatan.

The railroad from San Antonio station, on the Southern Railroad, to Chilchotla, State of Oaxaca, is completed and in operation. It is 54 kilometers (33½ miles) long and runs through a mountainous country. It opens up a rich coffee district. The work of laying the track on the Mexican International from Reata to Monterey was begun in July and is being rapidly pushed ahead. It is claimed that 112 kilometers (70 miles) of rail will be laid in ninety days. The extension of the Mexico, Cuernavaca and Pacific Railroad to Iguala was formally opened on July 16. The Monte Alto road has been completed for a distance of 20 kilometers (13 miles) and it is to be further extended. The work on the Chihuahua and Pacific Railroad was begun on March 25,

1898, and 1,000 men are now employed.   The contractors desire 2,000 more men, but suitable laborers are difficult to obtain.   By March 25, 1899, the road will be completed to Guerrero, a distance of 200 kilometers (125 miles).   The whole length of the road will be 600 kilometers (375 miles).   Several United States capitalists are stockholders.

The great tunnel that connects Catorce with Potrero has been completed.   The railroad line will shortly be laid, and the traffic of ore, merchandise, and passengers between the mountain city and the Mexican National Railroad will be greatly facilitated.   Catorce is one of the cities of the Republic that heretofore could be reached only on foot or by horseback.   All merchandise had to be carried upon the backs of animals, and all the products of the city's rich mines had to be brought down in the same manner, necessitating great expense.

The " Diario Oficial " publishes the full text of the concession granted by the Mexican Government to JOHN B. FRISBIE, representative of WILLIAM STEWART & Co., for the construction of a railroad in the States of Sinaloa and Durango, starting at the capital of Sinaloa and terminating at Villa de Tepia, in Durango. The concession is dated May 25, 1898, and besides the route mentioned the company is privileged to build another road from the capital of Sinaloa to Altata, or some point in that vicinity.

SYNOPSIS OF THE NATIONAL COPYRIGHT LAW.

Consul-General BARLOW sends the Department of State from the City of Mexico the following synopsis of the copyright laws of the country:

" The copyright law of Mexico establishes that for legal effect there will be no distinction between Mexicans and foreigners, provided the work in question be published in Mexico.   The author enjoys the copyright during his life; at his death it goes to his heirs.   Consequently it is a right which he can dispose of as any other kind of property in his possession is disposed of.   By prescription, however, his right expires in the course of ten years.

" The law concedes to the author the right of publishing translations of his works, but in this case he must declare whether he reserves his right to one or to all languages.   This right is granted for ten years to authors who do not reşide in Mexico, and who publish their works abroad.

" In order to acquire the copyright, the author, translator, or editor must apply personally or by his representative to the Department of Public Instruction, making note that he reserves his rights, and accompanying same with two copies of his work.

" All authors, translators, and editors should put their names, the date of publication, and notice of their copyright in a prominent place on said copies.

" If it be desired to obtain copyrights of some work of music, engraving, lithograph, or the like, two copies must also be sent. If it be a work of architecture, painting, or sculpture, a sample of the drawing or a plan, giving dimensions and all other details which characterize the original, shall be presented.

" A foreign author not resident in Mexico must send power of attorney, drawn before a notary public and certified by a Mexican consul. This in its turn has to be legalized by the State Department of Mexico and protocolized, duly translated. For these operations $25 is charged and $25 more for the work to be done in obtaining the copyright, including the value of Federal stamps, which have to be attached to the writing filed before the Department of Public Instruction. Hence, for the whole there is charged $50, Mexican currency."

AGRICULTURAL PROSPECTS.

There was never a time in the history of Mexico, says the editor of " El Comerciante," Mexico, when agriculture was as flourishing as now (August, 1898). This is not only the case with regard to coffee culture, which many people seem to think the principal occupation here, but likewise to the cultivation. of sisal grass (henequen), cotton, rubber, sugar cane, and hundreds of other tropical and semitropical products which can be success- ·fully raised in Mexico. Much of the agricultural prosperity of the Republic is derived from the fact that foreign colonists have introduced new methods, improved breeds of live stock, etc.

In reply to numerous inquiries on the subject, the same authority refers to the best paying agricultural products of the country as being dependent upon location and conditions. Corn pays as well as any other product in certain places, while in others coffee pays best.   Rubber undoubtedly has a big future, and its culture is unhesitatingly recommended.   It is true that under ordinary circumstances the planter has to wait nearly seven years for results from his rubber trees, but a method recently suggested is to plant from 1,000 to 2,000 or more trees to the acre and then thin them out yearly, beginning the second year.   The rubber is then to be extracted from the trees cut out.   In this manner an annual income of from $50 to $100 (Mexican currency) per acre may be easily secured, and a long delay is avoided.

Cotton is a profitable product, as there are now over 100 cotton manufactories in Mexico.   Mexican lands are very suitable for growing cotton, but over half of the cotton used by the mills is at present imported.

In some districts fruit growing would be remunerative.   The pineapple of Tehuantepec is one of the finest varieties in the world.   Proper facilities are about to be furnished for putting the Mexican pineapple in the United States markets.   An enterprising citizen of the United States is meeting with marked success in growing tomatoes near Tampico and shipping them across the border into his own country.

In other districts cattle raising can be safely recommended as a profitable investment, and in many the raising of marketable hogs pays well. · There is really no limit to the different agricultural possibilities in Mexico; all that is needed is intelligence in selection and sufficient capital for investment.

NICARAGUA.

FINDINGS OF THE CANAL COMMISSION.

The following extract from the " New York Tribune " of September 9, 1898, is published as being of special interest to trade connections of the American Republics:

No report on the Nicaragua Canal has yet been made by the Commission sent out to investigate the matter, of which Admiral WALKER is president and Professor HAUPT and General HAINS are members.   But the testimony of the members before the Senate select committee, on June 15–17, has been printed, and indicates clearly some of the results of the investigation.   The Commission

PERU.

EL SOL MATCH FACTORY.

The American Minister at Lima, Mr. DUDLEY, informs the Bureau that a company has been recently formed in that city under the name of " El Sol Match Factory," with a capital of 400,000 soles ($163,600), to engage in the manufacture of matches of all kinds, using the machines and patents of the well-known Diamond Match Company of Chicago, which has taken 50 per cent of the shares of the local factory.

The President of the new company is Don José PAYÁN, the Directors being Don FRANCISCO M. OLIVA and Don PABLO LA ROSA, with Don JUAN DUANY as Manager.

The stockholders of the enterprise are: LA SOCIEDAD MANUFACTURERA DE TABACOS, Messrs. JOSÉ PAYÁN, M. B. WELLS, ERNESTO AYULO, LORENZO DALAUDE, JOSÉ E. CASTAÑON, ROBERTO GANOZA, PABLO LA ROSA, OCTAVIO VALENTINI, HERMAN DENKS, JOAQUÍN GODOY, and FRANCISCO PÉREZ DE VELASCO.

The purpose is to locate the shops of the factory at Callao, but as yet no final resolution has been reached.

EXPORTS IN 1897 COMPARED WITH THOSE OF 1896.

Below is a synopsis of data regarding the exports from Peru in 1897 compared with those of 1896, as published in " El Comercio," Lima, June 27, 1898.

Articles.	1896.	1897.
	Kilos.	*Kilos.*
Sugar	71,735,473	105,463,238
Cotton	4,717,697	5,586,394
Borate	1,178,762	11,850,490
Cascarilla	16,489	62,261
Hides	1,331,689	1,710,206
Wool	2,543,641	3,767,799
Cotton-seed cake	1,048,456	1,007,527
Rice	2,803,640	4,221,835
Coffee	712,919	1,239,744
	Soles.	*Soles.*
Cochineal	32,070	2,407
Coca and cocaine	1,212,381	1,173,066
Coal and wood	97,429	93,307
Furniture and clothing	42,998	31,460
Gold, coined	59,321	104,524
Silver, coined	1,485,433	1,927,454

The customs receipts were $165,410 in excess of the previous year. Of the imports, 45 per cent of the total were from the United States.

The principal articles of export were: Sugar, 86,866,239 pounds; tobacco, 6,332,148 pounds; cocoa, 4,308,823 pounds; coffee, 2,437,400 pounds; divi-divi, 1,304,929 pounds; sugar-cane honey, 1,777,119 gallons; mahogany, 264,254 feet; 184,851 feet of whitethorn and cedar wood, and 14,710 tons of lignum-vitæ, logwood, etc.

The consul also reports that owing to more modern methods of cultivation agriculture has developed greatly within the past few years. The improvement in agricultural implements employed is very noticeable, while the cultivated area of the farms is enlarging yearly. These developments have been in a great measure the result of recently constructed railroads.

UNITED STATES.

TRADE WITH LATIN AMERICA.

STATEMENT OF IMPORTS AND EXPORTS.

Following is the latest statement, from figures compiled by the Bureau of Statistics, United States Treasury Department, O. P. AUSTIN, Chief, showing the value of the trade between the United States and the Latin-American countries. The report is for the month of June, corrected to July 27, 1898, with a comparative statement for the corresponding period of the previous year; also for the twelve months ending June, 1898, compared with the corresponding period of the fiscal year 1897. It should be explained that the figures from the various custom-houses, showing imports and exports for any one month, are not received at the Treasury Department until about the 20th of the following month, and some time is necessarily consumed in compilation and printing, so that the returns for June, for example, are not published until sometime in July.

EXPORTS OF DOMESTIC MERCHANDISE—Continued.

Articles and countries.	June— 1897.	June— 1898.	Twelve months ending June— 1897.	Twelve months ending June— 1898.
Animals—Continued.				
Horses (*Caballos; Cavallos; Chevaux*)—				
Central America	$200	$750	$38,172	$12,795
Mexico	1,120	7,425	88,978	85,490
South America			11,655	5,700
Sheep (*Carneros; Carneiros; Moutons*)—				
Mexico		238	11,877	9,748
South America	3,673	2,095	14,076	12,409
Books, maps, engravings, etc. (*Libros, mapas, grabados, etc.; Livros, mappas, gravuras, etc.; Livres, cartes de géographie, gravures, etc.*):				
Central America	8,923	433	69,564	34,264
Mexico	10,968	5,858	161,343	125,006
Santo Domingo	91	95	1,336	550
Argentina	1,245	1,422	25,313	26,614
Brazil	21,210	1,958	128,214	153,770
Colombia	145	559	72,389	17,484
Other South America	2,850	5,634	53,846	43,558
Breadstuffs:				
Corn (*Maíz; Milho; Maïs*)—				
Central America	9,185	4,576	50,421	70,965
Mexico	43,992	1,153	3,233,781	43,557
Santo Domingo	14		389	166
South America	2,337	1,343	13,921	38,186
Wheat (*Trigo; Trigo; Blé*)—				
Central America		4,015	71,236	43,808
South America	11,921	76,043	165,292	1,705,171
Wheat flour (*Harina de trigo; Farina de trigo; Farine de blé*)—				
Central America	103,503	86,881	1,190,324	1,183,182
Mexico	4,661	13,300	96,762	86,848
Santo Domingo	22,953	48,182	163,078	197,338
Brazil	186,711	229,701	3,541,579	3,240,362
Colombia	53,233	54,826	580,237	541,147
Other South America	137,345	157,329	1,500,624	1,740,204
Carriages, cars, etc., and parts of (*Carruages, carros y sus accesorios; Carruagens, carros e partes de carros; Voitures, wagons et leurs parties*):				
Central America	22,182	3,226	155,143	45,149
Mexico	274,801	25,550	615,468	508,680
Santo Domingo	1,591	737	20,588	24,111
Argentina	19,519	36,026	149,766	237,506
Brazil	1,208	30,786	119,334	564,773
Colombia	6,199	3,991	55,718	42,029
Other South America	4,427	2,451	47,042	79,934

EXPORTS OF DOMESTIC MERCHANDISE—Continued.

Articles and countries.	June—		Twelve months ending June—	
	1897.	1898.	1897.	1898.
Cycles and parts of (*Biciclos y sus accesorios; Bicyclos e accessorios; Bicyclettes et leurs parties*):				
Central America	$907	$934	$53,801	$8,267
Mexico	6,165	8,046	73,117	68,022
Santo Domingo	598	37	4,908	1,171
Argentina	3,768	9,600	42,091	90,229
Brazil	3,978	9,633	29,355	98,482
Colombia	2,671	653	24,290	15,684
Other South America	4,860	2,592	73,507	48,966
Clocks and watches (*Relojes de pared y de bolsillo; Relogios de parede e de bolso; Pendules et montres*):				
Central America	343	75	12,474	6,998
Mexico	2,317	1,443	25,116	20,128
Argentina	1,565	3,150	34,902	28,065
Brazil	2,201	2,205	59,520	40,898
Other South America	8,764	4,873	102,019	85,040
Coal (*Carbón; Carvão; Charbon*):				
Central America	798	200	28,000	19,335
Mexico	86,539	121,650	649,955	974,040
Santo Domingo	1,844	559	26,211	11,288
Brazil	27,505	19,182	88,080	93,778
Colombia	6,011	5,850	25,175	38,284
Other South America	2,238	2,125	32,548	20,425
Copper (*Cobre; Cobre; Cuivre*):				
Mexico	575	1,113	11,046	22,583
Cotton, unmanufactured (*Algodón no manufacturado; Algodão não manufacturado; Coton non manufacture*):				
Mexico	5,411	9,300	1,236,447	1,321,473
Cotton cloths (*Tejidos de algodón; Fazendas de algodão; Coton manufacture*):				
Central America	66,704	40,583	599,126	396,510
Mexico	25,881	36,079	366,753	415,910
Santo Domingo	5,684	28,973	92,831	120,167
Argentina	7,264	16,877	270,844	181,868
Brazil	51,222	80,474	607,019	565,921
Colombia	42,011	25,806	382,546	281,803
Other South America	78,626	124,462	1,364,903	1,126,871
Wearing apparel (cotton) (*Ropa de algodón; Roupa de algodão; Vétements en coton*):				
Central America	25,147	16,547	240,683	214,246
Mexico	22,879	43,432	346,139	334,663
Santo Domingo	1,048	596	31,012	18,491
Argentina	9,440	4,261	66,845	34,726
Brazil	3,281	4,603	67,975	50,828
Colombia	7,697	4,713	54,832	44,764
Other South America	8,585	2,619	56,683	35,410

EXPORTS OF DOMESTIC MERCHANDISE—Continued.

Articles and countries.	June—		Twelve months ending June—	
	1897.	1898.	1897.	1898.
Iron and steel, manufactures of— Continued.				
Typewriting machines and parts of (*Máquinas de escribir y accesorios; Machinas de escribir e accessorios Machines à écrire et leurs parties*).				
Central America................	$2,421	$;0	$13,270	$2,360
Mexico......	1,988	3,692	25,298	28,900
Santo Domingo...........	....	.....	267	90
Argentina....................	836	4,015	11,914	18,187
Brazil.......................	411	15	4,006	4,945
Colombia	647	145	3,995	4,228
Other South America..........	1,485	885	11,278	14,652
Leather, other than sole (*Cuero, distinto del de suela; Couro não para solas; Cuirs, autres que pour semelles*):				
Central America................	760	431	5,143	4,713
Mexico......................	1,740	711	16,456	9,310
Santo Domingo.................	169	....	1,177	569
Argentina.	150	....	4,055	4,360
Brazil.......................	1,500	2,833	18,914	54,022
Colombia	185	1,582	2,388	4,763
Other South America...........	524	466	14,242	12,658
Boots and shoes (*Calzado; Calçados; Chaussures*):				
Central America................	10,601	5,851	98,678	88,907
Mexico..............., ...	4,556	17,837	58,639	87,669
Colombia....................	4,239	4,315	42,719	41,735
Other South America..........	1,117	2,970	26,481	28,574
Naval stores: Rosin, tar, etc. (*Resina y alquitrán; Resina e alcatrão; Résine et goudron*):				
Central America................	2,228	990	24,151	15,459
Mexico......................	1,154	861	6,910	10,212
Santo Domingo............... ..	460	639	5,036	6,156
Argentina.................	17,919	22,841	75,851	95,161
Brazil	18,195	12,454	234,731	194,409
Colombia	1,696	2,060	19,163	13,102
Other South America	8,142	10,470	95,528	95,878
Turpentine, spirits of (*Aguarrás; Agua-raz; Térébenthine*):				
Central America....	365	217	4,346	3,029
Mexico......................	235	668	2,667	3,626
Santo Domingo.................	16	44	312	491
Argentina...................	1,650	18,841	50,264	129,506
Brazil......................	5,996	12,459	46,722	74,148
Colombia	314	473	5,781	4,513
Other South America...........	1,350	14,488	36,672	61,934
Oils, mineral, crude (*Aceites, minerales, crudos; Oleos, mineraes, crús; Huiles minérales, brutes*):				
Mexico......................	28,606	81	349,021	317,514

EXPORTS OF DOMESTIC MERCHANDISE—Continued.

Articles and countries.	June—		Twelve months ending June—	
	1897.	1898.	1897.	1898.
Oils, mineral, refined or manufactured (*Aceites minerales, refinados ó manufacturados; Oleos mineraes, refinados ó manufacturados; Huiles minérales, raffinées ou manufacturées*):				
Central America	$6, 578	$6, 363	$146, 789	$112, 834
Mexico	19, 798	16, 257	174, 107	184, 088
Santo Domingo	6, 253	267	52, 486	50, 051
Argentina	47, 399	104, 599	1, 060, 214	1, 007, 498
Brazil	183, 376	189, 998	1, 642, 912	1, 532, 231
Colombia	15, 141	11, 278	121, 861	103, 145
Other South America	63, 932	180, 191	990, 080	967, 067
Oils, vegetable (*Aceites vegetales; Oleos vegetaes; Huiles végétales*):				
Central America	79	154	4, 855	3, 080
Mexico	15, 260	7, 202	320, 496	328, 768
Santo Domingo	2, 230	7, 138	15, 616	27, 824
Argentina	623	1, 759	11, 594	5, 947
Brazil	19, 577	10, 728	172, 833	237, 065
Other South America	6, 221	13, 678	73, 379	104, 844
Paraffin and paraffin wax (*Parafina y cera de parafina; Paraffina e cera de parafina; Paraffine et cire faite de cette substance*):				
Central America	1, 687	2, 628	31, 083	19, 745
Mexico	4, 768	10, 632	144, 805	157, 863
Brazil	1, 185	844	13, 960	10, 968
Other South America	449		4, 733	5, 703
Provisions, comprising meat and dairy products:				
Beef, canned (*Carne de vaca en latas; Carne de vacca em latas; Bœuf conservé*)—				
Central America	4, 193	2, 472	37, 407	28, 584
Mexico	1, 048	991	14, 253	14, 232
Santo Domingo		7	72	40
Argentina		136	135	545
Brazil	648	1, 196	17, 610	17, 744
Colombia	415	368	6, 467	6, 623
Other South America	1, 052	2, 936	12, 750	14, 492
Beef, salted or pickled (*Carne de vaca, salada ó en salmuera; Carne de vacca, salgada ou em salmoura; Bœuf, salé ou en saumure*)—				
Central America	1, 593	1, 771	27, 921	39, 079
Mexico	56		250	492
Santo Domingo	392	1, 075	2, 612	2, 718
Brazil	150	125	3, 601	1, 237
Colombia	496	1, 740	12, 652	13, 240
Other South America	9, 284	24, 300	153, 416	175, 027

EXPORTS OF DOMESTIC MERCHANDISE—Continued.

Articles and countries.	June—		Twelve Months ending June—	
	1897.	1898.	1897.	1898.
Provisions, comprising meat and dairy products—Continued.				
Tallow (*Sebo; Sebo; Suif*)—				
Central America..............	$10,772	$7,800	$119,156	$95,679
Mexico	1,154	1,883	36,561	24,364
Santo Domingo..............	470	4,178	21,037	30,338
Brazil......................	2,835	....	9,256	25,070
Colombia	3,562	55	11,704	17,907
Other South America..........	862	8,057	13,126	20,033
Bacon (*Tocino; Toucinho; Lard fumé*)—				
Central America..............	2,217	1,716	19,248	16,692
Mexico	692	930	9,449	9,804
Santo Domingo..............	301	801	2,706	2,213
Brazil......................	95,617	11,176	1,013,182	508,171
Colombia	37	93	1,662	1,366
Other South America..........	3,211	3,257	21,593	29,223
Hams (*Jamones; Presunto; Jambons*)—				
Central America..............	3,351	1,914	33,654	28,291
Mexico.....................	1,882	3,543	28,976	23,790
Santo Domingo..............	607	1,316	7,316	6,716
Brazil......................	725	66	1,733	3,262
Colombia	1,080	981	14,969	13,805
Other South America..........	7,122	5,883	94,131	84,268
Pork (*Carne de puerco; Carne de porco; Porc*)—				
Central America..............	5,214	4,360	57,582	70,438
Santo Domingo..............	525	1,870	4,357	5,338
Brazil......................	412	90	17,684	2,045
Colombia	368	980	6,830	8,899
Other South America..........	14,610	27,192	175,566	18,508
Lard (*Manteca; Banha; Saindoux*)—				
Central America.....	17,475	20,059	111,747	156,161
Mexico	23,303	7,440	332,235	177,525
Santo Domingo	3,064	10,653	23,077	29,682
Argentina..................	107	179	4,665	3,133
Brazil......................	94,795	31,672	714,828	973,990
Colombia	14,989	10,258	152,501	120,436
Other South America..........	47,639	71,763	646,087	681,023
Oleo and oleomargarina; *Oleo e oleomargarina; Oléo et oléomargarine*)—				
Central America..............	185	248	261	1,254
Mexico	59	72	701	961
Colombia	691	1,110	7,513	8,400
Other South America..........	4,708	1,122	32,663	15,855
Butter (*Mantequilla; Manteiga; Beurre*)—				
Central America..............	5,010	3,817	45,737	48,631
Mexico	3,900	4,381	40,089	43,720
Santo Domingo.....	1,004	1,760	7,331	7,911
Brazil..............	5,922	5,318	40,303	92,191
Colombia	1,089	854	17,833	19,672
Other South America..........	7,335	11,593	87,960	91,622

EXPORTS OF DOMESTIC MERCHANDISE—Continued.

Articles and countries.	June—		Twelve months ending June—	
	1897.	1898.	1897.	1898.
Provisions, comprising meat and dairy products—Continued.				
Cheese (*Queso; Queijo; Fromage*)—				
Central America	$2,088	$1,381	$19,707	$17,721
Mexico	1,836	1,212	15,519	14,436
Santo Domingo	496	702	4,711	3,984
Brazil	132	....	212	257
Colombia	1,079	643	11,294	11,082
Other South America	2,388	1,211	16,142	17,079
Seeds (*Semillas; Sementes; Semence*)				
Central America	500	367	10,074	5,387
Mexico	126	393	20,085	29,472
Santo Domingo	114	122	538	864
Argentina	....	....	782	368
Brazil	5	....	1,583	858
Colombia	364	201	2,768	1,733
Other South America	311	339	4,905	2,345
Sugar, refined (*Azúcar refinado; Assucar refinado; Sucre raffiné*):				
Central America	3,491	2,920	59,695	50,408
Mexico	882	5,181	23,619	18,722
Santo Domingo	291	114	2,332	1,618
Colombia	2,879	1,302	44,386	26,815
Other South America	435	63	2,422	5,204
Tobacco, unmanufactured (*Tabaco no manufacturado; Tabaco não manufacturado; Tabac non manufacturé*):				
Central America	2,361	928	16,787	30,770
Mexico	1,515	6,073	109,152	135,636
Argentina	965	7,880	5,020	12,984
Colombia	49	839	2,405	8,057
Other South America	6,826	10,386	92,576	100,298
Tobacco, manufactures of (*Manufacturas de tabaco; Manufacturas de tabaco; Tabac fabriqué*):				
Central America	8,983	5,545	67,765	49,571
Mexico	262	8,189	13,235	25,914
Argentina	2,053	18	50,467	2,362
Brazil	....	....	1,355	560
Colombia	17	636	1,259	3,748
Other South America	6,538	8,837	65,412	82,015
Wood, unmanufactured (*Madera no manufacturado; Madeira não manufacturado; Bois brut*):				
Central America	8,153	642	145,861	49,526
Mexico	26,771	64,800	276,440	296,589
Argentina	....	4,643	33,799	11,728
Brazil	....	....	18,434	7,278
Colombia	1,021	....	21,294	23,737
Other South America	174	1,457	18,320	50,997

EXPORTS OF DOMESTIC MERCHANDISE—Continued.

Articles and countries.	June—		Twelve months ending June—	
	1897.	1898.	1897.	1898.
Lumber (*Maderas; Madeiras; Bois de construction*):				
Central America	$8,468	$3,190	$139,965	$38,469
Mexico	237,886	69,772	1,158,754	843,300
Santo Domingo	5,132	1,720	65,512	38,090
Argentina	49,395	46,365	999,491	876,362
Brazil	72,644	36,213	700,007	629,796
Colombia	6,192	2,561	58,211	56,838
Other South America	62,122	54,267	706,474	516,490
Furniture (*Muebles; Mobilia; Meubles*):				
Central America	20,562	3,070	156,364	74,586
Mexico	22,922	14,094	197,864	157,095
Santo Domingo	892	991	12,016	11,657
Argentina	10,263	2,257	89,638	62,224
Brazil	5,352	937	51,537	36,010
Colombia	4,759	2,027	40,831	33,410
Other South America	5,299	5,903	101,682	75,962
Wool, raw (*Lana cruda; Lã crúa; Laines brutes*):				
Mexico	6	....	140,609	10

CLASSIFICATION OF CALFSKINS AND HIDES.

A decision was rendered on August 27, 1898, by the United States Treasury Department, with reference to the classification of calfskins and hides, which places the dividing line between the two classes of goods at 12 pounds. This classification has met with the strong opposition of importers of hides and manufacturers of leather, and in Chicago and New York representatives of these business interests have been selected to present their side of the matter to the Secretary of the Treasury and ask for a reconsideration of the decision.

The full text of the decision referred to is as follows:

TREASURY DEPARTMENT, OFFICE OF THE SECRETARY,
Washington, D. C., August 27, 1898.

To Collectors and Other Officers of Customs:

For the purpose of securing uniformity of practice at the several ports in the classification of calfskins and hides under the provisions thereof, in the act of July 24, 1897, you are hereby directed to apply the following table of weights in determining the respective classifications, and to classify all skins of such weights or less as calfskins and all skins of greater weight as hides, viz:

	Pounds.
First. Wet or butcher's weight	12
Second. Wet salted	12
Third. Dry salted	7½
Fourth. Flint dry	5

W. B. Howell,
Assistant Secretary.

COINAGE BY THE MINT, AND BANK-NOTE CIRCULATION.

The report of the Director of the Mint for August, issued September 1, 1898, shows that the total coinage for the month was as follows: Gold, $9,344,200; silver, $2,350,000; minor coins, $163,786; total, $11,857,986.

The statement of the Comptroller of the Currency, issued on the same day and covering the same period, shows the total bank notes on September 1 to have been $227,178,615, an increase for the month of $481,745, and a decrease for the year of $3,329,909.

The circulation based on United States bonds was $196,775,704 an increase for the month of $1,083,019, and a decrease for the year of $9,013,022.

The circulation secured by lawful money amounted to $30,402,911; decrease for the month, $601,273, and an increase for the year of $5,650,363.

The United States registered bond deposits were as follows: To secure circulating notes, $220,496,160, and to secure public deposits, $46,860,660.

GOVERNMENTAL RECEIPTS AND EXPENDITURES DURING AUGUST, 1898.

The monthly comparative statement of receipts and expenditures of the Government was issued on September 1 by the Treasury Department.

The total receipts for August were $41,782,707.79, and the total expenditures were $56,260,717.80. The receipts in August, 1897, were $19,023,614.97, and the expenditures $33,588,047.41.

The receipts for August, 1898, were: From customs, $16,249,699; internal revenue, $24,015,934.08; miscellaneous, $1,517,073.81.

The expenditures were divided as follows: Civil and miscellaneous, $7,782,314.74; war, $25,163,235.94; Navy, $6,386,-
277.49; Indians, $766,084.26; pensions, $13,084,735.14; interest,
$3,078,070.30.

INTERNAL-REVENUE RECEIPTS, 1898.

The preliminary report of the Commissioner of Internal Revenue of the United States shows that the receipts from all
sources during the fiscal year ended June 30, 1898, amounted to
$170,869,519, an increase, as compared with the previous fiscal
year, of $24,249,925. The receipts from the several sources of
revenue during the year are given as follows: Spirits, $92,546,899
(increase, $10,538,356); tobacco, $36,230,622 (increase, $5,520,-
324); fermented liquors, $39,515,421 (increase, $7,043,259);
oleomargarine, $1,315,780 (increase, $281,650); filled ·cheese,
$16,518 (decrease, $2,473); banks and bankers, $1,180 (increase,
$1,094); miscellaneous, $1,243,096 (increase, $867,713).

The quantities of distilled spirits, fermented liquors, tobacco,
cigarettes, and cigars on which tax was paid during the year are
stated as follows: Spirits distilled from fruits, 1,411,448 gallons;
increase, 265,317 gallons; whisky and other spirits distilled from
materials other than fruit, 78,353,210 gallons; increase, 9,519,979
gallons; fermented liquors or beer, 37,486,156 barrels; increase,
3,063,062 barrels; cigars (number), 4,910,881,541; increase,
847,712,444; cigarettes (number), 3,753,539,534, a net decrease
of nearly 400,000,000; tobacco, 288,160,074 pounds; increase,
27,425,262 pounds; oleomargarine, 55,388,727 pounds; increase,
12,854,168 pounds; filled cheese, 1,412,923 pounds; decrease,
253,214 pounds.

The expenses incident to the collection of the internal-revenue
tax during the year were approximately $3,886,262. The States
paying the largest amounts of internal revenue are given as follows: Illinois, $39,658,686; New York, $21,058,569; Kentucky,
$18,228,918; Ohio, $16,436,908; Pennsylvania, $13,846,790;
Indiana, $10,022,274.

THE WOOL CLIP OF 1898.

Regarding the number of sheep in the flocks owned in the United States and the wool clip of 1898, the Boston "Commercial Bulletin" publishes the following statistics:

The total number of sheep in the country on January 1, 1898, was 37,656,960. The subsequent loss, as estimated by the Department of Agriculture, has been in the aggregate 1,985,046 sheep, leaving the size of the flock on April 1, 35,671,914 sheep. To ascertain the total yield of wool for the present year there are available only the figures arrived at last year in regard to the average weight of fleece, which will naturally render the estimate an approximate one. Taking, then, as the average weight of fleece 6.30 pounds, the total clip this year will amount to 224,733,058 pounds. Adding to this the estimated amount of pulled wool from skins—40,000,000 pounds—the total product for 1898 will be 264,733,058 pounds. The clip of 1897 was 259,153,251 pounds.

On April 1, 1897, the total number of sheep was 34,784,287, which, compared with the figures for this year, shows an increase of 887,627 sheep for 1898.

ELECTRICAL DEVELOPMENT.

It is figured that in 1884, according to the "Wall Street Journal," the total investment in electrical appliances throughout the United States did not aggregate much over $1,000,000, while to-day the capitalization of all the electrical concerns of the country is fully $1,900,000,000.

The watt is the electrical unit of power proposed by Dr. C. W. SIEMENS and so called after the distinguished scientist and mechanician JAMES WATT. One horse power is very nearly equal to 746 watts.

In 1884 a 50-kilo watt dynamo was considered a large machine, and the price of dynamos was about 20 cents per watt of output. At the present time the largest sized generator built is of nearly 5,000-watt capacity, and dynamos in comparatively small sizes, without switch boards, now cost about 2 cents per watt. It is estimated that about $600,000,000 has been invested in electric-lighting stations and plants in the United States. There are to-day in this country about 14,000 miles of electric railroad, with a nominal capital of about $1,000,000,000, which give employment to some 170,000 men. People can now actually converse at a distance of 1,800 miles, and conversations at a distance of 1,500 miles are common. There are at present over 1,000,000 telephones connected with the country's telephone service, employing a capitalization of about $100,000,000, with 40,000 stations and 900,000 miles of wire. Every day about 17,000 employees make on an average more than 3,000,000 telephone connections.

--- --- ---

URUGUAY.

PROPOSED HARBOR IMPROVEMENTS AT MONTEVIDEO.

In a recent consular report, ALBERT W. SWALM, United States Consul at Montevideo, informs the Government of contemplated improvements in the harbor of that city. This is of importance to contractors in the United States, as bids will be asked from firms in this country as well as from European contractors. The Consul's communication is as follows:

The Provisional Government of Uruguay has presented to the Council of State a scheme for the improvement of the harbor of Montevideo, which is sure to become a law, and which, when accomplished, will be hailed by all having to do with the commerce of this port as of the greatest possible benefit.

An appropriation of $15,400,000 is provided for, to be in 327,659 bonds of $47, or £10, each; interest to be 6 per cent per annum, payable quarterly, either at Montevideo or in some European financial center. As one of the items of the redemption fund, a tax of 2½ per cent is to be levied on all importations. All the new port dues are also set aside for the bonds and interest. A financial commission is to take charge of the matter, and within a year the bonds are to be on the local and general markets.

The scheme adopted is that known as the Kummer-Guerrard plan. The lowest water is to leave 7½ meters (24.52 feet) in the canal. A careening dock 200 meters (656.17 feet) long, and of corresponding width, with 8 meters (26.24 feet) of water on the lowest beams, is also provided for.

The Executive power is authorized to call for tenders for the construction of the work among capable and responsible European and American firms, reserving the right to reject all offers unless a suitable one is made. In case a contract is made an appointment of a technical commission is authorized to superintend the work. Should no general contract be made tenders for partial completion may be accepted. All payments for work done are to be in gold, and on monthly estimates to be made by the technical commission, and certified to in the usual way. When the sum of $15,000,000 shall have been expended, all contracts will be deemed canceled if the work is not completed, and no claim for damage in any way will be considered. I may add that the conditions of the harbor are not very dissimilar to those at Galveston, Texas.

The Government is able to enforce and carry out all engagements that may be entered into. There have been forced changes of government, but no alteration of the monetary basis.

RAILWAY SYSTEMS.

Mr. JUAN JOSÉ CASTRO, of Uruguay, has recently compiled a work on the railway systems of South America, dwelling particularly on the roads constructed and under contract in his own country. From this the following particulars as to the length of the roads and the capital stock of the companies have been obtained:

Name of road.	Length.	Capital.
	Kilometers.	
Central R. R...	321. 65	$13, 575, 000
Central, north extension	293. 34	7, 968, 700
Central, northeast extension............................	124. 30	3, 892, 000
Central, east extension..................	581. 20	14, 965, 000
Eastern..	419. 50	10, 233, 450
Midland...	317. 05	7, 711, 900
Northwestern R. R	178. 80	4, 944, 580
Northern R. R	114. 16	2, 771, 685
San Eugenio Branch	3. 00	73, 000
Western R. R	520. 10	11, 162, 500
Northern Branch	23. 00	671, 375
Interior R. R..	617. 70	15, 000, 000
Total	3, 513. 80	92, 969, 190

A kilometer is equal to 3,280 feet 10 inches, or 0.62137 of a mile, so that the total number of miles of railway in Uruguay is about 2,183.37. The capital stock, valued in the currency of the United States, is $26,458.30 per kilometer, or $42,117.32 per mile.

Compared with Uruguay, on January 1, 1897, the Argentine Republic had 9,041 miles (14,550 kilometers) of railway, representing a capital of $480,321,820, or $53,016.40 per mile. Brazil had 8,403 miles (13,523 kilometers), capitalized at $483,742,610, or $57,566.55 per mile. Chile had 2,490 miles (4,003 kilometers) with $107,030,000 capital, or $42,988 per mile.

The cost of construction per mile in the different countries has been as follows: Uruguay, $36,794; Argentina, $45,809; Brazil, $49,317; Chile (governmental), $43,225; Chile (private), $33,535; Peru, $134,141.

VENEZUELA.

IMPORTS THROUGH THE PORT OF LA GUAIRA DURING THE FIRST SIX MONTHS OF 1898.

Señor Dr. J. M. Rivas Mundaráin, collector of the port of La Guaira, has sent to the Bureau of American Republics, accompanied by a communication praising the services rendered the commercial interests of the continent by the Bulletin, statistical tables showing the imports of foreign merchandise introduced through the port of La Guaira from January 1 to June 30, 1898. The tables give the country of origin, the class of merchandise, number of packages with their gross weight in kilograms, duties collected, together with the 12½ per cent additional duty, and the general résumé of the import trade.

According to the work mentioned, the total imports for the six months were as follows: 427,845 packages, weighing 18,511,867 kilograms gross, with an invoice valuation of 12,315,929.95 bolivars (about $2,000,000), which paid 5,471,207.95 bolivars in duties. The countries represented were the following:

Countries.	Packages.	Declared value.
		Bolivars.
United States	165,837	3,680,800.58
Germany	66,690	2,178,460.52
France	36,298	2,223,397.75
England	119,513	2,127,912.80
Italy	10,683	591,898.75
Spain	18,626	832,004.35
Holland	10,191	676,722.20
Colombia	6	4,733.00

As may be seen, the United States occupies the first rank in the general imports of La Guaira, being followed, as regards quantity, by England, Germany, France, Spain, Italy, Holland, and Colombia; and as regards declared value, by France, Germany, England, Spain, Holland, Italy, and Colombia.

The status of the United States, by articles, was as follows: It had no competitors in the imports of kerosene oil, lard, photographic materials, and fresh fruits. It does not appear in the list of exporters of cotton goods in dress patterns, which are imported from France, Germany, and England; cardboard made up into different articles, which is imported from the same countries; felt and straw hats, which are imported from all the countries, and woolen goods, which are introduced from France, Germany, England, and Italy. The United States occupy the first rank in competition with the other countries named in the import of cordage and tackle, cereals, spices, sweetmeats, fruits in their own juices, hardware, cotton blankets, crackers, hams, wooden furniture, toys, and marble. It takes second place in the importation of baizes in bolts and spreads, preserved foods, cigarettes, tobacco, beer, salt beef, copper in various forms, drugs and medicines, agricultural implements and tools for the arts and trades, butter, paper of all kinds, and cotton cloths. It is third in stationery, railroad materials, household utensils, musical instruments, blank and printed books, cornstarch, samples, and perfumery; fourth in fancy articles, rice (unprepared), breadstuffs, coal and cement, stearine, lace embroideries, muslins, etc., linen and yarn, crockery and glassware, madapolams and trimmings; fifth in pickles and olives, cheese of all kinds, etc.; sixth in olive oil, silk ribbons, cloth, handkerchiefs, etc.; and seventh in imports of cotton undershirts and hose, and wines and liquors of all kinds.

COAL TRADE.

Writing from La Guaira, under date of June 15, Consul GOLD-SCHMIDT says, with reference to the fuel supply in Venezuela, that nearly all the coal consumed is of English origin and is mined in the vicinity of Cardiff, Wales, whence it generally comes in sailing vessels. The close proximity to the United States coal fields and the total absence of their product in this market have led him to investigate the subject, as the consumption of coal in that district is considerable.

The several railways, of which the La Guaira and Caracas and the Great German Railway, from Caracas to Valencia, are the largest, burn Cardiff fuel. All the coal retailed comes from the same source and is sold at a very high figure, evidently because of lack of competition. The retail price of coal by the ton of 2,240 pounds varies from 14 to 16 pesos ($11.20 to $12.80) in quantities from 1 to 20 tons, or even more.

One of the chief reasons why this coal is preferred is that it is put up by the Welsh miners into small bricks or "briquettes," 7 by 8 inches in thickness and about 11 inches long. This makes it very easy to handle on the railways, as the engines employed do not have a tender like the engines in the United States, but carry their fuel upon a small platform attached to the engine, where ordinary coal would roll off. Again, this kind of coal having been in use for some time, the grates in the boilers have been built to suit it, and loose coal might not answer as well.

The coal is pressed by means of tar, and is then brought on board the vessels, sometimes steaming hot, and for this reason frequently loses in weight during transportation by evaporation and drying, which loss is borne by the consignee.

Owing to the strikes in the coal mines of Wales, very little coal has arrived at La Guaira lately; but in spite of this fact no American coal has been landed at this port, except a special kind of hard coal used for the manufacture of gas.

There is an excellent opening there for United States coal, and no doubt the same holds good in many South American countries; but United States exporters must meet the demands of the trade.

The Consul is of the opinion that American coal could be landed in Venezuela and sold much cheaper than British coal and still leave an excellent profit for the shipper, and that any organization that will manufacture coal into bricks of the proper dimensions and send an able representative to introduce the article can find an excellent market. He also suggests that for this purpose a grade of soft coal can be used that is not always marketable in the United States.

Coal is mined in Venezuela close to the port of Barcelona, but the quality seems to be inferior, and it is not sold when other coal can be obtained. The Government of Venezuela collects no import duty from coal.

THE SULPHUR MINES OF CARUPANO.

The following condensed report of the sulphur deposits of Venezuela, which are described as so promising, but which as yet have been scarcely touched by their discoverer, is from an article taken from the "Venezuelan Herald," published at Caracas.

In a direction south-southeast from Carupano, at a distance of about 15 kilometers (9⅓ miles) as the crow flies, there are some immense deposits of sulphur mineral, located on the southern slope of the mountains, 300 meters (984 feet) above sea level. These deposits have remained unexplored until recently, owing to the great difficulty of transporting the mineral to the seashore.

The only method of transportation to the present time has been on the backs of mules and donkeys, which has made the cost of the product too great to permit its exportation to the markets of Europe and America. The present proprietor of the mines has, in a degree, overcome this difficulty by securing from the Venezuelan Government a concession to build a wire tramway from the deposits to one of the many caños (rivers) which flow into the Gulf of Paria, and to navigate those caños by means of lighters and tugboats which will carry the sulphur to vessels loading for foreign ports. The length of the tramway will exceed 10 kilometers (6¼ miles), and the river navigation is more than 30 kilometers (20 miles).

There are five large deposits of sulphur mineral, quite free of any overgrowth, presenting a surface area of about 300,000 square meters (9,113 square yards). Besides these there are a number of smaller deposits covered with overgrowth, which will gradually be cleared while working the larger areas. It has been found that all of the deposits penetrate to a great depth and are practically inexhaustible.

The quality of the mineral has been tested by London experts, five different samples giving an average of 62½ per cent of pure sulphur. A sample sent to a German chemist showed over 83 per cent pure sulphur. The richness of the deposits may be judged when it is known that the best Sicilian minerals never contain more than 40 per cent of pure sulphur and the average is but 25 per cent.

It is estimated that the cost of this sulphur on board ship will not exceed $4 per ton and that the cost laid down in the port of New York will not be in excess of $6 per ton.

THE COAL DEPOSITS OF COLOMBIA AND VENEZUELA.

To a recent number of "The Engineering and Mining Journal," of New York City, Mr. FRANCIS C. NICHOLAS, a mining expert, contributes an article on "The coal trade and lignite deposits of northern South America." As this is a subject of especial interest to several, if not all, of the American Republics, the principal portion of the writer's observations are reproduced here. Mr. NICHOLAS says:

The question of an economical fuel supply for northern South America, a region developing within easy reach of the commercial influence of the United States, has at times been discussed with some interest, and the fact that coal commands a high price there is frequently taken as a basis for the most exaggerated claims in regard to the value of certain lignite deposits found in South America, near the Caribbean Sea. These claims, however, are not based on a careful consideration of all conditions. Coal is expensive there because it is brought a long distance to a market with a present limited demand ; but this demand will increase, as development is natural for the country, and fuel will be required. This field seems an attractive one, even at a much lower calculation of values than the usual extravagant claims.

I have during the past few years examined all the seacoast from the Gulf of Darien to the mouth of the Orinoco River, and a number of times have been called to report on the various deposits found in those regions. These vary from an impure recent lignite to a good-appearing cretaceous brown coal, and are reported from the following places:

1. West of the Orinoco River in the State of Bermudez, Venezuela, a brown coal of apparently good quality.

2. In the regions back of Puerto Cabello, Venezuela, a brown coal, not so compact as that found in the State of Bermudez.

3. Near Maracaibo, in Venezuela, apparently a soft lignite.

4. In the low valleys back of Riohacha, Colombia, abundant deposits of soft lignite.

5. An irregular succession of deposits along the base of the Andes from the country back of Riohacha toward the interior.

6. An extensive bed of cretaceous coal, about one meter thick, near Bogota, in the Colombian Andes.

7. Considerable deposits in the State of Cauca, Colombia; apparently an impure cretaceous coal, accessible only from the Pacific.

8. Along the western side of the Magdalena River, in Colombia, thin strata of an impure lignite.

9. Near Santa Marta, in Colombia; an unimportant deposit of rather high-class lignite.

Bull. No. 3——4

10. On the upper Sinu River, Colombia; lignite, outcroppings apparently not very extensive.

11. Near the Chiriqui Lagoon, in Costa Rica and Panama; reported to be a high-grade coal, but important to the markets of Central, rather than of northern South America.

12. Near Barranquilla, in Colombia, there is an abundant supply of natural gas that can certainly be made available for fuel in that city.

Besides these sources of fuel, there are in the Island of Trinidad, in the State of Bermudez, near Maracaibo, in Venezuela, and in the upper regions of the Magdalena River, in Colombia, extensive asphalt deposits, with indications that petroleum and natural gas will be found in each country.

The term brown coal is intended to mean a more compact variety as distinguished from a very soft lignite that frequently crumbles in the hand and is quite characteristic of many of the South American deposits. From this list one might easily receive the impression that northern South America is unusually well supplied with fuel, but many of the deposits noted are hardly large enough to be of importance economically, and the region described is extensive, with a coast line equal to that of the United States from Portland, Me., to Charleston, S. C.

Of the coal formations of the interior those near Bogota, in Colombia, are the most important. There the coal is won by men working on their hands and knees, at great personal effort. The product is then loaded on flat cars, which are pushed out of the mine by men who creep after them. By such methods the output is not very large, but is sufficient to partially supply the wants of Bogota. The several workings have penetrated perhaps 1,200 feet, and are probably the most extensive coal-mining operations in northern South America.

The lignite deposits near the coast and accessible to commerce, or situated so as to compete in the development of the future coal trade in those countries, are more interesting economically. They are apparently of miocene formation, and had their origin in a series of shallow lagoons and river deposits of that period. They are exposed among miocene shales and lightly cemented sandstones, and are not favorably situated for working. How far they can be developed commercially it seems difficult to predict.

After the movements that finally formed the Andes Mountains in cretaceous times, the northern coast of South America presented a series of deep embayments represented now by the valleys of the Atrato, Magdalena, Rancheria, and Orinoco rivers, and the streams flowing into the Gulf of Maracaibo. These embayments penetrated far to the south, that of the Magdalena River perhaps 1,000 miles. The conditions for rapid sedementations could not have been more favorable, and sand bars, lagoons, and swamps, gradually working seaward, were natural points for plant accumulations, and formed a series of lignite beds generally only a few inches deep, but which at some places are apparently a very considerable accumulation.

At one point back of Riohacha, in Colombia, I opened a seam of very soft lignite, which exposed a deposit apparently about 8 feet thick, though this may have been the result of a thrust against the Andes Mountains, which had apparently disturbed that district and may have crowded several sections of a narrower seam one against the other. In the State of Bermudez, Venezuela, there are extensive deposits of a good quality of brown coal, resembling very much the cretaceous coals of the Andes in its general appearance as well as in the lithological characters of adjacent rocks and formations. The other coal deposits, found near the coast, excepting perhaps some in western Venezuela, are all in shales of soft sandstone, apparently formed out of miocene sediments.

In eastern Venezuela, where the rocks are firmer, a great deal of work has been done, and a short railroad has been constructed from the mines to Guanta, the seaport, where a plant is in operation for combining the coal with asphalt to make a patent fuel similar to the Cardiff blocks. So far the venture has not been a success.

At the mines in western Venezuela some effort has been made, but, though money has been spent in opening the properties, there are no practical results. In Colombia nothing has been done. Back of Riohacha there seems to be a great quantity of light, highly aqueous, free-burning lignite of fair quality. The economic prospects are perhaps better here because of the steamship travel on the Magdalena River, which is constantly increasing and dependent now on a diminishing supply of wood taken from the banks of the stream.

The other deposits of Colombia, except, perhaps, those up the Sinu River, are of scientific interest, but need scarcely be considered economically.

The deposits at Chiriqui I have not examined personally, but samples from there seem to indicate a better grade of coal, perhaps older than the tertiary formations, but this coal belongs to the markets of Central rather than those of South America.

The great quantities of asphalt found in Venezuela and Colombia will probably yield desirable material to mix with the lignite to form briquets, and may be the basis of a future important industry. In all this vast region, however, workable seams of lignite are indicated only at a few distant locations, and whatever may be the results obtained it is quite certain that with the development of these countries there will be an increasing demand for fuel, part of which at least will be supplied from the United States. As to what this demand will be worth it is hard to say. There is all the ocean steamship trade that now carries coal from a distance at the expense of freight capacity; there is the river steamboat trade on the Orinoco and Magdalena rivers, which combined may soon compare favorably with that on the Mississippi; there is an increasing railroad system to be supplied, and the growing demands of the cities of Caracas, La Guaira, Maracaibo, Cartagena, and Barranquilla, though this last will probably be supplied with fuel, in part at least, from its natural-gas well.

At present most of the coal used in northern South America is supplied from Cardiff, but some is purchased in the United States, and the future of the trade is well worth considering.

TRADE BETWEEN GREAT BRITAIN AND THE AMERICAN REPUBLICS, 1898.

An official publication of Great Britain, entitled "Accounts Relating to Trade and Navigation," issued August 4, 1898, gives interesting statistics with reference to imports from and exports to the several American Republics. The valuations are given in the accompanying tables for the first six months of 1898, and for the purpose of comparison the official returns for the same periods in 1897 and 1896 are shown. The values are expressed in pounds sterling, a pound being equal to $4.865 in United States currency.

Imports into Great Britain from the American Republics.

	1898.	1897.	1896.
United States	£68,729,114	£58,525,143	£51,872,954
Haiti and San Domingo	53,444	32,933	51,179
Mexico	147,755	302,739	352,439
Costa Rica	543,163	365,850	325,406
Guatemala	270,692	445,572	392,873
Honduras	4,965	635	3,587
Nicaragua	58,315	123,391	26,515
Salvador	184,397	121,186	136,223
Argentine Republic	4,854,019	3,570,885	4,947,443
Brazil	2,362,705	2,389,170	2,032,603
Chile	1,990,060	1,646,139	1,874,392
Colombia, Republic of	388,801	291,599	232,030
Ecuador	100,579	45,333	88,388
Peru	733,170	684,042	658,372
Uruguay	165,427	192,251	179,619
Venezuela	19,648	30,966	13,350
Total	80,606,254	68,767,834	63,187,372

Exports from Great Britain to the American Republics.

	1898.	1897.	1896.
United States	£7,438,955	£13,788,372	£11,252,506
Haiti and San Domingo	74,921	136,426	131,744
Mexico	822,060	717,137	774,785
Costa Rica	54,195	86,481	93,016
Guatemala	75,831	133,886	213,777
Honduras	10,855	21,537	21,584
Nicaragua	38,183	68,397	66,368
Salvador	41,737	153,240	174,164
Argentine Republic	2,435,871	2,338,248	3,146,416
Brazil	2,774,085	2,443,275	3,330,540
Chile	821,780	1,062,046	1,399,434
Colombia, Republic of	374,301	645,183	678,069
Ecuador	159,236	226,746	187,367
Paraguay	4,522	11,407	2,566
Peru	384,078	362,172	461,522
Uruguay	542,187	412,501	660,314
Venezuela	186,040	348,280	421,424
Total	16,238,837	22,955,434	23,015,596

RUBBER FROM INDIAN CORN.

An important development affecting the rubber trade has been recently made by a company operating the principal glucose plants of the United States, viz, the manufacture of a substitute for india rubber from corn oil. The company controls about 90 per cent of the total output of glucose for domestic and foreign consumption, and from a statement issued on August 1 it appears that its several mills had consumed since August 15, 1897, 20,616,000 bushels of corn, from which were produced 542,100,000 pounds of glucose, 120,572,000 pounds of starch, 98,382,000 pounds of sugar, 2,600,000 pounds of dextrine, and 151,788,000 pounds of residue.

The number of by-products manufactured is 40. Among these is the manufacture of a substitute for rubber. It is not intended to entirely take the place of rubber, but it is to be used as a mixer. The manufacturers are now selling the product at 4½ cents per pound, and the claim is made that rubber goods manufacturers, particularly those who make bicycle tires, are using it extensively. If its durability is proven it is thought that the rubber trade will be revolutionized.

This rubber substitute is made from corn oil by a vulcanizing process, the product closely resembling Para rubber in appearance and quality. It can be used, according to the statement of the company, in the manufacture of all grades of rubber goods, including sheet rubber, bicycle tires, rubber boots, rubber soles, waterproofing, linoleum, etc. The fact that corn oil does not oxidize readily makes this product of great value, since it also is not affected by oxidation, so that the products manufactured from it will always remain pliable and will not crack as those made from other substitutes made from rape-seed oil, linseed oil, etc. A mixture of 50 per cent pure rubber and 50 per cent rubber substitute will, it is claimed, remain soft and pliable and will not crack.

RUBBER, INCREASE IN OUTPUT, AND PRICE.

It is calculated that the world's production of crude rubber for the year ended June 30, 1898, was 94,000,000 pounds. This large quantity, however, is not enough to satisfy the increasing demands of manufacturers, and as a result the high price of $1.06 a pound was recently paid for the best grade of Para rubber.

The price of the crude product has advanced steadily since 1895, the highest price ever paid having been $1.25, and in view of the fact that the year which ended June 30, 1898, showed a falling off in production, as compared with the preceding year, it has been reported in some quarters that the rubber fields of the tropics were giving out, and that a continuous and disastrous advance in price would ensue.

The two principal sources from which the raw product comes are South America and Africa. Brazil last year exported 50,000,000 pounds, according to an accurate estimate from the reports of the customs department. The estimated output from Africa is 40,000,000 pounds. India produced about 1,000,000 pounds, while Central and South America, other than Brazil, are credited with about 3,000,000 pounds. The Brazilian crop returns show that fifty years ago the yearly shipments amounted to only about 1,000,000 pounds, which have increased at the rate of 1,000,000 pounds yearly.

A recent report to the British foreign office from its minister in Brazil estimates that the rubber territory yet untouched in South America amounts to 1,000,000 square miles. The principal difficulty in the exploitation of these tracts lies in limited population, it having been estimated that in one of the immense regions of Brazil, 1,000 by 500 miles, the total number of inhabitants is only 140,000.

The imports into the United States for the year just ended amounted to 45,000,000 pounds, at a value of $25,000,000. It is reported that one steamer within the last six months brought a cargo of crude rubber valued at $1,000,000. In spite of the big addition to the supply the market showed an advance in price from the day of its arrival. The crude product goes into an unlimited number of manufactured articles. All kinds of machinery require an extensive use of it, and the great demand for it in bicycles and other rubber-tired vehicles has opened a new field for it.

MINERAL RESOURCES OF CUBA.

The mineral wealth of the Island of Cuba is varied and abundant. Soon after its discovery, the island became famous not only for the quantity of gold which was found there, but also for the excellent character of that metal, which was deemed superior to that of Haiti. Silver is also found in several localities, and some mines which, up to a few years ago, were worked in the neighborhood of Santa Clara, are said to yield an average of 7½ per cent of pure metal. But the real mineral wealth of the Island of Cuba consists in its almost inexhaustible copper mines, most of them in the eastern part of the island, in the neighborhood of Santiago, where the majority of the ore extracted yielded an average of 60 per cent of pure metal, while in some localities the yielding goes as high as 75 per cent. In 1891 the total number of mining titles issued in the district of Santiago alone was 296, covering an area of 13,727 hectares. Not all these mines, however, were copper. Some of them were iron mines and some of them manganese. Iron is found almost without any trouble through the whole extent of the island from Bahia Honda to Baracoa. The Juragua mines are well known.

TRADE MISCELLANY.

BRAZIL.

Suggestions to manufacturers. The British consul at Para makes the following statement in the " British Trade Journal:" It is the custom to wear dark-colored cloth clothes, either because washing is expensive or because there are rapid changes of temperature, caused by the frequent rain, or perhaps both reasons combine to render it preferable to wear cloth instead of drill or linen, as in other tropical countries. Helmets are not used, but straw and felt hats are universally worn by men. Natives and the lower classes wear the same kind of clothes as the upper classes, and they invariably wear white linen shirts, boots, and shoes. The almost daily rainy weather makes it necessary for everyone to be provided with an umbrella. Iron fittings, oil, and distemper paints are in much use for houses, and, as every house has a long glass corridor, common glass for window panes is in good demand. Tarpaulins and waterproof canvas are in great request on account of the rainy climate. A clean, light waterproof, sewn throughout, might also find a good sale. Coal, machine oils, and paints are in good demand for the increasing number of river steamers.

BOLIVIA.

New Consul in Philadelphia. Mr. WILFRED H. SCHOFF has lately been appointed Bolivian consul in Philadelphia. In a recent published communication the new consul says that merchants and others may now obtain all necessary consular certificates on shipping documents, and that he will be pleased to furnish any information on the commerce and natural wealth of Bolivia.

COSTA RICA.

New consul-general in the United States. Dr. JUAN J. ULLOA G., ex-president of the Republic of Costa Rica, has been appointed as consul-general for Costa Rica in the United States, acting as consul in New York City, where he has his residence and consular office.

ECUADOR.

Rubber Concession in Tungurahua. The following statement is made in the "Boston Commercial Bulletin" in an article on the rubber production in Ecuador. The writer says: "In that country rubber has heretofore been obtained from wild trees, and the destruction of the plants by greedy seekers has played sad havoc with the trade of the coast. The people, however, are beginning to awaken to their opportunities. Evidence of this is to be found in the fact that an effort is being made to obtain from the Government an eight-year concession for the exploitation of rubber in a territory covering from 8 to 10 square leagues in the province of Tungurahua, and the hope is cherished that at some not far distant date the rubber yield will equal the cocoa and coffee crops, up to this time the chief products of the Republic."

HAITI.

Mining Enterprise in Haiti. In the advance sheets of Consular Reports, dated September 14, Minister POWELL writes from Port au Prince the following· "A rich vein of iron ore, almost pure metal, has recently been discovered in the northern section of this Republic. A concession has been obtained from the Government to mine the same, and an American company is being formed for this purpose."

HONDURAS.

Parcels Post Agreement. The statement is made in "The Manufacturer" that an agreement between Great Britain and the Republic of Honduras, for the exchange of postal parcels between the two countries, went into effect on September 1. Honduras is one of the few countries with which the United States has a parcels post service.

MEXICO.

Fireproof Safes. It is only in recent years that fireproof safes have become a necessity in Mexico. Formerly the buildings have been built with such enormous walls, cement floors, and with but little woodwork that only merchants who carried valuable and inflammable goods were obliged to have them. An extensive trade is carried on now with the United States and a profitable business being done in Mexico in this line, largely by Ohio firms who have adapted their goods to the needs of the country. The popular design of safe generally used on plantations by the average merchant and small manufacturers is hardly more than a big iron box, and is called a skeleton safe. It exceeds in capacity the regular fireproof safes, is strongly built and occupies only a small amount of space. The cost for exporting is less than the heavy safes, and it is the only possible safe when mules are used to convey it to its destination. The demand is constantly growing, many new buildings being erected and vaults placed within them in a greatly increased proportion.

Sewing and Knitting Machines. The United States has introduced sewing machines into Mexico with a great deal of success, having furnished as durable a machine of lighter weight than its competitors. In this way the duty has been lowered, and there is also less danger of breakage. Manufacturers have at last realized the necessity of sending agents who understand the language spoken by the great mass of the people, and also to have their illustrated circulars printed in that language. The great success an enterprising firm has met with in introducing their knitting machine demonstrates this fact.

Water-Power Machinery. Almost every large plantation in Mexico has water power, which is being developed in manufacturing the products of the country. New mills are being built continually, and thus far the cotton mills have been put in by English houses, who, until recently, have also furnished the coffee and sugar plants. United States firms are now offering a strong competition.

Manufacture of Boots and Shoes. A new industry recently established in Mexico is the manufacture of leather and machine-made shoes of United States patterns. If such an outfit is properly managed, the hides being cheap and the tanning material "Canaigre" (a root somewhat resembling a beet, which is indigenous to the soil) being plentiful, it should be successful and soon exclude what small importations are now being made.

Flour-Mill Machinery. With the increased use of modern appliances in the grain fields of Mexico, the increase in the number of flour mills is furnishing a good business to a United States concern which has an office in Mexico City and employs an expert to assist in selling and putting up such machinery. Excellent prices are obtained, and as the growing of wheat is increasing so largely, and as the advantages of grinding even imported wheat in Mexico are considerable, a brilliant prospect for the future is assured.

NICARAGUA.

Hardware The following extract is taken from a German official report from Leon-Managua: "Iron and steel goods come chiefly from Germany, whereas in former years English, and especially American, goods predominated. Only a few high-class tools now come from the United States, the principal articles of popular use, such as machetes and cutachas, all coming from Germany."

made in the United States, which is gradually displacing the massive mahogany desks, chairs, and tables so much in use here. Another fine brick edifice, St. Mary's School, which is nearing completion, will probably be equipped with United States school furniture. This will be an innovation here, for all the schools are fitted with the old-fashioned desks and 'forms,' as used in the English schools."

URUGUAY.

Increased Imports from Germany. Consul SWALM reports that Germans have made great inroads on the trade of Uruguay, heretofore almost wholly occupied by English manufacturers. For 1897 the British exports decreased in the following items: Woolen mixtures, 372,000 yards; worsted cloths, 267,000 yards; cotton cloths, 7,700,000 yards. In this last item the English exportations to Uruguay in 1896 were over 14,000,000 yards. The German goods, while cheaper, have also lacked the good qualities of those supplanted in very many lines, but the Germans have studied the market and met its demands, while the English manufacturers are too conservative to make changes. The Germans will necessarily improve the quality of their goods, in order to hold the market captured by them. The consul also says that in cotton goods the United States is making satisfactory advances, the manufacturers of this country having heeded the advice given by their consular officers.

Imports of Agricultural Implements. Writing from Montevideo under date of June 29, 1898, Consul SWALM says the present year will witness the largest importation of United States agricultural machinery yet recorded in Uruguay. Nearly all these machines have won their places on the market by sheer merit, being more serviceable, lighter, less liable to breakages, and better suited for the purposes intended. Intelligent agents have done excellent work in this line, and the machines will do their own talking in the harvest fields of this Republic in 1898. As long as the quality is maintained the exports in these lines from the United States will increase at the expense of those of other foreign make, some of which are rank counterfeits of United States goods.

Profit of the Meat-Extract Business. The thirty-second annual meeting of the English directory of the Liebig Meat Extract Company, Limited, held at Fra Bentos, has been the means of showing the profit that there is in the meat-extract business in Uruguay. For the year's work a balance of £122,376.10 ($595,545) was set aside. An ad interim dividend of 5 per cent was paid at one time, and 15 per cent at the close of the year—20 per cent net, free from all English income tax. After providing £15,000 ($72,997) for sundry expenditures, there was left £7,128 ($34,688) to carry forward into the new account of profit and loss for 1898. In transmitting this report to the Department of State, Consul SWALM says this company owns a large number of cattle and that it is considered one of the most profitable enterprises in South America.

Production of Gold in 1897. Consul SWALM reports to the Department of State that an official statement recently published shows that the amount of auriferous quartz crushed in the Republic in 1897 was 6,400,791 kilograms (14,111,183 pounds), and the yield of gold was 87,336 grams (3,527 ounces), which sold for $38,505.71. (The Uruguayan dollar equals $1.034 in United States currency). The reduction of the quartz is deemed wholly unremunerative, but there are hopes always of making a "big strike," and so the work is kept on. It may be added here that the gold-mining industry is handicapped by an old concession, more or less contested, which calls for a contribution of 25 per cent to the man claiming it. The courts have decided the question both ways, and there is always a lawsuit in sight for any company entering the field.

Exports of Wool. According to a report published in "The Review of the River Plate," the export of wool during the eight months ending May 31, 1898, amounted to 92,872 bales. Of these 18,077 bales were sent to Argentina, 456 to Brazil, and the balance to European countries. A bale of wool is equivalent to 470 kilograms, or 1,036.16 pounds.

Additional Import Tax. Consul SWALM writes from Montevideo July 27, 1898: "Beginning with August 1, an additional permanent tax of 2½ per cent on all imports into Uruguay is again in force. The proceeds are at first to be applied to the payment of outstanding treasury certificates, which are ten months behind, and will afterwards be devoted to the proposed harbor improvements. The tax is of especial significance to Americans interested in the exportation of lumber and refined oil, upon which the duty is already very heavy."

VENEZUELA.

Culture of Tobacco. The closing of the tobacco market in Cuba during the recent war excited great hopes in certain countries the climate and soil of which are propitious for the cultivation of tobacco. These hopes and expectations are so much more natural and rational because of the development of the tobacco trade in Mexico, where it had kept continually increasing, even at a time when Cuba was not prevented by hostilities from sending tobacco to the markets of other countries. Venezuela has been one of the first countries to realize the advantages of its splendid soil and climate in the development of the tobacco industry, and it was incited to it by the example of Mexico. In 1896 the United States imported $28,000 worth of Mexican tobacco, raw and manufactured, but in 1897 it imported $287,000 worth—a tenfold increase. The price also increased from 27 cents a pound, in the New York market, to 40 cents a pound. The "New York Tribune," in stating these facts, also adds that the Venezuelan papers suggest that their readers select proper seed, bring over specialists, choose suitable lands, and there will be no longer any necessity to import Venezuela's supply of tobacco from Cuba.

Salt Revenues for First Quarter of 1898. The Venezuelan Herald reports the salt revenues for the first quarter of the present year to be 370,682 bolivars ($71,541.57). The running expenses of the works amounted to 110,378 bolivars ($21,302.96), and the commissions paid to the bank of Venezuela aggregated 26,030 bolivars ($5,023.86), leaving a net balance of 234,273 bolivars ($45,214.75) to the Government.

BOLETÍN MENSUAL

DE LA

OFICINA DE LAS REPÚBLICAS AMERICANAS,

UNIÓN INTERNACIONAL DE REPÚBLICAS AMERICANAS.

VOL. VI.　　　　SETIEMBRE, 1898.　　　　No. 3.

EL DIRECTOR PROVISIONAL NOMBRADO DE NUEVO.

La Comisión Ejecutiva de la Unión Internacional de Repúblicas Americanas se reunió en el Salón de Recepciones del Departamento de Estado el martes, 27 de setiembre. Estuvieron presentes el Secretario de Estado interino, Señor ADEE, que presidió la reunión, el Señor ANDRADE, Ministro de Venezuela, y el Señor CALVO, Ministro de Costa Rica. El objeto de la reunión fué adoptar una resolución acerca del cargo de Director de la Oficina de las Repúblicas Americanas, en vista del hecho de que el período de Mr. FREDERIC EMORY como Director termina el 1º de octubre.

A moción del Señor ANDRADE, se volvió á nombrar á Mr. EMORY para el puesto de Director hasta el 1º de noviembre. Se cree que esta resolución ha sido adoptada á fin de que el nuevo Secretario de Estado, Mr. HAY, pueda ponerse al corriente de la condición de la Oficina en orden á que se resuelva algo definitivo respecto del cargo de Director.

Mr. EMORY, que es el Jefe de la Oficina de Comercio Extranjero del Departamento de Estado, fué designado para hacerse cargo de la Oficina de las Repúblicas Americanas á la muerte del último Director, Mr. JOSEPH P. SMITH, acaecida el 5 de febrero próximo pasado, y ha continuado desde entonces como Director Provisional, mediante decisiones adoptadas de tiempo en tiempo por la Comisión Ejecutiva.

REPÚBLICA ARGENTINA.

COMERCIO CON ALEMANIA.

El Cónsul MONAGHAN, de Chemnitz, Alemania, informa al Departamento de Estado, con fecha 23 de junio de 1898, que según la opinión de la prensa alemana ninguna de las repúblicas de la América del Sur puede hacer mayores compras que la Argentina, que en 1898 importó materias textiles, crudas y acabadas, por valor de 30,500,000 pesos contra 38,400,000 pesos en 1896. Esta baja se debió á las malas cosechas y también á que la república ha comenzado explotar dicha industria.

Los otros artículos importados por la Argentina fueron los siguientes:

Artículos	1897.		1896.	
	Pesos.	*Dollars.*	*Pesos.*	*Dollars.*
Medias ordinarias..........	823, 322	794, 495. 75	548, 408	529, 213. 70
Pañuelos	533, 986	515, 296. 50	341, 747	329, 785. 85
Algodones	12, 945, 132	12, 492, 441. 40	10, 594, 187	10, 223, 390. 55
Telas de medio hilo........	. 359, 078	348, 520. 25	236, 614	228, 333. 50
Tela para sacos............	5, 058, 161	4, 881, 125. 35	2, 700, 850	2, 606, 320. 25
Lona	644, 134	621, 589. 30	385, 915	372, 408. 00

Las importaciones de la Argentina en 1897 se efectuaron de los siguientes países: Inglaterra, 36,400,000 pesos; Alemania, 11,100,000 pesos; Francia, 11,000,000 pesos; Italia, 10,900,000 pesos; Estados Unidos, 10,100,000 pesos; Bélgica, 8,000,000 pesos. El verdadero comercio de Alemania es mucho mayor, pues por la vía de Amberes salen para la Argentina millares de pesos en mercancías.

EXPORTACIONES EN 1898.

La " Review of the River Plate " publica las siguientes estadísticas referentes al total de las exportaciones de la República

Argentina durante los cinco primeros meses de 1898, comparadas con las del período correspondiente de 1897:

Artículos.	1898.	1897.
Trigo...toneladas..	616, 923	73, 037
Maíz...idem..	75, 638	226, 272
Linaza.......................................idem..	136, 776	155, 423
Lana...pacas..	331, 024	308, 042
Harina.......................................toneladas..	12, 746	23, 306
Cueros.......................................número..	1, 402,599	1, 438, 936
Heno...fardos..	333, 603	359, 127
Carnes heladas...............................número..	1, 025, 237	800, 069
Caballos en pié..............................idem..	56, 387	59, 243
Ovejas en pié................................idem..	292, 948	226, 694

MERCADO DE TRIGO EN 1898.

El Cónsul americano, Mr. MAYER, de Buenos Aires, comunica al Departamento de Estado un interesante informe acerca de las fluctuaciones en el precio del trigo en la República Argentina durante el primer semestre de 1898. De los Informes Consulares para el mes de agosto tomamos lo siguiente:

La historia del mercado de trigo argentino durante la presente estación ha estado completamente llena de acontecimientos inesperados, los más de los cuales han sido poco agradables para los interesados en este comercio.

Al principio de la cosecha el estado de los negocios se presentó mal para aquéllos que prefieren negocios tranquilos á fluctuaciones violentas. La escasez de trigo á fines del año anterior había hecho subir los precios del mercado mucho más alto de lo que los exportadores podían pagar; la misma causa contribuyó á conservar los precios tan altos después de haberse comenzado á recojer la nueva cosecha, pero cuando los molineros habían comprado cuanto necesitaban comenzó una rápida baja en los precios.

Muchos exportadores habían hecho grandes contratos por toneladas del grano, en vista de la gran cantidad que había, pero las lluvias retardaron el transporte y los agricultores retuvieron sus productos. Vino luego una baja en fletes, subió el valor del oro, haciendo independiente la posición de los vendedores. Durante todo el mes de febrero y en marzo el mercado se mantuvo en este estado. En abril el mercado del país tomó un carácter más firme, debido á la escasez del grano, que se hacía cada día más aparente. Al declararse las hostilidades entre los Estados Unidos y España tuvo lugar una de las alzas más fenomenales de que hay noticia en el mercado de trigo. Para el 1º de abril el valor aquí era de $8.50; para el 15 era de $10; para el 22 era de $11, y para el 7 de mayo estaba de $12 50 á $13. Poco después de esta fecha se verificó un cambio en este mercado, que de quieto sufrió una depresión, pasando de la depresión al pánico. Los compradores se retiraron por completo y los precios han vuelto á ser más ó menos los mismos que regían en enero.

Hoy el mercado está casi paralizado por completo; y aunque hay por fuera una gran cantidad de grano, las ofertas son muy pocas. Todavía pueden sufrir las cosechas y el alza en el oro puede causar subida en el valor del papel. Por lo que respecta á embarques me inclino á calcularlos en 1,000,000 de toneladas para el año que termina el 31 de diciembre, incluyendo aquí los embarques del Uruguay. Exceptuando el año pasado, para el 30 de junio se han embarcado siempre las dos terceras partes de la cosecha argentina. Hasta el 18 del presente han salido de la Argentina 638,000 toneladas y cerca de 120,000 toneladas del Uruguay. Puede ser que el alza haya precipitado un poco los embarques, pero su duración no fué tal que produjera mucho efecto. Las existencias en Buenos Aires son grandes.

La langosta ha hecho su aparición temprano en este año y la Provincia de Santa Fé está completamente cubierta de ellas, que al principio produjeron beneficios impidiendo el crecimiento demasiado rápido de la planta; pero esta invasión de langostas quizás sea seguida de otras cuyos resultados pueden ser desastrosos para la cosecha.

EL PUERTO DE BUENOS AIRES.

Según un trabajo preparado por la Argentina para la Exposición de Paris, durante el año de 1897 las estadísticas del movimiento del puerto de Buenos Aires fueron como sigue:

El número total de las entradas y salidas de buques alcanzó á 20,884, con un tonelaje registrado de 7,365,405 toneladas; buques de vapor, 6,689, de 5,895,967 toneladas; buques de vela, 14,195, con 1,469,438 toneladas. El número de buques empleados en el comercio extranjero alcanzó á 2,025, cuyo tonelaje total fué de 2,984,208 toneladas, y el de los buques que hicieron el comercio de cabotaje alcanzó á 18,859, con 4,380,987 toneladas.

El número de buques abanderados argentinos fué de 16,745, cuyo tonelaje total llegó á 2,415,773; de estos 103, con 42,603 toneladas, hicieron el comercio extranjero, y 16,642, con 2,373,160 toneladas, se ocuparon del comercio de cabotaje. El número de buques abanderados argentinos fué de 3,389, cuyo tonelaje alcanzó á 1,392,441 toneladas, siendo 13,356 los buques de vela de un tonelaje de 1,023,322 toneladas.

Las entregas deben comenzar en las dos primeras semanas de enero de 1899 y terminar en diciembre del mismo año, reservando la compañía el derecho de rescindir el contrato en cualquier tiempo, en caso de que la entrega del carbón deje de verificarse por más de un mes ó de que se trate de entregar un artículo de inferior calidad, perdiendo de esta suerte el depósito que garantiza el cumplimiento del contrato, ó sea la suma de 40,000 milreis (cerca de $6,000) que debe depositar el contratista. También estipula el contrato que la falta de cumplimiento de cualquiera de las cláusulas da á la dirección del ferrocarril el derecho de imponer á los contratistas una multa de 2,000 á 20,000 milreis ($300 á $3,000), según la gravedad de la falta.

Los pagos se efectuarán en la tesorería del ferrocarril, en moneda nacional, dentro de los ocho días siguientes á la entrega de cada embarque, computando por tonelada inglesa de 1,050 kilogramos (2,237.66 libras) y calculada la libra esterlina á la rata de cambio del día anterior.

Las proposiciones deben ir acompañadas de certificados de depósito por la suma de 5,000 milreis (cerca de $750) como garantía, que quedará en la tesorería de la compañía del ferrocarril si después de aceptada la proposición el postulante rehusara firmar el contrato respectivo.

El Cónsul General SEEGER, con fecha 21 de agosto de 1898, dice, refiriéndose á esta oportunidad para los comerciantes americanos, que se pueden vender mensualmente á varios consumidores en grande escala de Río Janeiro de 1,000 á 2,000 toneladas de carbón, si es de buena calidad. La principal dificultad que se ha presentado ahora es que la mayor parte del carbón de los Estados Unidos no se puede emplear en los ferrocarriles sin cambiar las parrillas que hoy se usan.

CHILE.

EL MINISTRO MORLA VICUÑA PRESENTA SUS CREDENCIALES AL PRESIDENTE McKINLEY.

El Señor Don CARLOS MORLA VICUÑA, Enviado Extraordinario y Ministro Plenipotenciario ante el Gobierno de los Estados Unidos, llegó á Wáshington el 21 de agosto de 1898, y presentó sus credenciales al Presidente McKinley en la mañana del 26 del mismo mes. La ceremonia se verificó en el salón diplomático de la Casa Blanca, con las formalidades de costumbre.

El Señor Morla Vicuña puso en manos del Presidente la carta de retiro dando por terminado la misión del Señor Gana, y las credenciales que acreditan al nuevo Ministro en el mencionado carácter. El discurso del Señor Morla Vicuña fué altamente expresivo, y en él manifestó que su Gobierno desea estrechar más y más cada día las relaciones entre Chile y los Estados Unidos; dijo que el Gobierno y pueblo chilenos veían en la gran nación americana un modelo digno de imitarse, y habló con admiración del espíritu de tolerancia, de la actividad y energía que caracterizan al pueblo americano, agregando que desde los primeros años de su vida independiente, Chile ha sentido la benéfica influencia de los Estados Unidos en el sentido de conservar la paz ó de restablecerla cuando había sido interrumpida. Citó, como prueba de lo expuesto, el tratado de tregua indefinida celebrado en 1870 en la ciudad de Wáshington, y bajo los auspícios del Gobierno de los Estados Unidos, entre cuatro repúblicas sudamericanas y España, así como el tratado celebrado con la intervención de los representantes de este país en Santiago y en Buenos Aires, y que en 1881 sirvió para que se llegara á una solución pacífica de la cuestión de límites entre Chile y la República Argentina.

El Señor Morla Vicuña hizo referencia especial á las relaciones comerciales entre su país y los Estados Unidos, manifestando que, según la opinión de personas entendidas en el asunto, pueden desarrollarse considerablemente y sin dilación ninguna. Añadió el Señor Ministro que trae instruccíones para hacer todo lo posible á fin de obtener ese desarrollo, y que así lo hará, porque abriga la convicción de que los intereses económicos tienen cada vez mayor preponderancia en las relaciones internacionales.

Terminó el Señor Morla Vicuña su discurso expresando la esperanza de que encontrará en el Gobierno de los Estados Unidos la cooperación necesaria para llevar á cabo el objeto de su misión, y dijo que el Gobierno y pueblo chilenos estaban animados de los sentimientos más sinceros en pro del bienestar de los Estados Unidos y de la felicidad personal del Señor Presidente McKinley.

A tan cordiales palabras, el Presidente McKinley contestó de esta manera:

Señor Ministro: Con mucho gusto recibo de vuestras manos la carta en que se anuncia el retiro de vuestro honorable predecesor, Señor Don Domingo Gana, y las credenciales que os acreditan como Enviado Extraordinario y Ministro Plenipotenciario de la República de Chile ante el Gobierno de los Estados Unidos.

No puedo dudar que llevaréis á cabo el objeto de vuestra misión, que es de hacer más estrechos los lazos de amistad que han existido por largo tiempo entre vuestro país y el nuestro, tanto más que el Gobierno de los Estados Unidos se encuentra animado de los mismos elevados sentimientos, y á ese fin puedo aseguraros que contaréis con mi sincera cooperación y con la de mis asociados en la administración, en fiel cumplimiento de la voluntad del pueblo de los Estados Unidos, que desea vivir en paz, en amistad y en estrecha comunidad de intereses con las naciones vecinas del gran continente occidental.

De manera muy grata habéis hecho referencia á ocasiones en que el espíritu de cordialidad que anima á nuestro pueblo y Gobierno se ha manifestado con relación á los países de la América del Sur en beneficio de la paz y armonía, tanto entre ellos mismos, como entre ellos y las naciones extranjeras. Como ese espíritu cordial reconoce por causa una amistad desinteresada, no puede sino continuar en lo futuro como en lo pasado, siempre que se presente una ocasión oportuna de manifestarse, sin iniciativa ó solicitud de nuestra parte.

El desarrollo de las relaciones comerciales y económicas entre las naciones de este hemisferio, al cual habéis hecho referencia, es asunto de amistoso interés para el Gobierno y pueblo y de los Estados Unidos, cuyas leyes tienden á dar á este último participación en los beneficios que dicho desarrollo debe producir, y sobre bases de una reciprocidad mútua y equitativa, no solamente al tratarse de los países americanos, sino de los del mundo entero.

Al daros, Señor Ministro, una cordial bienvenida á esta tierra que volvéis á visitar como su digno huesped, deseo que vuestras relaciones personales con los empleados del Gobierno y con los habitantes del país, sean tan gratas como fueron las de vuestro digno predecesor, á fin de que podáis conocer los sentimientos de unos y otros en favor de vuestro país y los deseos que los animan respecto de su prosperidad y progreso. Confío en que haréis conocer estos sentimientos á vuestro Gobierno y á vuestros conciudadanos, y os ruego, al mismo tiempo, que impartáis al Señor Presidente de la República los votos personales que hago por su salud y bienestar.

CARRERA DIPLOMÁTICA DEL MINISTRO MORLA VICUÑA.

El Ministro Morla Vicuña comenzó su carrera diplomática en Wáshington en 1870 como Primer Secretario de la Legación chilena, y sirvió en ese carácter durante dos años. En seguida fué enviado á Londres. Más tarde, mientras desempeñaba el mismo cargo en la Legación en Paris, fué designado para encargarse de los asuntos económicos de Chile relacionados con las varias legaciones chilenas en Europa. En 1895 fué nombrado Enviado Extraordinario y Ministro Plenipotenciario á las repúblicas del Uruguay y Paraguay, y en 1896 pasó con el mismo carácter á la República Argentina. A fines de 1896 fué nombrado Ministro de Relaciones Exteriores en el gabinete chileno, y después de desempeñar ese cargo por diez meses, fué enviado como Ministro á los Estados Unidos.

Refiriéndose á su misión en este país, el Señor MORLA VICUÑA manifestó que tiene por objeto principal fomentar las relaciones de amistad entre los dos países y el desarrollo del comercio mutuo. Dijo que existe ahora una línea de vapores entre la costa occidental de la América del Sur y Nueva York, y que espera que el tráfico entre los dos países aumentará mucho en lo futuro. Agregó que los Estados Unidos van á llegar á ser uno de los primeros consumidores del salitre que Chile produce, y expresó deseos de que el pueblo americano conozca las ventajas que acarrea á la agricultura el uso del salitre.

Dijo también el Ministro de Chile que la exportación de salitre de su país á Europa asciende ahora á 1,250,000 toneladas, y que durante varios años ha venido aumentando constantemente de 5 á 7 por ciento, pero que en el año pasado el aumento fué de 10 á 12 por ciento. Opina el Señor MORLA VICUÑA que cuando se comprendan en los Estados Unidos las ventajas que resultan de hacer uso del salitre, la demanda aumentará notablemente. En Chile se usan en gran cantidad muebles, madera y maquinaria de los Estados Unidos, especialmente la maquinaria para agricultura, y últimamente ha comenzado en aquel país un gran comercio en géneros de algodón americanos. En este artículo los Estados Unidos compiten favorablemente, hasta cierto punto, con Inglaterra y Francia; pero el Ministro cree que esta clase de tráfico con los Estados Unidos está todavía en su infancia.

INDUSTRIA DE SALITRE.

La Asociación Salitrera de Propaganda acaba de publicar su informe relativo al primer trimestre de este año.

Contiene este informe un cuadro de la exportación de salitre durante el año de 1897, el cual es como sigue:

	Quintales españoles.		*Quintales españoles.*
Reino Unido ó Continente...	9, 631, 004	Honolulu	72, 723
Puertos directos del Reino		Islas de Mauricio	17, 549
Unido	266, 502	Puerto Elizabeth	42, 767
Alemania..................	6, 020, 064	Africa	39, 600
Suecia	74, 931	Guatemala.................	100
Holanda	1, 029, 613	Brasil.....................	147
Bélgica	1, 029, 428	Argentina	855
Francia	2, 192, 718	Ecuador...	60
Italia	310, 265	Perú	2, 684
Austro-Húngaro	46, 332	Bolivia..................	33
Estados Unidos...	2, 510, 203	Chile	42, 203
Martinica..................	24, 750		
Japón.....................	76, 082	Total....	23, 441, 613
Australia	11, 000		

Refiere á continuación los esfuerzos hechos en vista de la formación de una nueva sociedad para la limitación de la producción salitrera, y menciona la decisión adoptada por la asamblea general el 12 de abril de 1898, de no dar carácter oficial á las medidas que se tomen á fin de alcanzar este objeto tan deseado, y evitar así que se ejerza influencia sobre el mercado con la esperanza de un resultado favorable.

Los informes de varias comisiones de propaganda establecidas en Europa ocupan en dicho trabajo un lugar importante. Los resultados obtenidos justifican los sacrificios hechos en este sentido. La comisión permanente de Londres había recibido hasta el 18 de abril la cantidad de 8,091 libras esterlinas y 12 chelines, de la cual 5,000 libras provenían de la subvención oficial de 20,000 libras esterlinas, acordada por la ley de 7 de setiembre de 1897. Nada se ha omitido para asegurar al salitre nuevos mercados; las conferencias, los concursos con distribución de premios, las fundaciones de campos experimentales, las inserciones en las revistas se multiplican de día en día. El delegado para Francia habla con satisfacción de los resultados favorables de los experimentos hechos en el campo de Park au Prince, cerca de Paris, los cuales han demostrado la superioridad del salitre sobre el sulfato de amoniaco para el cultivo del maíz.

En Alemania, especialmente, es donde se necesita combatir la competencia del sulfato de amoniaco. Al buen éxito que ha obtenido este producto y á los ataques que sus fabricantes dirigen contra el salitre deben atribuirse la diminución de la importación de éste en Alemania, diminución que fué en este primer trimestre de 644,460 quintales españoles, comparado con el período correspondiente del año de 1897. De aquí la necesidad de adoptar definitivamente un método uniforme para mezclar el perclorato con el salitre. El método propuesto por el Dr. GILBERT ha sido objeto de informes favorables y parece que cuenta con la aprobación general.

Según una comunicación del agente de la Comisión, la producción anual de sulfato amoniaco tiene nécesariamente que limitarse á un máximum de 35,000 toneladas, por razón de que el cok fabricado en los hornos construidos para la elaboración de productos derivados no excede de 2,000,000 de toneladas; ahora bien, la cantidad de sulfato de amoniaco que una tonelada de cok produce no es más de 38 ó 40 libras. Por otra parte, no hay que temer que aumente el número de hornos de cok para la producción del sulfato de amoniaco, porque esto implicaría la transformación del material con un gasto enorme de capital, y, además, el cok así obtenido es de calidad muy inferior.

El consumo total de salitre en el mundo entero ha sido durante el primer trimestre, de 11,534,731 de quintales españoles, excediendo en 1,621,065 quintales el consumo durante el período correspondiente del año de 1897. En el cuadro que viene á continuación se dan las cantidades tomadas por los principales países, con indicación del aumento ó la diminución.

	Aumento.	Diminución.
Reino Unido	227,930	
Alemania		644,460
Francia	1,164,490	
Bélgica	214,360	
Holanda	224,020	
Italia	150,420	
Austro-Húngaro	78,890	
Suiza	11,500	
Dinamarca	89,700	
Estados Unidos (costa oriental)	212,082	
Estados Unidos (costa occidental)	65,844	
Países diversos	34,111	
Chile	4,422	

El muelle de Cartagena ha sido ensanchado, aumentando su largo 120 piés, de modo que las embarcaciones pequeñas no puedan impedir que atraquen las de mayor porte. También se han hecho trabajos importantes para rellenar y preparar los terrenos adyacentes al muelle con el objeto de construir vapores para el río Magdalena. Se han colocado rieles y desvíos y fabricado un buen almacén, habiéndose construido ya tres buques de vapor y una lancha.

EMPLEO DE BICICLETAS EN BARRANQUILLA.

El Cónsul SHAW, de Barranquilla, en una comunicación dirijida á una casa exportadora de Nueva York, dice que en aquella ciudad se hace poco uso de las bicicletas y que por consiguiente el comercio en este ramo ha aumentado poco. Esto se debe en gran parte al estado de los caminos, que son arenosos en el verano y pantanosos durante la estación de las lluvias. En Colombia no hay fábricas de bicicletas y las importadas se encuentran en los almacenes de ferretería y de mercancías en general. La mayor parte de las bicicletas importadas llegan de los Estados Unidos, pero un agente vendedor de bicicletas italianas ha estado viajando en el país en solicitud de pedidos.

El cónsul indica que el mejor modo de introducir bicicletas de los Estados Unidos es abrir una agencia bién surtida de mercancías baratas. La agencia debe hacerse cargo de las composiciones, las cuales se ejecutarán en la agencia misma. Las bicicletas importadas pagan derecho á razón de 70 centavos por kilógramo. Los comerciantes de Colombia acostumbran dar y recibir largos créditos, de seis, nueve y doce meses.

COSTA RICA.

EXPORTACIONES DURANTE EL PRIMER SEMESTRE DE 1897 Y 1898.

El Director General de Estadísticas de San José, se ha servido enviar á esta oficina un cuadro que demuestra el estado comparativo de las exportaciones habidas por los puertos de la República durante el primer semestre de 1898 é igual período de 1897.

Del trabajo en referencia tomamos los siguientes datos: Las exportaciones verificadas por Puerto Limón en el primer semestre de 1897 alcanzaron á 1,783 bultos con peso de 153,386 kilógramos, contra 2,081 bultos con 184,710 kilógramos en igual período de 1898. Las de Puntarenas fueron 31,849 bultos con peso de 3,564,113 kilógramos en 1897, contra 20,224 bultos pesando 2,761,134 kilógramos en igual período de 1898.

Los reembarques efectuados por Puerto Limón alcanzaron en los primeros seis meses de 1897 á 44 bultos con peso de 1,928 kilógramos, contra 182 bultos de 136,783 kilógramos de peso en 1898; los de Puntarenas fueron 229 bultos con peso de 14,178 kilógramos en 1897, contra 217 bultos pesando 15,751 kilógramos en 1898.

En resumen, el movimiento de exportación de ámbos puertos en los períodos indicados fué como sigue:

	1897.		1898.	
	Bultos.	Kilógramos.	Bultos.	Kilógramos.
PUERTO LIMÓN.				
Exportaciones varias.	1, 783	152, 386	2, 081	184, 710
Café en pergamino............	34, 767	1, 794, 874	105, 891	4, 428, 149
Café limpio......	164, 916	10, 139, 879	181, 029	11, 168, 992
Bananas	955, 106	27, 400, 966	1, 132, 811	34, 414, 609
Reembarques	44	1, 928	182	136, 788
Total	1, 156, 616	34, 491, 033	1, 421, 994	50, 333, 246
PUNTARENAS.				
Exportaciones varias..........	31, 849	3, 564, 113	20, 224	2, 761, 124
Café en pergamino............			428	16, 577
Café limpio........	27, 899	1, 653, 544	31, 465	1, 870, 280
Bananas				
Reembarques	229	14, 178	217	15, 751
Total	59, 977	5, 231, 835	52, 344	4, 663, 732

MEXICO.

PROGRESO EN LAS MANUFACTURAS.

En el solo ramo de manufacturas de algodón, México da pruebas de notables adelantos en el progreso industrial. De fuentes fidedignas se sabe que el país ha duplicado el número de sus telares de algodón durante los últimos años. En 1896 pagaban impuestos al Gobierno 107 fábricas de tejidos de algodón, de las cuales 3 eran telares, 6 eran fábricas de hilar, tejer é imprimir y 6 de imprimir telas. La fuerza motriz de estas fábricas alcanzaba á 13,826 caballos de fuerza, y la maquinaria constaba de 24 máquinas de imprimir, 13,600 telares y 448,156 husos; en ellas se empleaban 20,994 hombres, mujeres y niños y se consumían 53,273,397 libras de algodón en rama. La mitad del algodón empleado era de los Estados Unidos y el resto producto del país. Estas fábricas produjeron en 1896 7,116,547 piezas de algodón y 3,858,829 libras de filástica é hilo grueso.

Aun cuando la industria de la fabricación de telas de algodón en México tiene más de 60 años de establecida, pués el primer establecimiento de su clase se fundó en 1834, no ha sido sino en los últimos años que ha llegado á alcanzar un notable grado de desarrollo. Muchas otras son las empresas que marcan la nueva etapa del progreso industrial de México y que indican un cambio que habrá de producir paz y seguridad al mismo tiempo que dar impulso á la civilización del continente occidental.

La linaza, cuyo cultivo ha disminuido mucho en los Estados Unidos, se cultiva hoy en México no solamente para la extracción de su aceite, sino para la fabricación de telas de lino, industria que se explota con gran cuidado é interés en Cuernavaca y en San Luis Potosí, así como el yute, el cañamo y el algodón en Orizaba y Guadalajara, siendo ésta una industria que proteje decididamente la tarifa mexicana.

La mejor linaza mexicana posée el lustre y el aspecto sedoso característico de la irlandesa y crece en los alrededores de Cuernavaca. En esta ciudad hay un gran telar para lino, cuyo producto diario es de 2,500 metros. La potencia motriz empleada son el vapor y el agua y el producto es driles, holandas, coties, telas para sábanas, toallas, etc., que se venden en el país. El propietario de este telar tiene otro en la capital de México de igual capacidad productiva. En Orizaba están situados los telares de Río Blanco, que producen telas de hilo y de algodón, y en San Luis de Potosí hay una fábrica de origen inglés que fabrica telas para sábanas, telas blancas de calidad fina, driles finos, cuyo producto se vende de 40 centavos á $1.50 por metro. Todos estos productos se venden en la República.

Las telas de hilo hechas en México lo son por operarios del país, lo que demuestra que el artesano mexicano es susceptible de perfeccionarse en su arte; pronto aprenden á manejar la maquinaria y los aparatos americanos y cuando los fabricantes americanos en el ramo de maquinaria para hilar y tejer se resuelvan á introducir sus productos, remplazando los de origen inglés, se verá que el artesano mexicano puede manejar tan bién uno como otro. En 1829 se fabricaban en la República géneros de hilo, cuyo producto alcanzaba á 1,800 kilógramos, habiendo llegado en 1896 á 47,000 kilógramos.

LEY DE PROPIEDAD LITERARIA.

El Cónsul General, Mr. BARLOW, ha enviado al Departamento de Estado el siguiente extracto de la Ley de Propiedad Literaria vigente en México:

La Ley de Propiedad Literaria de México determina que, para los efectos legales, no habrá distinción entre los mexicanos y los extranjeros, siempre que las obras protegidas se publiquen en México. El autor goza por vida del derecho de propiedad, que á su muerte pasa á sus herederos, siendo éste un derecho de que se puede disponer como de cualquiera otra propiedad que se poséa. Dicho derecho caduca por prescripción á los 10 años.

La ley concede al autor el derecho de publicar traducciones de sus trabajos, pero en este caso debe declarar si reserva su derecho para uno ó para varios idiomas. Se concede este derecho por 10 años á los autores que no residen en México y que publican sus obras en el extranjero.

Para adquirir el derecho de propiedad, el autor, traductor ó editor debe hacer una solicitud, personalmente ó por medio de un representante, al Departamento de Instrucción Pública, consignando que reserva sus derechos y acompañando dos ejemplares de la obra.

Todos los autores, traductores y editores deben poner sus nombres, la fecha de publicación y el anuncio de sus derechos de propiedad literaria, en un lugar conspícuo de la obra.

Si se desea obtener derecho de propiedad sobre alguna obra de música, un grabado, litografía ú otras semejantes, también se deben consignar dos ejemplares de la obra. Si es de arquitectura, pintura ó escultura, debe enviarse una muestra del dibujo ó plano, dando las dimensiones y todos los otros detalles que caracterizan el original.

El autor extranjero que no resida en México debe enviar un poder otorgado ante un notario público y certificado por un cónsul mexicano. A su vez la certificación del cónsul será legalizada por el Departamento de Estado de México, protocolizada y debidamente traducida. Los derechos que se pagan por esto son 25 pesos y 25 pesos más por obtener el derecho de propiedad, incluyendo el valor de las estampillas federales que han de inutilizarse en el documento que se presente al Departamento de Instrucción Pública.

PORVENIR AGRÍCOLA.

Nunca en la historia de México, dice el redactor de "El Comerciante de México," ha habido una época en que el agricultura haya florecido como hoy (agosto, 1898). No sólo en cuanto se refiere al cultivo del café, que muchos creen es la principal ocupación de este país, sino también por lo que se refiere al cultivo del henequén, el algodón, el caucho, la caña de azúcar y un centenar más de otros productos tropicales y semitropicales que se pueden cultivar con éxito en México. La mayor parte de la prosperidad agrícola de la República depende de que los colonos extranjeros han establecido nuevos métodos, nuevas razas de ganado, etc.

En contestación á muchas preguntas acerca del asunto, la misma autoridad dice que los productos agrícolas que dan más resultado en el país son aquellos cuyo cultivo depende de la localidad y de ciertas condiciones. El maíz da tan buen resultado como cualquier otro producto en ciertos lugares, mientras que el café los da mejores en otras localidades. No hay duda de que el caucho tiene un gran porvenir y se recomienda grandemente su cultivo. Cierto es que en las circunstancias ordinarias el cultivador tiene que aguardar cerca de 7 años por el resultado de su siembra de caucho, pero un método reciente recomienda sembrar de 1,000 á 2,000 ó más árboles por acre y luego entresacarlos de año en año, comenzando desde el segundo año. El caucho se extrae de los árboles cortados y de esta manera se puede crear una renta de $50 á $100 moneda mexicana por acre, evitándose así la tardanza en el producto.

El algodón es otro cultivo conveniente, pués hoy hay más de 100 fábricas de telas de algodón en México, cuyo terreno es muy á propósito para el cultivo del algodón, del cual se importa hoy más de la mitad para el consumo de los telares.

En algunos lugares es remunerativo el cultivo de la fruta. La piña de Tehuantepec es una de las más finas que se producen en el mundo y parece que dentro de poco se tratará de importarla en los mercados de los Estados Unidos. Un ciudadano americano ha tenido muy buen éxito en el cultivo de tomates en los alrededores de Tampico, los cuales envía á su país por la frontera.

En otros distritos se puede recomendar como provechosa la cría de ganados y en otros lugares se crían marranos. En realidad no hay límite á las probabilidades de la agricultura en México y todo cuanto se necesita es inteligencia en escojer el cultivo y capital suficiente para su desarrollo.

NICARAGUA.

OPINIÓN DE LA COMISIÓN DEL CANAL.

A continuación aparece un extracto tomado del "New York Tribune" de 9 de setiembre de este año, que será sin duda interesante al comercio de las Repúblicas Americanas:

La Comisión enviada para estudiar el Canal de Nicaragua, de la cual es presidente el Almirante WALKER y miembros el Profesor HAUPT y el General HAINS, no ha presentado todavía su informe. El testimonio de los miembros de dicha Comisión ante el comité especial del Senado, en junio 15–17, ha sido impreso ya é indica claramente el resultado de aquel estudio. En ese trabajo se ocupó la Comisión por cerca de cuatro meses; su personal constaba de cerca de 250 hombres, de los cuales 80 eran ingenieros, acompañados de un geólogo é hidrógrafo competente y de los mejores instrumentos científicos para el objeto, incluyendo 10 aparatos para perforar. Los trabajos continúan todavía y la investigación hecha, que al parecer es la más completa que se ha verificado hasta ahora, ha demostrado que eran exactos los trabajos de Menocal, hasta donde llegaron, así como también muchos de los informes obtenidos posteriormente, y al mismo tiempo ha aclarado muchos puntos tan importantes como interesantes que parecen ser altamente favorables al proyecto.

Exámenes minuciosos han demostrado que la formación de roca, que según se creía haría necesaria la construcción de un grand y costoso tajamar para poder formar un puerto seguro en Brito, no existe. El Almirante WALKER dijo, y los otros miembros convenieron en ello, que se podría construir un puerto ancho y seguro con solo limpiar los mangles que están debajo de la costa de Brito, haciendo allí un pequeño dique. Por lo que se refiere á la variación de la profundidad del lago Nicaragua, que según se decía antes tenía como 15 piés, lo cual era una dificultad importante en los planos examinados hasta ahora, la Comisión no ha hallado pruebas de que la variación sea tan grande y su, peritos creen que el trabajo de regularizar la corriente de agua disminuirá mucho, ya sea usando las aguas del lago Managua ó quizás haciendo uso de una corriente que se pueda dirijir hacia él.

Más importante todavía es la conclusión, que parece ser opinión unánime de la Comisión, que se puede evitar el gran riesgo y el gasto que por lo general produciría la construcción de grandes represas á ambos lados. La opinión parece inclinarse á la construcción de un canal directo al lado occidental, que no esté unido al río; del lado oriental propónese construir una represa en Machuca, con un declive de 25 piés, de modo que la represa de Ochoa venga á quedar á una altura moderada. Las perforaciones hechas han sido causa de que desaparezcan las dudas que había, demostrando que los dos puntos donde se necesita construir las represas importantes tienen un fondo de roca sólida, como también lo tiene el terraplén en San Francisco, aun cuando sea más conveniente evitar esta costosa parte del trabajo haciendo un corte á traves de la línea divisoria. No se ha llegado á conclusiones finales, ni tampoco se han obtenido los informes necesarios acerca de estos puntos, pero la Comisión parece estar perfectamente satisfecha de que el trabajo puede terminarse con menos riesgo y probablemente con menos costo de lo que los presupuestos han indicado.

También se estudió la cuestión de puertos, resultando que del lado del este se pueden construir algunos, economizando así una distancia de dos á tres millas. En Greytown solo pueden salvarse las dificultades construyendo un dique de cerca de tres mil piés y otro más pequeño del lado opuesto, así como también por medio de trabajos constantes de draga como los necesarios para conservar los puertos de Galveston, la boca del Mississippi, y Port Said, pero la Comisión cree que es perfectamente practicable la construcción de puertos en los lugares donde son necesarios. Aun no se ha llegado á un presupuesto definitivo, pero el Profesor HAUPT cree firmemente que el trabajo puede terminarse por $90,000,000, mientras que los otros comisionados calcularon $125,000,000 y $140,000,000 como el máximum. Es interesante hacer notar que todos consideran que cualquiera diferencia en el costo, aun cuando llegase á $200,000,000, es de poca significación si se compara con el enorme valor que tendrá el Canal para este país y su comercio.

PERÚ.

FÁBRICA DE FÓSFOROS "EL SOL."

El Ministro americano en Lima, Mr. DUDLEY, informa á esta Oficina que se ha formado en aquella ciudad una compañía con este nombre, con S. 400,000 de capital, para dedicarse á la fabricación de fósforos de todas clases, explotando las máquinas y privilegios de la importante "Diamond Match Company," de Chicago, la cual ha tomado el 50 por ciento de las acciones de la fábrica de Lima. El presidente de la nueva fábrica es Don José PAYÁN; directores, Don FRANCISCO M. OLIVA y Don PABLO LA ROSA, y gerente, Don JUAN DUANY. Accionistas de esta empresa son: La Sociedad Manufacturera de Tabacos, Señores José PAYÁN, M. B. WELLS, ERNESTO AYULO, LORENZO DELAUDE, José E. CASTAÑÓN, ROBERTO GANOZA, PABLO LA ROSA, OCTAVIO VALENTINI, HERMANN DENKS, JOAQUÍN GODOY y FRANCISCO PÉREZ DE VELASCO.

Hay el propósito de establecer los talleres de esta fábrica en el Callao, pero todavía no se ha adoptado una resolución definitiva.

EXPORTACIONES DEL PERÚ EN 1897, COMPARADAS CON LAS DE 1896.

A continuación aparece un extracto sobre la exportación del Perú en 1897, comparada con la de 1896, publicada en "El Comercio" de Lima con fecha 27 de junio de 1898:

Artículos.	1896.	1897.
	Kilos.	*Kilos.*
Azúcar	71,735,473	105,463,238
Algodón	4,717,697	5,586,394
Borato	1,178,762	11,850,490
Cascarilla	16,489	62,261
Cueros	1,331,689	1,710,206
Lana	2,543,641	3,767,799
Pasta semilla algodón	1,048,456	1,007,527
Arroz	2,803,640	4,221,835
Café	712,919	1,239,744
	Soles.	*Soles.*
Cochinilla	32,070	2,407
Coca y cocaína	1,212,381	1,173,066
Carbón y leña	97,429	93,307
Muebles y ropa	42,998	34,460
Oro amonedado	59,321	104,524
Plata id	1,485,433	1,927,454
Minerales	4,576,511	6,448,567
Animales vivos	168,949	192,955
Ratania	20,673	11,180

Artículos.	1896.	1897.
	Soles.	*Soles.*
Semilla algodón..	69, 184	36, 156
Tabaco..	378, 439	27, 110
Cacao..	22, 581	32, 125
Cebollas, papas, etc..	173, 394	154, 345
Sal...	90, 141	120, 375
	Litros.	*Litros.*
Alcohol...	331, 020	255, 401
Aguardiente..	98, 302	68, 374
Cerveza..	54, 255	540
Vino...	289, 161	143, 095
Bitter ....docenas.	2, 029	40
Sombreros ....id . .	15, 408	13, 128

DESTINOS.

	Soles.	*Soles.*
Inglaterra..	10, 429, 386	15, 648, 310
Chile..	4, 599, 227	5, 753, 074
Alemania..	2, 231, 898	2, 322, 023
Estados Unidos......................................	1, 608, 900	1, 392, 623
Ecuador...	669, 276	1, 212, 497
Francia..	1, 508, 088	1, 181, 312
Colombia..	468, 536	447, 202
Bolivia..	120, 912	56, 683
Centro América......................................	125, 567	49, 546
Italia	35, 234	38, 964
China	31, 800	32, 660
España..	9, 657	11, 965
Brasil	2, 985	9, 010
Bélgica..		8, 786
Méjico..	9, 451	2, 871
Portugal...		500
Argentina		421
Iquitos..		2, 856, 929
Venezuela	8, 646	
Grecia...	2, 425	
Uruguay...	360	
	21, 862, 334	31, 025, 382

Saldo á favor de 1897, 9,193,047 soles.
En los datos remitidos por la aduana de Iquitos, no se expresan los países consumidores de los productos exportados.

SANTO DOMINGO.

SU DESARROLLO.

El Cónsul de Bélgica en Santo Domingo participa á su gobierno, en un informe reciente, que el comercio de la República en 1896–97 alcanzó á $4,535,380, moneda americana, de los cuales $1,824,375 representan las importaciones y $2,709,805 las exportaciones. Las entradas de aduana arrojaron $165,410 en exceso del año anterior. El cuarenta y cinco por ciento del total de las importaciones correspondió á los Estados Unidos.

Los principales artículos de exportación fueron azúcar, 86,866,239 libras; tabaco, 6,332,148 libras; cacao, 4,308,823 libras; café, 2,437,400 libras; dividivi, 1,304,929 libras; miel de azúcar, 1,777,119 galones; caoba, 264,254 piés; 184,851 piés de espino y cedro, y 14,710 toneladas de guayacán, campeche, etc.

También informa el cónsul que por razón de los métodos modernos que se emplean en la agricultura, ésta se ha desarrollado notablemente en los últimos años. Se hace muy notable el adelanto en el empléo de instrumentos de agricultura y aumenta de año en año el área de cultivo. Estos adelantos se deben en gran parte al establecimiento de líneas de ferrocarril.

ESTADOS UNIDOS.

CLASIFICACIÓN DE CUEROS Y PIELES.

Con fecha 27 de agosto de 1898, el Departamento del Tesoro de los Estados Unidos ha dispuesto, para la clasificación de las pieles y los cueros, un límite de doce libras. Esta clasificación ha sido mal recibida por los importadores y fabricantes de cuero. Dichos gremios de Chicago y Nueva York han nombrado representantes para que defiendan sus intereses ante el Ministro de Hacienda, pidiéndole vuelva á considerar la materia.

El texto de la disposición es como sigue:

DEPARTAMENTO DEL TESORO,
DESPACHO DEL SECRETARIO,
Washington, D. C., 27 de agosto, de 1898.

Á los directores y otros empleados de Aduana:

Con el objeto de dar uniformidad á la práctica establecida en los diferentes puertos para la clasificación de pieles y cueros, según lo dispuesto por la ley de 24 de julio de 1897, se ha ordenado la aplicación de la siguiente tabla de pesos para hacer las clasificaciones respectivas; y clasificar toda piel que llegue al límite del peso ó se acerque á él como pieles de ternero y todas las que pasen de dicho límite como cueros, de la manera siguiente:

Libras.

1º Cueros mojados ó peso de carnicero 12
2º Cueros mojados salados 12
3º Cueros salados secos 7½
4º Cueros secos al sol 5

W. B. HOWELL,
Sub-Secretario.

ACUÑACIÓN DE MONEDA Y PAPEL MONEDA EN CIRCULACIÓN.

El informe del Director de la Moneda, correspondiente al mes de agosto, y publicado el 1° de setiembre de 1898, demuestra que la cantidad total acuñada en aquel mes fué como sigue: oro, $9,344,200; plata, $2,350,000; moneda menuda, $163,786; total, $11,857,986.

El informe del Inspector de la Moneda, publicado en la misma fecha, y que abraza el mismo período, demuestra que la cantidad total de billetes de banco era el 1° de setiembre de $227,178,615, lo cual indica un aumento en el mes de $481,745 y una diminución en el año de $3,329,909.

La cantidad en circulación basada sobre bonos de los Estados Unidos, era de $196,775,704, lo que muestra un aumento para el mes de $1,083,019 y una diminución para el año de $9,013,022.

La cantidad en circulación garantizada con moneda legal, era de $30,402,911, ó sea un aumento para el mes de $601,273 y una diminución para el año de $5,650,363.

Los depósitos de bonos registrados de los Estados Unidos fueron como sigue: para garantizar los billetes en circulación, $220,496,160, y para garantizar los depósitos de fondos nacionales, $46,860,660.

INGRESOS Y EGRESOS DEL GOBIERNO DURANTE EL MES DE AGOSTO DE 1898.

El cuadro mensual comparativo de ingresos y egresos del Gobierno fué publicado el 1° de setiembre por el Ministerio de Hacienda.

Las entradas totales durante el mes de agosto fueron de $41,782,707.79, y el total de los gastos ascendió á $56,260,717.80. Los ingresos en agosto de 1897 fueron $19,023,614.97, y los gastos, $33,588,047.41.

Las entradas en agosto de 1898 fueron la siguiente: de las aduanas, $16,249,699; renta interna, $24,015,934.08; otras fuentes, $1,517,073.81.

Los gastos se dividieron así: servicio civil y otros, $7,782,314.74; guerra, $25,163,235.94; marina, $6,386,277.49; indios, $766,084.26; pensiones, $13,084,735.14; intereses, $3,078,070.30.

ENTRADAS DE LA RENTA INTERNA DE 1898.

El informe preliminar del Comisionado de la Renta Interna de los Estados Unidos muestra que las entradas provenientes de todas las fuentes, durante el año económico que terminó el 30 de junio de 1898, ascendieron á $170,869,519, ó sea un aumento, comparado con el año económico anterior, de $24,249,925. Las entradas de las diferentes fuentes, durante el año, fueron como sigue: licores, $92,546,899; aumento, $10,538,356; tabaco, $36,230,622; aumento, $5,520,324; bebidas fermentadas, $39,515,421; aumento, $7,043,259; oleomargarina, $1,315,780; aumento, $281,650; queso denominado "filled cheese," $16,518; diminución, $2,473; bancos y banqueros, $1,180; aumento, $1,094; otras fuentes, $1,243,096; aumento, $867,713.

Las cantidades de licores destilados, bebidas fermentadas, tabaco, cigarros y cigarrillos, que pagaron impuestos durante el año, fueron las siguientes: Licores destilados de frutas, 1,411,448 galones; aumento, 265,317 galones; whisky y otros licores destilados de otras sustancias y no de frutas, 78,353,210 galones; aumento, 9,519,979 galones; bebidas fermentadas ó sea cerveza, 37,486,156 barriles; aumento, 3,063,062 barriles; cigarros (número), 4,910,881,541; aumento, 847,712,444; cigarrillos (número), 3,753,539,534, diminución neta de cerca de 400,000,000; tabaco, 288,160,074 libras; aumento, 27,425,262 libras; oleomargarina, 55,388,727 libras; aumento, 12,854,168 libras; "filled cheese," 1,412,923 libras; diminución, 253,214 libras.

Los gastos ocasionados por la recaudación de la renta interna durante el año, ascendieron á cerca de $3,886,262. Los estados que pagaron la mayor cantidad de la renta interna fueron lo siguiente: Illinois, $39,658,686; New York, $21,058,569; Kentucky, $18,228,918; Ohio, $16,436,908; Pennsylvania, $13,846,790; Indiana, $10,022,274.

LA COSECHA DE LANA EN 1898.

Los datos estadísticos que siguen, relativos al número de ovejas que hay en los rebaños de los Estados Unidos y la cosecha de lana en 1898, aparecen en el " Boston Commercial Bulletin:"

El número total de ovejas en el país para el 1° de enero de 1898 fué 37,656,960. Las pérdidas ocurridas, según las calcula el Departamento de

URUGUAY.

MEJORAS DEL PUERTO DE MONTEVIDEO.

En un informe reciente el Cónsul de los Estados Unidos en Montevideo, Mr. ALBERT W. SWALM, participa á su Gobierno que se piensa ejecutar obras de mejora en el puerto de aquella ciudad. Esta es un materia importante para los contratistas de los Estados Unidos, pués se solicitarán proposiciones tanto de compañías de este país como de Europa. El Cónsul dice así en su comunicación :

El Gobierno Provisional del Uruguay ha presentado al Consejo de Estado un proyecto de mejora del puerto de Montevideo. Dicho proyecto probablemente pasará á ser ley, y cuando se haya llevado á cabo será considerado por el comercio de este puerto como un gran beneficio. Se propone votar la suma de $15,400,000 en 327,659 bonos de $47 ó sea £10 cada uno, al interés del 6 por ciento anual, pagadero por trimestre ó bien en Montevideo ó en cualquier centro financiero europeo. Se impondrá un derecho de 2½ por ciento en todas las importaciones para formar así el fondo de redención de la deuda. También se apartan todos los nuevos derechos arancelarios para atendor con ellos á los bonos y sus intereses. Una comisión financiera se hará cargo del asunto y dentro de un año los bonos deben estar colocados en ésta como en otras plazas.

El plan adoptado es él conocido aquí con el nombre de Kummer-Guerrard. El canal á la baja marea tendrá 7½ metros (24.52 piés) y se ejecutará un dique de 200 metros (656.17 piés) de largo y de un ancho correspondiente, con 8 metros (26.24 piés) de agua en las estacas más bajas.

El Poder Ejecutivo queda autorizado para oir proposiciones para la construc- ción del trabajo, presentadas por casas europeas y americanas de responsabilidad, reservándose el derecho de rechazar las proposiciones que no sean convenientes. En caso de hacer un contrato se nombrará una comisión técnica que dirija los tra- bajos, y en el caso de que no se pueda hacer un contrato general pueden aceptarse proposiciones parciales. Los pagos por el trabajo han de hacerse en oro, por presupuestos mensuales, lo cual queda á cargo de la comisión técnica que lo certi- ficará como de costumbre. Cuando se haya gastado la suma de $15,000,000 se considerarán como cancelados todos los contratos, si no está terminada la obra, sin que haya lugar á reclamaciones por daños y perjuicios. Debo añadir que las condiciones del puerto son bastantes semejantes á las del de Galveston, Texas.

SISTEMAS FERROCARRILEROS.

El Señor Don JUAN JOSÉ CASTRO, del Uruguay, ha hecho recientemente un trabajo sobre los sistemas ferrocarrileros de la América del Sur, con relación especial á los que en su país están en explotación ó en vía de construcción. Los informes que siguen, relativos á la extensión de los ferrocarriles y el capital en acciones de las compañías respectivas, han sido tomados de dicha obra:

Nombres de los Ferrocarriles.	Extensión.	Capital.
	Kilómetros.	
Ferrocarril Central	321. 65	$13, 575, 000
Extensión norte del Central..........................	293. 34	7, 968, 700
Extensión nordeste del Central	124. 30	3, 892, 000
Extensión este del Central	581. 20	14, 965, 000
Ferrocarril del Este.....	419. 50	10, 233, 450
Ferrocarril Midland	317. 05	7, 711, 900
Ferrocarril del Noreste	178. 80	4, 944. 580
Ferrocarril del Norte	114. 16	2, 771, 685
Ramal San Eugenio	3. 00	73, 000
Ferrocarril del Oeste	520. 10	11, 162, 500
Ramal del Norte	23. 00	671, 375
Ferrocarril Interior	617. 70	15, 000, 000
Total	3, 513. 80	92, 969, 190

Un kilómetro es igual á 3,280 piés 10 pulgadas, ó sea 162.37 de milla, de suerte que el número total de millas de ferrocarril en el Uruguay alcanza á cerca de 2,183.37. El capital en acciones, calculado en moneda de los Estados Unidos, alcanza á $26,458.30 por kilómetro, ó sea $42,117.32 por milla.

Para el 1 de enero de 1897 el Uruguay, compaɪado con la República Argentina, tenía 9,041 millas (14,550 kilómetros) de ferrocarril, que representan un capital de $480,321,820, ó sea $53,016.40 por milla. El Brasil tenía 8,403 millas (13,523 kilómetros), capitalizados en $483,742,610, ó sea $57,566.55 por milla. Chile tenía 2,490 millas (4,003 kilómetros), con un capital de $107,030,000, ó sea $42,988 por milla.

El costo de construcción por milla en los diferentes países fué como sigue: Uruguay $36,794; Argentina, $45,809; Brasil, $49,317; Chile: del Gobierno, $43,225; de empresas particulares, $33,535; Perú, $134,141.

VENEZUELA.

IMPORTACIONES HECHAS POR EL PUERTO DE LA GUAIRA DURANTE EL PRIMER SEMESTRE DE 1898.

El Doctor J. M. Rivas Mundaráin, Administrador de la Aduana Marítima de La Guaira, se ha servido enviar á la Oficina

las Repúblicas Americanas, acompañado de atenta comunica-
ón en la que hace justicia á los servicios que presta el BOLETÍN
os intereses comerciales del Continente, un cuadro estadístico que
muestra la importación de las mercancías extranjeras introducidas
r el puerto de La Guaira, del 1 de enero al 30 de junio de 1898.
icho cuadro expresa el país de procedencia, la clase de mercan-
ıs, el número de bultos con su peso en kilógramos brutos, el
lor declarado, los derechos arancelarios producidos, el de 12½
r ciento adicional, y el resumen general de este movimiento de
ıportación.

Según el trabajo en referencia, el total general de las impor-
ciones fué en esos seis meses como sigue: 427,845 bultos con
ı peso total de 18,511,867 kilógramos brutos, avaluados, según
ctura, en 12,315,929.95 bolívares (cerca de $2,000,000), que
odujeron derechos totales por la cantidad de 5,471,207.95
lívares. Los países representados son los siguientes:

Paises.	Bultos.	Valor decla-rado.
		Bolívares.
ados Unidos	165,837	3,680,800.58
? mania	66,690	2,178,460.52
ı ncia	36,298	2,223,397.75
? laterra	119,513	2,127,912.80
ıa	10,683	591,898.75
? aña	18,626	832,004.35
I anda	10,191	676,722.20
? ública de Colombia	6	4,733.00

Como se ve, correspondió á los Estados Unidos el primer
ʒar en las importaciones generales de La Guaira; síguenle en
ʒen á cantidad, Inglaterra, Alemania, Francia, España, Italia,
olanda y Colombia, y por lo que se refiere á valor declarado
;uen después de los Estados Unidos, Francia, Alemania,
ʒlaterra, España, Holanda, Italia y Colombia. .

La posición de los Estados Unidos por artículos fué así: No
ʋo competidores en la importación de aceite de kerosene,
ınteca de puerco, materiales de fotografía y frutas frescas. No
arece en la lista de los exportadores de confecciones de algodón,
ıe se introducen de Francia, Alemania é Inglaterra; cartón
anufacturado en formas diversas, que se importan de los mismos
ıíses; sombreros de fieltro y paja, que se importan de todos los
aíses, y telas de lana, que se introducen de Francia, Inglaterra,

Alemania é Italia. En competencia con los otros siete países mencionados, ocuparon los Estados Unidos el primer puesto en las importaciones de cordelería y jarcia, cereales en semilla, especias, dulces y frutas en su jugo, ferretería y quincalla, frazadas de algodón, galletas, jamones, madera en muebles, jugetes y mármol. Tocóle el segundo lugar en las introducciones de bayetas en piezas y cobijas, conservas alimenticias, cigarrillos, tabaco y picadura, cerveza, carnes saladas, cobre en formas diversas, drogas y medicinas, hierro en máquinas y en bruto, herramientas para agricultura y para artes y oficios, mantequilla, papel de todas clases, y telas de algodón. El tercer lugar le correspondió en artículos de escritorio, materiales para ferrocarriles, herramientas para uso doméstico, instrumentos de música, libros blancos é impresos, maicena y muestras y perfumería. Ocupó el cuarto lugar en artículos de fantasía, arroz en grano, cereales, carbón mineral y cimento, estearina, encajes, telas bordadas, muselinas, etc., hilo é hilaza, loza y cristalería, madapolanes y pasamanería; el quinto lugar en encurtidos y aceitunas, quesos de todas clases, etc.; el sexto en aceite de olivas, seda en cintas, telas, pañuelos, etc.; y el séptimo en las importaciones de almillas y medias de algodón y de vinos y licores de todas clases.

COMERCIO DE CARBÓN DE PIEDRA.

El Cónsul americano, Mr. GOLDSCHMIDT, escribe de La Guaira con fecha 15 de junio y dice, refiriéndose al combustible que se usa en Venezuela, que casi todo el carbón que se consume allí es de origen inglés, de las minas que quedan en los alrededores de Cardiff, Gales, de donde se envía por lo general en buques de vela. La proximidad de las minas de carbón de los Estados Unidos y la falta total de sus productos en aquel mercado, le indujeron á investigar la materia, pues el consumo de carbón en aquel distrito consular es de grande importancia.

Los diferentes ferrocarriles de la República, de los cuales el de La Guaira y Caracas y el Gran Ferrocarril Alemán que va de Caracas á Valencia son los más importantes, consumen carbón de Cardiff. Todo el carbón que se vende al detal viene de la misma procedencia y su precio es muy alto, probablemente á causa de la falta de competencia. El precio al detal del carbón, por tonelada

e 2.240 libras, varía de 14 á 16 pesos ($11.20 á $12.80) en can-
dades de 1 á 20 toneladas ó más.

Una de las razones principales porque este carbón es el prefe-
ido es por que los mineros lo preparan en pequeños panes ó
drillos de siete por ocho pulgadas de grueso y cerca de once
ulgadas de largo. Por esta razón se facilita su uso en los ferro-
arriles, pues las máquinas que usan en el país no tienen carbonera
omo las de los Estados Unidos, sino que llevan el combustible
n una pequeña plataforma unida á la máquina, en la cual el car-
ón ordinario no podría sostenerse; por otra parte, como hace
iucho tiempo que se viene usando esta clase de carbón, las parri-
as de las calderas han sido construidas con este objeto y no ser-
irían quizás para el carbón en pedazos.

El carbón se prensa por medio de alquitrán y se le lleva á bordo
e los buques muy caliente, á veces, y por esta razón pierde en el
eso durante la travesía á causa de la evaporación al secarse—pér-
ida que sufre el consignatario.

Por motivo de las huelgas en las minas de carbón en Gales ha
legado á La Guaira muy poco carbón últimamente; y esto no
bstante no se recibe carbón americano en ese puerto, con excepción
le una especie de carbón duro que se usa en la fabricación del gas.

Esta es una oportunidad excelente para introducir carbón de los
Estados Unidos y no es de dudarse que en otros países de Sud
América suceda lo mismo. Los exportadores de los Estados
Unidos deberían satisfacer las necesidades de este comercio.

El cónsul opina que el carbón americano se podría desembarcar
n La Guaira y venderse mucho más barato que el carbón inglés,
lejando todavía una buena ganancia al embarcador; y que cual-
uiera sociedad que fabrique el carbón en panes de las dimensiones
notadas y envíe un representante entendido que introduzca el
rtículo, puede encontrar allí un mercado excelente. También
ndica que para este objeto se puede emplear una especie de carbón
uave que no siempre tiene buena demanda en los Estados Unidos.

En Venezuela, cerca del puerto de Barcelona, hay minas de
arbón cuya calidad parece ser inferior y no tiene venta cuando
ueda conseguirse otra clase de carbón. El gobierno de Vene-
uela no cobra derechos de importación sobre el carbón.

MINAS DE AZUFRE DE CARÚPANO.

Los siguientes datos referentes á las minas de azufre de Venezuela, que según parece son muy ricas, aunque apenas han sido explotadas por el que las descubrió, han sido tomados del "Venezuelan Herald," de Caracas.

Al sudsudeste de Carúpano, como á 15 kilómetros en línea recta, hay unos inmensos depósitos de azufre mineral en la vertiente meridional de las montañas, á 300 metros sobre el nivel del mar. Estos depósitos hasta hace poco no habían sido explorados, á causa de la gran dificultad que había en el transporte del mineral hasta la orilla del mar.

El único medio de transporte empleado hasta ahora ha sido la carga en mulas y burros, lo cual ha aumentado tanto el costo del producto que ha impedido su exportación á los mercados de Europa y América. El dueño actual de las minas ha logrado en cierto modo vencer esta dificultad, obteniéndo del Gobierno de Venezuela una concesión para construir un ferrocarril de cable para el transporte del mineral desde los depósitos á uno de los muchos caños que desaguan en el Golfo de Paria y para hacer la navegación en dichos caños por medio de lanchas y remolcadores que llevarán el azufre hasta los buques que conducirán la carga á puertos extranjeros. La extensión del ferrocarril es de más de 10 kilómetros y la navegación por el río pasa de 30 kilómetros.

Existen cinco grandes depósitos de azufre mineral, libre de toda vegetación, cuya superficie abarca cerca de 300,000 metros cuadrados; además de estos hay un gran número de depósitos más pequeños cubiertos de una vegetación que se irá limpiando á medida que se trabaje en los otros depósitos. Se ha averiguado que todos los depósitos son muy profundos y prácticamente inagotables.

Peritos ingleses han examinado la calidad del mineral, encontrando en cinco muestras distintas, por término medio, 62½ por ciento de azufre puro. Una muestra examinada por un químico alemán dió más de 83 por ciento de azufre puro. Puede juzgarse de la riqueza de los depósitos al saber que los mejores productos de Sicilia no contienen más de 40 por ciento de azufre puro, ó sea 25 por ciento por término medio.

Se calcula que el costo de este azufre, puesto abordo, no pasa de $4 por tonelada y el costo, puesto en el puerto de Nueva York, no pasará de $6 por tonelada.

MINAS DE CARBÓN DE COLOMBIA Y VENEZUELA.

El "Engineering and Mining Journal," de Nueva York, publica un artículo de Mr. Francis C. Nicholas, que es persona entendida en minas, sobre el "Comercio de carbón y depósitos de lignito de los países septentrionales de la América del Sur." Como esta materia es de especial interés para algunas, si no todas, de las repúblicas americanas, se reproducen aquí las principales observaciones del autor.

Mr. Nicholas dice:

La cuestión de proveer de combustible económico la parte septentrional de la América del Sur, región que puede desenvolverse fácilmente dentro del alcance comercial de los Estados, ha sido discutida de cuando en cuando con algún interés; y el hecho de que el carbón obtiene altos precios en aquellos países, sirve de base con frecuencia á las más exajeradas apreciaciones sobre el valor de ciertos depósitos de lignito que se han encontrado en la América del Sur, cerca del mar Caribe. Pero al apreciar el valor de estas minas no se toman en consideración cuidadosa todas las circunstancias existentes, pues el carbón es caro en aquellos países, por cuanto están situados á larga distancia y la actual demanda de aquel artículo es en ellos limitada, pero esta demanda aumentará con el desarrollo natural del país. Estas minas, empero, parecen tener importancia aun bajo cálculos mucho menos extravagantes que los actuales.

Durante los últimos años he examinado toda la costa desde el Golfo de Darién hasta la boca del río Orinoco, y numerosas veces se me han pedido informes sobre los varios depósitos encontrados en aquellas regiones. El carácter de estos depósitos varía entre un lignito reciente, impuro, y un lignito (carbón pardo) cretáceo de buena apariencia, que se encuentran en los siguientes lugares:

1. Al oeste del río Orinoco, en el Estado Bermúdez, Venezuela, un carbón pardo con apariencia de buena calidad.

2. En las regiones situadas más allá de Puerto Cabello, Venezuela, un carbón pardo, no tan compacto como el que se encuentra en el Estado Bermúdez.

3. Cerca de Maracaibo, en Venezuela, aparentemente un lignito blando.

4. En los valles bajos á espaladas de río Hacha, Colombia, depósitos abundantes de lignito blando.

5. Una sucesión irregular de depósitos á lo largo de la base de los Andes, desde las tierras situadas á espaldas de río Hacha, hacia el interior.

6. Un extenso yacimiento de carbón cretáceo, como de un metro de espesor, cerca de Bogotá, en los Andes colombianos.

7. Considerables depósitos en el Estado de Cauca, Colombia, aparentemente de un carbón cretáceo impuro; accesible solamente por el Pacífico.

8. A lo largo del lado occidental del río Magdalena, en Colombia, estratos delgados de un lignito impuro.

9. Cerca de Santa Marta, en Colombia, un depósito poco importante de lignito de clase superior.

10. En la parte superior del río Sinú, en Colombia, hay un yacimiento de lignito cuyos estratos superficiales no parecen muy extensos.

11. Cerca de la laguna Chiriquí, en Costa Rica y Panamá, se dice que hay un carbón de clase superior, pero más importante para los mercados de la América Central que para los del norte de la América del Sur.

12. Cerca de Barranquilla, en Colombia, hay un depósito abundante de gas natural, que sin duda puede utilizarse como combustible en aquella ciudad.

Además de estas fuentes de combustible, en la isla inglesa de Trinidad, en el Estado Bermúdez y cerca de Maracaibo, en Venezuela, y en las regiones superiores del río Magdalena, en Colombia, hay extensos depósitos de asfalto con indicios de depósitos de petróleo y gas natural en ambos países.

El término "carbón pardo" se emplea para significar una variedad del lignito más compacto, que se distingue de uno muy blando que frecuentemente se desmorona en las manos y es característico de muchos de los depósitos de la América del Sur. Por esta lista, pudiera creerse fácilmente que la parte norte de la América del Sur está excepcionalmente bien surtida de combustible, pero muchos de los depósitos mencionados son apenas bastante grandes para tener importancia económica, y la región descrita es extensa, con un litoral que iguala al de los Estados Unidos, desde Portland, Maine, hasta Charleston, en la Carolina del Sur.

De las formaciones de carbón del interior, las que están situadas cerca de Bogotá, Colombia, son las más importantes. Allí el carbón se obtiene por medio del esfuerzo personal de los trabajadores. El producto se carga en carros planos que son sacados de las minas, empujándolos á mano. Por este procedimiento la extracción no es muy grande, pero si lo suficiente para abastecer en parte á Bogotá. Las excavaciones han penetrado tal vez 1,200 piés y son probablemente la explotación de carbón, en mayor escala que hay en el norte de la América del Sur.

Los depósitos del lignito cerca de la costa y accesibles al comercio, ó situados de manera que pueden competir en el desenvolvimiento del futuro comercio en carbón de aquellos países, son más interesantes desde el punto de vista económico. Aparentemente son de formación miocena y tienen su origen en una serie de bajas lagunas y depósitos fluviales de aquel período. Aparecen entre esquistos arcillosos del período mioceno, y piedras areniscas ligeramente cimentadas. Estos depósitos no están bien situados para la explotación y se hace difícil predecir hasta que punto se desenvolverán comercialmente.

Después de las convulsiones que finalmente formaron las montañas de los Andes, en los tiempos cretáceos, la costa norte de la América del Sur presentó

gar a espaldas de río Hacha, en Colombia, dori una veta del lignito

), la cual contenía un depósito como de unos ocho piés de espesor,
haber sido el resultado de una convulsión hacia las montañas de los
cuya consecuencia, tal vez, quedaron agrupadas entre sí varias sec-
una veta más delgada. En el Estado Bermúdez, Venezuela, hay
epósitos de carbón pardo de buena calidad, que se parece mucho á
s cretáceos de los Andes por su aspecto general y por el carácter
e las rocas y formaciones adyacentes. Los otros depósitos de carbón
encontrado cerca de la costa, con excepción tal vez de algunos
la parte occidental de Venezuela, se encuentran en esquistos de
isca blanda, formada aparentemente de sedimentos miocenos.
arte oriental de Venezuela, donde las rocas son más firmes, se han
abo considerables trabajos y se ha construido un corto ferrocarril de
Guanta, puerto de mar, en donde hay una planta en operación para
l carbón con asfalto y hacer un combustible semejante á los bloques
Hasta el presente la empresa no ha obtenido éxito.
echo algunos esfuerzos para la explotación de las minas de la parte
le Venezuela, y, aunque se ha gastado dinero en las obras, no se han
sultados prácticos. En Colombia no se ha hecho nada.
las de río Hacha parece que hay una gran cantidad de lignito de
lad, ligero, muy combustible y acuoso. El prospecto económico es
, á causa del tráfico por vapor en el río Magdalena, tráfico que está
onstantemente y que depende ahora de la madera que se extrae de
lel río, la cual está disminuyendo.
s depósitos de Colombia, con excepción tal vez de los del río Sinú,
rés científico, pero tienen poca importancia desde el punto de vista

ísitos de Chiriquí no los he examinado personalmente, pero algunas
arecen indicar que contienen un carbón de mejor clase, tal vez anterior
ciones terciarias; pero este carbón corresponde á los mercados de la
entral, más bien que á los de la América del Sur.

una creciente demanda de combustible, parte del cual será importado de los Estados Unidos.   Cual sea el valor de ésta demanda es difícil decir al presente. Hay todo el comercio de vapores del océano cuyo carbón es traido desde larga distancia á expensas de la capacidad para la carga; hay el comercio de vapores en los ríos Orinoco y Magdalena, que combinado puede compararse favorablemente con el comercio del Misisipí; hay que surtir un sistema de ferrocarriles de desarrollo creciente; y hay la creciente demanda de las ciudades de Caracas, La Guaira, Maracaibo, Cartagena y Barranquilla, aunque esta última se surtirá, en parte al menos, de su pozo de gas natural.

Al presente, la mayor parte del carbón que se usa en el norte de la América del Sur viene de Cardiff, pero también se importa alguno de los Estados Unidos, y el porvenir de este comercio bien vale la pena de ser considerado.

COMERCIO ENTRE LA GRAN BRETAÑA Y LAS REPÚBLICAS AMERICANAS EN 1898.

Una publicación oficial de la Gran Bretaña titulada " Informes acerca del Comercio y la Navegación," publicada el 4 de agosto de 1898, da informes estadísticos interesantes sobre las importaciones y las exportaciones de las varias repúblicas americanas.   En las tablas siguientes aparece el cómputo de los primeros seis meses de 1898, y por vía de comparación los guarismos oficiales relativos al mismo período en los años de 1897 y 1896.   Los valores están expresados en libras esterlinas, siendo el equivalente de una libra $4.865 en moneda americana.

Importaciones de productos de las Repúblicas Americanas á la Gran Bretaña.

	1898.	1897.	1896.
Estados Unidos	68, 729, 114	58, 525, 143	51,872. 954
Haití y Santo Domingo	53, 444	32,933	51, 179
México	147, 755	302, 739	352,439
Costa Rica	543, 163	365, 850	325, 406
Guatemala	270, 692	445, 572	392, 873
Honduras	4, 965	635	3, 587
Nicaragua	58, 315	123, 391	26, 515
Salvador	184, 397	121, 186	136. 223
República Argentina	4, 854, 019	3, 570, 885	4, 947. 443
Brasil	2, 362, 705	2, 389, 170	2, 032, 603
Chile	1, 990, 060	1, 646, 139	1, 874. 392
República de Colombia	388, 801	291, 599	232. 030
Ecuador	100, 579	45, 333	88, 388
Perú	733, 170	684, 042	658, 372
Uruguay	165, 427	192, 251	179, 619
Venezuela	19, 648	30, 966	13, 350
Total	80, 606, 254	68, 767, 834	63, 187, 372

Exportaciones de la Gran Bretaña para las Repúblicas Americanas.

	1898.	1897.	1896.
Estados Unidos	7,438,955	13,788,372	11,252,506
Haití y Santo Domingo	74,921	136,426	131,744
México	822,060	717,137	774,785
Costa Rica	54,195	86,481	93,016
Guatemala	75,831	133,886	213,777
Honduras	10,855	21,537	21,584
Nicaragua	38,183	68,397	66,368
Salvador	41,737	153,240	174,164
República Argentina	2,435,871	2,338,248	3,146,416
Brasil	2,774,085	2,443,275	3,330,540
Chile	821,780	1,062,046	1,399,434
República de Colombia	374,301	645,183	678,069
Ecuador	159,236	226,746	187,367
Paraguay	4,522	11,407	2,566
Perú	384,078	362,172	461,522
Uruguay	542,187	412,501	660,314
Venezuela	186,040	348,280	421,424
Total	16,238,837	22,955,434	23,015,596

CAUCHO DE MAIZ.

Una compañía que explota las principales fábricas de glucosa de los Estados Unidos ha logrado producir una sustancia que sustituirá al caucho. Dicha sustancia es un producto del aceite del maíz. La compañía dispone de cerca del 90 por ciento del producto total de la glucosa que se consume tanto en este país como en el extranjero, y según datos publicados el 1 de agosto, los diferentes molinos de dicha compañía han consumido 20,616,000 bushels de maís, de los cuales se extrajo 542,100,000 libras de glucosa, 120,572,000 libras de almidón, 98,382,000 libras de azúcar, 2,600,000 libras de dextrina, y 151,788,000 libras de residuo.

El número de los productos secundarios llega á 40, y entre estos se cuenta la fabricación del sustituto del caucho, que no llegará á ocupar enteramente el lugar de éste, sino que se empleará para mezclarlo con él. Los fabricantes del producto lo venden hoy á razón de 4½ centavos por libra y se dice que los fabricantes de efectos de caucho, especialmente los que fabrican llantas para bicicletas, emplean grandes cantidades de dicho producto. Su durabilidad está ya probada y se crée que causará una revolución en el comercio de caucho.

Este sustituto se fabrica del aceite de maíz, por medio de un procedimiento de vulcanización que da un producto muy seme-

jante en apariencia y en calidad al caucho de Pará.   Puede emplearse, según dice la' compañía, en la fabricación de toda clase de
objetos de caucho, entre otros, telas de caucho, llantas para bicicletas, botas de caucho, suelas de caucho, impermeables, linóleo, etc.
Como quiera que el aceite de maíz no se oxida con facilidad,
dicho producto es de gran valor, pues tampoco es afectado por la
oxidación, de modo que los productos que con él se hacen se conservan siempre suaves y elásticos y no se agrietan, como aquellos
en cuya composición entran el aceite de linaza y el de colza.
Una mezcla de 50 por ciento de caucho puro y 50 por ciento del
sustituto, según se dice, se conserva suave y elástica.

AUMENTO DEL PRODUCTO Y DEL PRECIO DEL CAUCHO.

El producto total del mundo en caucho crudo, para el año que
terminó el 30 de junio de 1898, se calculó en 94,000,000 de
libras.   Grande como es esta cantidad no es suficiente, sin
embargo, para satisfacer la demanda de los fabricantes y por consiguiente ha llegado á pagarse hasta la suma de $1.06 por una
libra de caucho de Pará de la mejor calidad.

Desde 1895 el precio del producto crudo ha ido aumentando
constantemente, llegándose á pagar hasta $1.25 por libra.   A
causa de que en el año que terminó el 30 de junio de 1898 la
producción fué menor que la del año precedente, ha corrido la
noticia de que se estaba agotando el caucho en los trópicos, de
lo cual resultaría una alza que se haría continuada y desastrosa
en los precios.

Africa y la América del Sur son las dos fuentes principales de
donde viene el caucho crudo.   Durante el año pasado el Brasil
exportó 50,000,000 de libras de caucho, según cálculos exactos
sacados de los informes del Departamento de Aduanas.   El producto de Africa se calcula en 40,000,000 de libras; la India produce cerca de 1.000.000 de libras, mientras que todos los países de
Centro y Sud América, con excepción del Brasil, dan cerca de
3,000.000 de libras.   La cosecha del Brasil era hace 50 años de cerca
de 1.000,000 de libras, á lo cual alcanzaban sus exportaciones anuales, que han aumentado á razón de 1.000,000 por año.

En un informe reciente, dirijido á la Oficina de Relaciones Extranjeras de Inglaterra por su Ministro en el Brasil, aparece el cálculo de que el terreno productor de caucho que todavía no se ha explotado en la América del Sur cubre una extensión de 1.000,000 de millas cuadradas. La dificultad principal que se presenta en la explotación de este territorio consiste en la escasez de la población, pués se ha calculado que en una de las inmensas regiones del Brasil, 1,000 por 500 millas, el número total de habitantes es 140,000.

Las importaciones hechas á los Estados Unidos durante el año que acaba de terminar alcanzaron á 45,000,000 de libras avaluadas en $25,000,000. Se dice que un vapor en el último semestre trajo un cargamento de caucho bruto avaluado en $1,000,000. No obstante tan grande refuerzo los precios del mercado continuaron subiendo desde el día de la llegada. El caucho en bruto se empléa en un número ilimitado de artículos; se usa en toda clase de maquinaria, y la fabricación de llantas para bicicletas y para otros vehículos de rueda ha aumentado su esfera de utilidad.

COMERCIO MISCELÁNEO.

BRAZIL.

Indicaciones á los Fabricantes. El Cónsul inglés en Pará hace las siguientes observaciones en el "British Trade Journal:" "Aquí se acostumbra á usar ropa de paño oscuro, ya sea porque el lavado es caro ó porque hay cambios rápidos de temperatura producidos por las frecuentes lluvias, ó quizás ambas razones hagan preferible usar ropa da paño en vez de dril ó hilo, como en otros países tropicales. No se usan cascos, sino sombreros de paja y fieltro. Los naturales del país y las clases bajas usan la misma clase de ropa que los de más alta posición, llevando invariablemente camisas de hilo blanco, botas ó zapatos. Las lluvias que son casi diarias, hacen obligatorio el uso de paraguas. Artículos de hierro y pinturas en aceite ó al destemple se emplean mucho en las casas, y como todas tienen largos corredores con vidrieras, el vidrio plano que se emplea para este efecto tiene gran demanda. También la tienen encerados y lona impermeable, á causa de las lluvias; por esta misma razón impermeables, ligeros de peso, pueden tener buena venta. A causa del aumento que hay en la navegación fluvial gozan de buena demanda el carbón, aceite para máquina y pinturas.

BOLIVIA.

Nuevo Cónsul en Filadelfia. Mr. WILFRED H. SCHOFF ha sido nombrado últimamente Cónsul de Bolivia en Filadelfia. En una comunicación recientemente publicada, el Cónsul informa que tanto los comerciantes como cualesquiera otras personas interesadas pueden obtener allí los certificados consulares necesarios en los documentos de embarque, y que tendrá gusto en dar todos los informes que se solicitan sobre el comercio y la riqueza natural de Bolivia.

COSTA RICA.

Nuevo Cónsul-General en los Estados Unidos. El Doctor Don JUAN J. ULLOA, G. ex-Presidente de la República de Costa Rica, ha sido nombrado Cónsul-General de aquella República en los Estados Unidos, y desempeña las funciones de Cónsul en la ciudad de Nueva York, donde tiene establecidas su residencia y su oficina consular.

ECUADOR.

Concesión para la Explotación del Caucho en Tungurahua. Los informes siguientes son de un artículo sobre la producción del caucho en Ecuador, que aparece en el "Boston Commercial Bulletin:" "Hasta ahora se ha obtenido el caucho en aquel país de árboles silvestres, y la destrucción de éstos por los explotadores ha hecho gran daño al comercio de la costa; pero ya la gente comienza á comprender el valor de las ventajas que se le ofrecen, como lo prueba el hecho de que se está haciendo un esfuerzo para conseguir del gobierno una concesión por ocho años para la explotación del caucho en un terreno de 8 á 10 leguas cuadradas, en la Provincia de Tungurahua, abrigándose la esperanza de que dentro de poco tiempo la cosecha del caucho iguale á las de café y cacao, que son hasta hoy los pricipales productos de la República."

HAITÍ.

Empresa Minera en Haití. En los Informes Consulares del 14 de setiembre, el Ministro americano, Mr. POWELL, comunica lo siguiente de Port-au-Prince: "En la parte norte de la República se ha descubierto últimamente un rico filón de mineral de hierro, que contiene el metal casi puro; se ha conseguido del Gobierno una concesión para explotar esa mina, con cuyo objeto se está formando una compañía americana."

HONDURAS.

Convenio sobre Paquetes Postales. El periódico "The Manufacturer" asegura que el convenio entre la Gran Bretaña y la República de Honduras para el cambio de paquetes postales entre los dos países, comenzó á regir el 1º de setiembre. Honduras es uno de los pocos países con los cuales los Estados Unidos tienen establecido el sistema de paquetes postales.

MÉXICO.

Cajas de Hierro á Prueba de Fuego. Solamente en los últimos años las cajas de hierro á prueba de fuego han llegado á ser una necesidad en México. Antiguamente los edificios eran construidos con enormes paredes y pisos de argamasa, y empleaban en ellos tan poca madera, que solamente los comerciantes que poseían objetos valiosos é inflamables se veían obligados á usar dichas cajas. Ahora se hace gran tráfico en estos artículos entre los Estados Unidos y México, y son principalmente algunas casas de Ohio las que se dedican á él, habiendo adaptado sus productos á las necesidades del país. Las cajas de hierro, que generalmente usan los comerciantes y manufactureros en pequeña escala, no son más que simples cajones de hierro, á los que se da el nombre inglés de "skeleton safe". Son más grandes que las cajas de hierro á prueba de fuego, y su construcción es sólida. Ocupan muy poco espacio. Su exportación cuesta menos que la de las cajas de hierro pesadas, y es la única clase posible cuando hay que hacer la transportación por medio de mulas. La demanda va en aumento; muchos edificios están en construcción y es mayor el número de bóvedas que en ellos se colocan.

Máquinas de Coser y de Tejer. Los Estados Unidos han introducido en México con muy buen éxito máquinas de coser, pues las hacen tan durables como las mejores de sus rivales y de menos peso. De esta manera se pagan menos derechos y hay menos peligro de que se rompan. Al fin y al cabo, los fabricantes han comprendido la necesidad de enviar agentes que entiendan el idioma que habla la gran masa del pueblo, y también publican en dicha lengua sus circulares ilustradas. El gran éxito alcanzado por una casa que ha introducido sus máquinas de tejer demuestra la verdad de lo dicho.

Maquinaria Hidráulica. Casi todas las grandes plantaciones de México disponen de agua como fuerza motriz, y se está desarrollando el uso de ésta en las manufacturas del país. Constantemente se levantan nuevas fábricas. Las de tejidos de algodón han sido fundadas hasta hoy por casas inglesas, que también poseían los establecimientos para la preparación de azúcar y café. En la actualidad algunas casas de los Estados Unidos están haciendo fuerte competencia.

Fábrica de Calzado. Una nueva industria recientemente establecida en México es la de cuero y la de calzado hecho por máquina, siguiendo el sistema americano. Bien administradas, estas manufacturas tienen que dar buenos resultados y acabarán en breve tiempo con las pequeñas importaciones que ahora se hacen, porque los cueros de res son baratos y la sustancia que se usa para curtir, llamada "Canaigre," y que es una raíz algo parecida á la remolacha, es indígena del suelo y muy abundante.

Maquinaria para Molinos de Harina. Con el aumento en el uso de sistemas modernos para disponer de los granos en México, se han establecido muchos molinos harineros, y esto proporciona excelente negocio á una casa de los Estados Unidos que tiene una oficina en la ciudad de México y un empleado experimentado para la venta y instalación de dicha maquinaria. Se obtienen excelentes precios, y como la producción de trigo está aumentando notablemente, y las ganancias que se alcanzan moliendo trigo, aun cuando sea importado, son considerables, se ofrece una brillante perspectiva para lo futuro.

NICARAGUA.

Ferretería. El siguiente extracto es tomado de un informe oficial alemán dirigido de León y Managua: "Los artículos de hierro y de acero vienen principalmente de Alemania, mientras que en años anteriores predominaban los efectos ingleses de esta clase y también los americanos. En la actualidad solamente vienen de los Estados Unidos unas pocas herramientas de calidad superior, pero los principales artículos de uso común, tales como machetes y cutachas, vienen todos de Alemania."

PERÚ.

Valor de la Renta de Sal. Las sesiones ordinarias del Congreso del Perú se abrieron el 28 de julio. Según dice el "South American Journal," el Presidente manifestó en su mensaje que el producto del monopolio de sal durante los dos años anteriores, ascendió á 734,000 soles ($306,812), lo cual permitió que se pagara inmediatamente 1,000,000 de soles ($418,000) como primera cantidad para el rescate de las ciudades de Tacna y Arica.

ESTADOS UNIDOS.

Bella Perspectiva en la Agricultura. El periódico "Age of Steel" dice que, según personas entendidas han podido calcularlo, la producción agrícola de los Estados Unidos en este año va á ser enorme. La cantidad de cereales producida ha sido muy grande y la demanda de ellos en el extranjero parece aumentar constantemente. Según informes oficiales, la cosecha de trigo de 1898 ascenderá á cerca de 700,000,000 bushels, y la de maíz será probablemente de 1,900,000,000 bushels. Se calcula que la cosecha de avena en 600,000,000 bushels, la de heno en 60,000,000 toneladas, y la de algodón en 10,000,000 fardos. Estas grandes cantidades dan un idea de la prosperidad nacional. Con el aumento constante del tráfico de exportación y con el desarrollo de la actividad industrial que cada día se hace notar más, los Estados Unidos poseen en sus graneros y almacenes una garantía segura de prosperidad en lo futuro.

URUGUAY.

Aumento en las Importaciones de Alemania. El Cónsul Swalm informa que los alemanes han aumentado mucho sus negocios con el Uruguay, cuyo tráfico estaba antes casi en su totalidad en manos de fabricantes ingleses. En 1897 las exportaciones de Inglaterra para este país disminuyeron de la manera siguiente: mezclillas de lana, 372,000 yardas; tela de estambre, 267,000 yardas; tejidos de algodón, 7,700,000 yardas. La exportación de este último artículo de Inglaterra á Uruguay en 1898 excedió de 14,000,000 yardas. Los géneros alemanes son más baratos, pero carecen de las buenas calidades de los que han venido á sustituir. Los alemanes han estudiado el mercado y satisfacen las necesidades de éste, mientras que los fabricantes ingleses no gustan de hacer cambios. Necesariamente, los alemanes tienen que mejorar la calidad de sus géneros en orden á conservar el tráfico que han obtenido. El Cónsul dice también que en el comercio de géneros de algodón los Estados Unidos progresan satisfactoriamente, porque los fabricantes de este país han seguido los consejos que les han dado los empleados consulares.

Importación de Instrumentos Agrícolas. Con fecha 29 de junio de 1898, el Cónsul Swalm escribe de Montevideo y dice que el año corriente verá la importación más grande en el Uruguay de maquinaria agrícola proveniente

e los Estados Unidos. Todas estas máquinas deben la buena reputación de
ue gozan en el mercado á su propio mérito, pues son más útiles, más ligeras y
nejor acondicionadas que otras, siendo, además, menos pesadas. Agentes de
econocida competencia han prestado muy buenos servicios en la introducción
.e este artículo, y las máquinas se recomendarán por sí mismas en el vasto
ampo agrícola que ofrece la República en 1898. Mientras se conserve la
·uena calidad de dichas máquinas, su exportación de los Estados Unidos
eguirá aumentando, con detrimento de las que fabrican en otros países, y que
io son sino una falsificación del artículo americano.

Ganancias en el Negocio de Extracto de Carne. La reunión trigésima segunda de la Junta Directiva de la
Liebig Meat Extract Company, Limited, que se verificó en
Fray Bentos, ha servido para demostrar las ganancias que se obtienen en el negocio
le extracto de carne en el Uruguay. El trabajo de un año arrojó un balance de
£122,376.10 ($595,545). Un dividendo ad interim de 5 por ciento se pagó de
ina vez, y otro de 15 por ciento al fin del año, dando un total neto de 20 por
iento, libre de los impuestos que en Inglaterra se cobran sobre las rentas particu-
ares. Después de dedicar £15,000 ($72,997) para varios gastos, quedaron
£7,128 ($34,688) para llevarlas á la cuenta de ganancias y pérdidas en el año de
898. Al transmitir este informe al Departamento de Estado, el Cónsul SWALM
lice que esta compañía posee una gran cantidad de ganado, y que es considerada
·omo una de las empresas más lucrativas en la América del Sur.

Producción de Oro en 1897. El Cónsul SWALM avisa al Departamento de Estado que
un informe oficial últimamente publicado, demuestra que la
:antidad de cuarzos auríferos molidos en la República durante el año de 1897,
ué de 6,400,791 kilogramos (14,111,183 libras), y el rendimiento de oro ascen-
lió á 87,336 gramos (3,527 onzas), que se vendieron por $38,505.71. (El peso
lel Uruguay vale $1.034 en moneda de los Estados Unidos.) Se considera
jue la molienda de cuarzos no es operación lucrativa; pero se tiene siempre la
:speranza de obtener una gran ganancia, y por esta razón es que se persiste en
:se trabajo. Conviene manifestar aquí que la explotación de minas de oro tropieza con un gran obstáculo en una antigua concesión, más ó menos disputada,
que impone una contribución de 25 por ciento á favor del supuesto dueño de la
misma. Los tribunales han emitido decisiones diversas acerca de este particular,
y toda compañía que se dedique á la explotación de minas está expuesta á un
litigio.

Exportación de Lana. Según un informe publicado en el periódico denominado
"The Review of the River Plate," la exportación de
lana durante los ochos meses que terminaron el 31 de mayo de 1898, ascendió á
92,872 fardos. De estos, 18,067 fardos fueron enviados á la Argentina, 456 al
Brasil, y el resto á Europa. Un fardo de lana equivale á 470 kilogramos, ó
sean 1,036.16 libras.

Impuestos Adicionales sobre la Importación en el Uruguay. Con fecha 27 de julio de 1898, el Cónsul SWALM escribe
de Montevideo lo siguiente: "A partir del 1° de agosto, se
cobrará otra vez el 2½ por ciento sobre todo lo que se
importe en el Uruguay. Al principio, la cantidad que se recaude se dedicará
al pago de los certificados del Tesoro, que están ya retrasados 10 meses, y más

tarde se empleará para mejoras en los puertos.   Este impuesto tiene gran significación para los comerciantes americanos que se dedican á la exportación de madera y aceite refinado, porque estos artículos pagan ya muy altos derechos.

VENEZUELA.

Cultivo de Tabaco.   El haberse cerrado el mercado de tabaco en Cuba durante la última guerra, hizo concebir grandes esperanzas en ciertos países cuyo clima y suelo son propios para el cultivo de tabaco.   Estas esperanzas son muy naturales y justas en presencia del desarrollo que ha alcanzado en México el tráfico de tabaco, que ha ido en aumento constante aun en la época en que Cuba, debido á la guerra, no podía enviar dicho artículo á los mercados de otros países.   Venezuela ha sido uno de los primeros países en comprender las ventajas que su espléndido suelo y su clima le ofrecen para el desarrollo de la industria de tabaco, y se ha dedicado á ella siguiendo el ejemplo de México. En 1896 los Estados Unidos importaron tabaco mexicano en rama y manufacturado por valor de $28,000, y en 1897 importaron por valor de $287,000, ó sea el décuplo.   El precio también aumentó de 27 centavos la libra, que era en el mercado de Nueva York, á 40 centavos.   El periódico "New York Tribune," al mencionar estos hechos, dice también que los periódicos venezolanos dicen á sus lectores que si escojen la clase de semilla aparente, hacen venir cultivadores expertos, y elijen terrenos adecuados, ya no habrá necesidad de importar tabaco de Cuba.

Renta de Sal en el Primer Trimestre de 1898.   El periódico "The Venezuelan Herald" dice que la renta de sal en el primer trimestre del presente año ascendió á 370,862 bolívares ($71,541.57).   Los gastos ocasionados por las salinas alcanzaron á la suma de 110,378 bolívares ($21,302.96), y las comisiones pagadas al banco de Venezuela representaron un valor total de 26,030 bolívares ($5,023.86), dejando á favor del Gobierno un balance neto de 234,273 bolívares ($45,214.75).

Boletim Mensal

DA

Secretaria das Republicas Americanas,

União Internacional das Republicas Americanas.

Vol. VI.   SETEMBRO de 1898.   No. 3.

NOMEAÇÃO DE NOVO DO DIRECTOR PROVISORIO.

A Commissão Executiva da União Internacional das Republicas Americanas se reuniu no salão de Recepção da Secretaria de Estado no dia quarta-feira, 27 de Setembro. Estiveram presentes o Secretario de Estado interino, Senhor Adee, que presidiu a reunião, o Senhor Andrade, Ministro de Venezuela, e o Senhor Calvo, Ministro de Costa Rica. O objecto da reunião foi adoptar uma resolução acerca do cargo de Director da Secretaria das Republicas Americanas, em vista do facto de que o periodo do Sr. Frederic Emory como Director termina no dia 1º de Outubro.

A moção do Senhor Andrade, se volveu a nomear o Sr. Emory para o posto de Director até o dia 1º de Novembro. Crê-se que esta resolução foi adoptada afim de que o novo Secretario de Estado, o Sr. Hay, possa informar-se da condição da Secretaria para que se resolva alguma cousa definitiva a respeito do cargo de Director. O Sr. Emory, que é o chefe da Repartição de Commercio Estrangeiro da Secretaria de Estado, foi designado para fazer-se cargo da Secretaria das Republicas Americanas á morte do ultimo Director, o Sr. Joseph P. Smith, occorrida no dia 5 de

ara os primeiros cinco mezes de 1898, em comparação com o periodo correspondente de 1897:

	1898.	1897.
Trigo ....toneladas..	616,923	73,037
Milho ....do....	75,638	226,272
Linhaça ....do....	136,776	155,423
Cã..fardos..	331,024	308,042
Farinha ....toneladas..	12,746	23,306
Couros ....num..	1,402,599	1,438,936
Feno..fardos.	333,603	359,127
Carneiros capados gelados ....num..	1,025,237	800,069
Novilhos vivos.............................. ....do..	56,387	59,243
Carneiros vivos ....do...	292,948	226,604

MERCADO DE TRIGO EM 1898.

O Sr. MAYER, Consul dos Estados Unidos em Buenos Aires, communica á Secretaria de Estado um interessante relatorio sobre as fluctuações no preço do trigo na Republica Argentina durante o primeiro semestre de 1898. Dos Relatorios Consulares para o mez de Agosto tomamos o seguinte :

A historia do mercado de trigo argentino durante a presente estação tem sido completamente cheia de acontecimentos inesperados, os mais dos quaes têm sido pouco agradaveis para os interessados neste commercio.

Ao principio da colheita o estado dos negocios se apresentou mal para aquelles que preferem negocios tranquillos a fluctuações violentas. A escassez de trigo em fins do anno anterior tinha feito subir os preços do mercado muito mais altos do que os exportadores podiam pagar ; a mesma causa contribuiu a conservar os preços tão altos depois de haver-se começado a recolher a nova colheita, mas quando os moleiros tinham comprado quanto necessitavam começou uma rapida baixa nos preços.

Muitos exportadores tinham feito grandes contractos por toneladas do grão em vista da grande quantidade que havia, mas as chuvas retardaram o transporte e os agricultores retiveram seus productos. Veio logo uma baixa em fretes, subiu o valor do ouro, fazendo independente a posição dos vendedores. Durante todo o mez de Fevereiro e em Março o mercado se manteve neste estado. Em Abril o mercado do paiz tomou um caracter mais firme, devido á escassez do grão, que se fazia cada dia mais apparente. Ao declararem-se as hostilidades entre os Estados Unidos e a Hespanha teve lugar uma alta no preço do trigo mais phenomenal de que ha noticia no mercado deste producto. No dia 1º de Abril, o valor aqui era de $8.50; no dia 15 era de $10; no dia 22 era de $11, e no dia 7 de Maio estava de $12.50 a $13. Pouco depois desta data se verificou uma mudança neste mercado, que de quieto soffreu uma depressão

passando da depressão ao panico.   Os compradores retiraram-se por completo
e os preços têm volto a serem mais ou menos os mesmos que regiam em Janeiro.

Hoje o mercado está quasi paralysado por completo; e ainda que ha por fora
uma grande quantidade de grão, as offertas são muito poucas.   Todavia podem
soffrer as colheitas e a alta no ouro pode causar subida no valor do papel.
Quanto aos embarques, me inclino a calculal-os em 1,000,000 de toneladas para
o anno que termina no dia 31 de Dezembro, incluindo aqui os embarques do
Uruguay.   Exceptuando o anno passado, para o dia 30 de Junho têm-se embarcado as duas terças partes da colheita argentina.   Até o dia 18 do presente
têm-se embarcado da Republica Argentina 638,000 toneladas e cerca de 120,000
toneladas do Uruguay.   Pode ser que a alta tenha precipitado um pouco os
embarques, mas sua duração não foi tal que produzisse muito effeito.   As
existencias em Buenos Aires são grandes.

Os gafanhotos têm feito sua apparição muito cedo neste anno, e a Provincia
de Santa Fé está completamente cuberta delles, que ao principio produziram
beneficios impedindo o crescimento demasiado rapido da planta; mas esta invasão
de gafanhotos seja seguida de outra cujos resultados podem ser desastrosos para
a colheita.

O PORTO DE BUENOS AIRES.

Segundo um trabalho preparado pela Republica Argentina para
a Exposição de Paris durante o anno de 1897, as estatisticas do
movimento do porto de Buenos Aires foram como se segue:

O numero total das entradas e sahidas de navios alcançou a
20,884, com uma tonelagem registrada de 7,365,405 toneladas ;
vapores, 6,689, de 5,895,997 toneladas; navios de vela, 14,195,
com 1,469,438 toneladas.   O numero de navios empregados no
commercio estrangeiro alcançou a 2,025, cuja tonelagem total foi
de 2,984,208 toneladas, e a dos navios que fizeram o commercio
de cabotagem alcançou a 18,859, com 4,380,987 toneladas.

O numero de navios que levaram a bandeira argentina foi de
16,745, cuja tonelagem total chegou a 2,415,773; destes 103, com
42,603 toneladas, fizeram o commercio estrangeiro, e 16,642, com
2,373,160 toneladas, se occuparam do commercio de cabotagem.
O numero de vapores que levaram a bandeira argentina foi de
3,389, cuja tonelagem alcançou a 1,392,441 toneladas, sendo
13,356 os navios de vela de uma tonelagem de 1,023,322 toneladas.

BRAZIL.

RIQUEZAS DA REPUBLICA.

ı Consul Geral dos Estados Unidos, Mr. Seeger, envia do de Janeiro, em data 3 de Agosto, 1898, um artigo sobre as liçōes economicos do Brazil, feito a seu requerimento por Mr. Lipman, autoridade reconhecida na materia. Mr. Lipman ressa-se como se segue:

Brazil tendo um muito extenso territorio situado nas zonas torrida e temda com grandes planaltos bastante elevados acima do nivel do mar e sendo ado em todos os sentidos e regado por innumeros cursos d'agua, muito dos :s navegaveis, possue todos os productos quer sob o ponto de vista do reino nal, quer sob o ponto de vista do reino vegetal ou mineral.

rico sob o ponto de vista animal; tudo ahi vive quasi que completamente :stado selvagem e não ha prova de que a mão de homen tenha-se feito sentir a melhorar e desenvolver as raças e as especies. O Brazil possue em todas zonas, com quanto muito espalhado o que não deixa de ser uma vantagem, or quantidade de gado do que a Republica Argentina, sendo uma grande parte lle em estado selvagem. A raça cavallar abunda principalmente no sul do :, mas encontra-se também nos estados do centro e do norte typos que são raordinariamente resistentes e que indicão por suas formas a nobreza do sangue ntal dos seus antepassados. A creação das mulas, que fazem quasi todo o iço de tracção animal, está bem desenvolvida e encontra-se nellas bellissimos os de formas e força. O gado suino cria-se em todos os Estados do Brazil e nvolve-se graças á natureza. Rebanhos de ovelhas apascentam ahi em ntidade. No interior do Norte vivem enormes quantidades de cabras que em para alimentação dos sertanejos. Encontra-se em todo o paiz as mais s e saborosas caças em quantidades inesgotaveis.

is aves de mais rica plumagem e mais mavioso canto ornam as suas tensas florestas virgens. Os mares que banham as suas costas de mais de e duzentas leguas de extensão e os innumeros cursos d'agua que serpentinam essa immensa região, são viveiros da mais rica fauna com que a natureza ouve dotar o mundo. Agassiz, por occasião da missão de que fora encarre-o pelo Governo dos Estados Unidos da America do Norte, reconheceu que una maritima e fluvial d'este paiz era incomparavel.

Jenhum paiz o iguala sob o ponto de vista vegetal. Todas as especies item ou podem ser ahi acclimatadas por causa da variedade do seu clima e qualidades das terras.

is madeiras de variadissimas qualidades e applicações industriães não têm ies, nem pela resistencia nem pela belleza; a sua exploração, bem como as résinas que muitas dellas contem e que são de subido valor, está ainda em do embrionario. Todos os fructos se pode colher ahi e dentro os indi-os de exquisito sabor, muito ha que são desconhecidos pelo velho continente.

.O Amazonas e quasi todos seus affluentes e confluentes, o Paraguay e o São Francisco, permittem a facil extracção do caoutchouc e de diversas especies de arvores existentes em tão enorme quantidade nessas florestas que, apezar de não serem cuidadas, parecem inesgotaveis; e do mesmo modo o cacao, as castanhas, etc.

É bastante conhecido pela sua riqueza mineral para que seja necessario estender-me sobre esse assumpto. O ouro, a prata, o mercurio, o ferro, o cobre, o topazio, os rubis, os marmores como os granitos de varias côres e qualidades, as agathas, o manganez, os phosphatos, o petroleo, a graphita, etc., sem contar os seus brilhantes da mais bella agua e os seus incomparaveis onyxs que são os mais bellos conhecidos, jazem em quantidade em toda a extensão d'esta magestosa e bizarra região; mas a exploração mineralogica que foi florescente nos tempos coloniaes quando se limitara aos processos rotineiros da exploração de que se achava quasi a superficie do sólo, não existe, á não ser a que é actualmente feita com resultados por algumas companhias inglesas. A monazite é encontrada em quantidade em diversas regiões. As areias do Frado na Bahia, muito proximo á costa, e de facillimo transporte, contêm 83 por cento de monazite. Outras menos ricas em monazite ou não analysadas são encontradas nos Estados de Minas, Goyaz, Matto-Grosso, Rio de Janeiro, Bahia e São Paulo. A exploração das minas de carvão de pedra está tambem em estado embrionario; segundo a opinião de NATHANIEL PLANT existem no Estado do Rio Grande do Sul minas de carvão igual ao melhor Cardiff.

Salvo a extracção da borracha, do cacao e da castanha que é favorecida por esta prodiga natureza, salvo a industria da canna e a industria do assucar, muito retrograda, salvo a cultura do algodão que póde ser produzido em quasi todo o paiz e que se acha em decadencia, salvo a cultura de fumo, salvo a cultura de cereaes em quantidade insufficiente para as necessidades do paiz, pode-se dizer que a unica cultura que existe é a do café, cuja producção se desenvolveu de tal modo que ja cria difficuldades, que não forão em tempo previstas pelos fazendeiros e principalmente pelos governos. É essa uma das causas da crise por que passa o Brazil.

Pode-se dizer que apenas tem sido feitos até hoje máos ensaios de colonização começados na zona torrida em lugar da temperada, sem a menor inquietação com as devastações que podiam produzir as febres. A riqueza dos differentes Estados é bem conhecida por todo o mundo, mas parece-me que se dever ia proceder com methodo para fazer practicamente a colonisação, isto é, começar na zona torrida pelo Estado de Minas Geraes e na temperada pelo Rio Grande do Sul.

Poder-se-ha talvez objectar-me que o Estado de São Paulo que pela iniciativa de seus habitantes havia já tomado a vanguarda no tempo do Imperio sobrepondo assim todas as provincias do Imperio, poderá ainda conservar a supremacia então adquirida. Infelizmente, para este Estado, todas as suas riquezas se acham accumuladas em uma unica especialidade—a cultura do café. Devia ter previsto o momento em que depois dos exitos obtidos com os ensaios feitos dessa cultura nas differentes possessões europeas na Asia, na Oceania, na America Central e na Africa que os preços baixos, conseguintes ao excessivo augmento

lo de Minas Geraes, ao contrario, e um dos Estados tropicaes, o que
igir de mais sadio, e tendo uma população de mais de quatro milhões
tes, tornar-se-ha seguramente, em futuro proximo, o mais bello florão
:ropical do Brazil. Situado no interior do paiz, ligado ao oceano
das de ferro dos Estados de S. Paulo, Rio de Janeiro e Bahia, gozando
1a delicioso e possuindo uma enorme riqueza mineral, vegetal e animal,
nvolvimento poderá ser muito rapido para collocal-o muito na van-
s outros Estados tropicaes. As culturas proprias ás zonas torrida e
podem ser ahi feitas; desde o caoutchouc do Amazonas, que pode
.roduzido, até o trigo, o milho e todos os outros cereaes, e sem contar
)lantas tuberculosas, muitas das quaes indigenas, e todos os legumes e
n como todas as flores, proprias ás duas zonas, podem ser ahi culti-
roduzidas em abundancia. Existem já algumas plantações de vinha
:rar que, com o tempo e com o desenvolvimento da industria viticola,
nacionães venhão supplantar em parte os vinhos importados.
1isação d'este Estado me parece não só facil, mas tambem indicada,
io só o colono não sente a differença de clima, mas tambem por causa
ctos naturães em estado selvagem, com insignificantes despezas, desde
ibelecido em suas terras, o colono, em certas regiões, antes de haver
essas terras, acharía uma renda quasi immediata, seja pela explo-
suas madeiras ou do caoutchouc do leite da Mangabeira, seja pela
) das plantas tuberculosas ou textis indigenas que ahi existem em
a. A maior parte do Estado se presta á criação; o gado que ahi
1almente poderá ser facilmente decuplado em alguns annos, do mesmo
a raça cavallar, lanigera, etc., sem contar a suina, cuja criação já
1ma industria mineira.
que é um poderoso auxiliar para a criação e para as industrias e que
da para as industrias textis que ahi existem, é limpida e magnifica e
toda a região em todos os sentidos e em abundancia extraordinaria, ora
cascatas que são aproveitadas como productoras de força para indus-
leslisando-se lentamente pelas extensas planaltos que rega.
1o do Rio Grande do Sul está situado na zona temperada e sua popu-

ninas de Cardiff ou de outras que produzem carvão de igual quali-
lade, devendo cumprir as seguintes condições; minado recente-,
nente; crivado tres vezes; não deve dar mais de 4 por cento de
:inza nem conter mais de nove-decimos de 1 por cento de enxofre,
: deve ter uma força calorifica não menor de 8,100 caloricas ao
gramma pelo calorimetro de Thomson; todo o que se averiguará
por meio de analyses e experiencias feitas pela administração da
:strada de ferro e por quemquer que ella designe. Estipula-se, de
nais, que o carvão deve-se prover em grandes peças, não admit-
:indo-se mais de 5 por cento de um tamanho menor de 30 pollegadas cubicas, e devendo-se prover em quantidades a razão de
19,000 toneladas mensalmente, não excedendo em qualquer dia
;oo toneladas, e com a estipulação expressa nos conhecimentos que
1 descarga por dia de trabalho não excederá 250 toneladas.

A entrega deve começar nas duas primeiras semanas de Janei-
o de 1899, e terminar em Dezembro do mesmo anno; e uma sus-
)ensão da entrega por mais de um mez, ou uma tentativa de pro-
/er um artigo de qualidade inferior, dará á companhia o direito
le abrogar o contracto, e tambem fará perder pelo contratador o
leposito que garante a execução do contracto, importando 40,000
nilreis (cerca $6,000). Dispõe-se tambem no contracto que a
alta de cumprir qualquer das condições estipuladas, dá aos
lirectores da estrada de ferro o direito de impôr aos contratadores
1ma pena de 2,000 a 20,000 milreis, segundo a gravidade da falta.

Fará-se pagamento na thesouraria da estrada de ferro, em moeda
1acional, dentro de oito dias depois da entrega de cada embarque,
;endo a tonelada ingleza de 1,015 kilogrammas (2,237.66 libras),
: a libra esterlina as bases de computação.

As propostas devem ser accompanhadas de um certificado de
leposito da somma de 5,000 milreis (cerca $750) como garantia,
1 que será vertida na thesouraria da companhia se, depois de feita
1 proposta, o lançador refusar de firmar o contracto segundo a
mesma.

O Consul-Geral SEEGER, em data de 21 de Agosto de 1898,
referindo a esta opportunidade para os commerciantes americanos,
diz que se poderião prover desde 1,000 até 2,000 toneladas de
carvão mensalmente a varios grandes consumidores em Rio, se se
provesse a propria qualidade. A principal difficuldade até agora

foi que a maior parte do carvão que vinha dos Estados Unidos não se podia usar pelas estradas de ferro sem uma mudança dos grades que se usão ordinariamente.

REPUBLICA DE COLOMBIA.

DESENVOLVIMENTO DAS ESTRADAS DE FERRO.

O Consul MADRIGAL, escrevendo de Cartagena á Repartição do Estado, inclue o relatorio annual da Companhia da Estrada de Ferro Cartagena-Magdalena para o anno de 1897. Esta companhia já comprou sete vapores de rio, com uma deslocação ou capacidade total de 950 toneladas. Estão-se construindo dous outros, com uma capacidade de 600 toneladas. Ella já possuia tres vapores de 700 toneladas, e terá agora, depois de acabados os dous vapores que se estão construindo, uma capacidade de umas 2,250 toneladas, além alguns rebocadores. Já podem-se despachar mercadorias de Cartagena para os armazens da companhia em Honda, o porto, La Dorado, distando umas 600 milhas.

Durante o anno de 1896, tanto o trafico de uma a outra extremidade da linha, como o trafico local, augmentou-se rapidamente, e é para lamentar que este augmento não continuou no anno proximo passado no trafico de uma a outra extremidade da linha como elle continuou no trafico local. A diminuição nos negocios occasionou uma diminuição de $33,226 (moeda de Colombia) nas receitas, a que compensou-se por uma diminuição de $77,569 nas despezas do serviço. As causas desta diminuição no trafico de uma a outra extremidade da linha são devidas quasi exclusivamente á falta de facilidades para o transporte no rio, sendo a frota da "Compañía del Dique" totalmente insufficiente para o cumprimento efficaz do serviço que se lhe exige. No decurso do anno, organizou-se a "Compañía Fluvial de Cartagena," com o fim de operar vapores no Rio Magdalena, e, durante estes ultimos mezes, ella pôz tres vapores no serviço—a Alicia, de 300 toneladas, a Helena, de 300 toneladas, e a Dorotea, de 100 toneladas. A Companhia de Cartagena encarregou-se desta empreza.

Já demonstraram-se as grandes vantagens conseguidas pela linha de Cartagena do serviço melhorado e accelerado fornecido por estes vapores, pelo augmento das exportações durante os primeiros mezes deste anno (1898).

O commercio geral de Colombia augmentou-se durante o anno proximo passado, apesar do estado pouco satisfactorio do mercado do café.

Fez-se uma addição ao caes em Cartagena, dando uma extensão maior de 120 pés, de maneira que os pequenos navios não impedirão o accesso dos grandes ao caes. Fez-se tambem uma obra importante com a preparação do terreno contiguo ao caes, com o fim de construir vapores para o Rio Magdalena. Collocaram-se trilhos e agulhas; edificou-se uma boa loja; e construiram-se tres vapores e um bote de descarga.

USO DAS BICYCLETTAS EM BARRANQUILLA.

Em uma communicação a uma casa de exportadores de New York, o Consul SHAW, de Barranquilla, diz que se usam pouco as bicyclettas naquella cidade; por conseguinte, ha havido pouco augmento no trafico. Isto é devido, em grande parte, ás estradas não macadamizadas, estando as ruas arenosas no tempo secco e decididamente molles na estação chuvosa. Não ha fabricantes de bicyclettas em Colombia, e as importadas vendem-se por quinquilheiros e pelos negociantes geraes. A maior parte das bicyclettas importadas vem dos Estados Unidos, mas um agente por uma bicycletta italiana tem estado viajando recentemente no paiz solicitando mandados.

O Consul suggere que o melhor modo de introduzir as bicyclettas dos Estados Unidos é o abrir uma agencia bem provida de bicyclettas baratas. As reparações deveriam incluir-se, e fazer-se na agencia. O direito aduaneiro para as bicyclettas importadas é de 70 centavos (23 cents) por kilogramma (2.2046 pounds). Os negociantes de Colombia são acostumados a dar e a receber longos creditos—seis, nove e doze mezes. O passatempo favorito dos jovens é o andar a cavallo. Um bom cavallo custa 200 pesos ($66), e póde-se manter por $5 mensalmente.

MEXICO.

O Mexico fornece, nas fabricas de algodão, sem mencionar as outras, clara evidencia de progressos industriaes. Autoridades fidedignissimas dão a aquelle paiz o credito de ter dobrado o numero das suas fabricas de algodão nos ultimos annos.

Em 1896 não menos de 107 fabricas de algodão pagaram impostos ao Governo. Destas, tres eram fabricas de fiação, seis eram fabricas de fiação, de tecidos e de chitas, e seis eram fabricas de chitas. A força motriz destas fabricas era a de 13,826 cavallos, e a sua equipação mechanica incluia 24 machinas de estampar, 13,600 teares e 448,156 fusos. Ellas empregavam 20,994 homens, mulheres e crianças, e consumiram 53,273,397 libras de algodão crú. A metade do algodão consumido veio dos Estados Unidos: o restante era de producção domestica. A producção destas fabricas em 1896 foi de 7,116,547 peças de panno e de 3,858,829 libras de filaça e de fio grosso.

Sem embargo de ter sido estabelecida a industria do algodão em Mexico ha mais de sessenta annos, tendo-se estabelecida a primeira fabrica em 1834, é só nos ultimos annos passados que se conseguiu qualquer gráo notavel de desenvolvimento. A nova era do Mexico industrial se marca por muitas outras emprezas, e é uma mudança feliz nos negocios que promove a paz e a segurança, e uma civilização accelerada no hemispherio occidental.

O linho, cuja cultura ha diminuido muito nos Estados Unidos, se está cultivando no Mexico, nao sómente para o producto de oleo, mas o panno de linho está fabricando em Cuernavaca e San Luis Potosi com tanta diligencia e cuidado quanto o estão a juta, o canhamo e o algodão em Orizaba e Guadalajara, sendo ella uma industria muito bem protegida pela tarifa Mexicana.

O melhor linho Mexicano possue aquella brandura e lustre que caracterizam o linho Irlandez, e cultiva-se perto de Cuernavaca. Ha naquella cidade uma grande fabrica de linho cuja producção diaria é de 2,500 metros. Tanto o vapor como a agua se empregam como força motriz. Fabricam-se riscados, Hollandas, cotins, fazendas para lenções, toalhas, etc., vendendo-se o tudo no paiz.

O mesmo proprietario tem uma fabrica na Cidade de Mexico de capacidade igual de producção.

Ha em Orizaba as fabricas Rio Blanco, que produzem fazendas de linho assim como de algodão, entretanto que ha em San Luis Potosi uma fabrica de origem Ingleza, a qual fabrica fazendas para lenções e pannos brancos de mais finas qualidades, riscados finos, e fazendas para vestidos, vendendo-se os pannos fabricados a 40 centavos até $1.50 por metro.   Vendem-se todos estes tecidos na Republica.

O linho tecido no Mexico é o producto do trabalho dos naturaes do paiz, demonstrando assim que o operario mexicano é susceptivel da melhor instrucção.   Os homens aprendem em breve tempo a manejar as machinas e apparelhos americanos, e quando os fabricantes americanos de machinas de fiação e de tecer se decidirão a introduzirem as suas machinas e a substituirem as inglezas, achar-se-há que o operario adaptivo mexicano é tanto habil com aquellas quanto com estas.

Em 1829 se fabricarão na Republica 1,800 kilogrammas de tecidos de linho, a qual quantidade augmentou-se em 1896 até 47,000 kilogrammas.

ESTRADAS DE FERRO, PROJECTADAS E CONSTRUIDAS.

A construcção de estradas de ferro acha-se num estado de grande actividade por toda a Republica, sendo as mais importantes estradas recentemente construidas e projectadas, as seguintes:

É projectada uma estrada de ferro de Cordova para o porto de Tehuantepec, estando o Engenheiro LOUIS B. CEBALLOS encarregado da empreza.   Uma companhia dos Estados Unidos recebeu uma concessão para construir uma estrada de ferro de Saltillo para Faredon, Trevino, ou qualquer outra ponta na Estrada de Ferro de Monterey para Mexico.   A estrada de ferro projectada de Mazatlan se extenderá até Rosario.   Señor ARTURO DE CIMA, que foi Vice-Consul dos Estados Unidos em Mazatlan, encarregou-se da empreza.   Entre os novos projectos, ha o de uma estrada de ferro de Mazatlan para Villa Union, no Estado de Sinaloa, donde ha grandes fabricas de algodão.   A cidade de Mazatlan e o Estado concorrerão com auxilio pecuniario.   Uma outra linha projectada, que tem uma boa perspectiva de ser construida, é a de Merida para Tuncas, em Yucatan.

LEI DE PROPRIEDADE LITTERARIA.

O Consul-Geral, Sr. BARLOW, remetteu á Secretaria de Estado o seguinte extracto da Lei de Propriedade Litteraria vigente no Mexico:

A Lei de Propriedade Litteraria do Mexico determina que, para os effeitos legaes, não haverá distincção entre os mexicanos e os estrangeiros, sempre que as obras protegidas se publiquem no Mexico. O autor goza por vida do direito de propriedade, que á sua morte passa a seus herdeiros, sendo este um direito de que se pode dispôr como de qualquer outra propriedade que se possua. O dito direito expira por prescripção aos 10 annos.

A lei concede ao autor o direito de publicar traducções de seus trabalhos, mas neste caso deve declarar si reserva seu direito para uma ou para varias linguas. Concede-se este direito por 10 annos aos autores que não residem no Mexico e que publicam suas obras no estrangeiro.

Para adquirir o direito de propriedade, o autor, traductor ou editor deve dirigir-se, pessoalmente ou por meio de um representante, ao Ministerio de Instrucção Publica, consignando que reserva seus direitos e acompanhando dous exemplares da obra.

Todos os autores, traductores e editores devem pôr seus nomes, a data de publicação e o annuncio de seus direitos de propriedade litteraria, em um lugar conspicuo da obra.

Si se desejar obter direito de propriedade sobre alguma obra de musica, um gravado, lithographia ou outros semelhantes, tambem deve consignar dous exemplares da obra. Si é de architectura, pintura ou esculptura, devem enviar-se uma amostra do plano, dando as dimensões e todos os outros detalhes que caracterisam o original.

O autor estrangeiro que não resida no Mexico deve enviar um poder outorgado perante um notario publico e certificado por um consul mexicano. A sua vez a certificação do consul será legalisada pelo Ministerio de Estado do Mexico, protocolisada e devidamente traduzida. Os direitos que se pagam por isto são 25 pesos e 25 pesos mais por obter o direito de propriedade, incluindo o valor dos sellos federaes que tem de inutilisar-se no documento que se apresentar ao Ministerio de Instrucção Publica.

Em outros districtos a criação do gado póde-se recommendar sem temor como emprego proveitoso de dinheiro, e em muitos, a criação de porcos para o mercado é muito lucrativa. Em realidade, não ha nenhum limite ás diversas possibilidades agricolas no Mexico; não se precisa senão intelligencia na selecção e bastante capital para o desenvolvimento.

NICARAGUA.

OPINIÃO DA COMMISSÃO DO CANAL.

Publicamos em seguida um extracto tomado do "New York Tribune" de 9 de Setembro deste anno, que será sem duvida de interesse especial ao commercio das Republicas Americanas:

A commissão enviada para estudar o Canal de Nicaragua, da qual é presidente o Almirante WALKER e membros o Professor HAUPT e o General HAINS, não tem apresentado ainda seu relaturio. O testimunho dos membros da dita commissão perante a commissão especial do Senado, nos dias 15-17 de Junho, foi impresso e indica claramente o resultado daquelle estudo. Neste trabalho occupou-se a commissão por cerca de quatro mezes; seu pessoal constava de cerca de 250 homens, dos quaes 80 eram engenheiros, acompanhados de um geologo e hydrographo competente e dos melhores instrumentos scientificos para o objecto, incluindo 10 apparelhos para perforar. Os trabalhos continuam ainda e a investigação feita, que parece a mais completa que se tem verificado até agora, tem demonstrado que eram exactos os trabalhos de MENOCAL até onde chegaram, assim como tambem muitas das informações obtidas posteriormente, e ao mesmo tempo tem aclarado muitos pontos tão importantes como interessantes que parecem ser altamente favoraveis ao projecto.

Exames minuciosos têm demonstrado que a formação de rocha, que segundo se creia faria necessaria a construcção de um grande e custoso quebra-mar para poder formar um porto seguro em Brito, não existe. O Almirante WALKER disse, e os outros membros concordaram com elle, que se poderia construir um porto largo e seguro com só limpar os brejos que estão debaixo da costa de Brito, fazendo alli um pequeno dique. Pelo que se refere á variação da profundidade do lago Nicaragua, que segundo se dizia antes tinha como 15 pés, o qual era uma difficuldade importante nos planos examinados até agora, a Commissão não tem achado provas de que a variação seja tão grande e seus peritos creem que o trabalho de regular a corrente de agua diminuirá muito, já seja usando das aguas do lago Managua ou talvez fazendo uso de uma corrente que se possa dirigir nelle.

Mais importante ainda é a conclusão, que parece ser opinião unanime da Commissão, que se pode evitar o grande risco e o gasto que produziria a construcção de grandes represas a ambos lados. A opinião parece inclinar-se á construcção de um canal directo ao lado occidental que não esteja unido ao rio; do lado oriental, propõe-se construir uma represa em Machuca, com um declive

ILO LA ROSA, OCTAVIO VALENTINI, HERMANN DENKS, Jo,
DOY, e FRANCISCO PEREZ DE VELASCO.
'ropõe-se estabelecer a fabrica em Callão, mas ainda não se
ptado uma resolução definitiva.

'ORTAÇÕES DO PERU EM 1897, COMPARADAS COM AS DE 18

)amos em seguida um extracto sobre a exportação do Peru e
7, comparada com a de 1896, publicada em " El Comercie
Lima em data de 27 de Junho de 1898:

Artigos.	1896.	1897.
	Kilos.	*Kilos.*
ıcar	71, 735, 473	105, 463, 238
ɔdão	4, 717, 697	5, 586, 394
ıto	1, 178, 762	11, 850, 490
ɛarilha	16, 489	62, 261
ros	1, 331, 689	1, 710, 206
	2, 543, 641	3, 767, 799
ısa de semente de algodão	1, 048, 456	1, 007, 527
ɔz	2, 803, 640	4, 221, 835
ɛ	712, 919	1, 239, 744
	Soles.	*Soles.*
ɛhinilha	32, 070	2, 407
ˈa e cocaina	1, 212, 381	1, 173, 066
vão e lenha	97, 429	93, 307
ˈeis e roupa	42, 998	34, 460
ˈcunhado	59, 321	104, 524
ˈcunhada	1, 485, 433	1, 927, 454
raes	4, 576, 511	6, 448, 567
aes vivos	168, 949	192, 955
hia	20, 673	11, 180
ˈte de algodão	69, 148	36, 156
ˈ	378, 439	27, 110
	22, 581	32, 125
ˈ, batatas, etc	173, 394	154, 345
	90, 141	120, 375
	Litros.	*Litros.*
	231, 020	255, 401
nte	98, 302	68, 374
	54, 255	540
	289, 161	143, 095
margas (duzias)	2, 029	40
duzias)	15, 408	13, 128

DESTINOS.

	Soles.	*Soles.*
	10, 429, 386	15, 648, 310
	4, 599, 227	5, 753, 074
	2, 231, 898	2, 322, 023
los	1, 608, 900	1, 392, 623
	669, 276	1, 212, 497
	1, 508, 088	1, 181, 312
	468, 536	447, 202

Artigos.	1896.	1897.
	Soles.	*Soles.*
Bolivia	120, 912	56, 683
America Central.................................	125, 567	49, 546
Italia...	35, 234	38, 964
China	31, 800	32, 660
Hespanha.......................................	9, 657	11, 965
Brazil	2, 985	9, 010
Belgica...		8, 786
Mexico...	9, 451	2, 871
Portugal..		500
Argentina.......................................		421
Venezuela	8, 646	....
Grecia	2, 425	....
Uruguay..	360	....
Nos dados remettidos pela alfandega de Iquitos não se indicam os paizes consumidores dos productos exportados........................ *?*	....	2, 856, 929
Total	21, 862, 334	31, 025, 382

Saldo a favor de 1897, 9,193,047.

SANTO DOMINGO.

SEU DESENVOLVIMENTO.

O Consul de Belgica em Santo Domingo, em um relatorio recente dirigido a seu governo, diz que o commercio da Republica em 1896–97 alcançou a $4,535,380, moeda americana, dos quaes $1,824,375 representam as importações e $2,709,805 as exportações. A renda aduaneira foi $165,410 em excesso do anno anterior. Quarenta e cinco por cento do total das importações correspondeu aos Estados Unidos.

Os principaes artigos de exportação foram assucar, 86,866,239 libras; tabaco, 6,332,148 libras; cacáo, 4,308,823 libras; café, 2,437,400 libras; dividivi, 1,304,929 libras; mel de assucar, 1,777,119 galões; mogno, 264,254 pés; 184,851 pés de espinho e cedro, e 14,710 toneladas de páu santo, páu campeche, etc.

Tambem informa o consul que por razão dos methodos modernos que se empregam na agricultura, esta tem sido desenvolvida notavelmente nos ultimos annos. É muito notavel o adiantamento no emprego de instrumentos de agricultura e augmenta de anno em anno a area de cultivo. Estes adiantamentos se devem em grande parte ao estabelecimento de linhas de estrada de ferro.

ESTADOS UNIDOS.

CLASSIFICAÇÃO DE COUROS E PELLES.

Em data de 27 de Agosto de 1898, a Secretaria do Thesouro dos Estados Unidos dispoz, para a classificação das pelles e os couros, um limite de doze libras. Esta classificação tem sido mal recebida pelos importadores e fabricantes de couro. Os importadores e fabricantes de couro de Chicago e Nova York têm nomeado representantes para que defendam seus interesses perante o Ministro da Fazenda pedindo-lhe que volva a considerar a materia.

O texto da disposição é como segue:

SECRETARIA DO THESOURO,
DESPACHO DO SECRETARIO,
Washington, D. C., 27 de Agosto de 1898.

Aos Directores e outros empregados de Alfandega:

Com o objecto de dar uniformidade á pratica estabelecida nos differentes portos para a classificação de pelles e couros segundo o disposto pela lei de 24 de Julho de 1897, tem-se ordenado a applicação da seguinte tabella de pesos para fazer as classificações respectivas, e classificar toda pelle que chegue ao limite do peso ou se acerque a elle como pelles de bezerro e todas as que passem do dito limite como couros, da maneira seguinte:

Libras.

1° Couros molhados ou peso de carniceiro.................................. 12
2° Couros molhados salgados............................. 12
3" Couros salgados seccos........ .... 7½
4° Couros seccos ao sol 5

W. B. HOWELL,
Sub-Secretario.

A COLHEITA DE LÃ EM 1898.

No "Boston Commercial Bulletin" se publicam os seguintes dados estatisticos relativos ao numero de ovelhas que ha nos rebanhos dos Estados Unidos e a colheita de lã em 1898:

O numero total de ovelhas no paiz para o 1° de Janeiro de 1898 foi 37,656,960. As perdidas occorridas, segundo as calcula a Secretaria da Agricultura, alcançam a 1,985,046 ovelhas, o que reduz o rebanho para o 1° de Abril a 35,671,914 rezes. Para calcular o rendimento total de lã no corrente anno têm-se empregado as quantidades do anno passado, no que se refere ao peso medio do tosão, pelo qual os calculos são necessariamente approximados. Calculando, pois, em 6.30 libras, termo medio do peso do tosão, a colheita total neste anno alcançará a 224,733,058 libras. Si a este se accrescentar o producto da lã arrancada—40,000,000 de libras—o producto total para 1898 será de 264,733,058 de libras.   A colheita de 1897 foi de 259,153,251 de libras.

Para o 1º de Abril de 1897, o numero total de ovelhas era 34,784,287, que comparado com os calculos feitos para este anno mostra um augmento de 887,627 ovelhas para 1898.

DESENVOLVIMENTO DA ELECTRICIDADE.

Calcula-se que em 1884, segundo diz o "Wall Street Journal," o total do capital empregado em negocios electricos em todos os Estados Unidos não passava de $1,000,000, emquanto que hoje a capitalisação de todas as companhias electricas do paiz alcança a $1,900,000,000.

Em 1884 se considerava que uma machina de 50 kilowatts era um dynamo de grandes proporções e o preço destes era como de 20 centavos por kilowatt de producto.   Hoje o mais grande dos generadores que se fabricam tem quasi uma capacidade de 5,000 kilowatts e os dynamos de tamanho relativamente pequeno, sem commutadores, custam approximadamente dous centavos por watt.   Calcula-se que nas estações de luz electrica e outras installações nos Estados Unidos tem-se empregado um capital de cerca de $600,000,000, e que ha hoje neste paiz cerca de 14,000 milhas de estradas de ferro electricas, com um capital nominal de cerca de $1,000,000,000, onde estão empregados 170,000 homens. Hoje pode-se fallar a uma distancia de 1,800 milhas.   O serviço de telephonos passa de 1,000,000 e o capital das companhias é de cerca de $100,000,000, com 40,000 estações e 900,000 milhas de arame.

URUGUAY.

MELHORAMENTOS DO PORTO DE MONTEVIDÉO.

Em um relatorio recente o Consul dos Estados Unidos em Montevidéo, o Sr. ALBERT W. SWALM, informa a seu Governo que se pensa executar obras de melhoramento no porto daquella cidade.   Esta é uma materia importante para os contratadores dos Estados Unidos, pois se solicitarão propostas tanto de companhias deste paiz como da Europa.   O Consul diz assim em sua communicação:

O Governo Provisorio do Uruguay apresentou ao Conselho de Estado um projecto de melhoramento do porto de Montevidéo.   O dito projecto provavelmente passará a ser lei, e quando se tenha levado a cabo, será considerado pelo ommercio deste porto como um grande beneficio. Propõe-se votar a somma e $15,400,000 em 327,659 bonos de $47 ou £10 cada um, ao juro de 6 por ento annual, pagavel por trimestre, ou em Montevidéo, ou em qualquer centro nanceiro europeo. Impor-se-há um direito de 2½ por cento em todas as imporações para forma. assim o fundo de resgate da divida. Tambem se apartam odos os novos direitos aduaneiros para attender com elles aos bonos e seus juros. Jma commissão financeira será encarregada do assumpto e dentro de um anno ›s bonos devem estar collocados nesta como em outras praças.

O plano adoptado é o conhecido aqui com o nome de Kummer-Guerrard.) canal á baixamar terá 7½ metros (24.52 pés) e se executará um dique de 200 netros (656.17 pés) de comprimento e de uma largura correspondente, com 8 netros (26.24 pés) de agua nas estacas mais baixas.

O Poder Executivo fica autorisado para solicitar propostas para a construcção do trabalho, apresentadas por casas europeas e americanas de responsabilidade, reservando-se o direito de rejeitar as propostas que não sejam convenientes. Em caso de fazer um contracto será nomeada uma commissão technica que dirija os trabalhos, e no caso de que não se possa fazer um contracto geral, podem ser aceitas propostas parciaes. Os pagamentos pelo trabalho têm de fazer-se em ouro, por presuppostos mensaes, o qual fica a cargo da commissão technica que o certificará como de costume. Quando se tenha gastado a somma de $15,000,000, se considerarão como cancellados todos os contractos, si não está terminada a obra, sem que tenha lugar a reclamações por damnos e prejuizos. Devo accrescentar que as condições do porto são muito semelhantes ás do de Galveston.

SYSTEMAS DE ESTRADAS DE FERRO.

O Sr. Don JUAN JOSÉ CASTRO, do Uruguay, fez recentemente ım trabalho sobre os systemas de estradas de ferro da America do ›ul, com relação especial ás estradas de ferro que em seu paiz stão em exploração ou em via de construcção. As seguintes ıformações relativas á extensão das estradas de ferro e o capital m acções das companhias respectivas foram tomadas da dita obra:

Nomes das Estradas de Ferro.	Extensão.	Capital.
	Kilometros.	
Strada de ferro Central	321.65	$13,575,000
Xtensão Norte do Central	293.34	7,968,700
Xtensão Nordeste do Central	124.30	3,892,000
Xtensão Este do Central	581.20	14,965,000
Strada de ferro de léste	419.50	10,233.450
Strada de ferro Midland	317.05	7,711,900
Strada de ferro do Noroeste	178.80	4,944,580
Strada de ferro do Norte	114.16	2,771,685
Ramal en San Eugenio	3.00	73,000
Estrada de ferro do Oeste	520.10	11,162,500
Ramal do Norte	23.00	671,375
Estrada de ferro Interior	617.70	15,000,000
Total	3,513.80	92,969,190

Um kilometro é igual a 3,280 pés 10 pollegadas, ou .62137 de milha, de modo que o numero total de milhas de estrada de ferro no Uruguay alcança a cerca de 2,183.37. O capital em acções, calculado em moeda dos Estados Unidos, alcança a $26,458.30 por kilometro, ou $42,117.32 por milha.

Para o 1° de Janeiro de 1897 o Uruguay, comparado com a Republica Argentina, tinha 9,041 milhas (14,550 kilometros) de estradas de ferro, que representam um capital de $480,321,820, ou $53,016.40 por milha. O Brazil tinha 8,403 milhas (13,523 kilometros), capitalisados em $483,742,610, ou $57,566,55 por milha. O Chile tinha 2,490 milhas (4,003 kilometros), com um capital de $107,030,000, ou $42,988 por milha.

O custo de construcção por milha nos differentes paizes foi como segue: Uruguay, $36,794; Argentina, $45,809; Brazil, $49,317; Chile (do Governo), $43,225; emprezas particulares, $33,535; Peru, $134,141.

VENEZUELA.

IMPORTAÇOES FEITAS PELO PORTO DE LA GUAIRA DURANTE O PRIMEIRO SEMESTRE DE 1898.

O Doutor J. M. Rivas Mundaráin, administrador da Alfandega de La Guaira, enviou á Secretaria das Republicas Americanas, acompanhado de uma communicação na qual faz justiça aos serviços que presta o Boletim aos interesses commerciaes do Continente, um quadro estatistico que mostra a importação das mercadorias estrangeiras introduzidas pelo porto de La Guaira, do 1° de Janeiro ao 30 de Junho de 1898. O dito quadro dá o país de procedencia, a classe de mercadorias, o numero de volumes, com seu peso em kilogrammas brutos, o valor declarado, os direitos cobrados, o direito addicional de 12½ por cento, e o resumo geral deste movimento de importação.

Segundo o trabalho em referencia, o total geral das importações foi nestes seis mezes como segue: 427,845 volumes com um peso total de 18,511,867 kilogrammas brutos, avaliados, segundo factura, em 12,315,929.95 bolivares (cerca de $2,000,000), que

·oduziram direitos totaes pela quantia de 5,471,207.95 bolivares.
s paizes representados são os seguintes:

Paizes.	Volumes.	Valor declarado.
		Bolivares.
;tados Unidos	165, 837	3, 680, 800. 58
llemanha	66, 690	2, 178, 460. 52
rança	36, 298	2, 223, 397. 75
iglaterra	119, 513	2, 127, 912. 80
alia	10, 683	591. 898. 75
·espanha	18, 626	832, 004. 35
lollanda	10, 191	676, 722. 20
.epublica de Colombia	6	4. 733. 00

Como se vê, os Estados Unidos occupam o primeiro lugar nas
mportações geraes de La Guaira; seguem-lhe em ordem quanto
. quantidade, Inglaterra, Allemanha, França, Hespanha, Italia,
Holanda e Colombia, e pelo que se refere ao valor declarado
;eguem depois dos Estados Unidos, França, Allemanha, Ingla-
:erra, Hespana, Hollanda, Italia e Colombia.

A posição dos Estados Unidos por artigos foi assim: Não teve
:oncorrentes na importação de kerosene, banha, materiaes photo-
graphicos e fructas frescas. Não apparece na lista dos exportadores de fazendas de algodão, que se introduzem da França,
Allemanha e Inglaterra; cartão manufacturado em formas
liversas, que se importam dos mesmos paizes; chapéos de feltro
palha, que se importam de todos os paizes, e telas de lã, que se
ttroduzem da França, Inglaterra, Allemanha e Italia.

Em concurrencia com os outros sete paizes mencionados os
:stados Unidos occuparam o primeiro lugar nas importações de
ordoalha e enxarcia, cereaes, especiarias, doces e fructas em seu
imo, ferragens, cobertores de algodão, biscoutos, presuntos, mo-
eis, brinquedos, e marmore. Occuparam o segundo lugar na
nportação de baietas em peças e colchas, conservas alimenticias,
garros, tabaco, cerveja, carnes salgadas, cobre em formas diversas,
rogas e remedios, ferro em machinas e em bruto, ferramentas para
griultura e para artes e industrias, manteiga, papel de todas as
lasses, e telas de algodão. O terceiro lugar lhe correspondeu em
rtigos de escriptorio, materiaes para estradas de ferro, ferramentas
)ara uso domestico, instrumentos de musica, livros brancos e impressos, amido de milho, amostras e perfumarias. Os Estados
Unidos occuparam o quarto lugar em artigos de fantasia, arroz em

grão, cereaes, carvão, mineral e cimento, estearina, bordados de renda, musselinas, etc., linho e filaça, louça e obras de vidro, madapolans e enfeites; o quinto lugar em conservas de vinagre e azeitonas, queijos de todas as classes, etc.; o sexto em azeite de azeitonas, seda em fitas, pannos, lenços, etc., e o setimo nas importações de camisas e meias de algodão e de vinhos e licores de todas as classes.

BORRACHA DE MILHO.

Uma companhia que explora as principaes fabricas de glucose dos Estados Unidos tem logrado produzir uma substancia que substituirá a borracha.   A dita substancia é o producto do oleo do milho.   A companhia dispõe de cerca de 90 por cento do producto total da glucose que se consome tanto neste paiz como no estrangeiro, e segundo dados publicados no 1º de Agosto, os differentes moinhos da dita companhia têm consumido 20,616,000 alqueires de milho, dos quaes se extrahiu 542,100,000 libras de glucose, 120,572,000 libras de amido, 98,382,000 libras de assucar, 2,600,000 libras de dextrina, e 151,788,000 libras de residuo.

O numero dos productos secundarios chega a 40, e entre estes se conta a fabricação do substituto da borracha, que não chegará a occupar inteiramente o lugar desta, mas que se empregará para mesclal-o com ella.   Os fabricantes do producto o vendem hoje á razão de 4½ centavos por libra e diz-se que os fabricantes de effeitos de borracha, especialmente os que fabricam aros para bicyclettas, empregam grandes quantidades do dito producto. Sua durabilidade está já provada e se crê que produzirá uma revolução no commercio de borracha.

Fabrica-se este substituto do oleo de milho, por meio de um processo de vulcanisação que dá um producto muito semelhante em apparencia e em qualidade á borracha de Pará.   Pode ser empregado, segundo diz a companhia, na fabricação de toda a classe de objectos de borracha, entre outros telas de borracha, aros para bicyclettas, botas de borracha, solas de borracha, mantas impermeaveis, linoleo, etc.   Visto que o oleo de milho não se oxyda com facilidade, o dito producto é de grande valor, pois tambem não é affectado pela oxydação, de modo que os productos que com elle se fazem se conservam sempre suaves e elasticos e não se quebram, como aquelles em cuja composição entram o oleo de linhaça e o de colza. Uma mistura de 50 por cento de borracha pura e 50 por cento do substituto, segundo se diz, se conserva suave e elastica.

—

AUGMENTO DO PRODUCTO E DO PREÇO DA BORRACHA.

A producção total de borracha crúa do mundo, para o anno findo em 30 de Junho de 1898, foi calculada em 94,000,000 de libras. Grande como é esta quantidade, não é sufficiente, comtudo, para satisfazer a procura dos fabricantes e por conseguinte tem chegado a pagar-se até a somma de $1.06 por uma libra de borracha de Pará da melhor qualidade.

Desde 1895 o preço do producto crú tem ido augmentando constantemente, chegando-se a pagar até $1.25 por libra. Em vista do facto de que no anno que terminou no dia 30 de Junho de 1898 a producção foi menor que a do anno precedente, tem corrido a noticia de que se estavam esgotando os seringaes nos tropicos, do qual resultaria uma alta continuada e desastrosa nos preços.

A Africa e a America do Sul são as duas fontes principaes de onde vem a borracha crúa. Durante o anno passado o Brazil exportou 50,000,000 de libras de borracha, segundo calculos exactos tirados dos relatorios da Repartição das Alfandegas. A producção da Africa se calcula em 40,000,000 de libras; a India produz cerca de 1,000,000 de libras, emquanto que todos os paizes da America Central e do Sul, com excepção do Brazil, dão cerca de 3,000,000 de libras. A colheita do Brazil era até 50 annos de cerca de 1,000,000 de libras, ao qual alcançavam suas exportações annuaes, que têm augmentado á razão de 1,000,000 por anno.

Em um relatorio recente, dirigido á Secretaria de Relações Exteriores da Inglaterra por seu Ministro no Brazil, apparece o calculo de que o terreno productor de borracha que ainda não se tem explorado na America do Sul cobre uma extensão de 1,000,000 de milhas quadradas. A difficuldade principal que se apresenta na exploração deste territorio consiste na escassez da população, pois tem-se calculado que em uma das immensas regiões do Brazil, 1,000 por 500 milhas, o numero total de habitantes é 140,000.

As importações feitas nos Estados Unidos durante o anno que acaba de terminar alcançaram a 45,000,000 de libras, avaliadas em $25,000,000. Diz-se que um vapor no ultimo semestre trouxe um carregamento de borracha crúa avaliada em $1,000,000. Não obstante tão grande reforço os preços do mercado continuaram subindo desde o dia da chegada. Emprega-se a borracha crúa em um numero illimitado de artigos; usa-se em toda a classe de machinas, e a fabricação de aros para bicyclettas e para outros vehiculos de roda tem augmentado sua esphera de utilidade.

COMMERCIO MISCELLANEO.

BRAZIL.

Suggestões aos Fabricantes. O Consul inglez em Pará faz as seguintes observações no "British Trade Journal": "Aqui se acostuma a usar roupa de panno escuro, já seja porque o lavado é caro, ou porque ha mudanças rapidas de temperatura produzidas pelas frequentes chuvas, ou talvez ambas razões façam preferivel usar roupa de panno em vez de riscados ou linho, como em outros paizes tropicaes. Usam-se chapéos de feltro e palha. Os naturaes do paiz e as classes baixas usam a mesma classe de roupa que os de mais alta posição, levando invariavelmente camisas de linho branco, botas ou sapatos. As chuvas que são quasi diarias fazem obrigatorio o uso de guarda-chuvas. Artigos de ferro e tintas a oleo são empregados muito nas casas e como todas têm largos corredores com vidraças, o vidro plano que se emprega para este fim tem grande procura. Tambem se procuram muito os encerados e lona impermeavel por causa das chuvas ; por esta mesma razão, impermeaveis, ligeiros de peso, podem ter boa venda. Por causa do augmento que ha na navegação fluvial gozam de boa venda o carvão, oleo para machinas e tintas."

BOLIVIA.

Novo Consul em Philadelphia. O Sr. WILFRED H. SCHOFF foi nomeado ultimamente Consul da Bolivia em Philadelphia. Em uma communicação recentemente publicada o Cónsul diz que os commerciantes e outras pessoas interessadas podem obter alli os certificados consulares necessarios nos documentos de embarque e que terá gosto em dar todas as informações que s solicitam sobre o commercio e a riqueza natural da Bolivia.

EQUADOR.

Concessão para a Exploração da Borracha em Tungurahua. As seguintes informações são de um artigo sobre a producção da borracha em Equador que apparece no "Boston Commercial Bulletin:" "Até agora se tem obtido a borracha naquelle paiz de arvores silvestres e a destruição destas pelo exploradores têm feito grande damno ao commercio da costa; mas já a gente começa a comprehender o valor das suas opportunidades como o prova o facto de que se está fazendo um esforço para conseguir do Governo uma concessão por oito annos para a exploração da borracha em um terreno de 8 a 10 leguas quadradas na Provincia de Tungurahua e se nutre a esperança de que dentro de pouco tempo a colheita da borracha iguale ás de café e cacáo que são até hoje os principaes productos da Republica."

HAITI.

Empreza Mineira em Haiti. Nas folhas avulsas dos Relatorios Consulares de data de 14 de Setembro, o Sr. Ministro POWELL communica o seguinte de Port-au-Prince: "Na parte norte da Republica tem-se descoberto ultimamente um rico veio de ferro, que contem o metal quasi puro; tem-se conseguido do Governo uma concessão para explorar essa mina, e já se está formando uma companhia americana para este fim.

HONDURAS.

Convenio sobre Volumes Postaes. O periodico "The Manufacturer" assegura que o convenio entre a de Gran Bretanha e a Republica de Honduras para a permuta de volumes postaes entre os dous paizes começou a reger no dia 1º de Setembro. Honduras é um dos poucos paizes com os quaes os Estados Unidos têm estabelecido o systema de volumes postaes.

MEXICO.

Caixas de Ferro á Prova de Fogo. Sómente nos ultimos annos as caixas de ferro á prova de fogo têm chegado a ser uma necessidade no Mexico. Anteriormente os edificios eram construidos com enormes paredes e soalhos de imento, e empregavam nelles tão pouca madeira que sómente os commerciantes ue possuiam objectos valiosos e inflammaveis se viam obrigados a usar as ditas aixas. Agora se faz grande trafico nestes artigos entre os Estados Unidos e Iexico, e são principalmente algumas casas de Ohio as que se dedicam a elle, m do adaptado seus productos ás necessidades do paiz.

As caixas de ferro, que geralmente usam os commerciantes e manufactureiros n pequena escala, não são mais que simples caixões de ferro aos quaes se da o rme inglez de "skeleton safe." São mais grandes que as caixas de ferro á ova de fogo e sua construcção é solida. Occupam muito pouco espaço. a exportação custa menos que a das caixas de ferro pesadas, e é a unica classe ssivel quando se faz o transporte por meio de mulas. A procura desta classe caixas vai augmentando; muitos edificios estão em via de construcção e é aior o numero de abobadas que nelles se collocam.

Machinas de Coser e de Tecer. Os Estados Unidos têm introduzido no Mexico com muito bom exito machinas de coser, pois as fazem tão uraveis como as melhores de seus rivaes e de menos peso. Desta maneira se agam menos direitos e ha menos perigo de que se quebram. Os fabricantes êm comprehendido, emfim, a necessidade de enviar agentes que entendam o idioma que falla a grande massa do povo, e tambem publicam na dita lingua suas circulares illustradas.   O grande exito alcançado por uma casa que tem introduzido suas machinas de tecer demonstra este facto.

Machinas Hydraulicas.   Quasi todas as grandes plantações do Mexico dispõem de agua como força motriz, e se está desenvolvendo o uso desta nas manufacturas do paiz.   Constantemente se levantam novas fabricas. As fabricas de tecidos de algodão têm sido fundadas até hoje por casas inglezas, que tambem possuiam os estabelecimentos para a preparação de assucar e café.   Na actualidade algumas casas dos Estados Unidos estão fazendo forte concurrencia.

Fabrica de Calçado.   Uma nova industria recentemente estabelecida no Mexico é a de couro e a de calçado feito por machina, seguindo o systema americano.   Bem administradas, estas manufacturas têm de dar bons resultados e acabarão em breve tempo com as pequenas importações que agora se fazem, porque os couros são baratos e a substancia que se usa para cortir, chamada "Canaigre," e que é uma raiz muito semelhante á beterraba, é indigena do solo e muito abundante.

Machinas para Moinhos de Farinha.   Com o augmento no uso de systemas modernos para dispor dos grãos no Mexico, têm-se estabelecido muitos moinhos de farinha, e isto proporciona excellente negocio á uma casa dos Estados Unidos que tem uma officina na cidade de Mexico, e um empregado experimentado para a venda e installação de ditas machinas.   Obtém-se excellentes preços, e como a producção de trigo está augmentando notavelmente, e as vantagens que se alcançam moendo trigo, ainda quando seja importado, são consideraveis, offerece-se uma brilhante perspectiva para o futuro.

NICARAGUA.

Ferragens.   O seguinte extracto é tomado de um relatorio official allemão dirigido de León e Managua: "Os artigos de ferro e de aço vêm principalmente da Allemanha, emquanto que em annos anteriores predominavam os effeitos inglezes desta classe e tambem os americanos· Na actualidade sómente vêm dos Estados Unidos umas poucas ferramentas de qualidade superior, mas os principaes artigos de uso commum, taes como machetes e cutachas, vêm todos da Allemanha."

ESTADOS UNIDOS.

Boa Perspectiva na Agricultura.   O periodico "Age of Steel" diz que, segundo os ꞓ culos de pessoas entendidas, a producção agricola ꞓ Estados Unidos neste anno vai a ser enorme.   A quantidade de cereaes p duzida tem sido muito grande e a procura delles no estrangeiro parece augme tar constantemente.   Segundo informações officiaes, a colheita de trigo de 18 ascenderá a cerca de 700,000,000 alqueires, e a de milho será provavelmente 1,900,000,000 alqueires.   Calcula-se a colheita de aveia em 600,000,000 alqueir a de feno em 60,000,000 toneladas, e a de algodão em 10,0 ɔ,000 fard Estas grandes quantidades dão uma idea da prosperidade nacional.   Com augmento constante do trafico de exportação e com o desenvolvimento da activ dade industrial que cada dia se faz notar mais, os Estados Unidos possuem ꞓ seus celleiros e armazens uma garantia segura de prosperidade no futuro.

URUGUAY.

Augmento nas Importações da Allemanha. O Consul SWALM informa que os allemães têm augmentado muito seus negocios com o Uruguay, cujo commercio estava antes quasi em sua totalidade em mãos de fabricantes inglezes. Em 1897 as exportações da Inglaterra para este paiz diminuiram do modo seguinte:

Misturas de lã, 372,000 varas; fazendas de estambre, 267,000 varas; tecidos de algodão, 7,700,000 varas. A exportação deste ultimo artigo da Inglaterra para o Uruguay em 1898 excedeu de 14,000,000 varas. Os generos allemães são mais baratos, mas carecem das boas qualidades dos que tem vido a substituir. Os allemães têm estudado o mercado e satisfazem as necessidades deste, emquanto que os fabricantes inglezes não gostam de fazer mudanças. Necessariamente os allemães têm de melhorar a qualidade de seus generos afim de conservar o trafico que têm obtido. O Consul diz tambem que no commercio de generos de algodão os Estados Unidos fazem um progresso satisfactorio, porque os fabricantes deste paiz têm seguido os conselhos que lhes têm dado os empregados consulares.

Importação de Instrumentos Agricolas. Em data de 29 de Junho de 1898, o Consul SWALM escreve de Montevidéo e diz que o anno corrente verá a importação mais grande no Uruguay de machinas agricolas provenientes dos Estados Unidos. Todas estas machinas devem a boa reputação de que gozam no mercado a seu proprio merito, pois são mais uteis, mais ligeiras e melhor acondicionadas que outras, sendo além disto menos pesadas. Agentes de intelligencia têm prestado muito bons serviços na introducção deste artigo, e as machinas se recommendarão por si mesmas no vasto campo agricola que offerece a Republica em 1898. Emquanto que se conservar a boa qualidade das ditas machinas, sua exportação dos Estados Unidos continuará augmentando, com detrimento das que se fabricam em outros pàizes e que não são senão uma falsificação do artigo americano.

Ganhos no Negocio de Extracto de Carne. A reunião trigesima segunda da Junta Directora da Liebig Meat Extract Company, Limited, que se verificou em Fray Bentos, tem servido para mostrar os ganhos que se obtêm no negocio de extracto de carne no Uruguay. Para o trabalho de um anno se ganhou a somma £123,376.10. Um dividendo ad interim de 5 por cento foi pago de uma vez, Outro de 15 por cento ao fim do anno, dando um total liquido de 20 por cento, é rc dos impostos que na Inglaterra se cobram sobre as rendas particulares. Depois de dedicar £15,000 para varios gastos, ficaram £7,128 para leval-as á conta de ganhos e perdas no anno de 1898. Ao transmittir este relatorio á Secretaria de Estado, o Consul SWALM diz que esta companhia possue uma grande quantidade de gado, e que é considerada como uma das emprezas mais lucrativas na America do Sul.

Producção de Ouro em 1897. O Consul SWALM avisa á Secretaria de Estado que um relatorio official ultimamente publicado mostra que a quantidade de quartzos auriferos moidos na Republica durante o anno de 1897 01 de 6,400,791 kilogrammas (14,111,183 libras), e o rendimento de ouro

BULLETIN MENSUEL

DU

JREAU DES REPUBLIQUES AMÉRICAINES,

UNION INTERNATIONALE DES RÉPUBLIQUES AMÉRICAINES.

| . VI. | SEPTEMBRE 1898. | No. 3. |

DIRECTEUR PROVISOIRE RENOMMÉ.

Le Comité Exécutif de l'Union Internationale des Républiques 1éricaines s'est réuni dans le salon diplomatique du Départe- nt d'Etat le mardi 27 septembre. Etaient présents: M. ADEE, :rétaire d'Etat interim, Président; Señor ANDRADE, Ministre du nézuéla et Señor CALVO, Ministre de Costa Rica. La réunion iit pour but de décider de la direction du Bureau des Répu- jues Américaines, vu que le terme de M. FREDERIC EMORY nme Directeur prendra fin le 1er octobre.

5ur une proposition de Señor ANDRADE, le terme de M. EMORY té prolongé jusqu'au 1er novembre. Il est entendu que cette olution a été prise afin de mettre le nouveau Secrétaire d'Etat, . HAY, en état de se mettre au courant des conditions du Bureau dans le but d'arriver à une décision définitive concernant la 'ection.

M. EMORY, qui est Chef du Bureau de Commerce Extérieur Département d'Etat, a été désigné pour prendre la direction du ıreau des Républiques Américaines à la mort de feu le Direc- ır M. JOSEPH P. SMITH, le 5 février dernier, où il a continué à nplir les fonctions de Directeur provisoire, à la suite de résolu- n prises de temps en temps par le Comité Exécutif.

RÉPUBLIQUE ARGENTINE.

COMMERCE AVEC L'ALLEMAGNE.

Le Consul MONAGHAN de Chemnitz, Allemagne, écrit au Ministère des Affaires Etrangères, en date du 23 juin 1898, que d'après l'opinion des journaux allemands, la République Argentine est le pays qui montre la plus grande habileté de toute l'Amérique du Sud pour faire des achats. En 1897 elle a acheté des textiles bruts et fabriqués pour une valeur de 30,500,000 de pesos ($29,432,500), contre une valeur de 38,400,000 de pesos ($37,056,000) en 1896. Cette diminution est due aux mauvaises récoltes et aussi à l'établissement de filatures dans cette république.

Les autres articles que la République Argentine a importés sont :

Articles.	1897.		1896.	
	Pesos.		*Pesos.*	
La bonneterie ordinaire	823, 322	$794, 495. 75	548, 408	$529, 213
Les mouchoirs de poche ...	533, 986	515, 296. 50	341, 747	329. 785
Les cotonnades....	12, 945, 132	12, 448, 440. 40	10, 594, 187	10, 223, 390
Les tissus de fil et de coton.	359, 078	4, 881, 125. 35	236, 614	228. 333
Les toiles à sacs..........	5, 058, 161	621, 589. 30	2, 700, 850	2, 606. 320
Les toiles à voiles	644, 134	....	385, 915	372. 408

En 1897 les importations de la République Argentine provenaient des pays suivants: Angleterre, 36,400,000 de pesos ($35,126,000); Allemagne, 11,100,000 de pesos ($10,715,000); France, 11,000,000 de pesos ($10,615,000); Italie, 10,900,000 de pesos; Etats-Unis, 10,000,000 de pesos ($9,746,500); Belgique, 8,000,000 de pesos ($7,720,000). Le commerce de l'Allemagne avec ce pays est bien plus important qu'on ne pourrait croire d'après les chiffres donnés plus haut, car des marchandises évaluées à des milliers de dollars sont expédiées à la République Argentine par le port d'Anvers.

EXPORTATIONS EN 1898.

La " Revue de la Rivière Plate" publie les statistiques suivantes sur le total des exportations expédiées de tous les ports de

République Argentine pendant les cinq premiers mois de 1898, comparées à celles de la même période de l'année 1897 :

Articles.	1898.	1897.
Blé..tonnes..	616, 923	73, 037
Maïs......................................do....	75, 638	226, 272
Graine de lin ....do....	136, 776	155, 423
Laine ....ballots..	331, 024	308, 042
Farine......... ....tonnes..	12, 746	23, 306
Cuirs ....nombre..	1, 402, 599	1, 438, 936
Avoine...................................ballots..	333, 603	359, 127
Viande de mouton frigorifié..................nombre..	1, 025, 237	800, 069
Bétail sur pied...............................do....	56, 387	59, 243
Moutons sur pied ....do....	292, 948	226, 604

MARCHÉ DE BLÉ EN 1898.

Le Consul MAYER à Buenos Ayres a envoyé au Ministère des Affaires Etrangères un rapport intéressant sur les fluctuations des prix du blé dans la République pendant le premier semestre de 1898. Voici ses observations telles qu'elles sont publiées dans les Rapports Consulaires du mois d'août.

Pendant la saison des expéditions le marché de blé a présenté des cas tout à fait inattendus dont la plupart ont lésé les intérêts des personnes qui sont engagées dans ce commerce.

Dès le commencement de la moisson, la situation des affaires existant alors ne promettait rien de bon à ceux qui préféraient des transactions tranquilles aux fluctuations violentes. La rareté du blé dans les derniers mois de l'année dernière avait fait hausser les prix locaux bien au-dessus de ceux que les exportateurs étaient à même de payer. C'est la raison pour laquelle la hausse s'est maintenue pendant quelque temps encore, même après le commencement de la moisson de la nouvelle récolte ; mais une fois que les meuniers en ont eu assez pour suffire à leurs besoins, une diminution rapide a eu lieu.

Beaucoup d'exportateurs avaient fait des contrats pour un tonnage considérable, en vue des grandes quantités de blé en perspective ; mais les pluies ont retardé le transport et les agriculteurs ont gardé leur blé. Il s'en est suivi une baisse dans les prix de transport, et l'or apprécié à sa juste valeur a rendu indépendante la position des vendeurs. Le marché a continué dans cette même condition pendant le mois de février et de mars. En avril, le marché est devenu plus ferme par suite de la disette apparente des provisions. Toutefois, les hostilités qui ont éclaté entre las Etats-Unis et l'Espagne ont été le signal d'une des hausses les plus étonnantes qui ait jamais eu lieu dans le marché de blé. Ici, le 1er avril, la valeur était de $8.50; le 15 elle était de $10; le 22 elle était de $11; et le 7 mai, elle était de $12.50 à $13. Peu de temps après cette date, un changement est survenu dans le pays. Le marché qui était calme a subi une dépression, et de la dépression à la panique il n'y avait qu'un pas. Les acheteurs se sont retirés entièrement et les prix sont revenus à peu près à la valeur constatée dans le courant de janvier.

A présent, le marché est presque entièrement paralysé. Bien qu'il y ait encore une assez grande quantité de grain dans le pays, les offres sont très rares. Il y a encore un espace de temps suffisant pour que les récoltes actuelles subissent des dommages, et une hausse dans le prix de l'or peut causer une augmentation dans les valeurs en papier.

Quant aux expéditions, je pense qu'on peut les estimer à un million de tonnes pour l'année se terminant le 31 décembre, y compris celles de l'Uruguay. A l'exception de l'année dernière, on a trouvé que deux tiers de la récolte de la République Argentine sont expédiés vers le 30 juin. Jusqu'au 18 du mois actuel, on avait expédié 638,000 tonnes de cette contrée et environ 120,000 tonnes de l'Uruguay. Il se peut que la hausse ait accéléré un peu les expéditions, mais elle n'a pas duré assez longtemps poir avoir eu beaucoup d'effet. Il y a un stock considérable à Buenos Ayres.

Les sauterelles ont paru de bonne heure cette année; la Province de Santa Fé en est infestée. Au commencement elles produiront un effet avantageux en empêchant la croissance trop rapide de la plante. Mais ces sauterelles peuvent être suivie par d'autres amenant des résultats désavantageux sur la moisson.

MOUVEMENT DU PORT DE BUENOS AYRES.

D'après un ouvrage préparé dans la République Argentine pour l'Exposition de Paris, il ressort que pendant l'année 1897 les statistiques sur le mouvement de la navigation dans le port de Buenos Ayres se répartissent comme suit:

Nombre total des entrées et sorties, 20,884; tonnage enregistré, 7,365,405 tonnes; vapeurs, 6,689, avec un tonnage de 5,895,967 tonnes; voiliers, 14,195, avec un tonnage de 1,469,438 tonnes.

Il y avait 2,025 bateaux engagés dans le commerce extérieur jaugeant 2,984,408 tonneaux, et 18,859 bateaux engagés dans le commerce de cabotage jaugeant 4,380,997 tonneaux.

Seize mille sept cent quarante-cinq bateaux, avec un tonnage total de 2,415,773 tonnes, portaient le drapeau Argentin. De ce nombre, il y avait 103 navires jaugeant 42,603 tonneaux qui faisaient le commerce extérieur, et 16,642 navires jaugeant 2,373,160 tonneaux qui faisaient le cabotage. Il y avait 3,389 vapeurs portant le drapeau Argentin, formant un tonnage de 1,392,441 tonnes, et 13,356 voiliers formant un tonnage de 1,023,332 tonnes.

BRÉSIL.

CHARBON POUR LE CHEMIN DE FER CENTRAL BRÉSILIEN.

Le Conseil des Directeurs du Chemin de Fer Central Brésilien a demandé des soumissions pour la fourniture de charbon à être employé sur la ligne pendant 1898. La quantité exigée est de 120,000 tonnes, pour lesquelles les soumissions seront reçues le 31 octobre prochain à une heure de relevée.

L'annonce, comme elle a été transmise au Département d'Etat par le Ministre BRYAN, spécifie que le charbon doit être de première qualité, provenant des mines de Cardiff ou d'autres, fournissant un article de la même qualité, et doit remplir les conditions suivantes : Avoir été retiré de la mine récemment, trois fois criblés, ne doit pas donner plus de 4 pour cent de cendres ni contenir plus de neuf dixièmes de 1 pour cent de soufre et avoir un pouvoir calorifique de pas moins de 8,000 calories par gramme, au calorimètre Thompson ; tout ceci sera verifié par une analyse et des expériences faites par l'administration du chemin de fer ou par la personne quelconque qu'elle pourrait désigner. Il est en outre stipulé que le charbon doit être fourni en gros morceaux et pas plus de 5 pour cent d'une grandeur plus petite que 30 pouces cubes ne sera admis, et doit être délivré en quantités correspondantes aux taux de 10,000 tonnes par mois, n'excédant en aucun jour 500 tonnes et avec la stipulation expresse dans les lettres de voitures que les chargements ne devraient pas dépasser 250 tonnes par jour ouvrable.

La livraison doit commencer dans les deux premières semaines de janvier 1899 et finir en décembre de la même année, et toute suspension de livraison pendant plus d'un mois ou toute tentative de fournir un article inférieur donnera à la compagnie le droit de résilier le contrat, et fera perdre aux soumissionaires les dépôts s'élevant à 40,000 milreis (environ $6,000), garantissant l'exécution du contrat. Il est aussi stipulé dans le contrat que la non-exécution d'une des conditions stipulées donne à la direction du chemin de fer le droit d'imposer aux soumissionaires une amende de 2,000 à 20,000 milreis ($300 à $3,000), selon la gravité du cas.

Les paiements seront effectués à la caisse du chemin de fer en monnaie nationale dans un délai de 8 jours après livraison de chaque chargement; la tonne anglaise de 1,015 kilogrammes (2,237.66 livres) et la livre sterling servira de base de calcul; cette dernière basée sur le change de jour précédent.

Des soumissions doivent être accompagnées d'un certificat de dépôt démontant de 5,000 milreis (environ $750) comme guarantie et qui sera déposé dans les coffres-forts de la compagnie du chemin de fer si, après que la soumission a été faite, les sousactionnaires refusent de signer le contrat.

Le Consul-Général SEGER, à la date du 21 août 1898, en parlant de cette occasion offerte aux négociants américains, dit que 1,000 à 2,000 tonnes de charbon pourraient être fournies chaque mois à divers grands consommateurs à Rio, si on fournissait une bonne qualité. La principale difficulté jusqu'ici a été que la plus grande partie du charbon provenant de Etats-Unis n'a pu être employée par la compagnie de chemin de fer sans apporter de changement aux grilles généralement en usage.

CHILI.

STATISTIQUE DE L'INDUSTRIE DU SALPÊTRE.

L'Association de propagande du salpêtre vient de publier son rapport relatif au premier trimestre de cette année.

Ce travail renferme tout d'abord le tableau rectifié de l'exportation du salpêtre pendant l'année 1897, qui est établit comme suit:

	Quintaux espagnols.		Quintaux espagnols.
Royaume-Uni ou continent ...	9, 631, 004	Honolulu	72, 723
Ports directs du Royaume-Uni	266, 502	Maurice....................	17, 549
Allemagne	6, 020, 064	Port-Elisabeth	42, 767
Suède.....................	74, 931	Afrique	39, 600
Hollande...................	1, 029, 613	Guatémala...................	100
Belgique	1, 029, 428	Brésil......................	147
France.....................	2, 192, 718	Argentine	855
Italie......................	310, 265	Equateur....................	60
Autriche-Hongrie........... .	16, 332	Pérou.......................	2, 684
Etats-Unis (Côte orientale)....	2, 021, 772	Bolivie.....................	33
San Francisco................	488, 431	Chili........	42, 203
Martinique	24, 750		
Japon......................	76, 082	Total..................	23, 441, 613
Australie...................	11, 000		

Il relate ensuite les efforts faits en vue de la formation d'une nouvelle association pour la limitation de la production (combinación salitrera), et mentionne la décision prise par l'assemblée générale du 12 avril 1898, de ne point donner un caractère officiel aux démarches entreprises pour atteindre ce but si désirable, afin d'éviter que le marché soit dès à présent influencé par l'expectative d'un résultat favorable.

L'exposé des travaux des divers comités de propagande installés en Europe tient dans le rapport une place considérable; les résultats obtenus justifient les sacrifices qui ont été faits de ce chef. Le comité permanent de Londres avait reçu au 18 avril une somme de 8,091 livres sterling 12, dont 5,000 provenant de la subvention officielle de 20,000 livres sterling, accordée par la loi du 7 septembre 1897. Rien n'est ménagé pour assurer au salpêtre de nouveaux débouchés: les conférences, les concours avec attribution de prix, les fondations de champs d'expériences, les insertions dans les revues se multiplient de jour en jour. Le délégué pour la France insiste avec complaisance sur les résultats favorables des expériences faites au champ du Parc au Prince, aux environs de Paris, et qui auraient démontré la supériorité du salpêtre sur le sulfate d'ammoniaque pour la culture du maïs.

C'est surtout en Allemagne qu'il importe de combattre la concurrence du sulfate d'ammoniaque. C'est au succès de ce produit et aux attaques dont le salpêtre a été l'objet de la part de ses fabricants qu'il faut attribuer la diminution de l'importation du salpêtre en Allemagne qui a été, dans ce premier trimestre, de 644,460 quintaux espagnols, comparativement à la période correspondante de l'année 1897. De là, la nécessité d'adopter définitivement une méthode uniforme de dosage du perchlorate dans le salpêtre; celle proposée par le Dr. GILBERT, qui a déjà fait l'objet de rapports favorables, paraît devoir réunir tous les suffrages.

D'après une communication de l'agent du comité en Angleterre, la production annuelle du sulfate d'ammoniaque serait d'ailleurs forcément limitée au maximum de 35,000 tonnes en raison de ce fait que le coke fabriqué dans les fours installés pour l'élaboration de produits dérivés n'excède pas 2,000,000 de tonnes; or, la quantité de sulfate d'ammoniaque que produit une tonne de coke n'est pas supérieure à trente-huit ou quarante livres. Il n'y aurait pas lieu de redouter, d'autre part, l'augmentation du nombre de fours à coke pouvant produire du sulfate d'ammoniaque parce que cette mesure impliquerait la transformation du matériel avec une dépense énorme de capital et que le coke ainsi obtenu est de qualité bien inférieure.

La consommation totale du salpêtre dans le monde entier a été, pendant ce premier trimestre, de 11,534,731 quintaux espagnols, dépassant de 1,621,065 quintaux la consommation de la période correspondante de l'année 1897.

· Le tableau suivant en donne la répartition dans les principaux pays, avec indication de l'augmentation ou de la diminution.

	Distribution.	Augmentation.	Diminution.
Royaume-Uni	864,110	227,930	
Allemagne	4,119,990		644,460
France	3,288,310	1,164,490	
Belgique	1,656,410	214,360	
Hollande	503,470	224,020	
Italie	197,800	150,420	
Autriche-Hongrie	163,990	78,890	
Suède			11,500
Danemark			89,700
Etats-Unis (côte orientale)	576,235	212,082	
Etats-Unis (côte occidentale)	109,844	65,844	
Pays divers	52,136	34,111	
Chili	2,386		4,422

Le stock disponible était évalué au 31 décembre 1897 à 17,255,501 quintaux espagnols, dont 9,687,701 sur les marchés étrangers et 7,567,800 en existence sur la côte.

Les tableaux qui précèdent permettent de se rendre compte de l'amélioration de la situation de l'industrie du saltpêtre qui est dû à l'augmentation de la consommation provoquée par une active propagande. Mais le défaut d'entente entre les producteurs n'a pas permis de tirer de ces résultats favorables tout le profit qu'on en aurait pu attendre. Ainsi que mes précédentes communications sur ce sujet le laissaient prévoir, les prix n'ont cessé de de baisser depuis 1895.

D'autre part, ainsi que les chiffres suivants permettent de le constater, la production augmente dans des proportions considérables par suite de l'échec de diverses tentatives faites pour la limiter.

Premier trimestre 1898... 6,934,853
Premier trimestre 1897... 3,885,316

    Augmentation.. 3,049,537

Quarante-quatre usines ont élaboré le salpêtre; leur nombre n'était que de trente pendant la période correspondante en 1897.

Enfin, l'exportation a suivi la même progression; elle a été de 5,593,390, dépassant de 1,766,474 celle du premier trimestre 1898. Elle s'est répartie de la façon suivante entre les divers pays:

Royaume-Uni ou continent	1,958,408
Ports directs du Royaume-Uni	245,845
Allemagne	1,224,985
Hollande	336,389
Belgique	133,133
France	899,540
Italie	41,623
Etats-Unis (côte orientale)	650,705
San Francisco (Californie)	48,240
Maurice	27,980
Indes occidentales (Barbade)	24,156
Chili	2,386
Total	5,593,390

RÉPUBLIQUE DE LA COLOMBIE.

EMPLOI DE BICYCLETTES EN BARRANQUILLA.

Le "Farm Implement" dit que dans une communication à une maison d'exportation à New York, le Consul Shaw de Barranquilla dit que les bicyclettes sont très peu employées dans cette ville. En conséquence, il n'a eu qu'une petite augmentation dans ce commerce. Ceci est dû dans une grande mesure aux routes nonmacadamisées, les rues étant très sablonneuses en temps secs et très molles pendant la saison des pluies. Il n'y a pas de manufactures de bicyclettes dans la Colombie et les bicyclettes importées sont vendues par les quincailliers et les négociants vendant des marchandises générales. La plupart des bicyclettes importées viennent des Etats-Unis, mais un agent pour une bicyclette italienne a récemment voyagé partout dans le pays et a solicité la clientèle.

Le consul propose que le meilleur moyen d'introduire les bicyclettes des Etats-Unis dans la Colombie est d'ouvrir une agence et de vendre une bonne qualité de marchandise à bas prix. Les réparations doivent y être comprises et faites à l'Agence. Les droits de douanes sur les bicyclettes importées sont de 70 centavos (23 cents) par kilogramme (2.2046 pounds). Les commerçants de la Colombie ont l'habitude de faire et de recevoir de longs crédits à six, neuf et douze mois. La récréation favorite des jeunes gens est l'équitation. Un bon cheval coûte 200 pesos ($66) et on peut le nourrir pour $5 par mois.

DÉVELOPPEMENT DES CHEMINS DE FER.

M. le Consul MADRIGAL, écrivant de Cartagena à la date du 10 juillet 1898, joint le rapport annuel de la compagnie du Chemin de Fer Cartagena Magdalena pour 1897. Cette compagnie vient d'acheter sept navires à vapeur pour la navigation fluviale d'une capacité de tonnage totale de 950 tonnes. Deux autres d'une capacité de 600 tonnes sont en voie de construction. Cette compagnie possédait déjà trois navires de 700 tonnes, et aura, quand ces deux navires à vapeur seront finis, une capacité de 2,250 tonnes de tonnage outre plusieurs remorqueurs. Les marchandises peuvent maintenant être expédiées directement de Cartagena aux entrepôts de la compagnie à Honda, le port La Dorada étant à 600 milles de distance.

Pendant l'année 1896 le commerce intérieur et extérieur a augmenté rapidement, et il est à regretter que cette augmentation n'ait pas continuée pendant l'année écoulée pour le transit comme pour le commerce local. Le dépérissement des affaires a eu pour résultat une diminution de $33,226 dans les recettes.

COSTA RICA.

EXPORTATIONS POUR LE PREMIER SEMESTRE DE 1897 ET 1898.

Le Directeur-Général des Statistiques à San José a envoyé à ce Bureau un rapport indiquant les exportations passant par les ports de la République pendant les premiers six mois de l'année 1898, comparées à la même période en 1897, et dont les données suivantes sont obtenues : Les exportations passant par Port Limon pendant les premiers six mois de 1897 s'élevaient à 1,783 colis pesant 153,386 kilogrammes, contre 2,081 colis pesant 184,710 kilogrammes pendant la même période en 1898. Les exportations de Puntarenas étaient de 31,849 colis pesant 3,564,113 kilogrammes en 1897, contre 20,224 colis pesant 2,761,134 kilogrammes pour les premiers six mois de 1898.

Les rechargements par Port Limon s'élevaient à 44 colis pesant 1,928 kilogrammes, pendant les premiers six mois de 1897, contre 182 colis pesant 36,788 kilogrammes en 1898; de Puntarenas il y avait 229 colis pesant 14,178 kilogrammes en 1897 et 217 colis pesant 15,751 kilogrammes en 1898.

Un résumé du commerce d'exportations passant par les deux ports pendant la même période est comme suit:

	1897.		1898.	
	Colis.	Kilos.	Colis.	Kilos.
PORT LIMON.				
Exportations miscellanées......	1,783	152,386	2,081	184,710
Café en parchemin.............	34,767	1,794,874	105,891	4,428,149
Café débarrassé de son parchemin ....:....	164,916	10,139,879	181,029	11,168,992
Bananes......................	955,106	27,400,966	1,132,811	34,414,609
Rechargements................	44	1,928	182	136,788
Total..................	1,156,616	34,491,033	1,421,994	50,333,246
PUNTARENAS.				
Exportations miscellanées......	31,849	3,564,113	20,224	2,761,124
Café en parchemin	....	....	428	16,577
Café débarrassé de son parchemin	27,899	1,653,544	31,465	1,870,280
Bananes	....	....	....	....
Rechargements...............	229	14,178	217	15,751
Total..................	59,977	5,231,835	52,344	4,663,732

MEXIQUE.

PROGRÈS DANS LES MANUFACTURES DU COTON.

Le Mexique donne, rien que dans les manufactures du coton, une preuve marquée de progrès industriel. Le "Boston Transcript" dit:

Des autorités présumées être dignes de confiance attribue à ce pays le mérite d'avoir doublé le nombre de ses fabriques de coton pendant ces dernières années.

Un bref résumé de faits est intéressant. En 1896 pas moins de 107 fabriques de coton ont payé une taxe au Gouvernement.   De celles-ci 3 étaient des filatures, 6 des filatures et des imprimeries et 6 des imprimeries.   La force motrice de ces fabriques était de 13,826 force cheval et leur outillage comprenait 24 machines à imprimerie, 13,600 métiers de tisserand et 448,156 fuseaux.   Elles ont employé 20,994 hommes, femmes et enfants, et ont consommé 53,273,397 livres de coton naturel.   La moitié du coton consommée a été importé des Etats-Unis et l'autre moitié était de production indigène.

Le rendement de ces fabriques en 1896, était de 7,116,547 pièces de drap et 3,858,829 livres de fil, et de gros fil de coton.

Quoique l'industrie de coton du Mexique a plus de soixante années d'existence, le premier établissement remontant à 1834, ce n'est que dans les années récentes qu'un degré marqué du developpement a été atteint.   La nouvelle époque de l'industrie du Mexique est marquée par plusieurs autres entreprises, et elle est un changement heureux dans les affaires qui ont pour but la paix, la confiance et la civilisation accélérée dans l'Hémisphère occidental.

Le lin, dont la culture a beaucoup décrue aux Etats-Unis, est cultivé au Mexique, non-seulement pour la production de l'huile, mais on fabrique aussi de la toile avec autant d'attention et de soin à Cuernavaca et San Luis Potosi qu'on on apporte à la fabrication du jute, du chanvre et du coton à Orizaba et Guadalajara, et cette industrie est fortement protégée par le tarif mexicain.

Le meilleur lin mexicain possède ce singulier lustre et cette singulière qualité soyeuse qui caractérisent le lin irlandais, et il est cultivé près de Cuernavaca.   Il y a dans cette ville une grande filature de toile dont la production quotidienne est de 2,500 mètres.   On emploie comme force motrice l'eau et la vapeur; du coutil, de la toile d'Hollande et de la toile à matelas, toile à draps de lit, des essuies-mains, etc., sont manufacturés et vendus dans le pays.   Le même propriétaire a une filature à Mexico d'une capacité de production égale.

A Orizaba il y a des filatures de Rio Blanco fabricant de la toile de lin, ainsi que des articles de coton.   A San Luis Potosi il y a une fabrique d'origine anglaise qui fait de la toile à draps de lit, des articles de blanc d'une qualité plus fine, du coutil fin, et des tissus de robes, le produit rapportant de 40 cents à $1.50 par mètre.   Tous ces articles sont vendus dans la République.

La toile de lin fabriquée à Mexico est des mains-d'œuvre indigènes, prouvant que l'ouvrier mexicain est susceptible de la meilleure éducation. Les ouvriers apprennent bientôt à diriger les machines et des appareils américains, et quand les fabricants américains d'une machine à tisser et à filer se décideront à introduire leurs produits pour remplacer celle de la fabrication anglaise, on trouvera que l'ouvrier mexicain se servira aussi bien des unes que des autres.

En 1829, la production de tissus dans la République s'élevait à 1,800 kilogrammes, et augmentait en 1896 à 47,000 kilogrammes.

MARCHÉ POUR LES MACHINES.

A la suite des efforts croissant de la part des Etats-Unis de trouver des débouchés étrangers pour leurs manufactures, il est important qu'ils ne perdent pas de vue le Mexique qui est tout à leur porte et les possibilités duquel ne peuvent pas être exactement déterminées par des statistiques donnant les importations pour ce pays en ce moment. Le "Modern Mexico" donne son avis basé sur une connaissance de la situation et un examen attentif des faits qu'à mesure que les qualités supérieures des machines et des manufactures modernes sont connues, et à mesure que les facilités pour leur transport aux différents endroits du pays s'améliorent, la demande pour ces machines augmentera au Mexique. L'extrait suivant donne l'avis de ce journal :

Des machines perfectionnées de tous genres ont été une des importations principales du Mexique pendant ces dernières années, et il y a toutes raisons de croire que l'augmentation dans ce genre de commerce va continuer pendant beaucoup d'années dans l'avenir. Il faudra des années avant que la République produira ces articles sur une grande échelle ; mais tous les jours l'extension des chemins de fer et le succès des méthodes modernes pour les industries, augmentent continuellement la demande pour les manufactures américaines. Et quand, dans le territoire déjà facilement accessible, une clientèle est sollicitée par les exportateurs américains, avec la moitié de l'attention donnée au commerce dans leur propre pays, le résultat sera étonnant. Au cours d'une promenade d'environ 15 minutes au centre de la ville de Mexico, on peut voir en usage le même genre de charrue en bois qu'a été employée au Mexique depuis l'époque de Cortez, et des centaines de mines partout au Mexique sont exploitées par des machines des plus primitives.

La demande du Mexique pour les manufactures modernes va continuer à augmenter pendant des années et beaucoup plus rapidement que les industries du pays ne pourront les exécuter. Tous les ans les choses qui ont été jusqu'ici du luxe pour des milliers de gens sont maintenant les nécessités de tous les jours. Ce pays riche de toutes les resources naturelles, et qui maintenant est en train de se développer vigoureusement, est bien attirant pour le manufacturier américain. Ce n'est pas un marché qui peut être obtenu en le demandant. Il faut faire une concurrence avec le commerce des nations d'Europe, mais la qualité supérieure des marchandises américaines et la proximité de la source des approvisionnements sont de très forts arguments. Il y a là un conseil que les manufacturiers américains devraient accepter avec empressement. Il n'y a aucune raison pourquoi ces commerçants ne puissent s'assurer la plus grande partie du commerce mexicain.

CHEMINS DE FER PROJETÉS ET CONSTRUITS.

La construction d'une voie ferrée est dans un état de grande activité partout dans la République. Les lignes les plus importantes récemment construites et projetées sont les suivantes:

Une voie ferrée est projetée de Cordova au port de Tehuantepec. c'est l'ingénieur Louis B. Ceballos qui est chargé des plans. Une compagnie des Etats-Unis a obtenu la concession de construire un chemin de fer de Satillo à Paredon. Trevino, ou n'importe quel autre point sur la ligne Monterey Mexican. La ligne projetée de Mazatlan sera poussée jusqu'à Rosario. Señor Arturo de Cima, ex-Vice-Consul des Etats-Unis, a l'affaire en main.

Parmi les nouveaux projets il y a une ligne de Mazatlan à Villa Union, dans l'Etat de Sinaloa, où il y a de grandes filatures de coton. La ville de Mazatlan et l'Etat donneront les secours financiers. Une autre ligne projetée qui a de bonne chance d'être construite est celle de Merida de Tuncas, à Yucatan.

La ligne de la station de San Antonio, sur la ligne de sud à Chichotla, dans Etat d'Oaxaca, est terminée et est en opération. Elle a 54 kilomètres de longueur (33½ milles) elle traverse un pays montagneux et ouvre un riche district de café. On a commencé à construire la voie du Mexican International de Reata, à Monterey, au mois de juillet, et les travaux sont poussés activement. On dit que 112 kilomètres (70 milles) de rails seront placés en 90 jours.

La ligne du chemin de Mexico Cuernavaca et Pacifique a été terminée sur une distance de 20 kilomètres (13 milles) et sera encore prolongée. Les travaux sur les chemins de fer Chihuahua et Pacifique ont été commencés le 25 mars 1898, et on y emploie à présent 1,000 hommes. Les entrepreneurs désirent encore 2,000 hommes, mais de bons ouvriers sont difficiles à trouver. A la date du 25 mars 1898, la voie sera complétée jusqu'à Guerrero, distance de 200 kilomètres (125 milles). La longueur totale de la ligne sera de 600 kilomètres (375 milles). Plusieurs capitalistes des Etats-Unis sont actionnaires.

Le grand tunnel reliant Catorce à Potreto est terminé. La voie sera posée prochainement et le trafic de minerai, marchandises et passagers entre la ville de Montagnes et le Chemin de Fer Mexicain National sera beaucoup facilité. Catorce est une des villes de la République qui jusqu'ici on ne pouvait atteindre qu'à pied ou à cheval.

On était obligé de transporter toute la marchandise au moyen de bêtes de somme et tous les produits des riches mines de la ville devraient être descendues de la même façon, ce qui nécessite de grandes dépenses.

Le "Diario Oficial" publie le texte complet de la concession accordée par le Gouvernement mexicain à JOHN A. FRISBIE, représentant de WILLIAM STEWART et CIE., pour la construction d'une ligne dans les Etats de Sinaloa et Durango, partant de la Capitale de Sinaloa et terminant à Villa de Tepia, en Durango. La concession est datée du 25 mai 1898, et outre la route mentionnée la compagnie a le privilège de construire une autre ligne de la Capitale de Sinaloa à Altata, ou quelque autre point dans cet voisinage.

RAPPORT SYNOPTIQUE DE LA LOI NATIONALE SUR LES DROITS D'AUTEUR.

Le Consul Général BARLOW envoie de la ville de Mexico au Département d'Etat le rapport synoptique de la loi sur les droits d'auteur de ce pays.

La loi sur les droits d'auteur du Mexique stipule qu'en ce qui concerne l'effet légal, il n'y aura pas de distinction entre les Mexicains et les étrangers pourvu que l'œuvre en question soit publiée au Mexique. L'auteur jouit des droits d'auteur pendant sa vie, à sa mort ils passent à ses héritiers. Par conséquent, c'est un droit dont il peut disposer comme de n'importe quelle autre propriété en sa possession. Mais ces droits expirent dans une période de dix ans.

La loi donne à l'auteur le droit de publier les traductions de son œuvre, mais dans ce cas il doit déclarer s'il réserve ses droits pour une ou toutes les langues.

Ces droits sont accordés pour une période de dix ans aux auteurs qui n'habitent pas le Mexique et qui publient leurs œuvres à l'étranger.

Pour obtenir les droits d'auteur, le traducteur ou l'éditeur doit faire la demande en personne ou par l'intermédiaire de son représentant au Département de l'Instruction Publique disant qu'il réserve ses droits, et il doit envoyer en même temps deux exemplaires de son œuvre.

Tout auteur, traducteur, ou éditeur doivent placer son nom, la date de publication, et l'avis de ses droits d'auteur à une place bien en vue desdites copies.

Si l'on désire obtenir les droits d'auteur pour une œuvre musicale, une gravure, une lithographie ou une œuvre semblable, deux exemplaires doivent être envoyées.   Si c'est une œuvre d'architecture, de peinture, ou de sculpture, une copie du dessin ou un plan donnant les dimensions et tous les autres détails qui caractérisent l'original doivent être présentés.

Un auteur étranger ne résidant pas au Mexique doit envoyer plein pouvoir rédigé par devant un notaire public et certifié par un consul mexicain.   Celui-ci doit à son tour être légalisé par le Département d'État du Mexique, et protocole doit en être fait dûment traduit.   Les frais de ces formalités s'élèvent à $25, et plus $25, pour les démarches à faire pour l'obtention des droits d'auteur, inclus la valeur des timbres fédéraux qui doivent être apposés aux documents enregistrés au Département de l'Instruction Publique.   Des frais totaux s'élèvent ainsi à $50, en argent Mexicain.

NICARAGUA.

RÉSULTATS DES RECHERCES FAITES PAR LA COMMISSION DU CANAL.

On publie l'extrait suivant, emprunté au "New York Tribune" du 9 septembre 1898 comme étant d'un intérêt spécial pour la prospérité des Républiques Américaines.

La Commission spéciale, chargée de faire des recherches au sujet du Canal de Nicaragua, ayant pour président l'Amiral WALKER et pour membres le Professeur

HAUPT et le Général HAINES, n'a fait jusqu'à présent aucun rapport sur le canal, mais on a publié le récit fait par les membres devant le comité choisi du Sénat les 15–17 juin, qui montre clairement quelques-uns des résultats de leurs recherches. Pendant quatre mois environ, la Commission a fait personnellement un examen approfondi. Comme personnel secondaire elle avait deux cent cinquante personnes, comprenant quatre-vingts ingénieurs, et un géologue compétent pouvant aussi s'occuper de travaux hydrauliques ; comme matériel elle possédait les meilleurs intruments pour les recherches scientifiques, comprenant dix perforateurs. La Commission poursuit encore ses travaux, mais les recherches les plus sérieuses qui ont été faites jusqu'ici, prouvent l'exactitude de l'arpentage fait par M. Menocal ainsi que des informations obtenues dernièrement, et elles ont mis en évidence des détails intéressants et importants qui paraissent très favorables au projet.

On a reconnu, après un examen sérieux, qu'il n'existe pas de formation rocheuse qui, croyait-on, rendrait nécessaire la construction d'un brise-lames étendu et coûteux afin de former un port sûr à Brito. M. l'Amiral WALKER et les autres membres certifient que pour construire un bon port il est seulement nécessaire de draguer le marais de mangliers au-dessous du Cap de Rito, et de construire à cet endroit une jetée relativement courte. Quant à la variation de la profondeur du Lac Nicaragua qui autrefois, dit-on, mesurait quinze pieds et qui était une des plus importantes difficultés des plans pris jusqu'ici en considération, la Commission ne trouve aucune preuve d'une aussi grande différence, et les hommes compétents faisant partie de la Commission croient que la difficulté de diriger l'écoulement des eaux sera grandement diminuée, aussi bien par l'établissement de la communication avec le Lac Managua que par l'établissement d'un courant d'eau qu'on pourra faire couler.

Plus important encore est la conclusion sur laquelle tous les membres de la Commission semblent être d'accord de savoir qu'on peut éviter les risques et les dépenses de la construction de môles extrèmement élevés de chaque côté. Ces messieurs pensent que pour le côté de l'ouest, il est préférable de continuer un canal direct sans communication avec la rivière. Du côté de l'est, on propose de construire à Machuco un môle ayant une pente de vingt-cinq pieds environ, donnant ainsi une hauteur modérée au môle d'Ochon. Les sondages qu'on a faits ont dissipé les doutes en faisant voir, comme aux digues de San Francisco, un fonds de roche solide aux deux endroits où les môles importants sont nécessaires, quoiqu'on trouve mieux d'éviter entièrement ce travail coûteux en coupant plus profondément cette partie.

On n'est arrivé à aucune solution définitive et on n'a pas pu obtenir toutes les informations sur ces détails, mais la Commission semble être entièrement satisfaite de voir qu'on peut accomplir le travail avec moins de risque et probablement avec moins de dépenses qu'on ne l'avait prévu.

On a examiné la question de construire des ports sur le lac et on a découvert qu'on peut choisir du côté comme un meilleur emplacement, épargnant ainsi une distance de deux ou trois milles. A Greytown on ne peut surmonter les difficultés que par la construction d'une jetée de plus de trois milles pieds et d'une autre plus courte du côté opposé, ainsi que par le dragage plus ou moins constant, tel qu'on le trouve nécessaire au port de Galveston, à l'embouchure du Mississippi et de Port Saïd ; mais la Commission trouve qu'il est très possible de construire des ports sûrs à tous les endroits où ils sont nécessaires. Jusqu'ici on n'a fait aucune estimation définitive sur les dépenses. M. le Professeur HAUPT croit fermement qu'on pourrait achever le travail avec une dépense de $90,000,000, mais les autres membres de la Commission estiment la dépense, l'un à $125,000,000 et l'autre à $140,000,000 comme maximum. Il est intéressant de constater que la Commission en entier considère que toute différence possible dans le coût, même si elle s'élevait à $200,000, est insignifiante, si on la compare à la valeur énorme qu'aurait le canal pour ce pays et pour son commerce.

PÉROU.

FABRIQUE D'ALLUMETTES DE EL SOL.

Le Ministre des Etats-Unis à Lima, M. DUDLEY, fait savoir au Bureau qu'on vient d'établir dans cette ville une compagnie intitulée "Fabrique d'Allumettes de El Sol," avec un capital de 400,000 de soles ($163,000), pour la fabrication d'allumettes de toutes sortes. On emploiera les machines et les brevets de la compagnie renommée de Chicago "Diamond Match," qui a pris 50 pour cent des actions de cette fabrique.

La compagnie a pour président, M. José PAYÁN ; pour directeurs, M. FRANCISCO M. OLIVA et M. PABLO LA ROSA, et pour régisseur, M. JUAN DUANY.

Les actionnaires de l'entreprise sont : LA SOCIEDAD MANUFACTURERA DE TABACOS, MM. José PAYÁN, M. B. WELLS, ERNESTO AYULO, LORENZO DELAUDE, José E. CASTAÑON, ROBERTO GANOZA, PABLO LA ROSA, OCTAVIO VALENTINI, HERMAN DENKS, JOAQUÍN GODOY et FRANCISCO PÉREZ DE VELASCO.

On propose d'établir les ateliers de la fabrique à Callao, mais jusqu'ici on n'est arrivé à aucune solution définitive.

EXPORTATIONS DE 1897 COMPAR ES AVEC CELLES DE 1896.

On donne ci-dessous un tableau synoptique concernant les exportations du Pérou en 1897, comparées à celles de 1896, telles qu'elles ont été publiées dans "El Comercio" à Lima, le 27 juin 1898.

Articles.	1896.	1897.
	Kilos.	*Kilos.*
Sucre	71, 735, 473	105, 463, 238
Coton	4, 717, 697	5, 586, 394
Borate	1, 178, 762	11, 850, 490
Cascarille...	16, 489	62, 261
Cuirs...	1, 331, 689	1, 710, 206
Laine	2, 543, 641	3, 767, 799
Tourteau de coton en coque............................	1, 048, 456	1, 007, 527
Riz...	2, 803, 640	4, 221, 835
Café	712, 919	1, 239, 744
	Soles.	*Soles.*
Cochenille..	32, 070	2, 407
Cocoa et cocaine......................................	1, 212, 381	1, 173, 066
Charbon et bois.......................................	97, 429	93, 307
Meubles et vêtements..................................	42, 998	34, 460
Or, monnayé..	59, 321	104, 524
Argent, monnayé......................................	1, 485, 433	1, 927, 454
Minéraux...	4, 576, 511	6, 448, 567
Animaux sur pied.....................................	168, 949	192, 955
Rotin	20, 673	11, 180
Coton en coque.......................................	69, 184	36, 156
Tabac	378, 439	27, 110
Cacao..	22, 581	32, 125
Oignons, pommes de terre, etc	173, 394	154, 345
Sel...	90, 141	120, 375
	Litres.	*Litres.*
Alcool	231, 020	255, 401
Rhum	98, 302	68, 374
Bière...	54, 255	540
Vin	289, 161	143, 095
Amers (douzaine).....................................	2, 029	40
Chapeaux (douzaine)..................................	15, 408	13, 128

PAYS DE DESTINATION.

	Soles.	*Soles.*
Angleterre	10, 429, 386	15, 648, 310
Chili	4, 599, 227	5, 753, 074
Allemagne	2, 231, 898	2, 322, 023
Etats-Unis	1, 608, 900	1, 392, 623
Equateur	669, 276	1, 212, 497
France	1, 508, 088	1, 181, 312
Colombie...	468, 536	447, 202
Bolivie	120, 912	56, 683
Amérique Centrale	125, 567	49, 546
Italie...	35, 234	38, 964
Chine	31, 800	32, 660
Espagne	9, 657	11, 965
Brésil	2, 985	9, 010
Belgique..	....	8, 786
Mexique..	9, 451	2, 871
Portugal..	....	500
République Argentine	....	421
Venezuela	8, 646	....
Grèce..	2, 425	....
Uruguay..	360	....
Envois de la Douane d'Iquitos (pays de destination n'étant pas donnés)	....	2, 856, 929
Total	21, 862, 334	31, 025, 382

Solde en faveur de 1897, 9,193,047 soles.

Le texte entier de la décision est comme suit :

DÉPARTEMENT DU SECRÉTAIRE DE LA TRÉSORERIE,
Washington, D. C., août 1898.

Aux Percepteurs et Fonctionnaires des Douanes.

Dans le but d'assurer une uniformité de pratique dans les différents ports dans la classification des cuirs de veau et des peaux sous ledit règlement de l'acte du 24 juillet 1897, vous êtes par la présente autorisés à employer le tableau suivant des poids en déterminant les classifications respectives, et de classifier toutes les peaux de tels poids ou de moins de ce poids comme cuirs de veau et toutes les peaux d'un poids plus grand comme peaux, savoir :

		Livres.
1.	Mouillés ou poids de boucher	12
2.	Mouillés et salés	12
3.	Sèches salés	7½
4.	Sèches	5

LA TONTE DES MOUTONS EN 1898.

"Le Bulletin Commercial" de Boston publie les statistiques suivantes ayant rapport au nombre de moutons qu'on possède aux Etats-Unis et à la tonte des moutons en 1898.

Le nombre total de moutons dans le pays au 1er janvier 1898 s'élevait à 37,656,960. D'après les estimations du Ministère de l'Agriculture, la perte subséquente a été en tout de 1,985,046 moutons, laissant, le 1er avril, un troupeau de 35,671,914 moutons. Pour savoir le total de la tonte de moutons pour l'année actuelle, on est forcé de se baser sur les chiffres de l'année dernière en prenant le poids moyen de la toison, ce qui donne seulement une estimation approximative. Prenant alores 6 livres 30 comme poids moyen de la toison, la tonte totale de cette année s'élèvera à 224,733,058 livres. En y ajoutant l'estimation totale de la laine prise sur les peaux, soit 40,000,000, la production totale pour 1898 sera de 264,733,058 livres. La tonte de 1897 était de 259,153,251 livres.

Le 1er avril 1897, le nombre total des moutons était de 34,784,287, soit, en comparaison avec les chiffres de cette année, une augmentation de 887,627 moutons pour 1898.

DÉVELOPPEMENT DE L'ÉLECTRICITÉ.

On constate, d'après le "Wall Street Journal," qu'en 1894 le total des appareils électriques placés dans tous les Etats-Unis était d'environ $1,000,000, tandis qu'aujourd'hui le capital employé dans toutes les entreprises électriques du pays est de $1,900,000,000 au moins.

En 1884 on considérait qu'un dynamo de 50 "kilowatts" était

une machine puissante et le prix des dynamos était d'environ 20 cents par "watt" de production. Actuellement la plus grande machine électrique qui ait été construite est d'une capacité d'environ 5,000 "watts," et les dynamos de volume assez petite coûtent maintenant environ 2 cents par "watt." On compte qu'environ $600,000,000 ont été placés dans les stations et des entreprises de lumière électrique aux Etats-Unis. Aujourd'hui, il y a dans ce pays 14,000 milles de chemins de fer électriques au capital nominal d'environ $1,000,000,000, employant 170,000 ouvriers. On peut maintenant se parler à une distance de 1,800 milles, et on communique très souvent à une distance de 1,500 milles. Il y a maintenant plus de 1,000,000 de téléphones dans le service téléphonique du pays, employant un capital d'environ $100,000,000, 40,000 bureaux et 900,000 milles de fil de fer. Chaque jour 17,000 employés font en moyenne plus de 3,000,000 de rapports téléphoniques.

URUGUAY.

AMÉLIORATIONS DU PORT À MONTÉVIDÉO.

Dans un rapport récent, M. ALBERT W. SWALM, Consul des Etats-Unis à Montévideo, informe son Gouvernement des améliorations contemplées dans le port de cette ville. Ceci est de très grande importance aux entrepreneurs des Etats-Unis car des soumissions seront demandées des commerçants dans ce pays aussi bien que des entrepreneurs européens. La communication du Consul est comme suit :

Le Gouvernement provisoire d'Uruguay a présenté au Conseil d'État un projet pour l'amélioration du port de Montévideo qui est certain de devenir loi, et qui sera considéré par tous ceux qui font des affaires commerciales dans ce port comme une entreprise de première utilité.

Une appropriation de $15,400,000 est déjà fournie d'être en obligations de $47 ou £10 chaque, intérêt 6 pour cent par an, payable chaque trimestre, soit à Montévidéo, soit sur n'importe quelle place commerciale d'Europe. Comme une des stipulations du fonds d'amortissement, une taxe de 2½ pour cent sera perçue sur toutes les importations. Tous les droits de port nouveaux sont retenus pour les obligations et l'intérêt. Une commission financière se chargera du projet et dans un an les obligations seront sur les marchés locaux et généraux.

Le projet adopté est connu sous le nom de plan Kummer-Guerrard. La plus basse eau laissera 7½ mètres (24.52 pieds) dans le canal. Un carénage de 200 mètres (656.17 pieds) de longueur et de largeur correspondante, avec 8 mètres (26.24 pieds) d'eau sur ses plus bas baux, est aussi stipulé.

Le pouvoir exécutif est autorisé de demander des soumissions pour l'exécution des travaux aux entrepreneurs capables et responsables en Europe et en Amérique tont en conservant le droit de refuser toutes les offres qui ne sont pas avantageuses. Dans le cas où un contrat est signé, une commission technique sera nommée pour surveiller les travaux. Tous les payements pour le travail fait doivent être en or. Quand la somme de $15,000 sera dépensée, tous les contrats seront résiliés si les travaux ne sont pas terminés. Les conditions dans ce port sont pareilles à celles de Galveston.

Le Gouvernement est bien capable de remplir tous ses engagements. Il y a eu des changements forcés dans son régime, mais l'unité monétaire reste la même.

RÉSEAUX DE CHEMINS DE FER.

M. Juan José Castro, de l'Uruguay, a compilé dernièrement un ouvrage sur les réseaux de chemins de fer de l'Amérique de Sud. Il s'occupe surtout des voies construites et sous contrat dans son pays. On a extrait de ce rapport les informations suivantes sur la longueur des routes et la situation financière des compagnies.

Routes.	Longueur.	Capital.
	Kilomètres.	
Chemin de fer Central...................................	321.65	$13,575,000
Chemin de fer Central—réseau du nord.................	293.34	7,968,700
Chemin de fer Central—réseau du nord-est.............	124.30	3,892,000
Chemin de fer Central—réseau de l'est..................	581.20	14,965,000
Chemin de fer de l'Est..............................	419.50	10,233,450
Chemin de fer du Centre	317.05	7,711,900
Chemin de fer du Nord-Ouest.........................	178.80	4,944,580
Chemin de fer du Nord...............................	114.16	2,771,685
Embranchement de San Engenho............	3.00	73,000
Chemin de fer de l'Ouest	520.10	11,162,500
Chemin de fer du Nord...............................	23.00	671,375
Chemin de fer de l'Intérieur	617.70	15,000,000
Total.............	3,513.80	92,969,190

Le kilomètre équivaut à 3,280 pieds 10 pouces, soit .62137 d'un mille, de sorte que le nombre total de milles de chemin de fer dans l'Uruguay est de 2,183.37 environ. Le stock capitalisé, évalué en monnaie des Etats-Unis, est de $26,458.30 par kilomètre, soit $42,117.32 par mille.

Le 1er janvier 1897, la République Argentine avait, en comparaison avec l'Urugua, 9,041 milles (14,550 kilomètres) de chemin de fer, représentant un capital de $480.321,820, soit $53,016.40 par mille. Le Brésil avait 8,403 milles (13,523 kilomètres) au capital de $483,742,610, soit $57,566.55 par mille.

Le Chili avait 2,490 milles (4,003 kilomètres) au capital de $107,030,000, soit $42,988 par mille.

Voici le prix de revient d'un mille de chemin de fer dans les différentes contrées: Uruguay, $36,794; Argentine, $45,809; Brésil, $49,317; Chili (chemins de fer de l'Etat), $43,225; Chili (chemins de fer appartenant aux compagnies particulières), $33,535; Pérou, $134,141.

VENEZUELA.

IMPORTATIONS PAR LE PORT DE LA GUAYRA POUR LE PREMIER SEMESTRE DE L'ANNÉE 1898.

Le Bureau des Républiques Américaines doit à l'amabilité de M. le docteur J. M. RIVAS MINDARÁIN, Receveur des Douanes du port de La Guayara, l'envoi de tableaux de statistiques montrant les importations de marchandises étrangères par le port de la Guayara du 1er janvier au 30 juin 1898. Ces tableaux sont accompagnés d'une communication faisant l'éloge des services que le BULLETIN a rendus aux intérêts commerciaux. Les tableaux désignent le pays d'origine, la classe des marchandises, le nombre de colis, avec le poids brut en kilogrammes, le montant des droits perçus, avec le 12½ pour cent en sus, et le résumé général du commerce d'importation.

D'après la publication ci-dessus, le total des importations pour les six mois en question était comme suit : 427,845 colis formant un poids brut de 18,511,867 kilogrammes ayant une valeur approximative de 12,315,929.95 de bolivars (environ $2,000,000) et dont les droits payés ont atteint 5,471,207.95 de bolivars. Les pays qui y étaient représentés étaient les suivants :

Pays.	Colis.	Valeur déclarée.
		Bolivars.
Etats-Unis	165, 837	3, 680, 800. 52
Allemagne	66, 690	2, 178, 460. 52
France	36, 298	2, 223, 397.75
Angleterre	119, 513	2, 127, 912. 80
Italie	10, 683	591, 898. 75
Espagne	18, 626	832, 004. 35
Hollande	10, 191	676, 722. 20
Colombie	6	4, 733. 00

Les Etats-Unis occupent, comme on peut le constater, le premier rang dans les importations générales de La Guayara, viennent ensuite, mais seulement au point de vue de la quantité, l'Angleterre, l'Allemagne, la France, l'Espagne, l'Italie, la Hollande et la Colombie, et au point de vue de la valeur déclarée, ce sont la France, l'Allemagne, l'Espagne, la Hollande, l'Italie et la Colombie qui suivent.

D'après les matières, voici la statistique des Etats-Unis. Pas de concurrents dans l'importation des articles suivants : Huile de pétrole, saindoux, appareils photographiques et fruits. D'exportation de cotonnades qui viennent de France, d'Allemagne et d'Angleterre : Le carton bristol fabriqué en articles divers qu'on importe de ces mêmes pays ; les chapeaux de feutre et de paille qu'on importe de tous les pays et les lainages qu'on fait venir de France, d'Angleterre, d'Allemagne et d'Italie.

Les Etats-Unis tiennent le premier rang dans la concurrence avec les sept autres pays cités, en fait d'importations de cordages et de cargues, de céréales, d'épices, de conserves et de fruits confits dans leur jus, de quincaillerie, de couvertures de coton, de biscuits, de jambons, de meubles en bois, de joujoux et de marbres. Ils tiennent le second rang dans les importations de baïetes en ballots, de couvertures, de conserves, de cigarettes, de tabac, de bière, de beuf salé, de cuivre sous différentes formes, de drogues, de médicaments, d'instruments agricoles, d'outils. Il en est de même pour l'industrie, les importations de beurre, de papier de toutes sortes et de cotonnades. Ils viennent en troisième lieu pour la papeterie, les matériaux de construction de chemins de fer, les instruments de cuisine, les instruments de musique, les livres, les carnets, l'amidon, les échantillons et la parfumerie. Ils occupent le quatrième rang pour les articles de fantaisie, le riz, non préparé, les céréales, le charbon, le ciment, la stéarine, les dentelles, les broderies, les mousselines, etc., le fil de lin, la laine à tricoter, les porcelaines et verrerie, les madapolams et les garnitures ; ils occupent le cinquième rang pour les légumes confits dans le vinaigre, les olives, les fromages de toutes sortes, etc.; le sixième pour l'huile d'olive, les rubans de soie, le drap, les mouchoirs de poche, etc.; le septième pour les importations de camisoles de coton, de bonneterie, de vins et liqueurs de toutes sortes.

Bull. No. 3——11

COMMERCE DE HOUILLE.

Ecrivant de La Guayra le 15 juin, le Consul GOLDSCHMIDT dit, concernant la quantité de combustible au Venezuela, que presque tout le charbon consommé est d'origine anglaise et provient du voisinage de Cardiff, dans le pays de Galles, d'où il vient généralement par les voiliers. La proximité des terrains houillers aux Etats-Unis et l'absence totale de leur produit sur ce marché, l'a poussé de faire des investigations sur ce sujet. La consommation de houille dans ce district est considérable.

Les divers chemins de fer dont La Guayra et Caruca et le Grand Chemin de fer allemand de Caraca à Valencia sont les plus grands, brûlent du combustible de Cardiff. Tout le charbon vendu au détail provient de la même source et est vendu à un prix très élevé, évidemment à cause du peu de concurrence. Le prix du charbon au détail par tonne de 2,240 livres varie de 14 à 16 pesos ($11.20 à $12.80), en quantité de 1 à 20 tonnes ou même plus.

Une des raisons principales pourquoi ce charbon est préferé, est qu'il est préparé par les mineurs Gallois en forme de briquettes de 7 à 8 pouces de longueur. Ceci le rend très facile à charger sur des chemins de fer, vu que les locomotives employées n'ont pas de *tender* comme celles des Etats-Unis, mais transportent leur combustible sur une petite plateforme attachée à la locomotive et d'où le charbon ordinaire pourrait très bien tomber. Ce genre de charbon ayant été employé pendant quelque temps, les grilles dans les chaudières ont été construites pour cette grandeur de houille et le charbon en morceaux ne conviendrait pas si bien.

Ce charbon est comprimé au moyen de goudron et est ensuite chargé sur les navires tout fumant, et pour cette raison il perd fréquemment en poids pendant le transport par l'évaporation et le séchage, et cette perte est à charge du consignataire.

Par suite des grèves dans les mines du pays de Galles, très peu de charbon est arrivé depuis peu; mais malgré ce fait aucun charbon américain n'a été déchargé dans ce port, excepté une espèce de charbon dur, employé dans la fabrication du gaz.

Il y a ici un débouché excellent pour le charbon des Etats-Unis, et sans doute il en est de même pour beaucoup de pays de l'Amérique du Sud, mais les exportateurs des Etats-Unis peuvent remplir tous les ordres.

Le consul est d'avis que la houille américaine pourrait être déchargée ici et vendue beaucoup meilleur marché que la houille anglaise et laisserait encore un beau bénéfice pour l'expéditeur. Il pense que n'importe quelle compagnie qui voudra manufacturer le charbon en briquettes de proportions commodes et envoyer un agent capable pour introduire cet article, trouvera un marché excellent. Le consul ajoute que pour ce but un charbon gras peut être employé qui ne trouve pas toujours un débouché aux Etats-Unis.

On retire du charbon dans ce pays près du port de Barcelona, mais la qualité semble être inférieure et il ne se vend pas quand on peut obtenir un autre charbon. Le Gouvernement du Venezuela ne prélève aucun impôt de douane sur le charbon.

MINES DE SOUFRE DE CARUPANO.

Le rapport synoptique qui suit sur les dépôts de soufre du Venezuela et qui y sont décrits comme ayant de si belles perspectives, mais qui jusqu'ici n'ont à peine été touchés par leur découvreur, est du "Herald" Venezuelien de Caracas.

Dans une direction sud-sudest de Carupano, à une distance d'environ 15 kilomètres (9⅓ milles) en ligne droite, il y a d'immenses dépôts de minerai de soufre situés sur la pente du sud des montagnes à 30 mètres (984 pieds) au-dessus du niveau de la mer. Ces dépôts sont restés inexplorés jusqu'à présent à cause des grandes difficultés de transporter le minerai aux bords de la mer.

La seule méthode de transport jusqu'ici a été à dos de mulets et d'ânes, ce qui a rendu le coût du produit trop grand pour en permettre l'exportation aux marchés d'Europe et d'Amérique.

Le présent propriétaire des mines a surmonté, dans une mesure, cette obstacle en obtenant du Gouvernement de Venezuela, une concession pour l'établissement d'un tramway aerien allant des dépôts à un des nombreux caños qui se jettent dans le Golfe de Parea, et de naviguer ces caños aux moyens de gabarres et de remorqueurs à vapeur qui transporteront le soufre aux navires chargeant pour des ports étrangers. La longueur du tramway

où la demande est très limitée. Mais cette demande va augmenter à mesure que le pays se développera et que l'on aura besoin de combustibles. Ce champ de spéculation est fort séduisant, même sur la base d'un calcul de valeur beaucoup plus bas que les prétensions ordinaires.

Pendant ces dernières années j'ai examiné toute la côte du Colfe du Darien jusqu'à l'embouchure du fleuve Orinoco, et plusieurs fois on m'a demandé de faire un rapport sur les divers dépôts existant dans cette région. Ces dépôts varient d'un lignite impur et récent à un lignite crétacé de bonne qualité et ils proviennent des places nommées ci-dessous.

1. A l'ouest du fleuve Orinoco dans l'Etat de Bermudez, Venezuela, un lignite de bonne qualité.

2. Dans la région derrière Puerto-Cabello, Venezuela, un lignite pas si compacte que celui trouvé dans l'Etat de Bermudez.

3. Près de Maracaïbo, en Venezuela, un lignite apparemment mou.

4. Dans les vallées basses derrière Richacha, Colombie, des dépôts abondants d'un lignite mou.

5. Une succession irrégulière de dépôts le long de la base des Andes, du pays situés derrière Rióchacha, vers l'intérieur.

6. Une couche de houille cretacée d'une grande étendue, d'à peu près un mètre d'épaiseur, près de Bogota, dans les Andes de la Colombie.

7. Dépôts considérables dans l'Etat de Cauca, de la Colombie, apparemment un charbon impur et cretacé accessible seulement du Pacifique.

8. Le long du rivage occidental du fleuve Magdalena, dans la Colombie, une mince couche de lignite impur.

9. Près de Santa Marta, dans la Colombie, un dépôt de lignite peu important mais d'une qualité de première classe.

10. Sur la partie supérieure du fleuve Sinu, de la Colombie, des affleurements en apparence pas très étendus.

11. Près de Chiriqui Lagoon en Costa Rica et en Panama; rapport d'une houille de première classe, mais importante aux marchés de l'Amérique Centrale plutôt qu'au nord de l'Amérique du Sud.

12. Près de Barranquilla dans la Colombie, il y a une quantité abondante de gaz naturel qui sera très util comme combustible dans cette ville.

Outre ces sources de combustibles, il y a sur l'île de Trinadad, dans l'Etat de Bermudez, près du Maracaïbo, en Venezuela, et dans les régions supérieures de la rivière Magdalena, dans la Colombie, des dépôts d'asphalte très étendus avec des indications que du pétrole et du gaz naturel existent dans ces pays.

L'expression "lignite" s'applique à une espèce de charbon compacte à la distinction d'un lignite qui s'émiette dans la main, qualité tout à fait particulière à beaucoup de dépôts de l'Amérique du Sud. De cette liste on pourrait très facilement conclure que le nord de l'Amérique du Sud est extraordinairement riche en combustibles, mais beaucoup de dépôts renommés ne sont pas assez grands pour être d'une importance économique, et la région décrite est très étendue, avec une côte égale à celle des Etats-Unis entre Portland, Me. et Charleston, S. C. Des dépôts houillers de l'intérieur, ceux près de Bogota sont les plus importants. Dans ce district le charbon est obtenu à grand effort par

Les perspectives économiques sont peut-être meilleures ici à cause du transport de passagers par bateau sur le fleuve Magdalena qui augmente continuellement, et dependant à present d'une quantité décroissante du bois pris des bords du fleuve.

Les autres dépôts de la Colombie, excepté peut-être ceux en amont du fleuve Sinu, présente un intérèt scientifique, mais ne valent guère d'être considerés au point de vue économique.

Je n'ai pas examiné les dépôts à Chiriqui, mais des échantillons de ce district semblent indiquer une meilleure qualité de houille, peut-être plus ancienne que les formations tertiaires, mais ce charbon appartient aux marchés de l'Amérique Centrale plutôt qu'à ceux de l'Amérique du Sud.

Des grandes quantités d'asphalte existant au Venezuela et dans la Colombie donneront, probablement, une bonne matière nécessaire au mélange avec le lignite pour en faire des briquettes et sera peut-être la base d'une industrie importante dans l'avenir. Dans toute cette étendue de territoire, cependant, les veines prêtes à l'exploitation se trouvent seulement aux endroits bien éloignés, et quelque soient les résultats obtenus, il est très certain qu'à mesure du dévelopment de ces pays la demande de combustibles augmentera, dont une grande partie au moins sera fournie par les Etats-Unis. Quant à la valeur de cette demande, il est difficile de la déterminer. Il y a tout le commerce des navires de mer qui à présent transportent la houille d'une grande distance et aux dépens de la capacité de chargement; il y a le commerce par navires sur les fleuves Orinoco et Magdalena, lesquelles, ensemble, pourront très bien ètre comparés favorablement avec celui du Mississippi. Il y a un réseau croissant de chemin de fer à approvisionner et les besoins croissants des villes de Caracas, La Guayra, Maracaïbo, Cartagena et Barranquilla, quoique cette dernière sera approvisionnée en partie de combustibles de ses puits de gaz naturel. En ce moment la plupart du charbon consumée dans le nord de l'Amérique du Sud vient de Cardiff, mais une partie est achetée aux Etats-Unis, et l'avenir de ce commerce vaut la peine d'être considéré.

COMMERCE ENTRE LA GRANDE BRETAGNE ET LES RÉPUBLIQUES AMÉRICAINES EN 1898.

Une revue officielle de la Grande-Bretagne intitulée "Rapports concernant le Commerce et la Navigation," publiée le 4 août 1898, donne des statistiques intéressantes concernant les importations des Républiques Américaines et les exportations des mêmes Républiques. Les évaluations sont données dans les tableaux ci-joints pour le premier semestre de 1898, et afin de pouvoir faire une comparaison, les données officielles pour les mêmes périodes de 1897 et 1896 sont données. Les évaluations sont données en livres "sterling," une livre étant égale à $4.865 en espèce des Etats-Unis.

emploie environ 90 pour cent de la production totale du glucose pour la consommation intérieure et extérieure. D'après un rapport publié le 1ᵉʳ août, il ressort que ces différentes fabriques ont consommé depuis le 15 août 1897 20,616,000 boisseaux de maïs, qui ont produit 542,100,000 livres de glucose, 120,512,000 livres d'amidon, 98,382,000 livres de sucre, 2,600,000 livres de dextrine et 151,788,000 livres de résidu.

Le nombre de produits secondaires qu'on a fabriqués est de 40. Parmi ceux-ci, on trouve un équivalent du caoutchouc. Ce produit n'est pas destiné à remplacer entièrement le caoutchouc, mais il peut être employé en qualité de mélange. Les fabricants vendent ce produit à 4 cents ½ la livre, et on affirme que les fabricants d'articles en caoutchouc, surtout ceux qui font les tubes de bicyclettes, s'en servent beaucoup. Si on peut en prouver la durée, il se peut que cette découverte révolutionne le commerce de caoutchouc. Cet équivalent du caoutchouc est fabriqué avec l'huile de maïs au moyen de la vulcanisation. Le produit ressemble de très près en apparence et en qualité au caoutchouc de Pará. D'après le rapport de la compagnie, on peut l'employer dans la manufacture de toutes les classes d'articles en caoutchouc, y compris le caoutchouc en feuilles, les tubes de bicyclettes, les chaussures en caoutchouc, les semelles en caoutchouc, les vêtements imperméables, la toile cirée, etc. L'huile de caoutchouc ne s'oxydant pas facilement, ce produit est d'une grande valeur, et par là même les produits qui en seront fabriqués resteront toujours souples et ne se fendront pas comme ceux qui sont faites avec d'autres substances tirées de l'huile de graine de navette, de l'huile de graine de lin, etc. On prétend qu'un mélange fait de 50 pour cent de caoutchouc pur et de 50 pour cent de remplaçant restera souple et pliant et ne se cassera pas.

Malgré la grande augmentation dans la quantité, le marché a subi une hausse dès le jour de son arrivée. Le produit brut est employé dans la manufacture des articles nombreux.

Une grande quantité de caoutchouc est employée pour toutes sortes de machines et la grande demande pour cet article dans la construction des bicyclettes et autres voitures où l'on emploie des bandes en caoutchouc pour les roues lui ont ouvert un nouveau débouché.

MISCELLANÉES COMMERCIALES.

RÉPUBLIQUE ARGENTINE.

Réduction des Salaires et Pensions. Le Journal de l'Amérique du Sud est autorité pour le rapport résolu par le Congrès Argentin que, du 1er juillet jusqu'au 31 décembre 1898, les salaires, pensions, subsides et subventions, etc., du Gouvernement seront réduits de 20 pour cent. La seule exception est pour la solde des soldats et des matelots de la flotte. Le Gouvernement espère épargner $5,000,000 par cette réduction.

Récolte de Céréales. Le 18 juin, WILLIAM GOODWIN, inspecteur autorisé des blés du fleuve Plate, écrivant de Buenos-Ayres, dit comme suit concernant la récolte de blé et de maïs en Argentine :

"Une prolongation du temps chaud et humide a eu un très mauvais effet sur les chargements de maïs, mais il n'y a aucune raison de craindre une trop abondante récolte de blé, le blé ayant été semé dans les conditions les plus favorables.

"La hausse du blé et du maïs est retarde par les marchés peu suivis, quoiqu'il y ait toujours une assez grande quantité de blé à exporter, et tous les rapports sont d'accord que la moisson de froment est sans doute la plus grande que l'on ait jamais récoltée, et l'on espère qu'elle sera plus tard de bonnes qualités pour les transports. Chaque année montre un grand avancement dans les méthodes d'agriculture en Argentine et surtout dans les soins que l'on prend des produits des champs au temps de la moisson. Mais il faut remarquer que la population agricole n'augmente pas rapidement, car très peu d'immigrants sont arrivés pendant les dernières années."

Importation d'Appareil Électrique. Pendant l'année 1897 la République Argentine a importé 16,081 tonnes de fil de fer galvanisé, évalué à $1,005,777 ; aussi 35,216 douzaines de lampes incandescentes, 5,123 caisses de matériel électrique général, 52 dynamos, 529 caisses de materiel télégraphique,

318 caisses de matériel de téléphone, ensemble avec d'autre appareil ; aussi l'évaluation du matériel des voies des lignes électriques, envoyé à l'Argentine par les manufacturiers des Etats-Unis, dépasse $2,000,000.

BRÉSIL.

Analyse de la Bière. Une loi a été récemment passée au Brésil, réglant l'analyse de la bière, dans le but d'y découvrir l'emploi des succédanés du houblon d'un caractère qui pourrait être nuisible au consommateur. La bière trouvée ainsi adultérée doit être réexportée sans être retirée de l'entrepôt ou détruite par l'importateur, et à défaut de se conformer aux termes de la loi, une forte amende sera imposée.

District de Caoutchouc de Para. Le consul du Brésil à Para écrit : " Quelques-uns supposent que la quantité de caoutchouc de l'Amazone pourrait s'épuiser dans un avenir prochain. Les autorités les plus compétentes ne sont pas toutes de cet avis, mais soutiennent que la quantité est inépuisable parce que l'"hevea" est continuellement reproduite par la nature. Il y a par-ci par-là des sections épuisées par avoir été trop travaillées, mais si elles ne sont pas dérangées pendant quelque temps, elles se remettront. Le district de Cametá, sur le fleuve Tocantins, a produit une excellente qualité de caoutchouc pour lequel il y avait des côtes spéciales. Ce district est à présent épuisé à cause que pendant environ 40 ans des milliers d'hommes ont entaillé les arbres. Tous les nouveaux arrivants sont allés en foule à Cametá pour y faire fortune. Il y a beaucoup de districts qui n'ont pas encore été exploités. Le territoire qui est renommé pour la production de caoutchouc de Para a une étendue de 1,000,000 de milles carrés. Une exploration plus étendue démontrera, sans doute, que ce territoire n'a pas été assez estimé."

Conseils aux Manufacturiers. Le Consul Anglais à Para fait le rapport suivant dans le " British Trade Journal : " C'est la coutume de porter des vêtements de drap foncé, soit parce que le blanchissage est cher ou parce qu'il y a de brusques changements de température causés par les pluies fréquentes ou peut-être pour les deux causes réunies, on a trouvé qu'il était préférable de porter du drap au lieu de coutil ou de la toile de lin comme dans les autres pays des tropiques. Les casques ne se portent pas, mais des chapeaux en paille et en feutre sont portés partout par les hommes. Les indigènes et les basses classes portent le même genre de vêtements que les hautes classes, et ils portent invariablement des chemises blanches de toile de lin et des bottes et des bottines. Les pluies presque quotidiennes obligent tout le monde de se fournir d'un parapluie. Des ferrures, de l'huile, et des couleurs à la détrempe sont fort demandées pour les maisons, et comme toutes les maisons ont un long corridor en verre, le verre ordinaire pour les carreaux est fort demandé. Les baches et la toile imperméable sont fort demandés à cause du climat pluvieux. Un imperméable propre et léger, entièrement cousu, pourrait se vendre facilement. Les charbons, les huiles à machine et les couleurs sont fort demandés pour le nombre augmentant des navires de fleuves.

BOLIVIE.

Nouveau Consul à Philadelphie. M. WILFRED H. SCHOFF a été récemment nommé consul de Bolivie à Philadelphie. Dans une communication récente, le nouveau consul dit que les commerçants et les autres personnes peuvent maintenant se procurer tous les certificats nécessaires sur les documents de rechargements, et qu'il sera très henreux de fournir n'importe quels renseignements sur le commerce et sur les ressources naturelles de son pays.

CHILI.

Concessions pour les Nouvelles Industries. D'après un rapport fourni par le Journal de l'Amérique du Sud, le Congrès National du Chili a récemment accordé des concessions pour l'établissement de plusieurs nouvelles industries à Santiago de Chili. Parmi ces industries est celle d'une fabrique pour le blanchissement, la teinture et l'impression des tissus de toile en pièce, et une autre industrie pour a fabrication d'acide sulfurique.

COSTA-RICA.

Nouveau Consul-Général aux Etats-Unis. Le Dr. JUAN G. ULLOA, ex-Président de la République de Costa-Rica, a été nommé Consul-Général aux Etats-Unis; il remplit les fonctions de consul à New-York, où il a élu domicile et où se trouve le Consulat.

ÉQUATEUR.

Concessions à la Compagnie Allemande de Navigation. Le Consul anglais à Guayaquil informe son Gouvernement que les lignes de bateaux de Kosmos et de Hambourg qui font le commerce entre Hambourg et Anvers, ainsi que les ports d'Espagne et d'Italie, et faisant de temps en temps des voyages à Londres, ont été récemment consolidées. Avant cela, en mai, la Compagnie Kosmos fit un contrat avec le Gouvernement d'Equateur pour transporter le courrier, sans paiement, entre les ports du pays et tous les autres ports où ses navires font escale. La compagnie consent aussi à transporter les passagers du Gouvernement et des immigrants pour l'Equateur entre les ports où ses navires font escale, avec une réduction de 30 pour cent du prix ordinaire, aussi de transporter, sans paiement, les premiers chargements d'échantillons des produits de l'Equateur à n'importe quelle exposition allemande. En compensation de ces services, le Gouvernement d'Equateur permet aux navires de la Compagnie d'entrer dans ses ports de mer, libres de tous paiements fiscaux, et fait une réduction d'une moitié sur les taux de pilotage. Le contrat a été approuvé par le Conseil d'Etat et restera en vigueur pendant quatre ans.

Récolte de Cacao pour 1897. La récolte de cacao de l'Equateur pour 1897 s'élevait à 14,800 tonnes ou 330,293 quintaux. Cette quantité ne peut pas être comparé favorablement avec la production des années récentes.

En 1896, la production fut de 15,300 tonnes, en 1895 de 16,000 tonnes, et en 1894 de 17,467 tonnes.

Concession de Caoutchouc dans la Province de Tungurahua.   La communication suivante est faite dans le "Boston Commercial World" dans un article sur la production de caoutchouc dans l'Equateur. Le Correspondent dit : "Dans ce pays, le caoutchouc jusqu'ici a été obtenu des arbres sauvages et la destruction des plantes par les chercheurs rapaces a fait énormément du tort au commerce de la côte.

"La population néanmoins commence à comprendre leurs intérêts. Ceci est démontré par le fait qu'on fait des efforts pour obtenir auprès du Gouvernement une concession de huit ans pour l'exploitation du caoutchouc sur un territoire couvrant de 8 à 10 lieues carrés dans la province de Tungurahua, et on entretient l'espoir qu'à une date peu éloignée le rendement de caoutchouc égalera les récoltes de cacao et du café qui était jusqu'ici les principaux produits de la République."

GUATÉMALA.

Occasions pour les Spéculateurs des Etats-Unis.   Un correspondant du "Manufacturier" (Philadelphie) écrivant de la ville de Guatémala le 25 juin 1898, dit : Le Gouvernement veut vendre le Chemin de Fer du Nord, et il est aussi désireux et presque obligé de le faire ; ceci, je pense, serait une belle occasion pour un syndicat Américain d'entrer en possession d'une bonne affaire.

Aujourd'hui on peut acheter cette ligne dans des conditions extrêmement favorables et avec les plus libérales concessions. Ceci s'applique aussi au chemin de Verapaz. Ensuite une ou plusieurs compagnies américaines pourraient acheter les plantations qu' elles désireraient à des prix purement nominaux. Et puis une compagnie américaine pourrait venir y établir une banque, ce qui serait très désirable, et elle ferait de bonnes affaires, tout en obtenant les plus belles sécurités.

Le Chemin de Fer du Nord, dont parle le correspondant, est projeté de Puerto Barrios, à la ville de Guatémala, capital de la République, et est maintenant terminé jusqu'à San Agustin, distance de 130 milles, ne laissant qu'une petite partie de la ligne à achever. Ceci est le projet de chemin de fer le plus important que l'on ait jamais entrepris dans l'Amérique Centrale, il fut aussi le projet favori du feu Président Barrios pour le développement des richesses de l'intérieur du Guatémala. Cette ligne ouvrira au commerce les terrains les plus riches en café et en minéraux de la République.

HAÏTI.

Entreprise d'Exploitation de Mines en Haïti.   Dans les premières pages des rapports consulaires du 14 septembre, M. le Ministre Powell écrit de Port au Prince comme suit :

"Une riche veine de minerai de fer de métal presque pur a été récemment découverte dans la section du nord de cette République. On a obtenu une concession du Gouvernement pour l'exploitation de cette veine et une compagnie américaine s'organise á cet effet."

MEXIQUE.

Perception des Douanes. Pendant le mois de juin les recettes totales de la République s'élevaient à $2,039,886.57. D'après les chiffres procurés des "Deux Républiques," ces recettes se divisent comme suit: Droits sur les importations, $1,879,919.44; droits sur les exportations, $55,478.60; droits de port, $55,478.60; arrérages, $1,281.79. Le port de Vera Cruz a perçu $956,042.20 et celui de Tampico $352,927.73, ou les deux ensemble presque 70 pour cent de la somme des droits d'importations.

Récolte de Blé pour 1898. La récolte de blé du Mexique pour 1898 dépasse de beaucoup la moyenne en qualité et quantité, mais cette année une partie de la récolte seulement est disponible pour l' exportation. Par suite, le Bulletin de la Société Agricole du Mexique dit que certains spéculateurs ont essayé de persuader le Gouvernement d'empêcher, même de défendre les exportations de blé. Mais ils n'ont pas réuissi, car le Secrétaire de la Trésorerie a fait annoncer qu'aucun droit d'entrée ou autre restriction ne sera imposé sur le blé venant du Mexique et pour lequel on a trouvé des acheteurs sur les marchés étrangers.

PARAGUAY.

Importation de Pétrole. Le Consul RUFFIN écrit au Département d'Etat d'Asuncion, disant que Paraguay est éclairé au pétrole importé des Etats-Unis, et qu'aucune lumière électrique ou de gaz n'est employée excepté celle produite par les manufactures privées. Le pétrole arrive dans des boîtes d'étain contenant 4 gallons, la forme des boîtes permettant un arrimage commode à bord des bateaux qui font le service entre Asuncion et Montevideo. Le Consul ajoute:

"Il me semble qu'il serait plus profitable d'envoyer des navires à réservoir qui diminueraient la dépense et par conséquent augmenteraient la vente. On vendrait les réservoirs immédiatement à cause de la grande demande pour cet article évitant ainsi la dépense de les renvoyer. Depuis la guerre avec l'Espagne, le prix du pétrole a augmenté de presque 50 pour cent, et il y a beaucoup de spéculation. Les Etats-Unis ont un monopole d'importation de pétrole, 40,648 gallons furent importés en 1897, à une valeur estimée à $19,511 d'or. Les droits d'entrée sont 25 pour cent ad valorem."

VÉNÉZUELA.

Nouveau Chemin de Fer Electrique. Le "Herald" de Venezuela parle d'une concession à une compagnie française pour une ligne de chemin de fer électrique de 70 kilomètres (43½ milles) de longueur. La ligne va relier Cumana

MONTHLY BULLETIN

OF THE

BUREAU OF THE AMERICAN REPUBLICS,

INTERNATIONAL UNION OF AMERICAN REPUBLICS.

VOL. VI.	OCTOBER, 1898.	No. 4.

COMMERCIAL CONDITIONS IN CUBA.

Hon. ROBERT P. PORTER, Special Commissioner appointed by the President to study commercial conditions in Cuba, has returned to the United States. His opinions, as published, are as follows:

The first problem to be grappled with in the industrial reconstruction of Cúba is that of labor, of which there is practically none available. With this question solved, Cuba will regain its prosperity in five or six years. Thousands of men are in demand, who could be put to work at once if they could be found. Employers of labor on plantations, mines, etc., prefer the Spanish, as they are hardworking and docile. A decree issued by General BLANCO, on October 5, provides that all of the Spanish soldiers who desire to remain in Cuba shall be discharged from the army. It is believed that a number will remain, as their prospects are better in Cuba than at home. Some have married there, and many have fraternized with the Cubans.

The work, in the plantations especially, is very hard. The hands are in the habit of going to the sugar fields at 4.30 in the morning, after a ration of coffee and bread. At 11 they breakfast, take a nap, and resume their labors at 1 p. m., working until sundown—say about 7 o'clock. The rations are eaten in the open air, and the men sleep in huts thatched with palms and bark.

The laborers never stop for the heaviest rains, and in the United States people do not know what such rains are. The wages are $16 to $20 (silver) per month, the silver dollar now being worth 65 cents; it will fall to 50 cents after the occupation. From this pay all rations are deducted. Food is very high, and it costs $8 to $9 per month for the farm laborer to live. In the mines the hours are not so long, although the pay is not high. The proprietors of El Cobre and other mines near Santiago want 1,000 miners and can not get them.

The tobacco crop is the most enduring product. Nothing can kill it off. The crop this year will be about one-half the average, while sugar will be only one-third. Tobacco raising does not call for such a heavy class of labor as sugar.

It has been decided to entirely revise the tariff adopted for Santiago before it is put in force for the whole island. The Santiago tariff was that which Spain enforced for merchandise coming from Spain, and was in favor of all articles produced in that country, or those which could be purchased from other countries, flour, for instance, when shipped from Spanish ports. On articles which Spain did not produce and could not import from other countries for export to Cuba, the rates have been found to be too high. The iron and steel schedule, for example, is as high as in the present Spanish tariff. Nearly all articles of railway supplies, including locomotives, rolling stock, iron, steel bridges, etc., are dutiable at almost 100 per cent.

This is practically an increase on the old tariff, as 20 per cent of the Spanish duties were payable in silver at 65 cents on the dollar, and 10 per cent in bank bills at 10 cents on the dollar. When revised, the tariff for Cuba will be harmonious and reasonable and will yield greater revenue, because the present high rates practically stop importation in many lines of industry. Under proper administration the annual customs revenues of Cuba will exceed $30,000,000. The tariff will be framed so as to bring in sufficient revenue and at the same time encourage in every possible way the importation of all articles that will help in the industrial and commercial reconstruction of the island. Provisions will come in cheaper, which will stop smuggling, increase the number of importers, and keep prices down through competition. An important order has recently been issued by the President, authorizing the admission into all ports of Cuba, duty free, of oxen for draft purposes, bovine animals for breeding and for immediate food supply; also, plows and other agricultural implements, not machinery. This will materially aid in the agricultural revival. In Matanzas Province to-day there are only 5,000 cattle, where there used to be 260,000 head.

Cuba will probably become one of the most prosperous parts of the earth's surface, and its commercial value to the United States will approach $200,000,000 annually.

FINANCIAL CONDITIONS IN CHILE.

In a dispatch to the Department of State, dated August 19, 1898, which is printed in full in advance sheets of Consular Reports, October 8, 1898, Hon. HENRY L. WILSON, United States Minister to Chile, gives an account of the recent financial changes in Chile. In 1895 the Government of Chile passed a resumption act, placing the currency of the country upon a gold basis. Mr. WILSON states that with the flexible character and ample guarantees of the law of 1895 its success would have been assured, and in fact the effect was to raise the value of the Chilean peso to a little over 17 pence, enabling importers, merchants, and bankers to make their calculations and estimates with reasonable accuracy. Credits were easy and extensive because of the faith that all current obligations would be met with dollars of equal value. Prices were low, because the merchant did not have to add to the value of his merchandise an estimate for the unknown depreciation of the money of liquidation. The law, therefore, did not fail to accomplish good results, and to measurably improve the condition of the commercial and industrial classes. Judged by these standards, adds Minister WILSON, it was a gratifying success.

In course of time, however, the law has failed to accomplish the results expected, for the reason, as stated by the Minister, that it was not fully carried out, and heavy expenditures were imposed upon the Treasury by the necessity of providing for a large increase of the military establishment. On the 8th of July, 1898, Minister WILSON telegraphed the Department of State that a severe financial crisis had been precipitated, and in his later report he states that the Chilean Congress, in July last, passed an act suspending payments or action at law for debts for 30 days. After the passage of this act the banks, which had closed their doors by consent of the Government, resumed business, paying to depositors such sums only as would relieve their actual necessities. On the 13th of July the President sent to Congress a message recommending the issue of 50,000,000 pesos of paper money as legal tender for the settlement of all obligations not specially contracted in gold. It was also recommended that the present issue of the banks be a part of the 50,000,000 pesos issued, the entire sum to be retired within a term of four years from the date of the act. July 22, 1898, the House of Deputies passed a bill for the emission of 50,000,000 paper pesos of 18 pence (36.5 cts.), but made many important departures from the recommendations in the President's message. This bill, after having been amended in the Senate, was adopted July 30, 1898.

Minister WILSON states that small tradesmen, artisans, and people of the working classes generally, opposed the issue of paper money and appeared to be universally in favor of the gold standard. The landholders, on the other hand, were in favor of the law for the issue of paper money. The explanation of this fact, Mr. WILSON finds, is the ability which the law conferred upon them to pay mortgages in depreciated currency. The report quoted further states that on the 1st of June, 1898, 45,000,000 pesos gold were in circulation in Chile, but shortly after the passage of the act the gold pesos disappeared absolutely from circulation, as gold had become a commodity, advancing by rapid stages from 6 per cent premium to as much as 40 per cent. A paper peso, according to the Minister's account, has depreciated something like 30 per cent from its face value. The chief burden of the depreciation, in his opinion, falls upon the small tradesmen and wage earners, owing to the fact that the former are unable to change their business methods promptly and are compelled to sell their wares at the prices ruling before the depreciation began, and the laborers are paid in currency, the purchasing power of which has decreased 30 per cent. The Government, on the other hand reaps some advantage from present conditions, owing to the fact that it "finds its coffers replenished temporarily with ample funds to meet its obligations of a domestic character." The wealthy proprietors of landed estates which are mortgaged find temporary relief in being enabled to pay their debts in money equal to only a little more than two-thirds of its face value.

With reference to Minister WILSON's statements and conclusions, it may be said that the Chilean Government has exhibited in recent years so much ability in dealing with difficult financial problems that it may be hoped the currency question will ultimately find a satisfactory solution, the objects of the resumption measure of 1895 having evidently been embarrassed by circumstances not then foreseen, which may disappear or be remedied by corrective legislation.

ARGENTINE REPUBLIC.

GENERAL ROCA INAUGURATED PRESIDENT.

Minister BUCHANAN telegraphed the Department of State on October 12 as follows: "General JULIO A. ROCA inaugurated President to-day. ALCORTA remains Minister of Foreign Affairs."

A press cablegram from Buenos Ayres states that General ROCA took the oath of office as President of the Republic and sent in his first message to Congress on the 12th inst. The dispatch briefly summarizes the President's address in the following words:

The President refers to the improvement in the relations with Chile, and declares that the maintenance of peace will allow the country to devote its energies to the amelioration of the financial situation. He proposes administrative reforms, a decrease in public expenditures, encouragement of immigration, and development in trade.

FOREIGN TRADE IN 1898.

The Director General of Statistics at Buenos Ayres has issued a report of the foreign trade of the Republic for the first six months of the current year. According to the official figures, the value of all imports, except bullion and specie, amounted to $49,553,375 (gold valuation), showing a decrease of $150,404 as compared with the same period in 1897.

During the same months the exports, exclusive of bullion and specie, were valued at $81,632,825 (gold), an increase of

$17,594,290; or a balance of trade in favor of Argentina of $32,079,450 in six months.

The showing of imports and exports in specie and bullion are also gratifying, as the former increased by $1,162,855 and the latter decreased by $1,075,240, as compared with the corresponding months for 1897.

INCREASE IN TARIFF RATES.

On September 23 Minister BUCHANAN wired the Department of State that, according to a law passed by the Argentine Congress September 22, in force from date of passage until December 31, customs duties are increased as follows: Ad valorem duties of 5 per cent and under, doubled; those above 5 per cent, subject to 10 per cent additional, and 10 per cent on customs law; value of article added on all specific duties.

The following are among the articles that come under the 5 per cent ad valorem classification in the Argentine tariff: Cork, jewelry, wire, twine, tin in sheets; iron, zinc, and lead in ingots or bars; sewing machines and parts of, tar oils, quicksilver, machinery for installation of electric plants or waterworks (except meters and electric fixtures), fire bricks and clay, wool-clipping machines, steam motors, gold and silver watches and plate, agricultural machinery, and wool yarn. Under the 2½ per cent rate come cotton in bales, zinc in sheets, wood pulp, hops, rabbit hair, gelatin, etc. Specific duties are charged on provisions, drinks, tobacco, collars and cuffs, hats and hat felts, matches, kerosene, grain bags, playing cards, stearin, linseed oil, etc.

CHANGES IN INTERNAL-REVENUE LAWS.

According to the "South American Journal," the Argentine Congress in secret session recently enacted several tax measures which were promulgated by the Executive. The Journal's correspondent adds that "The taxes are those planned for the 1899 budget, and the object of bringing them immediately into force is to prevent distillers and various other trades interested from forestalling the action of the Executive by laying in big stocks at the lower rates." The schedule furnished is as follows:

ALCOHOL.

From August 23, 1898, all alcohol imported or sold shall pay a tax of $1 per liter.

WINES.

1. From August 23, 1898, all natural wines produced in the Argentine Republic, as well as foreign wines, shall pay an internal consumption tax of 4 cents per liter.

2. All wines, irrespective of origin, will be considered natural when in following conditions:

(a) Exclusive product of the fermentation of the must (grape juice) of the fresh grape.

(b) Preparations indicated above which have been subjected to corrected processes usual in wine making for exclusive purpose of rectifying special defects in the crop.

(c) Preparations or mixtures of pure native wines or of the latter with foreign wines.

(d) Natural wines containing less than 24 per cent of dry extract, always provided that the owner proves to chemical officer and internal-revenue authorities that from their origin they are naturally poor in extract.

3. The rectifying processes alluded to in clause b can be made subject to prior permit of the internal-revenue office.

4. Wine made from raisins, Petiot wines, and all manufactured wines in general, which may be sold during period specified in article 1, shall pay, in addition to tax annually in force, an increase of 4 cents per liter.

HATS.

1. From August 23, 1898, manufacturers can not deliver nor can sales be made of hats, either of home or foreign manufacture, until following internal tax be paid in the form to be afterwards determined by the Executive.

(a) Hats and caps of woolen material or of straw, 30 cents each.

(b) Felt hats, rabbit-skin hats, or those of hare skin, beaver, or llama skin, etc., hard or soft, tall hats glazed for coachmen, 60 cents each.

(c) Tall hats in general, $1.20 each.

(d) Hats or bonnets for ladies, trimmed or not, $1 each

OILS.

All vegetable oils of home production or imported shall pay a tax of 5 cents per kilo.

TRADE OF THE PORT OF ROSARIO.

In a report recently issued by the vice-consul for France at Rosario, he gives some interesting information regarding the sources of supply for the imports to that port, and also makes valuable suggestions concerning the necessities of that locality. It appears that there is a large and increasing demand for fencing wire, resulting from the necessity of inclosing the immense properties of the country. This demand has been met in the past principally by Germany, but the United States and England have also entered into formidable competition with that country within the last year. The cheapness of the German article has heretofore given it the preference, though this wire was often of an inferior quality to the productions of other countries, but now that German manufacturers are producing the standard grade it will be impossible for them to maintain their former low prices, and the market will be open equally to all. Kitchen utensils of white metal are manufactured to some extent in the country, the supply being further supplemented from Germany, as is also the case with enameled ware.

The general usage of agricultural machines in Argentina causes them to be among the principal articles of importation to Rosario. The large German, American, Swiss, and Italian houses share this trade. Building materials come principally from England; and jewelry and metals, rough and worked, are supplied largely from France. Gold watches of a good quality come almost wholly from Switzerland, a few being also supplied by England, while a cheap article, in various metals, finds its sole source of supply in the United States. The clocks in general use come from the United States and Germany, a few French ones being seen in some of the shops. Plated ware comes mostly from the United States and Germany. According to the reports of various importers, the German metal is superior to the American; but, on the other hand, the workmanship of the American silver plater excels that of the German, so that practically the two classes are on a level.

The French vice-consul predicts a great future for the port of Rosario on account of its exceptionally advantageous location; situated, as it is, on the Parana River, in the center of the principal agricultural region of the Argentine Republic, accessible to commercial navigation and almost equidistant from the ports of Buenos Ayres and Montevideo. The improvements of the harbor of Montevideo will also have a beneficial effect upon

Rosario as the increased facilities for steamers and sailing vessels at Montevideo will advance the development of all adjacent ports, and Rosario will become, by force of circumstances, a great depot for the center of Argentina and Paraguay.

IMPORTS FROM THE UNITED STATES—DEMANDS OF TRADE.

Bulletin No. 22 of the United States Export Association contains the following items with reference to exports from the United States to the Argentine Republic:

Orders for electrical machinery and equipments continue to arrive in fairly large proportions. A Broad street, New York, concern recently received orders for $20,000 worth of these supplies. The future outlook for work of every sort in the electrical field in Argentina is very promising. The average value of the shipments of machinery and electrical supplies has reached from $7,000 to $10,000 for every steamer that has left the port of New York for the past three months.

The electric tramways of Argentina are supplied with equipments from the United States. During the past two months almost every vessel going to Buenos Ayres has taken at least $50,000 worth of car material. The Belgrano Tramway Company is said to be receiving a great deal of this material. The La Capital Company, with local offices in New York City, is an extensive shipper of all sorts of electrical appliances, including car equipments, for its own road. Early in November, it is said, the company will have ready for shipment 1,000 freight cars which have been constructed under contract.

The next largest shipments from New York City to Argentina are those of manufactured iron, the trade of which is gradually increasing, the last three steamers to Buenos Ayres having taken in all upward of $40,000 worth, principally harvesting machines.

Other articles in demand for Argentina have been rope, paper, hardware, box shooks, iron pipe, and domestics. A South Street (New York) firm has been informed that the field for glassware, lamp goods, oilcloths, linoleums, cheap carpets, and rugs is extensive. The correspondent also says that there is an opportunity for controlling a part of the market for sanitary appliances made in the United States. Advices from Argentina are to the effect that nearly every tramway company in Buenos Ayres will extend its line to near-by suburban towns, and the required equipments will be extensive.

The bark *Adam W. Spies*, recently loaded for Buenos Ayres, took a large amount of manufactured articles from the United States. Among these were $45,000 worth of agricultural machinery, $12,000 worth of sewing machines, and $10,000 worth of chairs and hardware. The steamer *Bellucia*, which also sailed for the same port, took $50,000 worth of agricultural machinery, and carriages valued at $5,000, and windmills invoiced at $10,971.

DISCOVERY OF COAL.

Commander NUNES, one of the officers of the Argentine navy has recently returned from Terra del Fuego with samples of coal discovered there. The samples he brought were tried with most satisfactory results in the locomotives in the port works at Buenos Ayres. It is only surface coal and the inference naturally is that if so good at the top it would prove the very best quality in depth. It only requires that these discoveries turn out well to launch this country into a manufacturing groove that may develop it more rapidly than its wheat growing. A short time only will be sufficient to test the real value of the coal.

The "Review of the River Plate," while admitting that this coal is of fair quality, does not indulge in rosy anticipations as to the quantity available. It says:

It is very pleasing to know that the samples of coal brought up from Terra del Fuego have given good results, better, we believe, than had been anticipated by anyone, whether connected with the discoveries or not. It is proposed to send down a certain amount of machinery, so as to ascertain the quantity of the mineral available. Even if it is found that the average quality is as good as that of the samples which have been tested, it is yet probable that the quantity may be so small as to render the deposit worthless for all time, or that the place where it exists in quantity may be commercially inaccessible.

Dr. KYLE made an analysis for the Government of two samples of lignite from the Slogget Bay mines in Patagonia, referred to above, and found them to vary greatly in value. Sample No. 1 was of a brilliant black color, both on the surface and in the interior when broken, and when pulverized the color of the powder was black. In burning, it gave off a short flame of little brilliancy; the products of distillation were decidedly acid, and the specific gravity was 1.273. No. 2 was of a dull reddish-brown color, and when pulverized the powder was of a coffee color. When burned it gave off a much larger flame than No. 1, but proved to be decidedly inferior as a heat producer. The analysis gave the following results:

	No. 1.	No. 2.
Water	26. 85	17. 00
Volatile matter	31. 63	31. 88
Fixed carbon	39. 47	18. 40
Ash	2. 05	32. 72
	100. 00	100. 00
Heat units	3, 482	2, 324

Neither sample would coke properly.   No. 1, according to the analysis, was an excellent quality of lignite, although much inferior to first-class grades of coal, which, weight for weight, possesses about double the heat-producing capacity.   No. 2 was of little value because of the great amount of ash.   It still remains to be seen if the deposits are of sufficient extent to pay for working.

NEW UNITED STATES COALING STATION.

An authentic dispatch from Norfolk, Va., states that the samples of Virginia coal sent to Argentina having proven satisfactory, other shipments will be made at once.   Messrs. CASTNER, CURRAN & BULLITT, of Philadelphia, agents for the Pocahontas Coal Company, have opened an agency at Buenos Ayres, with Mr. CARL H. ARNOLD in charge.   Mr. ARNOLD has for some time past been vice-consul at Norfolk for the Republics of Colombia and Venezuela.   It is also stated that a number of ships with cargoes of coal will shortly sail from Lamberts Point, Va., for Buenos Ayres, and are expected to return partially loaded, at least, with produce from the Argentine Republic.

BOLIVIA.

ABOLITION OF THE MATCH MONOPOLY.

Information has been received that the Bolivian Government has repealed the decree of March 14, last, in regard to the collection of duty on matches imported from abroad, and has suspended, provisionally, the law of November 18, 1896, which established a monopoly in the manufacture of matches in the Republic and subjected foreign matches to an additional import tax.

Hereafter, matches imported into Bolivia will pay only such import duty as has been specified in the general custom-house tariff.

WORK OF BOUNDARY COMMISSION.

While as yet there exists some anxiety as to the final outcome of the frontier disagreement between the Argentine Republic and Chile, though all the chances now seem to be in favor of a peaceful settlement, a similar work of delimitation is being carried on by Bolivia. The Government desires its frontier to be well defined on the Argentine side, so as to forever quiet counter claims of territory.

A Bolivian commission recently left Sucre, the capital, for the purpose of beginning its labors at La Quiaca. The surveys and studies which will be made by the Bolivians, in concert with a similar commission from Argentine, will be a preliminary affair. Only topographical observations will be noted preparatory to the work in ijoint convention of fixing the frontier definitely. The Bolivian commission, and likewise that of Argentine, will be divided into two sections. They will respectively study the ground on the east and on the west of the Quiaca. The two chiefs of the Bolivian parties are Muñoz D. Reyes, an expert engineer, and Colonel Muñoz, one of the foremost statesmen of the Republic.

BRAZIL.

THE COFFEE CROP OF 1898.

Consul General Seeger sends an interesting report of the production and movement of coffee in the Republic for the year ending June 30, 1898. From this the following statistics have been obtained:

RECEIPTS FOR THE YEAR.

	Bags.	Pounds.
Rio :		
Per railroad..	2, 300, 690	303, 691, 080
Per coast steamers...................................	840, 099	110, 893, 068
Per other craft.......................................	1, 163, 849	153, 617, 068
In transit..	232, 941	30, 748, 212
Total	4, 537, 579	598, 949, 428
Santos	6, 152, 594	812, 142, 408
Victoria (estimated)	400, 000	52, 800, 000
Bahia (estimated)	250, 000	33, 000, 000
Ceara (estimated)	20, 000	2, 640, 000
Grand total	11, 360, 173	1, 499, 531, 836

SHIPMENTS TO FOREIGN COUNTRIES.

	Bags.	Pounds.
United States	4, 740, 638	625, 746, 216
All Europe	5, 971, 468	770, 233, 776
Cape of Good Hope	149, 300	19, 707, 600
River Plate, etc	101, 533	13, 402, 356
Total	10, 962, 939	1, 429, 107, 948

Estimated at an average of $8.75 per bag (of 132 pounds), the value of this export amounts to $96,450,716.25.

During the last three calendar years the shipments of coffee from Brazil were as follows:

From—	1895.	1896.	1897.
	Bags.	*Bags.*	*Bags.*
Santos	3, 554, 696	4, 156, 567	5, 621, 762
Rio	2, 763, 720	2, 784, 958	4, 066, 734
Victoria	307, 438	273, 255	372, 221
Bahia	264, 775	260, 981	292, 480
Ceara	20, 202	6, 000	6, 568
Total	6, 910, 831	7, 418, 761	10, 359, 765

The New York prices per pound during the last crop year for quality No. 7 (spot) in New York decreased steadily from $7\frac{1}{16}$ cents on July 1, 1897, to $5\frac{7}{8}$ cents on May 1, 1898. On July 1, 1898, the price had advanced slightly, to $6\frac{1}{4}$ cents.

On June 30, 1898, the stock of 1,227,960 bags was distributed as follows: Rio, 268,167; Santos, 316,793; New York, Baltimore, and New Orleans, 643,000. On the same date the world's visible supply was calculated at 5,436,000 bags, which is an equivalent to about one-half a year's consumption.

Mr. SEEGER says there is a heavy overproduction of coffee at present, which has had a depressing influence on prices. This condition has made itself particularly felt during the last two years, although the cause of it dates much further back. During the ten years prior to 1897 the market price of coffee afforded an extraordinary large profit to the planters. The consequence was an enormous increase in the area of coffee plantations during the "boom." Now these additional millions of trees commence to bear, irrespective of demand and prices, and what was until recently an industry which sometimes yielded a profit of as much as 150 per

MONAZITE DEPOSITS.

According to the "Iron and Coal Trades Review," monazite sand, from which the incandescent oxides of thorium and cerium are procured, is obtained from North Carolina and Brazil. In the latter country it was discovered by SORCEIX, the director of the Oura Preto School of Mines, and is now found in the province of Bahia at Salabra and Caravellas; in the Minas Geraes district at Diamantina; in the provinces of Goyaz, Cuyaba, Sao Paulo, and Rio de Janeiro. The most extensive deposits occur in Bahia in the shape of sand banks at the edge of the ocean, particularly at the southern extremity of this province, near the island of Alcobaca. The continuous destruction of the rocks by the sea waves has gradually enriched the deposits, and the sands are quite rich in monazite, and are loaded directly upon the vessels, thus making the cost of manual labor and handling very low. This sand contains an average of 4 to 5 per cent of thorium oxide. The other localities in this country occur in the gold placer deposits and diamond fields of Minas Geraes, Cuyaba, and Goyaz, where the monazite exists in large nodules, colored a brilliant yellow by orangite. Monazite has also been discovered in the gold placers of Rio Chico, at Antioquia, in the United States of Colombia, and in the river sands of Buenos Ayres.

TO PARTICIPATE IN THE CELEBRATION.

The battle ships *Oregon* and *Iowa*, in company with the colliers *Celtic* and *Scindia*, started from New York for Honolulu on October 13. The *Abarenda* preceded the squadron by a few days. Before they started on their long journey, Hon. JOHN D. LONG, Secretary of the Navy, ordered Captain BARKER, commanding the *Oregon*, to reach Rio Janeiro with the two war ships before November 15, the anniversary of the establishment of the Republic of Brazil, that they might fittingly represent the United States Navy and participate in the celebration of the event. The vessels are expected to reach Rio about November 10.

STATISTICS OF IMMIGRATION.

During 1897 the number of immigrants arriving at the port of Rio de Janeiro was 44,225. Of these, 22,964 are reported to have received assistance or a monetary consideration for becoming citizens of Brazil, while 21,261 came voluntarily. As to sex, 29,634 were males and 14,621 were females. The nationalities represented were: Italians, 27,454; Portuguese, 7,423; Spaniards, 7,253; Germans, 420; Russians, 392; Syrians, 388; Armenians, 219; French, 215; Austrians, 132; all others, 329. A majority of these newcomers settled in the State of Minas Geraes.

CHILE.

COMMERCIAL STATISTICS FOR 1897.

The Chilian Times of August 31, says:

There has just been issued from the presses of the Universo Printing Office the volume of commercial statistics of the Republic for the year 1897. It is a portly tome of 700 pages, gotten up in irreproachable style, and the chief statist, Mr. WENCESLAO ESCOBAR, is to be congratulated on its appearance several months in advance of the usual time of publication. The contents of the volume comprise *Comercio Especial, Movimiento de la Navegación, Comercio Marítimo Interior, Estadística Retrospectiva*, and *Comercio de Tránsito*, the section entitled Comercio General, which has appeared in previous volumes, having been omitted as useless.

There was a very considerable falling off in the volume of trade in 1897 as compared with 1896. Before, however, proceeding to give the figures it will be well to point out that, as usual, the values are given in dollars of 38 pence. The value then of the imports was $65,502,805, and that of the exports $64,754,133. The total value of imports and exports was $130,256,938, or $18,185,281 less than the total in 1896. In this decrease of $18,185,281, imports figure for $8,580,000 and exports for $9,605,281. This was the fourth time in the history of the Republic since 1844, which was the year in which commercial statistics were first compiled, that the volume of trade of the country has shown a falling off to be compared with the decrease of 1897. The other times were the years 1877, 1885, and 1894. In the first of these years the falling off amounted to $14,211,411, in the second to $29,591,686, and in the third to $13,956,952.

The decrease in imports was principally in articles of food, raw materials, machines, machinery, and other articles for industrial purposes and for arts and trades, household effects, railway and telegraph articles, tobacco, articles connected with arts, science, and belles lettres, coal, shirtings, cotton trouserings, oils, and tallow.   Imports are divided into fifteen classifications, and in the following table there will be found the values of each in the years 1896 and 1897:

Classification.	1896.	1897.
Foods	$14,287,626	$13,926,523
Textiles	12,790,619	13,013,719
Raw materials	12,021,434	10,319,062
Clothing, jewelry, and articles of personal use	3,585,133	3,597,370
Machines, machinery, instruments, and other articles for industries, arts, and trades	9,710,679	9,156,614
Household effects	5,187,110	5,025,979
Railway and telegraph articles	2,347,432	1,073,744
Wines and liquors	934,649	1,178,878
Snuff, tobacco, etc	580,631	399,401
Ores and bullion	20,726	11,267
Articles for the arts, science, and belles lettres	1,297,941	1,089,023
Drugs and medicinal articles and for industrial purposes	1,179,509	1,113,469
Arms and their accessories	164,850	133,345
Miscellaneous	9,787,634	5,387,675
Specie and bank notes	186,832	76,733
Total	74,082,805	65,502,805

In exports, agricultural products, principally wheat, barley, nuts, hay, and pease, showed a decrease of $2,309,934.   Mineral products, principally nitrate, bar silver, borate of lime, silver ore, copper ore, and copper and silver regulus, showed a falling off to the amount of $6,160,600; while animal products, principally hides and wool and hams, showed a decrease of $549,065.

COLOMBIA.

ADVICE TO EXPORTERS.

The "Moniteur Officiel" of France publishes an extract from a local paper giving advice with regard to the methods for increasing the trade with the Republic of Colombia, and furnishing directions for packing merchandise destined for that country.   These are matters of interest to merchants in the United States, and are practically to the effect that of the two methods employed—advertising and traveling salesmen—the former should be considered only as a forerunner of the latter.   While prospectuses, market reviews, industrial bulletins, and commercial circulars are excellent means of preparing the ground and drawing attention to foreign products, they should be speedily supplemented by active, enterprising, Spanish-speaking agents, carrying with them sample cards and specimens of wares for sale—in fact, everything that might persuade the buyer and convince him of the superiority of the article offered.

It is not important that an agent should represent one branch of industry only, but in order to minimize the expense of travel he might represent several factories, and if he were well equipped could safely count upon a profitable result for the houses interested.

The writer considers that the establishment of sample warehouses at Bogota and Medellin would be attended with excellent results. These should be in the hands of confidential agents, capable of giving full information concerning the exhibits, and also of arranging suitable terms of sale.

In shipping merchandise it is important that it should be packed carefully, the packages not to exceed 80 centimeters (31½ inches) in length, 57 centimeters (22.44 inches) in breadth, and 55 centimeters (21.65 inches) in thickness, the average weight to be between 70 and 75 kilograms (154 and 166 pounds). If shipped in bundles, goods should be wrapped in several wrappings of paper and woolen cloths, the whole securely done up in metal bands. If boxes are used, care should be taken that they be of a material impervious to dampness, for fine wares are frequently ruined in transit by carelessness in this regard. Cases with an interlining of zinc are very good for this purpose, and in Colombia are objects of regular traffic. Casks should be inclosed in zinc sheeting. Heavy iron articles and machinery must be packed in strong cases, the heaviest portions detached from the machines, and the screws, clamps, and rivets shipped in barrels. Insurance by land and sea is worthy of attention, and increases the original cost of transportation but little.

LIQUOR TARIFF IN PANAMA.

Ordinance No. 39 of 1898, recently issued in the form of a decree by the Government, regulates the duties levied in the Department of Panama on "beverages not specified in Article 1 of Decree 289 of 1895," and is to take effect January 1, 1899. The duties are to be assessed at the following rates, calculated in Colombian silver:

Sirups	per kilo	$0.10
Bordeaux, Tinto, and other table wines	do	.06
Ale, beer, ginger ale, and cider champagne	do	.06
Malaga, sherry, port, sweet, and dry wines	do	.15
Champagne and other sparkling wines	do	.20
Patent medicated wines	do	.05
Essence of aniseed	per liter	20.00

Mineral waters are excepted from the payment of the duty on liquors, but medical wines are to pay 5 cents for each kilogram, gross weight (including the package). Articles which are to be used exclusively by the charity hospitals and similar institutions will be assessed only one-half of the above duties. Wines imported for use in St. Thomas Hospital at Panama are wnolly exempt from duty. Wines to be used by the ecclesiastical authorities in divine service, when certain formalities are complied with, are also exempted. The new items in this tariff are essence of aniseed and patent medicated wines. The increase in rates on malaga, sherry, port, etc., is 50 per cent; on champagne, etc., 100 per cent; on table wines, ale, beer, etc., 200 per cent; and on sirups, 400 per cent.

PROSPECTS OF THE PANAMA CANAL.

A number of the directors and representatives of the Panama Canal Company arrived recently in New York direct from Panama. One member of the party, Mr. R. G. WARD, seemingly voicing the opinions of all, stated publicly that in his opinion the present is a critical time in the affairs of the company, and suggested that "a definite business-like proposition be made looking to American participation in the completion and ownership of the canal." Mr. WARD evidently does not believe that the canal will ever be completed without assistance from the United States, and strongly advocates a canal across the Isthmus at Panama as against the proposed Nicaragua route.

COSTA RICA.

GOVERNMENT CONTRACT WITH TWO STEAMSHIP COMPANIES.

The Government of Costa Rica has entered into a contract with the representative of the Pacific Steam Navigation Company and the Compañía Sud Americana de Vapores (South American Steamship Company), the substance of which is as follows:

1. The steamers of both companies in their trips from Valparaiso, Chile, to Ocós, Guatemala, shall touch, both going north and returning, at least twice a month, at the port of Puntarenas or at Tivives, as soon as the latter is opened to commerce.

2. The steamers of both companies shall remain at the port of Puntarenas or at Tivives during the time required for the embarking and disembarking of passengers, mail, and freight, but in no case shall this detention exceed twenty-four hours, unless the companies should see fit to extend the time. However, should the Government demand it, the steamers shall remain in port during twelve hours of daylight.

3. The steamers shall carry, free of cost to the Government of Costa Rica, the mail and postal parcels coming from the post-offices of the Republic and destined to the terminal ports and to other ports along the route where the steamers call. They shall also carry the mail and postal parcels coming from said ports. The companies are obliged to receive and deliver the mail bags and postal packages at each port, at their own cost, through the respective post-offices, and at the same time to care for and preserve them on board. The companies shall deliver the mail bags and packages alongside of the steamers at their anchorage and shall receive them up to the hour of sailing. Employees of the companies are forbidden to carry letters outside of the mail bags, with the exception of those that are received after the latter have been closed or on the high seas; but in such cases said letters must be delivered to the proper employees of the Government, who shall collect whatever postage may be due. The companies may, however, carry letters or papers referring to their business to and from their agents and employees. Any violation of this article prejudicial to the Government of Costa Rica shall be punished with a fine of $100 each for the first and second offenses. These amounts shall be deducted from the subsidy granted by the present contract to the companies. Should the offense be repeated a third time, the Government reserves the right to declare the contract null and void. The companies bind themselves also to carry the mail bags and postal parcels coming from the United States and Europe which may be delivered to them at Panama by the respective postal employees.

4. The steamers shall carry as steerage passengers from one port to another of those at which they call, charging only 50 per cent of the regular rates for such passage, to artisans, farmers, laborers, and others who may emigrate to Costa Rica, provided they come under contract or agreement with the Government or its authorized agents.

5. The steamers shall carry all freight for the Government coming from or going to Puntarenas or Tivives, between the ports of Panama and Ocós, inclusive, at a reduction of 25 per cent of the regular rates.

6. The companies are obliged to inform the Government in due time of their rates for passengers and freight, the itinerary and connections of their lines, and of any changes made in the same.

7. The steamers are prohibited from carrying troops or ammunition from any port where they may touch to any port of the Republic of Costa Rica, unless they have been previously authorized by the Government to do so.

8. The steamers shall not take passengers or freight for Costa Rica at places against which quarantine has been established, and they must submit strictly, and without right of redress, to any measures that the Costa Rican Government may take upon this matter. These measures shall be communicated to the companies through their agent in the Republic.

The violation of this gives the Government of Costa Rica the right to impose upon the companies a fine of $500 for the first offense, and of $1,000 each for repeated offenses. These fine- shall be deducted from the monthly subsidy granted by the contract to the companies, but they do not exempt them from further responsibility.

The Government of the Republic of Costa Rica on its part pledges itself to the following:

9. To grant to the companies an annual subsidy of $5,000, Costa Rican currency, said amount to be paid in monthly installments, at the end of each month, to the agents of the companies in San José, Puntarenas, or Tivives. These sums, as well as those received for passages and freight, may be exported by the companies or its agents free of all duties or taxes. Should the steamers of the companies touch at Puntarenas or Tivives weekly, both ways, the Government will increase the subsidy to $7,500, payable in the same manner.

10. The steamers shall be exempted during the term of·this contract from the payment of any and all duties which now exist or may exist in the future, with the exception of the light-house duty; but this, in no case, shall exceed $100 annually for all the steamers that may touch at the port during the year.

11. If through mistake or carelessness the steamers of the companies should leave at Tivives or Puntarenas mail or freight intended for other ports, or if they should be obliged to land the same in order to have it reembarked in any other of their steamers, the Government of Costa Rica grants to the companies the right to do so without requiring them to pay any duty or charge.

12. The steamers of these companies are subject to all laws and regulations existing in the ports of the Republic, with the exception of those affected by the privileges granted by this contract.

13. The contract shall begin to be in force when the companies send the first steamer from Panama to the coast of Central America, as far as Ocós, inclusive, of which fact they must notify the Government in advance. The contract shall continue for two years from that date, and be considered as extended for two years longer if one or the other party does not give notice three months previous to the expiration of the term of its desire to rescind it.

14. Any differences between the Government of Costa Rica and the companies about the interpretation of this contract shall be decided by two arbitrators appointed one by each side, and should they fail to agree, by a third appointed by the other two, whose decision shall be final. The arbitrators must be citizens of Costa Rica.

15. The steamers of the companies shall enter the ports and be dispatched on Sundays and holidays the same as on ordinary days.

16. This contract, in order to be valid, must be ratified by the Costa Rican Congress.

CHANGES IN TARIFF.

According to advices received by the British Government from its consul at San José an import duty of 2 cents per kilogram had been placed on all lumber for building purposes and of

6 cents per kilogram on lumber for cabinet work imported by Port Limon for use in the Province of Limon, which heretofore when imported at Limon for use in the province had been allowed to enter duty free.

Also that the import duty on refined and white powdered sugars has been raised from 11 cents to 20 cents per kilogram and on all other grades of sugars from 7 to 15 cents. The duty on ground cocoa is raised from 13 to 20 cents per kilogram and that of cocoa in the bean from 7 to 15 cents per kilogram.

EXPORTS OF COFFEE IN 1897–98.

The Director of Statistics of the Republic has furnished the following figures relative to the exports of coffee for the fiscal year ending June 30, 1898; these show an increase of 2,000 bags (264,000 pounds) over 1896–97 and 6,000 bags (792,000 pounds) over 1895–96:

Routes.	Bags.	Kilograms.	Pounds.
To New York by Atlas Line	94,075	5,084,787	11,209,921
To England by Royal Mail Line	80,358	4,166,064	9,184,505
By Lyon and Cox Line	52,983	2,882,113	6,353,906
By the German Line	45,731	2,567,717	5,660,789
By the French Line	18,829	1,056,251	2,328,611
By other lines	5,515	328,257	723,675
Grand total	297,491	16,085,189	35,461,407

ECUADOR.

NEW MINISTRY.

Through the Department of State, this Bureau has been advised of the formation of the following cabinet at Quito:

Minister of Foreign Affairs.............Señor Don José PERÁLTA.
Minister of Interior ....Señor Don LINO CÁRDENAS.
Ministei of War ....Señor Don NICANOR ARELLANO.
Minister of Public Works...............Señor Don RICARDO VALDIVIESO.
Minister of Treasury ....Señor Don A. L. YEROVI.

NOTES FROM PRESIDENT'S MESSAGE.

President ALFARO delivered his annual message to Congress on the 9th of August From this it appears that the condition of the

MEXICO.

AN ATTRACTIVE FIELD.

The Mexican field is an attractive one for the American exporter because it is near at hand, and the demand, especially for manufactures, is large and growing. While the consumption of foreign products will increase handsomely during the next few years, American exporters must not overestimate the present possibilities of this market, says "Modern Mexico." In the first place, not more than one-fourth of the population of Mexico can to-day be taken into consideration when a calculation is made as to the possible consumption of imported products. In other words, at least 75 per cent of the population of Mexico is composed of Indians and peons that probably never, in the entire course of their lives, have the desire or the means to purchase a single imported article.

The number of small landed proprietors is very few when compared with United States proportions. Labor is cheap, and skilled labor capable of handling machinery is scarce, so that the general introduction of labor-saving machinery can not be as rapidly made there as in the United States. The bulk of Mexico's foreign trade can hardly be compared with the gigantic trade of the United States, but it is growing in the right direction, and the American manufacturers will find it much easier and much cheaper to secure Mexican trade now and grow with it than to get a foothold after imports have doubled.

A NEW CUSTOMS WHARF.

The new pier at Vera Cruz, though not quite completed, is now being used by the customs authorities. It is 580 feet long, 80 feet broad, and has 28 feet of water alongside at extreme low tide. The first ship to discharge its cargo at the new landing place was the West India and Pacific Steamship Company's vessel *Tampican*, of 3,126 net tons register, 430 feet long, drawing 17 feet 6 inches forward and 21 feet 3 inches aft, and the largest boat that visits the port. I is possible for another vessel of the same capacity to be discharged on the opposite side at the same time.

With the exception of coasting boats and colliers, this was the first time a ship has been able to discharge all classes of merchandise at the general wharf. The new facilities are of great importance to the port, opening up many possibilities for the speedy and more convenient dispatch of vessels and can not fail of increaseing trade.

TRADE WITH FRANCE.

The Mexican Consul at Havre, Señor COSTA Y NARVAEZ, has recently sent to his Government an extensive report on the commerce of Mexico and France, especial reference being made to the port of Havre. From this report it is learned that Mexican products were exported to France during the past year to the amount of 41,369,152 kilograms, 80 per cent of which were received at the port of Havre. The shipments of coffee are reported to be on the increase, 5,000 sacks of the Mexican product having passed through the Havre custom-house during the past year. This is the more remarkable as the Brazilian coffee crop was so largely in excess of demand that coffees from all countries felt the effect in a falling off of orders and a reduction in price. The dyewoods of Mexico are recognized in France as of superior quality, particularly is this the case with logwood from Laguna, which, on account of its fine qualities, is the first choice for fine dyes for silk goods, hats, gloves, etc. There is also a good market for woods from Yucatan, Tuxpan, Vera Cruz, and Tampico.

Building and cabinet woods are not shipped directly to French ports from Mexico, but pass through English ports first. The prices vary according to the dimensions and quality of the woods and according to their state of preservation, ranging from 20 to 28 francs per 50 kilos. Cedar employed in the manufacture of cigar boxes is reshipped to Belgium, Germany, Switzerland, and other countries where the Governments do not monopolize the tobacco trade, as is the case in France.

Mexican hemp and sisal grass go, in a great measure, to the port of New York and are then reshipped to London, Hamburg, and Havre, as American houses have practically monopolized the trade in these fibers and the benefits arising therefrom. The trade in skins between Mexico and France is comparatively small, the United States being preferably the market for such products.

Rubber from Mexico is in good demand and is identical with that received from Central America. The consul quotes the price obtained by recent shipments (8 francs the kilogram) as an incentive to further efforts in the production of this article, which, on account of the great industrial development of late years, is increasing in importance for the manufacture of bicycles, automobiles, etc.

All the sarsaparilla passes through United States markets before arriving in France, and the consul attributes to this fact the lack of consideration received by the Mexican product, as it loses in a great degree its true flavor by remaining in a foreign country. Honey finds a rival in the French product, for the protection of which an import tax of 15 francs per 100 kilos has been levied on foreign products.

SMELTING WORKS IN MONTEREY.

In his report on the industries of Monterey district, Consul-General POLLARD says:

There are two smelters in operation in the vicinity of this city, the larger having a daily capacity of 500 tons, which, in 1897, resulted in producing 7,076,544 ounces of silver, 23,830 ounces of gold (both troy weight), and 22,912 tons of lead. The smaller smelter has a capacity of 90 tons daily. The larger has ten blast furnaces, together with the necessary appurtenances for their operation, while the smaller has six "water-jacket" furnaces of a capacity of 90 tons daily and three revolving furnaces of 40 tons per day in the aggregate, with the necessary apparatus to operate them. The entire annual output of ore and constituents amounts to 112,000 tons.

Assay offices are connected with each of these establishments. Twenty thousand tons of coke and 5,000 tons of coal are annually consumed at the smaller smelter, and a proportionate amount at the larger. Of lead, 13,944,000 kilograms (30,740,942 pounds) were produced in the smaller smelter from May 1 to April 30, 1897-98, and 18,000 kilograms (39,683 pounds) of silver and 300 kilograms (661 pounds) of gold during the same period. From 400 to 500 men are annually employed at the smaller and about 700 at the larger smelter, the daily pay roll of the latter being about $1,000 in Mexican money ($452 in United States currency). Laborers at the smaller smelter receive from $1 to $5 daily in Mexican money (45 cents to $2.26), and are paid weekly. Skilled labor is paid monthly. Salaried officers receive from $100 to $600 in Mexican money ($45 to $271) monthly.

Both establishments do a large business with the United States, the products being shipped, and practically all supplies being obtained therefrom, the larger importing over 30,000 tons of coke alone during the year 1897. Smelting commenced here about 1891.   It has increased each year since, and, in view of the apparently inexhaustible supply of minerals in Mexico, it is only in its incipiency.

MINING INDUSTRY AND EXPORTS.

President DIAZ, in his annual message to Congress, which convened on September 16, devoted considerable space to the mining industries of the Republic.   In part he said:

The number of grants issued in the period that has elapsed since my last report is 837, covering an area of 7,820 pertenencias of 1 hectare each.   The development of the mining industry is further evidenced by the increase in the export of ore that has been observable for some time past.   According to data published by the Department of Finance with respect to the last fiscal year, the total value of the mineral products of all kinds passing through the custom-houses was $91,250,000, in round numbers, showing an increase of $10,500,000 over the value of similar products exported in the previous year.   Silver figures among such products to the value of $67,000,000; gold to the value of $16,000,000, silver valuation; copper to the value of $4,700,000; lead to the value of $3,000,000, and, on a smaller scale, antimony, zinc, plumbago, coal, sulphur, asphalt, and chalk.

NICARAGUA.

NEW TARIFF LAW.

Mr. M. J. CLANCY, United States consular agent at Bluefields, Nicaragua, writes to the Bureau under date of September 20, inclosing the latest tariff measure enacted for the Republic.   The full text of the previous tariff law is contained in BULLETIN No. 20, issued by this Bureau.

With reference to the present decree, Mr. CLANCY says:

By Presidential decree (a copy of which is inclosed herewith) a new tariff for the State of Nicaragua went into operation in the interior on the first instant, and became effective at this port and the department of Zelaya, by public proclamation, on the 17th instant.

The increase of duties on all imports will average 100 per cent over the former schedule.   Rice, beans, corn, and potatoes, that were formerly on the free list, will hereafter pay a duty of 10 cents Nicaraguan currency (4 cents gold) per kilo.   A kilo is equivalent to 2.20 pounds.   The reason for putting the above articles on the dutiable list is to foster the cultivation of the same in Nicaragua.   It is claimed that the products mentioned can be grown here in profusion with little or no exertion of labor.   Their cultivation will also tend to develop the agricultural resources of the country.

For some unaccountable reason the duty on soap is now only 2 cents Nicaraguan currency (0.08 cents gold) per kilo, while on the old list it paid 9 cents Nicaraguan currency (0.36 cents gold).

As Nicaragua is on a silver basis, an American dollar, either gold, paper or silver, possesses 2½ times the purchasing power that a silver peso, or sol, does, although each contains as much silver as does the dollar coined by the Government of the United States.

The rates on provisions, liquors, sugar, and beer are doubled. Paints of every description have been overlooked in the new tariff sheet. Heretofore in all invoices of foreign goods the weight was required to be designated in kilos, although the duty was paid by the pound, including the box, case, or wrapper that the articles are packed in. Now the duty will be collected on the basis of a kilo in weight. The following anomalous condition exists in Nicaragua to-day: All goods imported into San Juan del Norte (Greytown) are admitted free of duty, because it is what is termed a "free port," while goods brought to Bluefields, or Cape Gracias on the Atlantic coast, and Corinto, or San Juan del Sur on the Pacific side, pay the tariff as levied by the new schedule of imports.

The Presidential decree referred to by Mr. CLANCY contains the following articles:

THE PRESIDENT OF THE STATE,

Considering, That the tariff issued on the 25th of July, 1898, is inadequate to meet the present conditions of trade, since it does not include a number of new articles the importation of which has increased, and it has been found to contain many irregularities in the classification of merchandise of a certain class, all of which has caused an unjust distribution of the respective charges, by virtue of the authority conferred upon him by the constitutional amendment issued on the 15th of October, 1896,

DECREES:

ARTICLE 1. From the publication of the present decree the duties on the importation of merchandise shall be charged on each kilogram of the net weight in the following manner:

ART. 2. Articles not mentioned in the preceding classification shall pay the duty imposed on similar articles; but if they are composed of different materials, they shall pay the duty imposed upon the material that predominates.

ART. 3. Articles that have been omitted and that can not be classified according to the preceding article shall pay at the rate of 200 per cent upon their original value, according to the invoice. This duty shall be increased to 250 per cent on articles made from raw material produced in the country, and shall be decreased to 100 per cent on articles used in the arts and trades. These duties shall be paid in the currency of the country. If there is no invoice, the valuation of the articles shall be made by experts.

ART. 4. When a package contains articles paying different duties, the weight of the package shall be distributed in proportion to the net weights of the articles contained in the same.

The consul suggests that some manufacturer of the United States try the experiment of making shipments of butter to Paraguay. His idea is that by packing it in small cans (presumably one-pound cans), placing on each a picture of the President of Paraguay, or that of some of the leading statesmen of the country, and an old historic house or two, it will cause it to be talked about and give popularity to the brand. He thinks this would lead to quick and profitable sales, as no advertisements of that sort exist in that country.

What has been said of Paraguay may apply equally as well to nearly all the South American Republics, so far as the use, scarcity, and demand for butter is concerned. Proprietors of creameries in the United States might profit greatly by inquiring into the conditions existing, and catering to the demands of the trade.

THE NATIONAL DISH.

No product of the soil is more universally used in the Republic of Paraguay than mandioca. This is a product peculiar to tropical or semitropical regions. Every family, in all circumstances of life, has it upon the table. It is something like the sweet potato of the United States, though containing more starch and less sweetness. It is usually cooked with meat, together with corn, sweet potatoes, and other vegetables. This constitutes the national dish. It is also used in making starch, corn starch being an unknown commodity in Paraguay.

Mandioca is light brown in color and is from 18 inches to 2 feet in length, with a circumference of from 3 to 5 inches. It is planted in May, and during the winter months, June, July, and August, it is in the best condition to be marketed, although it grows the whole year around. For 5 cents (gold valuation) enough mandioca can be purchased to furnish the best part of a meal for a family of 5 or 6 persons. Consul RUFFIN reports the crop prospects for this year as good.

IMPROVEMENTS IN AGRICULTURE.

Consul RUFFIN states that the Agricultural Bank, a Government institution, has entire charge of the farming interests of the Republic. Modern agricultural methods and machinery are being

blacksmithing and roasting silver ore. The analyses Nos. 1 and 2, by A. S. McCreath, represent the coal from the regions referred to.

	Analyses—	
	No. 1.	No. 2.
Water	1.450	1.596
Volatile matter	5.633	3.030
Fixed carbon...	83.620	90.906
Sulphur..................	.554	.652
Ash	8.743	3.816
	100	100
Specific gravity	1.62	1.67

It will be noted that the coal of the northern field, as shown by analysis, is about the same quality as the average of Pennsylvania anthracite, while the second analysis shows the coal of quality far above the average, and perhaps superior to even our best Pennsylvania coal.

The Andes Mountains have evidently been intensely and uniformly heated throughout this whole region. It is reasonably certain, therefore, that these anthracites have a more or less uniform quality throughout, and are not liable to change to bituminous, as in Colorado. Surface deposits of lignite coal of a more recent age and of greater thickness are found in certain localities in the same district, but no bituminous coal. This latter field is well located and contains coal in sufficient abundance to warrant any expense that may be necessary for its development, having for a market the whole western coasts of South and North America, where coal commands an unusually high price, and this market will ere long be augmented by the coaling necessities of the Nicaragua Canal, which will doubtless be constructed in the near future and which this coal field is well located to supply.

About one-quarter of the fuel supply of the steamers which regularly ply between Panama and Valparaiso is brought as ballast from Wales and deposited in a coal bunker at port of Iquique, in northern Chile, by vessels engaged in the nitrate trade. The balance of the coal required on the South American coast is obtained from mines on the coast of Chile several hundred miles south of Valparaiso, to which point the steamers are obliged to go to coal, thus losing several days' time on each trip. An occasional cargo is also brought from Australia. This Chile product is a gas coal of very inferior quality for steam purposes, being very high in volatile matter, and, as ordinarily used, is very smoky, producing large percentage of ash and requiring excessive labor in firing; but, for want of something better, it has been in use for years, at a very high price, and has been the source of enormous wealth to the woman who owns the mines.

SALVADOR.

NEW TARIFF RATES.

Consul JENKINS sends from San Salvador, under date of August 11, 1898, copy of a decree of President GUTIERREZ, affecting duties on imports into Salvador. The principal articles are as follows:

ARTICLE I.

The duties upon imports shall be paid in the following manner:
Twenty per cent United States gold coin.
Twelve per cent United States gold coin for corporations.
Six per cent in silver in bonds of the French debt.

ARTICLE II.

The following articles shall continue paying duties as at present:
Artificial flowers in cotton or other matter not specified.

Baggage is free up to the weight of 100 kilograms per person, when the effects are for personal use; exceeding that weight without invoice shall pay $3 per kilogram.

Barrel staves, arches, and twigs for barrels; beers; bran (fine) and superfine flour; bricks of earth or other material; bronze and copper for steeples of churches; brooms and brushes of straw and hemp of all classes; essences; food, comfits, and pastes, chocolates, and other sweets; food, fruits preserved in spirits; food, sugared, of all classes; food in vinegar, sago, tapioca, and other paste goods, cocoa, sirups without alcohol, and nuts; food of wheat, oats, barley, and all other cereals not specified; ginger ale; hats, esparto grass, for ladies and children of whatever other class not specified; hats of junco or jipijapa; iron cradles, beds, cots, camp stools, sofas, and other articles of furniture; leather, dressed sheepskins, hides with hair, and fur robes; leather shoes and overshoes of whatever class not specified; leather soles for shoes, cowhides, and other leather not specified; leather in suspenders; leather visors for caps and the like; matches of all classes; materials for shawls and rebozos, plain, worked, or embroidered; pork lard, food and sauces, herring, cod and other fish not further prepared than dried, salted, or smoked; pumps, carts, wheelbarrows, pipes, beehives, wood for matches, and wheels for wagons and wheelbarrows, of 100 kilograms; silks in shawls and rebozos, plain, worked, or embroidered; smelling waters of any kind containing alcohol, such as Florida water or cologne, divina, kanga, lavender, and others of the same class; soap (common) without perfume; soda or potassium, caustic for industrial purposes; spirits, strong or sweet, as cognac, absinthe, rum, gin, cordials, whisky, rosoli, and others not specified, up to 22° Castier, 59 centigrades, in barrels or other vessel of more than 1 pint; spirits in ordinary bottles of more or less than 1

used with gratifying results. The consul believes that if its efficiency were generally known, United States machinery would revolutionize agriculture in Paraguay. It is suggested that the manufacturers send well-equipped salesmen to Asunción to establish agencies for the sale of articles of United States manufacture

---

PERU.

ANTHRACITE COAL AREA.

The BULLETIN for August contained a short article on the coal deposits of Peru, announcing that in 1892 a twenty-years concession for mining coal had been granted Mr. C. B. JONES. Since then two mining journals—"Mines and Minerals," of Scranton, Pa., and the "Association Letter," of the anthracite coal operators' organization—have published a description of the anthracite coal fields of Peru, prepared by WILLIAM GRIFFITH, a mining engineer, who, during the past year, visited and investigated the localities referred to. From this gentleman's descriptive article, the subjoined extracts are obtained:

The areas of anthracite coal in northern Peru are located in the lofty range of the Andes Mountains at various elevations from 7,000 to 13,000 feet above the sea, and on both sides of the Continental Divide. There are two notable localities, the most northern, in the department of Cajamarca, about 50 or 60 miles north of the ancient and historic city of the same name. At this point several seams of coal were noted outcropping in the nearly vertical cliffs, about 600 feet above the bottom of the valley, through which flows the roaring mountain torrent known as Rio Llaucon, a branch of the River Marinon, which forms the principal source of the main trunk of the Amazon River system. This locality is about 7,000 feet above tide, and perhaps 300 miles from navigable waters on the Amazon, and 150 miles from the Pacific. The coal measures here are composed of an altered sandstone or quartzite, over 2,000 feet in thickness, and extending over a large expanse of territory which has never been tested or prospected for coal. The workable seams which were exposed to view at the time of the visit were three in number, about 50 feet apart, and 5½, 3, and 6½ feet thick, respectively, with southwesterly dip of 22°, the strike being southeast and northwest parallel to the axis of a prominent anticlinal, which at this point elevates the coal measures. The formation covering the crest of the anticlinal has been eroded, and the valley thus formed is now occupied by a branch of the river, so that the mountains on either side of the valley are formed by the rocks of the coal formation which dip in opposite directions into the mountain side.

It is highly probable that other beds also might be found in the great thickness of overlying sandstone if carefully prospected. They contain interstratified slate and refuse in about the same proportions as is usually found in the beds of Pennsylvania anthracite.

The outcrops may be traced for some distance and the beds are exposed on the other side of the river, having nearly the same thickness as above sections, which are doubtless the continuation of the same seams. Good exposures in this region could only be noted in the nearly vertical cliffs, where the débris falling from above had small chance to lodge; elsewhere, the dense tropical foliage or surface wash hides the outcrop. The few natives who sparsely inhabit this wild region have absolutely no use for coal, and therefore no prospecting has been done by them.

The measures are exceptionally well disposed for water-level mining, and if the beds are as continuous as is usually the case with coal seams, hundreds of millions of tons could be mined entirely above water level. The outcrop of the coal-bearing sandstones may be traced for 15 or 20 miles or more on both sides of the valleys which are cut by the Llaucon River and its branches. The coal from this field must be raised over the Continental Divide to reach the Pacific coast. A descending grade could probably be secured, however, all the way to a navigable point on the Amazon River system. It is probable also that future investigations might result in finding workable coal beds in the southwestern outcrop of the same basin on the Pacific side of the divide, unless the volcanic disturbance which is predominant in the Andes should so disrupt the measures as to seriously affect or destroy the coal seams. This volcanic action seems to have been at a minimum in the locality above described, and the coal beds are very regularly disposed and apparently undisturbed.

The second field worthy of particular attention is situated 100 miles or more south of the region above mentioned, in the department of Libertad, near the source of the Chicama and Sanat rivers, which flow to the Pacific near the town of Trujillo and the Bay of Chimbote, respectively. The measures here are apparently of the same quartzite or altered sandstone and extend in a southeast and northwest direction. The coal seams have a southwest dip of about 75°, and some of the beds are very thick. The erosion of the outcrop, forming deep gulleys or trenches between the inclosing rocks of the veins, may be plainly noted like a great ditch crossing the rolling irregularities of the mountain. The principal bed is about 10 to 15 feet thick. Other sections quite similar to the second one were measured midway between.

The outcrop of this large bed and the measures which contain it can readily be traced for 15 or 20 miles. The first exposure visited was on the Pacific slope about 100 miles from the coast and elevated about 8,000 feet. Other exposures were inspected and samples taken at various points along the outcrop for 20 miles or more until it crossed the Continental Divide of the Andes at an elevation of 13,000 feet. Thinner beds from 2 to 4 feet in thickness were noted in this field. The outcrops, however, were usually so covered with a surface wash that few exposures could be found. This coal is used locally in a small way for

Bull. No. 4——3

IMPORTS OF MERCHANDISE—Continued.

Articles and countries.	July—		Seven months ending July—	
	1897.	1898.	1897.	1898.
India rubber, crude (*Goma elástica cruda; Borracha crua; Caoutchouc brut*):				
Central America	$21,892	$32,790	$256,070	$272,311
Mexico	2,760	1,158	21,974	29,137
Brazil	841,276	567,156	7,382,116	8,417,514
Other South America	22,768	84,031	210,851	387,127
Lead, in pigs, bars, etc. (*Plomo en galápagos, barras, etc.; Churiboem linguados, barras, etc.; Plomb en saumons, en barres, etc.*):				
Mexico	134,291	106,189	927,766	901,199
Sugar, not above No. 16 Dutch standard (*Azúcar, no superior al No. 16 de la escala holandesa; Assucar não superior ao No. 16 de padrão hollandez Sucre, pas au-dessus du type hollandais No. 16*):				
Central America	....	5,207	....	200,356
Mexico	523	1,401	10,274	42,058
Cuba	82,501	....	9,932,928	9,743,538
Brazil	....	47,253	1,839,639	2,350,166
Other South America	447,944	285,178	3,369,298	2,925,559
Hawaiian Islands	1,898,191	1,809,218	9,305,944	11,191,241
Philippine Islands	....	68,832	389,898	296,583
Tobacco, leaf (*Tabaco en rama; Tabaco em folha; Tabac en feuilles*).				
Mexico	18,101	16,409	179,067	97,418
Cuba	107,078	21,066	1,407,921	1,651,420
Wood, mahogany (*Caoba; Mogno; Acajou*):				
Central America	740	56,332	49,635	110,679
Mexico	17,678	25,983	191,645	141,563
Cuba	....	....	21,019	932
South America	778	737	18,948	34,000
Wool (*Lana; Lã; Laine*):				
South America—				
Class 1 (clothing)	91,860	9,668	4,685,452	530,732
Class 2 (combing)	9,391	....	1,183,201	19,020
Class 3 (carpet)	67,142	32,517	1,160,330	720,738

EXPORTS OF DOMESTIC MERCHANDISE.

Articles and countries.	July—		Seven months ending July—	
	1897.	1898.	1897.	1898.
Agricultural implements (*Instrumentos de agricultura; Instrumentos de agricultura; Machines agricoles*):				
Central America................	$463	$455	$14, 186	$1, 936
Mexico	10, 245	7, 149	81, 311	83, 388
Santo Domingo..................	170	....	985	266
Cuba..........................	1, 056	....	3, 690	2, 068
Porto Rico....................	120	....	1, 738	426
Argentina.....................	28, 479	53, 610	165, 465	219, 376
Brazil	993	2, 723	12, 546	16, 720
Colombia	493	66	1, 903	3, 156
Other South America	10, 315	24, 438	50, 236	114, 255
Animals:				
Cattle (*Ganado vacuno; Gado; Betai!*)—				
Central America..............	3, 001	....	11, 972	990
Mexico	4, 395	2, 390	18, 410	57, 951
South America	....	175	1, 228	5, 137
Hogs (*Cerdos; Porcos; Cochons*)—				
Mexico......................	255	20	67, 962	4, 568
Horses (*Caballos; Cavallos; Chevaux*)—				
Central America..............	1, 800	1, 200	9, 600	8, 395
Mexico......................	3, 370	1, 500	49, 938	62, 886
South America	....	....	2, 100	1, 850
Sheep (*Carneros; Carneiros; Moutons*)—				
Mexico......................	....	2, 040	2, 342	5, 855
South America	1, 637	285	11, 120	6, 338
Books, maps, engravings, etc. (*Libros, mapas, grabados, etc.; Livros, mappas, gravuras, etc.; Livres, cartes de géographie, gravures, etc.*):				
Central America..............	1, 688	645	25, 694	11, 389
Mexico	15, 652	5, 679	69, 703	52, 684
Santo Domingo................	37	....	606	262
Cuba........................	487	25	43, 915	2, 759
Porto Rico..................	69	....	2, 644	355
Argentina...................	316	1, 041	16, 745	14, 843
Brazil	21, 380	2, 587	117, 314	30, 162
Colombia	600	2, 085	20, 959	6, 536
Other South America	2, 171	4, 228	31, 568	28, 318
Breadstuffs:				
Corn (*Maíz; Milho; Maïs*)—				
Central America....	8, 307	4, 897	44, 428	42, 351
Mexico	28, 326	466	982, 501	6, 242
Santo Domingo....	40	....	379	61
Cuba	7, 713	688	136, 556	198, 703
Porto Rico..................	....	....	357	....
South America	4, 097	874	11, 826	9, 932
Wheat (*Trigo; Trigo; Blé*)—				
Central America.............	4, 861	1, 800	30, 380	23, 084
South America	310, 288	46	323, 530	385, 677

EXPORTS OF DOMESTIC MERCHANDISE—Continued.

Articles and countries.	July—		Seven months ending July—	
	1897.	1898.	1897.	1898.
Copper (*Cobre; Cobre; Cuivre*):				
Mexico......................	$690	$6,750	$9,891	$25,324
Cotton, unmanufactured (*Algodón no manufacturado; Algodão não manufacturado; Coton non manufacturé*):				
Mexico......................	....	....	390,752	561,331
Cotton cloths (*Tejidos de algodón; Fazendas de algodão; Coton manufacturé*):				
Central America................	48,612	29,332	314,200	239,980
Mexico	34,019	27,196	229,836	260,064
Santo Domingo................	7,459	22,838	46,698	90,778
Cuba	1,366	263	12,837	5,951
Porto Rico....................	228	....	3,055	1,023
Argentina.	10,754	22,926	63,647	99,485
Brazil	41,764	49,431	318,140	345,224
Colombia	19,401	25,401	217,402	155,480
Other South America...........	77,381	80,512	733,327	742,274
Wearing apparel (cotton) (*Ropa de algodón; Roupa de algodão; Vêtements en coton*):				
Central America......	20,911	12,133	141,268	139,980
Mexico.......................	20,867	37,326	181,448	227,590
Santo Domingo	657	1,853	14,406	11,622
Cuba	660	2,976	12,390	10,800
Porto Rico...................	142	....	2,205	746
Argentina..	1,108	5,238	29,161	24,197
Brazil	5,321	2,658	34,763	25,681
Colombia	3,816	2,266	29,954	23,789
Other South America...........	3,210	4,588	30,867	23,904
Fruits and nuts (*Frutas y nueces; Frutas e nozes; Fruits et noisettes*).				
Central America................	3,386	1,390	32,821	16,359
Mexico.......................	4,602	4,858	33,863	32,987
Santo Domingo................	12	87	503	273
Cuba	1,568	323	14,652	10,934
Porto Rico....	70	....	4,459	287
Argentina......	413	969	2,394	5,662
Brazil	513	1,050	3,625	3,611
Colombia	725	341	5,198	4,866
Other South America......	1,431	703	15,479	9,017
Hides and skins (*Cueros y pieles; Couros e pelles, Cuirs et peaux*):				
Central America................	....	....	543	....
Mexico	175	225	13,121	1,879
Hops (*Lúpulos; Lupulos; Houblon*):				
Central America................	236	410	2,337	2,552
Mexico.......................	113	332	55,596	7,472
Santo Domingo................	....	....	2	16
South America.......	31	89	885	863

EXPORTS OF DOMESTIC MERCHANDISE—Continued.

Articles and countries.	July—		Seven months ending July—	
	1897.	1898.	1897.	1898.
Iron and steel, manufactures of— Continued. Typewriting machines, etc.—C't'd				
Porto Rico			$110	
Argentina	$131	$1,465	3,541	$14,434
Brazil	676	131	1,602	2,548
Colombia	468	177	2,608	1,571
Other South America	478	1,592	6,495	8,917
Leather, other than sole (*Cuero, distinto del de suela; Couro não para solas; Cuirs, autres que pour semelles*):				
Central America		828	2,597	3,563
Mexico	885	460	7,364	4,112
Santo Domingo		106	747	186
Cuba	513	60	716	1,627
Porto Rico	12		221	708
Argentina		4,682	662	8,470
Brazil	4,850	3,889	15,578	37,716
Colombia	296	100	1,374	2,902
Other South America	728	1,686	5,271	8,736
Boots and shoes (*Calzado; Calçados; Chaussures*):				
Central America	5,704	2,438	51,303	45,121
Mexico	4,382	6,666	41,894	59,307
Colombia	2,797	3,187	26,382	22,817
Other South America	1,227	4,976	11,651	20,597
Naval stores: Rosin, tar, etc. (*Resina y alquitrán; Resina e alcatrão; Résine et goudron*:				
Central America	1,061	2,290	11,392	10,638
Mexico	1,067	961	4,401	6,678
Santo Domingo	695	125	2,721	3,219
Cuba	353		2,778	2,548
Porto Rico	44		711	281
Argentina	400	17,151	34,437	57,927
Brazil	19,358	19,628	103,654	92,355
Colombia	831	891	11,547	8,880
Other South America	4,626	3,360	43,193	47,037
Turpentine, spirits of (*Aguarras; Agua-raz; Térébenthine*):				
Central America	72	118	2,094	1,788
Mexico	105	352	1,804	2,719
Santo Domingo	47	37	226	272
Cuba	1,193		8,004	5,095
Porto Rico	28		1,651	583
Argentina	7,974	13,674	14,915	97,760
Brazil	4,181	5,546	33,656	48,509
Colombia	95	448	2,921	2,724
Other South America	5,111	3,973	23,049	46,129
Oils, mineral, crude (*Aceites minerales, crudos; Oleos mineraes, crús; Huiles minérales, brutes*):				
Mexico	30,979	57	204,322	152,003
Cuba	9,900		132,817	77,142
Porto Rico	13,635		25,793	19,477

EXPORTS OF DOMESTIC MERCHANDISE—Continued.

Articles and countries.	July—		Seven months ending July—	
	1897.	1898.	1897.	1898.
Provisions, comprising meat and dairy products—Continued.				
Beef, salted or pick ed—Cont'd.				
Brazil	$52	$42	$1,177	$648
Colombia	779	856	7,959	8,458
Other South America	9,656	14,988	51,801	106,685
Tallow (*Sebo; Sebo; Suif*)—				
Central America	7,292	7,878	56,130	58,386
Mexico	2,856	3,509	17,823	11,868
Santo Domingo	4,062	....	11,756	15,936
Cuba	650	....	6,892	5,465
Porto Rico	....	....	198	176
Brazil	4,190	2,395	10,857	3,475
Colombia	1,645	1,258	8,949	8,075
Other South America	426	622	6,648	15,048
Bacon (*Tocino; Toucinho; Lard fumé*)—				
Central America	2,325	1,659	13,144	8,318
Mexico	906	1,042	5,083	6,049
Santo Domingo	103	263	1,449	1,586
Cuba	70,316	14,243	373,863	338,937
Porto Rico	1,239	....	22,664	18,872
Brazil	102,979	35,365	800,015	209,431
Colombia	127	63	893	657
Other South America	1,970	2,701	14,519	14,093
Hams (*Jamones; Presunto; Jambons*)—				
Central America	3,040	1,331	20,638	14,102
Mexico	1,540	1,990	13,408	15,457
Cuba	23,822	7,054	185,687	161,699
Porto Rico	4,620	....	50,261	11,378
Santo Domingo	361	1,018	4,226	4,841
Brazil	6	....	1,306	2,079
Colombia	1,298	1,071	9,742	8,280
Other South America	6,100	4,814	50,546	37,916
Pork (*Carne de puerco; Carne de porco; Porc*)—				
Central America	4,392	4,890	36,537	46,463
Santo Domingo	157	557	2,277	4,560
Cuba	2,319	2,055	5,561	8,634
Porto Rico	15,247	....	103,748	68,951
Brazil	209	380	15,849	1,988
Colombia	548	643	4,488	5,733
Other South America	11,098	17,128	72,199	129,580
Lard (*Manteca; Banha; Saindoux*)—				
Central America	13,059	10,372	73,606	109,308
Mexico	16,645	6,135	202,279	84,709
Santo Domingo	1,673	5,928	15,690	24,735
Cuba	116,569	28,425	610,462	547,609
Porto Rico	12,378	....	142,090	85,627
Argentina	140	....	1,900	2,761
Brazil	78,781	64,902	577,383	523,439
Colombia	13,289	7,555	83,393	60,157
Other South America	54,484	49,019	344,132	403,105

EXPORTS OF DOMESTIC MERCHANDISE—Continued.

Articles and countries.	July—		Seven months ending July—	
	1897.	1898.	1897.	1898.
Provisions, comprising meat and dairy products—Continued.				
Oleo and oleo margarine (*Grasa y oleomargarina; Oleo e oleomargarina ; Oléo et oléomargarine*)—				
Central America................	$103	$24	$354	$1, 09:
Mexico.......................	....	54	283	823
Colombia	630	615	4, 010	5, 560
Other South America..........	2, 288	1, 607	15, 840	6, 983
Butter (*Mantequilla ; Manteiga ; Beurre*)—				
Central America................	4, 497	3, 529	28, 439	27, 857
Mexico.......................	3, 227	3, 822	25, 924	28, 703
Santo Domingo.................	495	2, 413	4, 675	7, 066
Cuba	394	584	6, 458	3, 803
Porto Rico...................	841	....	4, 772	420
Brazil.......................	4, 876	6, 464	26, 578	64, 174
Colombia	1, 987	1, 174	12, 236	9, 840
Other South America..........	9, 065	8, 983	52, 946	60, 297
Cheese (*Queso ; Queijo ; Fromage*)—				
Central America................	1, 733	1, 362	12, 786	10, 202
Mexico.......................	985	1, 093	8, 482	8, 730
Santo Domingo.................	200	495	3, 413	2, 973
Cuba.... ....:	1, 407	570	8, 392	13, 096
Porto Rico...................	92	....	2, 128	970
Brazil.......................	....	....	132	75
Colombia	1, 140	576	7, 240	5, 642
Other South America..........	1, 374	836	9, 666	9, 891
Seeds (*Semillas ; Sementes ; Semence*) :				
Central America	201	322	4, 163	4, 270
Mexico......	296	769	13, 131	23, 931
Santo Domingo.................	133	25	450	351
Cuba...	187	....	934	626
Porto Rico...................	....	....	131	....
Argentina....................	2	....	631	236
Brazil	11	....	1, 090	445
Colombia	137	12	1, 904	540
Other South America	106	128	1, 209	1, 425
Sugar, refined (*Azúcar refinado ; Assucar refinado ; Sucre raffiné*) :				
Central America................	4, 847	963	30, 783	23, 729
Mexico	1, 083	199	10, 944	9, 373
Santo Domingo.................	174	186	1, 436	697
Colombia	2, 258	1, 414	20, 649	12, 367
Other South America	679	33	1, 982	564
Tobacco, unmanufactured (*Tabaco no manufacturado ; Tabaco não manufacturado ; Tabac non manufacturé*) :				
Central America................	542	268	5, 368	17, 363
Mexico.......................	17, 011	8, 371	67, 327	73, 596
Argentina....................	....	.. ..	965	12, 489
Colombia	132	651	686	5, 708
Other South America	13, 907	4, 174	53, 353	58, 231

EXPORTS OF DOMESTIC MERCHANDISE—Continued.

Articles and countries.	July—		Seven months ending July—	
	1897.	1898.	1897.	1898.
Tobacco, manufactures of (*Manufacturas de tabaco ; Manufacturas de tabaco ; Tabac fabriqué*):				
Central America..............	$994	$3, 404	$39, 100	$33, 235
Mexico........................	757	2, 488	3, 526	22, 575
Cuba..........................	16, 800	1, 426	107, 188	76, 709
Argentina.....................	....	....	8, 813	910
Brazil	....	....	65	550
Colombia......	100	963	368	4, 040
Other South America...........	4, 573	8, 428	39, 883	49, 378
Wood, unmanufactured (*Madera no manufacturado ; Madeira não manufacturado ; Bois brut*):				
Central America..............	3, 341	7, 271	52, 592	21, 485
Mexico........................	16, 187	43, 628	136, 140	252, 912
Cuba	875	....	14, 245	12, 683
Argentina.....................	461	301	14, 140	6, 022
Brazil	480	....	9, 520	75
Colombia	1, 831	8, 370	19, 136	20, 838
Other South America...........	15, 015	....	27, 133	20, 353
Lumber (*Maderas ; Madeiras ; Bois de construction*)				
Central America..............	4, 940	3, 066	84, 545	19, 913
Mexico........................	68, 776	64, 780	844, 441	472, 400
Santo Domingo.................	5, 516	2, 922	57, 030	20, 713
Cuba..........................	25, 173	450	165, 016	105, 527
Porto Rico.......	4, 524	....	58, 081	19, 224
Argentina.....................	59, 228	68, 570	405, 081	524, 823
Brazil	64, 256	42, 333	381, 597	392, 039
Colombia......................	5, 321	7, 882	42, 037	31, 645
Other South America...........	50, 911	36, 479	361, 160	333, 558
Furniture (*Muebles ; Mobilia ; Meubles*):				
Central America..............	10, 759	1, 803	83, 306	25, 375
Mexico........................	10, 962	11, 238	117, 762	88, 901
Santo Domingo.................	2, 193	1, 201	7, 647	6, 545
Cuba	1, 674	12	20, 991	10, 119
Porto Rico....................	455	....	5, 487	2, 456
Argentina............	592	1, 659	36, 956	24, 673
Brazil.	1, 783	1, 046	26, 440	13, 530
Colombia	2 225	1, 346	24, 820	15, 831
Other South America...........	5, 536	4, 637	46, 729	43, 791
Wool, raw (*Lana cruda ; Lã crûa ; Laines brutes*):				
Mexico	....	....	30, 449	....

CONDITION OF THE TREASURY—MONEY IN CIRCULATION.

The following condensed statement of the condition of the United States Treasury at the close of business on September 30 was issued on October 1 : Available cash balance, $309,156,297 : free gold reserve, $243,327,379; net silver, $7,120,784; legal-tender notes in the Treasury, $36,454,266; Treasury notes of 1890, $1,751,950; total receipts for the month, $3,103,050; total receipts for the fiscal year, $128,510,936; total expenditures for the month, $2,281,000; total expenditures, fiscal year. $187,099,114; Treasury deposits in national banks, $82,344,416.

The statistics of money in circulation show a contrast to the two preceding months in exhibiting a net increase instead of a net decrease for the month, the net gain amounting to $24,499,847. Among the items showing a decrease, the most important was gold coin, which showed a falling off of $8,043,354.   Other items in which there was a decrease were currency certificates of 1872, $2,645,000, and gold certificates, $79,100.   The most notable increase was United States notes, amounting to $19,264,584.   The increase in national-bank notes amounted to $8,904,794.   Other increases were $3,050,515 in standard silver dollars, $1,828,417 in subsidiary silver, $453,362 in silver certificates, and $1,783,629 in Treasury notes of 1890.

A small net decrease is shown by the comparative statement, indicating the changes in money and bullion in the Treasury. Two items show an increase—the gain in gold coin amounted to $14,190,377, and bullion exhibited a gain of $11,123,581.   The most noteworthy decrease is one of $19,264,584 in United States notes, which corresponded with the increase in circulation mentioned above.   The general stock of money issued, the amount in the Treasury, and the amount in circulation are stated in the appended table:

	General stock, coined or issued.	In Treasury.	In circulation Oct. 1, 1898.
Gold coin	$785,041,686	$162,391,874	$622,649,812
Standard silver dollars	464,834,597	404,045,769	60,788,828
Subsidiary silver................	75,784,648	9,196,708	66,587,940
Gold certificates	36,990,799	1,596,890	35,393,909
Silver certificates...............	400,062,504	6,636,769	393,425,735
Treasury notes, act July 14, 1890..	98,549,280	1,844,997	96,704,283
United States notes	346,681,016	55,020,851	291,660,165
Currency certificates, act June 8, 1872	18,455,000	820,000	17,635,000
National-bank notes	235,439,985	3,689,265	231,750,720
Total	2,461,839,515	645,243,123	1,816,596,392

As compared with October 1, 1897, the amount of gold in circulation has increased by over $93,500,000. During the year the increase in United States notes was $39,800,000; silver certificates, $18,800,000; Treasury notes of 1890, about $6,900,000; subsidiary silver, over $5,400,000; national-bank notes, nearly $5,300,000, and standard silver dollars, over $3,600,000. There were decreases in only two items, each of about the same amount, $1,500,000. These were currency certificates of 1872 and gold certificates.

The grand total of money in circulation on October 1 amounted to $1,816,596,392. This represented an increase of over $137,750,000, as compared with October 1, 1897. The circulation per capita was $24.24, based by the Treasury expert on an estimated population of .74,925,000. This represents for the month of September an increase of 28 cents per capita and of $1.35 over October 1, 1897. It will be noted from the above statement that of the total amount of gold coin issued, nearly four-fifths was in circulation, while of standard-silver dollars over six-sevenths were in the Treasury vaults.

INTERNAL REVENUE RECEIPTS FOR AUGUST.

The statement of the collections of internal revenue for the month of August shows a net increase over August, 1897, of $11,006,235. The receipts from the several sources of revenue and the increase or decrease, as compared with August, 1897, are given as follows:

Spirits, $6,787,513; decrease, $207,645. Fermented liquors, $7,053,661; increase, $5,418,860. Oleomargarine, $131,354: increase, $64,923. Special taxes, not elsewhere enumerated, $1,289,335; miscellaneous, $3,098,510; increase, $3,072,036.

The several items from which special taxes were received were: .Bankers, $971,934; billiard rooms, $98,700; brokers, stocks, bonds, etc., $101,958; brokers, commercial, $48,123; brokers, custom-house, $2,202; brokers, pawn, $11,269; bowling alleys, $17,139; circuses, $6,058; exhibitions, not otherwise provided for, $12,039; theaters, etc., $19,908; mixed flour, $755; legacies, $5,057; documentary and proprietary stamps, $3,167,514; playing cards, $12,438; penalties, $12,266. The net increase

COTTON SUPPLY AND PRICES.

The phenomenally low price of cotton recently reported, said to be the lowest point reached in many years, lends special interest to a series of tables just compiled by the Bureau of Statistics of the Treasury Department, showing the remarkable increase in cotton productions and coincidental fall in price. These tables show that the United States, the chief cotton producer of the world, has quadrupled its cotton production since 1872, and that the price of cotton in the same period has fallen to about one-fourth the price which prevailed in that year. In 1872 the cotton crop of the United States is shown to have been 1,384,084,494 pounds, with an average price of 22.19 cents per pound; in 1898 the crop is reported at 5,667,372,051 pounds, with an average price of 6.23 cents per pound. Thus the production of 1898 is more than four times that of 1872, and the average price but a little over one-fourth of that of 1872.

When it is considered that the other cotton-producing countries of the world have not at all reduced their crops in the meantime, it is apparent that the increased cotton supply of the world in the quarter of a century under consideration has been very great and far in advance of the increase in population or power of consumption.

The United States, twenty-five years ago, produced 70 per cent of the cotton of the world; to-day it produces 85 per cent. This increase in the percentage has not been because of a reduction of the cotton produced in other parts of the world, but simply on account of the great increase in the United States. The cotton supply of the other producing sections of the world in 1872–73 was 1,667,000 bales, and in 1897–98, 1,665,000 bales. The average cotton production of other countries from 1872 to 1878 was 1,618,000 bales per annum, and from 1890 to 1897 was 1,924,000 bales per annum, showing that there has also been a slight growth in cotton production in other parts of the world, while our own production has been increasing enormously.

Not only has the price of cotton fallen at about the same rate that the production has increased, but there has also been a corresponding fall in the price of cloths manufactured from cotton.

BANKING INSTITUTIONS IN CUBA.

Heretofore the Bank of Spain and other European bankers have handled all the commercial paper called for by the requirements of the trade between the United States and Cuba, making discounts and collections, issuing letters of credit, buying and selling bills of exchange, and, in some cases, acting as commercial agents. The necessity for United States branch banking houses in Cuba (as is also the case in the American Republics) that will enable exporters to do business direct with their customers in that island is of course obvious.

Mr. S. M. JARVIS, vice-president of the North American Trust Company, has returned from Santiago de Cuba after establishing there the first United States branch bank in the West Indies. In an interview he said:

We have established and have in working order an agency in Santiago, which is purely a banking establishment, designed, first, to serve the needs of the United States Government and its fiscal agents; second, for the convenience of those who are conducting commercial operations there. To this latter end we are prepared to issue New York letters of credit to be used in Santiago either by travelers there or by importers of goods in that place; and in Santiago our agency is prepared to buy or sell exchange on New York and to handle shipping documents. At each of these points we are now prepared to furnish telegraphic transfers of money to the other. Similar agencies will be established in Havana, Matanzas, and such other points as we may hereafter select.

UNITED STATES OF CENTRAL AMERICA.

PROMULGATION OF THE NEW CONSTITUTION.

Under date of September 15, 1898, WILLIAM M. LITTLE, Consul at Tegucigalpa, Honduras, communicated officially with the Department of State relative to the new federation of Central American States, now (and until November 1, 1898) known as the Greater Republic of Central America. In his communication, Mr. LITTLE said:

I have the honor to inform you that this Government has officially published the political constitution of the United States of Central America (formerly called the Greater Republic of Central America), which was formed by the representatives of Honduras, Nicaragua, and Salvador, in Managua, Nicaragua,

into the territory of the Republic may be denied to a foreigner, or his expulsion ordered, on account of his being considered pernicious."

I believe that the faithful execution of this Constitution of the United Republic will greatly promote the establishment of permanent peace and order in the three States composing it.

URUGUAY.

CUSTOMS RECEIPTS IN MONTEVIDEO.

The customs receipts at the port of Montevideo for the month of July amounted to $1,005,007, as reported by the British consul. This is a remarkably large total when the fact that July in Uruguay is one of the dullest business months in the year is taken into consideration.

The consul attributes the unusual increase to the fact that in order to escape the additional 2½ per cent import duty, which came into force on August 1, merchants cleared goods from the custom-house in large quantities. Increased importations also were noticeable. The total for July, 1898, was $916,359, against a total of $583,000 in July, 1897.

According to the "Montevideo Times" the customs receipts for the first six months of 1898 amounted to $5,319,448, against $4,290,121 for the same period in 1897. The present year not only shows an enormous advance over the year of revolution, 1897, but also compares well with the first half of 1896, which was regarded commercially as very prosperous. Then the customs receipts amounted to $5,535,402, The figures for 1898, the Times states, are subject to revision, which will increase rather than lower them.

With reference to the additional 2½ per cent import duty on goods entering Uruguay, announcement of which was made in the September Bulletin, Consul SWALM reports that the Government has decided to devote the proceeds to the conversion of Treasury certificates until such times as they are needed for the new port works at Montevideo.

the various ports of embarkation; (2) to erect buildings for and furnish agricultural implements, and to supply them with food, clothes, and medicine until they shall have reaped their first crop, and also to build a church, public offices, and schools in each colony; (3) to establish a bimonthly service of steamships between Italy and Venezuela, touching at Barcelona de España, Teneriffe, and other ports, and terminating at La Guayra or Puerto Cabello, and also calling, if required, at any other ports subject to the fiscal laws of Venezuela; and to carry the mails to all such ports free of charge, the regular fare for passengers and freight not to exceed that charged by ships of like class and tonnage as those used by the company; and it agrees to charge only half fare to all employees of the diplomatic service (and their families) who use the ships, and to accord to them free passage if they officially reside or are going to reside abroad; (4) to establish in Caracas a bank institution, with branches in such districts of the Republic as may be deemed advisable, for the purpose principally of lending on mortgage security, to agriculturists and cattle breeders, the capital of such bank, to consist of 20,000,000 bolivars ($3,860,000), 12,000,000 of which shall be devoted to ordinary banking business and the remainder to lending as above mentioned; the two funds are to be kept separate and not allowed to entrench on each other; the interest on loans shall not exceed 7 per cent, and the bank has power to issue notes according to the provisions of existing banking laws; (5) to grant to the National Government the free use of all ways of traveling and communication it may construct; (6) to grant, after four years of cultivation, to each family a house of the colony, and to each colonist 3 hectares (14.8 acres) which shall have been allotted him for cultivation; (7) to deposit in the Bank of England, as a guaranty for the execution of this contract, and within three months from the date on which the same shall be approved by the National Congress, the sum of $200,000 bolivars ($38,000), which shall remain there until the company establishes the above-mentioned bank in Caracas and settles the first 500 families, and shall be forfeited to the Government of Venezuela in the event of the company failing to execute its contract.

" On the other hand, the Government undertakes (8) to grant to the company uncultivated land for the immigrants at the rate of

do so, and the Government will furnish land under the present immigration law, and when Congress sanctions the contract it shall have the benefit of its provisions; but that if Congress should not sanction it, the Government will pay the passages of the immigrants in accordance with the provisions of the present law. The Government reserves the right to enter into similar contracts with any other countries."

DECREES REGARDING MINES.

Consul PLUMACHER, of Maracaibo, under date of September 17, 1898, transmits to the Department of State copies of two Government decrees in regard to mines, translations of which are as follows:

DEPARTMENT OF AGRICULTURE, INDUSTRY, AND COMMERCE,

Caracas, August 6, 1898.

As the proprietors of mine concessions whose titles have been renewed according to prescriptions of the mining laws now in force have not complied with the duty of depositing their respective plans at this office, and this making the collection of mine taxes for areas of said concessions impracticable, the President of the Republic has decided that a period of ninety days, counting from this day, be granted to the interested parties to make and present said plans to this Department.

Let it be communicated and published.

For the National Executive.

NICOLAS ROLANDO.

Proofs existing at this Department that many mine concessionaries have obtained a definite title, and have permitted the five years mentioned in article 61 of the mining laws to pass without having put the mines in exploitation or stating that they have been abandoned, and this causing injury to the nation, as it prevents the working of this source of riches, the President of the Republic has decided that a period of sixty days, counting from this date, be given to the concessionaries for the payment of the taxes, which will grant them a prolongation of time, as specified in article 61 of the above-mentioned code.

Let it be communicated and published.

For the National Executive.

NICOLAS ROLANDO.

THE YUCCA PLANT.

In the Consular Reports for September, Mr. E. H. PLUMACHER, Consul at Maracaibo, makes the following statement:

The great staple of Venezuela is coffee; but, as the prices are now very low, it might be well if farmers would turn their attention to other plants which give a more lucrative return. The yucca appears to have a great future before it. It is a very productive plant, and, although well known in Venezuela, no one has yet taken especial pains to develop it. One hectare (2.471 acres) of land upon which yucca is grown will produce 150 quintals (15,000 pounds) of starch,

FARMERS' NATIONAL CONGRESS.

The eighteenth annual session of the Farmers' National Congress will be held at Fort Worth, Texas, from December 6 to 14, 1898, inclusive. The object of this organization, as is set forth in its constitution, is the advancement of the agricultural interests of the Union. Each State and Territory is entitled to as many delegates as it has representatives in both branches of the United States Congress, and, in addition, one delegate from each agricultural college; besides these, all heads of State and Territorial bureaus of agriculture are entitled to membership. The Governors of the several States and Territories are authorized to appoint the delegates other than those specially designated.

In speaking of the importance of this organization, the Hon. WILLIAM M. HATCH, for many years chairman of the House Committee on Agriculture, says that it had more influence with the Congress of the United States than all other agricultural organizations combined. It is the only farmers' assemblage whose transactions are reported in the American Cyclopedia.

In extending the Director of the Bureau of American Republics an invitation to be present at the meeting in December, Mr. D. O. LIVELY, of Fort Worth, the efficient secretary of the congress, writes:

I have, in my capacity as secretary of the Fort Worth Livestock Exchange, been for some time receiving a very valuable MONTHLY BULLETIN from the Bureau of which you are director, and I desire to call your attention to the meeting which will be held at Fort Worth, Texas, December 6 to 14 of this year, in which the Bureau of the American Republics, in my opinion, should be interested. In order that you may familiarize yourself with the character, scope, and importance of this organization, I have mailed you under separate cover a copy of the report of last year's meeting at St. Paul, to which I respectfully direct your earnest attention. You will observe that Señor ROMERO and Mr. SOTELDO were among the representatives at this meeting, and you will also note that many of the topics discussed had direct bearing upon the relations existing between the United States and other American Republics. As a result of a request made by the State Department at Washington, the Mexican Government has kindly consented to name official delegates to represent that country at the Fort Worth meeting.

It has occurred to me that if an invitation were extended through your BULLETIN, other American countries might see fit to name delegates to this congress. We realize the fact that it is a little bit late to have this matter go through the channels of the Department of State and from thence be referred to the separate

vernments. I defer to your judgment as to the possibility of having yo
ireau represented in an official capacity, and beg leave to assure you that suc
tion will meet with the sincere gratitude of everyone interested, and such
presentative will be accorded the consideration and honor his importance
serves.

It is to be regretted that this notice could not have been sent
the heads of the several governments some months ago, so that
ere would have been sufficient time for the selection of repre-
ntatives by the several American Republics, had they desired
take advantage of the opportunity.

IRRIGATION IN ARIZONA.

Mr. L. V. NAVARRO, representing the Mexican Government as
insul at Phœnix, Arizona, has courteously forwarded this BUREAU
portion of his annual report for 1897–98. This refers espe-
ally to the climatic conditions of Arizona and the benefits derived
om systematic irrigation. The future possibilities of the Terri-
ry, under an efficient scheme of irrigation such as is proposed,
, in the consul's opinion, exceedingly great. His report is as
lows:

he Territory of Arizona has an area of 113,000 square miles, most of
:h is mountainous. The tillable area, in comparison with the total area, is
small. Agriculture is confined in the main to the valleys of the Salt and
rivers and to the borders of the Colorado River.

ie general elevation of the Territory ranges from a little more than a
·ed feet above sea level at Yuma, on the Colorado River, to 13,000 feet
summit of San Francisco Mountain in the northern part of the Terri-
Of the total area, about 39,000 square miles lie at an altitude of 3,000
bout 27,000 lie between the contours of 3,000 and 5,000 feet, and
·7,000 lie above the elevation of 5,000 feet.

Territory is divided into two general climatic divisions by the trend
t of the great Colorado Plateau from the northwestern corner of the
·y to the southeasterly portion. This plateau slopes gently to the
rd, but on the southwestern side it breaks off abruptly through most of
:. For this reason, the low valleys which are found to the southwest
ateau have a climate semitropic in character, while but a few hours
will carry one to the higher elevations of the plateau, where a most
summer climate is encountered. To the north of this plateau the
much cooler, perpetual snow being found at the higher altitudes.
thern regions, on account of their rough contour, are given over to
ig and mining.

In the regions to the north of the plateau the precipitation from rain and snow is sufficient in quantity for successful agriculture, if the ground were tillable. This precipitation serves a beneficent purpose, however, in that it feeds the streams whence the waters for irrigation are drawn in the southern valleys, and the vast forests, the extent of which is not surpassed by any State in the Union, conserve this moisture, giving it out as needed to the Salt and Gila rivers. To the south of the plateau, in the valleys, the rainfall is very slight. At Phœnix it is not more than 8 or 10 inches per annum, and not more than 2 to 4 inches at Yuma.

For the purpose of farming and fruit raising, therefore, irrigation is absolutely necessary. Within the valley of the Salt River, the area of which, roughly speaking, is 100 by 20 miles, is found practically all the farming of any magnitude. Phœnix, the capital of the Territory (with a population of 12,000 people, of which number some 3,000 are of Mexican nativity), is situated near the center of this valley. Surrounding the town there are about 250,000 acres under irrigation. This is but a small percentage of the irrigable area of the valley, but the land now under cultivation absorbs all of the water of the Salt River in the summer season; hence it is impossible to extend the cultivated field in the absence of a greater water supply.

Irrigating canals of a total length of 72 miles, with a total of 600 miles of lateral ditches, supply the 250,000 acres above mentioned, and are capable of irrigating fully as much more if the water was at hand for them. This deficiency in the water supply greatly retards the development of the valley, and it is one great problem of interest for the people of the Territory, substantially all of whom draw their supplies from this valley. The soil of the valley, 20 feet and more in depth, is of the richest quality, and leaves nothing to be desired in that particular. It produces, with adequate water, almost every product of the temperate and semitropic zones in wonderful profusion. Abutting on this limited area of cultivation, where the improved lands are valued at $25 to $200 per acre, are thousands of acres of ground equally rich which are lying idle for want of water. These vacant lands are owned by the United States Government, and are open to settlement at the uniform price of $1.25 per acre, seven years being allowed to the settler in which to make his payments. That these vacant lands will be settled within a very few years now appears to be a certainty, since operations are on foot looking to a vast increase in the water supply of the valley.

This augmentation of the water supply will be through the storage of the flood waters of the Salt River. In the winter season, during the rains and snows in the mountains, 60 miles to the northward, Salt River carries a great volume of water, which is carried to the Gila River, thence to the Colorado, and thence to the Gulf of California, and thus wasted. It is estimated by the engineers of the United States Government that enough water thus goes to waste from the Salt River each winter to amply irrigate a million acres in the Salt River Valley throughout the year, were the water properly distributed.

It is purposed to store these winter floods, to be drawn from, as needed, during the summer months, by constructing a grand reservoir in the mountains, some 60 miles to the northeast of Phœnix. The project is very feasible from an engineering standpoint. As it traverses the mountains on its way to the valley, the Salt River passes through a great basin in the mountains, which has but one outlet, the canyon of the Salt River.

The United States Government has granted to the Hudson Reservoir and Canal Company this basin, known as the "Tonto Basin," to be used as a storage reservoir. The said company has completed all its engineering work, and plans and specifications for the dam have just been completed. It proposes to build a dam at the head of the canyon, where the river emerges from the basin, thus creating a lake which will cover 18 square miles to a depth of 100 to 200 feet. It will be necessary to build a dam 200 feet high and some 600 feet in length at the top, although the canyon is only 200 feet wide for the first 100 feet from the bottom. The Territory of Arizona has granted to the company the use of the channel of the Salt River in which to convey the waters thus stored to the valley below, and the stored waters will therefore be turned back into the channel as needed and conveyed through the canyon for a distance of 30 miles to the head of the valley, where the first diverting dam is found. To construct this great storage reservoir, which will be the largest in the world, will cost, it is estimated, about $2,500,000, and the company is now actively at work obtaining the necessary funds. It proposes to sell stored waters to the irrigating canal companies now doing business in the valley, and it is said these companies will be very willing to thus augment the limited supply which they now have ready for sale to the farmers.

Some of the canal companies have already entered into such contracts with the reservoir company. Farmers now pay for water at the rate of $1.25 to $2.25 per annum, and the canal companies, when they begin to furnish water from the reservoir, will charge the farmers an additional dollar per acre in order to reimburse themselves for their outlay to the reservoir company. It is said, however, that the farmers will be entirely willing to pay this additional price, as the increased water supply will enable them to harvest double the amount of their present crops. It can be seen, therefore, that when this immense undertaking has been accomplished, Arizona will have the greatest irrigation system in the world, and the harvest of farm products and fruits, already abundant in the valley, will go far toward making this one of the most prosperous regions on the globe.

SISAL, AND PROCESS OF PREPARATION.

Sisal, or sisal hemp, is the product of one of the numerous fibrous plants known as agaves. Nearly all the agave family bear a close resemblance, so that anyone having seen a specimen of the "century plant" can form a good idea of the general appearance of all other varieties of the genus. All the agaves are indigenous to the American Continent, and nearly all can be found in the Republic of Mexico. Only a few species flourish

Bull. No. 4——5

within the boundaries of the United States. While fiber can be derived from all these plants, only the quantity and quality obtained from a limited number of the species is such as to make them worthy of commercial attention. The *agave rigida*, variety *sisalona*, is one of the most valuable and yields fibrous raw material in abundance. No other plant has attracted so much attention among the manufacturers of cordage.

The leaves of this variety are of a dark green, from 4 to 6 feet in length, with a width of from 3 to 6 inches, and are covered with spines. The full-grown plant presents a striking if not beautiful appearance, bristling all over with its long spine-tipped leaves, thickly radiating from its short cylindrical trunk, which terminates in a short cone-like bud. In arriving at maturity the plant sends up its flower stalk, called the "mast," to a height of nearly 30 feet. The circumference of this mast is from 18 to 20 inches at the base, but it gradually grows smaller between that point and its termination. One of the peculiarities of the plant is that it seldom or never sets a seed. The flowers fall, carrying the ovary with them, then the young plants develop on the ends of the branches, which, when they have attained a height of from 3 to 4 inches, fall to the ground and take root. The old plants reproduce themselves by means of scions.

Sisal hemp is a distinct production of Yucatan. It takes its name from the town of Sisal, the second port in the province, located on the northwest side of the peninsula of Yucatan. Before the Spanish planted colonies on the American continent the natives had discovered its value, for when DE SOLIS and PIZON, the Spanish navigators, landed there in 1506, they found the Indians using crude cordage made from the agave fiber. Some years ago this particular variety of the agave family was introduced into the Bahamas, Cuba, Porto Rico, Jamaica, and even southern Florida, but in no place has the experiment proven a success. It is in Yucatan only that the plant found a congenial soil and climate. Sisal grows best on barren, rocky land that is useless for other agricultural purposes. Drought affects it but little, if at all. The yield is continual. An acre of plants yields a little over a ton of fiber. A correspondent of the "Farm Implement News" thus describes the process of obtaining the fiber:

When the state of flowering is reached the leaves are cut close to the trunk and are laid tip to butt in bundles of 50; then they are carted to the machines. The cutting of thirty bundles, or 1,500 leaves, is considered a good day's work. In order to save the cost of transportation, as the leaves yield but about 5 per cent of fiber, there is usually a machine to every 100 acres. The machine in use at the present time consists of a horizontal wheel, on the face of which brass strips are transversely placed, forming dull knives. The leaf is introduced so as to bring one side in contact with the revolving wheel, which is run by a small engine. A brake then presses the leaf against the scrapers, while the butt is firmly held by a pair of pinchers. The scrapers remove the outer surface and some of the soft tissues; then the leaf is taken out and turned and the other side undergoes the same operation, until only the fibers are left. These are then shaken out and hung in the sun for a few hours to dry. The result is a rather coarse fiber of much strength. The finest quality is nearly white, while the inferior grades are yellowish in color. In order to produce the best quality in fiber, the leaves must be cleaned as soon as possible after being cut. One of the principal obstacles in the way of cheaper fiber is the need of a good machine for decorticating. Although much skill and money have been spent in attempts to invent a better machine, as yet such efforts have been unsuccessful.

The English Admiralty Board adopted the cable made from sisal as superior to that made of manila hemp. It is necessary to "tar" a cable of the latter quality used on shipboard, but the smooth surface of the rope and the natural gum retained in the sisal does away with the necessity of this nasty remedy for protection from friction. Then again, sisal is superior to hemp because it is much lighter, the specific gravity being as 9 to 15.

In the fiscal year ending June 30, 1898, Mexico exported to the United States 68,432 tons of sisal, valued at $5,104,228, against 62,839 tons, valued at $3,809,415 in 1897. During the same period the United States imported from the Philippine Islands 48,541 tons of manila hemp, valued at $3,092,285, against 38,526 tons, valued at $2,701,651 in 1897.

The French Chargé d'Affaires in Mexico has recently addressed a report to his Government relative to the growing importance of the sisal fiber, which he states is very difficult for European houses to secure as the United States practically monopolizes the trade in this article. The principal Mexican States producing it are Tamaulipas, San Luis, Guerrero, Nuevo Leon, and Coahuila.

U of M

or 200 quintals (20,000 pounds) of tapioca. The plant is easily and cheaply cultivated. It will stand bad weather, and the dry season does not affect it, and it can be raised on any soil.

The yucca will thrive on the same soil as peas, corn, and beans, and ground so utilized becomes far more remunerative than land planted in coffee. One hectare of tilled soil will produce 1,600 coffee plants. Allowing the maximum yield of coffee per plant, a hectare will produce 8 quintals (800 pounds) of coffee, and on the same ground the yucca will yield 150 quintals (1,500 pounds) of starch, exclusive of other crops, from the same soil. These other crops will aggregate 12 bushels of peas and 12 bushels of beans. This will make land in which the yucca is planted from six to seven times as remunerative as when planted in coffee.

Means of cultivation are primitive. Plows and other modern American farming implements are almost unknown here. All the work is done with old-fashioned hoes, as neither men nor beasts have been trained to use modern plows.

TONNAGE DUES IN CUBA.

TARIFF CIRCULAR NO. 17.   ·

WAR DEPARTMENT,
Washington, October 11, 1898.

By direction of the President, paragraph 5, Tonnage Dues, on page 8 of the Customs Tariff and Regulations for Ports in Cuba in possession of the United States, is hereby amended to read as follows:

TONNAGE DUES.

5. At all ports or places in Cuba which may be in possession or under administrative control of the land or naval forces of the United States there shall be levied the following tonnage dues until further orders:

	Per net ton.
(*a*) On entry of a vessel from a port or place not in Cuba.	$0. 20
(*b*) On entry of a vessel from another port or place in Cuba, engaged at the time of entry in the coasting trade of Cuba.	.02

(*c*) The rate of tax on a vessel which enters or clears in ballast shall be one-half of the rate imposed by subdivision (*a*) or (*b*).

(*d*) A vessel which has paid the tonnage tax imposed on entry from a port or place not in Cuba shall not be liable to tonnage tax on entering another port or place in Cuba during the same voyage until such vessel again enters from a port or place not in Cuba.

(*e*) An express steamship engaged in carrying the mails in the service of a steamship line which is furnishing, under an agreement or contract with a government, a regular semimonthly mail service from a port not in Cuba to a port on the south coast of Cuba, or a regular semiweekly mail service from a port not in Cuba to a port on the north coast of Cuba, shall be exempt from tonnage taxes upon being furnished by the Secretary of War with a certificate that it is so employed.

(*f*) The tonnage tax on entries of a vessel from a port or place not in Cuba shall not exceed in the aggregate $2 per net ton in any one year, beginning from the date of the first payment.

The tonnage tax on entries of a vessel from other ports or places in Cuba, engaged at the time of entry exclusively in the coasting trade of Cuba, shall not exceed 40 cents per ton in any one year, beginning from the date of the first payment.

Upon receipt of this order by the officer in command of the United States forces at any port or place in the Island of Cuba in possession of the United States said order will be proclaimed and enforced.

R. A. ALGER,
Secretary of War.

THE LATE ALEJANDRO SANTOS.

The announcement on September 10 of the death at Short Hills, New Jersey, of Mr. T. ALEJANDRO SANTOS, consul of Bolivia at New York, was received with deep regret in circles interested in Latin-American trade and the development of closer relations between the South American Republics and the United States. Mr. SANTOS was the son of a wealthy merchant in Ecuador, and was born at Bahia de Caraques. He was a man of strict integrity, of varied accomplishments, and notable business sagacity. In youth he and his six brothers were sent to the United States in the care of a friend in Baltimore that they might be fitly educated. All but two were graduates of the College of St. James, near Hagerstown, Maryland, one of the brothers dying at this institution. The others returned to South America, four of them embarking in business in Ecuador, while ALEJANDRO and another brother conducted a mercantile establishment at Panama for several years.

Returning to the United States, ALEJANDRO was united in marriage with Miss MARY ONDERDONK LONG, of Baltimore. After a short residence in Maryland, Mr. SANTOS removed to New Jersey and established in New York City the firm of Santos & Co., importers of South American products, which has since conducted a prosperous business. Mr. SANTOS was a member of the International Postal Congress, and honorary consul in New York for Bolivia. He was particularly friendly to the Bureau of American Republics and was one of its chief authorities on matters relating to the South American countries with which he was more particularly identified.

port to Mobile, Alabama. The line is fitted both for passengers and freight. Messrs. ORR & LAUBENHEIMER controlled a line of steamships from Bluefields to Mobile previous to January, 1898, but upon the organization of the new company at that time the service was discontinued. Now that the line is again to be operated it will prove of considerable benefit to the lumber merchants of Mobile, as that is where nearly all the timber is purchased that is used in Bluefields and the territory surrounding it. The steamships engaged in this trade are the *Sunmia* and the *Tarl*.

Steel Railway Material. The "Boston Herald" states that a Norwegian fruit steamer recently arrived from Bluefields, Nicaragua, with a cargo of bananas and returned via Baltimore, loading steel at the latter port. This is believed to be the first full cargo of steel rails sent by the United States to Central America. It is said that the Carnegies have booked orders for several other cargoes.

PARAGUAY.

New Bureau of Information. A commercial chamber, or association, has been formed in the city of Asuncion, known as the "Centro Commercial del Paraguay." The object of this association is to give information on all points connected with the products, customs' laws, and commerce of the Republic, and to assist all persons desirous of entering into commercial relations with exporters and other business firms in Paraguay.

UNITED STATES.

Sugar Imports in September. The duties paid on sugars imported during September at the leading ports of the United States were $5,110,905, and the value of the 312,739,232 pounds withdrawn for consumption was $6,506,606. This was exclusive of the importations of sugar free of duty from the Hawaiian Islands, which were 35,723,373 pounds, valued at $1,280,369. The withdrawals of sugar from the warehouses for consumption were considerably larger during September than the entries for importation, which were 210,601,231 pounds, valued at $4,434,372. Even the general imports were more than double the figures for September of last year, which were 110,115,037 pounds, valued at $2,462,663. The bulk of the sugar withdrawn for consumption is now raw cane, of which the withdrawals during September last were 304,275,200 pounds, valued at $6,294,635. The withdrawals at New York were 199,148,986 pounds, valued at $4,250,246, and the withdrawals at Philadelphia were 82,720,001 pounds, valued at $1,607,610.

Book Tariff for Porto Rico. By order of the War Department, books printed in English are to be admitted into the ports of Porto Rico under the control of the United States at 2.50 pesos ($2.315) per 100 kilograms (220.46 pounds). Under Spanish rule a discriminating duty of 13 pesos ($12.038) per 100 kilograms was assessed on books printed in the English language.

Railroad Engines for Australia. According to a recent publication of the "Australian," bids have been accepted from United States firms for two narrow-gauge railroad engines, for a road connecting Wangaratta and Whitefield, Australia. The two engines will cost about $18,000. It is interesting to note that the price quoted was, according to the authority given above, $1,500 less than that of the next lowest English or Continental firm, also that the time required to complete the order was seventeen weeks in the United States, but was fifteen months in England.

The Production of Pig Iron in 1898.   Statistics published by the American Iron and Steel Association show that the production of pig iron in the United States for the first half of the current year amounted to 5,903,703 tons; while the returns compiled by the Iron Association of Great Britain show that the production of the same metal in the United Kingdom amounted to 4,432,893 tons, or for the half year a grand total of 10,342,596 tons. This is the largest production ever obtained in either of the two countries in any period of six months, and the total for the two is almost equal to the whole world's production in 1870. That year Great Britain produced 5,963,000 tons, the United States 1,865,000 tons, Germany 1,155,000 tons, and France, Belgium, Sweden, and Austria-Hungary together, 2,170,000 tons. The product of the United States for the present year, if maintained throughout the current six months, will be over 11,800,000 tons, which would far exceed the world's total output in 1865. The pig-iron product of the United States was 30 per cent more than the British output, showing a gain for the half year only of nearly 320 per cent over the total product for 1870.

VENEZUELA.

A fit Monument for Columbus.   The four hundredth anniversary of the discovery of Venezuela was celebrated as a public holiday throughout the Republic. On August 1, 1498, Columbus arrived at the Gulf of Paria, and, landing at a place called Macuro, took possession, in the name of his sovereign, of that portion of the new world now known as Venezuela. The present Government, in commemoration of the event, has decided to erect a light-house on the spot where the great discoverer landed.

Option for Mining Coal.   An option has been granted to an English syndicate for the purchase of the Curamichate coal mines. The "Herald" says that these mines are situated on the seacoast a few miles from Tucacas. Two special engineers are expected to inspect the mines in October, and if their report is favorable the plant will be purchased at a cash valuation of 250,000 bolivars ($48,250).

Vacation of Minister Loomis.   Hon. FRANK B. LOOMIS, United States Minister to Venezuela, is at present enjoying a vacation with his friends in the State of Ohio. Before going there from Washington he made an official visit to the Department of State. While here he was quoted in a newspaper interview as saying: "The Venezuelans are at present in just the mind to take the products of the United States. They need machinery, railroads, better wagons and streets, drainage systems, etc. There is one other thing I wish to speak of most emphatically. That is the exposition and warehouse opened by the National Association of Manufacturers at Caracas. Its usefulness is rapidly and justly increasing and should be encouraged for the sake of our own welfare."

BOLETÍN MENSUAL

DE LA

OFICINA DE LAS REPÚBLICAS AMERICANAS,

UNIÓN INTERNACIONAL DE REPÚBLICAS AMERICANAS.

VOL. VI. OCTUBRE, 1898. No. 4.

CONDICIONES COMERCIALES EN CUBA.

El Honorable ROBERT P. PORTER, Comisionado Especial nombrado por el Presidente para estudiar las condiciones comerciales en Cuba, ha regresado á los Estados Unidos. Su opinión sobre el particular, según ha sido publicada, es como sigue:

El primer problema con que se tropieza en la reconstrucción industrial de Cuba es el del trabajo, porque, en realidad, no se encuentran obreros disponibles. Una vez resuelta esta cuestión, Cuba recobrará su antigua prosperidad en cinco ó seis años. Se necesitan millares de trabajadores, que, si se encontraran, tendrían ocupación inmediatamente. Los que emplean operarios en las plantaciones, minas, etc., prefieren á los españoles, porque son muy activos y dóciles. El Capitán General Blanco emitió el 5 de octubre un decreto por el cual se dispone que todos los soldados españoles que deseen permanecer en Cuba, sean licenciados. Se cree que un número considerable de ellos va á quedarse en la isla, pues ella les ofrece mejor perspectiva que su propia patria. Algunos de estos soldados se han casado allí, y muchos de ellos han fraternizado con los cubanos.

El trabajo es muy duro, especialmente en las plantaciones, y los jornaleros tienen la costumbre de dar principio á sus faenas en el campo á las 4.30 de la mañana, después de haber recibido una ración de café y pan.   Almuerzan á las 11, duermen la siesta, y vuelven á la 1 al trabajo, que dura hasta la puesta del sol, esto es, como hasta las 7 de la noche.   Los operarios toman sus alimentos al aire libre y duermen en chozas hechas de palmas y cortezas de árboles.   Por fuertes que sean las lluvias, los jornaleros no suspenden su trabajo; y conviene observar que en los Estados Unidos no se sabe lo que es lluvia.   Los salarios varían de 16 á 20 pesos, plata, por mes.   El peso de plata vale ahora 65 centavos, y bajará á 50 después de la ocupación.   De este salario se deduce el valor de todas las raciones.   Los artículos de alimentación son muy caros, y á un jornalero le cuesta la vida de 8 á 9 pesos mensualmente.   En las minas, las horas de trabajo no son tan largas, aunque los salarios son mayores.   Los dueños de El Cobre y otras minas cerca de Santiago, han menester de 1,000 trabajadores, y no pueden encontrarlos.

La cosecha de tabaco es la más estable de todas, y nada puede destruirla.   En este año será como la mitad del promedio ordinario, mientras que la de azúcar ascenderá solamente á una tercera parte.

Se ha resuelto revisar por completo la tarifa aduanera adoptada para Santiago, antes de ponerla en vigor en toda la isla.   Dicha tarifa es la misma que España empleaba para las mercancías que venían de aquel país, y favorecía á todos los artículos producidos allá, y á los que se compraban en otros países, como harina, por ejemplo, cuando eran embarcados en puertos españoles.

Se ha podido observar que los derechos son demasiado altos sobre los artículos que España no produce y que no podía importar de otros países para exportarlos á Cuba.   Los derechos sobre hierro y acero, por ejemplo, son tan altos como en la actual tarifa española.   Casi todos los artículos para ferrocarriles, incluyendo locomotoras, material rodante, puentes de hierro y acero, etc., están gravados con un 100 por ciento.

Esto es prácticamente un aumento sobre la antigua tarifa española, pues, según ella, 20 por cento de los derechos se pagaba en plata, á razón de 65 centavos, oro, por peso, y 10 per ciento en billetes de banco, á razón de 10 centavos, oro, por peso.   Cuando la tarifa de aduanas que ha de regir en Cuba haya sido revisada, será justa y equitativa, y producirá mayores entradas, porque los altos derechos que ahora se cobran impiden la importación de muchos artículos. Con una buena administración, ia entrada anual de las aduanas de Cuba pasará de $30,000,000. La tarif será arreglada de manera que produzca una renta suficiente, y al miso tiempo fomente de todos modos la introducción de artículos que sirvan para la reconstrucción comercial é industrial de la isla. La introducción de provisiones costará menos, lo cual acabará con el contrabando, aumentará el número de los exportadores, y mantendrá bajo los precios por medio de la competencia. Últimamente, el Presidente ha emitido una orden muy importante, por la cual se admiten en los puertos de Cuba, libres de derechos, bueyes para el trabajo, animales de raza bovina para cría y para la alimentación, y arados y otros instrumentos de agricultura, pero no la maquinaria. Esto contribuirá notablemente á producir una gran reacción agrícola. En la provincia de Matanzas no hay en la actualidad sino 5,000 cabezas de ganado vacuno, mientras que antes había 260,000 cabezas.

Cuba llegará á ser, probablemente, uno de los parajes más florecientes de la tierra, y su comercio representará para los Estados Unidos cerca de 200,000,000 de pesos anualmente.

SITUACIÓN ECONÓMICA DE CHILE.

En un despacho dirigido al Departamento de Estado, con fecha 19 de agosto de 1898, que ha sido publicado íntegro en algunas hojas de los Consular Reports, impresas ya, que llevan la fecha de 8 de octubre de 1898, el Honorable HENRY L. WILSON, Ministro de los Estados Unidos en Chile, da cuenta de los últimos cambios económicos que se han verificado en esta República. En 1895, el Gobierno chileno emitió una ley restableciendo el patrón de oro en el país. El Señor WILSON dice que, dado el carácter flexible de la ley de 1895 y las amplias garantías que ofrecía, el buen éxito de la misma parecía asegurado y, en efecto, dió por resultado la elevación en el valor del peso chileno á algo más de 17 peniques, permitiendo así á los importadores, comerciantes y banqueros el hacer sus cálculos con bastante exactitud. Los créditos fueron más fáciles y extensos, porque se tenía fe en que todas las obligaciones serían satisfechas con pesos de igual valor. Los precios eran bajos, porque el comerciante no se veía obligado á agregar al valor de su mercancía algo más por la depreciación posible de la moneda. La ley, pues, no dejó de producir buenos resultados y de mejorar, hasta cierto grado, la condicíon de las clases comerciales é industriales. Si se la juzga por dichos resultados, agrega el Ministro WILSON, tuvo un éxito satisfactorio. Andando el tiempo, sin embargo, la ley no ha producido todo lo que de ella se esperaba, por razón de que, según asegura el Ministro WILSON, no se la puso en práctica en toda su amplitud, y porque la Tesorería tuvo que hacer frente á grandes gastos requeridos por el incremento dado á la organización militar

El 8 de julio de 1898, el Ministro WILSON telegrafió al Departamento de Estado que había ocurrido una seria crisis económica, y en un informe que envió, avisa que en el mes de julio próximo pasado, el Congreso chileno emitió una ley suspendiendo los pagos, así como toda acción judicial por deudas, durante treinta días. Después de la adopción de esta ley, los bancos, que se habían cerrado con el consentimiento del Gobierno, empezaron de nuevo sus negocios, pagando á los que habían depositado dinero, solamente las sumas necesarias para hacer frente á sus inmediatas necesidades. El 13 de julio, el Presidente dirigió al Congreso un mensaje recomendando la emisión de cincuenta millones de pesos en papel moneda, como moneda legal para la satisfacción de todas las obligaciones cuyo pago no se había estipulado que se haría en oro. También se recomendaba en dicho documento que la actual emisión de los bancos formase parte de los cincuenta millones de pesos emitidos, y que la cantidad fuese retirada de la circulación en su totalidad dentro del término de cuatro años, á contar de la fecha de la ley. El 22 de julio de 1898, la Cámara de Diputados adoptó un proyecto de ley para la emisión de cincuenta millones de pesos en papel moneda, á 18 peniques (36.5 centavos) el peso, pero hizo muchos cambios importantes á las recomendaciones contenidas en el mensaje del Presidente. Dicho proyecto de ley, después de haber sido enmendado en el Senado, fué adoptado el 30 de julio de 1898.

Dice el Ministro WILSON que los comerciantes en pequeña escala, los artesanos y las clases obreras en general, se oponían á la emisión del papel moneda, y parecían estar generalmente en favor del patrón de oro. Los dueños de tierras, por otra parte, estaban en favor de la ley para la emisión de papel moneda. La explicación de esto se encontraba, según el Señor WILSON, en el hecho de que la ley les permitía redimir las hipotecas con una moneda depreciada. Añade el informe mencionado, que el 1º de julio de 1898, había cuarenta y cinco millones de pesos, oro, en circulación en Chile, pero que poco después de la adopción de la citada ley, los pesos de oro desaparecieron por completo, porque este metal se había convertido en un artículo de comercio, y el premio que por él se pagaba avanzó rápidamente del 6 al 40 por ciento. Según el Ministro WILSON, un peso de papel perdía como 30 por ciento de su valor nominal, y en opinión de aquel funcionario, esta depreciación la sentían en primer lugar los comerciantes en pequeña escala y los trabajadores, debido á que los primeros no pueden cambiar de un momento á otro sus métodos comerciales, y tienen que vender sus mercancías á los precios que regían antes de que comenzara la depreciación, y á que á los segundos se les paga en moneda cuyo valor ha decaído un 30 por ciento. El Gobierno, por otra parte, saca algunas ventajas de las actuales condiciones, debido al hecho de que "encuentra sus arcas provistas temporalmente de los fondos suficientes para hacer frente á sus obligaciones de carácter nacional." Los dueños de ricas haciendas que se hallan hipotecadas, encuentran alivio temporal en la circunstancia de poder pagar sus deudas en una moneda que vale muy poco más de las dos terceras partes de su valor nominal.

Refiriéndose á lo que dice el Señor WILSON y á las conclusiones á que llega, se puede afirmar que, como el Gobierno chileno ha mostrado en los últimos años tanta habilidad para tratar difíciles problemas económicos, debe esperarse que se llegue á una solución satisfactoria de la cuestión monetaria, pues es evidente que la ley de 1895 tropezó con dificultades imprevistas para llevar á cabo el fin que se proponía, dificultades que pueden desaparecer ó ser obviadas por medio de disposiciones adecuadas.

REPUBLICA ARGENTINA.

INAUGURACIÓN DEL PRESIDENTE ROCA.

Un cablegrama de Buenos Aires anuncia que el General JULIO A. ROCA tomó posesión de la Presidencia de la República el 12 de octubre, y envió al Congreso su mensaje. He aquí como se compendian en ese despacho telegráfico las palabras del Presidente:

El Presidente hace referencia al hecho de que las relaciones con Chile se encuentran en mejor estado, y declara que el mantenimiento de la paz permitirá al país dedicar toda su energía al mejoramiento de la situación económica. Propone reformas administrativas, reducción en los gastos del Gobierno, fomento á la inmigración y desarrollo del comercio.

COMERCIO EXTERIOR EN 1898.

El Director General de Estadística en Buenos Aires ha publicado un informe sobre el comercio extranjero de la República durante los primeros seis meses del año corriente. Según los guarismos oficiales, el valor total de las importaciones, con excepción de metálico y moneda acuñada, alcanzó á $49,553,375 en oro, lo que demuestra una diminución de $150,404, comparado con el del mismo período en 1897.

Durante la misma época, las exportaciones, sin contar el metálico y la moneda acuñada, se calcularon en $81,632,825 en oro, lo que indica un aumento de $17,594,290, quedando así un balance á favor del comercio de la Argentina por la suma de $32,079,450 en seis meses.

El valor de las importaciones y exportaciones de metálico y moneda acuñada es halagador, pues aumentaron aquéllas en $1,162,855, al paso que éstas disminuyeron en $1,075,240, si se comparan con el correspondiente período de 1897.

AUMENTO DE LOS DERECHOS DE ADUANA.

El 23 de setiembre, el Ministro BUCHANAN telegrafió al Departamento de Estado que, de conformidad con la ley emitida por el Congreso argentino el 22 de ese mes, y vigente desde esa fecha hasta el 31 de diciembre, los derechos de aduana se aumentan de la manera siguiente: los derechos del cinco por ciento ó menos ad valorem se duplican. Los que exceden de 5 por ciento quedan sujetos á un 10 por ciento adicional, y á 10 por ciento más sobre el monto de los derechos aduaneros, añadiendo para el cobro de los derechos específicos, el valor de la mercancía.

Los siguientes artículos figuran entre los que caen bajo la clasificación de 5 por ciento ad valorem en la tarifa argentina: corcho, joyería, alambre, bramante, hoja de lata, hierro, zinc, plomo en lingotes y en barras, máquinas de coser y piezas de las mismas, esencia de alquitrán, azogue, maquinaria para instalaciones eléctricas é hidráulicas (con excepción de los medidores y de los accesorios eléctricos), ladrillos refractarios y de barro, máquinas de trasquilar, motores de vapor, relojes de oro, de plata y plateados, maquinaria para agricultura, é hilazas de lana. Bajo la clasificación de 2½ por ciento se encuentran los siguientes artículos: algodón en pacas, zinc en hojas, pulpa de madera, lúpulo, conejuna, gelatina, etc. Se cobran derechos específicos sobre las provisiones, bebidas, tabaco, cuellos y puños, sombreros y fieltro para sombreros, fósforos, kerosina, sacos de granos, naipes, estearina y aceite de linaza, etc.

COMERCIO DEL PUERTO DE ROSARIO.

En un informe del Vicecónsul francés en Rosario, recientemente publicado, se encuentran datos muy interesantes referentes á las fuentes de producción de las mercancías importadas en aquel puerto, al mismo tiempo que indicaciones de mucho interés sobre las necesidades del consumo local. Parece que aumenta la demanda de alambre de cerca, producida por la necesidad de cercar las grandes propiedades que hay en el país. Alemania hasta ahora ha atendido á ella, pero los Estados Unidos é Inglaterra han entrado á hacer una competencia formidable á aquel país, desde hace un año. No obstante la inferioridad de los productos alemanes y de otras nacionalidades en el ramo de alambres, lo barato del artículo producido en Alemania ha sido causa de que se le dé la preferencia; pero hoy que los fabricantes alemanes producen un alambre de la mejor calidad, les será imposible conservar los bajos precios que antes regían, y, por consiguiente, el mercado estará abierto para todos.

En el país se fabrica una buena cantidad de utensilios de cocina

un pedido por estos efectos eléctricos, cuyo monto alcanzó á $20,000. El porvenir de la electricidad aplicada á todos los ramos de la industria en la Argentina, está lleno de promesas. Por término medio el valor de los embarques de maquinaria y efectos eléctricos verificados en cada vapor de los que han salido del puerto de Nueva York en el último trimestre, se calcula de $7,000 á $10,000.

Los tranvías eléctricos de la Argentina están provistos de equipos de los Estados Unidos. Durante los últimos dos meses, casi todos los buques que han salido para Buenos Aires han llevado materiales para carros, valorados, por lo menos, en $50,000. La Compañía de Tranvías de Belgrano ha recibido la mayor parte de este material. La compañía llamada "The Capital Company," con oficinas establecidas en Nueva York, embarca grandes cantidades de efectos eléctricos, incluyendo equipos para los carros de su propia compañía de tranvías. Á principios de noviembre, según se dice, la compañía tendrá listos para embarcar 1,000 carros de carga, que han sido contruidos por contrata.

Siguen en importancia las exportaciones de hierro manufacturado que se hacen de Nueva York para la República Argentina, comercio que ha ido creciendo gradualmente. Los tres últimos vapores que salieron para Buenos Aires, llevaron más de $40,000, principalmente en agavilladoras.

Cordelería, papel, ferretería, cajas desarmadas, tubos de hierro y domésticos de algodón son otros de los artículos que tienen demanda en la Argentina. Una casa de South street ha recibido informes de que el mercado para cristalería, lamparería, hules, linóleo, alfombras y tapices baratos es bastante bueno. El corresponsal que envió los informes, añade que se presenta la oportunidad para hacer grandes negocios en artículos de uso sanitario fabricados en los Estados Unidos.

. Informes de la Argentina manifiestan que casi todas las compañías de tranvías de Buenos Aires extenderán sus líneas á pueblos cercanos y, por consiguiente, se harán grandes pedidos de materiales para el objeto.

La barca *Adam W. Spies*, que últimamente salió con carga para Buenos Aires, lleva una gran cantidad de artículos manufacturados en los Estados Unidos, entre otros, maquinaria agrícola por valor de $45,000, máquinas de coser por $12,000, y ferretaría y sillas por $10,000. El vapor *Bellucia*, que también salió con carga para aquel puerto, llevó $50,000 en maquinaria agrícola, $5,000 en carruajes, y molinos de viento por valor de $10,971.

DESCUBRIMIENTO DE MINAS DE CARBÓN.

El Comandante Nuñez, oficial de la Marina Argentina, de vuelta de la Tierra del Fuego, trajó consigo muestras de carbón descubierto allí, las cuales dieron los resultados más satisfactorios al ser probadas en las locomotoras que funcionan en los trabajos del puerto de Buenos Aires. El carbón ensayado es de formación superficial, de lo cual se deduce naturalmente que si es tan bueno en la superficie, mejor será su calidad, mientras más profundo sea el producto que se extraiga.

Bull. No. 4——6

orden que, á pesos iguales, tienen doble capacidad productora de calórico. La muestra número 2 fué de poco valor, á causa de la gran cantidad de cenizas que produjo. Falta ver si los depósitos son suficientemente grandes para compensar los trabajos de explotación.

ESTACIÓN CARBONERA DE LOS ESTADOS UNIDOS.

Un informe auténtico recibido de Norfolk, Virginia, dice que las muestras de carbón virginiano enviadas á la República Argentina han resultado satisfactorias y que se harán inmediatamente otros embarques. Los Señores CASTNER, CURRAN y BULLITT, de Filadelfia, agentes de la Pocahontas Coal Company, han establecido una agencia en Buenos Aires, á cargo de Mr. CARL H. ARNOLD. Este caballero ha sido por algún tiempo el Vicecónsul en Norfolk de las Repúblicas de Colombia y Venezuela. También se asegura que varios buques cargados de carbón están para salir de Lamberts Point, Virginia, con destino á Buenos Aires, y se espera que regresarán de allá cargados, aunque sea parcialmente, de productos argentinos.

BOLIVIA.

ABOLICIÓN DEL MONOPOLIO DE FÓSFOROS.

Se ha recibido noticia de que el Gobierno boliviano ha derogado el decreto de 14 de marzo último, relativo al pago de derechos sobre los fósforos importados, y ha suspendido provisionalmente la ley de 18 de noviembre de 1896, por la cual se estableció un monopolio de fósforos en la República y se impuso sobre el artículo extranjero un derecho adicional.

En adelante, los fósforos importados á Bolivia pagarán solamente los derechos especificados en la tarifa general de aduanas.

TRABAJOS DE LA COMISIÓN DE LÍMITES.

Aunque existe todavía alguna duda respecto del resultado final de la cuestión de límites entre la República Argentina y Chile, todo parece indicar una solución pacífica. También Bolivia está haciendo una demarcación de sus límites, y el Gobierno desea que queden bien definidos por el lado de la Argentina, en orden á poner término á toda clase de reclamaciones de territorio en lo futuro.

Una Comisión boliviana salió hace poco de Sucre, capital de la República, con el objeto de dar principio á sus trabajos en La Quiaca. Las medidas y estudios que dicha Comisión va á hacer, de acuerdo con otra Comisión argentina, serán de carácter preliminar. Se harán solamente observaciones topográficas, en calidad de obra preparatoria para los trabajos de la convención internacional que debe fijar definitivamente los límites. Tanto la Comisión boliviana como la argentina se dividirán en dos secciones, y estudiarán el terreno al este y al oeste de La Quiaca, respectivamente. Los dos jefes de las secciones bolivianas son el Señor Muñoz D. Reyes, ingeniero experimentado, y el Coronel Muñoz, uno de los primeros estadistas de la República.

BRASIL.

LA COSECHA DE CAFÉ EN 1898.

El Cónsul General americano, Mr. Seeger, de Rio Janeiro, ha enviado una interesante relación sobre el producto y el movimiento del café en la República durante el año que terminó el 30 de junio, 1898, donde aparecen los siguientes datos estadísticos:

ENTRADAS DURANTE EL AÑO.

	Sacos.	Libras.
Rio Janeiro:		
Por ferrocarril	2, 300, 690	303, 691, 080
Por vapores costaneros	840, 099	110, 893, 068
Otras embarcaciones	1, 163, 849	153, 617, 068
En tránsito	232, 941	30, 748, 212
Total	4, 537, 579	598, 949, 428
Santos	6, 152, 594	812, 142, 408
Victoria (calculados)	400, 000	52, 800, 000
Bahía (calculados)	250, 000	33, 000, 000
Ceara (calculados)	20, 000	2, 640, 000
Total general	11, 360, 173	1, 499, 531, 836

SALIDAS PARA EL EXTRANJERO.

	Sacos.	Libras.
Estados Unidos................................	4, 740, 638	625, 746, 216
Países de Europa..............................	5, 971, 468	770, 233, 776
Cabo de Buena Esperanza......................	149, 300	19, 707, 600
Río de la Plata, etc...........................	101, 533	13, 402, 356
Total	10, 962, 939	1, 429, 107, 948

Calculando á razón de $8.75, como término medio, por saco de 132 libras, el valor total de esta exportación alcanzó á $96,450,716.25

Durante los últimos tres años civiles, los embarques de café efectuados del Brasil fueron como sigue:

De—	1895.	1896.	1897.
	Sacos.	*Sacos.*	*Sacos.*
Santos	3, 554, 696	4, 156, 567	5, 621, 762
Rio Janeiro................................	2, 763, 720	2, 784, 958	4, 066, 734
Victoria...................................	307, 438	273, 255	372, 221
Bahía	264, 775	260, 981	292, 480
Ceara.....................................	20, 202	6, 000	6, 568
Total	6, 910, 831	7, 418, 761	10, 359, 765

El precio en Nueva York, durante la cosecha del año pasado, por café No. 7, al contado en dicha plaza bajó de $7\frac{1}{16}$ contavos por libra, que era el 1° de julio de 1897, á 5⅝ de centavo el 1° de mayo de 1898. En 1° de julio de 1898 el precio había subido hasta 6¼ centavos.

En el 30 de junio de 1898 las existencias eran de 1,227,960 sacos, como sigue: café de Rio, 268,167 sacos; Santos, 316,793 sacos; Nueva York, Baltimore y New Orleans, 643,000 sacos. En la misma fecha, las existencias á la vista en el mundo se calcularon en 5,436,000 sacos, lo que equivale á casi la mitad del consumo de un año.

En la actualidad, hay un excedente de café, lo cual ha producido una depreciación en los precios. Este estado de cosas se ha acentuado más durante los últimos dos años, aunque las causas á que obedece vienen de muy atrás. Durante la década anterior á 1897, los precios á que se cotizaba el café produjeron grandes ganancias á los agricultores de este fruto, dando por resultado, en consecuencia, un aumento enorme en el área cafetalera durante dicho período. Hoy esos millones de árboles que entonces se sembraron, comienzan á producir, y lo que hasta hace poco era una industria que á veces rendía hasta 150 por ciento al año, apenas da hoy con que sostenerse. Para el próximo año se espera que la cosecha sea mucho menor. El resultado de antiguo conocido se presenta otra vez; dos cosechas abundantes consecutivas dan, á causa de la condición exhausta de los árboles, una cosecha escasa.

Dos son los cálculos que se han hecho para la cosecha de 1898–1899, uno oficial y el otro comercial, cuya variación es notable. He aquí dichos cálculos:

Estado.	Oficial.	Comercial.
	Sacos.	*Sacos.*
Rio Janeiro	2, 500, 000	3, 000, 000
Santos	4, 500, 000	6, 000, 000
Total	7, 000, 000	9, 000, 000

De aquí se desprende que aun los cálculos más altos dan un millón de sacos menos que los producidos en la cosecha de 1897–1898.

Las plantaciones de café del Brasil han llamado últimamente la atención de los capitalistas europeos. Algunos sindicatos ingleses y belgas han comprado grandes plantaciones en los Estados de Minas Geraes y São Paulo. En Amberes se ha establecido una sociedad con agencia en Santos, con el objeto de comprar café de los agricultores directamente y de revenderlo en Europa sin emplear los servicios de un tercero.

En Rio Janeiro y en Santos se espera para fines de octubre una gran partida de ingleses, comerciantes, capitalistas, ingenieros y peritos en materias agrícolas, que viajarán por el interior del Brasil, con el objeto, según se dice, de comprar propiedades agrícolas é industriales cuyo precio haya sido rebajado. Aquellos á quienes se ofrezca hoy en venta dichas propiedades, pueden hacer buenos negocios, según la opinión de las personas mejor informadas en la materia, si los capitalistas no están obligados á esperar resultados inmediatos. Así pues, los ingleses, cuya posición en las finanzas .

y el comercio del Brasil es de primer orden, pueden llegar á alcanzar el dominio del comercio de café entre el Brasil y los Estados Unidos, ya sea por razón del cambio, ó bien por ser dueños de una gran parte del área de producción de aquel país, siempre que no intervenga una influencia extraña.

PRODUCTOS DE LAS ADUANAS Y DE LA RENTA INTERNA.

El Director de la Renta Interna de la República del Brasil rindió, con fecha de agosto 13, un informe, sujeto á enmienda, de las entradas producidas por los derechos de aduana y los impuestos internos durante el primer semestre de 1898, de cuyo trabajo han sido tomados los siguientes datos estadísticos.

Durante el primer semestre del año en curso, las entradas de aduana alcanzaron á 119,161,180 milreis, lo que arroja una diferencia de 3,742,896 milreis menos que durante igual período de tiempo en 1897, y de 23,302,261 milreis si se compara con los guarismos correspondientes á idéntico lapso de tiempo de 1896.

De estas entradas, corresponden al ramo de derechos de importación 102,933,069 milreis en la primera mitad de 1898, ó sea 9,670,101 milreis menos que en la de 1897, y 14,518,931 menos que en 1896.

Disminuyeron las entradas en 17 de las aduanas y aumentaron solamente en 6, en una de las cuales, la de Rio Grande do Sul, se debió el aumento á que fueron cerradas las aduanas de Porto Allegre y Pelotas.

Las entradas de la aduana de Rio Janeiro durante el primer semestre de 1898, fueron 6,554,537 milreis ó 16.02 por ciento menos que en 1897, y 13,174,340 milreis ó 32.17 por ciento menos que en 1896.

Los productos de la renta interna en los primeros seis meses de dichos años, se calcularon como sigue:

	Milreis.
1896	5,984,314.33
1897	6,659,984.33
1898	8,579,018.44

En las entradas ocurridas durante la primera mitad de 1898, están comprendidos los productos de los nuevos impuestos sobre fósforos y pólizas de seguro extranjeras, calculado en 745,073 milreis lo producido por aquéllos, y en 35,275 milreis el producto de éstas.

Aumentó considerablemente la renta del impuesto sobre tabaco y las bebidas, disminuyendo la renta producida por estampillas, traspaso de buques y bonos del Gobierno.

No es posible dar el valor correspondiente en moneda de los Estados Unidos, á causa de la gran depreciación que ha sufrido el milreis, que á la par se calcula en $0.546.

Á PARTICIPAR EN LA CELEBRACIÓN.

Los *acorazados Oregón* y *Iowa*, junto con los barcos carboneros *Celtic* y *Scandia*, salieron de Nueva York para Honolulu el 13 de octubre. El *Abarenda* partió primero que el escuadrón. El Honorable JOHN D. LONG, Ministro de Marina, ordenó al Capitán BAKER, Comandante del *Oregón*, que se encontrase en Rio Janeiro con los dos buques de guerra antes del 15 de noviembre, aniversario del establecimiento de la República del Brasil, á fin de que representasen dignamente á los Estados Unidos y participasen en la celebración de aquel acontecimiento. Se espera que los acorazados llegarán á Rio Janeiro cosa del 10 de noviembre.

CHILE.

ESTADÍSTICA COMERCIAL PARA 1897.

El "Chilean Times" del 31 de agosto dice lo siguiente :

Acaba de salir de la tipografía del Universo el volumen de estadística comercial de la República para el año de 1897. Es un libro de 700 páginas preparado con esmero. El jefe del Departamento de Estadística, Señor WENCESLAO ESCOBAR, merece que se le felicite por la aparición de ese volumen varios meses antes de la época en que generalmente se publica. La obra trata de las siguientes materias : Comercio Especial, Movimiento de la Navegación, Comercio Marítimo Interior, Estadística Retropectiva y Comercio de Tránsito. Se ha omitido la sección titulada Comercio General, que había figurado en los volúnenes anteriores, por considerársela inútil.

Hubo una diminución considerable en el tráfico en 1897, comparado con 1896. Antes de proceder á dar las correspondientes cifras, conviene manifestar que, como de costumbre, los valores se dan en pesos de treinta y ocho peniques. El valor de las importaciones fué de $65,502,805, y el de las exportaciones de $64,754,133. El valor de las importaciones y exportaciones fué de $130,256,-938, ó sea $18,185,281 menos que el total en 1896. En esta diminución de $18,185,281, las importaciones figuran por $8,580,000 y las exportaciones por

$9,605,281. Esta ha sido la cuarta vez en la historia de la República desde 1844, año en que se levantaron por primera vez estadísticas comerciales, en que el tráfico del país ha sufrido una reducción de esta magnitud. Los otros años fueron 1877, 1885 y 1894. En el primero de éstos, la diminución fué de $14,211,411; en el segundo, de $29,591,686; y en el tercero, de $13,956,952. La diminución de las importaciones fué principalmente en artículos de alimentación, materias primas, máquinas, maquinaria y otros artículos para industrias, artes y oficios, efectos de uso doméstico, artículos para ferrocarriles y telégrafos, tabaco, artículos relacionados con las artes, ciencias y letras, carbón, géneros para camisas, géneros de algodón para pantalonos, aceites y sebo. Las importaciones están divididas en 15 clases distintas, y en la tabla siguiente se encontrará el valor de cada una de ellas en los años de 1896 y 1897:

Clasificación.	1896.	1897.
	Valor.	Valor.
Artículos de alimentación	$14,287,626	$13,926,523
Materias textiles	12,790,619	13,013,719
Materias primas	12,021,434	10,319,062
Ropa, joyas y artículos para uso personal		
Máquinas, maquinaria, instrumentos y otros artículos para industrias, artes y oficios	3,585,133	3,597,370
	9,710,679	9,156,614
Artículos para uso doméstico	5,187,110	5,025,979
Artículos para ferrocarriles y telégrafos	2,347,432	1,073,744
Vinos y licores	934,649	1,178,878
Rapé, tabaco, etc.	580,631	399,401
Minerales y oro y plata en barras	20,726	11,267
Artículos para las artes, ciencias y letras	1,297,941	1,089,023
Drogas y artículos medicinales y para objetos industriales	1,179,509	1,113,469
Armas y sus accesorios	164,850	133,345
Artículos varios	9,787,634	5,387,675
Metálico y billetes de banco	186,832	76,733
	74,082,805	65,502,805

Se notó una diminución de $2,309,934 en la exportación de productos agrícolas, principalmente trigo, cebada, nueces, heno y guisantes. En cuanto á los productos minerales, hubo una diminución de $6,160,600, principalmente en salitre, plata en barras, borato de cal, mineral de plata y de cobre, y régulo de cobre y plata. Por lo que hace á los productos animales, los cueros, la lana y los jamones han mostrado una diminución que ascendió á $549,065.

REPÚBLICA DE COLOMBIA.

CONSEJOS Á LOS EXPORTADORES.

El "Moniteur Officiel" de Francia publica algunos consejos acerca de los métodos que deben emplearse para el desarrollo del comercio con la República de Colombia, dando direcciones en especial acerca de la manera de empacar mercancías con destino á este país. La materia es de interés para los comerciantes americanos, y prácticamente se resuelve teniendo en consideración que de los dos métodos empleados para aumentar el comercio, los anuncios y los agentes viajeros, aquél debe preceder á éste. Aun cuando los prospectos, las revistas del mercado, boletines industriales y circulares comerciales son métodos excelentes para preparar el terreno y llamar la atención á los productos extranjeros, su diseminación debe ser complementada por medio de agentes activos, emprendedores, que hablen el español y que lleven consigo muestras de todas las clases de mercancías que ofrecen en venta, así como todo aquello que pueda persuadir al comprador y convencerle de la superioridad del artículo que se le ofrece. No es de importancia que un agente represente sólo un ramo de la industria, pero para hacer menores los gastos de viaje, dicho agente puede representar varias fábricas, y si lleva un buen surtido de muestras, puede contar con seguridad que las casas que él represente· tendrán una buena ganancia.

El autor del artículo juzga que el establecimiento de almacenes de muestras en Bogotá y Medellín daría excelentes resultados; estos almacenes deben estar á cargo de agentes confidenciales, aptos para poder dar informes detallados con referencia á las muestras expuestas y, al mismo tiempo, arreglar condiciones convenientes para la venta de los artículos.

Es importante al embarcar mercancías, que éstas vayan empacadas con el mayor cuidado; los bultos no deben exceder de 80 centímetros de largo, 57 de ancho y 55 de espesor, siendo el peso por término medio de 70 á 75 kilógramos. Cuando las mercancías se embarcan en bultos, deben ir éstas bien envueltas en papel y telas de lana, todo muy bien sujeto por medio de bandas de metal. En el caso de emplear cajas, debe cuidarse de que éstas sean hechas de un material que impida la humedad, porque con frecuencia sucede que artículos finos se dañan en el tránsito á causa de descuidos en este particular. Para este objeto, son muy buenas, cajas con forro interior de zinc, las que en Colombia son artículo de comercio regular. Artículos pesados de hierro y maquinaria deben empacarse de suerte que las partes más pesadas estén separadas y los tornillos, las tuercas, etc., vayan en barriles. Bien vale la pena de asegurar las mercancías por mar y por tierra, aunque esto aumente un poco los gastos de trasporte.

PERSPECTIVA DEL CANAL DE PANAMÁ.

Algunos de los directores y representantes de la Compañía de Canal de Panamá llegaron últimamente á Nueva York, procedentes del istmo. Uno de ellos, Mr. R. G. WARD, hablando á lo que parece en nombre de todos, manifestó públicamente que, á su juicio, la situación actual de los negocios de la compañía es crítica, y sugirió el pensamiento "de hacer una propuesta definitiva que tenga por objeto el que los americanos cooperen á la conclusión del canal y sean en parte dueños de la obra." Es evidente que Mr. WARD no cree que el canal puede terminarse sin la ayuda de los Estados Unidos, y está decididamente en favor de la empresa por el Istmo de Panamá en oposición á la de Nicaragua.

— -

COSTA RICA.

CONTRATO CELEBRADO POR EL GOBIERNO CON DOS COMPAÑÍAS DE VAPORES.

El Gobierno de Costa Rica ha celebrado un contrato con el representante de la Pacific Steam Navigation Company (Compañía de Navegación por Vapor en el Pacífico) y la Compañía Sud Americana de Vapores, cuya sustancia es como sigue:

1. Los vapores de ambas compañías, en sus viajes de Valparaiso, Chile, á Ocós, Guatemala, tocarán, al menos dos veces al mes, tanto de ida como de vuelta, en el puerto de Puntarenas ó en el de Tivives, tan pronto quede éste habilitado como puerto de la República.

2. Los vapores de ambas compañías permanecerán en el puerto de Puntarenas ó Tivives el tiempo necesario para embarcar y desembarcar pasajeros, correspondencia y carga, pero en ningún caso excederá la detención de veinticuatro horas corridas, salvo la conveniencia de las compañías. Sin embargo, siempre que el Gobierno lo exigiere, los vapores permanecerán en el puerto durante doce horas de luz.

3. Los vapores conducirán, sin costo alguno para el Gobierno de Costa Rica, la correspondencia y envíos postales procedentes de las Oficinas de Correos de Costa Rica, destinados á los puertos terminales y de escala en toda la carrera de navegación de los vapores de ambas compañías. Asimismo conducirán á Costa Rica la correspondencia y envíos postales procedentes de dichos puertos. Es obligación de las compañías recibir y entregar por su cuenta las balijas y paquetes postales en cada puerto, por el intermedio de los empleados de correos respectivos, así como su cuidado y conservación á bordo. Las compañías entregarán

dichas balijas y paquetes al costado de los vapores en su fondeadero, y los recibirán hasta la hora de salida.

Es absolutamente prohibido á los empleados de las compañías recibir cartas fuera de las valijas, con excepción de las que sean entregadas en alta mar ó después de que aquéllas hayan sido cerradas; pero en tales casos dichas cartas serán entregadas á los funcionarios del Gobierno designados para recibirlas, y éstos colectarán el importe, si no estuviere pagado en sellos.   Las compañías pueden, sin embargo, conducir aparte las cartas ó papeles de ó para sus agentes y empleados, referentes á los negocios de ellas.   Cualquiera contravención á lo establecido en este artículo, que ceda en perjuicio de los intereses fiscales de Costa Rica, será penada con una multa de cien pesos por la primera vez é igual suma por la segunda; estas cantidades se deducirán de la subvención que por el presente contrato se concede á las compañías.   Si por tercera vez se repitiere la falta, el Gobierno se reserva desde ahora el derecho de declarar la caducidad de este contrato.   Las compañías se obligan igualmente á conducir las valijas y paquetes postales, procedentes de los Estados Unidos y de Europa, que les sean entregados en Panamá por los empleados postales respectivos.

4. Los vapores llevarán de uno á otro de los puertos en que toquen y por el cincuenta por ciento del precio de la tarifa ordinaria de pasajes de sobrecubierta, á los artesanos, labradores, trabajadores y demás que emigren para Costa Rica, · con tal que ellos vengan bajo contrato ó compromiso con el Gobierno ó con sus agentes autorizados.

5. Los vapores conducirán toda carga del Gobierno, procedente de ó para Puntarenas (ó Tivives) entre los puertos de Panamá y Ocós inclusive, con una reducción de veinticinco por ciento sobre la tarifa de fletes establecida.

6. Las compañías se comprometen á comunicar al Gobierno, con la debida anticipación, las tarifas de pasajes y fletes, itinerario de sus líneas y conexiones y á darle cuenta, con la debida anticipación, de las modificaciones que en unas y otros se hicieren.

7. Los vapores no podrán llevar tropas ni municiones de guerra de ningún puerto de aquellos en que toquen á puerto alguno de la República de Costa Rica, salvo en el caso de ser previamente autorizados por el Gobierno de esta última.

8. Los vapores no conducirán pasajeros ni mercaderías con destino á esta República, de procedencias para las cuales existiere prohibición, en virtud de cuarentena establecida en el puerto de Puntarenas (ó Tivives), y á sujetarse estrictamente, sin lugar á reclamo, á las disposiciones que sobre el particular dictare el Gobierno de Costa Rica, las que deberán comunicárse previamente á las compañías por medio de su representante en esta República.

La contravención á lo dispuesto en este artículo da derecho al Gobierno de Costa Rica para imponer á las compañías una multa de quinientos pesos por la primera vez y de mil pesos por la segunda y siguientes, multas que se deducirán de la subvención mensual que por este contrato concede el Gobierno á las compañías, sin perjuicio de las demás responsabilidades á que su procedimiento diere lugar.

El Gobierno de Costa Rica por su parte se obliga:

9. Á conceder á las compañía una subvención anual de cinco mil pesos ($5,000),

en moneda corriente de Costa Rica, en pagos mensuales que se harán al vencimiento de cada mes á los agentes de las compañías en San José, Puntarenas ó Tivives, y las sumas procedentes de esta subvención podrán exportarse por las compañías ó sus agentes, libres de todo derecho ó impuesto, así como también las sumas procedentes de pasajes y fletes. En caso de que los vapores de las compañías tocaren en Puntarenas ó Tivives semanalmente, tanto de ida al norte como de regreso para el sur, el Gobierno aumentará la subvención hasta siete mil quinientos pesos ($7,500), pagadera en la manera ya indicada.

10. Los vapores quedarán eximidos, durante todo el término de este contrato, del pago de cualquiera y de todos los derechos que actualmente existen ó que puedan ser establecidos en adelante, exceptuando el derecho de faro ; pero éste en ningún caso excederá de cien pesos anuales por todos los vapores que puedan tocar en el puerto durante el año.

11. Si por equivocación ó por olvido los vapores de las compañías dejaren en Puntarenas (ó Tivives) correspondencia ó mercaderías destinadas á otros puertos, ó se vieren obligados á desembarcarlas para ser embarcadas por cualquiera de sus otros vapores, el Gobierno de Costa Rica concede á las compañías la facultad de hacerlo sin que tengan que pagar por ello derecho ó contribución alguna.

12. Salvas las excepciones contenidas en este contrato, los vapores de las compañías quedan sujetos á todas las leyes y reglas vigentes en el tráfico marítimo de los puertos de Costa Rica.

13. El presente contrato principiará á surtir sus efectos desde la fecha en que las compañías mencionadas despachen el primer vapor desde Panamá á la costa de Centro América, hasta Ocós inclusive, de lo cual darán éstas aviso anticipado al Gobierno, y durará por dos años contados desde esa fecha y se considerará prorrogado por otros dos años más, si tres meses antes del vencimiento no se notifica la recisión por una ú otra parte.

14. Las diferencias que surgieren entre el Gobierno de Costa Rica y las compañías sobre la inteligencia y cumplimiento de este contrato serán decididas por medio de dos árbitros nombrados uno por cada parte y, en caso de discordia, por un tercero nombrado por aquéllos; su decisión será final y tendrá fuerza de cosa juzgada, como sentencia. Los árbitros deberán ser precisamente ciudadanos costaricenses.

15. Los vapores de las compañías serán recibidos y despachados los domingos y días festivos como en días ordinarios.

16. Este contrato queda sujeto para su validez á la ratificación del Poder Legislativo de Costa Rica.

MODIFICACIONES EN LA TARIFA DE ADUANAS.

Según informes recibidos por el Gobierno británico de su Cónsul en San José, se ha establecido un derecho de importación de 2 centavos por kilógramo sobre toda madera para construcción, y de 6 centavos por kilógramo sobre la madera de ebanistería que se introduzca por Puerto Limón para uso en la provincia de Limón. Antes de ahora, la madera introducida por Limón para uso en dicha provincia entraba libre de derechos.

Dice también el mencionado Cónsul que el derecho de importación sobre el azúcar refinado y pulverizado ha sido elevado de 11 centavos á 20 por kilógramo, y en otras clases de azúcares de 7 á 15 centavos. El derecho sobre el cacao molido ha sido elevado de 13 á 20 centavos por kilógramo, y el del cacao en grano de 7 á 15 centavos por kilógramo.

EXPORTACIÓN DE CAFÉ EN 1897-98.

El Director de Estadística de la República da las siguientes cifras relativas á la exportación de café durante el año económico que terminó el 30 de junio de 1898. Estas cifras muestran un aumento de 2,000 sacos (264,000 libras) sobre la exportación de 1896-97, y de 6,000 sacos (792,000 libras) sobre la de 1895-96:

Rutas.	Sacos.	Kilógramos.
Á Nueva York por la Línea Atlas	94,075	5,084,787
Á Ing'aterra por la Mala Real.	80,358	4,166,064
Á Inglaterra por la Línea Lyon y Cox	52,983	2,882,113
Á Inglaterra por la Línea Alemana	45,731	2,567,717
Á Inglaterra por la Línea Francesa	18,829	1,056,251
Á Inglaterra por otras líneas	5,515	328,257
Gran total	297,491	16,085,189

ECUADOR.
ALGUNOS PUNTOS DEL MENSAJE DEL PRESIDENTE.

El Presidente ALFARO presentó su mensaje anual al Congreso el 9 de agosto último. De lo que dice este documento, se desprende que la condición de la República del Ecuador mejora notablemente. Asegura el Presidente que el Departamento de Estadística de las Aduanas ha sido completamente reorganizado, y que los datos que ahora se dan pueden tenerse por fidedignos. Siendo esto el caso, anuncia él con satisfacción que las exportaciones en 1897 aumentaron cerca de 50 por ciento sobre las de 1896.

Las cantidades que el Presidente da en su mensaje son las siguientes: exportaciones en 1896, 21,862,324 sucres ($9,138,451.43); exportaciones en 1897, 31,025,382 sucres ($12,968,609.68); importaciones en 1897, 18,004,048 sucres ($7,525,692.06).

El Presidente dice que esta cantidad debe aumentarse en un

25 por ciento, porque las valuaciones contenidas en el informe de aduanas son indudablemente muy bajas. En consecuencia, el valor de las importaciones asciende, por lo menos, á 22,000,000 de sucres ($9,196,000). El Gobierno se propone elevar la valuación oficial sobre la cual se cobran los derechos, y á este efecto se ha nombrado una comisión.

GUATEMALA.

VALOR DEL CAPITAL ALEMÁN INVERTIDO EN GUATEMALA.

El periódico francés "Moniteur Officiel du Commerce" dice que durante varios años las exportaciones de Guatemala han sido mucho mayores que las importaciones. En 1896 la cantidad exportada representó un valor total de 23,085,000 pesos ($11,373,980), contra una importación por valor de 9,143,000 pesos ($4,503,756). Parece á primera vista ventajosa para Guatemala esta situación, pero el déficit anual que se nota demuestra lo contrario. Este estado anormal de cosas se debe al hecho de que la mayor parte de las plantaciones de café pertenecen á compañías alemanas, y las ganancias obtenidas por el capital invertido pasan á Alemania en la forma de dividendos. Se asegura que el capital alemán invertido en la República asciende á más de 150,000,000 marcos ($35,700,000), y, sin embargo, no hay más de 500 alemanes residentes en el país.

MÉXICO.

CAMPO HALAGÜEÑO.

México presenta un campo muy halagüeño al exportador americano, tanto por su proximidad como porque la demanda de toda clase de artículos, especialmente de manufacturas, es muy grande y aumenta cada día. El periódico "Modern México" dice que aunque el consumo de productos extranjeros aumentará notablemente durante los próximos años, los exportadores americanos no deben esperar demasiado de las oportunidades que dicho mercado ofrece en la actualidad. En primer lugar, al hacer un cálculo del consumo posible de artículos importados, no se debe tomar en consideración al presente más de la cuarta parte de la población de México.   En otras palabras, el 75 por ciento, por lo menos, de la población de México se compone de indios y de peones, que probablemente no han tenido en toda su vida ni el deseo ni los medios de comprar un sólo artículo importado.   El número de pequeños propietarios de terrenos es muy pequeño en proporción á los que hay en los Estados Unidos.   El trabajo es barato, pero son muy escasos los obreros hábiles, capaces de manejar máquinas, y por eso el uso general de éstas para ahorrar trabajo no puede hacerse en la escala en que se hace en los Estados Unidos.   El monto del comercio exterior de México apenas puede compararse con el inmenso tráfico de los Estados Unidos, pero va en aumento, y á los fabricantes americanos les sería más fácil y menos costoso tomar ahora una parte de ese comercio, y continuar haciéndolo á medida que se vaya desarrollando, que tratar de efectuarlo cuando las importaciones se hayan duplicado.

NUEVO MUELLE.

Aunque el nuevo muelle de Veracruz no está terminado todavía, ya está al servicio de la aduana.   Tiene 580 piés de largo y 80 de ancho.   En bajamar hay 28 piés de profundidad á lo largo de dicho muelle.   El primer buque que descargó en el nuevo desembarcadero fué el *Tampican*, de la West India and Pacific Steamship Company, barco de 3,126 toneladas de registro, y que mide 430 piés de largo y cala 17 piés 6 pulgadas á proa y 21 piés 3 pulgadas á popa.   Este buque es el más grande de los que entran á dicho puerto.   Es posible que otro barco de las mismas dimensiones descargue al otro lado del muelle y al mismo tiempo.

Con excepción de los barcos costaneros y de los carboneros, esta fué la primera vez que un buque pudo descargar toda clase de mercancías en el muelle general.   Las nuevas facilidades para el tráfico dan mayor importancia al puerto, y harán más pronto y más fácil el despacho de embarcaciones, lo cual, necesariamente, tiene que dar incremento al tráfico.

COMERCIO CON FRANCIA.

El Cónsul de México en el Havre, Señor Costa y Narvaez, ha enviado últimamente á su Gobierno un informe muy extenso sobre el comercio entre México y Francia, haciendo referencia especial al puerto del Havre. Se ve por dicho informe que los productos mexicanos exportados á Francia durante el año pasado ascendieron á 41,369,152 kilógramos, de los cuales 80 por ciento entraron al puerto del Havre. La exportación de café ha ido aumentando, pues por la aduana del Havre pasaron el año pasado 5,000 sacos, y esto es tanto más notable cuanto que la cosecha del Brasil excedió en mucho á la demanda, cosa que se sintió en todos los países productores de café, siendo menores los pedidos que se hicieron de este artículo y más bajo el precio que por él se pagó. Los palos de tinte de México son reconocidos en Francia como de superior calidad, particularmente el palo de campeche que viene de Laguna, el cual, debido á su buena calidad, es el que se usa en primer lugar para teñir artículos finos de seda, sombreros, guantes, etc. También hay bastante demanda de maderas de Yucatán, Tuxpan, Veracruz y Tampico.

Las maderas de construcción y de ebanistería no se mandan directamente de México á los puertos franceses, sino que van primero á los de Inglaterra. Los precios varían según las dimensiones y calidad de las maderas, y según su estado de preservación, siendo de 20 á 28 francos por cada 50 kilos. El cedro, que se emplea para hacer cajas de cigarros, es reembarcado á Bélgica, Alemania, Suiza y otros países donde el Gobierno no ha establecido, como en Francia, el monopolio de tabaco.

El cáñamo mexicano y el henequén van en grandes cantidades al puerto de Nueva York, y de allí son reembarcados á Lóndres, Hamburgo y el Havre, porque algunas casas americanas han monopolizado prácticamente estas fibras y las ventajas que se obtienen de su tráfico. El tráfico en pieles entre México y Francia es comparativamente pequeño, y el mercado principal para este producto son los Estados Unidos. El hule ó goma elástica de México se vende muy bien en Francia, y es idéntico al artículo que viene de la América Central. El Cónsul hace referencia al precio obtenido por los últimos cargamentos (8 francos el kilógramo) como un incentivo á nuevos esfuerzos para la producción de este artículo, el cual, debido al gran desarrollo industrial de los últimos años, ha adquirido mucha importancia en la manufactura de bicicletas, automóbiles, etc.

La zarzaparilla pasa por los mercados de los Estados Unidos

antes de llegar á Francia, y el Señor Costa y Narvaez atribuye á este hecho el que no sea muy apreciado este producto mexicano, porque pierde mucho de su verdadero sabor con la permanencia en un país extranjero. La miel de abejas tiene un rival en la que se produce en Francia, y á fin de proteger esta última, se ha impuesto un derecho de importación de 15 francos por cada 100 kilos sobre el artículo extranjero.

NICARAGUA.

NUEVA TARIFA.

El Agente Consular de los Estados Unidos en Bluefields, Nicaragua, Mr. M. J. Clancy, escribe á esta Oficina con fecha 20 de setiembre, al enviar la última ley de tarifa vigente en el país. El texto completo de la antigua tarifa se publicó en el número 20 del Boletín de la Oficina de las Repúblicas Americanas.

Refiriéndose al decreto vigente dice Mr. Clancy:

Por decreto del Presidente, cuya copia incluyo, la nueva tarifa que rije en Nicaragua entra en vigor el día primero del corriente en el interior del país y en este puerto y en el Departamento de Zelaya, por proclama, el 17 del corriente.

El aumento en los derechos de importación en todos los artículos que se introducen es como un ciento por ciento sobre los de la antigua tarifa. Arroz, frijoles, maíz y papas, que antes estaban en la lista de los productos libres de derecho, pagarán en lo adelante 10 centavos moneda de Nicaragua (4 centavos oro) por kilógramo. Un kilógramo es equivalente á 2.20 libras. Dichos artículos han sido pasados á la lista de los que pagan derecho, con el objeto de fomentar su cultivo en Nicaragua. Se dice que los productos mencionados pueden cultivarse aquí en grande escala con poco ó ningún trabajo. Su cultivo aumentará el desarrollo de las fuentes de riqueza agrícola del país.

Por razones que no puedo explicarme los derechos sobre el jabón son solamente 2 centavos, moneda nicaragüense, por kilógramo, mientras que en la lista antigua pagaba 9 centavos en moneda de Nicaragua.

Como la plata es el patrón de Nicaragua, el dollar americano, ya sea de oro, papel ó plata vale dos veces y media más que el peso ó el sol de plata, aun cuando cada uno de estos contiene tanta plata como el dollar acuñado por el Gobierno de los Estados Unidos.

Los derechos que afectan las provisiones, licores, azúcar y cerveza son dos veces mayores. En la nueva tarifa no aparecen pinturas de ninguna clase. Hasta hoy, en todas las facturas de mercancías extranjeras se requería que el peso fuese designado en kilógramos, aun cuando los derechos se pagaban por libra, incluyendo la caja ó envoltorio de los artículos. Hoy, se cobrarán los derechos tomando por base el kilógramo. En Nicaragua existe al presente la siguiente condición anómala: Todas las mercancías importadas á San Juan del Norte (Greytown) son admitidas libres de derecho por ser éste un puerto libre, mientras que las mercancías importadas á Bluefields ó Cabo Gracias en la costa del Atlántico, y Corinto ó San Juan del Sur en la del Pacífico, pagan los derechos requeridos por la nueva tarifa de importación.

El Decreto del Presidente, á que se refiere Mr. CLANCY, es como sigue:

EL PRESIDENTE DEL ESTADO,

Considerando: Que la tarifa de derechos de aduanas expedida el 25 de julio de 1898 no corresponde á las condiciones actuales del comercio; ya porque no comprende muchos artículos nuevos, cuya importación ha aumentado; ya porque la práctica ha hecho notar que contiene irregularidades en la clasificación de algunas mercaderías, de lo cual resulta falta de equidad en la distribución de los respectivos gravámenes: en uso de las facultades que le confiere la reforma constitucional expedida el 15 de octubre de 1896,

DECRETA:

ARTÍCULO 1. Desde la publicación del presente decreto, los derechos sobre la importación de mercancías se cobrarán por cada kilógramo de peso bruto con arreglo á lo siguiente:

ARTÍCULO 2. Los artículos no enumerados en la anterior clasificación pagarán el derecho de más semejante; pero si estuviesen compuestos de diversas materias se pagará el derecho señalado á la que más predomine en ellos.

ARTÍCULO 3. Las mercancías que se hayan omitido y que no puedan ser asimiladas conforme al artículo precedente se liquidarán al 200 por ciento sobre el valor principal de factura. Este derecho se elevará al 250 por ciento respecto de los artículos cuya materia prima se produzca en el país; y se rebajará al 100 por ciento respecto de los artículos de arte y oficios. Estos Ierechos se cobrarán en moneda corriente del país. A falta de factura, se procederá á valorar los artículos por peritos

ARTÍCULO 4. Cuando un mismo bulto contenga artículos que paguen derechos distintos, el peso del empaque se distribuirá en proporción á los pesos netos de los diferentes artículos contenidos en el bulto.

ARTÍCULO 5. La presente ley no comprende los artículos procedentes de los Estados centroamericanos cuya introducción sea libre ó esté gravada con derechos especiales conforme á los tratados vigentes.

ARTÍCULO 6. Los derechos liquidados conforme á la presente ley se pagarán en Tesorería General, del modo siguiente: 20 por ciento con órdenes contra las aduanas, creadas por decreto de 30 de octubre de 1896; 15 por ciento con órdenes contra las aduanas, creadas el 19 de junio de 1897; 15 por ciento en documentos de crédito público, legalmente liquidado y reconocido; y 50 por ciento en efectivo.

Esta disposición no afecta las pólizas de presente, ni los depósitos destinados actualmente á su amortización en los derechos marítimos.

ARTÍCULO 7. Los tenedores de órdenes al portador, creadas por decreto de 10 de noviembre de 1897, podrán pagar también con ellas el 5 por ciento de los derechos marítimos, sin recargo.

ARTÍCULO 8. Queda derogada la tarifa de 25 de julio de 1888 y cualquiera otra disposición que se oponga á lo dispuesto en el presente decreto.

PARAGUAY.

MERCADO PARA EL NEGOCIO DE MANTEQUILLA.

El Cónsul RUFFIN escribe de la Asunción que todo parece indicar una buena perspectiva en los mercados del Paraguay para la mantequilla de los Estados Unidos. Este artículo se encuentra en muy pequeña cantidad en esta República, aunque todos lo apetecen. La escasez debe atribuirse á la falta de establecimientos para su preparación y al reducido número de lecherías. Estas últimas se encuentran todas en el pequeño pueblo de San Bernardino, cuya población es casi exclusivamente alemana. Durante el año de 1897 se importaron como 2,500 libras de mantequilla, en latas de una libra. Dicha importación vino principalmente de Italia. La mantequilla que se hace en San Bernardino se vende al por menor á razón de 35 á 40 centavos, oro, la libra, y es la mejor que se puede obtener. El derecho sobre la mantequilla que se importa es de 50 por ciento ad valorem, y la renta que esto produce ascendió á $421, oro, el año pasado.

La mantequilla que se importa de Europa es de buena calidad, pero no es igual á la que se hace en los Estados Unidos. La superior calidad de esta última, que es de uso tan común en los Estados Unidos, facilitaría su inmediata salida en los mercados del Paraguay, con tal que se tuvieran en cuenta las peculiaridades de este pueblo. Muy poca mantequilla se consume en este país, y los hoteles que la usan cobran por ella una cantidad adicional.

Opina el Cónsul que sería conveniente que algún fabricante de los Estados Unidos hiciera la prueba de mandar mantequilla al Paraguay. Cree él que poniéndola en latas de una libra, con el retrato del Presidente del Paraguay ó de algún estadista notable del país, ó con un grabado que representara algún edificio histórico, se llamaría la atención del público y el artículo se volvería popular. El Cónsul piensa que en esta manera se obtendrían sin dilación ventas lucrativas, pues en el país no existe este sistema de anuncios.

Lo que se ha dicho del Paraguay puede aplicarse igualmente á las otras repúblicas americanas, en cuanto al uso, escasez y demanda de mantequilla. Los fabricantes de este artículo en los Estados Unidos podrían alcanzar grandes ventajas estudiando las condiciones existentes y adaptándose á las necesidades del tráfico.

EL ALIMENTO NACIONAL.

Ningún producto del suelo es más generalmente usado en la República del Paraguay que la mandioca. Es éste un producto peculiar á las regiones tropicales y semitropicales. La mandioca se encuentra en todas las mesas, y se parece algo á la batata de los Estados Unidos, aunque contiene más almidón y menos azúcar. Ordinariamente cocinan la mandioca junto con la carne, y le agregan maíz, batatas y otras legumbres, lo cual constituye el plato nacional. De la mandioca sacan el almidón, pues el almidón de maíz no se conoce en el Paraguay.

La mandioca es de color moreno claro y mide de 18 pulgadas á 2 pies de largo, con una circunferencia de 3 á 5 pulgadas. La siembran en mayo, y en los meses de junio, julio y agosto se encuentra en la mejor condición para el mercado, aunque crece durante todo el año. Con 5 centavos, oro, se puede comprar suficiente mandioca para una comida de una familia de 5 ó 6 personas. El Cónsul RUFFIN dice que la cosecha de este año será muy buena.

ADELANTOS EN LA AGRICULTURA.

El Cónsul RUFFIN avisa que el Banco Agrícola, que es una institución del Gobierno, tiene á su cargo todos los intereses agrícolas de la República. Se están usando con buenos resultados nuevos métodos de cultivo y maquinaria moderna.

Opina el Cónsul que si se comprendiera la importancia de la maquinaria americana se operaría en el Paraguay una revolución en la agricultura. Se aconseja á los fabricantes que manden agentes competentes á la Asunción á fin de establecer en aquella ciudad agencias para la venta de manufacturas americanas.

PERÚ.

EXTENSIÓN DE LOS DEPÓSITOS DE CARBÓN ANTRACITO.

El BOLETÍN correspondiente al mes de agosto publicó un corto artículo relativo á los depósitos de carbón del Perú, manifestando que en 1892 se había dado una concesión á Mr. C. B. JONES para explotar las minas de carbón durante 20 años. Desde entonces dos periódicos de minería, el "Mines and Minerals" de Scranton, Pa., y el "Association Letter," órgano de los explotadores de carbón antracito, han publicado descripciones de los terrenos carboníferos del Perú, preparados por WILLIAM GRIFFITH, ingeniero perito, que el año pasado visitó y estudió los lugares en referencia. De dicho artículo se han extractado los siguientes párrafos:

Los terrenos carboníferos de antracito del norte del Perú están situados en la magestuosa cadena de los Andes, á diferentes altitudes que varían de 7,000 á 13,000 piés sobre el nivel del mar y á ambos lados de aquella división del continente. Hay dos lugares notables; el más septentrional está situado en el Departamento de Cajamarca, 50 ó 60 millas al norte de la antigua é histórica ciudad del mismo nombre. En este lugar se notó la existencia de varias vetas de carbón en la superficie de barrancos casi verticales, como á 600 piés sobre el fondo del valle, por el cual corre el torrentoso río de la montaña, llamado Llaucón, ramal del Marañón que forma la fuente principal del cuerpo del río Amazonas. Este punto está cerca de 7,000 piés sobre la marea y como á 300 millas de las aguas navegables del Amazonas y 150 millas del Pacífico. Los lechos carboníferos en este lugar están formados de capas de cuarzita ó piedra caliza alterada de más de 2,000 piés de espesor, que se extienden por un grande espacio de terreno que jamás ha sido estudiado ni explorado en busca de carbón. Las venas explotables que estaban expuestas á la vista cuando se verificó la visita eran tres, como á 50 piés de distancia una de otra, cuyo espesor era 5½, 3, y 6½ piés, respectivamente, en dirección 22 grados al sur, siguiendo la dirección de la vena un paralelo al sudeste y al noroeste del eje de un plano inclinado en dirección opuesta, que en este punto hace subir el yacimiento de carbón. La formación que cubre la superficie superior de dicho plano inclinado ha sido desgastada y el valle que se formó de esta manera está hoy ocupado por un ramal del río, de modo que las montañas que quedan á cada lado del valle están formadas por las rocas de la formación carbonífera que corre en dirección opuesta en dichas montañas. Es muy probable que se encuentren también otros lechos carboníferos en las espesas capas de piedra arenisca, si se las examina con cuidado; dichas capas contienen estratificaciones de pizarra y desechos más ó menos en las mismas proporciones en que se encuentran en los yacimientos de carbón antracito de Pennsylvania.

Los yacimientos superficiales pueden seguirse por alguna distancia y los lechos están expuestos al otro lado del río, siendo casi del mismo espesor que el de las secciones arriba mencionadas, por lo que es de suponerse que sean de la misma vena. En esta región se pueden ver bien los yacimientos superficiales en los barrancos casi verticales, en donde los desechos que caen de arriba no se quedan, porque en otras partes el espeso follage tropical ó bien las lluvias han cubierto la vena Los pocos naturales que viven en esta región salvage no emplean el carbón en absoluto y de consiguiente no han hecho exploración alguna.

Las minas se prestan admirablemente para explotarlas por medio del agua y si los lechos son tan continuados como sucede generalmente con las venas carboníferas, se podrían extraer centenares de millones de toneladas, sobre el nivel del agua. Los yacimientos superficiales de la piedra carbonífera se pueden seguir por 15 ó 20 millas ó más á ambos lados de los valles por donde corren el río Llaucón y sus ramales. Para llevar el carbón de estas minas á la costa del Pacífico es necesario conducirlo por las montañas que sirven de línea divisoria. Es probable, sin embargo, que se pueda conseguir un descenso gradual hasta llegar á un punto navegable del río Amazonas; es probable, también, que los estudios que se hagan en el porvenir lleguen á dar por resultado el descubrimiento de lechos carboníferos de fácil explotación, situados al suroeste de la misma hoya, en la vertiente del Pacífico, á menos que las perturbaciones volcánicas que son tan frecuentes en los Andes hayan afectado ó destruido las venas carboníferas. Parece que esta acción volcánica no se ha hecho sentir mucho en la localidad descrita, pues los yacimientos de carbón al parecer están dispuestos con regularidad, sin que hayan sufrido perturbaciones.

El otro terreno carbonífero, digno de atención especial, está situado á 100 ó más millas al sur de la región ya mencionada, en el Departamento de la Libertad, cerca de las cabeceras de los ríos de Chicama y Sanat que desembocan en el Pacífico, cerca de la ciudad de Trujillo y la Bahía de Chimbote, respectivamente. Los lechos carboníferos parecen ser aquí de la misma formación de cuarzita y corren en dirección sudeste y noroeste. Las venas de carbón corren el sudoeste con una inclinación de 75 grados, aproximadamente, y algunos de los lechos tienen buen espesor. Se puede ver que el desgaste de los yacimientos superficiales ha formado profundas grietas entre las rocas carboníferas que siguen las irregularidades de la formación de la montaña. El lecho principal tiene de 10 á 15 piés de espesor. Se midieron otras secciones, bastante parecidas á la segunda, que quedan entre estas dos.

El yacimiento superficial de este gran lecho y la vena corbonífera que contiene se pueden seguir fácilmente por una distancia de 15 á 20 millas. El primer yacimiento superficial que se visitó está situado en la vertiente del Pacífico, cerca de 100 millas de la costa, á una altura de cerca de 8,000 piés. También se examinaron otros yacimientos, recogiéndose muestras á todo el largo de la vena por más de 20 millas, donde atraviesa la división continental do los Andes á una altura de 13,000 piés. También se observaron en esta sección lechos carboníferos más delgados, de 2 á 4 piés de espesor, cuyos yacimientos superficiales estaban por lo general tan cubiertos con depósitos acumulados en la superficie que muy poco se encontraba á flor de tierra. Este carbón lo emplean en la localidad en pequeña escala para trabajos de herrería y para quemar el mineral de plata. Los análisis números 1 y 2, hechos por A. S. McCreath, demuestran la calidad del carbón de las regiones antedichas:

	Análisis.	
	No. 1.	No. 2.
Agua..................................	1.450	1.596
Materias volátiles	5.633	3.030
Carbón fijo.................	83.620	90.906
Azufre......	.554	.652
Cenizas...................................	8.743	3.816
	100.000	100.000
Gravedad específica.......................	1.62	1.67

Es de notarse que el carbón de la región nordeste, como lo demuestra el primer análisis, es más ó menos de la calidad del carbón antracito de uso general en Pennsylvania, mientras que el segundo análisis demuestra que la calidad del carbón es muy superior al producto ordinario de Pennsylvania, y aun quizás muy superior también al de la mejor calidad de aquella región.

Es evidente que las montañas de los Andes han sido calentadas intensa y uniformemente por toda su extensión, de lo que se deduce casi con certeza que estos depósitos de antracito deben ser de calidad uniforme por toda la región carbonífera, no cambiándose en bituminoso como acontece en el Colorado. En ciertos lugares del mismo distrito se encuentran depósitos de carbón lignito de una edad más reciente y de gran espesor; pero no se halla carbón bituminoso alguno. Este último distrito está muy bien situado y contiene carbón en abundancia suficiente para compensar cualesquier gastos que sean necesarios para la explotación, pués es su mercado toda la costa occidental de Sur y Norte América, en donde este artículo por lo general tiene un alto precio; y no pasará mucho tiempo sin que éste se aumente por las necesidades de proveerse de carbón el canal de Nicaragua, el cual se construirá sin duda en adelante, siendo llamado á surtirse de carbón de dicho distrito.

La cuarta parte del combustible que usan los vapores que hacen viajes regulares entre Panamá y Valparaiso viene como lastre, desde Gales, y se deposita en las carboneras del puerto de Iquique, al norte de Chile, á donde es conducido por buques que hacen el comercio de nitrato. El resto del carbón que se consume en la costa de Sud América se obtiene de las minas de Chile, situadas centenares de millas al sur de Valparaiso, á cuyo punto los buques van á buscar carbón, perdiendo por consiguiente muchos días en cada viaje. De vez en cuando viene también un cargamento de Australia. Este carbón de Chile es carbón de gas de calidad muy inferior como combustible para vapor, pues contiene una gran cantidad de materias volátiles y como se usa de ordinario produce una gran cantidad de humo y deja una gran porción de cenizas al paso que da muchísimo trabajo para encenderlo. A falta de algo mejor se le ha venido usando hace años, aun cuando su precio es muy alto, y ha producido enormes riquezas á la señora dueña de las minas.

ESTADOS UNIDOS.

COMERCIO CON LA AMÉRICA LATINA.

RELACIÓN DE LAS IMPORTACIONES Y EXPORTACIONES.

En la página 617 aparece la última relación del comercio entre los Estados Unidos y la América Latina tomada de la compilación hecha por la Oficina de Estadística del Departamento del Tesoro de los Estados Unidos, cuyo ιjefe es Mr. O. P. Austin; estos datos se refieren al valor del comercio arriba mencionado. La estadística corresponde al mes de ιjuliö de 1898, corregida en setiembre 2 del mismo año, comparada con la del período correspondiente del año anterior y también comprende los datos referentes á los siete meses que terminaron en ιjulio de 1898 comparados con igual período de 1897. Debe explicarse que las estadísticas de las importaciones y exportaciones de las diversas aduanas referentes á un mes cualquiera no se reciben en el Departamento del Tesoro hasta el 20 del próximo mes,necesitándose algún tiempo para su compilación é impresión, de suerte que los datos estadísticos correspondientes al més de ιjulio, por ejemplo, no se publican sino en setiembre.

CONDICIÓN DEL TESORO—MONEDA EN CIRCULACIÓN.

Los siguientes datos sobre la condición del Tesoro de los Estados Unidos, al terminar las labores del 20 de setiembre, fueron publicados el 1º de octubre: fondos disponibles, en efectivo, $309,156,297; reserva en oro, $243,327,379; plata, $7.120,784; billetes de banco sobre el Tesoro, $36,454,266; billetes del Tesoro de 1890, $1,751,950; total de ingresos durante el mes, $3,103,050; ingresos totales durante el año fiscal, $128,510,936; total de egresos durante el mes, $2,281,000; total de egresos durante el año fiscal, $187,099,114; depósitos del Tesoro en bancos nacionales, $82,344,416.

Las estadísticas del dinero en circulación, comparadas con las de los dos meses anteriores, demuestran que˙ha habido un aumento neto que alcanzó á la suma de $24,499,837. De los ramos en donde ocurrió disminución, el principal es el oro acuñado, que alcanzó á $8,043,354; también la hubo en los certificados de moneda acuñada de 1872, por $2,645,000 y en los certificados de oro por $79,100. El aumento más notable ocurrió en los billetes de los Estados Unidos, que alcanzó á $19,264,584. El aumento en los billetes de banco nacionales alcanzó á $8,904,794; también hubo aumento de $3,050,515 en la moneda de plata de $1, $1,828,417 en monedas de plata subsidiarias, $453,362 en certificados de plata y $1,783,629 en billetes del Tesoro de 1890.

El cuadro comparativo que aparece más abajo indica la pequeña disminución en el metálico y oro acuñado del Tesoro. Nótase un aumento de $14,190,377 en oro acuñado y de $11,123,581 en metálico. La disminución más notable es de $19,264,584 en billetes de los Estados Unidos, que corresponde al aumento de circulación arriba mencionado. En el siguiente cuadro aparece todo el dinero emitido, la cantidad que existe en la Tesorería y la que está en circulación:

	Existencias acuñadas ó emisiones.	En Tesorería.	En circulación el 10 de octubre, 1898.
Oro acuñado..................	$785,041,686	$162,391,874	$622,649,812
Dollars de plata..................	464,834,597	404,045,769	60,788,828
Plata subsidiaria..................	75,784,648	9,196,708	66,587,940
Certificados de oro	36,990,799	1,596,890	35,393,909
Certificados de plata.............	400,062,504	6,636,769	393,425,735
Billetes del Tesoro, ley 14 de julio, 1890....................	98,549,280	1,844,997	96,704,283
Billetes de los Estados Unidos....	346,681,016	55,020,851	291,660,165
Certificados de curso legal, ley 8 de junio, 1872......	18,455,000	820,000	17,635,000
Billetes de los bancos nacionales ..	235,439,985	3,689,265	231,750,720
Total..................	2,461,839,515	645,243,123	1,816,596,392

La cantidad de oro en circulación, comparada con la que había el 1° de octubre de 1897, aumentó en más de $93,500,000. Durante el año el aumento en billetes de los Estados Unidos alcanzó á $39,800,000; certificados de plata, $18,800,000; billetes del Tesoro de 1890, cerca de $6,900,000; plata en pequeñas denominaciones, más de $5,400,000; billetes de los bancos nacionales, cerca de $5,300,000; monedas de plata de $1, más de $3,600,000. Las únicas disminuciones que ocurrieron, calculadas casi en la misma cantidad, $1,500,000, fueron en los certificados de moneda acuñada de 1872 y los certificados de oro.

El total general del dinero en circulación para el 1 de octubre alcanzó á $1,816,596,392, lo que indica un aumento de más de $137,750,000 comparado con el 1 de octubre de 1897. La circulación por cabeza se computó en $24.24 según cálculos de un perito de la Tesorería, hechos sobre una población de 74,925,000. Esto representa para el mes de setiembre un aumento de 28 centavos por cabeza, y para el mes de octubre de 1897 un excedente de $1.35. De lo antedicho se desprende que de la suma total de oro acuñado casi las cuatro quintas está en circulación, mientras que más de las seis séptimas partes de la cantidad de dollars de plata acuñados se conservaba en las cajas del Tesoro.

PRODUCTO DE LA RENTA INTERNA EN EL MES DE AGOSTO.

El informe sobre la recaudación de la renta interna durante el mes de agosto indica un aumento neto de $11,006,235, en comparación con el mismo mes en 1897. Las entradas de las diversas fuentes y el aumento y disminución comparados con los del mes de agosto de 1897 son como sigue:

Licores alcohólicos, $6,787,513; disminución, $207,645; bebidas fermentadas, $7,053,661; aumento, $5,418,860; oleomargarina, $131,354; aumento, $64,923; impuestos especiales no mencionados en otra parte, $1,289,335; diversos, $3,098,510; aumento, $3,072,036.

Las varias fuentes de donde provinieron las entradas fueron las siguientes: banqueros, $971,934; salas de billar, $98,700; corredores, acciones, bonos, etc., $101,958; corredores comerciales, $48,123; corredores de aduana, $2,202; prenderos, $11,269; juegos de bolos, $17,139; circos, $6,058; exhibiciones no mencionadas con especialidad, $12,039; teatros, etc., $19,908; harina mezclada, $755; legados, $5,057; sellos sobre documentos y artículos de comercio, $3,167,514; naipes, $12,438; multas, $12,266. El aumento neto durante los últimos dos meses sobre el período correspondiente de 1897 fué de $19,337,946.

GRAN INCREMENTO EN LA CONSTRUCCIÓN DE BUQUES.

Según los datos recibidos en la Oficina de Navegación, se ve que durante el año económico que terminó el 30 de junio de 1898, se construyeron y matricularon en los Estados Unidos 952

EXISTENCIA Y PRECIO DEL ALGODÓN.

El precio fenomenalmente bajo del algodón recientemente, que según se dice es el mínimum á que ha llegado en los últimos años, da especial interés á la série de cuadros estadísticos que acaba de preparar la Oficina de Estadísticas del Tesoro de los Estados Unidos y que demuestra el aumento notable alcanzado en la producción de este artículo y la baja de precios que coincidió con él. Demuestran los cuadros en referencia que los Estados Unidos, los primeros productores de algodón que hay en el mundo, han cuadruplicado su producción desde 1872 y que durante el mismo período el precio ha bajado á la cuarta parte de lo que era en dicho año. En 1872 la cosecha de algodón de los Estados Unidos fué 1,384,084,494 libras, cuyo precio, por término medio, era de 22.19 centavos por libra; en 1898, según informes, la cosecha se calcula en 5,667,372,051 libras, cuyo precio medio es de 6.23 centavos por libra. Como se ve, la producción en 1898 es más de cuatro veces mayor que la de 1872, y el precio medio poco más de la cuarta parte de lo que era en dicha fecha.

Cuando se considera que los otros países algodoneros del mundo no han disminuido sus cosechas durante este tiempo, se ve que el aumento de las existencias del algodón en el mundo, en el cuarto de siglo á que se hace referencia, ha sido muy grande y muy superior al aumento de la población y del consumo.

Hace veinticinco años que los Estados Unidos producían el 70 por ciento del algodón del mundo y hoy producen el 85 por ciento. Este aumento no obedece á la disminución de algodón en otras partes del mundo, sino al desarrollo de este país. La cosecha de dicho fruto en los otros países productores en 1872–73 alcanzó á 1,667,000 pacas y en 1897–98 á 1,665,000. El producto de los otros países puede calcularse por término medio de 1872 á 1878 en 1,618,000 pacas por año y de 1890 á 1897 en 1,924,000 pacas por año, lo que demuestra que también ha aumentado algo la producción de algodón en otras partes del mundo, al paso que la de los Estados Unidos ha tenido un enorme desarrollo.

No sólo el precio del algodón ha disminuido casi en la misma proporción que ha aumentado el producto, sino que también ha disminuido en proporción el precio de las telas de algodón. El

INSTITUCIONES BANCARIAS EN CUBA.

Hasta el día de hoy, todas las operaciones bancarias indispensables al tráfico entre los Estados Unidos y Cuba han sido hechas por el Banco de España y otras instituciones semejantes de Europa. Dichas operaciones han consistido en descuentos, recaudaciones, cartas de crédito y compra y venta de giros. En algunos casos aquellos bancos han servido como agencias comerciales. Es muy obvia la necesidad que existe de establecer bancos americanos en Cuba (otro tanto sucede en las repúblicas de la América latina) á fin de que los exportadores puedan negociar directamente con sus parroquianos en la isla.

Mr. S. M. JARVIS, Vicepresidente de la North American Trust Company, ha regresado de Santiago de Cuba, después de haber establecido la primera sucursal de un banco americano que se ha fundado en las Antillas. En una entrevista, dicho Señor se expresó de esta manera:

Hemos establecido y tenemos funcionando una agencia en Santiago, que es puramente una institución bancaria, destinada, en primer lugar, á satisfacer las necesidades del Gobierno de los Estados Unidos y de sus agentes fiscales, y, en segundo lugar, á facilitar las transacciones mercantiles de los que hacen negocios en aquel lugar. Con este último objeto, estamos listos para dar cartas de crédito sobre Nueva York, que puedan servir en Santiago á los viajeros y á los importadores de aquella plaza. Nuestra agencia en Santiago está lista para vender y comprar giros sobre Nueva York y para atender á los cargamentos de mercancías. En cada uno de estos puntos podemos hacer por telégrafo remesas de dinero para el otro. Agencias de esta clase se establecerán en la Habana, Matanzas, y otros puntos que elegiremos más tarde.

URUGUAY.

ENTRADAS DE ADUANA EN MONTEVIDÉO.

Según informa el Cónsul británico, las entradas de aduana en el puerto de Montevidéo durante el mes de julio subieron á $1,005,007. Si se toma en consideración el hecho de que julio es el mes en que los negocios están más deprimidos en el Uruguay, se convendrá en que dicha suma es muy considerable. El Cónsul atribuye este aumento extraordinario al hecho de que, á fin de no pagar el derecho de importación adicional de 2½ por

ciento que empezó á regir el 1º de agosto, los comerciantes introdujeron mercancías en grandes cantidades.   Fué notable también
el aumento en las importaciones.   El total de éstas en julio de
1898 tuvo un valor de $916,359, contra $583,000 en julio de 1897.

Según el "Montevideo Times," las entradas de aduana en los
primeros seis meses de 1898 ascendieron á $5,319,448, contra
$4,290,121 durante el mismo período en 1897.   Este año no solamente muestra un progreso enorme sobre 1897, que fué el año de
la revolución, sino que puede compararse favorablemente con la
primera mitad de 1896, que, desde el punto de vista comercial,
fué notablemente próspera.   En aquella época las entradas de
aduana llegaron á $5,535,402.   Dice el "Times" que las cifras
correspondientes al año de 1898 están sujetas á revisión, lo cual,
antes que reducirlas, las aumentará.

Refiriéndose al derecho de importación adicional de 2½ por ciento
sobre las mercancías que entran al Uruguay, de lo cual se dió
aviso en el BOLETÍN del mes de setiembre, dice el Cónsul SWALM
que el Gobierno ha resuelto dedicar el producto de este derecho á
la conversión de los bonos del Tesoro, hasta la época en que se le
necesite para los nuevos trabajos en el puerto de Montevidéo.

LOS ESTADOS UNIDOS DE CENTRO AMERICA.

PROMULGACIÓN DE LA NUEVA CONSTITUCIÓN.

Con fecha 15 de setiembre de 1898, Mr. WILLIAM M. LITTLE,
Cónsul de los Estados Unidos en Tegucigalpa, Honduras, comunica oficialmente al Departamento de Estado la nueva federación
de los países de Centro América, conocidos hasta hoy como La
República Mayor de Centro América, nombre que seguirán
llevando hasta el 1 de noviembre de 1898.   En la comunicación
precitada dice así Mr. LITTLE:

Tengo la honra de participar á usted, que este Gobierno ha promulgado
oficialmente la Constitución Política de los Estados Unidos de Centro América,
antes llamados La República Mayor de Centro América, documento preparado
por los representantes de Honduras, Nicaragua y Salvador, en Managua, Nicaragua, el 27 de agosto de 1898.   Adjunto un ejemplar de la Constitución.   Como
acabo de recibir dicho documento, no tengo tiempo de hacer una traducción

completa de él, por lo cual doy aquí un extracto de aquello que creo pueda interesar más á ese Departamento:

Los Estados Unidos de Centro América, formados por Honduras, Nicaragua y Salvador, constituyen una República Federal. Los departamentos de La Unión (Salvador), Chinandega (Nicaragua), Valle y Choluteca (Honduras), formarán temporalmente un Distrito Federal. El Poder Ejecutivo se instalará provisionalmente en Amapala, Honduras.

El Gobierno de la nación, que es una democracia representativa, se divide en tres poderes, Legislativo, Ejecutivo y Judicial.

El Congreso Federal se compone de dos Cámaras, la del Senado y la de Diputados; la primera consta de seis senadores por cada uno de los tres países y tres por el Distrito Federal, elegidos por el término de seis años por sus legislaturas respectivas. Por cada Estado y distrito habrá igual número de suplentes. Los diputados son elegidos uno por cada treinta mil habitantes. Hasta que se concluya el censo de la nueva República habrá 14 diputados por cada Estado y cuatro por el Distrito Federal é igual número de suplentes. Los diputados son elegidos por el término de cuatro años.

El Presidente de la República será elegido por votación popular, siendo su período de cuatro años, á partir del 15 de marzo. El primer período constitucional empieza el 15 de marzo de 1899, y hasta entonces habrá un Consejo Ejecutivo Provisional, compuesto de un delegado por cada uno de los tres Estados, que se instalará en Amapala el 1º de noviembre de 1898. El Consejo Ejecutivo adoptará las leyes de uno de los Estados para que rijan provisionalmente en el Distrito Federal, hasta que el Congreso determine una legislación definitiva. El primer Congreso Federal se instalará el 1º de marzo de 1899.

Referente á los extranjeros, dice el Cónsul que los extranjeros que aceptan puestos públicos á sueldo, con excepción del profesorado en las escuelas, serán considerados como naturalizados. Todo extranjero á su llegada al territorio de la República está en la obligación de respetar sus autoridades y cumplir sus leyes. Los extranjeros gozan en la República de los mismos derechos civiles que los hijos del país, y por consiguiente pueden adquirir toda clase de propiedades, estando sujetos, sin embargo, por lo que se refiere á ésta propiedad, al pago de los impuestos ordinarios y extraordinarios de carácter general que afecte la propiedad de los naturales del país. Los extranjeros no tienen derecho á reclamaciones ni indemnizaciones de la República sino en los casos y circunstancias en que los naturales del país gocen de estos privilegios. Los extranjeros no tendrán recurso á la intervención diplomática sino en el caso de denegación de justicia, no considerándose como tal el juicio adverso al reclamante. Si, en contravención de lo dispuesto, sus reclamaciones no pueden arreglarse amigablemente, causando así perjuicios al país, dichos contraventores perderán su derecho de domicilio en él. Las leyes pueden establecer la manera y los casos en que pueda negarse á un extranjero la entrada al territorio de la República, ó en los que se ordene su expulsión por considerarse pernicioso.

VENEZUELA.

FOMENTO DE LA INMIGRACIÓN ITALIANA.

El Ministro Loomis escribió últimamente de Caracas al Departamento de Estado, y remitió un recorte del "Venezuelan Herald" que contiene la traducción de un contrato celebrado entre el Gobierno venezolano y un sindicato de capitalistas italianos. Este contrato viene á sustituir la concesión Dotti, de que se trató con fecha 10 de enero.

La sustancia del contrato Dotti fué publicada en la página 1906 del Boletín correspondiente al mes de mayo.

Opina Mr. Loomis que el contrato es favorable á Venezuela, y que si se cumple en todos sus términos, dará por resultado el establecimiento en la República de 15,000 familias del norte de Italia. Estas familias recibirán protección de diversas maneras, y hasta se les dará auxilio pecuniario, con la esperanza de que desarrollen el cultivo de frutas y cereales, y dediquen especial atención á la vid y á la fabricación de vino. Después de la llegada de los inmigrantes, el éxito de la empresa dependerá de la construcción de caminos y ferrocarriles, que les permitan trasportar con poco gasto sus productos á los mercados del país y á la costa.

Dice el Ministro que el estudio de las condiciones actuales evidencia que, si la producción de frutas aumentara considerablemente, los cultivadores se verían obligados á buscar mercados en los Estados Unidos y en otros países extranjeros, pero que preferirían á los Estados Unidos, por razón de la proximidad de este país y de la gran demanda que hay en él de frutas tropicales. El recorte del periódico dice, entre otras cosas, lo siguiente:

El 1 de julio de 1898 el Gobierno celebró un contrato de inmigración sobre bases muy sólidas. Las partes contratantes son el Ministro de Agricultura, Industria y Comercio, autorizado al efecto por el Presidente de la República en Consejo de Ministros y con el consentimiento del Consejo de Gobierno, por una parte, y la Sociedad de Colonización Italiana por otra.

Según este contrato, la sociedad se compromete: 1º, á traer á Venezuela, en el curso de cada tres años, 3,000 familias europeas, principalmente de la raza latina, agricultoras y de reconocida buena conducta, todo lo cual ha de ser comprobado por medio de certificados de los cónsules en los diferentes puertos de embarco; 2º, á construir edificios para las mismas, proveerlas de instrumentos agrícolas, y darles alimento, ropa y medicinas hasta que hayan recogido la primera cosecha, y asimismo á levantar una iglesia, edificios para oficinas públicas y escuelas en cada colonia; 3º, á establecer un servicio bimensual de vapores entre Italia y Venezuela, tocando en Barcelona, España, en Tenerife y otros puertos, y cuyo término sea La Guaira ó Puerto Cabello; pero, si fuese necesario, dichos vapores tocarán en otros puertos, sujetos á las leyes fiscales de Venezuela; estos vapores llevarán las malas á todos los mencionados puertos sin remuneración, y no cobrarán por pasajeros y carga más de lo que cobran otros barcos de la misma clase y porte; la sociedad conviene en cobrar solamente medio pasaje á los empleados diplomáticos y sus familias y á darles pasaje libre cuando residan ó vayan á residir en el extranjero; 4º, á establecer en Caracas una institución bancaria, con sucursales en aquellos distritos de la República en que se crea conveniente tenerlas, siendo el objeto de la misma prestar dinero sobre hipotecas á los agricultores y criadores de ganado; el capital de dicho banco será de 20,000,000 bolívares ($3,860,000), de los cuales 12,000,000 se dedicarán á operaciones bancarias ordinarias y el resto á préstamos, según queda indicada; estos dos fondos deben mantenerse separados, sin confundirse jamás el uno con el otro; el interés sobre los préstamos no debe exceder de siete por ciento, y el banco tiene facultad de remitir billetes, de conformidad con lo que dispone la ley sobre bancos, vigente en la actualidad; 5º, á permitir al Gobierno nacional el uso libre de todos los medios de comunicación que establezca; 6º, á dar, al cabo de cuatro años de trabajos agrícolas, una casa á cada familia de la colonia y á cada colono tres hectáreas (14.8 acres), cuyo terreno será dedicado al cultivo; 7º, á depositar en el banco de Inglaterra, como garantía del cumplimiento de este contrato, y dentro de tres meses contados desde la fecha en que sea ratificado por el Congreso Nacional, la suma de 200,000 bolívares ($38,000), que permanecerá allí hasta que la sociedad funde en Caracas el banco mencionado y haya establecido á las primeras 500 familias; la sociedad perderá dicha suma á favor del Gobierno si no cumple con lo estipulado en el contrato.

Por otra parte, el Gobierno se compromete : 1°, á dar á la sociedad terrenos no cultivados para el uso de los inmigrantes, á razón de seis hectáreas (14.8 acres) por cabeza, y cada niño menor de 10 años que venga al país con una familia de inmigrantes, tendrá derecho, cuando llega su mayor edad, á todos los privilegios de que gocen los inmigrantes. 2°, á no celebrar en lo futuro contratos de esta naturaleza con ningún individuo ó compañía que desee traer agricultores directamente de Italia. 3°, á permitir la importación, libre de derechos, de instrumentos agrícolas y maquinaria para agricultura y para construcción de edificios y vías de comunicación, después que la sociedad haya cumplido con las condiciones impuestas por la ley. 4°, á dar á la sociedad la preferencia (ceteris paribus) en el desarrollo de todas las minas que se descubran en terrenos adyacentes á las colonias, y en el establecimiento de medios de comunicación entre las colonias y otras partes de la República. 5°, á pagar á la sociedad la suma de 18 bolívares ($3.47) anualmente durante la duración de este contrato (15 años) por cada inmigrante de 7 años de edad ó más que se traiga al país y se establezca en una colonia.

La sociedad se compromete también á vender al Gobierno nacional, cuando éste lo desee, todas las líneas telegráficas á un precio que será fijado por peritos; á traspasar al Gobierno sin indemnización el derecho de propiedad sobre dichas líneas después de 40 años; á trasferir á la municipalidad dentro de cuya jurisdicción estén situadas todas las líneas de teléfonos al cabo de 50 años, y al Gobierno nacional todos los ferrocarriles, tranvías, etc., á la expiración de un período de 90 años. La tarifa de lo que la sociedad cobrará por el uso de dichos medios de comunicación será establecida por medio de un convenio entre el Gobierno y la sociedad.

Los colonos pueden dedicarse á cualquier ramo de agricultura que prefieran, pero en aquellos terrenos adecuados al cultivo del trigo y de la vid los colonos estarán obligados á dedicar al mismo la tercera parte de los terrenos que se les concedan.

Este contrato permanecerá vigente durante 15 años, á contar desde la fecha en que sea ratificado por el Congreso, y es prorogable por un término igual y bajo las mismas condiciones, á no ser que haya sido denunciado antes de terminar el último año, ó en caso que la sociedad haya faltado en el cumplimiento de sus obligaciones y que el Gobierno le haya llamado la atención á dicha falta. Se estipula también que si la sociedad deseare introducir inmigrantes antes de que el Congreso haya ratificado el contrato, podrá hacerlo así, y el Gobierno le dará los terrenos necesarios de acuerdo con lo que dispone la ley sobre inmigración. Una vez que el Congreso haya ratificado el contrato, la sociedad gozará de todos los beneficios que de él se derivan; pero si el Congreso no ratificare el referido contrato, el Gobierno deberá pagar el valor de los pasajes de los inmigrantes de conformidad con las disposiciones de la presente ley.

El Gobierno se reserva el derecho de celebrar contratos semejantes con otros países.

LA YUCA.

En un informe de Mr. A. H. PLUMACHER, Cónsul en Maracaibo, publicado en los Informes Consulares correspondientes al mes de setiembre, se lee lo siguiente:

El principal producto de Venezuela es el café, pero, como el precio de este artículo es ahora muy bajo, los agricultores harían bien en dirigir su atención á otra planta cuyo cultivo da resultados más lucrativos. Según parece, la yuca promete mucho para lo porvenir. Es una planta muy productiva y, á pesar de ser muy bien conocida en Venezuela, nadie se ha ocupado especialmente en cultivarla. Una hectárea de tierra sembrada de yuca produce 150 quintales de almidón ó 200 quintales de tapioca. El cultivo de esta planta es fácil y barato. Soporta muy bien el mal tiempo, no sufre en la estación seca, y crece en todo terreno.

La yuca se da bien en el mismo suelo en que crecen los guisantes, el maíz y los frijoles, y un terreno sembrado de dicha planta rinde más que sembrado de café. Un hectárea de terreno bien cultivada puede llevar 1,600 cafetos. Tomando la producción máxima de cada árbol, una hectárea da 8 quintales de café, y la misma porción de terreno sembrada de yuca daría 150 quintales de almidón, fuera de otros productos que se obtendrían del mismo suelo, los cuales podrían ser, por ejemplo, 12 bushels de guisantes y 12 de frijoles. Esto demuestra que un terreno sembrado de yuca rinde 6 ó 7 veces más que sembrado de café. El sistema de cultivo es primitivo. Casi no se conocen los arados y otros instrumentos de agricultura de fabricación americana. Todo el trabajo se hace con azadas de antiguo estilo, pues ni los hombres ni las bestias han sido educados en el uso de los arados modernos.

DERECHOS DE TONELAJE EN CUBA.

CIRCULAR SOBRE DERECHOS DE TONELAJE, NO. 17.

MINISTERIO DE LA GUERRA,
Wáshington, 11 de octubre de 1898.

Por disposición del Presidente, el párrafo 5°, página 8, de la Tarifa de Aduanas y Reglamentos de los puertos de Cuba que están en posesión de los Estados Unidos y que trata de los derechos de tonelaje, queda enmendado como sigue:

DERECHOS DE TONELAJE.

5. En todos los puertos y lugares de Cuba que se encuentren en posesión ó bajo el domino administrativo de las fuerzas de mar y tierra de los Estados Unidos se cobrarán, hasta nueva orden, los derechos de tonelaje siguientes:

Por tonelada neta.

(*a*) Todo buque que arribe de un puerto ó lugar fuera de Cuba pagará........ $0. 20

(*b*) Todo buque que arribe de otro puerto ó lugar de Cuba, y que á la fecha de su llegada se ocupe en el tráfico de cabotaje en la isla.................. . 02

(*c*) Los buques que entren ó salgan en lastre pagarán la mitad de lo establecido en las cláusulas *a* y *b*.

(*d*) Cuando un buque haya pagado el derecho de tonelaje impuesto sobre las embarcaciones que arriban de puertos ó lugares fuera de Cuba, no estará obligado á pagar otros derechos de tonelaje al entrar en otro puerto ó lugar de Cuba durante el mismo viaje, pero sí pagará cuando vuelva á entrar procedente de un puerto ó lugar fuera de Cuba.

(*e*) Todo vapor expreso ocupado en llevar la correspondencia y al servicio de una línea de navegación que, bajo arreglo ó contrato con algún gobierno, haga un servicio regular bimensual de un puerto fuera de Cuba á un puerto en la costa meridional de la isla, estará exento del pago de derechos de tonelaje, tan luego obtenga del Ministro de la Guerra un certificado de que realmente está empleado en el servicio mencionado.

(*f*) El derecho de tonelaje impuesto á un buque que arribe de un puerto ó lugar fuera de Cuba, no excederá en su totalidad de $2 por tonelada neta durante un año, comenzando á contar desde la fecha en que se hizo el primer pago.
El derecho de tonelaje impuesto á un buque que llegue de puertos ó lugares de Cuba, y que se ocupe á la época de su llegada en el tráfico de cabotaje en la costa de la isla, exclusivamente, no excederá de 40 centavos por tonelada neta durante un año, comenzando á contar desde la fecha en que se hizo el primer pago.

Tan luego el jefe bajo cuyo mando estén las fuerzas de los Estados Unidos en cualquier puerto ó lugar de la isla de Cuba que se encuentre en posesión de los Estados Unidos recibiere esta orden, la hará promulgar y poner en vigor.

R. A. ALGER,
Ministro de la Guerra.

———

MUERTE DEL SEÑOR ALEJANDRO SANTOS.

La noticia publicada el 10 de setiembre de haber muerto en Short Hills, New Jersey, el Señor T. ALEJANDRO SANTOS, Cónsul de Bolivia en Nueva York, fué recibido con profundo pesar por todos los círculos interesados en el tráfico latino-americano y en el desarrollo de relaciones comerciales más estrechas entre las Repúblicas de la América del Sur y los Estados Unidos. El Señor SANTOS era hijo de un rico comerciante del Ecuador y nació en Bahía de Caracas. Era un hombre de acrisolada honradez, que poseía muchos conocimientos y estaba dotado de notable habilidad para los negocios. En sus mocedades fué enviado á los Estados Unidos junto con sus seis hermanos, y todos fueron puestos bajo los cuidados de un amigo de la familia, que residía en Baltimore, con el objeto de que recibieran una buena educación. Con excepción de dos de ellos, todos se graduaron en el colegio de St. James, cerca de Hagerstown, Maryland, y uno de los hermanos se murió en dicha institución. Los otros regresaron á la América del Sur, y cuatro de ellos se dedicaron á negocios en el Ecuador, mientras que ALEJANDRO y otro de los hermanos permanecieron por varios años en Panamá, donde establecieron una casa de comercio. .

ALEJANDRO regresó á los Estados Unidos y contrajo matrimonio con MISS MARY ONDERDONK LONG, de Baltimore. Después de haber residido por corto tiempo en el Estado de Maryland, el Señor SANTOS pasó al Estado de New Jersey y estableció en la ciudad de Nueva York la casa comercial de Santos y Compañía, importadora de productos sudamericanos, y que ha hecho excelentes negocios. El Señor SANTOS fué miembro del Congreso Postal Internacional y era Cónsul honorario de Bolivia en Nueva York. Estaba animado de los sentimientos más amistosos hacia la Oficina de las Repúblicas Americanas, y era una de las primeras autoridades en asuntos relacionados con los países sudamericanos, con los cuales se hallaba especialmente identificado.

CONGRESO NACIONAL DE AGRICULTORES.

La décima octava reunión del Congreso Nacional de Agricultores se verificará en Fort Worth, Texas, y durará del 6 al 14 de diciembre de 1898. El objeto de esta organización, según se expone en su constitución, es el desarrollo de los intereses agrícolas de los Estados Unidos. Cada Estado y Territorio tiene derecho á enviar tantos delegados como representantes manda á las dos cámaras del Congreso Nacional, y, además, un delegado por cada colegio de agricultura. Todos los jefes de oficinas agrícolas de los Estados y Territorios tienen derecho á ocupar asiento en aquella asamblea. Los gobernadores de los varios Estados y Territorios tienen facultad de nombrar delegados fuera de los especialmente designados. Al hablar de la importancia de esta organización, el Honorable WM. M. HATCH, que fué por muchos años presidente de la Comisión de Agricultura de la Cámara de Diputados, dice que goza de más influencia en el Congreso de los Estados Unidos que todas las otras organizaciones agrícolas combinadas. Es la única asamblea de agricultores de cuyas transacciones se da cuenta en la Encyclopedia Americana.

Al enviar al Director de la Oficina de las Repúblicas americanas una invitación para que asista á la reunión de diciembre, Mr. D. O. LIVELY, de Fort Worth, el activo secretario del congreso, escribe lo siguiente:

En mi carácter de secretario del Fort Worth Live Stock Exchange, he estado recibiendo por algún tiempo el importante BOLETÍN MENSUAL de la Oficina de que usted es Director, y deseo llamar su atención á la reunión que se verificará en Fort Worth, Texas, del 6 á 14 de diciembre de este año, y la cual, á mi juicio, debe interesar á la Oficina de las Repúblicas Americanas. A fin de que usted se familiarice con el carácter, propósitos é importancia de esta organización, le he remitido hoy, por el correo y bajo cubierta separada, una copia del informe sobre la reunión del año pasado en St. Paul, y me permito llamar la atención de usted á ese documento. Observará usted que los Señores ROMERO y SOTELDO estuvieron entre los representantes que asistieron á dicha reunión, y asimismo notará usted que muchos de los asuntos discutidos se rozan con las relaciones existentes entre los Estados Unidos y otras repúblicas americanas. Accediendo á una solicitud del Departamento de Estado de los Estados Unidos, el Gobierno mexicano ha consentido en nombrar delegados que oficialmente representen á aquel país en la reunión de Fort Worth.

Es mi opinión que si se dirigiera, por medio del BOLETÍN MENSUAL, una invitación, otros países de América quizás enviarian delegados á este congreso. Comprendemos bien que es ya un poco tarde para enviar esta invitación por conducto del Departamento de Estado á los diferentes gobiernos. Dejo al buen juicio de usted el resolver si es posible que esa Oficina se haga representar oficialmente, asegurándole que todos los interesados en el congreso agradeceríamos que tal cosa se hiciese, y que la persona que viniere investida con el carácter de representante recibirá una acogida digna de su importancia.

Es sensible que esta comunicación no haya llegado á la Oficina hace dos ó más meses á fin de que las diferentes repúblicas americanas, deseosas de aprovechar la oportunidad que se les ofrecía, hubieran tenido suficiente tiempo para elegir sus representantes.

IRRIGACIÓN EN ARIZONA.

El Señor Don V. L. Navarro, Cónsul del Gobierno de México en Phœnix, Arizona, ha tenido la amabilidad de enviar á la Oficina de las Repúblicas Americanas parte de su informe anual en 1897–98, en que hace referencia especial á las condiciones climatéricas de Arizona y los beneficios que se obtendrían con un sistema de irrigación regular. El fomento del territorio, si se implantase un sistema de irrigación tal y como lo propone es, en el sentir del Cónsul, de grandes promesas.

Del informe precitado extractamos lo siguiente :

El Territorio de Arizona ocupa una extensión de 113,000 millas cuadradas, en su mayor parte montañosa. El area de cultivo comparada con el area total es muy pequeña. El cultivo de la tierra está circunscrito por lo general á los valles de los ríos Salado y Gila y las márgenes del Colorado.

La elevación general del territorio varía entre cerca de 100 piés sobre el nivel del mar en Yuma, sobre el río Colorado, y 13,000 piés en la cima del monte San Francisco, en la parte septentrional del territorio. Como 39,000 millas cuadradas de la superficie total están á una altura de 3,000 piés ; como 27,000 quedan alrededor de 3000 á 5,000 piés y cerca de 47,000 están situadas á más de 5,000 piés de elevación.

El territorio está dividido en dos grandes porciones climatéricas por la gran meseta del Colorado, que va del extremo noroeste del territorio á la parte sudeste. Dicha meseta tiene una suave vertiente hacia el norte, mientras que hacia el sudoeste es quebrada en casi todo su trayecto. Por esta razón los valles bajos que se encuentran al sudoeste de esta meseta son semitropicales, por lo que se refiere al clima y á pocas horas de viaje se llega á la más alta elevación de la meseta, en donde reina una temperatura estival de lo más agradable. Al norte de la meseta la temperatura es mucho más fría, y en las altas latitudes se encuentran las nieves perpetuas. Por causa de lo quebrado del terreno estas regiones del norte se emplean para la cría y la minería.

En las regiones situadas al norte de la meseta, la precipitación de las lluvias y las nieves es suficiente para usos agrícolas, si se pudiese labrar la tierra. Esta precipitación produce excelentes resultados, pues alimenta las corrientes de donde se toma el agua para el riego de los valles del sur, y los inmensos bosques, cuya extensión no tiene rival en ningún otro Estado de la Unión, conservan la humedad, manteniendo así las fuentes de los ríos Salado y Gila. Al sur de la meseta, en los valles, las lluvias son escasas. En Phœnix no pasa de ocho á diez pulgadas por año y en Yuma no excede de dos á cuatro pulgadas.

De aquí resulta que el riego es de absoluta necesidad para la agricultura. Dentro de los límites del valle del río Salado, cuya extensión es aproximadamente de 100 por 20 millas, es donde se encuentra la mayor área de cultivo. Phœnix, que es la capital del territorio, con una población de 12,000 habitantes, entre los cuales se cuentan cerca de 3,000 naturales de México, está situada cerca del centro de este valle. En los alrededores de la codad hay cerca de 250,000 acres de terreno irrigadiu, lo cual representa una pequeña parte del área irrigable del valle; pero el terreno cultivado hoy emplea toda el agua del río Salado durante la estación del verano, y de aquí resulta que es imposible extender la superficie de cultivo por falta de fuentes de riego.

Los 250,000 acres mencionados son regados por medio de canales de irrigación, cuya extensión total es de 72 millas, con 600 millas de zanjas laterales, y podrían regar mayor extensión de terreno si hubiera agua suficiente. La falta de ésta retarda en gran manera el desarrollo del valle, y este es el gran problema que interesa á los habitantes del Territorio, que por lo general derivan sus medios de subsistencia de los productos de la tierra. El terreno del valle, que tiene hasta más de 20 piés de profundidad, es de riquísima calidad, no dejando nada que desear en el particular. Produce, con riego adecuado, casi todos los productos de las zonas templada y semitropical en profusión maravillosa. Contiguas á esta limitada superficie de cultivo, en donde los terrenos de riego valen de $25 á $200 por acre, hay millares de acres de terreno igualmente rico, inútiles por falta de agua. Dichos terrenos son propiedad del Gobierno de los Estados Unidos y han sido abiertos á la colonización al precio uniforme de $1.25 por acre, concediéndose al colono siete años para hacer los pagos. Hoy parece seguro que estos terrenos baldíos estarán colonizados dentro de pocos años, porque se están haciendo trabajos con el objeto de aumentar el abasto de agua del valle.

Este aumento del abasto de agua se efectuará por medio del estancamiento de las aguas de las crecientes del río Salado. En la estación del invierno, durante las lluvias y nieves de las montañas que se encuentran á 60 millas al norte, el río Salado lleva un gran volumen de agua que va al río Gila y de éste al Colorado, que á su vez las lleva al golfo de California, causándose de esta manera un gran desperdicio. Ingenieros del Gobierno de los Estados Unidos han calculado que el agua que se pierde del río Salado durante el invierno es bastante para regar un millón de acres en el valle de dicho río, durante todo el año, si la distribución del agua fuese como debe serlo.

Se ha hecho la proposición de estancar el agua de estas crecientes de invierno, para usarlas durante el verano á medida que las necesidades así lo exijan, construyendo un gran estanque en las montañas, como á 60 millas al nordeste de Phœnix. El proyecto, desde el punto de vista de la ingeniería, es hacedero. El río Salado, en su curso hacia el valle, atraviesa las montañas, pasa por la gran hoya que forman estas y que no tiene otra salida que el cañon que lleva el nombre del mismo río.

El Gobierno de los Estados Unidos ha concedido esta hoya, conocida con el nombre de "Tonto Basin," á la compañía "Hudson Reservoir and Canal Company" para ser empleado como un estanque de acumulación. Dicha compañía ha terminado ya todos sus trabajos de ingeniería, así como los planos y especificaciones para la construcción de la represa, proponiéndose construir una á la cabecera del cañon, en el lugar en donde el río sale de la hoya formando un lago que tendrá 18 millas cuadradas y una profundidad de cien á doscientos piés. Será necesario construir una represa de 200 piés de alto y cerca de 600 de largo en la parte superior, aunque el cañon solo tiene 200 piés de ancho por el primer centenar de piés de fondo. El Territorio de Arizona ha concedido á la compañía el empleo del canal del río Salado para llevar las aguas del estanque al valle abajo; dichas aguas volverán al canal cuando sea necesario y serán conducidas por el cañon por una distancia de 30 millas hasta la cabecera del valle, en donde se encuentra la primera represa de distribución. Para construir este grande estanque de acumulación, que será el más grande del mundo, se gastará según cálculos cerca de $2,500,000. La compañía se ocupa con actividad en conseguir los fondos necesarios. Existe el propósito de vender las aguas del estanque á las compañías del canal de irrigación que hoy explotan este negocio en el valle, y según se dice, dichas compañías están deseosas de aumentar de esta suerte la corta cantidad de agua que hoy pueden vender á los agricultores. Hay algunas de estas compañías que ya han hecho contratos con la del estanque. Los agricultores en la actualidad pagan á razón de $1.25 á $2.25 al año por agua, y las compañías del canal, cuando comiencen á repartir agua del estanque, cobrarán á los agricultores $1 más por acre, para compensar así el pago que han de hacer á la compañía del estanque. Dícese, sin embargo, que los agricultores pagarán de la mejor voluntad el precio adicional, pues el aumento del uso del agua les permitirá coger cosechas doble de lo que hoy recogen. Por eso se comprende que cuando se lleve á cabo esta inmensa empresa, tendrá Arizona el sistema de irrigación más grande del mundo y las cosechas de los productos agrícolas de esta región, que hoy son tan abundantes en el valle, la harán una de las más prósperas del mundo.

EL HENEQUÉN Y EL PROCEDIMIENTO DE SU PREPARACIÓN.

El Henequén, llamado también sisal, es el producto de una planta fibrosa de la numerosa familia de las agaves. Es indígena del continente americano y se encuentra en gran abundancia en México. En los Estados Unidos son muy escasas las especies que se dan. Aun cuando de todas ellas se puede extraer la fibra, sólo las que producen ciertas especies de la planta, tanto por su cantidad cuanto por su calidad, son dignas de atención por su valor comercial. El "agave rigida," de la variedad "sisalona," es una de las más valiosas, produciendo abundantemente dicha fibra. No hay otra planta que haya llamado más la atención de los fabricantes de cordelería.

Las hojas de la variedad de que se hace mención tienen un color rojo oscuro, miden de 4 á 6 piés de largo, tienen de 3 á 6 pulgadas de ancho y están cubiertas de espinas. Cuando la planta ha llegado á su completo desarrollo presenta una vista agradable aun cuando no es bella, con sus largas hojas lanceoladas, llenas de espinas que salen del tronco corto y cilíndrico. Á llegar al período de madurez la planta produce un alto tallo llamado el mástil, que alcanza una altura de cerca de treinta piés, y cuya circunferencia es de diez y ocho á veinte pulgadas en la base, disminuyendo hasta llegar á la cúspide; una de las particularidades de esta planta es que rara vez ó nunca da semilla. Al caerse las flores se llevan consigo el ovario; las plantas nuevas se desarrollan al extremo de las ramas, que cuando han llegado á un altura de tres ó cuatro pulgadas caen al suelo y echan raíces. Las plantas viejas se reproducen por medio de retoños.

El henequén es un producto peculiar de Yucatán, y toma el nombre de sisal de la ciudad del mismo nombre, que es el segundo puerto de la Provincia, situado del lado noroeste de la península. Antes que los españoles fundasen sus colonias en el continente americano ya los naturales habían descubierto el valor de esta planta; pues cuando DE SOLÍS Y PINZÓN, navegantes españoles, desembarcaron allí en 1506 encontraron que los indios hacían uso de cuerdas hechas de la fibra del agave. Hace algunos años que se introdujo en las Bahamas, Cuba, Puerto Rico, Jamaica, y aun en el sur de la Florida esta variedad especial del agave, pero hasta ahora no ha tenido éxito en ninguno de los lugares mencionados. Sólo en Yucatán es que la planta halla terreno y clima á propósito. El henequén crece mejor en lugares estériles y pedregosos que no sirven para otros usos agrícolas; las sequías no lo afectan, la cosecha es contínua y un acre sembrado de esta planta produce algo más de una tonelada de fibra. Un corresponsal del " Farm Implement News" describe de la manera siguiente el procedimiento de la extracción de la fibra:

Cuando la planta ha llegado al estado de floración se cortan las hojas muy cerca del tronco y se acomodan, en sentido inverso unas de otras, en háces de á cincuenta hojas, los cuales se llevan á las máquinas. El corte de cincuenta háces ó sean 1,500 hojas se considera un buen día de trabajo. Para economizar el costo de trasporte, como las hojas rinden como cinco por ciento de fibra, por lo general hay una máquina montada á cada cien acres de terreno. La máquina que hoy se usa consta de una rueda horizontal provista de tiras de latón, colocadas trasversalmente, formando cuchillas sin filo. Se introduce la hoja de modo que uno de sus lados venga en contacto con la rueda que gira impulsada por un pequeño motor. Por medio de una palanca se aprieta la hoja contra las cuchillas, mientras que la parte gruesa de ésta está sostenida por medio de un cepo. Las cuchillas separan la corteza y algunos de los tejidos más suaves; luego se saca la hoja volviéndosela del otro lado, que se somete á la misma operación, hasta que solo quedan las fibras, las cuales se sacuden y se cuelgan al sol por algunas horas para secarlas. El resultado de esta operación es una fibra de mucha resistencia. La de calidad más fina es casi blanca, mientras que las inferiores son de color amarillento. Para producir fibras de la mejor calidad es necesario limpiar las hojas lo más pronto posible después de haber sido cortadas. Uno de los obstáculos principales que impiden la producción más barata de la fibra es la falta de una máquina buena para la decorticación, y aunque se han empleado mucho tiempo y dinero tratando de inventar una, hasta ahora todos los esfuerzos hechos no han tenido éxito.

El Almirantazgo inglés ha adoptado el cable de henequén de sisal como superior al de cáñamo de Manila. Es necesario alquitranar el cable de Manila cuando se empléa abordo, pero la superficie suave y la resina natural que conserva el producto de sisal evitan la necesidad de este remedio para protegerlo contra la fricción. Por otra parte el sisal es superior al cáñamo, por que es mucho más ligero, siendo su gravedad específica como 9 es á 15.

Durante el año fiscal que terminó el 30 de junio de 1898, México exportó á los Estados Unidos 68,432 toneladas de sisal, valoradas en $5,104,228, contra 62,839 toneladas, calculadas en $3,809,415, en 1897. Durante el mismo período los Estados Unidos importaron de las islas Filipinas 48,541 toneladas de cáñamo de Manila, avaluadas en $3,092,285, contra 38,526 toneladas, valoradas en $2,701,651, en 1897.

El Encargado de Negocios de Francia en México envió recientemente á su Gobierno un informe sobre la creciente importancia de la fibra de sisal, que, según él dice, es muy difícil que puedan conseguir las casas europeas, pues los Estados Unidos prácticamente monopolizan el negocio en este ramo. Los principales Estados de México que producen el sisal son Tamaulipas, San Luís, Guerrero, Coahuila, y Nuevo León.

COMERCIO MISCELÁNEO.

REPÚBLICA ARGENTINA.

Principales Artículos Exportados al Brasil. Los principales artículos exportados de la República Argentina al Brasil durante la primera mitad del presente año fueron 1,868 pipas, 3,220 barricas y 6,837 bocoyes de sebo, 42,121 toneladas de trigo, 9,044 toneladas de maíz, 11,367 toneladas de harina, 3,160 toneladas de salvado, 1,655 sacos de semillas para pájaros, 327,446 fardos de heno, y 512 cajas de mantequilla. Solamente un fardo de lana figuró en la exportación.

BRASIL.

Importación de Carbón de los Estados Unidos. El periódico denominado "Black Diamond," que es el órgano oficial de la Asociación de Carboneros de Illinois y Wisconsin, hace notar el hecho de que un vapor, cargado de 3,000 toneladas de carbón, salió últimamente de Newport News para Rio Janeiro. Agrega dicha publicación que este barco es el primero de una línea de buques carboneros de igual porte que harán viajes semanales á Rio Janeiro, hasta que acaben de entregar á los traficantes brasileños en este artículo 150,000 toneladas de carbón que han sido contratadas. Este no es más que el principio del restablecimiento de las relaciones comerciales normales que fueron interrumpidas por la guerra con España. Según el "Black Diamond," este carbón fué vendido en competencia directa con el de Inglaterra, á pesar de que todas las condiciones mercantiles favorecían á los agentes británicos. Conviene observar que Inglaterra, Francia y Alemania están establecidas en los mercados brasileños y gozan de facilidades con que no cuentan los exportadores de los Estados Unidos, tales como sucursales de bancos, líneas directas de vapores y comunicación telegráfica. Todo esto debe ser establecido por los capitalistas americanos si quieren sacar ventajas del comercio extranjero.

Propuestas para la Construcción de Obras Hidráulicas. Hasta el 10 de noviembre se recibirán propuestas relativas al traspaso por el Gobierno del Estado de Para, del derecho exclusivo, por el término de sesenta años, prorogable por diez años más, bajo ciertas condiciones, de suplir de agua potable á la ciudad de Belem, capital del Estado. Se pueden obtener informes sobre este particular de los representantes del Brasil en los Estados Unidos.

ECUADOR.

Disminución de la Cosecha de Cacao. La cosecha de cacao de la República en 1897 fué de 14,800 toneladas, ó sea 330,293 quintales. Esta cantidad no se compara favorablemente con el producto de los últimos años, que en 1896 fué de 15,300 toneladas, en 1895 de 16,000 toneladas, y en 1894 de 17,467 toneladas.

MÉXICO.

Embarques de Plata á los Estados Unidos. El vapor *Acapulco*, en uno de sus últimos viajes de Mazatlán á San Francisco, llevó 140 barras de plata valoradas en $209,016.12; siete de oro con un valor de $47,344.88; siete cajas de mate, valoradas en $10,080.79; $150,000 en plata acuñada, y $2,846 en moneda de oro.

Nuevo Ferrocarril. El Cónsul Thompson escribe de Progreso, con fecha de 22 agosto, lo siguiente: "Los Estados de Yucatán y Campeche están ahora unidos por ferrocarril. Las ceremonias de la inauguración, que se verificaron el 29 de julio, fueron muy imponentes, y el banquete que se dió en esa ocasión fué presidido por el Ministro de Justicia de México, en representación del Presidente Díaz. La conclusión de este ferrocarril marca una era importante en la historia de ambos Estados."

Exportación de Goma Elástica ó Hule. La exportación de hule de México durante el año que terminó el 30 de julio de 1897 fué menor que en los cuatro años pasados, y ascendió solamente á 142,654 libras, con un valor de $63,126, plata.

Ganancias de los Ferrocarriles. La Compañía de Ferrocarril Mexicano da el siguiente informe sobre sus ganancias, en dinero mexicano, durante el mes de agosto: ganancias totales, $500,799; aumento, $663; gastos de explotación, $264,251; aumento, $22,397; ganancias netas, $236,548; disminución, $21,734; descuento, etc., $126,081; disminución, $12,859; excedente para el pago de bonos, $110,467; disminución, $8,875. La Compañía de Ferrocarril Mexicano dice que sus ganancias totales durante el mes de agosto alcanzaron á $281,491, ó sea un aumento de $46,744; gastos de explotación, $159,233; aumento, $2,147; ganancias netas, $122,258; aumento, $44,957.

NICARAGUA.

Nueva Línea de Vapores. El Agente Consular CLANCY escribe de Bluefields á la Oficina que á partir del 1° de octubre la Bluefields Steamship Company estableció un servicio de vapores entre aquel puerto y Mobile, Alabama, los cuales harán viajes tres veces al mes. Los barcos están arreglados para pasajeros y carga. Los Señores ORR y LAUBENHEIMER tenían antes del mes de enero de 1898 una línea de vapores entre Bluefields y Mobile, pero con el establecimiento de la nueva compañía aquélla suspendió su servicio. Ahora que va á establecerlo de nuevo será de mucha utilidad para los traficantes de madera de Mobile, porque es allí donde se compra casi toda la madera que se usa en Bluefields y en sus alrededores. Los vapores empleados en este tráfico son el *Sunmia* y el *Tarl*.

Rieles de Acero. Dice el Boston "Herald" que un vapor frutero noruego llegó últimamente de Bluefields, Nicaragua, con un cargamento de bananos y regresó vía Baltimore después de haber tomado un cargamento de rieles de acero en este último puerto. Se cree que este es el primer cargamento completo de rieles de acero que se envía de los Estados Unidos á la América Central. Asegúrase que la Compañía de Carnegie ha recibido otros pedidos.

PARAGUAY.

Nueva Oficina de Información. Se ha fundado en la ciudad de Asunción una cámara ó asociación comercial conocida con el nombre de Centro Comercial del Paraguay. El objeto de esta asociación es suministrar informes sobre todo lo que se relaciona con los productos, costumbres, leyes y comercio de la República, y ayudar á todas las personas que deseen establecer relaciones comerciales con los exportadores y otros hombres de negocios del Paraguay.

ESTADOS UNIDOS.

Derechos de Importación sobre los Libros en Puerto Rico. El Ministerio de la Guerra ha ordenado que los libros impresos en inglés sean admitidos en los puertos portorriqueños que se encuentran bajo el dominio de los Estados Unidos pagando un derecho de 2 pesos y medio ($2.315) por cada 100 kilógramos. Durante la dominación española, se imponía un derecho diferencial de 13 pesos (12.038) por cada 100 kilógramos sobre los libros impresos en lengua inglesa.

Locomotoras para Australia. Uno de los últimos números del "Australian" dice que se han aceptado propuestas de algunas casas de los Estados Unidos para la construcción de dos locomotoras para un camino de hierro de vía angosta entre Wangaratta y Whitefield, Australia. Las dos locomotoras costarán como $18,000. Es digno de notar el hecho de que el precio mencionado es, según el citado periódico, $1,500 más barato que el más bajo presentado

BOLETIM MENSAL

DA

SECRETARIA DAS REPUBLICAS AMERICANAS,

UNIÃO INTERNACIONAL DAS REPUBLICAS AMERICANAS.

Vol. VI.	OCTUBRO de 1898.	No. 4.

REPUBLICA ARGENTINA.

AUGMENTO DOS DIREITOS ADUANEIROS.

No dia 23 de Setembro, o Ministro BUCHANAN telegraphou á Secretaria de Estado que, de conformidade com a lei emittida pelo Congresso Argentino no dia 22 desse mez e vigente desde essa data até o 31 de Dezembro, os direitos aduaneiros se augmentam da maneira seguinte: Os direitos de cinco por cento ou menos se dobram; os que excedem de 5 por cento ficam sujeitos a um 10 por cento addicional, e a 10 por cento mais sobre a quantia total dos direitos aduaneiros, addicionando para a cobrança dos direitos específicos o valor da mercadoria.

Os seguintes artigos figuram entre os que caem sob a classificação de cinco por cento ad valorem na tarifa argentina: cortiça, joias, arame, barbantes, folha de lata, ferro, zinco, chumbo em linguados e em barras, machinas de coser e peças das mesmas, essencia de alcatrão, azougue, machinas para installações electricas e hydraulicas, com excepção dos medidores e dos accessorios electricos, tijolos refractarios e de barro, machinas de tosquiar lã, motores de vapor, relogios de vapor, relogios de ouro, de prata e de prateados, machinas para agricultura e filaças de lã. Sob a classificação de 2½ por cento se encontram os seguintes artigos: algodão em fardos, zinco em folhas, polpa de madeira, lupulo, pello de coelho, gelatina, etc.   Cobram-se direitos especificos sobre os viveres, bebidas, tabaco, collarinhos e punhos, chapéos e feltro para chapéos, phosphoros, kerosene, · saccos de grãos, cartas de jogar, estearina e oleo de linhaça.

DESCOBRIMENTO DE MINAS DE CARVÃO.

O Commandante Nuñez, official da Marinha Argentina, regressou recentemente da Terra do Fogo e trouxe comsigo amostras de carvão descoberto alli, as quaes deram os resultados mais satisfactorios ao serem provadas nas locomotivas que funccionam nos trabalhos do porto de Buenos Aires.   O carvão ensaiado é de formação superficial, do qual se deduz naturalmente que, si o carvão é tão bom na superficie, será muito melhor sua qualidade quando se extrae da formação mais profunda.

Si este descobrimento chega a dar os resultados que se esperam, o paiz entrará n'uma era de desenvolvimento manufactureiro que o fará mais rico ainda que o cultivo do trigo.   Necessitar-se-há pouco tempo para provar o verdadeiro valor do carvão.

A "Review of the River Plate" ainda quando admitte que o dito carvão seja de boa qualidade, não entretem illusões acerca da quantidade disponivel, e diz assim :

É muito agradavel saber que as amostras de carvão trazidas de Terra do Fogo tèm dado bons resultados, melhores talvez do que esperavam todos, quer si tivessem interesse nos descobrimentos ou não.   Propõe-se mandar machinas com o objecto de determinar a quantidade de carvão disponivel.   Ainda si se provar que a qualidade do mineral é tão boa como a das amostras que tèm sido submettidas á analyse, é provavel, todavia, que a quantidade seja tão pequena que os depositos não tenham valor, ou que o lugar onde se encontre o carvão em grandes quantidades seja sob o ponto de vista commercial, inaccessivel.

IMPORTAÇÕES DOS ESTADOS UNIDOS.

O Boletim No. 22 da Associação de Exportadores dos Estados Unidos contem as seguintes informações sobre as exportações dos Estados Unidos para a Republica Argentina:

Continuam chegando em grande numero pedidos por machinas e accessorios electricos.   Uma casa de Broad street, Nova York, recebeu recentemente um pedido por estes effeitos electricos no valor de $20,000.   O futuro da electricidade applicada a todos os ramos da industria na Republica Argentina é muito promettedor.   O valor médio dos embarques de machinas e effeitos electricos verificados em cada vapor dos que tèm sahido do porto de Nova York no ultimo trimestre, se calcula de $7,000 a $10,000.

Os tramvias electricos da Republica Argentina estão provistos de equipamentos dos Estados Unidos. Durante os ultimos dous mezes quasi todos os vapores que têm sahido para Buenos Aires têm levado pelo menos materiaes para carros, avaliados em $50,000. A Companhia de Tramvias de Belgrano tem recebido a maior parte deste material. A companhia chamada " La Capital Co.," com escriptorios estabelecidos em Nova York embarca grandes quantidades de apparelhos electricos, incluindo equipamentos para os carros de sua propria companhia de tramvias. Diz-se que em principios de Novembro, a companhia terá promptos para embarcar 1,000 carros de carga que foram construidos segundo contracto.

Seguem em importancia as exportações de ferro manufacturado que se fazem de Nova York para a Republica Argentina, commercio que tem ido augmentando gradualmente. Os tres ultimos vapores que sahiram para Buenos Aires levaram mais de $40,000, principalmente em machinas de ceifar.

Cordoalha, papel, ferragens, caixas abatidas, tubos de ferro e utensilios domesticos são outros dos artigos que tem procura na Republica Argentina. Uma casa de South street tem recebido informações de que o mercado para obras de vidro, artigos para lampadas, oleados, linoleo, tapetes e capachos baratos é muito bom. O correspondente tambem accrescenta que ha boa opportunidade para dominar o mercado em artigos de usos sanitarios fabricados nos Estados Unidos.

Segundo noticias recebidas da Republica Argentina; quasi todas as companhias de tramvias de Buenos Aires estenderão suas linhas á povoações vizinhas e por conseguinte se exigirá grande quantidade de materiaes para esse objecto.

A barca *Adam W. Spies* que ultimamente sahiu com carga para Buenos Aires levou uma grande quantidade de artigos manufacturados nos Estados Unidos, entre outros machinas agricolas no valor de $45,000, machinas de coser por $12,000 e ferragens e cadeiras por $10,000. O vapor *Ballucia* que tambem sahiu com carga para aquelle porto levou machinas agricolas no valor de $50,000, carruagens no de $5,000 e moinhos de vento por valor de $10,971.

NOVA ESTAÇÃO DE CARVÃO DOS ESTADOS UNIDOS.

Uma noticia authentica recebida de Norfolk, Va., diz que as amostras de carvão virginiano enviadas para a Republica Argentina têm resultado satisfactorias e que se farão immediatamente outros embarques. Os Senhores CASTNER, CURRAN e BULLITT, de Philadelphia, agentes da Pocahontas Coal Co., têm estabelecido uma agencia em Buenos Aires sob a direcção do Sr. CARL H. ARNAL. Este cavalheiro tem sido por algum tempo o vice consul em Norfolk das Republicas de Colombia e Venezuela. Tambem se assegura que varios navios carregados de carvão sahirão em breve de Lamberts Point, Va., com destino a Buenos Aires, e se espera que regressarão d'alli carregados, ainda que seja parcialmente, de productos argentinos.

BOLIVIA.

ABOLIÇÃO DO MONOPOLIO DE PHOSPHOROS.

Tem-se recebido informação de que o Governo boliviano tem revogado o decreto de 14 de Março ultimo, relativo á cobrança de direitos sobre os phosphoros que se importarem do estrangeiro, e tem suspendido provisoriamente a lei de 18 de Novembro de 1896, a qual estabeleceu um monopolio de phosphoros na Republica e impoz sobre os phosphoros estrangeiros um direito addicional.

D'aqui em diante, os phosphoros que se importarem na Bolivia pagarão sómente os direitos especificados na tarifa geral de alfandegas.

TRABALHOS DA COMMISSAO DE LIMITES.

Ainda que existe todavia alguma duvida a respeito do resultado final da questão de limites entre a Republica Argentina e Chile, tudo parece indicar uma solução pacifica. Tambem Bolivia está fazendo uma demarcação de seus limites, e o Governo deseja que fica bem definidos pelo lado da Republica Argentina em ordem a por termo a toda classe de reclamações de territorio no futuro.

Uma commissão boliviana sahiu ha pouco de Sucre, capital da Republica, com o objecto de dar principio a seus trabalhos em La Quiaca. As medidas e estudos que a dita Commissão vai a fazer de accordo com outra commissão argentina serão de caracter preliminar. Farão-se somente observações topographicas, em qualidade de obra preparatoria para os trabalhos da convenção internacional que deve fixir definitivamente os limites. Tanto a Commissão boliviana como a argentina se dividirão em duas secções e estudarão o terreno ao este e ao oeste de La Quiaca, respectivamente. Os dous chefes das secções bolivianas são o Senhor Muñoz D. Reyes, engenheiro experimentado e o Coronel Muñoz, um dos primeiros estadistas da Republica.

BRAZIL.

PARA ASSISTIR ÁS CEREMONIAS DO ANNIVERSARIO.

Os couraçados *Oregon* e *Iowa*, acompanhados dos carvoeiros *Celtic* e *Scindia*, sahiram de Nova York para Honolulu no dia 13 de Outubro. O *Abarenda* sahiu alguns dias antes da esquadra. Antes de sahirem os couraçados em sua longa viagem, o Ministro da Marinha, o Honrado JOHN D. LONG, deu ordens ao Capitão BARKER, Commandante do *Oregon*, que chegasse ao porto do Rio de Janeiro com os dous navios de guerra antes do dia 15 de Novembro, dia do anniversario do estabelecimento da Republica do Brazil, para que estes representem a marinha dos Estados Unidos e tomem parte na celebração desta data. Espera-se que os navios cheguem a Rio no dia 10 de Novembro.

A COLHEITA DE CAFÉ EM 1898.

O Consul Geral Americano, o Sr. SEEGER, de Rio Janeiro, enviou um interessante relatorio sobre a producção e o movimento do café na Republica do Brazil durante o anno que terminou em 30 de Junho de 1898, do qual tomam-se os seguintes dados estatisticos:

ENTRADAS DURANTE O ANNO.

Rio Janeiro.	Saccos.	Libras.
Por estrada de ferro	2, 300, 690	303, 691, 080
Por vapores de cabotagem	840, 099	110, 893, 068
Outras embarcações	1, 163, 849	153, 617, 068
Em transito	232, 941	30, 748, 212
Total	4, 537, 579	598, 949, 428
Santos	6, 152, 594	812, 142, 408
Victoria (calculados)	400, 000	52, 800, 000
Bahia (calculados)	250, 000	33, 000, 000
Ceará (calculados)	20, 000	2, 640, 000
Total geral	11, 360, 173	1, 499, 531, 836

SAHIDAS PARA O ESTRANGEIRO.

	Saccos.	Libras.
Estados Unidos	4, 740, 638	625, 746, 216
Paizes da Europa	5, 971, 468	770, 233, 776
Cabo de Boa Esperança	149, 300	19, 707, 600
Rio da Prata, etc	101, 533	13, 402, 356
Total	10, 962, 939	1, 429, 107, 948

Calculando á razão de $8.75 pela média, por sacco de 132 libras, o valor total desta exportação, alcançou a $96,450,716.25.

Durante os ultimos tres annos calendarios os embarques de café effectuados no Brazil foram como segue:

De—	1895.	1896.	1897.
	Saccos.	*Saccos.*	*Saccos.*
Santos	3, 554, 696	4, 156, 567	5, 621 762
Rio Janeiro.............................	2, 763, 720	2, 784, 958	4, 066, 734
Victoria.................................	307, 438	273, 255	372, 221
Bahia	264, 775	260, 981	292, 480
Ceara.................................	20, 202	6, 000	6, 568
Total	6, 910, 831	7, 418, 761	10, 359, 765

Os preços de Nova York durante a colheita do anno passado, por café No. 7, diminuiram de $7\frac{1}{16}$ centavos por libra, No. 1° de Julho de 1897, a $5\frac{7}{8}$ centavos em 1° de Maio de 1898. Para o 1° de Julho de 1898 o preço tinha subido até $6\frac{1}{4}$ centavos.

Para o 30 de Junho de 1898, as existencias eram de 1,227,960 saccos, como segue: Café de Rio, 268,197 saccos; Santos, 316,793 saccos; Nova York, Baltimore, e Nova Orleans, 643,000. Para a mesma data as existencias á vista no mundo calcularam-se em 5,436,000 saccos, o que equivale a quasi metade do consumo de um anno.

Na actualidade ha um excesso de café, o qual tem produzido uma depreciação nos preços. Este estado de cousas tem sido accentuado mais durante os ultimos dous annos, ainda que as causas a que obedece vêm de muito atraz. Durante a decada anterior a 1897, a cotação do café produziu grandes ganhos aos agricultores deste producto, dando em resultado um augmento enorme na area de plantações de café durante o dito periodo. Hoje estes milhões de arvores começam a produzir, e o que até ha pouco era uma industria que a vezes rendia até 150 por cento por anno, apenas dá hoje com que suster-se. Para o proximo anno se espera que a colheita seja muito menor. A experiencia de antigo conhecida apresenta-se outra vez; duas colheitas abundantes consecutivas dão, por causa da condição exhausta das arvores, uma colheita escassa.

Dous são os calculos que se têm feito para a colheita de 1898–99, um official e o outro commercial, cuja variação é notavel. Eis aqui os ditos calculos:

Estado.	Official.	Commercial.
	Saccos.	*Saccos.*
Rio Janeiro	2, 500, 000	3, 000, 000
Santos..	4, 500, 000	6, 000, 000
Total	7, 000, 000	9, 000, 000

De aqui se verá que ainda os calculos mais altos dão um milhão de saccos menos que os produzidos na colheita de 1897–98.

As plantações de café do Brazil têm chamado a attenção ultimamente dos capitalistas europeos. Syndicatos inglezes e alguns belgas têm comprado grandes plantações nos Estados de Minas Geraes e São Paulo. Em Antuerpia foi estabelecida. uma sociedade com agencia em Santos, com o objecto de comprar café dos agricultores directamente e de vendel-o por retalho na Europa sem empregar os serviços de um terceiro.

No Rio de Janeiro e em Santos se espera para fins de Outubro uma grande partida de inglezes, commerciantes, capitalistas, engenheiros e peritos em materias agricolas, que viajaram pelo interior do Brazil com o objecto, segundo se diz, de comprar propriedades agricolas e industriaes cujo preço tenha sido rebaixado. Aos preços que hoje se offerecem em venda as ditas propriedades, podem ser feitos bons negocios, segundo a opinião das pessoas melhor informadas na materia, si os capitalistas não estão obrigados a esperar resultados immediatos. Assim pois, os inglezes, cuja posição nas finanças e o commercio do Brazil é de primeira ordem, podem chegar a alcançar o dominio do commercio de café entre o Brazil e os Estados Unidos, já seja por razão do cambio, ou por serem donos de uma grande parte da area de producção daquelle paiz, sempre que não intervenha uma influencia estranha.

RECEITA DAS ALFANDEGAS E RENDA INTERIOR.

O Director da Renda Publica da Republica do Brazil, em data de 13 de Agosto, submetteu um relatorio (sujeito á revisão) das entradas produzidas pelos direitos de alfandega e os impostos internos durante o primeiro semestre de 1898. Deste relatorio extrahimos os seguintes dados estatisticos:

No primeiro semestre do exercicio corrente a receita de alfandega elevou-se a 119,161$180, a qual mostra uma diminuição de 3,742$896 comparada com a do primeiro semestre de 1897, e de 23,302$261 comparada com a do periodo correspondente de 1896.

Desta somma, a quantia correspondente aos direitos de importação foi de 102,933$069, no primeiro semestre de 1898, a qual é inferior á arrecadada em 1897, em 9,670$101, e á arrecadada em 1896, em 14,518$931.

A receita de 17 das alfandegas soffreu uma diminuição e notou-se um augmento de receita em só 6 alfandegas, numa das quaes, a de Rio Grande do Sul, este augmento se deveu a que foram cerradas as alfandegas de Porto Alegre e Pelotas.

A receita da alfandega de Rio de Janeiro para o primeiro semestre de 1898 foi inferior á de 1897 em 6,554$537 ou 16.02 por cento, e á de 1896 em 13,174$340 ou 32.17 por cento.

A renda interior no primeiro semestre dos tres annos de que se trata, foi como se segue :

```
1896...................................................................... 5,984,314$33
1897...................................................................... 6,659,984$33
1898...................................................................... 8,579,018$44
```

Nas entradas occorridas durante a primeira metade de 1898, estão comprehendidos os productos dos novos impostos sobre phosphoros e apolices de seguro estrangeiras, calculados em 745$073 producto daquelles, e em 35$275 o producto destas. Houve um augmento consideravel na renda produzida dos impostos sobre tabaco e as bebidas, e uma diminuição na renda produzida por sellos e trespasso de vapores e bonos do governo.

CHILE.

ESTATISTICA COMMERCIAL PARA 1897.

O "Chilian Times" de 31 de Agosto diz o seguinte:

Acaba de sahir da typographia do Universo o volume de estatistica commercial da Republica para o anno de 1897. È um livro de 700 paginas e preparado com cuidado. O chefe da Repartição de Estatistica, o Senhor WENCESLAO ESCOBAR, deve ser felicitado pela apparição desse volume varios mezes antes da epocha em que geralmente se publica. A obra trata das seguintes materias: commercio Especial, Movimento da Navegação, Commercio Maritimo Interior, Estatistica Retrospectiva e Commercio de Transito. Tem-se omisso a secção intitulada Commercio Geral, que tinha figurado nos volumes anteriores, por ser considerada inutil.

Houve uma diminuição consideravel no commercio em 1897, comparado com 1896. Antes de proceder a dar as cifras, convem notar que, como de costume, os valores são dados em pesos de trinta e oito pennys. O valor das importações foi de $65,502,805, e o das exportações, de $64,754,133. O valor total das importações e exportações foi de $130,256,938, ou $18,185,281 menos que o total em 1896. Nesta diminuição de $18,185,281, a somma de $8,580,000 corresponde ás importações, e a de $9,605,281 ás exportações. Esta foi a quarta vez na historia da Republica desde 1844, anno em que se levantaram por primeira vez estatisticas commerciaes, em que o commercio do paiz tem soffrido uma reducção desta magnitude. Os outros annos foram 1877, 1885 e 1894. No primeiro destes a diminuição foi de $14,211,441; no segundo, de $29,591,686; e no terceiro, $13,956,952.

A diminuição das importações foi principalmente em artigos de alimentação, materias primas, machinas e outros artigos para industrias e artes, artigos de uso domestico, artigos para estradas de ferro e telegraphos, tabaco, artigos relacionados com as artes, sciencias e lettras, carvão, fazendas para camisas, fazendas · de algodão para calças, oleos e sebo. As importações estão divididas em 15 classes distinctas, e na tabella seguinte se encontrará o valor de cada uma dellas nos annos de 1896 e 1897:

Classificação.	1896, valor.	1897, valor.
Artigos de alimentação	$14, 287, 626	$13, 926, 523
Tecidos	12, 790, 619	13, 013, 719
Materias primas....................................	12, 021, 434	10, 319, 062
Roupa, joias e artigos para uso pessoal................	3, 585, 133	3, 597, 370
Machinas, machinismos, instrumentos e outros artigos para industrias e artes	9, 710, 679	9, 156, 614
Artigos de uso domestico	5, 187, 110	5, 025, 979
Artigos para estradas de ferro e telegraphos	2, 347, 432	1, 073, 744
Vinhos e licores.................................	934, 649	1, 178, 878
Rapé, tabaco, etc................................	580, 631	399, 401
Mineraes e ouro e prata em barras................	20, 726	11, 267
Artigos para as artes, sciencias e lettras..........	1, 297, 941	1, 089, 023
Drogas e artigos medicinaes e para objectos industriaes..	1, 179, 509	1, 113, 469
Artigos diversos.....	164, 850	133, 345
Armas e seus accessorios	9, 787, 634	5, 387, 675
Moeda metallica e bilhetes de banco	186, 832	76, 733
Total.................................	74, 082, 805	65, 502, 805

Notou-se uma diminuição de $2,309,934 na exportação de productos agricolas, principalmente trigo, cevada, nozes, feno e ervilhas. Quanto aos productos mineraes, houve uma diminuição de $6,160,000, principalmente em nitrato, prata em barras, borato de cal, mineral de prata e de cobre, e regulo de cobre e prata. Tambem houve uma diminuição de $549,065 na exportação de productos animaes, principalmente em couros, lã e presuntos.

REPUBLICA DE COLOMBIA.

CONSELHOS AOS EXPORTADORES.

O periodico francez "Moniteur Officiel" publica um artigo sobre os methodos que se devem empregar para o desenvolvimento do commercio com a Republica de Colombia, dando instrucções acerca da maneira de empacotar mercadorias com destino a este paiz. O assumpto é de muito interesse para os commerciantes dos Estados Unidos e praticamente se resolve tendo em consideração que dos dous methodos empregados para augmentar o commercio, os annuncios e os agentes viajantes, aquelle deve ser considerado como o precursor deste. Ainda que os prospectos, as revistas do mercado, boletins industriaes e circulares commerciaes são methodos excellentes para preparar o terreno e chamar a attenção para os productos estrangeiros, estes devem ter como sup- plemento agentes activos e emprehendedores que fallem hespanhol e que levem comsigo cartões illustrados e amostras dos artigos que offerecem em venda, assim como tudo que possa persuadir ao comprador e convencel-o da superioridade do artigo que se lhe offerece. Não é de importancia que o agente represente um só ramo da industria, mas para reduzir as despezas de viagem, pode representar varias fabricas, e si leva um bom sortimento de amos- tras pode contar com segurança com lucros consideraveis para as casas interessadas.

O escriptor opina que bons resultados seguirão o estabelecimento de armazens de amostras em Bogota e Medellin. Estes devem estar a cargo de agentes de confiança, habilitados para dar informa- ções completas relativas aos artigos expostos e ao mesmo tempo arranjar condições convenientes para a venda dos artigos.

Quando se embarcam mercadorias é importante que sejam empacotadas com o maior cuidado; os volumes não devem exceder de 80 centimetros de comprimento, 57 de largura e 55 de espessura, sendo seu peso médio de 70 a 75 kilogrammas. As mercadorias que se embarcam em pacotes devem ser bem envoltas em papel e pannos de lã e depois asseguradas com bandas de metal. Si se empregarem caixas, deve cuidar-se de que estas sejam feitas de um material que impeça a humidade, porque com frequencia acontece que artigos finos soffrem prejuizos no transito por causa de descuidados neste particular: para o objecto ha muito boas caixas com forro interior de zinco, e na Colombia estas caixas são artigo de commercio regular Artigos pesados de ferro é machinas devem ser empacotados em caixas fortes de modo que as partes mais pesadas estejam separadas e os parafusos, arrebites, etc., vão em barris. Bem vale a pena assegurar as mercadorias por mar e por terra ainda que este augmenta um pouco os gastos de transporte.

PERSPECTIVA DO CANAL DE PANAMÁ.

Alguns dos directores e representantes da Companhia do Canal de Panamá chegaram ultimamente a Nova York, procedentes do Isthmo. Um delles, o Sr. R. G. WARD, fallando ao que parece em nome de todos, disse publicamente que, a sua opinião, a situação actual dos negocios da Companhia é critica, e suggeriu o pensamento "de fazer uma proposta definitiva, que tenha por objecto o que os americanos cooperem á conclusão do canal e sejam em parte donos da obra." É evidente que o Sr. WARD não crê que o canal pode ser terminado sem a ajuda dos Estados Unidos, e está decididamente em favor da empreza pelo Isthmo de Panamá em opposição á de Nicaragua.

COSTA RICA.

MUDANÇAS NA LEI ADUANEIRA.

Segundo informações recebidas pelo Governo britannico do seu Consul em San José, um direito de dous centavos por kilogramma foi imposto sobre todas as madeiras de construcção e um de seis centavos sobre as madeiras de marcenaria que se importarem em Porto Limon, para uso na Provincia de Limon, as quaes, quando se importaram anteriormente pelo Porto Limon para uso na provincia, entraram livres de direitos.

Tambem o direito de importação sobre assucar refinado e assucar branco pulverisado foi augmentado de 11 a 20 centavos por kilogramma e sobre assucar de todas as outras qualidades de 7 a 15 centavos. O direito sobre cacáo moido foi augmentado de 13 a 20 centavos por kilogramma e o direito sobre cacáo na casca, de 7 a 15 centavos por kilogramma.

EXPORTAÇÃO DE CAFÉ EM 1897-98.

O Director de Estatistica da Republica dá as seguintes cifras relativas á exportação de café durante o exercicio que terminou no dia 30 de Junho de 1898. Estas cifras mostram um augmento de 2,000 saccos (264,000 libras) sobre a exportação de 1896-97, e de 6,000 saccos (792,000 libras) sobre a de 1895-96.

Rotas.	Saccos.	Kilogrammas.
Para Nova York pela Linha Atlas	94,075	5,084,787
Para Inglaterra pela Linha Royal Mail	80,358	4,166,064
Para Inglaterra pela Linha Lyon e Cox	52,983	2,882,113
Para Inglaterra pela Linha Allemã	45,731	2,567,717
Para Inglaterra pela Linha Franceza	18,829	1,056,251
Para Inglaterra por outras linhas	5,515	328,257
Grande total	297,491	16,085,189

EQUADOR.

ALGUNS PONTOS DA MENSAGEM DO PRESIDENTE.

O Presidente Alfaro apresentou sua mensagem annual ao Congresso no dia 9 de Agosto ultimo. Segundo este documento, a condição da Republica do Equador está melhorando notavelmente. Assegura o Presidente que a Repartição de Estatisticas das Alfandegas tem sido completamente reorganisada, e que os dados que agora se dão podem ser considerados por fidedignos. Sendo isto o caso, elle annuncia com satisfação que as exportações em 1897 augmentaram cerca de 50 por cento sobre as de 1896.

Os algarismos que o Presidente dá em sua mensagem são os seguintes: Exportações em 1896, 21,862,324 sucres; exportações em 1897, 31,025,382 sucres; importações em 1897, 18,004,048 sucres.

O Presidente diz que esta quantia deve ser augmentada em 25 por cento, porque as avaliações dadas no relatorio de alfandegas são indubitavelmente muito baixas. Em consequencia, o valor das importações ascende, pelo menos, a 22,000,000 de sucres. O Governo propõe-se elevar a avaliação official sobre a qual se cobram os direitos, e para este fim tem-se nomeado uma commissão.

GUATEMALA.

VALOR DO CAPITAL ALLEMÃO EMPREGADO EM GUATEMALA.

O periodico francez, "Moniteur Officiel du Commerce," diz que durante varios annos as exportações de Guatemala têm sido muito em excesso das importações. Em 1896 a exportação representou um valor total de 23,085,000 pesos ($11,373,980), contra uma importação por valor de 9,143,000 pesos ($4,503,756). Parece á primeira vista vantajosa para Guatemala esta situação, mas o *deficit* annual que se nota mostra o contrario. Este estado anormal de cousas se deve ao facto de que a maior parte das plantações de café pertencem a companhias allemães, e os lucros obtidos pelo capital empregado passam á Allemanha na forma de dividendos. Assegura-se que o capital allemão empregado na

Republica ascende a mais de 150,000,000 marcos ($35,700,000), e, não obstante isso, não ha mais de 500 allemães residentes no paiz.

MEXICO.

MERCADO PROMETTEDOR.

O Mexico apresenta um campo muito promettedor ao exportador americano, tanto por sua proximidade, como porque a demanda de toda a classe de artigos, especialmente de manufacturas, é muito grande e augmenta cada dia. O periodico "Modern Mexico" diz que ainda que o consumo de productos estrangeiros augmentará notavelmente durante os proximos annos, os exportadores americanos não devem esperar demasiado das opportunidades que o dito mercado offerece na actualidade. Em primeiro lugar, ao fazer um calculo do consumo possivel de artigos importados, não se deve tomar em consideração ao presente mais da quarta parte da população do Mexico. Em outras palavras, 75 por cento, pelo menos, da população de Mexico compõe-se de indios e de peones que, provavelmente, não têm tido em toda sua vida, nem o desejo, nem os meios de comprar um só artigo importado. O numero de pequenos proprietarios de terrenos é muito pequeno, em proporção aos que ha nos Estados Unidos. O trabalho é barato, mas são muito escassos os operarios habeis, capazes de manejar machinas, e por isso o uso geral destas para economisar trabalho não pode fazer-se na escala em que se faz nos Estados Unidos. O total do commercio exterior do Mexico apenas pode ser comparado com o immenso commercio dos Estados Unidos, mas vai augmentando e aos fabricantes americanos seria mais facil e menos custoso tomar agora uma parte desse commercio, e continuar fazendo-o á medida que se va desenvolvendo, do que tratar de effectual-o quando as importações se tenham dobrado.

NOVO MOLHE.

Ainda que o novo molhe de Veracruz não está terminado todavia, já está ao serviço da alfandega. Tem 580 pés de comprimento e 80 de largura. Em baixamar ha 28 pés de profundi-

dade ao lado do dito mólhe. O primeiro navio que descarregou
no novo desembarcadouro foi o Tampican, da West India and
Pacific Steamship Company, barco de 3,126 toneladas de registro,
que mede 430 pés de comprimento e que tem 17 pés e 6 pollegadas de calado á próa e 21 pés 3 pollegadas á pôpa. Este navio
é o mais grande dos que entram ao dito porto. É possivel que
outro barco das mesmas dimensões descarregue ao outre lado e ao
mesmo tempo.

Com excepção dos barcos de cabotagem e dos carvoeiros, esta
foi a primeira vez que um navio poude descarregar toda a classe
de mercadorias no molhe geral. As novas facilidades para o commercio dão maior importancia ao porto, e farão mais prompto e
mais facil o despacho de embarcações, o qual, necessariamente, tem
de dar augmento ao commercio.

COMMERCIO COM FRANÇA.

O Consul de Mexico em Havre, Senhor COSTA Y NARVAEZ, tem
enviado ultimamente a seu Governo um relatorio muito extenso
sobre o commercio entre o Mexico e a França, fazendo referencia
especial ao porto de Havre. Deste relatorio se vê que os productos mexicanos exportados para a França durante o anno passado
ascenderam a 41,369,152 kilogrammas, dos quaes 80 por cento
entraram pelo porto de Havre. A exportação de café tem ido
augmentando, pois pela Alfandega de Havre passaram no anno
passado $5,000 saccos: isto é tanto mais notavel, quando se con-
sidera que todos os paizes productores sentiram uma diminuição
nos pedidos e uma baixa nos preços, como resultado do excesso de
producção no Brazil. Os páus de tinturaria do Mexico são reco-
nhecidos na França como de qualidade superior, particularmente o
páu de campeche que vem de Laguna, o qual, devido a sua boa
qualidade, é o que se usa em primeiro lugar para tingir artigos
finos de seda, chapéos, luvas, etc. Tambem ha grande demanda
de madeiras de Yucatán, Tuxpan, Veracruz e Tampica.

As madeiras de construcção e de marcenaria não se exportam
directamente do Mexico para os portos francezes, mas vão primeiramente para os portos da Inglaterra. Os preços variam segundo
as dimensões e qualidade das madeiras e segundo seu estado de
preservação, sendo de 20 a 28 francos por cada 50 kilos. O cedro

que se emprega na fabricação de caixas de cigarros, é reembarcado para Belgica, Allemanha, Suissa e outros paizes, onde o Governo não tem estabelecido, como na França, o monopolio de tabaco.

O canhamo e o hennequen vão em grandes quantidades ao porto de Nova York, e de alli são reembarcados para Londres, Hamburgo e Havre, porque algumas casas americanas têm monopolisado praticamente estas fibras e as vantagens que se obtêm de seu comercio. O comercio em pelles entre o Mexico e a França é comparativamente pequeno, e o mercado principal para este producto são os Estados Unidos. Vende-se muito bem na França a borracha que vem do Mexico, e é identica á que vem da America Central. O Consul faz referencia ao preço obtido pelos ultimos carregamentos (8 francos o kilogramma) como um incentivo a novos esforços para a producção deste artigo, o qual, devido ao grande desenvolvimento industrial dos ultimos annos, tem adquirido muita importancia na manufactura de bicyclettas, automobiles, etc.

A salsaparilha passa pelos mercados dos Estados Unidos antes de chegar á França, e o Senhor Costa y Narvaez attribue a este facto o que não seja muito appreciado este producto mexicano, porque perde muito de seu verdadeiro sabor com a permanencia em um paiz estrangeiro. O mel tem um rival no que se produz na França, e afim de proteger este ultimo, tem-se imposto um direito de importaço de 15 francos por cada 100 kilos sobre o artigo estrangeiro.

NICARAGUA.

NOVA LEI ADUANEIRA.

O Sr. M. J. Clancy, agente consular dos Estados Unidos em Bluefields, Nicaragua, communica á Secretaria em data de 20 de Setembro, remettendo-lhe copia da nova lei·aduaneira da Republica recentemente decretada. O texto completo da antiga lei aduaneira é dado no Boletim correspondente ao No. 20, publicação desta Secretaria.

Referindo-se ao presente decreto, o Sr. Clancy diz:

Por um decreto do Presidente, a nova lei aduaneira para o Estado de Nicaragua, copia da qual remetto junto, ficou vigente para o interior do paiz no dia 1º do corrente, e por proclamação publica foi declarada vigente para este porto e o Districto de Zelaya desde o dia 17 do corrente.

O augmento de direitos sobre todas as importações será pela média de 100 por cento sobre os da antiga lei aduaneira.   O arroz, feijão, milho e batatas que figuravam antigamente na lista dos artigos livres de direitos, pagarão d'ahi em diante um direito de dez centavos na moeda de Nicaragua (4 centavos ouro) por kilo.   Um kilo equivale a 2.20 libras.   A transferencia dos artigos mencionados para a lista dos sujeitos a direitos foi feita com o objecto de fomentar o cultivo destes em Nicaragua.   Diz-se que estes productos podem ser produzidos neste paiz em abundancia sem grande trabalho.   Tambem o cultivo destes productos dará em resultado o desenvolvimento dos recursos agricolas do paiz.

Por alguma razão inexplicavel, o sabão pela tarifa actual paga um direito de sómente 2 centavos na moeda de Nicaragua (.08 centavos ouro) por kilo, emquanto que pela antiga tarifa pagava 9 centavos em moeda de Nicaragua (.36 centavos ouro).

Como o padrão monetario de Nicaragua é de prata, pode se comprar com um dollar americano, quer de ouro, papel ou prata, por valor de duas e meia vezes mais do que com o peso ou sol de prata, ainda que cada um delles contem tanta prata como o dollar americano.

Os direitos sobre viveres, bebidas espirituosas, assucar e cerveja são dobrados. Na nova lei aduaneira não se dão os direitos sobre as tintas de diversas classes. Antes, nas facturas de mercadorias estrangeiras se dispoz que se designe o peso em kilos, ainda que os direitos foram pagos por libra, incluindo a caixa ou involtorio em que os artigos vêm empacotados.   Pela actual lei aduaneira os direitos serão cobrados sobre a base de um kilo de peso.   A seguinte condição anormal existe actualmente em Nicaragua.   Todas as mercadorias que se importam em San Juan del Norte (Greytown) entram livres de direitos, porque o porto é o que se chama um " porto livre," emquanto que as mercadorias que se importam em Bluefields ou Cape Gracias na costa do Atlantico, e em Corinto ou San Juan del Sur na costa do Pacifico pagam os direitos impostos de accordo com a nova tarifa de direitos sobre importações.

O Decreto do Presidente acima mencionado pelo Sr. CLANCY contem os seguintes artigos:

O PRESIDENTE DO ESTADO,

Considerando, Que a tarifa de direitos expedida no dia 25 de Julho de 1898, não corresponde ás condições actuaes do commercio, porque não comprehende muitos artigos novos, cuja importação tem augmentado, e porque a pratica tem feito notar que contem irregularidades na classificação de algumas mercadorias, do qual resulta falta de equidade na distribuição dos respectivos direitos; em uso das faculdades que lhe confere a reforma constitucional expedida no dia 15 de Outubro de 1896,

DECRETA:

ART. 1°. Desde a publicação do presente decreto, os direitos sobre a importação de mercadorias se cobrarão por cada kilogramma de peso bruto, do modo seguinte:

ART. 2°. Os artigos não mencionados na anterior classificação, pagarão os direitos que se cobram sobre artigos semelhantes; mas si forem compostos de diversas materias, pagarão os direitos que se cobram sobre a materia que mais predomine nelles.

ART. 3º. Os artigos que se tenham omisso e que não possam ser classificados conforme ao artigo precedente, pagarão á razão de 200 por cento sobre o valor principal de factura. Este direito será augmentado a 250 por cento sobre artigos cuja materia prima se produza no paiz; e será diminuido a 100 por cento sobre os artigos que se empregam nas artes e industrias. Estes direitos se cobrarão na moeda corrente do paiz. Si não houver factura, proceder-se-ha a avaliar os artigos por peritos.

ART. 4º. Quando um volume contiver artigos que paguem direitos distinctos, o peso do volume se distribuirá em proporção aos pesos netos dos differentes artigos contidos no volume.

ART. 5º. A presente lei não comprehende os artigos procedentes dos Estados da America Central, cuja introducção seja livre ou taxada com direitos especiaes conforme aos tratados vigentes.

ART. 6º. Os direitos impostos conforme á presente lei, serão pagos no Thesouro Geral, do modo seguinte: 20 por cento com ordens contra as alfandegas, creadas pelo decreto de 30 de Outubro de 1896; 15 por cento com ordens contra as alfandegas, creadas no dia 19 de Junho de 1897; 15 por cento em documentos de credito publico, legalmente liquidado e reconhecido; e 50 por cento em effectivo.

Esta disposição não affecta as facturas, nem os depositos destinados actualmente a sua amortisação nos direitos maritimos.

ART. 7º. Os possnidores de ordens pagaveis ao portador, creadas por decreto de 10 de Novembro de 1897, poderão pagar tambem com elles 5 por cento dos direitos maritimos, sem direito addicional.

ART. 8º. Fica revogada a tarifa de 25 de Julho de 1888 e qualquer outra disposição que se opponha ao disposto no presente decreto.

PARAGUAY.

MERCADO PARA O NEGOCIO DE MANTEIGA.

O Consul RUFFIN escreve de Assumpção que tudo parece indicar uma boa perspectiva nos mercados do Paraguay para a manteiga dos Estados Unidos. Encontra-se este artigo em muito pequena quantidade, ainda que todos appetecem. A escassez deve ser attribuida a falta de estabelecimentos para sua preparação e ao reduzido numero de queijeiras. Todas estas ultimas se encontram na pequena povoação de San Bernardino, cuja população é quasi exclusivamente allemã. Durante o anno de 1897 foram importadas umas 2,500 libras de manteiga em latas de uma libra. A dita importação veio principalmente da Italia. A manteiga que se faz em San Bernardino se vende ao retalho á razão de 35 a 40 centavos, ouro, por libra. e é a melhor que se pode obter. O direito sobre a manteiga que se importa é de 50 por cento ad valorem, e a renda que este produz montou a $42. ouro, no anno passado.

A manteiga que se importa da Europa é de boa qualidade, mas não é igual á que se faz nos Estados Unidos. A superior qualidade desta ultima, que é de uso tão commum nos Estados Unidos, facilitaria sua immediata sahida nos mercados do Paraguay, si se tomem em conta as peculiaridades deste povo. Consome-se muito pouca manteiga neste paiz, e os hoteis que a usam cobram por ella uma quantia addicional.

Pensa o Consul que seria conveniente que algum fabricante dos Estados Unidos fizesse a prova de mandar manteiga para o Paraguay. Cré elle que pondo-a em latas de uma libra, com o retrato do Presidente do Paraguay, ou de algum estadista notavel do paiz, ou com um gravado de algum edificio historico, se chamaria a attenção do publico e o artigo se volveria popular. O Consul pensa que nesta maneira se obteriam vendas promptas e lucrativas, pois no paiz não existe systema de annuncios.

O que se tem dito do Paraguay, pode applicar-se igualmente ás outras republicas americanas, em quanto ao uso, escassez e demanda de manteiga. Os fabricantes deste artigo nos Estados Unidos poderiam alcançar grandes vantagens, estudando as condições existentes e adaptando-se ás necessidades do commercio.

O ALIMENTO NACIONAL.

Nenhum producto do solo é mais geralmente usado na Republica do Paraguay que a mandioca. Este é um producto peculiar ás regiões tropicaes e semitropicaes. Encontra-se a mandioca em todas as mesas e é muito semelhante á batata doce dos Estados Unidos, ainda que contem mais amido e menos assucar. Ordinariamente cozinham a mandioca junto com carne, milho, batatas e outros legumes, o qual constitue o prato nacional. Da mandioca fazem o amido, pois o amido de milho não se conhece no Paraguay.

A mandioca é de cór morena clara e mede de 18 pollegadas a 2 pés de comprimento, com uma circumferencia de 3 á 5 pollegadas. A semeiam em Maio, e nos mezes de Junho, Julho e Agosto se encontra na melhor condição para o mercado, ainda que cresce durante todo o anno. Com 5 centavos, ouro, pode-se comprar sufficiente mandioca para uma comida de uma familia de 5 ou 6 pessoas. O Consul RUFFIN diz que a colheita deste anno será muito boa.

ADIANTAMENTOS NA INDUSTRIA AGRICOLA.

O Consul RUFFIN diz que o Banco Agricola, que é uma instituição do Governo, tem a seu cargo todos os interesses agricolas da Republica. Estão-se usando com bons resultados novos methodos de cultivo e machinas modernas. O Consul crê que si se comprehendesse a importancia das machinas americanas, se operaria no Paraguay uma revolução na agricultura. Convem que os fabricantes mandem agentes a Assumpção afim de estabelecer naquella cidade agencias para a venda de manufacturas americanas.

PERU.

EXTENSÃO DOS DEPOSITOS DE CARVÃO ANTHRACITE.

O BOLETIM correspondente ao mez de Agosto publicou um curto artigo sobre os depositos de carvão do Peru, dando noticia de que em 1892 foi dada uma concessão ao Sr. C. B. JONES para explorar as minas de carvão durante 20 annos. Desde então dous periodicos de mineração, o "Mines and Minerals" de Scranton, Pa., e o "Association Letter," orgão dos exploradores de carvão anthracite têm publicado descripções dos terrenos de carvão do Peru, preparadas por WILLIAM GRIFFITH, engenheiro perito, que no anno passado visitou e estudou os lugares em referencia. Do dito artigo, foi extrahido o seguinte:

Os terrenos de carvão anthracite do norte do Peru estão situados na magestosa cordilheira dos Andes, a differentes alturas que variam de 7,000 pés sobre o nivel do mar e a ambos lados daquella divisão do continente. Ha dous lugares notaveis; o mais septentrional está situado no Districto de Cajamarca, umas 50 ou 60 milhas ao norte da antiga e historica cidade do mesmo nome. Neste lugar se notou a existencia de varios veios de carvão na superficie de rochedos quasi verticaes, a 600 pés sobre o fundo do valle, pelo qual corre a impetuosa torrente da montanha, chamada Llaucon, ramal do Marañon que forma a fonte principal do corpo do rio Amazonas. Este ponto está cerca de 7,000 pés sobre a mare e a 300 milhas das aguas navegaveis do Amazonas e 150 milhas do

gráos, approximadamente, e alguns dos depositos têm boa espessura. Pode-se ver que a erosão das jazidas superficiaes tem formado profundos regos entre as rochas de carvão que seguem as irregularidades da formação da montanha. O deposito principal tem de 10 a 15 pés de espessura. Mediram-se outras secções, bastante parecidas á segunda, que ficam entre estas duas.

A superficie desta camada e o veio de carvão que contem se podem seguir facilmente por uma distancia de 15 a 20 milhas. A primeira jazida superficial que se visitou está situada na vertente do Pacifico, cerca de 110 milhas da costa, a uma altura de cerca de 8,000 pés. Tambem se examinaram outras jazidas, recolhendo-se amostras ao longo do veio por mais de 20 milhas, onde atravessa a divisão continental dos Andes, a uma altura de 13,000 pés. Tambem se observaram nesta secção jazidas de carvão mais delgadas, de 2 a 4 pés de espessura, cujas superficies estavam pelo geral tão cubertas com depositos que muito poucas podiam-se encontrar. Usa-se este carvão na localidade em pequena escala para trabalhos de ferraria e para queimar o mineral de prata. As analyses, numeros 1 e 2 feitas por A. S. McCREETH, mostra a qualidade do carvão das regiões acima mencionadas :

	Analyse.	
	No. 1.	No. 2.
Agua..	1.450	1.596
Materias volatis	5.633	3.030
Carvão fixo	83.620	90.906
Enxofre	.554	.652
Cinzas..	8.743	3.816
	100	100
Gravidade especifica..................................	1.62	1.67

É de notar-se que o carvão da região do norte, como o mostra a primeira analyse, é mais ou menos da qualidade do carvão anthracite de uso geral em Pennsylvania, emquanto que a segunda analyse mostra que a qualidade do carvão é muito superior ao producto ordinario de Pennsylvania, e ainda talvez muito superior ao da melhor qualidade daquella região.

É evidente que as montanhas dos Andes têm sido aquentadas intensa e uniformemente por toda sua extensão, do que se deduz quasi com certeza que estes depositos de anthracite devem ser de qualidade uniforme por toda a região de carvão, não mudando-se em betuminoso como acontece no Colorado. Em certos lugares do mesmo districto se encontram depositos de carvão lignito de uma idade mais recente e de grande espessura; mas não se encontra carvão betuminoso algum. Este ultimo districto está muito bem situado e contem carvão em abundancia sufficiente para compensar quaesquer gastos que sejam necessarios para a exploração, pois é seu mercado toda a costa occidental da America do Sul e do Norte, onde este artigo pelo geral tem um alto preço; e não passará muito tempo sem que este se augmente pelas necessidades de prover-se de carvão o canal de Nicaragua, o qual será construido sem duvida no proximo futuro.

A quarta parte do combustivel que usam os vapores que fazem viagens regulares entre Panama e Valparaiso, vem em navios que fazem o commercio de nitrato como lastro de Galles e se deposita nas carboneiras do porto de Iquique, ao norte do Chile. O resto do carvão que se consome na costa da America do Sul, se obtem das minas de Chile, situadas centenas de milhas ao sul de Valparaiso, a cujo ponto os navios vão a buscar carvão, perdendo por conseguinte muitos dias em cada viagem. De vez em quando vem tambem um carregamento de Australia. Este carvão do Chile é carvão de gaz de qualidade muito inferior como combustivel para vapor, pois contem uma grande quantidade de materias volatis e como se usa de ordinario produz uma grande quantidade de fumo e deixa uma grande porção de cinzas ao passo que dá muito trabalho para accendel-o. Mas por falta de carvão melhor, tem-se empregado por muitos annos, ainda quando seu preço é muito alto e tem sido fonte de enormes riquezas á senhora dona das minas.

ESTADOS UNIDOS.

COMMERCIO COM OS PAIZES LATINO-AMERICANOS.

RELAÇÃO MENSAL DAS IMPORTAÇÕES E EXPORTAÇÕES.

O quadro dado na pagina 617 é extrahido da relação compilada por O. P. Austin, chefe da Repartição de Estatistica do Ministerio da Fazenda, mostrando o commercio entre os Estados Unidos e os paizes latino-americanos. A relação corresponde ao mez de Julho de 1898, e é corrigida até o dia 2 de Setembro de 1898, com uma relação comparativa para o periodo correspondente do anno anterior, assim como para os sete mezes findos em Julho de 1898, comparados com os correspondentes de 1897. Deve-se explicar que os algarismos das varias alfandegas, mostrando as importações e exportações de um só mez não são recebidos no Ministerio da Fazenda até quasi o dia 20 do mez seguinte, e perde-se algum tempo necessariamente em sua compilação e impressão. Por conseguinte, as estatisticas para o mez de Julho, por exemplo, não são publicadas até os primeiros dias de Setembro.

CONDIÇÃO DO THESOURO—MOEDA EM CIRCULAÇÃO.

Os seguintes dados sobre a condição do Thesouro dos Estados Unidos ao terminar os trabalhos no dia 30 de Setembro foram publicados no dia 1° de Outubro: fundos disponiveis, em effectivo, $309,156,297; fundo de reserva em ouro, $243,327,379; prata,

$7,120,784; bilhetes de banco sobre o Thesouro, $36,454,266; bilhetes do Thesouro de 1890, $1,751,950; total da receita durante o mez, $3,103,050; receita total durante o anno fiscal, $128,510,936; total de despeza durante o mez, $2,281,000; total de despeza durante o anno fiscal, $187,099,114; depositos do Thesouro em bancos nacionaes, $82,344,416.

As estatisticas do dinheiro em circulação comparadas com as dos dous mezes anteriores mostram que houve um augmento neto que montou á somma de $24,499,837. Dos ramos em que occorreu diminuição o principal é o ouro cunhado, que alcançou a $8,043,354; tambem houve uma diminuição nos certificados de moeda cunhada de 1872 de $2,645,000 e nos certificados de ouro de $79,100. O augmento mais notavel occorreu nos bilhetes dos Estados Unidos que alcançaram a $19,264,584. O augmento nos bilhetes de banco nacionaes alcançou a $8,904,794; tambem houve augmento de $3,050,515 na moeda de prata, de $1,828,417 em moedas de prata subsidiarias, $453,362 em certificados de prata e $1,783,629 em bilhetes do Thesouro de 1890.

O quadro comparativo que apparece mais abaixo indica a pequena diminuição no metallico e ouro cunhado do Thesouro. Nota-se um augmento de $14,190,377 em ouro cunhado e de $11,123,587 em metallico. A diminuição mais notavel é de $19,264,584 em bilhetes dos Estados Unidos, que corresponde ao augmento de circulação acima mencionado. No seguinte quadro apparece todo o dinheiro emittido, a quantia que existe no Thesouro e a que está em circulação:

	Moeda cunhada ou emittida.	No Thesouro.	Em circulação no dia 10 de Outubro.
Ouro cunhado	$785,041,686	$162,391,874	$622,649,812
Dollars de prata.................	464,834,597	404,045,769	60,788,828
Moedas de prata subsidiarias	75,784,648	9,196,708	66,587,940
Certificados de ouro.............	36,990,799	1,596,890	35,393,909
Certificados de prata	400,062,504	6,636,769	393,425,735
Bilhetes do Thesouro de 14 de Julho de 1890..	98,549,280	1,844,997	96,704,283
Bilhetes dos Estados Unidos......	346,681,016	55,020,851	291,660,165
Certificados de moeda cunhada de 8 de Junho de 1872............	18,455,000	820,000	17,635,000
Bilhetes dos bancos nacionaes	235,439,985	3,689,265	231,750,720
Total	2,461,839,515	645,243,123	1,816,596,392

A quantia de ouro em circulação, comparada com a que havia no dia 1º de Outubro de 1897, augmentou em mais de $93,500,000.

Durante o anno o augmento em bilhetes dos Estados Unidos alcançou a $39,800,000; certificados de prata, $18,800,000; bilhetes do Thesouro de 1890, cerca de $6,900,000; prata em pequenas denominações mais de $5,400,000: bilhetes dos bancos nacionaes cerca de $5,300,000, moedas de prata de $1, mais de $3,600,000. As unicas diminuições que occorreram calculadas quasi na mesma quantia, $1,500,000, foram nos certificados de moeda cunhada de 1872 e os certificados de ouro.

O total geral do dinheiro em circulação para o 1º de Outubro alcançou a $1,816,596,392, o que indica um augmento de mais de $137,750,000 comparado com o 1º de Outubro de 1897. A circulação por cabeça foi de $24.24, segundo calculos de um perito do Thesouro, feitos sobre uma população de 74,925,000. Isto representa para o mez de Setembro um augmento de 28 centavos por cabeça, e para o mez de Outubro de 1897 um excesso de $1.35. Ver-se-ha do antedito que da somma total de ouro cunhado quasi as quatro quintas está em circulação, emquanto que mais das seis setimas partes da quantia de dollars de prata cunhados se conservava nas caixas do Thesouro.

AUGMENTO NA CONSTRUCÇÃO DE NAVIOS.

Segundo os dados recebidos na Repartição de Navegação, se vê que durante o exercicio findo em 30 de Junho de 1898, se construiram e matricularam nos Estados Unidos, 952 navios mercantes, com uma tonelagem total de 180,458 toneladas, contra 891 navios, com uma tonelagem total de 232,233 toneladas, construidos no anno anterior. A diminuição nas construcções está quasi inteiramente limitada aos grandes lagos, onde a tonelagem registrada chegou sómente a 54,084 toneladas, contra 116,937 toneladas no anno precedente. As construcções na costa do Pacifico representaram uma tonelagem total de 49,789 toneladas, contra 7,495 toneladas no exercicio anterior. Este augmento foi principalmente em vapores destinados ao commercio com Alaska pelo Pacifico e nos rios daquelle territorio. A decadencia nas construcções occorreu inteiramente na primeira metade do anno fiscal, epoca em que na Grã Bretanha e outras nações maritimas houve tambem uma diminuição de cerca de 20 por cento. Durante os mezes de Abril, Maio e Junho, que foram os da guerra com a Hespanha, os navios construidos e registrados nos Estados Unidos representaram uma tonelagem no dobro da dos mezes correspondentes de 1897.

Os navios construidos e formalmente enumerados durante o primeiro trimestre do exercicio corrente, trimestre que terminou no dia 30 de Setembro de 1898, ascenderam a 301, com uma tonelagem total de 83,191 toneladas, contra 97 navios, com uma tonelagem total de 26,805 toneladas, durante o trimestre correspondente do anno passado. Tudo parece indicar que neste anno as construcções serão maiores do que as de qualquer outro durante o ultimo quarto do seculo, exceptuando 1890–91.

O valor dos direitos sobre a tonelagem durante o exercicio que terminou no dia 30 de Junho, foi de $846,771, contra $731,770 no anno anterior, e $544,255 em 1896. Os navios inglezes pagaram $552,721; os allemães, $86,120; os americanos, $63,334; os noruegos, $47,070; e os hespanhóes, $17,521. Em Nova York se receberam $283,827, contra $237,778 no anno anterior; em Nova Orleans, $79,550, contra $65,948; em Philadelphia, $69,815, contra $62,354; em San Francisco, $32,330, contra $47,371. A importancia dos direitos cobrados durante o anno passado é maior do que a que se tem recebido em qualquer outro anno desde que se modificou a lei de direitos em 1884.

OS ESTADOS UNIDOS DA AMERICA CENTRAL.

PROMULGAÇÃO DA NOVA CONSTITUIÇÃO.

Em data de 15 de Setembro de 1898, o Sr. WILLIAM M. LITTLE, Consul dos Estados Unidos em Tegucigalpa, Honduras, communica officialmente á Secretaria de Estado a nova federação dos paizes da America Central, conhecidos até hoje como a Republica Maior da America Central, nome que seguirão levando até o 1º de Novembro de 1898. Na communicação citada o Sr. LITTLE disse:

Tenho a honra de participar-vos, que este Governo tem promulgado officialmente a Constituição Politica dos Estados Unidos da America Central, antes chamados a Republica Maior da America Central, documento preparado pelos representantes de Honduras, Nicaragua e Salvador, em Managua, Nicaragua, no dia 27 de Agosto de 1898. Remetto junto copia da Constituição. Como acabo de receber o dito documento, não tenho tempo de fazer uma traducção completa

de domicilio nelle. As leis podem estabelecer a maneira e os casos em que pode negar-se a um estrangeiro a entrada ao territorio da Republica, ou nos em que se ordena sua expulsão por considerar-se pernicioso.

———————

URUGUAY.

RECEITA ADUANEIRA DO PORTO DE MONTEVIDÉO.

Segundo um relatorio do Consul britannico, a receita aduaneira do porto de Montevidéo para o mez de Julho montou a $1,005,007. Essa somma é muito notavel quando se considera que no Uruguay não se fazem geralmente bons negocios durante o mez de Julho.

O Consul attribue esse extraordinario augmento ao facto de que os commerciantes retiraram da alfandega mercadorias em grandes quantidades, para que não fossem obrigados a pagar o direito addicional de 2½ por cento, que foi em vigor no dia 1° de Agosto. Tambem se notou um augmento na importação. O total da importação para o mez de Julho de 1898 foi de $916,359, contra um total de $583,000 para igual mez de 1897.

Segundo o "Montevidéo Times," a receita aduaneira para o primeiro semestre de 1898 ascendeu a $5,319,448, contra $4,290,121 de igual periodo de 1897. A receita do anno corrente não sómente accusa um enorme augmento sobre a de 1897, anno da revolução, mas tambem é muito a favor de 1898 quando comparada com a do primeiro semestre de 1896, anno que se considerou muito florescente sob o ponto de vista commercial. Neste anno a receita aduaneira montou a $5,535,402. Segundo o "Times," as estatisticas para 1898 são sujeitas á revisão, a qual contribuirá para augmental-as antes que diminuil-as.

Referindo-se ao novo direito addicional de 2½ por cento sobre as mercadorias que se importarem no Uruguay, do qual se deu noticia no BOLETIM correspondente ao mez de Setembro, o Consul SWALM diz que o Governo resolveu a dedicar o producto desse imposto á conversão dos certificados do Thesouro até que se necessitarem para a construcção das obras de melhoramento do porto de Montevidéo.

FOMENTO DA IMMIGRAÇÃO ITALIANA.

O Ministro Loomis, n'uma communicação dirigida ultimamente de Caracas á Secretaria de Estado, remette um recorte do "Venezuelan Herald," que contem a traducção do contracto celebrado entre o Governo venezuelano e um syndicato de capitalistas talianos. Este contracto vem a substituir a concessão Dotti, dei que se tratou em data de 10 de Janeiro. O resumo do contracto Dotti foi publicado na pagina 1906 do Boletim, correspondente ao mez de Maio.

O Sr. Loomis crê que o contracto é favoravel a Venezuela, e que si se cumprir devidamente o que dispõe, dará em resultado o estabelecimento na Republica de 15,000 familias do norte da Italia. Estas familias receberão auxilio pecuniario e serão auxiliadas de diversas maneiras, com a esperança de que desenvolvam o cultivo de fructas e cereaes, e dediquem especial attenção á cultura da vinha e á fabricação de vinho. Depois da chegada dos immigrantes, o exito da empreza dependerá da construcção de caminhos e estradas de ferro que lhes permittam transportar com pouco gasto seus productos aos mercados do paiz e á costa.

O Ministro diz que o estudo das condições actuaes faz evidente que, si a producção de fructas fôr augmentada consideravelmente, os cultivadores ver-se-hão obrigados a buscar mercados nos paizes estrangeiros e com preferencia nos Estados Unidos, por razão da proximidade deste paiz e da grande demanda que ha nelle de fructas tropicaes. O recorte do periodico diz, entre outras cousas, o seguinte:

No dia 1º de Julho de 1898, o Governo celebrou um contracto de immigração sobre bases muito solidas. As partes contractantes são o Ministro de Agricultura, Industria e Commercio, autorisado a isso pelo Presidente da Republica em Conselho de Ministros e com o consentimento do Conselho de Governo, por uma parte, e da Sociedade de Colonisação Italiana por outra.

Segundo este contracto, a sociedade compromette-se: 1º, a trazer a Venezuela, no curso de cada tres annos, 3,000 familias europeas, principalmente da raça latina, agricultores e de reconhecida boa conducta, todo o qual deve ser comprovado por meio de certificados dos consules nos differentes portos de embarque; 2º, a construir edificios para as mesmas, provel-as de instrumentos agricolas, e dar-lhes alimento, roupa e remedios, até que tenham recolhido a primeira colheita, e assim mesmo a levantar uma igreja, edificios publicos e escolas em cada colonia; 3°, a estabelecer um serviço bimensal de vapores entre a Italia e Venezuela, tocando em Barcelona, Hespanha, Teneriffe e outros portos, e cujo termino seja La Guaira ou Porto Cabello; mas, si fôr necessario, os ditos vapores tocarão em outros portos, sujeitos ás leis fiscaes de Venezuela; estes vapores levarão as malas a todos os mencionados portos sem remuneração e não cobrarão por passageiros e carga mais do que cobram outros barcos da mesma classe e tonelagem; a sociedade compromette-se a cobrar sómente meia passagem aos empregados diplomaticos e suas familias e a dar-lhes passagem livre quando residam ou vão a residir no estrangeiro; 4°, a estabelecer em Caracas uma instituição bancaria, com surccursaes naquelles districtos da Republica em que se creia conveniente tel-as, sendo o objecto da mesma prestar dinheiro sobre hypothecas aos agricultores e criadores de gado; o capital do dito banco será de 20,000,000 bolivares ($3,860,000), dos quaes 12,000,000 se dedicarão a operações bancarias ordinarias e o resto a emprestimos, segundo fica indicado; estes dous fundos devem manter-se separados, sem confundir-se jamais um com o outro; o juro sobre os emprestimos não deve exceder de sete por cento, e o banco tem faculdade de emittir bilhetes, de conformidade com o que dispõe a lei sobre bancos, vigente na actualidade; 5°, a permittir ao Governo nacional o uso livre de todos os meios de communicação que estabeleça; 6°, a dar, ao fim de quatro annos de trabalhos agricolas, uma casa a cada familia da colonia e a cada colono tres hectares, cujo terreno será dedicado ao cultivo; 7°, a depositar no banco de Inglaterra, como garantia do cumprimento deste contracto, e dentro de tres mezes, contados desde a data em que seja . ratificado pelo Congresso Nacional, a somma de 200,000 bolivares, a qual permanecerá alli até que a sociedade estabeleça em Caracas o banco mencionado e tenha estabelecido as primeiras 500 familias. A sociedade perderá a dita somma a favor do Governo si não cumprir com o estipulado no contracto.

Por outra parte, o Governo se compromette: 1°, a dar á sociedade terrenos não cultivados para o uso dos immigrantes, á razão de seis hectares por cabeça, e cada menino menor de 10 annos que venha ao paiz com uma familia de immigrantes, terá direito, quando che-

todos os beneficios que delle se derivam; mas si o Congresso não ratificará o referido contracto, o Governo deverá pagar o valor das passagens dos immigrantes de conformidade com as disposições da presente lei.

O Governo se reserva o direito de celebrar contractos semelhantes com outros paizes.

A YÚCCA.

Em um relatorio do Sr. A. H. PLUMACHER, Consul em Maracaibo, publicado nos Relatorios Consulares correspondentes ao mez de Setembro, se lê o seguinte:

O principal producto de Venezuela é o café, mas, como o preço deste artigo é agora muito baixo, os agricultores fariam bem em dirigir sua attenção para outra planta, cujo cultivo dá resultados mais lucrativos. Segundo parece, a yucca promette muito para o futuro. É uma planta muito productiva e apesar de ser muito bem conhecido em Venezuela, ninguem tem-se occupado especialmente em cultival-a. Um hectar de terra semeada de yucca produz 150 quintaes de amido ou 200 quintaes de tapioca. O cultivo desta planta é facil e barato. Supporta muito bem o mal tempo, não soffre na estação secca e cresce em todo terreno.

A yucca da-se bem no mesmo solo em que crescem as ervilhas, o milho e o feijão, e um terreno semeado da dita planta rende mais que semeado de café. Um hectar de terreno bem cultivado pode levar 1,600 cafeeiros. Tomando a producção maxima de cada arvore, um hectar dá 8 quintaes de café, e a mesma porção de terreno semeado de yucca daria 150 quintaes de amido, fora de outros productos que se obteriam do mesmo solo, os quaes poderiam ser, por exemplo, 12 alqueires de ervilhas e 12 de feijão. Isto mostra que um terreno semeado de yucca dá em rendimento 6 ou 7 vezes mais que semeado de café. O systema de cultivo é primitivo. Quasi não se conhecem os arados e outros instrumentos de agricultura de fabricação americana. Todo ó trabalho se faz com enxadas de antigo estylo, pois nem os homens nem as bestas têm sido educados no uso dos arados modernos.

CONGRESSO NACIONAL DE AGRICULTORES.

A decima oitava reunião do Congresso Nacional de Agricultores verificará em Fort Worth, Texas, e durará de 6 a 14 de Dezembro de 1898. O objecto desta organisação, segundo se expõe em sua constituição, é o desenvolvimento dos interesses agricolas dos Estados Unidos. Cada Estado e Territorio tem direito a enviar tantos delegados como manda representantes ás duas Camaras do Congresso Nacional, e, alem disto, um delegado

Les grandes maisons allemandes, américaines, suisses et italiennes se partagent ce commerce. Les matériaux de construction proviennent principalement d'Angleterre, tandis que la bijouterie et les métaux travaillés proviennent en grande partie de France. Les montres d'or de bonne qualité viennent presque toutes de la Suisse, l'Angleterre en fournissant quelques-unes, tandis que les articles bon marchés des divers métaux proviennent tous des Etats-Unis. Les pendules généralement en usage viennent des Etats-Unis et d'Allemange, mais on trouve quelquefois par-ci par-là quelques pendules françaises dans les magasins. Les articles argentés proviennent pour la pluspart des Etats-Unis et de l'Allemagne. D'après les communications de divers importateurs le métal allemand est supérieur au métal américain, mais d'autre part la main-d'œuvre de l'argenteur américain est supérieur à la main-d'œuvre de l'argenteur allemand, de sorte que les deux classes se trouvent être au même niveau.

Le consul français prédit un brillant avenir au port de Rosario à cause de sa position exceptionnellement avantageuse, situé comme il est sur le fleuve Parana, au centre de la principale région agricole de la République Argentine, accessible à la navigation commerciale et à distance égale des ports de Buenos Ayres et Montévidéo. Rosario profitera aussi des améliorations du port de Montévidéo à mesure que les plus grandes facilités pour les navires à vapeur et les voiliers avanceront le développement de tous les ports adjacents, et Rosario deviendra, par la force des circonstances, un grand dépôt pour le centre de la République Argentine et du Paraguay.

DÉCOUVERTE DE CHARBON.

Le Commandant Nuñez, officier de la marine Argentine, est revenu récemment de Terre de Feu avec des échantillons de charbon y découverts. Les échantillons qu'il a apportés ont été essayés dans les locomotives employées aux travaux du port de Buenos Ayres et ont donné les milleurs résultats. Il n'est que du charbon de surface et naturellement on a inféré que s'il est si bon à la surface il sera de toute première qualité dans les couches inférieures.

Il suffit que les espérances que ces découvertes ont données se réalisent pour lancer ce pays dans une voie manufacturière qui peut le développer plus rapidement que sa culture du blé. Il ne faudra que peu de temps pour déterminer la valeur réelle de ce charbon.

La "Review of the River Plate," tout en admettant que ce charbon est de bonne qualité, ne fait pas d'illusions concernant la quantité disponible. Elle dit:

Il est très agréable de savoir que les échantillons de charbon, apportés de la Terre de Feu, ont donné de bons résultats, dépassant, croyons-nous, les espérances de tout le monde, mêlé ou non à la découverte. On propose d'envoyer un certaiu nombre de machines afin de déterminer la quantité de minerai disponible. Même si l'on trouve que la qualité moyenne est aussi bonne que celle des échantillons essayés, il est encore possible que la quantité soit si petite qu'elle rendrait les dépôts inutiles pour toujours, ou que les lieux où le charbon se trouve en quantités soient commercialement inaccessibles.

IMPORTATIONS DES ETATS-UNIS EXIGENCES DE COMMERCE.

BULLETIN No. 22 de la Compagnie des Exportations des Etats-Unis contient les données suivantes concernant les exportations des Etats-Unis à la République Argentine:

Des commandes pour des machines et outillages électriques arrivent continuellement dans de grandes proportions. Une compagnie de Broad street, New York, a reçu récemment un ordre pour $20,000 de ces machines. Les perspectives de travail de toute sorte sur le terrain de l'électricité en Argentina sont très encourageantes. La valeur moyenne des chargements des machines et du matériel électriques s'est élevée de $7,000 à $10,000 pour chaque navire qui est sorti du port de New York pendant les trois mois écoulés.

Les tramways électriques d'Argentina sont fournis d'installations des Etats-Unis. Pendant les deux derniers mois presque tous les navires allant à Buenos Aires ont porté au moins de $50,000 de matériel de tramway. Une grande partie de ce matériel est destinée à la Compagnie de Tramway Belgrano. La Compagnie Capitale qui a des bureaux locaux à New York expédie sur une grande échelle toutes sortes de machines électriques, y compris les installations de tramways pour sa propre ligne. On dit qu'au commencement du mois de novembre, cette compagnie va expédier 1,000 wagons de marchandises, que l'on a construit sous contrat.

D'autres grands chargements de New York pour l'Argentina consistent de fer manufacturé dont le commerce augmente graduellement; les trois derniers navires pour Buenos Aíres ont emporté un total de $40,000 de machines, principalement des machines à moissonner.

D'autres articles fort demandés en Argentina sont de la corde, du papier, de la quincaillerie, du bois en paquets pour les caisses et des tuyaux en fer. On informe une maison de commerce de South street que la demande pour le cristal, la lampisterie, les toiles cirées, le linoléum et les tapis bon marchés est énorme.   On dit aussi qu'il y a une bonne occasion pour contrôler le commerce des articles sanitaires fabriqués aux Etats-Unis.

Des informations d'Argentina disent que presque toutes les compagnies de Tramways à Buenos Aires prolongeront leurs lignes jusqu'à toutes les villes des environs et les outillages nécessaires seront énormes.

La barque *Adam W. Spies* chargé récemment pour Buenos Aires a emporté une grande quantité d'articles fabriqués aux Etats-Unis.   De ces articles-ci, il y avait pour $45,000 de machines agricoles, pour $12,000 de machines à coudre et pour $10,000 de chaises et de quincaillerie.   Le navire *Bellucia* qui a aussi fait voile pour le même port a emporté pour $50,000 de machines agricoles et des voitures évaluées à $5,000 et des moulins à vent facturés à $10,971.

NOUVELLE STATION DE CHARBON AUX ETATS-UNIS.

Une dépêche authentique de Norfolk, Va., dit que des échantillons envoyés à Argentine ont donné de si bons résultats que d'autres chargements seront expédiés immédiatement.   MM. CASTNER, CORRAN et BULLITT de Philadelphie, agents pour le "Pocahontas Coal Company," ont établi une agence à Buenos Aires avec M. CARL H. ARNAL comme gérant.   M. ARNAL a été pendant quelque temps vice-consul des Républiques de Colombie et du Venezuela à Norfolk, Va.   On parle aussi d'un nombre de navires chargés de charbon qui partiront bientôt de Lamberts Point, Va., à Buenos Aires, et on s'attend que ces bateaux y repartiront à moitié chargés des produits de la République Argentine.

BOLIVIE.

ABOLITION DU MONOPOLE DES ALLUMETTES.

On envoie une communication que le Gouvernement Bolivien a abrogé le décret du 14 mars dernier concernant la perception des droits sur les allumettes importées de l'étranger et qu'il a suspendu, provisoirement, la loi du 18 novembre 1896, établissant un monopole sur la fabrication d'allumettes dans la République, et a prélevé sur les allumettes de l'étranger un impôt additionnel.

Désormais, les allumettes importées à la Bolivie ne payeront que le droit d'entrée spécifié dans le tarif de douane.

BRÉSIL.

RÉCOLTE DE CAFÉ DE 1898.

Le Consul Général Seeger envoie un rapport intéressant concernant la production et le transport de café dans la République pour l'année finissant le 30 juin 1898, et dont les statistiques suivantes ont été obtenues.

RECETTES POUR L'ANNÉE.

	Sacs.	Livres.
Rio :		
Par chemin de fer	2, 300, 690	303, 691, 080
Par cabotage	840, 099	110, 893, 068
Par d'autres bâtiments	1, 163, 849	153, 617, 068
En transit	232, 941	30, 748, 212
Total	4, 537, 579	598, 949, 428
Santos	6, 152, 594	812, 142, 408
Victoria (évalué)	400, 000	52, 800, 000
Bahia (évalué)	250, 000	33, 000, 000
Ceara (évalué)	20, 000	2, 640, 000
Grand total	11, 360, 173	1, 499, 531, 836

CHARGEMENTS POUR LES PAYS ÉTRANGERS.

	Sacs.	Livres.
Etats-Unis	4, 740, 638	625, 746, 216
Toute l'Europe	5, 971, 468	770, 233, 776
Cap de Bonne Espérance	149, 300	19, 707, 600
Rivière Plate, etc	101, 533	13, 402, 356
Total	10, 962, 939	1, 429, 107, 948

Evalué en moyenne à $8.75 par sac (132 livres), la valeur de cette exportation s'élève à $96,450,716.25.

Pendant les trois dernières années les chargements de café du Brésil furent comme suit:

De—	1895.	1896.	1897.
	Sacs.	Sacs.	Sacs.
Santos	3, 554, 696	4, 156, 567	5, 621, 762
Rio	2, 763, 720	2, 784, 958	4, 066, 734
Victoria	307, 438	273, 255	372, 221
Bahia	264, 775	260, 981	292, 480
Ceara	20, 202	6, 000	6, 568
Total	6, 910, 831	7, 418, 761	10, 359, 765

Les prix de New York par livre pendant la dernière année des récoltes pour qualité No. 7 ("spot") à New York ont diminués continuellement de 7$\frac{1}{16}$ cents le 1er juillet 1897, à 5$\frac{7}{8}$ cents le 1er mai 1898. Le 1er juillet 1898 les prix ont augmenté un peu jusqu'à 6$\frac{1}{4}$ cents.

Le 30 juin 1898 le stock de 1,227,960 sacs a été distribué comme suit: Rio, 268,167; Santos, 316,793; New York, Baltimore et la Nouvelle Orléans, 643,000; à la même date la quantité visible du monde a été calculée à 5,436,000 sacs, ce qui est un équivalent à environ la moitié de la consommation d'une année.

Il y a une trop grande production de café en ce moment et cela a déprécié les prix. Cette condition a existé surtout pendant les deux années écoulées, quoique la cause de cet état est d'une date plus éloignée. Pendant les 10 années précédant 1897, le prix courant du café a donné un bénéfice extraordinairement grand aux planteurs. Il en est résulté une augmentation énorme dans le territoire des plantations de café pendant la hausse. A présent, ces millions d'arbres commencent à porter des fruits malgré la demande et les prix, et ce qui était auparavant une industrie rapportant un profit de 150 pour cent par an, couvre à présent à peine les frais de production. Pour l'année prochaine, cependant, on s'attend à une récolte beaucoup plus petite.

Le résultat ordinaire va se répéter—deux abondantes récoltes successives suivies d'une production plus petite à cause de l'état épuisé des arbres.

Pour l'année de récoltes de 1898–99 il y a deux évaluations, l'évaluation officielle et l'évaluation commerciale, qui diffèrent considérablement. Les chiffres sont comme suit:

Etat.	Officiel.	Commerciale.
	Sacs.	Sacs.
Rio	2,500,000	3,000,000
Santos	4,500,000	6,000,000
Total	7,000,000	9,000,000

De là on verra que même les évaluations les plus élevées sont plus de 1,500,000 sacs moins que la récolte de 1897–98.

Récemment, les plantations de café du Brésil ont attiré l'attention des capitalistes européens. Plusieurs syndicats anglais et belges ont acheté de grandes plantations dans les Etats de Minas Geraes et São Paul. À Anvers une compagnie a été fondée ayant une agence à Santos, dans le but d'acheter le café directement des planteurs et de le vendre au détail en Europe sans intermédiaire.

On attend à Rio et Santos vers la fin d'octobre une groupe de négociants de capitalistes d'ingénieurs anglais et d'hommes expérimentés dans l'agriculture, qui ensuite traverseront l'intérieur, dans le but, dit on, de faire des occasions de propriétés agricoles et industrielles.

Les prix au quels de telles propriétés sont offertes en ce moment, des placements de profit peuvent être faits, d'avis des personnes les plus au courant, par les capitalistes qui ne sont pas obligés de compter sur les résultats immédiats. Ainsi les Anglais qui déjà occupent une place dominante dans les finances et le commerce brésiliens peuvent, par le change et par la possession d'une grande partie du territoire productif, gagner une grande influence sur le commerce de café entre le Brésil et les Etats-Unis, controlant entièrement ce commerce, à moins qu'une autre influence contraire intervienne.

RECETTES DES DOUANES ET DU REVENU INTÉRIEUR.

Le Directeur du Revenu Public de la République à la date du 13 août a soumis un rapport (sujet à révision) des recettes des droits de douane et du revenu intérieur pour le premier semestre de 1898. De ceci les statistiques ci-contre sont prises.

Dans la première partie de cette année les recettes de douane s'élevaient à $119,161,180 milreis, indiquant une diminution de 3,742,896 milreis comparée à celles de la première moitié de 1897, et de 23,302,261 milreis en comparaison avec celles de la période correspondante de 1896.

De ces recettes la somme dérivée des droits d'entrée s'est élevée à 102,933,069 milreis dans la première partie de 1898, faisant 9,670,101 milreis de moins que dans celle de 1897 et 14,518,931 de moins que dans celle de 1896.

À 17 des bureaux de douanes, les recettes ont diminué et il n'y avait une augmentation que dans 6 bureaux, un desquels, celui de Rio Grande de Sol, l'augmentation a été due à la fermeture des douanes de Porto Alege et Petotas.

En 1898, à la Douane Rio de Janeiro, les recettes pour la moitié de l'année étaient de 6,554,537 milreis, ou 16.02 pour cent de moins qu'en 1897, et 13,174,340 milreis, ou 32.17 pour cent de moins qu'en 1896.

Les recettes du revenu intérieur dans la première partie des trois années ont été comme suit:

	Milreis.
1896	5,984,314.33
1897	6,659,984.33
1898	8,579,018.44

Dans les recettes pour la première partie de l'année de 1898 sont compris le produit des nouvelles taxes sur les allumettes et les polices d'assurances étrangères qui s'est élevé à 745,073 milreis pour les premiers et à 35,273 milreis pour les derniers. Il y avait une augmentation considérable dans le revenu dérivé de l'impôt sur le tabac et les boissons, mais une diminution dans ceux obtenue des impôts sur les timbres et celui sur le transfer de navires et des obligations du gouvernement par suite de la dépréciation du milreis (qui au pair est $0.546 en or). Les valeurs correspondantes en espèces des Etats-Unis ne peuvent pas être données à ce point de vue.

CHILE.

STATISTIQUES COMMERCIALES DE 1897.

Le "Chilian Times" du 31 d'août dit:

Il vient d'être publié par les presses de l'Universo Printing Office le volume des statistiques commerciales de la République pour l'année 1897. C'est un grand tome de plusieurs centaines de pages, d'une exécution irréprochable, et le principal statisticien, M. WENCESLAO ESCOBAR, doit être félicité sur l'émission de ce volume plusieurs mois en avance sur l'époque de la publication ordinaire. Le contenu du volume comprend Comercio Especial, Movimiento de la Navegación, Comercio Marítimo Interior, Estadística Retrospectiva et Comercio de Tránsito. La partie intitulée "Comercio General" qui a paru dans le tome précédent, a été omise comme inutile.

Il y a eu une diminution considérable dans le chiffre d'affaires en 1897 comparée à 1896; cependant, avant de donner des chiffres, on fera bien de noter que comme d'habitude les évaluations sont données en dollars de trente-huit pence. L'évaluations alors des importations a été de $65,502,805 et celle des exportations de $64,754,133. La valeur totale des importations et des exportations a été de $130,256,930, ou $18,185,281 de moins que le total de 1896.

Dans cette augmentation de $18,185,281 les chiffres des importations sont de $8,580,000 et ceux des exportations de $9,605,281. Ceci est la quatrième fois dans l'histoire de la République depuis 1844, laquelle pour la première fois les statistiques commerciales furent compilées que le volume commercial du pays a indiqué une diminution comparée à la diminution de 1897. Les autres fois furent les années 1877, 1885 et 1894. Dans la première de ces années la diminution s'est élevée à $14,211,411, dans la seconde à $29,591,686, et dans la troisième à $13,956,952.

La diminution dans les importations a été principalement dans les denrées alimentaires, les matériaux bruts, les machines et articles d'industries, d'arts et de métiers, les objets de ménage, les articles de chemins de fer et de télégraphe, le tabac, les articles ayant rapport aux arts, aux sciences et aux belles lettres, le charbon, la toile à chemises, le coton pour pantalons, les huiles et le suif. Les importations se partagent en quinze classifications, et dans le tableau suivant on trouvera les évaluations de chaque article pour les années 1896 et 1897.

Classification.	Evaluations, 1896.	Evaluations, 1897.
Denrées alimentaires..............................	$14,287,626	$13,926,523
Textiles..........	12,790,619	13,013,719
Matériaux bruts..................................	12,021,434	10,319,062
Vêtements, bijouterie et articles d'usage personnel	3,585,133	3,597,370
Machines, instruments et autres d'industries d'arts et de métiers............	9,710,679	9,156,614
Objets de ménage	5,187,110	5,025,979
Articles de chemins de fer et de télégraphe	2,347,432	1,073,744
Vins et liqueurs..................................	934,649	1,178,878
Tabac à priser, tabac, etc.........................	580,631	399,401
Minerai et lingots................................	20,726	11,287
Articles d'arts, de sciences et de belles lettres........	1,297,941	1,089,025
Drogues et médicaments et articles industriels........	1,179,509	1,113,469
Armes et accessoires..............................	164,850	133,345
Miscellanées	9,787,634	5,387,675
Espèces et billets de banque.......................	186,832	76,733
Total	74,082,805	65,502,805

Dans les exportations de produits agricoles, principalement le blé, l'orge, les noix, le foin et les pois ont indiqué une diminution de $2,309,934. Les produits minéraux, principalement le nitrate, l'argent en barreau, le borat de chaux, le minerai de cuivre et le regulus en cuivre et en argent ont indiqué une diminution de $6,160,600, tandis que les produits animaux, principalement les peaux et de la laine et les jambons ont indiqué une diminution de $549,065.

COLOMBIE.

TARIF DES LIQUEURS À PANAMA.

L'ordonnance No. 39 de 1898 récemment publié par le Gouvernement sous forme de décret règle les droits perçus dans les Départements de Panama sur les boissons non-specifiées dans l'article 1 du Décret 29 de 1895 et doit entrer en vigueur le 1er janvier 1898. Les droits seront imposés aux taux suivants calculés en argent colombien :

Sirops	par kilo..	$0. 10
Bordeaux, Tinto, et autres vins de table	do...	.06
Ales, bière, ginger ale et cidre champagne	do...	.06
Malaga, xérès, porto, vins doux et mousseux	do...	.15
Champagne et autres vins mousseux	do...	.20
Vins médicamentés et brevetés	do...	.05
Essence d'anis	par litre..	20.00

Les eaux minérales sont exceptées de paiement de tous droits d'entrée sur les liqueurs, mais les vins médicamentés devront payer 5 cents par chaque kilogramme (y compris l'emballage). Les articles destinés à être employés exclusivement par les hôpitaux et semblables institutions ne seront imposées que pour la moitié des droits ci-dessus. Les vins importés à l'usage de l'Hôpital St. Thomas à Panama sont exempts de tous droits.

Vins pour l'usage des autorités ecclésiastiques dans les services réligieux sont aussi exempts de tous droits quand certaines formalités sont remplies. Les nouveaux articles sous ce tarif sont, essence d'anis et vins médicamentés et brevetés. L'augmentation des droits sur les vins de malaga, de xérès, porto, etc., est 50 pour cent, sur le champagne 100 pour cent, sur les vins de table, ale, bière etc., 200 pour cent et sur les sirops 400 pour cent.

PERSPECTIVES DU PANAMA CANAL.

Un nombre de directeurs et de représentants de la Compagnie du Panama Canal sont récemment arrivés à New York, tout direct, de Panama. Un membre de la compagnie, M. R. G. WARD, a dit publiquement que selon son avis et celui des autres que le présent est un moment bien critique dans les affaires de la compagnie, et il a proposé qu'une proposition définitive des affaires soit faite, s'adressant aux Américains, et invitant leur coopération dans l'achèvement et possession du canal. Evidemment, M. WARD ne croit pas que le canal sera jamais terminé sans la coopération des Etats-Unis et conseille fortement un canal traversant l'Isthme de Panama en préférence de celui de la route de Nicaragua.

COSTA RICA.

EXPORTATION DE CAFÉ EN 1897–98.

Le Directeur des Statistiques de la République a fourni les chiffres suivants concernant les exportations de café pour l'année fiscale finissant le 30 juin 1898. Ces chiffres indiquent une augmentation de 2,000 sacs (264,000 livres) sur ceux de 1896–97 et 6,000 sacs (792,000 livres) sur ceux de 1895–96.

Routes.	Sacs.	Kilogrammes.
Pour New York par Ligne Atlas	94,075	5,084,787
Pour l'Angleterre par Royal Mail	80,358	4,166,064
Par Ligne Lyon et Cox	52,983	2,882,113
Par Ligne Allemande	45,731	2,567,717
Par Ligne Française	18,829	1,056,251
Par d'autres	5,515	328,257
Grand total	297,491	16,085,189

ÉQUATEUR.

OBSERVATIONS PRISES DU MESSAGE DU PRÉSIDENT.

Président ALFARO a envoyé son message annuel au Congrès le 9 août. De ceci il parait que la condition de la République d'Equateur s'avance décidemment. Le Président dit que le Département Statistique de la Douane a été réorganisé au fond et que l'on peut accepter les statistiques fournies en ce moment en toute confiance. Ceci étant le cas, M. ALFARO est heureux à dire que les exportations de 1897 ont dépassé de presque 50 pour cent celles de 1896.

Les chiffres donnés dans le message du Président sont comme suit: Exportations de 1896, 21,862,324 sucres ($9,138,451.43);

exportations pour 1897, 31,025,382 sucres ($2,968,609.68); importations pour 1897, 18,004.48 sucres ($7,525,692.06).

Le Président dit que ce compte doit s'augmenter d'environ 25 pour cent, comme les valeurs officielles dans le rapport de la Douane sont de trop basses évaluations et que la valeur réelle des importations doit être au moins de 22,000,000 sucres ($9,196,000). Le Gouvernement propose d'augmenter l'évaluation officielle sur laquelle les droits furent estimés, et une commission a été nommé dans ce but.

GUATÉMALA.

VALEURS DES PLACEMENTS ALLEMANDS.

Le "Moniteur Officiel de Commerce Français" dit que pendant plusieurs années les exportations du Guatémala ont dépassé de beaucoup les importations. En 1896 les importations ont représenté un total de 23,085,000 piastres ($11,373,980), contre les importations évaluées à 9,143,000 piastres ($4,503,756). A première vue, la situation paraîtrait être avantageuse au Guatémala, mais les déficits annuels indiquent le contraire. Cette anormale condition des affaires est due au fait que la pluspart ` des plantations de café sont possédées par les Stock Compagnies Allemandes et les bénéfices rapportés par le capital employé vont à l'Allemagne en forme de dividendes. Les intérêts allemands dans la République, dit on, sont évalués à plus de 150,000,000 marks ($35,700,000), quoique le nombre d'Allemands résidant dans le pays ne dépasse pas 500.

MEXIQUE.

CHAMPS SÉDUISANT.

Le Mexique est un champ séduisant pour l'exportateur américain à cause de sa proximité et la demande pour les manufactures est grande et croissante. Le "Mexique Moderne" dit : Quoique la consommation de produits étrangers va augmenter dans les prochaines années, les exportateurs américains ne doivent pas se faire d'illusions concernant les présentes possibilités de ce marché. Premièrement pas plus qu'un quatrième de la population du Mexique ne doit être considérée en calculant la consommation possible des produits importés En d'autres mots, au moins 75 pour cent de la population du Mexique se compose d'Indiens et de péons qui n'achèteront jamais de leur vie un seul article importé. Le nombre de petits propriétaires est très petit comparé aux Etats-Unis. Le travail est bon marché et les ouvriers capables de diriger des machines sont rares, de sorte que l'introduction des machines destinées à économiser le travail ne sera pas aussi rapide qu'elle l'a été aux Etats-Unis. La plus grande partie du commerce étranger du Mexique ne peut guère être comparée au commerce énorme des Etats-Unis, mais ce commerce en augmentant suit une bonne voie et les manufacturiers américains trouveront qu'il est beaucoup plus facile et meilleur marché d'obtenir le commerce mexicain maintenant et de suivre son développement que d'assurer une entrée après que les importations auront doublées.

NOUVEAU DÉBARCADÈRE DE DOUANES.

Le nouveau débarcadère à Vera Cruz, quoique n'étant pas tout-à-fait terminé, est en usage maintenant par les autorités des douanes. Ce débarcadère a 580 pieds de longueur, 80 pieds de largeur et a 28 piéds de tirant d'eau sur les côtés à marée basse. Le premier navire qui déchargea sa cargaison au nouveau lieu de débarquement fut le *Tampican*, navire de la Compagnie des Indes occidentales et du Pacifique. Ce navire est enregistré à 3,126 tonnes de tonnage; il a 430 pieds de longueur, tirant 17 pieds 6 pouces à l'avant et 21 pieds 3 pouces à l'arrière; c'est le plus grand navire qui fait escale dans ce port. Un autre navire de la même capacité peut très bien faire son déchargement sur le côté opposé du débarcadère en même temps.

A l'exception des navires de cabotage et des houillers, ceci était la première fois qu'un navire ait pu décharger toute sa cargaison au débarcadère général. Ces nouvelles facilités sont d'une grande importance au port, présentant beaucoup de possibilités pour un plus rapide et plus facile départ des navires et elles ne peuvent pas manquer d'encourager et augmenter le commerce.

PARAGUAY.

COMMERCE DE BEURRE.

Le Consul Ruffin écrivant d'Asuncion dit qu'il y a des indications d'un bon marché pour le beurre fait aux Etats-Unis. Très peu de cet article se trouve dans la République, quoique tout le monde l'aime et qu'il est fort demandé. La rareté est due à l'absence de crameries et au petit nombre de laiteries. Ces dernières se trouvent toutes dans la petite ville de San Bernardino, dont la population est presque exclusivement allemande. En 1897 environ 2,500 livres ont été exportées venant principalement d'Italie dans des boîtes d'étain d'une livre. Le beurre provenant des laiteries de San Bernardino est vendu au détail de 35 à 40 cents en or par livre et est le meilleur qu'il soit possible d'obtenir. Les droits d'entrée sur le beurre importé sont 50 pour cent ad valorem et le revenu de cette source s'est élevé à $421 en or pendant l'année dernière.

Le beurre importé d'Europe est bon, mais il n'égale pas en qualité le beurre fait dans les laiteries des Etats-Unis. La qualité supérieure du beurre en consommation aux Etats-Unis garantira une vente rapide au Paraguay, pourvu qu'on tienne compte des-goûts et des coutumes des habitants. Le beurre n'est rarement sur la table et les hôtels qui en servent comptent un supplément aux voyageurs.

Le Consul propose que si les manufacturiers des Etats-Unis font l'essai d'envoyer des chargements de beurre au Paraguay en l'emballant dans de petites boîtes d'environ une livre et en y collant le portrait du Président du Paraguay ou d'un des hommes d'état en vue, et une ou deux maisons historiques, on en parlerait, et cela mettrait la marque en faveur auprès du public.

M. Ruffin pense que les ventes rapides et profitables en résulteront, comme aucune réclame de ce genre n'existe dans ce pays.

Ce qu'on dit du Paraguay peut s'appliquer également à toutes les Républiques de l'Amérique du Sud en ce qui concerne la consommation, la rareté et la demande du beurre. Les propriétaires des laiteries aux Etats-Unis profiteraient beaucoup d'un examen attentif des conditions existantes, et en pourvoyant aux exigences de ce commerce.

LA NOURRITURE NATIONALE.

Aucune production du sol n'est plus universellement en usage dans la République de Paraguay que le manioc. Ceci est une production particulière aux régions des tropiques. Chaque famille dans toutes conditions de la vie l'a sur la table. Il ressemble un peu à la patate des Etats-Unis, quoique possèdant plus d'amidon et moins de douceur. Ordinairement il est préparé avec de la viande ensemble avec le maïs des patates et d'autres légumes. Ceci compose le plat national du Paraguay. Le manioc est employé aussi dans la fabrication de l'amidon l'amidon de maïs, étant un article inconnu au Paraguay.

Le manioc est d'un brun clair; la plante atteint de 18 pouces à 2 pieds de hauteur avec une circonférence de 3 à 5 pouces. On la plante en mai et pendant les mois d'hiver. En juin, juillet et août il est dans la meilleure condition pour le marché, quoique poussant l'année entière. Pour 5 cents (valeur en or) on peut acheter une quantité suffisante de manioc pour fournir la partie la plus substantielle d'un repas pour une famille de 5 ou 6 personnes. Le Consul RUFFIN annonce les perspectives de récolte pour cette année comme étant bonnes.

ENCOURAGEMENT DE L'AGRICULTURE.

Le Consul RUFFIN envoie une communication concernant la Banque Agricole. Celle-ci est un établissement du Gouvernement et se charge des intérêts agricoles de la République. Les méthodes et machines agricoles modernes sont employées en ce moment avec de bons résultats. Le consul est d'avis que si la qualité supérieure des machines américaines était connue les machines des Etats-Unis révolutionneraient l'agriculture au Paraguay.

Les manufacturiers américains proposent d'envoyer des agents à Asuncion qui établiront des agences pour la vente des articles fabriqués aux Etats-Unis.

CONDITION DE LA TRÉSORERIE—ESPÈCES EN CIRCULATION.

Le rapport suivant sur la condition de la Trésorerie des Etats-Unis à la clôture des affaires du 30 septembre fut publié le 1er octobre: Balance en argent accessible, $309,156,297; réserve en or libre, $243,327,379; argent net, $7,120,784; billets en papier légal dans la Trésorerie, $36,454,266; billets de Trésorerie de 1890, $1,751,950; recettes totales pour le mois, $3,103,050; recettes totales pour l'année fiscale, $128,510,936; dépenses totales pour l'année fiscale, $187,099,114; dépôts de Trésorerie dans les banques nationales $83,344,416.

Les statistiques d'espèces en circulation indiquent une différence comparées avec celles des deux mois précédents et accusent une augmentation nette au lieu d'une diminution nette pour le mois, l'augmentation nette s'élevant à $24,499,847. Parmi les articles qui montrent une diminution la plus importante est la monnaie d'or qui indique une diminution de $8,043,354; d'autres articles qui ont subit une diminution étaient les certificats en espèces de 1872, $2,645,000, et certificats en or, $79,100. La plus remarquable augmentation a été dans les billets des Etats-Unis, s'élevant à $19,264,584. L'augmentation en billets de banque nationale s'est élevée à $8,904,794. D'autres augmentations étaient de $3,050,515 en dollars étalons d'argent, $1,828,417 en argent subsidiaire, $435,362 en certificats d'argent et $1,783,629 en billets du Trésor de 1890.

Une petite augmentation nette est indiquée par le rapport comparatif indiquant les changements en espèces et lingots dans la Trésorerie. Deux articles montrent une augmentation; le bénéfice en monnaie d'or s'est élevé à $14,190,377, et lingot $11,123,581. La diminution la plus notable est celle des billets des Etats-Unis qui a été proportionneé à l'augmentation en circulation mentionnée audessus. Le stock général d'argent employé, la quantité dans la Trésorerie, ainsi que la somme en circulation sont donnés dans le tableau ci-joint:

	Stock général en monnaie ou papier.	Dans la Trésorerie.	En circulation 1er octobre 1898.
Monnaie d'or	$785,041,686	$162,391,874	$622,649,812
Dollars en argent étalon.............	464,834,597	404,045,769	60,788,828
Argent subsidiaire	75,784,648	9,196,708	66,587,940
Certificats d'or....	36,990,799	1,596,890	35,393,909
Certificats en argent................	400,062,504	6,636,769	393,425,735
Billets de Trésorerie, acte 14 juillet 1890	98,549,280	1,844,997	96,704,283
Billets des Etats-Unis	346,681,016	55,020,851	291,660,165
Certificats en espèces, acte 8 juin 1872..	18,455,000	820,000	17,635,000
Billets de la Banque Nationale........	235,439,985	3,689,265	231,750,720
Total	2,461,839,515	645,243,123	1,816,596,392

Comparé au 1ᵉʳ octobre 1897, la quantité d'or en circulation est augmentée de plus de $93,500,000. Pendant l'année l'augmentation dans les billets des Etats-Unis étaient de $39,800,000; certificats d'argent, $18,800,000; billets de Trésorerie de 1890, environ de $6,900,000; argent subsidiaire, plus de $5,400,000; billets de la Banque Nationale, presque $5,300,000 et dollars étalons en argent plus de $3,600,000. Il n'y avait des diminutions que dans deux données chaque d'environ la même diminution de $1,500,000. Il y avait que des certificats de 1872 et des certificats d'or.

Le grand total d'argent en circulation le 1ᵉʳ octobre s'est élevé à $1,816,596,392. Ceci a représenté une augmentation de plus de $137,750,000, comparée au 1ᵉʳ octobre 1897. La circulation par habitant a été $24.24, basé par l'expert de la Trésorerie sur une population estimée à 74,925,000. Ceci représente pour le mois de septembre une augmentation de 28 cents par habitant et de $1.35 sur celle du 1ᵉʳ octobre 1897. On verra par rapport ci-dessus que de la quantité totale d'or émise presque quatre-cinquièmes a été en circulation, tandis que des dollars étalons en argent plus de six-septièmes étaient dans les caves de la Trésorerie.

RECETTES DU REVENU INTÉRIEUR POUR LE MOIS D'AOÛT.

Le rapport de la perception du revenu intérieur pour le mois d'août indique une augmentation nette sur celle du mois d'août 1897 de $11,006,235. Les recettes des différentes sources de revenu et l'augmentation ou diminution comparée au mois d'août 1897 sont données comme suit:

Spiritueux, $6,787,513; diminution, $207,645. Liqueurs fermentées, $7,053,661; augmentation, $5,418,860. Oléomargarine, $131,354; augmentation, $64,923. Impôts spéciaux pas autrement énumérés, $1,289,335. Miscellanée, $3,098,510; augmentation, $3,072,036.

Les différents articles dont les impôts spéciaux ont été obtenus étaient: Banquiers, $971,934; salles de billards, $98,700; courtiers, fonds publics obligations, etc., $101,958; courtiers de commerce, $48,123; courtiers en douane, $2,202; prêteurs sur gage, $11,269; jeux de quilles, $17,139; cirques, $6,058; expositions pas autrement désignées, $12,039; théâtres, etc., $19,908; farine mélangée, $755; legs, $5,057; timbres de documents de propriétés, $3,167,514; cartes à jouer, $12,438; amendes, $12,266. L'augmentation nette pour les deux derniers mois sur la période correspondante de 1897 a été $19,337,946.

ETATS-UNIS.

COMMERCE AVEC L'AMERIQUE LATINE.

RAPPORT SUR LES IMPORTATIONS ET EXPORTATIONS.

À la page 617, on trouvera le dernier rapport des chiffres compilés par le Bureau des Statistiques du Département de la Trésorerie des Etats-Unis dont M. O. P. AUSTIN est Chef. Ces chiffres démontrent les évaluations du commerce entre les Etats-Unis et les pays Américains-Latins. Le rapport est pour le mois de juillet 1898, corrigé jusqu'au 2 septembre 1898, avec un exposé comparé à la même période de l'année précédente, ainsi pour les sept mois finissant le mois de juillet 1898 comparé à la même période de 1897. On doit expliquer que les chiffres des diverses douanes démontrant les importations et exportations pour n'importe quel mois de l'année ne sont pas reçus au Département de la Trésorerie jusqu'au vingtième jour du mois suivant, et il faut nécessairement du temps pour la compilation et l'imprimerie, de sorte que les rapports pour le mois de juillet, par example, ne sont publiés qu'au mois de septembre.

GRANDE AUGMENTATION DANS LA CONSTRUCTION DE NAVIRES.

Un rapport au Bureau de Navigation montre que pendant l'année fiscale finissant le 30 juin 1898 on a construit et enregistré 952 navires marchands de 180,458 tonnes brutes comparés à 891 tonnes brutes pour l'année précédente. L'augmentation dans la construction est presque entièrement sur les Grands Lacs, où le tonnage enregistré dernièrement ne s'élevait qu'à 54,937 tonnes pour la fiscale année précédente. La construction sur la Côte Pacifique a été de 49,789, comparée à 7,495 tonnes pour l'année fiscale précédente, cette augmentation étant principalement des navires à vapeur destinés au commerce de l'Alaska Pacifique et du fleuve Alaska. La diminution dans la construction a été entièrement dans la première partie de l'année fiscale quand la construction des navires dans la Grande Bretagne et les autres nations maritimes a indiqué une diminution de 20 pour cent. En avril, mai et juin, les mois de la guerre avec l'Espagne, le tonnage construit et enregistré aux Etats-Unis a été le double de celui des mêmes mois de 1897.

Le tonnage construit et enregistré officiellement pendant le premier trimestre de l'année fiscale du mois courant finissant le 30 septembre comprend 301 navires de 83,191 tonnes, comparé à 97 navires de 26,805 tonnes pour le trimestre correspondant de l'année dernière. Il y a des indications que la construction pendant l'année présente dépassera celle de n'importe quelle année depuis vingt-cinq ans excepté la construction de l'année de 1890–91.

La taxe de tonnage perçue pendant l'année fiscale finissant le 30 juin s'élevait à $846,771, comparée à $731,770 pour l'année précédente et $544,255 pour 1896. Les navires anglais ont payé $552,721 ; les navires allemands, $86,120 ; les navires américains, $63,534 ; les navires norvégiens, $47,070, et les navires espagnols, $17,521. Les perceptions à New York étaient de $283,827, comparées à $237,778 pour l'année précédente ; la Nouvelle Orléans, $79,550, comparées à $65,948 ; Philadelphie, $69,815, comparée à $62,354 ; San Francisco, $38,330, comparée à à $47,371. La perception de douane pendant l'année écoulée dépasse celle de n'importe quelle année depuis le changement en 1884 de la loi sur les impôts.

BANQUES À CUBA.

Jusqu'ici la Banque d'Espagne et les banquiers européens se sont chargés de tout le papier commercial nécessaire aux exigences du commerce entre les Etats-Unis et Cuba, faisant escompte et l'encaissement, émettant des lettres de crédit, achetant et vendant des lettres de change et remplissant les fonctions d'agents commerciaux. Il est évident que les banques des Etats-Unis à Cuba, ce qui est aussi le cas dans les Républiques Américaines, sont nécessaires pour aider les exportateurs à faire des affaires directement avec leurs clients sur cette île.

M. S. M. JARVIS, vice-Président du "North American Trust Co.," est de retour de Santiago de Cuba après y avoir établi la première banque des Etats-Unis aux Indes occidentales. Dans une entrevue il a dit :

Nous avons établi à Santiago une agence prête à faire des opérations de commerce qui est purement un établissement de banque désigné en premier lieu à remplir les demandes du Gouvernement des Etats-Unis et ses agents fiscaux; secondement, pour la facilité de ceux qui y surveillent des opérations commerciales. Dans ce dernier but, nous sommes préparés à émettre des lettres de credit sur New York pour être employées à Santiago, soit par des voyageurs, soit par des importateurs de marchandises sur cette place, et à Santiago notre agence est prêt à acheter ou à vendre des lettres de change sur New York et nous nous chargeons des documents maritimes. Dans chacune de ces deux places nous sommes maintenant prêts à fournir des transfers d'argent télégraphiques sur l'autre place. Des agences semblables seront établies à la Havane, Maturzas et autres points à notre choix.

URUGUAY.

RECETTES DES DOUANES À MONTEVIDEO.

Les recettes des douanes de Montevideo pour le mois de juillet s'élevait à $1,005,007, selon le rapport du Consul anglais. Ceci est un total remarquable, quand on tient comptè que le mois de juillet est le plus mauvais à Montevideo.

Le consul attribue cette augmentation extraordinaire au fait que les négociants, pour ne pas payer le taux additionnel de 2½ pour cent, qui a été mis en vigueur le 1er août, ont retiré leurs marchandises des douanes en grandes quantités. Il y a eu aussi une augmentation des importations. Le total pour le mois de juillet 1898 s'élevait à $916,359, contre un total de $583,000 en juillet 1897.

D'après le Montévidéo "Times" les recettes des douanes pour es premiers six mois de 1898 s'élevaient à $5,319,448, contre $4,290,121 pour la même période en 1897. L'année présente montre non seulement une augmentation sur l'année de la révolution 1897, mais ne souffre pas de la comparaison avec la première partie de 1896, que l'on regardait comme une année prospère au point de vue commercial. Alors les recettes de douanes s'élevaient à $5,553,402. Les chiffres pour 1898 d'après le "Times" sont sujets à révision, qui les augmentera plutôt qu'elle ne les diminuera.

Concernant les additionnels 2½ pour cent droits d'entrée sur les marchandises entrant au Uruguay dont la publication fut faite dans le BULLETIN de septembre, le Consul SWALM dit que le

Gouvernement a décidé d'attribuer les recettes à la conversion des certificats du Trésor jusqu'à ce qu'on en aura besoin pour les nouvaux travaux à Montévidéo.

VENEZUELA.

IMPORTANCE DE LA COUR D'ARBITRATION.

L'approche de la réunion à Paris de la Cour d'Arbitration Anglo-Venezuelienne, dont les deux présidents, MM. FULLER et BREWER de la Cour Suprême des Etats-Unis, font partie en faveur du Venezuela, ne le cèdera en importance qu'à la réunion à la même ville de la Commission de Paix entre les Etats-Unis et l'Espagne, vu la crise que la question Venezuelienne amena entre les Etats-Unis et la Grande Bretagne, sous l'Administration de CLEVELAND, et vu jusqu'à quel point la question embrasse la Doctrine Monroe. Jusqu'ici on a décidé que la cour siègerait en séance préliminaire dans le courant du mois de janvier 1899, à laquelle époque le Juge BREWER se rendra à Paris; mais le Juge FULLER n'assistera pas, dit-on, à la première réunion, attendu que la Suprême Cour siègera à cette époque, il n'est pas possible que deux de ses membres soient absents en même temps. Le Juge BREWER proposera de remettre cette réunion jusqu'au mois de mai quand les deux juges seront libres et pourront s'occuper des questions importantes du tribunal.

Les cas et les contre-cas entre la Grande Bretagne et le Venezuela ont été terminés. Señor ANDRADE, Ministre du Venezuela à Washington, a soumis récemment à l'Embassade Anglaise à Washington le contre-cas de la République, et en même temps on a remis le contre-cas anglais à Dr. ROJAS, représentant Venezuelien à Paris. Les papiers forment une des discussions internationales les plus volumineuses qui ait jamais été soumise à l'arbitration. Le cas et contre-cas anglais remplissent onze grands volumes, un atlas et un nombre de cartes géographiques détachés, tandis que la question Venezuelienne remplit six volumes et trois atlas. Du moment que les archives sont complétées, il ne tient qu'au conseil des deux partis de soumettre leurs causes. La cause Venezuelienne sera préparée par l'ex-Président HARRISON, l'ex-

Secrétaire TRACY, des Etats-Unis, et M. MALET PROVOST. La cause anglaise sera présentée par les plus éminents avocats d'Angleterre, y compris Sir RICHARD WEBSTER. On croit que les Généraux HARRISON et TRACY seront présentés et qu'ils présenteront des arguments oraux quand la cour se réunira en mai. Ainsi les avocats aussi bien que des arbitres donneront une importance particulière à cette réunion; le Baron HERSCHEL, ancien chancelier d'Angleterre, est à la tête des arbitres anglais, avec lui se trouve Sir RICHARD HENN COLLINS.

Le cinquième arbitre qui occupe le rang de compromissaire est M. MARTENS, célèbre juriste russe et écrivain sur les questions de loi internationale. Il remplit les fonctions des arbitres jusqu'au moment de leur réunion, et on lui adresse tous les dossiers et autres actes et documents.

ENCOURAGEMENT DE L'IMMIGRATION ITALIENNE.

M. LOOMIS, Ministre à Caracas, a récemment envoyé une communication au Département d'Etat renfermant un extrait du " Herald " de Venezuela. Cet extrait est une traduction du contrat entre le Gouvernement du Venezuela et un Syndicat de Capitalistes Italiens. Ce contrat remplace la concession Dotti dont a parlé le 10 janvier. La partie essentielle du contrat Dotti fut publiée dans le BULLETIN du mois de mai, page 1906.

M. LOOMIS pense que le contrat est favorable aux intérêts du Venezuela, et si toutes ses conditions sont remplies fidèlement il en résultera l'établissement dans la République de 15,000 familles du nord de l'Italie. On leur donnera des secours financiers et dans le but de les encourager à développer la culture des fruits et des céréales et de s'occuper surtout de la viticulture et de la vinification.

Le succès du projet après l'arrivée des immigrants dépendra de la construction des chemins de fer afin de faciliter le transport de leurs produits à bas prix aux marchés locaux et à la côte.

Le Ministre dit que l'étude des conditions présentées prouve à l'evidence que si la production des fruits augmentait considérablement, les cultivateurs seraient obligés de chercher un débouché aux Etats-Unis ou dans d'autres pays étrangers, mais de préférance aux Etats-Unis, à cause de la proximité de ce pays et où

les fruits des tropiques sont fort demandés.   On a emprunté du
journal les observations suivantes :

Au 1ᵉʳ juillet le Gouvernement a fait un réel et effectif contrat d'immigration.
Les partis contractants sont lês Ministres de l'Agriculture, de l'Industrie et du
Commerce, autorisés par le Président de la République en conseil de ses minis-
tres et avec le consentement du Conseil du Gouvernement d'une part et la
Société de Colinisation Italienne d'autre part.

Par ce contrat la compagnie se charge de faire entrer au Venezuela, tous les trois ans, 3,000 familles européennes, principalement de la race latine, agriculteurs et de bonne conduite, ces faits
devant être certifiés par les Consuls des divers ports d'embarquement.   2. De construire des bâtiments et de fournir des outils
agricoles et de leur fournir de la' nourriture, des vêtements et des
médicaments jusqu'à ce qu'ils auront fait leur première récolte, et
aussi de construire une église, des bureaux publics et des écoles
dans chaque colonie.   3. D'établir un bi-mensuel service de navires
entre l'Italie et le Venezuela faisant escale à Barcelona, d'Espana,
Teneriffe et autres ports et terminant le voyage à La Guayra ou
Puerto Cabello, et aussi faisant escale, si nécessaire, dans n'importe
quel autre port sujet aux lois fiscales du Venezuela, et de faire le
transport du courrier à tous ces ports sans paiement, le prix établi
pour les passagers et les marchandises ne devant pas dépasser celui
demandé par des navires de la même classe et du même tonnage
que ceux employés par la compagnie, et elle consent à ne demander que la moitié du prix pour tous les employés du service
diplomatique et pour leurs familles qui se servent des navires et de
leur accorder le voyage sans paiement s'ils résident officiellement
à l'étranger ou ont l'intention d'y aller.   4. D'établir à Caracas une
banque avec des succursales dans tels districts de la République
où ceux-ci seront jugés utiles, principalement dans le but de prêter
de l'argent sur des hypothèques aux agriculteurs et aux éleveurs
de bétail.   Le capital de cette banque devait consister de
20,000,000 bolivars ($3,860,000), 12,000,000 duquel seront
employés pour les affaires ordinaires de la banque et le reste pour
les prêts mentionnés ci-dessus.   Ces deux fonds doivent être séparés
et l'un ne pourra pas empiéter sur l'autre.   L'intérèt sur les prêts ne
doit pas dépasser 7 pour cent et la banque a le droit d'émettre des
billets aux termes des présentés lois de banque.   5. D'accorder au Gouvernement National le libre service de toutes voies de transport et

de communication qu'elle pourrait construire. 6. D'accorder après 4 ans de culture, à chaque famille, une maison de la colonie et à chaque colon 3 hectares (14.8 acres) qui lui auront été assignés en culture. 7. De déposer à la banque d'Angleterre en garantie de l'exécution de ce contrat et dans la période de trois mois à partir de la date à laquelle le contrat sera approuvé par le Congrès National, la somme de 200,000 bolivars ($38,900) qui resteront dans la banque jusqu'au moment où la compagnie établira la banque mentionnée ci-dessus à Caracas, et qu'elle établira les premières 500 familles, et cette somme reviendra au Gouvernement du Venezuela en cas de non-exécution du contrat.

D'autre part le Gouvernement se charge d'accorder à la compagnie des terrains non-cultivés à raison de 6 hectares (14.8 acres) par personne, et tout enfant au-dessous de 10 ans amené dans le pays par une famille immigrante aura, en atteignant cet âge, les droits et privilèges d'un immigrant. 9. De ne faire aucun contrat futur de cette nature avec autre personne ou compagnie qui désirerait amener des agriculteurs directement de l'Italie. 10. De permettre l'importation sans droits d'entrée des outils agricoles et des machines employées dans la manufacture des produits et dans la construction des bâtiments et de toutes voies de communication après la compagnie aura rempli les conditions imposées par la loi. 11. D'accorder à la compagnie la préférence (ceteris paribus) dans le développement de toutes les mines découvertes sur les terrains à proximité des colonies et dans l'établissement de voies de communication entre les colonies et entre les autres parties de la République. 12. De payer annuellement à la compagnie la somme de 18 bolivars ($3.47) pendant le terme de (15 ans) ce contrat pour chaque immigrant de 7 ans et au-dessus amené dans le pays et attaché à la Colonie.

La compagnie se charge de vendre au Gouvernement National, quand il le désirera, toutes lignes télégraphiques à un prix estimé par des personnes expérimentées. 14. De rendre au Gouvernement sans indemnité la possession entière des dites lignes après une période de 40 ans; de rendre à la municipalité dans laquelle elles se trouvent toutes lignes de téléphone après une période de 50 ans, et au Gouvernement National à l'expiration de 90 ans, tous chemins de fer, tramways, etc. Les prix demandés par la compagnie pour le service de toutes les voies de communication mentionnées ci-dessus seront réglés par un arrangement réciproque entre le Gouvernement et la compagnie. Concernant les colons, il est stipulé qu'ils peuvent s'engager dans n'importe quelle industrie qu'ils préfèrent, mais quand les terrains sont adaptés à la culture du blé ou à la vigne les colons doivent réserver, dans ce but, la troisième partie des terrains à eux accordés.

Le contrat restera en vigueur pendant 15 ans à dater du moment où il a été approuvé par le Congrès et est prolongeable pour un terme semblable et dans les mêmes conditions, à moins qu'il n'ait été résilié avant le commencement de la dernière année ou à moins que la Société n'ait manqué de remplir ses obligations et le Gouvernement ne lui ait fait des observations sur la non-exécution des conditions. Il est aussi stipulé que si la Société désire faire entrer les immigrants avant que le Congrès ne donne son consentement à ce contrat, elle peut le faire et le Gouvernement accordera les terrains sous les présentes lois d'immigration, et quand le Congrès sanctionne le contrat la compagnie aura le bénéfice de ces articles. Mais au cas où le Congrès n'approuverait pas le contrat, le Gouvernement payera le voyage des immigrants selon les termes de la présente loi.

Le Gouvernement se réserve le droit d'entrer dans des contrats semblables avec d'autres pays.

CONGRÈS NATIONAL DES FERMIERS.

La 18me session annuelle du Congrès National des Fermiers sera tenue à Fort Worth, Texas, du 6 au 14 décembre 1898, inclusivement. Le but de cette organisation, comme il est formulé dans sa constitution, est l'encouragement des intérêts agricoles de l'Union. Chaque Etat et Territoire a droit à autant de délégués qu'il a de représentants dans les deux branches du Congrès des Etats-Unis, plus un délégué de chaque College Agricole, outre ceux-ci tous les Directeurs des Bureaux agricoles d'état et territoire sont autorisés de nommer des délégués autre que ceux spécialement désignés.

En parlant de l'importance de cette organisation, l'Hon. WM. M. HATCH, pendant beaucoup d'années Président du Comité d'Agriculture du Congrès, dit qu'elle a eu plus d'influence auprès du Congrès des Etats-Unis que toutes les autres organisations agricoles réunies. C'est la seule Union de Fermiers dont les transactions sont mentionnées dans l'Encyclopédie américaine.

En envoyant au Directeur, M. EMORY, une invitation d'être présent à la réunion de décembre, M. D. O. LIVELY de Fort Worth, l'efficient Secrétaire du Congrès, écrit :

En ma qualité du Secrétaire de "Live Stock Exchange" de Fort Worth, j'ai reçu, pendant quelque temps, un très utile Bulletin Mensuel du Bureau dont vous êtes le Directeur, et je désire attirer votre attention à la réunion qui aura lieu à Fort Worth du 6 au 14 décembre de cette année, et à laquelle, à mon avis, le Bureau des Républiques Américaines devrait s'intéresser. Afin de vous rendre compte du caractère du but et de l'importance de cette organisation, je vous ai envoyé par la poste sous envelope séparée une copie du rapport de la réunion de l'année dernière tenue à St. Paul, et pour laquelle je solicite respectueusement votre attention. Vous observerez que Señor ROMERO et M. SOTELDO étaient parmi les représentants qui ont assisté à cette réunion et vous noterez aussi que beaucoup des questions discutées se rapportaient directement aux relations existant entre les Etats-Unis et d'autres Républiques Américaines. A la suite d'une requête faite par le Département d'Etat à Washington, le Gouvernement Mexicain a bien voulu consentir à nommer des délégués officiels pour représenter ce pays à la réunion de Fort Worth.

J'ai pensé que si une invitation était lancée par votre BULLETIN d'autres pays américains pourraient trouver bon de nommer des délégués pour ce Congrès. Nous comprenons qu'il est un peu tard pour que cette affaire suive le chenal du Département d'Etat et que de là qu'elle soit référée au gouvernement séparé. Je m'en rapporte à votre jugement en çe que regarde la possibilité de faire représenter votre Bureau officiellement, et je me permets de vous assurer que toute action de cette nature vous assurera la sincère gratitude de toutes les personnes intéressées et que nous accorderons à ce représentant toutes les considérations et l'honneur que mérite son importance.

Il est à regretter que cet avis ne fut pas envoyé au Bureau il y a deux mois au plus, pour permettre le choix de représentants par plusieurs Républiques Américaines au cas où elles auront désiré proffiter de cette occasion.

MISCELLANÉES COMMERCIALES.

MEXIQUE.

Envois d'Argent aux Etats-Unis. Lors d'un récent voyage de Nazatlan à San Francisco le navire *Acapulco* transporta 140 lingots d'argent évalués à $209,016.12 ; 7 lingots d'or évalués à $47,334.88 ; 7 boîtes de matte évalués à $10,080.79 ; $150,000 en monnaie d'argent et $2,846 en monnaie d'or.

Nouveau Chemin de Fer en Mexique. Le Consul Thomson écrivant de Progresso à la date du 22 août dit: "Les Etats de Yucatan et de Campèche sont maintenant reliés par un chemin de fer. Les cérémonies d'inauguration qui eurent lieu le 29 juillet furent très imposantes et le banquet qui suivit fut présidé par M. le Président Diaz. L'exécution de ce chemin de fer marque une époque importante pour les deux Etats."

Exportation de Caoutchouc. Les exportations de caoutchouc du Mexique pendant l'année finissant le 30 juin ont été les moins importantes depuis quatre ans, ne s'élevant qu'à 142,654 livres, atteignant la valeur de $63,126 (argent).

Recettes de Chemin de Fer. La Compagnie Nationale Mexicain de Chemin de Fer fait sur ses recettes le rapport suivant (en espèces mexicaines) pour le mois d'août: Recettes totales, $500,799; augmentation, $663; frais d'exploitation, $264,251; augmentation, $22,397; bénéfices nets, $236,548; diminution, $21,734; escompte, addition, etc., $126,081; diminution, $12,859; excès pour obligations, $110,467; diminution, $8,875. La Compagnie Nationale Mexicaine de Chemin de Fer accuse pour le mois d'août, $281,491; de recettes totales, augmentation, $2,147; bénéfices nets, $122,258; augmentation, $44,957.

NICARAGUA.

Nouvelle Ligne de Navire à Vapeur. L'Agent Consulaire Clancy écrit de Bluefields au Bureau qu'à partir du 1er octobre la Compagnie de Navires à Vapeur de Bluefields a inauguré un service trimestriel de navires à vapeur de Bluefields à Mobile, Ala., le transport de passager et des marchandises. MM. Orr et Laubenheimer contrôlaient une ligne de navires à vapeur de Bluefields à Mobile avant le mois de janvier 1898, mais lors de l'organisation de la nouvelle compagnie vers cette époque le service cessa. Maintenant que la ligne entrera de nouveau en opération elle sera de grande utilité aux négociants en bois de Mobile, vu que c'est là qu'on achète presque tout le bois employé à Bluefields et dans le territoire environnant. Les navires à vapeur faisant ce commerce sont le *Sunmia* et le *Tarl.*

Matériel de Chemin de Fer en Acier. Le "Boston Herald" dit qu'un steamer Norvégien faisant le transport de fruit est arrivé dernièrement de Bluefields, Nicaragua, avec un chargement de bananes et est retourné par voie de Baltimore après avoir pris un chargement d'acier dans ce dernier port. On croit que c'est là le premier chargement complet de rails d'acier expédié par les Etats-Unis pour l'Amérique Centrale. On dit que la maison Carnegie ont des ordres pour plusieurs autres chargements.

PARAGUAY.

Nouveau Bureau de Renseignements. Une nouvelle chambre de commerce ou association vient d'être formée dans la ville d'Asuncion sous le nom de "Centro Commercial del Paraguay." Le but de cette association est de donner des renseignements sur toutes les choses ayant rapport aux produits, aux coutumes, aux lois et au commerce de la République, et de venir en aide à toutes personnes désireuses d'entrer en relation commerciale avec les exportateurs et autres maisons de commerce au Paraguay.

d'Etat. Pendant son séjour ici, un journal en rendant compte d'une intervue lui prête les propos suivants: "Les Venezueliens sont en ce moment très disposés d'accepter les produits des Etats-Unis. Ils ont besoin de machines, de chemins de fer, de meilleures voitures, de meilleures rues, des systèmes de colonisation, etc." Il y a encore une chose dont je voudrais parler en termes emphatiques. C'est l'exposition et l'entrepôt ouverts par l'Association Nationale des Manufacturiers à Caracas. Son utilité augmente tous les jours et nous devrions l'encourager pour des raisons d'intérêts personnels.

RÉPUBLIQUE ARGENTINE.

Exportations Principales au Brésil. Les exportations principales au Brésil pendant la première moitié de l'année courante ont été 1,860 pipes, 3,220 fûts, 6,837 hogsheads, 245 litres de suif, 42,121 tonnes de blé, 3,160 tonnes de son, 1,655 sacs de graines d'oiseaux, 327,446 bottes de foin, 512 caisses de beurre. Il n'y avait qu'une balle de laine comprise dans les exportations.

Industrie de Tonture des Moutons. Une dépêche annonce que la tonture des moutons en Argentine a commencé. On estime que l'augmentation de la production sur celle de 1897 s'élèvera à au moins 15 pour cent. Le marché s'est ouvert avec un bénéfice de 10 pour cent.

BRÉSIL.

Importations de Charbon des Etats-Unis. Le "Black Diamond," journal officiel de l'Association des Négociants de Charbon d'Illinois et Wisconsin, annonce qu'un steamer chargé de charbon est récemment parti de Newport News pour Rio de Janeiro. On ajoute que ce navire est le premier d'un service de houilleurs hebdomadaire d'une capacité égale qui feront le voyage à Rio jusqu'à ce que les 150,000 tonnes de charbon pour lesquelles l'on a fait contrat auront été expédiées aux négociants Brésiliens. Ceci n'est que le commencement de la reprise des relations commerciales qui ont été interrompues par la récente guerre avec l'Espagne. D'après le "Black Diamond," le charbon dont on parle a été vendu en concurrence directe avec le charbon anglais, malgré le fait que toutes les conditions du commerce paraissaient être en faveur des négociants anglais. On doit noter que l'Angleterre, la France, et l'Allemagne se sont établies sur les marchés Brésiliens et qu'elles ont des facilités dans ce pays que les exportateurs des Etats-Unis n'ont pas; des succursales, des lignes directes, et des communications télégraphiques. De pareilles institutions et lignes doivent être établies par les Etats-Unis s'ils désirent bénéficier du commerce étranger.

Soumissions pour les Eaux. Jusqu'au mois de novembre 10 le Gouvernement a demandé soumissions pour la cession pendant une période de soixante ans (à être prolongé sous certaines conditions pour un autre terme de dix ans), du droit exclusif de fournir l'eau nécessaire à Belem, la capitale de l'État. Les États-Unis peuvent obtenir d'autres renseignements des représentants du Brésil.

ECUADOR.

Diminution de Récolte du Cacao. La récolte du cacao de la République pour 1897 s'est élevée à 14,800 tonnes ou 330,293 quintaux. Cette quantité ne compare pas favorablement avec la production des années récentes. En 1896 la production totale a été de 15,400 tonnes et en 1895 de 16,000 tonnes et en 1894 de 17,467 tonnes.

MONTHLY BULLETIN

OF THE

BUREAU OF THE AMERICAN REPUBLICS,

INTERNATIONAL UNION OF AMERICAN REPUBLICS.

VOL. VI.   NOVEMBER, 1898.   No. 5.

FINANCIAL POSITION OF CHILE.

In the October number of the MONTHLY BULLETIN a summary was published of a report to the Department of State by the United States Minister at Santiago, Hon. HENRY L. WILSON, upon the recent financial changes in Chile. It is of interest to note, in this connection, that a pamphlet has been issued by the Chilean Legation in London, bearing date of August 8, 1898, upon the financial position of Chile. The author of the pamphlet is Señor Don RICARDO SALAS EDWARDS, First Secretary of the Legation. The pamphlet gives interesting details of the revenues and expenditures of Chile, the various changes in currency legislation, and particulars as to Chilean banking.

Another valuable publication on the subject is a letter from Señor Don ELIODORO INFANTE, Chargé d'Affaires for Chile, in the United States, dated August 24, 1898, addressed to the Secretary of the National Sound Money League at Chicago. This letter, which sets forth the conditions affecting the currency problem in Chile, is as follows:

DEAR SIR: I am in receipt of your letter, dated the 11th instant, in which you refer to statements made by some newspapers that "Chile has been compelled to abandon the gold standard," and request the Chilean Legation to inform you as to the actual facts concerning this matter. I hasten to comply with your

773

guaranteed by the State and by bonds deposited in the Public Treasury. These $50,000,000 in notes are redeemable in gold in the course of three and a half years. The law authorizing the issue provides that the Government is to invest every year, from June 1, 1899, $10,000,000 gold in foreign stocks for the purpose of redeeming the new issue on January 1, 1902. In the course of three and a half years $35,000,000 will thus have been invested. In the meantime the new issue will gradually acquire a gold basis at the rate of $10,000,000 gold per annum.

This arrangement gives the issue, although temporarily inconvertible, the character of a gold currency, as the security is based entirely on that metal. The present exceptional stress is thus being relieved by the issue of legal-tender notes based on gold securities. This issue, according to the private reports referred to, is to be made only to the banks upon securities. They will pay a moderate interest for the accommodation. As soon as the panic is allayed and confidence is restored by means of this issue the hoarded gold will reappear and business in Chile will return to its normal condition.

The gold standard, as you see by the foregoing narrative, has not been abandoned in Chile. The serious difficulties and the rude sacrifices which its introduction necessarily entails have been, in the case of Chile, considerably enhanced by the pending boundary question with the Argentine Republic. Fortunately for all concerned, this question is now in a fair way of a final and peaceful settlement. The experts for both countries have agreed to meet and discuss in Chile a general line of frontier. The differences that may arise between them are to be referred to their Governments. Should these not succeed in adjusting them, they are to be submitted immediately to the arbitration of Her Britannic Majesty's Government, according to the agreement of April 17, 1896.

The fact that Chile undertook in 1895 the establishment of the gold standard and the resumption of specie payments proves that she earnestly desires peace, that being essential to the success of her financial policy.

Since this letter was written the amicable settlement of the boundary question between Chile and the Argentine Republic, predicted in the same, has been happily reached.

The frontier line which is to be established between the two countries runs from parallel 23 to parallel 52 south latitude. On the 22d of September of this year the two Governments signed a protocol stating the differences existing between them in reference to said line, from parallel 27 to parallel 52 south latitude, and agreed to submit them at once to the arbitral decision of Her Britannic Majesty's Government. The commissioners who are to represent both countries before the arbitrator have been appointed, and are on their way to London.

In two protocols signed by both Governments on the 2d day of the current month (November), it has been agreed to submit the differences arising in regard to the demarcation of the frontier line betwen parallel 23 and 27 south latitude to the decision of a commission composed of five Chilean and five Argentine delegates, who must meet at Buenos Ayres during this month; and it has also been agreed that in case such commission could not arrive at an agreement, the differences shall be submitted to the final decision of a board composed of a Chilean citizen, an Argentine citizen, and Mr. Buchanan, envoy extraordinary and minister plenipotentiary of the United States of America to the Argentine Republic, which board shall meet at Buenos Ayres and give its decision in November.

The resolution adopted has entirely reestablished tranquillity in both countries, and the Government of Chile has already commenced to disarm, reducing its regular army, according to press dispatches. The war and navy appropriations will be considerably reduced, industry and commerce will develop rapidly in both countries, and the surplus in the Chilean budget will be again what it was before—about $10,000,000 gold yearly.

PROVISIONAL DIRECTORSHIP OF THE BUREAU.

The Executive Committee of the International Union of American Republics met in the diplomatic room of the Department of State at 11 o'clock, October 26, 1898. There were present:

The Secretary of State, Hon. John Hay, Chairman.
Mr. Andrade, Minister from Venezuela.
Mr. Mérou, Minister from the Argentine Republic.

The object of the meeting was to consider the question of appointing a Director of the Bureau of the American Republics, the term of the provisional director, Mr. Frederic Emory, expiring November 1. In view of the satisfactory condition of the Bureau and the progress recently made, the committee decided to reappoint Mr. Emory Director, subject to its future action. Mr. Calvo, Minister from Costa Rica, a member of the committee, who was unable to be present, sent a letter expressing his desire for Mr. Emory's continuance. No definite term was fixed, but it is understood that the present management will continue as long as the interests of the Bureau seem to require, it having received the unanimous indorsement of the representatives of the Latin American countries, as well as the approval of the Department of State. Mr. EMORY, who is the Chief of the Bureau of Foreign Commerce of the Department of State, has had charge of the Bureau of the American Republics since the death of the former Director, Mr. JOSEPH P. SMITH, on the 5th of February last. While continuing to serve as provisional director he will, as heretofore, remain in charge of the Bureau of Foreign Commerce, which is engaged in the publication of the commercial reports from diplomatic and consular officers to the Department of State.

THE BUREAU OF THE AMERICAN REPUBLICS AT THE TRANS-MISSISSIPPI AND INTERNATIONAL EXPOSITION AT OMAHA.

The International Exposition, held at Omaha, Nebraska, from June 1 to October 31, 1898, was invested with special interest as regards the Latin-American nations, since that event was a most propitious occasion for the presentation of their products and resources to the markets of the United States. The Bureau of the American Republics fully appreciated the importance of this gathering, and, being the official center of information regarding the commerce, production, industry, and material progress of the Repúblics forming the International Union of American Republics, arrangements were made whereby its exhibit should demonstrate this fact, and at the same time call closer attention to the commercial and industrial possibilities of Mexico, Central and South America, and the West Indies, by the distribution of bulletins and circulars on the subject.

The report of the representative of the Bureau is here published, showing the benefits, present and in prospect, growing out of the exhibit.

OMAHA, NEBR., *October 31, 1898.*

DIRECTOR OF THE BUREAU OF AMERICAN REPUBLICS:

Herewith I submit my report of the work done at the Trans-Mississippi Exposition by the Bureau of American Republics. The position occupied by the Bureau was most excellent. Located, as it was, on the ground floor of the Liberal Arts Building, with the Philadelphia Commercial Museum as next neighbor, it attracted universal attention. The exhibit was arranged by Mr.

JOHN M. BIDDLE, who had charge of the exhibit of the Department of State, and with artistic draping of the American Republics' flags, good hanging of numerous pictures illustrative of South American scenes, handsome furniture, and graceful palms, the whole effect was excelled by no other exhibit on the Exposition grounds.   By the more intelligent of the people who have visited the Exposition much interest has been shown in the Bureau and its workings.

The close proximity of the Commercial Museum, with many cases filled with South American products, as well as samples of goods manufactured in England and Germany, made a sort of object lesson to those genuinely interested in the purposes of the Bureau of the American Republics.

Twenty-one hundred copies of the MONTHLY BULLETIN of the Bureau have been distributed and the addresses and occupations of those to whom they were mailed have been kept.   As might be expected in this agricultural region, farmers lead in registration, with teachers second.   Every State and Territory in the Union, including Alaska, except New Hampshire, Vermont, Rhode Island, Delaware, and South Carolina, have had some representative to register, with Iowa leading and Nebraska next.   Guatemala, Nicaragua, Mexico, and France constitute the foreign addresses.   To manufacturers registering, I have sent several copies of the BULLETIN, hoping thereby to increase their desire for South American trade.   Many letters have been received from recipients of BULLETINS, stating benefit derived from perusal of same.   The Trans-Mississippi Exposition has been a grand success from every standpoint, and in no way has it been more successful than in showing the American people the practical working of the various departments of the United States Government.

Following is a list of the occupations of those to whom BULLETINS were sent by mail.   The other copies were taken personally.

Farmers	175
Teachers	170
Merchants	85
Newspaper men and publishers	80
Attorneys	70
Students	60
Real-estate men	35
Bankers	30
Railroad officials	30
Physicians	27
Ministers	25
Manufacturers and importers	18
Clerks	18
Agents	18

Architects, bookkeepers, students, statisticians, dentists, missionaries, and others of every occupation that could be imagined, have been supplied with from 1 to 15 each.

The number of registrations by States is as follows:

Iowa	331
Nebraska	318
Missouri	139
Kansas	138

Other States had fewer representatives.

MARY ALICE HARRIMAN.

ARGENTINE REPUBLIC.

GENERAL ROCA'S FIRST ADMINISTRATION.

In the BULLETIN for October it was noted that a cablegram from Minister BUCHANAN at Buenos Ayres announced the inauguration of General JULIO A. ROCA as President of the Argentine Republic on October 12. This information is supplemented by a communication from the Argentine legation at Washington in the form of an extract from "Il Corriere Mercantile," of Genoa, containing details in regard to the life and achievements of the new President. From this paper the following facts are obtained:

General ROCA was born in Tucumán in July, 1843, and received his education first in his native country and afterwards at the National College of Uruguay. During an interval of college life, in common with some fellow-students, he served in the Uruguayan army on the occasion of a revolution in that country, and on entering the military service of his native land passed with distinction through the successive ranks from lieutenant to general, receiving the last title on the battlefield of Santa Rosa in December, 1874, in recognition of his bravery. He subsequently filled the offices of Chief of the Frontier in Cordoba, San Luis, and Mendozo, and of Minister of War and Navy. In 1880 he was made lieutenant-general of the army, and finally President of the Republic on the 12th of October of the same year. His first administration was distinguished by a boundary treaty with Chile and the new impulse given to foreign immigration, while under his peaceful rule the wealth of the country was greatly developed.

The progress of Argentina during this administration can readily be seen by a comparison of statistics. From 1880 to 1886 the population increased over 33 per cent, while the yearly immigration trebled, reaching as high as 100,000 immigrants in one year. Foreign trade increased 80 per cent, its value in 1880 being estimated at 520,000,000 liras ($104,000,000), and in 1886 at 955,000,000 liras ($191,000,000). Shipping tonnage increased threefold; railroad mileage also trebled, being 2,300 kilometers in 1880 and 6,400 kilometers in 1886. The extent of cultivated land increased from 1,120,000 hectares to 1,920,000 hectares, and the currency circulation and general credit of the country advanced greatly.

Part of the interval since his retirement from office, in 1886, has been spent in foreign travel, and he enters upon the discharge of the duties of his second administration thoroughly imbued with modern progressive ideas for the advancement of his country and the development of its unbounded resources.

IMPORTS OF ELECTRICAL APPARATUS.

According to the official figures furnished by the Argentine customs officers, there has been a great increase in the use of electricity as a motive power and for lighting purposes within the bounds of the Republic for the first six months of 1898. The imports of all electrical apparatus and appliances during the period named, as well as their gold valuation, is given in the following table:

	Quantity.	Value.
Galvanized-iron wire..........................tons..	9, 523	$589, 115
Cables, wires, etc...........................do...	2, 090	524, 081
Electric-light material.......................		191, 565
Fittings for lights..........................tons..	38	55, 791
Dynamos...........................number..	38	28, 005
Incandescent lamps...................dozens..	4, 466	13, 398
Telegraph material.........................		11, 298
Telephone material		4, 533
Phonographs.............................		3, 200
Total		1, 420, 986

A large percentage of these supplies were purchased from firms in the United States.

PRINCIPAL ARTICLES OF EXPORT.

The "Review of the River Plate" publishes the accompanying list of the principal exports from Argentina for the months of July and August and for the first eight months of the current year.

Articles.	July.	August.	Eight months.
Dry oxhides.........................number..	92, 265	99, 465	1, 024, 392
Salt oxhides..... ....do...	127, 368	91, 530	1, 013, 339
Dry horsehides.....................do...	12, 249	5, 498	68, 632
Salt horsehides.........................do...	26, 742	7, 611	125, 789
Sheepskins.....................bales..	4, 375	4, 629	35, 673
Hair...................................do...	476	790	2, 833
Wheat.............................tons..	8, 700	4, 758	658, 856
Maize........................do...	109, 923	113, 195	359, 066
Linseed........................do...	4, 478	894	149, 802
Wool.............................bales..	9, 253	4, 317	361, 027
Hay ....do....	105, 499	49, 628	524, 611
Tallow...............................pipes..	3, 068	4, 047	25, 984
Do............................casks..	3, 323	1, 878	18, 599
Do...................hogsheads..	2, 376	4, 783	29, 798
Bran...............................tons..	6, 996	8, 613	36, 649
Quebracho (for tanning).....................do. .	23, 529	12, 801	98, 910
Frozen wethers ....number..	202, 362	154, 797	1, 581, 412
Birdseed ....bags..	784	....	2, 439
Tobacco..............................bales..	523	1, 153	4, 804
Goatskins......................do...	32	327	1, 975
Pollards ....bags..	1, 863	20, 406	77, 639
Oilseed ....do...	7, 637	5, 052	53, 444
Butter ....boxes..	281	420	10, 551
Sugar ....tons..	4, 635	138	10, 790
Flour.................................do...	2, 130	2, 679	16, 380

DESTRUCTION OF LOCUSTS.

The central commission for the extinction of the "langosta," or locusts, in Argentina, has made a very interesting report to the Minister of Agriculture of that Republic says "The Farm Implement News." The commission was appointed for the purpose of obtaining all the information possible regarding the locust, its habitat, procreation, migration, etc., and to inaugurate concerted efforts for its extinction. To this end the commission organized many local commissioners, and these again formed subcommissions, and all investigated and adopted such means of destruction as seemed most effective. The results are that the habits of the locust have been well studied and learned, enormous quantities of eggs and "saltonas" (locusts before they have wings) were destroyed, and the destruction of crops greatly lessened.

The means of extinction employed were, a preparation of zinc, various liquid extirpators, the plow, and fire. The quantities thus destroyed this year are estimated in thousands of tons weight, and the area of crops saved at hundreds of thousands of acres; and it is believed that if, with what has been learned, these organized efforts be assiduously continued, the locust can be controlled or its ravages greatly restricted. The arrest of the ravages of the locust, whether through the efforts mentioned or other causes, has greatly encouraged the agriculturists of Argentina and improved the general condition. According to late reports crops give great promise for the harvest now approaching, business has revived, and a return to normal prosperity is anticipated. That conditions in Argentina have very much improved this year is evidenced by the fact that the importations of farm machinery and vehicles have been greatly in excess of last year, those of the former in August having been over three times what they were in August, 1897.

BRAZIL.

STEAMSHIP COMMUNICATION WITH RIO DE JANEIRO.

Consul-General SEEGER forwards from Rio de Janeiro a list of steamship companies whose steamers call at that port. Mr. SEEGER also sends a list of port charges, together with a summary of the port regulations. He states that, owing to constant changes in rates, the steamship lines do not issue freight lists. Continuing, he says the several lines to and from the United States have formed a combination and adopted a uniform schedule of freight for the transportation of coffee from Santos and Rio to New York and New Orleans. Until recently they charged 40 cents per bag of 60 kilograms (132 pounds), then they reduced the rate to 15 cents, and for the two weeks prior to September 16, the rate was 10 cents.

The list of steamship companies, the nationalities of the flags they fly, etc., at the date of Mr. SEEGER's communication, September 16, 1898, were as follows:

Steamship lines.	Nationality.	Head office.	Time of sailing.	Destination.
Lamport & Holt..................	British	Liverpool	Fortnightly..	New York and New Orleans.
Prince	....do........	Newcastle-on-Tyne.	.....do........	New York.
Norton...........................	....do.......	Liverpool	.....do.......	Do.
Sloman	German......	Hamburg	Monthly	Do.
Chargeurs-Reunis................	French.......	Havre.	....do........	New Orleans.
Coast lines.				
Lloyd Brazileiro.................	Brazilian.....	Rio de Janeiro	Weekly	Northern and southern ports of Brazil.
Navegação Costeira Lage Irmãos.	....do.........	...do.........	...do........	Do.
Esperança Maritima	....do.......	...do.........	...do.......	Do.
Espirito Santence de Navegação a vapor.	....do.......	...do.......	...do.......	Do.
Companhia Pernambucana de Navegação.	....do.......	Recife........	...do.......	Do.
São Ivao da Barra e Campos	....do........	São Ivao da Barra.	....do........	Do.
Viação do Brazil.................	....do........	Rio de Janeiro	.....do........	River San Francisco and tributaries.

The port charges are: Light dues, 100 milreis, or £11 5s. ($54.74) in gold; hospital dues, 1.920 milreis (26 cents) for each man of the crew, including officers, and also 18 milreis ($2.70) for each vessel; pass fees, 9.800 milreis ($1.39); stamp duty on freight (outward), 4 per cent and 10 per cent. The charges, except light dues, are in paper currency. The paper milreis is now worth about 15 cents in United States currency.

The regulations of the port are these: A vessel entering has to wait at the free port for the visit of health and customs officials, who examine bills of health issued by the Brazilian consuls abroad and receive consular manifests and all other papers relating to the ship's cargo. When all is found in order, the captain is allowed to proceed to the final anchorage, where the discharge can begin as soon as all the custom-house papers are complete. Steamers belonging to regular lines and enjoying packet privileges can begin discharging and loading as soon as the inspectors have found the ship's papers in order, and need not wait until the customs papers are ready. In winter (from April to November) vessels are allowed to discharge and load alongside the wharves and warehouses. General cargo is almost always discharged into lighters and thence into the custom-house or warehouses, called "trapiches." Bulk articles are discharged on shore direct in winter. Coffee is received into lighters and transported to the vessels.

INTRODUCTION OF UNITED STATES PRODUCTS.

Consul-General SEEGER sends from Rio de Janeiro a translation of a letter from OTHON LEONARDOS, jr., a prominent Rio merchant, in regard to the introduction of United States products into Brazil. The letter reads, in part:

There is a large field here for the products of American industry. The two greatest impediments to the expansion of American trade in Brazil are poor transportation facilities and the want of direct representation of your manufacturers. As a rule, we have in Rio but two old and slow steamers a month from the United States, and their import trade with Brazil is so organized that there are no direct relations between the American manufacturer and the Brazilian merchant. Everything is done through more or less expensive commission men. The lack of an American bank here is also a general drawback. American manufacturers ought to have a bureau here in which there would be a permanent exposition of their products.

England, France, Germany, Portugal, Italy—all these countries have their lines of steamers and their banks here; their capital is being constantly invested in industrial and commercial enterprises. What does your country possess here? No line of steamers, no banks, no industrial enterprises; there is no investment of capital, with the exception of a few commercial houses.

In regard to the merchandise handled by our house (LEONARDOS & Co.), I will relate my personal experience concerning articles of American manufacture. My efforts to introduce these goods in the Rio market have been very successful. Cut and molded glass are of importance, and I will speak of them first. Cut glass from Fairpoint competes easily in quality and beauty with the English and French article. It is somewhat higher in price, but sells readily on account of its beautiful designs. The moldings and pressed glassware of certain American factories are as well made and as white as those we import from other countries; they are perhaps better, and, their price being lower, I think they will in time find a good market here. The same applies to bottles, jars, and other articles used by druggists. I think they can easily compete with products from other countries. Plated metals, silver and nickel plate, from the factories of Reed & Barton (Connecticut), Meriden Britannia Company, and others, are beginning to be favorably known in our markets, and, owing to their price, can well compete with the metals of Elkington (England), Christofle (Paris), Krupp (Austria), and others. I may remark in this connection that American plated ware pays only half the rate of duty that plated wares from other countries pay, copper entering into their composition, if at all, in a very small proportion. The importation of plated ware from the United States is susceptible of great development. American petroleum lamps are not known here, but their quality is superior to those we import from Belgium and Germany. Their price is the same, or even lower.

I have thus given an account as far as my own line of business is concerned. As to other American products, they are beginning to be well known in our market, but as yet are not largely exploited, for the reasons I have mentioned above. American leather, electrical appliances, photographic apparatus, agricultural implements, and all kinds of manufacturing machinery, bicycles, preserves, etc., are well known and greatly appreciated here. It only remains to strengthen the ties between our two countries by improving means of communication and securing for commerce and trade with the United States the proper representation here.

IMPORTS OF BREADSTUFFS AT RIO

According to "Handel's Zeitung," the imports of wheat flour into Rio Janeiro in 1897 were 39,402 barrels less than in the previous year, the actual figures being 336,533 barrels in 1897, against 375,935 in 1896. The principal decrease has been in Hungarian flour, which, in spite of its excellent quality, was only used for mixing purposes, on account of its dearness in the home ports. The statistics show that the imports last year were as follows: From the United States, 252,991 barrels; from the River Plate, 65,697 barrels; from Liverpool, 9,850 barrels; from Trieste and Fiume, 4,395 barrels, and from Chile 3,600 barrels, which make up the 336,533 barrels imported during the year. The diminution in the importation of bran in 1897 was due to the very active working of the English and Brazilian mills in Rio. The total imports during the year were 10,107 bags of 40 kilos (88 pounds)—all from the River Plate—against 62,374 bags in 1896, a difference of 52,267 bags, which is highly creditable to local enterprise. In the past year, too, the importation of macaroni, vermicelli, and the like, has considerably decreased, even more so than in previous years. In 1896, 7,941 cases were imported from Italy, but in 1897 only 1,227 were received. There is no doubt that the cause is due to the high perfection which the local factories are attaining, and it is certain that within a short time the imports of this article into Brazil will entirely cease. Indian corn is solely from the River Plate. This also suffered a diminution in 1897, as compared with the previous year, of 242,450 bags of 62 kilos (137 pounds), the receipts having been 1,254,097 bags, against 1,496,556 in 1896. As to rice, the imports from Europe increased, while those from India decreased.

The total amount which reached the Rio market was 1,237,277 bags of 60 kilos (132 pounds) each, against 1,240,833 bags in 1896, a decrease of 3,556 bags. The receipts for 1897 were made up of 134,359 bags from Europe and 1,102,918 from India.

PRODUCTION OF CARBONS.

Consul Furniss writes from Bahia transmitting to the Department of State a copy of a communication to a New York correspondent who asks about the carbon industry. In this he says that the claim is made that the State of Bahia is the sole seat of the carbon industry. Carbons have been found in Brazil for many years, but there has been no market until the commencement of the present decade, when, on account of their hardness, they were sought after by makers of so-called diamond drills. As the demand grew, the supply was found insufficient, and consequently prices advanced.

The stones are found in the interior of the State in a region reached only after a long and tiresome journey. The route is from Bahia by boat to St. Felix, and thence by rail to Bandeira de Mello. This is the edge of the diamond region, and carbons are always found near diamonds. The most productive territory is farther up the Paragassu River, and to reach it the traveler goes overland, carried by a mule, along a rough and hilly pack trail for two days. It is thought that diamonds and carbons are found all through this section; but, on account of the methods of obtaining them, only the bed of the Paragassu and its tributary, the San Antonio River, and the side range of mountains called Sierra das Lavras Diamantinas, are worked. Carbons are found in a kind of gravel called "cascalho" in the river bed beneath the silt and on top of a stratum of clay; in the mountains, beneath a stratum of rock and above the same clay stratum, and in the surrounding country, beneath several strata of earth.

To obtain those in the river bed, a place not more than 20 feet deep, where the current is not too rapid, is selected. A long pole is then planted, and the native diver climbs down this, taking along with him a sack held open by a ring. He first scrapes away the silt and then fills the sack with the underlying gravel, removing all down to the clay. As soon as a sack is full, the man above, in a native canoe made from a chiseled-out tree, is signaled. The bag is raised to the surface by the aid of the diver, taken to the shore, and dumped at a sufficient distance to prevent being washed away by any sudden rise in the river. This operation is repeated daily for the six months of the dry season. At the commencement of the rainy season, when diving necessarily has to be suspended, this gravel is washed and examined for carbons and diamonds. The divers are quite skillful, and many of them can remain below for a minute at a time; some as long as a minute and a half. The gravel again becomes covered with silt while at the surface, thus causing extra work, which could be avoided by more modern methods. At places where the river is very deep, it can not be worked at all.

The other method of mining consists in drilling through the rock in the mountain side, and, by means of a series of tunnels, removing the diamond and carbon bearing gravel. This is piled up in the dry season and washed out during the rainy season, by conveying the water down from above in sluices. More carbons are found in the mountains than in the river, because they are more accessible there. No mining of any consequence is attempted elsewhere except along the river banks. But here little is done, because the water comes in as soon as the carbon-bearing gravel is reached, and with their crude apparatus the natives can not bail it out fast enough to allow working. The reason why no mining is attempted in other localities is on account of the lack of water to wash the gravel. The idea seems never to have occurred to the natives to use modern mining machinery, or, if so, they have not sufficient capital to invest.

Carbons are found in all sizes, varying from that of a grain of sand to a single specimen of 975 carats weight. This large carbon was picked up in 1894 on a road where the gravel formation had become exposed, and was sold in Paris for 100,000 francs ($19,300). The most valuable and useful sizes are those weighing from 1 to 3 carats. Larger ones have to be broken, and thus there is always a great loss, as they have no line of fracture. For this reason the large carbon referred to, after having been broken into salable pieces, brought considerably less than its cost price. About two years ago there was a local combination to keep up prices, but the chief promoter failed, and there has since been no attempt to combine. The prevailing price is due entirely to the great demand, small supply, and the laborious plans of mining. The small supply on hand is attributed to the crude methods of obtaining them. Frequently a pair of workers will secure only 3 or 4 carbons as the result of their six months' work, and for these they expect and receive good prices.

The export dealers have their business in Bahia and their agents in the mining region, but as the miners keep posted as to prices, the dealers are little more than commission men. The largest exporter in Bahia, as reported by Mr. FURNISS, is THEOPHILO GOMES DE MATTOS, Rua Cons. Dantes. In July he was reported to have in stock about 125 carats of carbons of well assorted sizes. He will ship to the United States on the same terms as to European buyers. He says he has never sold to United States dealers because they insist on particular sizes, and he can not sell picked stones, but in lots, as he buys them. These are of sizes for which there is always a demand. The present price is about $5 per grain, making a carat worth $22.50, but the price fluctuates according to the supply and demand. Another firm in Bahia is FRANCISCO DE MELLO & Co., Rua Cons. Dantes. These dealers should be addressed by correspondents in Portuguese or French, though the first named reads German.

CHILE.

COAL MINING UNDER THE OCEAN.

In one of his interesting letters from the South American Republics, through which he is making a tour of observation, Mr. FRANK G. CARPENTER gives a description of the coal mines of Chile, which were first opened in 1855. He says:

These mines are exceedingly interesting. They are far different from any mines we have in the United States, and in some respects are far more difficult to work. The seam of coal, which is at its best about 5 feet thick, begins at the shore and runs down under the waters of the Pacific Ocean. The rock above it is slate and shale, so compact that the water does not drip through. The tunnels are so clean that you could walk through them in a dress suit without danger of getting dirty. They are worked with the latest machinery, and during my visit to them I had several experiences which it is hard to realize could take place in Chile. Think, for instance, of riding on an electric trolley coal train through a tunnel over a mile long under the Pacific Ocean at a speed of 20 miles an hour. Imagine mines lighted by electricity, forming a catacomb of corridors and chambers under the waves. Realize that just above you great steamships are floating and that the coal which is being taken out of this bed of the Pacific is being shoveled into them. Picture sooty miners, half naked, blasting out the coal and loading the cars, and follow the train carrying 27 tons of black diamonds to the shaft, where a mighty steam engine lifts four of them at one time to the surface, and you have some idea of what is going on at the Lota coal mines. These mines are now producing 1,000 tons of coal a day and 750 miners are employed within them. They pay a profit running high into the hundreds of thousands of dollars a year and are as carefully managed as any of the great coal properties of our country. I asked as to the pay of the miners and was told that they received from 90 cents to $1 Chilean, or from 31 to 35 cents of United States money. I wonder what our Pennsylvania miners would think of that? The Chileans, however, have their houses rent free and coal is furnished them at cost price.

COLOMBIA.

BUDGET 1899—RAILWAY STATISTICS—NEW LOAN.

A correspondent of " Le Nouveau Monde " (The New World), of Paris, France, states that the budget of receipts and expenditures of Colombia transmitted to Congress estimates the receipts of the fiscal year ending June 30, 1899, at $38,305,000. This is an increase of $3,944,000 over the fiscal year ending June 30, 1898, and is attributed to the match monopoly. As to the expenditures, it is estimated that, including the deficit for the past year and the present decreased value of paper currency, they will not exceed $34,000,000.

Under the preceding administration 242 kilometers (150.37 miles) of railroad were constructed, namely: From Cartagena to Calamar, 105 kilos; from Bogota to Zipaquira, 50 kilos; from Villamizar to Tachira, 16 kilos; from Yeguas to La Maria, 13½ kilos; from Puerto Camacho to Espinal, 11 kilos; from Bogota to Soácho, 11¼ kilos; continuation of the Antioquia line, 11½ kilos; continuation of Canca line, 6 kilos; and continuation of Santanda line, 17½ kilos. These improvements may be considered very satisfactory when it is remembered that they have

Bull. No. 5——2

been secured in spite of a financial condition that was very much depressed.

In order to obtain funds to meet the urgent demands of the Government, the Vice-President of the Republic, vested with executive power for the occasion, summoned the principal commercial representatives of the capital to meet him in council at the National Palace, on August 9. He then informed them that the Government proposed to issue a trade loan for commercial advantages. Those present manifested the utmost confidence in the Government, and at once agreed to take $166,000 of the new bonds.

MANUFACTURE AND PRICE OF SOAP.

A Colombian correspondent of a German trade paper, in a recent article, gives a description of the soap industry in Colombia, of which the following is a part:

There are only two works employing caustic alkalis and pure materials in the country—one in Barranquilla and the other in Bogota. A third is now being erected by an English company at Cartagena, and is expected to commence operations in the course of the present year. Formerly, a good deal of household soap was imported from the United States, but this trade is now prevented by the high protective duty imposed. In the same way the importation of toilet soaps and perfumes is killed by the duty, amounting to $1.20 per kilo (2.2046 pounds).

In the large soap works referred to, two chief grades of household soaps are produced from tallow and resin; the one, with 100 per cent of resin, being prepared on a pasty sublye. It is hardened with a solution of Glauber salts and crystal soda. The second grade is a paste soap with 90 per cent of resin, prepared by steam or fire heat, and also hardened by the aforesaid means if necessary, the cuttings being added after the soap is in the frames. The yield varies between 350 and 400 per cent.

Although these products lack the finish of European soaps, they wash well in cold water and satisfy the requirements of the consumer. For the first-named soap only best pale resin is used, but for the other grade a pitch-black resin is employed, in order to make it look like the jabon de tierra, since this is preferred by many to the yellow soap.

A little mottled and potash soap is also made, and toilet soap is prepared with French milling machines, the stock soap being made with 5 per cent of resin, owing to the poor quality of the native cocoanut oil. Medicinal and special (grease-spot) soaps are made by machinery, also cleansing soaps with levigated chalk for gold and silver, or with brick dust for iron; shaving soaps by the semi-warm process, from tallow and castor oil, with soda and potash lye, half and half. Glycerine soap in sticks, packed in cardboard boxes in the English style, is also in good demand. The perfumes most in favor are musk, patchouli, and heliotrope.

Prices rule higher than in Germany, household soap costing 8 cents per pound bar, or $6 per case of 88 bars wholesale; toilet soap, in 3 to 4 ounce cakes, 18 to 36 cents per tablet; highly filled soaps, weighing 1¾ to 2 ounces, 4 cents; medium qualities, 7 to 10 cents wholesale, with 20 per cent discount. Business is good, the home manufacturers being protected by the high tariff.

THE DARIEN GOLD-MINING REGION.

The region of Darien forms the southeastern portion of the Isthmus of Panama, in the Republic of Colombia, and extends from the Atlantic Ocean to the Pacific. It was from this region that Balboa, in his search for gold, discovered the Pacific Ocean, in September, 1513. The extensive gulf of San Miguel is situated about 100 miles southeast of Panama. The Tuira River empties into the Pacific in this gulf and is navigable for a distance of 50 miles. The swiftness of its current, in both directions, renders it difficult of navigation for sloops, except at intervals of six hours. This is due to the tide, the difference in the extremes between high and low tide in the gulf being 24 feet. The tidal effects are felt in diminishing ratio for 10 miles above Real de Santa Maria, the limit of navigation. A small steamboat, called the *Darien*, with a capacity of 20 tons of freight, makes the trip from Panama to Real de Santa Maria in twenty hours. It takes sloops from four to ten days to make the same voyage.

Between Real and Cana, where the mines are located, the trip has to be made by muleback over the mountains, and by canoe up the Cupe River. The road is exceedingly rough and dangerous, and the cost of transportation per ton is $50, Colombian currency (about $23 gold). In 1896 Eduardo J. Chibas located a route for a macadamized road, the construction of which is now well advanced. This will make possible the use of wagons at all seasons of the year, and will lower the freight rates to a nominal sum.

Balboa obtained considerable gold from the Indians, but not until more than a century later were attempts made at gold mining on the Isthmus. Then the Espiritu Santo gold mine was discovered and worked at Cana. According to Vincente Restrepo, of Bogota, this mine produced $30,000,000 in gold for the

Spaniards. It was successfully worked from 1680 to 1727, when the Indians revolted, one of the main galleries caved in, burying several laborers, and the disheartened miners withdrew and returned to Spain.

Not until a century and a half later were serious attempts made to work the mine. About 1878 a company was organized in New York, which spent $50,000 in opening a road and buying and transporting machinery. They abandoned the scheme in 1880, without having undertaken any actual mining.

In 1888 the present company was organized in Manchester, England, with a capital of $1,000,000. The difficulties encountered were almost insurmountable, as Cana is located on one of the spurs of the Andes, 2,000 feet above sea level. A 10-stamp mill was erected in 1889, but for many months the results were far from encouraging. The ore from the mine proved of poor quality, no signs of the wonderful riches were in sight, and the members of the company were almost wholly discouraged, when, in 1893, the miners accidentally struck the old Spanish workings, 90 feet below the surface. The accumulated waters in the old mine rushed into the new shafts, requiring additional labor and more capital to construct a tunnel to drain it off. This was finally accomplished and the mine is now yielding the coveted gold. During the years 1896 and 1897 the old workings have produced 10,528 ounces of gold, realizing in London £44,522 ($216,377). The average value of the rock treated has varied from 1 to 1½ ounces per ton. As all the mining has so far been confined to that part of the ore culled over by the Spaniards, a much larger yield is expected from the virgin lode, which is beginning to be worked to the lowest level. The results so far achieved point to the full realization of the expectation of the owners. They have spent vast sums on the latest machinery and improvements and deserve the greatest measure of success. Mr. CHIBAS, from whose interesting descriptive article in the current issue of the " Engineering Magazine " the foregoing facts are obtained, says:

The wealth of Darien is not limited to gold. It is very rich in valuable timber, and a considerable amount of mahogany has been exported. The palm-producing vegetable ivory is very abundant. The rubber industry was also very profitable at one time, but the inexcusable practice of the natives in cutting down the trees instead of tapping them to take out the rubber has greatly diminished the output. In spite of this wholesale destruction, however, a day hardly passed while we were surveying that we did not see rubber trees. They thrive so well in that locality that their planting and cultivation ought to prove a remunerative investment. When the rainy season was approaching we extracted rubber from some trees near one of the camps, and by use of a simple process adopted by the natives we rendered waterproof all the ordinary cloth bags that we had been using in carrying our clothes and instruments from camp to camp. We used them during the rainy season to our complete satisfaction. A coat treated in the same manner proved more impervious to water than the imported ones.

ECUADOR.

PROPOSED SOUTH AMERICAN CONFEDERATION.

" Le Nouveau Monde," of Paris, France, in its issue of October 8, published a dispatch from Guayaquil, dated October 1, 1898, which stated that Gen. ELOY ALFARO, President of the Republic, had just asked Congress for permission to propose an international conference to the Governments of Colombia and Venezuela.

This proposed conference, as explained by the President, will be for the purpose of examining into the expediency of preparing a new constitution for the old Republic of Colombia founded by BOLIVAR. That Republic was dissolved in 1830, and from its territory the Republics of Ecuador, Venezuela, and Colombia were formed. President ALFARO suggested that a resurrection of the old dissolved confederation would result in putting an end to the dissensions on the frontiers of the three integral factors; also that the three would constitute a formidable nation numbering about 8,000,000 inhabitants and embracing an immense, rich territory extending from the mouth of the Orinoco to the boundaries of Peru.

The correspondent adds that "it is not known how Venezuela and Colombia are disposed to look upon a proposition of this nature, which is a new manifestation of the tendency of Hispano-American Republics, as has just been the case with the three Republics of Central America, to group themselves into a confederation according to their affinities and their old historic limits."

HAITI.

REDUCTION OF DUTY ON SOAP.

Vice-Consul-General TERRES sends to the Department of State, from Port au Prince, October 7, 1898, a translation of a law recently passed by the legislature, as follows:

ARTICLE 1. Soap of all quality shall pay 50 cents per 100 pounds, without prejudice to the additional duties.

ART. 2. The surtax of 25 per cent provided by the law of December 16, 1897, shall not be deducted on soap.

ART. 3. The present law, which abrogates all laws and provisions of laws which are contrary to it, shall be executed at the diligence of the secretaries of state for finance and for commerce.

This, says Mr. TERRES, virtually reduces the duties on soap one-half.

MEXICO.

ANNUAL MESSAGE OF PRESIDENT DIAZ.

Following are extracts from the message addressed to the Nineteenth Mexican Congress, at its opening session on September 16, 1898, by President DIAZ:

DEPARTMENT OF ENCOURAGEMENT.

In the development of national industries mining plays the chief part. The number of grants issued in the period of time that has elapsed since the date of my last report is 837, covering an area of 7,820 pertenencias of one hectare each (2.471 acres). The total number of grants issued under the existing law of June, 1892, is 8,313, covering an area of 66,363 pertenencias of one hectare each, showing that the number of mining properties located in six years is almost four times the number of those held when the law in question was promulgated.

MINERAL EXPORTS.

The development of the mining industry is further evidenced by the increase in the exportation of ore that has been observable for some time past. According to data published by the Department of Finance with respect to the last fiscal year, the total value of the mineral products of all kinds passing through the custom-houses was $91,250,000 in round numbers, showing an increase of $10,500,000 over the value of similar products exported in the previous years. Silver figures among said products to the value of $16,000,000, silver valuation, copper to the value of $4,700,000, lead to the value of $3,000,000, and on a smaller scale antimony, zinc, plumbago, coal, sulphur, asphalt, chalk, and some other building materials.

PROGRESS OF AGRICULTURE.

Agriculture is also progressing, both the implements and methods of cultivation being improved and new lands being opened up for tillage. The good crops obtained last year permitted the exportation to Europe of agricultural products of the Central Plateau amounting to 7,150 tons during the months or June and July last, of which 4,398 tons were wheat, 2,273 barley, and the rest made up of rye and flour, according to data furnished to the Department or Encouragement by one of the exporting firms.

WATER POWER.

The increase in the number of applications in recent years for the utilization of water courses subject to Federal jurisdiction as motive power is worthy of note. By virtue of concessions granted by the Government to sundry enterprises, some important manufacturing establishments are in course of erection.

PUBLIC LANDS.

During the period covered by this report, 153,933 hectares (380,368 acres) of vacant and national lands have been reduced to private property by virtue of grants and sales, settlements with landowners for surplus area occupied by them, grants made to surveying companies by way of compensation for expenditures incurred, division of town commons into lots, and free donations to small farmers. The sales of land have been attended by the redemption of national securities to the value of $104,510.

RAILWAYS.

Between April and this date our railway system has increased by more than 314 kilometers (195 miles), of which 62½ appertain to the Mexico, Cuernavaca and Pacific Railroad; 60 to the Mexican Central in its branch from Jimenez to Hidalgo del Parral; 40 to the Mexican National between Patzcuaro and Uruapam; 25 to the International on its branch between Reata and Monterey, and the remainder to other lines, among which may be mentioned that which has lately joined the capitals of Yucatan and Campeche, an event which has with reason been celebrated with rejoicings by both States. To-day the line between San Juan Bautista and the Gonzalez River was inaugurated.

The railway system of the Republic now measures 12,403 kilometers (7,706 miles), including 235 kilometers 700 meters of State-owned tramways.

Some of the companies have either executed or have in preparation noteworthy works on their lines, such as the completion of the tunnel between Dolores and Catorce, which is 2 kilometers 212 meters in length; the permanent station building of the Mexican Southern at Oaxaca, and the plans for the introduction of electrical traction on certain of its lines presented by the Federal District Railway Company.

On account of the great damage periodically suffered by the provisional bridges of the Tehuantepec Railroad over the river of the same name a new location of the road at that point has been undertaken, so that the line may cross the river under favorable conditions and by a metallic bridge.

During the period covered by this report twelve new railway concessions have been granted and three have been declared forfeited.

TELEGRAPH LINES

Four new telegraph offices have been opened to the public; a new line has been strung between Esperanza and Tehuacan, and the lines between Banamichi and Arizpe and Teapa and Pichucalco have been incorporated into the Federal telegraph system. The advantage of constant telegraph service has been extended to thirty-six more towns. The total number of messages sent over the lines in the fiscal year 1897–98 was 2,086,050. During the half year from January to June, 1898, there was an increase of 24 per cent over the same period of last year.

A general map of the telegraph system for technical and managerial purposes having become a necessity, one was ordered made and it has now been completed. The substitution of copper for iron wire in the eastern section of the Republic has continued. The interior press service, which practically amounted to nothing at the date of last report, is now of considerable volume, and it may be said that its existence is now assured. On April 1 last the service of telegraph drafts was inaugurated, and the operations of this line are on the increase, amounting to $150,000 per month. In regard to the financial aspect of the telegraph lines, their proceeds increased in the year which has just ended to $850,000 from $698,000, which was their yield in the fiscal year 1896–97.

FEDERAL RECEIPTS.

The ordinary receipts of the Federation during the fiscal year 1897–98 amounted to $52,500,000, which is more than two millions in excess of the estimates of receipts for the same year, and is also greater than the authorized expenditure for that year in accordance with budget appropriations and subsequent additions.

LAW RELATING TO TONNAGE AND OTHER DUES.

Under date of July 1, 1898, the Mexican Government issued a decree relative to tonnage and other dues, from which the following is taken:

The following duties are abolished: The light-house duty, which was paid in accordance with article 17 of the general custom-house regulations; the harbor-masters' dues, which were levied according to the regulations of April 22, 1851, and the port dues established by decree of May 28, 1881. The decree also abolishes articles 16, 18, 19, and 20 of the general custom-house regulations relating to tonnage dues, which, in the future, shall be paid in the following manner: Sailing vessels, 10 cents per ton; steamers, 6 cents per ton. Steamers belonging to international lines making regular trips to the ports of the Republic, with fixed itinerary and days of sailing, shall be granted a reduction of the tonnage dues under these conditions:

On the Pacific coast, the reduction may amount to as much as 75 per cent for vessels engaged in the postal service of Mexico, without receiving any pecuniary aid from the Government on this account, nor exemption from other duties, and to 25 per cent only for vessels not engaged in the postal service, or if so engaged, receiving pecuniary assistance from the Government of Mexico, or exemption on this account from the payment of some tax. On the Atlantic coast, the reduction may be 50 per cent, and will apply only to such vessels as are engaged in the postal service, without receiving payment from the Mexican Government for this or for any other service, and are not subsidized or exempted from the payment of any duties.

In order to obtain these reductions, they must be requested, by those interested, from the Department of Communication and Public Works, and the latter shall fix the amount of such reductions. It is also necessary that the company should present its itineraries in due time to the department, and that the latter should accept them, declaring them to be in accordance with the conditions of the contract or of the permit granted.

Any vessel belonging to a company having the right to enjoy any of the reductions referred to, that may arrive at a Mexican port on the Atlantic, not included in the respective itinerary, shall pay in full the tonnage dues, if said port is the first of the Republic at which the vessel touches. If the same vessel, after having obtained a reduction when calling for the first time at a Mexican port included in its itinerary, should stop at another not included, it shall pay in the latter port a sum equal to the difference between the full value of the tonnage dues and the amount already paid. This shall be done even if the vessel should arrive at a port not included in its itinerary, with special permission of the Government.

wise trade, that may be embarked or disembarked at any improved port, whatever may be the circumstances under which these opera-tions are carried out, and even if the wharf or place at which this is done does not belong to the Federal Government. This duty shall be paid without any reduction and in the following manner:

Products and manufactures for exportation, merchandise car-ried in the coastwise trade, whether entering or leaving the port. Coal, lumber, or similar articles classified by the Government under this heading, shall pay the duty at the rate of 50 cents for each ton of 1,000 kilograms gross weight. Other articles not men-tioned above shall pay the duty at the rate of $1 for each ton of 1,000 kilograms gross weight. Merchandise that is transshipped from one vessel to another in a port and destined to other ports, and all freight embarked or disembarked on lighters, shall pay one-half the amounts mentioned above.

The additional tonnage dues shall not be paid by the following ships, whether national or foreign, sailing vessels or steamers: Men-of-war, vessels devoted exclusively to the fisheries, vessels whose gross tonnage is less than 10 tons, and those that are obliged to enter port through stress of weather or other cause.

The duty of loading and unloading shall not be paid by the following articles: Passengers' baggage; samples free of import duties; postal parcels; merchandise landed through mistake and which is to be embarked to its proper destination; products of the fisheries landed by vessels devoted to this industry; provisions, water, fuel, and naval stores taken on board by vessels lying in the port for their own use; any articles imported for the use of the Federal or State Governments and which are exempted from duty according to article 2 of the decree of June 6, 1898; and in the coastwise trade, all articles intended for the Federal Government.

The foreign vessels which, in accordance with the provisions of the custom-house ordinances, or from motive of contracts, or author-izations, or special permissions, conduct merchandise from one port of the Republic destined to another port or place of the country, if direct, or even through passing the merchandise in transit to a foreign country, will pay a duty called the duty on interior maritime traffic, the same to be charged by the ton of

1,000 kilograms gross weight of the merchandise carried, subject to the following tariff:

	On the Atlantic.	On the Pacific.
Between ports distant from each other 60 miles	$1.00	$1.00
Between ports distant from each other 60 to 360 miles	3.00	2.00
Between ports distant from each other 360 or more miles	5.00	3.00

The same duty and under the same conditions will be collected on foreign vessels that obtain special permission to discharge their cargo, or part of same, at a coastwise port or in any place which is not a port of entry, computing the duty according to the weight of the merchandise and the distance between the respective port of entry and the port of discharge.

This decree went into effect October 1, 1898.

VALUE OF IMPORTS AND EXPORTS.

The attached statement of imports and exports of the Republic for the past four years is taken from a report made by Consul CARDEN to the British Foreign Office, with the values reduced to United States currency:

Year.	Imports.	Exports.	Excess of exports.
1894	$29,372,819	$42,604,621	$13,231,802
1895	35,186,444	54,910,214	19,723,770
1896	45,224,958	57,090,415	11,865,457
1897	38,107,955	62,575,319	24,467,369
Total	147,892,176	217,180,669	69,288,398

Last year, it will be observed, there was a greatly increased excess of exports, more than double the excess of 1896, and a fourth more than in 1895, which previously had been the banner year. The exports have grown 46 per cent in four years, while the imports have expanded less than 30 per cent. Abundant crops on the one hand, and the steady decline in the value of silver on the other are credited with discouraging imports. Manufacturers of textiles in the United States will be interested to know the consul reports that the development of the textile industry in the

Republic "is not confined to cotton, but is being extended also to linen and woolen goods." He adds, however, that "there is still a good market for woolen and worsted tissues, especially those of a high quality." Among other articles for which there appears to be good openings for trade, he mentions mining, agricultural and industrial machinery in general, printing presses and type, high-class furnishing hardware, and paints.

Incidentally the consul refers to the annual excess of exports over imports, regarding which he says:

Of the £3,500,000 ($17,000,000) annual excess of imports over imports, £2,700,000 ($13,100,000) are accounted for by the remittances for the service of the debt and the earnings of railways, and the remaining £800,000 ($3,900,000), plus the amount of such foreign capital as may have been invested in any one year in Mexico, but was not remitted here in the form of specie or merchandise, must represent the interest on capital invested in commercial or industrial enterprises of all kinds by individuals or companies domiciled abroad.

IMPORTS OF COAL, COKE, AND IRON.

The importation of coal and coke into Mexico continues to increase very largely, the amount imported in 1897 being 460,000 tons or over, more than 35 per cent more than in 1896, which must be considered a healthy sign, as indicating a great advance in industrial enterprise. About three-fourths of the amount was coal and the remainder was coke. The imports of coal from the United States have nearly doubled in the past year, and now represent over 55 per cent of the total imports, the remainder coming largely from England. About 80 per cent of the coke is also from the United States. The price of American coal, or of Welsh coal of similar quality, has risen somewhat in the past few months. Toward the end of 1897 it was worth, in the capital, from $7.30 to $9.70 per ton. The decrease last year of $515,000 in the value of the imports of iron and steel into this country is to be attributed to the disinclination of buyers to order more goods than were absolutely necessary, under very adverse conditions of exchange, rather than to any special falling off in the demand. There was an increase of $165,000 (nearly 40 per cent) in the imports of corrugated-iron sheets and iron beams for roofing, which shows the activity in building, which is observable not only in the capital but also in many of the principal cities in the interior.

AN EXTENSIVE AGRICULTURAL SCHEME.

The "Financial Times," of London, is quoted as authority for the statement that Sir THOMAS J. LIPTON "meditates a new and important move in the direction of Mexico." According to this report, he proposes opening up some of the largest coffee plantations in the world, and also large areas for the cultivation of tobacco and cocoa.

The plan, which has reached an advanced stage, contemplates 10,000 acres in coffee, 10,000 acres in tobacco, and 5,000 acres in cocoa. The result will be watched with great interest, for Mexico possesses vast possibilities on these lines. Tobacco is commanding great attention in that country, and during the past four or five years large quantities of the weed have been sent from Mexico to be manufactured into Havana cigars, as little or no tobacco has been grown in Cuba during the civil war in the island that preceded the Hispano-American conflict. As a grower of coffee Mexico has also proved successful in the past, while the cocoa tree is indigenous to the country and is of the finest quality. If Sir THOMAS carries out this scheme of planting 25,000 acres, the matter will be one not only of importance to himself but to Mexico. It has always been the dream of President DIAZ to have as much as possible of the country under cultivation.

NICARAGUA.

NEW MINING ENTERPRISES.

The Bureau is in receipt of a letter from Señor DON ASCENCIÓN P. RIVAS, dated Rama, Nicaragua, October 18, 1898, in which Mr. RIVAS says that some months ago discoveries of rich gold veins in considerable quantity were made in that section of the Atlantic coast of Nicaragua called "Distrito del Sequia."

An account of these discoveries, written by Mr. J. P. MORGAN, was printed in the MONTHLY BULLETIN for August, 1898, page 291. In a note to the Director of the Bureau, dated October 15, 1898, Mr. MORGAN announces that there have been also found, close to the port of Rama, some coal beds believed to be quite extensive, and some good float of red oxide copper, the latter on the river Mico. Mr. MORGAN also says that the gold-mining district of the river Mico is opening up more richly than was expected; assays showing as high as 200 ounces to the ton and over 70 ounces silver.

In his communication to the Bureau, Mr. RIVAS says that the rivers crossing this territory, navigable by steamboats from the mouths at the sea up to the places where the minerals are found, afford unexceptionable facilities for the development of the mines. The principal rivers are the Siquia and the Mico. The large majority of those who, up to the present time, have made discoveries lack the necessary funds to develop the deposits, and Mr. RIVAS asks to be put in communication with persons in the United States who might furnish capital for mining enterprises.

NICARAGUA CANAL CONTRACTS.

Telegraphic dispatches from Managua, Nicaragua, announce that the Nicaraguan Congress has ratified the canal treaty entered into between the Government and two American citizens, Messrs. EYRE and CRAGIN, who represent a New York syndicate. As there exists a concession granted in 1888 to the Maritime Canal Company of Nicaragua, the new contract can not go into effect before the other concession has expired, which will be in 1899. It is well known that several bills for the construction of the canal have been presented to the Congress of the United States, but the matter is still pending. There is, perhaps, no enterprise that has attracted the attention of the world to such a degree during half a century as the opening of a water route between the Atlantic and Pacific through the Central American isthmus; but this subject has never before awakened so much interest as now, especially in the United States, due to the recent annexation of Hawaii, and to the long trip that the battle-ship *Oregon* was obliged to make in going from San Francisco to the West Indies.

The Nicaraguan route has been a matter of serious study, upon which the American Government, as well as the company, has spent considerable sums of money. A great deal has been written about the projected canal of Nicaragua, and it may be said that the subject is now practically exhausted. In the construction of this interoceanic communication it would be necessary to build locks, and this fact has been the pretext upon which M. DE LESSEPS based the opposition he always made to the Nicaraguan route, for he maintained that a canal between the two oceans must be a level canal, like the Suez, in order to meet all the requirements of commerce. However, the American engineers who have studied the project have demonstrated that the locks would not act as obstacles to the immense traffic that would pass through the Nicaraguan Canal, if it were opened, and the Panama Canal management, since the collapse of the DE LESSEPS enterprise, has itself adopted locks as necessary to the further prosecution of that work.

DEMARCATION OF BOUNDARY LINES.

According to the latest press dispatches the commission of engineers appointed by the Governments of Nicaragua and Costa Rica to determine and mark the boundary lines between the two Republics have again disagreed. and are preparing to submit the matter to the arbitrator, Gen. E. P. ALEXANDER.

On September 30, 1897, General ALEXANDER, appointed by President CLEVELAND as Engineer Arbitrator, submitted his report which is published in full in the BULLETIN for December, 1897. The terms agreed upon by the convention for the demarcation of the boundary lines are published in the BULLETIN for April, 1897. According to these terms General ALEXANDER has power to decide finally on points of difference that may arise in placing and marking out the boundaries between the two Republics. It is to be hoped that the representatives of the two Governments may be satisfied with the findings of General ALEXANDER with reference to the present difficulty.

PARAGUAY.

CODE OF COMMERCIAL NOMENCLATURE ADOPTED AS OFFICIAL TEXT.

Hon. WILLIAM R. FINCH, United States minister at Montevideo, informs the Department of State, under date of September 21, 1898, of the promulgation of an official decree by the Government of Paraguay, whereby the Code of Commercial Nomenclature prepared by the Bureau of the American Republics is adopted as official text for the designation of articles of commerce in the Spanish, Portuguese, and English languages. This action was taken in consequence of the commercial necessity for a common nomenclature, with other countries with which trade is maintained, for the merchandise exchanged, and on September 2, 1898, the decree covering the matter was ordered communicated, published, and given to the Official Register over the signatures of President EGUISGUIZA and Secretary GUILLERMO DE LOS RIOS.

The Treasury Department of the United States had previously taken similar action on January 22, 1898, by issuing a Department circular accepting the Code as a "proper reference book for the translation of commercial words and phrases for the use of this Department and of collectors of customs and appraisers of merchandise."

THE PRODUCTION OF COFFEE.

Among the recent reports from United States consuls is one from Mr. RUFFIN at Asunción with reference to the adaptability of the soil of Paraguay for the production of coffee. He says there are coffee plantations which have been in existence for many years, but they have not been cultivated, being left to some extent to the excellent climate. These plants produce a variety similar to that cultivated in Brazil and Bolivia, coming from the Arabian species. The production in this line is not extensive, and the consumption is local. The plantations which have been established of late years have proved profitable investments, as a market has been found in Paraguay for all the coffee produced. According to the statistics obtainable, Mr. RUFFIN places the number of coffee plants in the Republic at 343,407. He thinks all the products can be disposed of in the Asunción market, as "the people are great coffee drinkers."

The coffee plant thrives best in countries having a mean temperature of from 68° to 78° F. The official findings give Paraguay a temperature of from 58.42° in June to 84.45° in December, or a mean of 71.16°. The land is suitable for cultivation, as it is level and damp and can be worked easily. Among the many varieties of coffee, Mr. RUFFIN says that the most cultivated in Paraguay is the "yungas," because it originated in Bolivia, a country with much the same geographical position and a very similar soil. It is believed that this coffee can compete with the best known in the markets of Europe, where it already figures, though in small quantities. Authorities state that the yungas coffee of Peru and Guatemala is as good as any produced on the American Continent. The grain is well developed, of exquisite aroma, green-yellow in color, and in size and weight superior to Mocha coffee, which in general characteristics it resembles. The plant is vigorous, develops rapidly, and produces in three years.

MARKET FOR MANUFACTURED ARTICLES.

From the fact that the Republic of Paraguay is situated in the basin of the Paraná River, in the interior of the continent, with no seacoast of its own, it is commercially dependent on the Argentine Republic and Uruguay. But few transactions are made direct with Paraguay and there is scarcely ever a record of the exports to that country; nevertheless, it is a country rich in valuable territory and capable of large development. It is probably the richest known country in cabinet woods, as nearly 150 species of valuable trees are found in its forests.

Its consumption, while somewhat limited by the comparatively small number of its inhabitants, is of importance. There is no direct maritime communication between the United States and Paraguay, nor, in fact, between any of the great exporting countries and that Republic. Steamers will not book freight farther than Montevideo, Buenos Ayres, or Rosario, the important commercial cities of the La Plata Basin. The consequence is that Paraguayan merchants, when ordering foreign goods, are compelled to place their orders in one of the cities named, unless they have correspondents in those places who can attend to clearing and forwarding goods. This naturally enhances prices, for there are extra charges for handling or for commissions. There is also frequently great delay. As Paraguay has no gold or silver coins of its own stamping, it depends principally on the coinage of Argentina and Uruguay. In the former country, the currency has been of a fluctuating nature, causing the shipping companies to prefer Montevideo, where the gold standard prevails, as a port of transshipment for river traffic.

In reporting to the British Government, an official calls attention to the following lines of trade: Sewing machines are in great demand in the Republic, as indeed they are in every part of

South America; the cheapest kinds are the most salable, though a considerable number of high-class machines can also be placed. Most of those in the market are of German manufacture. There are a large number of stills in use, the greater part of which are imported from France. Small sizes, capable of distilling from 50 to 200 gallons per day of a strength of 18° (Cartier), are in most demand. They may be either simple or for continuous or semicontinuous distillation, but should be as little complicated as possible. There is little wine made in the country or any other liquor than caña (white rum). English manufacturers seem to have secured the full share of the trade in chemicals, and the same applies to surgical instruments and appliances. Mineral waters are in demand in Asuncion and the larger cities. Quite a number of portable iron sugar mills, suitable for working with oxen could be sold. A considerable amount of unrefined sugar is made in Paraguay, but nearly all on a small scale. However, the quantity is insufficient to meet the demand and the remainder is imported from Argentina, where there are some very large sugar works in the Chaco just across the river from Paraguay. Although the national drink of the country is maté (Paraguay tea), a good deal of tea is used, and the demand seems to be increasing. Any tea sent to the country should be of good quality. There is a large demand for textile fabrics, especially cheap cotton goods. The latter are sold by retailers at little or no profit to push the sale of other wares. In this line competition is keen, but English firms sell the greater proportion. Ponchos are largely sold and come from England. They are practically of the same sort as those sold to the Argentine Republic, but as the winters in Paraguay are somewhat warmer, the woolen sorts are not in so much demand.

The correspondent says that exchange shows a steady decline, having fallen fully 10 per cent during the last few months, and the tendency is to fall still lower. At present the premium on gold is 760, which means that the paper Paraguayan dollar is worth about 6½ pence (13 cents). He further states that foreign competition is keen in Paraguay, and the number of English firms very small, while German, French, and Italian houses are comparatively numerous. The English houses having dealings in Paraguay seem to be contented to work by means of agencies in Buenos Ayres, yet there is an opening in Asuncion and other towns for enterprising firms who make a specialty of the products of the country.

Attention is called to a paragraph in the BULLETIN for October which states that a commercial association had been formed in the city of Asuncion to give information on all points connected with the products, customs laws, and commerce of the Republic; also to assist all persons desirous of entering into commercial relations with exporters and other business firms in Paraguay. This association is known as the Centro Comercial del Paraguay.

REGISTRATION OF TRADE-MARKS.

According to the British Trade Journal, persons who wish to register trade-marks in Paraguay should apply to the Junto de Credito Publico, Asuncion. Protection is granted for ten years, and at the expiration of that term can be renewed for a further period of ten years. When transferred, trade-marks must be registered in the same office in which they were originally granted. Applications for registration must be accompanied by two copies of the trade-marks to be registered with duplicate inscriptions; a receipt showing that the amount of dues ($50) has been paid to the Junto de Credito Publico; and a power of attorney duly legalized, if the proprietor of the trade-mark does not apply personally. The power of attorney should be countersigned by the Paraguayan consul, and the name of the agent may be left in blank to be filled in later.

PRODUCTION OF ORANGES.

According to a recent report of Consul RUFFIN, the orange is one of the most generally used articles of food in Paraguay, forming a staple edible for the poor, particularly in the country. Hogs are also fattened on them, and orange-fed pork is considered a delicacy. The orange trees are of prolific growth, being found everywhere, either in orchards or in a wild state. They are cultivated on farms, growing from the seed and bearing when 5 years old. They flourish all the year except during the months of January, February, and March. A 7-year-old tree bears about 1,000 oranges. The fruit is about 3 inches in diameter, and the ordinary variety is very sweet. The mandarin orange is quite small and, while very pungent, is not so sweet as the kind first named, and is more expensive. There are not many of these raised, and most of them are sent to Buenos Ayres. Their sale is ready and the price remunerative. The third class is the sour or bitter orange, from whose skin marmalade is made, and an extract is also made from the blossoms. Some Frenchmen are engaged in this business, which is remunerative. The exportation of the crop commences about the end of May and lasts till November. The boats are loaded everywhere along the river, women with flat baskets on their heads carrying them on board. There is no export duty. Most of the fruit is sent to Buenos. Ayres and Montevideo. During the season an average of 300,000 oranges are exported.

INDUCEMENTS TO IMMIGRANTS.

In his communication to the Department of State, under date of September 2, 1898, JOHN N. RUFFIN, United States consul at Asuncion, says:

Allow me to state, for the benefit of those who contemplate entering this country for agricultural purposes, that the best sites would be along the river, accessible to boats which can carry produce to the markets of Buenos Ayres and Montevideo. There appears to be an opportunity for profitable investment in this line. The Government of Paraguay pays passage of immigrants from Buenos Ayres to the land on which it is desired to settle; furnishes oxen and agricultural implements, the latter to be paid for in labor or produce. Some agricultural implements, however, are loaned free of charge by officials of the colony. The point I hope to make clear is that what the Government furnishes is charged for, except the passage from Buenos Ayres. The land is good and fertile, and recommends itself to the favorable consideration of all.

UNITED STATES.

TRADE WITH LATIN AMERICA.

STATEMENT OF IMPORTS AND EXPORTS.

Following is the latest statement, from figures compiled by the Bureau of Statistics, United States Treasury Department, O. P. AUSTIN, Chief, showing the value of the trade between the United

States and the Latin-American countries. The report is for the month of August, corrected to September 29, 1898, with a comparative statement for the corresponding period of the previous year; also for the eight months ending August, 1898, compared with the corresponding period of the fiscal year 1897. It should be explained that tne figures from the various customhouses showing imports and exports for any one month are not received at the Treasury Department until about the 20th of the following month, and some time is necessarily consumed in compilation and printing, so that the returns for August, for example, are not published until some time in October.

IMPORTS OF MERCHANDISE.

Articles and countries.	August—		Eight months ending August—	
	1897.	1898.	1897.	1898.
Chemicals:				
Logwood (*Palo campeche; Páu campeche; Campêche*)—				
Mexico......................	$1, 002	....	$44, 028	$1, 792
Coal, bituminous (*Carbón bituminoso; Carvão betuminoso; Charbon de terre*):				
Mexico...	19, 645	$19, 385	166, 371	141, 039
Cocoa (*Cacao; Coco ou Cacão crú; Cacao*):				
Brazil............................	....	10, 753	151, 930	106, 977
Other South America	89, 087	109, 339	671, 111	890, 604
Coffee (*Café:*)				
Central America................	131, 133	236, 424	6, 093, 069	3, 852, 820
Mexico	171, 250	38, 259	4, 367, 934	2, 609, 316
Brazil.........................	3, 496, 245	2, 458, 830	31, 198, 633	22, 730, 349
Other South America...........	839, 774	470, 053	7, 033, 860	5, 401, 112
Cotton, unmanufactured (*Algodón en rama; Algodão em rama; Coton, non manufacturé*):				
South America.....................	....	451	73, 299	129, 225
Fibers:				
Sisal grass (*Henequén; Henquen; Hennequen*)—				
Mexico	321, 826	872, 956	2, 743, 551	5, 426, 326
Philippine Islands	199, 646	224, 919	2, 607, 394	2, 005, 977
Fruits:				
Bananas (*Plátanos; Bananas; Bananes*)—				
Central America..............	139, 672	171, 367	1, 149, 482	1, 191, 759
South America.................	50, 872	29, 803	535, 419	369, 580
Oranges (*Naranjas; Laranjas; Oranges*)—				
Mexico	1, 245	2, 035	18, 764	3, 730

IMPORTS OF MERCHANDISE—Continued.

Articles and countries.	August—		Eight months ending August—	
	1897.	1898.	1897.	1898.
Fur skins (*Pieles finas; Pelles; Fourrures*):				
South America	$12,457	$23,006	$19,706	$73,137
Hides and skins (*Cueros y pieles; Couros e pelles; Cuirs et peaux*):				
Central America...............	24,436	26,852	151,640	132,182
Mexico	77,563	119,105	1,431,199	1,223,493
South America	811,307	730,559	7,333,278	6,728,912
India rubber, crude (*Goma elástica cruda, Borracha crua; Caoutchouc brut*):				
Central America...............	22,525	50,592	278,595	322,903
Mexico	1,562	8,988	23,536	38,125
Brazil........................	614,669	727,571	7,996,785	9,145,085
Other South America...........	33,250	92,126	244,101	479,253
Lead, in pigs, bars, etc. (*Plomo en galápagos, barras, etc.; Chumbo em linguados, barras, etc.; Plombs en saumons, en barres, etc.*):				
Mexico	105,994	195,863	904,959	1,097,062
Sugar, not above No. 16 Dutch standard (*Azúcar, no superior al No. 16 de la escala holandesa; Assucar não superior ao No. 16 de padrão hollandez; Sucre, pas adu dessus du type hollandais No. 16*):				
Central America...............	....	2,156	....	202,512
Mexico	362	1,510	10,636	43,568
Cuba........................	....	154,214	9,932,935	9,897,752
Brazil	....	12,309	1,839,639	2,362,565
Other South America	41,966	201,599	3,411,264	3,127,158
Philippine Islands.............	....	436,617	389,898	733,200
Tobacco, leaf (*Tabaco en rama; Tabaco em folha; Tabac en feuilles*):				
Mexico.......................	25,779	39,633	213,883	137,051
Cuba........................	5,181	25,502	1,413,098	1,676,922
Wood, mahogany (*Caoba; Mogno; Acajou*):				
Central America...............	16,273	650	65,908	111,320
Mexico.......................	72,920	5,109	264,565	146,678
Cuba........................	....	....	22,019	933
South America	17,720	1,235	36,668	35,241
Wool (*Lana; Lã; Laine*): South America—				
Class 1 (clothing).............	....	3,616	4,705,452	534,348
Class 2 (combing)	....	9	1,183,201	19,029
Class 3 (carpet)...............	....	38,246	1,176,726	758,984

EXPORTS OF DOMESTIC MERCHANDISE.

Articles and countries.	August—		Eight months ending August—	
	1897.	1898.	1897.	1898.
Agricultural implements (*Instrumentos de agricultura; Instrumentos de agricultura; Machines agricoles*):				
Central America................	$4,731	$28	$18,917	$1,964
Mexico	10,180	15,353	91,491	98,741
Santo Domingo.....	18	38	1,003	304
Cuba........................	691	353	4,381	2,421
Porto Rico....................	60	....	1,798	426
.Argentina.....	48,843	150,630	214,308	370,006
Brazil	2,543	1,135	15,089	17,855
Colombia	625	739	2,528	3,895
Other South America	14,988	73,601	65,224	187,856
Animals:				
Cattle (*Ganado vacuno; Gado; Betail*)—				
Central America..............	1,020	1,175	12,992	2,165
Mexico	1,271	1,231	19,681	59,182
South America	1,100	....	2,328	5,137
Hogs (*Cerdos; Porcos; Cochons*)—				
Mexico	45	30	68,007	4,598
Horses (*Caballos; Cavallos; Chevaux*)—				
Central America..............	1,250	500	10,850	8,895
Mexico	2,200	2,879	52,138	65,765
South America	700	....	2,800	1,850
Sheep (*Carneros; Carneiros; Moutons*)—				
Mexico......................	260	90	2,602	5,945
South America	918	1,040	12,038	7,378
Books, maps, engravings, etc. (*Libros, mapas, grabados, etc.; Livros, mappas, gravuras, etc.; Livres, cartes de géographie, gravures, etc.*):				
Central America................	5,875	10,715	31,569	22,104
Mexico	5,204	2,564	74,907	55,248
Santo Domingo.................	24	592	630	854
Cuba........................	16,220	46	60,135	2,805
Porto Rico....................	15	10	2,659	365
Argentina....................	5,490	1,387	22,235	16,230
Brazil	23,260	2,292	140,574	32,454
Colombia	2,493	521	23,452	7,057
Other South America	2,372	4,421	33,940	32,739
Breadstuffs:				
Corn (*Maíz; Milho; Maïs*)—				
Central America....	3,258	1,409	47,686	43,760
Mexico......................	5,143	18	987,644	6,260
Santo Domingo....	....	2	379	63
Cuba........................	49,135	28,588	185,691	227,291
Porto Rico...................	....	....	357	....
South America	2,978	2,828	14,804	12,760
Wheat (*Trigo; Trigo; Blé*)—				
Central America..............	2,003	2,848	32,383	25,932
South America	232,221	56	555,751	385,733

EXPORTS OF DOMESTIC MERCHANDISE—Continued.

Articles and countries.	August—		Eight months ending August—	
	1897.	1898.	1897.	1898.
Breadstuffs—Continued.				
Wheat flour (*Harina de trigo; Farina de trigo; Farine de blé*):				
Central America.............	$73, 275	$77, 707	$796, 216	$856, 325
Mexico..................	11, 497	6, 651	67, 128	64, 129
Santo Domingo..............	10, 015	9, 085	119, 782	146, 912
Cuba	93, 211	133, 566	300, 607	824, 576
Porto Rico.................	39, 802	18, 155	411, 881	197, 576
Brazil	161, 718	270, 785	2, 388, 949	1, 980, 987
Colombia	46, 108	22, 933	354, 642	269, 322
Other South America...........	149, 711	104, 973	1, 014, 143	1, 022, 236
Carriages, cars, etc., and parts of (*Carruages, carros y sus accesorios; Carruagens, carros e partes de carros; Voitures, wagons et leurs parties*):				
Central America................	8, 170	9, 686	87, 935	34, 734
Mexico........................	43, 866	40, 307	530, 035	161, 550
Santo Domingo....	321	213	13, 118	10, 671
Cuba	124	1, 578	11, 013	19, 177
Porto Rico.	525	....	5, 842	1, 429
Argentina.....................	15, 436	113, 109	92, 005	426, 225
Brazil	7, 660	1, 042	107, 399	529, 304
Colombia	898	12, 511	30, 999	38, 065
Other South America.....	3, 632	2, 590	34, 762	65, 197
Cycles and parts of (*Biciclos y sus accesorios; Bicyclos e accessorios; Bicyclettes et leurs parties*):				
Central America................	732	1, 252	18, 242	4, 969
Mexico........	6, 272	3, 317	51, 464	45, 216
Santo Domingo................	71	21	3, 620	598
Cuba	2, 202	....	6, 366	3, 345
Porto Rico....................	280	24	2, 582	1, 230
Argentina.....	5, 031	1, 873	29, 810	70, 452
Brazil	....	7, 720	16, 620	76, 161
Colombia....................	2, 595	732	13, 942	6, 390
Other South America...........	1, 033	3, 457	42, 325	32, 376
Clocks and watches (*Relojes de pared y de bolsillo; Relogios de parede e de bolso; Pendules et montres*):				
Central America.....	149	151	7, 796	4, 082
Mexico......................	1, 913	2, 114	14, 230	13, 764
Argentina....................	977	3, 205	12, 500	22, 966
Brazil	3, 547	7, 686	18, 021	27, 071
Other South America..........	3, 877	7, 506	60, 366	58, 741
Coal (*Carbón; Carvão; Charbon*):				
Central America................	6, 370	1, 671	15, 635	6, 660
Mexico.....	73, 982	84, 725	563, 468	751, 674
Santo Domingo.............	....	1, 830	15, 533	6, 623
Cuba	38, 779	33, 238	396, 734	268, 000
Porto Rico..........	....	9, 069	35, 691	15, 098
Brazil......................	....	1, 666	82, 526	69, 987
Colombia	131	2, 511	30, 223	17, 147
Other South America...........	....	47, 967	24, 282	71, 637
Copper (*Cobre; Cobre; Cuivre*):				
Mexico.......................	563	585	10, 454	25, 909

EXPORTS OF DOMESTIC MERCHANDISE—Continued.

Articles and countries.	August—		Eight months ending August—	
	1897.	1898.	1897.	898.
Cotton, unmanufactured (*Algodón no manufacturado; Algodão não manufacturado; Coton non manufacturé*):				
Mexico	$7,042	$7,665	$397,794	$568,996
Cotton cloths (*Tejidos de algodón; Fazendas de algodão; Coton manufacturé*):				
Central America................	41,484	44,985	355,684	284,965
Mexico	39,886	34,158	269,722	294,222
Santo Domingo.................	7,727	15,521	54,425	106,299
Cuba	1,099	....	13,936	5,951
Porto Rico.	327	....	3,382	1,023
Argentina.....................	22,605	9,326	86,252	108,811
Brazil	59,965	40,974	378,105	386,198
Colombia	33,201	30,075	250,603	185,555
Other South America...........	38,371	104,446	771,698	846,720
Wearing apparel (cotton) (*Ropa de algodón; Roupa de algodão; Vêtements en coton*):				
Central America................	20,678	12,395	161,746	152,375
Mexico ....,.....	23,807	29,437	205,255	252,027
Santo Domingo	2,166	2,958	16,572	14,580
Cuba	782	55	13,172	10,855
Porto Rico....................	35	....	2,240	746
Argentina......	2,628	4,418	31,789	28,615
Brazil	4,910	3,699	39,673	29,380
Colombia	7,536	2,543	37,490	26,332
Other South America...........	1,973	2,995	32,840	26,899
Fruits and nuts (*Frutas y nueces; Frutas e nozes; Fruits et noisettes*):				
Central America................	3,301	1,606	36,122	17,965
Mexico	4,100	4,825	37,963	37,812
Santo Domingo...	30	179	533	452
Cuba	1,415	1,571	16,067	12,505
Porto Rico....................	87	....	1,546	287
Argentina.......	747	859	3,141	6,521
Brazil	283	1,340	3,908	4,960
Colombia	1,382	503	6,580	5,369
Other South America......	2,547	1,117	18,026	10,134
Hides and skins (*Cueros y pieles; Couros e pelles; Cuirs et peaux*):				
Central America................	....	....	543	....
Mexico	314	120	13,435	1,999
Hops (*Lúpulos; Lupulos; Houblons*):				
Central America................	195	383	2,532	2,935
Mexico	15,131	65	70,727	7,537
Santo Domingo.................	....	....	2	16
South America	27	92	882	955

EXPORTS OF DOMESTIC MERCHANDISE—Continued.

Articles and countries.	August—		Eight months ending August—	
	1897.	1898.	1897.	1898.
Instruments:				
Electric and scientific apparatus (*Aparatos eléctricos y científicos; Apparelhos electricos e scientificos; Appareils électriques et scientifiques*)—				
Central America	$3, 160	$7, 356	$66, 766	$43, 833
Mexico	20, 245	38, 285	210, 400	217, 086
Argentina	23, 247	23, 046	130, 656	97, 046
Brazil	5, 092	11, 203	87, 046	40, 144
Other South America	12, 375	10, 090	109, 925	74, 636
Iron and steel, manufactures of:				
Builders' hardware, and saws and tools (*Materiale de metal para construcción, sierras y herramientas; Ferragens, serras e ferramentas; Matériaux de construction en fer et acier, scies et outils*):				
Central America	6, 711	5, 902	86, 689	49, 711
Mexico	55, 467	15, 784	403, 139	264, 956
Santo Domingo	1, 403	1, 618	8, 553	8, 837
Cuba	2, 173	1, 280	42, 812	25, 304
Porto Rico	867	45	9, 487	3, 699
Argentina	6, 636	25, 239	121, 066	117, 446
Brazil	19, 058	21, 348	138, 231	115, 171
Colombia	8, 209	8, 623	72, 623	59, 044
Other South America	10, 698	22, 714	151, 763	132, 044
Sewing machines and parts of (*Máquinas de coser y accesorios; Machinas de coser e accessorios; Machines de d coudre et leurs parties*):				
Central America	4, 057	1, 988	55, 619	15, 254
Mexico	15, 227	17, 305	147, 328	150, 495
Santo Domingo	66	524	1, 246	1, 284
Cuba	1, 886	....	3, 418	27
Porto Rico	73	....	1, 774	1, 050
Argentina	16, 629	13, 356	58, 114	54, 953
Brazil	11, 234	5, 858	54, 933	67, 472
Colombia	11, 988	6, 499	76, 397	47, 538
Other South America	3, 273	15, 140	65, 439	76, 180
Typewriting machines and parts of (*Máquinas de escribir y accesorios Machinas de escribir e accessorios Machines à écrire et leur parties*):				
Central America	136	178	7, 167	868
Mexico	1, 462	2, 297	16, 196	23, 577
Santo Domingo	....	....	125	....
Cuba	257	78	1, 887	787
Argentina	2, 229	3, 441	5, 770	17, 875
Brazil	85	1, 001	1, 687	3, 549
Colombia	35	290	2, 643	1, 861
Other South America	683	522	7, 178	9, 439

EXPORTS OF DOMESTIC MERCHANDISE—Continued.

Articles and countries.	August—		Eight months ending August—	
	1897.	1898.	1897.	1898.
Leather, other than sole (*Cuero, distinto del de sueld; Couro não para solas; Cuirs, autres que pour semelles*):				
Central America.................	$451	$587	$3,048	$4,150
Mexico........................	647	395	8,011	4,507
Santo Domingo.................	....	172	747	358
Cuba........	210	....	926	1,627
Porto Rico.......	....	....	221	708
Argentina......	572	3,717	1,234	12,187
Brazil........................	1,761	3,076	17,339	40,792
Colombia	951	173	2,325	3,075
Other South America...........	743	1,785	6,014	10,521
Boots and shoes (*Calzado; Calçados; Chaussures*):				
Central America.................	10,113	3,249	61,416	48,370
Mexico.................. ...	9,655	7,509	51,549	66,816
Colombia	4,817	3,669	31,199	26,486
Other South America...........	1,955	4,371	13,606	24,968
Naval stores: Rosin, tar, etc. (*Resina y alquitrdn; Resina e alcatrão; Résine et goudron*):				
Central America.................	1,329	2,139	12,721	12,777
Mexico........................	256	189	4,657	6,867
Santo Domingo................ ..	542	75	3,263	3,294
Cuba.....	1,161	38	3,937	2,586
Porto Rico....................	16	....	727	281
Argentina.....................	15,135	722	49,572	58,649
Brazil	15,568	18,847	119,222	111,202
Colombia	941	391	12,488	9,271
Other South America	4,509	9,942	47,702	56,979
Turpentine, spirits of (*Aguarras; Agua-raz; Térébenthine*):				
Central America....	225	210	2,319	1,998
Mexico.........	58	228	1,862	2,947
Santo Domingo.................	31	63	257	335
Cuba..................... ..	1,788	100	9,792	5,795
Porto Rico....................	123	....	1,774	583
Argentina....	6,993	4,513	21,848	102,273
Brazil........................	3,242	5,791	36,898	54,300
Colombia	418	540	3,339	3,264
Other South America...........	331	4,202	23,380	50,331
Oils, mineral, crude (*Aceites minerales, crudos; Oleos mineraes, crús; Huiles minérales, brutes*):				
Mexico..................... ...	43,203	29,162	247,525	181,165
Cuba.........................	18,940	8,500	151,757	85,642
Porto Rico..	....	....	25,793	19,477
Oils, mineral, refined or manufactured (*Aceites minerales, refinados ó manufacturados; Oleos mineraes, refinados ó manufacturados; Huiles minérales, raffinées ou manufacturées*):				
Central America.................	7,654	9,053	82,107	78,879
Mexico	16,595	9,182	123,199	114,574
Santo Domingo.................	292	652	51,350	32,653

EXPORTS OF DOMESTIC MERCHANDISE—Continued.

Articles and countries.	August—		Eight months ending August—	
	1897.	1898.	1897.	1898.
Oils, mineral, refined or manufactured— Continued.				
Cuba	$232	$4,706	$4,356	$26,301
Porto Rico	5,547	222	23,565	9,832
Argentina	93,745	78,188	476,667	660,759
Brazil	119,906	149,942	1,235,507	1,013,741
Colombia	5,570	7,306	71,402	79,322
Other South America	51,497	61,216	610,152	733,835
Oils, vegetable (*Aceites vegetales; Oleos vegetaes; Huiles végétales*) :				
Central America	355	110	1,865	2,291
Mexico	8,858	29,976	191,492	219,343
Santo Domingo	2,005	3,891	13,296	25,491
Cuba	375	42	1,059	908
Argentina	457	2,381	3,092	8,356
Brazil	14,521	4,090	135,271	163,522
Other South America	7,785	3,050	47,686	77,343
Paraffin and paraffin wax (*Parafina y cera de parafina; Paraffina e cera de parafina; Paraffine et cire de cette substance*) :				
Central America		1,987	17,501	15,668
Mexico	13,789	15,453	79,450	101,848
Brazil	1,625	1,010	7,039	7,400
Other South America	249	1,737	2,178	5,115
Provisions, comprising meat and dairy products :				
Beef, canned (*Carne de vaca en latas; Carne de vacca em latas; Bœuf conservé*)—				
Central America	2,038	1,698	26,351	15,617
Mexico	1,166	1,447	8,316	9,261
Santo Domingo	12	3	40	26
Cuba	184	2,274	1,371	4,848
Porto Rico			178	
Argentina	50		425	505
Brazil	700	2,251	4,083	18,716
Colombia	886	242	5,213	3,582
Other South America	810	601	8,372	9,612
Beef, salted or pickled (*Carne de vaca, salada ó en salmuera; Carne de vacca, salgada ou em salmoura; Bœuf, salé ou en saumure*)—				
Central America	3,261	2,839	21,745	24,686
Mexico	12		209	190
Santo Domingo	265	79	1,593	2,999
Cuba	1,387	3,560	5,066	6,799
Porto Rico	176	120	4,621	140
Brazil	102	281	1,279	929
Colombia	966	713	8,925	9,171
Other South America	16,431	13,308	68,232	119,993
Tallow (*Sebo; Sebo; Suif*)—				
Central America	7,781	8,315	63,911	66,701
Mexico	2,478	4,086	20,301	15,954
Santo Domingo	2,439	82	14,195	16,018

EXPORTS OF DOMESTIC MERCHANDISE—Continued.

Articles and countries.	August—		Eight months ending August—	
	1897.	1898.	1897.	1898.
Provisions, comprising meat and dairy products—Continued.				
Tallow—Continued.				
Cuba	$1,160	....	$8,052	$5,465
Porto Rico	....	....	198	176
Brazil	2,831	$2,150	13,688	5,625
Colombia	2,266	174	11,215	8,249
Other South America	1,384	1,575	8,032	16,623
Bacon (*Tocino; Toucinho; Lard fumé*)—				
Central America	1,543	2,071	14,687	10,389
Mexico	508	1,739	5,591	7,788
Santo Domingo	175	336	1,624	1,922
Cuba	48,482	61,520	422,345	400,457
Porto Rico	495	2,128	23,159	21,000
Brazil	76,543	49,241	876,558	258,672
Colombia	243	21	1,136	678
Other South America	1,709	702	16,228	14,795
Hams (*Jamones; Presunto; Jambons*)—				
Central America	2,222	1,694	22,860	15,796
Mexico	1,454	2,172	14,862	17,629
Santo Domingo	470	607	4,696	5,448
Cuba	29,130	32,008	214,817	193,707
Porto Rico	3,614	....	53,875	11,378
Brazil	69	583	1,375	2,662
Colombia	1,033	1,017	10,775	9,297
Other South America	7,053	6,209	57,599	44,125
Pork (*Carne de puerco; Carne de porco, Porc*)—				
Central America	6,015	8,449	42,552	54,912
Santo Domingo	393	690	2,670	5,250
Cuba	2,245	995	7,806	9,629
Porto Rico	15,995	6,404	119,743	75,355
Brazil	82	2,150	15,931	4,138
Colombia	843	498	5,331	6,231
Other South America	20,485	18,783	92,684	148,363
Lard (*Manteca; Hanha; Saindoux*)—				
Central America	7,674	17,338	81,280	126,646
Mexico	17,146	7,473	219,425	92,182
Santo Domingo	2,211	2,943	17,901	27,678
Cuba	95,163	174,122	705,625	721,731
Porto Rico	16,058	10,193	158,148	95,820
Argentina	114	156	2,014	2,917
Brazil	81,821	128,645	659,204	652,084
Colombia	9,433	6,122	92,826	66,279
Other South America	50,384	44,487	394,516	447,592
Oleo and oleomargarine (*Grasa y oleomargarina; Oleo e oleomargarina; Oléo et oléomargarine*)—				
Central America	46	100	400	1,191
Mexico	....	137	283	960
Colombia	775	678	4,785	6,238
Other South America	4,165	1,031	20,005	8,014

EXPORTS OF DOMESTIC MERCHANDISE—Continued.

Articles and countries.	August—		Eight months ending August—	
	1897.	1898.	1897.	1898.
Provisions, comprising meat and dairy products—Continued.				
Butter (*Mantequilla ; Manteiga ; Beurre*)—				
Central America...............	$3, 484	$3, 433	$31, 923	$31, 290
Mexico	2, 841	2, 748	28, 765	31, 451
Santo Domingo...............	676	1, 701	5, 351	8, 767
Cuba	991	1, 316	7, 449	5, 119
Porto Rico....................	599	69	5, 371	489
Brazil.........................	2, 412	4, 953	28, 990	69, 127
Colombia	2, 406	1, 084	14, 642	10, 924
Other South America..........	7, 078	10, 894	60, 024	71, 191
Cheese (*Queso ; Queijo ; Fromage*)—				
Central America...............	1, 442	1, 550	14, 228	11, 752
Mexico	1, 047	1, 566	9, 529	10, 296
Santo Domingo...............	212	601	3, 625	3, 574
Cuba	1, 709	1, 001	10, 101	14, 097
Porto Rico....................	....	102	2, 128	1, 072
Brazil.........................	....	....	132	75
Colombia	896	786	8, 136	6, 428
Other South America..........	1, 864	1, 209	11, 530	11, 100
Seeds (*Semillas ; Sementes ; Semence*) :				
Central America	276	262	4, 439	4, 532
Mexico	379	480	13, 510	24, 411
Santo Domingo................	17	10	476	361
Cuba	665	280	1, 599	906
Porto Rico....................	....	....	131	....
Argentina.....................	35	9	666	245
Brazil	37	....	1, 127	445
Colombia	51	58	1, 955	598
Other South America	356	125	1, 565	1, 550
Sugar, refined (*Azúcar refinado; Assucar refinado ; Sucre raffiné*) :				
Central America...............	4, 733	1, 802	35, 516	25, 531
Mexico	2, 833	67	13, 777	9, 440
Santo Domingo................	49	273	1, 485	970
Colombia	3, 395	459	24, 044	12, 826
Other South America	....	436	1, 982	1, 000
Tobacco, unmanufactured (*Tabaco no manufacturado ; Tabaco não manufacturado ; Tabac non manufacturé*) :				
Central America................	3, 155	366	8, 523	17, 729
Mexico	5, 115	15, 246	72, 442	88, 842
Argentina.....................	495	750	1, 460	13, 239
Colombia.....................	1, 182	544	1, 868	6, 252
Other South America	8, 133	9, 775	61, 486	68, 006
Tobacco, manufactures of (*Manufacturas de tabaco ; Manufacturas de tabaco ; Tabac fabriqué*) :				
Central America...............	1, 310	4, 817	40, 410	38, 052
Mexico	398	1, 959	3, 924	24, 534
Cuba	14, 058	1, 557	121, 246	78, 266

EXPORTS OF DOMESTIC MERCHANDISE—Continued.

Articles and countries.	August—		Eight months ending August—	
	1897.	1898.	1897.	1898.
Tobacco, manufactures of—Cont'd.				
Argentina.............................	$360	$168	$9, 173	$1, 078
Brazil................................	....	....	65	550
Colombia.........	286	238	654	4, 287
Other South America...........	11, 908	3, 866	51, 791	53, 244
Wood, unmanufactured (*Madera no manufacturado; Madeira não manufacturado; Bois brut*):				
Central America.................	13, 783	420	66, 375	21, 905
Mexico.........................	13, 587	45, 026	149, 727	297, 938
Cuba..........................	755	....	15, 000	12, 683
Argentina......	343	385	14, 483	6, 407
Brazil	2, 060	....	11, 580	75
Colombia	468	173	19, 904	21, 011
Other South America...........	6, 806	150	33, 939	20, 503
Lumber (*Maderas; Madeiras; Bois de construction*):				
Central America.................	8, 636	3, 390	93, 181	23, 303
Mexico.........................	163, 966	66, 573	1, 408, 407	538, 973
Santo Domingo.................	2, 323	2, 286	59, 353	22, 999
Cuba..........................	36, 414	9, 844	201, 430	115, 371
Porto Rico....	8, 034	....	66, 115	19, 224
Argentina.......................	32, 008	87, 782	437, 489	612, 605
Brazil	38, 946	38, 162	420, 543	430, 201
Colombia	6, 517	888	48, 554	32, 533
Other South America...........	36, 748	55, 012	397, 908	388, 370
Furniture (*Muebles; Mobilia; Meubles*):				
Central America.................	8, 860	3, 598	92, 166	28, 973
Mexico.........................	10, 785	20, 762	128, 547	109, 663
Santo Domingo.................	375	380	8, 022	6, 925
Cuba..........................	4, 032	190	25, 023	10, 309
Porto Rico......................	967	....	6, 454	2, 456
Argentina.........	17, 553	12, 179	54, 509	36, 852
Brazil..........................	2, 973	2, 750	29, 413	16, 280
Colombia	2, 698	2, 348	27, 518	18, 179
Other South America...........	2, 934	8, 365	49, 663	52, 156
Wool, raw (*Lana cruda; La cría; Laines brutes*):				
Mexico	....	....	30, 449	....

ADDITIONAL PACIFIC STEAMSHIP LINE.

According to advices received and published by the "Chronicle," San Francisco, on October 11, San Francisco is to have further direct steamer communication with South American markets on both the west and east coasts. The Chargeurs-Réunis, one of the largest of the French steamship companies, is to establish a line of steamers between San Francisco and the following ports: Mazatlan and Acapulco, Mexico; Guayaquil, Ecuador; Callao, Peru; Valparaiso, Chile; Montevideo, Uruguay; Santos, Brazil; Liverpool, England; Havre, France, and possibly a Belgian port. The service is to begin next March and thereafter a monthly service is to be maintained between San Francisco and Liverpool with stoppages at the above-mentioned ports.

A representative of the company, now located in San Francisco, stated that for service in the Pacific, the company has now under construction three steamers which will have a length of 372 feet and a carrying capacity of 6,000 tons each.

FINANCIAL POSITION STRENGTHENED.

The accompanying statement, compiled from official records by the "Journal of Finance," showing the course of the imports and exports of the United States for the first eight months of the calendar years designated, demonstrates the extent to which this country, from its commercial operations with other countries (chiefly of Europe) and their dependencies, has strengthened its financial position in 1898:

	1898.	1897.	1896.
Merchandise:			
Imports	$426,412,038	$546,325,777	$471,232,299
Exports	778,674,025	641,697,330	580,930,792
Excess of exports	352,261,987	95,371,553	109,698,493
Gold:			
Imports	102,087,831	11,887,654	31,902,137
Exports	9,679,113	32,542,659	56,895,492
Excess of imports	92,408,718		
Excess of exports		20,655,005	24,993,355

The exports of merchandise have exceeded the imports by $352,261,987, while for the same months in 1897 the excess was $95,271,553, or a difference in favor of 1898 of $256,890,234. The creditor balance of this year has been offset by net gold imports amounting to $92,408,718, leaving a net balance on the commercial account of $259,853,069, or at the rate of $346,400,000 per annum.

Bull. No. 5——4

MARKS ON IMPORTED GOODS.

The following circular, issued by the Treasury Department, relating to the mark on goods imported into United States ports, was made public at the custom-houses on October 18:

In order to secure a more efficient enforcement of the provisions of section 8 of the act of July 24, 1897, requiring the marking of packages with the name of country of production and the quantity of their contents, and the marking and stamping of imported articles, it is directed that hereafter the appraising officer shall make examination of all merchandise in his hands for appraisement in order to ascertain whether the requirements of section 8 are fully complied with. Whenever he shall discover a failure to comply with such requirements, he shall call for the remaining packages of the invoice, and the importer shall be directed to mark the merchandise according to law. In default of such action by the importer, the goods shall. be under general order, and treated as unclaimed. The marking of such goods thus held in public stores shall be done by the importer, under the special supervision of an officer of the appraiser's department, and the expense of such supervision and all charges for cartage and labor shall be paid by the importer before the delivery of the merchandise.

----- --- -----

URUGUAY.

TRADE OF THE REPUBLIC DURING 1897.

The following extracts from the annual report of the British Consul, Mr. GREENFELL, have been forwarded from Montevideo to the Department of State by Mr. SWALM, United States Consul:

The total official value of the foreign commerce of the Republic for 1897 amounts to $49,492,305, of which $20,049,980 are imports, showing a balance of trade in favor of Uruguay. Customs receipts for 1897 have fallen off seriously, amounting to $8,175,442, or $2,424,558 less than those for 1896.

Great Britain has a monopoly of the importation of hams, tea, sacking, felt hats, sheepskins, hoes, rakes, thrashing machines, sewing thread, iron and lead piping, coal, galvanized-iron roof plates, tin plates, soda, jute, iron safes, and gunpowder, and stands first in imports of cotton articles, linen goods, mixed woolen goods, straw hats, linen socks, cotton handkerchiefs, mixed woolen and cotton blankets, windmill machinery, sulphate of copper, spades, carpenters' tools, twine, varnish, iron bands, iron bars and plates, paint, china and porcelain ware, saddlery and harness.

Germany has a monopoly of the importation of pianos, salt and dried codfish, and stands first in imports of refined sugar, flannels, ready-made clothes, cotton and linen shirtings, cuffs and collars, woolen singlets, cotton socks, pure and mixed woolen cloaks, cotton coverlets, towels, napkins, sewing machines, wire fencing, starch, bluing, printing paper, merceries, and house furniture.

France has a monopoly in kid skins and tiles, and stands first in woolen goods, pure and mixed silk stuffs, boots and shoes, cotton singlets, silk neckties, kid gloves, umbrellas, carriage springs, drugs, and perfumery.

Belgium has a monopoly in scythes, iron beams and pillars, zinc plates, and sporting guns, and stands first in mixed linen goods, blankets, plate and looking glass, table glass, window glass, Roman cement, white paper, and candles.

The United States has a monopoly in plows, pitchforks, and tar, and stands first in timber, reaping machines, binding twine, and axes; second in house furniture, third in sewing machines and sulphate of copper, and fifth in drugs and printing paper.

Mr. Swalm informs the Department that the trade of the United States, Germany, and France with Uruguay has greatly increased during the past year, largely at the expense of England. During the present year the decline in the importations of cotton goods from England has been most marked. Germany has beaten her competitors in cotton and linen shirtings, having put a cheap article on the market. The sewing machines sent from Germany, the consul notes, are cheap imitations of those manufactured in the United States.

PRINCIPAL ARTICLES OF EXPORT.

The exports of Uruguay are divided for statistical purposes into six classes, of which the principal item is "saladero and live-stock products." Under this head from 85 to 90 per cent of the valuation of outbound shipments are included. During the past ten years, according to the figures obtained from the Official Statistical Annuals, the exports of this class have amounted to $23,824,672 in 1889, $26,007,091 in 1890, $24,804,823 in 1891, $24,273,559 in 1892, $25,703,185 in 1893, $28,189,911 in 1894, $27,474,987 in 1895, $26,418,596 in 1896, $26,834,860 in 1897, and for the first six months of 1898, $14,922,467.

"Saladero and live-stock products" are divided into some forty items, which again are subdivided or otherwise distinguished. Of these the principal are: Horns, horsehair, bones and boneash, jerked beef (tasajo), preserved meats, meat extracts, liquid meat, salted oxhides, dried oxhides, salted calves' hides and kips, notato hides (skins of unborn calves), dried horsehides, salted horsehides, sheepskins, lambskins, hoofs, tallow (uncleansed, and tallow for culinary purposes), guano, wool, preserved tongues, hornpiths, entrails, sinews, and nerves.

Of all the above the most important item is jerked beef, known as "tasajo." The greatest quantity exported in a single year was $5,719,029 in 1894. In 1896, the latest statistics obtainable, the value of exports of this product was $4,561,799. Regarding its production and the adaptability of Uruguay for articles greatly superior to it in quality, the Montevideo Times says:

It is acknowledged that Uruguay is one of the finest beef-producing countries in the world, and the establishment here of so important an enterprise as Liebig's factories is a proof of this. Yet the greater part of the beef is converted into so wretched and primitive an article as tasajo, an article of food that scarcely merits the name of civilized, and which is only consumed by the lowest classes and the black population of Brazil and Cuba. It is impossible to believe that in these days of applied science nothing better can be made of the splendid Uruguayan beef, or that it can not be profitably prepared in such a manner as to find a wider and better market. Foreign beef is now largely consumed in England and other European countries, and it is exported in various forms by countries which have fewer facilities and advantages than Uruguay. * * * Being a pastoral country, Uruguay produces not only beef, but also mutton or an excellent quality. Up to the present, however, we are not aware that a single attempt has been made to utilize mutton as an article of export, although this has been done from Argentina. If space permitted, we might also deal with dairy and porcine products. For the preparation of both for export Uruguay is eminently fitted. The only thing wanted is enterprise, though we believe that, as regards pigs, there is some antiquated national or municipal law which places an exorbitant tax on their slaughter, and thus prevents the growth of what might be a very important industry. But with a progressive Government like the present it should not be difficult to obtain the repeal of this tax.

FINANCIAL AFFAIRS OF THE REPUBLIC.

Consul SWALM writes from Montevideo that the public debt of the Republic, bonded and floating, amounted to $140,000,000 on August 31, 1898. He also reports that the following amounts were appropriated for the support of the Government for the fiscal year 1898–99: Legislative power, $341,114; Presidency, $64,618; Ministry of Foreign Affairs, $149,089; Ministry of Government, $2,721,659; Ministry of Finance, $961,040; Ministry of Interior, $1,127,140; Ministry of War and Marine, $1,921,953; public debt, $5,329,662; railway guaranties, $884,770; pensions, $1,417,378; various purposes, $524,679; total, $15,434,003. This makes the per capita tax $18.24. The consul adds: "The Republic faithfully maintains its credit and has not repudiated a dollar of its debt."

In Uruguay, as Mr. SWALM notes, taxes are levied on exports

of animals and animal products, on land (at a very low rate), on notes, checks, etc. Licenses must be obtained for all kinds of business. The tobacco tax is levied under a system modeled on that of the United States, save that each cigar has a 2-mill stamp wrapped about it. Wax matches pay a tax of 5 mills on each box of 50. The city of Montevideo has bonds outstanding to the amount of $6,000,000. As an asset the city holds the electric-light plant, which yields a good revenue.

NEW MINISTER OF FOREIGN RELATIONS.

Consul-General Don PRUDENCIO DE MURGUIONDO has officially advised the Department of State of the United States that President CUESTAS has temporarily appointed Señor Don JACOBO A. VARELA as a minister in his cabinet. He takes the place of Señor Don DOMINGO MENDILAHARSU (resigned) as Minister of Foreign Relations.

VENEZUELA.

IMPORTANCE OF THE COURT OF ARBITRATION.

The approaching meeting in Paris of the Anglo-Venezuelan Court of Arbitration, of which Chief Justice FULLER and Justice BREWER, of the United States Supreme Court, are members in behalf of Venezuela, will be only second in importance to the meeting in the same city of the United States-Spanish Peace Commission, owing to the crisis which the Venezuelan question raised between the United States and Great Britain during President CLEVELAND's Administration and the extent to which the Monroe Doctrine is believed to be involved. The present plans are for the court to hold a preliminary session in January, 1899, when Justice BREWER will go to Paris. But Chief Justice FULLER is not likely to attend the first meeting, as the Supreme Court will be busy then, and two members can not be spared at the same time. Justice BREWER probably will arrange for a postponement until May, when both justices will be free to join the other arbitrators and take up the serious business of the tribunal.

The cases and counter cases between Venezuela and Great Britain have been completed. Minister ANDRADE, of Venezuela, recently submitted to the British embassy in Washington the counter case of the Republic, and at the same time the British counter case was handed to Dr. ROJAS, the Venezuelan agent in Paris. The papers make one of the most voluminous international controversies ever brought to arbitration. The British case and counter case fill eleven large volumes, one atlas, and a number of detached maps, while the Venezuelan case fills six volumes and three atlases. With the record all made up, it remains only with the counsel for the two parties to submit their briefs. The Venezuelan brief will be prepared by ex-President HARRISON and ex-Secretary TRACY, of the United States, and Mr. MALET-PROVOST. The British brief will be presented by the foremost lawyers of England, including Sir RICHARD WEBSTER. It is expected that Generals HARRISON and TRACY will be present and make oral arguments when the court assembles in May. Thus the personnel of the advocates, as well as the arbitrators, will give unusual importance to the hearing. The British arbitrators are headed by Baron HERSCHEL, formerly lord chancellor of England. Associated with him is Sir RICHARD HENN COLLINS. The fifth arbitrator, who occupies the attitude of an umpire, is the noted Russian jurist and writer on international law, M. MAARTENS. He is acting for the arbitrators up to the time of their meeting, receiving the papers, briefs, and other documents.

PURCHASES FROM THE UNITED STATES IN SEPTEMBER.

Mr. ANTONIO E. DELFINO, Consul-General of Venezuela in New York, has kindly furnished the Bureau of American Republics with the following statistical data relative to the exportations of merchandise from the port of New York to the several ports of Venezuela for the month of September, 1898:

The total number of packages shipped was 41,478, weighing, in kilograms, 2,195,375.30, in pounds, 4,839,924.39, and having a declared valuation of $199,831.62. The bulk of these goods went to La Guaira, 21,967 packages, valued at $120,764.62, having been shipped to that port. The value of the articles sent to Puerto Cabello was $36,745.39; to Ciudad Bolivar, $23,037.50; to Maracaibo, $9,746.11; to Carúpano, $5,276; to La Vela, $1,931; to Guanta, $1,880, and to Cumaná, $1,001.

The principal articles exported were: Wheat flour, $40,826.94; lard, $33,529.10; calicoes, $24,190.91; cotton goods, bleached and unbleached, $13,640.59; provisions, $15,069.06; drugs and perfumery, $10,668.83; miscellaneous goods, $11,140.92; butter, $8,558.11; kerosene, $7,889.15; hardware specialties, $6,262.24; canvas, $4,203.86; cordage, $2,932.10; cigarette tobacco, $2,943.80; barbed wire, $2,966.62; and electrical supplies, $2,675.41.

CONCESSION TO A PORCELAIN MANUFACTURER.

Under the administration of President ANDRADE, Venezuela seems to be making rapid strides forward, commercially and otherwise.   One of the chief aims of the Government is the encouragement of new enterprises, especially of those that will not only be of present benefit to the Government, but of future service to the people.   Recently there has been an unusual number of reports from United States consuls in Venezuela giving in detail the results of their observations on the new order of things.   Consul PLUMACHER, of Maracaibo, sends one of these reports, which contains a translation of the principal features of a concession granted Marquis GINO INCONTRI by the Minister of Agriculture, Industry, and Commerce for the manufacture of porcelain ware.   According to this, Signor INCONTRI is to—

Establish, within eighteen months, one or more factories of porcelain ware, but not of the sort already manufactured in the country.   The Government is not to make a similar grant for 10 years to any other person.   Congress is to be asked not to reduce the present duties on porcelain wares.   Materials for construction, machinery, etc., for the factory shall be exempt from duty, and the goods of the company shall not be taxed during the term of the contract.   Land (12 acres) is to be granted free to the company for the construction of the factories and 62 acres for the raw material.   The company is to pay into the treasury, one year after the execution of this contract, 10 per cent of the yearly profits, and will deposit in one of the banks of Venezuela 25,000 bolivars ($4,825) in gold or in Venezuelan or Italian bonds.   If the factories cease work for six consecutive months through the fault of the company, it must pay a fine of 20,000 bolivars ($3,860); should they remain idle another six months, this contract will be annulled.

ESTABLISHMENT OF A MECHANICS' BANK.

From Maracaibo, Consul PLUMACHER forwards to the Department of State a translation of a contract for the establishment of a mechanics' bank, which he thinks is a good enterprise.   This document is summarized thus:

The contractor binds himself to establish in this city a loan association, with the object of building houses in Caracas and other cities, advancing money and materials, secured by mortgage guaranty on the property, to be gradually repaid by the rents, so that in time the builder will acquire the absolute proprietorship of the house. The Mechanics' Bank will make loans at the rate of 70 per cent in materials for construction and 30 per cent in cash for payment of workmen, and will take a mortgage on the building, receiving 12 per cent in monthly payments. This 12 per cent is to be applied in the following manner: Six per cent interest on the capital employed in the work, 4 per cent for refunding of capital, 2 per cent for the current expenses of the bank. The concession will last fifteen years, and the bank is to be opened within one year after approval of the contract. The bank, as well as the houses it assists in building, until the mortgages are canceled, are to be exempted from municipal taxes.

SUGGESTIONS TO EXPORTERS.

M. QUIEVREUX, French Consul at Caracas, in a recent report to his Government, made several suggestions relative to the trade of the Republic, which ought to be valuable not only to his own countrymen, but to exporters to the United States. He said:

Purchases are made here in the Easter and Christmas seasons. These are the periods at which the Venezuelan consumer likes to make his provisions of all kinds. The fact that the Christmas festivities preceding the new year are coincident with the gathering of the coffee crop, the principal industry of the country, is sufficient reason why this date should be chosen. The choice of the Easter season is due only to motives of a religious order; the rainy season is then coming on, which will render transport into the interior difficult, the means of communication being reduced to bad tracks without bridges by which the rivers, transformed into impetuous torrents by the "aguaceros," have to be crossed. Apart from these two seasons the current of business does not display much activity; and our (French) exporters, to whom these observations are especially addressed on this subject, should always bear it in mind. By so doing they would enable the importers to avoid the unpleasantness of remaining with large stocks unsold, owing to the falling back in sales.

The requirements of the Venezuelan "Codigo de Haciendo," of which I have spoken, impose on manufacturers desirous of trading with this Republic the necessity of exercising precautions, of which I think it would be useful to give a summary. They must not forget, for example, to declare in Spanish, on the invoices, the merchandise shipped, and to declare it in the terms of the tariff. I have seen a fine of 125 bolivars inflicted on a merchant, who, having sent shapes of straw hats, had omitted to place on his declaration the translation, "sombreros de pajas sin ningun adorno," the expression used in the tariff. They must also not omit to consult the customs tariff beforehand and to specify exactly what class the merchandise shipped comes under, for payment of the import duties. It is also essential to remember that duty is charged on the gross weight of the merchandise. It is necessary in all shipments intended for Venezuela to use for packing only material that is both strong and light at the same time.

EXPORT BOUNTIES IN LATIN AMERICA.

In response to instructions sent by the Department of State of the United States to the various consular and diplomatic officers in foreign countries, reports have been furnished concerning bounties granted by the several Governments.

From Argentina, Minister BUCHANAN writes that the only article exported from the Argentine Republic on which a bounty is granted is sugar. The text of the sugar law is as follows:

TRANSLATION OF SECTIONS 3, 4, 5, AND 6 OF ARTICLE I OF THE INTERNAL TAX LAW FOR 1897.

SEC. 3. All sugars produced in the country from the date of the promulgation of this law, or which are imported up to December 31 proximo, will pay an internal tax of 6 centavos per kilogram, which will be paid by the producer or importer.

SEC. 4. In exchange for the tax referred to, the Executive power will deliver a certificate (drawback), which will give the holder the right to export 35 per cent of the sugar upon which he may have paid said tax and to receive in return 12 centavos moneda nacional per kilogram on such exported sugar.

SEC. 5. All sugar of national production existing in the country at the date of the promulgation of this law will pay an internal tax of 1 centavo moneda nacional per kilogram, which will be paid by the holder, to whom there will be repaid 4 centavos for each kilogram he exports; it being understood that the quantity exported shall not exceed 25 per cent of quantity upon which he may have paid the tax.

SEC. 6. Whenever the current wholesale price of sugar free on board at the point of production (including the tax paid) shall exceed $4 moneda nacional per 10 kilograms, the Executive power will suspend the delivery of the certificates mentioned in section 4.

Minister WILSON reports from Chile that the Government extends no grants or bounties of any kind to any article produced in the country or imported and subjected to further manufacture. The only Government protection afforded to native industries is given by the imposition of import duties on articles that are similar to those manufactured in the country.

With regard to Colombia, it is reported by Minister HART, from Bogotá, that no enactments which have the effect of extending bounties to any class of exports have been made by the Government.

In Ecuador the Government does not pay bounties on any class of exports, either directly or indirectly, in the crude or unmanufactured state. Minister TILLMAN reports that, on the contrary, a few of the chief products of the country have to pay an export duty, no matter to what country exported.

Sugar is the only article exported from Haiti on which a bounty is granted by the Government, but the chargé d'affaires ad interim, Dr. JOHN B. TERRES, writes to the Department of State that there have been no exports of that product for several years, the quantity produced being entirely consumed in the Republic. Consul GRIMKE reports that the Government of Santo Domingo has made no enactments extending bounties to any class of merchandise exported.

In Nicaragua an export tax of $1 gold per ounce on gold ingots and $2 per ounce on gold dust has been established, concerning which Mr. M. J. CLANCY reported to the United States Government on August 23, 1897.

Neither Paraguay nor Uruguay pays a bounty on home products, but both countries levy a tax on their principal exports.

Peru grants no bounties on any class of merchandise that may be exported.

PROMOTION OF IMMIGRATION IN SOUTH AMERICA.

In the course of an article on the future of South America the correspondent of the "London Morning Post" notes that quite recently there have been some attempts at organized emigration to South America. He calls attention to the contract made last July between the Government of Venezuela and the Italian Colonization Society, an account of which was published in the October BULLETIN. Further he says:

Negotiations are at present in progress for encouraging emigration to Brazil, and President-elect de CAMPOS SALLES is understood to have worked successfully toward this end during his visit to Berlin last month. The Von der Heydt rescript, by which all emigration to Brazil was forbidden, has now been substantially repealed. Germany is willing that her sons should settle in the Provinces of São Paulo, Rio Grande do Sul, Parana, and Santa Catarina provided that their perfect political independence is guaranteed. Brazil regards this requirement, not unnaturally, as amounting to a relinquishment of her own sovereignty, but it is nevertheless likely enough that some solution will be found of the difficulty, in which case it is expected that the plan adopted will be extended to Switzerland and Austria.

Germany aims to secure for her emigrants privileges they could not obtain in the British colonies or the United States, and the concession asked for would raise a serious question of principle. It is not easy to see how the Monroe

Doctrine would apply in such a case. That famous declaration asserts that the American continents are "not to be considered as subjects for further colonization by any European power," but much has occurred since "the era of good feeling," and modern diplomacy finds methods of obtaining concessions from weaker powers without resorting to the crude policy described by MONROE as "oppressing them or controlling in any other manner their destiny." In these days we deal in usufructs, but the substantial meaning of these words is not essentially different from that of the old-fashioned terms cession and conquest. The point is a nice one, but it seems certain to arise some time or other in connection with the inevitable development by colonization of South America, and the fact that France, Holland, and Great Britain hold territorial possessions in that country would not tend to simplify the controversy.

ARTICLES USED IN THE PHILIPPINES.

From Berne, Switzerland, Consul FRANKENTHAL writes the Department of State, giving the substance of an interview with a merchant of Manila. The consul does this with the hope that he may be able to enlighten United States exporters as to the requirements of the Philippine markets, and furnish certain points that may be of value to business men who contemplate entering the field at Manila or elsewhere in the islands. He says:

The Chinese, who are in the majority among the aliens, control the retail trade, while next to them come the Spanish dealers. It is estimated that there are about 300 other Europeans in business in the whole group of islands. The richest dealers are the "creoles" and "mestizos," a combination of Chinese and Tagalese.

In Manila there are many large cigarette factories, some of which employ as many as 4,000 hands. A few German, Swiss, and English firms have entered that field. There is also a sugar refinery, a steam rice mill, a Spanish electrical plant, a Spanish telephone exchange, a Spanish tramway, worked partly by steam and partly by horse power; rope factories, worked mainly by hand (a few use oxen); a Spanish brewery, which furnishes a good beer; a German cement factory, employing 70 hands; a Swiss umbrella factory; and a Swiss hat factory, which makes felt and straw articles, the latter out of Chinese straw braid. A cotton mill with 6,000 spindles and with a capital (English) of £40,000 ($194,600) is in process of construction. The European firms in Manila are divided as follows: 45 Spanish, 19 German, and 17 English; 2 English and 6 Swiss brokers; 2 French storekeepers, with large establishments; 1 Dutch firm and 1 Belgian firm. Small retail stores (40 in number) are kept by Chinese firms. The German and Swiss firms are general importers, while the export of hemp and sugar, the import of domestic dry goods, and the ship chandlery trade are in the hands of the English. Credit from one to three months and 5 per cent is given, while spot-cash sales command a discount of 7 per cent. Caution is advised in dealing with the Chinese merchants, as Manila has no mercantile register like Hongkong.

Cotton yarns are a heavy import article, so far mainly from Barcelona, by reason of the minimum Spanish tariff. The Spanish manufacturers have done what England, Germany, and Switzerland have always refused to do, and that is to renumber the yarns. In Manila, No. 10 is sold numbered 24, No. 16 numbered 30, No. 18 numbered 32, No. 22 numbered 49, No. 32 numbered 50, and No. 36 or 40 numbered 60. The orders given are for four-fifths unbleached and one-fifth bleached. Dyed yarn is bought in Nos. 20 and 32, in colors of orange, green, and rose. Turkey-red yarn, in the correct Nos. 20 to 40, especially 32, used to come from Elberfeld, but of late years Spain has managed to supply it. Bleached and unbleached shirtings and drills, from Manchester, are sold in large quantities, but of late the pieces have decreased in yards as well as in widths. The staples now are white shirtings, 26 inches wide and 36 yards long; gray T cloth, 25 inches wide and 21½ yards long; gray long cloth, 28 inches wide and 32 yards long, and gray drills, 25 inches wide and 27 yards long. Colored prints, 24 inches wide, with red ground and fancy crimps, are good sellers. Ginghams and challies for bed coverings, etc., common quality, in large patterns with red ground, some with yellow or blue squares, some with indigo ground, and a few in green, in pieces of 24 yards, find a good market, while cotton cassinette, in light weight and double width, for trousers, is in demand. Handkerchiefs, 17 by 18 inches and 22 by 22 inches, white, or white with colored borders, are the correct thing. Black cotton zanellas, 18½ inches wide, for the dresses of the country women, and aniline black satins, in 45-inch goods, are considered stylish. Woven cotton underwear is a great staple, and white cotton bed quilts, in fancy patterns, are used as ponchos, after a hole has been cut in the center. The consul says his informant estimates that 500,000 dozen undershirts are used annually—two-thirds with arms half-length, sizes 34 to 40, 27 inches long, bleached white, striped, printed, and net work. Men's cotton socks, 9 to 11, and ladies' cotton hose, 8 to 9½, are the right sizes. Cheap cotton lace pointed fichus are worn by all the women. Other articles which have a good sale are low-priced sewing machines, carriages and parts, enameled ware for cooking utensils, and, last but not least, American clocks, which now have a good foothold, and for which there is an increasing demand.

- - ———

TRADE MISCELLANY.

ARGENTINE REPUBLIC.

An Agricultural Adviser. The New Orleans Picayune says that Hon. J. STERLING MORTON, ex-Secretary of Agriculture of the United States, has been invited by the President of Argentina to spend the coming year in that country as an adviser of the Government in matters of agriculture, and the organization of an agricultural department. The Picayune adds that he may possibly accept the mission.

Wool-Shearing Industry. A telegram announces that wool shearing has begun in Argentina. It is estimated that the increased production over 1897 will amount to at least 15 per cent. The market opened with a gain of 10 per cent in prices.

BRAZIL.

Bids Asked for Draining. The Rio News announces that the department of public works of the State of Rio Janeiro is calling for tenders, which will be received up to the 17th of April, 1899, for draining the marshy districts in the basins of Lake Feia and rivers Macacú, Grandú, S. Joao, Macahé, and Iguassú, and their tributaries.

Immigration Statistics. During 1897 the number of immigrants arriving at the port of Rio Janeiro was 44,225. Of these, 22,964 received assistance or a monetary consideration for becoming citizens of Brazil, while 21,261 came voluntarily. As to sex, 29,634 were males, and 14,621 were females. The nationalities represented were: Italians, 27,454; Portuguese, 7,423; Spaniards, 7,253; Germans, 420; Russians, 392; Syrians, 388; Armenians, 219; French, 215; Austrians, 132; all others, 329. A majority of these newcomers settled in the State of Minas Geraes.

Exports from Para. The official valuation of articles subject to duty exported from Para in the fiscal year ending June 30, 1898, amounted to 76,454,035 milreis. This total included these items: Rubber, 70,109,749 milreis; cacào, 4,410,315 milreis; Brazilnuts, 1,331,387 milreis; hides, 364,751 milreis; isinglass, 193,446 milreis; heron feathers, 103,129 milreis; cumam, 8,226 milreis; tallow, 1,626 milreis.

The Carrapato Gold Mines. The Engineering and Mining Journal states that a company has been organized to work the old Carrapato gold mines, and that the stock is now being offered for sale in London and Paris. The authorized capitalization is $1,875,000, of which $1,500,000 is to be paid for the mines. The property includes a mining area of about 2,300 acres in the vicinity of the St. John del Rey mine. Part of this territory was previously mined, but was abandoned eighty to one hundred years ago owing to the hardness of the stone and to flooding. The primitive mining methods then in use were inadequate, besides the then Portuguese Government imposed so heavy a tax on the output that all the profits were consumed in that manner.

Manganese Ore Exchanged for Steel Rails. The South American Journal notes the fact that a greater part of the shipments of manganese ore from Brazil have been sent to the Carnegie Steel Works, in Pennsylvania. In return this company has recently unloaded on the Rio de Janeiro wharves a large shipment of steel rails for the Leopoldina Railway.

COLOMBIA.

Output of the Darien Gold Mines. The famous old Spanish Espiritu Santo gold mines in Darien are now being operated by a new mining company known as the Darien Gold Mining Company (limited). Recently the mines were equipped with a hydraulic pumping plant and other modern machinery. Work has been started in the lower level of the mines below the old Spanish workings, and a fine "stope" has been opened out, which will soon yield sufficient ore to keep the 20-stamp mill busy. The yield for August was 923 ounces of gold from 630 tons of material crushed, being an average of 1.47 ounces per ton.

Registry of Trade-Marks. A book for the official registry of trade-marks has been opened recently in the Ministry of Finance, and trade-marks may now be registered at Bogotá. This registration is not due to the passage of any special law on the subject, or Executive decree, but is the result of an order of the Minister of Finance, who by this means affords trade-mark owners a way of securing some official proof of the ownership of their trade-marks until Congress can pass a law upon the subject. The law is now being prepared, and it is expected will be passed at the coming session of Congress.

HAWAII.

Railway Earnings. According to the Railway Review, the principal rail-road in Hawaii is the Oahu Railway and Land Company line, which runs from Honolulu to Waianae, the total length, including sidings, being 38.5 miles. This road was opened for traffic July 1, 1890, since which time its business has shown a steady increase, both in its passenger and freight traffic. In 1897 the road carried 85,596 passengers, receiving a revenue of $30,993.50; 66,430 tons of freight were carried, earning $69,752.76.

MEXICO.

Postal Receipts in 1897-98. During the fiscal year 1897–98 the general post-office receipts amounted to $1,409,528, against $1,347,162 in 1896–97, an increase of $62,366. In the fiscal year 1894–95, the last in which the rate of letter postage was 10 cents, the receipts from stamp sales amounted to $1,309,905. Last year these amounted to $1,309,570. This demonstrates that the amount of mail matter distributed was more than doubled. There was also an increase of $31\frac{1}{2}$ per cent in the money orders over last year. The total sum distributed was $1,212,017.

New Construction for Tramway Company. The Riter-Conley Manufacturing Company, of Pittsburg, Pa. (U. S.), has the contract for the Mexico City Tramway Company, City of Mexico, for the erection of an engine and boiler house, a main building, and a cold-storage building. About 300 tons of structural steel will be required.

Activity in Railroad Building. A dispatch from Puebla, Mexico, says: "There is an unusual amount of activity in railroad building in Southern Mexico at present. In addition to the new lines already mentioned in press dispatches from Mexico is the road that is being built from Guadalajara to Ciudad Guzman. It is stated that this project is being backed by the governor of the State of Jalisco. Three capitalists subscribed $100,000 cash toward the construction of the road at the governor's solicitation. A company of Mexican capitalists has been organized to build a road from Cordoba, State of Vera Cruz, to Rio Tonto, by way of Motzerongo. The proposed line will pass through a rich coffee-raising section. A large force of men are at work constructing the Tuxtla Railroad. This line is to be built from Palo Harrado to Santiago Tuxtla, in the State of Vera Cruz."

New Railroad from Copper Mines. On October 13 the Government granted a concession for a standard gauge railroad, 150 kilometers (93 miles) maximum length, with 6,000 kilometers subsidy. The concessionaire is the Inguran Copper Mining Company, in which the ROTHSCHILDS of Paris are heavily interested. The railroad is being planned to connect the mines with the Bay of Zituataneza, on the Pacific coast, and will be an outlet for copper productions. The Inguran mines are believed to be the future rival of the Calumet and Hecla mines, the greatest known copper properties in the United States.

To move to Sonora. A dispatch from Denison, Tex., says it is stated on good authority that a contract has been concluded by Delaware Indians for the purchase of 550,000 acres of land in Mexico, and that as soon as they secure a settlement with the United States and the Cherokees they will remove there. It is thought that many of the full-blood Cherokees will accompany them. The tract purchased is on the Yagin River, State of Sonora, and is said to be fine land. Representatives of Mexican landholders were recently among the Cherokees.

The Inguran Copper Mines. It is reported that large numbers of engineers are going to Mexico from France to work the Inguran copper property recently bought by the ROTHSCHILDS and MIRBAUD, of Paris. The capital of the company will be $7,000,000 gold. By the first of the year a large amount of the preliminary work will be done and a railway to connect will have been fully surveyed. CARLOS EISENMAN, the former owner of the mines, retains half of the property.

PARAGUAY.

Navigation Opened. Notice has been received from Asuncion that a German steamboat line has been established on the Upper Paraguay River. The company has two steamers, which began carrying freight and passengers on September 18. It is now believed that both the exports and imports of the Republic will be increased. The German importers are expected to profit largely by this movement.

PERU.

The Borax Industry. The borax industry in Peru appears to be assuming some importance. In 1896, 7,350 tons, valued at $179,674, were exported, while in 1897, 12,464 tons, valued at $303,361, were shipped from Mollendo. The deposits are found about 20 miles in the interior from Arequipa.

UNITED STATES.

Largest Blast Furnaces. The two blast furnaces to be built by the Ohio Steel Company at Youngstown, Ohio, will, it is claimed, be the largest blast furnaces ever built in the world. All the dimensions have not been definitely decided upon, but the stacks will be 105 feet high and 23 feet at the bosh. The stoves will be on a lower level than the furnaces and will be 120 feet high. Some radical changes in blast-furnace practice are proposed when these stacks are ready for operation, by which maximum output will be secured. The two furnaces are expected to make not less than 1,200 tons of iron per day.

Nitrate Fertilizers. A new fertilizing material will shortly be put on the market by a California company. This company has secured an extensive deposit of metallic oxides near Lovelock, Nev. (only 10 miles from the railroad), from which they will extract niter, potash, and phosphate.

Exports of Gas Engines. On October 20 the Weber Gas and Gasoline Engine Company of Kansas City, Mo., informed the Bureau of American Republics that it had just shipped a carload of engines and hoists to New Zealand. A short time prior a shipment was made to Japan, and, at the date of communication, the company was preparing a shipment on an order from a firm in Ecuador.

Production of Copper and Aluminum. The official report of the mineral resources of the United States issued by the United States Geological Survey gives the production of copper for 1897 as 491,638,000 pounds, which is valued at $54,080,180, this being an increase of about 7½ per cent over the previous year. Of aluminum the production is given as 4,000,000 pounds, as against 1,300,000 pounds for the previous year, the value for 1897 being estimated at $1,500,000.

Great Mineral Resources. The reports of the United States Geological Survey for 1897, just completed, show a total of $632,312,347 worth of minerals and mineral products, principal among which were the following: Pig iron, 9,652,680 long tons, value $95,122,299; silver, 53,860,000 troy ounces, coinage value $69,637,172, commercial value $32,316,000; gold, 2,774,935 troy ounces, coinage and commercial value the same, $57,363,000; bituminous coal, 147,789,902 short tons, value $119,740,053; Pennsylvania anthracite, 46,814,074 long tons, value $79,129,126.

VENEZUELA.

Penalty for Careless Packing. The Venezuela Herald cites the case of a charge of 13,500 francs ($2,700) being recently imposed by the customs department, at La Guayra, on a shipment of paper from a Boston house. The firm had carelessly packed 20 kilos of samples of envelopes in printing paper. The result was that as the envelopes pay a duty of 20 francs per kilo, and the paper 5 cents, the customs directed that the whole weight should pay duty at envelope rates, which amounted to 13,500 francs—that is to say, more than thirty times the value of the shipment. Through the intervention of the United States legation at Caracas, which certified that no fraud was intended, the Government decided to remit the fine. Shippers should note the rule, and not put into the same case articles which are taxable at different rates.

Manual of Agriculture. The Minister of Agriculture, Industry, and Commerce is reported to have offered a prize of $400 for the best manual of elementary agriculture for use in the schools of the Republic. The treatises are to be sent to the Minister, who will declare the result of the competition on February 28, 1899.

New Government Building. The National Association of Manufacturers has secured the placing of a contract in the United States for the construction of a Government building at the port of La Guayra, Venezuela, for the use of the custom-house inspectors. A contract is also pending for the construction of a public market house in the city of Maracay, Venezuela, to cost about $40,000, and the contract will, it is thought, be placed in the United States.

BOLETÍN MENSUAL

DE LA

OFICINA DE LAS REPÚBLICAS AMERICANAS,

UNIÓN INTERNACIONAL DE REPÚBLICAS AMERICANAS.

VOL. VI.	NOVIEMBRE, 1898.	No. 5.

SITUACIÓN ECONÓMICA DE CHILE.

En el número del BOLETÍN MENSUAL, correspondiente al mes de octubre, se publicó una breve reseña del informe que acerca de los últimos cambios económicos de Chile, envió al Departamento de Estado el Honorable HENRY L. WILSON, Ministro de los Estados Unidos en Santiago. Con este motivo, no es fuera de lugar notar que el Señor Don RICARDO SALAS EDWARDS, Primer Secretario de la Legación de Chile en Londres, ha publicado un folleto, con fecha 8 de agosto de 1898, sobre la situación económica de su país, el cual contiene detalles interesantes acerca de los ingresos y egresos de la República, los cambios ocurridos en las leyes de moneda, y dando, además, informes sobre los bancos de Chile.

Otra publicación de no menos interés sobre la misma materia es una carta del Señor Don ELIODORO INFANTE, Encargado de Negocios de Chile en los Estados Unidos, fechada el 24 de agosto de 1898 y dirigida al Secretario de la "National Sound Money League," de Chicago, en la cual estudia las condiciones que afectan el problema monetario de Chile, y dice como sigue :

MUY SEÑOR MIO : He recibido su carta fechada á 11 de los corrientes, en la cual se hace referencia á las noticias publicadas en algunos periódicos, diciendo que "Chile se ha visto obligado á abandonar el patrón de oro," y desea que la Legación de Chile le informe acerca de lo concerniente á la materia. Con el mayor placer me apresuro á contestarle.

El Presidente de Chile en su mensaje de inauguración al Congreso, el 1 de junio último, dijo que podía considerarse como ya verificada la conversión del papel en metálico. Una ley dada el 11 de febrero de 1895 así lo disponía. Antes de aquella fecha, el circulante de Chile consistía en las siguientes emisiones: Papel moneda nacional, $29,459,364; vales del Tesoro, $8,901,728; emisión de los bancos, autorizada y garantizada, $20,993,330. Por consiguiente, en enero de 1895 el medio circulante alcanzaba en su totalidad á $59,354,422.

En enero de 1898 el Gobierno había redimido en oro y cancelado papel moneda nacional por la suma de $27,845,305, y vales del Tesoro por valor de $8,888,228. Los bancos habían redimido billetes de su emisión por valor de $3,448,858. Si deducimos estas tres sumas, que alcanzan en junto á $40,182,391, queda un residuo de $19,172,031 en papel moneda circulante de las clases mencionadas.

El remanente consistía en papel moneda nacional que no había sido presentado para su redención, probablemente destruido ó perdido, calculado en $1,614,059, y vales del Tesoro por pagar, por la suma $13,500. Los billetes de banco redimibles en oro alcanzaban á $17,544,472, lo que da un total de $19,172,031.

Los $40,182,391 retirados y redimidos habían sido reemplazados por moneda de oro y de plata acuñada en la casa de moneda nacional hasta el 31 de diciembre de 1897, en virtud de la ley de 11 de febrero de 1895. Dicha moneda acuñada alcanzó á $45,823,358, de suerte que en enero de 1898 el valor total de la moneda en papel y en metálico alcanzaba á $64,995,389. Este total de cerca de $65,000,000 puede considerarse por todos respectos como moneda de oro, pues las emisiones de los bancos estaban perfectamente garantizadas por bonos del Gobierno depositados en la Tesorería Nacional, comprometiéndose éste á pagar en oro los billetes de banco, si alguno de ellos dejare de verificarlo.

La inquietud producida por la enojosa cuestión de límites, pendiente entre Chile y la República Argentina, dió lugar, á principios de julio, á rumores de guerra que produjeron en Chile un pánico económico. El oro que circulaba libremente fué recogido y guardado, de suerte que muchos millones fueron retirados repentinamente de los bancos en donde estaban depositados. En Chile hay 20 bancos particulares; no hay bancos del Estado. Sus capitales, inclusa la reserva, alcanzan á cerca de $55,000,000. Los depósitos son algo más de $96,000,000, mientras que sus préstamos al público pasan de $120,000,000. El metálico en caja alcanza á cerca de $17,000,000. La proporción entre el capital y los depósitos—57 por ciento—era suficientemente sólida, pero la proporción entre el efectivo y los depósitos—17.30 por ciento—aun cuando habría sido suficiente en tiempos normales, era inadecuada durante un pánico. Los préstamos hechos al público no eran en su totalidad inmediatamente recobrables y de aquí que no siendo posible ya á los bancos resistir la repentina corrida sobre ellos, pidieran un mes de plazo para hacer frente á sus acreedores y al mismo tiempo solicitaran las medidas legales del caso.

El mes de gracia les fué concedido, y como era difícil conseguir oro en el extranjero, por motivo de los rumores de guerra, el Gobierno recibió del Congreso la autorización necesaria para emitir billetes fiduciarios con el objeto de mejorar la situación. Esta crisis es de carácter enteramente comercial, y la emisión de billetes por parte del Gobierno se efectuó con el objeto de ayudar á los bancos, suministrándoles circulante.

La nueva emisión, según informes particulares, será de $50,000,000, incluyendo las de los bancos, que aproximadamente alcazarán á $18,000,000, garantizadas por el Estado y por bonos depositados en la Tesorería Nacional. Estos $50,000,000 son redimibles en oro en el curso de tres años y medio. La ley que autoriza la emisión, dispone que el Gobierno invierta todos los años, á partir del 1º de junio de 1899, $10,000,000 en oro en bonos extranjeros, con el objeto de redimir la nueva emisión el 1º de enero de 1902. De esta suerte, en el curso de los tres años y medio, se habrán invertido $35,000,000 con el objeto indicado, y, mientras tanto, la nueva emisión adquirirá gradualmente una base de oro á razon de $10,000,000 en oro por año.

Por medio de este arreglo, la emisión adquiere el carácter de moneda de oro corriente, aunque sea temporalmente inconvertible. Así pues, la emisión de billetes de curso legal, basada en una garantía de oro, viene á mejorar la situación. Esta emisión, según los informes particulares á que se ha hecho referencia, se hará sólo para los bancos que den garantía; éstos paragán un moderado interés por el servicio. Tan luego como haya pasado el pánico y á favor de esta emisión se haya recobrado la confianza, volverá á circular el oro que hoy está atesorado, y volverán á su estado normal los negocios en Chile.

De lo anterior se desprende que el patrón de oro no ha sido abandonado. Las serias dificultades y los grandes sacrificios que la introducción del talón de oro trajo consigo, han sido mayores en Chile por motivo de la cuestión de límites pendiente con la República Argentina. Afortunadamente, esta cuestión está en camino de ser arreglada de una manera terminante y pacífica. Los peritos de ambos países han convenido en reunirse en Chile para discutir allí una línea general de fronteras; las diferencias que surjan han de ser sometidas á sus respectivos gobiernos. En caso que éstos no puedan arreglarlas, se someterán inmediatamente al arbitramento del Gobierno de S. B. M., de acuerdo con el convenio de 17 de abril de 1896.

El hecho de que en 1895 Chile emprendiera el establecimiento del patrón de oro y la reasunción de pagos en dinero sonante, prueba que desea ardientemente la paz, que es elemento esencial para el éxito de su política económica.

Soi de Vd. el atento servidor,

ELIODORO INFANTE,
Chargé d'Affaires de Chile.

En los meses trascurridos desde que esta carta fué escrita, la solución pacífica de la cuestión de límites entre Chile y la República Argentina, que ella preveía, se ha alcanzado felizmente.

La extensión de línea de frontera que está por demarcarse entre los dos países, corre desde el paralelo 23 hasta el 52 de latitud austral. Con fecha 22 de setiembre del presente año, en un acta suscrita por los dos Gobiernos, se han establecido las diferencias que existen entre ellos respecto de dicha línea desde el paralelo 27 hasta el paralelo 52 de latitud austral, y se ha convenido en someterlas á la decisión arbitral del Gobierno de Su Majestad Británica. Los Comisionados nombrados por uno y otro país para representarlos ante el árbitro han sido ya designados y se encuentran en camino para Londres.

En dos actas firmadas por ambos Gobiernos con fecha 2 del presente mes de noviembre, se ha convenido en someter las diferencias que se han suscitado en la demarcación de la línea de frontera entre los paralelos 23 y 27 de latitud austral, á la decisión de una comisión compuesta de cinco delegados chilenos y cinco argentinos, que deberán conferenciar al efecto en Buenos Aires en el curso de este mes, y se ha estipulado, asimismo, que en caso de que dicha comisión no llegase á un acuerdo, las mencionadas diferencias serán sometidas á la decisión final de una junta compuesta de un ciudadano chileno, uno argentino y el Señor Buchanan, Enviado Extraordinario y Ministro Plenipotenciario de los Estados Unidos de América en la República Argentina, junta que deberá funcionar igualmente en Buenos Aires y dictar su fallo en noviembre.

Con esta solución se ha restablecido totalmente la tranquilidad en ambos países y el Gobierno de Chile ha iniciado el desarme, según lo anuncia la prensa, reduciendo su ejército regular. Los Presupuestos de Guerra y Marina van á rebajarse considerablemente; la industria y el comercio van á adquirir en uno y otro país el vigor y vuelo que sus circunstancias permiten y los excedentes del presupuesto de Chile van á volver á ser lo que antes eran, de más de 10,000,000 de pesos oro, anualmente.

DIRECTOR PROVISIONAL DE LA OFICINA.

La Comisión Ejecutiva de la Unión Internacional de Repúblicas Americanas celebró una sesión en el Salón Diplomático del Departamento de Estado, el 26 de octubre de 1898 á las 11 de la mañana. Estuvieron presentes:

El Secretario de Estado, Hon. John Hay, Presidente;
El Señor Andrade, Ministro de Venezuela; y
El Señor Merou, Ministro de la República Argentina.

El objeto de la reunión fué tomar en consideración el asunto del nombramiento de un Director para la Oficina de las Repúblicas Americanas, porque el período provisional del Señor FRED-ERIC EMORY, como Director, terminaba el 1 de noviembre. En vista de la condición satisfactoria de la Oficina y de los progresos que últimamente se han hecho, la Comisión resolvió que el Señor EMORY continúe en el puesto de Director mientras no se tome otra disposición. El Señor CALVO, Ministro de Costa Rica y miembro de la Comisión, no pudo estar presente en la reunión, y dirigió una carta manifestando sus deseos de que el Señor EMORY continuase en su puesto. No se le fijó término definitivo, pero se entiende que las cosas seguirán como hasta ahora, mientras lo requieran los intereses de la Oficina, pues la actual administración de la misma cuenta con el apoyo unánime de los representantes de los paises latino-americanos, así como con la aprobación del Departamento de Estado. El Señor EMORY, que es el jefe de la Oficina de Comercio Extranjero en el Departamento de Estado, ha tenido á su cargo la Oficina de las Repúblicas Americanas desde la muerte de su antecesor, el Señor JOSEPH P. SMITH, acaecida el 5 de febrero último. Mientras continúe sirviendo como Director Provisional, el Señor EMORY tendrá á su cargo, como hasta ahora, la Oficina de Comercio Extranjero que se ocupa en la publicación de los Informes Comerciales que envían los empleados diplomáticos y consulares al Departamento de Estado.

LA OFICINA DE LAS REPÚBLICAS AMERICANAS EN LA EXPOSICIÓN TRANS-MISISIPIANA É INTERNACIONAL DE OMAHA.

La Exposición Internacional celebrada en Omaha, Nebraska, desde el 1 de junio hasta el 31 de octubre de 1898, ha revestido especial interés en cuanto á las naciones latino-americanas, pues ella ha ofrecido la ocasión propicia para hacer conocer los productos y recursos de aquellos países en los mercados de los Estados Unidos. La Oficina de las Repúblicas Americanas comprendió bien la importancia de esta Exhibición, y puesto que es el centro oficial de información en lo relativo al comercio, á la producción, á la industria y al progreso material de las repúblicas que forman la institución conocida con el nombre de Unión Internacional de Repúblicas Americanas, se hicieron los debidos arreglos para que á virtud de su exhibición quedase demostrado aquel hecho y para llamar al mismo tiempo una atención más detenida hacia las posibilidades comerciales é industriales de México, Centro y Sud América y las Antillas, por medio de la distribución de boletines y circulares sobre la materia.

El informe del representante de la Oficina se publica á continuación. En él se muestran los beneficios de presente y en perspectiva que se deben á la exhibición.

OMAHA, NEBRASKA, *Octubre 31 de 1898.*

DIRECTOR DE LA OFICINA DE LAS REPÚBLICAS AMERICANAS:

Adjunto presento mi informe relativo á los trabajos llevados á cabo por la Oficina de las Repúblicas Americanas en la Exposición del Trans-Misisipi. Lo posición ocupada por la Oficina fué excelente. Estaba situada en el piso principal del edificio de las Artes Liberales, al lado del Museo Comercial de Filadelfia, y atrajo universal atención. Los artículos exhibidos fueron puestos en orden por Mr. JOHN M. BIDDLE, á cuyo cargo estaba la exhibición del Departamento de Estado. La artística colgadura de las banderas de las Repúblicas Americanas, la apropiada colocación de numerosos cuadros ilustrativos de paisajes sud-americanas, los hermosos muebles y gentiles palmas, producían un efecto no superado por ninguna otra de las exhibiciones en los pisos de la Exposición. Las personas inteligentes que visitaron la Exposición mostraron gran interés por la Oficina y sus trabajos.

La estrecha proximidad del Museo Comercial con muchas cajas llenas de productos americanos así como muestras de géneros manufacturados en Inglaterra y Alemania, ofrecían una especie de lección objetiva á las personas realmente interesadas en los propósitos de la Oficina de las Repúblicas Americanas.

Se han distribuido 2,100 números del BOLETÍN MENSUAL de la Oficina y se han dejado consignadas las direcciones y las ocupaciones de aquellos á quienes han sido remitidos. Como puede suponerse, tratándose de esta región agrícola, los campesinos figuran los primeros en el registro y en segundo lugar los maestros. Cada Estado y Territorio de la Unión incluyendo Alaska, con excepción de New Hampshire, Vermont, Rhode Island, Delaware, y South Carolina, han registrado sus representantes con Iowa á la cabeza, y Nebraska en segundo término. Guatemala, Nicaragua, México, y Francia constituyen las direcciones extranjeras. A los fabricantes registrados he remitido varios números del BOLETÍN, esperando de esta suerte aumentar sus deseos por el establecimiento del comercio con la América del Sur. Se han recibido muchas cartas de personas á quienes se ha remitido el BOLETÍN, en las cuales hacen referencia al beneficio que han reportado de su lectura. La Exposición trans-misisipiana ha obtenido un gran éxito por todos conceptos, y este éxito ha consistido mayormente en mostrar al pueblo americano, en la práctica, el mecanismo de los diferentes departamentos del Gobierno de los Estados Unidos.

A continuación se publica una lista de las ocupaciones de aquellos á quienes se enviaron boletines por correo. Los otros números fueron tomados por los interesados en persona: .

Agricultores	175
Maestros	170
Comerciantes	85
Periodistas y editores	80
Abogados	70
Estudiantes	60
Corredores	35
Banqueros	30
Directores de Compañías ferrocarrileras	30
Médicos	27
Ministros	25
Fabricantes importadores	18
Dependientes	18
Agentes	18

Á los arquitectos, tenedores de libros, estudiantes, compiladores de estadísticas, dentistas, misioneros, y á todos las demas profesiones que pudieron imaginarse, se les remitieron también boletines en número entre 1 y 15 á cada una de ellas.

El número de inscripciones por estado es el siguiente:

Iowa	331
Nebraska	318
Missouri	139
Kansas	138
Illinois	69
South Dakota	40
Ohio	30
Minnesota	28
Wisconsin	25
Washington	15
Indiana	13
Pennsylvania	13

Los otros estados tuvieron menos representantes.

REPÚBLICA ARGENTINA.

PRIMER PERÍODO PRESIDENCIAL DEL GENERAL ROCA.

En el BOLETÍN de octubre se dió cuenta de un cablegrama del Ministro BUCHANAN, en Buenos Aires, en el cual anunciaba que el Gen. Don JULIO ROCA había tomado posesión del cargo de Presidente de la República Argentina. Esta noticia es suplementada por una comunicación de la Legación de la Argentina, en Washington, en forma de extracto que ha sido tomado de un artículo de "Il Corriere Mercantile" de Genova, con detalles relativos á la vida y trabajos del nuevo presidente. De este documento se toman los siguientes datos:

El General Roca nació en Tucumán en julio de 1843 y recibió su educación en su país natal primero y más tarde en el Colegio Nacional del Uruguay. Durante una de las vacaciones escolares sirvió, junto con algunos compañeros de estudio, en el ejército del Uruguay con ocasión de un movimiento revolucionario que tuvo lugar en el país, y durante su servicio militar, pasó con distinción, sucesivamente, del grado de teniente al de general, el que recibió en la batalla de Santa Rosa, en diciembre de 1894, en reconocimiento de su valor. Sirvió subsiguientemente los cargos de jefe de Frontera en Córdoba, San Luis y Mendoza, y de Ministro de Guerra y Marina. En 1880 fué hecho teniente general del ejército, y finalmente Presidente de la República el 12 de octubre del mismo año. Su primera administración se distinguió por un tratado de límites con Chile, y á virtud del impulso dado á la inmigración durante el período de su pacífico gobierno, obtuvo grande desarrollo la riqueza del país.

El progreso de la Argentina durante esta administración puede verse fácilmente si se comparan estadísticas. De 1880 á 1886, la población aumentó más de 33 por ciento, al paso que la inmigración anual se triplicó, llegando hasta 100,000 inmigrantes en un año. El comercio exterior aumentó 80 por ciento, siendo su valor en liras 520,000,000 en 1880 y 955,000,000 en 1886. El tonelaje de embarque tuvo un aumento del triple; la extensión de línea férrea construida también se triplicó, pues era de 2,300 kilómetros en 1880 y 6,400 en 1886. El área de cultivo aumentó de 1,120,000 á 1,920,000 hectáreas y la circulación monetaria y crédito general del país aumentaron grandemente.

Parte del tiempo, después de haber cesado en su primer término presidencial en 1886, el Presidente Señor Roca estuvo viajando en el extranjero, y entra ahora en el desempeño de los deberes de su segunda administración completamente imbuido de las modernas ideas de progreso para el adelanto de su país y el desarrollo de sus ilimitados recursos.

IMPORTACIÓN DE APARATOS ELÉCTRICOS.

Según las estadísticas oficiales publicadas por las aduanas de la Argentina durante el primer semestre de 1898, la electricidad como fuerza motriz y como alumbrado ha aumentado mucho en toda la República. Las importaciones totales de aparatos y accesorios para la electricidad durante el período mencionado, avaluadas en oro, aparecen en el cuadro siguiente:

	Cantidad.	Valor.
Alambre de hierro galvanizado...............toneladas..	9, 523	$589, 115
Cables, alambres, etc...........................idem..	2, 090	524, 081
Material para luz eléctrica...............................	....	191, 565
Accesorios para ésta.....................toneladas..	38	55, 791
Dinamos ....numero..	38	28, 005
Lámparas incandescentes, docenas......................	4, 466	13, 398
Material para telégrafos................................	....	11, 298
Material para teléfonos.....	....	4, 533
Fonógrafos.	....	3, 200
Total	....	1, 420, 986

La mayor parte de estos efectos fué comprada en los Estados Unidos.

DESTRUCCIÓN DE LA LANGOSTA.

Según dice el periodico "The Farm Implement News:" La comisión central para la extinción de la langosta en la República Argentina ha presentado un informe muy interesante al Ministro de Agricultura de aquella República. La comisión fué nombrada con el objeto de obtener todos los informes posibles respecto de este insecto, su procedencia, procreación, hábitos migratorios, etc., y á fin de hacer los esfuerzos necesarios para su extinción. Para obtener este resultado, la comisión organizó otras comisiones locales, y estas últimas establecieron subcomisiones, y todas se dedicaron á estudiar los medios que parecían más efectivos para la destrucción de la langosta, los que fueron adoptados. Los hábitos de este insecto fueron bien averiguados, y se destruyeron enormes cantidades de huevos y saltones, lo cual hizo que fuera menor el daño sufrido por las cosechas. Se emplearon como medios de destrucción una preparación hecha de zinc, varios extirpadores líquidos, el arado y el fuego. Se calcula que la

En la fecha en que .Mr. Seeger escribió su comunicación, 16 de setiembre de 1898, las compañías de navegación, sus nacionalidades y banderas eran como sigue:

Líneas de vapor.	Nacionalidad.	Oficina principal.	Fecha de salida.	Destino.
Lamport & Holt................	Inglesa.......	Liverpool .. .	Cada 15 días..	New York y New Orleans.
Prince...........................	...id	Newcastle-on-Tyne.	.....id	New York.
Norton	...id	Liverpool ...	.....id	Id.
Sloman..................	Alemania	Hamburg	Mensual-mente.	Id.
Chargeurs-Réunis................	Francesa.....	Havre...........	.....id	New Orleans.
Líneas costaneras.				
Lloyd Brazileiro..................	Brasileña	Rio Janeiro ..	Semanal-mente.	Puertos del norte y del sur del Brasil.
Navegação Costeira Lage Irmãos.	.....id	.....id	.....id	Id.
Esperança Maritima	.....id	.....id	.....id	Id.
Espirito Santence de Navegação a Vapor.	.....id	.....id	.....id	Id.
Companhía Pernambucana de Navegação.	.....id	Recife.........	.....id	Id.
São Ivao da Barra e Campos......	.....id	São Ivar da Barra.	.....id	Id.
Viação do Brazil....	.....id	Rio Janeiro ..	.....id	Río San Francisco y sus tributarios.

Los derechos de puerto son los siguientes: de faro, 100 milreis, ó sea £11 5 chilenas ($54.74) en. oro; de hospital, 1.920 milreis (26 centavos), por cada individuo de la tripulación, incluyendo los oficiales, y además 18 milreis ($2.70) para cada barco; derechos de entrada, 9.800 milreis ($1.39); derecho de timbre sobre la exportación, 4 y 10 por ciento. Estos derechos, con excepción de los de faro, se pagan en papel moneda. El milreis de papel vale como 15 centavos en moneda de los Estados Unidos.

Los reglamentos de puerto son los siguientes: todo buque al entrar al puerto debe esperar la visita de los empleados de la sanidad y de la aduana, quienes examinarán las patentes de sanidad dadas por los cónsules brasileños en el extranjero, y recibirán los manifiestos consulares y otros papeles relativos al cargamento de la embarcación. Si todo estuviere en orden, el capitán puede continuar su viaje hasta el lugar de anclaje, y allí dar principio á la descarga del buque, tan luego estén listos todos los papeles de la aduana. Los vapores que pertenecen á líneas regulares y que gozan de los privilegios de vapores-correos, pueden comenzar á cargar ó descargar tan luego los inspectores hubieren declarado que los papeles de dichos barcos están en orden, y sin necesidad de esperar que estén listos los documentos de la aduana. En el invierno (desde abril hasta noviembre) los buques pueden cargar y descargar á lo largo de los muelles y almacenes. La carga ordinaria se desembarca casi siempre por medio de lanchones que la llevan á la aduana ó á los depósitos, llamados "trapiches." Los artículos de mucho volumen son desembarcados directamente en la costa durante el invierno. El café es llevado en lanchones á bordo de los buques.

INTRODUCCIÓN DE LOS PRODUCTOS DE LOS ESTADOS UNIDOS.

El Cónsul General, Mr. SEEGER, remite de Rio de Janeiro la traducción de una carta de OTHON LEONARDOS, hijo, prominente comerciante de Rio, relativa á la introducción de productos americanos en el Brasil. Parte de la carta está escrita en los siguientes términos:

Hay aquí un gran campo para los productos de la industria americana. Los dos grandes obstáculos para la expansión del comercio americano en el Brasil son los malos medios de comunicación y la falta de representación directa de los fabricantes. Por regla general sólo tenemos en Rio dos vapores viejos y de andar lento que hacen el viaje mensual de los Estados Unidos y su comercio de importación con el Brasil está organizado de tal manera que hay relación directa entre los fabricantes americanos y los comerciantes brasileños. Todo se lleva á cabo por medio de comisionistas cuyos servicios son más ó menos costosos. La falta de un banco americano aquí constituye también una desventaja general. Los fabricantes americanos debieran tener una oficina aquí en la cual se expusieran sus productos permanentemente. Inglaterra, Francia, Alemania, Portugal, Italia, todos estos países tienen aquí sus líneas de vapores y sus bancos. Su capital es invertido constantemente en empresas industriales y comerciales. ¿Que es lo que vuestro país posee aquí? No tiene líneas de vapores, ni bancos, ni empresas industriales, ni hay inversión de capitales con excepción de unas cuantas casas de comercio.

En cuanto á las mercancías en que comercia nuestra casa (LEONARDOS Y CIA.), haré relación de mi experiencia personal relativa á los artículos de fabricación americana. Mis esfuerzos para introducir estos géneros en el mercado de Río han obtenido éxito. El cristal labrado y el cristal común son artículos de importancia y hablaré de ellos en primer lugar. El cristal labrado de Fairpoint, compite fácilmente en calidad y belleza con el inglés y el francés. El precio es algo más subido, pero se vende fácilmente á causa de sus hermosos grabados. Las molduras y el cristal común de ciertas fábricas americanas son de tan buena hechura y tan blancos como los importados de otros países; talvez son mejores y como su precio es más bajo, creo que encontrarán aquí un buen mercado. Lo mismo puede decirse de las botellas, potes, y otros artículos usados por los droguistas. Yo creo que pueden competir fácilmente con los productos similares de otros paises. Los artículos plateados y niquelados, procedentes de las fábricas de REED & BARTON, Connecticut; MERIDEN BRITANNIA Co., y otras, empiezan á ser conocidos favorablemente en nuestros mercados. Debido á su precio pueden competir con los metales de ELKINGTON, Inglaterra; CHRISTOFLE, Paris; KRUPP, Austria, y otros. Debo advertir á este respecto que los artículos enchapados americanos pagan sólo la mitad de los derechos que se cobran por los artículos semejantes procedentes de otros países; el cobre entra en su composición, si acaso, en muy pequeña proporción. La importación de artículos enchapados procedentes de los Estados Unidos es susceptible de gran desarrollo. Las lámparas de petróleo americanas no se conocen aquí, pero su calidad es superior á la de las importadas de Bélgica y Alemania. Su precio es el mismo y aún más bajo.

He hecho una relación de los artículos comprendidos en la clase de negocios á que me dedico. En cuanto á otros productos americanos, debo decir que empiezan á ser conocidos en nuestro mercado, pero no se les explota en grande escala por las razones que ya dejo mencionadas. El cuero americano, los aparatos eléctricos y fotográficos, los instrumentos agrícolas y toda clase de maquinaria para la fabricación, bicicletas, conservas, etc., son bien conocidos y grandemente apreciados aquí. Sólo queda estrechar más las relaciones entre los dos países, mejorando los medios de comunicación y asegurando para el comercio y la industria de los Estados Unidos una debida representación aquí.

IMPORTACIÓN DE CEREALES EN RIO JANEIRO.

Según el "Handels Zeitung," las importaciones de trigo en Rio Janeiro en 1897 alcanzaron á 38,402 barriles menos que en el año anterior, es decir 336,533 bariles en 1897 contra 375,935 en 1896. La mayor disminución ocurrió en harina húngara que, no obstante la excelencia de su calidad, sólo se emplea para mezclarla con otras á causa de lo alto de su precio en los puertos del Brasil. Las estadísticas demuestran que las importaciones del año pasado fueron como sigue: de los Estados Unidos, 252,991 barriles; del Río de la Plata, 65,697 barriles; de Liverpool, 9,850 barriles; de Trieste y Fiume, 4,395 barriles; y de Chile, 3,600 barriles, lo que hace un total de 336,533 barriles importados durante el año. La disminución en las importaciones de salvado ó afrecho en 1897 obedeció á los activos trabajos de los molinos ingleses y brasileros en Rio Janeiro. El total de las importaciones de este artículo durante el año llegó á 10,107 sacos de 40 kilógramos, del Río de la Plata, contra 62,374 sacos en 1896, ó sea una diferencia de 52,267 sacos, lo cual hace mucho honor á la empresa brasilera. En el año pasado las importaciones de macarrones, fideos y otros productos semejantes disminuyó notablemente, más aún que en los años anteriores; en 1896 se importaron de Italia 7,941 cajas, mientras que en 1897 sólo se recibieron 1,227 de la misma procedencia.   No hay duda que esto se debe á la perfección á que han llegado los productos de las fábricas del país y es casi cierto que dentro de poco tiempo cesarán por completo las importaciones de este artículo al Brasil.   El maíz importado es todo de procedencia del Río de la Plata.   Este grano sufrió también disminución en 1897 comparado con el año anterior, calculada en 242,450 sacos de 62 kilógramos, pues las importaciones alcanzaron en dicho año á 1,254,097 sacos contra 1,496,556 en 1896.   Por lo que toca á las importaciones de arroz, las de Europa aumentaron mientras que disminuyeron las de la India.   El número total de sacos que se introdujo á Río Janeiro fué 1,237,277 sacos de 60 kilógramos contra 1,240,833 sacos en 1896, ó sea una diferencia de 3,556 sacos.   Las importaciones de 1897 constaron de 134,359 sacos de Europa y 1,103,918 de la India.

PRODUCCIÓN DE CARBONES.

El Cónsul americano en Bahía ha trasmitido al Departamento de Estado copia de una comunicación, respuesta á un corresponsal de Nueva York, sobre la industria de los carbones.   En dicha comunicación dice el Cónsul que el Estado de Bahia es el único en donde existe la industria de los carbones que se han encontrado en el Brasil desde hace muchos años, pero que no han tenido demanda hasta á principios de la presente década cuando á causa de su dureza fueron solicitados por los fabricantes de los llamados taladros de punta de diamante.   Habiendo aumentado la demanda y siendo insuficiente la producción, los precios tuvieron un alza en consecuencia.

Las piedras de carbón se encuentran en el interior del Estado en una región á la cual se llega después de un viaje largo y cansado, partiendo de Bahía por embarcación hasta San Felix, y de allí por ferrocarril á Bandeira de Mello, que es el límite de la región de los diamantes, en cuyos alrededores se encuentran siempre estos carbones.   El territorio que produce mayor cantidad de ellos está más allá del río Paragassu y para llegar á él hay que viajar por tierra, en mula, durante dos días, por un camino de recua quebrado y montañoso.   Se crée que en toda esta sección se encuentran carbones y diamantes, pero á causa del método empleado para conseguirlos tan sólo se explotan el lecho del Paragassu y su tributario el San Antonio y la cadena de montañas llamada Sierra das Lavras Diamantinas. Los carbones se encuentran en una especie de arena gruesa llamada "Cascalho," en el lecho del río, debajo del fango y sobre una capa de arcilla; en las montañas, debajo de una capa de roca y sobre el mismo lecho de arcilla, y en los alrededores de estas debajo de varias capas de tierra.

Para extraer los carbones que están en el lecho del río se escoje un lugar de no más de 20 piés de profundidad, donde la corriente no es demasiado rápida. Se clava allí un largo palo por donde bajan los indígenas, llevando consigo un saco que se conserva abierto por medio de un anillo. Primero apartan el fango y llenan luego el saco de casajo, hasta llegar á la arcilla. Tan luego, como el saco está lleno se sube y en canoas se le conduce a la orilla en donde se vacia en un lugar á donde no llegan las aguas del río. Esta operación se ejecuta diariamente durante seis meses, que son los que dura la estación de la seca. Al comienzo de la estación lluviosa, cuando se hace necesario suspender la operación de bajar al río, se lava la arena, examinándosela en busca de carbones y diamantes. Los buzos que hacen esta operación son bastante hábiles y hay entre ellos quienes puedan mantenerse por un minuto y aún hasta minuto y medio debajo del agua. El cascajo vuelve á cubrirse de fango al aire libre, siendo necesario limpiarlo, lo que podría evitarse con el empleo de métodos modernos. Es imposible explotar los lugares en donde el río es más profundo.

El otro método que se emplea para explotar estos carbones es la perforación de las rocas de la montaña, sacando la arena en donde se encuentran los diamantes y los carbones por medio de túneles. Durante la estación de la seca se acumula la arena, que se lava en la estación de las lluvias con el agua que se hace bajar por medio de represas. En las montañas se encuentran carbones en mayor cantidad que en el río por ser más accesibles. Sólo á las orillas de los ríos es que se hace la explotación de este producto, y aún así poco se consigue porque el agua entra tan pronto como se ha llegado al cascajo carbonífero y con los aparatos primitivos que usan los indígenas no pueden sacarla tan rápidamente como se hace necesario para que la operación dé resultados. La falta de agua para lavar el cascajo es la causa de que en otros lugares no se explote este mineral.   Parece que nunca se ha empleado maquinaria moderna para efectuar este trabajo, ya sea porque los del país no saben donde se encuentra ó por que les falte capital suficiente que emplear en su industria.

El carbón referido se encuentra de distintos tamaños; los hay desde el de un grano de arena hasta de 975 quilates de peso Este gran pedazo de carbón fué recojido en 1894, en un camino en donde la formación de arena estaba expuesta y fué vendido en Paris por 100,000 francos ($19,300).   Los tamaños más útiles y valiosos son los de los carbones que pesan de uno á tres quilates, porque los más largos hay que quebrarlos causando así una gran pérdida, pues no tienen línea de fractura.   Por esta razón el carbón mencionado, despues de haber sido reducido á pedazos que se pudieran vender, produjo muchísimo menos de lo que se pagó por él.   Hace como dos años que se formó aquí una sociedad para conservar los precios altos, pero el promotor principal quebró y desde entonces no se ha tratado otra vez de entrar en nuevas combinaciones.   El precio que rige hoy se debe únicamente á la gran demanda, la escasez del producto y lo difícil de su explotación.   La pequeña existencia que hay en la actualidad se atribuye á los métodos primitivos empleados en la explotación.   Frecuentemente sucede que dos trabajadores logran conseguir sólo tres ó cuarto carbones como resultado de sus seis meses de trabajo y por los cuales esperan recibir muy buenos precios.

Los exportadores del producto tienen sus casas de comercio en Bahía y sus agentes en la región minera, pero como los mineros tienen siempre conocimiento de los precios, resulta que los exportadores vienen á quedar reducidos á desempeñar el papel de meros comisionistas.   Mr. FURNISS, el Consul, dice que el exportador en mayor escala de Bahía es THEOPHILO GOMES DE MATTOS, Rua Cons. Dantes.   Según informes, en el mes de julio se decía que tenía 125 quilates de carbones de buenos tamaños.   El Señor GOMES DE MATTOS está dispuesto á enviar carbones á los Estados Unidos á los mismos precios y en las condiciones que lo hace á Europa y dice que nunca ha vendido á los comerciantes de los Estados Unidos, porque estos insisten en comprar tamaños especiales; que él no puede vender piedras escojidas, sino en lotes como las compra, que son de los tamaños que siempre tienen demanda. En la actualidad el precio es como $5 por grano ó sea $22.50 por onza, pero el precio fluctúa según las necesidades del mercado y las existencias. Otra casa de Bahía es la de FRANCISCO DE MELLO Y COMPAÑA, Rua Cons. Dantes. Á ambos se les puede dirijir correspondencia en portugués ó francés, y á la primera casa mencionada se le puede escribir también en alemán.

CHILE.

MINAS DE CARBÓN EN EL FONDO DEL OCÉANO.

Mr. FRANK G. CARPENTER, en una de sus cartas escritas desde la América del Sur, por donde está haciendo un viaje de observación, describe las minas de carbón de Chile, las cuales fueron descubiertas en 1855:

Estas minas, dice, son en extremo interesantes; son diferentes á las minas de los Estados Unidos y más difíciles de explotar en muchos respectos. La vena de carbón que en su mayor parte es de unos cinco pies de espesor empieza en la orilla y se extiende debajo de las aguas del Océano Pacífico. La roca que la cubre es de pizarra tan compacta que por ella no filtra el agua. Las galerías son tan limpias que se puede caminar por ellas sin que se ensucie el traje. La explotación se lleva á cabo por medio de la mejor clase de maquinaria, y durante mi visita á estas minas, observé varios adelantos. Imagínese, por ejemplo, un viaje en ferrocarril eléctrico de trolley, con un tren cargado de carbón, á través de un túnel de mas de una milla de largo bajo el Océano Pacífico, á una velocidad de veinte millas por hora; imagínense minas alumbradas por la electricidad, formando una catacumba de corredores y cámaras bajo las aguas; imagínese que por encima de estas minas flotan vapores de grandes dimensiones y que el carbón que se extrae de aquéllas es embarcado en ellos; imagínense tiznados mineros, medio desnudos, extrayendo el carbón y cargando los carros; é imagínese, por último, el tren conduciendo veinte y siete toneladas de carbón hasta el elevador donde una poderosa máquina de vapor lo levanta hasta la superficie en lotes de cuatro carros á la vez, y se podrá formar una idea de las operaciones que tienen lugar en las minas de Lota.

Estas minas están produciendo 1,000 toneladas de carbón al día y están empleados en ellas 750 mineros. Dejan una ganancia anual de cientos de miles de dollars, y son tan bien manejadas como cualquiera de las minas de carbón de nuestro país. Pregunté cual era el salario de los mineros y se me dijo que recibían de 90 centavos á $1 en moneda chilena, ó de 31 á 35 centavos en moneda de los Estados Unidos. Yo quisiera saber que opinan de esto nuestros mineros de Pennsylvania. Los mineros chilenos, sin embargo, no pagan alquiler de casa y obtienen el carbón al costo.

Bull. No. 5——6

COLOMBIA.

PRESUPUESTO DE 1899—ESTADÍSTICAS DE FERROCARRIL— NUEVO EMPRÉSTITO.

Un corresponsal del "Nouveau Monde" de París, Francia comunica que el presupuesto de ingresos y gastos de Colombia, calcula los ingresos del año fiscal que termina el 30 de junio de 1899 en $38.305,000. Esta cantidad representa un aumento de $3,944,000 sobre el año fiscal que terminó el 30 de junio de 1898, y se atribuye al monopolio de los fósforos. En cuanto á los gastos, calcúlese que incluyendo el déficit del año pasado y el actual descenso en el valor del papel, no excederán de $34,000,000.

Durante la anterior administración se construyeron 242 kilómetros de ferrocarril, a saber: de Cartagena á Calamar, 105 kilómetros; de Bogotá á Zipaquira, 50 kilómetros; de Villamizar á Tachira, 16 kilómetros; de Yeguas á la María, 13½ kilómetros; de Puerto Camacho á Espinal, 11 kilómetros; de Bogotá á Soacho, 11½ kilómetros; continuación de la línea de Cauca, 6 kilómetros, y continuación de la línea de Santanda, 17½ kilómetros. Estos adelantos deben considerarse muy satisfactorios cuando se recuerda que se han obtenido á despecho de la situación económica, bastante deprimida.

Para obtener fondos con que atender á las urgentes necesidades del Gobierno, el Vicepresidente de la República, autorizado al efecto por el Ejecutivo, citó á los principales comerciantes de la Capital á una reunión en el Palacio Nacional el 9 de agosto. Les comunicó que el Gobierno se proponía hacer un empréstito para fines comerciales. Todos los individuos presentes manifestaron su absoluta confianza en el Gobierno, y suscribieron en el acto $166,000 de los nuevos bonos.

FABRICACIÓN Y PRECIO DEL JABÓN.

Un corresponsal colombiano de un periódico comercial alemán, en un artículo de fecha reciente, da una descripción de la industria de jabones en Colombia; parte de dicha descripción es como sigue:

Sólo hay dos fábricas que emplean álcali cáustico y materiales puros, una en Barranquilla y la otra en Bogotá. Se está estableciendo en Cartagena una tercera fábrica por una compañía inglesa, la cual comenzará sus operaciones dentro del presente año. Antes, se importaba de los Estados Unidos una gran cantidad de jabones, pero este comercio ha sido perjudicado por razón de los altos derechos proteccionistas impuestos. De igual suerte, la importación de jabones finos y perfumes ha sido grandemente perjudicada por aquellos derechos y ascienden á $1.20 por kilo.

En las fábricas de jabón mencionadas se fabrican dos clases principales de jabón común hecho de sebo y resina; el que contiene un ciento por ciento de resina se prepara con una lejía suave y espesa. Se enduerce con una solución de sal de Glauber y soda cristalizada. La segunda clase es una pasta de jabón con noventa por ciento de resina preparada al vapor ó al fuego y endurecida también, si es necesario, por los medios ya mencionados, agregando el álcali cuando ya el jabón está en los moldes. El rendimiento es de 350 á 400 por ciento.

Aunque estos productos no son tan acabados como el jabón europeo, dan buen resultado para el lavado en agua fría y llenan las exigencias del consumidor. Para el primer jabón mencionado sólo se usa la mejor clase de resina pálida, pero para la otra especie de jabón se emplea resina negra con el objeto de darle el aspecto de jabón de tierra, pues este es preferido al amarillo por muchos.

También se fabrica jabón veteado y jabón de potasa; el jabón fino se prepara en máquinas francesas, y el jabón de uso común se fabrica con cinco por ciento de resina, debido á la inferior calidad del aceite de coco del país. Los jabones medicinales y especiales se fabrican por medio de maquinaria y también jabones con yeso pulverizado para la limpieza de artículos de oro y plata ó con polvo de ladrillo para la limpieza de artículos de hierro; jabones para afeitar, por el procedimiento semicálido; de sebo y palma cristi con soda y lejía de potasa, por mitad. El jabón de glicerina en barras dispuesto en cajas de cartón al estilo inglés también obtiene buena demanda. Los perfumes que tienen más salida son el almizcle, el pachulí y el heliotropo.

Los precios son más altos que en Alemania, pues el jabón común cuesta ocho centavos la barra de una libra ó $6 por caja de 88 barras, al por mayor; los jabones finos de tres á cuatro onzas cuestan de 18 á 36 centavos; los jabones de gran consistencia que pesan de 1¾ á 2 onzas se venden á cuatro centavos; los de mediana calidad, de 7 á 10 centavos al por mayor con 20 por ciento de descuento. Los fabricantes de este artículo en el país hacen buenos negocios, pues están protegidos por una alta tarifa.

LA REGIÓN AURÍFERA DEL DARIÉN.

La región del Darien que forma la parte sudeste del Istmo de Panamá, en la República de Colombia, se extiende del Atlántico al Pacífico. Fué aquí que Balboa en setiembre de 1513, en busca de oro, descubrió el océano Pacífico. El extenso Golfo de San Miguel está situado como á 100 millas al sudeste de Panamá. El río Tuira desemboca en el Pacífico en este golfo y es navegable por una extensión de 50 millas. Lo rápido de su corriente en ambas direcciones hace difícil en él la navegación en chalupas, que sólo puede verificarse cada seis horas, á causa de la marea cuya diferencia entre la alta y la baja es de 25 pies en el golfo, efectos que disminuyen á 10 millas más allá de Real de Santa María, que es el límite de la navegación. Hay un pequeño bote de vapor, llamado *El Dariën*, de 20 toneladas de capacidad para carga, que hace el viaje de Panamá á Real de Santa María en 20 horas, mientras que una chalupa gasta de cuatro á diez días en efectuar el mismo viaje.

El viaje de Real á Cana, donde están situadas las minas, hay que hacerlo en mula por las montañas, y luego subir el río Cupe en canoa. El camino es extremadamente malo y peligroso y el costo de trasporte por tonelada es de $50 en moneda colombiana, ó sea cerca de $23 en oro americano. En 1896, EDUARDO J. CHIBAS trazó un camino para ser macadamizado, trabajo que ha adelantado bastante, facilitando cuando esté terminado el empleo de carros en todas las estaciones del año, lo cual rebajará los fletes á un precio nominal.

Balboa obtuvo gran cantidad de oro de los indios pero no fué sino un siglo después que se trató de explotar oro del Istmo. Fué entonces que se descubrió y comenzó á explotar la mina de oro del Espíritu Santo en Cana, que, según VICENTE RESTREPO, de Bogotá, produjo á los españoles $30,000,000. Se explotó con éxito desde 1680 hasta 1727, cuando los indios se alzaron, se hundió una de las galerías principales, sepultando varios trabajadores y los mineros, habiendo perdido sus esperanzas, volvieron á España.

Siglo y medio después se empezó á trabajar de nuevo seriamente en la explotación de la mina y para el año de 1878 se fundó una compañía en Nueva York que gastó $50,000 en abrir un camino y comprar y trasportar maquinaria; se abandonó el proyecto en 1880, sin que hasta entonces hubieran comenzado los verdaderos trabajos de explotación.

En 1888 la actual compañía fué organizada en Manchester, Inglaterra, con un capital de $1,000,000. Las dificultades con que se tropezó eran casi invencibles pues Cana está situado en uno de los estribos de los Andes á 2,000 piés sobre el nivel del mar. En 1889 se montó una maquinaria de diez bocartes, que durante muchos meses dió resultados poco satisfactorios. El mineral era de inferior calidad; á la vista no se presentaban señales de las marvillosas riquezas y los miembros de la compañía casi habían perdido todas sus esperanzas, cuando en 1893 los mineros accidentalmente se encontraron con los antiguos trabajos españoles á 90 piés de la superficie. Las aguas que se habían acumulado en la antigua mina se precipitaron á las nuevas galerías, siendo necesario más trabajo y más capital para construir un túnel de desagüe, lo que al fin se consiguió y hoy la mina produce el oro deseado. Durante los años de 1896 y 1897 la antigua mina española dió 10,528 onzas de oro, que produjeron en Londres £44,522 ($216,377). La roca sometida á tratamiento ha producido por término medio de 1 a 1½ onzas por tonelada. Como hasta ahora los trabajos de explotación se han circunscrito á aquella parte del mineral explotado por los españoles, se espera que la vena virgen, en la cual se comienza á trabajar, produzca mayores resultados. Hasta ahora parece que las esperanzas de los dueños de la mina se realizarán satisfatoriamente, pues han empleado grandes sumas de dinero en proveerse de la maquinaria más perfeccionada y merecen, por consiguiente, el mejor éxito. El Señor CHIBAS, de cuyo interesante artículo publicado en el último número del "Engineering Magazine," hemos recojido los datos que preceden, añade lo siguiente:

La riqueza del Darién no está circunscrita al oro, pues allí abundan maderas preciosas, exportándose una gran cantidad de caoba. Abunda también la palma que produce la tagua ó marfil vegetal. La extracción del caucho fué una industria que dió muy buenos resultados por algún tiempo, pero la costumbre imperdonable de los naturales de cortar los árboles en vez de sangrarlos para recojer la savia, ha hecho disminuir grandemente el producto. No obstante esta gran destrucción, no hubo un día mientras duraron nuestros trabajos de exploración en que no viéramos árboles de caucho, que se dan tan bien en aquel lugar que su cultivo debe ser muy remunerativo. Cuando se acercaba la estación de las lluvias sacamos caucho de unos árboles que estaban cerca del campamento y por medio de un simple procedimiento empleado por los naturales hicimos impermeables todos los sacos de uso ordinario que usábamos para llevar nuestras ropas y los instrumentos de uno á otro campamento, con los más satisfactorios resultados. Un vestido sometido al mismo tratamiento resultó más impermeable que los importados.

ECUADOR.

PROPUESTA CONFEDERACIÓN SUDAMERICANA.

Un periódico de Paris, " Le Nouveau Monde," en su número correspondiente al 8 de octubre de este año, publica un despacho de Guayaquil, fechado el 1° del mismo mes, en el cual se dice que el General ELOY ALFARO, Presidente de la República, acaba de pedir autorización al Congreso para proponer una conferencia internacional á los Gobiernos de Colombia y de Venezuela.

El objeto de esta conferencia, según lo expone el mismo Presidente, es averiguar si sería oportuna la reconstrucción de la antigua República de Colombia fundada por Bolívar. Dicha República fué disuelta en 1830, y de su territorio se formaron las Repúblicas del Ecuador, Venezuela y Colombia. Opina el Presidente ALFARO que el restablecimiento de la antigua Confederación pondría fin á las cuestiones sobre límites entre los tres países, y que unidos éstos constituirían una nación formidable, con cerca de 8,000,000 de habitantes y un inmenso y rico territorio, que se extendería desde las bocas del Orinoco hasta las fronteras del Perú.

El corresponsal del mencionado periódico agrega lo siguiente: "Se ignora en que disposición se encuentran Venezuela y Colombia respecto de este proyecto, que es una nueva manifestación de las tendencias de los Estados hispano-americanos á formar confederaciones, de conformidad con sus simpatías mútuas y en atención á sus antiguos límites, como acaba de suceder con tres repúblicas de la América Central."

HAITÍ.

REDUCCIÓN DE LOS DERECHOS SOBRE EL JABÓN.

El Vice-Cónsul-General TERRES envía al Departamento de Estado, desde Port au Prince, con fecha 7 de octubre de 1898, la traducción de una ley recientemente votada, la cual es como sigue:

ARTÍCULO 1. Los jabones de todas clases pagarán 50 centavos por cada 100 libras sin perjuicio de los derechos adicionales.

Artículo 2. El jabón no quedará exento del recargo de 25 por ciento establecido en la ley de 16 de diciembre de 1897.

Artículo 3. La presente ley, que deroga todas las leyes y disposiciones legales que le son contrarias, será ejecutada por los Ministros de Hacienda y Comercio.

Esto, dice Mr. Terres, reduce virtualmente á la mitad los derechos sobre el jabón.

MÉXICO.

MENSAJE DEL PRESIDENTE DIAZ.

A continuación aparecen extractos tomados del mensaje del Señor Presidente Diaz al abrirse el primer período de sesiones del 19° Congreso de la Unión el 16 de setiembre de 1898.

FOMENTO.

En el desarrollo de la industria nacional, ocupa el primer término la minería. El número de títulos expedidos en el período trascurrido desde la fecha de mi último informe asciende á ochocientos treinta y siete, que amparan siete mil ochocientas veinte pertenencias de una hectárea.   El total de los expedidos, con arreglo á la ley vigente de junio de 1892, asciende á 8,313 para 66,363 pertenencias de una hectárea; lo cual pone de manifiesto que el número de propiedades mineras adquiridas en seis años casi es el cuádruplo de las que existían al promulgarse dicha ley.

EXPORTACIÓN DE MINERALES.

Confirma el desarrollo de la industria minera el aumento de la exportación de minerales que se viene notando desde hace tiempo.   Según los datos publicados por la Secretaría de Hacienda, correspondientes al último año fiscal, el valor total de los productos minerales de todo género, presentados en las aduanas, fué de $91,250,000 en números redondos; lo cual significa un aumento de diez millones y medio de pesos sobre el valor de la misma exportación en el año fiscal precedente.   Entre esos productos figura la plata, con un valor de $67,-000,000; el oro, con el de $16,000,000, apreciado en pesos de plata; el cobre, con el de $4,700,000; el plomo, con el de $3,000,000 y en escala menor el antimonio, el zinc, la plombagina, el carbón de piedra, el azufre, el asfalto, yeso y algunos otros materiales de construcción.

AGRICULTURA.

La industria agrícola progresa, perfeccionando el material y los métodos de cultivo y abriendo nuevas tierras á la explotación.   Las buenas cosechas que se obtuvieron el año pasado han permitido exportar para Europa productos agrícolas de la Mesa Central, que ascendieron á 7,150 toneladas en los meses de junio y julio últimos; de las que 4,398 fueron de trigo, 2,273 de cebada, y el resto de centeno y harina de trigo, según datos ministrados á la Secretaría de Fomento por una de las empresas exportadoras.

AGUAS COMO FUERZA MOTRIZ.

Es de notarse en los últimos años el mayor número de solicitudes para aprovechar aguas de jurisdicción federal como fuerza motriz.   A virtud de las concesiones hechas por el Gobierno á diversas empresas, están en construcción algunos establecimientos importantes de manufacturas diversas.

TERRENOS BALDÍOS.

De terrenos baldíos y nacionales se han reducido á propiedad particular, en el período á que se refiere este informe, 153,933 hectáreas por adjudicación y venta, composición de demasías, compensación de gastos hechos por empresas deslindadoras, fraccionamiento de egidas de los pueblos y concesiones gratuitas á labradores pobres.   Los terrenos vendidos han causado la amortización de $104,510 en títulos de la deuda nacional.

FERROCARRILES.

De abril á la fecha, han aumentado en más de 314 kilómetros las vías férreas de los cuales corresponden 62½ al Ferrocarril de México á Cuernavaca y Pacífico; sesenta al Central Mexicano en su ramal de Jiménez á Hidalgo del Parral; cuarenta al Nacional Mexicano entre Pátzcuaro y Uruapam, veinticinco al internacional en sus ramas de Reato á Monterrey; y el resto á otras líneas, entre las que figura la que últimamente ha unido á las capitales de Yucatán y Campeche, unión justamente celebrada en estos días por ambos Estados.   Hoy se inaugura la línea de San Juan Bautista al Río González.

La red ferroviaria, en toda la extensión del país, mide 12,403 kilómetros, inclusos 235 kilómetros 700 metros pertenecientes á los tranvías propios de los Estados.

Algunas empresas han ejecutado ó preparado obras notables en sus líneas, como son la conclusión del túnel de Dolores á Catorce, que tiene un desarrollo de dos kilómetros doscientos doce metros, la estación definitiva del Ferrocarril Mexicano en Oaxaca y los planos para el establecimiento de la tracción eléctrica en algunas de sus líneas, presentados por la empresa de los ferrocarriles del Distrito Federal.

Con motivo de las periódicas y grandes averías que sufren los puentes provisionales del ferrocarril sobre el río de Tehuantepec, se está llevando á cabo la nueva localización de la vía, para que cruce dicho río en condiciones favorables, por medio de un puente metálico.   En este último período han sido otorgadas doce concesiones y declaradas tres caducaciones.

LÍNEAS TELEGRÁFICAS.

Cuatro oficinas telegráficas han sido abiertas desde el último informe; se ha construido una línea entre Esperanza y Tehuacán, y se han incorporado á la red federal las líneas de Banamichi á Arizpe y de Teapa á Pichucalco.

Se ha continuado la sustitución del alambre de hierro por el cobre fosforoso en la región oriental de la República. Haciendo falta una carta general técnico-administrativa de la red, se mandó construir y ha quedado terminada. El servicio permanente se ha extendido á treinta y seis poblaciones más del país. El número total de mensajes trasmitidos en el año fiscal de 1897–98 fué de 2,086,-050. En el semestre de enero á junio del presente año, hubo un aumento de veinticuatro por ciento respecto de igual período del año pasado. El servicio interior de la prensa, que en la fecha de mi informe anterior era casi nulo, hoy es considerable, pudiendo decirse que su existencia está asegurada. Con fecha 1º de abril último fué inaugurado el servicio de giros telegráficos, y sus operaciones van en aumento, no bajando ya su importe de $150,000. Por lo que hace á la cuestión económica de los telégrafos, me es grato manifestar que de $698,000 á que ascendieron sus productos en el año fiscal de 1896–97, se elevaron en el que acaba de fenecer á $850,000.

INGRESOS FEDERALES.

Los ingresos ordinarios de la Federación, durante el año fiscal de 1897–98, ascendieron á $52,500,000, cantidad que excede en más de dos millones á los cálculos sobre ingresos hechos para ese mismo año, siendo mayor también que el importe de los gastos autorizados por el presupuesto y los adicionales que decretó el Congreso durante el año expresado.

DECRETO SOBRE DERECHOS DE TONELADAS Y OTROS.

Con fecha 1º de julio de 1898, el Gobierno de México emitió un decreto sobre derechos de toneladas y otros, del cual se extracta lo siguiente:

Quedan derogados el derecho de faro, que se causaba con arreglo al artículo 17 de la Ordenanza General de Aduanas; el derecho de capitanías de puerto que se pagaba según el reglamento de 22 de abril de 1851, y los derechos de puerto establecidos por decreto de 28 de mayo de 1881. Igualmente quedan derogados los artículos 16, 18, 19 y 20 de la Ordenanza General de Aduanas, relativos al derecho de toneladas, que en adelante se cobrará de esta manera: los buques de vela pagarán diez centavos por tonelada, y los vapores seis centavos por tonelada. Los buques de vapor pertenecientes á líneas internacionales que hagan viajes regulares á puertos de la República, con itinerario fijo y días señalados para la salida, podrán disfrutar de una reducción del derecho de toneladas, en los casos y bajo las condiciones siguientes:

En el litoral del Pacífico, la reducción podrá ser hasta de un setenta y cinco por ciento, para los buques que hagan el servicio postal mexicano, sin recibir retribución pecunaria del Gobierno de México por este último concepto, ni dispensa de otros derechos; y hasta de un veinticinco por ciento, solamente, para los buques que no efectúen el servicio postal, ó que lo hagan mediante retribución pecuniaria del propio Gobierno, ó dispensa de alguno ó de algunos impuestos. En el litoral del Atlántico, la reducción podrá ser hasta de un cincuenta por ciento, y sólo se aplicará á los buques que hagan el servicio postal sin retribución del Gobierno mexicano, por ese concepto ni por ningún otro, y que no disfruten de subvención ó dispensa de alguno ó de algunos derechos.

Para que pueda disfrutarse de las reducciones mencionadas, se requiere que la empresa interesada las solicite de la Secretaría de Comunicaciones y Obras Públicas, y que ésta fije la proporción de las mismas reducciones. También será necesario, para disfrutar de la reducción, que la empresa presente sus itinerarios con la debida oportunidad á la mencionada Secretaría, y que ésta los autorice por estar de acuerdo con las condiciones del contrato ó con el permiso concedido.

Todo buque, perteneciente á una empresa que tenga derecho á disfrutar de alguna de las reducciones de que se habla atrás, y el cual buque arribe á un puerto mexicano situado en el Atlántico, y que no estuviese comprendido en el itinerario respectivo, causará íntegro el derecho de toneladas, si dicho puerto fuese el primero de los de la República á que arribare el buque en su viaje; y si el buque, después de haber disfrutado de una reducción al tocar primero en algún puerto mexicano de su itinerario, hiciese después escala en otro no comprendido en el mismo itinerario, causará en este último puerto el derecho de toneladas por el importe de la diferencia entre el derecho íntegro y el que hubiere pagado en el primer puerto. Lo prescrito se observará aun cuando el arribo ó escala extraordinarios de que se trata, los efectúe el buque con autorización especial del Gobierno.

No causarán el derecho de toneladas los buques procedentes directamente de puerto mexicano y que no se encuentren en el caso de que se trata arriba; los dedicados exclusivamente á la pesca; los de guerra; los dedicados al servicio postal, de faros, ó de otro género, del Gobierno de la República, ó de gobiernos extranjeros, y que no hagan, á la vez, ningún tráfico comercial, ya sea de pasajeros ó de carga; los de arribada forzosa; los *yachts* de placer, que no hagan tráfico comercial; y las embarcaciones menores que en los ríos limítrofes de la República hagan el tráfico internacional entre las poblaciones situadas en las fronteras.

En caso de que los buques vengan del extranjero destinados á dos ó más puertos de la República, la aduana que recaude el derecho de toneladas, además del correspondiente recibo de percepción, expedirá, de oficio, al capitán del buque respectivo, un certificado del pago, á fin de que ese documento le sirva de justificante en las demás aduanas. Por la falta de presentación de dicho documento, se causará de nuevo el impuesto; y sólo justificando ante la Secretaría de Hacienda el doble pago, se autorizará la devolución de lo cobrado de más por ese concepto.

En los puertos donde se hayan ejecutado ó se ejecuten obras que den abrigo, ó faciliten la entrada ó la carga y descarga á los buques, además del derecho de toneladas ya citado, se cobrarán á todo buque mercante, ya sea nacional ó extranjero, y de altura ó cabotaje, así como á las mercancías por ellos conducidas, los impuestos siguientes:

Un "derecho adicional de toneladas," aplicable á todo buque de cualquiera procedencia, nacional ó extranjera, que arribe al puerto mejorado. Este derecho se cobrará con sujeción á la misma base del derecho de toneladas atrás referido, ya sea que el buque cause en todo ó en parte dicho derecho de toneladas ó que no lo cause. El derecho adicional de toneladas lo fijará el Ejecutivo para cada puerto mejorado, sin que el monto pueda ser mayor del cincuenta por ciento de las cuotas señaladas arriba para el derecho de toneladas; y en ningún caso estará sujeto á las reducciones de que se habla después, ni á ninguna otra que pudiera recaer sobre el dicho derecho de toneladas.

Un "derecho de carga y descarga" que causará toda mercancía, ya sea de importación, exportación ó cabotaje, que se cargue ó descargue en el puerto mejorado, sean cuales fueren el lugar y forma en que se practiquen cualesquiera de esas operaciones, y aun cuando no pertenezca al Gobierno Federal el muelle ó lugar por donde se efectuaren. Este impuesto se causará también sin reducción alguna y en las proporciones siguientes:

Los productos y manfucturas de exportación, los efectos nacionales ó nacionalizados de cabotaje, ya sea de entrada ó de salida, el carbón de piedra, las maderas de construcción y los otros materiales y efectos que el Ejecutivo, por medio de reglamentos ó disposiciones agrupe á esta clase, causarán el derecho á razón de cincuenta centavos por cada tonelada de mil kilógramos del peso bruto de los efectos. Todas las demás mercancías no comprendidas en la anterior enumeración, causarán el derecho á razón de un peso por cada tonelada de mil kilógramos de peso bruto. Las mercancías que se trasborden de un buque á otro de los fondeados en el puerto, y las cuales vengan destinadas á otros puertos, así como los cargamentos que en su totalidad se carguen ó descarguen por medio de alijo, causarán la mitad de las cuotas de que se acaba de hablar.

El derecho adicional de toneladas no lo causarán los buques detallados á continuación, ya sean nacionales ó extranjeros, de vela ó de vapor: Los buques de guerra; los buques ó embarcaciones que se dediquen exclusivamente á la pesca; los buques ó embarcaciones con porte menor de diez toneladas brutas; los buques de arribada forzosa.

El derecho de carga y descarga sobre mercancías, no lo causarán: Los equipajes de pasajeros; las muestras que no causen derechos á su importación; los paquetes postales; los bultos de efectos desembarcados por equivocación y que sean reembarcados para su destino; los productos de la pesca que descarguen las embarcaciones dedicadas á esa industria; los víveres, aguada, pertrechos y combustible que embarquen, para su uso, los buques surtos en el puerto; los efectos que se importen para el servicio del Gobierno Federal ó el de los Estados y que estén exentos de derechos, conforme al art. 2° del decreto de junio 6 de 1898; en el tráfico de cabotaje, los efectos destinados al servicio del Gobierno Federal.

Los buques extranjeros que de acuerdo con las prevenciones relativas de la Ordenanza de Aduanas, ó por motivo de contratos, autorizaciones ó permisos especiales, conduzcan mercancías de un puerto de la República con destino á otro puerto ó lugar del país, ya sea directamente, ó bien pasando las mercancías en tránsito por país extranjero, pagarán un derecho llamado "Derecho de tráfico marítimo interior," el cual se causará por tonelada de mil kilógramos del peso bruto de las mercancías que conduzcan dichos buques extranjeros, sujetándose el cobro á la tarifa siguiente:

	En el Atlántico.	En el Pacífico.
Entre puertos que disten uno de otro hasta 60 millas marítimas.	$1.00	$1.00
Entre los que disten más de 60 y hasta 360 millas marítimas....	3.00	2.00
Entre los que disten más de 360 millas marítimas	5.00	3.00

El mismo derecho y bajo las mismas reglas lo causarán los buques extranjeros que obtengan permiso especial para descargar su cargamento, ó parte de él, en puerto de cabotaje ó en otro lugar que no sea puerto de altura; computándose el derecho sobre el peso de las mercancías que comprenda el permiso y según la distancia entre el respectivo puerto de altura y el lugar de la descarga.

Este decreto comenzó á regir el 1° de octubre de 1898.

LA INDUSTRIA DE LA GANADERÍA.

La industria pecuaria en México no está circunscrita á ninguna sección particular del país, dice el "Mexican Herald." Cuando las lluvias no son suficientemente abundantes para producir cosecha, como sucede en una gran extensión de los Estados de Chihuahua, Durango y Coahuila, la yerba que se da en cualquier año basta para pasto y aún para engordar el ganado. Sin embargo es más común que el ganado flaco de la parte norte de la República se lleve á engordar á las haciendas de la parte sur y del centro. De pocos años á esta parte se ha desarrollado una industria en la parte oriental de los Estados de San Luis Potosí, el sur de Tamaulipas y el norte de Veracruz, que aunque todavía está en la infancia, es sin embargo muy importante. Aprovechándose de las maravillosas propiedades de la yerba del Pará, los criadores de esta región compran ganado flaco en los pastos del norte y del este de la República para engordarlo para los mercados de Pachuca, Puebla, México y Yucatán. Puede comprarse ganado flaco á razón de $5 á $15 por cabeza, que cuando está gordo vale de $20 á $45 por cabeza. Se calcula que un acre de yerba del Pará en buena tierra, cortado para pienso, es bastante á alimentar dos cabezas de ganado durante todo el año; tres acres de pasto sirven para engordar cuatro animales. La yerba siempre está verde, crece abundantemente, es muy alimenticia y acaba con otra vegetación. Esta parte del país aunque se adapta admirablemente para engordar ganado no es tan favorable á la cría como las altas llanuras de Durango y Chihuahua, porque aquí las moscas y las garrapatas molestan mucho á los becerros. Pero aun cuando á mayores alturas se puede criar un gran número de cabezas de ganado, el pasto, á veces, hacia fines de la estación seca, es tan escaso que hay temor de que se pierda el ganado por falta de alimento si no se reparte para otros puntos.

VALOR DE LAS IMPORTACIONES Y EXPORTACIONES.

La adjunta estadística de las importaciones y exportaciones de la República durante los últimos cuatro años está tomada de un informe del Cónsul CARDEN dirijido á la Oficina de Relaciones Exteriores de la Gran Bretaña. Los valores han sido reducidos á moneda de los Estados Unidos:

Año.	Importaciones.	Exportaciones.	Exceso de las exportaciones.
1894	$29, 372, 819	$42, 604, 621	$13, 231, 802
1895	35, 186, 444	54, 910, 214	19, 723, 770
1896	45, 224, 958	57, 090, 415	11, 865, 457
1897	38, 107, 955	62, 575, 319	24, 467, 369
Total	147, 892, 176	217, 180, 669	69, 288, 398

Se obsevará que en el último año hubo un gran aumento en el exceso de exportación, más del doble del exceso de 1896, y una cuarta parte mayor que el de 1895, que antes había sido el año de mayor exportación. Las exportaciones han aumentado 46 por. ciento en cuatro años, mientras que la importación ha aumentado menos de 30 por ciento. El estado poco halagüeño de la importación se atribuye á las abuntantes cosechas por una parte y á la firme baja en el valor de la plata, por otra. A los fabricantes de tejidos de los Estados Unidos interesará saber que, según el informe del Cónsul, el desarrollo de la industria textil en la República no se limita al algodón, sino que está extendiéndose también á los géneros de hilo y de lana. El Cónsul agrega que todavía encuentra buen mercado el tisú de lana y estambre, especialmente el de calidad superior. Entre los otros ramos de la industria que parecen ofrecer buenos prospectos al comercio, el Cónsul menciona la minería, la maquinaria agrícola é industrial, máquinas de imprimir, artículos de metal de primera clase, y pinturas.

El Cónsul hace mención incidentalmente al exceso anual de la exportación sobre la importación, respecto del cual dice lo siguiente:

De los £3,500,000 ($17,000,000) exceso anual de la exportación sobre la importación, £2,700,000 ($13,100,000) constituyen el importe de las remisiones para el servicio de la deuda y las ganancias de los ferrocarriles; y las £800,000 ($3,900,000) restantes más el importe del capital extranjero que haya sido invertido en México, pero no remitido en forma de especie ó mercancía, representa el interés del capital invertido en empresas comerciales ó industriales de todas clases, por individuos ó compañías domiciliadas en el extranjero.

IMPORTACIÓN DE CARBÓN, COKE É HIERRO.

La importación de carbón y coke en México continúa aumentando mucho, pues la cantidad importada en 1897 fué de 460,000 toneladas, ó sea más del 35 por ciento sobre la cantidad importada en 1896, lo cual debe considerarse una buena señal, porque indica gran progreso en las empresas industriales. Como tres cuartas partes de toda la cantidad importada fueron de carbón y el resto de cok. La importación de carbón de los Estados Unidos casi se duplicó en el año pasado, y representa ahora más del 50 por ciento del total importado. El resto viene en su mayor parte de Inglaterra. Como el ochenta por ciento del cok viene también de los Estados Unidos. El precio del carbón americano y del de Gales de igual calidad ha subido algo en los últimos meses. A fines de 1897 la tonelada costaba en la capital de $7.30 á $9.70. La diminución por valor de $515,000 que ocurrió el año pasado en la importación de hierro y acero en este país, debe atribuirse á que los compradores no estaban dispuestos, bajo las desfavorables condiciones del cambio, á pedir sino los artículos que les eran absolutamente necesarios, y no á que la demanda haya sido menor. Hubo un aumento por valor de $165,000, ó sea cerca de 40 por ciento, en la importación de hierro corrugado y de vigas de hierro para techos, lo cual prueba mucho incremento en la construcción de edificios, cosa que se nota no solamente en la capital sino también en muchas de las principales ciudades del interior.

GRAN PROYECTO AGRÍCOLA.

Según el periódico "The Financial Times," de Londres, Sir Thomas J. Lipton "tiene en mira un nuevo é importante proyecto respecto de México." Parece que se propone formar algunas de las mayores haciendas de café del mundo, y cultivar también en grande escala el tabaco y el cacao.

Dicho proyecto, que está ya muy adelantado, comprende 10,000 acres de tierra para el cultivo del café, 10,000 para el tabaco y 5,000 para el cacao. Se espera con gran interés el resultado de esta empresa, porque México ofrece grandes ventajas para trabajos de esa clase. Mucha atención se está prestando en aquel país al cultivo del tabaco, y en los últimos cuatro ó cinco años, grandes cantidades de este artículo han sido exportadas de México para la fabricación de cigarros de la Habana, porque durante la guerra civil que precedió al conflicto hispano-americano, la isla de Cuba ha producido muy poco ó ningún tabaco. También en el cultivo de café se han obtenido en México muy buenos resultados en lo pasado, y por lo que hace al cacao, es indígena del país y su calidad es superior. Si Sir Thomas Lipton lleva adelante su pensamiento de cultivar 25,000 acres de tierra, el negocio será de gran importancia no solamente para él, sino también para México. El sueño del Presidente Díaz ha sido siempre desarrollar la agricultura hasta donde sea posible.

NICARAGUA.

NUEVO CONTRATO DEL CANAL.

Por despachos telegráficos llegados de Managua, Nicaragua, se sabe que el Congreso nicaragüense ratificó el contrato de canal celebrado últimamente entre el Gobierno y dos ciudadanos americanos, los Señores Eyre y Cragin, representantes de un sindicato de Nueva York. Existiendo, como existe, una concesión otorgada en 1887 á la Compañía de Canal Marítimo de Nicaragua, el nuevo contrato no puede comenzar á surtir sus efectos sino cuando haya expirado la referida concesión, lo cual será en octubre de 1899. Como es bien sabido, varios proyectos de ley para construcción del canal han sido sometidos al Congreso de los Estados Unidos, pero el asunto aun está pendiente. Quizá no hay una sola empresa que haya llamado tanto la atención del mundo durante medio siglo, como la de la apertura de una vía de comunicación entre el Atlántico y el Pacífico por el istmo centroamericano; pero jamás había despertado este asunto tanto interés como ahora, sobre todo, en los Estados Unidos, á causa de la anexión de las islas Sandwich (Hawaii) y del largo viaje que tuvo que hacer el acorazado *Oregón* para venir de San Francisco á las Antillas.

La ruta de canal por Nicaragua ha sido objeto de serios estudios, y tanto el Gobierno americano como la compañía concesionaria, han invertido en eso sumas de consideración. Mucho es lo que se ha escrito sobre el proyectado canal de Nicaragua, y puede decirse que el asunto está agotado. En la construcción de esta vía interoceánica habrá necesariamente que hacer uso de esclusas, y esto sirvió de pretexto para la oposición que M. DE LESSFPS hizo siempre á la ruta de Nicaragua, pues sostenía él que un canal entre los dos océanos tiene que ser á nivel, como el de Suez, á fin de que pueda responder á las necesidades del comercio. Sin embargo, los ingenieros americanos que han hecho los estudios del proyecto, han demostrado que las esclusas no serían impedimento al enorme tráfico que se haría por el canal de Nicaragua una vez que estuviera terminado. Además, después del fracaso del proyecto de LESSEPS, los directores de la empresa de Panamá han adoptado el sistema de esclusas como indispensable para llevar adelante la obra.

DELIMITACIÓN DE LAS LÍNEAS FRONTERIZAS.

Según los últimos despachos de la prensa, la comisión de ingenieros, nombrada por los Gobiernos de Nicaragua y Costa Rica para determinar y marcar las líneas fronterizas entre las dos Repúblicas, está en desacuerdo de nuevo, y se prepara para someter la decisión del asunto al arbitrador Gen. E. P. ALEXANDER.

El 30 de setiembre de 1897 el General ALEXANDER, nombrado Ingeniero Arbitrador por el Presidente CLEVELAND, presentó el informe que fué publicado literalmente en el BOLETÍN de diciembre de 1897. Los términos convenidos por la Comisión para la demarcación de las líneas fronterizas se publicaron en el BOLETÍN de abril de 1897. Según estos términos, el General ALEXANDER tiene la facultad de decidir en definitiva todos los puntos de diferencias que puedan surgir durante las operaciones de determinación y demarcación de las líneas fronterizas entre las dos Repúblicas. Es de esperarse que los representantes de los dos Gobiernos queden satisfechos con la opinión del General ALEXANDER con referencia á la actual dificultad.

Bull. No. 5——7

PARAGUAY.

EL CÓDIGO DE LA NOMENCLATURA COMERCIAL ADOPTADO COMO TEXTO OFICIAL.

El Honorable WILLIAM R. FINCH, Ministro de los Estados Unidos en Montevideo, comunica al Departamento de Estado con fecha 21 de setiembre de 1898, que el Gobierno del Paraguay ha promulgado un decreto oficial adoptando el Código de la Nomenclatura Comercial, preparado por la Oficina de las Repúblicas Americanas, como texto oficial para la designación de los artículos de comercio en español, portugués, é inglés. Esta disposición se dictó en consecuencia de la necesidad comercial de una nomenclatura común con otros países, para llevar á cabo el cambio de mercancías, y el 2 de setiembre de 1898 se dispuso que el mencionado decreto fuese comunicado, publicado y entregado en el Registro Oficial bajo las firmas del Presidente EGUISGUIZA y el Secretario GUILLERMO DE LOS RÍOS.

El Departamento del Tesoro de los Estados Unidos había dictado antes una disposición semejante con fecha 22 de enero de 1898, expediendo una circular en la cual se adoptaba el Código para la traducción de palabras y frases comerciales para el uso de aquel Departamento y para guía de los administradores y aforadores de aduana.

PRODUCCIÓN DE CAFÉ.

Entre los últimos informes de los cónsules de los Estados Unidos, figura uno suscrito por Mr. RUFFIN, Cónsul en Asunción, en el cual se trata de la adaptabilidad del suelo del Paraguay á la producción de café. Dice Mr. RUFFIN que hay en Paraguay plantaciones de café que cuentan muchos años de existencia, pero que no han sido cultivadas, sino que se las ha abandonado en cierto grado á la acción de su excelente clima. Los cafetos de estas plantaciones producen una variedad de café semejante al que se produce en Brasil y Bolivia, pues proceden de las especies arábigas. La producción en estas plantaciones no es extensa y el consumo es local. Las plantaciones que se han establecido en los últimos años han dado resultados favorables, pues todo el café producido ha encontrado salida en Paraguay. Según las estadísticas que Mr. Ruffin ha podido obtener, el número de cafetos de la República es de 343,407. Mr. Ruffin cree que toda la producción puede venderse en Asunción, pues los habitantes son "grandes tomadores de café."

El cafeto se da mejor en los países que tienen una temperatura media de 68° á 78° Fahrenheit. Según las observaciones oficiales, Paraguay tiene una temperatura de 58.42° en junio á 84.45° en diciembre con un promedio de 71.16°. El suelo es apropiado para el cultivo, pues el terreno es llano y húmedo y pueden llevarse á cabo fácilmente las operaciones de cultivo. Entre las muchas variedades de café la que más se cultiva en Paraguay, según Mr. Ruffin, es la "Yungas," porque procede de Bolivia que tiene casi la misma posición geográfica y un suelo de condiciones semejantes. Créese que este café puede competir con el mejor que se conoce en los mercados de Europa en donde ya se vende, aunque en pequeñas cantidades. Personas inteligentes en esta industria declaran que el café que se produce en Perú y Guatemala es tan bueno como cualquiera de las variedades que se cultivan en el continente americano. El grano está bien desarrollado, es de exquisito aroma y tiene un color verde-amarillo. En tamaño y peso es superior al café de Moca al cual se asemeja. La planta es vigorosa, se desarrolla rápidamente y da fruto en tres años.

MERCADO PARA ARTÍCULOS MANUFACTURADOS.

El hecho de que la República del Paraguay está situada en el valle del río Paraná, en el interior del continente, sin costas propias, hace que aquella República dependa comercialmente de las repúblicas de la Argentina y el Uruguay. Pero el comercio directo con Paraguay es reducido y apenas hay constancia de exportación alguna á esta República, pero el país es rico en valioso territorio y capaz de grande desarrollo. Es probable que sus bosques sean los que contienen las mejores maderas de ebanistería que se conocen, pues se encuentran en ellos cerca de 150 especies de árboles valiosos.

El consumo es de importancia, aunque algo limitado por razón del número relativamente pequeño de sus habitantes. No hay comunicación marítima directa entre los Estados y el Paraguay, ni tampoco entre esta República y los grandes países exportadores.

Los vapores no cargan mercancías á puntos más allá de Montevi
deo, Buenos Aires ó Rosario que son los ciudades de importancia
comercial del valle del río de la Plata. El resultado es que los
comerciantes del Paraguay al hacer sus pedidos de géneros extranjeros, se ven obligados á ordenar que las facturas vayan á alguna
de las ciudades nombradas, á menos que tengan agentes en aquellos lugares que atiendan al despacho y remisión de los géneros.
Esto naturalmente aumenta los precios, pues hay que hacer gastos
extraordinarios por concepto de despacho y comisiones. También
se da lugar de aquella suerte á frecuentes y dilatadas demoras.
Como el Paraguay no acuña moneda de oro ó de plata, circula en
el país la moneda de la Argentina y del Uruguay; y como en la
Argentina la base de la circulación ha sufrido fluctuaciones, los
cargadores han dado la preferencia á Montevideo, donde prevalece
el patrón de oro como puerto de reembarque para el tráfico por el
río.

En un informe dirijido al Gobierno británico por un corresponsal,
se llama la atención hacia los siguientes artículos de comercio:
Hay gran demanda de máquinas de coser en la República de igual
suerte que en toda la América del Sur; las clases mas baratas son
las que más se venden, aunque también ha encontrado salida un
gran número de máquinas de clase superior. La mayor parte de
las que existen en el mercado son de fabricación alemana. Hay
un gran número de alambiques en operación, la mayor parte de
los cuales se importa de Francia. Los de tamaño pequeño que
pueden destilar de 50 á 200 galones por día de 18° Cartier, son
los que obtienen mayor demanda. Pueden ser de destilación
sencilla, continua y semicontinua, pero deben ser lo menos complicado posible. En el país se fabrica poco vino y ningún otro
licor sino la caña ó aguardiente. Los fabricantes ingleses parece
que hacen toda la importación de productos químicos é instrumentos y aparatos de cirujía. Hay demanda de aguas minerales
en Asunción y las grandes ciudades. Podría venderse un número
considerable de trapiches de hierro portátiles propios para moverlos
por medio de bueyes. Se fabrica una cantidad considerable de
azúcar no refinado pero en pequeña escala. Sin embargo, la
cantidad que se produce es insuficiente para el consumo y el resto
se importa de la Argentina en donde hay grandes fábricas de
azúcar, en el Chaco, precisamente al otro lado del río, en dirección

opuesta á Paraguay. Aunque la bebida nacional del Paraguay es el mate (té del Paraguay), se consume una gran cantidad de té, y la demanda parece que aumenta. El té que se importa en Paraguay debe ser de superior calidad. Hay gran demanda de tejidos, especialmente de géneros baratos de algodón. Estos últimos son vendidos por detallistas con muy pequeña ó ninguna utilidad, pues solo lo hacen para facilitar la venta de otros artículos. La competencia es fuerte en este ramo, pero las casas. de comercio inglesas importan la mayor parte. Se vende gran número de ponchos, los cuales se importan de Inglaterra. Estos ponchos son de la misma clase que los que se venden en la República Argentina; pero como la temperatura del invierno en Paraguay es algo más cálida, los ponchos de lana no obtienen aquí tanta demanda.

Se llama la atención hacia un párrafo del BOLETÍN de octubre en el cual se da la noticia de haberse establecido en la ciudad de Asunción una asociación con el objeto de dar informes sobre todos los puntos que se relacionan con los productos, leyes de aduana y comercio de la República, así como también para ayudar á las personas que deseen entrar en relaciones comerciales con los exportadores y otras casas de negocios del Paraguay. Esta asociación es conocida con el nombre de Centro Comercial del Paraguay.

El corresponsal dice que el tipo del cambio acusa un firme descenso, pués ha bajado hasta el 10 por ciento durante los últimos meses, con tendencia á una baja mayor. En la actualidad el premio sobre el oro es de 760, es decir que el peso en billete del Paraguay vale unos 13 centavos. Dice además que la competencia extranjera es muy fuerte en el Paraguay y el número de las casas inglesas muy pequeño, mientras que el número de las casas alemanas, francesas é italianas es relativamente numeroso. Las casas inglesas que tienen comercio con el Paraguay parece que se conforman con hacer sus negocios por medio de agencias en Buenos Aires; hay, sin embargo, en Asunción y otros pueblos campo bastante para empresas que tengan por objeto principal la explotación de los productos del país.

INSCRIPCIÓN DE LAS MARCAS DE FÁBRICA.

Según el "British Trade Journal," las personas que deseen registrar marcas de fábrica en Paraguay deberán solicitarlo de la Junta de Crédito Público en Asunción. El privilegio se concede por diez años, y á la expiración de este término puede renovarse por diez años más. Las trasferencias deberán inscribirse en el mismo registro en donde consta inscrita la marca original. La solicitud de inscripción deberá acompañarse de dos copias de la marca de fábrica y la inscripción se hará por duplicado; también se presentarán un recibo de los derechos ($50) pagados á la Junta de Crédito Público y un poder debidamente legalizado si el propietario de la marca de fábrica no hace la gestión en persona. El poder deberá ser visado por el Cónsul de Paraguay, y el nombre del agente podrá dejarse en blanco para llenarlo más tarde.

PRODUCCIÓN DE NARANJAS.

Según un informe reciente del Cónsul RUFFIN, la naranja es uno de los productos que más se consumen en el Paraguay, y constituye un comestible para la clase pobre, especialmente en el campo. También se usa la naranja para la ceba de puercos, y la carne de estos animales así alimentados se considera muy buena. El naranjo crece profusamente y se encuentra en todas partes, ya sea en las huertas ó en los bosques. Su cultivo se lleva á cabo en las fincas. Esta planta nace de semillas y produce á los cinco años. Florece durante todo el año con excepción de los meses de enero, febrero y marzo. Una mata de siete años produce unas 1,000 naranjas. La fruta tiene unas tres pulgadas de diámetro y las naranjas de la clase común son muy dulces. La naranja de China es pequeña y no tan dulce como la de la clase antes mencionada; es también más cara que aquélla. No se cultiva gran número de esta clase de naranjas, y la mayor parte de las que se producen son exportadas á Buenos Aires. Se vende fácilmente y á precio remunerativo. La tercera clase es la naranja amarga de la cual se hace dulce; también se prepara un extracto con las flores. Algunos franceses se ocupan en este negocio que es lucrativo. La exportación de la cosecha comienza como á fines del mes de mayo y dura hasta noviembre. Los botes hacen las cargas en todos los lugares á lo largo del río y las naranjas son entregadas á bordo por mujeres que las llevan en cestos que cargan en la cabeza. No hay derecho de exportación. La mayor parte de esta producción es exportada á Buenos Aires y Montevideo. Durante la estación se exporta un promedio de 300,000 naranjas.

CONSEJOS A LOS INMIGRANTES.

Con fecha 2 de setiembre de 1898, Mr. JOHN N. RUFFIN, Cónsul de los Estados Unidos en la Asunción, escribe al Departamento de Estado lo que sigue:

Deseo manifestar en provecho de aquéllos que tienen la intención de venir á este país á dedicarse á empresas agrícolas, que las mejores localidades son las que quedan sobre el río, accesibles á las embarcaciones que pueden llevar los productos á los mercados de Buenos Aires y Montevideo. Parece que se presenta una buena oportunidad para la inversión de dinero en dichas empresas. El Gobierno del Paraguay paga el pasaje de los inmigrantes desde Buenos Aires hasta el punto donde deseen establecerse, y además les provee de bueyes y de instrumentos agrícolas, debiendo pagar por estos con su trabajo ó con los productos del suelo. Algunos de estos instrumentos, sin embargo, les son facilitados gratis por los empleados de la colonia. El punto que deseo establecer con toda claridad, es que tienen que pagar por todo lo que el Gobierno les proporciona, con excepción del pasaje desde Buenos Aires. Los terrenos son muy fértiles y merecen llamar la atención de todos.

ESTADOS UNIDOS.

COMERCIO CON LA AMÉRICA LATINA.

RELACIÓN DE LAS IMPORTACIONES Y EXPORTACIONES.

En la página 810 aparece la última relación del comercio entre los Estados Unidos y la América Latina tomada de la compilación hecha por la Oficina de Estadística del Departamento del Tesoro de los Estados Unidos, cuyo jefe es Mr. O. P. AUSTIN. Estos datos se refieren al valor del comercio arriba mencionado. La estadística corresponde al mes de agosto de 1898, corregida en setiembre 29 del mismo año, comparada con la del período correspondiente del año anterior, y también comprende los datos referentes á los ocho meses que terminaron en agosto de 1898, comparados con igual período de 1897. Debe explicarse que las estadísticas de las importaciones y exportaciones de las diversas aduanas referentes á un mes cualquiera no se reciben en el Departamento del Tesoro hasta el 20 del próximo mes, necesitándose algún tiempo para su compilación é impresión, de suerte que los datos estadísticos correspondientes al mes de agosto, por ejemplo, no se publican sino en octubre.

NUEVA LÍNEA DE VAPORES EN EL PACÍFICO.

Según informes recíbidos por el periódico de San Francisco, "The Chronicle," y que publicó en su número del 8 de octubre, aquel puerto va á tener otra línea directa de comunicación por vapor con los mercados sudamericanos, tanto en la costa occidental como en la oriental. Una de las compañías de navegación por vapor más fuertes que hay en Francia, Les Chargeurs Réunis, va á establecer una línea de vapores entre San Francisco y los puertos siguientes: Mazatlan y Acapulco, en México; Guayaquil, en el Ecuador; el Callao, en el Perú; Valparaíso, en Chile; Montevideo, en el Uruguay; Liverpool, en Inglaterra, y el Havre, en Francia. Es posible que los vapores toquen también en algún puerto de Bélgica. El servicio comenzará en marzo venidero, y después de esa fecha, continuará mensualmente entre San Francisco y Liverpool, con escala en los otros puertos mencionados.

Un representante de la compañía, que se encuentra ahora en San Francisco, asegura que para el servicio en el Pacífico la compañía tiene ahora en construcción tres vapores, que medirán 372 piés de largo, y cuyo porte será de 6,000 toneladas.

LA SITUACIÓN ECONÓMICA MUCHO MÁS FUERTE.

El cuadro que viene á continuación, formado con datos de origen oficial por el "Journal of Finance," y en el cual se dan las importaciones y exportaciones de los Estados Unidos durante los primeros ocho meses de los años civiles allí mencionados, demuestra hasta qué grado este país ha fortalecido su posición económica en 1898, mediante operaciones comerciales con otros paises, principalmente los de Europa y las dependencias de éstos:

	1898.	1897.	1896.
Mercaderías:			
Importaciones	$426,412,038	$546,325,777	$471,232,299
Exportaciones	778,674,025	641,697,330	580,930,792
Exceso de las exportaciones	352,261,987	95,371,553	109,698,493
Oro:			
Importaciones	102,087,831	11,887,654	31,902,237
Exportaciones	9,679,113	32,542,659	56,895,592
Exceso de las importaciones	92,408,718	. . . .	. . . .
Exceso de las exportaciones	. . . .	20,655,205	24,993,355

Las exportaciones de mercancías han excedido á las importaciones en un valor de $352,261,987, mientras que durante los mismos meses en 1897 el exceso fué de $95,271,553, ó sea una diferencia á favor de 1898 de $256,890,234. El balance á favor del país en este año ha sido compensado con una importación de oro por valor de $92,408,718, lo cual deja un balance neto de $259,853,069, ó sea en la proporción de $346,400,000 por año.

MARCAS EN LOS EFECTOS IMPORTADOS.

La siguiente circular expedida por el Ministerio de Hacienda, y referente á las marcas en los efectos que se importan en los Estados Unidos, fué publicada en las aduanas el 18 de octubre:

A fin de que se lleven á efecto con más eficacia las disposiciones de la sección 8ª de la ley de 24 de julio de 1897, referente á la marca de los bultos con el nombre del país de procedencia y con la cantidad de su contenido, así como á la marca y timbre de los artículos importados, se ordena al empleado aforador que en lo de adelante examine todas las mercancías existentes en su poder para ser aforadas, á fin de averiguar si se ha cumplido debidamente con lo que dispone la sección 8ª. Cada vez que dicho empleado descubra una falta en el cumplimiento de esas disposiciones, hará traer á su presencia todos los bultos mencionados en la factura y obligará al importador á que marque la mercancía conforme á la ley. Si el importador no llenare este requisito, la mercancía será almacenada y quedará en la condición de efectos no reclamados. Los artículos así guardados en almacenes públicos serán marcados por el importador bajo la vigilancia especial de un empleado del Departamento de Aforadores, y los gastos que ocasione esta vigilancia, así como los de carretaje y otros trabajos, serán pagados por el importador antes de la entrega de la mercancía.

URUGUAY.

COMERCIO DE LA REPÚBLICA EN 1897.

Los siguientes extractos tomados del informe anual del Cónsul británico, Mr. GREENFELL, han sido remitidos desde Montevideo al Departamento de Estado por Mr. SWALM, Cónsul de los Estados Unidos:

El total del importe oficial del comercio exterior de la República en 1897 asciende á $49,492,305, de los cuales $20,048,980 corresponden á la importación, acusando una diferencia en favor del Uruguay.

· Las entradas de aduana de 1897 han tenido un descenso notable y su importe es $8,175,442, ó $2,424,558 menos que las de 1896.

La Gran Bretaña tiene el monopolio en la exportación de jamones, té, sacos sombreros de paño, pieles de carnero, azadas, rastrillos, trilladoras, hilos de coser, tubos de hierro y plomo, carbón, planchas para techos, de hierro galvanizado, planchas de metal, soda, yute, cajas de hierro y pólvora, y ocupa el primer lugar en las importaciones de artículos de algodón, géneros de hilo, géneros de lana mezclada, sombreros de paja, medias de hilo, pañuelos de algodón, frazadas de algodón y de lana mezclada, molinos de viento, sulfato de cobre, azadones, herramientas de carpintería, bramante, barniz, aros de hierro, planchas y barras de hierro, pintura, porcelana, y artículos de talabartería.

Alemania tiene el monopolio de la importación de pianos, sal y bacalao seco, y ocupa el primer lugar en la importación de azúcares refinados, franelas, ropa hecha, camisas de algodón y de hilo, puños y cuellos, chalecos de lana, medias de algodón, capas de lana pura y mezclada, sobrecamas de algodón, toallas, servilletas, máquinas de coser, alambre para cercas, almidón, añil, papel para imprimir, mercerías y muebles.

Francia tiene el monopolio de cabritilla y telas, y ocupa el primer lugar en géneros de lana pura y mezclada y géneros de seda mezclada, botas y zapatos, chalecos de algodón, corbatas de seda, guantes de cabritilla, paraguas, muelles de carruaje, drogas y perfumería.

Bélgica tiene el monopolio de guadañas, vigas y pilares de hierro, planchas de zinc, y escopetas de caza, y ocupa el primer lugar en géneros de hilo mezclado, frazadas, vajilla y espejos, cristalería, vidrios para ventanas, cimento romano, papel blanco y velas.

Los Estados Unidos tiene el monopolio de arados, horquillas y alquitrán, y ocupa el primer lugar en madera de construcción, segadoras, bramante de engavillar y hachas; ocupa el segundo lugar en muebles, el tercer lugar en máquinas de coser y sulfato de cobre, y el quinto lugar en drogas y papel para imprimir.

Mr. SWALM informa al Departamento de Estado que el comercio de los Estados Unidos, de Alemania y de Francia con el Uruguay ha aumentado notablemente durante el último año á expensas de Inglaterra.   Durante el actual año el descenso en las importaciones de géneros de algodón procedentes de Inglaterra ha sido de lo más notable.   Alemania ha sobrepujado á sus competidores en camisas de algodón y de hilo, poniendo en el mercado un artículo barato de aquella clase.   El Cónsul hace notar que las máquinas de coser procedentes de Alemania son imitaciones baratas de las que se fabrican en los Estados Unidos.

PRINCIPALES ARTÍCULOS DE EXPORTACIÓN.

Las exportaciones del Uruguay están divididas, á los efectos estadísticos, en seis clases de las cuales la principal es la que figura bajo el rubro de "Saladero y productos del ganado."   Del 85 al

90 por ciento de la valuación de los cargamentos fletados para pases extranjeros, queda comprendido bajo este encabezamiento. Durante los diez últimos años las exportaciones de esta clase, según cifras obtenidas de los "Official Statistical Annuals," han aumentado hasta la cantidad de $23,824,672 en 1889; $26,007,091 en 1890; $24,804,823 en 1891; $24,273,559 en 1892: $25.703,185 en 1893; $28,189,911 en 1894; $27,474,987 en 1895; $26,418,596 en 1896; $26,834,860 en 1897; y por los seis primeros meses de 1898, $14,922,467.

Los productos de saladero y ganado se dividen en unas 40 clases que á su vez se subdividen ó de otra suerte se distinguen. De estas clases las principales son: cuernos, pelo de caballo, huesos y cenizas de hueso, tasajo, carnes en conserva, extractos de carne, carne líquida, cueros salados de buey, cueros secos, cueros salados de ternera, y cueros de añojo, cueros de novatos, cueros secos de caballo, cueros salados de caballo, pieles de carnero, pieles de cordero, cascos, sebo (no limpiado y para cocina), guano, lana, lenguas en conserva, médula de cuerno, entrañas, tendones, y nervios.

De todos estos productos el más importante es el tasajo. La mayor cantidad exportada durante un año fué de $5,719,029 en 1894. En 1896, fecha de la última estadística obtenible, el valor de la exportación de este producto fué de $4,561,799. Refiriéndose á esta producción del Uruguay y á la adaptabilidad del país para la producción de artículos de calidad muy superior al tasajo, el "Montevideo Times" dice lo siguiente:

Reconócese que el Uruguay es uno de los países que producen mejor carne de vaca y prueba de esto es el haberse establecido aquí una empresa tan importante como las fábricas de Liebig. Sin embargo, la mayor parte de la carne es convertida en artículo tan primitivo y detestable como el tasajo que escasamente merece que se le conserve en la lista de los alimentos de la gente civilizada, y que lo comen hoy solamente las clases bajas de la población del Brasil y de Cuba. Se hace imposible creer que en estos días en que se cuenta con los recursos de la ciencia aplicada, no se pueda hacer nada mejor con la esplendida carne del Uruguay, ó que no pueda prepararse en otra forma de modo que pueda encontrar un mercado más amplio y provechoso.

En Inglaterra se consume ahora gran cantidad de carne de vaca importada, y lo mismo ocurre en otros países extranjeros; y esta importación se hace por paises que tienen menos facilidades y ventajas que el Uruguay. Como país pastoral que es, en Uruguay se produce no sólo carne de vaca sino también excelente carne de carnero. Hasta el presente, sin embargo, no sabemos que se haya tratado de utilizar la carne de carnero como artículo de exportación, aunque ésto se ha hecho en la Argentina. Si el espacio lo permitiera, pudiéramos tratar también de los productos de lechería y del ganado de cerda para cuya preparación, á los efectos de la exportación, el Uruguay se presta admirablemente. Lo único que hace falta es el espíritu de empresa, aunque creemos que en cuanto al ganado de cerda existe cierta antigua ley municipal que grava la matanza con un impuesto exorbitante é impide así el crecimiento de lo que de otra suerte sería una industria muy importante. Pero con un gobierno progresista como el presente no sería deficil obtener la abolición de este impuesto.

SITUACIÓN ECONÓMICA DE LA REPÚBLICA.

El Cónsul Swalm escribe de Montevideo que la deuda pública de la República, en bonos y flotante, era de $140,000,000 en 31 de agosto de 1898. También comunica que se votaron, para el sostenimiento del Gobierno durante el año fiscal de 1898–99, las siguientes cantidades: Poder Legislativo, $341,114; Presidencia, $64,618; Ministerio de Relaciones Exteriores, $149,089; Ministerio de Gobierno, $2,721,659; Ministerio de Hacienda, $961,040; Ministerio de lo Interior, $1,127,140; Ministerio de Guerra y Marina, $1,921,953; Deuda Pública, $5,329,662; Garantías de ferrocarril, $884,770; Pensiones (clases pasivas), $1,417,378; varios, $524,679; total, $15,434,003. Estos gastos hacen ascender la contribución per capita á $18.24. El Cónsul agrega:

" La República mantiene fielmente su crédito, y no ha rechazado un solo peso de su deuda."

En Uruguay, como advierte Mr. Swalm, se pagan derechos de exportación sobre animales y sus productos y existe también un reducido impuesto sobre pagarés, cheques, etc. Es necesario obtener licencia para toda clase de negocios. El impuesto del tabaco está basado sobre un sistema tomado del de los Estados Unidos con la diferencia de que cada tabaco lleva un sello de $\frac{1}{5}$ de centavo (2-mill stamp). Los fósforos de cerilla pagan un impuesto de ½ centavo por cada caja de 50. La ciudad de Montevideo tiene emitidos bonos por la cantidad de $6,000,000. La ciudad cuenta con la planta de la luz eléctrica que le produce una buena renta.

NUEVO MINISTRO DE RELACIONES EXTERIORES.

El Cónsul General Don Prudencio de Murguiondo ha informado oficialmente al Departamento de Estado de los Estados Unidos de que el Presidente Cuestas nombró temporalmente al

Señor Don JACOBO A. VARELA miembro de su gabinete. Va á ocupar este caballero el lugar del Señor Don DOMINGO MENDILA-HARSU que renunció la cartera de Relaciones Exteriores.

VENEZUELA.

IMPORTANCIA DEL TRIBUNAL DE ARBITRAJE.

La reunión que pronto se verificará en París del Tribunal de Arbitraje Anglo-Venezolano, y del cual son miembros por Venezuela el Justicia Mayor FULLER y el Magistrado BREWER, del Tribunal Supremo de los Estados Unidos, es un acontecimiento casi tan importante como la reunión en la misma ciudad de la Comisión de Paz Hispano-Americana, por lo grave del incidente que la cuestión venezolana suscitó entre los Estados Unidos y la Gran Bretaña durante la administración de CLEVELAND, y la parte que en él le correspondió á la doctrina de Monroe. El tribunal tendrá una sesión preliminar en París en enero de 1899, á la cual asistirá el Magistrado BREWER; pero no es probable que se halle presente el Justicia Mayor FULLER en esa primera reunión, porque en esa época el Tribunal Supremo estará muy ocupado, y dos de sus miembros no podrían entonces ausentarse al mismo tiempo. Probablemente el Magistrado BREWER obtendrá un aplazamiento hasta el mes de mayo, y en esa fecha ambos magistrados estarán libres para ir á juntarse con los otros árbitros y dedicarse á los serios trabajos del tribunal.

Los alegatos y réplicas de Venezuela y de la Gran Bretaña están ya listos. El Ministro venezolano, Señor ANDRADE, presentó últimamente á la embajada británica en Wáshington la réplica de Venezuela, y al mismo tiempo la réplica de la Gran Bretaña fué entregada al Doctor ROJAS, agente del Gobierno venezolano en París. Los documentos forman un conjunto de lo más voluminoso que se ha visto nunca en una controversia internacional sometida á arbitraje. El alegato y réplica de la Gran Bretaña constituyen once grandes tomos, un atlas y varios mapas separados, mientras que el alegato de Venezuela se compone de seis volúmenes y tres atlas. Listos todos estos documentos, lo único que las partes tienen que hacer es presentar sus respectivos argumentos. El de Venezuela será preparado por el ex-Presidente de los Estados

Unidos, Mr. Harrison, por el ex-Ministro de Marina, Mr. Tracy, y por Mr. Mallet-Provost. El argumento de la Gran Bretaña va á ser presentado por los primeros abogados ingleses, incluyendo á Sir Richard Webster. Se cree que el General Harrison y el Señor Tracy se encontrarán presentes cuando el tribunal se reuna en mayo, y que harán argumentos orales. Por lo dicho, se ve que el personal de los abogados y el de los árbitros darán mucho interés á las sesiones. El primero de los árbitros ingleses es el Baron Herschel, antiguo Lord Canciller de Inglaterra. Asociado con él estará Sir Richard Henn Collins. El quinto árbitro, que tendrá el carácter de tercero en discordia, será el notable jurisconsulto ruso y escritor de derecho internacional, M. Maartens. Mientras se efectúa la reunión de los árbitros, él está encargado de recibir todos los papeles, argumentos, y otros documentos.

IMPORTACIÓN PROCEDENTE DE LOS ESTADOS UNIDOS EN SETIEMBRE DE 1898.

El Señor Don Antonio E. Delfino, Cónsul General de Venezuela en Nueva York, ha facilitado bondadosamente á la Oficina de las Repúblicas Americanas los siguientes datos estadísticos relativos á la exportación de mercancías del puerto de Nueva York, con destino á los varios puertos de Venezuela, en setiembre de 1898.

El número total de bultos embarcados fué de 41,478, con un peso de 2,195,375.30 libras y un valor de $199,831.62. La mayor parte de estos géneros fué á La Guayra, pues se embarcaron para este puerto 21,976 bultos valuados en $120,764.62. El valor de los artículos enviados á Puerto Cabello fué de $36,745.39; los enviados á Ciudad Bolívar, $23,037.50; á Maracaibo, $9,746.11; á Carúpano, $5.276; á La Vela, $1,931; á Guanta, $1,880; y á Cumaná, $1,001.

Los principales artículos exportados fueron: harina de trigo, $40,826.94; manteca, $33,529.10; zarazas, $24,190.91; driles de algodón blanqueados y crudos, $13,640.59; provisiones, $15,069.06; drogas y perfumería, $10,668.83; quincallería y miscelánea, $11,140.92; mantequilla, $8,558.11; kerosina, $7,889.15; ferretería, $6,262.24; lona, $4,203.86; cordelería, $2,932.10; picadura para cigarros, $2,943.80; alambre de puá, $2,966.62 y aparatos eléctricos, $2,675.41.

CONCESIÓN Á UN FABRICANTE DE PORCELANA.

Bajo la administración del Presidente ANDRADE, Venezuela parece estar haciendo rápidos progresos, tanto comercialmente como en otros sentidos. Uno de los objetos principales que el Gobierno se propone, es estimular nuevas empresas, especialmente aquellas que no solamente darán buenos resultados en la actualidad, sino que serán de utilidad pública en lo futuro. Últimamente se han recibido numerosos informes de los cónsules de los Estados Unidos en Venezuela, en los que ponen de manifiesto minuciosamente el resultado de sus observaciones en cuanto al nuevo orden de cosas. Uno de dichos informes ha sido enviado de Maracaibo por el Cónsul PLUMACHER, y en ese trabajo se encuentran traducidos los puntos principales de la concesión otorgada al Marques GINO INCONTRI por el Ministro de Agricultura, Industria y Comercio, para la manufactura de efectos de porcelana. Según esta concesión, el Señor INCONTRI debe establecer dentro de 18 meses una ó más fábricas de porcelana, pero no de la clase que se hace en el país. El Gobierno no otorgará durante 10 años á otra persona una concesión de esta clase, y se solicitará del Congreso que no rebaje los actuales derechos sobre los efectos de porcelana. Los materiales para construcción, la maquinaria, etc., para la fábrica quedarán exentos de derechos, y los efectos de la compañía no pagarán impuestos mientras dure la concesión. Doce acres de tierra se darán gratis á la compañía para la construcción de las fábricas, y 62 acres para las materias primas. Un año después de haber entrado en vigencia este contrato, la compañía pagará en la Tesorería el 10 por ciento de sus ganancias anuales, y depositará en algunos de los bancos de Venezuela 25,000 bolívares ($4,825) en oro, ó en bonos venezolanos ó italianos. En caso de que las fábricas suspendan sus trabajos por seis meses consecutivos, y por falta de la compañía, ésta pagará una multa de 20,000 bolívares ($3,860). Si la suspensión de los trabajos continuase por seis mesas más, el contrato será declarado nulo.

FUNDACIÓN DE UN BANCO DE ARTESANOS.

El Cónsul PLUMACHER ha enviado de Maracaibo al Departamento de Estado una traducción del contrato para el establecimiento de un banco de artesanos, empresa que él considera muy útil.   He aquí un extracto de ese documento:

El contratista se compromete á establecer en esta ciudad una sociedad de préstamos con el objeto de que se construyan casas en Caracas y en otras ciudades, adelantando dinero y materiales, con hipoteca de la propiedad como garantía, debiéndose pagar por ambas cosas con el valor de los alquileres, de modo que el constructor de la casa llegue con el tiempo á ser el verdadero propietario.   El banco de artesanos hará préstamos, dando el 70 por ciento en materiales de con strucción, y el 30 por ciento en dinero efectivo para el pago de los obreros, y tomará una hipoteca sobre el edificio, recibiendo el 12 por ciento en mensualidades.   Este 12 por ciento se aplicará á lo siguiente: 6 por ciento al pago de intereses sobre el capital invertido en la obra, 4 por ciento al fondo de amortización, y 2 por ciento para los gastos corrientes del banco.   La concesión durará 15 años, y el banco dará principio á sus operaciones un año después de haber sido aprobado el contrato.   Tanto el banco como las casas á cuya construcción coopere, quedarán exentos de impuestos municipales mientras las hipotecas no hayan sido canceladas.

INDICACIÓN Á LOS EXPORTADORES.

M. QUIEVREUX, Cónsul francés en Caracas, en un informe dirijido recientemente á su Gobierno, hace varias indicaciones sobre el comercio de la República de Venezuela, las c’ ales deben ser de importancia no sólo para sus compatriotas, sino también para los exportadores de los Estados Unidos.

M. QUIEVREUX se expresa de la manera siguiente:

Las compras se hacen aquí durante la Cuaresma y la Navidad.   Estas son las épocas del año en que el consumidor de Venezuela gusta de hacer sus provisiones de todas clases.   El hecho de que las fiestas de navidad coinciden con'la recolección de la cosecha de café, que es la principal industria del país, es razón suficiente para explicar aquella costumbre.   En cuanto á la cuaresma, su elección para las compras se debe exclusivamente á razones de orden religioso; luego viene la estación de las lluvias durante la cual el trasporte por el interior es difícil y los medios de comunicación quedan reducidos á malos senderos sin puentes, por los cuales hay que pasar los ríos, convertidos por los aguaceros en impetuosos torrentes.   Fuera de estas dos estaciones, la corriente de los negocios no ofrece mayor actividad; y nuestros exportadores, á quienes van dirijidas especialmente estas observaciones, deberán tener esto presente, pues así se evitará á los importadores el tener que conservar sus existencias sin venderlas, á causa del descenso en las ventas.

El Código de Hacienda de Venezuela impone á los fabricantes deseosos de comerciar con esta República la necesidad de tomar precauciones de las cuales creo que sería útil presentar un sumario.   No deben olvidar, por ejemplo, que deben declarar en las facturas, en castellano, las mercancías embarcadas, y hacer la declaración en los términos del arancel. Tampoco deben omitir consultar de antemano la tarifa de aduana y especificar exactamente la clase á que corresponde la mercancía embarcada, á los efectos del pago de los derechos de importación. Es también esencial que se recuerde que el derecho se cobra por el peso bruto de la mercancía. Es necesario usar en el embalaje de los cargamentos, con destino á Venezuela, sólo materiales que sean al mismo tiempo resistentes y lijeros.

CONCESIONES Á FAVOR DE LOS ARTÍCULOS DE EXPORTACIÓN EN LA AMÉRICA LATINA.

Consecuente á las instrucciones dadas por el Departamento de Estado de los Estados Unidos á los varios cónsules y empleados diplomáticos en los países extranjeros, se han recibido informes relativos á subvenciones concedidas por los diversos gobiernos.

El Ministro BUCHANAN escribe de la Argentina que el único artículo exportado de la República Argentina que obtiene prima, es el azúcar. A continuación se da el extracto de las secciones 3, 4, 5, y 6 del artículo primero de la ley de contribuciones de 1897:

SECCIÓN 3. Todos los azúcares que se produzcan en el país á contar desde la fecha de la promulgación de esta ley, ó que se importen hasta el 31 de diciembre próximo, pagarán un impuesto de 6 centavos por kilógramo, que será pagado por el productor ó el importador.

SECCIÓN 4. En cambio del impuesto ya mencionado, el Ejecutivo entregará un certificado el cual dará al tenedor el derecho de exportar el 35 por ciento de los azúcares sobre los cuales haya pagado el impuesto y á recibir en cambio 12 centavos en moneda nacional por kilógramo sobre el azúcar exportado.

SECCIÓN 5. Todos los azúcares de producción nacional que existan en el país á la fecha de la promulgación de esta ley, pagarán una contribución de 1 centavo en moneda nacional por kilógramo, el cual será pagado por el tenedor, á quién se le abonarán 4 centavos por cada kilógramo que exporte, entendiéndose que la cantidad exportada no habrá de exceder del 25 por ciento de la cantidad sobre la cual haya pagado el impuesto.

SECCIÓN 6. Cuando el precio corriente del azúcar al por mayor, libre á bordo en el lugar de su producción exceda de 4 pesos en moneda nacional por cada 10 kilógramos (incluyendo el impuesto pagado) el Poder Ejecutivo suspenderá la entrega de los certificados mencionados en la sección 4.

El Ministro WILSON informa desde Chile que el Gobierno no extiende concesiones ni concede premios á ninguna clase de artículo que se produzca en el país ó que se importe con el objeto de manufacturarlo. La única protección de las industrias nacio-

Bull. No. 5——8

nales consiste en la imposición de derechos de importación sobre artículos similares á los que se fabrican en el país.

En cuanto á Colombia el Ministro HART informa desde Bogotá que no se ha expedido ningún decreto haciendo concesiones de ninguna clase á la exportación.

En el Ecuador, el Gobierno no paga ninguna clase de primas sobre los artículos exportados, directa ni indirectamente, ya sean aquellos crudos ó manufacturados. El Ministro TILLMAN informa que, por el contrario, unos cuantos de los principales productos del país tienen que pagar derechos de exportación cualquiera que sea el país de su destino.

El azúcar es el único producto de Haití sobre el cual se concede una prima de exportación, pero el chargé d'affaires ad interim, Dr. JOHN B. TERRES, escribe al Departamento de Estado que no ha habido exportaciones de aquel producto en varios años, pues la pequeña cantidad que se produce se consume en el país. El Cónsul GRIMKE informa que el Gobierno de Santo Domingo no ha hecho concesión alguna á las mercancías que se exportan.

En Nicaragua se ha impuesto un derecho de exportación de $1 oro por onza sobre el oro en lingotes, y $2 por onza sobre el oro en polvo. Mr. M. J. CLANCY hace referencia á estos impuestos en un informe dirijido al Departamento de Estado con fecha 23 de agosto de 1897.

Ni el Paraguay ni el Uruguay pagan primas sobre los productos nacionales, y ambos paises imponen una contribución sobre sus principales productos de exportación.

El Perú no concede subvenciones sobre ninguna clase de mercancías que se exporten.

FOMENTO DE LA INMIGRACIÓN EN LA AMÉRICA DEL SUR

En un artículo sobre el porvenir de la América del Sur, el corresponsal del " London Morning Post " dice que últimamente se han hecho tentativas para organizar la emigración á la América del Sur. Menciona el contrato celebrado en el mes de julio próximo pasado entre el Gobierno de Venezuela y la Sociedad de Colonización Italiana, del cual se dió cuenta en el Boletín del mes de setiembre.

A continuación, el referido corresponsal se expresa así:

En la actualidad hay negociaciones pendientes para fomentar la emigración al Brasil, y se cree que el Presidente electo, Señor de Compos Salles, trabajó con buen éxito en este sentido durante su visita á Berlin el mes pasado. La disposición conocida con el nombre de Von der Heydt, que prohibía la emigración al Brasil, ha sido prácticamente derogada. La Alemania no se opone á que sus hijos vayan á establecerse á las provincias de Sao Paulo, Rio Grande do Sul, Paraná y Santa Catarina, con tal que se les garantize completa independencia política. El Brasil mira esto, y no sin razón, como una especie de abandono de su soberanía, pero es probable que se llegue á alguna solución de la dificultad, en cuyo caso se cree que el plan adoptado se extenderá á Suiza y Austria.

La Alemania desea obtener para sus súbditos que emigren á países extranjeros privilegios que no tendrían ni en las colonias británicas ni en los Estados Unidos, y la concesión que se pide promovería una cuestión de principios. No es difícil ver que la doctrina de Monroe tendría aplicación en semejante caso. Esa famosa declaración dice que el continente americano "no debe considerarse como sujeto al establecimiento de nuevas colonias europeas," pero muchas cosas han sucedido desde que se inició la "era de buena inteligencia," y la diplomacia moderna encuentra modos de obtener concesiones de los países débiles, sin necesidad de recurrir á la política descrita por Monroe como " tendente á oprimirlos ó á dominar de otra manera sus destinos." En estos tiempos lo que buscamos son usufructos, pero el significado sustancial de las palabras no es esencialmente diferente del que tenían los antiguos términos, cesión y conquista. La cuestión es delicada y tarde ó temprano se presentará en relación con el inevitable desarrollo de la América del Sur por medio de la colonización. El hecho de que Francia, Holanda y la Gran Bretaña tienen posesiones territoriales en aquella parte de América no tiende á simplificar la controversia.

MISCELANEA COMERCIAL.

REPÚBLICA ARGENTINA.

Consejero Agrícola. Dice el periódico "The New Orleans Picayune" que el Honorable J. Sterling Morton, ex-Ministro de Agricultura de los Estados Unidos, ha sido invitado por el Presidente de la República Argentina á pasar el año entrante en aquel país como consejero del Gobierno en asuntos agrícolas y en lo relativo á la organización de un departamento de agricultura. Agrega la mencionada publicación que es posible que el Señor Morton acepte la propuesta.

BRASIL.

Se Solicitan Propuestas para Trabajos de Drenaje. El periódico "The Rio News" anuncia que el Departamento de Obras Públicas del Estado de Rio Janeiro solicita propuestas, que se recibirán hasta el 17 de abril de 1899, para el drenaje de los distritos pantanosos que quedan en las inmediaciones del lago Feia y de los ríos Macacú, Grandú, S. Joao, Macahé, Iguassú y sus tributarios.

Estadística sobre Inmigración. El año de 1897 llegaron al puerto de Rio Janeiro 44,225 inmigrantes. De este número, 22,964 recibieron ayuda ó remuneración pecunaria á fin de que se hicieran ciudadanos del Brasil, y 21,661 se naturalizaron voluntariamente. Por lo que hace al sexo, 29,634 fueron hombres y 14,621 mujeres. He aquí las nacionalidades representadas por dichos inmigrantes: italianos, 27,454; portugueses, 7,423; españoles, 7,253; alemanes, 420; rusos, 392; siriacos, 388; arménios, 219; franceses, 215; austriacos, 132; de otros países, 329. La mayor parte de estos inmigrantes se estableció en el Estado de Minas Geraes.

Exportaciones del Pará. Según datos oficiales, los artículos exportados de la provincia del Pará durante el año económico que terminó el 30 de junio de 1898, y que pagaron derechos de exportación, representaron un valor de 76,454,035 milreis. En este total están incluidos los artículos siguientes: goma elástica, 70,109,749; cacao, 4,410,315 milreis; nueces del Brasil, 1,331,387 milreis; cueros, 364,751 milreis; colapez, 193,446 milreis; plumas de garza, 103,129 milreis; cumam, 8,226 milreis; sebo, 1,626 milreis.

Las Minas de Oro de Carrapato. El "Engineering and Mining Journal" dice que una compañía se ha organizado para la explotación de las antiguas minas de oro de Carrapato, y que las acciones de dicha corporación se hallan de venta ahora en Londres y en París. El capital autorizado es de $1,875,000, de lo cual $1,500,000 se invertirá en la compra de las minas. La pertenencia comprende un área de cerca de 2,300 acres en la vecindad de la mina de San Juan del Rey. Una parte de este territorio minero fué explotada en épocas pasadas, pero hace cosa de ochenta ó cien años la abandonaron á causa de la dureza del quijo y de las inundaciones. Los métodos primitivos que en aquel entonces se usaban eran en todo punto inadecuados, y, además, el Gobierno portugués imponía derechos tan fuertes sobre la producción que ellos consumían todas las ganancias.

Mineral de Manganeso en Cambio de Rieles de Acero. Dice el periódico "The South-American Journal" que la mayor parte del mineral de manganeso exportado del Brasil ha sido enviada á los talleres de CARNEGIE en Pennsylvania. En cambio, esta casa ha desembarcado últimamente en los muelles de Rio Janeiro un gran cargamento de rieles de acero para el ferrocarril de Leopoldina.

COLOMBIA.

Producción de las Minas de Oro de Darién. La compañía conocida con el nombre de "Darién Gold Mining Co." está explotando ahora las famosas viejas minas de oro del Espíritu Santo en Darién. Estas minas fueron provistas recientemente de una planta de bomba hidráulica y otras maquinarias modernas. Se han comenzado los trabajos en el bajo nivel de las minas, debajo de las antiguas excavaciones, y se ha abierto una excelente gradería que producirá suficiente mineral para mantener en operación la máquina trituradora. La producción por el mes de agosto fué de 923 onzas de oro extraidas de 630 toneledas de material triturado, lo cual da un promedio de 1.47 onzas por tonelada.

Inscripción de Marcas de Fábrica. En el Ministerio de Hacienda se ha abierto recientemente un libro para el registro oficial de las marcas de fábrica, y estas puedan inscribirse ahora en Bogotá. Esta inscripción no se debe á ninguna ley especial sobre la materia ó á ningún decreto del Ejecutivo, sino que es el resultado de una orden del Ministerio de Hacienda que de esta suerte facilita á los propietarios de marcas de fábrica la manera de obtener una prueba oficial de la propiedad de sus marcas, hasta que el Congreso vote una ley sobre la materia. Esta ley está ahora en proyecto y se espera que se vote en la próxima sesión del Congreso.

HAWAII.

Ganancias de los Ferrocarriles. Según el periódico "The Railway Review," el principal ferrocarril de Hawaii es el "Oóhu Railway and Land Company Line," que corre de Honolulu á Waianae, por una distancia de 38.5 millas, incluyendo cambiavías. Este ferrocarril fué abierto al tráfico el 1° de julio de 1890, y desde aquella fecha sus operaciones han aumentado constantemente, tanto en lo relativo á pasajeros como á carga. En 1897 este ferrocarril transportó 85,596 pasajeros, recibiendo por esto la suma de $30,993.50 como ganancias netas, y llevó 66,430 toneladas de carga, lo cual le produjo un beneficio de $69,752.76.

PERÚ.

La Industria de Bórax. Según parece, la industria de bórax en el Perú está tomando alguna importancia. En 1896, se exportaron 7,350 toneladas, valoradas en $179,674, mientras que en 1897 se embarcaron en Mollendo 12,464 toneladas, valoradas en $303,361. Los depósitos de bórax se encuentran en el interior, como á veinte millas de Arequipa.

PARAGUAY.

Establecimento de uma Linha de Navegação. Escriben de la Asunción que una línea alemana de navegación á vapor ha sido establecida en el alto Paraguay. La compañía tiene dos vapores que comenzaron á llevar pasajeros y carga el 18 de setiembre. Se cree que tanto el comercio de exportación como el de importación de la República aumentarán, y que de esto sacarán grandes ventajas los importadores alemanes.

MÉXICO.

Nuevo Edificio para una Compañía de Tranvías. La compañía denominada "The Riter-Conley Manufacturing Company," de Pittsburg, Pennsylvania, Estados Unidos, ha celebrado un contrato con la Compañía de Tranvías de la Ciudad de

México para la construcción de una casa de maquinaria, un edificio principal y un almacén de refrigeración. Se van á necesitar como 300 toneladas de acero de construcción.

Construcción de Nuevas Líneas Férreas. Un despacho de Puebla, México, dice lo siguiente : " Se nota una actividad extraordinaria hoy por hoy en la construcción de ferrocarriles en el sur de México. Además de las nuevas líneas ya mencionadas en despachos llegados de México, hay en construcción el ferrocarril de Guadalajara á Ciudad Guzmán. Se asegura que el Gobernador del Estado de Jalisco da su apoyo á esta empresa, pues á solicitud suya, tres capitalistas subscribieron $100,000 en dinero efectivo para la construcción de esta línea. Se ha organizado una compañía de capitalistas mexicanos para construir un ferrocarril desde Córdoba, en el Estado de Veracruz, á Río Tonto, pasando por Motzerongo. La propuesta línea atravesará una rica región cafetalera. Hay un número considerable de peones trabajando en el ferrocarril de Tuxtla. Esta línea irá de Palo Harrado á Santiago Tuxtla, en el Estado de Veracruz."

Emigración de Indios. Dice un despacho de Dennison, Texas, que se sabe de buena fuente que los indios Delaware han hecho un contrato para la compra de 550,000 acres de tierra en México, y que tan pronto como terminen un arreglo con el Gobierno de los Estados Unidos y con los indios Cherokees, se trasladarán á aquel país. Se cree que muchos de los Cherokees de raza pura se irán con ellos. Los terrenos que han sido comprados están situados sobre el río Yagin, en el Estado de Sonora, y se asegura que son muy fértiles. Algunos representantes de dueños de tierras de México estuvieron últimamente entre los Cherokees.

Las Minas de Cobre de Inguran. Se anuncia que muchos ingenieros de Francia vendrán pronto á Mexico á explotar las minas de cobre de Inguran, que acaban de ser compradas por ROTHSCHILD Y MIRBAUD de Paris. El capital de la compañía será de $7,000,000, en oro. A principios del año estará terminada ya una gran parte de los trabajos preliminares, y se habrán hecho los estudios para un ferrocarril. CARLOS EISEMAN, que era antes el dueño de estas minas, conservará la mitad de la propiedad.

Servicio de Correos 1897-98. Durante el año de 1897-98 lo recibido por la Oficina General de Correos alcanzó la suma de $1,409,528 contra $1,347,162 del año anterior, existiendo un aumento de $62,366. En el año fiscal de 1894-95, último año en que el precio del franqueo era de diez centavos, la venta de timbres llegó á $1,300,905. El año pasado, con el precio del franqueo á cinco centavos, la venta alcanzó la suma de $1,309,570. Esto demuestra que á los tres años la cantidad de artículos postales distribuidos fué más del doble. Hay también un aumento de treinta y uno y cuarto por ciento en los giros postales sobre el año anterior; la suma trasmitida alcanza en su totalidad á $1,212,017.

ESTADOS UNIDOS.

Producción de Cobre y Aluminio. En el informe oficial de los recursos minerales de los Estados Unidos, publicado por la Oficina de la Inspección Geológica de los Estados Unidos, se calcula la producción de cobre de 1897 en 491,638,000 libras, valuadas en $54,080,180, cantidad ésta que representa un aumento de un 7½ por ciento sobre el año anterior. La producción de aluminio se calcula en 4,000,000 de libras contra 1,300,000 libras en el año anterior, calculándose el valor de la producción de 1897 en $1,500,000.

Los Mayores Hornos de Fundición del Mundo. Los dos hornos de fundición que piensa construir la Ohio Steel Company en Youngstown, Ohio, serán los hornos de fundición más grandes del mundo. Todas las dimensiones no se han determinado todavía, pero la chimenea será de 105 piés de altura y 23 piés de atalaje. Las estufas quedarán á un nivel inferior al de los hornos y tendrán 120 piés de altura. Se proyectan cambios radicales en el manejo de estos hornos, en cuya virtud podrá obtenerse el máximum de trabajo. Se espera que los dos hornos trabajen 1,200 toneladas de hierro al día.

Abonos de Nitrato. Dentro de poco, una compañía de California presentará en el mercado un nuevo material para abono. Esta compañía ha obtenido un extenso depósito de óxidos metálicos, cerca de Lovelock, Nevada (á sólo diez millas del ferrocarril), del cual depósito se extaerá nitrato, potasa y fosfato. Incidentalmente, la compañía pondrá en el mercado una gran cantidad de materia fertilizante.

Máquina "Weber" en Demanda. La compañía denominada "Weber Gas and Gasoline Engine Company," de Kansas City, Missouri, comunicó á esta Oficina, con fecha 20 de octubre, que acababa de despachar un carro cargado de máquinas y cabrias con destino á Nueva Zelanda. Poco tiempo antes se despachó un cargamento para el Japón, y á la fecha de la comunicación, la compañía estaba preparando un cargamento á virtud de pedido hecho por una firma del Ecuador.

Grandes Recursos Minerales. Los informes de la Oficina de Inspección Geológica de los Estados Unidos, correspondientes á 1897, que acaban de terminarse, acusan una producción total de $632,312,347 de minerales y productos minerales, entre los cuales los principales son: hierro de lupia, 9,652,680 toneladas largas (2,240 libras), valuadas en $95,122,299; plata, 53,860,000 onzas de Troy (480 granos), de un valor monetario de $69,637,172 y un valor comercial de $32,316,000; oro, 2,774,935 onzas de Troy, con un valor monetario y comercial de $57,363,000; carbón bituminoso, 147,789,992 toneladas cortas (2,000 libras), con un valor de $119,740,053; antracita de Pennsylvania, 46,814,074 toneladas largas, con un valor de $79,129,126.

VENEZUELA.

Manual de Agricultura. Se dice que el Ministro de Agricultura, Industria y Comercio ha ofrecido un premio de $400 por el mejor manual de agricultura elemental para uso en las escuelas de la República. Los tratados deberán ser remitidos al ministro, quien decidirá la competencia en febrero 28 de 1899.

Nuevo Edificio del Gobierno. La Asociación Nacional de Fabricantes ha obtenido que se abra en los Estados Unidos la subasta de un contrato para la construcción de un edificio del Gobierno en el puerto de La Guayra, Venezuela, para el uso de los inspectores de aduana. También se halla pendiente un contrato para la construcción de un mercado público en la ciudad de

Maracay, Venezuela, que habrá de costar $40,000 y la subasta para el contrato, según se dice, será abierta en este país.

Multa por Descuido en el Embalaje.   El " Venezuela Herald " cita el caso de una multa de 13,500 francos, impuestos recientemente por el Departamento de Aduana de La Guayra, sobre un cargamento de papel procedente de una casa de Boston. Esta firma había empaquetado descuidadamente 20 kilos de muestras de sobres en papel de imprenta. El resultado fué que como los sobres pagan un derecho de 20 francos por kilo y el papel 5 centavos, la aduana dispuso que todo el peso debía pagar derecho al tipo señalado para los sobres. Estos derechos ascendieron á 13,500 francos, es decir, más de 30 veces el valor del cargamento. Por mediación de la legación de los Estados Unidos en Caracas, que certificó que no se había intentado fraude alguno, el Gobierno decidió condonar la multa. Los cargadores deben tomar nota de esto y no poner en la misma caja artículos que pagan diferentes derechos.

BOLETIM MENSAL

DA

SECRETARIA DAS REPUBLICAS AMERICANAS,

UNIÃO INTERNACIONAL DAS REPUBLICAS AMERICANAS.

Vol. VI. NOVEMBRO de 1898. No. 5.

SITUAÇÃO FINANCEIRA DO CHILE.

No numero do Boletim Mensal, correspondente ao mez de Outubro, se publicou um resumo do relatorio sobre as ultimas mudanças economicas do Chile, dirigido á Secretaria de Estado pelo Honrado Henry L. Wilson, Ministro dos Estados Unidos em Santiago. A este respeito, é de interesse notar que o Senhor Don Ricardo Salas Edwards, Primeiro Secretario da Legação do Chile em Londres, tem publicado um folheto, em data de 8 de Agosto de 1898, sobre a situação economica do Chile, o qual contem detalhes interessantes acerca da renda e despeza da Republica, as mudanças occorridas nas leis de moeda, dando, além disto, informações sobre os bancos do Chile.

Outra publicação de não menos interesse sobre este assumpto é uma carta do Senhor Don Eliodoro Infante, Encarregado de Negocios do Chile nos Estados Unidos, datada de 24 de Agosto de 1898 e dirigida ao Secretario da "National Sound Money League" de Chicago, na qual estuda as condições que affectam o problema monetario do Chile e diz como segue:

Estimado Senhor: Tenho recebido sua carta de data de 11 do corrente, na qual se faz referencia ás noticias publicadas em alguns periodicos dizendo que "o Chile tem-se visto obrigado a abandonar o padrão de ouro," e deseja que a Legação do Chile lhe dè informações relativas a esta materia. Com o maior prazer apresso-me a responder-lhe.

893

O Presidente do Chile, em sua mensagem de inauguração ão Congresso no dia 1º de Junho ultimo, disse que podia ser considerada como já verificada a conversão do papel em metallico. Uma lei dada no dia 11 de Fevereiro de 1895 assim o disponha. Antes daquella data, a moeda do Chile consistia nas seguintes emissões: papel moeda nacional, $29,459,364; bilhetes do Thesouro nacional, $8,901,728; emissão dos bancos, autorisada e garantida, $20,993,330. Por conseguinte, em Janeiro de 1895 o meio circulante alcançava em sua totalidade a $59,354,422.

Em Janeiro de 1898 o Governo tinha resgatado em ouro e cancellado papel moeda nacional pela somma de $27,845,305 e bilhetes do Thesouro nacional por valor de $8,888,228. Os bancos tinham resgatado bilhetes de sua emissão por valor de $3,448,858. Si deduzirmos estas tres sommas, que alcançam em junto a $40,182,391, fica um balanço de $19,172,031 em papel moeda circulante das classes mencionadas.

O resto da moeda consistia em papel moeda nacional que não tinha sido apresentado para seu resgate, provavelmente destruido ou perdido, calculado em $1,614,059, e bilhetes do Thesouro por pagar, pela somma de $13,500. Os bilhetes de banco resgataveis em ouro alcançavam a $17,544,472, o qual dá um total de $19,172,031.

Os $40,182,391 retirados e resgatados tinham sido substituidos por moeda de ouro e de prata cunhada na casa da moeda nacional, até o dia 31 de Dezembro de 1897, de accordo com a lei de 11 de Fevereiro de 1895. A dita moeda cunhada alcançou a $45,823,358, de sorte que em Janeiro de 1898, o valor total da moeda em papel e em metallico alcançava a $64,995,389. Este total de cerca de $65,000,000 pode ser considerado por todos respeitos como moeda de ouro, pois as emissões dos bancos estavam perfeitamente garantidas por apolices do Governo depositadas no Thesouro Nacional, compromettendo-se este a pagar em ouro os bilhetes de banco, si algum delles deixasse de verifical-o.

A inquietação produzida pela questão de limites pendente entre o Chile e a Republica Argentina, deu lugar, em principios de Julho a rumores de guerra que produziram no Chile um panico economico. O ouro que circulava livremente foi recolhido e guardado, de sorte que muitos milhões foram retirados repentinamente dos bancos em que estavam depositados. No Chile ha 20 bancos particulares; não ha bancos do Estado. Seus capitaes, inclusive o fundo de reserva, alcançam a cerca de $55,000,000. Os depositos são mais de $96,000,000, emquanto que seus emprestimos ao publico excedem de $120,000,000. O metallico em caixa alcança a cerca de $17,000,000. A proporção entre o capital e os depositos—57 por cento—era sufficientemente solida, mas a proporção entre o effectivo e os depositos, 17.30 por cento, ainda que teria sido sufficiente em tempos normaes, era inadequada durante um panico. Os emprestimos feitos ao publico não eram em sua totalidade immediatamente recobraveis e não sendo possivel aos bancos resistir a repentina corrida sobre elles, pediram um mez de prazo para fazer frente a seus credores e ao mesmo tempo solicitar as medidas legaes do caso.

O mez de graça lhes foi concedido, e como era difficil obter ouro no estrangeiro, por motivo dos rumores de guerra, o Governo recebeu do Congresso a autorisação necessaria para emittir bilhetes fiduciarios com o objecto de melhorar a situação. Esta crise é de caracter inteiramente commercial, e a emissão de bilhetes por parte do Governo se effectuou com o objecto de ajudar aos bancos subministrando-lhes fundos.

A nova emissão, segundo informações particulares, será de $50,000,000, incluindo os dos bancos, que aproximadamente alcançaram a $18,000,000 garantidas pelo Estado e por apolices depositadas no Thesouro Nacional. Estes $50,000,000 são resgataveis em ouro no curso de tres annos e meio. A lei que autorisa a emissão dispõe que o Governo empregue todos os annos, a partir do dia 1º de Junho de 1899, $10,000,000 em ouro em apolices estrangeiras, com o objecto de resgatar a nova emissão no dia 1º de Janeiro de 1902. Desta sorte, no curso de tres annos e meio, terão sido empregado $35,000,000 com o objecto indicado, e, entretanto, a nova emissão adquirirá gradualmente uma base de ouro á razão de $10,000,000 em ouro por anno.

Por meio deste arranjo, a emissão adquire o caracter de moeda de ouro corrente, ainda que seja temporalmente inconvertivel. Assim, pois, a emissão de bilhetes de curso legal, baseada em uma garantia de ouro, tende a melhorar a situação. Esta emissão, segundo as informações particulares a que se tem feito referencia, se fará sómente para os bancos que deem garantia e estes pagarão um moderado juro pelo serviço. Tão logo como tenha passado o panico e a favor desta emissão se tenha recobrado a confiança, volverá a circular o ouro que hoje está enthesourado, e volverão a seu estado normal os negocios no Chile.

Do anterior, se vê que o padrão de ouro não tem sido abandonado. As serias difficuldades e os grandes sacrificios que a introducção do padrão de ouro trouxe comsigo, têm sido maiores no Chile por motivo da questão de limites pendente com a Republica Argentina. Felizmente, esta questão está em via de ser arranjada de uma maneira pacifica e definitiva. Os peritos de ambos os paizes tem concordado em reunir-se no Chile para discutir alli uma linha geral de fronteira. As differenças que surgirem deverão ser submettidas a seus respectivos governos. Si estes não puderem arranjal-as, serão submettidas immediatamente ao arbitramento do Governo de S. B. M., de accordo com o accordo de 17 de Abril de 1896.

O facto de que em 1895, o Chile emprehendeu o estabelecimento do padrão de ouro e a reassumpção de pagamentos em dinheiro, prova que deseja ardentemente a paz, que é elemento essencial para o exito de sua politica economica.

Nos mezes transcorridos desde que esta carta foi escripta, a solução pacifica da questão de limites entre o Chile e a Republica Argentina, que ella previa, se tem alcançado felizmente.

A linha de fronteira que será estabelecida entre os dous paizes, corre desde o parallelo 23 até o 52 de latitude meridional. Em data de 22 de Setembro do presente anno, em um protocollo subscripto pelos dous Governos, têm-se estabelecido as differenças que existem entre elles a respeito da dita linha desde o parallelo 27 até o parallelo 52 de latitude meridional, e tem-se estipulado a obrigação de submettel-as á decisão, arbitral do Governo de Sua Magestade Britannica. Os commissarios nomeados por um e outro paiz para represental-os perante o arbitro foram já designados e se encontram em caminho para Londres.

Em dous protocollos firmados por ambos os Governos no dia 2 do corrente mez (Novembro) tem-se concordado em submetter as differenças que se têm suscitada na demarcação da linha de fronteira entre os parallelos 23 e 27 de latitude meridional, á decisão de uma commissão composta de cinco delegados chilenos e argentinos, que deverão reunir-se em Buenos Aires no curso deste mez, e tem-se estipulado, assim mesmo, que em caso de que a dita commissão não chegar a um accordo, as mencionadas differenças serão submettidas á decisão final de uma Junta composta de um cidadão chileno, um argentino e o Senhor BUCHANAN, Enviado Extraordinario e Ministro Plenipotenciario dos Estados Unidos da America na Republica Argentina, Junta que deverá funccionar igualmente em Buenos Aires e dar sua decisão em Novembro.

Com esta solução tem-se restabelecido totalmente a tranquilidade em ambos-os paizes e o Governo do Chile tem iniciado o desarme, segundo o annuncia a imprensa, reduzindo seu exercito regular. Os orçamentos de guerra e marinha serão reduzidos consideravelmente, a industria e o comercio serão desenvolvidos e os excedentes do orçamento de Chile volverão a ser o que antes eram, de mais de $10,000,000 ouro, annualmente.

DIRECTOR PROVISORIO DA SECRETARIA.

A Commissão Executiva da União Internacional das Republicas Americanas reuniu-se no salão diplomatico da Secretaria de Estado, no dia 26 de Outubro de 1898, ás 11 da manhã. Estiveram presentes:

O Secretario de Estado, o Honrado JOHN HAY, Presidente.
O Senhor ANDRADE, Ministro de Venezuela.
O Senhor MEROU, Ministro da Republica Argentina.

O objecto da reunião foi tomar em consideração o assumpto da nomeação de um Director para a Secretaria das Republicas

Americanas, porque o periodo provisorio do Senhor FREDERIC EMORY, como Director, terminava no dia 1° de Novembro. Em vista da condição satisfactoria da Secretaria e dos progressos que ultimamente têm-se feito, a Commissão resolveu que o Senhor EMORY continue no posto de Director, emquanto não se tome outra disposição. O Senhor CALVO, Ministro de Costa Rica e membro da Commissão, não poude comparecer e dirigiu uma carta manifestando seus desejos de que o Senhor EMORY continuasse em seu posto. Não se fixou termo definitivo, mas se entende que as cousas seguirão como até agora, emquanto que o requeiram os interesses da Secretaria, pois a actual administração da mesma conta com o apoio unanime dos representantes dos paizes latino-americanos, assim como com a approvação da Secretaria de Estado. O Senhor EMORY, que é o chefe da Repartição de Commercio Estrangeiro da Secretaria de Estado, tem tido a seu cargo a Secretaria das Republicas Americanas desde o fallecimento de seu predecessor, o Senhor JOSEPH P. SMITH, no dia 5 de Fevereiro ultimo. Emquanto que continue servindo como Director provisorio, o Senhor EMORY terá a seu cargo, como até agora, a Repartição de Commercio Estrangeiro, que se occupa na publicação dos Relatorios commerciaes que enviam os empregados diplomaticos e consulares á Secretaria de Estado.

A SECRETARIA DAS REPUBLICAS AMERICANAS NA EXPOSIÇÃO TRANS-MISSISSIPPIANA E INTERNACIONAL DE OMAHA.

A Exposição Internacional celebrada em Omaha, Nebraska, desde o dia 1° de Junho até 31 de Outubro de 1898, teve interesse especial em quanto ás nações latino-americanas, pois offerecem a occasião propicia para fazer conhecer os productos e recursos daquelles paizes nos mercados dos Estados Unidos. A Secretaria das Republicas Americanas comprehendeu bem a importancia desta exhibição, e por ser o centro official de informação sobre o commercio, a producção, a industria e o progreso material das republicas que formam a instituição conhecida com o nome de

União Internacional das Republicas Americanas, se fizeram os devidos arranjos para que em virtude de sua exhibição ficasse demonstrado aquelle facto, e para chamar ao mesmo tempo uma attenção mais detida para as possibilidades commerciaes e industriaes do Mexico, America Central, America do Sul e as Antilhas por meio da distribuição de boletins e circulares sobre a materia.

Publica-se em seguida o relatorio do representante da Secretaria, o qual mostra os beneficios de presente e em perspectiva que se devem á exhibição:

OMAHA, NEBRASKA, *31 de Outubro de 1898.*

DIRECTOR DA SECRETARIA DAS REPUBLICAS AMERICANAS:

Junto apresento meu relatorio relativo aos trabalhos levados a cabo pela Secretaria das Republicas Americanas na Exposição Trans-mississippiana. A posição occupada pela Secretaria foi excellente. Estava situada no sobrado principal do edificio das Artes Liberaes, ao lado do Muséu Commercial de Philadelphia, e attrahiu attenção universal. Os artigos exhibidos foram postos em ordem pelo Sr. JOHN M. BIDDLE, a cujo cargo estava a exhibição da Secretaria de Estado. A artistica colgadura das bandeiras das Republicas Americanas, a appropriada collocação de numerosos quadros illustrativos de paisagens sul-americanas, os formosos moveis e bellas palmas produziam um effeito não superado por nenhuma outra das exhibições da Exposição. As pessoas intelligentes que visitaram a Exposição mostraram grande interesse pela Secretaria e seus trabalhos.

A estreita proximidade do Muséu Commercial com muitas caixas cheias de productos americanos assim como amostras de generos manufacturados na Inglaterra, offereciam uma especie de lição objectiva ás pessoas realmente interessadas nos propositos da Secretaria das Republicas Americanas.

Têm-se distribuido 2,100 numeros do BOLETIM MENSAL da Secretaria e têm-se deixado consignadas os endereços e occupações daquelles a quem têm sido remettidos. Como se pode suppôr, tratando-se desta região agricola, os agricultores figuram os primeiros no registro e em segundo lugar os mestres. Cada Estado e Territorio da União incluindo Alaska, com excepção de New Hampshire, Vermont, Rhode Island, Delaware, e South Carolina, têm registrado seus representantes, com Iowa á cabeça e Nebraska em segundo lugar. Guatemala, Nicaragua, Mexico, e França constituem os endereços estrangeiros. Aos fabricantes registrados tenho remettido varios numeros do BOLETIM, esperando desta sorte a augmentar seus desejos pelo estabelecimento do commercio com a America do Sul. Têm-se recebido muitas cartas de pessoas a quem têm-se remettido o BOLETIM, nas quaes faz referencia ao beneficio que têm derivado de sua leitura. A Exposição Trans-mississippiana tem obtido um grande exito e este exito tem consistido maiormente em mostrar ao povo americano o mechanismo dos differentes ministerios da mais grande das Republicas da America.

Em seguida se publica uma lista das occupações daquelles a quem se enviaram

BOLETINS por correio. Os outros numeros foram tomados pelos interessados em pessoa:

Agricultores 175
Mestres 170
Commerciantes 85
Redactores e Editores. 80
Advogados 70
Estudantes. 60
Corretores 35
Banqueiros 30
Directores de Companhias de Estradas de Ferro. 30
Medicos. 27
Ministros. 25
Fabricantes Importadores. 18
Empregados 18
Agentes 18

Aos architectos, guardas-livros, compiladores de estatisticas, dentistas, missionarios e a todas as demais profissões, se remetteram tambem BOLETINS em numero de 1 a 15 a cada uma dellas.

O numero de inscripções por Estado é o seguinte:

Iowa 331
Nebraska 318
Missouri. 139
Kansas 138
Illinois. 69
South Dakota 40
Ohio 30
Minnesota 28
Wisconsin. 25
Washington. 15
Indiana. 13
Pennsylvania 13

Os outros estados tiveram menos representantes.

REPUBLICA ARGENTINA.

PRIMEIRA ADMINISTRAÇÃO DO GENERAL ROCA.

No BOLETIM correspondente ao mez de Outubro de 1898, se deu conta de um telegramma recebido do Ministro BUCHANAN em Buenos Aires, no qual annunciava que o General Don JULIO ROCA tinha tomado posse do cargo de Presidente da Republica Argentina. Esta noticia é supplementada por uma communicação recebida da Legação argentina em Washington, em forma de extracto que foi tomado de um artigo de "Il Corriere Mercantile" de Genoa, com detalhes relativos á vida e trabalhos do novo presidente.

O Géneral Roca nasceu em Tucuman em Julho de 1843 e recebeu sua educação em seu paiz natal primeiramente e mais tarde no Collegio Nacional do Uruguay. Serviu com distincção no exercito do Uruguay na occasião de uma revolução que teve lugar naquelle paiz e durante o serviço militar de seu paiz passou com distincção, successivamente, do gráo de tenente ao de general, o qual recebeu na batalha de Santa Rosa em Dezembro de 1894, em reconhecimento de sua bravura. Serviu subsequentemente os cargos de chefe de frontiera em Cordoba, San Luis e Mendoza e de Ministro da Guerra e Marinha. Em 1880 foi nomeado tenente general e finalmente no dia 12 de Outubro do mesmo anno Presidente da Republica. Sua primeira administração se distinguiu por um tratado de limites com o Chile e á virtude do impulso dado á immigração estrangeira durante o periodo de seu governo obteve grande desenvolvimento a riqueza do paiz.

Si se comparam as estatisticas, pode-se ver facilmente o progresso do paiz durante esta administração. De 1880 a 1886 a população augmentou mais de 33 por cento, emquanto que a immigração annual se triplicou chegando até 100,000 immigrantes em um anno. O commercio exterior augmentou 80 por cento, sendo no valor de $520,000,000 em 1880 e $955,000,000 em 1886. A tonelagem de embarques foi triplicada; a extensão de linha ferrea construida tambem se triplicou, pois era de 2,300 kilogrammas em 1880 e 6,400 em 1886. A area de cultivo augmentou de 1,120,000 a 1,920,000 geiras e a circulação monetaria e credito geral do paiz augmentou grandemente.

Parte do tempo depois de sua retirada do cargo de Presidente em 1886, o Presidente Roca esteve viajando no estrangeiro e entra agora no desempenho dos deveres de sua segunda administração completamente imbuido das modernas ideas de progresso para o adiantamento de seu paiz e o desenvolvimento de seus illimitados recursos.

DESTRUIÇÃO DOS GAFANHOTOS.

O periodico "The Farm Implement News" diz que a commissão central para a extincção dos gafanhotos na Republica

Argentina tem apresentado um relatorio muito interessante ao Ministro da Agricultura daquella Republica. A commissão foi nomeada com o objecto de obter todas as informações possiveis a respeito deste insecto, sua procedencia, procreação, habitos migratorios, etc., e afim de fazer os esforços necessarios para sua extincção. Para obter este resultado, a commissão organisou outras commissões locaes, e estas ultimas estabeleceram sub-commissões, e todas dedicaram-se a estudar os meios que pareciam mais effectivos para a destruição do gafanhoto, os quaes foram adoptados. Os habitos deste insecto foram bem estudados e se destruiram enormes quantidades de ovos, o qual fez que fosse menor o damno soffrido pelas colheitas.

Empregaram-se como meios de destruição uma preparação feita de zinco, varios extirpadores liquidos, o arado e o fogo. Calcula-se que a quantidade de gafanhotos destruida neste anno representa milhares de toneladas, e que as plantações que se têm salvado dos estragos do insecto cobrem centenas de milhares de geiras de terra. Crê-se que si, depois do que se tem descoberto acerca do gafanhoto, os esforços para destruil-o continuam com actividade, será muito menor o damno causado ás colheitas. A destruição do gafanhoto, já seja pelos meios mencionados ou por outros, tem servido de estimulo aos agricultores da Republica Argentina e tem melhorado as condições geraes da agricultura. Segundo as ultimas informações, parece que as proximas colheitas serão muito abundantes. Tem-se dado novo impulso aos negocios e se espera o restabelecimento da prosperidade nacional. Que a condição geral da Republica Argentina tem melhorado muito neste anno se evidencia pelo facto de que a importação de machinas e vehiculos para a agricultura tem sido muito maior do que no anno passado. Em Agosto deste anno se importaram tres vezes mais de machinas agricolas que no mesmo mez em 1897.

IMPORTAÇÃO DE APPARELHOS ELECTRICOS.

Segundo as estatisticas officiaes subministradas pelas alfandegas da Republica durante o primeiro semestre de 1898, a electricidade como força motriz e para a illuminação tem augmentado muito em toda a Republica. As importações totaes de apparelhos e accessorios para a electricidade durante o periodo mencionado, avaliadas em ouro, apparecem no quadro seguinte :

Artigos.	Quantidade.	Valor.
Arame de ferro galvanisado ... .toneladas..	9, 253	$589. 115
Cabos, arames, etc ....id....	2, 090	524, 081
Material para luz electrica..................................	... .	191, 565
Accessorios para luz electrica ....toneladas..	38	55, 791
Dynamos.......	38	28, 005
Lampadas incandescentes. ....duzias..	4, 456	13, 398
Material para telegraphos..................................	....	11. 298
Material para telephonos..................................	....	4. 533
Phonographos	....	3. 200
Total	....	1, 420, 986

A maior parte destes effeitos foram comprados nos Estados Unidos.

COMMERCIO ESTRANGEIRO EM 1898.

O Director Geral de Estatistica em Buenos Aires tem publicado um relatorio sobre o commercio estrangeiro da Republica durante os primeiros sete mezes do anno corrente. Segundo os algarismos officiaes o valor total das importações, com excepção de metallico e moeda cunhada, alcançou a $49,553,375 em ouro, o que mostra uma diminuição de $150,404 comparado com o mesmo periodo em 1897.

Durante a mesma epocha as exportações, sem contar o metallico e moeda cunhada, se calcularam em $81,632,825 em ouro, o que indica um augmento de $17,594,290, quedando assim um balanço a favor do commercio da Argentina pela somma de $32,079,450 em seis mezes.

O estado da importação e exportação de metallico e moeda cunhada é muito satisfactorio, pois augmentou aquella em $1,162,855 ao passo que esta diminuiu em $1,075,240, si se comparam com o correspondente periodo de 1897.

BRAZIL.

COMMUNICAÇÃO POR VAPOR COM RIO DE JANEIRO.

O Consul-Geral SEEGER tem remettido do Rio de Janeiro uma lista das companhias de navegação cujos vapores tocam naquelle porto. Tambem remetteu uma lista dos direitos de porto e um extracto dos regulamentos que regem nos portos daquelle paiz. Diz que, devido ás fluctuações nos preços dos fretes, as companhias não publicam listas sobre este particular, e accrescenta que varias linhas das que fazem viagens aos Estados Unidos têm concordado em adoptar uma tarifa uniforme de fretes para o café que transportam de Santos e do Rio de Janeiro aos Estados Unidos. Até ultimamente, cobravam 40 centavos por cada sacco de 60 kilogrammas. Depois reduziram o preço a 15 centavos, e durante as ultimas duas semanas têm cobrado 10 centavos.

Na data em que o Sr. Seeger escreveu sua communicação, 16 de Setembro de 1898, as companhias de navegação, suas nacionalidades e bandeiras eram como segue:

Linhas de vapor.	Nacionalidade.	Agencia principal.	Data de sahida.	Destino.
Lamport & Holt	Ingleza	Liverpool	Cada 15 dias.	Nova York, Nova Orleans.
Prince	id	Newcastle-on-Tyne.	id	Nova York.
Norton	id	Liverpool	id	Id.
Sloman	Allemã	Hamburgo	Mensalmente	Id.
Chargeurs-Reunis	Franceza	Havre	id	Nova Orleans.
LINHAS COSTEIRAS.				
Lloyd Brazileira	Braziliense	Rio de Janeiro	Semanalmente	Portos do norte e do sul do Brazil.
Navegação Costeira Lage Irmãos.	id	id	id	Id.
Esperança Maritima	id	id	id	Id.
Espírito Santence de Navegação a Vapor.	id	id	id	Id.
Companhia Pernambucana de Navegação.	id	Recife	id	Id.
São Ivão da Barra e Campos.	id	São Ivão da Barra.	id	Id.
Viação do Brazil	id	Rio de Janeiro	id	Rio São Francisco e seus affluentes.

Os direitos de porto são os seguintes: de pharol, 100 milreis ou £11-5 em ouro; de hospital, 1,920 milreis por cada individuo da tripulação, incluindo os officiaes, e além disto 18 milreis por cada barco: direitos de entrada, 9,800 milreis; direito de sello sobre a exportação, 4 e 10 por cento. Estes direitos com excepção dos de pharol, se pagam em papel moeda. O milreis de papel equivale a 15 centavos em moeda dos Estados Unidos.

Os regulamentos de porto são os seguintes: toda embarcação ao entrar ao porto, deve esperar a visita dos empregados da saude e da alfandega, os quaes examinarão as patentes de saude dadas pelos consules brazileiros no estrangeiro, e receberão os manifestos consulares e outros papeis relativos ao carregamento da embarcação. Si tudo estiver em ordem, o capitão pode continuar sua viagem até o lugar de atracação e alli dar principio á descarga do navio, tão logo que estiverem promptos todos os papeis da alfandega. Os vapores que pertencem a linhas regulares podem começar a carregar ou descarregar logo que os inspectores tiverem declarado que os papeis dos ditos barcos estão em ordem, e sem necessidade de esperar que estejam promptos os documentos da alfandega. No inverno (desde Abril até Novembro) os barcos podem carregar e descarregar ao longo dos molhes e armazens. A carga ordinaria se desembarca quasi sempre por meio de lanchões que a levam a alfandega ou aos trapiches. Os artigos de grande volume são desembarcados directamente na costa durante o inverno. O café é levado em lanchões a bordo dos vapores.

IMPORTAÇÃO DE CEREAES NO RIO DE JANEIRO.

Segundo o " Handels Zeitung," as importações de trigo no Rio de Janeiro em 1897 foram de 39,402 barris menos que no anno anterior, é dizer, 336,533 barris em 1897 contra 375,935 em 1896. A principal diminuição occorreu em farinha hungara que, não obstante a excellencia de sua qualidade, só se emprega para mesclal-a com outras por causa da alta de seu preço nos portos do Brazil. As estatisticas mostram que as importações do anno passado foram como segue: dos Estados Unidos, 252,991 barris; do Rio da Prata, 65,697 barris; de Liverpool, 9,850 barris; de Trieste e Fiume, 4,395, e do Chile, 3,000 barris, o qual faz um total de 336,533 barris importados durante o anno. A diminuição nas importações de farelo em 1897 se deve aos activos trabalhos dos moinhos inglezes e brazileiros no Rio de Janeiro. O total das importações deste artigo durante o anno chegou a 10,107 saccos de 40 kilogrammas, do Rio da Prata, contra 62,374 saccos em 1896, ou uma differença de 52,267 saccos, o qual faz muita honra á empreza brazileira. No anno passado as importações de macarrão, aletria e outros productos semelhantes diminuiram notavelmente, mais ainda que nos annos anteriores; em 1896 se importaram da Italia 7,941 caixas, emquanto que em 1895 só se receberam 1,227 da mesma procedencia. Não ha duvida que isto se deve á perfeição a que têm chegado os productos das fabricas do paiz e é quasi certo que dentro de pouco tempo cessarão por completo as importações deste artigo ao Brazil. O milho importado é todo de procedencia do Rio da Prata. O milho soffreu tambem diminuição em 1897 comparado com o anno anterior, calculada em 242,450 saccos de 62 kilogrammas, pois as importações alcançaram no dito anno a 1,254,097 saccos contra 1,496,656 em 1896. Quanto ás importações de arroz, as da Europa augmentaram, emquanto que diminuiram as da India. O numero total de saccos que se importou no Rio de Janeiro foi de 9,237,277 saccos de 60 kilogrammas contra 1,240,833 saccos em 1896, ou uma differença de 3,556 saccos. As importações de 1897 constaram de 134,359 saccos da Europa e 1,102,918 da India.

PRODUCÇÃO DE CARVÕES.

O Sr. Furniss, Consul americano em Bahia, remetteu á Secretaria de Estado copia de uma communicação, resposta a um correpondente de Nova York, sobre a industria dos carvões. Na dita communicação diz o Consul que o Estado da Bahia é o unico em que existe a industria dos carvões, que se têm encontrado no Brazil desde ha muitos annos, mas que não têm tido mercado até o principio da presente decada, quando por causa de sua dureza foram solicitados pelos fabricantes dos chamados furadores com ponta de diamante. Por ter augmentado a demanda e por ser insufficiente a producção, os preços tiveram uma alta.

Encontram-se as pedras de carvão no interior do Estado numa região á qual se chega depois de uma viagem longa e cançada, partindo da Bahia por embarcação até São Felix, e d'alli por via ferrea até Bandeira de Mello, que é o limite da região dos diamantes em cujos arredores se encontram sempre estes carvões. O territorio que produz maior quantidade delles está mais arriba do rio Paragassu e para chegar a elle tem de viajar por terra á costa de mula, durante dous dias por um caminho quebrado e montanhoso. Cré-se que se possam encontrar carvões e diamantes em toda esta secção, mas por causa do methodo empregado para conseguil-o, sómente se exploram o leito do Paragassu e seu affluente o São Antonio e a cadeia de montanhas chamada Serra das Lavras Diamantinas. Encontram-se os carvões numa especie de areia grossa chamada cascalho, no leito do rio, debaixo da lama e sobre a camada de argilla; nas montanhas debaixo de uma camada de rocha e sobre o mesmo leito de argilla, e nos arredores destes debaixo de varias camadas de terra.

Para extrahir os carvões que estão no leito do rio se escolhe um logar de não mais de 20 pés de profundidade, onde a corrente não é demasiado rapida. Planta-se alli um longo páu por onde baixam os indigenas, levando comsigo um sacco que se mantem aberto por meio de uma argola. Em primeiro logar tiram para fóra a lama e depois enchem o sacco de cascalho até que chegar á camada de argilla. Quando está cheio o sacco, faz-se elevar e se conduz para a terra onde se vazia em um lugar a onde não chegam as aguas do rio. Continua-se esta operação diariamente, durante os seis mezes da estação secca. Ao principio da estação chuvosa, quando se tem de suspender este trabalho necessariamente, se lava essa areia e se examina em busca de carvões e diamantes. Os mergulhadores são muito habeis e muitos delles podem manter-se debaixo da agua por um minuto e ainda até minuto e meio. A areia exposta na terra fica cuberta outra vez de lama, sendo necessario limpal-a, o que poderia evitar-se com o emprego de methodos mais modernos. Nos logares em que o leito do rio é muito profundo não se podem fazer explorações algumas.

O outro methodo que se emprega para excavar os carvões consiste em perforar as rochas da montanha, tirando a areia em que se encontram os diamantes e os carvões por meio de tunneis. Accumula-se essa areia durante a estação secca e se lava na estação chuvosa por meio da agua que se faz baixar por meio de represas. Encontra-se maior numero de carvões nas montanhas que no rio por serem mais accessiveis. Faz-se a exploração deste producto sómente nas margens dos rios, e ainda assim pouco se consegue porque a agua entra tão prompto como se tem chegado ao cascalho carbonifero. E com os apparelhos primitivos que usam os indigenas não podem removel-a tão rapidamente como se faz necessario para que a operação dê resultados. A falta de agua para lavar a areia é a causa por que não se fazem explorações em outras localidades. Parece que os indigenas nunca têm empregado machinas modernas para effectuar este trabalho, já seja porque não sabem onde se encontrem ou porque lhes falta capital sufficiente para compral-as.

Os carvões variam em tamanho de um grão de areia até um de 955 quilates de peso. Este grande carvão foi descoberto em 1894 em um caminho em que a formação estava exposta, e foi vendido em Paris por 100,000 francos. Os tamanhos mais uteis e valiosos são os dos carvões que pesam de um a tres quilates, porque os mais largos têm de ser quebrados, causando assim uma grande perda, pois não têm linha de fractura. Por esta razão o carvão mencionado, depois de ter sido reduzido a pedaços que se pudessem vender, produziu muito menos do que se pagou por elle. Ha dous annos que se formou aqui uma sociedade para conservar os preços altos, mas o promotor principal quebrou e desde então não se tem tratado outra vez de entrar em novas combinações. O preço que rege hoje se deve unicamente á grande demanda, á escassez de producto e á difficuldade de sua exploração. A pequena existencia que ha na actualidade se attribue aos methodos primitivos empregados na exploração. Frequentemente succede que dous trabalhadores obtém sómente tres ou quatro carvões como resultado de seus seis mezes de trabalho e pelos quaes esperam receber muito bons preços.

Os exportadores do producto têm suas casas de commercio em Bahia, e seus agentes na região mineira, mas como os mineiros têm sempre conhecimento dos preços, resulta que os exportadores estão reduzidos a desempenhar o papel de meros commissarios. O Consul FURNISS diz que o exportador em maior escala de Bahia é THEOPHILO GOMES DE MATTOS, Rua Cons. Dantes. Segundo informações, no mez de Julho se dizia que tinha 125 quilates de carvões de bons tamanhos sortidos. O Senhor GOMES DE MATTOS está disposto a enviar carvões aos Estados Unidos aos mesmos preços e nas condições que o faz á Europa e diz que nunca tem vendido aos commerciantes dos Estados Unidos porque estes insistem em comprar tamanhos especiaes; que elle não pode vender pedras escolhidas, excepto em lotes como as compra, que são os tamanhos que sempre têm demanda. O preço na actualidade é approximadamente de $5 por grão, ou $22.50 por quilate, mas o preço fluctua segundo as necessidades do mercado e as existencias. Outra casa de Bahia é a de FRANCISCO DE MELLO & Co., Rua Cons. Dantes. Pode-se dirigir-lhes correspondencia em portuguez ou francez, e á primeira casa mencionada se lhe pode escrever tambem em allemão.

CHILI.

MINAS DE CARVÃO NO FUNDO DO MAR.

O Sr. FRANK G. CARPENTER, em uma de suas cartas escriptas da America do Sul, por onde está fazendo uma viagem de observação, dá uma descripção das minas de carvão do Chile, as quaes foram descobertas em 1855. Elle diz:

Estas minas são muito interessantes; são differentes das minas dos Estados Unidos e mais difficeis de explorar em muitos respeitos. O veio de carvão que em sua melhor parte é de cinco pés de espessura, começa na margem e estende-se por baixo das aguas do oceano Pacifico. A rocha que o cobre é de ardosia tão compacta que por ella não filtra a agua. As galerias são tão limpas que se pode caminhar por ellas sem que se suje o vestido. A exploração se leva a cabo por meio da melhor classe de machinas, e durante minha visita a estas minas, observei varios adiantamentos. Imagine-se, por exemplo, uma viagem em via ferrea electrica de trolley, com um trem carregado de carvão, atravez de um tunnel de mais de uma milha de comprimento, debaixo do oceano Pacifico, a uma velocidade de vinte milhas por hora; imaginem-se minas illuminadas pela electricidade formando uma catacumba de corredores e camaras sob as aguas; imagine-se que por em cima destas minas fluctuam vapores de grandes dimensões e que o carvão que se extrahe daquellas é embarcado nelles; imaginem-se mineiros encarvoados, meio desnudos, extrahindo o carvão e carregando os carros; e imagine-se, por ultimo, o trem conduzindo vinte e sete toneladas de carvão até o elevador onde uma poderosa machina de vapor os levanta até a superficie, em lotes de quatro carros á vez, e se poderá formar uma idea das operações que têm lugar nas minas de Lota. Estas minas estão produzindo 1,000 toneladas de carvão por dia e estão empregados nellas 750 mineiros. Rendem annualmente centos de milhões de dollars e são tão bem dirigidas como qualquer das minas de carvão de nosso paiz. Perguntei qual era o salario dos mineiros e se me disse que recebiam de 90 centavos a $1 em moeda chilena, ou de 31 a 35 centavos em moeda dos Estados Unidos. Desejo saber o que opinam disto nossos mineiros de Pennsylvania. Os minerios chilenos, porem, não pagam aluguel e obtem o carvão ao custo.

COLOMBIA.

A REGIÃO AURIFERA DE DARIEN.

A região de Darien que forma a parte sudeste do Isthmo de Panamá, na Republica da Colombia, estende-se do Atlantico ao Pacifico. Foi desta região que Balboa em Setembro de 1513, em busca de ouro, descobriu o Pacifico. O extenso golfo de San Miguel está situado a umas 100 milhas ao sudeste de Panamá. O rio Tuira desemboca no Pacifico neste golfo e é navegavel por uma distancia de 50 milhas. A velocidade de sua corrente em ambas direcções faz difficil a navegação delle em chalupas, que só pode verificar-se cada seis horas, por causa da maré cuja differença entre a alta e a baixa é de 24 pés no golfo, effeitos que diminuem a 10 milhas mais arriba del Real de Santa Maria, que é o limite da navegação. Um pequeno bote de vapor, chamado o *Darien*, de 20 toneladas de capacidade para carga, faz a viagem de Panamá a Real de Santa Maria em 20 horas. Para fazer a mesma viagem as chalupas necessitam de 4 a 10 dias.

A viagem de Real a Cana, onde estão situadas as minas, tem de ser feita á costa de mula pelas montanhas e pelo rio Cupe em canoa. O caminho é muito máo e perigoso e o custo de transporte por toneladla é de $50 em moeda colombiana ou cerca de $23 em ouro americano. Em 1896, EDUARDO J. CHIBAS traçou um caminho para ser macadamisado, trabalho que está muito adiantado. Este caminho, quando for concluido, facilitará o emprego de carroças em todas as estações do anno, o qual diminuirá os fretos a um preço nominal.

Balboa obteve grande quantidade de ouro dos indios, mas não foi até um seculo depois que se tratou de explorar ouro do Isthmo. Foi então que se descobriu e começou a explorar a mina de ouro do Espirito Santo em Cana, a qual, segundo VICENTE RESTREPO, de Bogotá, produziu aos hespanhóes $30,000,000. Foi explorada com bom exito desde 1680 até 1727, quando os indios se revoltaram; cahiu uma das galerias principaes, sepultando varios trabalhadores, e os mineiros, perdendo suas esperanças, volveram á Hespanha.

Seculo e meio depois se começou a trabalhar de novo seriamente na exploração da mina, e em 1878 se organisou uma compannia em Nova York que gastou a somma de $50,000 em abrir um caminho e comprar e transportar machinas; mas abandonou-se o projecto em 1880, sem que até então tivessem começado os verdadeiros trabalhos de exploração.

Em 1888 a actual companhia foi organisada em Manchester, Inglaterra, com um capital de $1,000,000. As difficuldades com que se luctou eram quasi invenciveis, pois Cana está situado em um dos montes dos Andes a 2,000 pés sobre o nivel do mar. Em 1889 se montou uma machina de dez pilões, que durante muitos mezes deu resultados muito satisfactorios. O mineral era de inferior qualidade; á vista não se appresentavam signaes das maravilhosas riquezas e os membros da companhia quasi tinham perdido suas esperanças, quando em 1893 os mineiros por acaso encontraram os antigos trabalhos hespanhóes a 90 pés da superficie. As aguas que se tinham accumulado na antiga mina se precipitaram nas novas galerias, sendo necessario mais trabalho e mais capital para construir um tunnel para desaguar as aguas. Ao fim este tunnel foi construido e hoje a mina produz o ouro desejado. Durante os annos de 1896 e 1897 a antiga mina hespanhola deu 10,528 onças de ouro, que produziram em Londres £44,522. A rocha submettida a tratamento tem produzido pela média de 1 a 1½ onças por tonelada. Como até agora os trabalhos de exploração têm sido limitados áquella parte do mineral explorado pelos hespanhóes, espera-se que o veio virgem no qual se começa a trabalhar, produza maiores resultados. Julgando dos resultados já obtidos, parece que as esperanças dos donos da mina serão realizadas satisfactoriamente, pois têm empregado grandes sommas de dinheiro em proverem-se das machinas mais aperfeiçoadas e merecem por conseguinte o melhor exito. O Senhor CHIBAS, de cujo interessante artigo publicado no ultimo numero do "Engineering Magazine" temos obtido os dados precedentes, diz o seguinte:

A riqueza de Darien não está limitada ao ouro, pois alli abundam madeiras preciosas, exportando-se uma grande quantidade de mogno. Abunda tambem a palma que produz o marfim vegetal. A extracção da borrocha foi uma industria que deu muito bons resultados por algum tempo, mas o costume imperdoavel dos naturaes de cortar as arvores em vez de sangral-as para recolher a seiva, tem feito diminuir grandemente o producto. Não obstante esta grande destruição, não houve um dia emquanto que duraram nossos trabalhos de exploração em que não vimos arvores de borracha, que produzem tão bem naquelle lugar que sua semeada e cultivo deve ser muito remunerativo. Quando se acercava a estação das chuvas, extrahimos borracha de umas arvores que estavam cerca do acampamento e por meio de um simples processo empregado pelos naturaes fizemos impermeaveis todos os saccos de uso ordinario que usavamos para levar nossas roupas e os instrumentos de um outro acampamento com os mais satisfactorios resultados. Um vestido submettido ao mesmo tratamento resultou mais impermeavel que os importados.

MEXICO.

MENSAGEM ANNUAL DO PRESIDENTE DIAZ.

Damos os seguintes extractos da mensagem do Sr. Presidente Diaz ao abrir-se o primeiro periodo de sessões do 19° Congresso da União, no dia 16 de Setembro de 1898:

FOMENTO.

No desenvolvimento da industria nacional, occupa o primeiro lugar a mineração. O numero de titulos expedidos no periodo transcorrido desde a data de meu relatorio ascende a oitocentos trinta e sete, que comprehendem sete mil oitocentos e vinte pertenencias de um hectar. O total dos titulos expedidos de conformidade com a lei vigente de Junho de 1892 ascende a 8,313, comprehendendo uma area de 66,363 pertenencias de um hectar, o qual mostra que o numero de propriedades mineiras adquiridas em seis annos quasi é o quadruplo das que existiam ao promulgar-se a dita lei.

EXPORTAÇÃO DE MINERAES.

O desenvolvimento da industria mineira se evidencia pelo augmento da exportação de mineraes que se vem notando desde ha tempo. Segundo os dados publicados pela Secretaria da Fazenda, correspondentes ao ultimo anno fiscal, o valor total dos productos mineraes de todas as classes apresentados nas alfandegas foi de $91,250,000, em numeros redondos, o qual mostra um augmento de $10,500,000 sobre o valor da mesma exportação no anno fiscal anterior. Entre esses productos figura a prata, com um valor de $27,000,000, o ouro, com o de $16,000,000, apreciado em pesos de prata, o cobre, com o de $3,000,000, e em escala menor o antimonio, o zinco, a plombagina, o carvão de pedra, o enxofre, o asphalto, giz e alguns outros materiaes de construcção.

DESENVOLVIMENTO DA AGRICULTURA.

Tambem o estado da industria agricola está adiantado, sendo aperfeiçoados os instrumentos e os methodos de cultura e abertos novos terrenos á exploração. As boas colheitas que se obtiveram no anno passado, têm permittido exportar para a Europa productos agricolas da Mesa Central, que ascenderam a 7,150 toneladas nos mezes de Junho e Julho ultimos, das quaes 4,398 toneladas foram de trigo, 2,273 de cevada, e o resto de centeio e farinha de trigo, segundo dados subministrados á Secretaria de Fomento por uma das emprezas exportadoras.

AGUAS COMO FORÇA MOTRIZ.

É de notar-se nos ultimos annos o maior numero de pedidos para aproveitar aguas de jurisdicção federal como força motriz. Em virtude das concessões feitas pelo Governo a diversas emprezas, estão em via de construcção alguns estabelecimentos importantes de manufacturas.

TERRAS PUBLICAS.

No periodo a que se refere este relatorio, têm-se reduzido á propriedade particular 153,933 hectares de terrenos nacionaes, por concessões e vendas, compensação de demasias, compensação de gastos feitos por emprezas deslindadoras, concessões gratuitas a lavradores pobres, etc. Os terrenos vendidos têm causado a amortisação de $104,510 em titulos da divida nacional.

ESTRADAS DE FERRO.

De Abril á data, têm augmentado em mais de 314 kilometros as estradas de ferro, dos quaes 62 correspondem á Estrada de Ferro de Mexico, Cuernavaca e Pacifico; 60 á Central Mexicana em seu ramal de Jimenez a Hidalgo del Parral; 40 á Nacional Mexicana entre Patzcuaro e Urupam, 25 á Internacional em seu ramal de Reata a Monterrey, e o resto a outras linhas, entre as quaes figura a que ultimamente têm unido as capitaes de Yucatán e Campeche, união justamente celebrada nestes dias por ambos Estados. Hoje se inaugura a linha de San Juan Bautista ao Rio Gonzalez.

A rede de vias ferreas da Republica mede 12,403 kilometros, inclusos 234 kilometros setecentos metros, pertencentes ás tramvias proprias dos Estados.

Algumas emprezas têm executado ou preparado obras notaveis em suas linhas, como são a conclusão do tunnel de Dolores a Catorce, que tem dous kilometros duzentos e doze metros de comprimento, a estação definitiva da Estrada de Ferro Mexicana em Oaxaca e os planos para o estabelecimento da tracção electrica em algumas de suas linhas, apresentados pela empreza das estradas de ferro do Districto Federal.

Com motivo dos periodicos e grandes damnos que soffrem as pontes provisionaes da Estrada de ferro sobre o rio de Tehuantepec, se está levando a cabo a nova locação da via, para que cruze o dito rio em condições favoraveis, por meio de uma ponte metallica.

No periodo a que se refere este relatorio, têm sido feitas doze concessões de estradas de ferro e tres têm sido perdidas por confiscação.

LINHAS TELEGRAPHICAS.

Quatro officinas telegraphicas têm sido abertas desde o ultimo relatorio; tem-se construido uma linha entre Esperanza e Tehuacán, e têm-se incorporado na rede federal as linhas de Banamichí a Arizpe e de Teapa a Pichucalco. O serviço permanente tem sido estendido a trinta e seis povoações mais do paiz. O numero total de mensagens transmittidas no anno fiscal de 1897–98 foi de 2,086,050. No semestre de Janeiro a Junho do presente anno houve um augmento de vinte e quatro por cento respeito de igual periodo do anno passado.

Fazendo falta um mappa geral technico-administrativo da rede, se mandou construir e tem ficado terminado. Tem-se continuado a substituição do arame de ferro pelo de cobre na região oriental da Republica. O serviço interior da imprensa, que na data de meu relatorio anterior era quasi nullo, hoje é considerável, podendo dizer-se que sua existencia está assegurada. Em data de 1° de Abril ultimo foi inaugurado o serviço de lettras telegraphicas, e suas operações vão augmentando, já montando a $150,000 por mez. Quanto á questão economica dos telegraphos, seus productos que no anno fiscal de 1897–98 ascenderam a $698,000, se elevaram no que acaba de findar a $850,000.

RECEITA FEDERAL.

A receita ordinaria da Federação durante o anno fiscal de 1897–98 montou a $52,500,000, quantia que excede em mais de dous milhões o orçamento da receita para esse anno, sendo maior tambem que a importancia dos gastos autorisados pelo presupposto e os addicionaes que decretou o Congresso durante esse anno.

VALOR DAS IMPORTAÇÕES E EXPORTAÇÕES.

A seguinte estatistica das importações e exportações da República durante os ultimos quatro annos está tomada de um relatorio do Consul CARDEN dirigido á Secretaria de Relações Exteriores da Grã Bretanha. Os valores têm sido reduzidos á moeda dos Estados Unidos:

Anno.	Importacoes.	Exportações.	Excesso de exportações.
1894	$29,372,819	$42,604,621	$13,321,802
1895	35,186,444	54,910,214	19,723,770
1896	45,224,958	57,090,415	11,865,457
1897	38,107,955	62,575,319	24,467,369
Total	147,892,176	217,180,669	69,288,398

Observar-se-ha que no anno passado houve um grande augmento no excesso de exportação, mais do dobro do excesso de 1896 e uma quarta parte maior que o de 1895, que antes tinha sido o anno de maior exportação. As exportações têm augmentado 46 por cento em quatro annos, emquanto que as importações têm augmentado de 30 por cento. O estado pouco satisfactorio da importação se attribue ás abundantes colheitas, por uma parte, e a firme baixa no valor da prata, por outra. Os fabricantes de tecidos dos Estados Unidos serão interessados saber que segundo o relatorio do Consul, o desenvolvimento da industria textil na Republica não se limita ao algodão, mas que está estendendo-se tambem aos generos de linho e lã. Accrescenta o Consul que encontram bom mercado os tecidos de lã e estambre, especialmente os de qualidade superior. Outros artigos que encontram mercado são as machinas de mineração, agricultura e industria, machinas de imprimir, artigos de metal de primeira classe, e tintas.

O Consul menciona incidentalmente o excesso annual da exportação sobre a importação, respeito do qual diz o seguinte:

Dos £3,500,000, excesso annual da exportação sobre a importação, £2,700,000 constituem a importancia das remissões para o serviço da divida e as rendas das estradas de ferro; e as £800,000 restantes, mais a importancia do capital estrangeiro que tenha sido empregado no Mexico, mas não remettido em forma de especie ou mercadoria, representa o juro do capital empregado em emprezas commerciaes ou industriaes, de todas as classes, por individuos ou companhias domiciliadas no estrangeiro.

NICARAGUA.

NOVO CONTRACTO DE CANAL.

Telegrammas recebidos de Managua, Nicaragua, annunciam que o Congresso de Nicaragua ratificou o contracto de canal celebrado ultimamente entre o Governo e dous cidadãos americanos, os Senhores EYRE e CRAGIN, representantes de um syndicato de Nova York. Como existe uma concessão feita em 1887 á Companhia de Canal Maritimo de Nicaragua, o novo contracto não pode começar a vigorar antes que tenha expirado a referida concessão, o qual será em 1899. Como é bem sabido, varios projectos de lei para a construcção do canal têm sido submettidos ao Congresso dos Estados Unidos, mas o assumpto ainda está pendente. Talvez não ha uma empreza que tenha chamado tanto a attenção do mundo durante meio seculo, como a da abertura de um caminho maritimo entre o Atlantico e o Pacifico pelo Isthmo da America Central: mas nunca tem despertado este assumpto tanto interesse como agora, sobretudo nos Estados Unidos, por causa da annexação das ilhas de Hawaii, e da longa viagem que teve de fazer o couraçado *Oregon* para vir de San Francisco ás Antilhas.

A rota de canal por Nicaragua tem sido objecto de serios estudos, e tanto o Governo americano como a companhia concessionaria tem empregado neste sommas consideraveis. Tem-se escripto muito sobre o projectado canal de Nicaragua, e pode-se dizer que o assumpto está esgotado. Na construcção desta via interoceanica, seria necessario construir represas, e isto serviu de pretexto para a opposição que M. DE LESSEPS fez sempre á rota de Nicaragua, pois elle sustentava que um canal entre os dous oceanos tem de ser a nivel, como o de Suez, afim de que possa responder ás exigencias do commercio. Comtudo, os engenheiros americanos que têm feito os estudos do projecto, têm demonstrado que as represas não seriam impedimento ao enorme traffico que se faria pelo canal de Nicaragua uma vez que estivesse terminado. Além disso, depois do máo exito do projecto DE LESSEPS, os directores da empreza de Panamá têm adoptado o systema de represas como indispensaval para levar a cabo a obra.

PARAGUAY.

O CODIGO DA NOMENCLATURA COMMERCIAL ADOPTADO COMO TEXTO OFFICIAL.

O Honrado WILLIAM R. FINCH, ministro dos Estados Unidos em Montevideo, communica á Secretaria de Estado, em data de 21 de Setembro de 1898, que o Governo do Paraguay tem promulgado um decreto official adoptando o Codigo da Nomenclatura Commercial, preparado pela Secretaria das Republicas Americanas, como texto official para a designação dos artigos de commercio em hespanhol, portuguez, e inglez. Esta disposição foi dictada em consequencia da necessidade commercial de uma nomenclatura commum com outros paizes, para levar a cabo a troca de mercadorias, e no dia 2 de Setembro de 1898 se dispoz que o mencionado decreto fosse communicado, publicado e entregue no "Registro Official" sob as assignaturas do Presidente EGUISGUIZA e o Secretario GUILLERMO DE LOS RIOS.

A Secretaria do Thesouro dos Estados Unidos tinha dictado antes uma disposição semelhante com data de 22 de Janeiro de 1898, expedindo uma circular na qual se adoptava o codigo para a traducção de palavras e phrases commerciaes para o uso daquella Secretaria e para guia dos administradores e avaliadores de alfandega.

PRODUCÇÃO DE CAFÉ.

Entre os relatorios recebidos ultimamente dos consules americanos, figura um do Sr. Ruffin, Consul americano em Assumpção, no qual se trata da adaptabilidade do solo do Paraguay ao cultivo de café. Diz que ha cafezaes no Paraguay que têm sido estabelecidos por muitos annos e nunca têm sido cultivados, mas têm sido abandonados á acção do clima. Estes cafeeiros produzem uma variedade de café semelhante ao que se produz no Brazil e Bolivia, pois procedem das especies da Arabia. A producção do café não é extensa e o consumo é local. As plantações que se têm estabelecido nos ultimos annos têm dado resultados favoraveis, pois todo o café produzido tem encontrado um mercado no Paraguay. Segundo as estatisticas que o Sr. Ruffin tem podido obter, o numero dos cafeeiros na Republica é de 343,407. Crê que toda a producção pode ser vendida no mercado de Assumpção, pois os habitantes são "grandes bebedores de café."

O cafeeiro cresce melhor nos paizes que têm uma temperatura média de 68° a 78° Fahrenheit. Segundo as observações officiaes, o Paraguay tem uma temperatura de 58.42° em Junho a 84.45° em Dezembro, com uma média de 71.16°. O solo é apropriado para o cultivo, pois a terra é lhana e humida e pode ser lavrada com facilidade. Entre as differentes variedades de café a que mais se cultiva no Paraguay, segundo o Sr. Ruffin, é a "Yungas," porque procede da Bolivia, que tem quasi a mesma posição geographica e um solo de condições semelhantes. Crê-se que este café pode fazer concurrencia com o melhor que se conhece nos mercados da Europa, onde já se vende, ainda que em pequenas quantidades. Pessoas entendidas nesta industria declaram que o café que se produz no Peru e Guatemala é tão bom como qualquer das variedades que se cultivam no continente americano. O grão está bem desenvolvido e tem uma côr verde amarella. Em tamanho e peso é superior ao café de Mocha, ao qual muito se assimilha. A planta é vigorosa, se desenvolve rapidamente e dá fructo em tres annos.

MERCADO PARA OS ARTIGOS MANUFACTURADOS.

O facto de que a Republica do Paraguay está situada no valle do rio Paraná no interior do continente, sem costas proprias, faz que dependa commercialmente da Republica Argentina e do Uruguay. Mas o commercio directo com o Paraguay é reduzido e apenas ha estatistica da exportação para esta Republica, não obstante que o paiz é rico em valioso territorio e capaz de grande desenvolvimento. É provavel que suas florestas sejam as que contêm as melhores madeiras de marcenaria que se conhecem, pois se encontram nellas cerca de 150 especies de arvores valiosas.

O consumo é de importancia, ainda que um pouco limitado por razão do numero relativamente pequeno de seus habitantes. Não ha communicação maritima directa entre os Estados Unidos e o Paraguay, nem entre esta Republica e os grandes paizes exportadores. Os vapores não carregam mercadorias a pontos além de Montevideo, Buenos Aires ou Rosario, que são as cidades de importancia commercial do valle do Rio da Prata. O resultado é que os commerciantes do Paraguay, ao fazer seus pedidos de generos estrangeiros vêm-se obrigados a ordenar que as facturas vão a alguma das cidades nomeadas, a menos que tenham agentes naquelles lugares que attendam ao despacho e remissão dos generos. Isto naturalmente augmenta os preços, porque têm de fazer gastos extraordinarios por despacho e commissões. Tambem ha frequentes e grandes demoras. Como o Paraguay não acunha moeda de ouro ou de prata, depende da moeda da Republica Argentina e do Uruguay; e como na Republica Argentina a base da circulação tem soffrido fluctuações, os carregadores têm dado a preferencia a Montevideo—onde prevalece o padrão de ouro—como porto de reembarque para o trafico para o rio.

Em um relatorio dirigido ao Governo britannico por um correspondente, se chama a attenção para os seguintes artigos de commercio: Ha grande demanda de machinas de coser na Republica, de igual sorte que em toda a America do Sul; as classes mais baratas são as que mais se vendem, ainda que tambem tem encontrado sahida um grande numero de machinas de classe superior. A maior parte das que existem no mercado são de fabricação allemã. Ha grande numero de alambiques em operação, a maior parte dos quaes se importa da França. Os de tamanho pequeno que podem distillar de 50 a 200 galões por dia de 18° Cartier, são os que obtém maior demanda. Podem ser de distillação simples, continua ou semi-continua, mas devem ser o menos complicado possivel. No paiz se fabrica pouco vinho nem nenhum outro licor que a canna ou aguardente. Parece que os fabricantes inglezes fazem toda a importação de productos chimicos e instrumentos e apparelhos de cirurgia. Ha demanda de aguas mineraes em Assumpção e as grandes cidades. Poderia venderse um numero consideravel de engenhos de assucar portateis, proprios para movel-os por meio de bois. Fabrica-se uma quantidade consideravel de assucar não refinado mas em pequena escala; porem, a quantidade que se produz é insufficiente para o consumo e o resto se importa da Republica Argentina onde ha grandes fabricas de assucar, no Chaco, precisamente ao outro lado do rio, em direcção opposta ao Paraguay. Ainda que a bebida nacional do Paraguay é o matte, se consome uma grande quantidade de cha, e parece que a demanda augmenta. O cha que se importar no Paraguay deve ser de superior qualidade. Ha grande demanda de tecidos, especialmente de generos baratos de algodão. Estes ultimos são vendidos por commerciantes a retalho com muito pequena ou nenhuma utilidade, mas só o fazem para facilitar a venda de outros artigos. A concurrencia é forte neste ramo, mas as casas de commercio inglezas importam a maior parte. Vende-se grande numero de ponchos, os quaes se importam da Inglaterra. Estes ponchos são da mesma classe que os que se vendem na Republica Argentina, mas como a temperatura do inverno no Paraguay é um pouco mais quente, os ponchos de lã não obtêm aqui tanta demanda.

Chama-se a attenção para um paragrapho de Boletim de Outubro no qual se dá a noticia de ter-se estabelecido na cidade de Assumpção uma associação com o objecto de dar informações sobre todos os pontos que se referem aos productos, leis de alfandega e commercio da Republica, assim como tambem para ajudar ás pessoas que desejem entrar em relações com os exportadores e outras casas de negocios do Paraguay. Esta associação é conhecida com o nome de Centro Commercial do Paraguay.

O correspondente diz que o typo do cambio mostra um firme descenso, pois tem baixado até 10 por cento durante os ultimos mezes, com tendencia a uma baixa maior. Na actualidade o premio sobre o ouro é de 760, é dizer que o peso em bilhete do

Paraguay vale uns 13 centavos. De mais diz que a concurrencia estrangeira é muito forte no Paraguay e o numero de casas inglezas muito pequeno, emquanto que o numero das casas allemães, francezas e italianas é relativemente numeroso. As casas inglezas que tém commercio com o Paraguay fazem seus negocios por meio de agencias em Buenos Aires; ha, todavia, em Assumpção e outras povoações campo bastante para emprezas que tenham por objecto principal a exportação dos productos do paiz.

INSCRIPÇÃO DAS MARCAS DE FABRICA.

Segundo o "British Trade Journal" as pessoas que desejem registrar marcas de fabrica no Paraguay deverão solicital-o da Junta de Credito Publico em Assumpção. O privilegio se concede por dez annos e ao fim deste prazo pode renovar-se por dez annos mais. As transferencias deverão inscrever-se no mesmo registro em que consta inscripta a marca original. O pedido de inscripção deverá ser acompanhado de duas copias da marca de fabrica e a inscripção se fará por duplicado; tambem se apresentarão um recibo dos direitos ($50) pagos á Junta de Credito Publico e um poder devidamente legalisado, si o proprietario da marca de fabrica não pedir a inscripção em pessoa. O poder deverá ser assignado pelo Consul do Paraguay, e o nome do agente poderá ser deixado em branco para enchel-o mais tarde.

ESTADOS UNIDOS.

COMMERCIO COM OS PAIZES LATINO-AMERICANOS.

RELAÇÃO MENSAL DAS IMPORTAÇÕES E EXPORTAÇÕES.

O quadro dado na pagina 810 é extrahido da relação compilada por O. P. Austin, chefe da Repartição de Estatistica do Ministerio da Fazenda, mostrando o commercio entre os Estados Unidos e os paizes latino-americanos. A relação corresponde ao mez de Agosto de 1898, e é corrigida até o dia 29 de Setembro de 1898, com uma relação comparativa para o periodo correspondente do anno anterior, assim como para os oito mezes findos em Agosto de 1898, comparados com os correspondentes de 1897. Deve-se explicar que os algarismos das varias alfandegas, mostrando as importações e exportações de um só mez, são recebidos no Ministerio da Fazenda até quasi o dia 20 do mez seguinte, e perde-se algum tempo necessariamente em sua compilação e impressão. Por conseguinte, as estatisticas para o mez de Agosto, por exemplo, não são publicadas até os primeiros dias de Outubro.

NOVA LINHA DE VAPORES NO PACIFICO.

Segundo informações publicadas no "Chronicle" de San Francisco, em seu numero de 8 de Outubro, uma nova linha de vapores será estabelecida entre a cidade de San Francisco e os portos das costas de leste e de oeste da America do Sul. Chargeurs Reunis, importante companhia de vapores franceza, estabelecerá uma linha de vapores entre San Francisco, Mazatlan, Acapulco, Mexico; Guayaquil, Equador; Calláo, Peru; Valparaiso, Chile; Montevideo, Uruguay; Santos, Brazil; Liverpool, Inglaterra; Havre, França, e talvez um porto belgico. O serviço começará em Março proximo e d'aqui em diante um serviço mensal será mantido entre San Francisco e Liverpool, fazendo escalas nos portos supra mencionados.

O representante da companhia em San Francisco disse que estão em via de construcção tres vapores que se destinam ao serviço do Pacifico, cada um dos quaes é de 6,000 toneladas e tem 372 pés de comprimento.

MELHORAMENTO DA SITUAÇAO FINANCEIRA.

O seguinte quadro, compilado de estatisticas officiaes pelo "Journal of Finance," que dá a importação e exportação dos Estados Unidos durante os primeiros oito mezes dos annos designados, serve para mostrar quanto tem sido melhorada a situação financeira deste paiz em 1898, como resultado de suas operações commerciaes com os outres paizes (principalmente com os da Europa) e suas colonias:

	1898.	1897.	1896.
Mercadorias :			
Importações	$426,412,038	$546,325,777	$471,232,299
Exportações	778,674,025	641,697,330	580,930,792
Excesso das exportações	352,261,987	95,371,553	109,698,493
Ouro :			
Importações	102,087,831	11,887,654	31,902,137
Exportações	9,679,113	32,542,659	56,895,492
Excesso das importações	92,408,718		
Excesso das exportações		20,665,005	24,993,355

As exportações de mercadorias excederam ás importações em $352,261,987, emquanto que no periodo correspondente de 1897 o excesso foi de $95,271,553, ou uma differença a favor de 1898 de $256,890,234. Contra este balanço deve-se por o excesso das importações de ouro sobre as exportações deste metal que montou a $92,408,718, o qual deixa um balanço de $259,853,069, ou á razão de $346,400,000 por anno.

———

URUGUAY.

SITUAÇÃO ECONOMICA DA REPUBLICA.

O Consul SWALM escreve de Montevideo que a divida publica da Republica, em apolices e fluctuante, era de $140,000,000 em 31 de Agosto de 1898. Tambem communica que se votaram, para o sustento do Governo durante o anno fiscal de 1898–99 as seguintes sommas: Poder Legislativo, $341,114; Presidencia, $64,618; Ministerio de Relações Exteriores, $149,089; Ministerio de Governo, $2,721,659; Ministerio da Fazenda, $961,040; Ministerio do Interior, $1,127,140; Ministerio da Guerra e Marinha, $1,921,953; divida publica, $5,329,662; garantias de estradas de ferro, $884,770; pensões, $1,417,378; varios, $524,679; total, $15,434,003. Estes gastos fazem elevar a contribuição per capita a $18.24. O consul accrescenta: "A Republica mantem fielmente seu credito e não tem repudiado um só peso de sua divida."

No Uruguay se pagam direitos de exportação sobre animaes e seus productos e existe tambem um reduzido imposto sobre bilhetes, cheques, etc. É necessario obter licença para toda classe de negocios. O imposto do tabaco está baseado sobre um systema tomado do dos Estados Unidos com a differença de que cada charuto leva um sello de $\frac{1}{8}$ de centavo. Os phosphoros de cera pagam um imposto de $\frac{1}{2}$ centavo por cada caixa de 50. A cidade de Montevideo tem emittido apolices pela quantia de $6,000,000. A cidade conta com o estabelecimento da luz electrica que lhe produz uma boa renda.

PRINCIPAES ARTIGOS DE EXPORTAÇÃO.

As exportações do Uruguay estão divididas para os fins estatisticos em seis classes, das quaes a principal é a que figura sob a rubr:ca de " Salgadeiro e productos do gado." De 85 a 90 por cento da avaliação dos carregamentos fretados para paizes estrangeiros fica comprehendido sob este encabeçamento. Durante os dez ultimos annos as exportações desta classe, segundo cifras obtidas dos "Official Statistical Annals," foram no valor de $23,824,672 em 1889; $26,007,091 em 1890; $24,804,823 em 1891: $24,273,559 em 1892; $25,703,185 em 1893: $28,189,911 em 1894; $27,474,987 em 1895: $26,418,596 em 1896: $26,834,860 em 1897; e pelos seis primeiros mezes de 1898, $14,922,467.

Os productos de salgadeiro e gado dividem-se em umas 40 classes que a sua vez se subdividem ou de outra sorte se distinguem. Destas classes as principaes são: chifres, pello de cavallo, ossos e cinza de osso, xarque, carnes em conserva, extractos de carne, carne liquida, couros de boi salgados, couros de boi seccos, couros de bezerro salgados, e couros de novilho, couros de nonatos, couros seccos de cavallo, couros salgados de cavallo, pelles de carneiro, pelles de cordeiro, cascos de gado, sebo (não limpado e para cozinha), guano, lã, linguas em conserva, medulla de chifre, entranhas, tendões e nervos.

De todos estes productos o mais importante é o xarque. A maior quantidade exportada durante um anno foi de $5,719,029 em 1894. Em 1896, data das ultimas estatisticas, o valor da exportação deste producto foi de $4,561,799. Referindo-se a esta producção do Uruguay e á adaptabilidade do paiz para a producção de artigos de qualidade superiores ao xarque, o " Montevideo Times " diz o seguinte:

Reconhece-se que o Uruguay é um dos paizes que produzem melhor carne de vacca e a prova disso é o ter-se estabelecido aqui uma empreza tão importante como as fabricas de Liebig. Sem embargo, a maior parte de carne é convertida em artigo tão primitivo e detestavel como o xarque que apenas merece que se o conserve na lista dos alimentos da gente civilisada e que o comem ha sómente as classes baixas e a população negra do Brazil e de Cuba. Faz-se impossivel creer que nestes dias em que se conta com os recursos da sciencia applicada, não se possa fazer nada melhor com a esplendida carne do Uruguay, ou que não possa ser preparada em outra forma de modo que possa encontrar um mercado mais amplo e proveitoso. Na Inglaterra se consome agora grande quantidade de carne vacca importada, e o mesmo occorre em outros paizes estrangeiros; e esta importação faz-se por paizes que têm menos facilidades e vantagens que o Uruguay. Como é paiz pastoril, no Uruguay se produz não sómente carne de vacca mas tambem excellente carne de carneiro. Até o presente, sem embargo, não sabemos que se tenha tratado de utilisar a carne de carneiro como artigo de exportação, ainda que isto tem-se feito na Republica Argentina. Si o espaço o permittisse, poderiamos tratar tambem dos productos de queijeira e do gado de porco para cuja preparação para exportação o Uruguay se presta admiravelmente. O unico que falta é o espirito de empreza, ainda que crêmos que em quanto ao gado de porco existe certa antiga lei municipal que grava a matança com um. imposto exorbitante e impede assim o crescimento do que de outra sorte seria uma industria muito importante. Mas com um Governo progressivo como o presente não seria difficil obter a abolição deste imposto.

COMMERCIO DA REPUBLICA EM 1897.

O Sr. SWAIM, Consul americano em Montevideo, remetteu á Secretaria de Estado o seguinte extracto do relatorio annual do Sr. GREENFELL, Consul da Inglaterra :

O total do commercio estrangeiro da Republica em 1897 foi no valor de $49,492,305, dos quaes $20,049,980 correspondem ás importações, o qual mostra um balanço de commercio a favor do Uruguay. As rendas aduaneiras montaram a $8,175,442, ou a $2,424,558 menos que as de 1896.

A Grã Bretanha tem o monopolio da importação de presuntos, cha, generos para saccos, chapeos de feltro, pelles de carneiro, enxadas, ancinhos, machinas de debulhar, fios de costura, tubos de ferro e chumbo, carvão, chapas de ferro galvanizado para telhados, chapas de estanho, soda, juta, caixas de segurança de ferro e polvora, e occupa o primeiro lugar na importação de artigos de algodão, fazendas de linho, fazendas de lã mixta, chapeos de palha, meias curtas de linho, lenços de algodão, cobertores de algodão e lã, machinas para moinhos de vento, sulphato de cobre, pás de cavar, instrumentos de carpinteiro, barbantes, verniz, bandas de ferro, barras e chapas de ferro, tintas, porcellana, obras de selleiro e arreios.

A Allemanha tem o monopolio da importação de pianos, bacalhau salgado e secco e occupa o primeiro lugar na importação de assucar refinado, flanelas, roupa feita, fazendas de algodão e de linho para camisas, punhos e collarinhos, camisas de lã, meias curtas de algodão, mantos de lã e de lã mixta, cobertores de algodão, toalhas, guardanapos, machinas de coser, cercas de arame, amido, azul, papel de imprimir, mercearias e mobilia.

A França tem o monopolio da importação de pelles de cabrito e telhas, e occupa o primeiro lugar na importação de fazendas de lã, fazendas de seda e de seda mixta, calçado, camisas de meia de algodão, gravatas de seda, luvas de pelle, guarda-chuvas, molas para carruagens, drogas e perfumarias.

A Belgica tem o monopolio na importação de fouces, vigas e columnas de ferro, chapas de zinco e espingardas de caça ; occupa o primeiro lugar na importação de fazendas de linho mixto, cobertores, vidro comprimido, vidro para espelhos e para a mesa, cimento romano, papel branco e velas.

Os Estados Unidos têm o monopolio na importação de arados, forcados para feno e alcatrão; occupam o primeiro lugar na importação de madeiras de construcção, machinas de ceifar, barbantes de engavelar e machados, e segundo lugar em mobilia, terceiro lugar em machinas de coser e sulphato de cobre e quinto em drogas e papel de imprimir.

O Sr. SWALM informa á Secretaria que o commercio dos Estados Unidos, Allemanha e França com o Uruguay tem augmentado consideravelmente durante o anno passado com prejuizo á Inglaterra. Durante o anno corrente houve diminuição consideravel na importação de generos de algodão da Inglaterra. As fazendas de algodão e de linho para camisas foram importadas em maior quantidade da Allemanha por serem estas mais baratas. O Consul accrescenta que as machinas de coser importadas da Allemanha são inferiores ás fabricadas nos Estados Unidos.

NOVO MINISTRO DE RELAÇÕES EXTERIORES.

O Senhor Don PRUDENCIO DE MURGUIONDO, Consul Geral do Uruguay junto a este Governo, informa officialmente á Secretaria de Estado 'dos Estados Unidos que o Presidente CUESTAS tem nomeado interinamente o Senhor Don JACOBO A. VARELA para o cargo de Ministro de Relações Exteriores. Preenche a vaga occasionada pela demissão do Senhor Don DOMINGO MENDILAHARSU.

VENEZUELA.

IMPORTANCIA DO TRIBUNAL DE ARBITRAMENTO.

A reunião que logo se verificará em Pariz do Tribunal de Arbitramento Anglo-Venezuelano, e do qual são membros por Venezuela o Justiça Maior FULLER e o Magistrado BREWER do Tribunal Supremo dos Estados Unidos, é um acontecimento quasi tão importante como a reunião na mesma cidade da Commissão de Paz Hispano-Americana, pela gravidade do incidente que a questão venezuelana suscitou entre os Estados Unidos e a Grã Bretanha durante a administração de CLEVELAND, e a parte que nelle lhe correspondeu á doutrina de Monroe. O tribunal terá uma sessão preliminar em Pariz em Janeiro de 1899, á qual assistirá o Magistrado BREWER; mas não é provavel que se ache presente o Justiça Maior FULLER nessa primeira reunião, porque nessa epocha o Tribunal Sepremo estará muito occupado, e dous de seus membros não poderiam ausentar-se ao mesmo tempo. Provavelmente, o Magistrado BREWER obterá um adiamento até o mez de Maio, e nessa data ambos magistrados estarão livres para ir a juntar-se com os outros arbitros e dedicar-se aos serios trabalhos do tribunal.

Os allegados e replicas de Venezuela e da Grã Bretanha estão ja promptos. O Ministro venezuelano, Senhor ANDRADE, apresentou ultimamente á embaixada britannica em Washington a replica de Venezuela, e ao mesmo tempo a replica da Grã Bretanha foi entregue ao Doutor ROJAS, agente do Governo venezuelano em Pariz. Os documentos formam um conjuncto do mais voluminoso que se tem visto nunca em uma controversia internacional submettida ao arbitramento. O allegado e replica da Grã Bretanha constituem onze grandes volumes, um atlas e varios mappas separados, em quanto que o allegado de Venezuela compõe-se de seis volumes e tres atlas. Promptos todos estes documentos, o unico que as partes têm de fazer é apresentar seus respectivos argumentos. O de Venezuela será preparado pelo ex-Presidente dos Estados Unidos, Mr. HARRISON, pelo ex-Ministro da Marinha, Mr. TRACY, e por Mr. MALLET-PROVOST. O argumento da Grã Bretanha vai a ser apresentado pelos primeiros advogados inglezes, incluindo Sir RICHARD WEBSTER. Crê-se que o Genéral HARRISON e o Sr. TRACY estarão presentes quando o tribunal se reuna em Maio, e que farão argumentos oraes. Pelo dito, se vê que o pessoal dos advogados e o dos arbitros darão muito interesse ás sessões. O primeiro dos arbitros inglezes é o Barão HERSCHEL, antigo Lord Chanceller da Inglaterra. Associado com elle será Sir RICHARD HENN COLLINS. O quinto arbitro, que terá o caracter de terceiro em discordia, será o notavel jurisconsulto russo e escriptor de direito internacional, M. MAARTENS. Emquanto que se effectua a reunião dos arbitros, elle está encarregado de receber todos os papeis, argumentos e outros documentos.

SUGGESTÕES AOS EXPORTADORES.

M. QUIEVREUX, Consul francez em Caracas, em um relatorio dirigido recentemente a seu Governo, faz varias suggestões sobre o commercio da Republica, as quaes devem ser de importancia não sómente para seus compatriotas mas tambem para os exportadores dos Estados Unidos. Elle diz:

As compras se fazem aqui durante a quaresma e o Natal. Estas são as epocas do anno em que o consumidor de Venezuela gosta de fazer suas provisões de todas as classes. O facto de que as festas do Natal coincidem com a collecta da colheita do café, que é a principal industria do paiz, é razão sufficiente para explicar aquelle costume. Quanto á quaresma, sua eleição para as compras se deve exclusivamente a razões de ordem religiosa; logo vem a estação das chuvas durante a qual o transporte pelo interior é difficil e os meios de communicação ficam reduzidos a máos caminhos sem pontes, pelos quaes ha que passar os rios, convertidos pelos aguaceiros em impetuosas torrentes. Fora destas duas estações, a corrente dos negocios não offerece maior actividade; e nossos exportadores, a quem estão dirigidas especialmente estas observações, deverão ter isto presente, pois assim evitarão o ter de conservar suas existencias sem vendel-as, por causa da diminuição nas vendas.

O "Codigo de Hacienda" de Venezuela impõe aos fabricantes desejosos de commerciar com esta Republica a necessidade de tomar precauções das quaes creio que seria util apresentar um summario. Não devem olvidar, por exemplo, que devem declarar nas facturas, em hespanhol, as mercadorias embarcadas, e fazer a declaração nos termos da tarifa. Não devem omittir consultar de antemão a tarifa de alfandega e especificar exactamente a classe a que corresponde a mercadoria embarcada, aos effeitos dos direitos de importação. É tambem essencial que se lembre que o direito se cobra sobre o peso bruto da mercadoria. É necessario usar no enfardamento dos carregamentos com destino a Venezuela, sómente materiaes que sejam ao mesmo tempo resistentes e ligeiros.

PREMIOS DE EXPORTAÇÃO NA AMERICA LATINA.

Em consequencia das instrucções dadas pela Secretaria de Estado dos Estados Unidos aos varios consules e empregados diplomaticos nos paizes estrangeiros, tem-se recebido informações relativas a subvenções concedidas pelos diversos governos.

O Ministro BUCHANAN escreve da Republica Argentina que o unico artigo exportado da Republica que obtem premio é o assucar. Dá-se em seguida o extracto das secções 3, 4, 5 e 6 do artigo primeiro da lei de contribuições de 1897:

SECÇÃO 3. Todos os assucares que se produzirem no paiz a contar da data da promulgação desta lei, ou que se importarem até o dia 31 de Dezembro proximo, pagarão um imposto de 6 centavos por kilogramma, o qual será pago pelo productor ou importador.

SECÇÃO 4. Em troca do imposto já mencionado, o executivo entregará um certificado o qual dará ao possuidor o direito de exportar 35 por cento dos assucares sobre os quaes tenha pago o imposto e de receber em troca 12 centavos em moeda nacional por kilogramma sobre o assucar exportado.

SECÇÃO 5. Todos os assucares de producção nacional que existirem no paiz á data da promulgação desta lei pagarão uma contribuição de 1 centavo em moeda nacional por kilogramma, o qual será pago pelo possuidor, a quem far-se-ha um reembolso de 4 centavos por cada kilogramma que exportar, ficando entendido que a quantidade exportada não excederá de 25 por cento da quantidade sobre a qual tenha pago o imposto.

SECÇÃO 6. Quando o preço corrente do assucar por maior, livre a bordo no lugar de sua producção, exceder de $4 em moeda nacional por cada 10 kilo-grammas (incluindo o imposto pago), o poder executivo suspenderá a entrega dos certificados mencionados na secção 4.

O Ministro WILSON informa de Chile que o Governo não dá concessões nem concede premios a nenhuma classe de artigo que se produza no paiz ou que se importe com o objecto de manu-factural-o. A unica protecção das industrias nacionaes consiste na imposição de direitos de importação sobre artigos semelhantes aos que se fabricam no paiz.

Quanto á Republica da Colombia, o Ministro HART informa de Bogotá que não se tem expedido nenhum decreto fazendo con-cessões de nenhuma classe á exportação.

No Equador, o Governo não paga nenhuma classe de premios sobre os artigos exportados, directa nem indirectamente, já sejam elles crús ou manufacturados. O Ministro TILLMAN informa que, pelo contrario, alguns dos principaes productos do paiz têm de pagar direitos de exportação, qualquer que seja o paiz de seu destino.

O assucar é o unico producto de Haiti sobre o qual se concede um premio de exportação, mas o encarregado de negocios interino, Dr. JOHN B. TERRES, escreve á Secretaria de Estado que não têm havido exportações daquelle producto em varios annos, pois a pequena quantidade que se produz se consome no paiz. O Consul GRIMKE informa que o Governo de Santo Domingo não tem feito concessão alguma ás mercadorias que se exportam.

Em Nicaragua, tem-se imposto um direito de exportação de $1 ouro por onça sobre o ouro em linguados e $2 por onça sobre o ouro em pó. O Sr. M. J. CLANCY faz referencia a estes impostos em um relatorio dirigido á Secretaria de Estado em data de 23 de Agosto de 1897.

Nem o Paraguay nem o Uruguay pagam premios sobre os pro-ductos nacionaes, e ambos paizes impõem uma contribuição sobre seus principaes productos de exportação.

O Peru não concede subvenções sobre nenhuma classe de mercadorias que se exportem.

FOMENTO DA IMMIGRAÇÃO NA AMERICA DO SUL.

Em um artigo sobre o porvenir da America do Sul, o correspondente do "London Morning Post" diz que ultimamente têm-se feito tentativas para organisar a emigração para a America do Sul. Menciona o contracto celebrado no mez de Julho proximo passado entre o Governo de Venezuela e a Sociedade de Colonisação Italiana, do qual se deu conta no BOLETIM do mez de Setembro. Elle diz:

Na actualidade ha negociações pendentes para fomentar a emigração para o Brazil, e se crê que o Presidente eleito, Senhor de CAMPOS SALLES, trabalhou com bom exito neste sentido, durante sua visita a Berlim no mez passado. A disposição conhecida com o nome de VON DER HEYDT, que prohibia a emigração para o Brazil, tem sido practicamente revogada. A Allemanha não se oppõe a que seus filhos vão a estabelecer-se nas provincias de São Paulo, Rio Grande do Sul, Paraná e Santa Catharina, com a condição de que se lhes garanta completa independencia politica. O Brazil considera isto, e não sem razão, como uma especie de abandono de sua soberania, mas é provavel que se chegue alguma solução da difficuldade, em cujo caso se crè que o plano adoptado se estenderá á Suissa e Austria.

A Allemanha deseja obter para seus subditos, que emigrem para os paizes estrangeiros, privilegios que não teriam nem nas colonias britannicas, nem nos Estados Unidos, e a concessão que se pede promoveria uma questão de principios. Não é facil ver que a doutrina de Monroe teria applicação em semelhante caso. Essa famosa declaração diz que o continente americano "não deve ser considerado como sujeito ao estabelecimento de novas colonias europeas;" mas muitas cousas têm occorrido desde que se iniciou a "era de boa intelligencia," e a diplomacia moderna encontra modos de obter concessões dos paizes debis, sem necessidade de recorrer á politica descripta por Monroe como "tendente a opprimil-os ou a dominar de outra maneira seus destinos." Nestos tempos, o que buscamos são usufructos, mas o significado substancial das palavras não é essencialmente differente do que tinham os antigos termos, sessão e conquista. A questão é delicada e cedo ou tarde se apresentará em ralação com o inevitavel desenvolvimento da America do Sul por meio da colonisação. O facto de que a França, Hollanda e a Gra Bretanha têm possessões territoriaes naquella parte da America não tende a simplificar a controversia.

COMMERCIO MISCELLANEO.

REPUBLICA ARGENTINA.

Conselheiro Agricola. Diz o periodico "The New Orleans Picayune" que o Honrado J. STERLING MÒRTON, Ex-Ministro da Agricultura dos Estados Unidos, tem sido convidado pelo Presidente da Republica Argentina a passar o anno vindouro naquelle paiz como conselheiro do Governo em assumptos agricolas e no relativo á organisação de um ministerio de agricultura. Accrescenta a mencionada publicação que é possivel que o Senhor Morton aceite a proposta.

BRAZIL.

Solicitam-se Propostas para Trabalhos de Drenagem. O "Rio News" annuncia que o Ministerio de Obras Publicas do Estado de Rio Janeiro solicita propostas, que se receberão até o dia 17 de Abril de 1899, para a drenagem dos districtos pantanosos que estão situados nos valles do lago Feia e dos rios Macacú, Grandú, S. João, Macahé, Iguassú e seus tributarios.

Estatistica sobre Immigração. No anno de 1897 chegaram ao porto de Rio Janeiro 44,225 immigrantes. Deste numero, 22,964 receberam ajuda ou remuneração pecuniaria afim de que se fizeram cidadãos do Brazil, e 21,661 se naturalisaram voluntariamente; 29,634 foram do sexo masculino e 14,621 do sexo feminino. As nacionalidades representadas pelos immigrantes foram : italianos, 27,454 ; portuguezes, 7,423 ; hespanhóes, 7,253 ; allemães, 420 ; russos, 392 ; syriacos, 388 ; armenios, 219 ; francezes, 215 ; austriacos, 132 ; de outros paizes, 329. A maior parte destes immigrantes se estabeleceu no estado de Minas Geraes.

Exportações do Pará. Segundo dados officiaes, os artigos exportados do estado do Pará durante o anno fiscal findo em 30 de Junho de 1898, e que pagaram direitos de exportação, representaram um valor de 76,454,035 milreis. Neste total estão incluidos os artigos seguintes : borracha, 70,109,749 milreis; cacáo, 4,410,315 milreis; nozes do Brazil, 1,331,387 milreis ; couros, 364,751 milreis ; mica, 193,446 milreis ; pennas de garça, 103,129 milreis ; cumam, 8,226 milreis ; sebo, 1,626 milreis.

PARAGUAY.

Estabelecimento de Uma Linha de Navegação. Segundo informações recebidas de Assumpção, uma linha allemã de navegação a vapor foi estabelecida no alto Paraguay. A companhia tem dous vapores que começaram a levar passageiros e carga no dia 18 de Setembro. Crê-se que tanto o commercio de exportação como o de importação da Republica augmentarão e que disto receberão grandes vantagens os importadores allemães.

PERU.

A Industria de Borax. Parece que a industria de borax no Peru está tomando alguma importancia. Em 1896, se exportaram 7,350 toneladas, no valor de $179,674, emquanto que em 1897, se embarcaram em Mollendo 12,464 toneladas, no valor de $303,361. Encontram-se os depositos de borax no interior, a vinte milhas de Arequipa.

COLOMBIA.

Producção das Minas de Ouro de Darien. A companhia conhecida com o nome de Darien Gold Mining Company (anonyma) está explorando agora as famosas minas de ouro do Espirito Santo em Darien. Estas minas foram providas recentemente de bombas hydraulicas e outras machinas modernas. Têm-se começado os trabalhos no baixo nivel das minas, debaixo das antigas excavações, e tem-se aberto um excellente veio que produzirá sufficiente mineral para manter em operação a machina trituradora. A producção no mez de Agosto foi de 923 onças de ouro, extrahidas de 630 toneladas de material triturado, o qual dá uma média de 1.47 onças por tonelada.

MEXICO.

Novo Edificio para uma Companhia de Tramvias. A companhia denominada "The Ritter-Conley Manufacturing Company," de Pittsburg, Pennsylvania, tem celebrado um contracto com a Companhia de Tramvias da Cidade de Mexico, para a construcção de uma casa de machinas, um edificio principal e um armazem de refrigeração. Para estas obras necessitar-se-hão umas 300 toneladas de aço de construcção.

Construcção de Novas Linhas Ferreas. Um despacho de Puebla, Mexico, diz o seguinte. "Na actualidade se nota uma actividade extraordinaria na construcção de estradas de ferro no sul do Mexico. Além das novas linhas já mencionadas em despachos chegados de Mexico, ha em construcção a estrada de ferro de Guadalajara a Ciudad Guzmán. Diz-se que o governador do Estado de Jalisco dá seu apoio a esta empreza, pois á sua solicitude, tres capitalistas subscreveram $100,000 em dinheiro effectivo para a construcção desta linha. Tem-se organisado uma companhia de capitalistas mexicanos para construir uma estrada de ferro desde Cordoba, no Estado de Veracruz, a Rio Tonto, passando por Motzerongo. A projectada linha atravessará uma rica região productora de café. Ha um numero consideravel de trabalhadores empregados na construcção da estrada de ferro de Tuxtla. Esta linha estenderá de Palo Harrado a Santiago Tuxtla, no Estado de Veracruz."

ESTADOS UNIDOS.

Producção de Cobre e Aluminio. No relatorio official dos recursos mineraes dos Estados Unidos publicado pela Repartição da Inspecção Geologica dos Estados Unidos, se calcula a producção de cobre de 1897 em 491,-638,000 libras, no valor de $54,080,180, o qual mostra um augmento de 7½ por cento sobre o anno anterior. A producção de aluminio é calculada em 4,000,000 libras contra 1,300,000 libras no anno anterior, calculando-se o valor da producção de 1897 em $1,500,000.

Os Maiores Fornos de Fundição do Mundo. Os dous fornos de fundição que serão construidos pela "Ohio Steel Company" em Youngstown, Ohio, serão os fornos de fundição mais grandes do mundo. Todas as dimensões não tem sido determinadas ainda mas a chaminé será de 105 pés de altura. As estufas estarão a um nivel inferior ao dos fornos e terão 120 pés de altura. Projectam-se mudanças radicaes no manejo destes fornos, em cuja virtude poderá ser obtido o maximum de trabalho. Espera-se que os dous fornos trabalhem 1,200 toneladas de ferro por dia.

VENEZUELA.

Manual de Agricultura. Diz-se que o Ministro de Agricultura, Industria e Commercio tem offerecido um premio de $400 pelo melhor manual de agricultura elementar para uso nas escolas da Republica. Os tratados deverão ser remettidos ao Ministro, que decidirá a concurrencia em 28 de Fevereiro de 1899.

BULLETIN MENSUEL

DU

BUREAU DES REPUBLIQUES AMÉRICAINES,

UNION INTERNATIONALE DES RÉPUBLIQUES AMÉRICAINES.

VOL. VI. NOVEMBRE 1898. No. 5.

SITUATION FINANCIÈRE DU CHILI.

Dans l'édition du BULLETIN MENSUEL pour le mois d'octobre il a été publié un résumé du rapport de l'Hon. HENRY L. WILSON, Ministre des Etats-Unis à Santiago, au Département d'Etat, sur les changements financiers au Chili. Il est intéressant à noter concernant ce sujet qu'une brochure a été publiée par la Légation Chilienne à Londres portant la date du 8 août 1898 sur la situation financière de Chili. L'auteur de la brochure est Señor Don RICARDO SALAS EDWARDS, Premier Secrétaire de la Légation. La brochure donne des détails intéressants sur le revenu et les dépenses du Chili, les changements divers dans la législation, les espèces et des détails sur les banques du Chili.

Une autre publication de valeur sur ce sujet est une lettre de Señor Don ELIODORO INFANTE, Chargé d'Affaires du Chili aux Etats-Unis, sous date du 24 août 1898 et adressée au Secrétaire de la "National Sound Money League" à Chicago. Cette lettre qui décrit les conditions touchant le problème financier au Chili est comme suit:

CHER MONSIEUR: J'ai l'honneur d'accuser réception de votre lettre sous date du 11 du courant et dans laquelle vous faites allusion aux assertions publiées par des journaux que le "Chili a été obligé d'abandonner l'étalon d'or," et dans laquelle vous priez la Légation Chilienne de vous informer des faits actuels concernant ce sujet.

931

C'est avec le plus grand plaisir que je me rends à votre désir. Le Président de Chili a annoncé dans son message inaugural au Congrès le 1ᵉʳ du mois de juin dernier que l'on pourrait considérer le remboursement d'espèces monnayées comme un fait accompli.

Cet article fut ordonné par une loi datée le 11 février 1895. Avant cette date les espèces du Chili étaient composé des émissions suivantes :

Espèces en papier national, $29,459,364 ; billets de la Trésorerie Nationale, $8,901,728 ; émissions de banque autorisées et garanties $20,993,330. La somme totale d'espèces en circulation, en janvier, 1895 a été ainsi de $59,354,422.

En janvier 1898 le Gouvernement a remboursé en or et a fait rentrer des espèces en papier national jusqu'à concurrence de $27,845,305, ainsi que des billets de la Trésorerie Nationale, s'élevant à $3,888,228. Les banques ont remboursé $3,448,858 de leurs billets. En déduisant ces trois sommes, le total s'élève à $40,182,391, indiquant une balance de $19,172,031 en espèces en papier sur le total d'espèces en circulation. Le restant en espèces qui consistent en monnaie de papier national non présenté au remboursement et probablement détruit ou perdu s'élèvent à $1,614,069 et $13,500 en billets des émissions des banques remboursables en or s'élevaient à $17,544,472, faisant un total de $19,177,031.

Les $40,181,391 retirés et remboursés ont été remplacés en monnaie d'or et d'argent (monnaie d'argent) émise par la Monnaie Nationale jusqu'au 31 décembre 1897 d'après la loi du 11 février 1895. Ces espèces métalliques s'élevaient à $45,823,358 Les espèces totales en métal et en papier au mois de janvier 1898 s'élevaient à $64,995,389. Ce total de presque $65,000,000 a été sous tous les rapports une monnaie d'or ; comme les émissions des banques ont été entièrement garanties par les obligations du Gouvernement déposées dans la Trésorerie Nationale le Gouvernement se charge de rembourser en or les billets de banque en cas où les banques manqueraient de le faire.

La peur d'une guerre résultant de l'inquiétude produite par la prolongation de la question pendante des frontières entre le Chili et la République Argentine a occasionné une panique financière. L'or en circulation libre fut amassé et beaucoup de millions furent retirés subitement des dépôts de la banque. Il y a vingt banques au Chili. Toutes ces banques sont des établissements privés, car il n'y a pas de banque d'Etat. Leurs capitaux et leurs réserves s'élèvent à presque $55,000,000. Leurs dépôts dépassent un peu $96,000,000, tandis que leurs prêts au public dépassent $120,000,000. L'espèce en métal accessible est moins de $17,000,000. La proportion entre le capital et les dépôts, 57 pour cent, a été assez solide, mais la proportion entre l'argent comptant et les dépôts, 17.30 pour cent, bien que suffisante dans des circonstances ordinaires, a été insuffisante dans un moment de panique. Les prêts au public ne donnant à ce moment aucun bénéfice, par conséquent les banques ne purent résister à ces subites invasions. Elles ont demandé un mois pour faire face aux créanciers et pour l'aide législatif nécessaire. Un mois de grâce fut accordé. Comme il était difficile de trouver de l'or à l'étranger à cause des bruits de guerre qui couraient, le Gouvernement a été autorisé par le Congrès d'émettre des billets fiduciaires à fin d'améliorer la situation. Cette crise est entièrement commerciale et l'émission de billets par le Gouvernement est faite pour aider les banquiers en leur fournissant des espèces. La nouvelle émission, d'après des informations particulières, sera de $50,000,000, y compris les émissions des banques, s'élevant à environ $18,000,000, qui sont guaranties par l'Etat et par les obligations déposées dans la Trésorerie publique. Ces $50,000,000 en billets sont remboursables en or dans le courant de trois années et demie. La loi autorisant l'émission stipule que le Gouvernement doit placer chaque année, à partir de juin 1899, $10,000,000 d'or en stocks étrangers, dans le but de rembourser la nouvelle émission au 1er janvier 1902. Dans l'espace de trois ans et demie $35,000,000 auront ainsi été placé. Dans l'intervalle la nouvelle émission acquerra une base d'or pour la somme de $10,000,000 d'or par an.

Cet arrangement donne à l'émission, quoique pour le moment inconvertible, le caractère d'espèces en or, comme la quantité est basée entièrement sur ce métal. Cette inquiétude exceptionnelle est améliorée par l'émission d'argent en papier légal basé sur les quantités en or. Cette émission d'après les rapports particuliers, dont on a parlé, doit être faite seulement aux banques sur garanties. Elles payeront un intérêt modéré pour l'accomodement. Aussitôt que la panique sera calmée et la confiance sera rétablie par cette émission, l'or amassé va reparaitre et les affaires au Chili reprendront leur condition normale.

L'étalon d'or, comme on voit par le compte rendu ci-dessus, n'a pas été abandonné au Chili. Les difficultés sérieuses et les sacrifices que son introduction nécessairement occasionneront ont été dans le cas du Chili considérablement augmentées par la question pendante des frontières avec la République Argentine. Heureusement pour tous les intéressés, cette question est entrée, à présent, dans une voie d'arrangement pacifique. Les experts dans les deux pays ont convenu de se réunir au Chili et de discuter une ligne générale de frontière. Les différences qui peuvent se présenter entre eux doivent être soumises aux gouvernements. Si les gouvernements ne peuvent pas arriver à une solution des difficultés, elles doivent être immédiatement soumises au Gouvernement de Sa Majesté Britannique selon la convention du 17 avril 1896.

Le fait que le Chili a entrepris en 1895 l'établisement d'un étalon d'or et la reprise de paiement en espèce indiquent qu'elle désire sincèrement la paix, celle-ci étant essentielle au succès de sa politique financière.

Depuis la réception de cette lettre un arrangement amical de la question de frontière entre le Chili et la République Argentine, prédit dans la même lettre, a été heureusement terminé.

La ligne de frontière qui sera établie entre les deux pays s'étend du parallèle 23 au parallèle 52 latitude du sud. Le 22 septembre de cette année les deux gouvernements ont signé un protocole indiquant le différend existant entre eux concernant ladite ligne, entre les parallèles 27 et 52 latitude du sud, et ils ont convenu de soumettre la question au Gouvernement de Sa Majesté Britannique. Les Commissaires qui vont représenter les deux pays devant l'arbitre ont été nommés et sont en route pour Londres.

Dans les deux protocoles signés par les deux Gouvernements le 22 novembre courant, il a été convenu de soumettre ce différend, résultant de la démarcation de la ligne de frontière entre les parallèles 23 et 27 latitude du sud, à la décision d'une commission composée de cinq délégués d'Argentine et cinq délégués du Chili qui doivent se réunir à Buenos Aires dans le courant de ce mois, et il est aussi convenu que dans le cas que ladite commission n'arriverait pas à décider cette question, elle sera soumise à la décision définitive d'un Comité dont les membres seront un citoyen Chilien, un citoyen Argentin et Mr. BUCHANAN, Envoyè Extraordinaire et Ministre Plenipotentiaire des Etats-Unis de l'Amérique, auprès de la République Argentine. Cette Commission se réunira à Buenos Aires et fera connaître sa décision en novembre.

Cette résolution adoptée a rétabli entièrement, d'après les dépêches des journaux, la tranquilité dans les deux pays, et le Gouvernement du Chili a déjà commencé à désarmer son armée régulière. Le budget de la guerre et de la marine sera considérablement diminué. L'industrie et le commerce vont se développer rapidement dans les deux pays, et l'excédent du budget Chilien sera le même qu'avant, c'est à dire environ $10,000,000 en or par an.

DIRECTEUR PROVISOIRE DU BUREAU.

Le Comité Exécutif de l'Union Internationale des Républiques Américaines s'est réuni au Salon Diplomatique du Département d'Etat à 11 heures le 26 octobre 1898. Étaient présents:

L'Honorable JOHN HAY, Secrétaire d'Etat, Président.
Señor ANDRADE, Ministre du Venezuela.
Señor MÉROU, Ministre de la République Argentine.

La réunion avait pour but la nomination du Directeur du Bureau des Républiques Américaines, le terme de Mr. FREDERIC EMORY, comme Directeur provisoire, expirant le 1er novembre. Vu la condition satisfaisante du Bureau et le progrès fait récemment, le comité a décidé de renommer Mr. EMORY comme Directeur, sujet à une autre résolution. Señor CALVO, Ministre de Costa Rica, membre du Comité, n'ayant pu être présent, a envoyé une

lettre exprimant son désir pour la prolongation du terme de Mr.
EMORY. Aucune date n'a été fixée, mais il est entendu que la présente direction sera prolongée tant que les intérêts du Bureau
l'exigent, cette résolution ayant été soutenue par les représentants
des pays Américains-Latins, ainsi qu'ayant reçue l'approbation
du Département d'Etat. Mr. EMORY, qui est chef du Bureau de
Commerce Étranger au Département d'Etat, a dirigé le Bureau
des Républiques Américaines depuis la mort du Directeur précédent, Mr. JOSEPH P. SMITH, survenue le 5 février dernier. Pendant
son terme de Directeur provisoire, Mr. EMORY continuera ses
fonctions comme Chef du Bureau de Commerce Etranger qui
s'occupe de la publication des rapports commerciaux des Bureaux
diplomatiques et consulaires au Département d'Etat.

BUREAU DES RÉPUBLIQUES AMÉRICAINES À L'EXPOSITION TRANS-MISSISSIPPIENNE ET INTERNATIONALE À OMAHA.

L'Exposition Internationale qui a été tenue à Omaha, Nebraska,
du 1er juin au 31 octobre 1898 a présenté un intérêt particulier
pour les nations Américaines-Latines, comme cette évènement fut
une bonne occasion de présenter leurs produits et leurs ressources
aux marchés des Etats-Unis. Le Bureau des Républiques Américaines a apprécié pleinement l'importance de cette réunion, et étant
le centre officiel d'information concernant le commerce, la production, l'industrie et le progrès matériel des Républiques composant
l'Union Internationale des Républiques Américaines, des arrangements furent faits pour que son exposition démontrât ce fait et
attirât en même temps davantage l'attention sur les possibilités
commerciales et industrielles du Mexique, de l'Amérique du Sud
et Centrale et les Indes occidentales par la distribution de bulletins
et circulaires sur ce sujet.

Le rapport des représentants du Bureau est publié ici et montre
les avantages présents et futurs qui résulteront de l'Exposition.

OMAHA, NEBR., 31 octobre 1898.

DIRECTEUR DU BUREAU DES RÉPUBLIQUES AMÉRICAINES:

Ci-joint je soumets mon rapport sur le travail fait à l'Exposition Trans-
Mississippienne par le Bureau des Républiques Américaines. La place occupée par

le Bureau était excellente.   Etant situé au rez-de-chaussée du Bâtiment des Arts Libéraux, et ayant pour voisin le Musée Commercial de Philadelphia, il a attiré l'attention universelle.   L'exposition a été arrangée par Mr. John M. Biddle, qui s'est chargé des objets exposés par le Département d'Etat, et avec des draperies artistiques de drapeaux des Républiques Américaines et un bon arrangement de nombreux tableaux représentant des scènes de l'Amérique du Sud, de beaux meubles et de gracieux palmiers, l'ensemble a surpassé toutes les autres expositions dans les jardins de l'Exposition.   Les personnes intelligentes qui ont visité l'Exposition ont pris beaucoup d'intérêt au Bureau et ses opérations.

La proximité du Musée Commercial au grand nombre de caisses pleines de produits de l'Amérique du Sud, ainsi que d'échantillons de marchandises fabriquées en Angleterre et en Allemagne, était une espèce de leçon objective pour ceux qui s'intéressent, au but du Bureau des Républiques Américaines.

Vingt-et-un cents exemplaires du Bulletin Mensual du Bureau ont été distribués et les adresses ainsi que les occupations de ceux auxquels ils ont été enregistrés.   Comme on devait s'y attendre dans cette région agricole, les fermiers viennent en premier lieu dans l'enregistrement ; viennent ensuite les professeurs.   Chaque province et territoire dans l'Union, y compris l'Alaska, à l'exception de New Hampshire, Vermont, Rhode Island, Delaware, et South Carolina, a eu un représentant à enregistrer, l'Iowa étant le premier et le Nebraska le second.   Le Guatémala, le Nicaragua, le Mexique et la France fournissent les adresses étrangères aux manufacturiers qui se sont inscrits.   J'ai envoyé plusieurs exemplaires du Bulletin, espérant par cela d'augmenter leur désir d'obtenir le commerce de l'Amérique du Sud.   Nous avons reçu beaucoup de lettres des personnes auxquelles nous avons adressé des Bulletins, témoignant deavantages dérivés de la lecture de ceux-ci.   L'Exposition Trans-Mississippienne a pleinement réussi à point de vue et son succès a été surtout éclatant en démontrant aux Américains le fonctionnement des départements divers du Gouvernement des Etats-Unis.

Ci-dessous se trouve une liste des occupations de ceux à qui l'on a envoyé les Bulletins par la poste.   Les autres copies ont été demandées par les intéressés en personne :

Fermiers	175
Professeurs	170
Négociants	85
Journalistes	80
Avocats	70
Etudiants	60
Propriétaires	35
Banquiers	30
Employés de chemins de fer	30
Médecins	27
Ministres	25
Manufacturiers et importateurs	18
Commis	18
Agents	18

On en a aussi envoyé au nombre de 1 à 15 à des architectes, des comptables, des étudiants, des statisticiens, des dentistes, des missionnaires, ainsi qu'à des personnes exerçant toutes les professions imaginables.

Le nombre d'inscriptions par Etats est comme suit :

Iowa.... 331
Nebraska 318
Missouri 139
Kansas 138
Illinois ....,...... ... 69
South Dakota 40
Ohio.. 30
Minnesota 28
Wisconsin 25
Washington.. 15
Indiana..,............ 13
Pennsylvania.. 13

Les autres Etats avaient moins de représentants.

RÉPUBLIQUE ARGENTINE.

PREMIÈRE ADMINISTRATION DE PRÉSIDENT ROCA.

Dans le BULLETIN pour octobre 1898 on a remarqué qu'un cablegramme de M. le Ministre BUCHANAN, à Buenos Aires, annonçait l'inauguration du Général JULIO ROCA comme Président de la République Argentine le 12 octobre. Outre cette information, on a reçu une communication de la Légation Argentine à Washington, sous forme d'un extrait du "Corriere Mercantile" de Geneva, contenant des détails concernant la vie et la carrière du nouveau Président:

Le Général ROCA est né à Tucaman en juillet 1843, et a fait ses études, premièrement, dans son pays, et ensuite au Collège National d'Uruguay. Il a servi avec honneur dans l'armée d'Uruguay pendant quelque temps, à l'époque d'une courte révolution dans ce pays, et en entrant dans l'armée de son pays avec le grade de lieutenant, il est en peu de temps devenu Général, obtenant le dernier grade sur le champs de bataille de Santa Rosa, en décembre 1894, en reconnaissance de sa bravoure. Il a ensuite rempli les fonctions de Chef de Frontière à Cordoba, San Luis et Mendoza et a occupé le poste de Ministre de la Guerre et de la Marine. En 1880 il fut nommé Lieutenant-Général, et enfin Président de la République le 12 octobre de la même année. Sa première administration fut remarquable par le traité avec le Chili et par la nouvelle impulsion donnée à l'immigration étrangère. Pendant son administration pacifique les richesses du pays se développèrent grandement.

On peut facilement déterminer le progrès du pays pendant cette administration par une comparaison des statistiques. De 1880 à 1886 la population a augmenté de plus de 33 pour cent, tandis que l'immigration annuelle a triplé, s'élevant aux chiffres de 100,000 immigrants. Le commerce extérieur a augmenté de 30 pour cent, sa valeur en 1880 étant estimée à 520,000,000 et a plus de 955,000,000 en 1886. Le tonnage maritime a triplé; le nombre de voies ferrées a aussi triplé, étant à 2,300 kilomètres, estimes à 2,300 kilomètres en 1886. La quantité de terre cultivée a augmenté de 1,120,000 à 1,920,000, et les espèces en circulation et le crédit général du pays ont beaucoup augmentés.

M. Roca a passé une partie de l'intervalle depuis sa retraite de la vie publique en 1886, voyageant à l'étranger, et il entre en fonctions pour remplir les charges de sa seconde administration, inspiré d'idées modernes et progressives pour l'amélioration de son pays et le développement de ses ressources illimitées.

IMPORTATIONS D'APPAREILS ÉLECTRIQUES.

D'après les chiffres officiels fournis par les fonctionnaires des douanes, l'électricité a fait de grand progrès comme force motrice et pour l'éclairage dans la République Argentine pour les premiers six mois de 1898. Les importations de tous appareils et machines électriques pendant la période mentionnée, ainsi que leurs évaluations en or, sont données dans le tableau ci-joint:

	Tonnes.	Valeur.
Fil de fer galvanisé	9, 523	$589, 115
Cables fil de fer, etc.	2, 090	524, 081
Matériel d'éclairage		191, 565
Articles d'éclairage	38	55, 791
Dynamos	38	28, 005
Lampes incandescentes (douz.)	4, 466	13, 398
Matériel télégraphique		11, 298
Matériel de téléphone		4, 533
Phonographes		3, 200
Total		1, 420, 986

Une grande partie de ces articles a été achetée des maisons de commerce aux États-Unis.

BRÉSIL.

IMPORTATIONS DE CÉRÉALES À RIO.

D'après le "Handel-Zeitung," les importations de blé à Rio
Janeiro en 1897 ont été de 39,402 barils moins que dans l'année
précédente, les chiffres actuels étant 336,553 barils en 1897 contre
375,935 en 1896. La diminution principale a été dans le blé
hongrois, lequel, malgré sa qualité excellente, n'a été employé que
pour faire des mélanges à cause de son haut prix dans les ports
indigènes. Les statistiques indiquent que les importations de
l'année dernière ont été comme suit: des Etats-Unis, 252,991
barils; de la Rivière Plate, 65,697 barils; de Liverpool, 9,850
barils; de Trieste et Fiume, 4,395 barils; et de Chili, 3,600 barils,
lesquels composent les 336,533 barils importés l'année dernière.
La diminution dans l'importation de son en 1897 a été due aux
opérations très actives des moulins anglais et brésiliens. Les
importations totales pendant l'année ont été de 10,107 sacs de 40
kilos (88 livres), tous de la Rivière Plate, contre 62,374 sacs en 1896,
une différence de 52,267 sacs (qui est très favorable à l'enterprise
locale). Aussi pendant l'année passée l'importation de macaroni,
vermicelli et d'articles semblables a diminué considérablement
plus que dans les années précédentes. En 1896 7,941 caisses
furent importées d'Italie, mais en 1897 seulement 1,227 caisses
ont été reçues. Il n'y a aucun doute que la cause est due à la
haute perfection des fabriques locales, et il est certain que dans peu
de temps l'importation de cet article au Brésil cessera entièrement.
Le maïs vient seulement de la Rivière Plate. Celui-ci a souffert
aussi d'une diminution de 242,450 sacs de 62 kilos (137 livres),
les recettes ayant été de 1,254,097 sacs contre 1,496,556 en 1896.
Quant au riz, les importations d'Europe ont augmenté, tandis
que celles des Indes ont diminué. La quantité totale de sacs qui
sont arrivés sur le marché de Rio a été de 1,237,277 sacs de 60
kilos (13 livres) chaque, contre 1,240,833 sacs en 1896, une
diminution de 3,556 sacs. Les recettes pour 1897 se composent
de 134,359 sacs d'Europe et 1,102,919 sacs des Indes.

PRODUCTION DE CARBONES.

Le Consul Furniss écrit de Bahia et transmet au Département d'Etat la copie d'une communication à un correspondant de
New York qui demande des détails sur l'industrie de carbone.
Dans cette communication il dit que l'Etat de Bahia prétend être
le seul lieu de l'industrie du carbone.   On a trouvé des carbones
au Brésil pendant plusieurs années, mais il y a dix ans il n'y avait
aucune demande jusqu'au moment quand à cause de leur dureté
ils furent recherchés par les fabricants de forets.   Comme la
demande a augmenté la quantité est insuffisante, et par conséquent
les prix sont montés.

Les pierres se trouvent dans l'intérieur de l'Etat dans une
région atteinte seulement après un long et fatiguant voyage.   La
route est de Bahia par bateau à St. Félix et alors par chemin de
fer à Bandeira de Mello.   C'est là le bord de la région des diamants et on trouve toujours des carbones près des diamants.   Le
territoire le plus productif est plus en aval sur la rivière Paragassu
et pour l'atteindre le voyageur s'y rend à dos de mulets en suivant
pendant deux jours un sentier de montagnes escarpé.   On pense
qu'il y a des diamants et des carbones dans toute cette section,
mais à cause des méthodes employées pour les obtenir on n'exploite que le lit du fleuve Paragassu et ses tributaires, le fleuve
San Antonio et une chaine de montagnes nommée Sierra das
Laviras Diamantinas.   Des carbones se trouvent dans un espèce
de gravier nommé "cascalho" dans le lit de la rivière dessous la
boue et au-dessus une couche d'argile dans les montagnes dessous
une couche de rocher et au-dessus de la même couche d'argile et
dans le pays environnant sous plusieurs couches de terre.

Pour obtenir les carbones du lit de la rivière on choisit une
place n'ayant pas plus de 20 pieds en profondeur où le courant
n'est pas trop rapide.   Une longue perche est ensuite enfon-
cée dans l'eau et les plongeurs indigènes descendent emportant un sac tenu ouvert par un anneau.   Ils enlèvent d'abord la
boue et remplissent ensuite le sac de gravier sousjacent enlevant
tout jusqu'à l'argile.   Aussitôt qu'un sac est plein on donne un
signal à l'homme qui se trouve au-dessus dans un canot indigène
construit d'une seule pièce d'un arbre.   Le sac est amené à la
surface avec l'aide d'un plongeur transporté au rivage et déchargé

à une distance suffisante pour l'empêcher d'être emporté par l'eau au cas où la rivière montait subitement. Cette opération se répète tous les jours pendant les 6 mois de la saison sèche. Au commencement de la saison des pluies, quand les plongeurs sont forcés de cesser leurs opérations, ce gravier est examiné et lavé et on y cherche des carbones et des diamants. Les plongeurs sont très adroits et beaucoup peuvent rester sous l'eau pendant une minute, d'autres pendant une minute et demie. Pendant que le gravier gît à la surface il se couvre de nouveau de boue, occasionnant un surcroit du travail que l'on pourrait empêcher par des méthodes plus modernes. Aux endroits où la rivière est très profonde l'exploitation n'est pas possible.

Une autre méthode d'exploitation consiste à percer le rocher sur les pentes des montagnes d'enlever au moyen d'une succession de tunnels, le gravier contenant des diamants et des carbones. Le gravier est accumulé pendant la saison des pluies en amenant de l'eau dans les écluses. On trouve plus de carbones dans les montagnes que dans la rivière à cause de la facilité de les atteindre. Aucune exploitation d'importance n'est essayée autrepart excepté le long des bords des fleuves. Mais ici même on exploite peu parce que le gravier contenant le scarbones est atteint et avec leurs appareils primitifs les indigènes ne peuvent pas enlever l'eau des mines assez rapide pour en permettre exploitation. La raison que l'on ne fait pas d'essais d'exploitation dans les autres endroits est le manque d'eau pour laver le gravier. Il paraît que les indigènes n'ont jamais eu l'idée d'employer des machines modernes ou s'ils l'ont eu ils n'avaient pas de capitaux suffisants.

On trouve des carbones de tous grandeurs, variant de la grandeur d'un grain de sable à un seul échantillon de 975 carats. Ce grand carbone fut trouvé en 1894 sur un chemin où la couche de gravier était exposée et il fut vendu à Paris pour 100,000 francs ($19,300). Les grandeurs les plus utiles et présentant la plus grande valeur sont celles pesant de 1 à 3 carats. Il faut casser les plus grands, ce qui occasionne de grande perte, vu qu'ils n'ont pas de ligne de fracture. Pour cette raison le grand carbone cité plus haut, après avoir été cassé en plusieurs morceaux pour la vente, a rapporté un prix beaucoup plus bas que son prix d'achat. Il y a environ deux ans il y a eu une combinaison locale pour maintenir les prix, mais le membre le plus important de la compagnie a fait faillite et il n'y a pas eu d'autre essai depuis. Les prix du marché sont dus à la grande demande—la rareté de cet article et les méthodes difficiles d'exploitation. Souvent une couple de mineurs ne trouvent que 3 ou 4 carbones comme résultat d'un travail de 6 mois, et ils espèrent alors en obtenir des prix élevés.

Les exportateurs font affaires à Bahia et leurs agents dans la région des mines, mais comme les mineurs s'informent toujours des prix, ces commerçants ne sont plus que des maisons de commission; le plus grand exportateur à Bahia d'après M. Furniss est M. Theophilo Gomes de Mallos, Rua Cons. Dantes. En juillet on dit qu'il avait en stock environ 125 carats de carbones de grandeurs bien assortis. Il expédiera aux Etats-Unis aux mêmes conditions qu'aux acheteurs européens. Il dit qu'il n'a jamais vendu aux acheteurs des Etats-Unis parce qu'ils exigent les grandeurs particulières et il ne peut pas vendre des pierres choisies, mais en quantités comme il les achète. Ces pierres-là sont d'une grandeur pour lesquelles il y a une forte demande. Le prix à présent est d'environ $5 par grain portant la valeur d'un carat à $22.50, mais le prix varie selon la quantité et la demande. Une autre maison de carbones à Bahia est celle de M. Francisco de Mello & Co., Rua Cons. Dantes. On doit adresser ces messieurs en portugais ou en français, quoique le premier lise l'allemand.

CHILI.

EXPLOITATION DES MINES SOUS L'OCÉAN.

Frank G. Carpenter, dans une de ses lettres intéressantes sur les Républiques de l'Amérique du Sud, à travers lesquelles il fait en ce moment un voyage d'observation, donne une description des houillères du Chili qui furent exploitées pour la première fois en 1855. Il dit que ces mines sont très intéressantes. Elles sont tout à fait différentes de n'importe quelles mines aux Etats-Unis, et sous certains rapports sont beaucoup plus difficiles à exploiter. La couche de houille qui est la meilleure à présent est de 5 pieds en profondeur. Elle commence à la côte et s'étend sous les vagues de l'Océan Pacifique. Le rocher au-dessus est d'ardoise et de schiste si compacte que l'eau ne dégoutte pas à travers.

Mr. Carpenter dit·—Les tunnels sont si propres que l'on pourrait y circuler en habit sans danger de se salir. On les exploite avec les machines les plus récentes, et pendant ma visite j'ai eu plusieurs aventures qu'on croirait difficilement, pouvaient, m'arriver au Chili. Pensez, par exemple, de faire un voyage sur un train électrique de charbon à travers un tunnel de plus d'un mille de long sous l'Océan Pacifique à une vitesse de vingt milles par heure. Imaginez-vous les mines éclairées par l'électricité, formant des catacombes de corridors et chambres sous les vagues. Pensez que juste au-dessus de vous de grands navires à vapeur flottant et que le charbon qu'on retire de cette couche du Pacifique s'entasse dans leurs cales.

Figurez-vous des mineurs couverts de suie et de fumée à moitié nus qui font sauter du charbon qui chargent des wagons et qui suivent le train emportant vingt-sept tonnes de diamant noir au puits où une gigantique machine à vapeur enlève à la fois quatre tonnes à la surface et vous avez une idée de ce qui se fait dans la Mine Lota. Ces mines rendent en ce moment 1,000 tonnes de charbon par jour et 750 mineurs y sont employés. Elles rapportent un bénéfice qui s'élève à des centaines de mille dollars par an et on les surveille aussi soigneusement que n'importe quelle grande propriété houillère de notre pays. J'ai demandé des renseignements concernant les salaires des mineurs et on m'a dit qu'on les paye de 90 cents à $1 Chilien ou de 31 à 35 cents en argent des Etats-Unis. Je me demande ce que nos mineurs de Pennsylvania penseront de cela. Les Chiliens cependant ont leurs loyers libres et le charbon leur est fourni au prix de revient.

COLOMBIE.

BUDGET DE RECETTES DE 1899—STATISTIQUES DES CHEMINS DE FER—NOUVEAU EMPRUNT DANS LE COMMERCE.

Un correspondant français du "Nouveau Monde" de Paris dit que le budget de recettes et dépenses de Colombie comme soumis au Congrès calcule les recettes pour l'année finissant le 30 juin 1899 à $38,305,000. Ceci est une augmentation de $3,944,000 sur l'année fiscale finissant le 30 juin 1898 et est due au monopole des allumettes. Quant aux dépenses il est estimé que le déficit,

passer les montagnes à dos de mulets et de remonter le fleuve Cupe en canots. La route est extrèmement difficile et dangereuse et le prix de transport s'élève par tonne à $50 en espèces colombiennes (environ $23 en or). En 1896, E. J. CHIBAS a fait le tracé d'une route macadamisée dont la construction est fort avancée. Ceci rendra possible l'emploi de wagons dans toutes les saisons de l'année et réduira le prix du transport de marchandises à une somme nominale.

Balboa obtint une quantité considérable d'or des Indiens, mais ce ne fut qu'un siècle plus tard que l'on essaya l'exploitation des mines d'or sur l'Isthme. A cette époque la mine d'or d'Espíritu Santo fut découverte et exploitée à Cana. D'après VINCENTE RESTREPO, de Bogata, les Espagnols ont retiré $30,000,000 d'or de cette mine. Elle a été exploitée avec succès de 1680 à 1727 quand les Indiens se revoltèrent; une des galeries principales s'écroula, enterrant plusieurs mineurs et les autres découragés se retirèrent et retournèrent en Espagne.

Il s'écoula un siècle avant qu'on fît des essais sérieux d'exploitation de cette mine. Vers 1878 une compagnie fut fondée à New York qui dépensa $50,000 pour la construction d'un chemin et pour l'achat et la transportation de machines. Elle renonça au projet en 1880 sans avoir entrepris aucune exploitation réelle.

En 1888 la compagnie actuelle fut fondée à Manchester, Angleterre, avec un capital de $1,000,000. Les difficultés qu'on rencontra furent presque insurmontables, vu que Cana est situé à 2,000 pieds au-dessus du niveau de la mer. Une usine de dix bocards fut construite en 1889, mais pendant plusieurs mois les résultats furent loin d'être encourageants. Le minerai de la mine était d'une qualité inférieure; aucun signe de ces richesses merveilleuses n'était en vue, et les membres de la compagnie étaient tout à fait découragés lorsqu'en 1893 les mineurs par hazard rencontrèrent les anciennes galeries espagnoles à 90 pieds de la surface. L'eau accumulée dans l'ancienne mine se précipita dans les nouvelles galeries, ce qui exigea un travail supplémentaire et plus de capital afin de construire un tunnel pour les vider. A la fin ceci fut fait et la mine donne à présent l'or tant désiré. Pendant les années 1896 et 1897 les anciennes galeries ont donné 10,525 onces d'or, qui ont été rendues en argent réel, £44,522 ($216,377). La valeur moyenne du rocher exploité a varié de 1 à 1½ onces par tonne. Comme toute l'exploitation a été limitée à la partie du minerai recueilli par les Espagnols, on s'attend à une plus grande production de la veine vierge que l'on commence à exploiter jusqu'au plus profond niveau. Les résultats obtenus jusqu'ici indiquent la pleine réalisation des espérances des propriétaires. Ils ont dépensé des sommes énormes pour des machines perfectionnées et pour des améliorations et ils méritent le plus grand succès.

M. CHIBAS dans son intéressant article dans l'édition courante de la "Engineering Magazine," auquel les faits ci-dessus sont empruntés, dit :

Les richesses de Darien ne sont pas limitées à l'or. Cette région est très riche en bois de construction d'une grande valeur et l'on a exporté une quantité considérable d'acajou. Le palmier produisant l'ivoire végétable y est très abondant. L'industrie du caoutchouc y a été aussi très importante dans le passé, mais la pratique des indigènes d'abattre les arbres au lieu de les entailler, a fortement diminué le rendement. Malgré cette énorme destruction il ne s'est pas passé un seul jour que nous n'ayons au cours de notre arpentage vu des arbres à caoutchouc. Ils poussent si bien dans cette région que leur plantation et leur culture promettent un placement rémunératif. A l'approche de la saison des pluies nous avons extrait du caoutchouc des arbres près d'un des camps et à l'aide d'un procédé simple employé par les indigènes nous rendimes imperméable à l'eau tous les sacs de drap dont nous nous étions servis pour transporter nos effets et nos instruments d'un camp à l'autre. Nous nous en sommes servis pendant la saison des pluies à notre plus grande satisfaction. Un paletot soumis au même procédé était plus imperméable à l'eau que les paletots importés.

HAITI.

RÉDUCTION DE L'IMPÔT SUR LE SAVON.

Le Vice-Consul Général TERRES à Port au Prince envoie au Département d'Etat le 7 octobre 1898, une traduction d'une loi récemment faite par la législature. Elle est comme suit :

ARTICLE 1. Les savons de toutes qualités doivent payer 50 cents par 100 livres sans préjudices aux impôts additionnels.

ARTICLE 2. La surtaxe de 25 pour cent établie par la loi du 16 décembre 1897 ne sera pas déduite sur le savon.

ARTICLE 3. La loi actuelle qui abroge toutes les lois et les dispositions des lois qui y sont contraires sera exécutée à la diligence des Secrétaires d'Etat pour la Finance et le Commerce.

Ceci, dit M. TERRES, réduit virtuellement les impôts sur le savon de moitié.

MEXIQUE.

VALEURS DES IMPORTATIONS ET EXPORTATIONS.

Le rapport ci-joint des importations et exportations de la République pour les quatre années passées est emprunté à un rapport fait par M. CARDEN, consul anglais au Mexique et envoyé au Bureau des Affaires Etrangères de son Gouvernement. Les évaluations sont exprimées en espèces des Etats-Unis.

Année.	Importations.	Exportations.	Augmentation des importations.
1894	$29, 372, 819	$42, 604, 621	$13, 231, 802
1895	35, 186, 444	54, 910, 214	19, 723, 770
1896	45, 224, 958	57, 090, 415	11, 865, 457
1897	38, 107, 955	62, 575, 319	24, 467, 369
Total	147, 892, 176	217, 180, 669	69, 288, 398

Il est à noter que l'année dernière il y eut une grande augmentation sur les exportations, dépassant deux fois celle de 1896 et quatre fois celle de 1895, qui jusqu'ici a été l'année de prime. Les exportations ont augmentées de moins de 30 pour cent. Ces importations décourageantes sont dues à des récoltes abondantes de blé d'un côté et la diminution dans la valeur de monnaie d'argent d'un autre. Il sera important pour les manufacturiers de textiles aux Etats-Unis de savoir que l'industrie des textiles dans la République n'est pas limitée au coton, mais que son développement va comprendre des articles en lin et en laine. M. CARDEN ajoute, pourtant, qu'il y a toujours un bon débouché pour les tissus en laine et en fil de laine, surtout celles d'une bonne qualité. Parmi d'autres articles fort demandés sont les machines pour l'exploitation de mines, des machines agricoles et industrielles en général, des presses et caractères d'imprimerie, de la quincaillerie de bonne qualité et des couleurs.

Incidemment M. le Consul parle de l'augmentation des exportations sur les importations. Il dit:

Des £3,500,000 ($17,000,000) d'excédent annuel des exportations sur les importations, £2,700,000 ($13,100,000) sont dus aux remises pour le service de la dette, et les bénéfices des chemins de fer et les £800,000 ($3,900,000) qui restent, plus la somme du capital étranger qu'a pu être placé dans n'importe quelle année au Mexique, mais qui ne fut pas remis ici sous forme d'espèces ou de marchandise, doit représenter l'intérêt sur le capital placé dans les entreprises commerciales et industrielles de tous genres par les organisations, ou les personnes domiciliées à l'étranger.

NICARAGUA.

NOUVELLE ENTREPRISE D'EXPLOITATION DES MINES.

Le Bureau accuse réception d'une lettre de Señor Don Ascencion P. Rivas à Rama, Nicaragua, datée du 18 octobre 1898, dans laquelle il dit qu'il y a quelques mois qu'on a découvert des veines riches en or en quantités considérables dans la section de la côte Atlantique du Nicaragua, appelée " Distrito del Sequia."

Une description de ces découvertes a été publiée dans le Bulletin Mensuel du mois d'août 1898 à la page 291 par Mr. J. P. Morgan. Dans une lettre au Directeur du Bureau à la date du 15 octobre 1898, Mr. Morgan annonce qu'on a trouvé près du port de Rama des couches de houille très étendues et du bon flot d'oxide de cuivre rouge, ce dernier sur la rivière Mico. Mr. Morgan dit aussi que le district aurifère de la rivière Mico se développe mieux qu'on ne croyait, des épreuves donnant jusqu'à 200 onces d'or à la tonne et plus de 70 onces d'argent.

Dans sa communication au Bureau, Mr. Rivas dit que les fleuves traversant ce territoire, et qui sont navigables pour bateaux à vapeur depuis leurs embouchures à la mer jusqu'aux endroits où se trouvent les minéraux, offrent des facilités exceptionnelles pour le développement des mines. Les fleuves principaux sont le Siquia et le Mico. La plupart des personnes qui jusqu'à présent ont fait des découvertes n'ont pas les capitaux nécessaire pour développer les dépôts, et Mr. Rivas désire communiquer avec des personnes aux Etats-Unis qui voudraient fournir les capitaux nécessaire pour l'exploitation des mines.

NOUVEAU CONTRAT DU CANAL.

Des dépèches télégraphiques de Managua, Nicaragua, annoncent que le Congrès Nicaraguien a ratifié le traité conclu entre le Gouvernement et deux citoyens américains, MM. Eyre et Cragin, représentant un syndicat de New York. Comme il existe déjà une concession accordée en 1888 à la Compagnie du Canal Maritime du Nicaragua, le nouveau contrat ne peut entrer en vigueur avant l'expiration de l'autre concession qui expirera en 1899. Il est bien connu que plusieurs bills pour la construction du canal ont été présentés au Congrès des Etats-Unis, mais le sujet est toujours pendant.

Il n'y a pas d'entreprise qui ait à tel point attiré l'attention du monde pendant un demi siècle que l'ouverture d'une route entre l'Atlantique et le Pacifique à travers l'Isthme de l'Amérique Centrale, mais ce sujet n'a jamais excité tant d'intérêt qu'en ce moment, surtout aux Etats-Unis, par suite à l'annexion récente d'Hawaii et du long voyage que le vaisseau de guerre, *Oregon*, fut obligé de faire pour se rendre de San Francisco aux Indes occidentales.

La route Nicaraguienne a été un sujet d'étude sérieuse sur lequel le Gouvernement Americain, ainsi que la Compagnie, a dépensé des sommes considérables. On a beaucoup écrit à propos de ce canal projeté de Nicaragua, et on peut dire que le sujet à présent est pour ainsi dire épuisé. En établissant cette communication interocéanique, il faudra construire des écluses, et ce fait a été le prétexte sur lequel M. de Lesseps a basé l'opposition qu'il a toujours fait à cette route, car il a soutenu qu'un canal entre les deux océans doit être un canal à niveau comme le Suez pour répondre à toutes les exigences du commerce. Cependant les ingénieurs américains qui ont étudié le projet ont démontré que des écluses ne seront pas des obstacles au trafic énorme qui passera par cette route si le canal venait à être construit, et la Compagnie du Canal de Panama, depuis l'insuccès de l'entreprise de Lesseps, a elle-même adopté les écluses comme nécessaires à la continuation de ce travail.

PARAGUAY.

CODE DE NOMENCLATURE COMMERCIALE ADOPTÉ COMME TEXTE OFFICIEL.

L'Honorable William R. Finch, Ministre des Etats-Unis à Montévideo, informe le Département d'Etat, à la date du 21 septembre 1898, de la promulgation d'un décret officiel par le gouvernement du Paraguay d'après lequel le Code de Nomenclature

Commerciale préparé par le Bureau des Républiques Américaines est adopté comme texte officiel pour la désignation de commerce en espagnol, portugais et anglais. Cette action fut prise en conséquence de la nécessité commerciale d'une nomenclature commune avec d'autres pays avec lesquels des relations de commerce existent, et entre lesquels il y a échange de marchandises, et le 2 septembre 1898 le décret comprenant l'affaire fut ordonné, communiqué, publié et donné au Registre Officiel sur les signatures du Président EGUISGUIZA et Secrétaire GUILLERMO DE LOS RIOS.

Le Département de la Trésorerie des Etats-Unis avait auparavant pris action semblable le 22 janvier 1898, par l'émission d'une circulaire du Département acceptant le code comme un livre particulier des références à l'usage de ce département pour la traduction des mots et des phrases pour les Officiers des Douanes et pour les estimateurs de marchandises.

PRODUCTION DE CAFÉ.

Parmi les rapports récents des consuls des Etats-Unis, il y en a un de Mr. RUFFIN, à Asuncion, concernant l'adaptabilité du sol du Paraguay à la production de café. Il dit qu'il y a des plantations de café qui existent depuis de nombreuses années, mais qu'elles n'ont pas été cultivées et qu'on les a laissées aux hasards du climat excellent. Ces plantes produisent une variété de café semblable à celle cultivée au Brésil et en Bolivie provenant de l'espèce arabe. La production dans cette direction n'est pas grande et la consommation est locale. Les plantations qui ont été établies pendant les dernières années ont eu pour résultat des placements de profit, comme on a trouvé un marché à Paraguay pour tout le café produit. D'après les statistiques qu'on peut se procurer, Mr. RUFFIN calcule le nombre des plantes à café dans la République à 343,407. Il pense que tous les produits seront disponibles sur le marché d'Asuncion, comme les habitants sont de grands buveurs de café.

La plante de café pousse mieux dans les pays ayant une température moyenne de 68° à 78° Fahrenheit. Les chiffres officiels donnent à Paraguay une température 58.42° en juin à 84.45° en décembre, et une moyenne de 71.16°. La terre est propre à la culture car elle est plate et humide et on peut la travailler facilement.   Parmi les grands nombres de variétés de café, Mr. RUFFIN dit que la plus cultivée au Paraguay est le "Yungas," parcequ'elle est indigène à la Bolivie, pays occupant la même position géographique et ayant un sol semblable.   On croit que ce café peut entrer en concurrence avec celui le plus connu en Europe, où on en trouve déjà quoique en petites quantités.   Les autorités affirment que le café Yungas du Pérou et Guatémala est aussi bon que n'importe quel autre produit sur le continent Américain.   La graine est bien développée, d'un arôme exquis d'un jaune-vert et en grandeur et poids supérieur au café Moca dont il a les caractéristiques générales.   La plante est vigoureuse, se développe rapidement et porte après trois ans.

MARCHÉ POUR LES ARTICLES FABRIQUÉS.

Par le fait que la République du Paraguay est située dans le bassin de la rivière Parana, dans l'intérieur du Continent ne possédant pas de côte a elle, elle dépend commercialement de la République Argentine et de l'Uruguay.   Mais peu de commerce est fait directement avec le Paraguay et on n'enregistre presque jamais d'exportations pour ce pays.   Malgré cela le Paraguay est un pays riche en territoire de grande valeur, et est capable d'un grand développement.   La République est sans contredit le pays le plus riche en bois d'ébénisterie, vu qu'il y a environ 150 variétés d'arbres de grande valeur dans ses forêts.

Sa consommation quoique un peu limitée par le petit nombre d'habitants est d'une grande importance.   Il n'y a aucune communication maritime entre les Etats-Unis et le Paraguay, ni en effet entre aucun des grands pays d'exportation et cette République. Les navires n'enregistrent pas leurs cargaisons plus loin que Montevideo, Buenos Aires ou Rosario, les trois villes d'importance commerciale du bassin de La Plata.   La conséquence est que quand les négociants du Paraguay commandent des marchandises étrangères, ils sont obligés de placer leurs ordres dans une des villes mentionnées ci-dessus, à moins qu'ils aient des correspondants dans ces places pouvant surveiller l'enlèvement et l'expédition des marchandises.   Ceci, bien entendu, augmente les prix parce qu'il y a d'autres frais de maniement ou de commissions.   Il y a très souvent de longs délais.   Comme le Paraguay n'a pas de monnaie d'or ou d'argent frappée dans le pays, elle dépend principalement de monnaies d'Argentine et d'Uruguay. Dans le premier pays l'argent a été fluctueux, faisant préférer aux Compagnies Maritimes, le Montevideo, où l'étalon d'or est en usage, comme port de transbordement pour le trafic des fleuves.

Dans un rapport au Gouvernement Anglais un correspondant attire l'attention sur les articles suivants: Les machines à coudre sont fort démandées dans la République, comme elles le sont d'ailleurs dans les autres parties de l'Amérique du Sud. Les qualités à meilleur marché sont le plus demandées, bien qu'un nombre considérable de machines de bonne qualité se vendent facilement. La plupart de celles sur le marché sont de fabrication allemande. Il y a un grand nombre d'alambics en usage, dont la plus grande partie est importée de France. Les petits alambics capables de distiller de 50 à 200 gallons par jour et d'une force de 18° (Cartier) sont les plus demandés. Ils peuvent être simples ou pour la distillation continuelle ou semi-continuelle, mais ils doivent être le moins compliqués possible. On fabrique très peu de vin dans le pays, ainsi que toute autre liqueur, excepté le Cana (vin blanc).

Les fabricants anglais semblent avoir obtenu la plus grande partie des produits chimiques ainsi que les instruments de chirurgie. Les eaux minérales sont fort demandées à Asunción, et dans les grandes villes un nombre considérable de moulins à sucre en fer portatifs, pouvant être travaillés par des bêtes de somme, pourraient se vendre facilement. Une grande quantité de sucre non-raffiné est fabriqué, tout sur une petite échelle. Cependant la quantité ne suffit pas aux demandes, et le reste est importé d'Argentine où il y a de très grandes fabriques de sucre au Chaco, de l'autre coté de la rivière du Paraguay. Bien que la boisson nationale du Paraguay soit le " mate " (thé de Paraguay), les habitants consomment une grande quantité de thé et la demande pour cet article augmente continuellement. Le thé envoyé ici doit être de bonne qualité. Il y a une grande demande pour les tissus, surtout les articles bon marchés fabriqués en coton. Ceux-ci sont vendus par les détaillants avec un très petit bénéfice afin d'encourager la vente d'autres marchandises. Il y a une grande concurrence dans ce genre de commerce, mais les maisons anglaises font le plus d'affaires. Les ponchos se vendent beaucoup et viennent d'Angleterre. Ils sont de la même espèce que ceux vendus dans la République Argentine, mais comme les hivers au Paraguay sont un peu plus chauds, les articles en laine ne sont pas fort demandés.

Le correspondant dit que le change accuse une diminution d'au-moins 10 pour cent pendant les derniers mois et tend à diminuer toujours. En ce moment la prime sur l'or est de 760, ce qui veut dire que le dollar en papier Paraguayien est d'une valeur d'envi-ron 6½ pence (13 cents). Il ajoute plus loin que la concurrence étrangère est très vive au Paraguay et que le nombre de maisons anglaises est très petit, tandis que les maisons allemandes, françaises et italiennes sont relativement nombreuses. Les maisons anglaises qui font des affaires au Paraguay se contentent de faire des affaires par des agences à Buenos Aires, mais il y a toujours des occasions à Asuncion et dans les autres villes pour des maisons entreprenantes qui auraient la spécialité des produits du pays.

Un paragraphe dans le BULLETIN pour le mois d'octobre annonce qu'une association commerciale a été organisée dans la ville d'Asun-cion pour donner des renseignements sur tous les points concernant les produits, les régulations des douanes et le commerce de la République d'aider aussi toutes les personnes désireuses d'entrer en relations commerciales avec les exportateurs et autres maisons de commerce au Paraguay. Cette association est connue sous le nom de Centro Comercial du Paraguay.

ENREGISTREMENT DES MARQUES DE FABRIQUES.

D'après le " British Trade Journal," les personnes qui désirent enregistrer des marques de fabriques au Paraguay doivent s'adresser à la Junta de Crédito Público d'Asuncion. Les droits sont sauve-gardés pour une période de dix ans. En cas de remise d'une marque de fabrique, celle-ci doit être enregistrée au même bureau qui l'a accordée. Toute demande d'enregistrement doit être accompagnée de deux exemplaires de la marque de fabrique à enregistrer avec des inscriptions en double, d'un reçu prouvant que le montant des droits ($50) a été payé à la Junta de Crédito Público, ainsi que de plein pouvoir dûment légalisé si le pro-priétaire de la marque de fabrique n'a pas fait la demande per-sonnellement. Les pleins pouvoirs devraient être contresignés par le Consul du Paraguay et le nom de l'agent peut être laissé en blanc ou être rempli plus tard.

PRODUCTION D'ORANGES.

D'après un rapport récent du Consul RUFFIN, l'orange est un des articles de nourriture le plus général en usage au Paraguay, et est un des principaux aliments des pauvres, surtout dans la campagne. On engraisse aussi les cochons avec des oranges et les porcs nourris d'orange sont considérés très bons. Les orangers produisent énormément et se trouvent partout, soit dans les vergers soit à l'état sauvage. Il y a des fermes cultivant des orangers qui poussent des pépins et portent des fruits après 5 ans. Ils poussent bien toute l'année pendant les mois de janvier, février et mars. Un arbre de 7 ans porte environ 1,000 oranges. Le fruit a environ 3 pouces de diamètre et la variété ordinaire est très douce. Les mandarines sont petites, et bien que très piquantes ne sont pas si douces que les oranges et sont plus chères. On n'en cultive pas beaucoup et la plupart sont expédiées à Buenos Aires. Elles se vendent facilement à des prix rémunératifs. La troisième classe est l'orange âcre ou amère avec l'écorce de laquelle on fait de la marmelade et on fait aussi un extrait de fleurs. Des Français sont engagés dans cette industrie qui est très rémunératrice. L'exportation de la récolte commence vers la fin de mai et dure jus'qu'à novembre. Les bateaux sont chargés partout le long de la rivière, les femmes portant des paniers plats sur la tête les apportent à bord.

Il n'y a aucun droit d'entrée. La plus grande partie est envoyée à Buenos Aires et Montévideo. Pendant la saison on exporte une moyenne de 300,000 oranges.

ETATS-UNIS.

COMMERCE AVEC L'AMÉRIQUE LATINE.

RAPPORT SUR LES IMPORTATIONS ET EXPORTATIONS.

A la page 810 on trouvera le dernier rapport des chiffres compilés par le Bureau des Statistiques du Département de la Trésorerie des Etats-Unis dont O. P. AUSTIN est chef. Ces chiffres démontrent les évaluations du commerce entre les Etats-Unis et les pays Américains-Latins. Le rapport est pour le mois d'août 1898, corrigé jusqu'au 29 septembre 1898, avec un exposé comparé à la même période de l'année précédente, ainsi pour les huit mois finissant le mois d'août 1898 comparé à la même période de 1897. On doit expliquer que les chiffres des diverses douanes démontrant les importations et exportations pour n'importe quel mois de l'année ne sont pas reçus au Département de la Trésorerie jusqu'au vingtième jour du mois suivant, et il faut nécessairement du temps pour la compilation et l'imprimerie, de sorte que les rapports pour le mois d'août, par exemple, ne sont publiés qu'au mois de septembre.

AMÉLIORATIONS DES CONDITIONS FINANCIÈRES.

Le rapport ci-joint, compilé des chiffres officiels du " Journal des Finances," montrant le mouvement des importations et exportations des Etats-Unis pour les premiers huit mois des années indiquées, démontre le degré auquel ce pays de ses opérations commerciales avec d'autres pays (principalement avec l'Europe) et leurs dépendances a amélioré son état financier en 1898:

	1898.	1897.	1896.
Marchandise :			
Importations	\$426, 412, 038	\$546, 325, 777	\$471, 232, 299
Exportations	478, 674, 025	641, 697, 330	580, 930, 792
Excédent des exportations	352, 261, 987	95, 371, 553	109, 698, 493
Or :			
Importations	102, 087, 831	11, 887, 654	31, 902, 137
Exportations	9, 679, 113	32, 542, 659	56, 895, 492
Excédent des importations	92, 408, 718	. . . .	. . . .
Excédent des exportations	. . . .	20, 655, 005	24, 993, 355

Les exportations de marchandises ont dépassé les importations par \$352,261,987, tandis que pour les mêmes mois en 1897 l'augmentation a été \$95,271,553, ou une différence en faveur de 1898 de \$256,890,234. La balance du crédit pour cette année a été compensée par les importations en or net s'élevant à \$92,408,718, et laissant une balance nette dans les comptes commerciaux de \$259,853,069, ou à raison de \$346,400,000 par an.

UNE AUTRE LIGNE DE BATEAU DU PACIFIQUE.

D'après les communications reçues et publiées par le "Chronicle" de San Francisco le 11 octobre, San Francisco possèdera une autre ligne directe de communication avec les marchés de l'Amérique du Sud sur les côtes de l'Est et de l'Ouest. Les Chargeurs Réunis, une des plus grandes compagnies de navires français va établir une ligne de bateaux entre San Francisco et Mazatlan, Acapulco, Mexique; Guayaquil, Ecuador; Callas, Pérou; Valparaiso, Chili; Montévideo, Uruguay; Santos, Brésil; Liverpool, Angleterre; Havre, France; et peut-être un port belge. Le service commencera au mois de mars prochain, et alors un service mensuel sera établi entre San Francisco et Liverpool, les navires faisant escale dans les ports mentionnés ci-dessus.

Un représentant de la compagnie, domicilié à présent à San Francisco, a trois navires en voie de construction qui auront une longueur de 372 pieds et une capacité de 6,000 tonnes chacun.

AUGMENTATION DES EXPORTATIONS D'HUILE D'ÉCLAIRAGE.

Malgré l'avis fréquemment exprimé que la grande production de pétrole en Russie et aux Indes orientales hollandaises, et l'emploi croissant de l'électricité pour l'éclairage, diminuerait les exportations d'huilés d'éclairage des Etats-Unis, l'année qui vient d'ecouler a montré la plus grande exportation de cet article. Les chiffres pour le moi d'août montrent, d'ailleurs, les plus grandes exportations d'huiles pour n'importe quel mois enregistré. Les rapports du Bureau des Statistiques de la Trésorerie indiquent que les exportations d'huiles minérales pendant l'année fiscale de 1898 ont dépassé d'un billion de gallons le total, y compris toutes les classes, étant 1,034,269,676 gallons contre 973,614,946 gallons en 1897 et 890,458,994 gallons en 1896.

Le tableau ci-dessous montrant les pays auxquels l'huile a été exportée en 1897–98 indique la distribution énorme de cet article.

EXPORTATIONS D'HUILE MINÉRALE RAFFINÉE.

Exportations pour—	1897.	1898.
	Gallons.	*Gallons.*
Royaume-Uni..............................	213,627,168	212,265,563
France	9,065,114	12,835,631
Allemagne..................................	124,261,435	152,203,222
Autre Europe...............................	244,336,854	260,431,316
Amérique du Nord Britannique.............	10,013,517	11,087,502
Etats de l'Amérique Centrale et Honduras Anglais....	1,256,760	1,064,980
Mexique......................	836,628	1,106,853
Saint-Domingue............................	526,671	579,825
Cuba.......................................	68,474	243,202
Porto-Rico.................................	276,195	200,542
Autres Indes Occidentales et Bermuda......	4,224,737	4,108,714
Argentine.	10,394,716	11,099,132
Brésil	20,503,693	20,561,084
Colombie........	1,245,285	1,069,622
Autre de l'Amérique du Sud................	10,213,795	11,283,540
Chine	12,627,184	44,523,552
Indes Orientales d'Angleterre	21,361,346	35,152,592
Japon	47,411,176	53,398,185
Australasie Britannique....................	16,837,914	20,495,398
Autre d'Asie et Océanie	46,111,698	34,353,636
Afrique....................................	10,474,918	12,222,744
Autres pays................................	63,548	42,020

URUGUAY.

AFFAIRES FINANCIÈRES DE LA RÉPUBLIQUE.

Le Consul Swalm écrit de Montevideo que la dette publique de la République en obligations et en dettes flottantes s'élevaient à $140,000,000 le 31 août 1898. Il dit aussi que les sommes suivantes furent consacrées au soutien du Gouvernement pour l'année fiscale 1898-99: Pouvoir législatif, $341,114; Présidence, $64,618; Ministère des Affaires Etrangères, $149,089; Ministère du Gouvernement, $2,721,659; Ministère des Finances, $961,040; Ministère de l'Intérieur, $1,127,140; Ministère de la Guerre et de la Marine, $1,921,953; dette publique, $5,329,662; garanties de chemins de fer, $884,770; pensions, $1,417,378; miscellanées, $524,679; total, $15,434,003. Cela fait $18.24 de contributions par habitant. Le Consul ajoute: La République maintient son crédit fidèlement et n'a pas répudié un dollar de sa dette.

Dans l'Uruguay, comme M. Swalm note, les droits d'entrée sont prélevés sur les exportations d'animaux sur les terres (très bas taux), sur les notes, checks, etc. On doit se procurer une patente pour tous genres de commerce. L'impôt sur le tabac est prélevé d'après un système semblable à celui des Etats-Unis, excepté que chaque cigare porte un timbre de 2 mills. Les allumettes paient un impôt de 5 mills sur chaque boîte de 50. La ville de Montévideo a des obligations non ⋅ payées jusqu'à, concurrence, de $6,000,000. Comme actif, la ville possède l'installation d'éclairages électrique qui rapporte un bon revenu.

NOUVEAU MINISTÈRE DES AFFAIRES ÉTRANGÈRES.

Le Consul-Genéral Don PRUDENCIO DE MURGUIONDO a informé officiellement le Département d'Etat des Etats-Unis que le Président CUSTAS a nommé Señor Don JACOBO A. VARELA Ministre provisoire dans son cabinet. Il remplace Señor Don DOMINGO MENDILAHARSU (qui a donné sa démission) comme Ministre des Affaires Etrangères.

COMMERCE DE LA RÉPUBLIQUE PENDANT L'ANNÉE 1897.

Les extraits suivants du rapport annuel du Consul Anglais, Mr. GREENFELL, ont été envoyés de Montévideo au Département d'Etat par Mr. SWAIM, Consul des Etats-Unis.

La valeur officielle du commerce extérieur de la République pour l'année 1897 s'élève à $49,492,305, dont $20,049,980 sont des importations, montrant une balance commerciale en faveur de l'Uruguay.

Les recettes des douanes pour l'année 1897 ont diminué sérieusement, s'élevant à $8,175,442, ou $2,424,558 de moins que celles de 1896.

La Grande Bretagne a le monopole des importations des jambons, de thé, de toile à sacs, des chapeaux en feutre, des paux de moutons, des houes, des râteaux, des batteuses mécaniques, du fil à coudre, des tuyaux en fer et en plomb, du charbon, des platines pour les toits en fer galvanisé, des platines en étain, du soudre, du chanvre, des coffres-forts en fer, de la poudre à canon. Elle tient premier rang dans l'importation des articles en coton, en lin, en laine mélangée, des chapeaux de paille, des chaussettes en lin, des mouchoirs en coton, des couvertures de lit en laine et en coton mélangés, des machines pour moulins à vent, du sulfate de cuivre, des bêches, des outils de charpentiers, de la ficelle, du verni, des bandes de fer et des platines de fer, des articles en porcelaine de Chine, de la sellerie et des, harnais.

L'Allemagne a le monopole de l'importation des pianos, de la morue sèche, et elle occupe le premier rang dans les importations du sucré raffiné, des flanelles, des vêtements confectionnés, des tissus de coton et de lin pour chemises, des cols et des manchettes, des chaussettes en coton, des manteaux en laine pure et en laine mélangée, des couvertures de lit en coton, des essuies-mains, des serviettes de table, des machines à coudre, du fil de fer pour barrières, de l'amidon, des bleus, du papier à imprimer, des articles de merceries et des meubles.

La France a le monopole des peaux de chèvre et des toiles, et elle occupe le premier rang dans les articles en laine et en soie melangée, les bottes et les chaussures, les cravates en soie, les gants, de chevreaux, les parapluies, les ressorts de voitures, les drogues et les parfums.

La Belgique a le monopole des faux, des poutres en fer, des platines en zinc et des fusils de sport, et elle occupe le premier rang en articles de lin melangés, de couvertures de lit, de platines, de miroirs, de cristeaux des table, de vitraux, de ciment romain, de papier blanc et de bougies.

Les Etats-Unis ont le monopole des charrues, des fourches de fer, du goudron, et ce pays occupe le premier rang dans les importations du bois de construction, des machines à moissonner, de la ficelle et des haches; les Etats viennent second en importations de meubles, troisième en machines à coudre et sulfate de cuivre et cinquième en drogues et en papier d'imprimerie.

Mr. Swalm informe le Département que le commerce des Etats-Unis, de l'Allemagne et de la France avec l'Uruguay a augmenté beaucoup pendant l'année passée, grandement aux dépens de l'Angleterre. Pendant l'année présente la diminution dans les importations des articles en coton d'Angleterre a été très remarquable. L'Allemagne a occupé le premier rang dans une concurrence de toile de lin et de coton pour chemises, ayant mis un article peu couteaux sur le marché. Les machines à coudre envoyées d'Allemagne, dit le Consul, sont des imitations bon marché de celles manufacturées aux Etats-Unis.

PRIMES D'EXPORTATIONS DANS L'AMÉRIQUE-LATINE.

En réponse aux instructions envoyées par le Département d'Etat des Etats-Unis aux bureaux diplomatiques et consulaires des pays étrangers, on a fourni des rapports concernant les primes d'exportations accordées par les divers gouvernements.

Le Ministre BUCHANAN écrit d'Argentine que le seul article exporté de la République sur lequel une prime d'exportation est accordée est le sucre.   Le texte de la loi concernant le sucre est comme suit:

Traductions des sections 3, 4, 5, et 6 de l'article 1 de la loi sur l'impôt intérieur pour 1897.

SECTION 3. Tous les sucres produits dans le pays à partir de la date de la promulgation de cette loi, ou tous les sucres importés jusqu'au 31 décembre prochain, doivent payer une taxe intérieure de 6 centavos par kilogramme qui sera payée par le producteur ou l'importateur.

SECTION 4. En échange de cette taxe dont on a parlé, le Pouvoir Executif délivrera un certificat (retrait) qui donne au propriétaire le droit d'exporter 35 pour cent du sucre sur lequel il pourrait avoir payé ladite taxe, et de recevoir en échange 12 centavos, monnaie nationale, par kilogramme sur tel sucre exporté

SECTION 5. Tout sucre de production nationale existant dans le pays à la date de la promulgation de cette loi payera une taxe intérieure de 1 centavo, monnaie nationale, par kilogramme, qui sera payée par le propriétaire, et qu'il sera remboursé la somme de 4 centavos par chaque kilogramme exporté; et il est convenu que la quantité exportée ne doit pas dépasser 25 pour cent de la quantité sur laquelle il aurait pu payer la taxe.

SECTION 6. Quand le prix courant en gros du sucre, franco à bord au point de production (y compris la taxe payée), dépassera $4, monnaie nationale, par 10 kilogrammes, le Pouvoir Exécutif doit suspendre la remise des certificats mentionnés dans la section 4.

M. le Ministre WILSON a envoyé un rapport du Chili dn s lequel il dit que le Gouvernement n'accorde aucune prime d'exportation d'aucune sorte sur les articles produits dans le pays sujets à d'autre fabrication.   La seule protection du Gouvernement accordée aux industries indigènes est la perception des droits d'importation sur les articles semblables à ceux fabriqués dans le pays.

Concernant la Colombie, M. le Ministre HART dit, dans son rapport de Bogota, qu'aucun décret ayant pour résultat d'accorder des primes à n'importe quelle classe d'exportations, n'a été publié par le Gouvernement.

En Ecuador, le Gouvernement ne paye de primes sur aucune classe d'articles, soit directement ou indirectement, pouvant être classés comme article brut ou manufacturé. M. le Ministre Tillman fait un rapport dans lequel il dit qu'au contraire on est obligé de payer un droit sur plusieurs des articles principaux, quelque soit le pays pour lequel ils sont exportés.

Le sucre est le seul article exporté d'Haïti sur lequel une prime est accordée par le Gouvernement, mais le Chargé d'Affaires ad interim, le Dr. John B. Terres, écrit au Département d'Etat qu'il n'a pas eu d'exportations de ce produit pendant plusieurs années, la petite quantité produite étant consommée dans le pays. Le Consul Grimke fait un rapport que le Gouvernement de Saint Domingue n'a publié aucun décret accordant des primes à aucune classe de marchandise exportée.

Au Nicaragua un impôt de $1 par once en ingots d'or et de $2 par once en poussière d'or a été établi, et concernant lequel Mr. M. J. Chancey a fait un rapport au Gouvernement des Etats-Unis le 23 août 1897.

Ni le Paraguay ni l'Uruguay payent de prime sur les produits indigènes, mais les deux pays imposent une taxe sur les exportations principales.

Le Pérou n'accorde de prime sur aucune classe de marchandise exportée.

MISCELLANÉES COMMERCIALES.

RÉPUBLIQUE ARGENTINE.

Conseiller Agricole. La "New Orleans Picayune" annonce que l'Hon. J. Sterling Morton, ex-Secrétaire de l'Agriculture aux Estats-Unis, a été invité par le Président de l'Argentine de passer la prochaine année dans ce pays comme conseiller du Gouvernement concernant l'agriculture et l'organisation d'un département agricole. Le "Picayune" ajoute que Mr. Sterling Morton acceptera peut-être la mission.

BRÉSIL.

Soumission de Canalisation. Le "Rio News" annonce que le département des travaux publics de la province de Rio Janeiro demande des soumissions qui seront reçues jusqu'au 17 avril 1899 pour la canalisation des districts marécageux dans les bassins du lac Feia et des rivières Macacu Grandu, San Joao Macahe et Iguassu, et leurs tributaires.

Statistiques d'Immigration. Pendant l'année 1897 le nombre d'immigrants arrivés au port à Rio Janeiro étaient de 44,225. De ceux-ci 22,924 ont reçu des secours ou une compensation pécunière pour être devenus citoyens du Brésil, tandis que 22,261 sont venus volontairement. De ces immigrants il y avait 29,634 hommes et 14,621 femmes. Les nationalités représentées étaient : Italiens, 27,454 ; Portugais, 7,423 ; Espagnols, 7,253 ; Allemands, 420 ; Russes, 392 ; Syriens, 388 ; Arméniens, 219 ; Français, 215 ; Autrichiens, 132 ; autres nationalités, 329. La majorité de ces nouveaux arrivés se sont établis dans la province de Minas Geraes.

COLOMBIE.

Rendement des Mines d'Or de Darien. Les fameuses anciennes mines d'or espagnoles d'Espiritu Santo, dans la province de Darien, sont maintenant exploitées par une nouvelle compagnie minière connue sous le nom de Darien Gold Mining Company (limited) ; dernièrement ces mines ont été pourvues de machines hydrauliques d'épuisement et autres machines modernes. On a commencé le travail dans le niveau inférieur des mines, au dessous de l'ancienne exploitation espagnole, et une belle veine a été ouverte qui donnera bientôt suffisamment de minerais à 2 obocards. Le rendement pour le mois d'août a été de 923 onces d'or provenant de 630 tonnes de matière broyée, ce qui fait une moyenne de 1.47 onces par jour.

Enregistrement de Marques de Fabrique. Un livre pour l'enregistrement officiel des marques de fabrique a été ouvert dernièrement au Ministère des finances et les marques de fabrique peuvent maintenant être enregistrées à Bogota. Cet enregistrement n'est dû à aucune loi spéciale ni aucun décret exécutif, mais est le résultat d'un ordre du Ministre des finances qui par cela désire accorder aux propriétaires de marque de fabrique un moyen d'obtenir une preuve officielle de la propriété de leurs marques de fabrique jusqu'à ce que le Congrès puisse faire une loi concernant cetta question. Cette loi est maintenant en préparation et on espère qu'elle passera à la prochaine session du Congrès.

MEXIQUE.

Nouvelle Construction pour Compagnie de Tramways. La Riter Conley Manufacturing Co., de Pittsburg, Pennsylvanie (Etats-Unis), a obtenu le contrat pour la compagnie des tramways de Mexico pour la construction d'une maison devant abriter les machines et les chaudières, un batiment principal et un batiment frégorifique. Environ 300 tonnes de construction en acier seront nécessaires.

Activité dans la Construction de Voies Ferrées. Une dépêche de Puebla Mexique, dit qu'il règne en ce moment dans le sud du Mexique une activité extraordinaire dans la construction de voies ferrées. Outre les nouvelles voies déjà mentionnés dans des dépèches venant du Mexique et envoyées à la presse, il y a une ligne en voie de construction de Guadalajara à Ciudad Guzman. On dit que ce projet est favorisé par le gouverneur de la province de Jalisco. Trois capitalistes ont souscrit $100,000 en espèces pour la construction de la ligne à la demande du gouverneur. Une compagnie de capitalistes Mexicains a été fondée pour la construction d'une ligne de Cordoba, province de Vera Cruz à Rio Tonto en passant par Motzerongo. La ligne projetée traversera une riche région de plantations de café. Un grand nombre d'ouvriers sont en train de construire le chemin de fer de Tuxtla. Cette ligne sera construite de Palo Harrado à Santiago, Tuxtla, province de Vera Cruz.

PARAGUAY.

Ouverture de Navigation. On a reçu avis d'Asuncion qu'une ligne de navires à vapeur allemande a été établie en amont sur la rivière Paraguay. La compagnie a deux navires à vapeur qui ont fait le trafic de passagers et de cargaison au 18 septembre. On croit que maintenant les exportations et les importations de la République augmenteront. Les importateurs allemands feront de grands bénéfices par ce mouvement.

PÉROU.

Industrie de Borax. L'industrie de borax au Pérou paraît être d'une grande importance. En 1896, 7,350 tonnes, évaluées à $179,674, ont été exportées, tandis qu'en 1897 12,464 tonnes, évaluées à $303,361, ont été expédiées de Mollendo. Les dépôts se trouvent à environ vingt milles d'Arequipa dans intérieur.

ETATS-UNIS.

Production de Cuivre et d'Aluminum. Le rapport officiel des ressources minérales des Etats-Unis, publié par le Geological Survey des Etats-Unis, donne la production de cuivre pour 1897 à 491,638,000 livres qui sont évaluées à $54,080,180, cela étant une augmentation d'environ 7½ pour cent sur celle de l'année précédente. La production d'aluminum est donnée à 4,000,000 livres contre 1,300,000 livres pour l'année précédente, la valeur pour 1897 étant estimée à $1,500,000.

Grandes Ressources Minérales. Les rapports du Geological Survey des Etats-Unis pour 1897 indiquent une production totale de $632,312,347 de minéraux et de produits minéraux, parmi lesquels les principaux produits sont comme suit :

Saumon de fonte, 9,652,680 tonnes de 2,240 livres, évaluées à $95,122,299 ; argent, 53,860,000 onces " troy," valeur en monnaie $69,637,172, valeur commerciale $32,316,000 ; or, 2,774,935 onces " troy," valeur de monnaie commerciale la même ; charbon de terre bitumineux 147,789,902 tonnes de 2,000 livres, évaluées à $119,740,053 ; anthracite de Pennsylvanie 46,814,074 tonnes de 2,240 livres, évaluées à $79,129,126.

Plus Grand Haut Fourneau. Les deux hauts fourneaux construits par la Compagnie d'Acier à Youngstown, Ohio, seront les plus grands qu'on ait jamais construits. Toutes les dimensions n'ont pas été définitivement arrêtées, mais les souches auront 105 pieds de hauteur et 23 pieds à la base. Les poêles seront sur un niveau plus bas que les fourneaux et auront 120 pieds de hauteur. On se propose de faire des changements radicaux dans les opérations des hauts fourneaux quand ces souches seront prêtes à opérer, par lesquels on obtiendra un rendement maximum. On croit que ces deux fourneaux ne produiront pas moins de 1,200 tonnes de fer par jour.

Emploi de Nitrate pour la Fertilisation. Une nouvelle matière pour la fertilisation sera bientôt mise sur le marché par une compagnie de Californie. Cette compagnie a trouvé des dépôts très étendus d'oxides métalliques près de Lovelock, Nev. (à seulement 10 milles du chemin de fer.), et desquels elle retirera le nitre, la potasse et le phosphate. Incidemment, cette compagnie mettra une grande quantité de matière de fertilisation peu coûteuse sur le marché.

Demande pour les Machines Weber. Le 20 octobre, la Weber Gas and Gasoline Engine Company de Kansas City, Mo., a informé ce Bureau qu'elle venait d'expédier un train chargé de machines et des grues à la Nouvelle-Zélande. Peu de temps avant, un chargement fut expédié au Japon, et à la date de communication la compagnie préparait un chargement sur une commande d'une maison d'Ecuador.

VENEZUELA.

Manuel d'Agriculture. On dit que le Ministre d'Agriculture, d'Industrie et de Commerce a offert un prix de $400 pour le meilleur manuel d'agriculture élémentaire à l'usage des écoles de la République. On enverra ses traités au Ministre qui décidera le résultat du concours le 28 février 1899.

Amende pour négligence d'emballage de Marchandises. Le "Venezuela Herald" cite le cas d'une amende de 13,500 francs imposée récemment par le Département des Douanes à La Guayra sur un chargement de papier expédié par une maison à Boston. La maison avait emballé 20 kilos d'échantillons d'enveloppes dans le papier d'imprimerie. Il en résulta que comme les enveloppes paient un impôt de 20 francs par kilo, et le papier 5 cents par kilo, les officiers de douanes ont ordonné que le chargement entier fut imposé aux taux d'enveloppes qui s'élevait à 13,500 francs, c'est à dire à plus de 30 fois la valeur du chargement. Par l'intervention de la légation des Etats-Unis à Caracas qui a certifié qu'il n'y avait aucune intention de fraude, le Gouvernement a décidé de faire remise de l'amende. Les expéditeurs doivent faire attention à cette règle, et on ne doit pas mettre dans la même caisse les articles qui sont sujets à des impôts différents.

Nouveau Bâtiment du Gouvernement. L'Association Nationale des Manufacturiers a conclu un contrat avec les Etats-Unis pour la construction d'un bâtiment du Gouvernement au port de la Guayra, Venezuela, pour être employé par les inspecteurs des douanes. Un contrat est aussi pendant pour la construction d'une halle dans la ville de Maracay, Venezuela, qui coûtera environ $40,000, et le contrat sera placé, on pense, dans ce pays.

SENOR DON MATIAS ROMERO.

See pages 975, 1040, 1090, and 1126.

Monthly Bulletin

OF THE

Bureau of the American Republics,

International Union of American Republics.

Vol. VI.   DECEMBER, 1898.   No. 6.

VISIT OF THE PRESIDENT OF COSTA RICA.

Don Rafael Iglesias, President of the prosperous Republic of Costa Rica, arrived in Washington on the 23d of November, and was the guest of the Government of the United States at the Arlington Hotel. Soon after his arrival President McKinley called, and the same afternoon Señor Iglesias returned the visit at the White House. During his stay in the capital he was visited by almost every member of the diplomatic corps, as well as by Senators, Members of Congress, and other distinguished persons. He is still a very young man, being only 38 years of age, and is now serving his second term as President of Costa Rica. When he arrived in New York, he was met by Col. W· R. Carter, of the United States Army, who went from Washington as the personal representative of President McKinley to welcome Señor Iglesias to this country. The President of the United States, on the 29th of November, gave à dinner in honor of President Iglesias, at which all the Latin-American diplomats and other people of prominence were present. On the 30th another banquet was given by the Secretary of State, in honor of President Iglesias, at which, as at the one given in the White House, all the members of the Cabinet, Assistant Secretaries, Senators, Representatives, and other persons of political, personal, and social prominence were in attendance.

The Director of the Bureau of the American Republics, Mr. FREDERIC EMORY, accompanied by the Secretary, Dr. HORACIO GUZMAN, called on President IGLESIAS on the 25th of November and tendered a breakfast at the Shoreham on the following Monday, November 28. The President accepted the invitation, and the company included Hon. DAVID J. HILL, Assistant Secretary of State; Mr. CALVO, Minister from Costa Rica; Mr. MÉROU, Minister from the Argentine Republic; Mr. PONTE, Chargé d'Affaires of Venezuela; Mr. RENGIFO, Chargé d'Affaires of Colombia; Col. W. R. CARTER, U. S. A., President McKINLEY'S representative in attendance upon President IGLESIAS, Dr. HORACIO GUZMAN, Secretary of the Bureau of the American Republics, and Mr. QUESADA, Secretary to President IGLESIAS.

At the close of the breakfast Director EMORY proposed the health of the President of Costa Rica. In doing so, he said it gave him special pleasure to express his sense of obligation, and that of the Bureau of the American Republics, to the Government of Costa Rica for the active interest it had always shown in the welfare of the Bureau, and particularly for the zealous coöperation of the able and efficient Minister of Costa Rica, Mr. CALVO. He closed by asking the company to join him in drinking to the prosperity and happiness of the President of Costa Rica and of his country.

In responding, President IGLESIAS said:

I desire to thank very sincerely the Director of the Bureau of the American Republics for tendering me this breakfast, an attention that I appreciate most highly, and, at the same time, I wish to say that it has afforded me the greatest pleasure to meet the members of the Executive Committee of the International Union of American Republics. This institution is of the utmost importance for the development of the commercial relations between our nations of Latin America and the Republic of the United States, and no country is more aware of this fact than the Republic of Costa Rica. The publications of the Bureau of the American Republics are read with the greatest interest by our public men, as they serve to convey to them an exact idea of the advancement and progress of all the nations of our continent. As the Chief Magistrate of Costa Rica, I shall always do everything in my power to foster the interests of the Bureau of the American Republics, and I entertain no doubt that the Administration that will follow mine will do so as well.

Gentlemen, I propose the health of the Director of the Bureau of the American Republics, Mr. EMORY.

The Director thanked the President for his courtesy.

Mr. Mérou, Minister from the Argentine Republic, spoke as follows:

. As a member of the Executive Committee of the Bureau of the American Republics, and in the absence of my distinguished colleagues the Ministers of Mexico and Venezuela, it gives me pleasure to express my thanks to the President of Costa Rica for the interest he shows in the work of the Bureau, and for the importance he attributes to it. Justly speaking, all the credit for the efficient work of the Bureau belongs to its distinguished Director, Mr. Emory. It is due to his indefatigable activity and wise administration that that institution is now giving such valuable results, and it affords me great satisfaction to avail myself of this opportunity to add my congratulations to those he has received from His Excellency, Señor Iglesias.

Being by chance the senior member of the Executive Committee, permit me now to propose a toast to the eminent Chief Magistrate of the United States, the Hon. Mr. McKinley, who so wisely conducts the affairs of this great nation, and to express, in the names of my colleagues here present, our most sincere wishes for his personal happiness, for the glory of his Government, and for the prosperity of the American people.

Director Emory said he wished to express the regret of the Secretary of State at his inability to be present, owing to a previous engagement, and to ask the Assistant Secretary to respond to the toast of "The President of the United States."

In reply Hon. David J. Hill, Assistant Secretary of State, in a graceful speech, said he was sure that if the President of the United States were present he would express his cordial sympathy in the purposes of the International Union and his desire for the cultivation of closer relations among the various Republics of this hemisphere. The Assistant Secretary described the similarity in the political institutions of the American Republics as having their origin in the same system of political philosophy, and said the Republics of North America, Central America, and South America had many purposes in common and were attracted to each other by the prospect of the development of commercial intercourse, which in this case was bounded not by lines of latitude, but rather by lines of longitude, two great oceans separating this hemisphere from the rest of the world, and thus securing the three Americas a certain solidarity of interests. He was sure the President of the United States had the promotion of the general tendency toward a closer union between the United States of America and the various Latin American Republics very much at heart, and it therefore gave him special pleasure to acknowledge the compliment, so graciously expressed by the Minister from the Argentine Republic, to the Chief Magistrate of the United States.

Director EMORY said he had one more toast to propose, and would ask the company to join him in drinking to the future prosperity of the International Union and the continued development of the generous purposes of its founders, the distinguished members of the International American Conference, which met in Washington in 1889–90. He requested the Minister from Costa Rica to say a few words in response.

Mr. CALVO, Minister from Costa Rica, said that, although the Bureau of the American Republics is in its ninth year of existence, it is the first time that its Director meets the Chief Magistrate of one of the countries forming the Union, and that he felt himself very happy for the distinction Costa Rica enjoyed at this moment.

He, personally, as well as his Government, had always felt the deepest interest in the success of the plan outlined by the International American Conference, and was convinced that the Bureau of the American Republics was earnestly striving to give effect to the intentions of the Conference. He wished more particularly, although this might not be the most fitting occasion, to express his appreciation of the attentions which had been shown to the President of Costa Rica by the President, Cabinet, and various officials of the Government of the greatest and most important of the nations forming the union of the American Republics. The courtesies extended to the President of Costa Rica in Washington were extremely gratifying, and in acknowledgment of them, he desired again to propose the health of the President of the United States.

After drinking this toast the company separated.

The day before he left Washington President IGLESIAS called at the Bureau of the American Republics, accompanied by the Minister from Costa Rica, Mr. CALVO, and was received by the director of the bureau, Mr. FREDERIC EMORY, and the secretary, Dr. HORACIO GUZMAN. In honor of the visit the building was decorated with the flags of Costa Rica and the United States. The President spent over an hour examining its practical workings, and said it would give him pleasure upon his return to Costa Rica to do everything in his power to promote the work of the Bureau.

PRESIDENT McKINLEY'S MESSAGE.

President McKINLEY's annual message was sent to the Fifty-fifth Congress of the United States at the opening of its final session, December 5, 1898. The major part of the message is, in effect, a dispassionate, comprehensive, and concise record of the events of the past year in so far as they are involved in Government affairs. Naturally, the first place is given to the causes of and conduct of the war with Spain, in which all who were engaged in any manner on behalf of the United States are given their just meed of praise. There is no undue exultation over the victories achieved on sea and on land by the forces of the United States, but there is throughout a vein of sympathy and respect for the defeated Spanish forces. The President congratulates the country because, "with the one exception of the rupture with Spain, the intercourse of the United States with the great family of nations has been marked with cordiality, and the close of the eventful year finds most of the issues that necessarily arise in the complex relations of sovereign States adjusted or presenting no serious obstacles to a just and honorable solution by amicable agreement."

Referring to the government of Porto Rico and the Philippines, the President says:

I do not discuss at this time the government or the future of the new possessions which will come to us as the result of the war with Spain. Such discussion will be appropriate after the treaty of peace shall be ratified. In the meantime and until the Congress has legislated otherwise, it will be my duty to continue the military governments which have existed since our occupation, and give to the people security in life and property and encouragement under a just and beneficent rule.

INDEPENDENCE OF CUBA.

With respect to the government of Cuba the following was said:

As soon as we are in possession of Cuba and have pacified the island it will be necessary to give aid and direction to its people to form a government for themselves. This should be undertaken at the earliest moment consistent with safety and assured success. It is important that our relations with this people shall be of the most friendly character and our commercial relations close and reciprocal. It should be our duty to assist in every proper way to build up the waste places of the island, encourage the industry of the people, and assist them to form a government which shall be free and independent, thus realizing the best aspirations of the Cuban people. Spanish rule must be replaced by a just, benevolent, and humane government, created by the people of Cuba, capable of performing all international obligations, and which shall encourage thrift, industry, and prosperity, and promote peace and good will among all of the inhabitants, whatever may have been their relations in the past. Neither revenge nor passion should have a place in the new government. Until there is complete tranquillity in the Island and a stable government inaugurated military occupation will be continued.

References and recommendations with regard to the Nicaraguan Canal, the other American Republics, and the Bureau of the American Republics, are contained in the following extracts:

ARGENTINE-CHILEAN ARBITRATION.

A long unsettled dispute as to the extended boundary between the Argentine Republic and Chile, stretching along the Andean crests from the southern border of the Atacama Desert to Magellan Straits, nearly a third of the length of the South American continent, assumed an acute stage in the early part of the year, and afforded to this Government occasion to express the hope that the resort to arbitration, already contemplated by existing conventions between the parties, might prevail despite the grave difficulties arising in its application. I am happy to say that arrangements to this end have been perfected, the questions of fact upon which the respective commissioners were unable to agree being in course of reference to Her Britannic Majesty for determination. A residual difference touching the northern boundary line across the Atacama Desert, for which existing treaties provided no adequate adjustment, bids fair to be settled in like manner by a joint commission, upon which the United States Minister at Buenos Aires has been invited to serve as umpire in the last resort.

UNIFORM CABLE RATES.

I have found occasion to approach the Argentine Government with a view to removing differences of rate charges imposed upon the cables of an American corporation in the transmission between Buenos Aires and the cities of Uruguay and Brazil of through messages passing from and to the United States. Although the matter is complicated by exclusive concessions by Uruguay and Brazil to foreign companies, there is strong hope that a good understanding will be reached and that the important channels of commercial communication between the United States and the Atlantic cities of South America may be freed from an almost prohibitory discrimination.

In this relation, I may be permitted to express my sense of the fitness of an international agreement whereby the interchange of messages over connecting cables may be regulated on a fair basis of uniformity. The world has seen the postal system developed from a congeries of independent and exclusive services into a well-ordered union, of which all countries enjoy the manifold benefits.

It would be strange were the nations not in time brought to realize that modern civilization, which owes so much of its progress to the annihilation of space by the electric force, demands that this all-important means of communication be a heritage of all peoples, to be administered and regulated in their common behoof. A step in this direction was taken when the International Convention of 1884 for the protection of submarine cables was signed, and the day is, I trust, not far distant when this medium for the transmission of thought from land to land may be brought within the domain of international concert as completely as is the material carriage of commerce and correspondence upon the face of the waters that divide them.

EVENTS IN CENTRAL AMERICA.

The year's events in Central America deserve more than passing mention.

A menacing rupture between Costa Rica and Nicaragua was happily composed by the signature of a convention between the parties, with the concurrence of the Guatemalan representative as a mediator, the act being negotiated and signed on board the United States steamer *Alert*, then lying in Central American waters. It is believed that the good offices of our envoy and of the commander of that vessel contributed toward this gratifying outcome.

In my last annual message the situation was presented with respect to the diplomatic representation of this Government in Central America, created by the association of Nicaragua, Honduras, and Salvador under the title of the Greater Republic of Central America and the delegation of their international functions to the Diet thereof. While the representative character of the Diet was recognized by my predecessor and has been confirmed during my Administration by receiving its accredited envoy and granting exequaturs to consuls commissioned under its authority, that recognition was qualified by the distinct understanding that the responsibility of each of the component sovereign Republics toward the United States remained wholly unaffected.

This proviso was needful inasmuch as the compact of the three Republics was at the outset an association whereby certain representative functions were delegated to a tripartite commission, rather than a federation possessing centralized powers of government and administration. In this view of their relation, and of the relation of the United States to the several Republics, a change in the representation of this country in Central America was neither recommended by the Executive nor initiated by Congress; thus leaving one of our envoys accredited as heretofore separately to two States of the Greater Republic, Nicaragua and Salvador, and to a third State, Costa Rica, which was not a party to the compact, while our other envoy was similarly accredited to a union State—Honduras—and a nonunion State—Guatemala. The result has been that the one has presented credentials only to the President of Costa Rica, the other having been received only by the Government of Guatemala.

Subsequently the three associated Republics entered into negotiations for taking the steps forecast in the original compact. A convention of their delegates framed for them a Federal constitution under the name of the United States of

Central America, and provided for a central Federal Government and legislature. Upon ratification by the constituent States, the 1st of November last was fixed for the new system to go into operation. Within a few weeks thereafter the plan was severely tested by revolutionary movements arising, with a consequent demand for unity of action on the part of the military power of the Federal States to suppress them. Under this strain the new Union seems to have been weakened through the withdrawal of its more important members. This Government was not officially advised of the installation of the federation, and has maintained an attitude of friendly expectancy, while in nowise relinquishing the position held from the outset, that the responsibilities of the several States toward us remained unaltered by their tentative relations among themselves.

THE NICARAGUA CANAL COMMISSION.

The Nicaragua Canal Commission, under the chairmanship of Rear-Admiral John G. Walker, appointed July 24, 1897, under the authority of a provision in the sundry civil act of June 4 of that year, has nearly completed its labors, and the results of its exhaustive inquiry into the proper route, the feasibility, and the cost of construction of an interoceanic canal by a Nicaraguan route will be laid before you. In the performance of its task the commission received all possible courtesy and assistance from the Governments of Nicaragua and Costa Rica, which thus testified their appreciation of the importance of giving a speedy and practical outcome to the great project that has for so many years engrossed the attention of the respective countries.

As the scope of the recent inquiry embraced the whole subject, with the aim of making plans and surveys for a canal by the most convenient route, it necessarily included a review of the results of previous surveys and plans, and in particular those adopted by the Maritime Canal Company under its existing concessions from Nicaragua and Costa Rica, so that to this extent those grants necessarily hold as essential a part in the deliberations and conclusions of the Canal Commission as they have held and must needs hold in the discussion of the matter by the Congress. Under these circumstances and in view of overtures made to the Governments of Nicaragua and Costa Rica by other parties for a new canal concession predicated on the assumed approaching lapse of the contracts of the Maritime Canal Company with those States, I have not hesitated to express my conviction that considerations of expediency and international policy as between the several Governments interested in the construction and control of an interoceanic canal by this route require the maintenance of the status quo until the Canal Commission shall have reported and the United States Congress shall have had the opportunity to pass finally upon the whole matter during the present session, without prejudice by reason of any change in the existing conditions.

Nevertheless, it appears that the Government of Nicaragua, as one of its last sovereign acts before merging its powers in those of the newly formed United States of Central America, has granted an optional concession to another association, to become effective on the expiration of the present grant. It does not appear what surveys have been made or what route is proposed under this contingent grant, so that an examination of the feasibility of its plans is necessarily not embraced in the report of the Canal Commission. All these circumstances suggest the urgency of some definite action by the Congress at this session, if the labors of the past are to be utilized and the linking of the Atlantic and Pacific oceans by a practical waterway is to be realized. That the construction of such a maritime highway is now more than ever indispensable to that intimate and ready intercommunication between our eastern and western seaboards demanded by the annexation of the Hawaiian Islands and the prospective expansion of our influence and commerce in the Pacific, and that our national policy now more imperatively than ever calls for its control by this Government, are propositions which I doubt not the Congress will duly appreciate and wisely act upon.

CHILEAN CLAIMS COMMISSION.

A convention providing for the revival of the late United States and Chilean Claims Commission and the consideration of claims which were duly presented to the late commission, but not considered because of the expiration of the time limited for the duration of the commission, was signed May 24, 1897, and has remained unacted upon by the Senate. The term therein fixed for effecting the exchange of ratifications having elapsed, the convention falls, unless the time be extended by amendment, which I am endeavoring to bring about, with the friendly concurrence of the Chilean Government.

EXTRADITION CONVENTION WITH MEXICO.

The interpretation of certain provisions of the extradition convention of December 11, 1861, has been at various times the occasion of controversy with the Government of Mexico. An acute difference arose in the case of the Mexican demand for the delivery of JESÚS GUERRA, who, having led a marauding expedition near the border with the proclaimed purpose of initiating an insurrection against President DIAZ, escaped into Texas. Extradition was refused on the ground that the alleged offense was political in its character, and therefore came within the treaty proviso of nonsurrender. The Mexican contention was that the exception only related to purely political offenses, and that as GUERRA's acts were admixed with the common crime of murder, arson, kidnaping, and robbery the option of nondelivery became void, a position which this Government was unable to admit in view of the received international doctrine and practice in the matter. The Mexican Government, in view of this, gave notice January 24, 1898, of the termination of the convention, to take effect twelve months from that date, at the same time inviting the conclusion of a new convention, toward which negotiations are on foot.

THE MEXICAN FREE ZONE.

The problem of the Mexican Free Zone has been often discussed with regard to its inconvenience as a provocative of smuggling into the United States along an extensive and thinly guarded land border. The effort made by the joint resolution of March 1, 1895, to remedy the abuse charged by suspending the privilege of free transportation in bond across the territory of the United States to Mexico failed of good result, as is stated in Report No. 702 of the House of Representatives, submitted in the last session, March 11, 1898. As the question is one to be conveniently met by wise concurrent legislation of the two countries looking to the protection of the revenues by harmonious measures operating equally on either side of the boundary, rather than by conventional arrangements, I suggest that Congress consider the advisability of authorizing and inviting a conference of representatives of the Treasury Departments of the United States and Mexico to consider the subject in all its complex bearings, and make report with pertinent recommendations to the respective Governments for the information and consideration of their Congresses.

MEXICAN WATER BOUNDARY COMMISSION.

The Mexican Water Boundary Commission has adjusted all matters submitted to it to the satisfaction of both Governments save in three important cases; that of the "Chamizal" at El Paso, Texas, where the two Commissioners failed to agree and wherein, for this case only, this Government has proposed to Mexico the addition of a third member; the proposed elimination of what are known as "Bancos," small isolated islands formed by the cutting off of bends in the Rio Grande, from the operation of the treaties of 1884 and 1889, recommended by the Commissioners and approved by this Government, but still under consideration by Mexico; and the subject of the "Equitable Distribution of the Waters of the Rio Grande," for which the Commissioners recommended an international dam and reservoir, approved by Mexico, but still under consideration by this Government. Pending these questions it is necessary to extend the life of the Commission, which expires December 23, next.

ABROGATION OF TREATY.

The Government of Peru has given the prescribed notification of its intention to abrogate the Treaty of Friendship, Commerce, and Navigation concluded with this country August 31, 1887. As that treaty contains many important provisions necessary to the maintenance of commerce and good relations, which could with difficulty be replaced by the negotiation of renewed provisions within the brief twelve months intervening before the treaty terminates, I have invited suggestions by Peru as to the particular provisions it is desired to annul, in the hope of reaching an arrangement whereby the remaining articles may be provisionally saved.

THE VENEZUELAN-BRITISH ARBITRATION TREATY.

The arbitral tribunal appointed under the treaty of February 2, 1897, between Great Britain and Venezuela, to determine the boundary line between the latter and the colony of British Guiana, is to convene at Paris during the present month. It is a source of much gratification to this Government to see the friendly resort of arbitration applied to the settlement of this controversy, not alone because of the earnest part we have had in bringing about the result, but also because the two members named on behalf of Venezuela, Mr. Chief Justice FULLER and Mr. Justice BREWER, chosen from our highest court, appropriately testify the continuing interest we feel in the definitive adjustment of the question according to the strictest rules of justice. The British members, Lord HERSCHELL and Sir RICHARD COLLINS, are jurists of no less exalted repute, while the fifth member and President of the Tribunal, M. F. DE MARTENS, has earned a world-wide reputation as an authority upon international law.

THE BUREAU OF THE AMERICAN REPUBLICS.

I have the satisfaction of being able to state that the Bureau of the American Republics, created in 1890 as the organ for promoting commercial intercourse and fraternal relations among the countries of the Western Hemisphere, has become a more efficient instrument of the wise purposes of its founders, and is receiving the cordial support of the contributing members of the International Union which are actually represented in its board of management. A commercial directory, in two volumes, containing a mass of statistical matter descriptive of the industrial and commercial interests of the various countries, has been printed in English, Spanish, Portuguese, and French, and a Monthly Bulletin published in these four languages, and distributed in the Latin-American countries as well as in the United States, has proved to be a valuable medium for disseminating information and furthering the varied interests of the International Union.

SEÑOR ROMERO AN AMBASSADOR.

Señor Don MATIAS ROMERO, Envoy Extraordinary and Minister Plenipotentiary to the United States from the Republic of Mexico, has returned to Washington after a somewhat prolonged visit to the Mexican capital. Soon after his arrival, the Minister informed the Secretary of State of the United States that his official rank had been advanced to that of Ambassador. This information was received with great satisfaction both at the State Department and in diplomatic circles, and Señor ROMERO was warmly congratulated at this mark of the esteem of his Government.

As the law provides that the United States Government may advance to the rank of Ambassador any of its ministers, when the country to which he is accredited takes the first step in this direction with its own representative, General POWELL CLAYTON, at present Minister of the United States to Mexico, has accordingly become Ambassador to that Republic, his nomination having been sent to the Senate December 6 and confirmed by that body two days later.   This provision of the law governing the diplomatic service was enacted less than six years ago and there was at that time no diplomat in the United States of a higher rank than Minister, and the United States had no representative abroad of ambassadorial rank.   Since then six countries have . given the credentials of an Ambassador to their envoys in Washington.   The Governments so represented are: Great Britain, Italy, Germany, France, Russia, and Mexico   The latter country is the first American Republic to confer so distinguished an honor upon its diplomatic representative in Washington.

Señor ROMERO is one of the most eminent statesmen, writers, and diplomats of Mexico.   He was born in the city of Oaxaca, February 24, 1837.   He received his first education in his native place, and finished it at the capital of the Republic, where he received his diploma as a lawyer.   In 1855, he first entered the Foreign Office, although still pursuing his legal studies.   In 1857, when President COMONFORT made his *coup d'etat*, forcing President JUAREZ to leave the capital, Senor ROMERO accompanied him to Vera Cruz where he continued in the service of the Department of Foreign Relations.   In December, 1859, he came to Washington as First Secretary of the Mexican Legation, and remained here in that capacity until August, 1860, when, in the absence of the Minister, he became Chargé d'Affaires.   He returned to Mexico in 1863, to take part in the war against the French, and was appointed Colonel by the President.   General PORFIRIO DIAZ then appointed him as his chief of staff.   Soon after that, President JUAREZ accredited him as Envoy Extraordinary and Minister Plenipotentiary to Washington.   He remained at this post from October, 1863, until January, 1868, having rendered most important services to his country.

On his return to Mexico, he was appointed Secretary of the Treasury, but was obliged, on account of ill health, to give up that office in 1872.   For three years he remained in Soconusco, devoting himself to agricultural pursuits, and from 1877 to 1878 was again Secretary of the Treasury.   In 1880, he served as Postmaster-General.   In March, 1882, he came back to Washington as Envoy Extraordinary and Minister Plenipotentiary, and has remained in that capacity ever since, with an interruption of only ten months, in 1892, when, for the third time, he was called to serve as Secretary of the Treasury. As representative of his country in the United States, Señor ROMERO has shown himself a most efficient and able diplomat. His efforts have been most successful in strengthening the friendly ties between the two nations, and with this object in view he has written a great deal, his productions always receiving the highest encomiums from the press of the United States and other countries.

Señor ROMERO was a member of the International American Conference, and in that body served with great distinction, having been one of its two vice-presidents. As representative of Mexico in the conference he voted for the establishment of the Bureau of the American Republics, and ever since its organization has shown an active and zealous interest in its progress. He was a member of the executive committee of the Bureau when that body was first organized, and on every occasion has lent his valuable aid to the work of the International Union of American Republics.

THE LATE DR. WILLIAM PEPPER.

MEMORIAL MEETING IN THE CITY OF MEXICO—TRIBUTE OF MINISTER ROMERO.

At a meeting which took place in the City of Mexico on September 12, 1898, in honor of the memory of the late Dr. WILLIAM PEPPER, with the attendance of President DIAZ, of Mexico, Señor Don MATIAS ROMERO, Minister from Mexico to the United States, delivered the following address:

Mr. PRESIDENT, LADIES, AND GENTLEMEN: I have been requested to announce to this audience that Dr. EDUARDO LICEAGA has been asked through the cable by the provost of the University of Pennsylvania, of which the late Dr. PEPPER was dean for several years, to represent on this occasion that very important institution of learning, one of the highest standard in the United States of America. So the University of Pennsylvania takes an active part in this evening's proceedings to honor the memory of one of its honored heads and benefactors. The cablegram alluded to reads as follows:

PHILADELPHIA, PA., *September 9, 1898.*

Prof. E. LICEAGA, *México:*

Please represent University of Pennsylvania at to-morrow's memorial meeting.

CHARLES C. HARRISON, *Provost.*

After having read the above message, Señor ROMERO continued:

The desire of paying a sincere though feeble tribute to the distinguished merit of a man who was noted for the high personal traits that adorned his character and for the good which he did to his fellow men during his passage through this life, and who was, moreover, a sincere friend of our country, causes me to emerge for an instant from the retirement into which I have been forced by the most severe bereavement that can befall a man.

I thought it was not improper for me to attend this meeting because its object being to mourn for the demise of a friend recently departed from this life and honor his memory, it is in keeping with my present feelings and with what I have been recently doing on account of the great personal and grevious loss I have experienced.

In the address I delivered in Philadelphia at the inauguration of the Commercial Museums, to which I have already alluded, I could not help making the following allusion to the gentleman to whom their organization was due:

"I beg to be allowed to make a personal allusion referring to one of Philadelphia's foremost citizens, Dr. WILLIAM PEPPER, through whose instrumentality the Philadelphia Commercial Museums has been so successfully established. I do not need to praise Dr. PEPPER before a Philadelphia audience, where he is so well known, and I will only say, what everybody knows here, that he is always ready to promote anything which is for the welfare of his city, his country, and humanity, as when he, at his own and his friends' expense, among whom are several public-spirited ladies, undertakes anthropological and archæological researches throughout the world for the advancement of science, which must necessarily redound to the benefit of all nationalities. The high qualities of Dr. PEPPER are appreciated not only in his own country, but also in foreign lands."

Before his death Dr. PEPPER had succeeded in securing the funds necessary not only to sustain the museum permanently, but also to build for it a suitable edifice at a cost of several millions of dollars.

I also had an opportunity of becoming acquainted with another of the good works of this good man, having a connection, like the former, with our country. There lives in Washington during the winter and in California during the summer a distinguished lady, who not long ago visited this country, leaving behind her a luminous trail in the form of kindnesses done to persons in need, who delights in employing her large fortune in founding colleges and in other useful undertakings having for their object the promotion of science and the good of mankind in general. All my hearers will understand that I refer to Mrs. PHOEBE A. HEARST. Dr. PEPPER, who used to apply to this philanthropical lady for the funds necessary for his noble undertakings, arranged with her to send to Mexico a scientific commission to engage in archæological and anthropological studies in some of the States of the Republic, with a view to the advancement of science; and, as is characteristic of people who do good for the sake of the satisfaction which they derive therefrom and not for vain display, this fact would have been unknown to me, in spite of my personal acquaintance with both of the prime movers, had it not been for the necessity of obtaining the consent of the Mexican Government to the sending of the commission, thus constraining them to communicate their plans to me. I believe that Mexico was not the only country to which they sent a commission for a like purpose. I therefore regard as laudable the exercises held to-night for the purpose of paying a tribute to the memory of a man whose life was an honor to humanity.

I had the good fortune to know Dr. WILLIAM PEPPER personally in his own country and an opportunity of appreciating his conspicuous merits. Unlike the other speakers who will deliver his panegyric to-night, I did not know him in his capacity as a physician, high as were his attainments in that province, but in his capacity as an altruist, determined to do all the good that he could to his fellow-men and devoting his time to beneficent works to which he applied his own fortune without any other recompense than the satisfaction that comes from the consciousness of doing good. He also availed himself of the advantageous position which he occupied in the United States to secure the funds necessary to carry out great and beneficial undertakings, and, in a country where there are so many philanthropists, he always succeeded.

Dr. WILLIAM PEPPER was one of those luminous bodies that visit our planet in human form, to do good to their fellows, to serve as an example for present and future generations, to elevate and improve the condition of humanity. I will not attempt, nor would it be possible, to give at this moment even a summarized biographical sketch of Dr. PEPPER, and all that I propose to do is to relate briefly the circumstances under which I made his acquaintance, circumstances that brought the most admirable features of his character into relief.

Desiring to promote the trade of the United States with the other nations of the American continent, he conceived the project of establishing at Philadelphia, his native city, a commercial museum or museums for the exhibition of samples of the natural and manufactured products of each of the Republics of America, so that the manufacturers of his own country, if so desiring, might examine the raw material which we produce, with a view to its employment for their manufactures. This was a colossal undertaking for a single individual to attempt, involving as it did the necessity of a large building, a staff of scientific employees, a considerable force of clerks, and other adjuncts requiring heavy expenditure. The energy of Dr. PEPPER was not daunted by these difficulties, and overcoming all of them he succeeded in establishing the commercial museums, which were solemnly inaugurated at Philadelphia, in the presence of the President of the United States of America, on June 3, 1897.

Dr. PEPPER desired, for the better success of his undertaking, to secure the cooperation of the Governments of the other nations of America, interested as they are also in such success, and as I was the senior diplomatic representative in Washington, he applied to me with a view to effecting arrangements to that end, and thus it was that I had the good fortune to make his acquaintance. He often came to Washington to confer with us, and we also, invited by him, went to Philadelphia on several occasions to visit the museums and also to take part in their dedication, at which ceremony I, on behalf of the Latin-American diplomats, and of the diplomatic council of the museums, which he had organized, delivered an address. On December 11, 1897, the diplomatic representatives in question held a meeting at the Mexican legation at Washington, which was the last that Dr. PEPPER attended.

GOLD AND SILVER PRODUCTION IN 1897.

UNITED STATES COINAGE—WORLD'S COINAGE.

In his report to the Secretary of the Treasury, the Director of the Mint deals not only with the production of precious metals in the United States during the calendar year 1897, but also with the production in all foreign countries where these metals are found. The totals form a basis for comparisons between the leading producing nations, as the sources from which the information was obtained were the most authentic and reliable and the figures are as nearly accurate as it was possible to obtain them.

The value of the gold produced in the United States in 1897 was $57,363,000. This amount was surpassed by but one other country—the South African Republic, which produced $58,306,600. Combined Australasia produced $55,684,182, and Russia, the next country in order, $23,245,763. The South African Republic made the most remarkable gain of the year—$13,854,192. Australasia's increased supply of gold was valued at $10,502,249; that of the United States at $4,974,800, and that of Russia at $1,709,970.

The United States during the year produced 53,860,000 fine ounces of silver and the Republic of Mexico produced 53,903,180 fine ounces. This was a decrease for the former of 4,974,800 fine ounces and an increase for the latter of 8,256,756 fine ounces. In the United States the number of fine ounces of gold was 2,774,935. The coinage value of the silver produced in the United States was $69,637,172. While many of the silver mines, which in the past were most productive, were closed down, the increased production of lead and copper ore in which there was an admixture of silver has, to a great extent, offset this loss. During 1897, gold was obtained in twenty-five States and Territories in the United States, ranging in amounts of from $100, in each of four States, to $19,104,200 in the State of Colorado. California produced $14,618,300; South Dakota, $5,694,900; Montana, $4,373,400; Nevada, $2,976,400; Arizona, $2,895,900; Alaska, $1,778,000; Utah, $1,726,100; Idaho, $1,701,700, and Oregon, $1,353,100. No other State produced as much as $500,000.

The world's production of silver, by the report of the Director of the Mint, is shown to be largely in excess of any previous year. The next largest yield was in 1895, when it was 167,509,960 ounces. The world's product of gold and silver in 1897 is given in the appended table:

Countries.	Gold Dollars.	Silver. Fine Ounces.	Silver, Coinage Value.
United States..........................	$57,363,000	53,860,000	$69,637,200
Mexico.............................	9,436,300	53,903,181	69,693,000
Central American States.............	470,500	1,546,875	2,000,000
Argentine Republic................	137,600	383,470	495,800
Bolivia............................	750,000	15,000,000	19,393,900
Brazil.............................	1,204,200	....	....
Chile..............................	928,600	6,440,569	8,327,200
Colombia..........................	3,000,000	1,687,950	2,182,400
Ecuador...........................	132,900	7,734	10,000
Peru..............................	628,000	9,784,680	12,650,900
Uruguay	38,500	....	....
Venezuela.........................	948,500	....	....
The Guianas.......................	4,324,300	....	....
Dominion of Canada...............	6,027,100	5,558,446	7,186,700
European Countries................	27,175,600	16,464,108	21,286,900
British India......................	7,247,500	....	....
Japan	713,300	2,507,532	3,242,100
China.............................	2,209,100	....	....
Korea.............................	733,100	....	....
Borneo	45,900	....	....
Africa............................	58,306,600	....	....
Australasia	55,684,200	15,951,546	20,624,200
Total........................	237,504,800	183,096,091	236,730,300

The total value of gold deposited at the United States mints and assay offices during the year was $87,924,232, consisting of $67,923,535 domestic and $20,000,597 foreign. The value of silver deposited at the same institutions for returns in fine bars, which were used in the industrial arts or exported, was $12,707,128, of which amount $11,847,530 was domestic and $859,598 foreign. The United States coinage during the year was of gold, $76,028,485, and of silver, $18,487,297, of which amount $12,651,731 was in standard silver dollars, coined from silver purchased under act of July 14, 1890, prior to November 1, 1893, the date of the repeal of the purchasing clause of said act. The world's coinage during the year, including recoinages, was gold, $437,719,342; silver, $142,380,588, or a total of $580,099,930.

The highest London price for silver 0.925 fine, British standard, during the year was 29 13-16 pence, the lowest 23¾ pence, and the average price 27 9-16 pence, equivalent to $0.60449 in United States money per ounce fine.   At the average price of silver for the year tne bullion value of the silver dollar was $0.467.   The net value of the gold exports from the United States for the year was $512,609, and the net value of the silver exports of the country for the same period was $26,287,612.

There was consumed in the industrial arts in the United States during the calendar year 1897, gold to the value of $11,870,231 and silver to the value of $11,201,150.   The world's consumption of the precious metals in the industrial arts during the same period was: Gold, $59,005,980;   silver, $40,435,577.

On January 1, 1898, the metallic stock of the United States consisted of gold, $745,245,953;   silver, $635,310,064;   or a total of $1,380,556,017.

THE SPANISH LANGUAGE IN LATIN-AMERICAN TRADE.

Mr. Abraham Christiani writes the Bureau from Comitan, State of Chiapas, the southeasternmost province of the Republic of Mexico, calling attention to the uselessness of sending communications and advertising matter written or printed in the English language to the citizens of that section of the Republic. It may be well again to remind exporters, advertisers, and others desiring to enter into commercial relations with the citizens of any part of Mexico (except known English-speaking firms) that they should conduct all correspondence in Spanish and send all catalogues and other descriptive matter printed in the same language.   These might as well be printed in French, German, or Italian as in English; just as many people would then be reached, for there are about as many residents of each of those nationalities in Mexico as there are English-speaking people.   As but comparatively few persons engaged in trade in the United States can speak and understand Spanish, so in Mexico the percentage of English-speaking natives is proportionately as small.   What has been said in regard to Mexico is equally true of all the Central

American States and all the South American Republics except Brazil, where Portuguese is the language of the people. In Haiti the French language prevails.

Mr. CHRISTIANI's communication is as follows:

We see with satisfaction that the MONTHLY BULLETIN of the American Republics, under your direction, which circulates in the United States, Mexico, and other countries of America, is published in four different languages. We regret to say, however, that most of the letters and catalogues which we receive from manufacturers of machinery in the United States are written in English, and, as we are not acquainted with the language, we are unable to inform ourselves of their contents. We consider it opportune to call your attention to this fact, taking the liberty to suggest to you that, if you deem it advisable, you will cause an article to be published in the BULLETIN to the effect that the only language spoken in this city is the Spanish language, in order that they may take notice of it in foreign countries.

Quite a number of the trade journals of the United States are advocating the teaching of Spanish in the high schools of the country. The manner in which the language should be taught, and the reason why its study should be added to the curriculum of the schools designated, is set forth in the following extract from "American Trade":

The attention which Cuba, Porto Rico, and the Philippines are attracting as fields for the extension of American trade gives increased interest to the Spanish tongue as a language of commerce. The importance of Spanish in our commercial relations with the outer world has been increasing with the development of our trade interests in Latin-America, and the possibility of American ownership or control of colonies that are peopled by Spanish-speaking races brings the business man of the United States more squarely face to face with the need of a knowledge of this language than ever before. From a commercial standpoint, the Spanish language is of vast importance to the business interests of the United States, and the necessity for familiarity with this tongue will not be diminished for many years to come. The sooner our young men get right down to work in the study of Spanish the more quickly they will be equipped to get out and hunt for business in the countries to the south of us. There is no need of overburdening the already crowded courses of the public schools of the lower grades. There is abundant place for the teaching of Spanish in the commercial courses that are being added rapidly to the schools of the higher grade. Every business college and every educational institution that aims to fit young men for commercial pursuits should give proper place to the teaching of Spanish. The ignorance or imperfect knowledge of this tongue retards the growth of our trade with the Spanish-speaking countries far more than is generally known or recognized.

TRADE OF SPAIN WITH MEXICO AND SOUTH AMERICA.

The Spanish Government has recently taken an important step relating to trade. A royal order was issued in September creating a special or subdepartment of foreign affairs, for the purpose of supplying commercial information and statistics, and of rendering assistance to exporters and business men in general. This new bureau is to be under the direction of the commercial bodies and consular department, and to have a special government officer to oversee it. Mexico and the South American Republics are to receive especial attention from this bureau. They are thought to offer special inducements to Spanish exporters by reason of similarity of race, language, and customs. It is believed by the Government that Spanish manufactures of boots and shoes, gloves, silks, fans, lace, and cordage would have no difficulty in competing in Mexico and South America with like manufactures of other countries. The first movement to obtain a foothold for these goods and all others of Spanish origin in Mexico, the Argentine Republic, Brazil, Uruguay, and Chile has been the appointment of a commercial attaché for each country to reside respectively in Vera Cruz, Buenos Aires, Rio de Janeiro, Montevideo, and Valparaiso. These officers are expected to be ready at all times to render practical assistance to merchants.

DISSOLUTION OF THE UNITED STATES OF CENTRAL AMERICA.

The MONTHLY BULLETIN for October contained a communication from Mr. WILLIAM M. LITTLE, United States Consul at Tegucigalpa, Honduras, relative to the formation of the Government of the United States of Central America. Mr. LITTLE's letter was accompanied by a translation of the articles of the constitution respecting the rights of foreigners residing within the jurisdiction of the Union. This constitution was to take effect on November 1, 1898. The new Government was one, however, of but short duration. According to a dispatch received from Nicaragua on December 1, 1898, the success of the revolution in Salvador and the overthrow of President GUTIERREZ led to a meeting of the three commissioners who formed the executive head of the Union until a President could be elected, and they decided to abandon the new form of government. This decision of the commissioners, Messrs. GALLEGO, MATUS, and AGNOLUGARTE, left as the only alternative to the three States of Honduras, Nicaragua, and Salvador each to resume its former status as an independent nation. As a result of the collapse of the Union, Messrs. BONILLA, ZELAYA, and REGALADO became Presidents of the respective countries, the latter as the successor of President GUTIERREZ—according to the press dispatches. The Department of State of the United States has been advised by Minister MERRY, and also by one of the consular officials, that the uprising in Salvador was successful and that peace was restored after much disorder.

ARGENTINE REPUBLIC.

GENERAL ROCA'S CABINET.

Hon. WILLIAM I. BUCHANAN, Minister of the United States at Buenos Ayres, has officially advised the Department of State of the inauguration, on October 12, of Gen. JULIO A. ROCA as President and Señor Don NORBERTO QUIRNO COSTA as Vice-President of the Republic. President ROCA has appointed the following cabinet:

Minister of Interior..........................Dr. FELIPE YOFRE.
Minister of Foreign Relations.................Dr. AMANCIO ALCORTA.
Minister of Finance..........................Dr. JOSÉ MARIA ROSA.
Minister of Justice and Public Instruction........Dr. OSWALDO MAGNASCO.
Minister of War ....Gen. LUIS MARIA CAMPOS.
Minister of Marine ....Com. MARTIN RIVADAVIA.
Minister of Public Works.....................Dr. EMILIO CIVIT.
Minister of Agriculture......................Dr. EMILIO FRERS.

EFFORTS TO SUBDUE THE LOCUST PLAGUE.

Writing from Buenos Aires, under date of October 12, United States Consul MAYER says:

The locust advices are not reassuring, as, though the extinction goes on briskly the invasions are tremendous, and it is apprehended that they will soon be in the province of Buenos Aires. Entre Rios and parts of Santa Fé and Cordoba are overrun. In the first three days of October, 398 tons of locusts were gathered in Entre Rios alone; but the subcommissions complain that in some quarters the inhabitants refuse to work at the extinction, and that the police does not lend its authority to compel them. The central commission has issued a circular urging that prompt notice be given of all desoves (egg depositing) and samples sent in, with dates and all other pertinent particulars. The news from Paraguay is that the locusts are thick there and doing wholesale damage. In the colonies south of Santa Fé there have been no invasions as yet, and farmers are of the opinion that if they escape until the 15th both wheat and linseed will be safe. * * * The work of extinction is being briskly pushed in other provinces and giving good results.

A correspondent of the "Chilian Times" at Bahia Blanca says:

The Argentine Government is making great efforts, for the first time, to combat the ever enormously increasing plague of locusts, and has made their destruction compulsory. Besides having devoted large sums of money for the purpose, and appointing a central and local committee all over the Republic, the Government imposes fines for infractions of the law, and these sums, together with private aid from those most interested, form a very good working basis. There is no doubt that the number destroyed has been enormous, and it remains to be seen what ameliorating effect will be produced as a result. The locust winters in the northern and warmer provinces, flies southward in the spring, lays its eggs to the amount of about eighty, and dies. These eggs hatch out in about forty days, and the tiny insect, which has no serviceable wings at its birth, at once begins its devastating march, growing larger and larger, and shedding its skin some five times until, in about forty days from its birth and after its final shedding, it becomes fully fledged and full sized, and continues for some days committing its ravages in a flying state. Suddenly all take flight northward, where the winter is passed, and the process goes on *ad infinitum*. The method adopted for the destruction of these insects is as follows : Lengths of tin one foot high are extended for hundreds of yards, and pits are dug at intervals of fifty yards. The locust comes to the tin barrier, can not surmount it, and skirting the tin hops into the pit. At the end of each day the victims are covered up with earth, and are so destroyed. These are the hoppers (saltona), and require very little driving.

BOLIVIA.

FISCAL REVENUES OF 1897 AND BUDGET FOR 1898.

Señor GUITERREZ, Minister of Finance, has made a report to the National Congress, now in session, of the receipts of the Republic of Bolivia for the fiscal year 1897. The receipts of the country are divided into national and department or provincial revenue.

These are given in bolivianos, a silver dollar nearly similar in size and assay to the United States dollar, but at the present price of silver its exchange value, according to the report of the Treasury Department, is $0.436 United States currency.

The Minister reports the national revenue of Bolivia in 1897 as 4,840,300.56 bolivianos. The several sources of revenue were:

	Bolivianos.
Customs duties	2,691,722.71
Silver bullion and minerals	679,581.85
Duty on liquors	406,281.00
Revenue and postage stamps	238,890.45
Rubber exports and patents	149,002.92
Nickel money	149,000.00
Tin, copper, and bismuth	97,632.13
Tax on companies' patents	86,732.79
Consular invoices	75,543.76
Mint revenues	58,960.83
Mining patents	52,589.43
Duty on cattle and tolls	51,417.49
Duty on coca	40,000.00
Bills and mortgages	39,447.45
Duty on matches	14,085.67
Interest and items not specified	9,082.28
Gold	289.80
Trade-marks	40.00

The budget for 1898 estimates the amount to be expended at 5,714,793.80 bolivianos. These are distributed as follows:

	Bolivianos.
Instruction and public works	1,817,489.80
Finance Department	1,571,482.50
War Department	1,519,218.50
Foreign Affairs	389,817.00
Home and Justice Department	260,182.00
Legislative service	159,604.00

It is worthy of notice that more than one-third of the expenditure is now appropriated for popular instruction and public works, whereas, in the recent past, a much larger share of general expenditure was chargeable to the War Department. It will be noticed also that the revenue for 1897 falls short of the proposed expenditures for 1898.

The provincial revenue amounts to about 600,000 bolivianos. This is used in maintaining the provincial government and in executing works of local character.

The internal debt, acquired since the formation of the Republic, amounts to 3,707,541.20 bolivianos, but the Government is under

no immediate obligation to redeem this until Congress decides the
manner in which it is to be done.   The only other debt recognized
by the Government is one to Chilean creditors, to the payment of
which 40 per cent of the custom-house duties acquired in Arica
is devoted.   The original amount of this debt was about 6,500,000
bolivianos, on which 5,415,444.86 bolivianos had been paid at the
close of the fiscal year 1897.   The Bolivian custom-house agency
at Antofogasta produces about 1,300,000 bolivianos per year.   The
national mint at Potosi issues on an average 1,500,000 bolivianos
silver coin yearly.   Notwithstanding this, and 6,600,000 bolivianos in bank notes in circulation, there has been recently great
complaint of the scarcity of circulating medium.

RUBBER CULTURE.

In an interview, ALBERTO VIERLAND, an Austrian, residing at
La Paz, gives some facts about the condition of the india-rubber
business in Bolivia, of which the following is a summary:

All the best lands have been taken up, but are mainly in the
hands of people who have not capital to develop them, but who
are anxious to sell.   The gathering of rubber is very costly.   The
Indians who do the work demand high wages and insist on being
paid in advance.   They will work only for a limited time, being
afraid of climatic sickness.   The regions are always unhealthful,
as the rubber tree grows only in a low, marshy soil, with its roots
under water for a part of the year.   There is a profusion of rubber trees in the Bolivian forests, but Mr. VIERLAND knew of but
one cultivated plantation, and that contained only 100 trees.   The
trees usually grow in the valleys below the eastern slopes of the
Andes, and in the forests as many as 6,000 trees to the square
mile are found.   There are groves estimated to contain 10,000
trees.   These trees are of all sizes, from the very small to the
giant of the forest, 150 feet high and so large that it is said three
men joining hands could not reach around it.   A great deal of
money can be made out of the rubber business, but only by the
use of large capital.   A producer can not do much without
$25,000 or $50,000 capital, and he will make much more proportionately if he has $100,000 to invest.   With this amount
Mr. VIERLAND thinks he ought to net from 60 to 70 per cent a

year. Capitalists can secure rubber forests easily, as the best of the lands upon which such trees grow are now in the hands of "Cholos," or Bolivians with an admixture of Indian blood, who have taken up Government lands and have not the money to work them. The crude rubber from the producing district is conveyed on the backs of mules to La Paz, or to Chililaya, on Lake Titicaca, finding its way in time to Mollendo, on the Pacific coast, whence it goes to Liverpool, where it is marketed as "Mollendo" rubber, at prices only a little lower than for the best grades of "Bolivian."

BRAZIL.

THE NEW PRESIDENT.

Mr. M. F. DE CAMPOS SALLES, the new President of the United States of Brazil, who was inaugurated on November 15, has had a long and interesting political career. The following brief outline of his public services is compiled from reliable sources:

Before the rise of the Republican party, Dr. CAMPOS SALLES, then a very young man, belonged to what was called the Liberal party. In 1870, however, some leading Liberals organized the Republican party of Brazil, which assumed control of the Government in 1889. CAMPOS SALLES became one of the leaders of the new party in his own province, the present State of São Paulo. Previous to this, the Liberals had elected him deputy of the province of São Paulo, in which capacity it soon became evident that he was an orator and politician of considerable ability.

In 1884, despite very strong opposition on the part of the Imperialists, he was elected Deputy to the General Assembly, which corresponds to the present Federal Congress. It is a curious fact that, of the two Republican deputies then elected, one was the present President of the Republic and the other the President who has just retired, Dr. PRUDENTE DE MORAES. In the Imperial Parliament, Dr. CAMPOS SALLES made several speeches which were published and widely read throughout Brazil.

The Republic which was proclaimed on November 15, 1889, was for eighteen months under the direction of a provisional government, pending the drafting and adoption of the constitution.

The Republicans decided to extend the period of the provisional government in order to afford time for the establishment of various electoral reforms.   Dr. CAMPOS SALLES was a member of this provisional government during almost the whole of its existence, holding the Portfolio of Justice, in which he labored actively and zealously.   Himself a jurist, he surrounded himself with jurists and completed the reform of the judiciary, harmonizing the laws with the form of government.   Everything in the new constitution with reference to the judiciary is his work.

At the first general election of the Republic, Dr. CAMPOS SALLES was chosen Senator from his native State.   His work in the Senate corresponded with his past record, and he was considered one of its leading members.   On leaving the Senate, he was elected Governor of the State of São Paulo, holding the office until he was elected President, March 1, 1898.

The selection of Dr. CAMPOS SALLES as a candidate marks the decided distinction of parties in Brazil.   Previously, there had been various divergencies among the Republicans, but no distinct party differences.   But at that time there arose a party advocating the selection of a candidate who would favor the national against the foreign (naturalized) element; one who would have influence with the few remaining advocates of the monarchial government; who would give preference to a military over a civil government; finally, one who would introduce into the government the system called "Jacobinism," a designation which the new party did not refuse to accept.   Dr. CAMPOS SALLES was the candidate of the moderate Republicans or Conservatives, who were organized under the name of the Republican party, with a platform demanding respect for the constitution and declaring for the institution of such reforms as only reason and time should dictate.   The sympathies of the conservative element and of foreigners who had interests in the country were with the candidate of this party and gave him their support.

The election of Dr. CAMPOS SALLES inspired renewed confidence in the stability of Brazil, a confidence which was at once manifested by the higher quotation of the national bonds, by an advance in the rate of exchange, and by greater activity in business throughout the country.   Brazil, in spite of all hindrances, has prospered since 1889.   In proof of this, the citation of only two facts is sufficient: (1) In the nine years of the Republic the railway mileage has been doubled; (2) the largest coffee crop during the Empire (coffee was always the principal source of the country's wealth) was about 4,000,000 bags of 60 kilos (132 pounds), while the coffee crop of last year was more than 11,000,000 bags of the same weight. It is not the fault of the Republic that it has received as an inheritance from the Empire the system of inconvertible paper money, or that the net price of a bag of coffee has fallen everywhere, and that in Brazil it has dropped from (£4) $19.44 to (£1) $4.86. The country has immense resources other than coffee, and it is believed that a wise and energetic administration, such as the past official career of Dr. CAMPOS SALLES would indicate, must at least restore the wealth and credit of the Republic to its normal state.

Dr. CAMPOS SALLES is a descendant of one of the oldest families of the country and is about 55 years old. He is a native of the city of Campinas, State of São Paulo, to which State also belongs the retiring President, PRUDENTE DE MORAES. He is temperate and methodical in his manner of living, and to this is probably due that enviable physical strength which has enabled him to sustain the burdens of an active career. He has practiced the profession of law for many years and is a graduate of the Law School of São Paulo, which is one of the leading institutions of the country. His family has always enjoyed great wealth, derived principally from coffee plantations, and he himself has always been and still is the owner of fine coffee estates.

IMPORTS OF SHOES AND LEATHER.

The Republic of Brazil is a free importer of shoes and leather and buys directly of those countries to which the United States ships large quantities of leather and shoes. This being the case, it is logical to suppose that if the United States can supply the countries from which Brazil buys, it could compete with those countries in the markets of Brazil. The fact remains that the contrary is the case. In the fiscal year ending June 30, 1897, the shipments of shoes from the United States to Brazil amounted to $2,427; in the same period Germany sent $200,000 worth, England exported more than this amount, and France and Belgium enjoyed appropriate proportions of the business. The

English goods predominate over the German and Belgian articles. The French supply most of the high-priced women's shoes and the Austrians most of the low-priced women's goods. Of the leather and leather goods shipped to Brazil, England sent nearly $1,000,000 worth ; Germany, $650,000 worth, and France and Belgium likewise large shipments. The United States exports of leather goods amount to scarcely more than $33,000. Brazilians tan considerable quantities of leather, most of it being the product of the southern States. The quality of the leather, however, is not of the first class, and there is an opportunity for the sale of better grades on the part of the United States. In the manufacture of shoes the Republic has made some headway during the last few years, but the output is confined mainly to medium and low grades of men's shoes. One factory in Bahia turns out $1,000,000 worth of stock yearly.

IMPORTANCE OF THE RUBBER INDUSTRY.

That Brazil is a country of vast natural resources is a fact that can not be questioned. The great variety of its soil and the great climatic variation adapts its territory to nearly all the products of the temperate and torrid zones, yet despite this the Republic is best known to the commercial world through two articles—coffee and india rubber. Of these, especially the latter, it has had almost a monopoly. One is the product of the field, the other of the forest—the cultivated and the uncultivated. Formerly more attention was paid to the production of coffee, but in recent years, because of the increase of area devoted to it and the growing competition of other countries, prices have steadily declined until almost all the profit in coffee plantations has vanished. It is not so with rubber, for while the production of this forest tree, indigenous to almost the whole country, has increased with astonishing rapidity, prices have not only been maintained, but have gradually moved steadily upward.

The Government has not been slow to recognize this fact, and to note the increased amount of money brought into the country from its sale. Explorers say there is an abundant supply in the yet almost wholly unknown forests of the interior. But the Government is not satisfied to rest content with such evidence, and is working to acquaint the people with the habits of the several varieties of the rubber tree, the best means of cultivation, the adaptability of certain species to the soil of the different States, and the manner of preparing the crude product for the markets of the world. The growing use and availability of rubber in almost every industry has not escaped attention, and the product of cultivated plantations no doubt will soon supplement the yield from the forest trees. Even the wild trees are not to be neglected, for the Government proposes to prevent useless waste in that direction.

Recently, Consul CLARK at Pernambuco and Acting Vice-Consul RONSHEIM at Santos have made reports to the Department of State of the United States regarding the varieties of rubber, the quantities produced, and their value in the different States of Brazil. Mr. CLARK's communication treats of "maniçoba" and Mr. RONSHEIM's of "mangabeira rubber."

The former says the maniçoba plant is grown in the north of Brazil, especially in Ceara and Rio Grande do Norte and Parahyba. In price this is second to the "seringueira" or Para rubber, and for certain classes of work is preferred.

The interest in the growth of the plant is steadily increasing through the three States, and is also extending rapidly throughout Pernambuco, Alagoas, and Bahia, giving better results with less labor than almost any other agricultural pursuit. The seed is planted at the beginning of the winter, red or brown soil giving the best results. At the time of planting, the soil should be neither excessively dry nor wet. Once the tree has reached the age of two years it can resist any weather; but, of course, the amount of milk will always more or less depend on the climatic influence.

At 6 years the plant will have reached its maturity, which is the time best suited for tapping, though this may be begun at the age of 2 years. After 6 years the trees will produce annually, until the age of 30 years, from 2 to 5 kilograms (4.4 to 11 pounds) of rubber, if in good condition. After 30 years the yield will slightly decrease, the life being at least a century under fair conditions. The sap is prepared in exactly the same manner as the seringueira of Para, but is of a deeper brown color after smoking. The way the greater part of the maniçoba rubber is produced in the States named is simply to cut the bark of the tree, letting the sap run in drops to the base, where, by the action of the sun's rays, it coagulates and forms an irregular solid mass, which is gathered by the natives and sold to the middlemen, by whom it is shipped to America and Europe. The price per kilogram ranges in these States from 2 to 5 milreis (28 to 70 cents per 2.2046 pounds) according to the quality. Besides the maniçoba, these States produce a great quantity of mangabeira rubber, which is of an inferior grade and is used for covering cables, etc.

Mr. CLARK gives the following table of the rubber export from Ceara for the years 1893 to 1897, inclusive:

Year.	Quantity.	Value.	
	Kilos.*	Milreis.	
1893	135, 569	1, 129, 742	† $259, 840. 66
1894	146, 627	1, 221, 892	242, 378. 40
1895	146. 627	1, 592, 567	302, 587. 73
1896	324, 327	2, 702, 725	486, 490. 50
1897	475, 693	3, 964, 108	594, 616. 20

* 1 kilogram = 2.2046 pounds.
† The paper milreis estimated as follows: 1893, 23 cents; 1894, 20 cents; 1895, 19 cents; 1896, 18 cents; 1897, 15 cents. See Commercial Relations for 1896-97, vol. 1, p. 798.

In his report, Mr. RONSHEIM notes that during the last six months several consignments of mangabeira rubber arrived in Santos from the interior, and were quietly shipped to Europe. The results being fair, other expeditions were sent to the interior and the arrivals of rubber are increasing daily, promising to be an important source of revenue for this State, which, so far, has had to rely solely upon the export of coffee.

Among the many articles in the native press which have recently appeared on this subject, the Consul calls attention to one from the "Deutsche Zeitung," of São Paulo, of August 11, 1898, of which he gives this translation:

Brazilian rubber is extracted from trees belonging to three distinct families—
(1) *Hevea brasiliensis* Müll Arg. or seringueiro of the Amazon (Para rubber).
(2) *Manihot glaziovii* Müll Arg. or manicoba of Ceara (Ceara scraps).
(3) *Hancornia speciosa* Gom. or mangabeira (mangabeira rubber).

The first and second kinds do not concern São Paulo, as nothing has resulted from the seeds distributed by the Government among farmers. The third is found in the western part of São Paulo. It does not thrive in the east and on the coast, probably on account of the moisture or some condition of the soil.

Formerly, mangabeira rubber brought only about half as much as that of

Para, but the price has risen. It is said to be much harder and therefore preferable for certain purposes.

The newspapers say that during the first six months of 1898, 76,498 kilograms (168,647 pounds) have been transported by the Magyana Railroad. Experienced workmen from the State of Bahia are tapping the trees, the owners receiving one-third of the net profit, while buyers pay about 75 milreis per arroba (at the present rate of exchange about $11 for 33 pounds). One man is said to be able to extract as much as 3 kilograms (6.6 pounds) daily.

The Government is desirous of fostering the cultivation of this useful tree, and is considering the payment of subsidies to farmers occupied in this industry.

The "South American Journal," of October 8, states that the State of São Paulo has passed a law offering two premiums of 25,000 milreis each, and four of 15,000 milreis each, for the cultivation of mangabeira rubber; also that a premium of 15,000 milreis is offered for the best process of extracting the gum, and one of 10,000 milreis for the acclimatization of other rubber-producing trees. The "Journal" does not give whether these prizes are at gold or silver valuation. The gold milreis is estimated by the Treasury Department of the United States at $0.546.

CHILE.

INDUSTRIAL DEVELOPMENT OF THE REPUBLIC.

Chile is a country that buys merchandise of good quality and its markets are therefore worth cultivating by the manufacturers of the United States. The following brief résumé of the resources of the Republic is condensed from the complete descriptive account to be found in the Commercial Directory issued by the Bureau of the American Republics:

Chile has a length of 600 miles and a width varying from 50 to 200 miles. PEDRO DE VALDIVIA, the second Spanish invader, likened it to the blade of a sword, because of its great length and narrowness. Its area is 293,970 square miles, and, according to the census of 1895, the population was 2,766,747, or 9.2 inhabitants per square mile. The number of inhabitants now probably exceeds 3,300,000. Of this number, about one-half are engaged in agriculture, producing annually 28,500,000 bushels of wheat and 8,500,000 bushels of other cereals, besides vegetables, fruits, etc. More than 500,000 head of cattle and 2,000,000 goats, etc., are raised in the country each year. The mineral products, such as nitrate, copper, silver, gold, coal, manganese, etc., are extensive. Chile's nitrate fields cover an area of about 220,356 acres, estimated to contain 2,316,000 metric quintals (228,000,000 tons) of nitrate, being the most extensive in the world. The total product from these fields in 1897, as stated in a recent BULLETIN, was 1,040,000 tons.

An idea of the industrial development of Chile may be gained from the fact that in 1895, in the department of Valparaiso, with a population of less than 200,000, there were 417 industrial establisements, equipped with 162 steam engines, having a total of 1,766 horsepower, which during the year employed 12,616 operatives. Among these establishments were gas works, breweries, sugar refineries, carriage and wagon works, sawmills, factories for mineral and aerated waters, etc. Tanneries form a flourishing branch of the manufacturing industry.

Chile was the first country in South America to construct railroads. At the beginning of 1897 the total length of railways in the Republic was stated by Consul DOBBS to have been over 1,300 miles, completed and in course of construction, owned and worked by the State. There were also 938 miles owned and operated by private corporations, mainly English. The leading line is the Grand Central, belonging to the State, which is composed of three divisions, from Valparaiso to Santiago, and thence to Melipilla; from Santiago to Talca, from San Fernando to Alcones, and from Pelequen to Peumo; from Talca to Talcahuano, San Rosendo to Traiguen, Santa Fé to Los Angeles, and Robleria to Victoria—a total of 766 miles. Work on the Transandine Railway is now being vigorously prosecuted. According to the statistics obtained for the Commercial Directory, there are 25,000 miles of public roads and 2,875 miles of waterway in the country. At the end of 1895 the length of the State telegraph lines was 6,965 miles, with 8,330 miles of wire. There were also 4,500 miles of lines belonging to railways and private corporations.

Chile's merchant navy consisted in 1896 of 188 vessels, with a tonnage of 105,642 tons. Forty-two of these vessels were steamers. English, German, and French lines of steamships ply regularly between the coasts of Chile and Europe, through the Straits of Magellan, and constant and direct communication is maintained by Chilean and foreign steamship lines along the coast as far as Panama, there connecting with steamers for the Atlantic, Pacific, and Gulf ports of the United States and for Europe. Chile imports the bulk of the manufactured goods consumed, but the Government offers inducements for the establishment of new industries, and is anxious to promote manufactures. Congress is reported to have recently appropriated $500,000 to foster iron and steel enterprises, it having been demonstrated that a high grade of iron ore exists in abundance in the country. In 1897 the value of the imports into Chile amounted to $65,502,805 and the exports to $64,754,133.

IMPORTATIONS FROM FOREIGN COUNTRIES.

Mr. THOMAS WORTHINGTON, who was appointed by the Board of Trade, in December, 1897, on the suggestion of the Associated Chambers of Commerce of Great Britain, to inquire into the prospects of British trade in South America, has just presented reports on Chile to the board. Mr. WORTHINGTON states that the Government imports its own arms and ammunition. KRUPP has an agent in the country, and most of the Government supply in 1896 came from Germany. In regard to explosives, the shipment from the Continent is reported to be less hampered than from England. The coal consumption is about 1,200,000 tons per annum, of which about half is native and one-sixth West Hartley and other English coal. Much of this fuel comes to the nitrate ports in French vessels. In cast-iron goods the tinned ware is practically obsolete; and in enameled articles the British make is almost entirely superseded by that of Germany, owing solely to the much lower cost of the latter, but in quality the German is very inferior to the British. The German wrought-iron enameled ware has far outstripped the British, and now the United States is also competing. In iron—pig, bar, angle, and bolt—England still has the great bulk of the trade, but the Continental imports have made a great advance, while the English have stood still; the cheaper freight rates from Antwerp and Hamburg tell against the English. Iron pipes, anchors and chains, are practically all English. In cut iron nails the United

States manufactures seem to give the best satisfaction; the latter's nails are considered to be better proportioned, and less likely to turn over or to split the wood in driving. England practically holds the market in brass, iron, and steel screws.

EXPORTS OF NITRATE IN 1898.

The exports of nitrate, from Chile, for the current year are estimated at from 1,203,000 to 1,228,000 tons, as against 1,040,000 tons in 1897, 1,210,000 in 1896, and 1,075,000 in 1895. The total shipments from June 1 to November 1, were: For Europe, 745,000 tons; for North America, 122,000 tons, and for all other countries, 11,000 tons, making a total of 878,000 tons. The November and December shipments are expected to amount to between 300,000 and 350,000 tons. Assuming that these shipments do not exceed 325,000 tons, the total exports for 1898 will amount to 1,203,000 tons, or about 26,464,000 Spanish quintals. This will be 1,464,000 quintals more than the Minister of Finance of Chile calculated upon when his budget estimates for 1898 were sent to Congress.

The export duties received by Chile, including increased exports of nitrate, will, it is believed, amount to $41,729,777, as against the estimate of $41,000,000 in the budget for 1898.

COLOMBIA.

TRADE WITH NEW ORLEANS.

The Consul of the Republic of Colombia at New Orleans, Señor ESCRIPCIÓN CANAL, reports to his Government concerning the trade of his consular district with Colombia for the year 1897. From this it is learned that Colombian exports for the year, amounting to $947,717.20, consisted principally of bananas.

The exports to Colombia, via New Orleans, destined in great part for the port of Bocas del Toro, amounted to $155,219.77, the principal shipments being made in March, April, and November. The leading articles were rice, sugar, meats (canned), fish, liquors, hams, fowls, eggs, barley, onions, beans, soap, sperm candles, lard, butter, flour, corn, potatoes, bread, and crackers.

Agricultural implements, lumber, paints, drugs, and medicines, house and office furniture, writing materials, shoes, hats, ready-made clothes, crockery and glass were also exported in smaller quantities.

The consul notes that there is a balance of $792,497.43 in favor of Colombian trade, owing largely to the great exportation of bananas from the Island of Bocas del Toro. This port, which is the point of shipment for a very fertile agricultural district, only lacks appropriate and better methods for the exploitation and export of this and other products to become an important trade center.

The valuations given in this report are in Colombian currency, the silver peso or dollar being equivalent to $0.418.

THE NEW PANAMA CANAL.

In the course of a contribution to the " Forum," Gen. H. L. Abbott gives a description of the present condition of the Panama Canal, from which the following extracts are taken:

The entire length of the canal is 46 miles, of which about 15 miles on the Atlantic side and 7½ miles on the Pacific side, or about one-half of the whole distance, will be at sea level. Of this distance 18 miles, or about two-fifths of the entire route, is to-day essentially completed, so that at a moderate outlay for dredging it will be made at once serviceable. We have, therefore, only to consider the 23½ miles between Bujio on the Atlantic side and Miraflores on that of the Pacific. Two excellent harbors, which will demand no outlay for protection, are available; and the Panama Railroad skirts the canal throughout its entire route, to be availed of in construction.

By careful technical studies the company has succeeded in provisionally adjusting the project so that a choice between the best three different summit levels may be reserved, to be decided by actual experience in conducting the work upon a grand scale. These projects are designated as "Level 96⅓ feet," "Level 69 feet," and "Level 32⅓ feet," the figures indicating the elevation in feet of the bottom of the canal and its highest level above mean tide, which is found at practically the same absolute level in both oceans, although the tidal range at Colon is only a few inches, while at Naos at times it reaches 20 feet. A comparison of the estimated cost of construction, properly so called, has established that, as between larger excavations on the one hand and more locks and higher dams, etc., on the other, there will be nearly a balance of expenditure. The cost of either of the plans is estimated at $100,000,000.

COSTA RICA.

MODIFICATIONS OF TARIFF.

The Bureau of the American Republics has been furnished by the Government of Costa Rica with a special copy of the "International Customs Journal," containing the text of the laws modifying existing tariff rates. The first is the law of July 22, 1898, modifying the duties leviable on sugar and cocoa and prohibiting the importation of alcohol, as follows:

ART. 1. Numbers 85, 87, and 88 of Class IX of the customs tariff of September 7, 1885, are modified as follows:

		Cents.
White sugar of all kinds	kilog..	20
All other sugar	do...	15
Cocoa in powder	do...	20
Cocoa in the bean	do...	15

ART. 2. The importation of alcohol is prohibited.

ART. 3. The present law shall enter into force on the day of its publication.

The second is the law dated August 2, 1898, which amends the duty on starch.

ART 1. Numbers 27 and 85 of Classes III and IX of the customs tariff are modified as follows:

		Cents.
Starch	kilog..	15

ART. 2. The present law shall enter into force on the day of its publication.

The third, a law of the same date, establishes a monopoly for manufactured tobacco:

ART. 1. The importation of cigarettes, cigars, snuff, and tobacco, cut or otherwise manufactured, shall form a monopoly.

ART. 2. The Executive is authorized to procure the above-mentioned tobacco through private persons offering the same, provided that the latter undertake to place the tobacco at the disposal of the public at their own expense and discharge the principal value of the goods and the expenses resulting from their importation into the country and, prior to withdrawing the tobacco from the customs warehouses of the Republic, pay into the treasury a duty of 2 pesos 20 centavos per kilog. gross weight.

ART. 3. The present law shall enter into force on the day of its publication.

HONDURAS.

EXPERIENCE OF AN AGRICULTURIST.

The BULLETIN for July, 1898, contained an article on the people, climate, resources, etc., of Honduras. Incidentally, the name of W. M. BAMBERGE was mentioned by the writer. A copy of the BULLETIN was sent to Mr. BAMBERGE, who did not entirely agree with the statement made in the sketch, and subsequent correspondence led up to the following communication, under date of October 23, 1898, which portrays in an interesting manner the agricultural resources of the Republic as observed by a practical tiller of the soil:

I beg to submit the following as the result of five years' experience as an agriculturist in the Sula Valley, Honduras. I give you the facts, because you say "Honduras is the subject of numerous inquiries at this office," and I believe it best that the actual truth should be told those who design coming here. If my statements are not in harmony with those made by your correspondents, you can attribute the discrepancy to just that difference which exists between "the man who has wielded the hoe and followed the plow" and the man who has "farmed by word of mouth in the village store."

The immigrant on entering Honduras is struck with the luxuriant vegetation which clothes the landscape from the tops of the mountains to the lowest valleys and he immediately assumes the soil is rich, and, to use a stereotyped expression, "will grow anything." Without investigating, he floods the mails with letters to his family, friends, and home newspapers, and the subject matter of this correspondence is "eternal verdure," "richest soil on earth," "vegetation running riot," "terrestrial paradise," "spontaneous growth," and their changes. If agriculturally inclined, he gets some land, hires labor (if he can get it) and goes to work. In a few months, he sells out, if he can, or gives his place away if he can not sell, and goes back to the United States a poorer man and devotes his leisure time to cursing Honduras. Now, the fault does not lie in the country. Honduras is all right, and its soil and climate will produce just those articles which nature designed should thrive under its peculiar climatic conditions. Were a Hondurean to emigrate to the United States and settle in Ohio and there attempt the cultivation of the plantain, the banana, the mango, the papayo, the cashero nut, or any other tropical product, he would do just what the immigrant from the United States does who comes to Honduras and attempts the cultivation of those vegetables and fruits which thrive only in the temperate zone, and that is, make a complete failure. I admit that a few temperate-zone vegetables can be grown here, but it can only be done by giving them artificial conditions, and there is no market at prices which will justify this labor and expense. The time will come when such a market will exist, but not in the immediate future, I believe.   It is a fact that nothing in the line of economic vegetation (not indigenous to the tropics) grows here as rapidly as it would grow in the United States, nor do such plants produce as well here.   Sweet potatoes (*Convolvulus batata*) under the best cultivation, produce about 1,000 pounds to the acre.   Irish potatoes (*Solanum tuberosum*) will not return seed.   Tomatoes do not pay cost of staking and training the vines.   Taking one variety with another, a pound to the vine is an outside yield.   I have tried some twenty varieties and find the "Dwarf Champion" the most satisfactory.   Eggplants (*Solanum melongena*), if highly manured, yield fairly well.   Cabbage, by shading, manuring, and watering can be made to produce fair heads.   If bone meal and cotton-seed meal could be admitted to the farmer absolutely free of duty, cabbage growing could be made fairly remunerative.   Radishes do fairly well in sandy soils during the months of November, December, and January.   Lettuce requires much shading and care, and even then yields poorly.   Shallots and garlic do well during the rainy season.   Cucumbers, in a propitious season, make fairly well, but "propitious seasons" come so infrequently as to make the culture very precarious.   Okra (*Hibiscus esculentus*) does well and is remunerative.   Cantaloupes and watermelons will mature, but lack the flavor of those produced in the United States.   In five years we have failed to grow even a medium-sized onion, though both seeds and sets were tried of every variety that could be obtained.

Even were the conditions of climate favorable to the growth of the above-named vegetables, the insect enemies are so numerous and the cost of insecticides is so great as to eliminate any margin to the grower.   The most inveterate foe to agriculture is the leaf-bearing ant, known as "Saüba" to naturalists.   This destructive insect is found in every part of Honduras, from the highest mountain peaks to the deepest valleys, and seems to be increasing as rapidly as only ants and termites can multiply.   It is especially destructive to orange and mango trees and to cabbage and onion or shallot beds.   I have known them to completely denude a 10-year-old orange tree in a single night, and then continue their depredations upon the same tree until they killed it.   I also have known them to completely clean up a shallot patch of half an acre in a single night, while the quantity of cabbage they will carry off in the same time is only equaled by the size of the planted field.   BATES, the naturalist, mentions large tracts of land in Brazil upon which not even coffee can be grown owing to the ravages of this "Saüba," but I only know of one instance here when the leaf-carrying ant has attacked coffee.   Were the Government to enact laws looking to the extermination of this pest, and it appears to me this could be done economically and in a comparatively short time, the culture of oranges, lemons, and other citrus fruits could be made a profitable industry.   I have found bisulphide of carbon the most effective agent for the annihilation of the ant, but its excessive cost prohibits its use.

Now, if you will bear with me, I will present the other side and mention some things in which energetic Americans may make money in Honduras.   I do not mention everything, because I have not yet experimented sufficiently, but enough is spoken of to make wealthy all those who come here and work intelligently. Three or four men can combine their labor and profitably grow plantains and bananas. There is a steady local demand for plantains at from 50 cents to 75 cents per 100, while the steamships pay 31¼ cents (silver) per racimo (bunch) of bananas delivered anywhere alongside the railroad track. Banana suckers planted in April, May, and June will commence yielding the following April, and thenceforward cuttings can be made every week, provided the place is kept clean and the right kind of soil has been selected. Intending banana growers will find it money in their pockets to plant their own places, instead of buying one already planted. The culture of bananas is very simple. All the necessary information can be imparted in a few minutes, while the result will be in exact proportion to the labor performed.

Sugar cane once planted will produce an annual crop for from eight to twelve years with comparatively little labor. The juice can be converted into "dulce," which finds a ready sale among the natives. On our "finca" we convert our cane into sugar by the evaporating pan, which is similar to, but much more rapid than, the old-fashioned "open kettle" process. We produce an extremely light-colored sugar, for which we find a ready sale. There are no large sugar plantations in Honduras (to my knowledge), but this does not signify that many would not pay. My opinion is that sugar making on a large scale would prove profitable, even though it was found necessary to bring the labor from the United States.

There are hundreds of spots within reasonable distance of the railroad that have virgin soil, shady, and well drained, which is essential to the profitable cultivation of cocoa (it is the fruit of this tree from which chocolate is made), and which only await the introduction of brain and brawn to convert their unprofitable stillness into the hum of commercial prosperity. The tree should bear its first crop in three years from seed, and should continue bearing for twenty-five years. There is a steadily increasing demand for the product at remunerative prices.

The tree yielding the rubber of commerce, so far as I have observed, has no insect enemies. Like all other tropical plants, it improves under intelligent cultivation. Once planted under proper conditions and properly cared for until firmly established will yield its annual product for years. The rubber tree will grow almost anywhere in the Republic, but it is only in rich, moist, well-drained soils that its culture will prove profitable. I have planted only for experimental purposes, yet I have demonstrated to my perfect satisfaction that rubber trees properly planted and cared for have made treble the growth of those planted in the woods, "native style." Native rubber tappers do not approve of tapping trees under 8 years of age. Next August my cultivated rubber trees will be three years from seed, when I shall tap them and give you the result. From my investigations I am confident that there is more sure money to the average American in rubber planting than in any other class of investment possible in Honduras. I will cheerfully give estimates to anyone caring to investigate.

We are possibly too far distant (time used in transportation considered) to profitably ship pineapples to the United States at present, but there is no earthly reason why a company should not grow the fruit here and ship the canned product. It is not necessary that the company should be a very strong one financially; on the contrary, a mutual or cooperative company would make a more certain success than one backed by money solely. From the planting of the "slips," which form at the base of the fruit, to the maturing of the fruit, is from eighteen to twenty months; after that each plant will produce 2 or 3 fruits, which grow on the suckers, so called, which spring from the stem of the original plant. I think that the best results are obtained by setting the plants 4 feet apart in the rows and the same distance between rows. A little shade is beneficial to pines here. By planting at the distance above stated, you have 4,692 plants to the "manzana," which, after the first crop, will yield, at a minimum estimate, 9,000 fruits per annum. We grow three varieties here, the favorite being the "sugar loaf," which not only attains a very large size, but is very sweet and melting. JEAN DE LERY, who described the pineapple over three hundred years ago, said; "It should only be gathered by the hand of Venus, and fed alone to the gods." JEAN must have tasted a sugar loaf.

The indigenous vanilla, if carefully cured, has a very pleasant aroma and should have a commercial value. I have made an extract from the native bean (curing it as is done in Mexico) and found it very good for family use. I had no means of determining the quantity or percentage of the active principle of the bean. There is no doubt the vanilla will produce freely, and by cultivating (that is reducing the overhead shade and thinning out the undergrowth to permit free circulation of air) a longer and more profitable bean will result. The natives do not seem to care to give the curing of the product the attention necessary to produce a commercial commodity.

Lemons grow rapidly, producing fruit three years from seed. This citrus fruit has, so far as I have observed, few, if any insect enemies. There is not sufficient grown here to justify exportation, but there is no doubt that there will be some attention given this most profitable article in the near future. California and Florida have not sufficient area, were they planted wholly in lemon trees, to supply the United States, and Honduras can supply the deficiency.

The very best coffee I have seen of Honduras growth was grown in the Sula Valley (altitude about 200 feet above the sea level), with plantains for shade. I know that coffee growers claim that coffee can only be grown at an altitude of between 2,500 and 5,000 feet, but circumstances alter cases, and where the conditions for the growth of coffee exist, there coffee will be grown, be the altitude one foot or 10,000 feet. The only impediment to the growth of coffee is the difficulty of obtaining labor at the time needed and at fair wages. At the present time "mozos" (unskilled farm laborers) are difficult to get at $1.50 (silver) per day of eight hours' work. This is more than coffee growers or farmers can afford to pay. I am told that wages are much lower in the interior, but the difficulty of obtaining labor is about the same. Coffee has not had a profitable crop the past season, though it will, no doubt, pay better in the future, for an increased acreage and close grading will give Honduras coffee a classing on its merits, which the limited quantity now exported does not justify.

But I have written at a greater length than I intended and have not mentioned many products in which both the large and small grower can make money. In a future communication I will mention other fruits and fiber and medicinal plants.

MEXICO.

STATISTICS OF FOREIGN TRADE.

The Mexican fiscal statistics for the year ending June 30, 1898, were issued by the finance department in October and present a showing especially favorable to the Government. The imports show an increase over those of 1896 of $1,399,397. Among the articles whose importation increased to the greatest extent are the following: Machinery for mining and industrial purposes, material for railways, cotton manufactures, and crude, bleached, and printed cotton goods. The items which show a decrease are maize, lard, flour, and foodstuffs in general.

The total amount of exports is $128,972,749, which, a few years ago, would have been considered almost incredible. This sum was principally made up of ores which contained the precious metals, being valued at $75,042,332, leaving the amount from all other articles at $53,930,417. The total compared with the total of the previous year, $111,346,494, shows an increase of $17,626,255. Compared with the year 1896, the increase in exports has been $9,859,235 in precious metals and ores and $8,767,020 in all other articles.

The following list gives the countries from which the greatest amount of imports were received, and also the valuation of the exports to those countries:

	Importations.	Exportations.
United States	$21,490,604	$94,974,616
England...	8,105,696	14,775,638
France...	5,435,698	5,320,016
Germany...	4,781,821	6,995,733
Spain...........	2,039,132	1,231,342
Belgium...	590,196	1,556,090
Italy	186,273	30,600
Switzerland..........................	156,732	200
Austria	125,144	....
Holland...	103,913	719,322
Brazil...	8,658	....
Colombia........	24,127	2,260
Ecuador...	73,681	342
Guatemala...	14,950	846,016
Cuba...	1,130	2,152,544
Peru	314	7,999
Salvador...	3,648	21,191
Santo Domingo	38	50,720
Venezuela...	36,963	170
Russia	19,644	270,370

BUREAU OF INFORMATION.

It is stated in the "American Manufacturer" that Governor
TEODORO A. DEHESA, of the State of Vera Cruz, has established in
Xalapa a special bureau of information, through which it is proposed to furnish to such persons as may be interested any general
specific information that may be desired respecting the State of
Vera Cruz. The State is well provided with railroads and, in the
lower levels, with numerous navigable rivers, by which the producer
finds easy access to the seaports of the Gulf coast and to Salina
Cruz on the Pacific, while, by different lines of railway, the interior
of the country can be quickly and cheaply reached. The State
is also well provided with water power furnished by the numerous
perennial mountain streams that descend to the coast, and is sufficient for manufactories or industries of any description or magnitude. The State is developing rapidly and is about to receive
fresh·impetus through the projection of several new lines of railway and through the improvements to the harbors of Vera Cruz,
Coatzacoalcos, and Salina Cruz. That of Vera Cruz is almost
completed, vessels being now able to receive and discharge cargo
from the city's wharves. The design of the bureau is to furnish,
without charge, reliable information from official sources to any
who may wish to acquaint themselves with the advantages offered
by the State of Vera Cruz, with the view of investing in lands,
engaging in agricultural or mechanical pursuits, opening channels
of trade, or developing in any form the resources of the State, and
also to advise with those who may visit the State for such purposes. Inquiries may be addressed to ALEXANDER M. GAW,
Special Agent, Xalapa, State of Vera Cruz, Mexico.

RECENT MINERAL DISCOVERIES.

A large deposit of copper and silver ore has been discovered
a short distance from the terminus of the Rio Grande and Pacific
Railroad. In the State of Durango a new silver mine has been
discovered and is being opened at Coneto Camp. A valuable
gold deposit has been opened at Sauçes Camp, and the old Santa
Fe mine at the same point is again being worked. THOMAS
WARK and others have opened up the Eureka mine near Canatlan, and half a mile southeast of Gavalon mines a new mine of

valuable silver has been opened up.   In the State of Sonora the Mesa Quemada mines are producing good results.   In working in the tunnel to communicate with the Guillermina mine a rich vein of high-grade silver ore was discovered by the operators.   The placer mines of Palomas are reported as producing many nuggets of fine gold.   In the State of Guerrero a new silver mine has been discovered on the banks of the Hueymatla River, near Taxco el Viejo.   Engineer WILLIAM BAKER has reported the discovery of a valuable vein of gold ore at a point close to Los Ollos, in the State of Michoacan.   The "Weekly Herald" reports the sale of the valuable San Juan and Santo Domingo mines near Etzatlan, in the State of Jalisco, to an American company.   In the State of Tepic, the Tajitos mine near Santa Maria del Oro is again being worked by Mexican capital.   The ore contains iron, gold, and silver.   In the State of Hidalgo a new silver mine has been recently opened near Mineral del Oro.

At Sonora, Mexico, a deposit of sodium carbonate has been discovered 2 miles inland from Adair Bay, an indentation from the Gulf of California, 100 miles south of the mouth of the Colorado River.   The deposit is said to cover an area of about 70 acres, in the center of which are several flowing springs, the water being strongly impregnated with the salts.   This water has spread over the surrounding area, and evaporation has formed a crust of the crystallized salts of from 1 to 3 feet in thickness, beneath which is 12 or 18 inches of water   As this crust is excavated and taken away the water from below quickly fills its place, and very shortly, by evaporation, the crust is completely renewed, making the deposit practically inexhaustible.   It is estimated that there are at present fully 100,000 tons available in the deposit, and a trial shipment to San Francisco yielded handsome returns. Sodium carbonate is used in the manufacture of acids, glass, bicarbonate of soda, etc., and there is a steady demand for it for these purposes.

It is stated in the "Le Monde Economique" that several deposits of tin have been discovered in Mexico, principally in the States of Guanajuato, San Luis Potosi, and Sonora.   The heights of the Sierra de la Estanera, in the mining district of Comanja (State of San Luis Potosi), contain tin ore which assays from 70 to 75 per cent of metal.   In the State of Durango also tin is met with in considerable quantities, which, if properly treated, would yield from 35 to 75 per cent of metal, often under the form of oxides. If the deposits prove to be extensive, the production of tin will undoubtedly be a source of revenue for the Government.

NICARAGUA.

TARIFF CHANGES.

The Bureau of the American Republics has just received information from Mr. M. J. Clancy, United States Consular Agent at Bluefields, that the new tariff which went into operation last September proved so unsatisfactory, that the Government has revoked it, so that all merchandise now at the custom-house at Bluefields and subsequent importations will pay duty according to the tariff and special enactments relating thereto that were in operation on the 30th of August, 1898.

The new tariff to which Mr. Clancy refers was published in the Monthly Bulletin for October of this year, in the form of a decree, by which the duties on all imports averaged 100 per cent over the former schedule. Some articles, such as rice, beans, corn, and potatoes, that were formerly on the free list had to pay, according to this new tariff, 10 cents per kilo in Nicaraguan currency (4 cents gold). All duties were to be paid on each kilogram of net weight. Some articles were taxed as high as 250 per cent upon their original value. The duties imposed by this new tariff were to be paid at the general treasury in the following manner: Twenty per cent in orders against the custom-houses established by decree of October 30, 1896; 15 per cent in orders against the custom-houses established June 19, 1897; 15 per cent in Government obligations, duly liquidated and acknowledged, and 50 per cent in currency.

According to the tariff of 1888, which was published by this Bureau in 1892 in the Handbook of Nicaragua, duties are assessed on the gross weight, no deduction being made for the package.

POSTAL CONVENTION.

The Diet of the Greater Republic of Central America, in behalf of the State of Nicaragua, has entered into a postal convention with the French Government for the exchange of postal parcels. This agreement was made in Paris on the 12th of June, 1897, between the Representative of the Diet and the Minister of Foreign Affairs of France. The exchange of the ratifications took place in the same city, June 8, 1898.

Among the provisions of this convention, the following are found:

The postal parcels to be mailed without declaration of their value from France and Algiers to Nicaragua, or from Nicaragua to France and Algiers, may weigh as much as 5 kilograms. The French post-office guarantees the transportation of postal parcels between France and the port of Colon by the French mail steamers. For each package sent from France and Algiers to Nicaragua the French post-office shall pay Nicaragua a territorial duty of 50 centimes and a duty of 50 centimes for the maritime transit between Panama and Corinto or San Juan del Sur. For each parcel sent from Nicaragua to France or Algiers the Nicaraguan post-office shall pay France a territorial duty of 50 centimes and a maritime duty of 2 francs for the transportation between France and Colon. The post-office of Nicaragua is authorized to collect from the sender, in case of parcels sent from France to Nicaragua, the expense of railway transportation between Panama and Colon. The two contracting parties reserve the right to collect 25 centimes for postal parcels sent from continental France to Nicaragua, and vice versa.

The country of destination reserves the right to collect from the person receiving the parcel a fee not exceeding 25 centimes per parcel for the delivery of it and for compliance with custom-house regulations. Packages containing letters or notes having the character of correspondence, or objects the admission of which is not authorized by the laws or regulations of the custom-house or other laws, shall not be sent by the mails under this contract. Except in case of force majeur, when a postal parcel has been miscarried, damaged, or lost, the sender, and in case he fails to make the demand, the addressee, has the right to an indemnity covering the damage or loss. This indemnity, however, must not exceed 15 or 25 francs, if the package does not weigh more than 3 kilograms. When a package is lost, the sender has the right to the return of fees paid.

The obligation to pay the indemnity devolves upon the post-office department of the country to which the office sending the package belongs, but this department has the right to claim the reimbursement of the amount from the post-office of the other country, when the damage or loss of the package has occurred within its jurisdiction. Until the contrary is proven, the responsibility falls upon the post-office department that, having received the package, can not prove that it has been delivered to the addressee or forwarded elsewhere. The payment of the indemnity by the office from which the package was sent must be made as soon as possible, and not later than one year from the date of the presentation of the claim. The office responsible for the loss or damage must return without delay to the office sending the package the amount of the indemnity paid by the latter.

It is understood that the claim can not be presented after the expiration of a year from the date of the delivery of the package at the post-office.   After this period the claimant shall have no right to indemnity.   If the loss or damage occurs in transit between the two countries and it is impossible to fix the responsibility, each country shall be responsible for one-half.   Should extraordinary circumstances justify it, either of the post-office departments may suspend the postal-parcel service partially or entirely, but under the condition that the other shall be immediately advised, by telegraph if necessary.

This convention shall remain in force until one of the parties shall have informed the other, one year in advance, of its intention to abrogate it.

PARAGUAY.

EXPERIENCE OF A UNITED STATES IMMIGRANT.

A few months since Mr. I. WAVRUNK wrote to the Bureau of the American Republics asking for information concerning the inducements offered by Paraguay to immigrants.   The Bureau communicated with Hon. W. R. FINCH, United States Minister to Paraguay, asking for the latest immigration laws of the country, and upon being received a copy was sent to Mr. WAVRUNK, who availed himself of the opportunities offered.   Recently he has written to Mr. FINCH, detailing his experiences.   From his letter, dated September 23, 1898, and forwarded to the Bureau through the courtesy of the Minister, the following extracts are taken:

I deem it my duty to inform you that I have finally located on a piece of land near the Colonia Gonzales, and that I am well satisfied with the selection. Before settling here I visited three other colonies in Paraguay, but found that the advantages in Colonia Gonzales overbalanced all the others.   I was fortunate in securing an allotment of 62 acres, upon which there were considerable improvements made by a former occupant.   About 15 acres are cultivated, 3½ or 4 of which have been planted in sugar, and the same number in mandioca. There are 43 orange trees, 30 banana plants, 30 grapevines, etc., most of which will bear fruit this year.   There is a running spring on the place and other advantages, not the least of which is that the railway station is less than two miles distant.   The Government has been extremely liberal, having furnished me free transportation to the colony, and men and teams to put my effects upon the land.   It furnished me with a cow and calf and all the necessary tools and seeds for planting.   In short, the officials did all they could to help me.   In consideration of the improvements, I assumed a debt upon the premises to the amount of 1,130 pesos ($1,130), but as this is not to be paid before ten years, without interest, it is practically nothing.   We are delighted with the country and climate, but miss the English language, which we seldom hear spoken.   This colony consists principally of Germans and French, but the people are all kind and generous.

UNITED STATES.

STATISTICS OF IMMIGRATION.

The annual report of the Commissioner-General of Immigration, Hon. T. V. Powderly, has been submitted to the Secretary of the Treasury, and shows that the decrease in the number of immigrants arriving during the fiscal year ending June 30, 1898, as compared with the year previous, was only 1,533, the total arrivals being 229,299.   Of this number, 135,775 were males and 83,524 females.   Italy contributed the largest number, viz, 58,613; followed by Russia with 27,221; Ireland, 25,128; Germany, 17,111; Sweden, 12,398; and England, 9,877.   Those debarred from landing represented a total of 3,030, or about 1⅓ per cent.   Of this number, 2,261 were paupers, and not acceptable because of their liability to become public charges.   Those coming under the ban of contract laborers were 417.   Those returned on account of diseases were 258.

Although during the heavy immigration months, the United States was on the verge of, or engaged in, war, this did not deter immigration, and it is to be assumed that, unless the laws are further amended at the present session of Congress, the number of new arrivals will exceed during the next year those of the current year.   The Commissioner advances several ideas with regard to amendments of the laws.   For instance, he favors an increase of the per capita tax from $1 to $2, his purpose being to provide a fund which will enlarge the usefulness of the Bureau of Immigration with respect to increasing the facilities for greater protection against the admission of criminal and other undesirable classes.   The repeal of the law prohibiting the expenditure of a larger sum for the care of immigration at any one port than may have been collected at such port is also recommended.

TRADE WITH LATIN AMERICA.

STATEMENT OF IMPORTS AND EXPORTS.

Following is the latest statement, from figures compiled by the Bureau of Statistics, United States Treasury Department, O P. AUSTIN, Chief, showing the value of the trade between the United States and the Latin-American countries. The report is for the month of September, corrected to October 28, 1898, with a comparative statement for the corresponding period of the previous year; also for the nine months ending September, 1898, compared with the corresponding period of the fiscal year 1897. It should be explained that the figures from the various customhouses showing imports and exports for any one month are not received at the Treasury Department until about the 20th of the following month, and some time is necessarily consumed in compilation and printing, so that the returns for September, for example, are not published until some time in November:

IMPORTS OF MERCHANDISE.

Articles and countries.	September—		Nine months ending September—	
	1897.	1898.	1897.	1898.
Chemicals:				
Logwood (*Palo campeche; Pâu campeche; Campêche*)—				
Mexico..........................	....	$7, 849	$40, 028	$9, 641
Coal, bituminous (*Carbón bituminoso; Carvão betuminoso; Charbon de terre*):				
Mexico...	$16, 045	18, 319	182, 416	159, 358
Cocoa (*Cacao; Coco ou Cacáo crú; Cacao*):				
Brazil	13, 349	30, 890	165, 279	137, 867
Other South America	115, 963	34, 496	787, 074	925, 100
Coffee (*Café*):				
Central America...............	121, 793	145, 009	6, 214, 862	3, 997, 829
Mexico	206, 318	113, 939	4, 574, 252	2, 723, 255
Brazil........................	3, 546, 204	3, 472, 271	34, 744, 837	26, 202, 620
Other South America...........	861, 986	483, 559	7, 892, 718	5, 884, 671
Cotton, unmanufactured (*Algodón en rama; Algodão em rama; Coton, non manufacturé*):				
South America.................	....	1, 933	73, 299	131, 158

IMPORTS OF MERCHANDISE—Continued.

Articles and countries.	September—		Nine months ending September—	
	1897.	1898.	1897.	1898.
Fibers:				
Sisal grass (*Henequén; Henequen; Hennequen*)—				
Mexico	$218,542	$196,749	$2,962,093	$5,623,075
Philippine Islands	27,827	127,460	2,635,221	2,133,437
Fruits:				
Bananas (*Plátanos; Bananas; Bananes*)—				
Central America	118,860	151,715	1,230,992	1,343,474
South America	34,276	39,229	607,045	408,809
Hawaiian Islands	4,647	2,829	37,249	32,286
Oranges (*Naranjas; Laranjas; Oranges*)—				
Mexico	3,680	340	22,444	4,070
Fur skins (*Pieles finas; Pelles; Fourrures*):				
South America	5,314	....	25,020	73,137
Hides and skins (*Cueros y pieles; Couros e pelles; Cuirs et peaux*):				
Central America	12,237	27,221	163,877	159,403
Mexico	106,474	83,258	1,488,283	1,306,751
South America	347,944	578,655	7,681,222	7,307,567
India rubber, crude (*Goma elástica cruda; Borracha crua; Caoutchouc brut*):				
Central America	30,943	53,713	309,538	376,616
Mexico	2,535	2,538	26,071	40,663
Brazil	1,213,863	634,115	9,210,648	9,779,200
Other South America	40,771	87,002	284,872	566,255
Lead, in pigs, bars, etc. (*Plomo en galápagos, barras, etc.; Chumbo em linguados, barras, etc.; Plombs en saumons, en barres, etc.*):				
Mexico	200,748	106,120	1,234,508	1,237,086
Sugar, not above No. 16 Dutch standard (*Azúcar, no superior al No. 16 de la escala holandesa; Assucar não superior ao No. 16 de padrão hollandez; Sucre, pas au dessus du type hollandais No. 16*):				
Central America	....	3,807	....	206,319
Mexico	....	351	10,636	43,919
Cuba	356	1,124,029	9,933,284	11,021,781
Brazil	....	24,321	1,839,639	2,386,886
Other South America	25,508	475,838	3,436,772	3,602,996
Hawaiian Islands	1,101,708	1,280,369	12,664,769	14,328,404
Philippine Islands	....	90,033	389,898	823,233
Tobacco, leaf (*Tabaco en rama; Tabaco em folha; Tabac en feuilles*):				
Mexico	80,653	64,227	285,499	201,278
Cuba	578,855	205,084	1,991,957	1,882,006

Bull. No. 6——4

IMPORTS OF MERCHANDISE—Continued.

Articles and countries.	September—		Nine months ending September—	
	1897.	1898.	1897.	1898.
Wood, mahogany (*Caoba; Mogno; Acajou*):				
Central America	$14,596	$35,058	$80,504	$146,378
Mexico	25,479	68,209	290,044	214,887
Cuba	606	....	22,625	933
South America	984	....	37,652	35,241
Wool (*Lana; Lã; Laine*):				
South America—				
Class 1 (clothing)	210,320	22	4,873,326	534,370
Class 2 (combing)	....	....	1,183,201	19,029
Class 3 (carpet)	40	657	1,176,766	759,641

EXPORTS OF DOMESTIC MERCHANDISE.

	September—		Nine months ending September—	
Agricultural implements (*Instrumentos de agricultura; Instrumentos de agricultura; Machines agricoles*):				
Central America	$660	$3,326	$19,577	$5,290
Mexico	7,957	17,390	99,448	116,131
Santo Domingo	52	50	1,055	354
Cuba	784	129	5,165	2,550
Porto Rico	437	....	2,235	426
Argentina	25,321	435,505	239,629	805,511
Brazil	2,233	983	17,322	18,838
Colombia	397	....	2,925	3,895
Other South America	36,018	36,171	101,242	224,027
Animals:				
Cattle (*Ganado vacuno; Gado; Betail*)—				
Central America	1,590	....	14,582	2,165
Mexico	305	6,945	19,986	66,127
South America	200	1,766	2,528	6,903
Hogs (*Cerdos; Porcos; Cochons*)—				
Mexico	167	135	68,174	4,733
Horses (*Caballos; Cavallos; Chevaux*)—				
Central America	1,400	2,020	12,250	10,915
Mexico	2,610	11,801	54,748	77,566
South America	....	173	2,800	2,023
Sheep (*Carneros; Carneiros; Moutons*)—				
Mexico	1,805	2,857	4,407	8,802
South America	601	875	12,639	8,253
Books, maps, engravings, etc. (*Libros, mapas, grabados, etc.; Livros, mappas, gravuras, etc.; Livres, cartes de géographie, gravures, etc.*):				
Central America	1,196	1,044	32,765	23,148
Mexico	7,286	5,989	82,193	61,237
Santo Domingo	36	4	666	858

EXPORTS OF DOMESTIC MERCHANDISE—Continued.

Articles and countries.	September—		Nine months ending September—	
	1897.	1898.	1897.	1898.
Books, maps, engravings, etc.—C't'd.				
Cuba	$500	$2,729	$60,635	$5,534
Porto Rico		957	2,659	1,322
Argentina	641	1,803	22,876	18,033
Brazil	27,518	4,197	168,092	36,651
Colombia	6,525	507	29,977	7,564
Other South America	2,401	4,516	36,341	37,255
Breadstuffs:				
Corn (*Maíz; Milho; Maïs*)—				
Central America	4,283	2,060	51,969	45,820
Mexico	1,785	724	989,429	6,984
Santo Domingo			379	63
Cuba	30,428	9,861	216,119	237,152
South America	1,251	1,579	16,055	14,339
Wheat (*Trigo; Trigo; Blé*)—				
Central America	4,180	6,923	36,563	32,855
South America	367,467	44	923,218	385,777
Wheat flour (*Harina de trigo; Farina de trigo; Farine de blé*):				
Central America	90,649	86,365	886,865	942,690
Mexico	2,433	7,501	69,561	71,630
Santo Domingo	11,909	898	131,691	147,810
Cuba	53,416	121,425	354,023	946,001
Porto Rico	46,510	59,267	459,391	256,843
Brazil	342,937	258,792	2,731,886	2,239,779
Colombia	74,021	20,744	428,663	290,066
Other South America	203,432	125,404	1,217,575	1,147,640
Carriages, cars, etc., and parts of (*Carruages, carros y sus accesorios; Carruagens, carros e partes de carros; Voitures, wagons et leurs parties*):				
Central America	2,631	1,904	90,566	36,636
Mexico	134,569	45,409	664,604	206,959
Santo Domingo	359		13,477	10,671
Cuba	333	384	11,346	19,561
Porto Rico	1,040	16	6,882	1,445
Argentina	16,327	28,280	108,332	454,505
Brazil	17,187	19,096	124,586	548,400
Colombia	5,972	1,184	36,971	39,249
Other South America	5,058	1,768	39,820	66,965
Cycles and parts of (*Biciclos y sus accesorios; Bicyclos e accessorios; Bicyclettes et leurs parties*):				
Central America	466	585	18,708	5,554
Mexico	4,648	5,735	56,112	50,951
Santo Domingo	102		3,722	598
Cuba	593	61	6,959	3,406
Porto Rico	522	124	3,104	1,354
Argentina	6,314	8,579	36,124	79,031
Brazil	6,833	5,879	23,453	82,040
Colombia	1,788	503	15,730	6,893
Other South America	4,334	2,142	46,659	34,518

EXPORTS OF DOMESTIC MERCHANDISE—Continued.

Articles and countries.	September—		Nine months ending September—	
	1897.	1898.	1897.	1898.
ches (*Relojes de pared Relogios de parede e de bolso; Pendules et montres*):				
Central America............	$266	$66	$8,062	$4,148
Mexico......................	2,297	1,419	16,527	15,183
Argentina...................	1,651	....	14,151	22,966
Brazil	2,223	6,103	20,244	33,174
Other South America..........	5,096	6,436	65,462	65,177
Coal (*Carbón; Carvão; Charbon*):				
Central America...............	1,992	1,094	17,627	7,754
Mexico......................	64,622	76,453	628,090	828,127
Santo Domingo.................	225	1,198	15,758	7,821
Cuba	23,369	52,268	420,103	320,268
Porto Rico..................	1,906	....	37,597	15,098
Brazil........................	....	55,618	82,526	125,605
Colombia	19	184	30,242	17,331
Other South America..........	5,695	28,982	29,977	100,619
Copper (*Cobre; Cobre; Cuivre*):				
Mexico......................	1,098	799	11,552	26,708
Cotton, unmanufacture 1 (*Algodón no manufacturado; Algodão não manufacturado; Coton non manufacturé*):				
Mexico......................	14,179	54,543	411,973	623,539
Cotton cloths (*Tejidos de algodón; Fazendas de algodão; Coton manufacturé*):				
Central America...............	40,523	64,504	396,207	349,469
Mexico	23,054	39,541	292,776	333,763
Santo Domingo.................	4,701	5,224	59,126	111,523
Cuba	201	241	14,137	6,192
Porto Rico..................	73	143	3,455	1,166
Argentina...................	9,328	12,725	95,580	121,536
Brazil	35,655	37,657	413,760	423,855
Colombia	24,742	19,773	275,345	205,328
Other South America..........	91,705	71,576	863,403	918,296
Wearing apparel (cotton) (*Ropa de algodón; Roupa de algodão; Vêtements en coton*):				
Central America...............	9,371	12,845	171,117	165,220
Mexico·.....................	16,827	26,570	222,082	278,597
Santo Domingo	1,006	1,299	17,578	15,879
Cuba	520	1,169	13,692	12,024
Porto Rico..................	68	85	2,308	831
Argentina......	7,274	4,056	39,063	32,671
Brazil	4,705	2,889	44,378	32,269
Colombia	2,667	2,134	40,157	28,466
Other South America..........	2,623	5,017	35,463	31,916
Fruits and nuts (*Frutas y nueces; Frutas e nozes; Fruits et noisettes*):				
Central America...............	2,565	2,385	38,687	20,350
Mexico......................	3,111	6,056	41,074	43,883
Santo Domingo.................	99	23	632	475

EXPORTS OF DOMESTIC MERCHANDISE—Continued.

Articles and countries.	September—		Nine months ending September—	
	1897.	1898.	1897.	1898.
Fruits and nuts—Continued.				
Cuba	$3,742	$4,942	$19,809	$17,447
Porto Rico	128	244	1,674	531
Argentina	883	155	4,024	6,676
Brazil	16	1,374	3,924	6,324
Colombia	386	356	6,966	5,725
Other South America	2,311	1,672	20,337	11,806
Hides and skins (*Cueros y pieles; Couros e pelles; Cuirs et peaux*):				
Central America			543	
Mexico	183	210	13,618	2,209
Hops (*Lúpulos; Lupulos; Houblons*):				
Central America	195	230	2,727	3,165
Mexico	9,612	98	80,339	7,635
Santo Domingo			2	16
South America	77	22	959	977
Instruments:				
Electric and scientific apparatus (*Aparatos eléctricos y científicos; Apparelhos electricos e scientificos; Appareils électriques et scientifiques*)—				
Central America	3,560	10,705	70,326	54,538
Mexico	18,420	7,323	228,820	224,409
Argentina	2,117	32,140	132,773	129,186
Brazil	5,451	13,121	92,497	53,265
Other South America	18,518	6,197	128,443	80,833
Iron and steel, manufactures of:				
Builders' hardware, and saws and tools (*Materiales de metal para construcción, sierras y herramientas; Ferragens, serras e ferramentas; Matériaux de construction en fer et acier, scies et outils*):				
Central America	7,534	6,332	94,223	56,043
Mexico	20,797	21,414	423,936	286,370
Santo Domingo	1,294	10	9,847	8,847
Cuba	4,266	9,493	47,078	34,797
Porto Rico	1,003	688	10,490	4,387
Argentina	9,106	20,998	130,172	138,444
Brazil	12,095	20,325	150,326	135,496
Colombia	6,301	7,317	78,924	66,361
Other South America	20,734	8,319	172,497	140,363
Steel rails (*Carriles de acero, trilhos de aço; rails d'acier*).				
Central America		7,124	20,274	18,475
Mexico	9,484	32,986	299,500	539,020
South America	3,300	31,210	35,692	292,613
Sewing machines and parts of (*Máquinas de coser y accesorios; Machinas de coser e accesorios; Machines à coudre et leurs parties*):				
Central America	2,952	2,152	58,571	17,406
Mexico	17,306	7,401	164,634	157,896

EXPORTS OF DOMESTIC MERCHANDISE—Continued.

Articles and countries.	September—		Nine months ending September—	
	1897.	1898.	1897.	1898.
Iron and steel, manufactures of— Continued. Sewing machines, etc.—Continued.				
Santo Domingo	$56	$63	$1,302	$1,347
Cuba		252	3,418	279
Porto Rico	863		2,637	1,050
Argentina	5,575	9,608	63,689	64,561
Brazil	7,394	4,639	62,327	72,111
Colombia	6,012	7,204	82,409	54,742
Other South America	7,749	3,689	73,188	79,869
Typewriting machines and parts of (*Máquinas de escribir y accesorios; Machinas de escribir e accessorios; Machines à écrire et leurs parties*):				
Central America	320	253	7,487	1,121
Mexico	589	725	16,785	24,302
Santo Domingo			125	
Cuba	40	123	1,927	910
Argentina	897	2,777	6,667	20,652
Brazil	359	75	2,046	3,624
Colombia	647	43	3,290	1,904
Other South America	374	1,633	7,552	11,072
Leather, other than sole (*Cuero, distinto del de suela; Couro não para solas; Cuirs, autres que pour semelles*):				
Central America	254	564	3,302	4,714
Mexico	255	708	8,266	5,215
Santo Domingo	217		964	358
Argentina		1,433	1,234	13,620
Brazil	2,298	495	19,637	41,287
Colombia	130		2,455	3,075
Other South America	306	1,053	6,320	11,574
Boots and shoes (*Calzado; Calçados; Chaussures*):				
Central America	3,957	6,191	65,373	54,561
Mexico	6,169	7,138	57,718	73,954
Colombia	2,408	1,078	33,607	27,564
Other South America	1,874	2,378	15,480	27,346
Naval stores: Rosin, tar, etc. (*Resina y alquitrán; Resina e alcatrão; Résine et goudron*):				
Central America	1,001	640	13,722	13,417
Mexico	599	571	5,256	7,438
Santo Domingo	28		3,291	3,294
Cuba	1,070	1,595	5,009	4,181
Porto Rico	149	40	876	321
Argentina		1,025	49,572	59,674
Brazil	31,195	18,445	150,417	129,647
Colombia	895	241	13,383	9,512
Other South America	6,707	1,274	54,409	58,253
Turpentine, spirits of (*Aguarras; Agua-raz; Térébenthine*):				
Central America	263	408	2,582	2,406
Mexico	236	373	2,098	3,320

EXPORTS OF DOMESTIC MERCHANDISE—Continued.

Articles and countries.	September—		Nine months ending September—	
	1897.	1898.	1897.	1898.
Turpentine, spirits of—Continued.				
Santo Domingo	$17	$25	$274	$360
Cuba	1,478	2,297	11,270	8,092
Porto Rico	506	166	2,280	749
Argentina	4,370	2,734	26,218	105,007
Brazil	7,332	1,560	44,230	55,860
Colombia	530	337	3,869	3,601
Other South America	2,211	519	25,591	50,850
Oils, mineral, crude (*Aceites minerales, crudos; Oleos mineraes, crús; Huiles minérales, brutes*):				
Mexico	29,775	29,593	277,300	210,758
Cuba	29,998	12,963	181,755	98,605
Porto Rico	....	......	25,793	19,477
Oils, mineral, refined or manufactured (*Aceites minerales, refinados ó manufacturados; Oleos mineraes, refinados ó manufacturados; Huiles minérales, raffinées ou manufacturées*):				
Central America	9,305	11,072	91,412	89,951
Mexico	9,981	7,213	133,180	121,787
Santo Domingo	804	443	52,154	33,096
Cuba	289	6,697	4,645	32,998
Porto Rico	1,309	6,372	24,874	16,204
Argentina	51,753	71,299	528,420	732,058
Brazil	190,109	98,246	1,425,616	1,111,987
Colombia	9,027	4,013	80,429	83,335
Other South America	46,888	16,622	657,040	750,457
Oils, vegetable (*Aceites vegetales; Oleos vegetaes; Huiles végétales*)				
Central America	88	111	1,953	2,402
Mexico	7,603	27,261	199,095	246,604
Santo Domingo	1,419	337	14,715	25,828
Cuba	380	303	1,439	1,211
Argentina	....	903	3,092	9,259
Brazil	5,670	11,165	140,941	174,687
Other South America	5,156	4,061	52,842	81,404
Paraffin and paraffin wax (*Parafina y cera de parafina; Paraffina e cera de paraffina; Paraffine et cire de cette substance*):				
Central America	2,938	4,022	20,439	19,690
Mexico	24,086	9,002	103,536	110,850
Brazil	830	1,442	7,869	8,842
Other South America	82	....	2,260	5,115
Provisions, comprising meat and dairy products:				
Beef, canned (*Carne de vaca en latas; Carne de vacca em latas; Bœuf conservé*)—				
Central America	1,650	1,304	28,001	16,921
Mexico	710	1,894	9,026	11,155
Santo Domingo	....	....	40	26
Cuba	3,109	255	4,480	5,103

EXPORTS OF DOMESTIC MERCHANDISE—Continued.

Articles and countries.	September—		Nine months ending September—	
	1897.	1898.	1897.	1898.
Provisions, comprising meat and dairy products—Continued.				
Beef, canned—Continued.				
Argentina........................	....	....	$425	$505
Brazil...........................	$590	$962	4, 673	19, 678
Colombia	290	515	5, 503	4, 097
Other South America...........	763	319	9, 135	9, 931
Beef, salted or pickled (*Carne de vaca, salada ó en salmuera; Carne de vacca, salgada ou em salmoura; Bœuf, salé ou en saumure*)—				
Central America...............	4, 095	3, 271	25, 840	27, 957
Mexico.........................	130	....	339	190
Santo Domingo	95	....	1, 688	2, 999
Cuba...........................	2, 737	2, 568	7, 803	9, 367
Porto Rico.....................	50	31	4, 671	171
Brazil	26	476	1, 305	1, 405
Colombia	757	682	9, 682	9, 853
Other South America	15, 507	14, 020	83, 739	134, 013
Tallow (*Sebo; Sebo; Suif*)—				
Central America...............	10, 106	6, 746	74, 017	73, 447
Mexico.....	3, 610	1, 797	23, 911	17, 751
Santo Domingo.................	210	....	14, 405	16, 018
Cuba...........................	1, 582	4, 499	9, 634	9, 964
Porto Rico.....................	....	....	198	176
Brazil..........................	2, 535	731	16, 223	6, 356
Colombia	2, 215	769	13, 430	9, 018
Other South America...........	670	560	8, 702	17, 183
Bacon (*Tocino; Toucinho; Lard fumé*)—				
Central America...............	1, 665	1, 754	16, 352	12, 143
Mexico	586	972	6, 177	8, 760
Santo Domingo.................	142	....	1, 766	1, 922
Cuba...........................	66, 394	48, 164	488, 739	448, 621
Porto Rico.....:..............	2, 340	7, 064	25, 499	28, 064
Brazil..........................	43, 240	74, 357	919, 798	333, 029
Colombia	59	95	1, 195	773
Other South America...........	4, 493	919	20, 721	15, 714
Hams (*Jamones; Presunto; Jambons*)—				
Central America...............	2, 625	2, 491	25, 485	18, 287
Mexico	1, 225	3, 104	16, 087	20, 733
Santo Domingo.................	458	....	5, 154	5, 448
Cuba...........................	29, 406	26, 400	244, 223	220, 107
Porto Rico.....................	7, 531	3, 301	61, 406	14, 679
Brazil..........................	730	655	2, 105	3, 317
Colombia	924	973	11, 699	10, 270
Other South America...........	7, 085	6, 181	64, 684	50, 306
Pork (*Carne de puerco; Carne de porco; Porc*)—				
Central America...............	5, 998	5, 546	48, 550	60, 458
Santo Domingo.................	248	300	2, 918	5, 550
Cuba...........................	762	2, 040	8, 568	11, 669
Porto Rico	20, 283	25, 686	140, 026	101, 041
Brazil..........................	29	73	15, 960	4, 211
Colombia	651	508	5, 982	6, 739
Other South America...........	30, 218	11, 844	122, 902	160, 207

EXPORTS OF DOMESTIC MERCHANDISE—Continued.

Articles and countries.	September—		Nine months ending September—	
	1897.	1898.	1897.	1898.
Provisions, comprising meat and dairy products—Continued.				
Lard (*Manteca; Banha; Saindoux*)—				
Central America	$7,685	$10,115	$88,965	$136,761
Mexico	10,652	14,300	230,077	106,482
Santo Domingo	1,833	298	19,734	27,976
Cuba	75,701	90,303	781,326	812,034
Porto Rico	19,800	46,746	177,948	142,566
Argentina		54	2,014	2,971
Brazil	102,850	112,197	762,054	764,281
Colombia	15,256	5,729	108,082	72,008
Other South America	47,278	39,643	441,794	487,235
Oleo and oleomargarine (*Grasa y oleomargarina; Oleo e oleomargarina; Oléo et oléomargarine*)—				
Central America	22	119	422	1,310
Mexico		49	283	1,009
Colombia	400	710	5,185	6,948
Other South America	273	1,476	20,278	9,490
Butter (*Mantequilla; Manteiga; Beurre*)—				
Central America	4,388	4,261	36,311	35,551
Mexico	2,087	3,628	30,852	35,079
Santo Domingo	519		5,870	8,767
Cuba	644	2,892	8,093	8,011
Porto Rico	515	707	5,886	1,196
Brazil	4,617	2,647	33,607	71,774
Colombia	1,517	678	16,159	11,602
Other South America	5,600	9,736	65,624	80,927
Cheese (*Queso; Queijo; Fromage*)—				
Central America	1,471	1,554	15,699	13,306
Mexico	958	1,077	10,487	11,373
Santo Domingo	307	42	3,932	3,616
Cuba	1,658	3,634	11,759	17,731
Porto Rico	200	495	2,328	1,567
Brazil	135		267	75
Colombia	895	497	9,031	6,925
Other South America	975	497	12,505	11,597
Seeds (*Semillas; Sementes; Semence*):				
Central America	278	189	4,717	4,721
Mexico	786	505	14,296	24,916
Santo Domingo	154		630	361
Cuba	158	1,215	1,757	2,121
Argentina			666	245
Brazil	20	95	1,147	540
Colombia	256	103	2,211	701
Other South America	91	48	1,656	1,598
Sugar, refined (*Azúcar refinado; Assucar refinado; Sucre raffiné*):				
Central America	3,796	1,963	39,312	27,494
Mexico	189	58	13,966	9,498
Santo Domingo	180		1,665	970
Colombia	1,412	1,252	25,456	14,078
Other South America	1,223	83	3,205	1,083

EXPORTS OF DOMESTIC MERCHANDISE—Continued.

Articles and countries.	September—		Nine months ending September —	
	1897.	1898.	1897.	1898.
Tobacco, unmanufactured (*Tabaco no manufacturado ; Tabaco não manufacturado ; Tabac non manufacturé*):				
Central America..............	$534	$579	$9,057	$18.308
Mexico	10,165	7,926	82,607	96 768
Argentina...................	....	....	1,460	13.239
Colombia....................	913	....	2,781	6,252
Other South America	9,002	5,731	70,488	73,737
Tobacco, manufactures of (*Manufacturas de tabaco ; Manufacturas de tabaco ; Tabac fabriqué*):				
Central America...............	3,762	4,949	44,172	43,001
Mexico	315	79	4,239	24,613
Cuba.......................	7,458	6,605	128,704	84,871
Argentina...................	....	704	9,173	1,782
Brazil	....	....	65	550
Colombia...................	....	1,057	654	5,344
Other South America......... ..	12,097	3,707	63,888	56,951
Wood, unmanufactured (*Madera no manufacturado ; Madeira não manufacturado ; Bois brut*):				
Central America..............	1,492	352	67,867	22,257
Mexico	12,215	29,571	161,942	327,509
Cuba.......................	53	....	15,053	12,683
Argentina...................	1,929	679	16,412	7,086
Brazil	2,213	....	13,793	75
Colombia	776	4,131	20,680	25,142
Other South America...........	....	400	33,939	20,903
Lumber (*Maderas ; Madeiras ; Bois de construction*):				
Central America...............	1,149	7,428	94,330	30,731
Mexico	71,385	36,658	1,079,792	575 631
Santo Domingo.................	317	931	59,670	23,930
Cuba.......................	14,495	34,611	215,925	149,982
Porto Rico........	5,100	20	71,215	19,244
Argentina...............	65,386	71,131	502,475	683,736
Brazil	47,413	23,669	467,956	453,870
Colombia	8,280	3,086	56,834	35,619
Other South America............	50,705	16,720	448,613	405,090
Furniture (*Muebles ; Mobilia ; Meubles*):				
Central America...............	10,726	3,421	102,892	32,394
Mexico	12,999	17,939	141,546	127,602
Santo Domingo.................	835	72	8,857	6,997
Cuba	1,846	951	26,869	11,260
Porto Rico...................	833	514	7,287	2,970
Argentina...................	2,815	4,635	57,324	41,487
Brazil.....................	2,981	2,595	32,394	18,875
Colombia	4,013	1,314	31,531	19,493
Other South America............	5,116	2,254	54,779	54,410
Wool, raw (*Lana cruda ; La crïa ; Laines brutes*):				
Mexico	10	....	30,459	....

VENEZUELA.

IMPORTS FROM THE UNITED STATES IN OCTOBER.

The Consul-General of Venezuela at New York, Mr. ANTONIO E. DELFINO, has furnished the Bureau the following statistical information regarding the merchandise shipped to Venezuelan ports from the port of New York during the month of October, 1898: The total number of packages was 54,520, weighing 6,390,591 pounds (2,898,753 kilos), with a declared valuation of $311,532.17, a net increase of $76,592.72 over October, 1897. The great proportion of the goods exported went to the ports of La Guaira and Maracaibo, the value of shipments being respectively $156,036.63 and $70,439.77. Next in order were Puerto Cabello, $29,700.21; Ciudad Bolivar, $26,409.39; La Vela, $17,805.15; Carúpano, $8,136.75; Guanta, $1,620.27; Cumá, $737; and Caño Colorado, $647. The principal articles shipped were: Flour, $44,029.06; gold ore and coin, $43,082; lard, $41,686.06; calicoes, $25,628.03; drillings, bleached and unbleached, $25,556.83; groceries, $21,688.64; drugs and perfumery, $14,591.13; kerosene, $10,964.41; lumber, $9,557.17; butter, $8,387; sewing machines and attachments, $8,384.35; hardware, $7,158.51; notions, etc., $6,385; cigarettes and cigarette tobacco, $6,260; sailcloth, $5,486.12; cordage, $5,188.53.

EXPORTS OF CATTLE TO CUBA.

The "Venezuela Herald" predicts that Venezuela will soon become a great exporter of cattle. The fact is noted that a contract was entered into in October by five large stock raisers of the State of Miranda for the supply of 24,000 head of cattle. These are destined for Cuba and will be delivered at the rate of 2,000 per month. The contract provides that the animals shall be shipped at the rate of 2½ cents gold per pound, to be delivered at a station named Gonzalito, situated on the German railroad, a short distance from Maracay. The cost of transportation from this station to Puerto Cabello, the port of embarkation, will be borne by Mr. ROJAS, the Cuban contractor. During the last week of October 533 oxen, weighing from 400 to 650 pounds each, were shipped to Havana. A similar contract has been entered into between Mr. Rojas and a breeder of Guanta, who shipped in in the same week 800 head. It will require from six to seven days to deliver the cattle in Havana from Puerto Cabello. Consul Ellsworth, at Puerto Cabello, reports the following additional shipments: 750 head of cattle to Santiago, and 300 head to Manzanillo.

TARIFF CLASSIFICATION OF WIRE BOX STRAPS.

In consequence of a decision requested by the collector of the custom-house at Maracaibo concerning the duty leviable upon the article known in trade as "wire box straps" (flejes de alambre de hierro torcido), the President of Venezuela, on the 29th of September, 1898, directed that it be placed in class 3 of the tariff, under section 147 of the same. This is a very important article of trade in Venezuela, being used instead of bands and ropes to bind cases and packages for transport, and consists of two iron wires intertwined, forming a durable and flexible cordage. According to the custom-house tariff in force in Venezuela, articles in class 3 pay an import tax of 5 centavos per kilogram (5 cents per 2.2046 pounds). Exporters from the United States should note that Venezuela buyers prefer packages that are bound with this twisted wire to those that are protected by flat band iron or packages simply bound with rope, because the wire is so little worn on arrival that it can be used again for binding packages for transportation into the interior.

FREE ENTRY OF STATIONERY FOR VENEZUELAN CONSULAR OFFICERS.

Treasury Department Circular No. 196, Division of Customs, issued November 23, 1898, and bearing the signature of W. B. Howells, Assistant Secretary, reads as follows:

To Collectors and other Officers of the Customs:

The Department having been advised that stationery supplies for consuls of the United States in Venezuela will hereafter be admitted free of duty, supplies of this character for consuls of Venezuela in the United States will hereafter be admitted free of duty. Circular No. 175, dated September 26 last, is modified accordingly.

TRADE MISCELLANY.

BOLIVIA.

Great Silver Producing Mines. The Campañía Huanachaca de Bolivia has had the operation of its mines seriously interfered with for the last two years by water and other mishaps. Nevertheless, its production in 1897 was 151,995 kilograms, or 4,886,673 ounces, of silver. But this was not much more than one-half of the maximum output which was reached in 1893, and was 281,007 kilograms, or 9,034,385 ounces.

BRAZIL.

Bids for Waterworks. In the October BULLETIN there was an item stating that the Government of the State of Para invited bids to supply the city of Belem with portable water. The contract was to have been awarded on November 10, but the Government has deferred the date of presenting tenders for the lease of the waterworks until March 15, 1899. Tenders can be presented on a gold basis and also for the collection of the water rate in gold, and the Governor has arranged that such propositions shall receive favorable consideration.

New Mines Discovered. The "South American Journal" reports the discovery of several mines, said to be very rich. These are in the gold mines near Minas Novas and diamond mines near Sacramento, in the State of Minas Geraes.

Exportation of Manganese Ore. A shipment of 891 tons of manganese ore has been recently made from Bahia to the United States. The mineral was extracted from a mine near Nazareth, and was exported from Itaparica.

German Activity in Trade. Consul-General SEEGER writes from Rio that December is the best month in which to visit the State of Parana. He also states that he has received a communication from Mr. THON, a prominent United States merchant located at Curityba, urging that United States manufacturers increase their efforts to secure the trade of Brazil. The Germans are very active in behalf of their countrymen. About the 15th of October the new German consul arrived at Curityba, which will mean additional energy on their part. Plans are being made by the Germans for the colonization of the Inaguassú region, for the building of railroads, for obtaining concessions of lands, etc.

CHILE.

Parcels-Post Treaty with the United States. On the 6th of December the new Minister from Chile, Señor DON CARLOS MORLA VICUÑA, concluded with Hon. CHARLES EMORY SMITH, Postmaster-General, a convention for the establishment of the parcels-post system of exchanges between the two countries. The provisions of the convention are, in the main, identical with the convention entered into with Honduras, except that the rates of postage are increased from 12 cents to 20 cents a pound for packages sent from the United States to Chile, and to 50 cents, instead of 25 cents, a pound on packages originating in Chile which are sent to the United States. The increased rates are due to the distance between the two countries. By the treaty articles of merchandise permissible in the mails, not exceeding 11 pounds (or 5 kilograms) in weight, and of no greater length in any direction than 3 feet 6 inches (105 centimeters), and whose greatest length and girth combined do not exceed 6 feet (180 centimeters), which are so wrapped as to be easily examined by the postal authorities, are to be speedily forwarded to their destination, subject to the payment of the prescribed customs duties. The exchanges of mails are to be effected between the exchange post-offices of New York, New Orleans, and San Francisco, in the United States, and Valparaiso, in Chile.

Money Order Exchange. The United States Post-Office Department has been informed of the recent ratification by the Chilean Government of the convention for the exchange of money orders between Chile and the United States, which was negotiated in August, 1897. Under this convention, which is to take effect January 1, 1899, postal orders may be issued in Chile to the amount of $100 each, and in the United States to the amount of 100 pesos each.

New Consular Office. President McKinley has appointed John W. Lutz Consul of the United States at Arica, Chile, he being the first incumbent of the office. Heretofore the affairs of the United States have been in the hands of a vice-consul, David Simpson, a Scotchman residing in Chile.

MEXICO.

New Monthly Bulletin. The Bureau of the American Republics is in receipt of a monthly publication issued at the capital of the Mexican Republic, under the title of "Boletin de la República Mexicana." This new periodical is edited by Señor Don José M. Romero, and is devoted to the diffusion of information in foreign countries concerning the actual state of development, both material and intellectual, of the Republic, the industries that may be successfully established, the enterprises requiring large capital, and the advantages and inducements offered by the soil and climate of the country and the legislation applicable to immigrants, either agricultural or industrial. The Boletin is published in four languages—Spanish, English, French, and Italian—and contains valuable data and useful information for all classes of readers.

Contract for Mexico City Waterworks. The correspondent of the National Association of Manufacturers at Mexico City reports that the contract for the cast-iron pipe for the waterworks has been secured by the American Pipe and Foundry Company, Chattanooga, Tenn. It will amount to about 18,000 gross tons, and the first installment, valued at about $250,000, is now under way. The general contractors, Vezin & Co., called for tenders from several European countries, and while the matter was subjected to forceful competition it was won by a United States firm, and a large factor in their favor was having a representative constantly on the ground. The contract will be handled by the firm of G. & O. BRANIFF & Co., and rapidly pushed to a conclusion.

Excellent Site for Milling Purposes. It is claimed by parties who have investigated the subject that the State of Tlaxcala possesses special advantages for the raising of flax and hemp of a superior quality, states Modern Mexico. GERARDO EMILIA HERRERIAS, of that State, writes that a large flax mill near the city of Tlaxcala, where water power could easily be obtained and building material and labor are plenty, would prove a paying investment. He believes that linen of as good a quality as the best European product could be produced and enter into active competition with cotton goods for domestic consumption.

New Biscuit Factory. A corporation recently organized in Mexico, under the laws of the State of Maine, to operate on an extensive scale, is the Compania Bizcochera Mexicana. The company is now erecting a fine establishment in Mexico City for the purpose of manufacturing candies and crackers. The Mexican duty on candies is 75 cents per kilo, and on crackers 15 cents gross per kilo, prohibiting foreign goods from that market. There is a strong demand for both lines in the Republic, and the promoters of the new company see a great future before it. The president of the company is H. M. DINGLEY, of Lewiston, Me.; treasurer, W. S. LIBBY, of Lewiston, Me.; manager, EMIL ARNER, formerly representative in Mexico for the National Biscuit Company. The output will necessitate a large number of employees.

NICARAGUA.

Republication of Bureau Handbook. In the "Diario Oficial of Nicaragua," the official organ of the Government, the Department of Public Instruction is publishing a translation in Spanish of the Handbook of Nicaragua, issued by the Bureau of the American Republics.

PARAGUAY.

New Steamship Service. There are large German settlements throughout Paraguay, and German exporters command much of the foreign trade of the country. Recently Consul-General SEEGER, of Rio de Janeiro, Brazil, reported to the Department of State that a new line of steamships had been established between Germany and Paraguay, through the steamers *Arsy* and *Kurt*.

PERU.

Japanese Agricultural Laborers. According to the Rio News, the Japanese Minister in Lima has completed the necessary arrangements with the Peruvian Minister of Foreign Relations for enabling a large number of Japanese emigrants to go to Peru to engage in agricultural pursuits. The News adds that the same Minister is to proceed to Mexico immediately, with a view to making similar arrangements with the Mexican Government.

SANTO DOMINGO (DOMINICAN REPUBLIC).

United States Capital Desired.   Mr. E. LECROIX, a French citizen of Port au Prince, Haiti, informs the Bureau of the American Republics that he and a Mr. JULIEN have obtained an important concession from the Government of the Dominican Republic for the erection of one or several "fecula" or tapioca factories, and that they desire to interest United States capitalists in the enterprise. Hon. ALEJANDRO WOZ Y GIL, who is stationed in New York as Consul-General for the United States for the Dominican Republic, confirms Mr. LECROIX's statement as to the concession, stating that the agreement was published in the Official Gazette under date of September 23, 1898. Mr. LECROIX has forwarded the following to this Bureau: The official journal containing the clauses of the concession, printed in the Spanish language; a commentary on the different clauses; notes on the yucca or manioc, from which the "fecula" or tapioca is obtained; a table of estimates for the establishment of the first manufactory; an approximate estimate of the trade; a sample of fecula obtained by hand from manioc. The estimated capital required for four or five factories is $250,000, but the statement is made that an excellent start could be made with $40,000 capital.

UNITED STATES. .

National Convention of Manufacturers.   The fourth annual convention of the National Association of Manufacturers of the United States will be held at Cincinnati, Ohio, January 24, 25, and 26, 1898. This promises to be one of the most important conventions ever held by the organization. The association was organized in Cincinnati and held its first session there in 1896. It is said that the present membership is nearly 1,000, including many of the largest manufacturers of the country, representing nearly all branches of productive industry.

Exports of Mineral Oil.   Exports of mineral illuminating oil from the United States in the fiscal year 1875 amounted to 221,955,308 gallons; in the year ended June 30, 1898, they aggregated 1,034,269,676 gallons.

URUGUAY.

Products of Hides and Leather.   The Republic of Uruguay. imports about $200,000 worth of leather annually, of which scarcely $4,000 worth is bought from the United States, though the United States buys from Uruguay $2,000,000 worth of hides and skins yearly. What Uruguay requires from the United States is mainly tanned kid, calf, and sheep skins. Of French kid alone about $46,000 worth is imported annually. It is estimated that in the Republic there are 380,000 hides tanned, of these 160,000 are calf, 150,000 sheep, 48,000 cow, and 40,000 kid hides. A good reciprocal trade ought to be developed between the two Republics.

BOLETÍN MENSUAL

DE LA

OFICINA DE LAS REPÚBLICAS AMERICANAS,

UNIÓN INTERNACIONAL DE REPÚBLICAS AMERICANAS.

VOL. VI. DICIEMBRE, 1898. No. 6.

VISITA DEL PRESIDENTE DE COSTA RICA.

El 23 de noviembre llegó á Wáshington el Presidente de la próspera República de Costa Rica, Señor Don RAFAEL IGLESIAS, á quién el Gobierno de los Estados Unidos ofreció hospedaje en el hotel Arlington. Poco después de su llegada, el Presidente McKINLEY pasó á saludarle, y en aquella misma tarde el Señor IGLESIAS le devolvió la visita en la Casa Blanca. Durante su permanencia en la capital, el Presidente IGLESIAS fué visitado por casi todos los miembros del cuerpo diplomático, así como por senadores, diputados, y otras personas distinguidas. El Señor IGLESIAS es todavía muy joven, pues sólo tiene treinta y ocho años de edad y está ahora sirviendo el segundo término como Presidente de Costa Rica. Á su llegada á Nueva York, fué recibido por el Coronel del Ejército de los Estados Unidos, Mr. W. R. CARTER, que fué desde Wáshington como representante personal del Presidente McKINLEY á darle la bienvenida. El 29 de noviembre el Presidente de los Estados Unidos dió una comida, en honor del Presidente IGLESIAS, á la cual asistieron todos los diplomáticos latino-americanos y otras personas prominentes, y el 30 el Secretario de Estado dió otro banquete en su honor, en el cual, como en el de la Casa Blanca, estuvieron presentes todos los miembros del Gabinete, Subsecretarios, Senadores, Representantes, y otras personas prominentes política y socialmente.

El Señor Director de la Oficina de las Repúblicas Americanas acompañado del Señor Secretario, Dr. HORACIO GUZMÁN, visitó al Presidente IGLESIAS el 25 de noviembre y le manifestó sus deseos de obsequiarle con un almuerzo en el hotel Shoreham el lunes siguiente, 28 de noviembre; el Presidente aceptó la invitación y asistieron á esta solemnidad los Señores siguientes: Honorable DAVID J. HILL, Subsecretario de Estado; Señor CALVO, Ministro de Costa Rica; Señor MÉROU, Ministro de la República Argentina; Señor PONTE, Encargado de Negocios de la República de Venezuela; Señor RENGIFO, Encargado de Negocios de la República de Colombia; Coronel W. R. CARTER, del Ejército de los Estados Unidos, que asistió en representación del Presidente McKINLEY; Dr. HORACIO GUZMÁN, Secretario de la Oficina de las Repúblicas Americanas, y el Señor QUEZADA, Secretario del Presidente IGLESIAS.

A la conclusión del almuerzo, el Director, Mr. EMORY, propuso un brindis á la salud del Presidente de Costa Rica. Al ofrecer este brindis, el Señor EMORY manifestó que sentía especial placer en expresar su gratitud personal y la de la Oficina de las Repúblicas Americanas hacia el Gobierno de Costa Rica por el activo interés que siempre ha mostrado en todo lo concerniente á la prosperidad de la Oficina, y particularmente por la celosa cooperación del distinguido y eficaz Ministro de Costa Rica, Señor CALVO. Terminó pidiendo á los comensales que se le unieran en el brindis que ofrecia á la prosperidad y dicha del Presidente de Costa Rica y su país.

Al contestar, el Presidente IGLESIAS se expresó en los siguientes términos:

Deseo dar las más sinceras gracias al Director de la Oficina de las Repúblicas Americanas por este almuerzo con que se sirve distinguirme, atención que aprecio en el más alto grado; y deseo expresar al mismo tiempo el gran placer con que he saludado á los miembros de la Comisión Ejecutiva de la Unión Internacional de Repúblicas Americanas. Esta institución es de la mayor importancia por cuanto tiende al desarrollo de las relaciones comerciales entre las naciones de la América Latina y la República de los Estados Unidos; y ningún país aprecia mejor este hecho que la República de Costa Rica. Las publicaciones de la Oficina de las Repúblicas Americanas son leidas con el mayor interés por nuestros hombres públicos, pues sirven para dar á éstos una idea exacta del adelanto y progreso de todas las naciones del continente. Como primer Magistrado de la República de Costa Rica, siempre haré todo cuanto esté en mi poder por alentar los intereses de la Oficina de las Repúblicas Americanas, y no abrigo duda alguna de que la administración que suceda á la mía abrigará los mismos sentimientos.

Señores, yo propongo un bríndis por la salud del·Director de la Oficina de las Repúblicas Americanas, Mr. EMORY."

El Director dió las gracias al Presidente por esta cortesía.

El Señor MÉROU, Ministro de la República Argentina, dijo:

Como miembro del Comité Ejecutivo del Bureau de las Repúblicas Americanas y en ausencia de mis distinguidos colegas los Ministros de México y de Venezuela, me cabe el placer de agradecer en esta ocasión al Señor Presidente de Costa Rica, el interés que manifiesta en las labores de aquella Oficina y la importancia que atribuye á sus trabajos. · A decir verdad, todos los honores de la acción eficiente del Bureau, corresponden á su distinguido Director, el Señor EMORY. Es debido á su infatigable actividad y á su acertada administración que aquella institución está dando ahora tan valiosos frutos, y en este sentido me es especialmente satisfactorio unir las mías á las felicitaciones que ha recibido de su Excelencia el Señor IGLESIAS.

Séame permitido ahora, invocando los mismos títulos de antigüedad accidental á que me he referido antes, pedir que me acompañeis á brindar por el eminente Presidente de los Estados Unidos, Honorable Señor McKINLEY, que con tanto acierto dirije los destinos de esta Gran República y espresar en nombre de mis colegas aquí presentes, nuestros más sinceros votos por su felicidad personal, por la gloria de su Gobierno y por la prosperidad del pueblo americano.

El Director, Mr. EMORY, manifestó que lamentaba la ausencia del Señor Secretario de Estado que no había podido asistir por tener una cita convenida con anterioridad á la invitación para esta fiesta, y pidió al Subsecretario de Estado que contestara al brindis hecho en honor del Presidente de los Estados Unidos.

El Honorable DAVID J. HILL, Subsecretario de Estado, contestó en un elegante discurso. Dijo que estaba seguro de que, si el Presidente de los Estados Unidos estuviera presente, expresaría su cordial acuerdo con los propósitos de la Unión Internacional y su deseo de estrechar más las relaciones entre las varias repúblicas de este hemisferio. El Subsecretario de Estado hizo mérito de la semejanza de las instituciones políticas de las repúblicas americanas, pues que tienen su origen en el mismo sistema de filosofía política, y dijo que las repúblicas de Norte, Centro y Sud América tienen muchos propósitos en común y se encuentran atraidas entre sí por el prospecto de un desarrollo comercial que en este caso no está limitado por líneas de latitud sino más bien por líneas de longitud, por cuanto dos grandes océanos separan á este hemisferio del resto del mundo, obteniendo así las tres Américas cierta solidaridad de intereses. Estoy cierto, dijo, que el Presidente de los Estados Unidos muestra grande empeño por alentar la tendencia general hacia una unión más estrecha entre los Estados Unidos de América y las varias repúblicas de la América Latina, y, por tanto, tengo especial placer en reconocer la atención extendida al Primer Magistrado de los Estados Unidos por el Señor Ministro de la República Argentina.

El Director EMORY dijo que tenía que ofrecer un brindis más y, en consecuencia, pidió á los concurrentes que brindaran con él por la futura prosperidad de la Unión Internacional y por el continuo desarrollo de los generosos propósitos de sus fundadores, los distinguidos miembros de la Conferencia Internacional Americana que estuvo reunida en Wáshington de 1889 á 1890. Mr. EMORY pidió al Señor Ministro de Costa Rica que dijera algunas palabras en contestación. El Señor CALVO dijo que aunque la Oficina de las Repúblicas Americanas se encuentra en el noveno año de su existencia, aquella era la primera vez que su Director se encontraba con el primer magistrado de uno de los paises que forman la Unión, y dijo que era motivo de gran placer para él la distinción que en aquel momento se hacía á Costa Rica. Manifestó el Señor CALVO que él y su Gobierno habían sentido siempre el más profundo interés en el éxito del plan que se propuso la Conferencia Internacional Americana y que él estaba convencido de que la Oficina de las Repúblicas Americanas trataba con decidido empeño de llevar á la práctica los propósitos de la Conferencia. El Señor CALVO expresó sus deseos, aunque, según dijo, talvez no fuese aquella la ocasión más propicia, de dar las gracias más sentidas por las atenciones con que había sido obsequiado el Presidente de Costa Rica por el Presidente, Gabinete y varios otros funcionarios del Gobierno de la más grande é importante de las naciones que forman la Unión de Repúblicas Americanas. Las cortesías, dijo, de que ha sido objeto el Presidente de Costa Rica en Wáshington, han sido de lo más halagador y, en su reconocimiento, el Señor CALVO propuso de nuevo un brindis á la salud del Presidente de los Estados Unidos.

Con este bríndis terminó aquella festividad.

El día antes de su partida, el Señor Presidente IGLESIAS hizo una visita á la Oficina de las Repúblicas Americanas acompañado del Ministro de Costa Rica, Señor Calvo, y fué recibido por el Director de la Oficina, Mr. Frederic Emory y el Señor Secretario, Dr. Horacio Guzmán. En obsequio á la visita, se adornó el edificio con las banderas de Costa Rica y de los Estados Unidos. El Presidente estuvo más de una hora examinando los trabajos prácticos de la Oficina y manifestó que le sería grato, á su regreso á Costa Rica, hacer todo cuanto estuviese en su poder en obsequio á los fines de aquella institución.

EL MENSAJE DEL PRESIDENTE McKINLEY.

El mensaje anual del Presidente McKinley fué enviado el día 5 de diciembre de 1898 al quinquagésimo quinto Congreso de los Estados Unidos, en la apertura de sus últimas sesiones. La mayor parte del mensaje es una reseña imparcial, comprensiva y concisa de los acontecimientos del año pasado, por cuanto se relacionan con los asuntos del Gobierno. Como es natural, se da el primer puesto á las causas que produjeron la guerra con España y la manera como ésta fué dirigida, y se hace merecida alabanza á los que en ella tomaron parte á favor de los Estados Unidos. No hay en el documento muestras de indebida satisfacción por las victorias que, por tierra y por mar, alcanzaron las fuerzas de los Estados Unidos, pero sí vibra en toda la pieza una nota de simpatía y respeto por las derrotadas fuerzas españolas. El Presidente felicita al país, "porque con la sola excepción de la ruptura con España, las relaciones de los Estados Unidos con la gran familia de las naciones ha sido señalada por la cordialidad, y al terminar el año tan lleno de acontecimientos, la mayor parte de los asuntos que necesariamente se desprenden de las relaciones complejas entre estados soberanos están arreglados ó no presentan serios obstáculos para llegar á una solución justa y honorable por medio de arreglos amistosos."

Con referencia al Gobierno de Puerto Rico y las Filipinas, el Presidente se expresa así:

"No discutiré por ahora el gobierno ó el porvenir de las nuevas posesiones que serán nuestras como resultado de la guerra con España. Después de la ratificación del tratado de paz, habrá tiempo para tratar de estas cuestiones. Mientras tanto, y hasta que el Congreso no dé leyes en contrario, mi deber será continuar los gobiernos militares que han existido desde nuestra ocupación y dar al pueblo garantías de vida y propiedad y estimularle bajo un gobierno justo y benigno."

INDEPENDENCIA DE CUBA.

Refiriéndose á Cuba, dice:

Tan pronto como estemos en posesión de Cuba y hayamos pacificado la isla, será necesario ayudar y dirigir al pueblo en la formación de un gobierno propio. Esto debe llevarse á cabo lo más pronto posible, sin perder de vista las consideraciones de seguridad y de buen éxito.   Es importante que nuestras relaciones con aquel pueblo sean de lo más amistosas y nuestro comercio sea estrecho y recíproco.   Es nuestro deber favorecer de todos modos el fomento de los lugares devastados de la isla, estimulando la industria y ayudando á formar un gobierno libre é independiente, realizando de esta manera las más altas aspiraciones del pueblo cubano.   El dominio español debe ser reemplazado por un gobierno justo, benévolo y humano, creado por el pueblo de Cuba, capaz de cumplir con todas sus obligaciones internacionales y que sepa estimular el trabajo, la industria y la prosperidad, fomentando la paz y la buena voluntad entre todos sus habitantes, cualesquiera que hayan sido sus relaciones en el pasado.   Ni la venganza ni la pasión deben tener cabida en el nuevo gobierno.   Continuará la ocupación militar hasta que se haya restablecido completamente la tranquilidad de la isla y se haya inaugurado una forma estable de gobierno.

En los siguientes párrafos se hace referencia y recomendaciones acerca del Canal de Nicaragua, las otras Repúblicas del continente, y la Oficina de las Repúblicas Americanas:

ARBITRAMENTO ARGENTINO-CHILENO.

La disputa de largo tiempo pendiente acerca de los límites entre la República Argentina y Chile, que se extienden por las cimas de los Andes desde el límite meridional del Desierto de Atacama hasta el Estrecho de Magallanes, casi una tercera parte del largo del continente sud-americano, llegó á un período agudo á principios del año, permitiendo á este gobierno la ocasión de expresar la esperanza de que se recurriera al arbitramento, en el cual se había pensado en las reuniones celebradas entre las partes interesadas y que esto se llevara á cabo, no obstante las graves dificultades que se presentaban para su aplicación.   Me complace decir que se han hecho arreglos con este objeto, habiéndose referido á su Majestad británica la determinación de las cuestiones de hecho en que no podían convenir los comisionados respectivos.   La diferencia que existe relativa á la línea limítrofe del norte, á través del Desierto de Atacama, de cuyo arreglo no se trataba en los convenios existentes, parece que se determinará de igual modo por una comisión mixta habiéndose invitado al Ministro de los Estados Unidos en Buenos Aires para servir de árbitro en último caso.

UNIFORMIDAD EN LA TARIFA DE CABLES.

He tenido oportunidad de dirigirme al Gobierno Argentino con el bjeto de hacer desaparecer las diferencias de la tarifa impuesta á la línea calográfica de una corporación americana al trasmitir telegramas entre Buenos Aires y las ciudades del Uruguay y del Brasil dirigidos á los Estados Unidos ó procedentes de aquí. Aunque el asunto es complicado, á causa de las concesiones exclusivas hechas por el Uruguay y el Brasil á compañías extranjeras, hay grandes esperanzas de que se llegue á un acuerdo y de que quede libre de una discriminación casi prohibitiva esa importante vía de comunicación comercial entre los Estados Unidos y las ciudades de Sud-América sobre el Atlántico.

Con este motivo me permito expresar mi idea acerca de lo apropiado de un convenio internacional, que regule el intercambio de telégramas por cables que se conectan, partiendo de una base uniforme y equitativa. El mundo ha visto salir el sistema postal de manos de una reunión de individuos independientes y exclusivistas y convertirse en una unión bien organizada cuyos múltiples beneficios gozan todos los pueblos. Estraño sería que las naciones no llegasen á convencerse de que la civilización moderna—cuyo progreso debe tanto á la desaparición del espacio por medio de la potencia eléctrica—exije que este medio de comunicación tan importante sea herencia de todos los pueblos, administrada y dirigida para el común beneficio. Se dió un paso en esta vía cuando la Convención Internacional de 1884, para la protección de los cables submarinos, fué firmada; y espero que no esté lejano el día en que este vehículo para la trasmisión del pensamiento de una á otra tierra caiga bajo el dominio de un concierto internacional, de manera tan completa como el transporte del comercio y de la correspondencia sobre la superficie de las aguas.

ACONTECIMIENTOS DE CENTRO AMÉRICA.

Los acontecimientos ocurridos en Centro América durante el año merecen que se haga de ellos mención señalada:

La ruptura que amenazaba tener lugar entre Costa Rica y Nicaragua se pudo arreglar felizmente por medio de una convención entre las partes interesadas, con la asistencia del representante de Guatemala como mediador, habiéndose preparado y firmado el acta á bordo del vapor de los Estados Unidos "Alert," que á la sazón estaba en aguas centro-americanas. Existe la creencia de que los buenos oficios de nuestro Enviado y el Comandante de aquel buque contribuyeron al resultado de tan grato arreglo.

En mi último mensaje anual se hizo referencia á la representación diplomática de este gobierno en Centro América, con motivo de la asociación de Nicaragua, Honduras y Salvador bajo el título de República Mayor de Centro América y la delegación hecha de sus funciones internacionales en la Dieta. No obstante haber sido reconocido por mi antecesor, y confirmado durante mi administración, el carácter representativo de la Dieta, recibiendo á su Enviado acreditado y concediendo exequatur á los cónsules nombrados por su autoridad, dicho reconocimiento fué hecho en la inteligencia clara de que la responsabilidad de cada una de las Repúblicas soberanas que la componen, para con los Estados Unidos, quedaba sin ser afectada en absoluto.

Esta salvedad se hacía necesaria, tanto más cuanto que la combinación de las tres Repúblicas fué en su principio una asociación por la cual se delegaban en una comisión triple ciertas funciones representativas, más bien que una federación que poseyese autoridad centralizada de gobierno y administración. En vista de sus relaciones entre sí y las de los Estados Unidos para con las diversas Repúblicas, el Ejecutivo no recomendó, ni el Congreso indicó, cambios en la representación de este país en Centro América, dejando así uno de nuestros enviados acreditado como hasta ahora ante los Estados de la República Mayor, Nicaragua y Salvador y también Costa Rica, que no tomó parte en el convenio, mientras que otro enviado estaba igualmente acreditado ante un Estado de la Unión, Honduras, y otro que no pertenecía á ella, Guatemala. El resultado ha sido que uno ha presentado sus credenciales solamente al Presidente de Costa Rica y el otro ha sido recibido tan sólo por el Gobierno de Guatemala.

Más tarde las tres Repúblicas asociadas entraron en negociaciones con el objeto de llevar á cabo lo propuesto en el convenio original. Una convención de sus delegados preparó una constitución federal para los Estados Unidos de Centro América, en la cual se disponía la forma de centralización federal para el gobierno y la legislatura. Ratificada esta por los Estados constituyentes, se fijó el primero de noviembre último para que entrase en operación el nuevo sistema. Pocas semanas después el plan fué sometido á prueba por los movimientos revolucionarios que tuvieron lugar y que exijían por consecuencia unidad de acción de parte del poder militar de los Estados confederados para suprimirlos. Esta prueba parece haber debilitado la Unión, á causa de la separación de sus miembros más importantes. Este Gobierno no recibió aviso oficial de la instalación de la federación y ha mantenido una actitud de amistosa expectativa, al paso que de ninguna manera ha abandonado la actitud que desde un principio ha conservado de que la responsabilidad de cada uno de los Estados para con los otros no sufría alteración por causa de las relaciones que existiesen entre ellos.

COMISIÓN DEL CANAL DE NICARAGUA.

La Comisión del Canal de Nicaragua, nombrada el 24 de julio de 1897 por virtud de la cláusula del "Sundry Civil Act" de 4 de junio de aquel año, cuya presidencia desempeña el Contra-almirante JOHN G. WALKER, ha terminado casi sus labores y someterá el resultado de sus minuciosas investigaciones acerca de la vía adecuada, lo hacedero del trabajo y el costo de la construcción de un canal interoceánico por Nicaragua. En el desempeño de sus labores la Comisión fué objeto de la mayor cortesía de los gobiernos de Nicaragua y Costa Rica, que le prestaron todo género de auxilios, demostrando de esta manera cuanto aprecian la importancia de terminar, tan pronto como sea practicable, el gran proyecto que durante tantos años ha ocupado la atención de los países respectivos.

Como el programa de la reciente investigación abarcaba todo el asunto, con el objeto de hacer planos y trazos para un canal construido por la vía más conveniente, necesariamente comprendía un examen de los resultados de los trazos y planos anteriores y en particular de los que había adoptado la Compañía del Canal

Marítimo, por virtud de las concesiones que posee de Nicaragua y Costa Rica, de suerte que éstas concesiones son de necesidad parte esencial de las deliberaciones y deducciones de la Comisión del Canal, como han sido y deben ser parte de las discusiones de la materia en el Congreso. Dadas estas circunstancias, y en vista de los ofrecimientos hechos á los gobiernos de Nicaragua y Costa Rica por otros individuos, referentes á una concesión para un nuevo canal fundada en la supuesta próxima caducidad de los contratos celebrados entre la Compañía del Canal Marítimo y aquellas naciones, no he titubeado en expresar mi convicción de que razones de conveniencia y de política internacional entre los diferentes gobiernos interesados en la construcción y jurisdicción de un canal interoceánico por esta vía exijen la conservación del *statu quo*, hasta que la Comisión del Canal haya presentado su informe y que el Congreso de los Estados Unidos haya tenido la oportunidad de aprobarlo durante las presentes sesiones, sin perjuicios por razón de cualesquier cambios ocurridos en las condiciones existentes.

Sin embargo, parece que el gobierno de Nicaragua como uno de sus últimos actos de soberanía, antes de traspasar sus poderes al de los nuevos Estados de Centro América, hizo un concesión condicional á otra sociedad la cual entraría en vigor tan pronto como feneciese la presente concesión. No aparece cuales trazos hayan hecho, ni cual sea la vía propuesta en esta concesión contingente, de modo que en el informe de la Comisión del Canal no está necesariamente incluido el examen de lo practicable de los planos. Todas estas circunstancias sugieren la urgencia de que el Congreso tome una medida definitiva en estas sesiones, si los trabajos del pasado han de ser utilizados y si se ha de realizar la unión de los océanos Atlantico y Pacífico por medio de una vía acuática practicable. Que la construcción de semejante vía marítima es al presente más indispensable que nunca para la comunicación íntima y fácil entre nuestras costas del oriente y del occidente, como lo piden la anexión de las Islas del Hawaii y la futura expansión de nuestra influencia y de nuestro comercio en el Pacífico; y que nuestra política nacional exije hoy más imperativamente que nunca que este gobierno la domine, son consideraciones que no dudo que el Congreso sepa apreciar debidamente, procediendo en ello de una manera sabia.

COMISIÓN DE RECLAMACIONES CHILENAS.

La convención que dispone el restablecimiento de la fenecida Comisión de Reclamaciones de los Estados Unidos y Chile y el examen de aquellas que fueron debidamente presentadas á la dicha Comisión, pero que no se estudiaron á causa de haber expirado el tiempo limitado para su duración, fué firmada el 24 de mayo de 1897 y el Senado no ha dado ningún paso en el asunto. El término fijado en aquélla para efectuar el cambio de ratificaciones ha expirado y la convención dejará de existir á menos que se prorogue el tiempo, introduciendo la reforma, lo que estoy tratando de conseguir con la cooperación amistosa del gobierno de Chile.

TRATADO DE EXTRADICIÓN CON MÉXICO.

La interpretación de ciertas disposiciones contenidas en el tratado de extradición de 11 de diciembre, 1861, ha sido en varias ocasiones motivo de controversia con el Gobierno de México.   La solicitud del Gobierno mexicano para la entrega de Jesús Guerra, que había conducido una expedición de merodeo cerca de la frontera, con el propósito declarado de iniciar una insurrección contra el Presidente Díaz, y que escapó á Texas, trajo la cuestión á un periódo agudo.   Se rehusó la extradición basándose en que el delito alegado era de carácter político y por consiguiente estaba comprendido en lo dispuesto en el tratado acerca de la no entrega.   México alegaba que la excepción sólo se refiere á los crímenes políticos y que como los actos de guerra estaban acompañados de los delitos comunes de asesinato, incendiarismo, secuestro y robo, no era aplicable la no entrega, argumento que este Gobierno no pudo admitir, en vista de la doctrina internacional y la práctica en estos casos.   El Gobierno de México con este motivo anunció el 24 de enero de 1898, la terminación del tratado, que tendría lugar doce meses después de aquélla fecha, solicitando al mismo tiempo la celebración de un nuevo tratado cuya negociación nos ocupa actualmente.

LA ZONA LIBRE MEXICANA.

El problema de la Zona Libre mexicana ha sido discutido frecuentemente por motivo de su inconveniencia, como que invita á introducir contrabando en los Estados Unidos por toda la frontera, que está escasamente custodiada.   Como se dijó en el Informe No. 702 de la Cámara de Representantes, presentado á la última sesión el 11 de marzo de 1898, las providencias contenidas en la resolución mixta del 1 de marzo de 1895 para remediar el abuso suspendiendo el privilegio de libre trasporte, en tránsito, por el territorio de los Estados Unidos con destino á México, no han dado buenos resultados.   Como quiera que la cuestión puede arreglarse, más bien que por convenios, por leyes al efecto dadas por ambos paises, con el objeto de proteger las rentas por medio de medidas que tengan igual fuerza á ambos lados de la frontera, indico al Congreso que estudie la conveniencia de autorizar una conferencia de representantes de los departamentos del Tesoro de los Estados Unidos y de México para examinar la materia en todos sus puntos y presentar un informe haciendo recomendaciones pertinentes á los gobiernos respectivos, para la consideración y estudio de los respectivos congresos.

COMISIÓN DELIMITADORA DEL LÍMITE FLUVIAL DE MÉXICO.

La Comisión delimitadora del límite fluvial de México ha terminado á la satisfacción de ambos gobiernos todas las materias que le fueron sometidas, con excepción de tres casos importantes—el de "Chamizal" en El Paso, Texas, en que no pudieron convenir los dos comisionados, por cuyo motivo, este Gobierno ha propuesto al de México el nombramiento, para este caso nada más, de un tercer miembro; la propuesta eliminación de los llamados "Bancos," isletas aisladas formadas por el corte de los codos del Río Grande, según los tratados de 1884 y 1889, recomendada por los comisionados y aprobada por este Gobierno, pero que todavía está sometida á la consideración de México; y el asunto de la distribución equitativa de las aguas del Río Grande, para cuyo efecto los comisionados recomendaron la construcción de una represa y un estanque internacional, lo cual fué aprobado por México y todavía está sometido á la consideración de este Gobierno. Dadas estas circunstancias es necesario prorogar el término de la Comisión que fenece el 23 de diciembre próximo.

RESCISIÓN DE UN TRATADO.

El Gobierno del Perú ha hecho la notificación de ley de su intención de rescindir el Tratado de Amistad, Comercio y Navegación firmado con este país el 31 de agosto de 1887. Como dicho tratado contiene muchas disposiciones importantes, necesarias para la conservación del comercio y de las buenas relaciones, que sería difícil reemplazar con la negociación de nuevas cláusulas dentro del breve período de 12 meses, que termina el tratado, he invitado al Perú para que indique cuales son las disposiciones que desea anular en particular, con la esperanza de llegar á un arreglo por el cual puedan salvarse provisionalmente los otros artículos.

EL TRIBUNAL ARBITRAL ANGLO-VENEZOLANO.

El Tribunal Arbitral nombrado por virtud del Tratado de 2 de febrero de 1897, celebrado entre la Gran Bretaña y Venezuela, para determinar la línea limítrofe entre ésta y la Colonia de la Guayana Inglesa, se reunirá en París durante el presente mes. Es motivo de mucha complacencia para este Gobierno ver que se ha hecho uso del amistoso recurso del arbitramento para el arreglo de esta controversia, no sólo por la parte interesada que hemos tenido en que se llegase á este resultado, sino también porque dos de los miembros nombrados por parte de Venezuela, el Justicia Mayor, Mr. FULLER y el Justicia Mr. BREWER, han sido escojidos de entre los que forman nuestro más alto tribunal, lo cual demuestra el interés continuado que tenemos en el arreglo definitivo de la cuestión, según las reglas más estrictas de la justicia. Los miembros británicos, Lord HERSCHELL y Sir RICHARD COLLINS son jurisconsultos de no menos alta reputación, mientras que el quinto miembro y Presidente del Tribunal, M. F. de MARTENS, ha adquirido fama universal como autoridad en derecho internacional.

LA OFICINA DE LAS REPÚBLICAS AMERICANAS.

Tengo la satisfacción de poder manifestar que la Oficina de las Repúblicas Americanas, creada en 1890 como órgano para fomentar las relaciones comerciales y fraternales entre los países del hemisferio occidental, ha llegado á ser instrumento de la mayor eficacia para la consecución de los sabios propósitos de sus fundadores y recibe la ayuda cordial de todos los miembros de la Unión Internacional que á ella contribuyen y que están representados en su Junta Directiva. Ha publicado en inglés, español, portugués, y francés un Directorio Comercial, en dos volúmenes, que contiene gran acopio de informes estadísticos relativos á los intereses industriales y comerciales de los distintos países de que trata, y publica en estos cuatro idiomas un BOLETIN MENSUAL, que se distribuye en los países latino-americanos y en los Estados Unidos y que ha demostrado ser un valioso medio para la deseminación de informes y el fomento de los varios intereses de la Unión Internacional.

EL SEÑOR ROMERO NOMBRADO EMBAJADOR.

El Señor Don MATÍAS ROMERO, Enviado Extraordinario y Ministro Plenipotenciario de México en los Estados Unidos, ha regresado á Wáshington después de una visita algo dilatada á la capital de su país. Poco después de su regreso, el Ministro informó al Secretario de Estado de los Estados Unidos de que había sido elevado al grado de embajador. Esta noticia fué recibida con gran satisfacción tanto en el Departamento de Estado como en los círculos diplomáticos, y el Señor ROMERO fué objeto de sinceras congratulaciones por la muestra de aprecio que ha recibido de su Gobierno.

Como existe una ley que dispone que el Gobierno de los Estados Unidos puede elevar al grado de embajador á cualquiera de sus ministros cuando el país donde está acreditado toma la iniciativa en este asunto, confiriendo esa dignidad á su propio representante, el Gen. POWELL CLAYTON, en la actualidad Ministro de los Estados Unidos en Mexico, ascenderá á la categoría de embajador, y ya su nombramiento fué enviado al Senado el 6 de este mes. Esta disposición relativa al servicio diplomático fué emitida hace menos de seis años, y en aquella época no había en los Estados Unidos representante diplomático de grado más elevado que el de ministro, ni este país tenía en el exterior un solo embajador. Desde aquella fecha seis naciones han acreditado embajadores en Wáshington, y son las siguientes : la Gran Bretaña, Italia, Alemania, Francia, Rusia, y México. Esta última nación es la primera república americana que confiere esa distinción á su representante diplomático en Wáshington.

El Señor ROMERO es uno de los estadistas, escritores, y diplomáticos más distinguidos de México. Nació en la ciudad de Oaxaca el 24 de febrero de 1837. Principió su educación en el lugar de su nacimiento, y la terminó en la capital de la República donde se recibió de abogado. En 1855 entró por primera vez en la Secretaría de Relaciones Exteriores, pero siguió dedicado á sus estudios jurídicos. Cuando en 1857 el Presidente COMONFORT dió el golpe de Estado y el Señor JUAREZ se vió precisado á salir de la capital, el Señor ROMERO le acompañó hastá que llegó al puerto de Veracruz. Allí prestó sus servicios como oficial de la misma Secretaría de Relaciones Exteriores. En diciembre de 1859 vino á Wáshington como Primer Secretario de la Legación mexicana, y permaneció en esta capital con ese carácter hasta agosto de 1860, cuando, por ausencia del Ministro, quedó de Encargado de Negocios. Regresó á México en 1863 para tomar parte en la guerra contra los franceses, y nombrado Coronel por el Presidente JUAREZ el Gen. Don PORFIRIO DÍAZ le designó como su Jefe de Estado Mayor. Poco después, el Presidente JUAREZ le nombró Enviado Extraordinario y Ministro Plenipotenciario en Wáshington, cargo que desempeñó hasta enero de 1868, y en el cual prestó importantes servicios á su país. De regreso á México, fué nombrado Ministro de Hacienda, pero se vió obligado, debido á su quebrantada salud, á separarse de ese empleo en 1872. Vivió por tres años en Soconusco, dedicado á trabajos agrícolas, y después volvió á desempeñar la cartera de Hacienda en 1877 y 1878 y fué también Alministrador General de Correos en 1880. En marzo de 1882 regresó á Wáshington con el carácter de Enviado Extraordinario y Ministro Plenipotenciario, y desde entonces hasta la fecha ha seguido desempeñando ese cargo, con solo la interrupción de unos diez meses en 1892, cuando por tecera vez estuvo al frente de la Secretaría de Hacienda. En su carácter de representante de su país en los Estados Unidos, el Señor ROMERO ha demostrado que es un diplomático muy hábil. Sus esfuerzos para estrechar más y más cada día los amistosos lazos que unen á las dos naciones han sido coronados del mejor éxito, y con tal objeto en mira ha publicado muchos escritos que le han valido los mayores elogios, tanto por parte de la prensa de los Estados Unidos como por la de otros países.

El Señor ROMERO fué miembro de la Conferencia Internacional Americana, en la que sirvió con gran distinción, habiendo sido uno de los dos vicepresidentes de aquel cuerpo. Como delegado de México en la Conferencia, votó por el establecimiento de la Oficina de las Repúblicas Americanas, y desde que ésta se estableció, ha mostrado mucho interés en su desarrollo. Fué miembro de la Comisión Ejecutiva de la Oficina cuando por primera vez fué organizada aquélla, y ha prestado en toda ocasión su valiosa ayuda á los trabajos de la Unión Internacional de Repúblicas Americanas.

EL DOCTOR WILLIAM PEPPER.

VELADA FÚNEBRE EN LA CIUDAD DE MÉXICO—DISCURSO DEL SEÑOR ROMERO.

En una reunión que tuvo lugar en la ciudad de México el 12 de setiembre de 1898 en honor á la memoria del Doctor WILLIAM PEPPER, á la cual asistió el Presidente de México Don PORFIRIO DIAZ, el Señor ROMERO, Ministro de México en los Estados Unidos, pronunció el siguiente discurso:

Señor PRESIDENTE, SEÑORAS Y CABALLEROS. Se me ha suplicado que anuncie al auditorio que el Señor Doctor DON EDUARDO LICEAGA ha recibido un cable-grama del Director de la Universidad de Pensilvania, de cuyo establecimiento fué el Dr. PEPPER director por varios años, para que represente en esta ocasión á aquel distinguido colegio, uno de los principales y más notables de los Esta-dos Unidos. De esta manera la Universidad de Pensilvania se asocia á los procedimientos de esta noche en honor de la memoria de uno de sus más distin-guidos directores y benefactores. El cablegrama á que me he referido dice así:

FILADELFIA, *Setiembre 9 de 1898.*

Profesor E. LICEAGA, *México:*

Sírvase Vd. representar á la Universidad de Pensilvania en la velada con-memorativa de mañana.

CHARLES C. HARRISON, *Provost.*

Después de leido el presente cablegrama, el Sr. ROMERO leyó la alocución siguiente:

El deseo de pagar un merecido aunque débil tributo al mérito distinguido de un hombre notable por las bellas condiciones personales que lo adornaron y por el bien que hizo á sus semejantes durante su tránsito por la vida humana, y que á la vez era amigo sincero de nuestro país, me hacen salir siquiera por un instante del retraimiento en que me ha colocado la más terrible de las desgracias que pueden afligir á un hombre.

He creido que no sería impropio de mi parte concurrír á esta velada y tomar parte activa en ella, porque teniendo un carácter funebre, supuesto que su objeto es expresar condolencia por la pérdida de un amigo que ha partido reciente-mente de esta vida, y honrar su memoria, ella está en consonancia con el actual estado de mi ánimo y con lo que yo he estado haciendo recientemente con motivo de la grande desgracia personal que acabo de sufrir.

Tuve la fortuna de conocer personalmente y en su propio país al Dr. WILLIAM PEPPER, y la oportunidad de apreciar sus altas cualidades. A diferencia de los demás oradores que hacen su panegírico esta noche, no lo conocí en su carácter de médico, aunque fué excelso su mérito en ese ramo, sino como altruista, empe-ñado en hacer todo el bien posible á sus semejantes, consagrando todo su tiempo á empresas benéficas, á las que contribuía con sus propios recursos sin obtener más recompensa que la satisfacción de hacer el bien. Se aprovechaba de la muy ventajosa posición de que gozaba en los Estados Unidos, para allegar los recursos necesarios á fin de llevar á cabo grandes y benéficas empresas, lo cual se le facilitaba en ese país en que hay tantos filántropos.

El Dr. WILLIAM PEPPER era uno de esos astros luminosos que vienen á nuestro planeta en forma humana, para hacer el bien á sus semejantes y para servir de ejemplo á los contemporáneos y á las generaciones futuras, con el fin de elevarlas y mejorar la condición de la humanidad.

No intento, ni me sería posible hacer aquí ni ligeramente, la biografía del Dr. PEPPER y tan solo me propongo referir á grandes rasgos, la manera como lo conocí, que hace resaltar algunas de sus más bellas cualidades.

Deseando el Dr. PEPPER promover el comercio de los Estadados Unidos de América con las demás naciones del continente americano, concibió el proyecto de establecer en Filadelfia, su ciudad natal, unos Museos comerciales en que se reunieran muestras de los productos naturales y manufacturados de cada una de las repúblicas americanas, á fin de que los fabricantes de su país, que lo desearan, pudieran examinar allí las materias primas que producimos con objeto de usarlas en sus artefactos. Empresa colosal era esta para ser acometida por un particular, pues se necesitaba un gran edificio, un cuerpo científico de empleados, un número considerable de dependientes y otros servicios que requieren fuertes gastos. La energía del Dr. PEPPER no desmayó ante esas dificultades, y salvandolas todas, llegó á establecer los Museos comerciales, que fueron inaugurados solemnemente en Filadelfia, con asistencia del Presidente de los Estados Unidos de América, el 3 de Junio de 1897.

El Dr. PEPPER deseaba para el mejor éxito de su empresa, contar con la cooperación de los gobiernos de las demás naciones americanas interesadas también en su buen resultado, y siendo yo el más antiguo de sus representantes diplomáticos en Wáshington, ocurrió á mi para concertar lo referente á este asunto, y así fué como tuve la fortuna de conocerlo. Con frecuencia pasaba á Wáshington á conferenciar con nosotros, y á nuestra vez y por invitación suya, fuimos también en varias ocasiones á Filadelfia, ya para visitar los museos, ya para concurrir á su formal inauguración en la cual llevé la voz de los representantes latinoamericanos, pronunciando una alocución á nombre del consejo diplomático de los museos que él había organizado. El 11 de diciembre de 1897 tuvimos esos mismos representantes, una reunión en la legación mexicana, en Wáshington, que fué la última á que concurrió el Dr. PEPPER.

En la alocución que pronuncié en Filadelfia al inaugurarse el Museo Comercial de aquella ciudad y á la cual acabo de aludir, no pude menos que hacer la siguiente alusión al caballero á quien especialmente se debió la organización del museo:

"Deseo que se me permita hacer una alusión personal, mencionando el nombre del Dr. WILLIAM PEPPER, uno de los más notables ciudadanos de Filadelfia, á cuyos esfuerzos se debe el que el Museo Comercial de Filadelfia, haya quedado establecido con tantísimo éxito. No necesito elogiar al Dr. PEPPER ante una concurrencia compuesta de residentes de Filadelfia, en donde es tan bien conocido. Solamente diré lo que todo el mundo sabe aquí, esto es, que siempre está dispuesto á impulsar todo lo que redunde en bien de esta ciudad, de su país y de la humanidad, como por ejemplo cuando emprende con fondos propios y de sus amigos entre los que se cuentan varias Señoras de ideas elevadas, investigaciones arqueológicas y antropológicas por todo el mundo en pro del adelantamiento de las ciencias y que indudablemente redundarán en provecho de todas las naciones. Las elevadas cualidades del Dr. PEPPER son apreciadas no solamente en su propio país, sino también en el extranjero."

Antes de su muerte el Dr. PEPPER había logrado reunir los fondos necesarios no sólo para sostener permanentemente el museo, sino también para construir un gran edifico adecuado, con el costo de varios millones de pesos.

Tuve además ocasión de conocer otra de las buenas obras de este buen hombre, que también se relaciona con nuestro país. Vive en Wáshington durante el invierno y en California durante el verano una distinguida dama—que hace poco estuvo entre nosotros, dejando en pos de sí un reguero de luz en forma de beneficios á personas necesitadas—que se complace en emplear la gran fortuna que posee en establecer colegios y en hacer otras obras benéficas para el desarrollo de las ciencias y en general para el bien de la humanidad. Todas las personas que me escuchan comprenderán que me refiero á la Sra. PHOEBE A. HEARST.

El Dr. PEPPER que ocurría á esta filantrópica dama en solicitud de fondos para sus nobles empresas, concertó con ella el envío á México, de una comisión científica encargada de hacer estudios arqueológicos y antropológicos de algunos de nuestros Estados en beneficio de la ciencia, y como toda persona que hace el bien por la satisfacción que ello le causa y no por un vano alarde, esto habría pasado desapercibido para mi sin embargo de conocer bien á ambos protagonistas, á no haber sido por la circunstancia de que necesitándose el consentimiento del Gobierno de México para el envío de la comisión, tuvieron que comunicarme sus propósitos. Entiendo que no es á México al único punto del globo adonde enviaron comisiones con un objeto semejante.

Considero por lo mismo muy loable la celebración de esta velada para honrar por nuestra parte, la memoria de un hombre cuya vida hace honor á la humanidad.

DISOLUCION DEL GOBIERNO DE LOS ESTADOS UNIDOS DE LA AMÉRICA CENTRAL.

En el BOLETÍN MENSUAL del mes de octubre se publicó una comunicación de Mr. WILLIAM M. LITTLE, Cónsul de los Estados Unidos en Tegucigalpa, Honduras, relativa á la formación del Gobierno de los Estados Unidos de la América Central. La carta de Mr. LITTLE venía acompañada de una traducción de los artículos de la constitución referentes á los derechos de los extranjeros que residen dentro del territorio de la Unión. Esta constitución había de empezar á regir el 1° de noviembre de 1898. El nuevo

Gobierno ha sido, empero, de muy corta duración. Según despacho recibido de Nicaragua en 1º de deciembre de 1898, el éxito de la revolución del Salvador y la deposición del Presidente GUTIERREZ dieron margen á una reunión de los tres jefes que formaban el núcleo ejecutivo de la Unión, y decidieron abandonar la nueva forma de gobierno. Como resultado de esta decisión de los Señores SALLEGO, MATUS, y AGNOLUGARTE, los tres Estados de Honduras, Nicaragua, y Salvador han reasumido su primitivo estado como naciones independientes.

Disuelta la Unión, los Señores BONILLA, ZELAYA, y REGALADO han venido á ocupar la presidencia de sus respectivos paises, el último como sucesor del Presidente GUTIERREZ, según los despachos de la prensa. El Ministro, Mr. MERRY, y también uno de los agentes consulares, han comunicado al Departamento de Estado de los Estados Unidos que el levantamiento en el Salvador ha obtenido éxito y·que la paz ha sido establecida tras considerable desorden.

COMERCIO DE ESPAÑA EN MÉXICO Y LA AMÉRICA DEL SUR.

El gobierno español ha tomado recientemente un puesto avanzado en materias de comercio. En setiembre se dictó una Real Orden en la cual se creaba un departamento especial de Relaciones Exteriores con el objeto de suministrar informes comerciales y estadísticos y de asistir á los exportadores y hombres de negocios en general. Esta nueva oficina habrá de estar bajo la dirección de los cuerpos comerciales y del Departamento consular y se nombrará también un empleado del gobierno para que la inspeccione. México y las repúblicas sudamericanas recibirán atención especial de esta oficina. Piénsase que estos gobiernos ofrecerán ventajas especiales á los exportadores españoles por razón de la igualdad de raza, idioma y costumbres. El gobierno cree que los fabricantes españoles de botas, zapatos, guantes, sedas, abanicos, encaje, y cordelería no encontrarán dificultad ninguna en la competencia de otros países en México y Sud America. El primer paso que se ha dado al objeto de obtener mercado para estos artículos, y los demás de origen español, en México, la República Argentina, Brasil, Uruguay y Chile, ha sido el nombramiento de un delegado comercial para cada uno de aquellos paises, los cuales residirán respectivamente en Veracruz, Buenos Aires, Río de Janeiro, Montevideo, y Valparaiso. Estos delegados habrán de estar dispuestos en todo tiempo á prestar asistencia práctica á los comerciantes.

PRODUCCIÓN DE ORO Y PLATA EN 1897.

MONEDA DE LOS ESTADOS UNIDOS—MONEDA DEL MUNDO.

El Director de la Casa de Moneda, en su informe al Secretario del Tesoro trata no sólo de la producción de metales preciosos en los Estados Unidos durante el año común de 1897, sino que habla también de la producción en todos los países extranjeros donde se encuentran estos metales. Las cantidades totales forman una base para hacer comparaciones entre las principales naciones productoras, pues las fuentes de las cuales se obtuvo la información eran de lo más fidedigno y las cifras son tan exactas como fué posible.

El valor del oro producido en los Estados Unidos en 1897 fué $57,363,000. Este importe sólo es inferior al correspondiente á la República del Sur de Africa, que produjo $58,306,600. Australasia produjo $55,684,182, y Rusia, el otro país que le sigue en órden $23,245,763. La República del Sur de Africa presenta el aumento más notable del año que es de $13,854,192. La producción aumentada de Australasia fué calculada en $10,502,249; la de los Estados Unidos en $4,974,800, y la de Rusia en $1,709,970.

Los Estados Unidos, durante el año, produjeron 53,860,000 onzas de plata fina y la República de México produjo 53,903,180 onzas. Esto representa una baja en la producción de los Estados Unidos ascendente á 4,974,800 onzas finas y un aumento en la producción de México de 8,256,756 de onzas finas. En los Estados Unidos el número de onzas de oro fino fué de 2,774,935. El valor monetario de la plata producida en los Estados Unidos fué de $69,637,172. A tiempo que las minas de plata que eran las más productivas dejaron de explotarse, la mayor producción de plomo y cobre, mezclados con plata, ha compensado hasta cierto punto aquella pérdida. En 1897 se obtuvo oro de 25 Estados y

Territorios en los Estados Unidos y las cantidades fluctúan entre $100 en cada uno de cuatro Estados y $19,104,200 en el Estado de Colorado. California produjo $14,618,300; South Dakota, $5,694,900; Montana, $4,373,400; Nevada, $2,976,400; Arizona, $2,895,900; Alaska, $1,778,000; Utah, $1,726,100; Idaho, $1,701,700, and Oregon $1,353,100. Ningún otro Estado produjo la cantidad de $500,000.

La producción de plata del mundo según informe del Director de la Casa de Moneda excede con mucho á la de los años anteriores. La mayor producción después de la mencionada ocurrió en 1895 y fué de 167,509,960 onzas. El producto de oro y plata del mundo en 1897 es como sigue :

Países.	Pesos en oro.	Plata, onzas finas.	Plata, valor monetario.
Estados Unidos......................	$57,363,000	53,860,000	$69,637,200
México............................	9,436,300	53,903,181	69,693,000
Centro America....................	470,500	1,547,875	2,000,000
República Argentina................	137,600	383,470	495,800
Bolivia...........................	750,000	15,000,000	19,393,900
Brasil............................	1,204,200	....	....
Chile	928,600	6,440,569	8,327,200
Colombia	3,000,000	1,687,950	2,182,400
Ecuador..........................	132,900	7,734	10,000
Perú.............................	628,000	9,784,680	12,650,900
Uruguay..........................	38,500	....	....
Venezuela........................	948,500	....	....
Las Guyanas......................	4,324,300	....	....
Dominio del Canadá.............. .	6,027,100	5,558,446	7,186,700
Países Europeos...................	27,175,600	16,464,108	21,286,900
India Británica...................	7,247,500	....	....
Japón.......................... .	713,300	2,507,532	3,242,100
China...........	2,209,100	....	....
Korea...........................	733,100	....	....
Borneo...........................	45,900	. . ..	....
Africa	58,306,600	....	....
Australasia................	55,684,200	15,951,546	20,624,200
Totales.................	237,504,800	183,096,091	236,730,300

El valor total del oro existente en las casas de moneda y oficinas de ensayo de los Estados Unidos, durante el año, fué de $87,924,232, de los cuales $67,923,535 son moneda nacional y $20,000,597 moneda extranjera. El valor de la plata depositada en los mismos establecimientos para devolución en barras finas, que fueron usadas en las artes industriales, ó exportadas, fué de $12,707,128, de los cuales $11,847,530 corresponden á la producción doméstica y $859,598 á la extranjera. La acuñación de moneda de los Estados Unidos durante el año fué de $76,028,485 oro, y $18,487,297, de cuya cantidad $12,651,731 eran del valor legal corriente, acuñados con plata procedente de la compra que se hizo por virtud de la disposición de 14 de julio de 1890, anterior al 1° noviembre de 1893, fecha en que se revocó la cláusula de aquella disposición, relativa á la compra. La acuñación de moneda en el mundo durante el año, incluyendo reacuñaciones fué de $437,719,342 oro; $142,380,588 plata, ó sea un total de $580,099,930.

El precio mayor, en Londres, de la plata de .925 de ley, patrón inglés, durante el año, fué de 59 10-16 centavos (29 13-16 pence) y el más bajo 47½ centavos (23¾ pence), con un precio medio de 55⅛ centavos (27 9-16 pence), equivalente á $0.604449 en moneda de los Estados Unidos por onza fina. Al precio medio de la plata durante el año, el valor en barra del peso de plata fué de $0.467. El valor de la exportación neta de oro de los Estados Unidos durante el año fué de $512,609 y el valor de la exportación neta de plata del país durante el mismo período fué de $26,287,612.

Durante el año común de 1897 se consumió en las artes industriales de los Estados Unidos, oro por valor de $11,870,231, y plata por valor de $11,201,150. El consumo en el mundo de metales preciosos en las artes industriales, durante el mismo período, fué de $59,005,980 oro, y $40,435,577 plata.

El 1 de enero de 1898, la existencia metálica de los Estados Unidos consistía en $745,245,953 oro, y $635,310,064 plata, ó sea un total de $1,380,556,017.

EL CASTELLANO PARA EL COMERCIO CON LA AMÉRICA LATINA.

Mr. ABRAHAM CRISTIANI escribe á esta Oficina desde Comitán, Estado de Chiapas, la provincia más meridional de la República de México, y llama la atención hacia la inutilidad de enviar comunicaciones y anuncios escritos ó impresos en inglés á los ciudadanos de aquella sección de la República. A este respecto, conviene recordar á los exportadores, anunciadores y demás personas que deseen entablar relaciones comerciales con los habitantes de cualquiera parte de México (con excepción de las casas de comercio donde se habla el inglés) que deben escribir toda la correspondencia en castellano y enviar los catálogos y demas materia descriptiva impresos en el mismo idioma. La misma razón habría para imprimir estas materias en francés, alemán ó italiano que en inglés, pues hay en México tantos residentes que pertenecen á aquellas nacionalidades como personas que hablan el inglés. Así como en los Estados Unidos hay relativamente pocas personas que conozcan el castellano, de igual suerte en México el tanto por ciento de personas que saben hablar el inglés, es relativamente pequeño. Lo que se ha dicho respecto de México es cierto también respecto de Centro América y de las Repúblicas Sud Americanas, con excepción del Brasil en donde el portugués es la lengua del pueblo. En Haití y Santo Domingo prevalece el francés.

En su comunicación Mr. Cristiani dice que vé con satisfacción que el BOLETIN MENSUAL de la Oficina de las Repúblicas Americanas, el cual circula en los Estados Unidos, México y otros países de América, se publica en cuatro idiomas. Lamenta, sin embargo, que la mayor parte de las cartas y catálogos que se reciben de los fabricantes de maquinaria de los Estados Unidos están escritos en inglés, y como no todos conocen el idioma, no pueden informarse de su contenido. Considera oportuno llamar la atención de la Oficina hacia este hecho y sugiere que se publique un artículo en el BOLETIN al objeto de hacer saber que el único idioma que se habla en los países hispano-americanos es el castellano, de modo que se pueda tomar nota de este hecho en los países extranjeros.

Un gran número de los periódicos comerciales de los Estados Unidos están abogando por la enseñanza del idioma castellano en las escuelas superiores del país. La manera como debe enseñarse aquel idioma y las razones que abonan su inclusión en el plan de estudio de las escuelas designadas, se consignan en el siguiente extracto tomado del "American Trade," aunque se advertirá que el escritor ha omitido una de las razones más poderosas, que es la creciente importancia del comercio de los Estados Unidos con las Repúblicas de la América del Sur:

La atención que están despertando Cuba, Puerto Rico, y las Filipinas como campos para la extensión del comercio americano dá mayor interés á la lengua castellana como idioma comercial. La importancia del castellano en nuestras relaciones comerciales con el extranjero ha venido creciendo con el desarrollo de nuestro comercio con la América Latina; y la posibilidad del dominio ó de la protección de los Estados Unidos sobre colonias habitadas por individuos que hablan el castellano hace hoy más necesario que nunca para los hombres de negocios de los Estados Unidos el conocimiento de este idioma. Desde el punto de vista comercial, el idioma castellano es de vasta importancia para los intereses generales de los Estados Unidos, y la necesidad de familiarizarse con este idioma no dejará de sentirse por muchos años. Mientras más pronto se dediquen nuestros jóvenes al estudio del castellano, tanto más pronto podrán contar con los medios que aquel conocimiento les ofrecerá para la persecución de los negocios en los países situados al sur del nuestro. No hay necesidad de sobrecargar los ya nutridos cursos de las escuelas públicas primarias, pues el estudio del castellano puede muy bien incluirse en los cursos comerciales que se están agregando cada día á las escuelas superiores. Todas las escuelas mercantiles é instituciones docentes que tienen por objeto la preparación de los jóvenes para el comercio, debieran dar cabida en su plan de estudio á la enseñanza del castellano. La ignorancia ó el conocimiento imperfecto de este idioma retarda el crecimiento de nuestro comercio con los países donde se habla el castellano mucho más de lo que se supone ó reconoce.

REPUBLICA ARGENTINA.

GABINETE DEL GENERAL ROCA.

El Honorable WILLIAM I. BUCHANAN, Ministro de los Estados Unidos en Buenos Aires ha dado cuenta oficialmente al Departamento de Estado de la inauguración el 12 de octubre del Gen. JULIO ROCA como Presidente y del Señor Don NORBERTO QUIRNO COSTA como Vicepresidente de la República. El Presidente ROCA ha constituido su gabinete con los siguientes señores:

Ministro de lo Interior..................Dr. Don FELIPE YOFRE;
Ministro de las Relaciones Exteriores.......Dr. AMANCIO ALCORTA;
Ministro de Hacienda....................Dr. José MARÍA ROSA;
Ministro de Justicia é Instrucción Pública....Dr. OSWALDO MAGNASCO;
Ministro de la Guerra....................Gen. LUIS MARÍA CAMPOS;
Ministro de Marina......................Comandante MARTÍN RIVADAVIA;
Ministro de Obras Públicas...............Dr. EMILIO CIVIT;
Ministro de Agricultura..................Dr. EMILIO FRERS.

LA PLAGA DE LA LANGOSTA.

El Cónsul americano, Mr. MAYER, en Buenos Aires, con fecha 12 de octubre, ha enviado un informe relativo á la destrucción causada por la plaga de langosta que en años anteriores ha producido grandes estragos en las cosechas y en la vegetación en general de la República. El cónsul dice que las noticias recibidas acerca de esta plaga no son satisfactorias, pues aunque el trabajo de destruir la langosta continúa sin descanso, tan inmensas son las invasiones del insecto que mucho se teme que pronto lleguen á la provincia de Buenos Aires.

Entre Rios y parte de las provincias de Santa Fé y Córdoba están cubiertas de la plaga. En los tres primeros días de octubre, se recojieron en Entre Rios solamente 398 toneladas de langostas; pero las comisiones encargadas del trabajo se quejan de que en algunos lugares los habitantes rehusan cooperar en la extinción de la plaga y que la policía no hace uso de su autoridad para obligarlos á hacerlo. La Comisión Central ha publicado una circular pidiendo que sin pérdida de tiempo se le notifique de todos los nidos de huevos que existan, enviando muestras acompañadas de fechas y cualesquier otros informes pertenecientes á la materia. Noticias del Paraguay informan que abunda allí la langosta y que hace grandes estragos. En las colonias que se encuentran al sur de Santa Fé no ha habido invasiones todavía, y los agricultores creen que si para el 15 de este mes han escapado de la plaga tanto el trigo como la linaza se salvarán. Las colonias hebreas de Villaguay han sido invadidas y destruidos los cultivos. La compañía colonizadora posee allí 70,000 hectáreas de terreno, de las cuales están cultivadas de 25,000 á 30,000, de suerte que fácil es imaginarse cual será la pérdida de los agricultores si la cosecha no se da otra vez y para esto las lluvias son de absoluta necesidad. Los agricultores nada han hecho para enfrentarse con la plaga y la subcomisión recomienda á la comisión principal que sea inexorable en imponer multas. El trabajo de destrucción de la plaga continúa sin descanso en otras provincias, alcanzándose buenos resultados.

Un corresponsal del "Chilian Times" escribe de Bahía Blanca acerca del mismo asunto y dice que el Gobierno de la Argentina, por la primera vez está haciendo grandes esfuerzos para combatir la plaga de langosta cada vez más grande y ha hecho obligatoria la destrucción del insecto. Además de haber votado una gran cantidad de dinero con este objeto y de haber nombrado comisiones centrales y locales en toda la República, el Gobierno impone multas por infracción de la ley y estos fondos junto con los que contribuyen los particulares vienen á formar una buena base para el trabajo. No hay duda de que ha sido enorme el número de langostas destruidas y sólo falta ver cuales son los resultados y que ventajas pueden traer estos esfuerzos. La langosta inverna en los climas cálidos de las provincias del norte, viaja al sur en la primavera, pone hasta 80 huevos y muere. Estos huevos producen á los 40 días y el insecto que nace de ellos no tiene alas pero comienza inmediatamente su marcha desvastadora; va creciendo, muda de piel como cinco veces hasta que á los 40 días de haber nacido llega á adquirir todo su tamaño y continúa por algunos días su obra destructora; de pronto todas las langostas vuelan hacia el norte donde pasan el invierno y el procedimiento se repite hasta el infinito. Unos de los métodos empleados para la destrucción de estos insectos es el siguiente: Tiras de estaño como de un pié de alto se colocan por centenares de yardas y se hacen perforaciones ó zanjas á intervalos de 50 yardas. Le langosta llega á la barrera de estaño, no puede salvarla y cae en las zanjas. Al termino del día de trabajo, se tapan las zanjas de tierra, destruyendo así las saltonas.

BOLIVIA.

INGRESOS FISCALES EN 1897 Y PRESUPUESTO DE 1898.

El Señor Gutiérrez, Ministro de Hacienda, ha dirigido un informe al congreso nacional, ahora en sesión, sobre los ingresos de la República durante el año fiscal de 1897. Las entradas están divididas en ingresos nacionales y departamentales ó provinciales. Las cantidades están expresadas en bolivianos, peso de plata semejante en tamaño y ley al dollar de los Estados Unidos; pero dado el actual precio de la plata su valor en cambio según el informe de Departamento de Hacienda, es de $0.436 en moneda de los Estados Unidos.

Según el informe del Ministro los ingresos nacionales de Bolivia en 1897 fueron de 4,840,300.56 bolivianos. Las varias fuentes de ingresos fueron:

	Bolivianos.
Derechos de aduana	2,691,722.71
Plata en barra y minerales	679,581.85
Impuesto sobre licores	406,281.00
Sellos de larenta interior y de correos	238,890.45
Exportación de goma elástica y patentes	149,002.92
Moneda de niquel	149,000.00
Estaño, cobre y bismuto	97,632.13
Contribución sobre patentes de compañías	86,732.79

	Bolivianos.
Facturas consulares	75,543.76
Ingresos de la casa de moneda	58,960.83
Patentes de minería	52,589.43
Derechos sobre el ganado y portazgo	51,417.49
Derechos sobre la coca	40,000.00
Hipotecas	39,447.45
Impuesto sobre los fósforos	14,085.67
Interés y partidas no especificadas	9,082.28
Oro	289.80
Marcas de fábrica	40.00

En el presupuesto de 1898 se calculan los gastos en 5,714,-793.80 bolivianos. Estos gastos están distribuidos de la manera siguiente:

	Bolivianos.
Instrucción y obras públicas	1,817,489.80
Departamento de hacienda	1,571,482.50
Departamento de guerra	1,519,218,50
Relaciones exteriores	389,817.00
Departamento de lo interior y de Justicia	260,182.00
Servicio legislativo	159,604.00

Es de notarse que más de una tercera parte de los gastos se dedica á instrucción pública y obras públicas, mientras que antes una gran parte de los gastos se cargaban al Departamento de la Guerra. Se advertirá que los ingresos de 1897 son menores que los gastos presupuestos para 1898. Los ingresos provinciales ascienden á unos 600,000 bolivianos. Esta cantidad se emplea en el mantenimiento del gobierno provincial y en la ejecución de obras de carácter local.

La deuda interior contraida desde que se constituyó la República, es de 3,707,541.20 bolivianos; pero el Gobierno no está en la obligación inmediata de redimirla hasta que el Congreso decida la manera en que ha de hacerse. La otra única deuda reconocida por el Gobierno pertenece á acreedores chilenos á cuyo pago se dedica el 40 por ciento de los derechos de aduana que se cobran en Arica. La deuda original es de unos 6,500,000 bolivianos de los cuales se han de pagar 5,415,444.86 bolivianos al terminar el año fiscal de 1897. La Agencia aduanera de Bolivia en Antofogasta produce como 1,300,000 bolivianos por año. La casa de moneda nacional de Potosí acuña anualmente un promedio de 1,500,000 bolivianos de plata. .'. pesar de esto y de los 6,600,000 bolivianos en billetes de banco en circulación, ha habido recientemente gran descontento á causa de la escasez del medio circulante.

CULTIVO DEL CAUCHO.

En una entrevista, ALBERTO VIERLAND, austriaco, residente en La Paz, se expresa acerca de la condición del negocio del caucho en Bolivia en términos más ó menos como sigue:

Los mejores terrenos están todos ocupados en su mayor parte por personas que no tienen capital para explotarlos y están deseosas de venderlos. La colecta del caucho es muy costosa. Los indios que trabajan en este ramo exijen grandes jornales é insisten en recibir el pago por adelantado. Trabajan sólo por poco tiempo, temerosos de las enfermedades que produce el clima. Las regiones en donde se produce el caucho son siempre mal sanas, pues el árbol se da en lugares bajos y pantanosos conservando las raices bajo el agua durante parte del año. En los bosques de Bolivia hay gran variedad de árboles de caucho, pero Mr. VIERLAND sólo sabe que hay una hacienda en cultivo que tiene como cien árboles. Los árboles, por lo general, crecen en los valles que están más abajo de la vertiente oriental de los Andes, y en los bosques se encuentran hasta 6,000 árboles por milla cuadrada, y hay lugares que contienen hasta 10,000 árboles. Estos árboles los hay de todos tamaños, desde los más pequeños hasta aquellos que llegan á 150 piés de alto y tan anchos que según dicen tres hombres tomados de las manos no pueden rodear su tronco. El negocio del caucho puede producir mucho dinero para aquellos que tengan un gran capital.

No se puede hacer mucho si no se tiene un capital de $25,000 á $50,000, siendo las ganancias mucho más grandes en proporción si se dispone de un capital de $100,000, suma que en la opinión de Mr. VIERLAND debe producir una ganancia líquida de 60 á 70 por ciento anual. Los capitalistas pueden obtener fácilmente el derecho de explotación de los bosques de caucho, pues los mejores terrenos en donde se produce la planta están hoy en manos de los "Cholos," es decir Bolivianos mestizos que ocupan los terrenos baldíos; pero carecen de dinero para explotarlos.

El caucho bruto que se recoje en aquellos distritos es transportado en mula á La Paz, ó á Chililaya sobre lago Titicaca, de donde va á Mollendo, en la costa del Pacífico, y de allí á Liverpool, donde se vende bajo la nominación de "caucho de Mollendo " á precios muy poco más bajos que aquel á que se cotiza la clase más fina del caucho "boliviano."

BRASIL.

EL NUEVO PRESIDENTE.

El Señor Don M. F. DE CAMPOS SALLES, nuevo Presidente de los Estados Unidos del Brasil, que fué inaugurado el 15 de noviembre, ha tenido una carrera política tan larga como interesante.

De fuentes fidedignas se ha extractado lo siguiente en relación á sus servicios publicos:

Antes de formarse el partido republicano el Dr. CAMPOS SALLES, á la sazón muy joven, pertenecía á lo que se llamaba entonces el partido liberal. En 1870 los cabecillas de dicho partido organizaron el llamado republicano que entró á figurar en 1889. CAMPOS SALLES llegó á ser unos de los principales miembros del nuevo partido en su provincia, que es hoy el Estado de São Paulo. Ya antes los liberales le habían elegido como diputado por dicha provincia demostrando en el desempeño de su cargo que era un orador y político de grande habilidad.

No obstante la fuerte oposición que le hizo el partido de los imperialistas fué elegido en 1884 diputado á la Asamblea General, que corresponde á lo que hoy es el Congreso Federal. Es un hecho curioso que de los dos republicanos elegidos uno fué el que es hoy Presidente de la República y el otro el que acaba de desempeñar tan alto puesto, el Dr. PRUDENTE DE MORAES. En el Parlamento Imperial el Dr. CAMPOS SALLES pronunció varios discursos que fueron publicados y leidos en todo el Brasil.

La República que fué proclamada el 15 de noviembre de 1889 estuvo durante diez y ocho meses bajo la dirección de un gobierno provisional mientras se preparaba y adoptaba la constitución. Los republicanos decidieron extender el período del gobierno provisional con el objeto de dar tiempo para implantar varias reformas electorales. El Dr. CAMPOS SALLES fué uno de los miembros de dicho gobierno provisional durante casi todo el tiempo que existió y en él desempeñó la cartera de justicia con actividad y empeño. Siendo jurisconsulto, se rodeó de hombres del foro llevando á cabo la reforma de la judicatura, harmonizando las leyes con la nueva forma de gobierno; todo lo que en la nueva constitución se refiere á leyes es obra suya.

En la primera elección general de la República el Dr. CAMPOS SALLES fué escojido senador por su Estado natal, y sus labores en el senado correspondieron á lo que ya antes se sabía de él, llegando á considerársele uno de sus miembros más notables. Al salir del senado, fué electo gobernador del Estado de São Paulo, cargo que desempeñó hasta su elección á la presidencia el 1° de marzo de 1898.

La elección del Dr. CAMPOS SALLES como candidato marca la distinción notable que existe entre los partidos políticos del Brasil. Antes había habido varias divergencias entre los republicanos sin que existieran diferencias de partido; pero para entonces se levantó un partido que abogaba por la elección de un candidato que favoreciera al elemento natural ó del país contra el extranjero ó naturalizado, que tuviese influencia con los pocos que quedaban de aquellos que eran partidarios del gobierno monárquico, que diera preferencia al gobierno militar sobre el civil y por último un candidato que introdujera en el nuevo gobierno el sistema llamado "jacobinismo," título que el nuevo partido no rehusó aceptar. El Dr. CAMPOS SALLES era el candidato de los republicanos moderados ó conservadores que se organizaron con el nombre de partido republicano y cuya plataforma pedía respeto para la constitución, declarándose á favor de la implantación de aquellas reformas que el buen juicio y el tiempo dictasen. Las simpatías del elemento conservador y de los extranjeros que tenían intereses en el país estaban con el candidato de este partido al cual prestaron su apoyo.

La elección del Dr. CAMPOS SALLES inspiró nueva confianza en la estabilidad del Brasil, confianza que se manifestó inmediatamente por el alza del valor de la deuda nacional, en el tipo de cambio y la mayor actividad en los negocios por todo el país.

El Brasil, no obstante todos los obstáculos que se le han presentado, ha prosperado desde 1889. Para probar esto basta solamente citar dos hechos: (1) En los nueve años de la República el número de millas de ferrocarril ha aumentado; (2) la mayor cosecha de café en tiempos del Imperio (el café ha sido siempre la principal fuente de riqueza del país), fué de cerca de 4,000,000 de sacos de 60 kilógramos, mientras que la del año pasado pasó de 11,000,000 de sacos de igual peso. No puede culparse á la República de haber recibido como herencia del Imperio el sistema de papel moneda incontrovertible, ó que el precio neto del saco de café haya bajado en todas partes y que en el Brasil haya tenido una baja de $19.44 á $4.86. El país posee además del café otras inmensas fuentes de riqueza y se cree que una administración sabia y enérgica, tal y como la pasada carrera oficial del Dr. CAMPOS SALLES parece prometerla, debe devolver otra vez á la República su riqueza y crédito.

El Dr. CAMPOS SALLES desciende de una de las familias más antiguas del país y cuenta cerca de 55 años. Nació en la ciudad de Campinas, Estado de São Paulo, al cual pertenece también el Presidente saliente Don PRUDENTE DE MORAES. Es de hábitos temperados y metódico en su manera de vivir y á esto debe probablemente esa envidiable fuerza física que le ha permitido soportar el peso de una activa carrera. Por muchos años, ejerció la profesión de abogado habiéndose graduado en la escuela de jurisprudencia de São Paulo que es una de las primeras instituciones del país. Su familia ha sido siempre rica, fortuna que procede principalmente de sus haciendas de café y el mismo Dr. CAMPOS SALLES ha sido siempre y es todavía dueño de magníficas plantaciones de este fruto.

IMPORTANCIA DE LA INDUSTRIA DEL CAUCHO.

Es incuestionable que el Brasil es un país de inmensas fuentes de riquezas naturales. La gran variedad de su suelo y de sus condiciones climatéricas le adaptan especialmente á la producción de todos los frutos de las zonas templada y tórrida, y esto no obstante, en el mundo comercial, dicha República más que por otra cosa es conocida por dos de sus productos—el café y el caucho. Puede decirse que ejerce el monopolio de ambos, especialmente el de este último. Aquél es producto del campo, éste de los bosques; el uno es producto del cultivo, el otro es producto natural. Antes se cuidaba más de la producción del café, pero en los últimos años por razón de la extensión consagrada á su cultivo y la competencia creciente de otros países, los precios que alcanzaba este producto han ido bajando hasta que casi ha desaparecido la ganancia que producían las haciendas de café. No sucede lo mismo con el caucho, porque aunque la producción de este árbol, que es indígena á casi todo el país, ha aumentado con asombrosa rapidez, no sólo se han conservado los precios sino que también han ido subiendo paulatinamente.

El Gobierno no ha tardado en reconocerlo así y en observar el aumento del dinero que traía al país la venta de este producto. Los exploradores afirman que en el interior del país hay una inmensidad de árboles de caucho en bosques casi inexplorados. El Gobierno, sin embargo, no está satisfecho con esto y se ocupa en enseñar al pueblo las particularidades de las distintas variedades que existen del árbol del caucho, el mejor método de cultivo, la adaptabilidad de ciertas especies al suelo de los diferentes estados, y la manera de preparar el producto bruto para los distintos mercados del mundo.

Habiendo comprendido la aplicación y utilidad del caucho en casi todas las industrias, el cultivo de la planta vendrá á ser una nueva industria cuyo producto aumentará la cosecha del caucho. Esto no obstante, no se piensa descuidar el caucho de los bosques y el Gobierno se propone impedir los daños que hasta ahora se han hecho á estos.

Recientemente el Cónsul americano en Pernambuco, Mr. CLARK, y el Vice-cónsul interino en Santos, Mr. RONSHEIM, han informado al Departamento de Estado de los Estados Unidos acerca de las variedades del caucho, la cantidad que se produce, y su valor en los diferentes estados del Brasil. Mr. CLARK, en su comunicación, habla del "maniçoba" y Mr. RONSHEIM del "mangabeira." Dice el primero que el caucho llamado "maniçoba" crece en la parte norte del Brasil, especialmente en Ceara, Rio Grande del Norte, y Parahyba; su precio sigue al del "seringueira" ó caucho del Pará, siendo preferido el producto para ciertos trabajos.

El interés despertado en el cultivo de la planta sigue aumentando en dichos tres estados y se extiende rápidamente por Pernambuco, Alagoa, y Bahia, dando mayor resultado con menos trabajo que cualquier otro producto agrícola. A principios del invierno se siembra la semilla, que da mejor resultado en tierra roja ó prieta. Al tiempo de sembrar, la tierra no debe estar ni demasiado seca ni demasiado humeda, y una vez que el árbol ha llegado á la edad de dos años ya puede resistir cualquier cambio de clima; pero por supuesto la cantidad de leche siempre dependerá más ó menos de las influencias del clima.

A los seis años la planta ha llegado á su madurez y este es el mejor tiempo para sangrarla, aunque esta operación puede comenzarse á ejecutar cuando la planta tiene dos años. Después de los seis años el árbol produce anualmente hasta los treinta años, de dos á cinco kilógramos de caucho si el árbol se ha conservado en buena condición. Después de los treinta años, la cosecha comienza á disminuir un poco, y en buenas condiciones la vida del árbol puede llegar á un siglo. La savia se prepara lo mismo que la de la "seringueira" de Pará, pero después de haber sido ahumada toma un color prieto oscuro. La manera como en los estados antedichos se produce el caucho "maniçoba" consiste en cortar la corteza del árbol, dejando que la savia gotee hasta la base, en donde por la acción de los rayos del sol se coagula, formando una masa sólida é irregular, que recojen los naturales y venden á los comerciantes, que luego la embarcan para los Estados Unidos y Europa. El precio por kilógramo varía en estos estados de 2 á 5 milreis, según la calidad.

Además del "maniçoba" estos Estados producen gran cantidad de caucho "mangabeira," que es de inferior calidad y se emplea para cubrir cables, etc.

Mr. CLARK envía el siguiente cuadro de las exportaciones de Ceara en los años de 1893 á 1897, inclusive:

Años.	Cantidad.		Valor.
	Kilos.	*Milreis.*	
1893	135, 569	1, 129, 742	$259, 840. 66
1894	146, 627	1, 221, 892	242, 378. 40
1895	146, 627	1, 592, 567	302, 587. 73
1896	324, 327	2, 702, 725	486, 490. 50
1897	475, 693	3, 964, 108	594, 616. 20

En su informe Mr. RONSHEIM hace notar que durante los últimos seis meses llegaron á Santos, procedentes del interior, varios cargamentos de caucho "mangabeira," los cuales fueron embarcados para Europa. Habiendo sido buenos los resultados obtenidos, se enviaron al interior otras expediciones y las llegadas de cargas de caucho aumentan diariamente, prometiendo producir una importante renta á este Estado, que hasta ahora no ha tenido otras sino las provenientes de las exportaciones de café.

Entre los muchos artículos publicados en la prensa brasilera últimamente sobre esta materia, el Cónsul llama la atención al del "Deutsche Zeitung" de São Paulo, de fecha 11 de agosto de 1898, cuya traducción envía y es como sigue:

El caucho del Brasil se extrae de los árboles que pertenecen á tres familias distintas:

(1) *Hevea brasiliensis*, Müll Arg. ó seringueiro del Amazonas (Caucho del Pará).

(2) *Manihot Galsiovii*, Müll Arg. ó maniçoba de Ceara (Retazos de Ceara).

(3) *Hancornia speciosa* Gom. ó mangabeira (Caucho mangabeira).

Las dos primeras clases no se refieren á São Paulo, pus ningún resultado se ha obtenido de las semillas distribuidas por el Gobierno á los agricultores; la tercera clase se encuentra en la porción occidental de São Paulo. No se da en el Este ni en la costa, quizas á causa de la humedad ó de otras condiciones del terreno.

Antes el caucho "mangabeira" producía como la mitad de lo que rendía el precio del Pará, pero el valor ha subido. Se dice que es mucho más duro y por consiguiente preferible para ciertos usos.

Dice la prensa que durante el primer semestre de 1898 el ferrocarril de Magyana transportó 76,498 kilógramos de caucho. Operarios experimentados del Estado de Bahía se emplean para sangrar los árboles. Los propietarios reciben la tercera parte del producto neto, mientras que los compradores pagan cerca de 75 milreis por arroba. Se dice que un hombre puede extraer hasta tres kilógramos por día.

El Gobierno desea fomentar el cultivo de este árbol tan útil y estudia el plan de pagar una prima á los campesinos que se ocupen en esta industria.

El "South American Journal" de octubre 8, dice que el Estado de Sao Paulo ha promulgado una ley por la que ofrece dos premios de 25,000 milreis cada uno y cuatro de 15,000 milreis cada uno para el cultivo del caucho mangabeira. Ofrece también una prima de 15,000 milreis por el mejor procedimiento para extraer la resina y otra de 10,000 milreis para la aclimatación de otros árboles de caucho. El periódico en referencia no dice si estos premios son en oro ó plata. El Departamento del Tesoro de los Estados Unidos calcula el milreis de oro en $0.546.

CHILE.

DESARROLLO INDUSTRIAL DE LA REPÚBLICA.

Chile compra mercancías de buena calidad y vale la pena de que los fabricantes de los Estados Unidos cultiven aquel mercado. El siguiente breve resumen de los recursos de la República está extractado del Directorio Comercial publicado por la Oficina de las Repúblicas Americanas.

Chile tiene una longitúd de 600 millas y su anchura varía entre 50 y 200 millas. PEDRO DE VALDIVIA, el primer español invasor la comparó á la hoja de una espada á causa de su gran longitud y su angostura. Su área es de 293,970 millas cuadradas y según el censo de 1895 la población era de 2,766,747 ó sea 9.2 habitantes por milla cuadrada. El número de habitantes excede ahora probablemente de 3,300,000. De este número, la mitad se dedica á la agricultura. Prodúcense en el país 28,500,000 fanegas de trigo y 8,500,000 fanegas de cereales, además de legumbres, frutas, etc. Se crían más de 500,000 cabezas de ganado vacuno y 2,000,000 de chivos anualmente. Abundan los productos minerales como nitrato, cobre, plata, oro, carbón, manganeso, etc. Los depósitos de nitrato de Chile cubren un área de unos 220,356 acres que se calcula que contienen 2,316 quintales métricos de nitrato, y son los más extensos del mundo. La producción total de estos depósitos en 1896, según se consigna en un BOLETÍN de fecha reciente, era de 1,092,000 toneladas.

Puede formarse una idea del desarrollo industrial de Chile si se considera que en 1895, en el Departamento de Valparaiso, con una población de menos de 200,000 almas, había 417 establecimientos industriales, provistos de 162 máquinas de vapor de un total de 1,766 caballos de fuerza, los cuales dieron empleo durante el año á 12,616 operarios. Entre estos establecimientos figuraban fábricas de gas, cervecerías, refinerías de azúcar, fábricas de carruajes y carros, asserraderos, fábricas de aguas minerales y gaseosas, etc. Las tenerías constituyen un ramo floreciente de la industria del país.

Chile fué el primer país de la América del Sur que construyó ferrocarriles. A principios de 1897, la extensión total de ferrocarriles en la República era, según el Cónsul DOBBS, de más de 1,300 millas, concluidas y en construcción. Estas líneas eran propiedad del Góbierno, el que también las explotaba. Había también 938 millas de propiedad de particulares y corporaciones, principalmente inglesas. La línea principal es la Gran Central que pertenece al Estado y comprende tres secciones; de Valparaiso á Santiago y de este punto á Melipilla; de Santiago á Talca, de San Fernando á Alcones y de Pelequen á Peomó; de Talca á Talcahuano, San Rosendo á Traguen, Santa Fé á Los Angeles, y Roblería á Victoria, un total de 766 millas. Los trabajos del ferrocarril trasandino se están haciendo ahora con gran actividad.

Según las estadísticas tomadas del Directorio Comercial, hay 25,000 millas de caminos públicos y 2,875 de vías de agua. A fines de 1895 la extensión de las líneas telegráficas del Estado era de 6,965 millas con 8,330 millas de alambre. Había también

Bull. No. 6——7

4,500 millas de línea telegráfica pertenencientes á ferrocarriles y á corporaciones privadas.

La marina mercante de Chile consistía en 1896 de 188 buques con un tonelaje de 105,642 toneladas. Cuarenta y dos de estos buques eran vapores. Líneas de vapores inglesas, alemanas y francesas hacen viajes regulares entre las costas de Chile y Europa por el Estrecho de Magallanes, y hay comunicación directa y constante por medio de líneas de vapores chilenos y extranjeros que viajan á lo largo de la costa hasta Panamá en donde conectan con vapores que van para puertos de los Estados Unidos en el Pacífico, Atlántico y Golfo de México, y para Europa.

Chile importa la mayor parte de los géneros manufacturados que se consumen en el país, pero el Gobierno ofrece alicientes para el establecimiento de nuevas industrias y está ansioso del fomento de empresas manufactureras. Se dice que el Congreso ha votado recientemente $500,000 para fundiciones de hierro y acero, pues está demostrado que existe mineral de hierro en abundancia en el país. En 1897, el valor de las importaciones en Chile fué de $65,502,805, y el de las exportaciones $64,754,133.

EXPORTACIÓN DE NITRATO EN 1898.

La exportación de nitrato de Chile durante el presente año se calcula entre 1,203,000 y 1,228,000 toneladas, contra 1,040,000 toneladas en 1897, 1,210,000 en 1896, y 1,075,000 en 1895. El importe de los cargamentos del 1° de noviembre, fué: para Europa, 745,000 toneladas; para la América del Norte, 122,000 toneladas, y para los demás países 11,000 toneladas, haciendo un total de 878,000 toneladas. Se espera que en noviembre y diciembre los cargamentos lleguen á 300 ó 350,000 toneladas. Suponiendo que estos cargamentos no excedan de 325,000 toneladas, el total de exportaciones de 1898 ascenderá á 1,203,000 toneladas ó unos 26,464,000 quintales. Esta cantidad representará 1,464,000 quintales más que la cantidad calculada por el Ministro de Hacienda de Chile en el presupuesto de 1898. Los derechos de exportación recibidos en Chile, incluyendo las aumentadas exportaciones de nitrato, serán de $41,729,777 contra $41,000,000, cantidad en que los calcula el presupuesto de 1898.

COLOMBIA.

COMERCIO CON NUEVA ORLEANS.

El Cónsul de la República de Colombia en Nueva Orleans, Señor ESCRIPCIÓN CANAL, ha remitido á su Gobierno un informe en el cual trata del comercio de su distrito consular con Colombia durante el año de 1897. Se ve por este informe que las exportaciones de Colombia durante aquel año, fueron por valor de $947,717.20 y consistieron principalmente en plátanos.

Las exportaciones á Colombia vía Nueva Orleans, con destino en gran parte á Bocas del Toro, fueron por valor de $155,219.77 y los principales cargamentos se hicieron en marzo, abril, y noviembre. Los principales artículos fueron arroz, azúcar, carnes, pescado, licores, jamones, aves, huevos, cebada, cebollas, frijoles, jabones, velas de esperma, manteca, mantequilla, harina, maíz, patatas, pan, y galletas. También se exportaron en menos cantidades instrumentos de agricultura, madera de construcción, pinturas, drogas, y medicinas, muebles para casas y oficinas, artículos de escritorio, zapatos, sombreros, ropa hecha, loza, y cristalería.

El Cónsul hace notar que hay un balance de $792,497.43 en favor del comercio colombiano, debido principalmente á la gran exportación de plátanos de la Isla de Bocas del Toro. Este puerto, que es el punto de embarque de un fértil distrito agrícola, sólo necesita mejores medios de explotación y exportación de este y otros productos para que venga á ser un importante centro comercial. Los valores que se consignan en este informe, están expresados en moneda colombiana, cuyo peso es equivalente á $0.418 en moneda de los Estados Unidos.

EL NUEVO CANAL DE PANAMÁ.

El Gen. H. L. ABBOTT, en un artículo publicado en el "Forum" dá la siguiente descripción del estado actual del Canal de Panamá:

La longitud del canal es de 46 millas de las cuales unas 15 por el lado del Atlántico y 7½ por el del Pacífico, ó sea como la mitad de toda la distancia, quedarán al nivel del mar. De esta distancia están ya esencialmente terminadas 18 millas ó sean unos dos quintos de toda la ruta, de modo que con un pequeño desembolso para llevar á cabo el drenaje, quedará desde luego utilizable. Por consiguiente, sólo tenemos que considerar las 23¾ millas entre Bujio en el lado del Atlántico y Miraflores en el del Pacífico. Hay dos excelentes puertos utilizables que para hacerlos puertos protegidos no sería necesario hacer desembolso alguno; y el ferrocarril de Panamá que borda toda la ruta del canal, podrá utilizarse en la construcción de éste. En muchos lugares se han preparado ya alojamientos en bastante buenas condiciones para el número crecido de trabajadores. Estas ventajas son inmensas donde el tiempo tiene tanta importancia.

Hay otra ventaja no menos importante á mi juicio. Por medio de cuidadoso estudio técnico la compañía ha podido ajustar provisionalmente el proyecto de modo que quede reservada la elección entre los tres mejores niveles, elección que tendrá lugar prácticamente al llevar á cabo los trabajos en gran escala. Estos proyectos están designados de la manera siguiente: "Nivel de 96¼ piés;" "nivel de 69 piés;" y "nivel de 32¼ piés." Las cifras indican la elevación en pies del fondo del canal á su mayor nivel sobre la marea media que se encuentra prácticamente al mismo nivel absoluto en ambos océanos, aunque la oscilación de la marea en Colón es sólo de unas cuantas pulgadas, mientras que en Naos alcanza hasta 20 piés. De la comparación de los presupuestos·de construcción resulta que los gastos del canal serían casi los mismos, ya se hicieren mayores excavaciones ó ya esclusas y represas. El costo de uno ú otro de los planes se calcula en $100,000,000.

COSTA RICA.

MODIFICACIONES DEL ARANCEL.

La Oficina de las Repúblicas Americanas ha recibido del Gobierno de Costa Rica un número especial del Boletin Internacional de Aduanas en el cual se publican tres leyes modificativas del arancel vigente. La primera ley es la de fecha 22 de julio de 1898, modificando los derechos aplicables al azúcar y al cacao y prohibiendo la importación de alcoholes. El texto de esta ley es como sigue:

ART. 1º.—Las partidas nᵒˢ 85, 87 y 88, clase 9ª del Arancel de Aduanas de 7 de setiembre de 1885, quedan reformadas en lo conducente, según los términos siguientes:

Azúcar blanco, en cualquier forma.................................kilogr.. $0. 20
Azúcar de otras clases ....id.... 15
Cacao molido........................ .. ..id.... 20
Cacao en grano...id.... 15

ART. 2º.—Prohíbese la introducción de alcoholes.
ART. 3º.—Esta ley empezará á regir desde el día de su publicación.

La segunda ley es la de 2 de agosto de 1898, modificando los derechos aplicables á los almidones:

ART 1º.—Las partidas nᵒˢ 27 y 85, clases 3ª y 9ª del Arancel de Aduanas, quedan reformadas en lo conducente, en los siguientes términos:

Almidones ... .kilogr. $0. 15

ART. 2º.—La presente ley empezará á regir desde el día de su publicación.

La tercera ley es de igual fecha que la anterior, y en ella se declara monopolio fiscal la importación del tabaco elaborado.

ART. 1º. Declárase monopolio fiscal la importación del tabaco elaborado en cigarrillos, puros, rapé, picadura, ó en otra forma.

ART. 2º. Facúltase al Poder Ejecutiva para que se provea de estos artículos por medio de los particulares que lo soliciten, siempre que éstos se encarguen de expenderlos al público por su propia cuenta, de tomar á su cargo el pago del valor principal y gastos que ocasione la introducción de dichos artículos al país, y paguen al fisco, previamente al desalmacenaje de los mismos en las aduanas de la República, $2.20 por kilógramo de peso bruto.

ART. 3º. La presente ley empezará á regir desde el día de su publicación.

HONDURAS.

EXPERIENCIA DE UN AGRICULTOR.

El BOLETÍN del mes de julio de 1898 contiene un artículo sobre la población, el clima, los fuentes de riqueza, etc., de Honduras. El autor del artículo mencionó incidentalmente el nombre de W. M. BAMBERGE, á quien se remitió una copia del BOLETÍN. Mr. BAMBERGE no se mostró de acuerdo por completo con las declaraciones hechas en aquel bosquejo, y la correspondencia que subsiguientemente tuvo lugar dió margen á la siguiente comunicación de fecha de 23 de octubre de 1898, en la cual se trata por manera interesante de las fuentes agrícolas de la República según lo observado por un cultivador práctico del suelo:

Permítame presentar los siguientes hechos como el resultado de cinco años de experencia en mis trabajos de agricultura en el Valle de Sula, en Honduras. Doy á V. estos datos, porque V. dice que "en esa Oficina se reciben numerosas solicitudes de informes acerca de Honduras," y yo creo que debe decirse la verdad á aquellos que tienen el propósito de venir aquí. Si mis declaraciones no están en harmonía con las de los corresponsales de V., puede V. atribuir la discrepancia á la diferencia que existe entre el hombre que ha manejado la azada y dirigido el arado y el que de palabra ha dirigido las faenas agrícolas desde la ciudad.

El inmigrante, al entrar en Honduras, es sorprendido por la lujuriosa vegetación desde las cumbres de las montañas hasta los más bajos valles, é inmediatamente supone que el suelo es rico y que puede producir cualquier cosa. Sin más investigaciones, el inmigrante escribe numerosas cartas á su familia, á sus amigos, y á los periódicos del lugar de su procedencia, y el asunto de estas cartas se traduce en "eterna verdura," "paraíso terrenal," "vegetación expontánea," etc. Si siente afición por la agricultura, obtiene algún terreno, contrata trabajadores (si puede obtenerlos) y empieza á trabajar. En pocos meses vende la propiedad, si puede, ó la abandona y se vuelve pobre á los Estados Unidos, en donde dedica sus ratos de ocio á maldecir á Honduras. Pero la falta no es de este país; el suelo y clima de Honduras dan aquellos productos adaptables á sus condiciones peculiares. Si un hondureño emigrase á los Estados Unidos y se estableciese en Ohio tratando de cultivar allí plátanos, mangos, papayas, ó cualquier otro producto tropical, haría lo mismo que hace el emigrante de los Estados Unidos que viene á Honduras y trata de cultivar aquellas legumbres y frutas que sólo se producen en la zona templada; y el resultado sería un fiasco completo.

Admito que se pueden cultivar aquí algunos vegetales de la zona templada, pero esto sólo puede hacerse dándoles condiciones artificiales, y no se encuentran mercados donde obtener precios que justifiquen el trabajo y los gastos. Vendrá un tiempo en que se encontrarán tales mercados, pero no creo que sea en un futuro próximo. Es un hecho que en materia de vegetación económica, ninguna planta (que no sea indígena de los trópicos) crece aquí tan rápidamente como crecería en los Estados Unidos ni produciría en tan buenas condiciones. El buniato (*convolvulus batata*) produce bajo el mejor cultivo unas 1,000 libras por acre. La patata (*solanum tuberosum*) no se reproduciría. El tomate no paga los gastos del estacado y de la guía de la planta. Entre una y otra variedad se puede calcular como límite de producción una libra por cada cepa. Yo he hecho experimentos con unas veinte variedades y encuentro que el "champión enano" es la más satisfactoria. La berengena (*solanum melongena*) rinde bastante con buenos fertilizadores. La col, si se le proporciona sombra y se la abona y riega, puede producir buenos repollos. Si el hueso molido y la harina de semilla de algodón fueran obtenidos por el cultivador absolutamente libres de derecho, el cultivo de la col podría hacerse bastante remunerativo. El rábano se da bastante bien en suelo arenoso durante los meses de noviembre, diciembre, y enero. La lechuga requiere mucha sombra y mucho cuidado y aun con todo esto produce poco. El chalote y el ajo se dan bien durante la estación de la lluvia. El pepino, en estación propicia, se produce bastante bien, pero las "estaciones propicias" se presentan con tan poco frecuencia que aquel cultivo es por demás precario. El hibisco comestible (*hibiscus esculentus*) se produce bien y es remunerativo El melón y la sandía alcanzan el período de madurez, pero carecen del sabor que tienen los que se producen en los Estados Unidos. En cinco años de cultivo no hemos podido lograr siquiera una cebolla de tamaño mediano por más que se han empleado simientes y posturas de todas las variedades obtenibles.

Aunque las condiciones climatológicas fueran favorables al cultivo de las plantas mencionadas, los insectos enemigos son tan numerosos y el costo de los insecticidas tan grande que aquellos cultivos no dejarían provecho alguno al cultivador. El enemigo más inveterado de la agricultura es la hormiga conocida por los naturalistas con el nombre de "Sauba." Este destructor insecto se encuentra en todas partes de Honduras, desde los picos más altos hasta los valles más profundos, y parece aumentar tan rápidamente como solamente las hormigas pueden reproducirse. Son especialmente destructoras para el naranjo y el mango y también para la col y la cebolla ó tablas de chalote. Yo he visto que han desnudado por completo un naranjo de un año en una sola noche y han continuado su obra de destrucción sobre el mismo árbol hasta matarlo. También las he visto destruir una tabla de chalotes de un área de extensión en una sola noche, mientras que la cantidad de col que cargan consigo en el mismo tiempo es sólo igualada por el tamaño de toda la extensión cultivada. El naturalista Bates hace mención de grandes extensiones de tierra en el Brasil en las que ni siquiera se da el café á causa de los estragos de la "Sauba," pero yo sólo conozco de un caso aquí en que este insecto haya atacado el café. Si el Gobierno dictara leyes tendentes al exterminio de esta plaga (y yo creo que esto podría hacerse económicamente y en un período relativamente corto), el cultivo de naranjas, limones, y otras frutas de la misma familia podría ser una industria provechosa. Yo he encontrado que el bisulfuro de carbono es el más eficaz agente para el aniquilamiento de la hormiga, pero su excesivo costo prohibe su uso.

Ahora bien, contando con la indulgencia de V. presentaré el otro lado de la cuestión y mencionaré algunos ramos en que un americano activo puede hacer dinero en Honduras. No menciono todas las industrias, porque todavía no he obtenido suficiente experiencia, pero ya se ha dicho lo bastante para que se comprenda que pueden hacerse ricos aquí todos cuantos vengan á trabajar inteligentemente. Tres ó cuatro personas pueden combinar su trabajo y sembrar con provecho plátanos de todas clases. Hay en el país una demanda firme de plátanos de 50 á 75 centavos el ciento, mientras que los vapores pagan 31¼ centavos (plata) por el racimo de plátanos entregado en la línea del ferrocarril. Las cepas que se siembran en abril, mayo y junio comienzan á producir en el siguiente abril, y en lo adelante pueden hacerse cortes cada semana con tal que el lugar se conserve limpio y se elija un suelo apropiado. Los que tengan el proyecto de cultivar plátanos, encontrarán que es gran economía sembrar ellos mismos la planta en lugar de comprar terreno ya sembrado. El cultivo del plátano es muy sencillo. Todos los informes necesarios pueden obtenerse en pocos minutos, y el resultado será en exacta proporción al trabajo empleado.

La caña de azúcar una vez sembrada produce una cosecha anual por ocho ó doce años con trabajo relativamente pequeño. El jugo puede convertirse en "dulce" que encuentra fácil salida entre los naturales. En nuestra finca convertimos nuestra caña en azúcar por medio de la evaporación que es semejante al antiguo proceso de tachos abiertos, pero mucho más rápida. Nosotros elaboramos un azúcar de color extremadamente claro, la cual se vende fácilmente. No hay grandes plantaciones de azúcar en Honduras, que yo sepa, pero esto no quiere decir que si hubiera muchas no fueran productivas. Yo opino que la fabricación de azúcar en grande escala sería productiva, aunque fuese necesario traer los trabajadores de los Estados Unidos.

Hay cientos de lugares á buena distancia del ferrocarril con suelo virgen, buena sombra y buen desagüe,—condiciones esenciales al provechoso cultivo del cacao—los cuales lugares sólo aguardan por la acción de la inteligencia y el trabajo para convertirse en centros de propiedad comercial. Este árbol produce en tres años y continúa produciendo por 25 años más. Hay una creciente y firme demanda de este producto el cual se vende á precios remunerativos. El árbol que produce la goma del comercio, no tiene, por lo que hasta el presente he observado, insectos enemigos. Al igual de las demás plantas tropicales, se mejora bajo un cultivo inteligente.   Una de estos árboles, sembrado en las propias condiciones y debidamente atendido, daría su producto anual por muchos años.   El hule puede crecer casi en cualquier punto del país, pero su cultivo sólo será provechoso en terrenos ricos, húmedos y en buenas condiciones de drenaje.   Yo he sembrado solamente con un propósito experimental, pero he demostrado á mi entera satisfacción que el hule propiamente sembrado y cuidado ha crecido á un tamaño triple del de los sembrados en el monte "estilo nativo." Los explotadores nativos del hule no opinan por la extracción de la goma de árboles que tengan menos de 8 años de edad.   El próximo agosto, mis hules cultivados tendrán tres años; por aquella época les extraeré la goma y comunicaré á V. el resultado.   Estoy convencido, por el resultado de mis investigaciones, de que la generalidad de los americanos sacarán más beneficio de la plantación del hule que de ninguna otra inversión de dinero en Honduras.   Con mucho gusto daré presupuestos á todo el que desee investigar sobre este punto.

Probablemente estamos demasiado lejos (tomando en consideración el tiempo empleado en el trasporte) de embarcar, con utilidad, piñas de los Estados Unidos al presente, pero no hay razón ninguna para que una compañía no cultive aquí el fruto y lo exporte en latas.   No es necesario que la compañía sea acaudalada, sino que, antes al contrario, una compañía mutua ó cooperativa obtendría éxito más seguro que una que contara con dinero solamente.   Desde que se siembra el renuevo que se forma en la base de la fruta hasta que esta se madura, trascurren de 18 á 20 meses; después, cada planta produce dos ó tres frutas que crecen en las cepas que brotan del tronco de la planta.   Yo creo que los mejores resultados se obtienen colocando las plantas á cuatro piés de distancia unas de otras en los surcos y á la misma distancia entre éstos.   Un poco de sombra es beneficiosa para el cultivo de la piña aquí.   Sembrando á la distancia mencionada, se pueden plantar 4,692 matas en cada manzana, las cuales rendirán después de la primera cosecha un minimum de 9,000 frutas por año. Cultivamos aquí tres variedades de esta planta, pero la de mayor preferencia es la piña "pan de azúcar" que no sólo alcanza gran tamaño, sino que es también muy dulce y jugosa.   JEAN DE LERY, que describió la piña hace más de 300 años, dice : "debiera ser recogida solamente por la mano de Venus y servida sólo á los diosos."   Probablemente JEAN probó de la piña "pan de azúcar."

La vainilla indígena cuidadosamente curada tiene un aroma muy agradable y debiera tener valor comercial.   Yo he hecho un excelente extracto del fruto del país (curándolo, como se hace en México) y lo encontré muy bueno para el uso de las familias.   No tuve los medios de determinar la cantidad ó tanto por ciento de principio activo del fruto.   No hay duda de que la vainilla daría una producción abundante, y cultivándola (es decir, reduciendo el follaje que le dá sombra, y la maleza, para que circule libremente el aire) se obtendría un fruto más largo y productivo.   Los nativos parece que no tienen mayor interés en dar la atención necesaria á la preparación de este producto y hacer de él un artículo de comercio.

El limón crece rápidamente y produce en tres años.   Este fruto, por lo que hasta el presente ha sido observado tiene muy pocos insectos enemigos, si es que los tiene.   No se produce en número suficiente para justificar la exportación, pero sin duda se dará alguna atención á este importantísimo producto en un futuro cercano. California y la Florida no tienen área suficiente, aunque toda ella estuviera sembrada de limones, para surtir de este producto á los Estados Unidos, y Honduras podría suplir la deficiencia.

El mejor café que he visto en Honduras se cultiva en el valle de Sula (á una altura de 200 pies sobre el nivel del mar) y se le proporciona sombra por medio de matas de plátanos. Sé que los cultivadores de café sostienen que este grano sólo se dá á una altura entre 2,500 y 5,000 piés, pero las circunstancias alteran los casos, y en los puntos en donde existen condiciones para el crecimiento de aquella planta, su producción tendrá lugar ya sea la altura de uno ó ya de diez mil piés. El único obstáculo para el crecimiento del café es la dificultad de obtener trabajadores á salarios moderados y en oportunidad. Al presenta es difícil obtener "mozos" (trabajadores inexpertos) por $1.50 por día de ocho horas de trabajo, y esto es más de lo que puede pagar el cultivador. Se me dice que los salarios son más bajos en el interior, pero la dificultad de obtener braceros es poco más ó menos la misma. La cosecha de café no ha dejado mayor utilidad en la pasada estación, pero es indudable que aquella será mejor en el futuro, pues el aumento del área de cultivo y una mejor selección del grano, darán al café de Honduras un lugar de importancia en el mercado por razón de su mérito que no puede hacerse patente en la actualidad á causa de la limitada cantidad que se produce.

Pero he escrito más extensamente de lo que me proponía, y no he mencionado muchos productos en los cuales los cultivadores ya en mayor ó ya en menor escala, pueden hacer dinero. En otra comunicación haré referencia á otros frutos así como á ciertas plantas textiles y medicinales.

MEXICO.

ESTADÍSTICA DEL COMERCIO EXTERIOR.

La Estadística Fiscal Mexicana correspondiente al año que terminó el 30 de junio de 1898 fué publicada por el Departamento de Hacienda en octubre y acusa un resultado especialmente favorable al Gobierno. En las importaciones se advierte un aumento sobre las de 1896 de $1,399,397. Entre los artículos cuya importación aumentó en mayor escala se encuentran los siguientes: maquinaria para minería é industria, materiales para ferrocarriles, manufacturas de algodón y géneros de algodón crudos, blanqueados, y estampados. Las partidas que acusan una baja comprenden el maíz, la manteca, la harina, y los alimentos cereales en general.

El importe total de las exportaciones es de $128,972,749, lo que unos cuantos años ha se habría considerado casi increíble.

Esta suma se componía en su mayor parte de minerales contentivos de metales preciosos, valuados en $75,042,332, quedando el importe de los otros artículos á un valor de $53,930,417. El total comparado con el del año anterior $111,346,494 acusa un aumento de $17,626,255. Comparado con el año de 1896, el aumento en las exportaciones ha sido $9,859,235 en metales preciosos y minerales y $8,767,020 en los otros artículos.

La siguiente lista contiene los nombres de los países de los cuales se recibió la mayor parte de las importaciones y también el valor de las exportaciones hechas á los mismos.

	Importación.	Exportación.
Estados Unidos	$21,490,604	$94,974,616
Inglaterra	8,105,696	14,775,638
Francia	5,435,698	5,320,016
Alemania	4,781,821	6,995,733
España	2,039,132	1,231,342
Bélgica	590,196	1,556,090
Italia	186,273	30,600
Suiza	156,732	200
Austria	125,144	
Holanda	103,913	719,322
Brasil	8,658	
Colombia	24,127	2,260
Ecuador	73,681	342
Guatemala	14,950	846,016
Cuba	1,130	2,152,544
Perú	314	7,999
Salvador	3,648	21,191
Santo Domingo	38	50,720
Venezuela	36,963	170
Rusia	19,644	270,370

NUEVOS ARTÍCULOS DE EXPORTACIÓN.

El Vicecónsul de México en Cardiff, Gales, ha dirigido una nota consular á su gobierno en la que llama la atención hacia la demanda en su distrito consular del artículo conocido en el comercio con el nombre de cera de Campeche. Esta cera de Campeche, que se considera como una de las mejores variedades, obtiene buen precio en todos los mercados del Reino Unido. Se obtiene en México á poco costo y se vende en Europa para uso en las industrias y artes con gran provecho de los productores mexicanos.

Otro artículo de comercio que se produce en México con gran abundancia, y que pudiera venderse en el extranjero á buenos precios, es el que comunmente se conoce con el nombre de aceite de pie de buey. El aceite mexicano, que comercialmente se considera como el menos adulterado, obtiene mejor precio que el de los otros paises, pues su origen garantiza su pureza. Como este aceite se considera que es uno de los mejores lubricantes para toda clase de maquinaria, su explotación y embarque en grandes cantidades constituirán una fuente considerable de ingresos.

OFICINA DE INFORMACIÓN.

Dice el "American Manufacturer" que el Gobernador TEODORO A. DEHESA, del Estado de Veracruz, ha establecido en Jalapa una oficina especial de información por medio de la cual se darán informes sobre el Estado de Veracruz. Este Estado está bien provisto de ferrocarriles y de numerosos ríos navegables. Los productores encuentran fácil acceso á los puertos del golfo, y á Salina Cruz, en el Pacifico, á paso que puede llegarse rápidamente y barato al interior del país, merced á las líneas de ferrocarril. El Estado está también provisto de agua utilizable como fuerza motriz, suministrada por numerosas perennes corrientes de las montañas que descienden á la costa. Agua en abundancia, utilizable como fuerza motriz, puede obtenerse por toda clase de fabricantes ó industriales. Este Estado está desarrollándose rápidamente, y está á punto de recibir nuevo impulso á virtud de nuevas líneas de ferrocarril y de las mejoras en las bahías de Veracruz, Coatzacoalcos, y Salina Cruz. Los trabajos de la bahía de Veracruz están casi terminados y los buques pueden cargar y descargar en los muelles de la ciudad.

El propósito de la Oficina es suministrar gratuitamente informes exactos tomados de datos oficiales á los que quieran familiarizarse con las ventajas que ofrece el Estado de Veracruz al objeto de invertir dinero en tierras ó de establecer empresas agrícolas ó mecánicas, desenvolviendo el comercio ó de alguna suerte desarrollando las fuentes de riqueza del Estado; así como también aconsejar á aquellos que visiten el Estado con aquellos propósitos. Los informes podrán pedirse á ALEXANDER M. GAW, Agente Especial, Jalapa, Estado de Veracruz, México.

ÚLTIMOS DESCUBRIMIENTOS MIN

Se ha descubierto un gran depósito de mine
á corta distancia de la estación terminal del
Grande y el Pacífico.   También se ha descubi
de plata en el Estado de Durango, en Coneto
depósito de oro ha sido abierto en Sauces Cam
de Santa Fé, del mismo punto, se está ex|
THOMAS WARK y otros han abierto la mina
Canatlan, y otra valiosa mina de plata ha s
milla al sudeste de las minas de Gavalón.
Sonora, las minas de Mesa Quemada están
tados.   Trabajando en el túnel que comuni
Guillermina, se descubrió por los mineros una
de plata de calidad superior.   Según se di
Palomas producen muchas pepitas de oro fino
Guerrero se ha descubierto una nueva mina
genes del río Hueymatla, cerca de Taxco el V
WILLIAM BAKER, ha dado cuenta del descubrim
vena de mineral de oro en un punto cerca de Lo
de Michoacán.

El "Weekly Herald" da noticia de la v
minas de San Juan y Santo Domingo, cerc;
Estado de Jalisco; esta venta fué hecha á una
en el Estado de Tepic; la mina de Tapitos, c
de Oro, está de nuevo en explotación con cap
mineral contiene hierro, oro y plata.   En el E
ha abierto recientemente cerca de Mineral
mina de plata.   En Sonora, se ha descubie
carbonato de sodio, á dos millas de la bahía
interior, una indentación del Golfo de Calif
Sur de la Boca del río Colorado.   El depós
unos 70 acres en cuyo centro hay varias corrie
está fuertemente impregnada de sales.   Esta a
sobre las tierras vecinas y se ha formado, por ev;
de las sales cristalizadas, de uno á tres pies de
esta costra hay un pie ó dieciocho pulgadas de a¡
esta costra, que es el producto, es excavada y re
su lugar y muy pronto, por evaporación, qued

mente renovada, resultando así el depósito prácticamente inagotable. Calcúlase que hay 100,000 toneladas utilizables en el depósito, y un cargamento que por vía de ensayo se hizo á San Francisco, dejó considerable ganancia. El carbonato de sodio se usa en la fabricación de ácidos, cristales, bicarbonato de soda, etc., y su demanda es firme.

Dice "Le Monde Economique" que hay varias minas de estaño en México, principalmente en los Estados de Guanajato, San Luis Potosí, y Sonora. Las alturas de la Sierra de la Estanera, en el distrito de Comanja (Estado de San Luis Potosí), contienen mineral de estaño con un 70 á 75 por ciento de metal. En el Estado de Durango también se encuentra estaño en considerables cantidades que, propiamente tratado, rendiría de 35 á 75 por ciento de metal, á menudo bajo la forma de óxidos. Si estos depósitos resultan ricos, la producción de estaño será indudablemente una fuente de ingresos para el Gobierno.

NICARAGUA.

CAMBIOS EN LA TARIFA DE ADUANAS.

Mr. M. S. CLANCY, Agente Consular de los Estados Unidos en Bluefields, ha dirigido últimamente una carta á la Oficina de las Repúblicas Americanas, en la cual manifiesta que no habiendo dado resultados satisfactorios la nueva tarifa de aduanas promulgada en el mes de setiembre próximo pasado, el Gobierno la ha derogado, de suerte que todas las mercancías que ahora existen en la aduana de Bluefields y las que más tarde se importen pagarán derechos conforme á la tarifa y á las disposiciones especiales sobre la materia que se hallaban vigentes el 30 de agosto de 1888.

La nueva tarifa de aduanas á que Mr. CLANCY hace referencia fué publicada en el BOLETÍN MENSUAL correspondiente á octubre de este año, en la forma de un decreto por el cual los derechos de importación se elevaban á un ciento por ciento, por término medio, sobre los de la antigua tarifa. Algunos artículos, tales como arroz, frijoles, maíz, y patatas, que antes estaban en la lista de los productos libres de derecho, debían pagar, conforme á esta nueva tarifa, 10 centavos por kilógramo en moneda de Nicaragua (4 centavos oro). Todos los derechos debían cobrarse por cada kiló-gramo de peso bruto. Algunos artículos tenían que pagar hasta 250 por ciento sobre su valor primitivo. Los derechos debían pagarse en la Tesorería General del modo siguiente: 20 por ciento con órdenes contra las aduanas creadas por decreto de 30 de octubre de 1896; 15 por ciento con órdenes contra las aduanas creadas el 19 de junio de 1897; 15 por ciento en documentos de crédito público, legalmente liquidados y reconocidos; y 50 por cientos en efectivo.

Según la tarifa de aduanas de 1888, que fué publicada por esta Oficina en el Manual de Nicaragua en 1892, los derechos se cobran sobre el peso bruto, sin hacer reducción alguna por los embalajes.

CONVENIO POSTAL.

La Dieta de la República Mayor de Centro América, en nombre del Estado de Nicaragua, ha celebrado un convenio con el Gobierno francés para el cambio de paquetes postales. Este contrato fué hecho en París el 12 de junio de 1897 entre el repre-sentante de la Dieta y el Ministro de Relaciones Exteriores de Francia, y el canje de las ratificaciones se verificó en la misma ciudad el día 8 de junio de 1898.

Entre las disposiciones de este convenio, se hallan las siguientes:

Los paquetes postales que se expedirán sin declaración de valor, tanto de Francia y Argelia para Nicaragua como de Nicaragua con destino á Francia y Argelia, podrán pesar hasta 5 kilógramos. La Administración de Correos de Francia asegura el trasporte de los paquetes postales entre la Francia y el puerto de Colón por medio de los buques-correos franceses. Por cada paquete expedido de Francia y de Argelia con destino á Nicaragua, la Administración de Cor-reos de Francia paga á la de Nicaragua un derecho territorial de 50 céntimos y un derecho de 50 céntimos por el tránsito marítimo entre Panamá y Corinto ó San Juan del Sur. Por cada paquete expedido de Nicaragua con destino á Fran-cia y Argelia, la Administración de Correos de Nicaragua paga á la Francia un derecho territorial de 50 céntimos y un derecho marítimo de 2 francos por el trasporte entre la Francia y Colón. La Administración de Correos de Nicara-gua está autorizada para cobrar del expedidor en los casos de encomiendas enviadas de Nicaragua á Francia, y del destinatario en los casos de encomiendas enviadas de Francia á Nicaragua, en valor de los gastos de tránsito por el ferro-carril entre Colón y Panamá. Las dos partes contratentes se reservan la fa-cultad de percibir un recargo de 25 céntimos por los paquetes postales enviados de la Francia continental á Nicaragua y recíprocamente.

El país del destino queda facultado para percibir del destinatario, por la distri-bución y cumplimiento de formalidades de aduana, un derecho cuyo importe total no puede exceder de 25 céntimos por paquete. Queda prohibido expedir por la vía del correo paquetes que contengan cartas ó notas con carácter de correspondencia, ú objetos cuya admisión no está autorizada por las leyes ó reglamentos de aduana ú otros. Salvo el caso de fuerza mayor, cuando un paquete postal ha sido extraviado, averiado ó expoliado, el expedidor, y á falta ó á pedido de éste, el destinatario, tiene derecho á una idemnización correspondiente al importe real de la pérdida, de la avería ó de la expoliación. Sin embargo, esta indemnización no podrá exceder de 15 á 25 francos, según que el peso del paquete no exceda ó pase de 3 kilógramos. El expedidor de un paquete perdido tiene derecho, además, á la restitución de los gastos de expedición. La obligación de pagar la indemnización incumbe á la administración de la que depende la oficina expedidora.

Queda reservado á esta administración el recurso contra la administración correspondiente, cuando la pérdida, la avería ó la expoliación ha ocurrido en el territorio ó en el servicio de esta última administración. Hasta prueba de lo contrario, la responsabilidad incumbe á la administración que, habiendo recibido el paquete, no puede comprobar ni la entrega al destinatario, ni la expedición del paquete. El pago de la indemnización por la oficina expedidora debe hacerse lo más pronto posible y, á más tardar, dentro del plazo de un año, á partir del día de la reclamación. La oficina responsable está obligada á reembolsar, sin demora, á la oficina expedidora, el importe de la indemnización pagada por ésta. Queda entendido que la reclamación no será admitida sino dentro del plazo de un año, á partir de la fecha del depósito del paquete en el correo. Pasado este plazo, el reclamante no tiene derecho á ninguna indemnización. Si la pérdida, la avería ó la expoliación ha ocurrido durante el trasporte entre las oficinas de cambio de los dos países, sin que sea posible establecer en cual de los servicios se ha verificado el hecho, las dos administraciones son responsables del daño por mitad. En el caso de circunstancias extraordinarias que justifiquen la medida, cualquiera de las administraciones de correos puede suspender temporalmente el servicio de paquetes postales, ya sea de una manera general ó parcial, pero á condición de dar aviso inmediatamente á la otra administración interesada, por telégrafo si fuere necesario.

Este convenio continuará en vigor hasta que una de las dos partes contraantes haya anunciado á la otra, con un año de anticipación, su intención de hacer cesar sus efectos.

PARAGUAY.

EXPERIENCIA DE UN INMIGRANTE DE LOS ESTADOS UNIDOS.

Hace unos cuantos meses que Mr. I WAVRUNK escribió á la Oficina de las Repúblicas Americanas pidiendo informes relativos á las ventajas que el Paraguay ofrece á los inmigrantes. La Oficina dirigió una comunicación al Hon. W. R. FINCH, Ministro de los Estados Unidos en Paraguay, pidiéndole las últimas leyes de aquél país sobre la inmigración, y la Oficina recibió del referido

Mr. Finch, un ejemplar de aquellas leyes que fué remitido á Mr. Wavrunk quien se aprovechó de las oportunidades que en dichas leyes se ofrecen. Recientemente, Mr. Wavrunk ha escrito á Mr. Finch detallando sus experiencias. De esta carta, fechada el 23 de setiembre de 1898, y obtenida por cortesia de Mr. Finch, se extracta lo siguiente:

Considero que es mi deber informar á usted que al fin me he instalado en un pedazo de tierra cerca de la Colonia Gonzales y que estoy bien satisfecho de la elección. Antes de establecerme aquí, visité otras tres colonias en Paraguay, pero encontré que la Colonia Gonzales ofrecía más ventajas que las otras. Tuve la fortuna de obtener una extensión de 62 acres de tierra en los cuales encontré considerables mejoras que había hecho un arrendatario anterior. Hay unos 15 acres cultivados, 3½ ó 4 sembrados de caña de azúcar y el mismo número de mandioca. Hay 43 naranjos, 30 matas de plátanos, 30 vides, etc. La mayor parte de estas plantas darán fruto este año. Hay un arroyo en este lugar así como otras ventajas, de las cuales no es la menos importante una estación de ferrocarril que está á menos de dos millas de distancia. El Gobierno ha sido liberal en extremo, pues ha concedido libre trasporte á la colonia y ha facilitado hombres y vehículos para llevar mis efectos á la finca. Me proveyó de una vaca y un ternero y todas las herramientas necesarias y semillas para la siembra; en resumen, las autoridades hicieron todo lo posible para ayudarme en mi empresa. En compensación de las mejoras yo reconocí una deuda sobre la finca ascendente á 1,130 pesos, pero como ésta cantidad no ha de pagarse antes de diez años y no gana interés, es realmente de ninguna importancia. Nos agrada en extremo el país y el clima, pero echamos de menos el idioma inglés que muy pocas veces oimos hablar. La Colonia consiste principalmente en alemanes y franceses, pero la gente es bondadosa y generosa.

ESTADOS UNIDOS.

COMERCIO CON LA AMÉRICA LATINA.

RELACIÓN DE LAS IMPORTACIONES Y EXPORTACIONES.

En la página 1012 aparece la última relación del comercio entre los Estados Unidos y la América Latina tomada de la compilación hecha por la Oficina de Estadística del Departamento del Tesoro de los Estados Unidos, cuyo jefe es Mr. O. P. Austin. Estos datos se refieren al valor del comercio arriba mencionado. La estadística corresponde al mes de setiembre de 1898, corregida en octubre 28 del mismo año, comparada con la del período correspondiente del año anterior, y también comprende los datos referentes á los nueve meses que terminaron en setiembre de 1898, comparados con igual período de 1897. Debe explicarse que las estadísticas de las importaciones y exportaciones de las diversas aduanas referentes á un mes cualquiera no se reciben en el Departamento del Tesoro hasta el 20 del próximo mes, necesitándose algún tiempo para su compilación é impresión, de suerte que los datos estadísticos correspondientes al mes de setiembre, por ejemplo, no se publican sino en noviembre.

ESTADÍSTICA DE INMIGRACIÓN.

El informe anual de la Comisión General de Inmigración, hecho por el Honorable T. V. POWDERLY, ha sido remitido á la Secretaría del Tesoro, y en él se vé que la baja en el número de inmigrantes durante el año fiscal que terminó el 30 de junio de 1898, con relación al año anterior, fué sólo de 1,533 y el total de 229,299. Del número total de inmigrantes 135,775 eran varones y 83,524 hembras. De Italia vino el mayor número, que fué de 58.613. Rusia ocupó el segundo lugar con 27,221. De Irlanda vinieron 25,128; de Alemania, 17,111; de Suecia, 12,398, y de Inglaterra 9,877.

El número de inmigrantes á quienes no se permitió desembarcar fué de 3,030 ó sea como el 1⅓ por ciento. De este número 2,261 eran individuos completamente destituidos de recursos é inadmisibles por temor de que se convertieran en carga pública. El número de obreros que vinieron bajo contrato fué de 417. Los que regresaron por razón de enfermedad fueron 258.

Aunque durante los meses de nutrida inmigración los Estados Unidos estaban ó á punto de entrar en guerra ó ya empeñados en ella, esta circunstancia no perjudicó la inmigración, y es de suponerse que á menos que las leyes no sufran alteración en la actual sesión del Congreso, el número de inmigrantes en el próximo año excederá al del presente año. El Comisionado expresa varias ideas relativas á la modificación de las leyes. Se declara en favor, por ejemplo, de un aumento de la contribución per capita de uno á dos pesos, con el propósito de obtener un fondo á virtud del cual pueda ensancharse la esfera de utilidad de la Oficina de Inmigración respecto al aumento de facilidades para la mayor protección, en el sentido de impedir la entrada de criminales y otras clases perniciosas. También se recomienda la propagación de la ley que prohibe gastar, por concepto de emigración, en puerto alguno, una cantidad mayor de la que se recaude en aquél.

VENEZUELA.

IMPORTACIÓN PROCEDENTE DE LOS ESTAODS UNIDOS EN EL MES DE OCTUBRE.

El Cónsul-General de Venezuela en Nueva York, Don Antonio E. Delfino, ha remitido á la Oficina de las Repúblicas Americanas los siguientes informes estadísticos sobre las mercancías
embarcadas en Nueva York en octubre de 1898 con destino á
los puertos de Venezuela.

El número total de paquetes fué de 54,520, que pesaban 6,390,-
591 libras (2,898,753 kilos), con un valor declarado de $311,532.17,
un aumento neto de $76,592.72 sobre el mes de octubre de 1897.
La mayor parte de las mercancías se exportaron con destino á los
puertos de La Guaira y Maracaibo; el valor de los cargamentos
fué respectivamente de $156,036.63 y $70,439.77. Siguió en
orden de importancia Puerto Cabello, con un importación de
$29,700.21; Ciudad Bolivar, con $26,409.39; La Vela, $17,805.15;
Carúpano, $8,136.75; Guanta, $1,620.27; Cuma, $737, y Caño
Colorado, $647.

Los principales artículos embarcados fueron: harina, $44,029.06;
oro acuñado, $43,082; manteca, $41,686.06; zarazas, $25,628.03;
driles, crudos y blanqueados, $25,556.83; víveres, $21,688.64;
drogas y perfumería, $14,591.13; kerosina, $10,964.41; madera
en bruto, $9,557.17; mantequilla, $8,387; máquinas de coser y
accesorios, $8,384.35; ferretería, $7,158.51; quincallería y miscelánea, $6,385; picadura para cigarrillos, $6,260; lona, $5,486.12;
cordelería, $5,188.53.

LOS ARTÍCULOS DE PAPELERÍA PARA LOS CÓNSULES VENE-ZOLANAS, LIBRES DE DERECHO DE ENTRADA.

La Circular del Departamento del Tesoro, No. 196, Sección
de Aduanas, publicada el 23 de noviembre de 1898, con la firma
de W. B. Howells, subsecretario, dice así:

A los administradores y otros oficiales de aduana:

Habiéndose comunicado á este Departamento que los artículos de papelería
para el uso de los cónsules de los Estados Unidos en Venezuela serán admitidos
en lo adelante libres de derechos, se dispone que los artículos de esta clase
destinados al uso de los cónsules de Venezuela en los Estados Unidos serán en
lo sucesivo admitidos libres de derechos. La Circular No. 175, fechada en 26
de setiembre último, se modifica de acuerdo con aquella disposición.

EXPORTACIÓN DE GANADO Á CUBA.

El "Venezuela Herald" predice que Venezuela será pronto un gran país exportador de ganado. Menciónase el hecho de que cinco ganaderos de importancia del Estado de Miranda celebraron un contrato en octubre con el objeto de entregar 24,000 cabezas de ganado. Este ganado se destina á Cuba y será entregado en partidas de 2,000 cabezas por mes. En el contrato se estipula que el ganado será embarcado á razón de dos y medio centavos oro por libra y que será entregado en una estación llamada Gonzalito, situada en la línea del ferrocarril alemán, á corta distancia de Maracay.

El costo del trasporte desde esta estación hasta Puerto Cabello, que es el puerto de embarque, será sufragado por el Señor Rojas, que es el contratista cubano. Durante la ultima semana de octubre se embarcaron para la Habana 533 reses con un peso de 400 á 650 libras cada una. Se ha celebrado también un contrato de menos importancia entre el Señor Rojas, y un ganadero de Guanta que embarcó en la misma semana 800 cabezas. Se necesitarán de seis á siete días para hacer llegar el ganado de Puerto Cabello á la Habana. El Cónsul ELLSWORTH, en Puerto Cabello, informa que han tenido lugar los siguientes embarques adicionales: 750 cabezas de ganado para Santiago y 300 para Manzanillo.

CLASIFICACIÓN ARANCELARIA DE LOS FLEJES DE ALAMBRE DE HIERRO.

Como resultado de una consulta hecha por el administrador de la aduana marítima de Maracaibo, sobre la clase arancelaria en que debía aforarse el artículo conocido en el comercio con el nombre de flejes de alambre de hierro torcido, el Presidente de Venezuela ha dispuesto que dicha mercadería se afore por las Aduanas de la República en la 3ª clase arancelaria como comprendida en el número 147 del arancel vigente. Este es un artículo de comercio muy importante en Venezuela y se emplea en lugar de flejes y de mecate para asegurar las cajas y fardos de mercaderías que se trasportan y se compone de dos alambres de hierro enlazados y torcidos de consistencia flexible y de duración.

Según la tarifa de aduanas vigente en Venezuela, los artículos de la clase 3ª pagan un derecho de importación de cinco centavos por kilógramo.

Los exportadores en los Estados Unidos debieran notar que

los compradores de Venezuela prefieren este alambre torcido á las bandas de hierro ó á los mecates, para el embalaje de mercancías, porque el alambre es tan perfecto que puede usarse de nuevo en el embalaje de las mercancías destinadas al interior.

COMERCIO MISCELÁNEO.

BRASIL

Subasta para un Acueducto. En el BOLETÍN del mes de octubre se publicó la noticia de que el gobierno del Estado de Para sacaba á subasta el contrato para la provisión de agua potable, en la ciudad de Belem El contrato debía adjudicarse el 10 de noviembre, pero el gobierno ha deferido la presentación de las proposiciones para el arrendamiento del acueducto hesta el 15 de marzo de 1899. Pueden presentarse proposiciones á base de oro, y también para la recaudación del precio del agua en oro ; y el gobierno ha dispuesto que tales proposiciones reciban favorable consideración.

Nuevas Minas. El "South American Journal" anuncia el descubrimiento de varias minas que, según se dice, son muy ricas ; estas minas están en las minas de oro cerca de Minas Novas y de las minas de diamantes cerca de Sacramento, en el Estado de Minas Geraes.

Exportación de Manganeso. Recientemente se ha despachado en Bahía un cargamento de 891 toneladas de mineral de manganeso, con destino á los Estados Unidos. El mineral fué extraído de una mina cerca de Nazareth, y exportado de Itaparica.

Actividad Comercial. El Cónsul General Mr SEEGER escribe desde Río que el mes de diciembre es la mejor época para visitar el Estado de Paraná. También dice que ha recibido una comunicación de Mr THOM, ciudadano de los Estados Unidos y comerciante prominente de Curityba, Brasil, en la cual manifiesta que es urgente que los fabricantes de los Estados Unidos redoblen sus esfuerzos por obtener el comercio del Brasil. Dice que los alemanes se muestran muy activos en obsequio de sus compatriotas. Por el 15 de octubre llegó el nuevo cónsul alemán, lo cual significa nuevos esfuerzos en favor del comercio alemán. Proyéctase por los alemanes la construcción de ferrocarriles, obtención de concesiones de tierras, colonización de la región Irraguassú, etc.

CHILE.

Tratado sobre el Cambio Postal de Paquetes. Con fecha 6 de diciembre, el nuevo Ministro de Chile, Señor DON CARLOS MORLA VICUÑA, celebró con el Honorable CHARLES EMORY SMITH, Administrador General de Correos, un convenio para el establecimiento de un sistema para el cambio postal de paquetes entre los dos países. Las disposiciones de este convenio son, en lo esencial, idénticas á las de la convención celebrada con Honduras, con la diferencia de que los tipos del franqueo han sido aumentados de 12 á 20 centavos la libra para los paquetes enviados de los Estados Unidos á Chile, y 50 centavos la libra en lugar de 25 centavos sobre paquetes procedentes de Chile con destino á los Estados Unidos. El aumento en el tipo se debe á la distancia entre los dos países. Según el tratado, los artículos de mercancías admisibles en el correo, que no excedan de 11 libras, que no tengan de extensión más de tres pies y seis pulgadas (105 centímetros), cuyas mayores longitud y extensión circunferencial combinadas no excedan de seis pies (180 centímetros), que estén envueltos de modo que las autoridades postales puedan examinarlos fácilmente, deberán ser remitidos prontamente á su destino, sujetos al pago de los correspondientes derechos de aduana. Los cambios postales deberán efectuarse entre las oficinas postales de cambio de Nueva York, Nuevo Orleans, y San Francisco, en los Estados Unidos, y de Valparaiso, en Chile.

Ordenes Postales. El Departamento de Correos de los Estados Unidos ha sido informado de la ratificación hecha recientemente por el Gobierno chileno del convenio relativo al cambio de órdenes postales entre Chile y los Estados Unidos que fué negociado en agosto de 1897. Según este convenio, que ha de empezar á regir el 1° de enero de 1899, las órdenes postales pueden emitirse en Chile y en los Estados Unidos hasta la cantidad de 100 dollars y 100 pesos respectivamente.

Nueva Oficina Consular. El Presidente McKinley ha nombrado á W. Lutz, Cónsul de los Estados Unidos en Arica, Chile. Hasta el presente, los negocios de los Estados Unidos habían estado en manos de un vicecónsul, David Simpson, que es un escocés residente en Chile.

Nueva Fábrica de Galletas. Una asociación, conocida con el nombre de Compañía Bizcochera Mexicana, se ha organizado recientemente en el Estado de Maine, E. U., con el objeto de dedicarse á la fabricación de galletas en grande escala. La compañía está construyendo ahora un buen edificio en la ciudad de México para la fabricación de confituras y galletas. Los derechos mexicanos sobre las confituras son de 75 centavos por kilo, y los derechos sobre las galletas son de 15 centavos por kilo. Este impuesto es prohibitivo. Hay en la República una gran demanda de aquellos dos artículos y los iniciadores de la nueva compañía se prometen un gran éxito. El Presidente de la Compañía es H. M. Dingley de Lewiston, Me.; el Tesoro, W. S. Libby de Lewiston, Me., y el administrador, Emil Arner, anterior representante en México de la "National Biscuit Company." La producción hará necesario un gran número de empleados.

Nueva Fábrica. En Santa Julia, barrio de la ciudad de México, se ha abierto recientemente un establecimiento para la preparación de productos químicos y farmacéuticos. La máquina de vapor y maquinaria para la preparación del algodón absorbente son de fabricación inglesa y la maquinaria para la preparación de productos farmacéuticos es de fabricación francesa. La maquinaria fué instalada por un ingeniero mecánico mexicano.

Contrato para el Acueducto de la Ciudad de México. El corresponsal de la Asociación Nacional de Fabricantes en la ciudad de México comunica que el contrato para suministrar la tubería de hierro fundido para el acueducto, ha sido adjudicado á la "American Pipe and Foundry Company," de Chattanooga, Tennessee. Este material ascenderá á unas 18,000 toneladas brutas, y la primera entrega valuada en unos $250,000 está ya en camino. Los contratistas generales Vezin & Co. solicitaron proposiciones de varios paises europeos, y aunque hubo gran competencia, una compañía americana obtuvo al fin el contrato, habiéndole favorecido grandemente el hecho de haber tenido constantemente un representante sobre el terreno. El contrato estará á cargo de la casa de G. & O. Braniff & Co., la que pronto lo llevará á cabo.

Nuevo Boletín Mensual. La Oficina de las Repúblicas
una publicación mensual, edita
República Mexicana, bajo el título de "Boletín de la
Este nuevo periódico es dirigido por el Señor Don José
á difundir informes en los países extranjeros sobre el
rrollo material é intelectual de la República, las indust
cerse con éxito, las empresas que requieren gran capital
que ofrecen el suelo y clima del país, y la legislación ;
sea con propósito agrícola ó industrial.   El Boletín se pul
español, inglés, francés, é italiano—y contiene valiosos
para toda clase de lectores.

NICARAGUA.

Reproducción del Manual de la Oficina. En el "Diario Oficial," que es (
Nicaragua, el Ministerio de Insti
ciendo publicar la versión castellana del Manual de Ni(
Oficina de las Repúblicas Americanas.

PARAGUAY.

Nuevo Servicio de Vapores. Hay grandes colonias alemana:
los exportadores alemanes disfr
comercio del país.   El Cónsul-General de Río de Janei:
recientemente al Departamento de Estado de que se ha
línea de vapores entre Alemania y Paraguay por medi(
Kurt.

ESTADOS UNIDOS.

Exportación de Aceite Mineral. La exportación de aceite minei
el año fiscal de 1875 fué de 221,(
año que terminó el 30 de junio de 1898 fué de 1,034,26

Convención Nacional de Fabricantes. La cuarta reunión anual de la
Fabricantes se celebrará en Cinci
días 24, 25, y 26 de enero de 1899.   Promete ser una
importantes que jamás ha celebrado aquella corporac(
organizó en Cincinnati y celebró su primera sesión en
número de miembros es de cerca de 1,000, incluyendo n
más importantes del país, representado casi todos los ra

URUGUAY.

Cueros y Pieles. La República del Uruguay im
$200,000 anuales entre cueros
los cuales apenas unos $4,000 proceden de los Esta(
Estados Unidos compran del Uruguay por valor de {
pieles anualmente.   Lo que Uruguay requiere de los Es
palmente cabritilla, becerro, y pieles de carnero.   De
mente se importa cada año por valor de unos $46,0(
República hay 380,000 cueros curtidos.   De estos,
150,000 piel de carnero, 48,000 cueros de vaca, y
b'ien comercio debiera establecerse recíprocamente entre

Boletim Mensal

DA

Secretaria das Republicas Americanas,

União Internacional das Republicas Americanas.

| Vol. VI. | DEZEMBRO de 1898. | No. 6. |

`A MENSAGEM DO PRESIDENTE McKINLEY.

A mensagem annual do Presidente McKinley foi enviada no dia 5 de Dezembro de 1898 ao Quinquagesimo-quinto Congresso dos Estados Unidos na abertura de suas ultimas sessões. A maior parte da mensagem é uma relação imparcial, comprehensiva e concisa dos acontecimentos do anno passado em quanto se referem aos assumptos do governo. Como é natural, o primeiro logar é dado ás causas que produziram a guerra com a Hespanha e a maneira como esta foi dirigida e dão-se merecidos louvores aos que tomaram parte nella a favor dos Estados Unidos. Não se nota indevida satisfação pelas victorias que por terra e por mar alcançaram as forças dos Estados Unidos, mas ha em todo o documento uma veia de sympathia e respeito pelas derrotadas forças hespanholas. O Presidente felicita o paiz "porque, com a só excepção da ruptura com a Hespanha, as relações dos Estados Unidos com a grande familia das nações têm sido assignalado pela cordialidade e ao terminar do anno cheio de acontecimentos a maior parte dos assumptos que necessariamente se suscitam das relações complexas entre estados soberanos estão ajustados ou não apresentam serios obstaculos para chegar a uma solução justa e honrosa por meio de arranjos amistosos."

Referindo-se ao governo de Porto Rico ‹
Presidente exprime-se assim: ‑

Não discutirei por ora o governo ou o futuro das no\
nossas por resultado da guerra com a Hespanha.   D‹
tratado de paz, haverá tempo para tratar destas questõ
Congresso não dê leis em contrario, meu dever será con
tares que têm existido desde de nossa occupação e da!
vida e propriedade e estimulal-o sob um governo justo e

INDEPENDENCIA DE CUB*

Com relação a Cuba, diz: Tão logo como estejamos
tenhamos pacificado a ilha será necessario adjudar e dir
cimento de um governo proprio.   Isto deve ser levado
possivel tomando em consideração a segurança e o bor
que nossas relações com esse povo sejam das mais am
commerciaes estreitas e reciprocas.   É nosso dever ajud
restabelecimento dos logares devastados da ilha, dando
povo e ajudando-o a formar um governo livre e indeper
maneira as mais altas aspirações do povo cubano.   O ‹
ser substituido por um governo justo, benevolo e human
Cuba, capaz de cumprir com todas suas obrigações intern
o trabalho, a industria e a prosperidade fomentando a pa
todos seus habitantes quaesquer que sejam suas relaçõ
vingança nem a paixão devem ter logar no novo gove
restabelecido completamente a tranquillidade da ilha e s‹
forma estavel de governo continuará a occupaçaõ milirar

Nos seguintes paragraphos se faz referencia
acerca do Canal de Nicaragua, ás outras R‹
nente e á Secretaria das Republicas American

ARBITRAMENTO ARGENTINO-CH

A questão por muito tempo pendente dos limites entr‹
e o Chile que se estendem pelas cimas dos Andes desd‹
Deserto de Atacama até o Estreito Magalhães, quasi um‹
primento do continente sul-americano, chegou a um pe‹
do anno permittindo a este Governo a occasião de expr‹
se recorresse ao arbitramento no qual se tinha pensado
entre as partes interessadas, e que isto se levasse a cab‹
difficuldades que se apresentavam para sua applicação.
que se têm feito arranjos com este objecto, havendo-se r
britannica a determinação das questões de facto em qu‹
commissarios respectivos.   A differença que existe relati
norte atravez do Deserto de Atacama de que não se

existentes com referencia a seu arranjo, parece que será determinada de igual modo por uma commissão mixta, tendo sido convidado o Ministro dos Estados Unidos em Buenos Aires como arbitro em ultimo caso.

UNIFORMIDADE NA TARIFA DE CABOS.

Tenho tido occasião de dirigir-me ao Governo argentino com o objecto de fazer desapparecer as differenças nas taxas impostas sobre os telegrammas por cabo de uma corporação americana ao transmittil-os entre Buenos Aires e as cidades do Uruguay e do Brazil, despachados ou dirigidos dos Estados Unidos. Ainda que o assumpto é complicado por causa das concessões exclusivas feitas pelo Uruguay e o Brazil a companhias estrangeiras, ha grandes esperanças de que se chegue a um intendimento e que fiquem livres de uma discriminação quasi prohibitiva essas importantes vias de communicação commercial entre os Estados Unidos e as cidades da America do Sul sobre o Atlantico.

Com este motivo permitta-me exprimir minha idea acerca da conveniencia de um convenio internacional em virtude do qual a troca de telegrammas por cabos que se enlaçam, regule-se sobre uma base uniforme equitativa. O mundo tem visto o systema postal sahir de mãos de uma reunião de individuos independentes e exclusivos e convertir-se em uma união bem organisada cujos multiplos beneficios gozam todas as nações. Seria estranha si as nações não chegassem a convencer-se de que a civilisação moderna, cujo progresso deve tanto á desapparição do espaço á força electrica, exige que este meio de communicação tão importante seja herançã de todos os povos, administrada e dirigida para o commum beneficio. Deu-se um passo neste sentido quando a Convenção Internacional de 1884 para a protecção dos cabos submarinos foi assignada e espero que não esteja longe o dia quando este vehiculo para a transmissão do pensamento de uma a outra terra caia sob o dominio de concerto internacional de uma maneira tão completa como o transporte do commercio e da correspondencia sobre a superficie das aguas que as separa.

ACONTECIMENTOS DA AMERICA CENTRAL.

Os acontecimentos occorridos na America Central durante o anno merecem que se faça delles menção especial :

A ruptura que ameaçava ter lugar entre Costa Rica e Nicaragua foi tranquillisada felizmente pela firma de uma convenção entre as partes interessadas, com a assistencia do representante de Guatemala como arbitro, tendo-se preparado e firmado o auto a bordo do vapor dos Estados Unidos *Alert* que então estava em aguas da America Central. Acredita-se que os bons officios de nosso enviado e o commandante daquelle vapor contribuiram ao este resultado satisfactorio.

Em minha ultima mensagem se fez referencia á representação diplomatica deste governo na America Central, por causa da associação de Nicaragua, Honduras e Salvador sob o titulo de Republica Maior da America Central e a delegação feita de suas funcções internacionaes na Dieta. Não obstante haver sido reconhecido por meu antecessor e confirmado durante minha administração o caracter representativo da Dieta, recebendo seu Enviado acreditado e concedendo exequatur aos consules nomeados por sua autoridade, o dito reconhecimento foi feito com o intendimento claro de que a responsabilidade de cada uma das republicas soberanas que a compõem para com os Estados Unidos ficava sem ser affectada em absoluto.

Esta estipulação se fazia necessaria tanto mais quanto que a combinação das tres republicas foi em seu principio uma associação pela qual se delegavam em uma commissão triple certas funcções representativas, antes que uma federação que possuisse autoridade centralisada de governo e administração. Em vista de suas relações entre si e as dos Estados Unidos para com as diversas Republicas, o Executivo não recommendou nem o Congresso indicou mudanças na representação deste paiz na America Central, deixando assim um de nossos enviados acreditado como até agora aos Estados da Republica Maior, Nicaragua e Salvador e tambem a Costa Rica, que não tomou parte no convenio, emquanto que outro enviado estava igualmente acreditado a Honduras, um Estado da União, e a outro que não pertencia a ella, Guatemala. O resultado tem sido que um delles tem apresentado suas credenciaes sómente ao Presidente de Costa Rica e o outro tem sido recebido sómente pelo Governo de Guatemala.

Mais tarde as tres Republicas associadas entraram em negociações com o objecto de levar a cabo o proposto no convenio original. Uma convenção de seus delegados preparou uma constituição federal para os Estados Unidos da America Central na qual se dispunha a forma de centralisação federal para o Governo e a legislatura. Ratificada esta pelos Estados constituintes se fixou o primeiro de Novembro ultimo para que entrasse em operação o novo systema. Poucas semanas depois o plano foi submettido a prova pelos movimentos revolucionarios que tiveram logar e que exigia por consequencia unidade de acção por parte do poder militar dos Estados confederados para supprimil-os. Esta prova parece ter debilitado a União por causa da separação de seus membros mais importantes. Este Governo não recebeu aviso official da installação da federação e tem mantido uma attitude de amistosa expectativa ao passo que de nenhuma maneira tem abandonado a posição que desde o principio tem sustentado de que a responsabilidade de cada um dos Estados com os Estados Unidos não soffriam alteração por causa das relações que existissem entre elles.

COMMISSÃO DO CANAL DE NICARAGUA.

A Commissão do Canal de Nicaragua nomeada no dia 24 de Julho de 1897, por virtude da clausula do "Sundry Civil Act" de 4 de Junho daquelle anno, cuja presidencia desempenha o Contra-almirante JOHN G. WALKER, tem concluido quasi seus trabalhos e vos será submettido o resultado de suas minuciosas investigações acerca do caminho adequado, a possibilidade do trabalho e o custo da construcção de um canal interoceanico por Nicaragua. No desempenho de seus trabalhos a Commissão foi objecto da maior cortezia e recebeu auxilio dos Governos de Nicaragua e Costa Rica que desta maneira demonstraram quanto apreciam a importancia de terminar de uma maneira tão prompta como pratica o grande projecto que durante tantos annos tem occupado a attenção dos paizes respectivos.

Como o escopo da recente investigação abraçava todo o assumpto com o objecto de fazer planos e estudos para um canal construido no caminho mais conveniente, comprehendia necessariamente uma exame dos resultados dos estudos e planos anteriores e especialmente dos que tinha adoptado a Companhia do Canal Maritimo por virtude das concessões feitas por Nicaragua e Costa Rica, de sorte que estas concessões são necessariamente parte essencial das deliberações e deducções da Commissão do Canal como tem sido e devem ser parte das discussões da materia no Congresso. Dadas estas circumstancias e em vista dos offerecimentos feitos aos governos de Nicaragua e Costa Rica por outros individuos referentes a uma concessão para um novo canal fundada na supposta proxima caducidade dos contractos celebrados entre a Companhia do Canal Maritimo e aquellas nações, não tenho hesitado em exprimir minha convicção de que razões de conveniencia e de politica internacional entre os differentes governos interessados na construcção e jurisdicção de um canal interoceanico por esta via exige a conservação do *statu quo* até que a Commissão do Canal tenha apresentado seu relatorio e que o Congresso dos Estados Unidos tenha tido a opportunidade de approval-o durante as presentes sessões, sem prejuizos por razão de quaesquer mudanças occorridas nas condicões existentes.

Comtudo, parece que o Governo de Nicaragua como de seus ultimos actos de soberania antes de trespassar seus poderes aos dos novos estados da America Central, fez uma concessão condicional a outra associação a qual entrará em vigor ao terminar o prazo da presente concessão. Não parece que estudos tenham feito nem qual seja o caminho proposto nesta concessão contingente de modo que no relatorio da Commissão do Canal não está necessariamente incluido o exame da possibilidade dos planos. Todas estas circumstancias suggerem a urgencia de que o Congresso tome medida definitiva nestas sessões si os trabalhos do passado têm de ser utilisados e si tem de realizar a união dos oceanos atlantico e pacifico por meio de um caminho maritimo praticavel. Que a construcção de semelhante caminho maritimo é hoje mais indispensavel que nunca para a communicação intima e facil entre nossas costas do oriente e do occidente que exige a annexação das Ilhas de Hawaii e a futura expansão de nossa influencia e de nosso commercio no Pacifico; e que nossa politica nacional exige hoje mais imperativamente que nunca que este Governo o domine, são considerações que não duvido que o Congresso appreciará devidamente e tomará medidas sabias procedendo nelle de uma maneira sabia.

COMMISSÃO DE RECLAMAÇÕES CHILENAS.

A convenção que dispõe o *restabelecimento da Commissão de Reclamações dos Estados Unidos e Chile e o exame das que foram devidamente apresentadas á dita commissão, mas não foram estudadas por ter expirado o tempo limitado para sua duração, foi firmada no dia 24 de Maio de 1897 e o Senado não tem dado neuhum passo no assumpto. O periodo fixado naquella para effeituar a troca de ratificações tem expirado e a convenção deixará de existir a menos que se prorogue o prazo, introduzindo uma emenda, o que estou tratando de conseguir com a cooperação amistosa do Governo do Chile.

TRATADO DE EXTRADICÇÃO COM O MEXICO.

A interpretação de certas disposicões contidas no tratado de extradicção de 11 de Dezembro, de 1861, tem sido em varias occasiões motivo de controversia com o Governo do Mexico. O pedido do Governo mexicano pela entrega de JESUS GUERRA que tinha conduzido uma expedição de pilhagem cerca da fronteira, com o proposito declarado de iniciar uma insurreição contra o Presidente DIAZ, e que escapou a Texas, troux a questão a um periodo agudo. Recusou-se a extradicção, baseando-se esta acção em que o delicto allegado era de caracter politico e por conseguinte estava comprehendido no disposto no tratado acerca da não entrega. O Mexico allegava que a excepção só refere-se aos crimes politicos e que como os actos de guerra estavam acompanhados dos delictos communs de assassinio, incendiarismo, sequestro e roubo, não era applicavel a não entrega, argumento que este Governo não poude admittir, em vista da doutrina internacional e a pratica nestes casos. O Governo do Mexico com este motivo annuncio no dia 27 de Janeiro de 1898, a terminacão do tratado que terá lugar doze mezes a contar daquella data, solicitando ao mesmo tempo a celebração de um novo tratado cuja negociação nos occupa actualmente.

A ZONA LIVRE MEXICANA.

O problema da Zona Livre Mexicana tem sido discutido frequentemente por motivo de sua inconveniencia, como que invita a introducção do contrabando nos Estados Unidos por toda a fronteira, que está escassamente custodiada. Como se disse no Relatorio No. 702 da Camara de Representantes, apresentado á ultima sessão no dia 11 de Março de 1898, as providencias contidas na resolução mixta de 1º de Março de 1895 para remediar o abuso suspendendo o privilegio de livre transporte, em transito, pelo territorio dos Estados Unidos com destino ao Mexico, não têm dado bons resultados. Como é uma questão que pode ser arranjada, mais bem que por convenios, por leis dadas por ambos os paizes com o objecto de proteger as rendas por meio de medidas que tenham igual força a ambos os lados da fronteira, indico ao Congresso que considere a conveniencia de autorisar e convidar uma conferencia de representantes dos Departamentos do Thesouro dos Estados Unidos e do Mexico para examinar a materia em todos seus pontos e apresentar um relatorio fazendo recommendações pertinentes aos governos respectivos, para a consideração e estudo de seus respectivos Congressos.

COMMISSÃO DE LIMITES FLUVIAES DO MEXICO.

A Commissão de Limites Fluviaes do Mexico tem terminado á satisfacão de ambos os Governos todas as materias que lhe foram submettidas com excepção de tres casos importantes: o de "Chamizal" em El Paso, Tex., em que não pouderam convir os dous commissarios, por cujo motivo este governo tem proposto ao do Mexico a nomeação, para este caso nada mais, de um terceiro membro; a proposta eliminação dos chamados "Bancos," pequenas ilhas isoladas formadas pelo corte das curvas do Rio Grande, segundo os tratados de 1884 e 1889, recommendado pelos commissarios e approvado por este Governo, mas que ainda está submettido á consideração de Mexico; e o assumpto da distribuição equitativa das aguas do Rio Grande, para cujo effeito os commissarios recommendaram a construcção de uma represa e um estanque internacional, o qual foi approvado pelo Mexico e ainda está submettido á consideração deste Governo. Dadas estas circumstancias é necessario prorogar o prazo da Commissão que termina no dia 23 de Dezembro proximo.

ABROGAÇÃO DE UM TRATADO.

O Governo do Peru tem annunciado sua intenção de rescindir o tratado de amizade, commercio e navegação celebrado com este paiz a 31 de Agosto de 1887. Como o dito tratado contem muitas disposições importantes, necessarias para a conservação do commercio e das boas relações, que seria difficil reestabelecer com a negociação de novas clausulas dentro do breve periodo de 12 mezes, que termina o tratado, tenho convidado o Peru para que indique quaes são as disposições que deseja annullar em particular, com a esperança de chegar a um arranjo pelo qual possam ser salvados provisoriamente os outros artigos.

TRIBUNAL ARBITRAL ANGLO-VENEZUELANO.

O Tribunal Arbitral nomeado por virtude do Tratado de 2 de Fevereiro de 1897, celebrado entre a Grã Bretanha e Venezuela para determinar a linha limitrophe entre este paiz e a Colonia da Guyana Ingleza, reunir-se-ha em Pariz durante o presente mez. É motivo de muita satisfação para este Governo ver que se tem feito uso do amistoso recurso do arbitramento para o arranjo desta controversia, não só pela parte interessada que temos tido em que se chegasse a este resultado, mas tambem porque dous dos membros nomeados por parte de Venezuela, o Juiz Maior, Mr. FULLER e o Juiz Mr. BREWER, têm sido escolhidos de entre os que formam nosso mais alto tribunal, o qual demonstra o interesse continuado que temos no arranjo definitivo da questão, segundo as regras mais estrictas da justiçã. Os membros britannicos, Lord HERSCHELL e Sir RICHARD COLLINS, são jurisconsultos de não menos alta reputação, emquanto que o quinto membro e Presidente do Tribunal, M. F. DE MARTENS, tem adquirido fama universal como autoridade em direito internacional.

A SECRETARIA DAS REPUBLICAS AMERICANAS.

Tenho a satisfação de poder manifestar que a Secretaria das Republicas Americanas, creada em 1890 como orgão para fomentar as relações commerciaes e fraternaes entre os paizes do hemispherio occidental, tem chegado a ser instrumento da maior efficacia para a consecução dos sabios propositos de seus fundadores e recebe o apoio cordial de todos os membros da União Internacional que a ella contribuem e que estão representados em seu Junta Directora. Tem publicado em inglez, hespanhol, portuguez e francez um Directorio Commercial, em dous volumes, que contem grande quantidade de dados estatisticos relativos aos interesses industriaes e commerciaes dos varios paizes de que trata, e publica nestes quatro idiomas um BOLETIM MENSAL que se distribue nos paizes latino americanos e nos Estados Unidos e que tem demonstrado ser um valioso meio para a disseminacão de informações e o fomento dos varios interesses da União Internacional.

––––––––––

O SENHOR ROMERO ELEVADO Á DIGNIDADE DE EMBAIXADOR.

O Senhor Don MATIAS ROMERO, Enviado Extraordinario e Ministro Plenipotenciario da Republica do Mexico junto aos Estados Unidos, tem regressado a Washington depois de ter feito uma visita demorada á capital mexicana. Logo apos sua chegada, o Ministro avisou o Secretario de Estado de que tinha sido promovido a embaixador. Esta noticia foi recebida com muita satisfação tanto na Secretaria de Estado como nas rodas diplomaticas e o Sr. ROMERO recebeu sinceras felicitações por esta prova de consideração por parte do seu Governo.

Como fica estipulado no regulamento do serviço diplomatico que o Governo dos Estados Unidos pode promover á dignidade de embaixador qualquer de seus ministros quando o paiz a que elle esteja acreditado tomar a iniciativa neste assumpto, conferindo essa dignidade a seu proprio representante, o General POWELL CLAYTON, actual Ministro dos Estados Unidos junto ao Mexico, é promovido a Embaixador, sua nomeação tendo sido submettida ao Senado para sua approvação no dia 6 de Dezembro. Esta disposição da lei que regula o serviço diplomatico foi approvada ha menos que seis annos e naquella epoca não era acreditado aos Estados Unidos nenhum diplomata de grão superior ao de Ministro, e os Estados Unidos não tinham representante no estrangeiro da dignidade de embaixador. Desde então, seis paizes têm conferido as credenciaes de embaixador a seus enviados em Washington. Os Governos assim representados são: a Grã Bretanha, Italia, Allemanha, França, Russia e Mexico. O Mexico é a primeira das Republicas Americanas que tem concedido honra tão distincta a seu representante diplomatico em Washington.

O Senhor ROMERO é um dos estadistas, jornalistas e diplomatas mais proeminentes do Mexico. Nasceu na cidade de Oaxaca no dia 24 de Fevereiro de 1837. Educou-se em sua cidade natal e mais tarde na capital da Republica onde recebeu seu diploma de advogado. Em 1855 entrou para a diplomacia como addido á Secretaria de Relações Exteriores. Quando em 1857, o Presidente

COMONFORT deu seu golpe de Estado, obrigando o Senhor JUAREZ a retirar-se da capital, o Senhor ROMERO o acompanhou ao porto de Veracrux. Alli exerceu o mesmo cargo official na Secretaria de Relações Exteriores. Em Dezembro de 1859 foi promovido a Secretario da Legação Mexicana em Washington e continuava no exercicio deste cargo até o mez de Agosto de 1860, quando na ausencia do Ministro, servio de Encarregado de Negocios. Em 1863 voltou ao Mexico para tomar parte na guerra contra os francezes e foi nomeado coronel pelo Presidente. Depois, foi nomeado pelo General PORFIRIO DIAZ, chefe do seu Estado-Maior. Logo depois foi acreditado por Presidente JUAREZ Enviado Extraordinario e Ministro Plenipotenciario em Washington, commissão que exerceu até o mez de Janeiro de 1868, tendo prestado relevantissimos serviços ao seu paiz.

Á sua volta ao Mexico foi nomeado Secretario do Thesouro, mas foi obrigado a pedir sua demissão em 1872 por estar de má saude. Durante tres annos vivia em Soconusco dedicando-se á agricultura. Serviu como Secretario do Thesouro de 1877 a 1878 e em 1880 como Director Geral dos Correios. Em Março de 1882 regressou a Washington para servir como Enviado Extraordinario e Ministro Plenipotenciario, cargo que tem desempenhado desde então com uma interrupção de só dez mezes em 1892, quando, pela terceira vez, foi mandado servir como Secretario do Thesouro. O Sr. ROMERO, como representante do seu paiz nos Estados Unidos, tem-se mostrado um diplomata habil e competente. Os esforços que tem feito para promover relações amistosas entre o Mexico e os Estados Unidos têm tido muito bom exito, e com este motivo tem escripto grande numero de artigos, os quaes têm sido sempre elogiados tanto pela imprensa dos Estados Unidos como pela de outros paizes.

O Senhor ROMERO foi membro da Conferencia Internacional Americana e servio com grande distincção, tendo sido nomeado um dos seus vice-presidentes. Como representante do Mexico na Conferencia, deu o seu voto a favor do estabelecimento da Secretaria das Republicas Americanas e desde sua organisação, tem-se mostrado activo e zeloso pelo seu bom exito. Fez parte da Commissão Executiva da Secretaria desde sua organisação e sempre tem prestado valiosos serviços á União Internacional das Republicas Americanas.

PRODUCÇÃO DE OURO E PRATA EM 1897.

MOEDA DOS ESTADOS UNIDOS—MOEDA DO MUNDO.

O Director da Casa da Moeda em seu relatorio annual ao Secretario da Fazenda, trata não sómente da producção de metaes preciosos nos Estados Unidos durante o anno de 1897, mas tambem da producção de todos os paizes em que se encontram estes metaes. Os totaes da producção formam uma base para fazer comparações entre as principaes nações productores, pois as fontes das quaes se obtiveram os dados eram muito fidedignas e os algarismos são tão exactos como foi possivel.

O ouro que se produziu nos Estados Unidos em 1897 foi no valor de $57,363,000. O unico paiz, cuja producção excedeu a esta somma, foi a Republica da Africa do Sul, que produziu no valor de $58,306,600. A Australasia produziu no valor de $55,684,182 e a Russia, que lhe segue em ordem, no valor de $23,245,763. O augmento na produção da Republica da Africa do Sul, que foi de $13,854,192 foi o mais notavel do anno. O augmento na producção de ouro da Australasia foi de $10,502,249; o dos Estados Unidos, de $4,974,800 e o de Russia, $1,709,970.

Durante o anno os Estados Unidos produziram 53,860,000 onças de prata fina e a Republica do Mexico, 53,903,180 onças. Isto mostra uma diminuição na producção dos Estados Unidos de 4,974,800 onças e um augmento na producção do Mexico de 8,256,756 onças finas. Nos Estados Unidos o numero de onças de ouro fino foi de 2,774,935. O valor monetario da prata produzida nos Estados Unidos foi de $69,637,172. Não obstante que muitas das minas de prata que outr'ora eram as mais productivas deixaram de explorar-se, o augmento na producção de chumbo e cobre, mixtos com prata, contrabalançou esta diminuição. Durante o anno de 1897, se obteve o ouro em 25 Estados e Territorios dos Estados Unidos em quantidades que variam de $100 em cada um de quatro Estados a $19,104,200 no Estado de Colorado. A California produziu no valor de $14,618,300; South Dakota no de $5,694,900; Montana, $4,373,400; Nevada, $2,976,400; Arizona, $2,895,900; Alaska, $1,778,000; Utah, $1,726,100; Idaho, $1,701,700 e Oregon, $1,353,100. Nenhum outro estado produziu no valor de $500,000. A producção de prata do mundo segundo relatorio do Director da Casa da Moeda excede á dos annos anteriores, A maior producção depois da mencionada occorreu em 1895 e foi de 167,509,960 onças. A producção de ouro e prata do mundo em 1897 é como segue:

Paizes.	Dollars em ouro.	Prata, onças finas.	Prata, valor monetario.
Estados Unidos	$57,363,000	53,860,000	$69,637,200
Mexico	9,436,300	53,903,181	69,693,000
America Central	470,500	1,547,875	2,000,000
Republica Argentina	137,600	383,470	495,800
Bolivia	750,000	15,000,000	19,393,900
Brazil	1,204,200		
Chile	928,600	6,440,569	8,327,200
Colombia	3,000,000	1,687,950	2,182,400
Equador	132,900	7,734	10,000
Peru	628,000	9,784,680	12,650,900
Uruguay	38,500		
Venezuela	948,500		
As Guyanas	4,324,300		
Dominio do Canada	6,027,100	5,558,446	7,186,700
Paizes Europeos	27,175,600	16,464,108	21,286,900
India Britannica	7,247,500		
Japão	713,300	2,507,532	3,242,100
China	2,209,100		
Korea	733,100		
Borneo	45,900		
Africa	58,306,600		
Australasia	55,684,200	15,951,546	20,624,200
Totaes	237,504,800	183,096,091	236,730,300

O valor total de ouro existente nas casas de moeda e officinas de ensaio dos Estadas Unidos durante o anno foi de $87,924,232, dos quaes $67,923,535 são moeda nacional e $20,000,597 moeda estrangeira. O valor da prata depositada nos mesmos estabelecimentos para devolução em barras finas, que foram usadas nas artes industriaes ou exportadas, foi de $12,707,128, dos quaes $11,-847,530 correspondem á producção domestica e $859,598 á estrangeira. A cunhagem de moeda dos Estados Unidos durante o anno foi de $76,028,485 ouro, e $18,487,297 prata, de cuja quantia $12,651,731 eram do valor legal corrente, acunhados com prata procedente da compra que se fez por virtude da disposição de 14 de Julho de 1890, anterior ao 1° de Novembro de 1893, data em que se revocou a clausula daquella disposição relativa á compra. A cunhagem de moeda no mundo durante o anno, incluindo recunhagens, foi de $437,719,342 ouro; $142,380,588 prata, ou um total de $580,099,930.

Bull. No. 6——9

O preço maior, em Londres, da prata de .925 de lei, padrão inglez, durante o anno foi de 29⅛ pence, e o mais baixo 23¾ pence, com um preço médio de 27⁹⁄₁₆ pence, equivalente a $0.604449 em moeda dos Estados Unidos por onça fina. Ao preço médio da prata durante o anno, o valor em barra do dollar de prata foi de $0.467. O valor da exportação neta de ouro dos Estados Unidos durante o anno foi de $512,609 e o valor da exportação neta de prata do paiz durante o mesmo periodo foi de $26,287,612.

Durante o anno commum de 1897 se consumiu nas artes industriaes dos Estados Unidos ouro por valor de $11,870,231 e prata por valor de $11,201,150. O consumo no mundo de metaes preciosos nas artes industriaes durante o mesmo periodo foi de $59,005,980 ouro e $40,435,577 prata.

No dia 1° de Janeiro de 1898, a existencia metallica dos Estados Unidos consistia em $745,245,953 ouro e $635,310,064 prata, ou um total de $1,380,566,017.

O IDIOMA HESPANHOL NO COMMERCIO LATINO-AMERICANO.

O Sr. ABRAHAM CRISTIANI escreve a esta Secretaria de Comitan, Estado de Chiapas, Mexico, chamando a attenção para a inutilidade de enviar aos cidadãos daquella secção da Republica communicações e annuncios escriptos ou impressos em inglez. A este respeito, convem lembrar aos exportadores, annunciantes e outros que desejam estabelecer relações commerciaes com os cidadãos de qualquer parte do Mexico (com excepção das casas inglezas) que toda a sua correspondencia deve ser escripta em hespanhol e todos os catalogos e demais materia descriptiva devem ser impressos no mesmo idioma. Haveria a mesma razão para imprimir estas materias em francez, allemão ou italiano que em inglez, pois ha no Mexico tantos residentes que pertencem áquellas nacionalidades como pessoas que fallam o inglez. Assim como nos Estados Unidos ha relativamente poucas pessoas que conhecem o idioma hespanhol, de igual sorte no Mexico a porcentagem de pessoas que sabem fallar o inglez é relativamente pequena. O que se tem dito respeito do Mexico, é certo tambem respeito da America Central e das Republicas Sul-Americanas, com excepção do Brazil, onde o portuguez é a lingua do povo. Em Haiti e Santo Domingo prevalece o francez.

A communicação do Sr. CRISTIANI é como segue :

Vemos com satisfação que o BOLETIM MENSAL da Secretaria das Republicas Americanas, sob vossa direcção, o qual circula nos Estados Unidos, Mexico e outros paizes da America, se publica em quatro idiomas. Lamentamos, portanto, que a maior parte das cartas e catalogos que recebemos dos fabricantes de machinas dos Estados Unidos vem escriptos em inglez, e como não conhecemos o idioma, não podemos informar nos de seu conteúdo. Consideramos opportuno chamar a attenção de V. S. para este facto, e tomamos a liberdade de suggerir que si V. S. o estima conveniente faça publicar um artigo no BOLETIM com o objecto de fazer saber que o unico idioma que se falla nesta cidade é o hespanhol, de modo que se possa tomar nota deste facto nos paizes estrangeiros.

Um grande numero dos periodicos commerciaes dos Estados Unidos estão advogando pelo ensino do idioma hespanhol nas escolas superiores do paiz. A maneira como deve ensinar-se aquelle idioma e as razões que justificam sua inclusão no plano de estudo das escolas designadas, se consignam no seguinte extracto tomado do "American Trade," ainda que se observará que o escriptor tem omisso uma das razões mais poderosas que é a crescente importancia do commercio dos Estados Unidos com as Republicas da America do Sul :

A attenção que estão despertando Cuba, Porto Rico e as Fillippinas como campos para a extensão do commercio americano, dá maior interesse á lingua hespanhola como idioma commercial. A importancia do hespanhol em nossas relações commerciaes com o estrangeiro, tem ido augmentando com o desenvolvimento de nosso commercio com a America Latina, e a possibilidade do dominio ou da protecção dos Estados Unidos sobre colonias habitadas por individuos que fallam o idioma hespanhol, faz hoje mais necessario que nunca para os homens de negocios dos Estados Unidos, o conhecimento deste idioma. Sob o ponto de vista commercial, o idioma hespanhol é de vasta importancia para os interesses geraes dos Estados Unidos, e a necessidade de familiarizar-se com este idioma não deixará de sentir-se por muitos annos. Mais prompto que se dediquem nossos jovens ao estudo do hespanhol, tanto mais prompto poderão contar com os meios que aquelle conhecimento lhes offerecerá para a perseguição dos negocios nos paizes situados ao sul do nosso. Não ha necessidade de sobrecarregar os já nutridos cursos das escolas publicas primarias, pois o estudo do hespanhol pode muito bem incluir-se nos cursos commerciaes que se estão aggregando cada dia ás escolas superiores. Todas as escolas mercantis e instituições docentes que têm por objecto a preparação dos jovens para o commercio, deverão incluir no seu plano de estudo a lingua hespanhola. A ignorancia ou o conhecimento imperfeito desde idioma, retarda o crescimento do nosso commercio com os paizes onde se falla o hespanhol muito mais do que se suppõe ou reconhece.

COMMERCIO DE HESPANHA CO
E A AMERICA DO SU

O Governo hespanhol tem tomado recenten
avançada em materias de commercio. Em Se|
uma Ordem Real na qual se creava uma Rep
Relações Exteriores com o objecto de submi·
commerciaes e estatisticas e de ajudar os exp·
de negocio em geral. Esta nova repartição ser:
corpos commerciaes e do departamento consul
tambem um empregado do Governo para que
Mexico e as republicas sul-americanas receberá
desta repartição. Crê-se que estes governos of
especiaes aos exportadores hespanhóes por razão ‹
de raça, idioma e costumes. O Governo crê
hespanhóes de botas e sapatos, luvas, sedas, leqɩ
alha não encontrarão difficuldade nenhuma na
manufacturas semelhantes de outros paizes no
do Sul. O primeiro passo que se tem dado
obter mercado para estes artigos, e os demais
nhola no Mexico, a Republica Argentina, Brazi·
tem sido a nomeação de um delegado commer
daquelles paizes, os quaes residirão respectivam
Buenos Aires, Rio de Janeiro, Montevideo e
delegados haverão de estar dispostos em todo ɩ
commerciantes.

REPUBLICA ARGENTII

GABINETE DO GENERAL ROC

O Honrado WILLIAM I. BUCHANAN, Min
Unidos em Buenos Aires, informou officialme
Estado da inauguração no dia 12 de Outubro
A. ROCA como Presidente e do Senhor Don I
COSTA como Vice-presidente da Republica. ‹
tem constituido seu gabinete com os seguintes

Ministro do Interior ....Dr. Don FEL
Ministro das Relações Exteriores.........Dr. AMANCIC

Ministro da Fazenda.................Dr. José María Rosa.
Ministro da Justiça e Instrucção Publica...Dr. Oswaldo Magnasco.
Ministro da Guerra...................Gen. Luis María Campos.
Ministro da Marinha.................Commandante Martin Rivadavia.
Ministro das Obras Publicas.............Dr. Emilio Civit.
Ministro da Agri ultura ....Dr. Emilio Frere.

A PRAGA DOS GAFANHOTOS.

O Consul americano Sr. MAYER, em Buenos Aires, em data de 12 de Outubro apresenta o seguinte relatorio relativo á devastação causada pelos gafanhotos que em annos anteriores têm produzido grandes estragos nas colheitas e na vegetação em geral da Republica. O Consul diz que as noticias da praga não são satisfactorias.

Pois, ainda que os trabalhos de destruir o gafanhoto continuam, tão immensas são as invasões do insecto que se teme que prompto cheguem á provincia de Buenos Aires. Entre Rios e partes das provincias de Santa Fé e Cordoba já estão invadidas pelos gafanhotos. Nos primeiros tres dias de Outubro, se recolheram em Entre Rios sómente 398 toneladas de gafanhotos; mas as sub-commissões queixam-se de que em alguns lugares os habitantes recusam cooperar na extincção e que a policia não faz uso de sua autoridade para obrigal-os a fazel-o. A Commissão Central tem publicado uma circular pedindo que se lhe notifique promptamente de todos os nirhos de ovos que existam, enviando amostras acompanhadas de datas e quaesquer outras informações a proposito da materia. Noticias do Paraguay informam que abundam alli os gafanhotos e que fazem grandes estragos. Nas colonias que se encontram ao sul de Santa Fé não tem havido invasões ainda e os agricultores creem que si o trigo e a linhaça escaparem da praga até meiados deste mez serão salvos. As colonias judiacas de Villaguay têm sido invadidas e destruidas as colheitas. A companhia de colonisação possue alli 70,000 hectares de terreno dos quaes estão cultivados de 25,000 a 30,000, de sorte que facil é imaginar-se qual será a perda dos agricultores si a colheita não se dá outra vez e para isto as chuvas são absolutamente necessarias. Os agricultores nada têm feito para combater a praga e a sub-commissão recommenda á commissão principal que seja inexoravel em impor mulctas. O trabalho de destruição da praga continua sem descanço em outras provincias, alcançando-se bons resultados.

Um correspondente do "Chilean Times," tratando deste assumpto diz:

O Governo da Republica Argentina pela primeira vez está fazendo grandes esforços para combater a praga de gafanhotos cada vez mais grande e tem feito obrigatorio a destruição do insecto. Além de ter votado grande verba com este objecto e de ter nomeado commissões centraes e locaes em toda a Republica, o Governo impõe mulctas por infracção da lei, e estes fundos juntamente com os que contribuem os particulares vem a formar uma boa base para o trabalho. Não

ha duvida de que tem sido enorme o numero de gafanho
ver quaes são os resultados e que vantagens podem tr;
gafanhoto inverna nos climas quentes das provincias d
primavera, põe até 80 ovos e morre. Estes ovos pro
pequeno insecto, que não tem azas, começa immediatarr
tadora; vai cresendo, muda de pelle cinco vezes até que a
chega a adquirir todo seu tamanho e continua por alguns
ção. De prompto todos os gafanhotos voam para o nort;
e este procedimento se repete *ad infinitum*. Um dos
para a destruição destes insectos é o seguinte: Tiras de
altura são collocadas por centenares de jardas e fazem-s¡
50 jardas. Os gafanhotos chegam á barreira de estanh
caem nas covas. Á conclusão do dia de trabalho se co
assim destruindo os gafanhotos.

BOLIVIA.

RENDAS FISCAES EM 1897 E ORÇAMEN

O Senhor GUTIERREZ, Ministro da Fazend
relatorio ao Congresso Nacional, agora em ses
da Republica durante o anno fiscal de 1897.
se em rendas nacionaes e departamentaes o¡
quantias estão expressadas em bolivianos, dol
hante em tamanho e lei ao dollar dos Estados
actual preço da prata seu valor em cambio, seg
Ministerio do Thesouro, é de $0.436 em 11
Unidos.

Segundo o relatorio do Ministro, as rendas 1
em 1897 foram de 4,840,300.56 bolivianos.
rendas foram:

Direitos de alfandega . . . .
Prata em barras e mineraes . . . .
Impostos sobre licores . . . .
Sellos de renda interior e de correios . . . .
Exportação de borracha e patentes . . . .
Moeda de nickel . . . .
Estanho, cobre e bismutho . . . .
Contribuição sobre patentes de companhias . . . .
Facturas consulares . . . .
Rendas da casa de moeda . . . .
Privilegios de mineração . . . .
Direitos sobre o gado e portagem . . . .
Direitos sobre a coca . . . .
Hypothecas . . . .

	Bolivianos.
Imposto sobre os phosphoros	14, 085. 67
Juros e verbas não especificadas	9, 082. 28
Ouro	289. 80
Marcas de fabrica	40. 00

A despeza de 1898 é orçada em 5,714,793.80 bolivianos, que estão distribuidos da maneira seguinte:

	Bolivianos.
Instrucção e obras publicas	1, 817, 489. 80
Ministerio da Fazenda	1, 571, 482. 50
Ministerio da Guerra	1, 519, 218. 50
Relações Exteriores	389, 817. 00
Ministerio do Interior e da Justiça	260, 182. 00
Serviço legislativo	159, 604. 00

Gonvem notar que mais de uma terceira parte da despeza é dedicada á instrucção publica e obras publicas, emquanto que antes uma grande parte dos gastos se carregavam ao Ministerio da Guerra. Ver-se-ha que a renda de 1897 é menor que a despeza orçada para 1898. As rendas provinciaes attingem á somma de 600,000 bolivianos. Emprega-se esta quantia na manutenção do Governo provincial e na execução de obras de caracter local.

A divida interior contraida desde que se constituiu a Republica é de 3,707,541.20 bolivianos, mas o Governo não está na obrigação immediata de resgatal-a até que o Congresso decida a maneira em que tem de fazer-se. A unica outra divida reconhecida pelo Governo pertence a credores chilenos, a cujo pagamento se dedica 40 por cento dos direitos de alfandega que se cobram em Arica. A divida original é de uns 6,500,000 bolivianos, dos quaes foram pagos 5,415,444.86 bolivianos ao terminar o anno fiscal de 1897. A agencia aduaneira de Bolivia em Antofogasta produz uns 1,300,000 bolivianos por anno. A casa de moeda nacional de Potosi acunha annualmente uma média de 1,500,000 bolivianos de prata. Apezar disto e dos 6,600,000 bolivianos em bilhetes de banco em circulação, tem havido recentemente grande descontento por causa da escassez do meio circulante.

CULTIVO DA BORRACHA.

Em uma entrevista, ALBERTO VIERLAND, austriaco, residente em La Paz, expressa-se acerca da condição da industria da borracha na Bolivia nos termos seguintes:

Todos os melhores terrenos estão occupados em sua maior parte por pessoas que não dispõem de capital para exploral-os e estão anciosos de vendel-os. A collecta da borracha é muito custosa. Os indios que se empregam neste tra-

balho exigem grandes salarios e insistem em receber o pagamento em adiantamento.   Trabalham só por pouco tempo, receosos das enfermidades que produz
o clima.   As regiões em que se produz a borracha são sempre insalubres, pois a
arvore de borracha dá-se sómente em lugares baixos e pantanosos, conservando
suas raizes debaixo da agua durante parte do anno.   As arvores de borracha
abundam nos mattos da Bolivia, mas o Sr. Vierland só sabe que ha uma fazenda
em cultivo que tem apenas cem arvores.   As arvores pelo geral crescem nos
valles mais abaixo da vertente oriental dos Andes e nos mattos se encontram até
6,000 arvores por milha quadrada, e ha lugares que contêm até 10,000 arvores.
Estas arvores são de todos os tamanhos desde as mais pequenas até aquellas que
chegam a 150 pés de altura, e tão largas que segundo dizem tres homens com as
mãos juntas não podem rodear seu tronco.   O negocio da borracha pode produzir muito dinheiro para aquelles que tenham um grande capital.

Não se pode fazer muito si não se tem um capital de $25,000 ou $50,000,
sendo os ganhos muito mais grandes em proporção, si se dispõe de um capital
de $100,000, somma que na opinião do Sr. Vierland deve produzir um ganho
liquido de 60 a 70 por cento annualmente.   Os capitalistas podem obter facilmente os terrenos productores de borracha, pois os melhores terrenos estão hoje
em mãos dos "Cholos," é dizer Bolivianos mixtos, que occupam as terras do
Governo mas carecem de dinheiro para exploral-as.

A borracha bruta que se recolhe nos districtos productores é transportada á
costa de mula a La Paz, ou a Chililaya, no Lago Titicaca, de onde vai a Mollendo, na costa do Pacifico, e d'alli a Liverpool, onde se vende com o nome de
"borracha de Mollendo" a preços um pouco mais baixos que aquelle a que se
vende a classe mais fina da borracha "boliviana."

BRAZIL.

O NOVO PRESIDENTE.

O Sr. M. F. De Campos Salles, o novo Presidente que tomará
o governo da grande Republica Sul Americana a 15 de Novembro,
tem atraz de si uma larga historia politica, de que não daremos
aqui senão os dados culminantes, sem commentarios.

Antes da fundação do partido puramente republicano, o Dr.
Campos Salles, ainda muito moço, fez parte do chamado partido
Liberal.   D'esse partido Liberal sahiram na sua quasi totalidade
os homens que formaram em 1870 o partido Republicano, que
devia vencer em 1889.

Campos Salles esteve com os primeiros fundadores do novo
partido na sua provincia natal, o actual Estado de São Paulo.
Antes d'isso, porém, chegou a ser eleito deputado provincial pelos

Liberaes paulistas. Já nessa qualidade revelou aptidões apreciaveis de orador e homem politico.

No partido Republicano da então provincia de São Paulo occupou sempre logar no Conselho dirigente. Foi mais de uma vez eleito deputado provincial pelo novo partido, ainda durante o Imperio. Em 1884, apezar da mais encarniçada opposição dos imperialistas, foi eleito deputado á assemblea geral, que correspondia ao actual Congresso Federal. É curioso que, tendo sido eleitos apenas dois deputados republicanos nessa occasião, fossem um delles o actual Presidente da Republica e o outro o presidente que deixa o poder, o Dr. PRUDENTE DE MORAES. Na Camara imperialista, CAMPOS SALLES pronunciou alguns discursos notaveis, sobresahindo nelles a ausencia de violencia de linguagem, a par de grande logica e clareza nos raciocinios. Os seus discursos foram publicados e muito lidos em todo o Brazil.

A Republica, proclamada em 15 de Novembro de 1898, foi durante um anno e alguns mezes dirigida por um governo provisorio, emquanto não se votava a constituição. Os republicanos brasileiros entenderam conveniente fazer extenso o periodo do governo provisorio, para dar tempo á implantação de varias reformas que anticipassem e facilitassem a obra da Constituinte. D'esse governo provisorio fez parte, até quasi ao fim, o Dr. CAMPOS SALLES, a quem tocou a pasta da Justiça. O seu trabalho foi, então, activo e fecundo. Cercando-se de jurisconsultos de nota e sendo tambem elle jurisconsulto, emprehendeu e completou a reforma da administração judiciaria brasileira, pondo-a de accordo com as novas instituições. Tudo quanto está na actual constituição com referencia ao judiciario é obra d'elle. Ao deixar o seu logar, nenhuma voz se levantou para o accusar de perseguições ou injustiças, aliás tão difficeis de evitar, nas circumstancias em que elle governou.

Nas primeiras eleições para os corpos representativos da Republica o Sr. CAMPOS SALLES foi escolhido Senador pelo seu Estado natal. A sua presença no Senado correspondeu ao seu passado, sendo elle considerado alli o *leader* do seu partido.

Do Senado sahiu para o cargo de governador de São Paulo, que estava exercendo quando foi escolhido candidato á presidencia da Republica e eleito a 1° de Março d'este anno, por uma grande maioria.

A eleição do Sr. Campos Salles marcou a definitiva discriminação dos partidos no Brazil. Até então tinha havido varias divergencias entre os republicanos, mas nenhuma differenciação partidaria definitiva se tinha estabelecido. Nas vesperas, porém, da escolha de candidatos á presidencia da Republica, apresentou-se um partido exaltado, preguando pela eleição de um candidato que favorecesse o elemento nacional contra o extrangeiro, que exercesse pressão sobre os poucos representantes que ainda restam da opinião monarchica, que désse preponderancia aos militares sobre os civis, que, finalmente, traduzisse no governo o systema historicamente conhecido com o nome de "jacobinismo," nome que os membros do partido não desdenhavam acceitar para si. O Sr. Campos Salles foi o candidato da corrente opposta, isto é, dos republicanos moderados, ou conservadoras, que se organisaram sob o nome de Partido Republicano, declarando que o seu programma era o respeito da Constituição, com os melhoramentos que só a razão e o tempo aconselhassem. Todos os elementos conservadores do paiz e os extrangeiros que nelle tinham interesses sympathisaram grandemente com esta candidatura e deram-lhe o seu apoio.

A eleição do Sr. Campos Salles foi um novo elemento de confiança para o Brazil, confiança que se manifestou logo na melhor cotação dos titulos da divida nacional, na alta do cambio e na maior actividade em todos os negocios.

O Brazil, apezar de tudo o que dizem os inimigos da Republica, tem prosperado muito durante este regimen. Basta apresentar dois factos para o provar: 1º, nos 9 annos da Republica a extensão das estradas de ferro foi duplicada; 2º, a maior colheita de café no Imperio (e o café foi sempre a mais consideravel fonte de riqueza do paiz) foi de perto de quatro milhões de saccos de 60 kilos, ao passo que a colheita do anno passado foi de mais de onze milhões de saccos de 60 kilos. Não é culpa da Republica que o Imperio lhe deixasse, como herança, o regimen do papel moeda inconvertivel, nem que o preço liquido de um sacco de café deixasse de ser £4 para ser agora £1. O paiz, porém, dispõe de immensos recursos, e todos esperam que uma administração sabia e energica, como todos os antecedentes do Sr. Campos Salles autorisam a esperar d'elle, ha de restaurar a normalidade da riqueza e do credito.

Terminaremos esta rapida noticia com alguns dados pessoaes relativos ao novo presidente do Brazil.

O Sr. CAMPOS SALLES tem hoje cerca de 55 annos de idade. É natural da cidade de Campinas, Estado de São Paulo, Estado a que tambem pertence o presidente PRUDENTE DE MORAES, que conclue agora o seu periodo. Gosa o novo presidente de muita saude, é muito sobrio e methodico na sua vida, e d'ahi lhe vem a invejavel robustez physica, que lhe tem permittido grande energia de acção e uma apparencia de bem estar e tranquillidade de consciencia que não é o menor dos seus attractivos. Exerceu por muito tempo a profissão de advogado e é graduado em direito pela faculdade de São Paulo, a mais afamada do paiz. A sua familia desfructou sempre de grande fortuna, ganha nas plantações de café, e elle mesmo foi sempre e ainda é possuidor de bellos cafesaes. É descendente de uma das mais antigas familias do paiz.

IMPORTAÇOES DE CALÇADO E DE COURO.

A Republica do Brazil importa em grandes quantidades calçado e couro que compra directamente daquelles paizes aos quaes os Estados Unidos embarcam estes productos em grandes quantidades. Sendo isto assim é logico suppôr que, si os Estados Unidos abastecer aquelles paizes dos quaes o Brazil faz suas compras, podem fazer concurrencia com elles nos mercados do Brazil. Isto não obstante os factos provam o contrario.

Durante o exercicio que terminou em 30 de Junho de 1897, os embarques de calçado feitos dos Estados Unidos para o Brazil montaram a $2,427. No mesmo periodo a Allemanha exportou, para a dita Republica, calçado por valor de $200,000; as exportacões da Inglaterra excederam a esta quantia e as da França e Belgica foram em proporção. O producto inglez tem preponderancia sobre o allemão e o belga. Os francezes enviam a maior parte do calçado caro de senhora e os austriacos os mais baratos desta classe. Quanto ao couro e seus productos à Inglaterra exportou para o Brazil no valor de $1,000,000, Allemanha, $650,000, e França e Belgica tambem gozaram de grandes exportações. As exportações de couro dos Estados Unidos apenas alcançaram a $33,000. No Brazil se corte couro em grandes quantidades, especialmente nos estados do sul. O couro, porém, não é da melhor qualidade a ha opportunidade para a venda dos

productos superiores dos Estados Unidos. Na fabricação de
calçado a Republica tem feito muito progresso durante os ultimos
annos, mas a producção é limitada a artigos de qualidade mediana
e inferior. Em Bahia ha uma fabrica que produz $1,000,000 de
calçado por anno.

IMPORTANCIA DA INDUSTRIA DA BORRACHA.

Que o Brazil é um paiz de grandes riquezas naturaes é um
facto que não se pode disputar. Não obstante que por causa da
grande diversidade de seu solo e clima o seu territorio é adaptado
ao cultivo de quasi todos os productos das zonas temperada e
torrida, a Republica é conhecida ao commercio por dous de seus
productos, o café e a borracha. Destes artigos, e especialmente do
ultimo, tem tido quasi um monopolio. Um é producto do
campo, outro das florestas. Um é producto do cultivo, o outro é
producto natural. Antes, se dedicava muita attenção ao cultivo
do café, mas nos ultimos annos, devido á extensão consagrada a
seu cultivo e á concurrencia crescente de outros paizes, os preços
têm soffrido uma diminuição constante até que quasi têm desappa-
recido os ganhos que produziam as fazendas de café. Não succede
o mesmo com a borracha, porque, apesar da crescente producção
desta arvore, que é indigena a todo o paiz, os preços não sómente
têm sido mantidos mas têm ido subindo paulatinamente.

, O Governo não tardou em reconhecer este facto e em notar o
augmento do dinheiro que trazia ao paiz a venda deste producto.
Os exploradores affirmam que no interior do paiz ha uma immen-
sidade de arvores de borracha em florestas quasi inexploradas.
Mas o Governo não está satisfeito com isto, e occupa-se em
instruir o povo nas particularidades das differentes variedades da
arvore da borracha, o melhor methodo de cultivo, a adaptabilidade
de certas especies ao solo dos differentes estados, e o modo de
preparar o producto para os mercados. Havendo comprehendido
a utilidade da borracha em quasi todas as industrias, o cultivo da
planta virá a ser uma nova industria cujo producto augmentará a
colheita da borracha. Isto não obstante, não se pensa descuidar
a borracha das florestas e o Governo propõe-se impedir os damnos
que até agora têm-se feito a estas.

Recentemente o Consul americano em Pernambuco, o Sr. CLARK,

e o Vice-consul interino em Santos, o Sr. RONSHEIM, remetteram á Secretaria de Estado relatorios sobre as variedades de borracha, a quantidade que se produz e seu valor nos differentes Estados do Brazil. A communicação do Sr. CLARK trata da "Maniçoba" e a do Sr. RONSHEIM da "Mangabeira." Diz o Consul CLARK que a borracha chamada "Maniçoba" cresce na parte septentrional do Brazil, especialmente no Ceará e Rio Grande do norte e Parahyba. Seu preço segue ao da "Seringueira" ou borracha do Pará, sendo preferido o producto para certos trabalhos.

O cultivo desta planta vai augmentando constantemente em todos os tres Estados, e tambem estende-se rapidamente por todo o Estado de Perambuco, Alagoas e Bahia, dando maior resultado com menos trabalho que qualquer outro producto agricola. Semeia-se a semente no principio do inverno, dando o melhor resultado em terra vermelha ou parda. Ao semear a planta, a terra não deve estar muito secca nem muito humida; quando a planta tem dous annos de idade pode resistir qualquer mudança de clima, mas a quantidade do sumo dependerá mais ou menos das influencias do clima,

Aos seis annos a planta tem chegado a sua madureza e este é o melhor tempo para cortal-a ainda que esta operação pode fazer-se quando a planta tem dous annos. Depois dos seis annos a arvore produz annualmente, até os 30 annos, de 2 a 5 kilogrammas de borracha, si a arvore tem sido conservada em boa condição. Depois dos trinta annos a colheita começa a diminuir um pouco e em boas condições a vida da arvore pode chegar a um seculo. Prepara-se o sumo mesmo que se prepara o da "seringueira" do Pará, mas sua côr, depois de ser exposto o sumo ao fumo, é mais escura. Para obter a borracha nos Estados mencionados, corta-se a casca da arvore, deixando sahir o sumo, o qual pela acção dos raios do sol coalha ao pé da arvore e forma uma massa solida, que recolhem os indigenas e vendem aos commissarios, os quaes a embarcam para os Estados Unidos e a Europa. O preço por kilogramma varia nestes Estados de 2 a 5 milreis por 2.2046 libras, segundo a qualidade.

Alem da "Maniçoba," estes Estados produzem grande quantidade de borracha de "Mangabeira," que é inferior em qualidade e se usa para cobrir cabos, etc.

O Sr. Clark dá o seguinte quadro da exportação da borracha do Ceará para os annos de 1893-1897.

Anno.	Quantidade.	Valor.	
	Kilos.	*Milreis.*	
1893	135, 569	1, 129, 742	$259, 840. 66
1894	146, 627	1, 221, 892	242, 378. 40
1895	146, 627	1, 592, 567	302, 587. 73
1896	324, 327	2, 702, 725	486, 490. 50
1897	475, 693	3, 964, 108	594. 616. 20

O Sr. Ronsheim, no seu relatorio, diz que durante os ultimos seis mezes, varios carregamentos de borracha "Mangabeira" chegaram a Santos procedentes do interior, os quaes foram embarcados para a Europa. Tendo sido bons os resultados obtidos, outras expedições foram enviadas para o interior e as chegadas de cargas de borracha augmentam diariamente, promettendo produzir uma importante renda a este Estado que até agora não tem tido outras senão as provenientes das exportações do café.

Entre os muitos artigos que têm sido publicados recentemente na imprensa nacional sobre este assumpto, o Consul chama a attenção para um publicado no "Deutsche Zeitung" de São Paulo, no seu numero de 11 de Agosto de 1898, do qual dá a seguinte traducção:

Extrae-se a borracha do Brazil das arvores que pertencem a tres familias distinctas.

1. *Hevea brasiliensis* Müll Arg. ou seringueiro do Amazonas.
2. *Manihot glaziovii* Müll Arg. ou maniçoba do Ceará.
3. *Hancornia speciosa* Gom. ou mangabeira.

As duas primeiras classes não se referem a São Paulo, porque nenhum resultado tem-se obtido das sementes distribuidas pelo Governo aos cultivadores. Encontra-se a terceira especie na parte occidental de São Paulo. Não cresce bem na parte oriental e na costa, provavelmente por causa da humidade ou alguma condição da terra.

Antes, a borracha "mangabeira" produzia como a metade do que rendia o preço do Pará mas o valor tem subido. Diz-se que é muito mais dura e por conseguinte preferivel para certos usos. Diz a imprensa que durante o primeiro semestre de 1898 a estrada de ferro de Mogyana transportou 76,498 kilogrammas de borracha. Operarios experimentados do Estado da Bahia se empregam para cortar as arvores. Os proprietarios recebem a terceira parte do producto neto, emquanto que os compradores pagam cerca de 75 milreis por arroba. Diz-se que um homem pode extrahir até tres kilogrammas por dia.

O Governo deseja fomentar o cultivo desta arvore, e está considerando a conveniencia de pagar um subsidio aos cultivadores que se occupem nesta industria.

O "South American Journal" de Outubro diz que o Estado de São Paulo tem promulgado uma lei pela qual offerece dous premios de 25,000 milreis cada um e quatro de 15,000 milreis cada um para o cultivo da borracha mangabeira.   Offerece tambem uma prima de 15,000 milreis pelo melhor processo para extrahir a resina e outra de 10,000 milreis para a acclimatisação de outras arvores de borracha.   O periodico em referencia não diz si estes premios são em ouro ou prata.   A Secretaria do Thesouro dos Estados Unidos calcula o milreis de ouro em .546.

CHILE.

DESENVOLVIMENTO INDUSTRIAL DA REPUBLICA.

O Chile é um paiz que compra mercadorias de boa qualidade e, por conseguinte, os seus mercados merecem que os fabricantes dos Estados Unidos cuidem nelles.   O seguinte breve resumo dos recursos da Republica é extrahido do Directorio Commercial publicado pela Secretaria das Republicas Americanas.

O Chile tem um comprimento de 600 milhas e sua largura varia de 50 a 200 milhas.   PEDRO DE VALDEIRA, o segundo invasor hespanhol, o comparou á folha de uma espada por causa de seu grande comprimento e sua estreiteza.   Sua area é de 293,970 milhas quadradas, e, segundo o recenseamento de 1895, a população era de 2,766,747, ou á razão de 9.2 habitantes por milha quadrada.   O numero de habitantes excede agora provavelmente de 3,300,000.   Deste numero, quasi a metade se dedica á agricultura.   Produzem-se annualmente no paiz 28,500,000 alqueires de trigo e 8,500,000 alqueires de cereaes, além dos legumes, e fructas, etc.   Criam-se mais de 500,000 cabeças de gado vaccum e 2,000,000 de cabras.   Abundam os productos mineraes como nitrato, cobre, prata, ouro, carvão, manganez, etc. Os depositos de nitrato do Chile cobrem uma area de umas 220,356 'geiras, que se calcula que contém 2,316,000 quintaes metricos de nitrato, e são os mais extensos do mundo.   A producção total destes depositos em 1896, segundo se consigna em um numero recente do BOLETIM, era de 1,092,000 toneladas.

Pode-se formar uma idea do desenvolvimento industrial do Chile do facto de que em 1895, no districto de Valparaiso, com

uma população de menos de 200,000, havia
industriaes providos de 162 machinas de va
1,766 cavallos de força, os quaes deram emp
a 12,616 operarios.   Estes estabelecimentos
·ricas de gaz, fabricas de cerveja, fabricas de
ricas de carruagens e carros, fabricas de sen
mineraes e gazosas, etc.   As fabricas de cortir
florescente da industria do paiz.

O Chile foi o primeiro paiz da America
estradas de ferro.   Em principios de 1897,
estradas de ferro na Republica era, segundo
mais de 1,300 milhas, concluidas e em consti
eram propriedade do Governo.   Havia tan
propriedade de particulares e corporações, pri
A linha principal é a Grande Central que
comprehende tres secções: de Valparaiso a S:
a Melipilla; de Santiago a Talca, de San I
de Pelequen a Feumo; de Talca a Talcah
Traiguen, Santa Fé a Los Angeles, e Rol
total de 766 milhas.   Os trabalhos da estrac
dina se estão fazendo agora com grande acti
estatisticas tomadas do Directorio Commerc
de caminhos publicos e 2,875 de vias de agua
a extensão das linhas telegraphicas do Estad·
com 8,330 milhas de arame.   Havia tamb
linhas pertencentes a estradas de ferro e a cor

A marinha mercante·do Chile consistia e
barcações com uma tonelagem de 105,642
e dous destas embarcações eram vapores.
inglezas, allemães e francezas fazem viagei
costas do Chile e a Europa pelo Estreito de
municação directo e constante por meio de li·
nas e estrangeiras que viajam ao longo da cc
fazem connexão com vapores que vão para
Unidos no Atlantico, Pacifico e Golfo de Me:

O Chile importa a maior parte dos artigos
se consomem no paiz, mas o Govero favore
de novas industrias e deseja fomentar as empi

Diz-se que o Congresso votou recentemente a verba de $500,000 para fundições de ferro e aço, pois tem sido demonstrado que existe mineral de ferro em abundancia no paiz. Em 1897, o valor das importações no Chile foi de $65,502,805, e o das exportações, $64,754,133.

EXPORTAÇÃO DE NITRATO EM 1898.

A exportação de nitrato do Chile durante o presente anno é calculada entre 1,203,000 e 1,228,000 toneladas, contra 1,040,000 toneladas em 1897, 1,210,000 em 1896, e 1,075,000 em 1895. O total das exportações do dia 1° de Junho ao 1° de Novembro foi: para a Europa, 745,000 toneladas; para a America do Norte, 122,000 toneladas, e para os demais paizes, 11,000 toneladas, fazendo um total de 878,000 toneladas. Espera-se que em Novembro e Dezembro os carregamentos cheguem a 300,000 ou 350,000 toneladas. Suppondo que estes carregamentos não excedam de 325,000 toneladas, o total de exportações de 1898 ascenderá a 1,203,000 toneladas, ou uns 26,464,000 quintaes. Esta quantidade representará 1,464,000 quintaes mais que a quantidade calculada pelo Ministro da Fazenda do Chile no orçamento de 1898.

Os direitos de exportação recebidos por Chile, incluindo as augmentadas exportações de nitrato, serão de $41,729,777 contra $41,000,000, quantia que os calcula o orçamento de 1898.

COLOMBIA.

COMMERCIO COM NOVA ORLEANS.

O Senhor ESCRIPCIÓN CANAL, consul da Republica da Colombia em Nova Orleans, tem remettido a seu Governo um relatorio sobre o commercio do seu districto consular com a Republica da Colombia no anno de 1897. Por este relatorio se vê que as exportações da Colombia durante aquelle anno foram no valor de $947,717.20, e consistiram em bananas.

As exportações para a Colombia via Nova Orleans, com destino em grande parte ao porto de Bocas del Toro, foram no valor de $155,219.77, e os principaes carregamentos se fizeram em

Março, Abril e Novembro. Os principaes artigos foram arroz, assucar, carnes (conservadas), pescado, licores, presuntos, aves domesticas, ovos, cevada, cebolas, feijão, sabão, velas de esperma, banho, manteiga, farinha, milho, batatas, pão e biscoutos. Tambem se exportaram em menores quantidades instrumentos agricolas, madeiras de construcção, tintas, drogas e remedios, moveis para casas e escriptorios, artigos de escriptorio, sapatos, chapéos, roupa feita, louça de barro e obras de crystal.

O consul faz notar que ha um balanço de \$792,497.43 em favor do commercio colombiano, devido principalmente á grande exportação de bananas da ilha de Bocas del Toro. Este porto, que é o ponto de embarque de um fertil districto agricola, só necessita melhores meios de exploração e de exportação deste e outros productos para que venha a ser um importante centro commercial.

Os valores que se dão neste relatorio estão expressados em moeda colombiano, cujo peso equivale a \$0.418 em moeda dos Estados Unidos.

MEXICO.

ESTATISTICA DO COMMERCIO EXTERIOR.

A Estatistica Fiscal Mexicana correspondente ao anno que terminou em 30 de Junho de 1898 foi publicada pelo Ministerio da Fazenda em Outubro e mostra um resultado especialmente favoravel ao Governo. Nas importações houve um augmento sobre as de 1896 de \$1,399,397. Entre os artigos cuja importação augmentou em maior escala, se encontram os seguintes: machinas para mineração e industria, materiaes para estradas de ferro, manufacturas de algodão e generos de algodão crús, branqueados e estampados. Houve uma diminuição na importação de milho, banha, farinha e productos alimenticios em geral.

O valor total das exportações foi de \$128,972,749, o qual ha poucos annos teria sido considerado quasi incrivel. Esta somma se compunha em sua maior parte de mineraes que continham metaes preciosos, avaliados em \$75,042,332, ficando a quantia de \$53,930,417 que corresponde ao valor dos outros artigos. O total comparado com o total do anno anterior, que foi de \$111,346,494.

mostra um augmento de $17,626,255. Comparado com o anno de 1896, o augmento nas exportações foi de $9,859,235 em metaes preciosos e mineraes e de $8,767,020 nos outros artigos.

A seguinte lista contem os nomes dos paizes dos quaes se recebeu a maior parte das importações e tambem o valor das exportações feitas aos mesmos:

	Importação.	Exportação.
Estados Unidos	$21,490,604	$94,974,616
Inglaterra	8,105,696	14,775,638
França	5,435,698	5,320,016
Allemanha	4,781,821	6,995,733
Hespanha	2,039,132	1,231,342
Belgica	590,196	1,556,090
Italia	186,273	30,600
Suissa	156,732	200
Austria	125,144	
Hollanda	103,913	719,322
Brazil	8,658	
Colombia	24,127	2,260
Equador	73,681	342
Guatemala	14,950	846,016
Cuba	1,130	2,152,544
Peru	314	7,999
Salvador	3,648	21,191
Santo Domingo	38	50,720
Venezuela	36,963	170
Russia	19,644	270,370

AGENCIA DE INFORMAÇÕES.

Diz o "American Manufacturer" que o Governador TEODORO A. DEHESA, do Estado de Vera Cruz, tem estabelecido em Xalapa uma agencia especial de informação, por meio da qual se darão informações sobre o Estado de Vera Cruz. O Estado está bem provido de estradas de ferro e de numerosos rios nevegaveis. Os productores encontram facil accesso aos portos do Golfo e a Salina Cruz no Pacifico, ao passo que pode chegar-se rapidamente e barato ao interior do paiz por differentes vias ferreas. Ha no Estado numerosas correntes que descendem á costa, as quaes podem ser utilisadas como força motriz. Pode-se obter agua em abundancia como força motriz por toda a classe de fabricas ou industrias. Este Estado está desenvolvendo-se rapidamente, e está a ponto de receber novo impulso em virtude de novas linhas de estradas de ferro e dos melhoramentos nos portos de Vera Cruz, Coatzacoalcos e Salina Cruz. Os tralbalhos do porto de Vera

Cruz estão quasi concluidos e os vapores podem carregar e descarregar nos cáes da cidade.

O proposito da agencia é fornecer gratuitamente informações exactas, tomadas de dados officiaes, aos que quizerem familiarizar-se com as vantages que offerece o Estado de Vera Cruz, com o objecto de empregar dinheiro em terras ou de estabelecer emprezas agricolas ou mechanicas, desenvolvendo o commercio ou de alguma sorte desenvolvendo as fontes de riqueza do Estado; assim como tambem aconselhar aquelles que visitarem o Estado com aquelle objecto. Para informações dirijam-se ao Sr. ALEXANDER M. GAW, Agente Especial, Xalapa, Estado de Vera Cruz, Mexico.

PARAGUAY.

EXPERIENCIA DE UM IMMIGRANTE DOS ESTADOS UNIDOS.

Ha alguns mezes que o Sr. I. WAVRUNK escreveu á Secretaria das Republicas Americanas pedindo informações relativas ás vantagens que o Paraguay offerece aos immigrantes. A Secretaria dirigiu uma communicação ao Honrado W. R. FINCH, Ministro dos Estados Unidos junto ao Paraguay, pedindo-lhe as ultimas leis daquelle paiz sobre a immigração, e ao receber um exemplar daquellas leis, a Secretaria o remetteu ao Sr. WAVRUNK, quem se aproveitou das opportunidades offerecidas. Recentemente o Sr. WAVRUNK escreveu ao Sr. FINCH dando conta detalhada de suas experiencias. Desta carta, datada de 23 de Setembro de 1898 e remettida a esta Secretaria por cortezia do Ministro FINCH, extrahimos o seguinte:

Julgo que é meu dever informar-vos que emfim me tenho estabelecido em um terreno cerca da Colonia Gonzales, e que estou bem satisfeito da selecção. Antes de estabelecer-me aqui, visitei outras tres colonias no Paraguay, mas encontrei que a Colonia Gonzales offerecia mais vantagens do que as outras. Tive a fortuna de obter uma extensão de 62 geiras de terra nas quaes encontrei consideraveis melhoramentos que tinha feito um arrendatario anterior. Ha umas 15 geiras de terra em cultivo, das quaes 3½ ou 4 são semeades de canna de assucar e o mesmo numero de mandioca. Ha 43 laranjeiras, 30 bananeiras, 30 vinhas, etc., etc. A maior parte destas plantas darão fructo este anno. Ha um arroio na fazenda assim como outras vantagens, das quaes não é a menos importante uma estação de estrada de ferro que está a menos de duas milhas de distancia. O Governo tem sido extremamente liberal, pois tem concedido livre transporte á colonia e tem facilitado homens e vehiculos para levar meus effeitos á fazenda. Me proveu de uma vacca e uma vitella e todas as ferramentas necessarias e sementes para a semeada; em resumo, as autoridades fizeram tudo possivel para ajudar-me. Em compensação dos melhoramentos eu reconheci uma divida sobre a fazenda na importancia de 1,130 pesos, mas como esta quantia não tem de ser paga antes de dez annos e não ganha juro, é realmente de nenhuma importancia. Estamos muito contentes com o paiz e o clima, mas sentimos a falta do idioma inglez que muito poucas vezes ouvimos fallar. Esta colonia consiste principalmente em allemães e francezes, mas a gente é bondosa e generosa.

ESTADOS UNIDOS.

COMMERCIO COM OS PAIZES LATINO-AMERICANOS.

RELAÇÃO MENSAL DAS IMPORTAÇÕES E EXPORTAÇÕES.

O quadro dado na pagina 1012 é extrahido da relação compilada por O. P. Austin, chefe da Repartição de Estatistica do Ministerio da Fazenda, mostrando o commercio entre os Estados Unidos e os paises latino-americanos. A relação corresponde ao mez de Setembro de 1898, e é corrigida até o dia 28 de Outubro de 1898, com uma relação comparativa para o periodo correspondente do anno anterior, assim como para os nove mezes findos em Setembro de 1898, comparados com os correspondentes de 1897. Deve-se explicar que os algarismos das varias alfandegas, mostrando as importações e exportações de um só mez, são recebidos no Ministerio da Fazenda até quasi o dia 20 do mez seguinte, e perde-se algum tempo necessariamente em sua compilação e impressão. Por conseguinte, as estatisticas para o mez de Setembro, por exemplo, não são publicadas até os primeiros dias de Novembro.

ESTATISTICA DE IMMIGRAÇAO.

O relatorio annual do Commissario Geral de Immigração, Honrado T. V. Powderly, tem sido submettido á Secretaria do Thesouro e nelle se vê que a diminuição no numero de immigrantes durante o anno fiscal findo em 30 de Junho de 1898, com relação ao anno anterior, foi só de 1,533 e o total foi de 229,299. Do numero total de immigrantes 135,775 eram do sexo masculino e 83,524 do sexo feminino. Da Italia veiu o maior numero que foi de 58,613; a Russia occupou o segundo lugar com

27,221; da Irlanda vieram 25,128; da Allem
Suecia, 12,398 e da Inglaterra 9,877. O nume
a quem não se permittiu desembarcar foi de
cento. Deste numero 2,261 eram pobres e
temer de que se convertessem em carga public
trabalhadores que vieram sob contracto, foi d
regressaram por razão de enfermidade foram de

Ainda que durante os mezes de maior immi
Unidos estavam ou a ponto de entrar em gu
nhados nella, esta circumstancia não prejudicou
de suppôr-se que a menos que as leis não so
actual sessão do Congresso, o numero de immig
anno excederá ao do presente anno. O com
varias ideas relativas á modificação das leis. F
rece um augmento da contribuição per capita, (
lars, com o proposito de obter um fundo em vir
ser estendida a esphera de utilidade da Repartiçi
respeito ao augmento de facilidades para a m
sentido de impedir a entrada de criminaes e ot
ciosas. Tambem se recommenda a revogação (
hastar para a immigração, em porto algum, uma
que se recebe naquelle.

VENEZUELA.

EXPORTAÇÃO DE GADO PARA (

O "Venezuela Herald" prediz que Venezuel:
grande paiz exportador de gado. Nota-se o fa
criadores de gado do Estado de Miranda celebr:
em Outubro para o supprimento de 24,000 ca
quaes são destinadas a Cuba e 2,000 cabeças s
mez. Segundo as estipulações do contracto o ga
á razão de dous e meio centavos ouro por libra (
uma estação chamada Gonzalito, situada na
allemá, a curta distancia de Maracay.

O custo de transporte desde esta estação al
que é o porto de embarque, será por conta do
o contractante cubano. Durante a ultima sem:
embarcaram 530 bois, pesando de 400 a 650 lil

Tambem foi celebrado outro contracto entre o Sr. Rojas e um criador de gado de Guanta, que embarcou na mesma semana 800 cabeças. Necessitar-se-hão seis ou sete dias para transportar o gado de Puerto Cabello a Habana.

CLASSIFICAÇÃO NA TARIFA DE TIRAS DE ARAME DE FERRO TORCIDO.

Como resultado de uma consulta feita pelo administrador da alfandega de Maracaibo sobre a classe da tarifa em que devia figurar o artigo conhecido no commercio com o nome de tiras de arame de ferro torcido, o Presidente de Venezuela dispoz que a dita mercadoria se avalie pelas alfandegas da Republica na 3ª classe da tarifa sob a secção 147 da mesma. Este é um artigo de commercio muito importante em Venezuela e se emprega em lugar de bandas e de cordas para assegurar as caixas e fardos de mercadorias que se transportam, e se compõe de dous arames de ferro enlaçados e torcidos de consistencia flexivel e de duração. Segundo a tarifa aduaneira vigente em Venezuela, os artigos da classe 3ª pagam um direito de importação de cinco centavos por kilogramma.

Os exportadores dos Estados Unidos devem notar que os compradores de Venezuela preferem este arame torcido ás bandas de ferro ou ás cordas no enfardamento de mercadorias, porque o arame é tão perfeito que pode usar-se de novo no enfardamento das mercadorias destinadas ao interior.

COMMERCIO MISCELLANEO.

BOLIVIA.

Grandes Minas de Prata. A Companhia Huanachaca de Bolivia tem soffrido serias interrupções na exploração de suas minas nos ultimos dous annos, com motivo da agua e outros accidentes. Não obstante isto, sua producção em 1897 foi de 151,995 kilogrammas, ou 4,886,673 onças de prata. Mas isto não foi muito mais da metade do maximum de exportação alcançado em 1873 e que foi de 281,007 kilogrammas ou 9,034,385 onças.

BRAZIL.

Propostas para o Serviço do Abastecimento de Agua. No Boletim do mez de Outubro se publicou a noticia de que o Governo do Estado de Pará receberá propostas para o serviço do abastecimento de agua da cidade de Belem. O contracto devia ser concedido no dia 10 de Novembro, mas o Governo prorogou a apre-

sentação das propostas para o arrendamento do serviç
agua até o dia 15 de Março de 1899. Podem-se apres
de ouro, e tambem para a cobrança da taxa de agua em
disposto que taes propostas recebam favoravel considera

Novas Minas.   O South American Journal am
de varias minas, que, segundo se
estas minas estão nas minas de ouro cerca de Minas Ne
mantes cerca de Sacramento no Estado de Minas Geraes

Exportação de Manganez.   Um carregamento de 891 ton
manganez foi despachado recent
destino aos Estados Unidos. O mineral foi extrahid
Nazareth e exportado de Itaparica.

Actividade Commercial dos
Allemães.   O Consul Geral Seeger escrev
Dezembro é o melhor para visita
Tambem diz que tem recebido uma communicação do
Estados Unidos e commerciante proeminente de Curityb
selha que os fabricantes dos Estados Unidos redobram se
commercio do Brazil. Diz que os allemães mostram-se
resse de seus compatriotas. O novo Consul allemão che
qual significa novos esforços em favor do commercio alle
allemães a construcção de estradas de ferro, obtenção e
colonisação da região de Iguassú, etc.

COLOMBIA.

Inscripção de Marcas de
Fabrica.   No Ministerio de Fazenda tem-
um livro para o registro official e
estas podem ser inscriptas agora em Bogotá. Esta ins
nenhuma lei especial sobre a materia ou a nenhum decr
é o resultado de uma ordem do Ministerio de Fazenda qu
proprietarios de marcas de fabrica a maneira de obter um
priedade de suas marcas, até que o Congresso vote uma lei
lei está agora em projecto e se espera que se vote na proxi

HAWAII.

·Rendas das Estradas de
Ferro.   Segundo o periodico The Rail
pal estrada de ferro de Hawaii é
Land Company Line, que corre de Honolulu a Waiana
38.5 milhas, incluindo as vias lateraes. Esta estrada
trafico no dia 1º de Julho de 1890, e desde aquella da
augmentado constantemente tanto no que refere a pas
Em 1897, esta estrada de ferro transportou 85,596 pass
isto a somma de $30,993.50, e levou 66,420 toneladas d
ziu uma renda de $69,752.70.

MEXICO.

Lugar Excellente para o Esta-
belecimento de Fabricas.   Diz o Modern Mexico que, a
que têm investigado o assumpto,
offerece vantagens especiaes para o cultivo de linho e

superior. O Sr. GERARDO EMILIA HERRERIAS escreve daquelle Estado que, na sua opinião, o estabelecimento de uma grande fabrica para a manufactura do linho cerca da cidade de Tlaxcala, onde se pode obter facilmente agua como força motriz e onde abundam materiaes de construcção e trabalhadores, seria uma empreza lucrativa. Elle crê que poderão ser fabricados generos de linho de tão boa qualidade como os melhores productos europeos, e que poderão fazer concurrencia com os generos de algodão no consumo local.

Nova Estrada de Ferro que se Estenderá das Minas de Cobre de Inguran ao Pacifico. No dia 13 de Outubro, o Governo concedeu uma concessão para a construcção de uma estrada de ferro de bitola ordinaria, a qual terá 150 kilometros de extensão, com um subsidio de 6,000 kilometros. O concessionario é a Inguran Copper Mining Company, na qual os Srs. ROTHSCHILD de Paris tem grandes interesses. A projectada linha porá as minas em communicação com a Bahia de Zituatanega, no Pacifico, e dará sahida aos productos de cobre. Assegura-se que as minas de Inguran rivalisarão com as de Calumet e Hecla, as mais conhecidas minas de cobre nos Estados Unidos.

Immigração para o Estado de Sonora. Um despacho recebido de Dennison, Texas, informa que um contracto tem sido celebrado com os indios Delaware para a compra de 550,000 geiras de terra no Mexico e que logo que fizerem arranjos com os Estados Unidos e os Cherokees, irão a este paiz. Crê-se que muitos dos Cherokees os acompanharão. Diz-se que o terreno comprado, queestá situado no rio Yagin, no Estado de Sonora, é muito fertil. Os representantes dos proprietarios de terras mexicanos estiveram recentemente com os Cherokees.

As Minas de Cobre de Inguran. Annuncia-se que muitos engenheiros de França virão logo ao Mexico para explorar as minas de cobre de Inguran, que acabam de ser compradas por ROTHSCHILD E MIRBAUD de Paris. O capital da companhia será de $7,000,000, em ouro. A princípios do anno estará terminada uma grande parte dos trabalhos preliminares e se terão feito os estudos para uma estrada de ferro. CARLOS EISENMAN, que era antes dono destas minas, conservará a metade da propriedade.

NICARAGUA.

Reimpressão do Manual de Nicaragua, publicado pela Secretaria. No Diario Oficial de Nicaragua, orgão official do Governo, se está publicando uma traducção em hespanhol do Manual de Nicaragua, publicado pela Sectetaria das Republicas Americanas.

PARAGUAY.

Novo Serviço de Vapores. Ha grandes colonias allemães em todo o Paraguay e os exportadores allemães gosam de grande parte do commercio do paiz. O Consul-Geral SEEGER, do Rio de Janeiro, participou recentemente á Secretaria de Estado que foi estabelecida uma nova linha de vapores entre a Allemanha e o Paraguay por meio dos vapores *Arsy* e *Kurt*.

PERU.

Trabalhadores Agricolas Japonezes. Segundo o Rio News, o Ministro japonez em Lima tem feito os arranjos necessarios com o Ministro peruano de Relações Exteriores para facilitar a immigração no Peru de um grande

numero de immigrantes japonezes, que se dedicarão á
ado periodico accrescenta que o Ministro japonez irá a(
com o objecto de celebrar igual convenio com o Gove

ESTADOS UNIDOS.

Nova Associação Industrial.   Foi organisada em Omaha,
nacional que tem por objecto :
modernos ao cultivo e preparação do linho, canhamo, r
Unidos a legislação apropriada tanto nacional como d
adiantamento destes interesses em todos os modos poss
J. STERLING MORTON, Nebraska, ex-secretario de Agri
dos, presidente; a senhora do Governador LORD, O
Mrs. O. N. OLBERG, Minnesota, thesoureiro.

Machinas de "Weber" em   A companhia denominada \
Demanda.   Engine Company de Kansas
nicou a esta Secretaria, em data de 20 de Outubro, q
um carro carregado de machinas e elevadores com d
Pouco tempo antes se despachou um carregamento
communicação, a Companhia estava preparando um
de pedido feito por uma casa do Equador.

Convenção Nacional de   A quarta reunião annual d:
Fabricantes.   Fabricantes terá lugar em Cin
dias 24, 25, e 26 de Janeiro de 1899. Promette ser um:
tantes que jamais tem celebrado aquella corporação.
em Cincinnati e celebrou sua primeira sessão em 1
numero de membros é de cerca de 1,000, incluindo m
importantes do paiz, e representando quasi todos os r:

Exportação de Oleo Mineral.   A exportação de oleo miner
exercicio de 1875 foi de 221,ç
findo em 30 de Junho de 1898 foi de 1,034,269,676 g

URUGUAY.

Couros e Pelles.   A Republica do Uruguay im
$200,000 annualmente, dos q
procedem dos Estados Unidos, ainda que os Estados I
guay couros e pelles no valor de $2,000,000 annualm
requer dos Estados Unidos são principalmente pelle:
de carneiro. Importam-se annualmente pelles de cab
$46,000. Calcula-se que na Republica ha 380,000
160,000 são couros de bezerro; 150,000 couros de
de vacca e 40,000, couros de cabrito. Um bom comm
reciprocamente entre os dous paizes.

BULLETIN MENSUEL

DU

BUREAU DES REPUBLIQUES AMÉRICAINES,

UNION INTERNATIONALE DES RÉPUBLIQUES AMÉRICAINES.

VOL. VI.   DÉCEMBRE 1898.   No. 6.

MESSAGE DU PRÉSIDENT McKINLEY.

Le message annuel du Président McKINLEY fut envoyé au Cinquante-cinquième Congrès des Etats-Unis, à l'ouverture de sa session finale le 5 décembre 1898. La partie principale du message est en effet une histoire autoritative et une exposition impassionnée et compréhensive des événements de l'année écoulée en tant qu'ayant rapport aux affaires du Gouvernement. Naturellement la première place est donnée aux causes et à la conduite de la guerre avec l'Espagne, et la juste part des éloges est accordée à tous ceux qui y ont pris part, à quelque titre que ce soit, pour les Etats-Unis. Cependant il n'y a pas d'exultation exagérée sur les victoires remportées par les forces militaires des Etats-Unis sur mer et sur terre, mais il y a partout dans ce discours une veine de sympathie et de respect pour l'Espagne vaincue. Le Président félicite le pays parce que, à l'exception de la rupture avec l'Espagne, les relations des Etats-Unis avec la grande famille des nations ont été empreintes de cordialité, et à la fin de l'année, si pleine d'événements, la plupart des questions résultant nécessairement des relations compliquées des états souverains sont réglées ou ne présente aucun obstacle à une juste et honorable solution par une entente amiable.

1119

Concernant le Gouvernement de Porto Rico et des Philippines, le Président dit :

Je ne discute pas en ce moment le Gouvernement ni l'avenir des nouvelles possessions qui nous reviendront à la suite de la guerre avec l'Espagne. De telles discussions seront à propos après que le traité de paix aura été ratifié. Dans l'intervalle et jusqu'à ce que le Congrès ait décidé autrement, il sera mon devoir de continuer les gouvernements militaires qui ont existé depuis notre occupation et d'assurer au peuple la sécurité de la vie et de la propriété et de l'encourager par un Gouvernement juste et bienveillant.

INDÉPENDANCE DE CUBA.

Les observations concernant Cuba sont comme suit :

Dès que nous serons en possession de Cuba et que nous aurons fait la paix dans l'Ile, il sera nécessaire d'aider et de conseiller ses habitants pour former un Gouvernement. Cela doit être entrepris dès que les circonstances sembleront en assurer la sûreté et le succès. Il est important que nos relations avec ce peuple soient d'une nature des plus amicales et que nos relations commerciales soient intimes et réciproques. Il doit être de notre devoir d'aider, par tous les moyens possibles, à reconstruire les terres ruinées de l'Ile, d'encourager l'industrie des habitants et de les aider à organiser un gouvernement qui sera libre et indépendant et qui réalisera les meilleures aspirations du peuple Cubain. Le Gouvernement espagnol doit être remplacé par un Gouvernement juste, bienveillant et humain, créé par le peuple de Cuba, qui est capable de remplir toutes les obligations internationales, et qui encouragera la frugalité, l'industrie et la prospérité, et d'avancer la paix et la bienveillance parmi tous les habitants quelqu'ait été leurs relations dans le passé. Ni la revanche ni la passion ne doit avoir place dans le nouveau Gouvernement. Tant que la tranquillité complète ne règnera pas dans l'Ile, et tant qu'il n'y aura pas de Gouvernement établi, l'occupation militaire sera continué.

Les extraits suivants contiennent des observations et recommendations concernant le Canal de Nicaragua, les autres Républiques Américaines, le Bureau des Républiques Américaines et le Bureau de Commerce Etranger.

LA COMMISSION DE FRONTIÈRE ENTRE LA RÉPUBLIQUE ARGENTINE ET LE CHILI.

Une discussion longue et encore pendante concernant la frontière s'étendant entre la République Argentine et le Chili et suivant la crête des Andes des bords du sud du Désert Atacama au Détroit de Magellan, un tiers environ de la longueur du continent de l'Amérique du Sud, est entré dans une phase critique au commencement de l'année et a donné à ce Gouvernement l'occasion d'exprimer l'espoir que le recours à l'arbitration déjà contemplée par les conventions existantes entre les parties pourraient dominer malgré les graves difficultés se présentant dans son application. Je suis heureux de dire que des arrangements dans ce sens ont été pris, les questions de fait sur lesquelles les commissaires respectifs n'ont pu s accorder ont été référées à sa Majesté Britannique pour être résolues. Il restait un différend touchant la ligne de frontière du nord traversant le Désert Atacama, concernant lequel les traités ne contiennent aucune disposition, et sera sans doute arrangé de la même manière par une commission mixte, à laquelle le Ministre des Etats-Unis à Buenos Ayres a été invité de remplir les fonctions d'arbitre au dernier ressort.

TAÜX DE CABLES UNIFORMES.

J'ai trouvé occasion d'entretenir le Gouvernement Argentin dans le but d'écarter la différence des taux imposés sur les câbles des compagnies américaines pour la transmission entre Buenos Aires et les villes de l'Uruguay et du Brésil des messages envoyés directs de et aux Etats-Unis. Quoique le sujet soit compliqué par des concessions exclusives de l'Uruguay et du Brésil aux compagnies étrangères, on espère toujours qu'on arrivera à une bonne entente et que les voies de communication commerciales entre les Etats-Unis et les villes Atlantiques de l'Amérique du Sud pourront être libérées de taux presque prohibitoires.

Dans cette circonstance, je me permets d'exprimer mes idées sur l'opportunité d'un arrangement international par lequel l'échange des messages par les câbles reliant les différents pays pourrait être reglé sur une base d'uniformité. Le monde a vu le système postal, une masse informe des services indépendants et exclusifs se développe dans une union dont tous les pays jouissent des multiples avantages. Il serait étrange si les nations ne reconnaissaient bientôt que la civilisation moderne qui doit tant de son progrès à l'annihilation de l'espace par la force électrique, demande que ce-tout-puissant moyen de communication soit un héritage de tous les peuples devant être administrés et reglés à leur avantage commun. Un pas dans cette direction fut pris lors de la signature de la Convention Internationale de 1884 pour la protection des câbles sous-marins, et le jour n'est, j'espère, pas très éloigné quand ce moyen de transmission des idées de pays à pays fera partie du domaine international aussi complètement que dans ceux employés dans les relations de commerce et de correspondance sur les mers qui les séparent.

ÉVÉNEMENTS DANS L'AMÉRIQUE CENTRALE.

Les événements dans l'Amérique Centrale méritent plus qu'une simple mention :

Une rupture menaçante entre le Costa Rica et le Nicaragua a été heureusement terminée par la signature d'une convention entre les partis avec l'appui du Représentant Guatémalien comme médiateur, l'acte ayant été négocié et signé à bord du navire Alert des Etats-Unis, alors sur les eaux de l'Amérique Centrale. On pense que les bons offices de notre Envoyé et du Commandant du navire ont contribué à cet heureux résultat

Dans mon dernier message annuel j'ai présenté la situation de la représentation diplomatique de ce Gouvernement dans l'Amérique Centrale créée par l'Association du Nicaragua, Honduras et Salvador sous le titre de la plus grande

République de l'Amérique Centrale et la délégation de leurs fonctions internationales à la Diète du même pays. Quoique le caractère représentatif à la Diète fut reconnu par mon prédécesseur et a été confirmé pendant mon administration par la réception de son Envoyé accrédité et accordant l'exéquatur aux Consuls commissionnées sous son autorité, cette reconnaissance a été qualifiée par la convention distincte que la responsabilité de chacune des Républiques souveraines envers les Etats-Unis ne serait affectée.

Cette condition a été nécessaire d'autant plus que le contrat des trois Républiques a été au commencement une association par laquelle certaines fonctions représentatives furent déléguées à une tripartite commission plutôt qu'une fédération possédant des pouvoirs centralisés de gouvernement et d'administration. Au point de vue de leurs relations et de la relation des Etats-Unis aux diverses républiques, un changement dans la représentation de ce pays dans l'Amérique Centrale n'a été ni conseillé par le Pouvoir Exécutif ni initié par le Congrès, laissant ainsi un de nos Envoyés accrédité comme auparavant, séparément aux deux Etats de la plus Grande République, le Nicaragua et le Salvador, et a un troisième Etat, Costa-Rica, qui n'était parti au contrat, tandis que notre autre Envoyé a été semblablement accrédité à un Etat de l'Union, le Honduras, et un Etat, Guatemala, ne faisant pas parti de l'Union. L'un a présenté des lettres de créance seulement au Président de Costa Rica, et l'autre n'a été reçu que par le Gouvernement de Guatémala.

Subséquemment, les trois Républiques associées sont entrées en négociations pour prendre les mesures prévues dans le contrat original. Une convention de leurs délégués a rédigé pour eux une constitution fédérale sous le nom d'Etats-Unis de l'Amérique Centrale, et ont pris des dispositions pour un gouvernement et une législature centrale fédérale. Lors de la ratification par les Etats constituants, il fut décidé que le nouveau système devait entrer en vigueur le 1er novembre écoulé. Après quelques semaines le plan fut mis a une sévère épreuve à la suite des agissements révolutionnaires, rendant nécessaire l'action commune du pouvoir militaire des Etats-Unis fédéraux pour les supprimer. Sous cette tension la nouvelle Union paraît s'être affaiblie par la retraite de ses membres les plus importants. Ce Gouvernement n'a pas été informé officiellement de l'installation de la fédération et a maintenu une attitude d'attente amicale, bien que ne renonçant aucunement à la position prise dès le commencement que la responsabilité des divers Etats envers nous est restée la même que par leurs tentatives entre eux.

COMMISSION DU CANAL NICARAGUIEN.

La Commission du Canal de Nicaragua, sous la présidence du Contre-Amiral JOHN G. WALKER nommé le 24 juillet 1897, par l'autorité d'une stipulation dans l'acte civil du 4 juin de cette année, a presque terminé son travail, et les résultats de son enquète approfondie sur la route la plus commode, la possibilité et le coût de la construction d'un canal interocéanique traversant le territoire Nicaraguien vous seront soumis. Dans l'accomplissement de sa tâche, la Commission a reçu tous les égards et tout l'aide possible des Gouvernements de Nicaragua, et de Costa Rica, ce qui a prouvé leur appréciation de l'importance d'un résultat prompt et pratique du grand projet qui a, pendant tant d'années, attiré l'attention des pays respectifs. Comme l'enquête récente a embrassé le sujet entier dans le but de faire les plans et l'arpentage pour un canal par la route la plus commode, elle a nécessairement inclu un résumé des résultats des plans et des arpentages, et surtout ceux adoptés par la "Maritime Canal Company" sous ses concessions existantes du Nicaragua et de Costa Rica ainsi sous ce rapport ces concessions tiennent nécessairement la place dans les délibérations et les conclusions de la Commission du Canal qu'elles ont tenues et doivent tenir dans la discussion du sujet par le Congrès.

Dans ces circonstances, et en vue des ouvertures faites aux Gouvernements de Nicaragua et de Costa Rica par des autres compagnies pour une nouvelle concession du Canal annoncé sur la supposition de l'expiration des contrats de la "Maritime Canal Company" avec ces Etats, je n'ai pas hésité d'exprimer mes convictions que les considérations d'utilité et de politique internationale existant entre les divers gouvernements intéressés dans la construction et le contrôle du canal interocéanique par cette route, exigent le maintien du status quo jusqu'à ce que la Commission du Canal ait fait son rapport et le Congrès des Etats-Unis ait eu le temps de voter sur cette question pendant la session présente, sans préjudice à la suite de changements dans les conditions existantes.

Cependant il paraît que le Gouvernement du Nicaragua, comme un de ces derniers actes souverains avant d'unir ses pouvoirs avec ceux des Etats-Unis de l'Amérique Centrale nouvellement formés, a accordé une concession facultative à une autre association devenant effective à l'expiration de la présente concession. Le rapport ne constate pas quels arpentages ont été faits ou quelle route on propose sous cette concession extraordinaire, ainsi un examen de la possibilité de ses plans est nécessairement pas compris dans le rapport de la Commission du Canal. Toutes ces circonstances démontrent l'urgence d'une action définitive par le Congrès pendant cette session si les travaux du passé doivent être utilisés et si l'on veut voir se réaliser l'union des Océans Atlantique et Pacifique, par une voie d'eau.

Que la construction d'une grande route maritime est en ce moment plus que jamais indispensable et que l'intercommunication prête entre nos côtes de l'Est et de l'Ouest demandée par l'annexion des Îles Hawaïennes et l'expansion future de notre influence et de notre commerce sur le Pacifique et que notre politique nationale en ce moment exige plus impérativement que jamais le contrôle de Gouvernement, sont des propositions que je ne doute pas le Congrès va dûment apprécier et sur lequel il votera sagement.

COMMISSION DES DEMANDES DU CHILI.

Une convention stipulant le renouvellement de la récente Commission des demandes des Etats-Unis et du Chili et la consideration des prétensions qui furent dûment presentées à la récente Commission mais qui ne furent pas pris en considération à cause de l'expiration du temps limité pour la durée de la Commission fut signée la 24 mai 1897 mais n'a pas été votée par le Sénat. La période fixée pour l'échange des ratifications étant écoulée la convention sera

abandonée à moins que le terme soit prolongé par un
en ce moment à arranger avec le concours amical du (

CONVENTION D'EXTRADITION AVE

L'interprétation de certaines stipulations de la C(
11 décembre 1861 a été à diverses époques l'occa
Gouvernement Mexicain.   Un différend sérieux
demande d'extradition par le Mexique de Jesus Gui
expédition de maraude près de la frontière dans l
insurrection contre le Président Diaz se refugia au
refusée pour le motif que l'offense en question avait
par conséquent était prévue dans la clause de non ex

Le Gouvernement Mexicain soutenait que l'excep
offenses politiques et qu'il entrait dans les actes de
de meutre, d'incendie par malveillance et de vol, le ref
recevable, interprétation que le Gouvernement ne l
la doctrine internationale admise et pratiquée à cei
Mexicain en vue de ceci a donné avis le 24 janvier i
convention, à prendre effet à douze mois de cette dat
la nomination d'une nouvelle convention pour laque
voie en ce moment.

ZONE LIBRE DU MEXIQ

Le problème de la Zone Libre du Mexique a été
de vue de sa provocation à la contrabande aux Etats-
étendue et mal gardée.   Les efforts faits de commu
pour porter remède à cet abus par la suspension de
territoire des Etats-Unis des marchandises pour le
comme il est constaté dans le Rapport 702 de la
soumis dans la dernière session du 11 mars 1898.   C
resolue par une sage legislation concourante des deu
des revenus par des mesures harmonieuses opérant é
la frontière plutôt que par des arrangements conver
Congrès considère l'opportunité d'autoriser et de p
représentants du Départements de la Trésorerie des
pour étudier le sujet dans toutes ces portées compl
des recommandations pertinentes aux Gouvernement
tion et la consideration de leurs Congrès.

COMMISSION DE FRONTIÈRE MARITI

La Commission de la Frontière Maritime a tranché
ont été soumises à la satisfaction des deux Gouvernei
ants : celui du " Chamizal " à El Paso, Tex., où les d
tomber d'accord et dans lequel, pour ce cas seulemen
posé au Mexique l'addition d'un troisième membre ;
ce qui est connu comme les " Bancos," petites îles isolé
de coudes du fleuve Rio Grande de l'opération de
recommendées par les Commissaires et approuvées l

toujours en considération par Mexique; et le sujet de la " Distribution Equitable des Eaux du Rio Grande " pour lequel les Commissaires ont recommandé une digue et un reservoir international, approuvé par le Mexique mais toujours en considération par ce Gouvernement. Pour résoudre ces questions il est nécessaire de prolonger le terme de la Commission lequel expire le 23 décembre prochain.

ABROGATION DE TRAITÉ.

Le Gouvernement du Pérou a donné les notifications préscrites de son intention d'abroger le traité d'amitié, de commerce et de navigation conclu avec ce pays le 31 août 1887. Comme ce traité contient beaucoup de stipulations importantes nécessaires à la continuation du commerce et de bonnes relations qui pourront avec difficulté être remplacés par la négociation à court espace de douze mois qui nous séparent de l'expiration du traité, j'ai invité le Pérou à faire des propositions concernant les articles particuliers que ce pays désire abroger, dans l'es poir d'arriver à un arrangement par lequel les autres articles pourraient être provisiorement conservés.

TRIBUNAL D'ARBITRATION DU VENEZUELA ET LA GRANDE BRÉTAGNE.

Le tribunal d'arbitre, nommé sous le traité du 2 fevrier 1897 entre la Grande Brétagne et le Venezuela pour déterminer la ligne de frontière entre le dernier pays et la Colonie de la Guyanne Anglaise, va se réunir à Paris au cours de ce mois. C'est une grande satisfaction pour ce Gouvernement de voir l'arbitration amicale appliquée à l'arrangement de différend non seulement à cause de l'importance de notre concours pour arriver à ce résultat mais aussi à cause des deux membres nommés par le Venezuela—Mr. FULLER, Premier Juge et le Juge BREWER choisis de notre Cour Suprême, attestent le désire que nous avons de voir la question définitivement réglée selon les plus strictes règle de justice. Les membres anglais, Lord HERSCHELL et Sir RICHARD COLLINS, sont des juristes de non moins de renom tandis que le cinquième membre et Président du Tribunal, M. F. de MARTENS s'est fait une réputation univeselle comme autorité sur la loi internationale.

BUREAU DES RÉPUBLIQUES AMÉRICAINES.

Je suis heureux de dire que le Bureau des Républiques Américaines créé en 1890 comme organe pour l'avancement des relations commerciales et fraternelles entre les pays de l'hemisphère occidentale, est devenu un instrument plus · efficient du but prévoyant de ceux qui l'ont fondé et reçoit l'appui cordial des membres contribuants de l'union internationale qui sont actuellement représentés dans son Comité Executif. Un Annuaire Commercial, en deux volumes, contenant une masse de statistiques déscriptives des intérêts commerciaux et iadustriels des différents pays, a été imprimé en anglais, espagnol, portuguais et français et un BULLETIN MENSUEL publié dans ces quatre langues, et envoyés dans les pays de l'Amérique-Latine ainsi qu'aux Etats-Unis, ont grandement contribué à répandre d'utiles informations commerciales aussi qu'à l'avancement des divers intérêts de l'Union Internationale.

SEÑOR ROMERO, AMBAS!

Señor Don Matías Romero, Envoyé Exti
Plénipotentiare de la République du Mexic
Unis, vient de rentrer à Washington après u
longée à la capitale mexicaine.   Peu de ter
le Ministre a informé le Secrétaire d'Etat
son rang officiel avait été élevé au titre d'.
nouvelle a été reçue avec grande satisfact
d'Etat et dans le monde diplomatique, et
chaudement félicité de cette marque d'estir
Gouvernement.

Comme la loi stipule que le Gouverne:
peut élever au rang d'Ambassadeur, n'impor
tres, quand le pays auprès duquel il est accr
pas dans cette direction concernant son proj
le Général Powell Clayton, en ce moment
est devenu Ambassadeur auprès de cette Répi
ayant été envoyée au Sénat le 6 décemb
cette assemblée deux jours après.   Cette
règlant le service diplomatique fut établie i!
avait alors aucun diplomate aux Etats-Unis
que Ministre, et les Etats-Unis n'avait a
l'étranger du rang d'Ambassadeur.   Depui
donné des lettres de créance d'Ambassade
Washington.   Ces gouvernements ainsi r
Grande Bretagne, l'Italie, l'Allemagne, la F
Mexique.   Ce pays est la première Répu
conférer un tel honneur à un de ses représen

Señor Romero est un des plus éminents
vains et diplomates du Mexique.   Il est né c
le 24 février 1837.   Il a fait ses première
natale et a fini son éducation dans la capita
où il a reçu sou diplôme d'avocat.   En 1:
mièrement au Ministère des Affaires Etra
tinuant toujours ses études de droit.   En 185
Comonfort fit son coup d'état et Señor J

de la Capitale, SeñorRomero l'accompagna á Vera Cruz et prêta son concours au Département des Relations Etrangères. En décembre 1859 il vint à Washington comme premier secrétaire de la 'Légation mexicaine et y resta dans cette capacité jusqu'au mois d'août 1860, et dans l'absence du Ministre il devint Chargé d'Affaires. Il retourna au Mexique en 1863 pour prendre part à la guerre contre la France et fut nommé Colonel par le Président; le Général Porfirio Diaz alors le nomma son chef d'état major. Peu de temps après le Président Juarez l'accrédita Envoyé Extraordinaire et Ministre Plénipotentiaire à Washington. Il remplit ces fonctions jusqu'en janvier 1868 et rendit des services très importants à son pays. A son retour au Mexique, il fut nommé Secrétaire de la Trésorerie, mais il fut obligé de renoncer à ce poste en 1872 pour cause de mauvaise santé. Pendant trois années il resta à Soconusco s'occupant d'agriculture et fut nommé de nouveau Secrétaire de la Trésorerie de 1877 à 1878; il a aussi rempli les fonctions de Directeur Général des Postes en 1889. En mars 1882 il revint à Washington comme Envoyé Extraordinaire et Ministre Plénipotentiaire et depuis il y est toujours resté au même titre à l'exception d'un intervalle de dix mois en 1892, quand pour la troisième fois son Gouvernement le rappela pour remplir les fonctions de Secrétaire de la Trésorerie. Comme représentant de son Gouvernement aux Etats-Unis, Senor Romero s'est montré diplomate de premier ordre. Ses efforts, tendant à resserrer les relations amicales entre les deux pays, ont toujours été très heureux, et avec cet objet en vue il a beaucoup écrit, ses écrits obtenant toujours les plus hauts éloges des journaux des Etats-Unis et d'autres pays.

Señor Romero fut membre de la Conférence Américaine Internationale et dans cette assemblée a servi avec grande distinction, ayant été un de ses vice-présidents. Comme représentant du Mexique à la Conférence il vota pour l'établissement du Bureau des Républiques Américaines, et depuis son organisation a montré un intérêt actif et ardent dans le progrès du Bureau. Il fut membre du Comité Exécutif du Bureau quand celui-ci fut organisé, et en toute occasion il prêta son concours précieux à la cause de l'Union Internationale des Républiques Américaines.

FEU LE DR. WILLIAM PEPPER.

RÉUNION COMMÉMORATIVE DANS LA VILLE DE MEXICO— HOMMAGE DU MINISTRE ROMERO.

A la réunion qui eut lieu dans la ville de Mexico le 12 septembre 1898, pour honorer la mémoire de feu le Dr. WILLIAM PEPPER, étaient présents le Président DIAZ de Mexico et Señor Don MATÍAS ROMERO, Ministre du Mexique aux Etats-Unis, qui a prononcé le discours suivant:

Monsieur le Président, Mesdames et Messieurs, on m'a prié de vous annoncer que le président de l'Université de Pennsylvanie a demandé par câblegramme que M. le Dr. E. LICEAGA représente en cette occasion ce grand établissement d'enseignement, un des premiers en Amérique et dont le Dr. PEPPER fut doyen pendant plusieurs années. Et l'Université de Pennsylvanie se joint à vous pour honorer la mémoire d'un de ces chefs et bienfaiteurs. Le câblegramme en question est comme suit:

PHILADELPHIE, LE 9 SEPTEMBRE 1898.

Professeur E. LICEAGA, *Mexico:*

Représentez, s'il vous plait, l'Université de Pennsylvanie à la Réunion Commémorative de demain.

CHARLES C. HARRISON, *Président.*

Après avoir lu le message ci-dessus, M. ROMERO a prononcé le discours suivant:

Le désir de rendre un sincère quoique faible hommage au mérite distingué d'un homme qui a été remarquable par ses hauts traits personnels de caractère et pour le bien qu'il a fait à ses semblables penaant sa vie et qui a été de plus, un ami sincère de notre pays, m'engage de sortir pour un moment de la retraite dans laquelle j'ai dû me retirer à la suite d'une des plus grandes douleurs qui puisse frapper un homme.

J'ai donc pensé que je pouvais assister à cette réunion, et comme nous sommes ici pour pleurer la mort d'un ami récemment parti de cette vie et d'honorer sa mémoire, elle est en harmonie avec mes sentiments du moment et de ce que j'ai fait récemment à cause de la grande perte personnelle que j'ai éprouvé.

Dans le discours que j'ai fait à Philadelphie à l'inauguration des Musées Commerciaux dont j'ai déjà parlé je n'ai pu m'empêcher de faire les allusions suivan:es à l'homme à qui l'on doit l'organisation du Musée:

"Permettez moi de dire quelques mots sur un des premiers citoyens de Philadelphie, le Dr. WILLIAM PEPPER, à l'influence duquel on doit le Musée Commercial de Philadelphie qui a été couronné d'un si grand succès. Je n'ai pas besoin de faire les éloges du Dr. PEPPER devant une auditoire de Philadelphie où il est si bien connu, et je dirai seulement ce qui tout le monde ici sait, qu'il est toujours prêt à encourager n'importe quelle entreprise pour le bien de sa ville, de son pays, et de l'humanité. Comme à ses propres frais et aux frais de ses amis parmi lesquels se trouvent plusieurs dames philanthropiques, il entreprend des recherches et des investigations anthropologique et archéologiques dans le monde entier pour l'avancement des sciences qui doivent contribuer au bien de toutes les nationalités. Les hautes qualités du Dr. PEPPER sont appréciées non seulement dans son propre pays mais aussi dans les pays étrangers."

Avant sa mort le Dr. PEPPER a réussi à obtenir l'argent nécessaire pour non seulement entretenir le Musée définitivement mais aussi pour construire un bâtiment convenable coûtant plusieurs millions de dollars.

J'ai aussi eu occasion de connaître une autre bonne œuvre de cet homme ayant rapport comme la première avec notre pays. Une dame distinguée, habitant Washington pendant l'hiver et la Californie pendant l'été, a visité dernièrement ce pays, laissant derrière elle une suite de bienfaits sous forme d'actions généreuses temoignées à des personnes qui en avaient besoin, et cette dame est enchantée d'employer sa fortune à fonder des collèges et d'autres entreprises ayant pour but l'avancement des sciences et le bien de l'humanité en général. Tous mes auditeurs vont comprendre que je parle de Mme. PHŒBE A. HEARST. Le Dr. PEPPER, qui autrefois s'adressa à cette dame philanthropique pour l'argent nécessaire pour ses nobles entreprises, a fait un arrangement avec elle pour envoyer au Mexique une commission scientifique chargée de faire des études archéologiques et anthropologiques dans plusieurs Etats de la République pour l'avancement des sciences, et comme il est caractéristique des personnes qui font le bien pour la satisfaction qu'elles en ont et non pour faire parade de leurs bontés, ce fait serait resté inconnu pour moi malgré mes rapports personnels avec les deux premiers promoteurs de cette œuvre, si ce n'avait été la nécessité d'obtenir le consentement du Gouvernement mexicain d'envoyer la commission. C'est ainsi qu'ils arrivèrent à me communiquer leurs projets. Je crois que le Mexique n'a pas été le seul pays auquel ils ont envoyé une commission dans un but semblable. Je considère alors, comme louable les fonctions qui ont lieu ce soir dans le but d'honorer la mémoire d'un homme dont la vie fait honneur au genre humain.

J'ai eu le bonheur de connaître le Dr. WILLIAM PEPPER personnellement dans son pays et j'ai eu l'occasion de reconnaitre et apprécier ses mérites remarquables. A l'opposé d'autres personnes qui vont prononcer ses louanges ce soir, je ne l'ai pas connu en sa capacité de médecin, grande comme a été son abilité dans cette partie, mais en qualité d'altruist déterminé de faire du bien au genre humain, et donnant tout son temps aux œuvres de bienfaisance auxquelles il a donnè sa propre fortune sans autre récompense que la satisfaction d'avoir fait le bien. Il se prévalut aussi de la position avantageuse qu'il occupait aux Etats-Unis pour obtenir l'argent nécessaire d'accomplir de grandes et utiles entreprises et dans un pays où il y a tant de philanthropes, il a toujours réussi.

Le Dr. WILLIAM PEPPER a été un de ces corps lumineux qui visite notre planète sous forme humaine pour faire du bien à ses semblables et de servir comme modèle pour les générations présentes et futures et pour élever et améliorer la condition du genre humain. Je ne veux pas tenter ici, ni sera-t-il possible de donner en ce moment même une courte esquisse du Dr. PEPPER, et tout ce que je me propose de faire est de raconter brièvement les circonstances dans

lesquelles j'ai fait sa connaissance, circonstances qui on
plus admirables de son caractère.

Désirant développer le commerce des Etats-Unis a
continent americain il conçut le projet d'établir à Ph
un musée commercial pour l'exposition des échantill
manufacturés de chacune des républiques americaines
riers de son pays puissent examiner les matières brutes
le but de les employer dans leurs manufactures.   C
gigantesque pour un seul homme d'attaquer compre
nécessité d'un grand bâtiment, un groupe d'hommes
considérable de commis et divers autres associés nécess
L'énergie du Dr. Pepper n'a jamais été abattue.   Il ;
cles et a réussi à établir des Musées Commerciaux
beaucoup de pompe et de solennité à Philadelphie en
Etats-Unis d'Amérique le 3 juin 1897.

Le Dr. Pepper a désiré, pour assurer le succès complet (
la coopération des gouvernements des autres pays ou
téressés comme ils le sont toujours dans sa réussite
doyen des représentants diplomatiques à Washington
but de faire des arrangements à cette fin et c'est de ce
bonne fortune de faire sa connaissance.   Il est venu t
pour conférer avec nous et nous sommes allés très sou
visiter les Musées et aussi pour assister dans leur dedic
moi, comme représentant diplomatique de l'Amérique
matique des Musées qu'ils avaient organisés, j'ai fait un (
1897, les représentants diplomatiques en question eurent
mexicaine à Washington, qui fut la dernière à laquelle

PRODUCTION D'OR ET D'ARG

MONNAIE DES ETATS-UNIS—MONNAIE D

Dans son rapport au Secrétaire de la Tres
la Monnaie parle non seulement des métaux
Unis pendant l'année 1897 mais aussi de la
les pays étrangers où ces métaux se trouve
ment une base de comparaison entre les princ
santes comme des sources dont on a obten
étaient les plus authentiques et dignes de ce
sont aussi justes qu'il a été possible de les
d'or produit aux Etats-Unis en 1897 a
Cette quantité n'a été dépassée que par u
République de l'Afrique du Sud qui a

Toute l'Australasie a produit $56,684,182 et la Russie, qui vient après, $23,245,763. La République de l'Afrique du Sud a fait la plus rémarquable augmentation de l'année, $13,854,192. L'augmentation en or d'Australasie a été évaluée à $10,502,249; celle des Etats-Unis à $4,974,800, et celle de la Russie à $1,709,970.

Les Etats-Unis pendant l'année ont produit 53,860,000 onces d'argent fin et la République du Mexique en a produit 53,903,180. Ceci a été une diminution de 4,974,800 onces fines pour le premier pays et une augmentation de 8,256,756 onces pour le Mexique. Aux Etats-Unis le nombre d'onces d'or fin a été de $69,637,172. Quoique beaucoup de mines d'argent qui autrefois étaient très productives ont cessé leurs opérations, l'augmentation dans la production du minerai de plomb et de cuivre dans lequel il y avait un alliage d'argent a, à un grand dégré, compensé cette diminution. Pendant l'annee 1897 on obtint de l'or dans 25 Etats et Territoires aux Etats-Unis, allant de $100 dans chacun des quatre Etats à $19,104,200 dans l'Etat de Colorado. La Californie a produit $14,618,300, South Dakota $5,694,900, Montana $4,373,400, Nevada $2,976,400, Arizona $2,895,900, Alaska $1,778,000, Utah $1,726,100, Idaho $1,701,700, et Oregon $1,353,100. Aucun autre Etat n'a produit $500,000. La production d'argent du monde entier, d'après le rapport du Directeur de la Monnaie, indique une grande augmentation sur celle de n'importe quelle autre année. La deuxième grande production a été en 1895, quand elle s'élevait à 167,509,960 onces. La production d'or et d'argent du monde entier en 1897 est indiquée dans le tableau ci-joint:

Pays.	Dollars en or.	Onces d'argent fin.	Valeur en monnaie d'argent.
Etats-Unis	$57,363,000	153,860,000	$69,637,200
Mexique	9,436,300	58,903,180	69,693,000
Etats de l'Amérique Centrale	470,500	1,546,875	2,000,000
République Argentine	137,600	383,470	495,800
Bolivie	750,000	15,000,000	19,393,900
Brésil	1,204,200		
Chili	928,600	6,440,569	8,327,200
Colombie	3,000,000	1,687,950	2,182,400
Equateur	132,900	7,734	10,000
Pérou	628,000	9,784,680	12,650,900
Uruguay	38,500		
Venezuela	948,500		
Guyane Française	4,324,300		
Dominion du Canada	6,027,100	5,558,446	7,186,700

Pays.	Dollars en or.	Onces d'argent fin.	Valeur en monnaie d'argent.
Pays Européens	$27, 175, 600	16, 464, 108	$21, 286, 900
Indes Anglaises....	7, 247 500	....	....
Japon	713, 300	2, 507, 532	3, 242, 100
Chine	2, 209, 100	....	....
Corée	733. 100	....	....
Borneo......................·....	45, 900	....	....
Afrique	58, 306, 600	.. . .	... .
Australasie	55. 684. 800	15. 951, 546	20. 624, 200
Total	237, 504, 800	183, 096, 091	236, 730, 300

La valeur totale d'or déposée dans la Monnaie des Etats-Unis et aux bureaux d'essai a été $87.924.232, consistant de $67,923,535 d'or indigène et $20,000,597 d'or étranger. La valeur d'argent déposé dans les mêmes établissements pour être coulé en barres fines, employées dans les arts industriels ou exportées, a été de $12,707,128, de laquelle quantité $11,847,530 a été d'indigène et $859,598 étrangère. La monnaie des Etats-Unis pendant l'année a été or $76,028,485 et argent $18,487,297, de cette quantité $12,651,731 ont été en dollars étalons d'argent frappés d'argent acheté sous l'acte du 14 juillet 1890 avant le 1 novembre 1893, date de la révocation de la clause d'achat du dit acte. Le monnayage du monde entier pendant l'année, y compris les réfontes a été or $437,719,342; argent, $142,380,588, ou un total de $580,099,930.

Le prix le plus élevé à Londres pour l'argent 0.925 de finesse étalon anglais pendant l'année a été 29 13·16 pence. Le plus bas prix 23¾ pence, et le prix moyen 27 9-16 pence, équivalent à $0.60449 argent des Etats-Unis par once fine. Au prix moyen de l'argent pour l'année la valeur en lingot du dollar en argent a été $0.467. La valeur en or net des exportations des Etats-Unis a été $512,609 et la valeur en argent net des exportations de ce pays pour la même période a été de $26,287,612. La consom mation d'or dans les arts industriels aux Etats-Unis pour l'année 1897 a été or à la valeur de $11,870,231 et argent à la valeur de $11,201,150. La consommation des métaux précieux dans les arts industriels pendant la même période a été or, $59,005,980; argent, $40,435,577. Le 1 janvier 1890 le stock métallique des Etats-Unis a consisté: or, $745,245,953; argent, $635,310,064, ou un total de $1,380,556,017.

LANGUE ESPAGNOLE DANS LE COMMERCE AMÉRICAIN-LATIN.

M. ABRAHAM CHRISTIANI écrit au Bureau, de Comitan, province de Chiapas, la province le plus au sudest de la République du Mexique, pour attirer l'attention sur l'inutilité d'envoyer des communications imprimées, et des annonces, en anglais. Sous ce rapport il sera bien de rappeler aux exportateurs et courtiers d'annonces et autres personnes désireuses d'entrer en relations commerciales avec les citoyens de n'importe quelle partie du Mexique (excepté les maisons où l'on parle anglais) qu'ils doivent faire toutes leurs correspondances en espagnol et envoyer tous les catalogues et autre matière descriptive dans la même langue. On pourrait tout aussi bien imprimer ces communications en français, en allemand, ou en italien qu'en anglais et elles seraient lues par autant d'habitants, car il y a autant de résidents de chacune de ces nationalités au Mexique qu'il y a d'anglais. Comme très peu de personnes engagées dans le commerce aux Etats-Unis parlent et comprennent l'espagnol de même au Mexique le pour cent d'indigènes parlant l'anglais est très petit en proportion. Ce qu'on a dit concernant le Mexique est également vrai de tous les Etats de l'Amérique Centrale et de toutes les Républiques de l'Amérique du Sud, excepté le Brésil où le portugais est la langue des habitants, et à Haïti et à San Dominique où le français est la langue de ces pays.

La communication de M. CHRISTIANI est comme suit :

> Nous voyons avec beaucoup de satisfaction que le BULLETIN MENSUEL des Républiques Américaines sous votre direction, qui est distribué dans les Etats-Unis, au Mexique et dans les autres pays de l'Amérique, est publié en quatres langues différentes. Nous regrettons à dire, pourtant, que la plupart des catalogues que nous recevons des manufacturiers de machines aux Etats-Unis sont écrits en anglais, et comme nous ne comprenons pas cette langue nous ne pouvons pas nous rendre compte de leur contenus. Nous pensons qu'il est bien alors, d'attirer votre attention sur ce fait en prenant la liberté de vous conseiller que si vous le jugez opportun vous ferez en sorte qu'un article à cet effet paraisse dans votre BULLETIN que la seule langue parlée dans cette ville est la langue espagnole afin qu'on en prenne note à l'étranger.

Un grand nombre de journaux commerciaux des Etats-Unis conseillent l'enseignment de la langue espagnole dans les écoles supérieures du pays. La méthode d'après laquelle la langue devrait être enseignée et la raison pourquoi cette étude doit être ajoutée au cours des écoles en question, sont expliqués dans l'extrait emprunté au "American Trade," mais on notera qu'une des raisons plus importantes—l'importance croissante du commerce des Etats-Unis avec les Républiques de l'Amérique du Sud—a été omise par l'auteur:

L'attention que Cuba, Porto-Rico et les Philippines attirent en ce moment comme champs d'extension du commerce américain donne plus d'intérêt à la langue espagnole comme langue de commerce. L'importance de l'espagnol dans nos relations commerciales avec le monde extérieur a augmenté à mesure du développement de nos intérêts commerciaux dans l'Amérique-Latine et la possibilité du contrôle des colonies qui sont habitées par les races parlant l'espagnol rameuèrent les commerçants des Etats-Unis plus que jamais face à face avec le besoin de la connaissance de cette langue. D'un point de vue commercial la langue espagnole est de grande importance aux intérêts commerciaux des Etats-Unis, et la necessité d'une connaissance de cette langue ne diminuera pas pendant beaucoup d'années à venir. Le plus, tôt que nos jeunes gens commenceront d'étudier sérieusement l'espagnol le plus-tôt ils serons prêts à aller à la recherche des affaires dans les pays au sud de nous. On n'a pas besoin de surcharger les cours déjà encombrés des classes élémentaires des écoles publiques. Il y a assez place pour l'enseignment de l'espagnol dans les cours commerciaux que l'on ajoute rapidement aux écoles supérieures. Chaque collège commercial et chaque institution d'education qui a pour objet de préparer les jeunes gens pour le commerce, doivent donner une place à l'espagnol. Le fait de ne connaitre pas ce langue retardera le progrès de notre commerce avec ces pays où l'on parle espagnol plus qu'on ne croit généralement.

ENCOURAGEMENT D'IMMIGRATION DANS L'AMERIQUE DU SUD.

Dans une communication sur l'avenir de l'Amérique du Sud, le correspondant du "London Morning Post" dit que tout récemment on a fait des essais d'immigration organisée vers l'Amérique du Sud. On parle surtout du contrat fait en juillet dernier entre le Gouvernement du Venezuela et la Société de Colonisation Italienne, dont un compte rendu fut publié dans le BULLETIN du mois de septembre.

Le correspondant ajoute:

Des négotiations sont en voie en ee moment pour encourager l'immigration au Brésil, et le Président-élu, DE CAMPOS SALLES, a fait, dit-on, des projets dans ce but, et pendant un séjour à Berlin le mois passé. "Le Von der Heydt" Rescrit par lequel toute immigration au Brésil est défendue, est maintenant, pour ainsi dire, abrogé. L'Allemagne veut bien que ses fils s'établissent dans les Provinces de São Paulo, Rio Grande do Sul, Parana et Santa Catarina, pourvu que leur indépendance politique soit assurée. Le Brésil regarde cette exigence naturellement comme une rénonciation de sa propre souveraineté, mais il est pourtant très probable que l'on trouvera une solution quelconque pour se tirer de la difficulté ; dans ce cas on s'attend à ce que le projet adopté sera applicable à la Suisse et à l'Autriche.

L'Allemagne tient à obtenir pour ses immigrants des privilèges qu'ils n'obtiendraient pas dans les Colonies Britanniques ou aux Etats-Unis. Il n'est facile de voir comme la Doctrine Monroe puisse s'appliquer dans un tel cas et la concession demandée pourrait soulever une sérieuse question de principe. Cette fameuse déclaration stipule que les Continents Américains ne seront pas considérés comme sujets à la colonisation d'aucun pouvoir étranger, mais beaucoup d'évènements ont eu lieu depuis. L'époque de bons sentiments et de la diplomatie moderne trouvent movens d'obtenir des concessions des pouvoirs faibles sans avoir recours à la simple politique qualifiée. Monroe, comme opprimant ou contrôlant en aucune manière leur destiné. De nos jours nous traitons en " usufruits," mais la vraie signification de ces mots n'est pas différente de celle des vieilles expressions, cession et conquête. La distinction est fine, mais elle est certaine de se présenter un de ces jours en vue du développement inévitable par la colonisation de l'Amérique du Sud, et le fait que la France, la Hollande et la Grande Bretagne possèdent des territoires dans ce pays, ne rendra pas les discussion plus simple.

RÉPUBLIQUE ARGENTINE.

CABINET DU GÉNÉRAL ROCA.

L'Honorable WILLIAM I. BUCHANAN, Ministre des Etats-Unis à Buenos Ayres, a envoyé une communication officielle au Département d'Etat comme suit :

L'innauguration du Général JULIO A. ROCA comme Président de la République a eu lieu le 12 octobre, et Señor Don NOBERTO QUIRNO COSTA, Vice-President. Le President ROCA a nommé son Cabinet comme suit :

Ministre d'Intérieur . . . . Dr. FELIPE YOFRE.
Ministre des Affaires Étrangères . . . . Dr. AMANCIO ALCORTA.
Ministre des Finances . . . . Dr. JOSÉ MARÍA ROSA.
Ministre de la Justice et de l'Instruction Publique . . Dr. OSWALDO MAGNASCO.
Ministre de la Guerre . . . . Gen. LUIS MARÍA CAMPOS.
Ministre de la Marine . . . . Com. MARTIN RIVADAVIA.
Ministre des Travaux Publics . . . . Dr. EMILIO CIVIT.
Ministre de l'Agriculture . . . . Dr. EMILIO FRERS.

BOLIVIE.

REVENUS FISCAUX POUR 1897 ET BUDGET DE 1898.

Señor Gutierrez, Ministre des Finances, a fait un rapport au Congrès National actuellement en session sur les recettes de la République pour l'année fiscale 1897. Les recettes du pays sont devisées en revenus nationaux et départementaux et provinciaux, Les recettes sont divisées en bolivianos similaires en grandeur et pureté aux dollars des Etats-Unis mais au prix actuel de l'argent sa valeur au change d'après le rapport du Département de la Trésorerie est $0.436 en monnaie des Etats-Unis.

Le Ministre dans sons rapport place le revenu national en 1897 à 4,840,300.56 bolivianos. Les diverses sources de revenu étaient:

	Bolivianos.
Droits d'entré	2,691,722.71
Argent en barres et minéraux	679,581.85
Droits sur les spiritueux	406,281.00
Timbres et timbres à poste	238,880.45
Exportation de caoutchouc et patentes	149,002.92
Monnaie de nickel	149,000.00
Fer blanc, cuivre et bismuth	97,632.13
Taxe sur patentes de compagnies	86,732.79
Factures consulaires	75,543.76
Revenus de la monnaie	58,960.83
Patentes minières	52,589.43
Droits sur bestiaux et péage	51,417.49
Droits sur cacao	40,000.00
Billets de hypothèques	39,447.45
Droits sur les allumettes	14,085.67
Intérêt et articles non-specifiés	9,082.28
Or	289.80
Marques de fabriques	40.00

Le budget pour 1898 estime les dépenses à 5,714,793.80 bolivianos. Ceci sont distribués comme suit:

	Bolivianos.
Instruction et travaux publiques	1,817,489.80
Département de Finance	1,571,482.50
Département de la Guerre	1,519,218.50
Affaires Étrangères	389,817.00
Département de l'Interieur et de la Justice	260,182.00
Service legislatif	159,604.00

Il est à remarquer que plus d'un tiers des dépenses est appropriée à l'instruction publique et aux travaux publiques alors que dans le passé une plus grande part allait au Département de la Guerre. On remarquera que les revenus de 1897 ne s'élèvent pas aux dépenses proposées pour 1898.

Les revenus provinciaux s'élèvent à 600,000 bolivianos. Cette somme est employée au maintien du gouvernement provincial et pour l'exécution de travaux de nature locale.

La dette intérieure encourue depuis le formation de la République s'élève à 3,707,541.20 bolivianos, mais le Gouvernement n'est placé dans aucune obligation immédiate de payer cette dette avant que le Congrès ne decide de quelle manière elle sera payée. La seule autre dette reconnue par le Gouvernement est une dette envers les créanciers Chiliens à laquelle on consacre 40 pour cent des droits de douane prétés à l'Arica.

La dette était de 6,500,000 bolivianos, dont 5,415,444.86 bolivianos ont été payés à la fin de l'année fiscale 1897. La douane bolivien à Antofogasta a rapporté environ 1,300,000 bolivianos par an. La monnaie nationale à Potosi a mis en circulation une moyenne de 1,500,000 bolivianos en argent par an. Malgrès cela et malgrès 6,600,000 bolivianos en billets de banque en circulation il y a eu dernièrement de nombreuses plaintes sur la rareté d'espèces.

BRÉSIL.

LE NOUVEAU PRÉSIDENT.

Le Dr. M. F. Campos Salles, le nouveau Président des Etats-Unis du Brésil et qui a été installé le 15 novembre, a eu une carrière politique longue et intéressante. La courte esquisse suivante de ces services publiques est empruntée à des sources dignes de confiance.

Avant l'arrivée au pouvoir Républicain le Dr. Campos Salles, alors très jeune, était membre du parti Libéral. En 1870 des Libéraux influents organisaient ce qui est connu comme le parti Républicain du Brésil qui en 1889 prit les rênes du Gouvernement. Campos Salles devint un des "leaders" du nouveau parti dans sa propre province, le présent Etat de São Paulo. Avant cette époque les Libéraux l'avaient nommé Député de la Province de São Paulo. Dans cette capacité il devint bientôt évident qu'il était un orateur et politicien rémarquable. En 1884, malgré une forte opposition de la part des Impérialistes, il fut nommé Député à l'Assemblée Générale qui correspond au présent Congrès Féderal. Il est un fait curieux que des deux députés républicains alors élus, un était le présent Président de la République et l'autre le Président qui vient de se retirer de la vié publique, le Dr. PRUDENTE DE MORAES. Au Parlement Impérial, le Dr. CAMPOS SALLES a fait plusieurs discours très rémarquables qui ont été publiés et lus partout au Brésil.

La République qui a été proclamée le 15 novembre 1889 était pendant dix-huit mois sous la direction d'un gouvernement provisoire pendant la rédaction et l'adoption de la Constitution. Les Républicains ont décidé de prolonger la période du gouvernement provisoire afin d'avoir le temps pour faire diverses réformes électorales. Le Dr. CAMPOS SALLES a été membre de ce gouvernement provisoire pendant toute la période de son existence, tenant le portefeuille de la justice; pendant qu'il occuppait ce post il a travaillé avec diligence et enthousiasme. Lui-même juriste il s'entoura de juristes et acheva la réforme judiciàre, mettant les lois en harmonie avec la nouvelle forme de gouvernement. Toute dans la présente constitution se rapportant à la procédure est son travail. A la première élection générale de la République le Dr. CAMPOS SALLES fut nommé Sénateur de son Etat natal. Son travail au Sénat est d'accord avec son récente carrière et on le considérait un de ses plus illustres membres. En quittant le Sénat il fut nommé Gouverneur de l'État de São Paulo, remplissant ces fonctions jusqu'à ce qu'il fut élu Président le 1 mars 1898.

Le choix du Dr. CAMPOS SALLES comme candidat indique la distinction marquée des partis au Brésil. Auparavant il y avait diverses lignes de divergence parmi les Républicains mais aucune différence distincte de partis. Mais à cette époque il se forma un parti conseillant la choix d'un candidat qui eût faveur de l'élément national contre l'élément étranger ou naturalisé; d'un candidat qui aurait de l'influence auprès des quelques partisans du gouvernement monarchique qui restaient et qui donneraient la préférence à un gouvernement militaire sur un gouvernement civil eu fin, un candidat qui introduirait dans le gouvernement le système nommé Jacobinism, designation qui le nouveau parti n'a pas réfuser. Le Dr. CAMPOS SALLES fut le candidat des Républicains modérés ou conservateurs qui furent organisés sous le nom de parti Républicain, avec un programme demandant le respect de la Constitution et se déclarant pour les réformes que seulement le temps et la raison dicteraient. Les sympathies de l'élément conservateur et étranger qui a des intérêts dans le pays, sont allés aux candidat de cet parti et l'en ont donné leur appui.

L'élection du Dr. Campos Salles ainspiré de nouveau la confiance dans la stabilité du Brésil—confiance qui s'est tout de suite manifestée par la cotisation plus élevée des obligations nationales; par une augmentation dans la valeur du change, et par une plus grande activité commerciale dans tout le pays.

Le Brésil malgré tous les obstacles a prospéré beaucoup depuis 1889. Ces deux faits le prouvent suffisamment: (1) Dans les neuf années de la République le nombre de milles de chemin de fer a doublé; (2) la plus grande récolte de café (la récolte du café ayant été toujours la source principale des richesses du pays) a été d'environ 4,000,000 sacs de 60 kilos (132 livres), tandis que la récolte du café de l'année dernière a été plus de 11,000,000 sacs du même poids. Ce n'est pas la faute de la République qu'elle a reçu comme héritage de l'Empire le système de monnaie en papier inconvertible ou que le prix net d'un sac de café a diminué de \$19.44 à \$4.86. Mais le pays a des ressources immenses autre que le café, et on croit qu'une administration sage et énergique telle que la carrière officielle de Dr. Campos Salles promet, doit au moins rétablir les richesses et le crédit de la République à son état normal.

Le Dr. Campos Salles descend d'une des plus anciennes familles du pays et a environ 55 ans. Il est né dans la ville de Campinas, Etat de São Paulo, d'où était aussi le Président précédent, Prudente de Moraes. Il est tempéré et méthodique dans sa manière de vivre, et c'est là sans doute la raison de cette force physique enviable et qui l'a permis de supporter les fardeaux d'une carrière active. Il a pratiqué le droit pendant de nombreuses années et est sorti de l'École de Droit de São Paulo qui est une des premières institutions du pays. Sa famille a toujours jouit d'une grande fortune, obtenue principalement des plantations de café, et lui-même a toujours été et est encore propriétaire d'une grande plantation de café.

IMPORTANCE DE L'INDUSTRIE DU

Que le Brésil est un pays de grandes ress
fait incontestable.   La grande variété du s(
tions du climat rendent son territoire apte
productions des zones temperées et torride
République est plus renommée dans le mor
deux articles, le café et le caoutchouc.   De
tout du dernier, ce pays a eu presque un 1
production des champs, l'autre de la forêt—
cultivé. Autrefois plus d'attention fut appo
café mais dans les années récentes, à cause
territoire consacré à sa culture et la concurrer
pays, les prix ont diminué continuellement
tout le bénéfice des plantations de café a ce
même du caoutchouc, car pendant que la ¡
de futaie, indigène à presque tout le pays,
rapidité étonnonte, les prix ne se sont nor
mais ont augmenté continuellement.

Le Gouvernement n'a pas manqué de r
noter l'augmentation dans la quantité d'arge
la suite des ventes de caoutchouc.   Les e1
y en a une quantité abondante dans les foré
de l'intérieur.   Mais le Gouvernement n'es
cette evidence mais fait toujours des efforts ¡
habitants les caractéristiques des différen
caoutchouc, les meilleures méthodes de cr
certains arbres au sol, des divers états et l
l'article brut pour les marchés du monde e
sant et l'adaptabilité du caoutchouc à presq
n'a pas échapé l'attention du monde et les
tions cultivées supplémenterons le rendeme
Même les arbres, sauvages ne doivent pɛ
Gouvernement se propose d'empêcher les p
direction.

Récemment le Consul CLARK, à Pernam
à Santos, ont fait des rapports au Départe
Unis concernant les variétés du caoutchouc,

et leur valeur dans les différents Etats du Brésil. La communication de M. CLARK est au sujet de "maniçoba" et celui de M. RONSHEIM de "mangabeira." Le premier dit que la plante maniçoba est cultivée au nord du Brésil, surtout dans les provinces de Ceara et Rio Grande de Norte et Parahyba. Au point de vue du prix il vient après le "seringueira" ou caoutchouc de Pará et pour certains genres d'industrie il est préférable. L'intérêt dans la culture de cette plante est croissante partout dans les trois provinces et s'étende rapidement partout dans les provinces de Pernambuco, Alagoas, et Bahia, et donne les meilleurs résultats avec moins de travail que dans n'importe quelle autre industrie agricole. On plante les graines au commencement de l'hiver, le sol rouge ou brun donnant les meilleurs résultats. Au moment de la plantation le sol ne doit être excessivement sec ni excessivement mouillé. Quand l'arbre a atteint l'âge de 2 ans il peut résister à n'importe quel temps mais naturellement la quantité du fluide dépendra plus ou moins des influences du climat.

A six ans la plante aura atteint sa maturité, qui est le meilleur moment pour faire les incisions, quoiqu'on puisse déjà commencer à l'âge de 2 ans. Après 6 ans les arbres produiront tous les ans jusqu'à l'âge de 30 ans de 2 à 5 kilogrammes (4.4 à 11 livres) de caoutchouc s'il sont en bon état. Après 30 ans la production diminuera un peu la vie de l'arbre étant d'un siècle au moins dans de bonnes conditions. La sève est préparée exactement de la même manière que le seringueira de Pará mais elle est d'une couleur brun plus foncé après le fumage. La plus grande partie du caoutchouc maniçoba est produite dans les Etats mentionnés, d'après la manière suivante : On coupe l'écorce de l'arbre laissant la sève tomber goutte à goutte au pied de l'arbre où par l'action du soleil elle se coagule et forme une accumulation solide et irregulière qui est ramassée par les indigènes et vendue aux intermédiaires qui l'expédie en Amérique et en Europe. Le prix par kilogrammes varie dans ces provinces de 2 à 5 milreis (28 à 70 cents par 2.2046 livres) selon la qualité.

Outre le maniçoba ces provinces produisent une grande quantité de caoutchouc mangabeira qui est d'une qualité inférieure et est employé pour recouvrir les cables, etc.

M. CLARK donne la table suivante des e:
chouc de Ceara pour les années 1893 à 1897

Année.	Quantité.
	Kilos.
1893	135, 569
1894	146, 627
1895	146, 627
1896	324, 327
1897	475, 693

Kilogramme = 2.2046 livres.

Dans son rapport M. RONSHEIM note que
six mois plusieurs consignations de caoutch
arrivés à Santos de l'intérieur et ont été tran
en Europe.   Les résultats etant bons, d'autr
envoyées à l'intérieur et les arrivages de cao
tous les jours et promettent de devinir ur
importante pour cet Etat qui jusqu'ici a é
exclusivement du café pour la plus part de ses
le grand nombre d'articles qui ont paru réce
du pays à ce sujet le Consul attire l'attenti
"Deutsche Zeitung" de São Paulo du 11 ao
cette traduction: .

Le caoutchouc Brésilien est extrait des arbres appar
tinctes—

1. *Hevea brasiliensis* Müll Arg. ou seringueiro d
Pará).

2. *Manihot glaziovii* Müll Arg. ou maniçoba de C

3. *Hancornia speciosa* Gom. ou mangabeira (caout

La première et séconde espèce ne concernent pas à l
comme aucun résultat n'a été obtenu des graines dist
ment parmi les fermiers.   La troisième variété se trou
tale de São Paulo.   Il ne pousse pas bien dans l'Est e
cause de l'humidité ou d'une condition quelconque du
chouc mangabeira a rapporté seulement la moitié du p
prix s'est élevé.   On dit que ce caoutchouc est plus d
férable pour certains usages.

Les journaux disent que pendant les premiers six m
grammes (168,647 livres) ont été transportées par le
Les travailleurs experimentés de l'Etat de Bahia
moment, les propriétaires recevant un troisième des b
les acheteurs paient environ 75 milreis par arroba (

$11 pour 33 livres). On dit qu'un homme peut extraire jusqu'à 3 kilogrammes (6.6 livres) par jour. Le Gouvernement est désireux d'encourager la culture de cet arbre utile et considére en ce moment le paiement de subsidies aux fermiers engagés dans cette industrie.

Le "Journal de l'Amérique du Sud" du 8 octobre dit que l'Etat de São Paulo a établi une loi offrant deux prix de 25,000 milreis chacun et quatre prix de 15,000 milreis chacun pour la culture du caoutchouc mangabeira; ainsi qu'un prix de 15,000 milreis offert por la meilleure méthode d'extraire la gomme et un prix de 10,000 milreis pour l'acclimatation d'autres arbres produisant du caoutchouc. Le "Journal" ne dit pas si ces prix sont en argent, ou en or. Le milreis en or est estimé par le Département de la Trésorerie des Etats-Unis à $0.546.

PAPETERIE ET FOURNITURE DE BUREAUX.

Le Consul anglais, à Rio Grande du Sud, présente les observations suivantes concernant la demande de papeterie dans cette ville. Les envelopes sont demandées par boîtes de 100, et non en paquets de 250, lesquels s'abiment dans les magazins et dans les entrepôts de douanes. Tout papier doit être mis en paquets de 400 feuilles et non en paquets de 480 feuilles qui est le nombre ordinaire. Le papier à lettre doit plié par cinq feuilles, pas davantage, et doit être emballé en boîtes ensemble avec les envelopes. Le papier à lettre pour usage officiel doit mesurer 22 par 33 centimètres (environ 8⅔ par 13 pouces). Le papier tellière ne se vend pas. Celui des dimensions 22 par 33 centimètres est aussi employé par les négociants et il est sub-divisé par les imprimeurs et par d'autres. Toutes sortes de papier sont à présent importés presque exclusivement d'Autriche. Le papier de soie en couleurs est très employé pour la décoration. Bien que fabriqué en Angleterre on le fait venir principalement d'Hambourg, où les agents de commerce trouvent moyen de fournir le même article 2½ pour cent meilleur marché que les importateurs anglais ne peuvent l'acheter à Londres.

En expédiant les factures, le poids des parties qui composent l'article, de quelle classe, de quelle máteriel, etc., ne sont pas spécifiés par beaucoup d'exportateurs anglais, occasionnant par cela des dépenses suplémentaires aux importateurs, parcequ'aux termes des lois de douanes brésiliennes, chaque partie paye un impôt différent. Les allemands sont généralement très attentif à cet égard, et cela porte les importateurs à acheter par l'entremise de maisons allemandes.

CHILI.

DEVELOPPEMENT INDUSTRIEL DE LA RÉPUBLIQUE.

Le Chili est un pays qui achète des marchandises de bonne qualité et ses marchés sont par conséquent dignes d'être recherchés par les manufacturiers des Etats-Unis. Le Chili a une longeur de 600 milles et une largeur de 50 à 200 milles. PEDRO DE VALDEVIA, le second envahisseur espagnol, a comparé le Chili a une lame d'épée à cause de sa grande longeur et de son peu de largeur. Son superficie est de 293,970 milles carrés et d'après le recensement de 1895 la population était de 2,766,747 ou 9.2 habitants par mille carré. Le nombre d'habitants en ce moment dépasse probablement 3,300,000. De ce nombre la moitié environ s'occupent d'agriculture, produisant annuellement 28,500,000 boisseaux de blé et 8,500,000 boisseaux de céréales outre des légumes, des fruits, etc. Plus de 500,000 bêtes à cornes et 2,000,000 chèvres, etc., ont été élevés dans le pays chaque année. Les produits minéraux comme le nitrate, le cuivre, l'or, le charbon, la manganèse, etc., sont abondants. Les champs de nitrate du Chili s'étendent sur un superficie d'environ 220,356 acres, estimés contenir 2,316,000 quintaux métriques (228,000,000 tonnes) de nitrate le plus grand du monde entier. La production totale de ces champs en 1896, d'après un des récents BULLETINS MENSUELS a été de 1,092,000 tonnes.

On peut se faire une idée du développement industriel du Chili du fait qu'en 1895, dans le Département de Valparaiso d'une population de moins de 200,000 habitants, il y avait 417 établissements industriels possedant 162 machines à vapeur, ayant une force totale de 1,766 chevaux, qui pendant l'année ont employé 12,616 machines ouvriers. Parmi ces établissements il y avait les usines à gaz, des brasseries, des raffineries de sucre, des fabriques de voitures et de wagons, des scieries, des fabriques d'eaux minérales et aérées, etc. Les tanneries forment une branche florissante de l'industrie.

Le Chili a été le premier pays dans l'Amérique du Sud qui ait construit des chemins de fer.   Au commencement de 1897 la longeur totale des voies ferrées dans la République, d'après le Consul DOBBS, était de plus de 1,300 milles achevés et en voie de construction, possédés et opérés par l'Etat.   Il y avaient aussi 938 milles possédés et opérés par des compagnies privées principalement des compagnies anglaises.   La ligne principale est le Grand Central appartenant à l'Etat, et qui est composé de trois divisions de Valparaiso à Santiago et de là à Melipilla; de Santiago à Talca, de San Fernando à Alcones et de Pelequen à Peumo; de Talca à Talcahuano, San Rosendo à Traiguen, Santa Fé à Los Angeles, et Robleria à Victoria; totale de 766 milles.   Le travail sur le Chemin de Fer Transandin est maintenant poussé vigoureusement.   D'après les statistiques de l'Annuaire Commercial il y a 25,000 milles de routes publiques et 2,875 milles de voies d'eau dans la République.   À la fin de 1895 la longeur des lignes télégraphiques était de 6,965 milles, avec 8,330 milles de fil.   Il y avaient aussi 4,500 milles de voies appartenant à des compagnies de chemins de fer et à des compagnies privées.

En 1896 la marine marchande du Chili consistait de 188 bâtiments avec une tonnage de 105,642 tonnes.   Quarante-deux de ces bâtiments étaient des navires à vapeur   Les lignes anglaises, allemandes et françaises font le service regulier entre les côtes du Chili et l'Europe par le Détroit de Magellan, et des lignes de navire à vapeur chiliennes et étrangères maintiennent des communications constantes et directes le long la côte jusqu'à Panama, ayant correspondance à cet endroit avec les navires à vapeur pour les ports des Etats-Unis sur l'Atlantique le Pacifique et le Golfe et pour l'Europe.   Le Chili importe la plupart des marchandises fabriquées consommées, mais le Gouvernement offre des encouragements pour l'établissement de nouvelle industries et est désireux d'avancer les manufactures.   On dit que le Congrès a récemment voté $500,000 pour l'encouragement des entreprises métallurgiques, vu qu'on a démontré qu'une bonne qualité de minérai de fer se trouve en grandes quantités dans le pays.   En 1897 la valeur des importations au Chili s'élevait à $65,502,805 et les exportations à $64,754,133.

EXPORTATIONS DE NITRATE EN 1898.

Les exportations de nitrate du Chili pour l'année présente sont évaluées de 1,203,000 tonnes à 1,228,000 tonnes contre 1,040,000 tonnes en 1897, 1,210,000 en 1896 et 1,075,000 en 1895. Les chargements totaux du 1er juin au novembre 1er ont été pour l'Europe 745,000 tonnes; pour l'Amérique du Nord, 122,000 tonnes, et pour tous les autres pays 11,000 tonnes, faisant un total de 878,000 tonnes. On croit que les chargements pour les mois de novembre at décembre s'éleveront de 300,000 à 350,000 tonnes. En supposant que ces chargements ne dépassent pas 325,000 tonnes, les exportations totales pour 1898 s'éleveront à 1,203,000 tonnes ou à environ 26,464,000 quintaux espagnols, ce qui fera 1,464,000 quintaux de plus que le Ministre des Finances au Chili a calculé quand ses estimations du budget pour 1898 furent envoyés au Congrès. Les droits d'exportation reçus par le Chili y compris l'augmentations dans les exportations de nitrate, s'élveront à $41,729,777 contre l'estimation de $41,000,000 dans le budget pour 1898.

COLOMBIE.

COMMERCE AVEC LA NOUVELLE ORLÉANS.

Le Consul de la République de Colombie, Señor Escripción Canal, à la Nouvelle Orléans, envoie à son Gouvernement un rapport sur le commerce de son district consulaire avec la Colombie pour l'année 1897. De ce rapport on apprend que les exportations colombiennes pour l'année, s'elevant à $947,717.20, consistaient principalement de bananes. Les exportations pour la Colombie, par voie de la Nouvelle Orléans, destinées pour la plupart au port de Bocas del Toro, s'élevaient à $155,219.77, les principaux chargements ayant été faits en mars, avril et novembre. Les principaux articles étaient du riz, du sucre, des viandes en boites de fer blanc, du poisson, des liqueurs, des jambons, du gibier, des œufs, de l'orage, des ognons, des haricots, du savon, des bougies de cachalot, du saindoux, du beurre, de la farine du maïs, des pommes de terre, du pain et des biscuits, des outils agricoles, du bois de construction, des couleurs, des drogues et des médecines, des articles d'ameublement et de bureau, des fournitures de bureaux, des chaussures, des chapeaux, des vêtements confectionnés, de la poterie et des cristaux furent aussi exportés en plus petites quantités.

Le Consul note qu'il y a une balance de $792,497.43 en faveur du commerce colombien qui est dû, grandement, aux grandes exportations de bananes de l'Île de Bocas del Toro. Ce port, qui est le point d'embarquement d'un très riche district agricole, ne manque de méthodes plus perfectionnées pour l'exploitation et exportation de ce produit aussi que d'autre pour devenir un centre commercial de très grande importance. Les évaluations données dans ce rapport sont en monnaie colombienne, le dollar ou peso en argent équivalent à $0.418.

MEXIQUE.

BUREAU DE RENSEIGNEMENTS.

On annonce dans le "American Manufacturer" que le Gouverneur TEODORO A. DEHESA, de l'Etat de Vera Cruz, a établi à Xalapa un bureau spécial de renseignements par lequel on se propose de fournir aux personnes qui pourraient s'intérsser au pays, n'importe quelle information générale spécifique qu'elles pourraient désirer concernant la Province de Vera Cruz. La Province possède de nombreux chemins de fer et dans les parties plus basses il y a de nombreuses rivières navigables par lesquelles le producteur trouve un accès facil aux ports de la côte du Golfe et de Salina Cruz sur le Pacifique, tandis que par les différentes voies de chemin de fer on arrive rapidement à l'intérieur du pays à très bas prix. La Province est aussi bien fournie des force hydrauliques venant des nombreux courants perpétuels des montagnes qui descendent à la côte. Des forces hydrauliques abondantes peuvent être obtenues pour des fabriques ou des industries de n'importe quelle importance. La Province se développe rapidement et est en train de recevoir une nouvelle impulsion par la construction projetée de plusieurs nouvelles lignes de chemins de fer et par les améliorations apportées aux ports de Vera Cruz. Le port de Vera Cruz est presque terminé, les navires pouvant être maintenant chargés et déchargés de leurs cargaisons sur les quais de la ville. Le but du Bureau est de fournir gratis des renseignements sérieux des sources officielles à n'importe quelle personne qui désirerait de s'informer des avantages offerts par l'Etat de Vera Cruz, dans le but de faire de placements dans des industries mécaniques ou agricoles, d'ouvrir des voies de commerce ou de developper de n'importe quelle façon les ressources de la Province aussi que de délibérer avec ceux qui pourraient visiter la Province dans ce but.   Toutes communications peuvent être adressées à M. ALEXANDER M. GARR, agent spécial, Xalapa, Etat de Vera Cruz, Mexique.

NOUVEAUX ARTICLES D'EXPORTATION.

Le Vice-Consul mexicain à Cardiff, pays de Galles, a adressé une communication à son Gouvernement attirant l'attention sur la demande dans son district consulaire pour l'article connu dans le commerce sous le nom de cire de Campéche.   Cette cire qu'on considère comme une des meilleures variétés du monde atteint un haut prix sur tous les marchés du Royaume Uni.   Elle est importée du Mexique à un prix modéré et quand elle est vendue dans les pays européens pour être employée dans les industries et les arts, c'est un article très compensatoire pour les exportateurs Mexicains.

Un autre article de commerce qui est produit au Mexique en grandes quantités et qui pourrait trouver un bon débouché à l'étranger, est ce qu'on nomme ordinairement "neat's-foot oil" (huile de pied de bœuf).   L'huile mexicaine, qui est considérée commercialement comme l'huile le moins adulterée sur le marché, atteint un meilleur prix que celle de n'importe quel autre pays, son origine garantissant sa pureté.   Comme cette huile est considerée une des meilleures pour huiler toutes genres de machines, son exploitation et expédition en grandes quantités sera une source de revenu considérable.

RÉCENTES DÉCOUVERTES MINÉRALES.

Un grand dépôt de minerai de cuivre et d'argent a été découvert une petite distance des termini des chemins de fer Rio Grande et Pacifique.   Dans l'Etat de Durango une nouvelle mine d'argent a été découverte et ouverte à Coneto Camp.   Un dépôt d'or de grande valeur a été ouverte a Sauces Camp, et l'ancienne mine de Santa Fé au même endroit est de nouveau exploitée.   THOMAS WARK et d'autres personnes ont ouvert la mine Eureka près de

Canatlan et à un demi-mille au sud-est des mines Gavalon une nouvelle mine d'argent de grande valeur a été découverte.   Dans l'Etat de Sonora les mines Mesa Quemada donnent de bons résultats.   En travaillant dans le tunnel pour communiquer avec la mine Guillermina une veine riche de minerai d'argent de première qualité fut découverte par les mineurs.   On dit que les gisements aurifères de Palomas donnent beaucoup de pépites d'or fin.   Dans l'Etat de Guerrero, on a découvert une nouvelle mine d'argent sur les bords de la rivière Hueymatla, près de Taxco el Vrejo.   L'Ingenieur WILLIAM BAKER a annoncé la découverte d'une veine de minerai d'or de grande valeur à un endroit près de Los Ollos, dans l'Etat de Michoacan.   Le " Herald Hebdomadaire " annonce la vente des riches mines de San Juan et Santo Domingo, près d'Etzatlan dans l'Etat de Jalisco, á une compagnie americaine.   Dans l'Etat de Tepic on exploite de nouveau la mine Tajitos avec des capitaux mexicains prés de Santa Maria del Oro.   Le minerai contient du fer de l'or et de l'argent.   Dans l'Etat d'Hidalgo on a récemment découvert une nouvelle mine près de Mineral del Oro.

À Sonora, Mexique, on a découvert un dépôt de carbone de sodium à 2 milles à l'interieur du Golfe d'Adair, une baie du Golfe de Californie à 100 milles au sud de l'embouchure du fleuve Colorado.   Le dépôt s'étend sur une superficie de 70 acres au centre de laquelle se trouvent plusieurs sources dont l'eau est fortement impregnée de sels.   Cette eau est repandue sur les terrains voisins et l'évaporation a formé une croûte de sels cristalisés d'un profondeur de 1 à 3 pieds, au-dessous desquels il y a d'un pied à 18 pouces d'eau.   A mesure qu'on creuse et qu'on emporte cette croûte qui est le produit, l'eau qui se trouve au dessous remplie vite les vides, et bientôt, par l'évaporation, ils sont complètement renouvelés rendant de la suite le dépôt en réalité inépuisable.   On estime qu'il y a au moins 100,000 tonnes accessibles dans le dépôt et un chargement pour San Francisco a donné de beaux bénéfices.   De carbonate de sodium est employé dans la fabrication d'acides du verre et du bi-carbonate de soude, etc., la demande pour cet article est continuelle.

On annonce dans " Le Monde Économique " que plusieurs dépôts d'étain ont été formés au Mexique, principalement dans les Etats de Guanajuato, San Luis Potosí, et Sonora.   Les hauteurs de la Sierra de la Estanera, dans le district aurifère de Comanja (Etat de San Luis Potosí) contiennent du minerai d'étain qui donne à l'épreuve de 70 pour cent à 75 pour cent de métal. Dans l'Etat de Durango on trouve aussi de l'étain en quantités considérables qui, si bien exploités, rendrait de 35 à 75 pour cent de métal, souvent sous la forme d'oxides. Si on trouve que les dépôts sont très étendus, la production d'étain sera sans doute une source de revenu pour le Gouvernement.

PARAGUAY.

EXPÉRIENCE D'UN IMMIGRANT DES ETATS-UNIS.

Il y a quelques mois M. I. WAVRUNK a écrit au Bureau des Républiques Américaines demandant des renseignements concernant l'encouragement offert par le Paraguay aux immigrants. Le Bureau a communiqué avec l'Honorable W. R. FINCH, Ministre des Etats-Unis au Paraguay, demandant les plus récentes lois sur l'immigration et au reçu de cette lettre une copie fut envoyée a Mr. WAVRUNK qui profita de cette occasion. Il a écrit récemment a Mr. FINCH énumérant ses éxpériences. De sa lettre datée le 23 septembre 1898 et envoyée par le Ministre FINCH les extraits suivants sont pris:

Je considère comme mon devoir de vous informer que j'ai acquis un terrain près de la Colonie Gonzales, et que je suis fort content de mon choix. Avant de m'établir ici j'ai visité trois autres colonies au Paraguay, mais j'ai trouvé que les avantages de la Colonie Gonzales surpassaient tous les autres. J'ai eu la chance d'obtenir 62 acres qui avaient été considérablement améliorés par le premier occupant. Environ 15 acres sont cultivés, dont 3½ ou 4 ont été plantés de sucre et le même nombre de manioc. Il y a 43 orangers, 30 plantes de bananes, 30 vignes, etc., dont la plupart portera des fruits cette année. Il y a une source sur ces terres et d'autres avantages, entre autres la station de chemin de fer qui est a moins de deux milles de distance. Le Gouvernement a été extrèmement généreux, payant mon voyage jusqu'à Colon et m'ayant fourni des hommes et des chevaux pour transporter mes effets sur mon terrain.

Il m'a fourni une vache et un veau et tous les outils nécessaires ainsi que des graines pour la plantation, en un mot, les fonctionnaires ont fait tout leur possible pour m'aider. En considération des améliorations, j'ai reconnu une dette sur les terres pour la somme de 1,130 pesos, mais comme je ne suis obligé de payer cette somme qu'après une période de dix ans sans intérêt, la dette est pour ainsi dire, rien. Nous sommes enchantés du pays et du climat mais nous regrettons la langue anglaise que l'on entend rarement. Cette colonie consiste principalment d'allemands et de français mais les gens sont tous bons et généreux.

ETATS-UNIS.

COMMERCE AVEC L'AMÉRIQUE LATINE.

RAPPORT SUR LES IMPORTATIONS ET EXPORTATIONS.

A la page 1012 on trouvera le dernier rapport des chiffres compilés par le Bureau des Statistiques du Département de la Trésorerie des Etats-Unis dont O. P. Austin est chef. Ces chiffres démontrent les évaluations du commerce entre les Etats-Unis et les pays Américains-Latins. Le rapport est pour le mois de septembre 1898, corrigé jusqu'au 28 octobre 1898, avec un exposé comparé á la même période de l'année précédente, ainsi pour les neuf mois finissant le mois de septembre 1898 comparé à la même période de 1897. On doit expliquer que les chiffres des diverses douanes démontrant les importations et exportations pour n'importe quel mois de l'année ne sont pas reçus au Département de la Trésorerie jusqu'au vingtième jour du mois suivant, et il faut nécessairement du temps pour la compilation et l'imprimerie, de sorte que les rapports pour le mois de septembre, par exemple, ne sont publiés qu'au mois d'octobre.

STATISTIQUES D'IMMIGRATION.

Le rapport annuel du Commissaire Général d'Immigration, l'Hon. T. V. Powderly, a été soumis au Secrétarie de la Trésorerie, et indique que la diminution dans le nombre d'immigrants arrivés pendant l'anneé fiscale, finissant le 30 juin, 1898, comparé avec l'année précédente a été seulement 1,535, le total étant 229,299. Du nombre arrivé il y avait 133,775 hommes et 83,524 femmes. L'Italie a contribué le plus grand nombre, ou 58,613; suivit par la Russie qui a contribué 27,221; l'Irlande, 25,128; l'Allemagne, 17,111; la Suède, 12,398, et l'Angleterre, 9,877. Ceux défendus de débarquer a représenté un total de 3,030, ou environ 1⅓ pour cent. De ce nombre 2,261 étaient des pauvres et pas admis, à cause de la possibilité qu'ils tomberaient à la charge publique. Ceux classés comme ouvriers de contrat s'élevaient à 417; ceux renvoyés à cause de maladies s'elevaient á 258.

Quoique pendant les mois de plus grande immigration les Etas-Unis se préparaient pour la guerre, ceci n'a pas empêché l'immigration, et on peut bien supposer qu'à moins que le Congrès, pendant sa session présente, n'amende pas davantage les lois, le nombre de nouveaus arrivés dépassera celui de l'année présente. La Commission avance plusieurs idées concernant les amendements de la loi. Par example elle conseille une augmentation de taux per capita de $1 à $2, son intention étant d'obtenir des fonds qui avanceront l'utilité du Bureau d'Immigration concernant les facilités pour la plus grande protection contre l'admission des classes criminelles et d'autres classes peu désirables. La révocation de la loi prohibant la dépense d'une somme d'argent plus grande pour soigner les immigrants à un seul port que l'on aurait pu percevoir à tel port, est aussi recommandé.

VENEZUELA.

EXPORTATION DU BÉTAIL À CUBA.

"Le Herald" du Venezuela deviendra, un de ces jours, un grand exportateur de bétail. Le fait est notable qu'un contrat fut établi en octobre par cinq grands éleveurs de bétails de la province de Miranda pour 24,000 bêtes à cornes. Ces bêtes sont destinées à Cuba et seront livrées au nombre de 2,000 par mois. Le contrat stipule que les animaux soient expédiés au prix de 21 cents en or par livre, et soient livrés à une station appelée Gonzalito, située sur le Chemin de Fer Allemand, près de Maracay. Le prix de transport de cette station à Puerto Cabello, le port d'embarquement, sera à charge de M. Rojas, l'entrepreneur Cubain. Pendant la dernière semaine d'octobre 530 bœufs, pesant de 400 à 650 livres chacun, furent expédiés à la Havane. Un contrat semblable a été fait entre M. Rojas et un éleveur de Guanta qui a expédié dans la même semaine 800 bêtes à cornes. Il faudra de six à sept jours pour livrer les bêtes à la Havane de Puerto Cabello. Le Consul ELLSWORTH à Puerto Cabello a fait un rapport des chargements additionnels de 750 bêtes à cornes à Santiago et de 300 à Manzanillo.

CLASSIFICATION DES DOUANES POUR LES BANDES EN FIL DE FER POUR BOÎTES.

A la suite d'une décision demandée par le percepteur des douanes de Maracaïbo concernant les droits imposés sur l'article

connu dans le commerce comme "bandes en fer pour boîtes"
(flejes de alambre de hierro torcido), le Président du Venezuela
a ordonné le 29 septembre 1898 de le classer dans la Clause 3
du Tarif sous la section 147 de la même. Cet article est très
important au Venezuela, étant employé au lieu de bandes et de
cordes pour envelopper les caisses et les paquets à transporter, et
consiste de deux fils de fer entrelacés qui forment un cordage
durable et flexible. D'après le tarif des douanes qui est en
vigueur au Venezuela, des articles de la classe 3 paient un droit
de cinq centavos par kilogramme (5 cents par 2.2046 livres). Les
exportateurs des Etats-Unis devraient noter que les acheteurs du
Venezuela préfèrent des paquets qui sont liés avec ce fil de fer
entrelacés à ceux qui sont protégés par les bandes en fer ou à des
paquets liés tout simplement avec des cordes, parce que le fil de
fer est si parfait qu'il peut être utilisé de nouveau pour lier des
paquets à transporter dans l'intérieur.

MISCELLANÉES COMMERCIALES.

BRÉSIL.

Exportations de Para. L'estimation officielle des articles soumis aux droits
d'exportations de Para pour l'année fiscale finissant le 30
juin 1898, s'élevait à 76,454,035 milreis. Ce total comprend ces articles:
Caoutchouc, 70,109,749 milreis; cacao, 4,410,315 milreis; noix de Brésil,
1,331,387 milreis; peaux, 364,751 milreis; colle de poisson, 139,446 milreis;
plumes de heron, 103,129 milreis; cuman, 8,226 milreis; suif, 1,626 milreis.

Mines d'Or de Carrapato. Le "Engineering and Mining Journal" dit qu'une
compagnie a été formée pour exploiter les vieilles mines
d'or de Carrapato et que ces titres sont offerts en vente à Londres et à Paris.
La capitalisation autorisée est de $1,875,000, dont $1,500,000 sera employé à
l'achat des mines. La propriété comprend une superficie d'environ 2,300 ares
à proximité de la mine St. John del Rey. Une partie de ce territoire a déjà été
exploitée, mais fut abandonnée il y a 90 ou 100 ans à cause des inondations et
de la dureté de la pierre. Les procédés d'exploitation alors en usage ne répondant pas aux exigences imposa de si lourds impôts sur le rendement que tous
les bénéfices furent absorbés.

Echange de Minerai de Manganèse contre des Rails d'Acier. Le "South American Journal" constate le fait que
la plus grande partie des chargements de minerai de
manganèse du Brésil ont été expédiés aux Aciéries Carnegie en Pennsylvanie. En échange cette compagnie a récemment déchargé sur
les quais de Rio Janeiro un grand chargement de rails d'acier pour le chemin de
fer Leopoldine.

BOLIVIE.

Mines d'Argent de Grands Rendements. Les exploitations de mines de la " Compagnie Huana-chaca " de Bolivie ont été sérieusement retardées pendant les deux dernières années par l'eau et par d'autres accidents.   Malgré cela, sa production en 1897 a été de 151,995 kilogrammes, ou 4,886,673 onces d'argent. Mais cette quantité n'a été que la moitié du rendement maximum de 1893 qui s'élevait à 281,007 kilogrammes, ou 9,034,385 onces.

HAWAÏ.

Bénéfices des Chemins de Fer. D'après le " Railway Review," le chemin de fer principal au Hawaï est le Chemin de Fer Ochu et la ligne de la Land Company, qui s'étend de Honolulu à Waianae et qui a une longueur de 38.5 milles, y compris les voies de garage.   Cette ligne a été ouverte au trafic le 1ᵉʳ juillet 1890; depuis cette époque ses affaires ont montré une augmentation continuelle dans le trafic de marchandises et de passagers.   En 1897, 85,596 passagers ont voyagé sur cette ligne, et la compagnie a reçu un revenu de $30,993.50; 66,430 tonnes de marchandises furent transportées avec un bénéfice de $69,752.76.

MEXIQUE.

Exposition Proposée des Produits Mexicains. Le Consul-Général du Mexique, Señor Vigo Limon, qui représente son Gouvernement auprès de la France, propose à son Gouvernement l'établissement d'une exposition permanente à Paris pour les produits Mexicains.   Le Gouvernement, dit-on, regarde cette proposition comme très favorable.   On se propose qu'à l'Exposition de Paris en 1900, où il y aura sans doute une belle exposition de produits Mexicains, de saisir cette occasion pour construire un entrepôt d'échantillons.

Force Motrice par l'Air Comprimé. Le premier système de force motrice par l'air comprimé au Mexique vient d'être fini aux mines Rincon près de Temascaltepec, dans l'Etat de Mexico.   L'installation a coûté $10,000, les machines ayant été achetées aux Etats-Unis.

Nouveau Chemin de Fer des Mines de Cuivre. Le 13 octobre le Gouvernement a accordé la concession pour un chemin de fer à voie ordinaire d'une longueur maximum de 150 kilomètres (93 milles) avec un subside de 6,000,000 kilomètres. La compagnie des mines de cuivre d'Inguran, dans laquelle les Rothschilds de Paris ont de grands intérêts, en est concessionnaire.   Ce chemin de fer sera construit afin de relier les mines à la baie de Zituataneza sur la côte Pacifique et sera un débouché pour les productions de cuivre ; on pense que les mines Calumet et Hecla sont les plus grandes mines de cuivre aux Etats-Unis.

Départ pour Sonora. Une dépêche de Dennison, Texas, dit qu'on tient de bonne autorité qu'un contrat a été conclu par des Indiens de Delaware pour l'achat de 550,000 ares de terrain au Mexique, et dès qu'ils auront établi leurs comptes avec les Etats-Unis et les Cherokees, ils se rendront sur ces terres.   On pense que beaucoup de Cherokees pur sang les accompagneront. Les terrains qu'ils ont acquis sont situés sur la rivière Tagin, province de Sonora, et on dit que ces terres sont très bonnes.

Mines de Cuivre d'Inguran. On dit qu'un grand nombre d'ingénieurs se rendent de France au Mexique pour exploiter les mines de cuivre acquises dernièrement par les Rothchilds et Mirbaud de Paris. Le capital de la compagnie sera de $7,000,000 en or. Pour la fin de la première année une grande partie des travaux préliminaires sera terminée et on aura fait l'arpentage d'une voie ferrée les reliant. CARLOS EISEMAN, l'ancien propriétaire des mines, conserve la moitié de la propriété.

PÉROU.

Ouvriers Agricoles Japonnais. D'après le " Rio News," le Ministre qui représente le Japon à Lima a terminé les arrangements nécessaires avec le Ministre Péruvien des Affaires Etrangères pour aider un grand nombre d'immigrants Japonnais à aller au Pérou pour s'engager dans les industries agricoles. Le "News" ajoute que le même Ministre se mettra immédiatement en route pour le Mexique, dans le but de faire des arrangements semblables avec le Gouvernement Mexicain.

SAINT DOMINGUE (RÉPUBLIQUE DOMINICAINE).

Demande de Capital des Etats-Unis. M. E. LACROIX, citoyen français de Port-au-Prince, Haïti, informe le Bureau des Républiques Américaines que lui et M. JULIEN ont obtenu une concession de trente ans du Gouvernement de la République Dominicaine pour la construction d'une ou plusieurs fabriques de fécule ou tapioca, et qu'ils désirent la coopération des capitalistes des Etats-Unis dans l'entreprise. M. ALEJANDRO WOZ Y GIL, Consul-Général des Etats-Unis auprès de la République Dominicaine, confirme les assertions de M. LECROIX et une annonce a été publiée dans la Gazette Officielle disant que le Gouvernement lui a accordé cette concession le 29 septembre 1896. M. LECROIX envoie au Bureau les devis suivants : Le Journal officiel contenant les clauses de la concession en langue espagnole ; un commentaire sur les différentes clauses ; notes sur le yuca ou manioc duquel le fécule ou tapioca est obtenu ; un tableau de devis pour l'établissement de la première fabrique ; un devis approximatif du commerce ; un échantillon de fécule obtenu du manioc, travail fait à la main. Le capital nécessaire pour 4 ou 5 fabriques est $250,000, mais on dit qu'un commencement peut être fait avec $40,000.

THE STANLEY

New Britain, Conn.,
79 Chambers Street,
New York, N. Y., U. S. A.

Soporte de anaquel de acero forjado con contra-esquineros

BISAGRAS DE ACERO FORJADO, GOZNES, . . .
CERROJOS DE PUERTA, SOPORTES DE ANAQUEL, ETC.

Goznes ornamentales y soportes de anaquel T.

COLW

Lam
tod

TAMBIÉN HACEMOS los

CELEBRADOS INODOROS de
que son los mejores de su precio. Ha
toda clase de Artículos de Latón, Cañe
Hierro Forjado al natural ó galvani
lesagües. Tinas de baño, y toda clase
instaladores de Cañerías de Vapor, Gas
Miembros de la Asociación Nacional de Fabricantes de los Esta

Bacín de Porcelana del Inodoro de "Clase"

UNGÜENTO CRESÍLICO I

O mata-sarna para la destrucción de aradores en la piel y cu
Este ungüento es inmejorable para mataduras, llagas, etc., en
También toda clase de Jabones de Tocador de Ácido Fénico, p

CARBOLIC SOAP CO.
New Yo

Hágase pedidos por conducto de cualquier casa exportadora de

LA PRINCIPAL COMPAÑÍA FABRICANTE DE TI
EN LOS ESTADOS UNIDOS ES LA

FREDK. H. LEVEY CO., 59 Beekman

TINTAS DE IMPRENTA, NEGRA Y
Hechas Especialmente para los Clima

Las principales revistas en Papel del Estucado en la Century, Harp
en fotolitografía. Se recomiendan para toda clase de trabajo especialmente todo

---

SEPARADORAS DE CREMA DE FUERZA CE
Las Separadoras de Crema Mejoradas de Sharples son
Desnatar más Perfectas.

P. M. SHARPLE
WEST CHESTE

LLANTAS OF DUNLOP

be ich ta
pevistas
S die tos
reglas, et
de los va
bles de
The A

Monthly Bulletin

OF THE

Bureau

OF THE

American Republics.

INTERNATIONAL UNION OF AMERICAN REPUBLICS.

———

FREDERIC EMORY, DIRECTOR.

———

DECEMBER, 1898.

———

WASHINGTON, D. C., U. S, A.:
GOVERNMENT PRINTING OFFICE,
1898.

WILLIAM CRAMP & SONS SHIP AND ENGINE BUILDING

WM. T. MALSTER,
President and General Manager.

JAS. F. LYND,
Secretary and Treasurer.

THE
COLUMBIAN IRON WORKS AND
DRY DOCK COMPANY

OF BALTIMORE CITY,

Ship Builders in Iron and Steel.

COMPOUND AND TRIPLE EXPANSION ENGINES.

BOILERS, IRON AND BRASS CASTINGS OF EVERY DESCRIPTION.

Unequalled facilities for docking and repairing vessels afforded by the dry dock of 450 feet length. Ample wharf accommodations whilst vessels are repairing.

OFFICES AND WORKS AT

LOCUST POINT,

BALTIMORE, MD.

Telephone No. 370.

U.S. CRUISER MONTGOMERY, BUILT BY THE COLUMBIAN IRON WORKS & DRY DOCK CO.

WM. T. MALSTER,
Presidente y Administrador General.

JAS. F. LYND,
Secretario y Tesorero.

THE
COLUMBIAN IRON WORKS AND
DRY DOCK COMPANY

DE LA CIUDAD DE BALTIMORE,

CONSTRUCTORES DE NAVÍOS DE HIERRO Y DE ACERO.

MÁQUINAS DE VAPOR DE DOS CILINDROS Y DE TRIPLE EXPANSIÓN.

Ingenieros y Maquinistas. Calderas, Fundiciones de Hierro y de Bronce de Toda Clase.

El dique seco, que tiene 450 piés de largo, presenta facilidades sin rival para meter allí navios y repararlos. Se ofrecen amplios alojamientos en los muelles mientras se reparan los navios.

OFICINA Y TALLERES EN

LOCUST POINT,

BALTIMORE, MD.

Número del Teléfono: 370.

		Precio en los Estados Unidos.
KODAKS DE BOLSILLO (pequeñas, pero de calidad inmejorable).		
Para Cartuchos de película y placas de vidrio, 1½ x 2 pulgadas, · · · ·		$5.00
Cartuchos á prueba de luz, 12 exposiciones, 1½ x 2 pulgadas, · · · ·		.25
KODAKS FALCON No. 2.		
Para Cartucho de película, 3½ x 3½ pulgadas, con lente acromático, · · · ·		5.00
Cartucho á prueba de luz, 12 exposiciones, 3½ x 3½ pulgadas, · · · ·		.60
KODAKS BULL'S-EYE No. 2.		
Para Cartucho de película, 3½ x 3½ pulgadas, con lente acromático, · · ·		8.00
Cartucho á prueba de luz, 12 exposiciones, 3½ x 3½ pulgadas, · · · ·		.60
KODAKS BULLET No. 2.		
Para Cartuchos de película y placas de vidrio, 3½ x 3½ pulgadas, con lente acromático, ·		10.00
Cartucho á prueba de luz, 12 exposiciones, 3½ x 3½ pulgadas, · · · ·		.60
KODAKS BULL'S-EYE No. 4.		
Para película, 4 x 5 pulgadas, con lente acromático, · · · · ·		12.00
Cartucho á prueba de luz, 12 exposiciones, 4 x 5 pulgadas, · · · ·		.90
KODAKS BULLET No. 4.		
Para Cartuchos de película y placas de vidrio, 4 x 5 pulgadas, con lente acromático, ·		15.00
Cartucho á prueba de luz, 12 exposiciones, 4 x 5 pulgadas, · · · ·		.90
KODAKS DE CARTUCHO No. 4 (Dobladiza).		
Para Películas de cartucho y placas de vidrio, 4 x 5 pulgadas, con lente rápido rectilíneo y pantalla pneumática con obturadores de iris de diafragma, · · ·		25.00
Cartuchos de película á prueba de luz, 12 exposiciones, 4 x 5 pulgadas, · · ·		.90

Ningún comerciante en materiales fotográficos tiene un surtido completo sin las arriba mencionadas. Droguistas, Detallistas de juegos de diversión, Joyeros, Ópticos y Comerciantes en general, encuentran la venta de Kodaks muy ventajosa en conexión con sus negocios.

Descuentos Ventajosos á los Comerciantes.

Suplimos gratis á los agentes anuncios impresos en español.
Ejecutamos órdenes directas ó por conducto de exportadores de reputación.
Escríbasenos directamente por Catálogos y descuentos.

EASTMAN KODAK COMPANY,
Rochester, N. Y., U. S. A.

COME AND SEE WHERE AN EMPIRE IS BUILDING

Kansas City, Pittsburg and Gulf R. R. Co.

"PORT ARTHUR ROUTE."

Offers the Investor and Home Seeker advantages perhaps superior to any other railroad or proposition of this kind on the American continent. Starting from Kansas City with feeders from Omaha and Quincy in the very heart of the best agricultural country in the world, reaching the semitropical termini at Port Arthur, on the Gulf of Mexico.

From Kansas City south, the road passes through an agriculturist's paradise; also through fine cotton fields, an inexhaustible supply of pine timber, and a fruit country unexcelled in America.

This company is building an inland locked harbor, and will have steamship and commercial relations with Old Mexico, South America, West Indies, and Europe.

This line is destined to be the great highway from central United States territory to Hot Springs, Houston, Galveston, New Orleans, and the Gulf of Mexico.

The Passenger Equipment is modern, and the service equal to any on the continent, including Dining Cars with meals served on the Café plan.

For information concerning lands and investments, address:

F. A. HORNBECK, H. C. ORR,
Land Commissioner. Gen. Pass. Agt.

ROBERT GILLHAM, A. E. STILWELL,
General Manager. President.

KANSAS CITY, MISSOURI

LA SEPARADORA,

Y CLASIFICADORA

DE CAFÉ "EUREKA."

Separa el café y lo clasifica mejor que cua quiera otra máquina y es la única de su cla que tenga cedazos de limpieza automática, funcione sin producir polvo. Se fabrica seis tamaños, cuya capacidad varía de dos treinta sacos por hora.

PRECIOS: $225.00 Á $500.00
(ORO AMERICANO)

ENTREGADAS LIBRE DE GASTOS ABORDO EN NEW YORK.

ÚNICOS FABRICANTES DE LA MAQUINARIA

"EUREKA,"

PARA LIMPIAR GRANOS.

Fabricantes de maquinaria especial para limpiar arroz, café y semillas.

Dirigirse en solicitud de informes más extensos á

THE S. HOWES COMPANY
SILVER CREEK, N. Y., U. S. A.

THE NATIONAL BISCUIT COMPANY

U. S. A.

Benjamin T. Crawford, President.
H. V. Veries, 1st Vice-President.
Frank O. Lowden, 2d Vice-President.
C. E. Rumsey, Secretary and Treasurer.

CAPITAL,
$55,000,000.00

Esta compañía abarca todas las principales fábricas de galletas y galletitas de los Estados Unidos. El capital de $55,000,000.00 y las facilidades sin igual que posee para la fabricación de estos productos la hacen superior á todas las fábricas de galletas y galletitas que hay en el mundo. La fama de que gozan las marcas de esta compañía hace que sea ventajoso para los comerciantes en el ramo traficar en los productos de esta fábrica.

La compañía más grande que hay en el mundo para la fabricación de galletitas.

LA FÁBRICA EN NUEVA YORK.

Esta compañía fabrica las siguientes clases de galletitas cuya fama es universal . . . .

VANDERVEER & HOLMES, NEW YORK.
HOLMES & COUTTS, NEW YORK.
AMERICAN BISCUIT COMPANY, NEW YORK.
F. A. KENNEDY & CO., BOSTON.
TREADWELL & HARRIS, NEW YORK.
HETFIELD & DUCKER, NEW YORK.
LANGLES & CO., NEW ORLEANS.
LOOSE BROTHERS, KANSAS CITY, MO.
J. D. MASON & CO., BALTIMORE, MD.

Dirigirse á la

NATIONAL BISCUIT COMPANY,

en cualquiera de las ciudades arriba mencionadas.

Una Gran Oportunidad de Hacer Dinero

está en el empleo de las muchas cascadas que hay, para transmitir la fueza por medio de la electricidad á cualquier ciudad
cercana, en donde se puede utilizar para el alumbrado ó como
portencia motriz.

Hoy se puede transmitir la potencia así hasta 100 millas de
distancia.

El sistema de multiple fase de Westinghouse para la Trans-
mision Eléctrica está ya completamente desarrollado.

Los interesados pueden escribirnos.

Westinghouse Electric

& Mfg. Co., Pittsburg, Pa., U. S. A.

120 Broadway, New York, U. S. A.

Westinghouse.

La Máquina de
Westinghouse es la más propia
para la Exportación

por que es la que menos necesita del cuidado
peritos. Está provista de un lubricador automá
tico que conserva inalterables las funciones de
máquina y frios los soportes.   Todas las piez
son de tamaño normal, permutables y se
volver á colocar fácilmente.

Por la manera económica de ejecutar el
bajo, la máquina de vapor no condensadora, compuestá, de Westinghouse, ocupa el primer lugar
el mundo.   También fabricamos máquinas de gas para todos usos.

Westinghouse Machine Company,	Westinghouse, Church, Kerr & C
PITTSBURG, PA., U. S. A.,	NEW YORK, N. Y., U. S. A.,
FABRICANTES.	INGENIERO(

Dirijanse á la casa arriba mencionada, ó á

Westinghouse Electric Co., Ltd., London, England.   Eduardo Chaiaux, Barcelona, Spain.
Rogers & Boulte, Paris, France.   Agar Cross & Co., Buenos Ayres, Argentina.
Dikema & Chabot, Rotterdam, Holland.   I. K. Robinson, Iquique, Chile.
G. Blumcke, Hamburg, Germany.   Frazar & Co., Yokohama and Kobe, Japan.

Westinghouse
Air Brake Co.,

Wilmerding, Pa., U. S. A.

EL TRANSPORTE CON TODA FELICI-
DAD DE ¾ DE UN MILLÓN DE LA CARGA,
PASAGEROS, CARROS DE FERROCARRIL
Y LOCOMOTORAS SE DEBE Á LOS

Frenos Neumáticos de Westinghouse.

Con una hora de aviso se pueden despachar pedidos por 1,000 juegos.

Las Lámparas (Eléctricas Incandescentes) de Sawyer-Man

han sido adoptadas universalmente por razón de

LO LARGO DE SU DURACIÓN.
LO EFICAZ DE SUS FUNCIONES.
LO EXCELENTE DE SU CONSTRUCCIÓN.

Sawyer-Man Electric Co.,

ALLEGHENY, PA., U. S. A.

120 Broadway, New York.   Mills B'ld'g, San Francisco.

Todas casas de primer órden.

A. ESTEP, Presidente y Tesorero.   J. R. McGINLEY, Vicepresidente.   THOMAS FAWCUS, Superintendente.

R. D. NUTTALL COMPANY,

ALLEGHENY, PA., U. S. A.

Poleas (Trolleys), Engranajes, Piñones y Cojinetes,

Para toda clase de Sistemas Eléctricos.

ENGRANAJES DE RUEDA RECTA, CÓNICOS Y DE ÁNGULO,

Para toda clase de Usos Mecánicos.

MEDIUM GRADE AUTOMATIC.

HIGH GRADE AUTOMATIC

AMES . . .
IRON . . .
WORKS,

OSWEGO, N. Y.,

U. S. A.

OFICINA PARA LA VENTA:

38 Cortlandt Street, New York.

8 Oliver Street, Boston, Mass.

716 Fidelity Mutual Building,
Philadelphia, Pa.

Se solicita correspondencia.

T^{he} Carnegie Steel Company,

Limited,

FABRICANTE DE ACERO.

**Oficinas Principales: CARNEGIE BUILDING, PITTSBURG, PA., U. S. A.
Agencias para la venta en todas partes del Mundo.**

FABRICA y Vende Planchas de Blindaje;
Lingotes (de 1½ pulgadas para arriba),
Lupias, Planchas, Cok; Ferromanganeso, Hierro
Especular, Goas; Forjaduras, tales como Ejes,
Barras de Unión, Eslabones, Pasadores y otras
Forjaduras para Carros, Barras de Conexión,
Ejes de Manubrio, Armaduras de Locomotoras,
Barras de Ojo; Planchas para Calderas, Puentes,
Navíos y Tanques; Rieles de Acero, de 16 á 100
libras de peso la Yarda, Barras de Eclisa de Acero
(Rectas y de Codo) para Cualesquiera Secciones
de Rieles; Formas Laminadas para Construc-
ciones, de Codo, Redondas, Chatas, Cuadradas y
Ovaladas, Vigas en forma de I, Acanaladuras,
Baos para Cubiertas de Buques, Viguetas en
forma de T, de Z, etc., y Obras para Construc-
ciones, como Puentes, Edificios, Ferrocarriles
Elevados, Tiantres, Columnas, etc. . . . . . .

T^{he} Carnegie Steel Company,

PITTSBURG, PA., U. S. A.

FORT WAYNE ELECTRIC CORPORATION

Fort Wayne, Indiana, U. S. A.

APARATO

SUCURSALES EN TODAS LAS CIUDADES PRINCIPALES. OFICINA PARA LA EXPORTACION 115 BROADWAY NEW YORK, E.U. DE A.

Dinamo de Arco "Wood" No. 10.   El dinamo más grande
para luz de arco que hay en el mundo.

METRIC WEIGHTS AND MEASURES.

METRIC WEIGHTS.

Milligram (1/1000 gram) equals 0.0154 grain.
Centigram (1/100 gram) equals 0.1543 grain.
Decigram (1/10 gram) equals 1.5432 grains.
Gram equals 15.432 grains.
Decagram (10 grams) equals 0.3527 ounce.
Hectogram (100 grams) equals 3.5274 ounces.
Kilogram (1,000 grams) equals 2.2046 pounds.
Myriagram (10,000 grams) equals 22.046 pounds.
Quintal (100,000 grams) equals 220.46 pounds.
Millier or tonneau—ton (1,000,000 grams) equals 2,204.6 pounds.

METRIC DRY MEASURE.

Milliliter (1/1000 liter) equals 0.061 cubic inch.
Centiliter (1/100 liter) equals 0.6102 cubic inch.
Deciliter (1/10 liter) equals 6.1022 cubic inches.
Liter equals 0.908 quart.
Decaliter (10 liters) equals 9.08 quarts.
Hectoliter (100 liters) equals 2.838 bushels.
Kiloliter (1,000 liters) equals 1.308 cubic yards.

METRIC LIQUID MEASURE.

Milliliter (1/1000 liter) equals 0.0388 fluid ounce.
Centiliter (1/100 liter) equals 0.338 fluid ounce.
Deciliter (1/10 liter) equals 0.845 gill.
Liter equals 1.0567 quarts.
Decaliter (10 liters) equals 2.6417 gallons.
Hectoliter (100 liters) equals 26.417 gallons.
Kiloliter (100 liters) equals 264.17 gallons.

METRIC MEASURES OF LENGTH.

Millimeter (1/1000 meter) equals 0.0394 inch.
Centimeter (1/100 meter) equals 0.3937 inch.
Decimeter (1/10 meter) equals 3.937 inches.
Meter equals 39.37 inches.
Decameter (10 meters) equals 393.7 inches.
Hectometer (100 meters) equals 328 feet 1 inch.
Kilometer (1,000 meters) equals 0.62137 mile (3,280 feet 10 inches)
Myriameter (10,000 meters) equals 6.2137 miles.

METRIC SURFACE MEASURE.

Centare (1 square meter) equals 1,550 square inches.
Are (100 square meters) equals 119.6 square yards.
Hectare (10,000 square meters) equals 2.471 acres.
The metric system has been adopted by the following-named countries: Argentine Republic, Bolivia, Brazil, Chile, Costa Rica, Ecuador, Mexico, United States of America, and United States of Colombia.

Hampden Woolen Co.

DALTON,

MASS., U. S. A.

FABRICANTES DE

Cheviots e Casimiras

Finos e de Moda,

ASSIM COMO DE

Pannos para Sobretudos.

FABRICA EM DALTON, MASS.

FÁBRICA DE TEJIDOS DE MANCHESTER

TODA CLASE DE TELAS ESTAMPADAS.

ORGANDÍES DE CLASE . . . . SUPERIOR.

LINONES DE FANTASÍA Y LOS LLAMADOS

"LAPPETTS,"	PERCALES,
TELA "GALATEA,"	
CHEVIOTS CRUZADOS.	

MINOT, HOOPER & CO.,

40 Thomas Street,

NEW YORK, N. Y., U. S. A.

xvi BUREAU OF AMERICAN REPUBLICS—*Aavertisements.*

See that this trade-mark is on every roll.
Cuidese de ver que cada rollo lleva esta marca de fábrica.
Cubiertas "Neponset" para Techos y para Paredes.
Impermeables, Duraderas, Baratas.
Las cubiertas "Red Rope" para techos y paredes en quintas, edificios de minas y casas de campo de todas clases; son fuertes, flexibles, bonitas, impermeables y herméticas.
Ligeras de peso, compactas, de fácil trasporte. Siempre listas, siempre dignas de confianza.
Papel Aislador Neponset.
Impermeable, Hermético, Inodoro.
Para forrar y aislar almacenes de refrigeración, neveras y carros refrigeradores. Con este papel se pueden hacer las más perfectas cámaras herméticas.
Escríbase en solicitud de muestras é informes detallados á
F. W. BIRD & SON,
Fabricantes de papel,
East Walpole, Mass., U. S. A.

NEPONSET RED ROPE ROOFING

AND SIDE COVERING.

WATERPROOF, DURABLE, CHEAP.

Neponset Red Rope Roofing is a tough, flexible, handsome, air and water tight covering for roofs and sides for farm, mining, and camp buildings of every kind. Very light in weight, compact, easily transported. Ever ready. Always reliable. Very low in price. Sun will not melt it. Frost will not crack it. Rain and wind will not go through it.

Any man with a hammer and a pocket knife can put it on. Every roll carries enough nails and tin caps to apply it.

Rolls 36 inches wide, 500 square feet in each roll.

NEPONSET INSULATING PAPER

WATERPROOF, AIR-TIGHT, ODORLESS.

For lining and Insulating Cold Storage Warehouses, Ice Boxes and Refrigerator Cars. With this paper the most perfect dead air chambers can be made. Will not become hard, brittle, or decay, but permanently retain its high insulating qualities.

This paper is the standard of excellence in America. Rolls 36 and 80 inches wide, 1,000 square feet in each roll. Write for samples and full information.

F. W. BIRD & SON,

Paper Makers,

EAST WALPOLE, MASS., U. S. A.

SPECIAL PAPER FOR SPECIAL PURPOSES.

LA BATERÍA DE EDISON-LALANDE ES LA BATERÍA IDEAL.

Se emplea por las principales compañías de Ferrocarril y Telégrafos, Sistemas de Alarma para Incendios, Fabricantes de Máquinas de Gas y Compañías de Teléfonos. Fuerza Electro-Motriz Alta y Constante. Resistencia Interior Baja. No hay pérdida á causa de circuito abierto.
Escríbase por el Catálogo M. B.

EDISON MANUFACTURING CO., St. James Building, Broadway and 26th Street, **NEW YORK, U. S. A.**

SCARRITT-COMSTOCK FURNITURE CO.,

Establecida durante 60 años.
Manufactureros de MUEBLES.
Especialidad del Comercio de Exportación.
Un inmenso Surtido de Toda Clase de Muebles.

La Más Antigua Casa Exportadora en ST. LOUIS,
Que es la Tercera Ciudad Manufacturera de los Estados Unidos.
Ventas por Mayor y por Menor.

3 GRANDES FÁBRICAS.

Se suministran Catálogos que contienen Precios y Peso de las Mercancías. Se solicita correspondencia.

ESTAMOS LISTOS PARA TOMAR

Contratos de Gobiernos para Uniformes y Fornituras Militares.

INSIGNIAS, ADORNOS Y DIPLOMAS MASÓNICOS.

Se Solicita Correspondencia.

DIRÍJANSE Á

THE PETTIBONE BROS. MFG. CO., Cincinnati, Ohio, U. S. A.

ESTABLECIDA EN 1863.

CARLOS KAESTNER Y CIA

Fabricante de maquinaria para hacer cerveza, fermentar los granos, para la destilación y para hacer almidón. Se garantizan la capacidad y el costo. Máquinas, Calderas.

ALPHABETICAL LIST OF ADVERTISERS.

For English and Spanish List of Articles Advertised, See Pages LVIII–LXXXII.

LAS PLUMAS DE EST
—SON DE—
CALIDAD SUPERIOR.
NÚMEROS POPULARES: O48, 14, 130, 239, 284, 313, 792.
GRAN VARIEDAD DE LAS OTRAS CLASES, PARA TODOS LOS USOS.
ENVIADAS POR EL INTERMEDIO DE CASAS COMISIONISTAS.
THE ESTERBROOK STEEL PE
96 JOHN STREET, NEW YORK, U. S. A.

JOSEPH DIXON CRUCIBLE CO.
(COMPANHIA DE CRYSOES JOSÉ DIXON.)
JERSEY CITY, N. J., U. S. A.
MINEIROS, IMPORTADORES E FABRICANTES DE
GRAPHITO, PLOMBAGINA, LAPIS, CRYSOES, LUSTRE PARA FOGÕES, LUBRIFIGANTES E PRODUOTOS DE GRAPHITO DE TODA A SORTE.
SOLICITA-SE CORRESPONDENCIA.

LA PRENSA PERFECCIONADA DE GORDO
DE
CHANDLER & PRICE

HAY MÁS DE 9,000 QUE TRABAJ Á PLENA SATISFACCIÓN.

Tanto la demanda extran jera como la del país, po estas prensas, aumenta co rapidez, porque son:

1ª. Más resistentes y más fuertes que las de cualquiera otra fábrica. La palanca ó brazo lateral y el eje son de forjado, sin suturas ó soldaduras. Los rodillos de leva son de acero templado del que se usa para herramientas. saca-pliegos es seguro de acción y fácil de manejar. No tiene resortes, abrazaderas ó retenes. Las manillas no pu meterse debajo de los rodillos. Las abrazaderas de la rama son fuertes, sencillas y funcionan instantáneamente.

2ª. Sea cual fuese la clase de impresión, trabajan fácil, silenciosa y rápidamente. Ninguna otra maquina posee novísimas mejoras que ésta tiene para la distribución de la tinta. El engranaje de estas prensas está arreglado de suerte que pueden funcionar con tanta rapidez como se haga la alimentación, sin sacudimientos ni deterioración La platina horizontal de larga base las hace aparentes para que la alimentación sea rápida y fácil.

THE CHANDLER & PRICE CO., Fabricantes de Maquinaria para Imprimir CLEVELAND, OHIO, U. S.

H. K. PORTER & CO.
540 WOOD STREET,
PITTSBURG, PA., U. S.
Fabricantes de Locomotoras Ligeras de Vapor, Neumáticas y Eléctri para Vías de Cualquier Ancho, Pesando de 3 á 45 Toneladas.
NOTA: Remitiremos un folleto ilustrado á cualquier corresponsal interesado en ferrocarriles, minas, haciendas, ingea tranvías, ferrocarriles urbanos, cortes de madera, trabajos de contratista, obras públicas ó manufacturas de hierro, ú otras en que se puedan emplear nuestras locomotoras. Se ruega á nuestros corresponsales mencionen este Boletin.

ESTABLECIDOS EN 1873.   CONSTITUIDOS LEGALMENTE EN 1
THE WYOMING SHOVEL WORKS
Fabrican toda clase de
PALAS, AZADAS, ACHICADORES, HERRAMIENTAS PARA ZANJAS

WHEELER REFLECTOR C

BOSTON, MASS., U. S. A.

LOS REFLECTORES MÁS GRANDES
QUE SE FABRICAN EN EL MUNDO.

Centenares de Modelos para
Todos los Usos Imaginables.

Para Luces de Petróleo, Gas
y Eléctricas.

Se envian Catálogos gratis.

Linternas Eléctricas, de Petróleo y de Gas para Locomotoras.

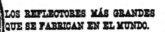

NAIPES ESPAÑOLE

Núm. 71. Los Leones.

Naipes españoles. Pergamino legítimo; tienen todas las calidades de
los mejores naipes españoles; colores
permanentes; esquinas cuadradas ó
redondas; se fabrican de tres tamaños
—2⅝ x 3½, 2⁷⁄₁₆ x 3¹¹⁄₁₆, y 2¼ x 3½;
pulimento de superficie dura; barajas
completas de 48 naipes. la calidad,
la gruesa, 144 barajas, $27.00.

Genuine parchment stock; possesses
all the finest Spanish qualities; permanent colors; square or round
corners; made in three sizes—
2⅝ x 3½, 2⁷⁄₁₆ x 3¹¹⁄₁₆ and 2¼ x 3½;
hard surface finish; full packs, 48
cards. Per gross, $27.00.

Núm. 81.

Colombiano

Naipes Españoles.

Los de figura grabados especialmente al estilo de los que se
usan en Colombia y en los países
adyacentes. Tienen todas
las calidades superiores de la
marca arriba, No. 71; se fabrican
de los tres tamaños arriba
indicados; pergamino legítimo;
esquinas cuadradas ó redondas;
pulimento de superficie dura;
barajas completas de 48 naipes.
la calidad, la gruesa, 144
barajas, $27.00.

Specially engraved faces, after
the style used in Colombia and
adjacent countries; all the superior
qualities of brand No. 71; made in
the three sizes same as brand
No. 71; genuine parchment stock;
square or round corners; hard
surface finish; 48 cards.
Per gross, $27.00.

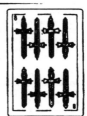

Núm. 95. Spanis

Fáciles de barajar y distribuir;
gada fábrica del papel mas fino
pergamino con pulimiento de su
ficie dura; puntas perfectamen
esactas y redondeadas; superic
á los mas finos naipes de Barce
Hacemos otros naipes españole:
pedido de los compradores. la
dad, la gruesa, 144 barajas, $24

Barcelona size, 2⅜ x 3½; finest
ment paper; hard surface
full packs, 48 cards; for M
and other Spanish games.
Per gross, $24.00.

Condiciones: efectivo después de haberlos entregado á bordo del buque en Nueva York por pedidos de tres
gruesas cuando ménos.

Vése el anuncio de naipes con figuras americanas en la próxima tira de este periodico.

Los fabricantes más
importantes de naipes del mundo.

The United States Playing Card Com

CINCINNATI, U. S. A.

Apagador de Incendios "Stempel

Este Apagador no tiene rival por la sencillez de
construcción y por la seguridad, prontitud y poder c
que funciona. Cada Apagador es sometido, á fin de probarlo
una presión de 400 libras.

Aprobado por la Asociación de Seguros contra Incendios de Filadelfia. Lo usan la
sylvania Railroad Company; el Hospital de Pennsylvania; la Academia de Bellas Artes; la Esc
de Artes y Oficios; el Arsenal del Schuylkill, del Ejército de los Estados Unidos; el Arse
Frankford, del Ejército de los Estados Unidos; la Biblioteca Pública de Filadelfia; la U
Traction Company; los Corrales para Ganado de West Philadelphia; John Wanamaker; el Co
de Girard; el Colegio de Medicina y el Hospital de Jefferson; los Cuarteles del 1º y del 2º Regim
de la Guardia Nacional de Pennsylvania; Geo. V. Cresson Co.; Harrison Bros. & Co., y milla
otros establecimientos públicos y privados, así como fábricas. Pida Usted por medio de su
en los Estados Unidos, un Apagador, como muestra, especificando que el que desea es el "
pel." Se remitirán Catálogos y descripciones á los que los pidan.

H. R. BENNETT,

CONTENTS.

COMPANY

26 and 28 FERRY STREET, NEW YORK CITY, U. S. A.

Cable Address, "UNIT, NEW YORK."

ALSO

BOSTON,   CINCINNATI,   CHICAGO.

MANUFACTURERS OF

HEMLOCK SOLE LEATHER,
From domestic and foreign dry and green salted hides.

UNION TANNED SOLE LEATHER,
In backs from green salted hides.

PURE OAK TANNED SOLE LEATHER,
In sides, backs, and bends.

PURE OAK TANNED BELTING BUTTS.

OAK UNION AND HEMLOCK OFFAL.
Particular care taken in manufacturing to suit export trade.

FABRICANTES DE

SUELA CURTIDA CON CORTEZA PINO DEL CANADÁ,
Empleamos cuero seco y cuero salado del país y del tranjero.

SUELA GRUESA Y CURTIDA,
Hecha de cuero salado.

CUERO DE COSTADO Ó MEDIO CUE
Curtido puramente al roble, y suela gruesa y de calidad, curtida también al roble.

CORREAS DE CUERO SÓLIDO DE I
Curtido al Roble, y Cuero de Desperdicio al Roble, por Fermentación y con de Pino del Canadá.
Se dedica particular atención á los pedidos extran

UNITED STATES

MONSANTO y Cía,

Introducers of

United States Manufactures

Into

MEXICO.

NEW YORK:

96 Broadw

MEXICO CITY

6 Puente de San Francis

CON EL BACALAO SHREDDE

(DESMENUZADO)

de Beardsley se prepara en diez minutos un plato delicioso. No que remojarlo ó que hervirlo. No despide olor alguno ni causa m tia. Se conserva bien en cualquier clima.

J. W. BEARDSLEY'S SONS, New York, U. S. A.

TUBOS REMACHADOS EN ESPIRAL DE ROO

Negros, Galvanizados ó Asfaltados,
Diámetro, de 3 á 24 pulgadas.

Hechos de Acero ó de Hierro Afinad
Hasta de 25 piés de largo.

Para Riego, Cañerías, Trabajos Hidráulicos en Minas, Granjas, etc.

Cada tubo es sometido á la última prueba posible.
Conexiones y Accesorios necesarios para cualquier servicio.

Gran resistencia al mismo tiempo que peso muy

comerciantes en grande y casas de abastecimientos especiales en cualquier parte. Pídanse

DROTH & ROOT MFG. CO., 28 Cliff Str NEW YORK,

ÍNDICE.

BICICLETAS DE . .

CRAWFORD

Fabricadas por

THE CRAWFORD MFG. CO.,

HAGERSTOWN, MARYLAND, U. S. A.

Se envía el Catálogo gratis.

AMERICAN
BOOT AND SHOE
MFG. CO.,

118-120 Duane Street,
NEW YORK, U. S. A.

FACTORIES:
Poughkeepsie, N. Y.
Farmington, N. H.
Rochester, N. H.

Send for samples.   Solicitense muestras.

✦ HAUTHAWAY'S ✦
Peerless Gloss
For Ladies' and Children's Boots and Shoes.
Contains nothing injurious to leather.

Sold by all New York Commission Houses.

C. L. HAUTHAWAY
& SONS,
346 Congress Street,
BOSTON, MASS., U. S. A.

EL LUSTRE
SIN RIVALD E
Hauthaway
...PARA...
Calzado de Señoras y Niños.
No contiene cosa alguna que
pueda dañar el cuero.
Lo venden todas las casas comisionistas de Nueva York.

C. L. HAUTHAWAY & SONS,
346 Congress Street, BOSTON, MASS., U. S. A.

¿TIENE VD. UNA TIENDA

en conexión con su mina, fábrica ó hacienda?

Si es así, lo que necesita Vd. son nuestros

LIBROS DE CUPONES

Empleando éstos se evitan las cuentas, errores y
pérdidas debidas al olvido de asentar partidas. No
hay que llevar libros ni que hacer cambio. Reducen
al mínimo el trabajo de llevar los libros de la tienda.
Fabricamos libros que contienen desde $1 hasta $25,
compuestos de cupones que representan desde 1 centavo
hasta 1 peso, y en los idiomas inglés y castellano.
Para un libro de muestra y una circular que lo describe
y contiene los precios, diríjanse á

ALLISON COUPON COMPANY,   INDIANAPOLIS, IND., U. S. A.

INDICE.

THE "LAKE"
Portable Key-Seater

With this tool it is possible to quickly and perfectly cut a straight and central key-seat, of any width or depth, in a steel shaft, without removing the shafting from hangers. It is a time and money saver wherever machinery is used; is portable, inexpensive, and will soon save its cost. Can be purchased of machinery supply houses in any part of the world, through importers, and direct from us.

Descriptive Circulars and Prices on application.

**Máquina Po
Encajar Cha**

Con ayuda de este instr

**MÁQUINAS DE ENCAJAR
CHAVETAS "LAKE."**

A solicitud se envían Ci

LAKE BROS., PHILAD

TABLE DES MATIÈRES.

THE PERKINS-CAMPBELL CO.,
CINCINNATI, OHIO, U. S. A.

Fabricantes en mayor escala en los Estados
Unidos de Arneses, Sillas de Montar, Colleras,
Portarriendas, Cojinetes de Colleras, etc.

Á solicitud se envían *gratis* Catálogos y Listas de Precios en
Español, Inglés y Alemán.
Se solicitan contratos con los Gobiernos ó con particulares.

Joseph Bancroft & Sons Company,

WILMINGTON, DELAWARE, U. S. A.,

✦ ✦ ✦ ✦ ✦ ✦

FABRICAN, BLANQUEAN ✦✦✦
Y TIÑEN CON PERFECCIÓN

✦ ✦ ✦ ✦ ✦ ✦

Holandas para Cortinas de Ventana,
CORTINAS DE VENTANA,
TELAS DE ENCUADERNAR Y GÉNEROS PARA CAMISAS.

PRESIDENTS OF THE AMERICAN REPUBLICS.

Countries.	Names.	Executive residence.
Argentine Republic	Señor Don Julio A. Roca	Buenos Aires.
Bolivia	Señor Don Severo Fernandez Alonso	Sucre.
Brazil	Senhor Don M. F. de Campos Salles	Rio de Janeiro.
Chile	Señor Don Federico Errázuris	Santiago.
Colombia	Señor Don Miguel Antonio Caro	Bogotá.
Costa Rica	Señor Don Rafael Iglesias	San José.
Ecuador	Señor Don Eloy Alfaro	Quito.
Guatemala	Señor Don Manuel Estrada Cabrera	Guatemala City.
Haiti	Monsieur T. Simon Sam	Port au Prince.
Honduras	Señor Don Policarpo Bonilla	Tegucigalpa.
Mexico	Señor Don Porfirio Diaz	City of Mexico.
Nicaragua	Señor Don José Santos Zelaya	Managua.
Paraguay	Señor Don Juan B. Egusquiza	Asunción.
Peru	Señor Don Nicolás de Piérola	Lima.
Salvador	Señor Don Rafael Antonio Gutierrez	San Salvador.
Santo Domingo	Señor Don Ulises Heureaux	Santo Domingo.
United States	Mr. William McKinley	Washington, D. C.
Uruguay	Señor Don Juan Lindolfo Cuestas	Montevideo.
Venezuela	Senor Don Ignacio Andrade	Caracas.

CHILE.—Señor DON CARLOS MORLA VICUNA,
  1800 N street, Washington, D. C.
COLOMBIA.—Señor DON JOSÉ MARCELINO HURTADO. (Absent.)
  Señor DON JULIO RENGIFO, Chargé d'Affaires *ad interim*,
  1728 I street, Washington, D. C.
ECUADOR.—Señor DON LUIS FELIPE CARBO,
  The Arlington, Washington, D. C.
GREATER REPUBLIC OF CENTRAL AMERICA.—Señor DON JOSÉ DOLORES R
  (Absent.)
  Señor DON LUIS F. COREA, Secretary of Legation and Cha
  ad interim,
  1537 I street, Washington, D. C.
GUATEMALA.—Señor DON ANTONIO LAZO ARRIAGA,
  1312 Twenty-first street, Washington, D. C.
HAITI.—Mr. J. N. LÉGER,
  1461 Rhode Island avenue, Washington, D. C.
MEXICO.—Señor DON MATÍAS ROMERO,
  1413 I street, Washington, D. C.
PERU.—Señor DON VICTOR EGUIGUREN,
  2025 Hillyer Place, Washington, D. C.
VENEZUELA.—Señor DON JOSÉ ANDRADE,
  2 Iowa Circle, Washington, D. C.

MINISTER RESIDENT.

COSTA RICA.—Señor DON JOAQUIN BERNARDO CALVO,
  2111 S street NW., Washington, D. C.

CHARGÉ D'AFFAIRES.

SANTO DOMINGO.—Señor DON ALEJANDRO WOZ Y GIL,
  31 and 33 Broadway, New York City, N. Y.

CONSULS-GENERAL.

PARAGUAY.—Honorable JOHN STEWART,
  28 I street NE., Washington, D. C.
URUGUAY.—Señor DON PRUDENCIO DE MURGUIONDO,
  309 North avenue east, Baltimore, Md.

Executive Committee of the Bureau of the American Rep

Somos los Mayores Exportadores de Vehiculos, Arneses y Sillas de Montar en el Mundo.

Carros, $13.85; Carretones de Camino, $19.75; Calesines con Fuelles, $29.85; Faetones, $54.90; Carros Ligeros de Cuatro Ruedas, llamados Surreys, $58; Carretones de Repartir Mercancías, $39.75; Arneses para Un Solo Animal, $4.25; Arneses para Dos Animales, $12.75; Sillas de Montar, $1.97.

Un surtido completo de materiales rodantes á precios tan bajos como los anteriores.

VEHÍCULOS.

"MURRAY."

ARNESES.

WILBER H. MURRAY MFG. CO.,

Dirección Cablegráfica:
"WILBER," Cincinnati.

CINCINNATI, OHIO, U. S. A.

Enviamos grátis por el correo nuestro Grande y Hermoso Catálogo.

MYRON C. WICK, Presidente.   F. L. CLARK, Gerente y Tesorero.   C. A. PAINTER, Secretario.

EXPORT IRON AND STEEL CO.,

Fabricante de la marca "BATTLE AXE."

BATTLE   AXE.

OFICINAS PRINCIPALES:

LEWIS BUILDING, PITTSBURG, PA., U. S. A.

Dirección por Cable:
"Export Pittsburg."

Arcos de Barril, Barrica, Tanque, Cubas, Mantequeras y Baúles; Flejes para Pacas de Algodón y Lana; Hojas para Sierras de Cantero; Tiras para Bisagras, Tachuelas y Cerraduras; Arcos Galvanizados y Estañados.

Arcos para Toda Clase de Tonelería, Embalaje y Necesidades Manufactureras.

TALLERES PARA LA MANUFACTURA DE EFECTOS DE HIERRO DE

MILLIKEN BROTHERS,

INGENIEROS Y CONTRATISTAS.

Establecidos en 1857.

Fabrican efectos de Hierro y de Acero de Construcción y Ornamento, así como Obras de Latón, Bronce y Electro-plateadas para Edificios; Puentes, Techos, Vigas de Acero Cilindrado, Columnas de Hierro Fundido y Batido, Escaleras y Armazones para Elevadores, Armaduras y Cuartones Remachados. Se hace una especialidad en la Construcción de Armazones para Edificios Incombustibles de Acero y de Cobertizos de Hierro para los Países del Sur. Techos Encarrujados y Galvanizados para Edificios.

Fabricantes privilegiados de los Postes Patentados de Acero de Milliken para Tranvías Eléctricas del Sistema de Poleas (Trolley), Telégrafos y Teléfonos. También fabrican el Taladro Bicicleta, Portátil, Patentado de Milliken, los Arcos Incombustibles Patentados de Milliken para Pisos y las Grúas de Botalón Mecánicas Patentadas de Milliken.

TALLERES: OFICINA:
Bryant and Clinton Streets,   **39 Cortlandt Street,**
        Brooklyn, N. Y.   **New York City, U. S. A.**

DUQUESNE

BICICLETA DE SUPERIOR CALIDAD BAJO TODOS CONCEPTOS.

DE hermosa apariencia, acabada y provista de todo lo necesario. Perfecta en cuanto á su hechura y cojinetes. Famosa por la facilidad y suavidad con que se mueve.

Separadora y Clasificadora de Café "Monitor."

La "Monitor" es la clasificadora de café perfecta que se ha construido hasta hoy.

Separa los granos con mucha limpieza, q tando todos los fragmentos y las materi extrañas, clasificándolos en cinco clases tintas, que son: grano ancho de tamañ grande, mediano y pequeño; caracolillo gran y pequeño.

Se fabrican de 5 tamaños, con capaci para preparar de 60 á 80 sacos por h Precios de $350 á $600 libre de gastos á bor del ferrocarril en la ciudad de Nueva Yor N. Y.

Las Separadoras de Arroz "Monitor" modelos en su clase y son las que casi exclusi mente se usan en los Estados Unidos.

Fabricamos un surtido completo de Limpiadoras de Granos y de Semillas. Escríbase en solicitud de informes detallados.

HUNTLEY MFG. CO.,
SILVER CREEK, N. Y., U. S. A.

A. G. SPALDING & BROS.,
LOS MAYORES FABRICANTES DE BICICLETAS Y SAVI PARA ATLETAS EN EL MUNDO. . . . .

LA BICICLETA "NYACK."

Elegantemente esmaltada de diferentes colores, verde Brewster, negro ó castaño oscuro. La armadura es hecha de tubos sin soldar. Los soportes son de acero tan fino como el que se usa para herramientas; los cubos son cortados de una barra sólida del mismo metal; los rebordes son de madera, y las chumaceras tienen esferas metálicas. Los mangos ó hacia arriba ó hacia abajo; la corona es de una pieza, y todas las partes de que se compone la bicicleta, con excepción de la armadura, son de cobre niquelado y muy hermosas. Se entrega completa, incluyendo un de herramientas. Las sillas son de las denominadas "Christy."

Los Avíos para el Juego de Pelota (Base Ball) de Spalding son los que se usan modelo donde quiera que existe dicho juego. La marca de fábrica de Spalding, en quier artículo que se compra, es una garantía de que dicho artículo es de la mejor cali

AVÍOS PARA LOS JUEGOS DE RAQUETA (TENNIS), VILORTA (CRICKET) Y GOLF, Y PARA ATLETAS Y GIMNASIOS. . . . . .

Pídanse los Precios y el Catálogo.

A. G. SPALDING & BROS.,
Chicago.
Philadelphia. 132 Nassau Street, New York, U. S.

UNITED STATES CONSULATES.

Frequent application is made to the Bureau for the address of United States consuls in the South and Central American Republics. Those desiring to correspond with any consul can do so by addressing "The United States Consulate" at the point named. Letters thus addressed must be delivered to the proper person. It must be understood, however, that it is not the duty of consuls to devote their time to private business, and that all such letters may properly be treated as personal, and any labor involved may be subject to charge therefor.

The following is a list of United States consulates in the different Republics:

ARGENTINE REPUBLIC—
Buenos Aires.
Cordoba.
Rosario.

BOLIVIA—
La Paz.

BRAZIL—
Bahia.
Para.
Pernambuco.
Rio Grande do Sul.
Rio de Janeiro.
Santos.

CHILE—
Antofagasta.
Arica.
Coquimbo.
Iquique.
Talcahuano.
Valparaiso.

COLOMBIA—
Barranquilla.
Bogotá.
Cartagena.
Colón (Aspinwall).
Medellin.
Panama.

COSTA RICA—
San José.

DOMINICAN REPUBLIC—
Puerto Plata.
Samana.
Santo Domingo.

ECUADOR—
Guayaquil.
Bahia de Caraques.
Esmeraldas.
Manta.

GUATEMALA—
Guatemala.

HAITI—
Cape Haitien.

HONDURAS—
Ruatan.
Tegucigalpa.

MEXICO—
Acapulco.
Chihuahua.
Durango.
Ensenada.
Guaymas.
La Paz.
Matamoros.
Mazatlan.
Merida.
Mexico.
Monterey.
Nogales.
Nuevo Laredo.
Paso del Norte.
Piedras Negras.
Progreso.
Saltillo.
Tampico.
Tuxpan.
Vera Cruz.

NICARAGUA—
Managua.
San Juan del Norte.

PARAGUAY—
Asunción.

PERU—
Callao.

SALVADOR—
San Salvador

URUGUAY—
Colonia.
Montevideo.
Paysandu.

VENEZUELA—
La Guayra.
Maracaibo.

"CONSTRUIDA COMO UN RELOJ."

"Sterling" y "Strength"

=== SON SINÓNIMOS. ===

LA BELLEZA DE LA BICICLETA "STERLING" ES EVIDENTE.

LA VELOCIDAD DE LA BIC CLETA "STERLING" PRUEBA FÁCILMENT

"STERLING"

Son de la Mejor Clase. Su Baratura Maravillosa, dada su Buena Calidad

Precios para el '98: Modelos para paseo, de $60 á $75. Para carreras, $55. Sin cad $125. "Tandems," $125. Los Catálogos se remiten gratis y franqueados.

Bicicletas de Primera Clase al alcance de todo el Mundo.

Sterling Cycle Werks, 274, 276, 278 Wabash Aven CHICAGO, ILL., U. S. A.

THE
BROWN HOISTING & CONVEYING MACHINE CO

CLEVELAND, OHIO, U. S. A.,

INGENIEROS, DIBUJANTES Y FABRICANTES DE

ESTABLECIMIENTOS COMPLETOS PARA EL ACARREO DE MATERIALES.

MAQUINARIA PARA EL ACARREO DE CARBÓ Y METALES.

GRÚAS DE TODAS CLASES—ELÉCTRICAS, DE VAPOR Y DE MANO.

Maquinaria para Astilleros; para el Manojo de

THE ·

COMMERCIAL DIRECTORY

OF THE AMERICAN REPUBLICS.

The Bureau of the American Republics has published in two volumes a comprehensive and reliable COMMERCIAL DIRECTORY of the American Republics and European dependencies in Central and South America and the West Indies. The work is the most complete and accurate ever issued in any of the countries to which it relates. It consists of two handsome quarto volumes, 9 by 12 inches in size, containing about 2,500 pages, and is sold at five dollars ($5.00) per volume. The first volume was issued November 11, 1897. The second volume is now ready for distribution. The DIRECTORY embraces in its contents the following information:

1. Reliable descriptive, geographical, industrial, commercial, and statistical data of each country, and the latest maps.

2. The addresses and lines of business of nearly one hundred thousand commercial houses of Latin America and the Hawaiian Islands.

3. The names of over ten thousand representative manufacturers, merchants, shippers, and bankers of the United States interested in foreign trade, classified under their respective business designations.

4. The names of the commercial and trade organizations and associations of the countries embraced in the International Union of the American Republics.

5. Valuable data of transportation companies and trade routes by land and water; railroad, telegraph, and cable facilities; particulars as to shipping, port regulations, tariffs, and customs; patent, trade-mark, and copyright laws; commercial licenses; passport and postal regulations.

The above information has been secured from the most reliable sources, with a view to accuracy and completeness, and it will undoubtedly meet specific requirements in the conduct of the foreign trade in the Western Hemisphere.

The cooperation of business men generally throughout the United States is requested for this work, which is recognized as being, not only of practical utility, but of international importance.

Copies may be examined at the Bureau of the American Republics, 2 Jackson Place, Washington, D. C., and purchased only upon application to the Director. The practice of soliciting for subscriptions upon commission was discontinued February 28, 1898. No advertisements are inserted in the DIRECTORY. The offer to insert names of subscribers in the lists of business houses, being in conflict with the original plan of the work as outlined by the late Director of the Bureau, Mr. Joseph P. Smith, which contemplated the publication of lists of representative firms without charge, was withdrawn. Contracts entered into under the former arrangement have been fulfilled, but the Bureau has not considered itself bound to insert any names for pecuniary consideration, nor does it assume any responsibility of guaranteeing the business standing of firms.

FREDERIC EMORY,
Director.

FRANK M. PIERCE, COMPAÑÍA DE INGENIEROS.

INGENIEROS CONTRATISTAS.

Se preparan planos de Establecimientos de Fuerza Motriz para Luz Eléctrica, Ferrocarriles y Fábricas. Se suministran los equipos y se colocan. Se entregan funcionando perfectamente al vapor.

MÁQUINAS Y CALDERAS

DE PRIMERA CLASE, DE TODOS TAMAÑOS Y DISEÑOS. APARENTES PARA TODA CLASE DE FINES.

FRANK M. PIERCE ENGINEERING COMPANY,
26 CORTLANDT STREET,

PÍDASE EL CATÁLOGO. **NEW YORK, N. Y., U. S. A.**

EL ·

DIRECTORIO COMERCIAL
.—DE LAS REPÚBLICAS AMERICANAS.

La Oficina de las Repúblicas Americanas ha publicado en dos tomos el DIREC-
TORIO COMERCIAL de las Repúblicas Americanas y de las colonias europeas en la
América Central y del Sur, así como en el Mar de las Antillas. La obra es la
más completa y perfecta que se haya publicado jamás en país alguno de los de que
trata. Consta de dos hermosos tomos en cuarto, de 12 pulgadas de largo y 9 de
ancho, que contienen cerca de 2,500 páginas. La obra se vende á razón de cinco
pesos ($5.00) cada tomo. El primer tomo se publicó el 11 de noviembre de 1897.
El segundo tomo está ya listo para ser distribuido.

El DIRECTORIO contiene las siguientes materias:

1. Datos fidedignos descriptivos, geográficos, industriales, comerciales y estadísticos sobre cada país, así como los últimos mapas.

2 Las señas de cerca de 100,000 casas comerciales de la América Latina y de
las Islas de Hawaii, lo mismo que los negocios á que se dedican.

3.· Los nombres de más de ·10,000 fabricantes, comerciantes, armadores y banqueros prominentes de los Estados Unidos que se interesan en el tráfico extranjero.
Dichos nombres serán clasificados según los negocios á que los respectivos individuos se dedican.

4. Los nombres de las corporaciones y asociaciones comerciales en los países
comprendidos en la Unión Internacional de Repúblicas Americanas.

5. Datos importantes acerca de las compañías de trasporte y de las rutas
comerciales por tierra y por agua, lo mismo que sobre ferrocarriles, medios de
comunicación por telégrafo y por cable, trasportes marítimos, reglamentos de
puerto, aranceles y aduanas, marcas de fábrica y leyes relativas á la propiedad
literaria, patentes comerciales, pasaportes y reglamentos postales.

Todos los datos á que se ha hecho referencia han sido obtenidos de las fuentes
más fidedignas, con la mira de que fueran completos y exactos, y es seguro que
responderán á las necesidades especiales del comercio extranjero en el Hemisferio
Occidental. Se solicita la cooperación de los hombres de negocios de los Estados
Unidos á una obra que no solamente es de utilidad práctica, sino de importancia
internacional.

Se pueden ver ejemplares de esta obra en la Oficina de las Repúblicas Americanas, 2 Jackson Place, Washington, D. C., y para comprarla es preciso dirigirse
al Director. El método que antes se usaba y que consistía en solicitar suscripciones, pagando una comisión, fué abolido el 28 de febrero de 1898. No hay
anuncios insertos en el Directorio. El ofrecimiento de poner los nombres de los
suscritores en la lista de las casas de comercio fué retirado, porque es contrario
al plan primitivo de la obra, tal como fué adoptado por el difunto Director de la
Oficina, Mr. Joseph P. Smith, y de acuerdo con el cual se debían publicar gratis
listas de las principales casas comerciales. Los contratos celebrados de conformidad con el ofrecimiento anterior han sido cumplidos; pero la Oficina no se ha
considerado obligada á insertar ningún nombre por consideraciones pecuniarias, ni
asume la responsabilidad de garantizar la posición de ninguna casa comercial.

FREDERIC EMORY,
Director.

El Cerrador de Puertas Sin Ruido.

EL

"NORTON"

Sujeta-Puertas
y Resorte.

Usado en los edificios del Gobierno y en los municipales.
· Premiado con medalla y diploma en la Exposición Universal Colombina en 1893.

Diríjanse á

THE NORTON DOOR CHECK & SPRING CO.

EDIFICIO SEARS,

BOSTON, MASS., U. S. A.

THE WHITMAN & BARNES MFG. CO.,

NEW YORK, N. Y., U. S. A.

EXPORTADORES EN GENERAL,

COMISIONISTAS Y FABRICANTES.

MARCAS DE
FÁBRICA.

FABRICANTES DE

HACHAS, HACHUELAS Y MARTILLOS.

Taladros Salomónicos.

Llaves Inglesas de Todas Clases.

Secciones, Cuchillas, Hoces y Guardas para toda clase de Segadoras y Agavilladoras.

O Directorio Commercial

.... das Republicas Americanas.

A Secretaria das Republicas Americanas tem publicado, em dous volumes, um comprehensivo Directorio Commercial das Republicas Americanas e das colonias europeas na America Central e do Sul e nas Antilhas.   A obra é a mais completa e perfeita que se tem publicado jamais em paiz algum dos de que trata, e se compõe de dous elegantes tomos de 12 pollegadas de comprimento e 9 de largura, que contem cerca de 2,500 paginas.   Vende-se a obra pela somma nominal de cinco pesos ($5.00) cada tomo, que é apenas o valor da impressão e encadernação   O primeiro volume salim á luz no dia 11 de Novembro de 1897.   O segundo volume acaba de ser publicado.

O Directorio contem as seguintes materias:

1. Dados descriptivos, geographicos, industriaes, commerciaes, e estatisticos sobre cada paiz, assim como os ultimos mappas.

2. Os endereços de cerca de cem mil casas commerciaes da America Latina e das ilhas de Hawaii, assim como os negocios a que se dedicam.

3. Os nomes de mais de dez mil fabricantes, commerciantes, embarcadores, e banqueiros proeminentes dos Estados Unidos, que se interessam no commercio estrangeiro.   Ditos nomes serão classificados segundo os negocios a que os respectivos individuos se dedicam.

4. Os nomes das corporações e associações commerciaes nos paizes comprehendidos na União Internacional das Republicas Americanas.

5. Dados importantes acerca das companhias de transportação e dos caminhos commerciaes por terra a por agua, assim como os sobre estradas de ferro, vias de communicação por telegrapho e por cabo, transportações maritimas, regulamentos de porto, direitos das alfandegas, marcas de fabrica e leis relativas a propriedade litteraria, licenças commerciaes, passaportes e regulamentos postaes.

Todos os dados acima mencionados têm sido obtidos das fontes mais fidedignas. São completos e exactos e, sem duvida, responderão as necessidades especiaes do commercio estrangeiro no Hemispherio Occidental.   Solicita-se a cooperação dos homens de negocios nas Republicas Americanas, n'uma obra que não sómente é de utilidade pratica, mas de importancia internacional.

Podem-se ver exemplares do Directorio Commercial na Secretaria das Republicas Americanas, 2 Jackson Place, Washington, D. C., e para compral-os é preciso dirigir-se ao Director.   O methodo que antes se usava e que consistia em solicitar assignaturas, pagando uma commissão, foi abolido a 28 de Fevereiro de 1898. Não ha annuncios inseridos no Directorio.   O offerecimento de pôr os nomes dos assignantes na lista das casas de commercio tem sido retirado, porque é contrario ao plano primitivo da obra, que foi adoptado pelo finado Director da Secretaria, o Sr. Joseph P. Smith, e pelo qual se propunha publicar gratis listas das principaes casas commerciaes.   Os contractos celebrados de conformidade com o offerecimento anterior, têm sido cumpridos; mas a Secretaria nao se considerou obrigada a inserir nenhum nome por considerações pecuniarias, nem assume a responsabilidade de garantir a posição de nenhuma casa commercial.

FREDERIC EMORY,
Director.

WELLS FILING CABINETS.

ARMARIOS DE WELLS PARA ARCHIVAR PAPELES.

──FOR FILING──

Letters,

  Invoices,

    Catalogues,

      Price Lists,

        · Documents (flat),

Documents (folded),

  Legal Blanks,

    Any Kind of Sheet,

      Any Size of Sheet.

More than Fifty Different Styles and Sizes constantly on hand.

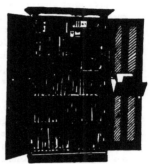

"Special Combination," for Letters, Invoices, Cards, Documents, Catalogues, Price Lists, etc.

STRONG POINTS.

Quick Reference.	No Waste Room.
Rapid Filing.	Labor Saving.

Adjustability.
(Keep the adjustable feature in mind.)

Combination.
(One cabinet can be arranged to do all work mentioned above.)

Will file anything, from a newspaper clipping to a 1000-page catalogue.

Shelf removed from Catalogue Cabinet, showing method of indexing.

NO WASTE ROOM.

The Shelves are Adjustable.

The Partitions are Adjustable.

The Files will expand from one inch to five inches, as case may require.

Special sizes and styles made to order.

Send for Catalogue showing different styles and sizes.

Section of Shelf, showing method of Adjustment and Indexing.

Our system is a radical departure from the old drawer system, enabling one to file data of all kinds in one cabinet.

CATALOGUE FREE.

A. J. WELLS MANUFACTURING CO.,

SYRACUSE, N. Y., U. S. A.

L'Annuaire du Commerce

...des Républiques Américaines.

Le Bureau des Républiques Américaines a publié en deux tomes l'Annuaire détaillé et authentique du commerce des Républiques Américaines et des dépendances européennes dans l'Amérique du Centre et du Sud et les Indes Occidentales. Ce travail est le plus complet et le plus exact qui ait jamais été publié par aucun des pays décrits dans cet ouvrage; il consiste de deux beaux volumes in-4 de 9 par 12 pouces de grandeur, et contenant 2,500 pages environ. Il se vend à cinq dollars ($5.00) le tome. Le premier volume a paru le 11 novembre 1897. Le second volume est maintenant prêt à être distribué.

La table des matières de l'Annuaire contient la liste d'informations suivantes:

1. Données authentiques relatives à la géographie, à l'industrie, au commerce et aux statistiques de chaque pays, accompagnées des dernières cartes.

2. Adresses et genre du commerce de près de cent mille maisons commerciales de l'Amérique Latine et des Iles Hawaï.

3. Noms de plus de dix mille manufacturiers, commerçants, expéditeurs et banquiers importants des Etats-Unis engagés dans le commerce extérieur, classés sous les désignations commerciales respectives.

4. Noms des organisations et associations commerciales des pays qui appartiennent à l'Union Internationale des Républiques Américaines.

5. Données utiles relatives aux compagnies de transport et aux routes commerciales par vois terrestres et maritimes; aux facilités de chemins de fer, de télégraphe et de câble; aux affaires maritimes, aux tarifs et aux douanes; aux brevets d'invention, aux marques de fabrique et à la propriété littéraire; aux patentes commerciales; aux règlements de passeports et de la poste.

Les informations ci-dessus indiquées ont été obtenues des sources les plus authentiques afin d'assurer leur exactitude et de suppléer aux exigences particulières dans la conduite du commerce extérieur de l'Hémisphère Occidental.

La coopération des commerçants en général des Etats-Unis est sollicitée avec empressement pour ce travail, qui est reconnu être, non seulement d'une utilité pratique, mais d'une importance internationale.

Des exemplaires pourront être examinés au Bureau des Républiques Américaines, No. 2 Jackson Place, Washington, D. C., où ils pourront être achetés sur demande seulement au Directeur. Le système de sollicitation d'abonnements, moyennant commission, fut supprimé le 28 février 1898. L'Annuaire ne renferme aucune annonce. La proposition d'insérer les noms d'abonnés dans la liste des maisons commerciales, étant en opposition au plan original, tracé par feu le Directeur du Bureau, M. Joseph P. Smith, qui proposait la publication gratuite des noms de maisons commerciales importantes, a été retirée. Les contrats conclus sous cet arrangement ont été remplis, mais le Bureau ne s'est pas considéré obligé à insérer des noms pour des considérations financières, et les noms sont donnés à titre de simple indication et sans aucune responsabilité pour le Bureau, quant à la condition des maisons de commerce.

FREDERIC EMORY,
Directeur.

Thom & Bayley,

NEW YORK CITY, U. S. A.,

Fabricantes y Exportadores.

SOMBREROS DE PIELES,
SOMBREROS DE LANA,
SOMBREROS DE PAJA,

para Hombres y Muchachos.

PRODUCCIÓN DE LAS FÁBRICAS, 2,500 DOCENAS POR DÍA.

Se venden solamente en su empaque original.

Sombreros de Pieles, 3 docenas en cada caja.
Sombreros de Lana, 6 docenas en cada caja.
Sombreros de Paja, de 3 á 30 docenas en cada caja.
Sombreros Suaves de Piel de Todos Colores, de $9 á $30 la docena.
Sombreros Duros de Pieles de Todos Colores, de $9 á $30 la docena.
Sombreros Suaves de Lana de Todos Colores, de $3.50 á $9 la docena.
Sombreros de Paja, de 75c. á $48 la docena.

Miembros de la Asociación Nacional de Fabricantes.

* Estos estilos son muy populares en los Estados Unidos.

•53.

•54.

•55.

ADVERTISEMENTS . .

•——IN THE MONTHLY BULLETIN.

The policy of the Bureau of the American Republics in regard to advertisements was announced in a circular letter under date of March 5, 1898, which was sent to advertisers in the MONTHLY BULLETIN, organized trade bodies, trade newspapers, and prominent business men. This letter was also published in the March (1898) issue of the BULLETIN.

The contract which had existed with an advertising agent was terminated February 28, 1898, since it had been found that the method of obtaining advertisements and subscriptions by means of agents on commission not only entailed an outlay largely in excess of the immediate returns, but brought the BULLETIN into conflict with the interests of trade newspapers and publishing houses of the United States.

Advertisements will be received as heretofore, but application for space must be made to the Director of the Bureau of the American Republics, Washington, D. C.

The object in accepting these advertisements is:

First. To further the interests of manufacturers and others in the various American Republics, by permitting them to use the columns of the MONTHLY BULLETIN for the purpose of calling attention to their business in the manner which seems to them most practical in an international publication of wide circulation in the Western Hemisphere.

Second. To obtain for the Bureau of the American Republics a revenue to increase its usefulness without entailing additional expense upon the Governments interested.

It is hoped the efforts of the Bureau will receive the support not only of firms seeking markets in Latin American countries, and of exporters in the latter who wish to sell their goods in the United States, but of all interests that would be benefited by an increase in the volume of Latin American trade.

THE ONLY MAKERS OF . . .
ALBANY GREASE.

No FREEZING OF OIL.   Self-acting.
MOST ECONOMICAL LUBRICANT ON THE MARKET.
ALBANY GREASE is the only safe lubricant for electrical machinery of all kinds and is used by all the large plants and every street railway in the U. S. A.
Where oil is used we can save you from one-fourth to one-half in the cost of lubrication. Catalogues, giving full information, sent free with samples.
The only lubricant recognized by the United States Government as the "STANDARD" of lubricants.

Albany Lubricating Compound & Cup Co.,
ADAM COOK'S SONS,
313 West Street, NEW YORK, U. S. A.
Address: "BUCOLIC," New York.

COMPAÑÍA DENOMINAD
REMINGTON MACHI
WILMINGTO , DELAWARE, E.

Fabricante de Maquinaria de Refrigeración por el de compresión de amoniaco.
SIMPLE, SEGURO, EFICAZ.
Constituyen una especialidad de esta Fábrica las completas de maquinaria de esta clase de pequeña dad.
Se tiene un surtido de estas máquinas cuya capac varía desde ½ de tonelada hasta 10 toneladas. Las tengan desde 11 hasta 60 toneladas se construirán se encarguen.
Se enviarán catálogos al que escriba pidiéndolos dirección arriba indicada.

ANUNCIOS . . . .

✳——— EN EL BOLETÍN MENSUAL.

La conducta que ha de observar la Oficina de las Repúblicas Americanas en cuanto á anuncios, fué explicada en una carta circular de fecha 5 de marzo de 1898, que fué remitida á los que se anuncian en el BOLETÍN MENSUAL, así como á las asociaciones de comercio, periódicos comerciales y comerciantes prominentes. La carta se publicó además en el número del BOLETÍN correspondiente al mes de marzo de 1898.

El contrato, que se había celebrado con un agente de anuncios, fué revocado en 28 de febrero de 1898, pues se encontró que el sistema de obtener anuncios y suscripciones por medio de agentes en comisión no sólo causaba gastos mucho mayores que el importe del producido inmediato, sino que dió márgen á conflictos entre el BOLETIN y los periódicos comerciales y casas editoriales de los Estados Unidos.

Se seguirá recibiendo anuncios como antes, pero la solicitud de espacio en el BOLETÍN deberá ser dirigida al Director de la Oficina de las Repúblicas Americanas, Washington, D. C.

Los propósitos en la aceptación de estos anuncios són :

Primero. Extender los intereses de los fabricantes y de otras personas en las varias Repúblicas de la América, facilitándoles las columnas del BOLETÍN MENSUAL al objeto de llamar la atención hácia sus negocios, de la manera que les parezca más práctica, en una publicación internacional de grande circulación en el Hemisferio Occidental.

Segundo. Obtener para la Oficina de las Repúblicas·Americanas una entrada con que aumentar su utilidad, sin causar gastos adicionales á los Gobiernos en ella representados.

Se espera que los esfuerzos de la Oficina recibirán el apoyo no sólo de las firmas interesadas en la adquisición de los mercados de los países de la América Latina y de los exportadores de aquel Continente que deseen vender sus géneros en los Estados Unidos, sino también de todos cuantos obtendrían beneficio con el aumento del comercio en la América Latina.

IMPRENTA BARATA

Prensas de mano de fácil manejo por hombre ó niño. Se hace fácil la composición por las plenas instrucciones impresas que se envían.

¡ Haced Vuestros Trabajos Tipográficos !

La Prensa de 5 x 8 pulgadas para imprimir tarjetas, circulares, etc., con 7 clases de tipos, tinta, etc., precio $40.

La Prensa de 10 x 15 pulgadas, con 10 clases de tipos, tintas, etc., $125, ó con más tipos, reglas, etc., para imprimir un periódico, $200.

La Prensa "O. K." Una rápida y moderna máquina rotatoria, la mejor del mundo. Rama 9 x 13 pulgadas. Precio, con 15 clases de tipos y todos los accesorios para una imprenta general, $200. Prensas mayores de estilo semejante, rama 11 x 17 pulgadas, $400, incluyendo equipo completo.

Cortadores para Papel y Cartón.—Máquinas de Mano, Cuchillas de Acero de 24½ pulgadas, $12.

PRENSAS DE CILINDRO

Para periódicos, libros, anuncios grandes, platina 29 x 43 pulgadas.

Precio, $500,

Incluyendo 300 libras de tipos pequeños, 25 clases de tipos surtidos, tintas, reglas, etc., para periódico. Todos nuestros equipos son completos y listos para emplearse en seguida.

Sírvanse pedir por correo el Catálogo Ilustrado de Prensas, Tipos, Papel, etc., dirigiéndose á nuestra fábrica cerca de New York.

ANNUNCIOS . . . .

—^{NO} BOLETIM MENSAL.

O systema que a Secretaria das Republicas Americanas adoptou relativo aos annuncios foi explicado n'uma circular em data de 5 de Março de 1898, a qual foi remettida aos annunciantes no BOLETIM MENSAL, assim como ás juntas commerciaes, periodicos commerciaes e negociantes proeminentes. Esta circular foi publicada tambem no numero do BOLETIM correspondente ao mez de Março de 1898.

O contracto que se tinha celebrado com um agente de annuncios, foi revogado a 28 de Fevereiro de 1898, por se ter visto que o methodo de obter annuncios e assignaturas por meio de agentes em commissão, não sómente causava gastos muito em excesso das receitas, mas tambem punha em conflicto os interesses das publicações commerciaes e casas editoras dos Estados Unidos com esta Secretaria.

Se seguirá recebendo annuncios como antes, mas a solicitação de espaço no BOLETIM deverá ser dirigida ao Director da Secretaria das Republicas Americanas, Washington, D. C.

O objecto de aceitar estes annuncios é:

Primeiro. Promover os interesses dos fabricantes e outras pessoas nas varias Republicas Americanas, facilitando-lhes as columnas do BOLETIM MENSAL afim de chamar a attenção para suas industrias do modo que lhes parecer mais pratico n'uma publicação internacional de grande circulação no Hemispherio Occidental.

Segundo. Obter para a Secretaria das Republicas Americanas uma renda com que augmentar sua utilidade sem causar gastos addicionaes aos governos interessados.

Espera-se que os esforços da Secretaria receberão o apoio não só das casas commerciaes que procuram mercados nos paizes latino-americanos e dos exportadores daquelle continente que desejem vender suas mercadorias nos Estados Unidos, mas de todos quantos obteriam beneficio com o desenvolvimento do commercio na América Latina.

GANANCIAS COMPUESTAS.

LA PRENSA "TRIUNFO."

Todo impresor debe comprender la manera como se hacen ganancias compuestas en el ramo de imprenta. De no comprender ésto claramente, no se entiende como es que una prensa que cuesta lo mismo que otra, es más valiosa que ella.

Tomemos, por ejemplo, la prensa **"TRIUNFO"** de Cottrell. Con las formas más pesadas trabaja con facilidad á la velocidad de 1,500 impresiones por hora. No hay otra prensa de la misma clase ó del mismo precio que haga más de 1,000 impresiones por hora.

A primera vista se diría que con la prensa **"TRIUNFO"** de Cottrell se gana 50 por ciento más dinero porque hizo un trabajo 50 por ciento mayor. Pero no es de esta manera que se hacen las ganancias compuestas. Pensemos por un momento. Todos los gastos deben salir de los primeros 1,000 ejemplares, sueldo del prensista, sueldo del que la alimenta, tinta, aceite, alquiler, calefacción, alumbrado, impuestos, aseguro, etc.

No hay, sin embargo, para que sacar los gastos de los 500 ejemplares adicionales. Estos son ganancia neta; el primer millar ha pagado todos los gastos.

Así, pues, si las ganancias en la prensa que imprime 1,000 ejemplares por hora es de 25 por ciento, quiere decir que bastaron 800 impresiones para pagar los gastos. Por consiguiente las ganancias en la prensa Cottrell, que hace 1,500 impresiones por hora, es de 87½ por ciento! Calcúlese!

Es ésta la razón porque la prensa **"TRIUNFO"** de Cottrell vale tanto. Su producción de 50 por ciento adicional no significa ganancias 50 por ciento más grandes, sino **250 por ciento más en las ganancias!**

Y esto no obstante, esta prensa no cuesta más que cualquiera otra. Solicítense nuestros Catálogos Ilustrados de estas prensas, en Español. Háganse los pedidos por conducto de casas comisionistas de responsabilidad.

C. B. COTTRELL & SONS CO.,
41 PARK ROW, NEW YORK, U. S. A.

Annonces . . . . .

*———— DANS LE Bulletin Mensuel.

Le système du Bureau des Républiques Américaines relativement aux annonces a été publié dans une lettre circulaire, datée du 5 mars 1898, et envoyée à ceux qui annoncent dans le BULLETIN MENSUEL, aux organisations commerciales, aux journaux commerciaux et aux commerçants importants. Cette lettre a été publiée aussi dans l'édition du BULLETIN pour le mois de mars 1898.

Le contrat conclu avec un agent d'annonces a pris fin le 28 février 1898, parce qu'on a trouvé que le système de la sollicitation d'annonces et d'abonnements par le moyen d'agents commissionnaires entrainait, non seulement à une dépense bien au-dessus des revenus, mais aussi parce qu'il mettait le Bureau en conflit avec les intérêts des journaux de commerce et des maisons de publication des Etats-Unis.

Les annonces seront reçues comme autrefois, mais les demandes de place devront être adressées au Directeur du Bureau des Républiques Américaines, Washington, D. C.

Les raisons pour l'insertion d'annonces dans le BULLETIN sont les suivantes :

1º. Servir les intérêts des manufacturiers et autres dans les différentes Républiques Américaines, en leur permettant de se servir des colonnes du BULLETIN MENSUEL pour attirer l'attention sur leur commerce, selon la manière qui leur semble la meilleure, dans une publication internationale ayant une grande circulation dans l'Hémisphère Occidental.

2º. Augmenter les revenus du Bureau des Républiques Américaines, afin d'accroître son utilité sans entraîner à des dépenses additionnelles les gouvernements intéressés.

Il est à espérer que les efforts du Bureau recevront le soutien, non seulement des maisons cherchant des débouchés dans les contrées de l'Amérique Latine, et de tous les exportateurs dans ses dernières qui désirent vendre leurs marchandises aux Etats-Unis, mais de tous les intérêts qui doivent profiter d'une augmentation dans le volume du commerce latin américain.

 **CAÑONES** **N**

DE TIRO R/

GRUESO CA

CON MONTAJES PARA TODO GÉNERO DE

MUNICIONES DE TODA CLASE. . . . .

***

DEPARTAMENTO COMERCI

WEIGHTS AND MEASURES.

The following table gives the chief weights and measures in commercial use in Mexico and the Republics of Central and South America, and their equivalents in the United States:

Denomination.	Where used.	United States equivalents.
Are	Metric	0.02471 acre.
Arobe	Paraguay	25 pounds.
Arroba (dry)	Argentine Republic	25.3175 pounds.
Do	Brazil	32.38 pounds.
Do	Cuba	25.3664 pounds.
Do	Venezuela	25.4024 pounds.
Arroba (liquid)	Cuba and Venezuela	4.263 gallons.
Barril	Argentine Republic and Mexico	20.0787 gallons.
Carga	Mexico and Salvador	300 pounds.
Centavo	Central America	4.2631 gallons.
Cuadra	Argentine Republic	4.2 acres.
Do	Paraguay	78.9 yards.
Do	Paraguay (square)	8.077 square feet.
Do	Uruguay	2 acres (nearly).
Cubic meter	Metric	35.3 cubic feet.
Fanega (dry)	Central America	1.5745 bushels.
Do	Chile	2.575 bushels.
Do	Cuba	1.599 bushels.
Do	Mexico	1.54728 bushels.
Do	Uruguay (double)	7.776 bushels.
Do	Uruguay (single)	3.888 bushels.
Do	Venezuela	1.599 bushels.
Frasco	Argentine Republic	2.5096 quarts.
Do	Mexico	2.5 quarts.
Gram	Metric	15.432 grains.
Hectare	do	2.471 acres.
Hectoliter (dry)	do	2.838 bushels.
Hectoliter (liquid)	do	26.417 gallons.
Kilogram (kilo)	do	2.2046 pounds.
Kilometer	do	0.621376 mile.
League (land)	Paraguay	4,633 acres.
Libra	Argentine Republic	1.0127 pounds.
Do	Central America	1.043 pounds.
Do	Chile	1.014 pounds.
Do	Cuba	1.0161 pounds.
Do	Mexico	1.01465 pounds.
Do	Peru	1.0143 pounds.
Do	Uruguay	1.0143 pounds.
Do	Venezuela	1.0161 pounds.
Liter	Metric	1.0567 quarts.
Livre	Guiana	1.0791 pounds.
Manzana	Costa Rica	1.5-6 acres.
Marc	Bolivia	0.507 pound.
Meter	Metric	39.37 inches.
Pie	Argentine Republic	0.9478 foot.
Quintal	do	101.42 pounds.
Do	Brazil	130.06 pounds.
Do	Chile, Mexico, and Peru	101.61 pounds.
Do	Paraguay	100 pounds.
Do. (metric)	Metric	220.46 pounds.
Suerte	Uruguay	2,700 cuadras (*see* Cuadra).
Vara	Argentine Republic	34.1208 inches.
Do	Central America	38.874 inches.
Do	Chile and Peru	33.367 inches.
Do	Cuba	33.384 inches.
Do	Mexico	33 inches.
Do	Paraguay	34 inches.
Do	Venezuela	33.384 inches.

lii   BUREAU OF THE AMERICAN

LAS BALANZAS DE TORSIÓN,

construidas según un sistema patentado, son las mejores balanzas que hay para pesar con exactitud. Como no tienen filo de ninguna clase nunca son inexactas.

Siempre son sensibles y exactas.

Se emplean en número enorme por los fabricantes, droguistas, especieros, etc. Solicítese nuestro Catálogo profusamente ilustrado.

92 Reade St.,

The Springer Torsion Balance Co., New York, U. S. A.

LA "BRADBURY"

Máquina remendadora de calzado.

Esta máquina sirve para toda clase de remiendos en el calzado. Es la máquina más completa y expedita que se fabrica. Rapidez, buen trabajo y fácil manejo.

FABRICADA POR

DUNLAP MACHINERY CO.,
(LIMITED)

9 SPRUCE STREET, NEW YORK, U. S. A.

R. R. FOGEL & CO.,

177 & 179 Broadway, New York, U. S. A.

Fabricantes de

JOYERÍA

DE TODAS CLASES.

Únicos Agentes de los **RELOJES** "American Waltham," "Sol" y "Cronómetro Victoria." Útiles y Herramientas para Relojeros. Lentes y Espejuelos.

Se enviarán Catálogos Ilustrados, en castellano á los del giro.

NIAGARA MACHINE & TOOL WORKS,

Buffalo, N. Y., U. S. A.

FABRICANTE DE

HERRAMIENTAS
Y MÁQUINAS

Para Trabajadores de Metal en Hojas.

Herramientas para Hojalatero, Cizallas, Prensas y Discos.

Aparatos Completos para hacer Artículos de Hoja de Lata, Latas y otros Artículos de Metal en Hoja.

Se envía el Catálogo

FABRICANTES DE

LÁMPARAS Y LINTERNAS TUBULAR
DECHADOS EN SU CLASE.

Steam Gauge and Lantern

MANUFACTURERS

Standard Tubular Lamps and Lante

SYRACUSE, N. Y., U. S. A.

GLOBE STREET LAMP.
No. 3 Burner.   3-Inch
Price, $3.00 Each.

VICTOR LANTERN.
No. 1 Burner.   No. 0 Glo
Price, $3.85 per Dozen.

BUCKEYE SIDE AND DASH LAM
Bull's-Eye Lens.   Price, $5.65 per Dozen.

IRONCLAD RAILROAD LANTERN
Price, $5.00 per Dozen.

PUBLICATIONS.

The Bureau of the American Republics was established as the official agency of the Republics of Central and South America, Mexico, and the United States for the collection and prompt distribution of commercial information, and to foster inter-trade relations in these countries. In pursuance of this purpose the Bureau has published for distribution a number of Bulletins, Handbooks, Reports, Codes of Commercial Nomenclature (three large volumes), and a Commercial Directory of the American Republics, including the European dependencies in Central and South America and the West Indies—two handsome quarto volumes of about 2,500 pages.

In addition to the general information embraced in the Handbooks, etc., each issue of the Monthly Bulletin, a magazine of 300 pages, contains special current articles and items of interest relating to the various countries represented by the Bureau. It has been greatly enlarged and improved during the current year.

Payment is required to be made in cash, money orders, or by bank drafts on banks in New York City or Washington, D. C., payable to the order of the BUREAU OF THE AMERICAN REPUBLICS. *Individual checks on banks located outside of New York or Washington, or postage stamps, can not be accepted.*

PRICE LIST OF PUBLICATIONS.

No.		Price.
3	Patent and Trademark Laws of America	$0.05
4	Money, Weights, and Measures of the American Republics	.05
6	Foreign Commerce of the American Republics	.10
7	Handbook of Brazil. (Out of print. Undergoing revision.)	
9	Handbook of Mexico. (Out of print. Undergoing revision.)	
31	Handbook of Costa Rica. (Out of print. Undergoing revision.)	
33	Handbook of Colombia. (Out of print. Undergoing revision.)	
34	Handbook of Venezuela. (Out of print. Undergoing revision.)	
42	Newspaper Directory of Latin-America. (See Bulletin No. 90.)	
44	Import Duties of the United States (1890). (See also Vol. 5, Part 3, Reprints of Publications)	.05
51	Handbook of Nicaragua. (See also Vol. 3, Reprints of Publications)	.35
52	Handbook of Santo Domingo. (See also Vol. 2, Reprints of Publications)	.35
54	Handbook of Paraguay. (See also Vol. 2, Reprints of Publications)	.30
55	Handbook of Bolivia. (See also Vol. 4, Reprints of Publications)	.40
57	Handbook of Honduras. (See also Vol. 3, Reprints of Publications)	.35
58	Handbook of Salvador. (See also Vol. 3, Reprints of Publications)	.35
60	Handbook of Peru. (See also Vol. 4, Reprints of Publications)	.25
61	Handbook of Uruguay. (See also Vol. 3, Reprints of Publications)	.35
62	Handbook of Haiti. (See also Vol. 2, Reprints of Publications)	.35
63	How Markets of Latin-America may be Reached	.30
64	Handbook of Ecuador. (See also Vol. 4, Reprints of Publications)	.35
65	Handbook of the Spanish Colonies. (In course of preparation.)	
66	Handbook of the British Colonies. (In course of preparation.)	
67	Handbook of the Argentine Republic. (See also Vol. 2, Reprints of Publications)	.35
68	Handbook of Guatemala. (Revised edition)	.25
70	Import Duties of Peru (1890)	.65
71	United States Tariff Act of 1894	.05
75	Import Duties of United States, 1897 (English)	.10
76	Import Duties of United States, 1897 (Spanish)	.10
77	Import Duties of United States, 1897 (Portuguese)	.10
78	Import Duties of United States, 1897 (French)	.10

BUFFALO DENTAL MANUFACTURING CO.

587 and 589 Main Street,
Corner of Chippewa,
BUFFALO, N. Y., U. S. A.

Fabricantes de y Comerciantes en

ARTÍCULOS DE TODAS CLASES . . .

. . . . . . PARA DENTISTAS.

LOS QUE PRIMERO FABRICARON

VULCANIZADORES PARA . . . . .

DENTISTAS Y ORIFICADORES . .

AUTOMATICOS . . . .

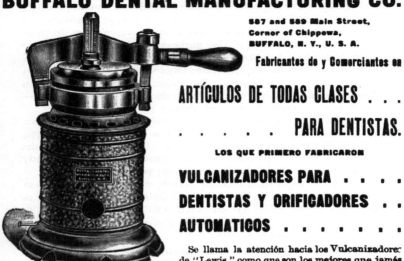

El Vulcanizador de "Lewis" con palanca atra-
vesada y aparato para calentar con gas.
Patentado el 2 de octubre de 1894.

Se llama la atención hacia los Vulcanizadores
de "Lewis," como que son los mejores que jamás
se han fabricado.

Se envían catálogos al que los pida. Se solicita
correspondencia.

PUBLICATIONS NOT NUMBERED.

REPRINTS OF PUBLICATIONS BOUND TOGETHER IN PAPER.

NOTE.—The publications of this Bureau are sent free of postage throughout the United States, Canada, Costa Rica, Ecuador, Guatemala, Haiti, Honduras, Mexico, Nicaragua, and Venezuela, and in these countries the Bulletin will be furnished to subscribers at $2.00 per annum.

FREDERIC EMORY,

Director.

JEFFREY

Cadenas de Acero ú Otras
Especiales, con Rodillos

— PARA —

ELEVADORES y CONDUCTORES

De Toda Clase de Materias, tales como

Caña de Azúcar, Bagazo, Granos,
Café, Carbón, Minerales,
Barriles, Cajas,
Tozas, Madera, Desperdicios, etc.

Maquinaria para Minas de Carbón.

Conductores
con Cable de
Alambre

Para Distancias Largas y Cortas.

THE JEFFREY MFG. CO.,
Columbus, Ohio, U.S.A.

THE IOWA FARMING TOOL COMPANY, MAKERS.

FREE
CATALOGUE
ON
APPLICATON.   FORT MADISON, IOWA, U.S.A.

La COMPAÑÍA de HERRAMIENTAS
PARA AGRICULTORES de IOWA, F

FORT MADISON, IOWA, U

Horquillas, Azadas, Se en
Rastrillos, Etc.   que

MARCA DE
GOND
FÁBRICA.

Las Baterías de Circuito
son las Primeras del

Medalla de oro en Paris,
Primer premio en Chicago.

Las Únicas Pilas Legítil
Leclanché y la Mejor
Todas las Baterías de
Circuito Abierto.

Pidanse Circulares y Listas de Precios.

THE LECLANCHÉ BATTERY COMP

111 to 117 East 131st Street, NEW YORK, U.S.

UTICA STEAM COTTON MILLS—INCORPORATED 1848.

También se fabrica en los mismos establecimientos una clase MUY FINA y al mismo tiempo DE MUCHO CUERPO de géneros blanqueados de hacer CAMISAS. Estos géneros son de calidad superior, y se llama particularmente hacia ellos la atención de todos. Además de llevar el nombre del establecimiento en que se fabrican, se les designa también con los de "NONPAREILS," "ACME" y "ONE, TWO, THREE."

LAWRENCE, TAYLOR & CO., Agentes para la venta, New York, E. U. de A.

FABRICAS DE TECIDOS DE ALGODÃO DENOMINADAS
"THE UTICA STEAM COTTON MILLS" e
"MOHAWK VALLEY COTTON MILLS."

AS FAZENDAS PARA LENÇÓES E CAMISAS fabricadas nos estabelecimentos acima ditos recommendão-se em alto grao pelo sen grande peso, pela finura e perfeição de sen fio, e a uniformidade do tecido. Resulta disto, como podem attestal-o os numerósos consumidores que têm con hecido e apreciado estas fazendas, que são SUPERIORES a todas as demais do mercado por razão de sua CONTEXTURA e DURACAO.

MOHAWK VALLEY MILLS.

Fabrica-se tambem nos mesmos estabelecimentos uma sorte de fazendas branqueadas FINISSIMAS, e no mesmo tempo DE MUITO CORPO, para CAMISAS. Estas fazendas são de qualidade superior, e chamase a ellas particularmente a attenção do publica. Alem de se chamar pelo nome do estabelecimento em que se fabricão, designão-se tambem pelos nomes de "NONPAREILS," "ACME" e "ONE, TWO, THREE."

LAWRENCE, TAYLOR & CO., Agentes o para a venda, New York, E. U. de A.

ENGLISH AND SPANISH LIST OF ARTICLES ADVERTISED.

Soportes Colgantes para Árboles de Trasmision

De Acero y de Forma
Tubular; Lubricación Cir-
cular; de Ajuste Automá-
tico. Estos soportes son fuertes
y firmes, pero al mismo tiempo
ligeros. Las piezas son permutables; tienen
chumaceras largas de metal de Babbitt;
abrazaderas dobles; se abren en forma de
yugo y tienen bases perfectamente planas;
pueden usarse en forma de poste, ó aplicarse á la pared, ó ponerse en el suelo. Son
de ajuste automático á manera de la arti-
culación de bola y encastre. Se pueden
montar de diversos modos para usarse en
todas direcciones. Se tiene siempre un surtido de todos los tamaños principales. Se
desea establecer correspondencia con todas
aquellas personas que emplean fuerza motriz, así como con
las que negocian en maquinaria y sus accesorios.
T. C. DILL MACHINE CO. (legalmente constituida),
2756 á 2800 Mascher St., Philadelphia, Pa., U. S. A.

THE GENESE
ROAD CA
BEST
TOP AND OPEN C
ON EARTH.
Rides as Easy as a Buggy
SALE. Free
culars for A

D. F. SARG
& SO
GENESE
Henry C
gastos á bord
ork.

LA NUEVA
LÁMPARA
"ROCHESTER"
Cinco Millones en Uso.
COMPAÑÍA DENOMINADA:
THE
ROCHESTER LAMP CO.
NEW YORK, U. S. A.

SEMBRADERA Á VOLEO DE PEA
MEJORADA SOBRE LA DE CAHOON.

150,000 están en
Siembra toda clase de
y semillas de yerba
pina.
Hace el trabajo de 5 ho
y economiza una t
parte de las semillas
Es duradera y no pue
componerse. Cual
puede manejarla.

PRECIO: $30 LA DOC
Puesta á bordo en New

Se solicitan pedido
medio de cualquie
comisionista respon

GOODELL COMPANY, Antrim, N. H., U. S.

ENGLISH AND SPANISH LIST OF ARTICLES ADVERTISED.

PAGE.

ENGLISH AND SPANISH LIST OF ARTICLES ADVERTISED.

ENGLISH AND SPANISH LIST OF ARTICLES ADVERTISED.

CONFITES, CARAMELOS, CHOCOLATES,
LOS MEJORES DEL MUNDO.

Solicitamos correspondencia con aquellas personas que
deseen articulos de primera calidad.

Quaker City Chocolate and Confectionery Co.,
PHILADELPHIA, PA., U. S. A.

DR. W. F. DAVENPORT,
DENTIST,
NO. 503 FIFTH AVENUE,
NEW YORK.

Office Hours,
9 a. m. to 5 p. m.

ENGLISH AND SPANISH LIST OF ARTICLES ADVERTISED.

A. FRENCH, Presidente.
J. E. FRENCH, Vicepresidente.
GEO. W. MORRIS, Admor. Gral.
D. C. NOBLE, Srio. y Tesorero.
P. N. FRENCH, Supte. Gral.

A. FRENCH SPRING CO.,
FABRICANTES DE

RESORTES
DE TODA CLASE,

PITTSBURG, PA., U. S. A.
Sucur- {New York, 109 Boreel Building.
sales:- {Chicago, 1414 Fisher Building.
         {St. Louis, 505 Union Trust Bldg.

BROWN'S BRONCHIAL TROCHES

BROW OCHES." A world-renowned remedy for COUGHS, COLDS, BRONCHITIS, Asthma, Catarrh, the *Hacking Cough* in Consumption, and numerous affections of the THROAT, giving *immediate relief.* They have received the sanction of physicians generally and testimonials from eminent men throughout the world. All dealers in medicines and proprietary goods can recommend them with confidence. Sold only in boxes or bottles, with *facsimile* of the proprietors on outside wrapper of the package.
Foreign Depot: THE ANGLO-AMERICAN DRUG CO. (Ltd.), LONDON, ENGLAND.
JOHN I. BROWN & SON, PROPRIETORS, BOSTON, MASS., U. S. A.

FOR COUGHS AND COLDS

"Tablillas Bronquiales de Brown." Un medicamento de fama universal para la Tos, os Resfriados, la Bronquitis, el Asma, el Catarro, la Tos de la Tisis y numerosas afecciones de la garganta. Producen un alivio amediato. Han sido aprobadas por los médicos en general y hombres notables en todo el mundo han certificado sus buenos factos. Todos los que trafican en medicinas y en preparaciones de patente pueden recomendarlas con toda confianza. Solamente e venden en cajas ó botellas con el facsímile de los propietarios en la parte exterior del paquete.
JOHN I. BROWN & SON, PROPIETARIOS, BOSTON, MASS.,U. S. A.
Depósito Extranjero: THE ANGLO-AMERICAN DRUG CO. (Ltd.), LONDON, ENGLAND.

TURBINAS
Y
MÁQUINAS
DE
VAPOR.

CAÍDAS DE 3 Á 2000 PIES.
35 años de experiencia nos ponen en capacidad de construir ruedas de la mayor excelencia y adaptadas á toda especie de aplicaciones.

MÁQUINAS Y CALDERAS
Automáticos y Sencillas, Válvulas Corredizas.
Todas las obras construídas con los mejores materiales, con partes de remuda. Folletos de las ruedas de agua ó de las máquinas se reparten y remiten gratis. Dígasenos la especie de aplicación que se desea.
JAMES LEFFEL & CO. Sprin field, Ohio, E. U. de A.

EDISON PHONOGRAPH AGENCY, Edison Building,
New York, N. Y., U. S. A.
F. M. PRESCOTT Manager.

FONÓGRAFO DE EDISON para
Familias. Graba y Raspa el Cilin-
dro y reproduce los Sonidos.
Mueve 3 cilindros con solo
darle cuerda una sola vez.

Precio, - - $20,
oro americano.

Cilindros de música,
50 centavos cada uno,
$5 por docena.
Pídanse por escrito ca-
tálogos en inglés y en
español, y clave telegrá-
fica impresa que compren-
den todos los productos de
EDISON, tal como FONÓ-

New Edison
Standard
Phonograph

As per illustration,
records, reproduces,
and shaves cylinders;
operates 3 cylinders
with one winding of
the spring.

Price, $20.
Musical Records, 50
cents each; $5 per

Níquel Maleable,

PROYECTILES, PLANCHAS, LINGOTES, BARRAS, LÁMINAS, ALAMBRE.

Las mejores clases para Anodos,
Plata Alemana y Acero-Níquel.

ORFORD COPPER CO.,
37 WALL STREET,
NEW YORK, N. Y., U. S. A.

THE CANADIAN COPPER CO.,
12 WADE BUILDING,
CLEVELAND, OHIO, U. S. A.

PANCOAST VENTILATORS.

Handsome, Strong, Durable, Efficient.

Leads them all in giving the Best of Ventilation.

Houses, Mills, Factories, School Houses, Churches, Refineries, and Foundries use them with perfect results. Architects in preparing plans for buildings should always specify the PANCOAST VENTILATOR. Send for testimonials and discounts. Made in all sizes from two inches to ten feet, and guaranteed absolutely storm proof.

Broken View.

Manufactured and sold by

PANCOAST VENTILATOR CO., Inc.

Main Office, 316 Philadelphia Bourse, PHILA., PA.

SEMBRADERA "CROWN."

Armazón de hierro.   Tolva, 14 por 16 piés.

Liviana, fuerte, duradera.   La atmósfera no afecta al agitador de alambre como afectaría á uno de cuerda. Rueda de hierro de 30 pulgadas de diámetro, con canto ancho hecho como el de las ruedas de bicicleta.

SEMBRADERA "CROWN" PARA HACER SURCOS, etc.—Las dos ruedas son motrices. No hay cambio de engranajes. Es el mejor distribuidor de abono que se ha hecho jamás.

Alimentador de fuerza eficaz para granos, semillas de yerba y abonos.

Enviese por circulares y condiciones á

CROWN MFG. CO., Phelps, N. Y., U. S.

Maquinaria para Hacer Cajas de Cartón.

Máquina para eforzar las esquinas de las cajas.

KNOWLTON & BEACH,

ROCHESTER, N. Y., U. S A.,

Fabrican maquinaria completa perfeccionada para hacer Cajas de Cartón con la cual se economiza trabajo. Dicha maquinaria comprende Máquinas para Cortar, Rayar, Formar y Cubrir, y para Reforzar las Esquinas de las Cajas.

Pídanse Catálogos

American Railway Supply Co.

24 PARK PLACE, NEW YORK,

FABRICANTES DE

CHEQUES PARA EQUIPAJE,
ARMARIOS PARA BILLETES,
SACABOCADOS y FECHADORES para los mismos.

Únicos fabricantes del **Fechador de Billetes locales con tipo de acero de Jones,** y éste estampa la fecha en relieve con el tipo. No se necesitan ni tinta ni cinta.

KEYSTONE DRY PLATE AND FILM WORKS,

Wayne Junction, Philadelphia, Pa., U. S. A.

JOHN CARBUTT, Propietario.

Fabricante de

PLANCHAS SECAS Y PELÍCULAS . .
FOTOGRÁFICAS DE CELULOIDE . . .

para uso en la Fotografía.

Tomado en una Plancha Ortocromática de Carbutt por Alois Beer, Fotógrafo del Emperador de Austria.

La Película en forma de cinta, positiva y negativa, llamada Eureka, para Máquinas en que se ven figuras animadas. . . . .
Se solicita correspondencia.

Se llama la atención á las Planchas y Películas fabricadas especialmente para uso en la América del Sur.

RANDOLPH & CLOWES,

Waterbury, Conn., U. S. A.

Tubos de Cobre Puro
Estirado sin Costuras.

Diámetro, de $\frac{1}{8}$ de pulgada á 32 pulgadas.

Tubos de Latón sin Costura.

Diámetro, de $\frac{1}{8}$ de pulgada á 32 pulgadas.

Canales, Molduras y Tubos de Acero Bronceado, Bronce ó Cobre.

Bronce en Hojas y Metal Amarillo.

Varillas de Bronce.

Especialidades de Plomeros.

Calderas de Cobre para Fogones de los Hermanos Brown.

ENGLISH AND SPANISH LIST OF ARTICLES ADVERTISED.

Facsimile del paquete.

Preparado
exclusivamente por

===== THE =====

National Starch Mfg. Co.,

Sucesora de la

GLEN COVE MFG. CO. (Los Sres. Duryea).

LA MAIZENA es empacada en cajas de 40 y 20 libras, en paquetes de 1. ½ y ¼ de libra, y puede obtenerse por medio de todas las casas importadoras de la América Central y del Sur, así como por conducto de todas las exportadoras de los Estas Unidos.

ENGLISH AND SPANISH LIST OF ARTICLES ADVERTISE

CHRISTOPHER CUNNINGHAM & SON,
FÁBRICA DE CALDERAS DE VAPOR "NOVELTY.
OFICINA Y TALLERES:
BROOKLYN. Greenpoint Avenue and Newtown Creek. **NEW YOR**
Fabricantes de Calderas de Vapor Marinas y Fijas, Cubas de Mezcla, Tinas
Cervecero de Fondo Postizo, Pailas y Resfriaderas para Azúcar, Alambiques
Refinar Petróleo, Tanques para Aceite, Melaza y Agua.
Se dedica especial atención para complacer al tráfico de exportación.

West Virginia Pulp and Paper Co

309 Broadway, New York.

FABRICANTES DE

PULPA CON EL USO DE SULFITOS, BLANQUEADA Y SIN BLANQUEAR

PAPEL PARA LITOGRAFÍA Y SATINADO
DE SUPERIOR CALIDAD PARA LIBROS,
HECHO CON PERFECCIÓN POR
MÁQUINAS DE PRIMERA CLASE.
PAPEL DE FIBRA PARA ENVOLVER.

LA FÁBRICA PUEDE HACER 150 TONELADAS AL DÍA

NIVE
Patentado
COO

En Madera y en Hierro. | Se despachan pedidos || fabricad

The Rock Island Plow Co.

ROCK ISLAND, ILL., U. S. A.

Fabricantes en gran escala de Instrumentos de Agricultura de todas clases, incluyendo

Arados de Acero,

Rastros de Disco con Sembradoras,

Arados con Asiento,

Arados

Arados de Fundición Enfriada,

Múltiples

DE TODOS TAMAÑOS Y MODELOS.

Se envían los precios al que los pida.

Los efectos se entregan embalados á bordo de los navíos en New York, libres de gastos.

Comprendemos muy bien las necesidades del comercio extranjero.

SE SOLICITA CORRESPONDENCIA.

Fabricantes de Mostruarios de todas clases. Mostradores Patentados de Heurich, de respaldo que se abre en secciones y de respaldo inclinado. Mostradores de vidrio desarmados, especialidad para la exportación. Solicítese el Catálogo Ilustrado de la

EXHIBITION SHOW CASE CO.,
ERIE, PA., U. S. A.

F. E. BRANDIS, SONS & CO.,
FABRICANTES DE
Instrumentos para Ingenieros y Agrimensores,
814 Gates Avenue, Borough of Brooklyn,
NEW YORK, N. Y., U. S. A.

Extracto del "U. S. Government Advertiser," 8 de setiembre de 1887: El Cuerpo de Ingenieros de los Estados Unidos en Willets Point, dirigió una invitación á los fabricantes de instrumentos para que presentaran muestras de los mismos, y *once fabricantes* la aceptaron. Tres peritos fueron designados para que hicieran cuidadosamente una lista de dichas muestras y el resultado fué que se escogieron los instrumentos hechos por Mr. F. E. BRANDIS, 55 Fulton Street, New York, *por ser muy ligeros, exactos en sumo grado y de un trabajo excelente.*

PELÍCULAS Y MÁQUINAS DE
TAMBIÉN FONÓGRAFOS Y TODA CLASE DE MÁQ

KINETOSCOPIO PROYECTOR DE

(Edison Projecting Kinetoscope.

Con este aparato y
las películas de Edi-
son y Lumiere se
pueden presentar
figuras de tamaño
natural y reproducir
los movimientos y,
en general, todos los
caractéres distin
tivos de vitalidad,
ofreciendo así el
espectáculo más in-
teresante y maravi-
lloso.

Nuestro surtido de
artículos para exhibi-
ción es el más com-
pleto. Somos los que
trafican en mayor
escala en el mundo
en máquinas de pro-
yección y películas,
duplicados inútiles.

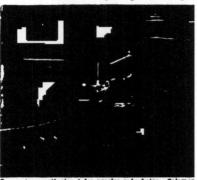

Los mejores artículos á los precios más bajos. Solamen
Las películas para el Drama de la Pasión, están ya terminad

MAGUIRE & BAUCUS, 44 F
(LIMITED.) NE\

4 & 5 WARWICK COURT W. C., LONDON, ENGLAND.

Aparatos para Bucear.
Materiales para Bomberos.

A. J. MORSE & SON.

DIVING APPARATUS

140

CONGRESS ST. BOSTON.

140 Congress Street, Boston, Mass., U. S. A.

J. F. CAVAGNARO,
216 Centre St., New York, U.S.A.
Fabricante de la Maquinaria Mejorada
la mas Adelantada de hacer

Fideos, Macarrones, Pastas de Sopa
y demas pastas de cualquiera clase.

Fabricamos máquinas de hacer pasta de toda clase—como prensas, amasadoras, mezcla-tiras, cortadoras—y de varios tamaños, desde las pequeñas movidas por mano ó fuerza mecanica, hasta las mayores movidas por motor de magrv, de agua, de vapor, ó electrico.

Nuestras máquinas incluyen todos los últimos adelantos conocidos en Europa como en America. Están construidas en las mejores condiciones, bajo todo concepto, se pueden desarmar para cargar á lomo de mulo. Con cada máquina se manden indices mas detallados para armar y operarse.

Suministramos presupuestos para máquinas sueltas, o plantas completas, hasta con fuerza motriz. Máquinas para acabar, pulir, estinar y estampar tejidos de seda, y maquinaria especial para cualquier uso.

Catálogo ilustrado se manda gratis, con lista de precios, á quien lo pida.

ENGLISH AND SPANISH LIST OF ART

YO CURO LA SORDERA y los ruidos de o
Tubulares de P
fectamente restituye el oído, lo mismo que las gafas y esp
los demás medios y remedios han sido infructuosos. El pacien
colocados **no se notan desde el exterior.** Envío inst
tratamiento propios de cada caso particular. Los pedi
comisionistas ó por las compañías de expresos. El precio es de
en la extranjera. Al hacer un pedido, dígase la edad, el sexo,
alrededor de la cabeza. Téngase cuidado en solicitar los **Tim
way, New York ;** y no se admitan otros en su lugar; pues so
eficaz de su clase para curar la sordera. No tengo agentes; po
folleto ilustrado de pruebas, **gratis.** Dirección: F. HISC

H. M. NEWHAL

ENGLISH AND SPANISH LIST OF ARTICLES ADVERTISED.

ENGLISH AND SPANISH LIST OF ARTICLES ADVERTISED.

Herman Kohlbusch, Sr.

Establecido en 1859.

Fabricante de Balanzas Finas y Pesos para todos los usos que requieran la exactitud.

59 Nassau Street,
Corner Maiden Lane,
New York.

Pidase el Catálogo.

BAY STATE CUT SOLE CO.

Suelas Cortadas para Fabricantes de Zapatos y Zapateros,

del Mejor Cuero Preparado en Curtidurias de la "Unión."

**No. 180 Purchase Street,
BOSTON, MASS., U. S. A.**

GOLD PENS

MABIE, TODD & BARD,

FABRICANTES DE LAS

Plumas "Swan,"

con Depósito de Tinta;

Y FABRICANTES DE

Plumas de Oro, Lápices, etc.

**130 Fulton Street,
New York, U. S. A.**

Se remite la Lista de Precios al que la pida.

ADVERTISING RATES.

MONTHLY BULLETIN

OF THE

BUREAU OF THE AMERICAN REPUBLICS,

INTERNATIONAL UNION OF AMERICAN REPUBLICS.

1 page	8 x 5 inches	- - -	$50.00 per month.	Net,	$450.00 per annum.
$\frac{1}{2}$ "	4 x 5 or 8 x 2$\frac{1}{2}$ inches	30.00 " "		"	270 00 " "
$\frac{1}{4}$ "	2 x 5 " 4 x 2$\frac{1}{2}$ "	20.00 " "		"	180.00 " "
$\frac{1}{8}$ "	1 x 5 " 2 x 2$\frac{1}{2}$ "	10.00 " "		"	90.00 " "
*$\frac{1}{16}$ "	$\frac{1}{2}$ x 5 " 1 x 2$\frac{1}{2}$ "	5.00 " "		"	45.00 " "

* Professional Cards.

Inside Covers and Pages facing beginning and ending of text are double above rates. Other pages facing reading matter are one and one-half above rates. Outside Back Cover Page is treble above rates. "Three Months' Contracts" are entitled to 10 per cent, "Six Months' Contracts" to 15 per cent, and "Annual Contracts" to 25 per cent discounts. In the above per annum column the 25 per cent discount is deducted.

ADDRESS

ADVERTISING DEPARTMENT,

BUREAU OF THE AMERICAN REPUBLICS,

WASHINGTON, D. C.

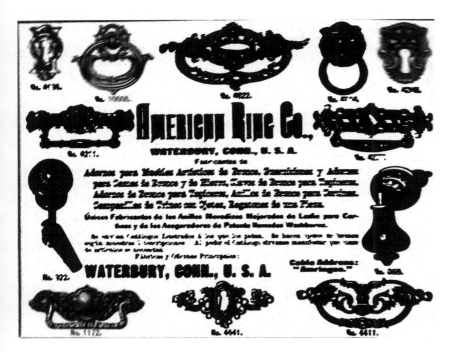

VALUE OF AMERICAN COINS.

The following table shows the value, in United States gold, of coins representing the monetary units of the Central and South American Republics and Mexico, estimated quarterly by the Director of the United States Mint, in pursuance of act of Congress:

ESTIMATE OCTOBER 1, 1898.

Countries.	Standard.	Unit.	Value in U. S. gold or silver.	Coins.
ARGENTINE REPUBLIC.	Gold and silver.	Peso	$0.965*	Gold—Argentine ($4.824) and ½ Argentine. Silver—Peso and divisions.
BOLIVIA	Silver	Boliviano	.436	Silver—Boliviano and divisions.
BRAZIL	Gold	Milreis	.546*	Gold—5, 10, and 20 milreis. Silver—½, 1, and 2 milreis.
CENTRAL AMERICAN STATES— Costa Rica	Gold	Colon	.465	Gold—2, 5, 10, and 20 colons ($9.307). Silver—5, 10, 25, and 50 centimos.
Guatemala Honduras Nicaragua Salvador	Silver	Peso	.436	Silver—Peso and divisions.
CHILE	Gold	Peso	.365	Gold—Escudo ($1.825), doubloon ($3.650), condor ($7.300). Silver—Peso and divisions.
COLOMBIA	Silver	Peso	.436	Gold—Condor ($9.647) and double condor. Silver—Peso and divisions.
CUBA	Gold and silver.	Peso	.926*	Gold—Centen ($5.017). Silver—Peso.
ECUADOR	Silver	Sucre	.436	Gold—Condor ($9.647) and double condor. Silver—Sucre and divisions.
HAITI	Gold and silver.	Gourde	.965	Silver—Gourde.
MEXICO	Silver	Dollar	.474	Gold Dollar ($0.983), 2½, 5, 10, and 20 dollars. Silver—Dollar (or peso) and divisions.
PERU	Silver	Sol	.436	Silver—Sol and divisions.
URUGUAY	Gold	Peso	1.034	Gold—Peso. Silver—Peso and divisions.
VENEZUELA	Gold and silver.	Bolivar	.193*	Gold—5, 10, 20, 50, and 100 bolivars. Silver—5 bolivars.

* Fixed.

Paraguay has no gold or silver coins of its own stamping. The silver peso of other South American Republics circulates there, and has the same value as in the countries that issue it.

STANDARD MANUFACTURING CO.,

PITTSBURG, PA., U. S. A.

Bañaderas de Hierro Colado con Esmalte de Porcelana, y Otros Efectos Higiénicos.

Bañadera de hierro colado, esmaltado en blanco, del modelo "Perfecto" con borde arrollado de 2½ pulgadas, esmaltado, provisto de accesorio de bronce para el abastecimiento del agua, colocado en el fondo en forma de campana; válvulas de compresión con llave de seis rayos; tubos de bronce para el abastecimiento del agua que van hasta el piso, provisto de rebordes para sujetarlos al suelo y tubo de desagüe "Imperial" de bronce. La bañadera descansa sobre patas artísticas, que representan una garra sujetando una bola. Todos los accesorios están pulidos y niquelados. El acabado es hermoso, en blanco de marfil con filetes de oro. Bañadera de 5 pies; largo desde los bordes, 5 pies 1 pulgada; ancho desde los bordes, 22 pulgadas. **PRECIO, $50.00**

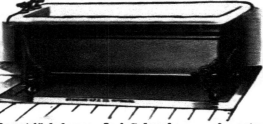

Bañadera de hierro colado, esmaltado en blanco, del modelo "Madeline," con borde arrollado de 3 pulgadas, esmaltado, provisto de accesorio de bronce para el abastecimiento del agua, colocado en el fondo en forma de campana; válvulas de compresión con llave de seis rayos; tubos de bronce para el abastecimiento del agua que van hasta el piso, provisto de rebordes para sujetarlos al suelo, y tubo de desagüe "Imperial" de bronce. La bañadera descansa sobre patas artísticas que representan una garra sujetando una bola. Todos los accesorios están pulidos y niquelados. El acabado exterior es hermoso, en blanco de marfil con filetes de oro. Bañadera de 5 pies; largo desde los bordes 5 pies 6 pulgadas; ancho, desde los bordes, 31 pulgadas. **PRECIO, $73.65**

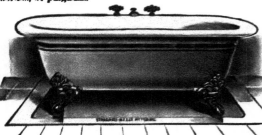

Bañadera de hierro colado, esmaltado en blanco, del modelo "Albion" con borde arrollado de 4½ pulgadas, esmaltado, provisto de accesorio de bronce para el abastecimiento del agua, colocado en el fondo en forma de campana; válvulas de compresión con llaves de seis rayos; tubos de bronce para el abastecimiento del agua, que van hasta el piso, provistos de rebordes para sujetarlo al suelo y tubo de desagüe "Imperial" de bronce. La bañadera descansa sobre patas artísticas que representan una garra sujetando una bola. Todos los accesorios están pulidos y niquelados. El acabado exterior es hermoso, en blanco de marfil con filetes de oro. Bañadera de 5 pies; largo desde los bordes, 3 pies 9½ pulgadas; ancho desde los bordes, 34½ pulgadas. **PRECIO, $91.00**

Los Precios Mencionados están sujetos á Descuentos Liberales.

Fabricamos un surtido completo de Bañaderas, Excusados, Lavamanos, Sumideros y otros efectos higiénicos de todos tamaños y modelos. Nos será grato dar informes detallados á quienes los soliciten. Somos en el mundo los que fabricamos en mayor escala artículos de ésta especie, teniendo inmensas facilidades para proveer al comercio de exportación á los precios más satisfactorios. Solicitamos correspondencia en cualquier idioma.

STANDARD MANUFACTURING CO.,

PITTSBURG, Pa., U. S. A.

United States Representatives in the Latin-American Republics.

ARGENTINE REPUBLIC.—WILLIAM I. BUCHANAN, Buenos Ayres.

BOLIVIA.—GEORGE H. BRIDGMAN, La Paz.

BRAZIL.—CHARLES PAGE BRYAN, Rio de Janeiro.

CHILE.—HENRY L. WILSON, Santiago.

COLOMBIA.—CHARLES BURDETT HART, Bogota.

COSTA RICA.—WILLIAM L. MERRY, San José.

ECUADOR.—ARCHIBALD J. SAMPSON, Quito.

GREATER REPUBLIC OF CENTRAL AMERICA.—(See Guatemala, and Honduras.)

GUATEMALA.—W. GODFREY HUNTER, Guatemala City.

HAITI (also Chargé d'Affaires, SANTO DOMINGO).—WILLIAM F. POWELL, Port au Prince.

HONDURAS.—(See Guatemala.)

MEXICO.—POWELL CLAYTON, City of Mexico.

NICARAGUA.—(See Costa Rica.)

PARAGUAY.—WILLIAM R. FINCH, Montevideo, Uruguay.

PERU.—IRVING B. DUDLEY, Lima.

SALVADOR.—(See Costa Rica.)

URUGUAY.—(See Paraguay.)

VENEZUELA.—FRANCIS B. LOOMIS, Caracas.

¡DIEZ MIL VACAS!

Suministran la leche que
se requiere para la

Marca de la Cruz Roja

MEJOR
QUE
UNA
VACA.

CUATRO VECES
MÁS RICA QUE
LA LECHE
ORDINARIA.

Leche Condensada

**Preparada en el célebre Valle de Mohawk, Nueva York,
con leche absolutamente pura y el mejor
azúcar de caña.**

✦ ✦ ✦

VENTAJAS:

1. Conserva su fluidez por más tiempo que la de cualquier otra marca.
2. Está preparada especialmente para todos los climas.
3. Es de gran valor como alimento para los niños y enfermos.

Precio, $4.25 por caja de 48 latas del tamaño regular, entregada á bordo de los navios en Nueva York libre de todo gasto. Se reciben pedidos por conducto de todas las casas comisionistas de los Estados Unidos. Sírvanse enviar por la circular descriptiva.

MOHAWK CONDENSED MILK CO.,

ROCHESTER, N. Y., U. S. A.

FLINT EDDY & CO.,

Nos. 66 y 68 Broad Stroot, NEW YORK, U. S. A.

EXPORTAN

Artefactos Norte-Americanos, Maquinaria, Material para Ferrocarriles, Hierro y Acero, Provisiones, Géneros de Algodón, etc.

PRESUPUESTOS SOBRE MAQUINARIA ESPECIAL.
PUENTES, VAPORES, INSTALACIONES DE VAPOR Y ELÉCTRICAS . . . .
EDIFICIOS DE HIERRO Y ACERO, ETC. . . . .

IMPORTAN

Cueros, Pieles, Lana, Café, Caucho, Caoba, Cedro, Cacoa, Nitrato de Soda, etc.

ADELANTOS LIBERALES SOBRE CONSIGNACIONES.

BRASIL.
Eddy, Mascarenhas y Guerín, - - - - Río Janeiro.

REPÚBLICA ARGENTINA.
Eddy, Hall y Ca., - - - - - - Buenos Ayres.

CHILE.
Beéche y Ca., - - - - - Valparaíso y Santiago.

PERÚ.
Beéche y Ca., F. L. Crosby, Agente, - - - - - Lima.

ECUADOR.
E. Pavía, - - - - - - - - - Guayaquil.

CUBA.
Luís de Olazarra, - - - - - - - Habana.

MÉJICO.
Frank G. Senter, - - - - - - - Méjico.

SUR DE AFRICA.   AUSTRALIA.

WEST COAST LINE,
VAPORES PARA
CHILE, PERÚ Y ECUADOR.

FLINT EDDY & CO.,
Nos. 66 y 68 Broad Street, New York, U. S. A.

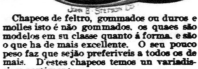

SOMBREROS
DE
STETSON.

Sombreros de fieltro, engomados ó duros y suaves ó sin engomar, que son modelos en su clase en cuanto á la forma, y de calidad superior. Su reducido peso los hace preferibles á todos los otros. Los tenemos en gran variedad.

Enviaremos á todo el que los desee catálogos ilustrados y también listas de precios. En la badana interior de todos los sombreros hechos por nosotros, van estampadas las palabras "JOHN B. STETSON CO." ó "JOHN B. STETSON & CO." que constituyen nuestra marca de fábrica.

Chapeos de feltro, gommados ou duros e molles isto é não gommados, os quaes são modelos em su classe quanto á forma, e são o que ha de mais excellente. O seu pouco peso faz que sejão preferiveis a todos os de mais. D'estes chapeos temos un variadissimo sortimento.

Enviaremos a todo aquelle que os desejar, catalogos illustrados e a nossa lista de preços. Na tira interior de cada um dos chapeos feitos por nósoutros vão estampadas as palavras "JOHN B. STETSON Co." ou "JOHN B. STETSON & CO." Estas palavras constituem a nossa marca de fabrica.

JOHN B. STETSON CO.

MIEMBROS DE LA ASOCIACIÓN NACIONAL DE FABRICANTES.

Fábrica y Establecimiento de Venta: North Fourth Street and Montgomery Avenue,

PHILADELPHIA, PA., U. S. A.

EN NEW YORK, No. 750 BROADWAY.

F. E. REED COMPANY,

WORCESTER, MASS., U. S. A.,

COMPAÑÍA FABRICANTE DE MAQUINARIA PARA

LABRAR EL HIERRO.

Nuestra especialidad son los Tornos Mecánicos . . .
. . . con un vuelo de 10 hasta 30 pulgadas, inclusives.

Citaremos lo que dice acerca de nuestros tornos el Diploma que nos fué otorgado en la

EXPOSICIÓN COLOMBINA DE CHICAGO DE 1893.

"Son hechos especialmente para el trabajo ordinario y para proporcionar al comprador una máquina muy buena á un precio notablemente bajo, problema difícil de resolver con acierto. A fin de llenar este requisito, estas máquinas son sencillas en cuanto á su construcción y movimiento, y están arregladas de tal modo que no pueden romperse á causa de descuidos por parte del que las maneja." Estos tornos son hechos de conformidad con las reglas establecidas y su trabajo es de superior calidad.

DURANTE LOS ÚLTIMOS CINCO AÑOS SE VENDIERON

350,000 ══════

BICICLETAS ✳ ✳

✳ ✳ "CRESCENT"

**POR EL PRECIO, ES LA BICICLETA MÁS PREFERIDA
Y NO HAY OTRA MEJOR Á NINGÚN PRECIO. . . .**

───────────

LAS BICICLETAS "CRESCENT"

se adaptan á todo género de personas, ya sean jóvenes ó
viejos, gordos ó flacos, grandes ó chicos . . . .

───────────

**DONDE QUIERA QUE SE LAS CONOCE . .
LAS BICICLETAS "CRESCENT"
SON LAS MÁS ACREDITADAS . : . .**

**SE GARANTIZA EL PRECIO . : . .
TANTO COMO LA CALIDAD . . . .**

WESTERN WHEEL WORKS,

CHICAGO, ILL., U. S. A.

R. G. DUN & CO.,

The Mercantile Agency.

(LA AGENCIA MERCANTIL.) NEW YORK, N. Y., U. S. A.

Establecida en 1841

PARA LA PROTECCIÓN Y EL . .
DESARROLLO DEL COMERCIO.

Informamos acerca de la posición comercial y del crédito de que gozan comerciantes, negociantes, manufactureros, etc., de todas partes del mundo.

Sucursales en todas las ciudades principales de los Estados Unidos, Canadá, y Europa. . . . .

También tenemos representantes en todas las Repúblicas de Sur y Centro América, y en Asia, Africa, y Australia. . . . .

El Grabado que acompaña á este anuncio representa el

CARGAMENTO MAYOR DE ESTUFAS DE PETRÓLEO
QUE SE HA DESPACHADO JAMÁS DE UNA VEZ

Un tren entero, compuesto de QUINCE grandes carros de carga,

LLENOS DE **ESTUFAS DE COCINA DE PETRÓLEO,**

Fué enviado á Siracusa, Estado de Nueva York, el 1.° de Marzo de 1906.

Fabricamos las Estufas de Cocina de Petróleo más modernas y perfeccionadas, conocidas con el nombre de

Blue Flame,

así como los

CALENTADORES DE PETRÓLEO DE ALUMINIO.

Novelty Manufacturing Co.,

JACKSON, MICH., U. S. A.

En todas estas Estufas se usa el keroseno ordinario (petróleo refinado).

Enviamos directamente pidiéndonos Listas de Precios é Informes, á no ser que no tengan Agentes en este país.

Nuestras Estufas son tan sencillas que un niño pudo manejarlas.

En caso de preferencia escríbannos ó háganos el pedido á su comisionista en Nueva York.

Lightning Source UK Ltd.
Milton Keynes UK
UKHW051712280219
337881UK00017BB/1065/P